DEFORESTING THE EARTH

DEFORESTING THE EARTH

From Prehistory to Global Crisis

M ICHAEL W ILLIAMS

The University of Chicago Press   *Chicago and London*

Michael Williams is professor of geography at the University of Oxford and a Fellow of Oriel College. He is the author of *Americans and Their Forests: A Historical Geography* (Cambridge University Press) and *The Making of the South Australian Landscape* (Academic Press); editor of *Wetlands: A Threatened Landscape* (Blackwell); joint editor of *A Century of British Geography* (British Academy and Oxford University Press); and author of numerous papers and chapters on changing landscapes.

The University of Chicago Press, Chicago 60637
The University of Chicago Press, Ltd., London
© 2003 by The University of Chicago
All rights reserved. Published 2003
Printed in the United States of America

12 11 10 09 08 07 06 05 04 03   1 2 3 4 5
ISBN: 0-226-89926-8 (cloth)

Library of Congress Cataloging-in-Publication Data

Williams, Michael, 1935–
    Deforesting the earth : from prehistory to global crisis / Michael Williams.
        p. cm.
    Includes bibliographical references and index.
    ISBN: 0-226-89926-8 (cloth : alk. paper)
    1. Forests and forestry—History. 2. Clearing of land—History.
    3. Deforestation—History. I. Title
SD131.W53 2002
333.75′137—dc21

                                                2001007754

♾ The paper used in this publication meets the minimum requirements of the American National Standard for Information Sciences—Permanence of Paper for Printed Library Materials, ANSI Z39.48-1992.

For Loré
once again

CONTENTS

ILLUSTRATIONS

PLATES

FIGURES

TABLES

PREFACE

> Probably the most important single factor that has changed the European landscape (and many other landscapes also) is the clearing of the woodland.
> —H. Clifford Darby to Paul Fejos, 19 July 1954

> There are many gaps in the evidence—dark ages in time and dark areas in space.
> —E. Estyn Evans, "The Ecology of Peasant Life in Western Europe" (1956)

The thinning, changing, and elimination of forests—deforestation, no less—is not a recent phenomenon; it is as old as the human occupation of the earth, and one of the key processes in the history of our transformation of its surface. More than forty years ago H. Clifford Darby suggested that "probably the most important single factor that has changed the European landscape (and many other landscapes also) is the clearing of the woodland," and he may well have been right.[1] Indeed, perhaps more of the earth's surface has been affected by this process than by any other single resource-converting activity.

This book is about how, why, and when humans eliminated trees and changed forests, and so shaped the economies, societies, and landscapes that lie around us. For as long as I can remember, I have been curious about the fashioning of the landscape and the creation of the visual world, and the way that humanized landscapes reinforce and reproduce social culture. I think that this curiosity got focus and structure when as a geography student I was introduced by my tutor Frank Emery to Darby's unassumingly simple but deeply scholarly essay, "The Clearing of the Woodland in Europe," and William Hoskins's evocative account of *The Making of the English Landscape,* both of which had only recently appeared.[2] From then on I was firmly hooked on what Hoskins called "the logic that lies behind the beautiful whole"; first I worked on wetland landscapes changed through draining, and then on forested landscapes changed through clearing.

The clearing of the forest is an intensely geographical phenomenon but self-evidently a historical process too. Whether this makes it historical geography or environmental history seems less debatable to me than the importance of the topic being investigated. Perhaps one should not worry, because such pigeonholes of classification seem to be of dwindling significance as modern scholarship increasingly sees geography and history for what they are: complementary and interdependent enterprises that are inseparable. Such

xxi

an approach is not new: in 1677 Richard Blome wrote, "Without . . . Geography all History is a thing of little use, the affinity between them both being such, that they seem to centre both in one."[3] It is that centering of time and space "both in one" that gives this book its special flavor; and given my inclination and training to be interested in places, localities, regions, and landscapes, it is what I would like to call historical geography.

So this book is not a history of forests or forestry, less still one about lumbering and land settlement, although all figure in it; it is not a history of industrial and domestic fuel use, although they enter into the picture; nor is it a history of conservation and environmental concern, although these loom large toward the end. It is a book about the clearing of trees, and the changes wrought in the visible biotic landscape as humans have made new worlds around themselves, and in so doing transformed the face of the earth.

The cutting down of trees is universal if only because wood, like water, is one of the necessities of everyday life. Every society in every age has used wood for fuel to keep warm, to prepare food, and to provide shelter. That these self-evident needs contribute to deforestation requires little explanation. But other human activities that affect the forest are more complex: agriculture, smelting, shipbuilding, trade, war, territorial expansion, and an attitude of either aversion to or reverence for trees. To understand these factors, one must understand something of the social, economic, and political motives and processes of the society in which people are acting out their ideas and technologies.

Consequently, deforestation is as much, if not more, about the people that do the clearing as about the number of hectares or acres cleared. There is a need for each deforestation story to be firmly rooted in an intellectual and scholarly context that helps explain the society of the age in which it occurred. In the long view, of crucial importance are the different driving forces and "cultural climates" of past ages that influence and direct human action. Just as events must be situated in space, so they must be related to the times in which they occurred. These events are discussed in the individual chapters, but those at the beginning of the early modern era circa 1500, the modern industrial era circa 1800, and to a certain extent the immediate post–World War II decades were so fundamental, extensive, and far reaching for the forest that I have devoted chapters 6, 9, and 13 to them exclusively. Having said all that, however, it is one of my aims to calibrate, however crudely, the extent of deforestation in the past in order to give concrete meaning to the many vague generalizations about the process and to show that deforestation is not a new phenomenon. The area cleared since 1950 has still not come near the amount cleared before that.

And yet, for all the widespread geographical and historical importance and magnitude of deforestation there is much about it that is not known. It may be about as old as the human occupation of the earth itself—controlled fire being perhaps coterminous with the emergence of *Homo erectus* some five hundred thousand years ago—but there are enormous gaps in our knowledge of the where and the when of the process, and equally large problems of interpretation of evidence. Deforestation is characterized by "dark ages in time and dark areas in space," especially in what may be termed the "deep" past before, say, 1500.[4] Even today, for all the outpouring of literature on tropical deforestation, the process is surrounded by much debate, uncertainty, confusion, and even obscurity.[5] If that is true about the present, then how much more so must it be about the past?

The "darkness" that envelops the ages and areas of the forest of the past consists broadly of two elements. First, there are the problems intrinsic to forests as living ecosystems or entities; many of these are still more or less uncertain and murky. Second, and mainly, there are the difficulties of knowing what human activity took place. But in recent years there has been much work in history, archeology, anthropology, and paleobotany that has lifted the gloom from some of the deeper recesses of space and time, particularly in Europe and the Americas, so that the prehistoric is illuminated by reinterpretation, the classical by greater detail, and the medieval by both of these advancements together with new insights into motivation. We also appreciate much better the global impacts of European expansion in the early modern world.

Nonetheless, the evidence is still fragmentary, so one must infer much. There are great gaps that cannot be filled, there is widespread ignorance of what does exist, and there are very few statistics that are wholly reliable. Much evidence is also highly prejudiced, or used for purposes quite different from those for which it was written. The evidence of deforestation is a little like Charles Darwin's metaphoric description of the evidence of the geological record for his theory of the origin and evolution of species: "I look at the geological record as a history of the world imperfectly kept, and written in a changing dialect; of this history we possess the last volume alone, relating to only two or three countries. Of this volume, only here and there a short chapter has been preserved; and of each page, only here and there a few lines." [6] *Deforesting the Earth* is also a history "imperfectly kept," and we too look at odd volumes, separated chapters, and isolated lines, written in strange dialects, in the hope that these fragments make some overall sense about the process.

Where this work has a Eurocentric focus that is quite deliberate I would maintain that the history of the world during the last five centuries has of necessity been a history in very large measure of the things which Europeans (and North Americans) did to themselves and to others, and how non-Europeans reacted to them and were frequently adversely affected. That, after all, is what the rest of the world thinks is wrong and criticizes. I know that my point of view is not shared by all. This book could have been written in a more overtly theoretical way with a greater emphasis on marxist, postmodernist, or political ecological approaches. But I have to say that it is not my inclination, preferring, as I do, to eschew all such structures. Those who want to infer or interpret other meanings in what I have written can easily do so.

This book was written in the old-fashioned way; not by a team of research workers but by the lone scholar trying to make sense of an enormous literature. However, like many solo practitioners I have had the benefit of talking to many people, more than I can faithfully recall. However, I am indebted to John Richards, Norman Myers, Pete Steen, Richard Tucker, Stephen Pyne, Andrew Sherratt, David Lowenthal, Andrew Goudie, Phil Stott, and many students who have knowingly, and sometimes unknowingly, been the foil for my ideas. Sheryl Oakes, librarian of the Forest History Society, Durham, North Carolina, was assiduous and cheerful in finding references and photographs for me, and John Perlin was particularly helpful in supplying illustrations. I owe a particular thanks to Penny Kaiserlian, formerly associate director of the University of Chicago Press, who put the idea of this book to me over lunch in the Quadrangle Club on campus many years ago. I rejected it initially; it was, I protested, simply too big for one person, encompassing as it would the whole earth through all time. A fortnight or so later she returned to the idea and suggested that I might know more about it than many. I agreed to try, having become convinced in the meantime that while it was probably a topic too big to be mastered, it was one that was too compelling to be ignored. I hope the result justifies her support and patience in a project interrupted by irksome administrative and heavy teaching duties. Although planned originally as a short survey, this book has in the course of elaboration become much larger; given the scope and scale of the enquiry it cannot be otherwise.

In addition, staff at the Press have eased the birth of this volume in many ways. My copy editor, Sandy Hazel; my illustrations editor, Jennifer Howard; and my editor, Christie Henry, have performed their tasks with skill, efficiency, and not a little grace, and made this a far less painful experience than I anticipated.

The British Academy has generously supported this work with its incomparable "small personal" grants scheme, a godsend for the individual scholar. I would like to thank Nick Entriken of the Geography Department in UCLA for offering hospitality and facilities while on a visit there, and Tom Vale and David Ward of the University of Wisconsin-Madison for my election as Brittingham Distinguished Visitor during most of 1994 and early 1995, which allowed me to get this project truly off the ground. In the School of Geography and the Environment in Oxford, Jane Battersby did wonders with the tables and bibliography, and Ailsa Allan skillfully and patiently produced the many maps, which are a special feature of this book.

But above all I am particularly indebted to the University of Oxford and the provost and fellows of Oriel College for giving me that most precious of commodities for research and reflection—contiguous time to travel, to think, and to write. Oriel College has made one other, though totally unintentional contribution. Among the portraits in the Hall and Common Room of the college are those of many of its past students who have made their mark on the world during Oriel's astounding nearly 700 years of existence. Three, in their various ways, encapsulate some of the themes of this book. There is a large oil painting of a swaggering and swashbuckling Walter Ralegh, discoverer of new worlds in the era of rambunctious European expansion (and also the author of the first "History of the World"); another oil is of a successful and smug-looking Cecil Rhodes, maker of empires in the era of high imperialism at the end of the nineteenth century; and there is a small, simple, pen and ink sketch of an altogether gentler, more scholarly person: Gilbert White, country parson and a true product of the Enlightenment. He was the author of the celebrated *Natural History of Selbourne,* and he is widely credited with being the father of ecology. Once this trilogy of *Orielensis* and their significance as discover of worlds, maker of empires, and inquirer of nature's relationships entered my consciousness, their presence and silent gaze acted as a sort of reminder, goad, and admonishment to complete the task.

Finally, my deepest thanks to Loré, my dearest companion and most discerning critic, who has always attempted to make me write better by insisting that I say what I really mean and mean what I say. She has kept the whole enterprise afloat; without her none of this would have been possible.

MEASURES, ABBREVIATIONS, AND ACRONYMS

AREA

The most common measure in this book relates to area. Metric measures of hectares and square kilometers dominate the world of international land use and land cover literature, and I have tried to keep to these. However, acres are commonly used in the United States and until recently in Britain, and certainly were the common measures historically. Occasionally I have inserted equivalents. In order to facilitate comparisons, a few equivalents are listed below.

> 1 ha = 2.47105 acres
>
> 100 ha = 1 km², or 247.105 acres
>
> 1000 ha = 10 km² or 2471.05 acres (or 3.86 mi²)
>
> 1,000,000 ha = 10,000 km² or 2,471,050 acres (or 3861 mi²)

Reversing the conversion:

> 1 acre = 0.404686 ha
>
> 100,000 acres = 40,468 ha, or 404.68 km²
>
> 1,000,000 acres = 404 686 ha, or 4046.8 km²

TIMBER/LUMBER VOLUME

Contemporary timber/lumber volumes are similarly expressed as cubic meters (m³); 1 m³ = 1.308 yd³.

An older measure common in the United States is the board foot (bf): 1 ft × 1 in. 12 bf equals 1 ft³, and 1 million bf = 2,360 m³.

One cord of wood (a common measure for fuelwood) = 4 × 4 × 8 ft, a total of 128 ft³, or 3.625 m³.

Reversing the conversions, 1 ft³ = 0.028313 m³, and 1000 ft³ = 28.317 m³.
mbf = 1,000 bf

OTHER ABBREVIATIONS AND ACRONYMS

      t/yr =tons per year
        BP = Before Present (conventionally taken as 1950 AD)
   CLIMAP = Climate: Long-Range Investigation, Mapping, and Prediction
       GIS = Geographical Information Systems
       IBP = International Biological Programme
 LANDSAT = Land surveillance satellite
       FAO = Food and Agricultural Organization (Rome)
       PIN = Program for National Integration (Brazil)
     SPVEA = Superintendency for the Economic Valorization of the Amazon (Brazil)
    SUDAM = Superintendência de Desenvolvimento da Amazônia (Brazil)
     UNEP = United Nations Environment Programme
      WRI = World Resources Institute (Washington, D.C.)

PART I

CLEARING IN THE DEEP PAST

Chapter 1

The Return of the Forest

Ever since the dawn of Holocene time, when global conditions remotely like those of the present-day first evolved from the ice ages, humans have always impacted the natural environment.
—WILLIAM R. DICKINSON, "The Times Are Always Changing: The Holocene Saga" (1995)

PROLOGUE: THE END OF THE ICE AGE

If ever there was a beginning to the modern forest it was at the end of the Ice Age just over 10,000 years ago when the great sheets of ice that covered the Northern Hemisphere began to melt and retreat. Then the Holocene, or most recent age of the Quaternary, was born, and the modern forest began to emerge around the world. Almost immediately humans began adapting and changing the evolving physical landscape.

Before the thawing began, a wintry blanket had held the world in its grip for over 10,000 years during the Pleistocene. Ice over 4 km thick covered both North America and northern Europe, and smaller ice caps existed in the Alps, the southern Andes, and even parts of eastern Asia, all surrounded by a deep girdle of land in which periglacial processes were at work. Most of northern Asia was too dry for ice sheets to form, and Siberia also experienced intensive periglacial activity. The border between land and water was dynamic as temperatures fluctuated and water became locked up in the ice sheets. Generally, the global sea levels were lower than today, by up to 100 m. Land bridges were exposed between Britain and Europe, Alaska and Asia, and the islands of Southeast Asia were joined to the mainland, allowing humans to migrate between land masses.

Then, about 16,000 years before the present (hereafter BP), the great sheets of ice that covered the Northern Hemisphere began to melt slowly and retreat. A new map of the vegetation of the world began to emerge. Europe had no forests except in isolated pockets or refugia in Iberia and southeastern Europe. A wide tundra zone covered most of the Continent, in which the predominant vegetation was shrubs and steppelike grasses capable of surviving the harsh climate. Forests did occur, however, in Japan, and in the pine and spruce woodland of eastern United States. A tundra zone also existed in North America, but in contrast with Europe it was much narrower, being only 100 km–200 km broad.

If the temperate areas were colder then the tropical areas were drier, and with the southward advance of drier conditions existing sand deserts expanded. Ancient sand seas (ergs) extended to places where there is tropical and subtropical forest today, for example in western Africa and Florida, and great dust plumes swept out to sea to leave revealing depositional sequences on the ocean bed. Throughout Africa and Latin America aridity reduced the extent of the rain forest and left it as a series of isolated refugia where, it is thought, they may have developed their amazing biodiversity, but there is no agreement about this. Most rain forest existed in Southeast Asia, and surprisingly, in the currently arid Southwest of the United States. The effect of lowering temperatures of at least 5°C was to bring montane biomes down from 1,500 m to approximately 500 m.[1]

When the ice began to melt about 16,000 BP the change was not sudden, and during the next 8,000 years temperatures moved slowly upward by some 4° or 5°C to become something like those of today. What caused the climate to change then, or at other times before in geological history, is difficult to know. There are a number of hypotheses, the most likely being the Milankovitch hypothesis based on the regular variations in the earth's orbital geometry, which fluctuates as it circles the sun.[2] In addition, toward the end of the Ice Age, the sheer bulk of the ice would have created anticyclonic conditions that would have deflected the moisture-bearing winds fueling the supply of snow for the ice away from the ice itself. Also the large quantities of cold freshwater on the ocean surface would have acted like a lid over the denser seawater, thus reducing evaporation in summer and leading to thick layer of ice in winter.[3] Thus, climatic influences and then ice-ocean interactions created a negative feedback mechanism that worked either singly or together to destroy the source of nourishment for the ice. The ice sheets became thinner, the ocean rose, large blocks broke off and floated far afield, and by about 13,000 BP the edge of the ice began its long retreat.

The retreat was not even; oscillating climatic conditions, particularly in northwest Europe, caused it to advance again many times, only to retreat even further later, always accompanied by changes in sea level. The water that had been locked in the ice began to melt and form huge rivers that gouged river channels across the northern continents, which must have had to cope with volumes of water up to 20 times that of modern rivers. The result was sandy and gravelly outwash plains that spread over vast areas, and a reduction in the salinity of the ocean. The resultant outwash plains were subject to wind erosion and deflation; and wind-borne dust and sand were lifted from the edge of the ice front to be carried many thousands of miles away to create the enormous, thick loess deposits stretching from northern Europe into Central Asia and China, in the pampas of Argentina and Uruguay, and in the Great Plains of the United States, with pockets in Washington and Idaho. In the tropics greater humidity acting on unconsolidated and unvegetated soils caused massive erosion to produce the greatest sediment yields of the age.

In short, the end of the Ice Age heralded a new era in the history of the world. Its physical, surface geography was largely made anew and the landscape began to take on something like its appearance today, although its climate kept on fluctuating.[4] Likewise, the mantle of vegetation began to move as opportunistic species colonized the new land, and with what seems to have been a bewildering speed and kaleidoscopic complexity, the forest returned to something like its old, though now radically changed, habitats. And humans were not far behind, showing an equal speed and flexibility in adapting to changing habitats.

WRITING THE BIOGRAPHY OF THE FOREST

It is a common notion that the world—nature, the environment, call it what one will—was a stable, pristine place before the industrial age. It is a deeply rooted myth in the Western psyche and its culture that nature is a passive, harmonious, God-given backdrop against which the drama of human life is played out; the "sound and fury" of human existence contrasting strongly with the notion that "earth abides." But it is a myth. When George Perkins Marsh made the revolutionary and unfashionable statement in *Man and Nature* in 1864 that "man is everywhere a disturbing agent. Wherever he plants his foot, the harmonies of nature are turned to discords," it was rarely believed.[5] How could the humans of the past with such low levels of culture and technology radically alter the natural world around them?

But for the forest nothing could be further from the truth. It has never been still. Not only is it a living, ever-changing, dynamic entity that is affected directly by both short- and long-term environmental changes, particularly climate, but it is also severely affected by quite minor human disturbances. Agriculture, domestication, and the control of fire have all been roughly coincident with the formation of the modern forests during the last 10,000 years, and their interaction is inseparable.

Consequently, if we want to understand how humans have changed the present forest mantle of the earth, we need to travel back along the distant corridors of time to when the forest was being formed after the end of the Ice Age. Just as people have biographies, so forests have their own histories that can be unraveled and documented. But unlike human biographies the writing of forest histories needs something more than words alone. Pollen analysis and radiocarbon dating are essential components of the language of those histories.

Pollen analysis, or palynology, entails the counting of grains of different tree-pollen types preserved at a variety of levels in peat deposits or lake and riverine sediments. The quantities are indicative of the past vegetation communities and, by implication, of past environmental conditions, even those produced by human disturbances. These data are usually presented in the form of pollen diagrams showing the concentration of the percentage values of the various pollen and spore types in the individual samples, arranged stratigraphically.[6]

Pollen emissions can be prolific; for example, in areas of temperate vegetation they can reach up to 10 metric tons annually per square kilometer of land. Some trees produce more than others; beech *(Fagus)* produces twice as much pollen as lime *(Tilia)*; elm *(Ulmus)* and spruce *(Picea)* twice as much again as beech; and alder *(Alnus)*, birch *(Betula)*, pine *(Pinus)*, oak *(Quercus)*, and hazel *(Corylus)* twice as much again as elm or spruce; in other words, eight times that of lime, the variability having to be corrected statistically in any sample.[7]

While the samples usually show a clear relative sequence of different pollens, an absolute chronology is difficult unless the samples are interbedded with datable human

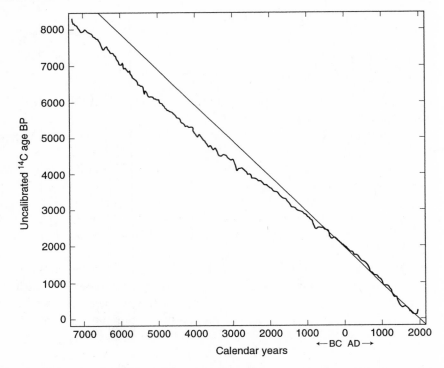

Figure 1.1 The radiocarbon calibration curve for the last 9,000 years, based on Irish oak annual ring sequence (*Source:* after Zohary and Hopf, 1993: 13). If the radiocarbon age corresponded exactly to the calendar and dendrological age, the two lines would be coincident, but the gradual falloff of ^{14}C after about 2,500 years is evident.

artifacts. The advent of radiometric techniques, largely pioneered by Willard Libby of Chicago in the mid-1950s, gave palynology a new certainty.[8] Most natural, living elements (e.g., wood, charcoal, peat, seeds, bone, shell, cloth, rope, or soil) absorb a mixture of isotopes, of which the most common is radiocarbon (^{14}C). But following the death of the plant or animal, ^{14}C decay occurs at a fixed and known rate. Hence the measurement of the ^{14}C remaining in the fossil will provide an age for the death of that organism. Results are usually expressed as an age in years before present (BP)—present being AD 1950—with a standard deviation appended. Thus a date of 5000 ± 50 indicates that there is a 68 percent probability that the date is in the range 4950–5050.

The method works well in most cases, with one exception. Because the amount of carbon in the atmosphere has varied over the course of the Holocene, ^{14}C tends to underestimate samples. Precise dates can be achieved by plotting ^{14}C dates against the sequence of annual rings in wood remains in trees (e.g., Irish bog oaks, or Californian bristlecone pines) over the last 9,000 years. If, as in figure 1.1, the radiocarbon age corresponds exactly to the calendar and dendrochronological age, the two lines coincide and lie on the straight line, but the gradual falloff of ^{14}C after 2,500 years is evident. By 5000 BP the actual calendar age should be about 5,800 years.[9] However, throughout this book the convention of quoting dates in an unadjusted, uncalibrated form is used.

THE RETURN OF THE FOREST

Armed with these techniques, sufficient data had been accumulated by the 1980s for the scattered information to be collated into continental histories of forest distribution and change. In Europe, Brian Huntley and Harry Birks compiled fossil-pollen data for 843 sites, mapping them by means of isopolls (lines of equal pollen) and the percentage of key taxa, and by using Principal Components Analysis to reconstruct the vegetation for the last 13,000 years.[10] In North America, Hazel and Paul Delcourt mapped changes in the relative dominance of major biomes and many tree taxa from 162 sites over the last 40,000 years, and Thompson Webb and others have done similar work.[11] Others have attempted to model the climatic changes that went with these vegetational distributions and shifts in both the Northern Hemisphere and the tropics.[12]

Although the two continental analyses are not strictly comparable in terms of methods and detail, the overall conclusions stand close comparison. Vegetation belts migrated over several hundreds, if not thousands, of kilometers in response to fluctuating climate, and followed a roughly similar sequence.

Europe

At 10,000 BP ice sheets still dominated Fennoscandia, Iceland, and a small ice sheet was present in Scotland. Europe's tundra, steppe, and birch-conifer boreal forest remained largely unchanged and dominated most of the lowlands of northern Europe, although some deciduous trees were beginning to move out of their southern refugia (fig. 1.2A). Around the Mediterranean herb-dominated steppe was being colonized by the typical mediterranean plants, like olive, pistachio, and evergreen oak, which were emerging from refugia in the Levant.[13]

Then, with a rapid climate amelioration during the next 1,000 years, there were dramatic changes in vegetation everywhere, and by 9000 BP the outlines of the modern forest were becoming evident. Most of the Continent saw the replacement of the tundra, first by open grassland, then by dwarf shrub heath with juniper *(Juniperus)* and willow *(Salix)*, and then by birch *(Betula)* and hazel *(Corylus)*, all with astonishing rapidity. As deciduous tree taxa migrated northward at rates of up to 1000 m per year most of Europe, both north and south, became dominated by mixed deciduous forest with some pine *(Pinus)* mixture in the north, grading to birch forest (fig. 1.2B). The herb steppe of the Mediterranean disappeared.

By 8000 BP the transition was complete; the mixed deciduous forest had moved from Spain and southern France to dominate the land area of the British Isles, Spain, France, central north Europe, and southern Scandinavia. In extreme southern Europe the deciduous forest gave way to the first substantial manifestations of a typical mediterranean evergreen oak and pine forest. The boreal (birch-conifer) forest was pushed northward to northern Scandinavia and Russia, and tundra and steppe all but disappeared, as had all permanent ice (fig. 1.2C).

During the next 4,000 years the vegetation change slowed down as temperature changed less, with the exception of the development of a well-marked western alpine zone

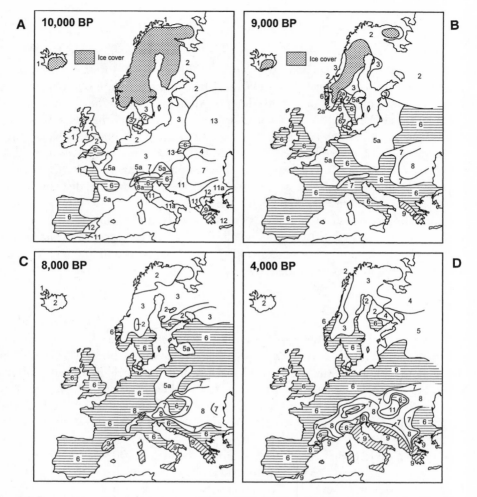

Figure 1.2 Europe: reconstructed vegetation, 10,000, 9000, 8000, and 4,000 BP (*Source:* after Huntley and Birks, 1983): 1. Tundra; 2. Birch forest; 3. Birch-conifer forest; 4. Spruce dominated forest; 5. Northern mixed conifer-deciduous forest; 5A. Northern mixed conifer-deciduous forest (*pinus* variety); 6. Mixed deciduous forest (horizontal shading); 7. Montane mixed conifer-deciduous forest; 8. Montane mixed-conifer forest; 9. Mediterranean forest (diagonal shading).

of montane forest and the expansion of the mediterranean vegetation mix over much of Italy and the coastal littoral of the Balkan peninsula. Thus, by 4000 BP the distribution of trees was looking remarkably like that of today as the climate took on a contemporary complexion (cf. figs 1.2C and 1.2D). But while the distribution of the main biomes was similar to that of today, their composition was not. New trees, such as oak *(Quercus)*, lime *(Tilia)*, alder *(Alnus glutinosa)*, and ash *(Fraxinus excelsior)*, invaded and dominated locally. Hazel *(Corylus avellana)* and elm *(Ulmus)* spread even more rapidly. Other trees, such as spruce *(Picea)*, did not expand to their present distribution until a slight deterioration of climate, which was noticeable by 2000 BP. Between 2000 BP and the present, there has, if anything, been slightly more cooling and the further expansion of boreal forest.[14]

North America

Although glacial conditions were more fully developed in North America than in Europe, the absence of any marked thermal oscillations during the Holocene meant that the return of the temperate forests began earlier and was more even, although in some places adjustment did not finish until later. At its maximum extent in 18,000 BP the Laurentide ice spread as far south as about latitude 40°, and a narrow belt of tundra separated it from a quite broad band of boreal forest. The temperate mixed forest was confined to the warm Gulf and south Atlantic plains.

By 14,000 BP (fig. 1.3A) the distribution of the forest had not changed significantly, because warming had led to the thinning, but not yet to the retreat, of the ice. But after 14,000 BP the retreat accelerated and there was a marked northward shift of temperate deciduous forest and mixed coniferous/northern hardwood forest, which pushed boreal forest and tundra ahead of them, with a corresponding expansion of the southern

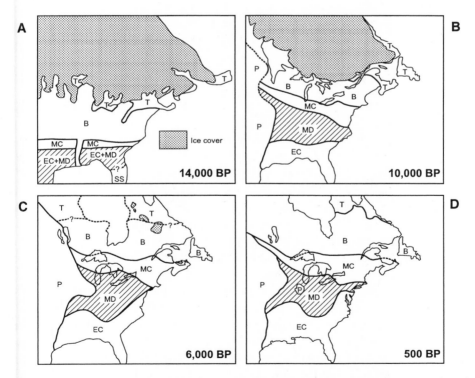

Figure 1.3 Eastern North America: Paleovegetation, 18,000, 10,000, 6000, and 500 BP (*Source:* adapted from Delcourt and Delcourt, 1981): *T*, Tundra; *B*, Boral forest; *MC*, Mixed conifer forest; *EC*, Oak-hickory–Southern pine forest; *MD*, Mixed deciduous forest; *SS*, Southern evergreen forest; and *P*, Prairie.

evergreen (pine) forests on their southern margin. By 10,000 BP the distribution of the forest was getting a decidedly modern appearance, although the ice still sat firmly over what is now the Canadian Shield (fig. 1.3B).

By 6000 BP the ice was all but gone and the forest had extended to very nearly its modern limits (fig. 1.3C). Like Europe, this mesocratic stage in the deciduous forest was marked by the progressive invasion of new species; for example, oak *(Quercus),* hemlock *(Tsuga),* hickory *(Carya),* and sweet chestnut *(Castanea Sativa),* with consequent changes in its composition. It is thought that unlike Europe, where northward migration was rapid because of the transport of pollens and seeds by generally north-flowing rivers, American vegetation migration was slower because the wide distribution of pollens was inhibited by the dominantly east–west trending rivers.

The general northward movement of vegetation assemblages was accompanied by another trend, which was the progressive eastward shift of the prairie/woodland ecotone (not shown), which reached its maximum eastward extent about 6000 BP, only to retreat somewhat in more recent times (fig. 1.3D).

This generalized analysis of biome distribution in the eastern United States of the past can be backed up by detailed work on the reconstruction of the distribution and behavior of individual tree taxon for 1,000-year intervals going back to 18,000 BP (fig. 1.4).[15] The postage stamp–sized maps spread across the page, for all the world like the repetitious but slightly varied frames of a typical Andy Warhol painting. But they illustrate clearly the dynamism of vegetation taxa in the continent as it adjusted to the retreating ice and changing temperatures.

The Tropical World

The temperate world was not the only part of the globe where vegetation was radically affected by climatic change during the last 10,000 years. Probably equally dramatic changes occurred in the tropics, but we know less about them. The concentration of intellectual effort on the temperate zones has many explanations. They were the areas of glaciation, and there existed tangible and visible evidence and remains of change in the form of, for example, meltwater channels, moraines, outwash plains, and boulder clay deposits. In addition, the focused research to unravel the past in Europe and North America by glaciologists, geologists, palynologists and archeologists, to mention only a few disciplines, has been formidable. Consequently, the low latitudes have been neglected and dismissed as being in an almost permanent state of aridity and desiccation.[16]

But the story is vastly more complex than thought. Since the 1950s evidence has been accumulating for some tropical pollen sites, which, taken together with high lake levels, sediments, and artifactual data from Africa in particular,[17] show that aridity was replaced by increasing moisture, and that low temperatures were giving way to higher temperatures. This puts pay to the idea of postglacial desiccation, Neil Roberts going so far as to suggest that the Sahara did not exist during most of the early Holocene (9000–5000 BP).[18] This climatic change allowed the tropical forest to expand—both laterally so as to reclaim areas of fossil sand dunes, as in West Africa,[19] and vertically so that montane vegetation climbed back up the mountains by as much as 1,500 m–2,000 m—especially in

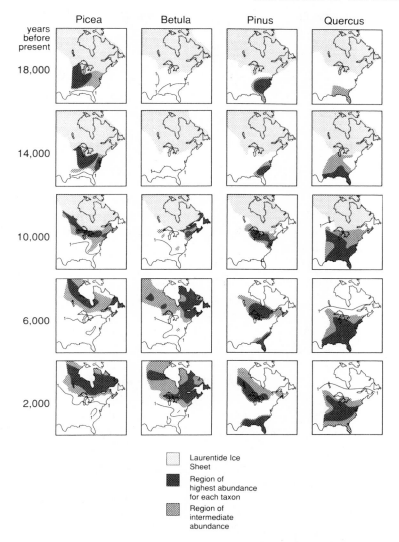

Figure 1.4 Distribution of contours of equal pollen frequency in North America for spruce *(Picea)*, birch *(Betula)*, pine *(Pinus)*, and oak *(Quercus)*, at 4,000-year intervals from 18,000 years ago to the present (500 years ago). *Source:* McDowell et al., 1990, after Webb, 1988.

East Africa, New Guinea, and the Andes when glaciers melted and retreated.[20] The long isolation of species in the remnant refugia of Latin America which had encouraged speciation and marked difference now ended with the onset of warm, pluvial conditions, so that a vast reservoir of biodiversity was created that still exists today.

But the low latitudes were far from stable, and it is possible that climatic deterioration 3,000–4,000 years ago led to increasing dryness. The tropical forest may have become less extensive with the reduction of temperatures and rainfall, but the net effect has probably not been great enough to cause major changes.

THE HUMAN IMPACT

As the forest changed, so humans colonized the newly vegetated land with remarkable rapidity, doing all those things that humans do: foraging, firing, hunting, selecting species and rejecting others, turning the soil, fertilizing it, trampling it, and mixing it. In the course of this manipulation of the biota some tree taxa moved, flourished, or were eliminated, just as surely as if they had been affected by changing climate. So, even as the forests were changing in the climatic see-saw of the millennia of the early Holocene era— slowly assuming their modern, historical distribution and form—the people who witnessed and survived that Ice Age were in the active process of changing their composition and density. From the boreal forests of the cold north of Canada and Siberia, to the hot, humid rain and monsoon forests and savannas of the tropics, via the intermediate mixed deciduous, pine, and mediterranean forests and prairie, steppe, and pampas of the temperate middle belt, hunters and foragers were changing the distribution, density, and composition of biomes just as surely as was the climate. It was a coevolution.

Thus, during the last 6,000 years, if not longer, many of the changes in vegetation reflect adjustments to human disturbances, brought about by the increasing density and spread of population, the use of fire, technological advances, the cultivation of exotic plant species, and the introduction of grazing animals. In Europe, forest clearing, cultivation, the cutting of tree sprouts and limbs for fodder, and the localization and intensification of grazing all had their effects on opening up the forest canopy and thus creating opportunities for invasion by early succession forest taxa, such as fir *(Abies)*, birch *(Betlua)*, spruce *(Picea)*, and particularly the mediterranean pine (Haploxylon *Pinus*).[21] The deliberate clearing of the forest accompanied by cultivation of cereals by Neolithic and post-Neolithic peoples led to forest fragmentation, the introduction and inadvertent spread of disturbed-ground weeds and ruderals, like plantain *(Plantago)*.[22] Some trees such as the walnut *(Juglans)*, the olive *(Olea europaea)*, and the pistachio *(Pistachia* spp.) became naturalized well beyond their native ranges as cultivation and grazing eliminated native plant competitors, and they were even deliberately spread and planted for their food value.

Disturbance may even have promoted the spread of selective pathogens. For example, the progressive diminishing of the elm *(Ulmus* spp.) in southeastern Europe between 7000 and 6500 BP and its replacement by beech *(Fagus)* and hornbeam *(Carpinus)* continued across central Europe between 6500 and 5500 BP, to be succeeded by early succession taxa including birch *(Betula)* and hazel *(Corylus)*.[23]

Similarly, in North America humans played an important part in shaping the vegetational development, quite contrary to some ecological accounts that see change as a purely post-Columbian event. Bottomland forests in the central Mississippi, lower Illinois, and Tennessee river valleys were cleared extensively as cultivation expanded along floodplains and lower terraces. The cultivation of squash *(Cucurbita pepo)* began as early as 7000 BP, to be followed by other exotics such as the sunflower *(Helianthus annus)* and bottle gourd *(Lagenaria siceraria)*, and later still by exotic cultigens such as maize *(Zea mays)* and beans *(Phaseolus vulgaris)*, and useful fruit- and nut-bearing trees were protected and hence propagated.[24] The story of weeds and ruderal invasions paralleled that of Europe. Other changes, far greater than are generally acknowledged, occurred in the forests at the oak–savanna transition, the forest generally being eliminated by fire to be replaced by more valuable grasses.

Less is known about the tropical world, but all the indications are that the impact was no less. The changes affected the forest in all continents, and are explored in greater detail in the following two chapters.

In sum, then, in addition to the natural, climatically induced changes, the human impact was early, widespread, and significant, and the forests of the world changed accordingly. Across the globe the first halting steps toward deforestation were under way. In the space of 10,000 years (a mere five hundred generations) humans were going to have an effect on global vegetation only slightly less dramatic and widespread than that of the Ice Age in the 100,000 years before.

Chapter 2

Fire and Foragers

Wherever primitive man has had the opportunity to turn fire loose on a land, he seems to have done so, from time immemorial; it is only civilized societies that have undertaken to stop fires.
—Carl Sauer, "The Agency of Man on Earth" (1956)

By the time of European arrival, North America was a manipulated continent. Indians had long since altered the landscape by burning or clearing woodland for farming and fuel. Despite European images of an untouched Eden, this nature was cultural not virgin, anthropogenic not primeval.
—Shepard Krech, *The Ecological Indian: Myth and History* (1999)

There are no virgin . . . forests today, nor were there in 1492.
—William M. Denevan, "The Pristine Myth: The Landscape of the Americas in 1492" (1992)

EVEN BEFORE the climate, vegetation, and landscape had achieved their modern character, humans were at odds with nature, changing it, manipulating it, and attempting to tame it. Vast areas of forest and grassland were burned, vegetation was altered irretrievably, soils were changed, and fauna were eliminated. Indeed, it is increasingly difficult to think that any forests, from the tundra margins to the tropics, were ever pristine and untouched; all were being changed in form and composition.

However, the long-held view has been that prehistoric peoples were a nonfactor in environmental change and degradation. Their numbers and densities were too low to bring about significant change; their technology was insufficient to cause alteration; and their livelihood (particularly that of non-Western "primitive" peoples) was in perfect harmony with nature: "we must understand, in their minds, all aspects of life are harmonized into a whole," Janaki Ammal asserted of early India. Not all agreed: Carl Sauer was more realistic, and had no doubt that widespread fire was endemic and integral to early human life, and that with domestication "the natural land became deformed, as to biota, surface, and soil, into unstable cultural landscapes."[1]

Of course, some of the changes may well have been natural as the forest adjusted to the climatic shifts associated with the last convulsions of the retreating ice. But no one is sure if natural vegetation acts as it is thought to theoretically, by achieving, eventually, a climax state. Some vegetation is disturbance dependent and thrives on frequent perturbations like cutting and fire.[2] Even if the climax state is true, only one factor has to change significantly to upset that state and start the forest working toward a new climax. For example, the soils that were exposed after the ice retreated would have taken many hundreds—even thousands—of years to weather enough to support a full vegetation succession (by which time the climate may have changed again anyhow). In contrast, abandoned agricultural clearings could have grown back in about 100 years to reestablish something like the original woodland.[3] Another complication is that even under stable environmental conditions, a forest community may experience change as it matures. Such "retrogressive succession" could be confused with human action, although that may well have accelerated the change. Additionally, natural occurrences like lightning fire, wind throw, disease, and frost, which are so important in forest dynamics, find little place in the traditional models of succession and climax, which make these models very incomplete.[4]

Whatever the true character of the natural mechanisms of succession, climax, and vegetational change, the role of humans in bringing about change in the "deep" past should not be in doubt. Each shift in the complexity and sophistication of technique and culture merely made the human impact more certain and more pronounced. And even the mildest and slowest change could be cumulative, leading to dramatic long-term effects. At the very simplest level, hunter-foragers manipulated vegetation by fire in order to round up and slaughter game, causing irreversible change to forest extent and composition. The hunter-foragers gave way to agricultural and/or complex irrigation societies that deliberately manipulated the soil and water supply, thereby radically altering and replacing one vegetation cover by another. In turn these gave way to urban/industrial societies that sent out shock waves of innovation, modernization, and change into their surrounding hinterlands in the form of fuel demands, crop productivity, and land use change.

In many ways the distinction used in this and the next chapter between foraging and farming as a means of altering the forest is a difficult one to sustain. In many societies there was, and is, a seamless continuity between the two, with the validity of the distinction decreasing the nearer it comes to the present. In reality, both used fire, the foragers, almost certainly more than the farmers. Nevertheless, it is a convenient distinction which underlines a particular emphasis in the subsequent account.

FIRE: "THE FIRST GREAT FORCE"

Fire was, in the words of Omer Stewart, "the first great force employed by man," and it was crucial in the story of deforestation Along with stone tools and language, fire was the first nonhuman force incorporated into human society, and one of the key features that distinguished humankind from the rest of the primates as they evolved from the beginning of the Pleistocene. With fire humans accomplished the first great ecological transformation of the earth, to be followed much later by two others of the same order of magnitude: the development of agriculture and animal husbandry 10,000 years ago, and the rise of large-scale industrial production a little less than 200 years ago. Humans assimilated fire into their biological heritage, thereby gaining access to the world's biota, and the biota, in turn, acquired a new regimen of fire transformed by human society. Fire, suggests Stephen Pyne, was the first of "humanity's Faustian bargains." [5]

So much must be supposed, but imagination and logic suggest that before "natural" or wildfire was domesticated by developing tools to create new, controlled fire, much thought and energy must have been used to preserve fire rather than to extinguish it. There is no evidence in the ethno-historical literature of past and contemporary aboriginal societies of a conscious effort to extinguish opportunistic fire, or concern to protect vegetation. Fires would be left to burn and smolder for days on end. [6] In areas of seasonal drying and strong winds, fire must have ranged far and wide, with dramatic effect on the vegetation.

Wildfire is a great modifier and has its own ecology that upsets traditional models of vegetation succession, leading to a single climatic climax. If fires are frequent and regular enough, vegetation adapts by shifting toward species (pyrophytes) that can regenerate after a fire or even withstand it. [7] For example, many plants have a thick, fire-resistant bark or buds that tolerate high temperatures, or they reproduce belowground. Other trees and shrubs have seeds that are stimulated by the heat of fire, their serotinous cones or fruit dehiscing in response to heat. Without heat the trees cannot germinate and they die. [8] While repeated burning discourages certain woody plants that cannot adapt or regenerate, it encourages a greater growth of herbs and grasses, both annual and perennial, through structural change and the fertilizing effect of the proteins and minerals left on the ground. After a burn, the forage available in deciduous woodlands may increase many times over for a number of years; the incentive to burn in order to encourage game is obvious.

To the early hominids, fire was complex, subtle, and dynamic; it was also destructive, irreversible, purposeless, and self-generating. But they also were to learn that the many negative qualities of this destructive force could be turned to positive and productive uses (fig. 2.1).

First and foremost, if humans could mimic nature's own fire drives caused by windstorm and lightning, the world was made more habitable and usable. Land was cleared and plant and animal resources were increased (see plate 2.1). Even the most primitive of aboriginal peoples seemed to grasp intuitively the idea that deliberate burning improved vegetation by promoting and maintaining the growth of favored plants such as grasses, forbs, tubers, wild fruits, wild rice, hazelnuts, sunflowers, cama, bracken, cassava, and blueberries. The yields of all these plants increased, which encouraged greater numbers and densities of animals. Burning also helped to control the distribution of animals, making hunting more predictable and thus more efficient because less time and energy were expended on stalking individual animals into areas of dense forest. From a wide variety of evidence Paul Mellars suggests that controlled burning could not only alter species variety, but increase the yields of browse and herbaceous forage in deciduous forests by between 300 and 700 percent, with a corresponding increase of animal populations of up to 400 percent. Additionally, fire opened up the tangle of woodland and jungle by removing the dense understory of brush and small trees, so that visibility was improved,

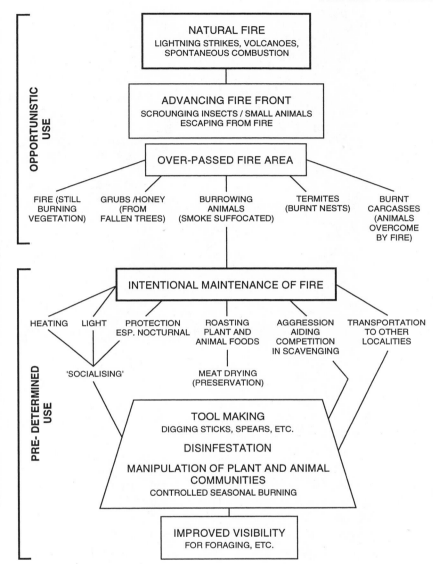

Figure 2.1 Possible uses of natural fire by early hominids. *Source:* after Clark and Harris, 1985.

travel facilitated, and surprise attack from animals and other humans minimized. Simply put, widely spaced trees and clear meadows offered greater mobility, and more productive and safer hunting.[9]

The reduction of vegetational cover for rousing and driving game is one of the most frequently cited reasons for deliberate burning throughout the historical aboriginal world, and it seems reasonable to suppose that the further back one extends into the past, the more frequently it would have been used. Anything to facilitate the hunt was desirable. Early hominids had only sharpened and fire-hardened wooden spears for hunting; not

Plate 2.1 Using fire to clear vegetation is a practice as old as humankind. Firing vegetation for cropping, Central African Republic. (Mathieu Labourer, Still Pictures.)

until later, when the more versatile and long-range bow and arrow were perfected, could the task have become more efficient and safer.

Not only were large mammals "flushed out" by fire, so too were nutritious insects, lizards, and rodents from trunks, holes, caves, and burrows, and even honey could be safely collected from combs. Night fishing by torch was very productive. The opposite was also true of fire: it had a purgative effect, ridding the ground of poisonous snakes, scorpions, and spiders and a host of ticks and bugs, while many peoples in the Americas learned to live in perpetual smoke to ward off flies and mosquitos.[10]

One also can speculate as to whether more accessible herds allowed a selective culling of animals, which might ultimately have affected the age, sex, and species components of herds. Such deliberate manipulation might have been the first step in the herding-husbanding-domestication of animal populations and would have contributed to the emergence of concepts of ownership and territoriality.[11]

Further, there are few foods that do not benefit from the application of heat. Therefore, the second great benefit of fire was in cooking and boiling, which leached out toxins, softened tough fibers, and reduced bacteria and fungi, extending the range of foods available and leading, presumably, to better health. In addition, it does not take too much imagination to realize that cooking became the model for ceramics and metallurgy.

Finally, fire became embedded in human cognition and sociocultural behavior. It is, says Pyne, "a maddening amalgam of human and ecological history." Fire could be used for protection as well as aggression; it accompanied ceremonies and entered belief systems as a purifier and atoner through sacrifice and ordeal; it has entered into concepts of creation and damnation in many religions. Certainly it made life more comfortable and sociable, and contributed to civilization. Fire was a source of heat and light, giving protection against cold and darkness and warning off predators, thus facilitating territorial expansion and population increase. Because of the comfort and security it offered it became a focus for group and community life, and enhanced communication and solidarity. Fire may have encouraged such practices as meat eating, food sharing, the division of labor, and new forms of sexual behavior, thereby helping to weld early groups into coherent units. It is most likely responsible for the formation of the characteristics of the family unit in society, the hearth being a potent image of (and in) family life and sedentariness, and the focal point for gathering, discussion, and dissemination of group wisdom.[12]

Johann Goudsblom suggests that learning to control and domesticate fire inevitably involved foresight, cooperation, the renunciation of "primary impulses," and the exercise of discipline in the tasks of gathering fuel, keeping it dry, and feeding the fire with it. Thus, he goes so far as to suggest that the care of fire was a cultural mutation that required a civilizing process. Moreover, the taming of the wild force of fire must be the first example of the tending, guarding, and exploitation of a natural force. Once fire was incorporated into human life, it was a natural progression to think of extending care and control over other nonhuman resources by selecting plants and animals, and guarding and protecting them against competing species and parasites. If that is so, then the use and control of fire may have initiated the second great ecological transformation of the earth—plant and animal domestication—giving it a significance way beyond the mere burning of vegetation for hunting. It was an integral part of civilizing and civilization.[13]

Be that as it may, all the practical benefits enumerated led to repeated and regular use of fire in most societies in the world, creating high concentrations of plants and animals that could provide humans with useful products, primarily food. The human monopoly of fire separated *homo sapiens* from all other beings, and made them the dominant species on the earth and its ecological manipulators. The implications for deforestation were enormous.

BEFORE THE ICE: PREHISTORY "CAUGHT ALIVE"

The obvious advantages of fire as a facilitator of life and provider of food are well attested by examples of vegetational changes from around the world. Just as the multitude of ethno-historical studies show the significance of fire during the last few hundred years, there is no reason to suppose that it would not have applied with equal or even greater force in the deep past of prehistory. Fire use is ancient, and we know that the end of the Ice Age was not the beginning of the human impact through fire. Australophitecines, the ancestor of modern humans, go back at least 1.5 million years to the celebrated sites such as Olduvai Gorge in the East African Rift Valley, and it is very likely that these early hominids used fire.[14] However, it was only with the migration of the descendants, *homo erectus,* out of the African heartland about one million years ago into Europe and Asia that we get very clear evidence of the human control of fire. Sites in such places as Torralba-

Ambrona in Spain (400,000 BP), Zhoukoudian in China (400,000 BP), Terra Amata on the French Mediterranean coast (300,000 BP), Vertesszollos in Hungary (400,000 BP), and Westbury-sub-Mendip in Britain (500,000–400,000 BP) all have definite signs of fire in association with animal bones. There is also evidence of the use of fire to harden bone and wood for implements, particularly hunting spears. Undoubtedly too, fire would have helped people to keep warm in the colder area into which they had moved, especially with the recurring advances of ice during the mid-Pleistocene.[15]

That the finds are at settlement sites suggests that the fires were not caused naturally by, for example, lightning strikes, which are universal and widespread,[16] or volcanoes or spontaneously combustible coal seams or peat beds, which are locationally specific. Nevertheless, to find unequivocal evidence of the deliberate use of fire to manipulate vegetation solely to facilitate hunting activities—particularly in the period around the Pleistocene–Holocene transition or before—is difficult. Fire-sticks (kindling sticks) leave little archeological evidence, unlike the clues of crop and weed pollen and erosion that accompany agricultural clearing. But there is a clue to vegetational change—and that is the animals that were killed, and their abundant skeletal remains.

Sometime during the late Paleolithic/early Mesolithic, between 16,000 and 10,000 BP, there was a massive decline in large mammals, such as mammoths, mastodons, woolly rhinoceros, giant deer, and cave bears, the so-called Pleistocene overkill. The decline was most noticeable in North America, where some 33 out of 45 genera of large mammals disappeared between 11,500 and 11,000 BP. South America lost 46 out of 58 genera while Europe and north Asia lost 7 out of 24 as cave bears, lions, hyenas, mammoths, and woolly rhinos disappeared abruptly by 12,000 BP. South Asia and sub-Saharan Africa were relatively immune: only 2 out of 44 genera disappeared, their large beasts stocking the zoos of the world today.[17]

The cause of this dramatic decline is a mystery. Epidemic disease and cosmic accidents are ruled out, and the conventional explanation has been that climatic change caused a readvancement of the forests, which reduced the open, vegetation-rich grasses and herbs of the northern plains, while changing sea levels hindered animal migration away from the areas of stress. More recently others have noted the almost perfect coincidence of the decline in North America with the emergence of "anatomically" modern humans, the Clovis people, a late Paleolithic hunting culture with a distinctive technology of flaked stone spears. They have postulated that vast numbers of large mammals, tame and unwary of humans, were butchered, leading to an overkill and eventual extinction.[18]

Neither climatic nor vegetational change alone account for all the observed facts. The most likely explanation is that a combination of two forces worked together, namely, human predation reduced animal populations already stressed by a reduced geographical range. But many questions remain. Even in such conditions, could Upper Paleolithic peoples have been capable of totally exterminating so many species? Why did so many of the species killed in North America not feature significantly in the human diet? Why did humans technically similar to the Clovis people, present in Europe since circa 35,000 BP, not kill off the mammals well before the classic overkill phase? Also remarkable is the fact that during the subsequent 10,000 years of the Holocene very few species have become totally extinct until the relatively recent rise in global population, the extension of human land uses, the reduction of natural habitats, and the advent of firearms.[19]

Another and more likely explanation for the loss of animal species is that as humans struggled to maintain open habitats for hunting in the face of forest advance they severely modified the structure and stability of the ecosystems by fire. Now the mammals were more vulnerable to the stresses of the physical and human environment around them. The likelihood of this scenario is bolstered by the striking historical analogy of the destruction of large fauna in the Pacific Islands by the seafaring, immigrant Polynesians during the first millennium AD. Here, in the words of archaeologist Jack Golson, prehistory has been "caught alive."[20]

The Polynesians reached Madagascar between about AD 100 and 500, Easter Island about AD 400, Hawaii about AD 800, and New Zealand between AD 900 and 950.[21] In the 117 km² of Easter Island, clearing for agriculture, firewood, and large timbers for moving the *moai,* or massive stone face statutes, together with frequent fire, resulted in "[a] deforestation which must surely be one of the most extreme examples of its kind anywhere in the world," leaving scarcely a single tree.[22] Dramatic as it was, however, this deforestation came nowhere near the destruction by fire "of almost half of the forest" in New Zealand by the Maoris.[23] The Maoris brought no plants with them and came as hunter-gathers. The moa, a large, ostrichlike, flightless bird standing up to 16 ft high, was their principal source of protein, without equal in any of the Pacific Islands. Moas also provided material for clothing and for most implements, so much so that they were known as *kuranui,* "the great treasure" or "primary source." In the absence of any large predators moas were present in vast numbers, tending to congregate on the forest edges and clearings. The Maori soon learned the value of fire in pushing back the forest edge and in driving the moas to places where they could be slaughtered more easily. Once started, the fires were fanned by the desiccating nor'westers that then, as now, sweep from the mountain across the foothills and the rain-shadow plains on the eastern side of the South Island during the hot, dry summers. The mixed broadleaf-conifer forests (dominant species, *Northofagus* and *Podocarpus* varieties) were completely destroyed. It could not withstand fire, did not regenerate, and was replaced by bracken, fern, tussock, and scrub. The denudation initiated the first great cycle of humanly induced soil erosion that buried old forests near present-day Christchurch under 12 ft of detritus. About a hundred years later the interior beech forests went the same way. By 1250 there were barely any moa left to hunt, and by the time of European colonization they were extinct. Thus, by the mid-thirteenth century a mere 8,000–12,000 people in South Island had destroyed "not less than 8 million acres of . . . forest," and driven the moa to the verge of extinction (fig. 2.2).[24] By the time of the fairly precise European vegetation surveys of circa 1800, the forest, particularly in the North Island, had been reduced even further; subsequent clearing for extensive agriculture and sheep grazing completed the task of denudation begun 1,500 years earlier by the Maoris (fig. 2.3).

With such evidence, one can well believe Captain James Cook's comment during the 1770s that throughout his voyages between the Pacific Islands "we saw either smoke by day and fires by night, in all parts of it." However, because of the prevailing myth of the

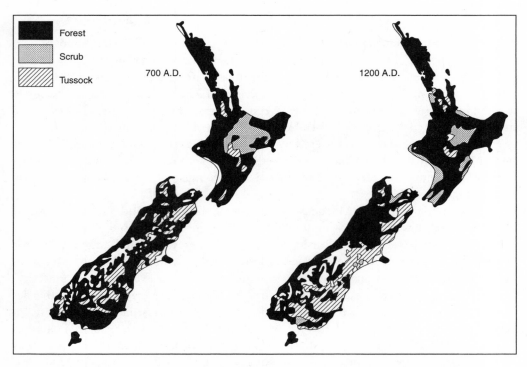

Figure 2.2 New Zealand vegetation: "Pre-Polynesian, AD700" and "Pre-Classical Maori, AD 1200." *Source:* Cochrane, 1977.

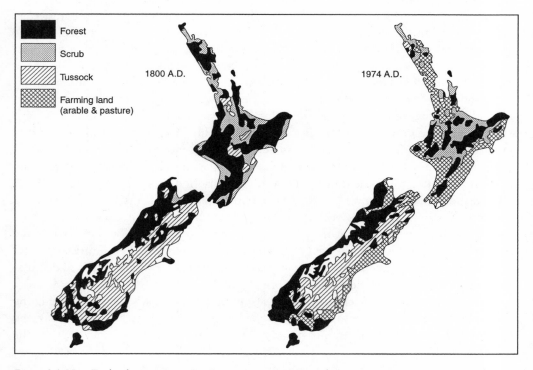

Figure 2.3 New Zealand vegetation: "Pre-European, AD 1800"; and "Present, AD 1974." *Source:* Cochrane, 1977.

harmony of preindustrial peoples with nature there has been a "marked reluctance to accept" what he saw and its consequences.[25]

Just as near-temperate New Zealand experienced acute deforestation with the influx of the hunter Maoris, so did near-tropical Madagascar during the early phase of the Polynesian immigration, circa AD 100–500. At least 14 species of large lemur, large avifauna, aardvark, and pygmy hippopotamus became extinct in the western forests.[26] From charcoal layers in pollen remains it is clear that fire was used extensively both in natural grasslands and in forested lands. The extinction spasm was over by circa AD 900, when hunting-gathering was replaced by cattle pastoralism and swidden farming, known as *tavy,* both maintained through the succeeding centuries by an endless cycle of fire. By the time of European contact in the late eighteenth century, over three-quarters of the central plateau was in grassland, and fire was common.[27]

Whether before the Ice Age or after, the dramatic decline of large fauna is a direct result, and surrogate measure, of the ability of humans to alter their forest environment by fire. We have to concede that the Pleistocene "overkill" was more likely to have been a Pleistocene "overburn."

AFTER THE ICE: EUROPE

The South Pacific excepted, in more recent times it is only from about 6000 BP in Europe, about the same time in South America and elsewhere, and probably only from about 1000 BP in eastern North America, that clear evidence comes to light that hunter-foragers were playing an active role in the transformation of the forest.

In Europe the evidence of vegetation manipulation is patchy before 5000 BP. In the forests of what is now Poland, a phase of disturbance with charcoal tissues of wood appears in lake sediments sometime between 6700 and 6100 BP and another from 6000 to 5600 BP.[28] In Britain the evidence is much clearer, as Mesolithic foragers attempted to open up the thickening vegetation in order to encourage red deer and wild pig. As the climate warmed after the glacial retreat the tundra-conifer vegetation of pine and birch was gradually replaced by a thicker deciduous mixed forest of mainly oak, alder, and lime. There are many patches of charcoal in association with lithic remains, soil erosion, and an increased prevalence of pollen from hazel *(Corylus)* as well as alder *(Alnus)* that could only have come about with burning, as they are shade-intolerant plants.[29]

But the picture gets clearer for the period after 5000 BP, when the forest thickened even more and there was an almost total cover of closed-canopy deciduous high forest, especially lime, the shade of which significantly hindered the growth of grasses and herbs.[30] Foraging groups must have been aware of the effect of sunlight on the greater productivity in the openings and edges of the forest, and of the cessation of the vernal efflorescence of the forest floor with the closing of the overhead canopy in late spring.

Over 100 sites in the Pennines and North York Moors show repeated fires associated with layers of charcoal, lithic remains, and some animal bones. Frequent lightning strikes in one spot is unlikely; in any case, as Ian Simmons points out, the damp forest is "about as likely to burst into flames after a lightning strike as a sackful of wet socks."[31] Most of the fires were on the forest edge or openings, and areas as large as 5 km in diameter were affected. The shade-tolerant oak and ash cease to dominate the pollen count, and their place is taken by scrubby hazel, with lesser quantities of rowan and bramble, and substantial amounts of grasses and herbs. Even nettles *(Urtica),* a sure sign of disturbed ground, appear. The net ecological effect was to replace the high, mixed deciduous forest with a mosaic of open-canopy woodland with grassy clearings near water sources, the ideal hunting ground.[32] As a consequence of the repeated burning the lower edge of the forest appears to have retreated upward to a higher altitude than might otherwise have been expected.

The less-dense plant communities had an unforeseen consequence: the hydrological balance may have been altered. Trees no longer transpired water that then collected, and upland peat beds were formed, often 3 m–4 m thick, in which many of the remains of the trees have been preserved.[33]

It is puzzling that there is a relative lack of similar evidence elsewhere in Europe. In nearby Denmark, for example, Johannes Iversen's 1941 view—that there was no clearing in the pre-Neolithic forest because people were forced to give way to dense forest advance and seek the "open" coastal fringes during the Atlantic period of climatic optimum—has been influential, and has colored generations of subsequent work. "Large parts of the country must have been almost empty of human beings," he wrote, and his coworker, Jorgen Troels-Smith, went so far as to make the incredible suggestion that "scarcely 30 people divided among 5 or 6 families probably constituted the entire population of Denmark at that time."[34]

But it is far more likely that the deliberate use of fire to clear woodland undergrowth has been underestimated, the evidence of extensive ungulate and human occupation has been ignored, and that the mechanisms of the dispersal and uneven distribution of pollen due to variable wind speed in the forest has not been understood fully.[35] Nonetheless, despite these probabilities and the evidence of burning and clearing leaving charcoal remains in pollen diagrams in Sweden and Finland, there is still nothing like the evidence accumulated for Britain.

Yet Mesolithic foraging groups certainly inhabited northern, western, and parts of Mediterranean Europe in reasonably well-defined "social territories." Their logistically organized subsistence systems revolved around seasons of exploitation, which depended on the availability of game, fish, and forage.[36] The degree to which the forest was a barrier to penetration and manipulation depended on the type of forest prevalent at the time. The damp boulder clays and silts of the northern European plain would have been dominated by dense lime forest that would have provided little opportunity for burning except around its edges and in clearings; but the sandy and gravelly outwash soils to the south, and the extensive friable loess soils in particular, would have dried out enough in summer to provide ample opportunity for deliberate firing.

Perhaps the most persuasive evidence of the intensity of the Mesolithic impact is the widespread and sharp decline in elm *(Ulmus)* pollen across the Continent. This remarkable feature of the paleological record first appeared in approximately 6400–6300 BP in southern and southeastern Europe and culminated between approximately 5000–5200 BP in Britain. Various hypotheses, both anthropogenic and natural, have been put forward. Deteriorating, colder climate at the end of the Atlantic and beginning of the Sub-

Boreal phases has been suggested, but the decline is not synchronous over large areas as might be expected. Moreover, the onset of greater coolness, wetness, or continentality does not seem possible, as the pollen of ash *(Fraxinus excelsior),* a very cold-sensitive tree, remains constant.[37] The onset of a devastating fungal pathogen outbreak has also been invoked, but again, this seems unlikely: once established, tree diseases have never shown any propensity to go away, and elm recovered in later centuries.[38]

The most popular explanation of the elm decline is anthropogenic. In a few places the decline is considered to accompany the initial appearance of Neolithic agriculture and the rise in the pollen record of typical disturbance- and open habitat–indicator plants like Ribwort Plantain *(Plantago Lanceolata),* two factors associated with Iversen's classic *landnam* (literally, "taking of land") model of clearing and vegetation regeneration.[39] But these are rarely coeval, and there is confusion. For example, in northern Poland the annually stratified sediments of Lake Gosciaz give a fine and precise record of changes. Between 5400/5280 and 4470 BP there was a complex interplay of pollens, suggesting disturbance; but it is only in the later phase from 4900 to 4700 that *Ulmus* drops sharply and is accompanied by what seems to be increased soil erosion. Elsewhere in Poland, the greatest declines are in regions characterized by fertile, loessic chernozum soils, and coincide with concentrations of pottery by middle Neolithic cultures (5500 to 4500 BP).[40] While clearing seems an obvious answer, the fact that elm pollen declined by one half while other tree taxa pollens stayed more or less constant suggests a curious selective clearing strategy. Linking elm decline with Iversen's *landnam* model of forest clearance is usually erroneous, says Peter Bogucki, as *landnam* "represents an episode of land clearance usually several centuries *later* than the elm decline and is characterized by displacements in whole groups of plant species."[41]

The most widely cited anthropogenic explanation is that put forward by Troels-Smith: in the absence of winter grassland pastures in a continuous forest canopy, the nutritious elm leaves and small branches (together with ivy and mistletoe) were collected and used for stall-fed cattle in the semiagrarian communities that were emerging in Denmark and the north European plain. Excessive pollarding every two or three years prevented regeneration and altered the forest. However, evidence of such practices does not exist and the scale of the operation would have to have been enormous and synchronous to produce the result that the pollen diagrams reveal. Revealingly, Peter Rowley-Conwy calculated that it would take the pollarding of between 47 million and 80 million trees in Denmark alone to cause a 50-percent decline in pollen there, and that would have supported between 190,000 and 400,000 cattle—for which there is no evidence. In another calculation Oliver Rackham estimated that it would have taken half a million people in Mesolithic Britain to have pollarded the 4 million ha of elm that had to be affected in order to account for the decline. Such cattle and population figures were not attained until many centuries, if not millennia, later.[42] Put another way, the decline normally predated the appearance of the earliest domesticated animals and plants in areas where it occurs by several centuries.[43]

It is possible that to some degree all these explanations could have worked together to produce change, but given the evidence of deliberate burning in foraging societies, it is much more likely that differences in burning regimes accounted "for variations in the timing and magnitude of the elm decline,"[44] especially in loessic areas. Elms are often located in desirable lower areas with only shallow groundwater—though near bodies of water—areas favorable to vegetation manipulation. Once affected by fire, elms do not regenerate easily or quickly. Rather than being dominated by the forest and a "passive beneficiary of its largesse," Bogucki suggests that the Mesolithic foragers "played an active role in the modification of the ecosystem to suit their own needs."[45]

The deliberate burning and elimination of the forest was not the only manipulation of the resource. Wood was the most valuable and versatile raw material available in the past. Not only did it furnish shelter and heat, but also the material for a vast range of tools and weapons necessary for survival. Given its importance, it is ironic that wood has played little part in the traditional, outmoded, but convenient Three Ages system of European prehistory—Stone, Bronze, and Iron. There is barely a tool or weapon that did not have a wooden part, and the latter two ages would not have existed without the wood for smelting ore. The organic nature and perishability of wood, contrasted to the permanence of stone, metal, and pottery, have led to its neglect.

Yet Mesolithic societies had acquired considerable knowledge and appreciation of the qualities of different timbers and their suitability for different functions—the elm and yew for bow staves, pine for arrow shafts, hazel for spear shafts, and tough root wood for ax hafts. Bark quality was also understood: the resistance of birch bark to water and its usefulness for hut floor insulation and net-float construction; the use of its pitch for caulking artifacts and preparing leather; and the use of willow bark to provide the thread for making the nets. Even tree fungus *(Fomes fometarius)* was stripped of its outer skin and used for tinder.[46]

John Coles, S. V. E. Heal, and Bryony Orme instance over 600 different types of wooden artifacts from about 200 sites in Ireland and Britain, ranging from the Mesolithic to the Neolithic. The dugout canoes, kegs, bowls, boxes, and baskets, as well as the more usual weaponry and tools, such as ax hafts, bows, spear and arrow shafts, sheaths, scabbards, shields, clubs, hammers, forks, knives, looms, and wheels, form an impressive array of artifacts that came from wood. Because of their organic nature, many are well preserved in wetland locations.[47]

This catalogue excludes the palisades and structures in forts, and the worked rods, brushwood hurdles, pegs, and planks that went to make up the prehistoric trackways and platforms that straddled the low-lying wetlands in the Somerset Levels and the Fens—literally millions of pieces. Perhaps even more impressive than the intricacy and magnitude of these trackways is the evidence of the conscious management of the surrounding woodlands by coppicing to stimulate the growth of long, straight poles from the trees' stools.[48]

All the evidence of clearing and wood use points to the fact that a greater continuity of technology occurred between the Mesolithic and Neolithic than is often supposed. The later Mesolithics were not, as Gordon Childe thought, the primitive fag end of the hunting and gathering Paleolithic age who became absorbed by the superior new Neolithic agriculturalists; rather, they were the sophisticated and innovative precursors who not only heralded the Neolithic agricultural age but hastened its establishment. Indeed, Mesolithic and Neolithic are "definitional nightmares" that are more likely to obscure than to clarify. As far as the clearing of the forest is concerned, these "ages" mask a continuity of ceaseless change and modification that began over 6,000 years ago.[49]

AFTER THE ICE: NORTH AMERICA

The Forest or Eastern Woodland cultures of pre-Columbian North America may be separated by up to 5,000 years from the forest economies of Mesolithic Europe, but there were many parallels. There were also differences. In Europe, evidence depends almost entirely on archeological techniques for retrieval and interpretation, whereas in North America, an inquisitive audience of literate and artistically inclined newcomers left a record for all to read and see. The New World they found filled them with curiosity and awe, and although they did not, by any means, understand or appreciate what they found, their accounts and sketches bring Indian forest use vividly alive.

Despite the eyewitness accounts and the rapidly accumulating botanical and archeological evidence, the impact of the Indian on the forest—even of his existence—has been strenuously denied in the past, and still is by some. The denial, particularly in the eastern woodlands, has a long history. During the nineteenth century writers such as Longfellow, Thoreau, Parkman, and Fenimore Cooper, and painters of the Hudson River school and it descendants, such as Cole, Catlin, and Church, extolled the idea of an untouched, virgin, and virtually uninhabited forest wilderness. Such a Romantic vision served as a stark contrast to heighten the heroic struggle of the pioneer farmers, who were subduing the unending forest by clearing. These pioneers were replacing wilderness with a "made," humanized landscape, darkness with light, and fear and evil with hope, redemption, and civilization. This vision has become a part of the American heritage.[50]

The idea of a nonhumanized "presettlement" landscape/ecology is equally attractive for many modern-day ecologists, anthropologists, biogeographers, and "wilderness" enthusiasts, for it acts as a benchmark against which to measure subsequent change, as well as a datum toward which conservation policy must aim and against which societal change can be measured. Thus they would prefer using the concept of "pre-European" landscapes as "natural analogues against which modern environmental impacts can be judged."[51] In their concept of conservation the past (and even present) rural populations are missing.[52] The celebrations—or commiserations, depending on one's point of view—to mark the quincentennial of the Columbian landfall have similarly, but for entirely different reasons, created a vision of a virtually untouched paradise in which the Native American was more readily admitted, but who lived benignly and in harmony with nature.[53] Somehow, in this naive view, they were always "natural ecologists" whose mental constructs precluded cultural activities that would be destructive to the environment. Pre-Columbian America

> was still the First Eden, a pristine natural kingdom. The native people were transparent in the landscape, living as a natural element of the ecosphere. Their world, the New World of Columbus, was a world of barely perceptible human disturbance.[54]

It was the blundering European who transformed, destroyed, and devastated it all. Such views tend to be accepted uncritically by nonscientific audiences with a conservation agenda.[55]

The unintentional alliance among mid-nineteenth-century romantics, contemporary ecologists/conservationists, and latter-day politically corrects has obscured the fact that, first, there was an impact, and second, as William Denevan has said, it was "neither benign nor localized and ephemeral, nor were resources always used in a sound ecological way." On the contrary, there is abundant evidence that by 1492 by burning, clearing, and foraging, the Indian had modified the extent and composition of the forest, creating forests in many stages of ecological succession, making and expanding grasslands, and otherwise engaging in the first steps towards deforesting the landscape.[56]

For the "deniers," ancient and modern alike, ignorance or willful omission of the true magnitude and effect of Indian numbers has played a part in their views. Rather than the 8 million to 15 million native peoples present in all the Americas just prior to 1492 as was previously thought, modern biological and archival reconstruction has put the number at between 43 million and 65 million, some even suggesting double that figure. Denevan conservatively calculates a figure of 57.9 million: 3.0 million for North America, 17.2 million for Mexico, 5.6 million for Central America, 3.0 million for the Caribbean, 15.7 million for the Andes, and 17.2 million for the lowlands of South America. Such numbers *must* have meant extensive ecological transformations. Subsequent devastating pandemic diseases of common Old World pathogens like measles and influenza, as well as a host of more virulent diseases like smallpox, cholera, dysentery, and yellow fever to which native Americans had no immunity, led to a demographic collapse, so that perhaps only 5.6 million people remained by 1650—a mere million of which were in North America.[57]

Because forest disturbance is largely an outcome of human numbers, and given the high total number and density of the original population, it would not be surprising that the first Europeans found a profoundly manipulated landscape. However, because of the rapid decline of native human numbers through disease, the humanly modified landscape physically receded before forest re-advance, and also figuratively "receded" in the collective consciousness. Human transformation has been increasingly discounted to a point where it has been almost denied. Indeed, despite the in-migration of perhaps 2 million Europeans by the middle of the eighteenth century, it is probable that the forest landscape of 1750 was less humanized than that of 1492, when Indian numbers and their impact was at their peak. With such evidence the terms *presettlement* and *postsettlement* should be consigned to the intellectual trash can. Concepts of "natural" and "equilibrium" have probably not existed since the end of the Ice Age.

In the Eastern Woodland cultures, fire use was an integral part of the economy, not only for hunting and foraging but also for cultivation. Many Indian tribes moved easily and smoothly between the two modes of production, so that there is no clear distinction between them. The Penobscots of Maine, for example, had a two-part existence, being big-game hunters of moose inland during the winter and returning downstream to plant maize on the river islands during the summer. Thus, the criteria by which we make distinctions and judge cultural achievement in the Old World Neolithic, such as domestication, agricultural control, sedentariness, pottery, and trade, simply do not apply to the American Indian. After reviewing the diverse evidence, Joan Taylor concludes that the Indians remained a

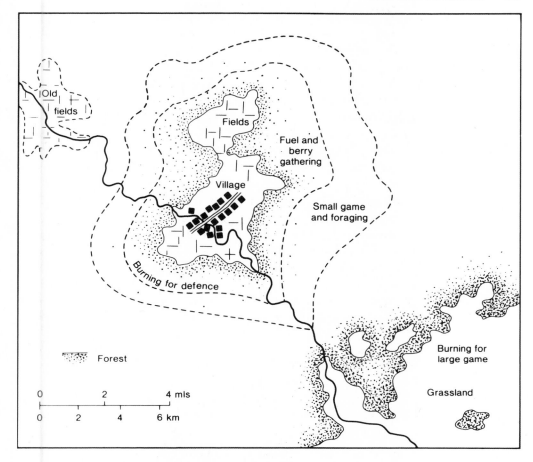

Figure 2.4 Zonation of Indian forest use. *Source:* after Williams, 1989.

much more diverse population of varying achievement right up to the arrival of the Europeans. Here man seemed to resist a settlement economy and retain his hunting ties while living in village complexes.[58]

This complexity is represented, perhaps, by Richard MacNeish's D1 path of domestication. (See fig. 3.4 below.)

In many settlements (such as those of the Huron, Iroquois, and Cherokee) there was a hierarchy of fire uses in the forest that had a rough locational expression. There was a core of fire-cleared ground for fields and cultivation. Beyond this was a zone of intensive fuel, berry, and nut gathering, which merged into a more extensive, distant zone that was periodically opened up by fire to extend open grassland, promote the growth of fresh grasses; and encourage small game and foraging. Beyond that was an area in which wildfire burning was common for driving or encouraging large game. (See fig. 2.4.) Fire created a favorable environment, especially on the mixed forest-grassland edge, where returns of game and cultivated foods could be maximized.

The extent, frequency, and impact of Indian burning is not without controversy. Hugh Raup thought climate more important than anthropogenic effects, and Emily Russell has argued that although increasing Indian numbers may have led to an increase in the frequency of fires, which in turn might have had a marginal effect on the forest, there is no conclusive evidence that "Indians purposely burned large areas . . . frequently"; climate and soil "probably played the greater role in determining the pre-colonial forests." Thus, widespread and regular burning was "an unlikely hypothesis." [59]

But the evidence of human modification of the forest is early, stark, and clear, especially when taken in conjunction with the experience of similar societies elsewhere in the world. The Native Americans were careful stewards of fire as a tool to manage the land and to promote their welfare. Cereal grasses were fired annually, basket grasses and nuts about every three years, brush and undergrowth in the forest about every 15 to 30 years or more; and annual broadcast fire in the fields got rid of vermin, disease, weeds, and regrowth.[60] Fire for defense and hunting occurred as needed. As in most economically primitive societies, fire was a natural and integral—even sacred—part of the Indian landscape and livelihood.[61] The contemporary record of the nature, purpose, and effect of Indian fire for foraging is rich and quite conclusive, and only a fraction of the evidence can be selected.[62] Fire alone, without any other activity, produced three major changes in the forest: opening up the forest, creating grasslands, and altering the composition and range of trees.

The Opening of the Forest

The repeated use of broadcast fire on the forest to free it of underbrush affected the density of trees. Many Europeans approaching the eastern coast had seen evidence of great conflagrations even before they landed. Mark Catesby said of the Carolinas in 1747,

> In *February* and *March* The inhabitants have the custom of burning the woods, which causes such a continual smoke, that not knowing the cause it might be imagined to proceed from fog, or a natural thickness of the air.[63]

Thomas Morton, who had lived in New England for several years by 1627, made the connection between vegetation type and fire:

> The Salvages are accustomed to set fire of the Country in all places where they come, and to burne it twize in the yeare, viz; as the Spring and the fall of the leaf. The reason that mooves them so to doe so, is because it would other wise be so overgrowne with underweedes that it would be all coppice wood, and the people would not be able in any wise to passe through the Country out of a beaten path.

This repeated broadcast firing of the undergrowth

> destroyes the underwoods and scorcheth the elder trees that it shrinkes them, and hinders their growth very much; so that hee that will looke to finde large trees and good tymber, must not depend upon the help of a woodden prospect to finde them on the upland ground; but must seeke for them . . . in the lower grounds, where the grounds are wett.

The result was to open out the forest and to create a sort of ecological secondary association: "The trees growe here and there as in our parks; and makes the Country very beautifull and commodious," Morton wrote.[64]

Elsewhere similar landscapes were encountered. The area around Salem, Massachusetts, was described by Francis Higginson as being "open plains, in some places five hundred acres, some places more, some lesser, not much troublesome for to cleere for the plough to goe in," while the forest around the Roanoke River in Virginia had become so open and parklike that William Byrd could say, "There is scarce a shrub in view to intercept your prospect, but grass as high as a man on horseback." Again, Andrew White, on an expedition along the Potomac in 1633, said that the forest was "not choked up with undergrowth of brambles and bushes, but as if laid out by hand in a manner so open, that you might freely drive a four horse chariot in the midst of the trees"; and a little earlier John Smith in Virginia had commented that "a man may gallop a horse amongst these woods any waie, but where the creekes and Rivers shall hinder." [65] The ability to ride a horse or drive a horse and carriage between and under the trees became a favourite literary topos to describe the open nature of the fire-burned forest, but it was, nonetheless, true. If the opening-out went far enough, then small meadows—or prairies, as they were called later—resulted, evoking another set of typical descriptive comments. As early as 1654 Edward Johnson had observed that the thinness of the timber in parts of New England made the forest "like our Parkes in England"; and Adam Hodgson, on a journey from Natchez through central Mississippi, found that the forest was "delightful, open and interspersed with occasional small prairies and had the appearance of an English Park." [66] While these were mainly aesthetic judgments on the type of landscape the observers liked and found to be familiar, nevertheless they were also comments on the type of fire-opened forest encountered, and which we know were far more common than the dense, impenetrable, dark woods beloved of the Romantic imagination.

The Creation of Grasslands

Wherever fire was more frequent and devastating, completely open ground was the result, even though rainfall was sufficient to support trees. The sparsely growing, parklike forest gave way to what were variously called plains, barrens, openings, deserts, prairies, or, particularly in the South, savannas—all individual patches of open grassland in the main body of the forest, varying from a few acres to many thousands of square miles. Their location and extent varied, but the further west one moved the more frequent the clearings became, and they merged into the true treeless prairies. But one did not have to go that far west to find large "openings" in the forest. Some of the first major prairies encountered were on the Rappahannock River in Virginia, and particularly along the Potomac to the Shenandoah Valley. Traveler after traveler through the valley commented on the "large level plains," "the large spots of meadows and savannas wherein are hundreds of acres without any trees at all," and the "firing of the woods by the Indians." Similarly, the enormous and anomalous openings of the bluegrass country of western Kentucky, later invaded by the European plant *Poa pratensis,* excited much comment,[67] as did other openings in eastern New York that the Iroquois kept open by repeated firing in order to promote grass growth for game.[68] There were further examples in the "prairie belt" of Alabama and adjacent parts of Missouri.[69] Over a century ago, Asa Gray, the noted botanist, was convinced that all the openings east of the Mississippi and of the Missouri up to Minnesota "have been either greatly extended or were even made treeless under Indian occupation and annual burnings."[70]

Burning promoted the browse for the three major animal food species: the bison, the elk, and the white-tailed deer, the latter being the major food source in the eastern forests from the beginning of human occupation.[71] "The aborigines of New England," said Timothy Dwight in 1821, "customarily fired the forests that they might pursue their hunting with advantage." Dozens of other commentators and eyewitnesses from John Smith in the early seventeenth century onward described, in various ways and with various details, what Mark Catesby witnessed in 1747 in the coastal plains and "desserts" of Florida and Carolina every October, when "deers, bears and other animals are drove by the raging fire and smoak, and being hemm'd in are destroyed in great numbers by their guns."[72]

The destruction of the forest by fire and the creation of individual openings did not approach in either impact or extent the destruction of the forest along its whole western edge. From Wisconsin south to Texas repeated firing by the nomadic hunting cultures of the Plains Indians sustained the grassland vegetation against forest encroachment and extended the grassland at the expense of the forest. Their object was to extend the range of game by continually burning the forest edge in order to prevent timber regeneration, as well as setting massive wildfires to drive the buffalo to convenient slaughtering places. Fire was of critical significance in altering faunal habitats, and as the forests were burned and opened out the buffalo, for example, spread throughout the continent, crossing the Mississippi via newly formed openings in about AD 1000, entering the South by the fifteenth century, and penetrating as far east as Pennsylvania and Massachusetts by the seventeenth century.[73]

Climatic conditions alone cannot be evoked to explain the origin and peculiar purity of the prairie grassland as a climax vegetation, just as it cannot be evoked to explain the expansion of the buffalo.[74] When fire was suppressed with European settlement, the forest began to encroach on these openings. For example, the "oak openings" of southwestern Wisconsin were reckoned to have decreased by nearly 60 percent between 1829 and 1854 following the control of fire; Herbert Gleason calculated that the oak-hickory forest advanced into the Illinois grasslands at between 1 and 2 mi in 30 years after fire ceased; and there were many other examples.[75] Not until there was complete occupation of the prairies for agriculture and the suppression of wildfires did the advance of the forest stop on its western edge. Most ecologists are now prepared to support the bold and unequivocal statement of Roger Anderson that the eastern prairies would have disappeared and have been replaced by forests "if it had not been for the nearly annual burning of these grasslands by the North American Indians" during the last 5,000 years.[76]

Altering the Forest Composition and Range

Frequent burning had one other permanent and far-reaching effect: it altered the composition and range of species in the forest by reducing their number and simplifying their biological components. For example, the extensive open loblolly *(Pinus taeda)*, longleaf *(P. palustris)*, and slash pine *(P. elliottii)* forests of the Southeast are thought to be a human-induced fire subclimax within the general deciduous region of the eastern woodlands. The repeated firing in the past had tended to propagate pyrophytic deformations with the characteristic needle-leafed adaptation, and cones that only opened with the heat of fire. Fire suppression has led to the invasion of the southern pine forest by hardwoods, such as oak and hickory, and the pines have reached the last stage of their succession, have declined, and are being replaced by relatively stable hardwood communities.[77] The southern pines are only one example of many tree species, as widely distributed as sequoia, Douglas fir *(Pseudotsuga menziesii),* and ponderosa pine *(P. ponderosa)* in the West, to red and eastern white pine *(P. resinosa and P. strobus)* in the North, that while not strictly fire types, require fire to hasten and ensure their reproduction.[78]

At the same time, fire encouraged fire-tolerant and sun-loving species along with the conditions favorable for the growth of edible, gatherable foods, such as strawberries, blackberries, and raspberries, all of which fostered human occupation and made further alteration of the forest composition more likely. Moreover, native plants like ground nuts and leeks were dispersed more widely.[79]

Everywhere in the forests of North America, fire setting together with other modification activities represented a "long and steady pressure by human action on plant assemblages."[80]

AFTER THE ICE: THE TROPICS

The forests of the tropics, no less than those of the temperate world of Europe and North America, bear unmistakable signs of human manipulation and change. Yet even as late as the 1950s their reputation for being untouched and pristine was as strong as it was in 1450. In 1958 the celebrated tropical botanist-ecologist, Paul Richards, thought that until recently humans had had "no more influence on the vegetation than any of the other animal inhabitants," which produced the counterargument by Carl Sauer that humans had "been around from the beginning" and that burning, swiddens, and the manipulation of species had modified the forest extensively everywhere to make it largely anthropogenic in form and composition. Similarly, a few years earlier, Gerardo Budowski had stuck his neck out and declared the adjacent and intermingled tropical savannas were the result of a "sequence of forest felling and repeated burnings."[81]

The palynological and historical record of the tropical forest is complicated by many factors, particularly by the type of *forest* and the type of *disturbance,* as well as by there simply being less information. No forest is uniform, and the tropical forest is strikingly not so. Broadly speaking, there are humid, moist forests where the fire record is quickly obliterated by rapid and luxuriant growth, and on their margins there are seasonally dry forests or savannas where seasonal droughts and frequent natural fires complicate the record of change. It is likely that these latter forests would have been much more extensive in the drier past, extending into areas that are now moist forest. Second, even more than in the temperate forests of the Northern Hemisphere, pure foraging without some sort of cultivation was rare, and consequently to attribute anthropogenic disturbance to hunter-gatherers alone while ignoring slash-and-burn activities is erroneous.

Despite all the complications, tropical forest pollen diagrams everywhere show a reduction of primary forest taxa, and a rise in secondary (often ephemeral) forest taxa and other elements of seral vegetation such as tree ferns and Gramineae (grasses).[82] There is no way of knowing conclusively whether the cause of the change is natural, by lightning strikes for example, or tree falls, which are very common, or if it is humanly induced. Thus, fires in the northern Amazon basin at 6000 BP and southeastern Venezuela at circa 3500 BP that have thinned and altered the forest may be a result of either natural or human activities, but are often associated with human settlement. On the other hand, John Flenley quotes abundant evidence of disturbance by burning in the Americas and in West and East Africa for 3000 BP; Sumatra, 6000 BP; Taiwan, 4000 BP; Fiji, 3000 BP; and New Guinea, 6000–9000 BP, all accompanied by agricultural activity.[83]

In the south and central Amazon basin there is widespread evidence of charcoal, so much so that Christopher Uhl would go so far as to say that "it is difficult to find soils that are not studded with charcoal." It is possible, of course, that some of this is a result of natural lightning fires, but it is more likely to be clearing for swiddens and the manipulation of the forest for useful plants (see chapter 3).[84] Indeed, ethnobotanists like Darrell Posey, William Balée, Anna Roosevelt, and Laura Rival assert that much of the Amazonian forest is a "cultural artefact" or "anthropogenic," as native peoples have developed successive resource management strategies to cope with fluctuations in population dynamics and disturbances. It is a mosaic of different ages, compositions, and structures made all the more complex by the propagation of useful tree crops like nuts, palms, and bamboo, so that plant diversity has increased. Posey concludes that even in areas where Indians have disappeared, "the hand of human manipulation and management may still be evident." Similar arguments for human manipulation can be made for the Maya lowlands and other parts of tropical Central America.[85] It is estimated that today up to 40 percent of the tropical forest is secondary forest resulting from periodic clearing, and almost all the remainder has suffered from some sort of modification.[86]

Evidence of the modification of forest on the tropical savanna-forest interface by fire, and the probable extension of grassland at the expense of forest, is widespread, with good examples coming from Australia and Africa.[87] And even better examples are the grasslands and forests of the humid tropics in Central and South America. In a review of the human impact in these ecotones, Denevan presents an account of changing forest composition, forest opening, and lack of forest "purity" that parallels the story of temperate North America.[88] For example, the extensive pine forests of the cooler upland regions of Nicaragua, Guatemala, and Mexico are analogous to the pines of the U.S. South. If the seedlings escape destruction by fire during their first 3–7 years, the trees grow and are fire resistant; but if fire is subsequently absent, as happened with the abandonment of land with the Indian decline, then the forest is invaded by mixed hardwoods that gradually replace the pines. The pines, therefore, are a humanly induced fire species.

Similarly, many of the savannas and small openings of South America are humanly induced. Putting aside the extensive *campas cerrado* of Brazil which are partially produced by reason of being on toxic oxisols developed on peneplains, or the *llanos* of the Orinoco lowlands which are periodically inundated floodplains or consist of soils of impeded drainage, there is evidence that the edges of many savannas are affected by anthropogenic action.[89] J. G. Myers went so far as to say, "I have never seen in South America a savanna, however small and isolated or distant from settlement which did not show signs of more or less frequent burning," although that might include "natural" burns.[90]

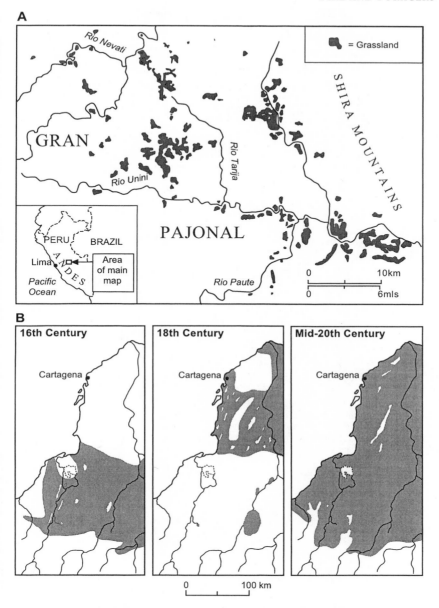

Figure 2.5 The creation of grasslands: *A, pajonales* in Peru; and *B,* savannas in Colombia. *Source:* based on Scott, 1977, and Gordon, 1957.

However, it is in the smaller "openings" that there is clear documentation of human origin. The small, scattered grasslands, or *pajonales,* on the Andean foothills of east-central Peru were created, maintained, and extended by the Campa Indians (fig. 2.5). They are probably abandoned dooryard swiddens, but repeated burning is practiced because the low grass cover is of more immediate use close to home (as well as for all the defensive, game, antipest, and foraging reasons noted before) than is the rank secondary forest growing on exhausted soils.[91]

Further north in the Andean foothills of northwestern Colombia, there is clear documentary evidence that in the basins of the San Jorge, Cauca, and Sinu rivers, the open savanna that greeted the first Europeans in the early sixteenth century had reverted to forest by 1750 with Indian decline, except around a few surviving settlements (fig. 2.4). Then the emergence of European settlement and cattle ranching around the growing colonial settlement of Catagena in the north created new savannas. Eventually, both the Indian and European savannas became one large cleared area by the mid-twentieth century.[92]

Nearly half a century ago Grahame Clark suggested fancifully that if one could have flown over northern Europe during Mesolithic times it would have been doubtful if

> more than an occasional wisp of smoke from some camp fire, or maybe a small cluster of huts or shelter by a river bank or old lake bed, would have advertised the presence of man: in all essentials the forest would have stretched unbroken, save only by mountain, swamp or water, to the margins of the sea.[93]

But the chances are that one would have seen something very different: massive smoke plumes, and clearings, and mosaics of different age planting and structures in a forest that was anything but unbroken and uninhabited. The same would have been even truer over the forested areas of the Americas at any time before 1492. Perhaps, then, one can agree with Denevan, who concludes that in Latin America "there are no virgin tropical forests today, nor were there in 1492."[94] Whether it was Europe, the Americas, Australia, New Zealand, or Asia, it was a far more altered world than we have ever thought.

Chapter 3

The First Farmers

It is almost incredible, in retrospect, how rapidly people seized the opportunities afforded by post glacial conditions.
—WILLIAM R. DICKINSON, "The Times Are Always Changing: The Holocene Saga" (1995)

There is reason to believe that the surface of the habitable earth, in all climates and regions which have been the abodes of dense and civilized populations, was, with few exceptions, already covered with a forest growth when it first became the home of man."
—GEORGE PERKINS MARSH, *Man and Nature* (1864)

THE CHANGES in the forest achieved by fire and foraging were extended and multiplied by agriculture, which, more often than not, destroyed trees—not necessarily forever, but certainly in the short run. Yet one can suppose that early humans did not want to labor at chopping down trees in order to get enough food to live. The evidence is that hunter-gathers had enough food to eat, and that their diet was much more varied and nutritious than is commonly thought. Fire had added a certain predictability to productivity, and waterside locations were particularly favorable with their yield of shellfish, fish, and fowl. Life was anything but hand-to-mouth; not the "brutish nightmare it seemed to many nineteenth century observers," but secure, easy, and productive.[1]

In fact, agriculture was more time consuming and labor intensive than hunting and foraging, with its multitude of essential tasks such as tree felling, soil preparation, weeding, manuring, and irrigation. How laborious is difficult to assess, but we get a clue from the number of person-days required to clear forest of different biomass densities (and hence ages) in western Africa (fig. 3.1). Obviously there are many caveats relating to what is meant by "clearing"—the hardness of the timber, the degree to which fire can be incorporated into the operation, and the type of agricultural regime in question. But all the indications are that clearing land took up much of the laboring year, and that it was anything but an incidental and leisurely task.[2]

Nonetheless, agriculture had many advantages, one of the most important of which was that it freed people from their perpetual quest for food and released their energies to pursue other occupations. No civilization, past or present, has existed without a sound agricultural base. Hence it was agriculture and, in time, its associated integrated pastoral

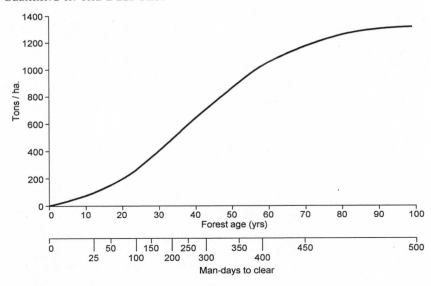

Figure 3.1 Approximate amount of labor required (in person-days) to clear forest of varying age and associated density (in tons moist weight/ha), West Africa. *Source:* based on Wilks, 1978: 504.

sector, that made the greatest and most permanent impact on the world's forests because it led to the replacement of one vegetation cover by another. The appearance of the plow and other soil-breaking instruments in the late fourth millennium BC marked a major shift toward increased clearing. Additionally, in the Old World, a number of in-built feedback loops, primarily those related to traction and the controlled manipulation of stock, were set in motion that had far-reaching effects.[3]

But it is difficult to ascertain the impact of the First Farmers on the forest. Evidence of clearing is fragmentary because it has usually been regarded as the incidental accompaniment of agriculture. Often, and certainly in earliest times, there are no literary sources; and, as has been emphasized before and will continue to be throughout this book, clearing leaves nothing in its place and very few remains from which to reconstruct events. In addition, it is difficult to summarize meaningfully the multitude of individual events that took place over such a vast sweep of space and time. It is truly a case of what Estyn Evans called "dark ages in time and dark areas in space."[4] But having said that, archeological, pollen, and macro-plant remains (plant remains larger than pollen grains and phytoliths) do exist in sufficient abundance for one to build up a general picture of considerable environmental impact and change.

DOMESTICATION AND CENTERS OF AGRICULTURE

The process of domestication that ultimately led to agriculture (and hence clearing) and a more sedentary existence is a mystery: little is known about how, when, where, and why it happened.[5] There was no "big bang" when the supposed meat-eating diet of "primitive" hunting humans was replaced by a more omnivorous diet of plant foods. All the evidence points to a gradual change that upsets the traditional ideas of, for example, Gordon Childe's concept of a "Neolithic Revolution," a rapid transition from food procurement to food production, and of the deeply-ingrained Western ideas about discrete "stages of civilization."[6]

From the very beginning of evolution, diet was mixed and plant and *not* animal sources of food were primary.[7] Similarities appear to be present between primates and early hominids in the diet and subsistence patterns that affected the collection, selection, dispersal, and storage of seeds and fruits, as well as in the gender division of hunting and gathering activities. Given these similarities, the idea of early *Homo sapiens* as solely a big-game hunter has fallen out of favor in recent years; human diet was not qualitatively different from primate diet. Also, like primate behavior, human food preferences and behavior patterns would have favored certain plants around camps. Natural vegetation would be disturbed and enriched, which encouraged the coevolution of species. A symbiosis developed between the ecological needs of plants and the food requirements of humans. It must have seemed, said Jacquetta Hawkes, "little short of miraculous" to preagricultural man to find that "the plants needed for food sprang up by his very huts and paths."[8]

In particular, hybrids thrive in niches created by dump heaps and on cleared land, where the "natural" successional process is disturbed and competition reduced.[9] Selection will favor those plants possessing parts that are both attractive to humans and easy to gather. Even before planting was practiced, the "unconscious selection by man of the plants with less efficient dispersal methods took place, since it was the seeds of these that were automatically more efficiently gathered." In this way, gathering changed imperceptibly into harvesting, and the first stages in the development of agriculture occurred involving the colonization of plants that were useful and had weedy tendencies; in other words, an ecological adaption—even toleration—to "open" situations, and to disturbed or unstable habitats of bare soil with few competitors.[10]

An important factor in the domestication process was defecation. The seeds of sweet corn, tomatoes, lemons, cucumbers, and many more edible plants, as well as the fruits of shrubs and trees, can pass intact through the human as well as animal gut (it may even enhance their reproductive vigor), and can be subsequently dispersed and reproduced. In the case of humans the peripheral latrine areas common to virtually all societies would become new gardens in time.[11]

Unconscious as well as conscious selection promoted useful plants, and the greater the size of the population the greater its effectiveness as a modifying and dispersal agent. Thus, *incidental domestication,* the coevolutionary, "selective" relationship between a nonagricultural society and the plants on which it fed, gave way to *specialized domestication,* in which humans were directly interacting with the plants on which they fed, for example by either aiding dispersal or destroying unwanted plants, thus establishing a symbiotic relationship with a community of coevolved plants. This finally culminated in *agricultural domestication* with conscious actions like plant selecting, the destruction of the forest clearing by fire or ax, weeding, and irrigating.[12] Even the cutting of nonvalued trees for firewood created a gap for competing species to flourish.

It goes without saying that large-scale agricultural domestication not only altered and often degraded ecosystems but also led to a system of management that increased the

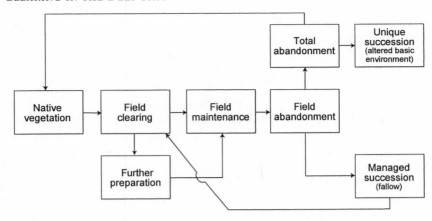

Figure 3.2 Effect of agricultural disturbance on natural vegetation. *Source:* Minnis, 1978: 349.

yield of energy available to the cultivators. This set in motion a whole range of related changes. Most agricultural systems (simple or complex), says Paul Minnis, "share a similar general model of effects on local vegetation" (fig. 3.2). First the "pristine" vegetation is cleared by chopping and burning, and the soil is broken and disturbed with deliberate agricultural engineering ranging from plowing, to terracing, to making mounds for tubers. Next the artificial, often less diverse, and consequently less stable ecosystem of cultivated fields must be maintained. Because it is a simplified ecosystem more human energy has to be bestowed on it in order to maintain fertility, check erosion, and combat disease. Third, after the termination of maintenance (with either abandonment or fallow) a successional cycle is set in motion. If initial disturbance has not been too radical or extensive, then the successional cycle of regenerated vegetation may be similar to the natural pattern; but because agriculture is so often characterized by overexploitation, the ecosystem is usually degraded and changed irreversibly. Each stage of exploitation leaves clues as to the human impact in the form of pollens, seeds (cultigens and weeds), charcoal, and soil degradation, in addition to humanly manufactured artifacts such as dwellings, tools, and shards.[13] All this is crucially important in understanding the deforestation process.

Thus, given the ubiquity and complex interactive cultural nature of the plant domestication processes, it is now thought that the centers of agriculture were multiple and widespread, and not a single "hearth" in the Middle East as postulated by Gordon Childe in his riverine-oasis thesis.

In the quest for beginnings Alphonse de Candolle's original observation in 1855 that agriculture originated in the three regions of "China, the south-west of Asia (with Egypt), and inter-tropical America," from which it then spread, was perceptive; it has been the basis of much contemporary thinking. Later, Nikolai Vavilov enlarged these regions to eight independent "hearths of domestication" (fig. 3.3). He reasoned that the regions of today that have the greatest number of varieties of edible plant species are likely to be the areas of that plant's original domestication. But he was never able to prove either that domestication had taken place or when or how it had occurred, other than to hypothesize that an increasing population needed more food.

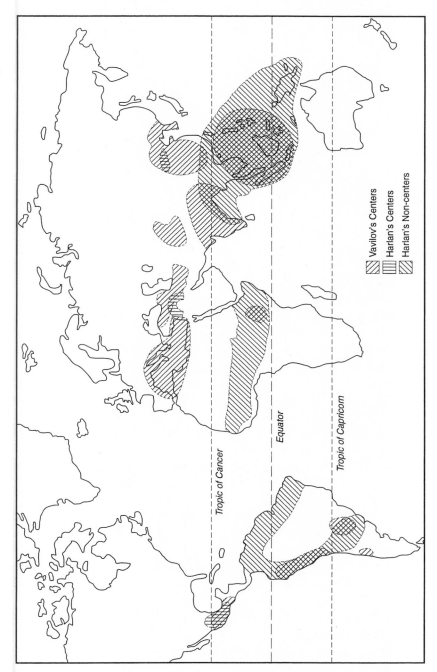

Figure 3.3 Centers of crop origin as suggested by Vavilov (1926), and Centers and Non-centers by Harlan (1971) and MacNeish (1992). *Source:* Harlan, 1971, and MacNeish, 1992.

Other hypotheses followed. Carl Sauer thought the origin of *all* agriculture was in the tropical woodlands of Southeast Asia, which seems unlikely. More recently, Jack Harlan has suggested that de Candolle got it just about right, and that there were just three small, clearly demarcated Centers of origin where a number of plants were domesticated in situ: in Mesoamerica (southern Mexico), the Near East (the Fertile Crescent), and northern China (Yangshao), all of which were "very definable in time and space." From these centers of abundance domestication dispersed over wide distances to places that had hitherto been defined as Centers but which Harlan designated "Non-Centers" on biological and archeological grounds. These were relatively large regions that consisted of important domesticated species from Centers and the other domesticated plants in situ. These included Andean and Amazonian South America, Egypt, and sub-Saharan Africa, and Southeast Asia and the South Pacific. In subsequent times Center and Non-Center may well have interacted with each other, but again, how and why is not clear. Harlan's three Centers are adhered to by Richard MacNeish, with one extra one in the Andean area. But his Non-Centers are slightly different.[14] The debate is not closed yet, as evidence that surfaced during the late 1980s suggests that the eastern woodlands of North America could well have been an additional independent center of plant domestication.

But such definitions of *Center* and *Non-Center* are of limited use because they say nothing about the temporal dimensions of change. In the most comprehensive and thorough review of the evidence in recent years, MacNeish proposed a complex explanatory model which he calls his Trilinear theory of primary, secondary, and tertiary developments.[15] Within the framework of four primary Centers (the Near East, the Far East, Mesoamerica, and the Andean region), where the majority of plants were initially domesticated, there were three hypothetical models of development (fig. 3.4). Starting from Hunting-Collecting Bands (System A) in Stage 1 at the top of the diagram, it is possible to reach the ultimate Stage 3 of the Agricultural Villager (System E), through the transitional Stage 2, via a variety of different routes (1–17) and their associated different intermediate Systems. For example, Horticultural Villagers (System C2) and Efficient Foraging Bands (System D) are just two possible intermediate Systems along the routes of development in the Secondary and Tertiary Models, and there could be much criss-crossing of routes. It recognizes the possibility that a forest foraging economy can exist in a number of different guises and can coexist with, or lead to, an agricultural economy.

It is not our task here to argue the pros and cons of Centers-of-Origin theories, or even MacNeish's Trilinear Model. Suffice it to say, earlier work is under attack as being simplistic and reductionist, and as subordinating the question of how and why domestication occurred to where and when it occurred. Domestication is not simply a biological phenomenon alone; it is inextricably bound up with broader issues of contingent and mutually dependent sets of specializations and technologies (with all their positive and negative feedback loops) that go to make up cultures and economies. Simply put, the process of plant domestication has taken a long time and has been gradual; there have been multiple origins and multiple paths of change; parallelism of farming innovation was not accompanied by simultaneous development; and cultural/economic change is not in synchrony with chronological change the world over.

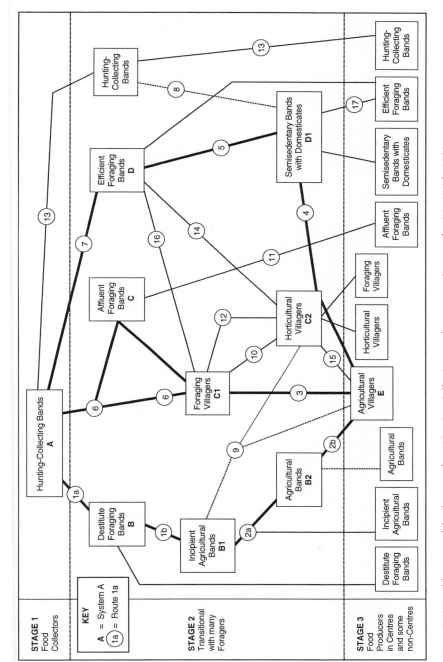

Figure 3.4 Possible routes of development from Hunting-Collecting to other systems. *Source:* after MacNeish, 1992.

More important for this study of global deforestation is that multiple evolutions of domestication occurred, with specific impacts on the surrounding forest vegetation of those regions. The nucleus of the Near East spread, in time, to the forested lands of temperate Europe; the nucleus of Mesoamerica (and the Andean Region?) spread into the tropical forested lands of South America and, possibly, in time to those of North America; and the nucleus of North China spread into the temperate and tropical forested lands of eastern and southeastern Asia, all with devastating effect. Sub-Saharan Africa was another Non-Center. We know a great deal about the first two Centers, but very little about the latter two.

Domestication was the beginning of agriculture and settled life. Next to the control of fire it was the start of the second great cultural revolution in human affairs and the prelude to the first great attack on the forests.

THE NEOLITHICS AND FOREST CLEARING

While the Mesolithic foragers were successfully manipulating European vegetation to cope with the dual problems of increasing population and increasing forest density during the warm, moist Atlantic period, the agricultural innovations of the "Neolithic" were emerging many thousands of miles away. From the core of the Middle East the agriculturalists spread spectacularly, first into Anatolia, Greece, between 7000 and 6000 BC and then in spurts and halts into forested central and western Europe after circa 5600–5500 BC[16] (fig. 3.5).

The economic and social complexity of this punctuated movement into the European "peninsula" is best understood by dividing it into the useful generic terms of the "Primary" and "Consequent" Neolithic. The "Primary Neolithic" ran from about 5500–4400 BC. The early farmers were known as the Linear Pottery Culture (*Linearbandkeramik,* or LBK) because of the distinctive material cultural trait of simple, round ceramics decorated with incised and later punched linear, ribbonlike ornament. Then, from circa 4400–3300 BC there followed the "Consequent Neolithic" into the rest of northern and western Europe and the Alpine Lake region, represented primarily by the Funnel Beaker Culture (*Trichterrandbecher,* or TRB) farmers, so called because of their distinctive pottery, which featured a flared rim. They displaced–or, far more likely, absorbed—the Mesolithic indigenous peoples who adopted agricultural techniques.[17] Both groups displayed a great variety of form and organization as they progressed from simple food collection, through sedentary agriculture with associated foraging, to more recognizable agricultural villages, as suggested in Stages 1 and 2 in MacNeish's Trilinear Model (fig. 3.4).

The original idea that the early Neolithics practiced a swidden regime of rotational burning and cropping (*Wanderbauertum* or *Brandwirtschaft*), never staying in the same area for more than a few years because of soil exhaustion, is now discredited. The idea started with V. Gordon Childe, who labeled the primary Neolithics "primitive agriculturalists" who, therefore, must have practiced "primitive agriculture" as did "shifting agriculturalists" in the contemporary tropics. The hypothesis was supported by the influential archeologist Grahame Clark, who stated categorically that

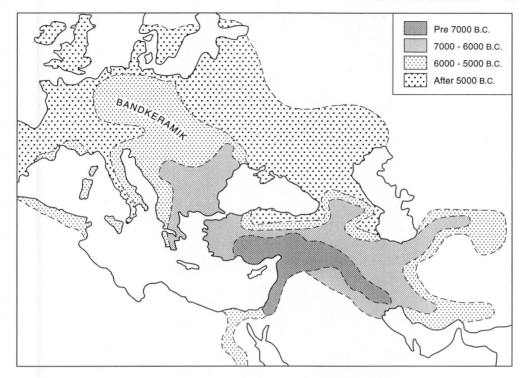

Figure 3.5 Spread of agriculture/settlement in Europe and western Asia during the early Holocene. *Source:* after Sherratt, 1980: 108.

> [there could be] no question of initiating systematic, permanent clearance and the forma-
> tion of settled fields. Their approach was tentative and their agriculture extensive. Patches
> of forest would have been cleared, sown, cropped, and after a season or two allowed to re-
> vert to the wild, while the farmers took in a new tract.[18]

Pollen profiles of anthropogenic indicator species interbedded with charcoal from Denmark in Johannes Iversen's classic *landnam* (literally, "taking of land") example (discussed
below) seemed to verify this hypothesis, and the later vogue of Ester Boserup's thesis of
the intensification of agrarian systems with population pressure bolstered the hypothesis
intellectually.[19] However, recent research shows that settlement was far more sedentary
and stable than once thought, with lasting effects on the forests and soils.

Primary Neolithic Settlement, circa 5500–3500 BC

First settled were the fertile, glacially derived, well-drained, windblown fine soils—the
loess—which spread in a broad but intermittent band across the Continent from northern France to the Ukraine, with a large outlier in the Hungarian Basin. The loess did not
have an open, steppelike vegetation as free from forest "as the prairies of North America," as was once thought by Robert Gradmann and many others. It was covered with a

mixed deciduous forest of mainly oak mixed with lime and beech, with greater proportions of lime in the north and oak in the south. In places the forest presented a dense,
closed canopy through which little sunlight penetrated for most of the year, and the
autumnal fall of leaf litter gave dense layers of humus. Admittedly, the permeable, dry
character meant that much of it was probably only lightly wooded even during the Atlantic period of thickening cover, though the riverside sites would have supported a dense
forest.[20]

It was this varied mosaic of different forest densities on the flat to gently rolling topography of the loess that was attractive to the Linear Pottery Culture, because when
cleared its natural fertility made it especially suited to wheat and barley. Colonization
proceeded by a careful use of restricted niches favorable for settlement—the *Siedlungs-
kammern*—each new cell probably a kin-related daughter settlement created as population increased, or migrated through the motivations and aspirations of households. It did
not occur in a continuous wave moving at a steady 18 km per 25 years across the face of
Europe, and channelled into the supposed forest-free sites, as implied in earlier accounts.[21] The evidence of the reassessment of Neolithic settlement stability and its consequent impact on the forest is threefold: the stability and longevity of settlements; the
complexity of farming; and the sustaining of crop yields.

Typically, settlements consisted of substantial timber-framed and -clad longhouses,
about 6 m wide and 8 m–50 m long, occupied by both humans and animals; livestock
were often stall fed, as there was little open ground for grazing. The longhouse timbers
were split by stone wedges, and the rigidity of the structure achieved by setting uprights
in deep postholes. The farmstead houses were clustered in groups of between a dozen to
40 or 50, sometimes surrounded by a ditch, bank, and even palisade, surrounded in turn
by fields in which was cultivated wheat (mainly einkorn and emmer), with lesser amounts
of barley, peas, lentils, and flax.[22] Groups of clusters were strung out in a roughly linear
fashion alongside watercourses, each group forming a cell that was separated from the
next one by areas of lower fertility.[23] Until the 1970s the significance of these longhouses
was ignored. Yet excavations show that some had been occupied continuously for several
hundred if not a thousand years.[24] The stability and longevity of the habitations is simply not consistent with shifting agriculture.

The houses and field clusters were overwhelmingly located on the high-quality loessic
soils, with 85 percent of 1,142 neolithic sites in eight sample areas in southern and central Germany being so placed, the proportion never falling below two thirds in any area.
In many cases the clusters were strung out alongside streams on flat terrain or at the transition between floodplain and lower watershed slopes, habitats that maximized soil mixtures and water supply.[25]

The floodplains had a dense timber cover, and the trees were chopped down with flint
and polished stone axes, which modern experiments show were quite efficient.[26] All but
the most desirable timber, which would be reserved for the construction of the elaborate
longhouses and palisades, would, presumably, have been burned in situ, the addition to
the soil of ash and residual nutrients being a positive advantage to cultivation. Although
not a part of some migratory cycle, periodic slash-and-burn clearing in the surrounding
forests would have provided browse, and even the ground for an occasional crop. If burn-

ing and animal grazing were intensive enough, they would have thinned and ultimately eliminated forests in some areas, processes which continued unabated until the early Bronze Age (circa 1000 BC).

Second, the evidence of sustained, mixed farming bolsters the ideas of stability and hence impact. The slash-and-burn hypothesis was based on the assumption that the first farmers could not clear enough forest to grow the amount of grain they needed, and that continuous cultivation could not be sustained. However, the large number of cattle found at many sites (outnumbering all other stock by 2:1) suggests that food risk was diversified and diet was supplemented by animal products, such as meat, milk, blood, and cheese. Meat is an obvious enough product from cattle at this time, but milk is not. This is where the contingent technologies mentioned earlier were important. Andrew Sherratt suggests that milk was an early manifestation of the "Secondary Products Revolution." The lactose intolerance of much of world's populations has been assumed (erroneously) to apply to early Neolithic populations. However, a vitamin D deficiency in a cereal-based diet in areas of low sunlight (leading to rickets) would have given a selective advantage to those who had the ability to consume milk. Milking presented "an advantageous way of using the rich pasture grasses that would have colonised abandoned fields in temperate Europe." Moreover, milk is a highly efficient form of animal exploitation, giving four to five times the amount of protein and energy from the same amount of feed as would the exploitation of meat.[27] With the conversion of milk to cheese, yogurt, and other products, the problem of digestion was mitigated further, and there is considerable artifactual evidence that cheese making was practiced.

Livestock, far from being few in number and playing a minor role in the economy, as Childe suggested, were numerous and important. If the general reproductive dynamics of livestock are considered in detail, and the depredations of disease, predation, and escape are taken into consideration, then large numbers were needed in order to have sufficient breeding stock to make it economically feasible to extract milk and meat products, have available some working beasts, and ensure reproduction. Herds of between 10 and 20 are too small; 30 to 50 are more realistic.[28] Again, this has implications for forest clearance; the grazing, browsing, and trampling effects of herds of this size on forest composition and wildlife must have been considerable.

The role of livestock in subsistence is substantiated by an investigation of optimal farming strategies. Susan Gregg's simulation model of the crop yields and dietary requirements of a typical primary Neolithic village of six households, incorporating various assumptions on yields and consumption, shows that the optimal strategy was for grain to provide between 50 and 70 percent of the calorific intake, which could be achieved on plots of between 0.35 and 0.45 ha. A greater dependence on grain would have meant larger allotments and therefore excessive labor inputs. Also, in good years there would have been unabsorbable surpluses that could not be disposed of by consumption or exchange; but by the same token the probability of crop failure would also have increased, leading to potential famine. The likelihood is, then, that within certain limitations of time, labor, and availability of seed, the farmers assumed a "worst case" scenario and overproduced. Any shortfall in diet was made up by animal products and foraging for wild products.[29]

Finally, continuous cropping on loess and deep humus- and nutrient-rich soils was sustained with only a slight reduction in yields over long periods. There was some appreciation of the benefits of alternating cereals with legumes and intermingling stock and the fertilizing effects of the nutrient-rich autumn river floods, as well as taking advantage of the downwash of fertile soils from gently sloping surrounding hills.[30]

In summary, rather than being shifting cultivators, the first Neolithic farmers were intensive floodplain hoe horticulturalists, who also pastured adjacent meadows and ran stock in the surrounding forest. Seasonal shortfalls could be combated by diversification, the wild products of the forest (e.g., hazelnuts, beechnuts, berries) being abundant and crucial. It is possible that the original foraging Mesolithics were not eliminated but integrated into the new economic system, providing foraging "know-how" and labor during the critical agricultural periods of late winter and early spring, and exchanging forest-gathered wild crops.

Consequent Neolithic Settlement, 4400–3300 BC

By about 4400 BC or a little earlier, and for at least another thousand years, growing numbers of Neolithic farmers and stockherders (the Funnel Beaker Pottery, or TBR [*Trichterrandbecher*] Culture) spread further west and north onto the complex mixture of glacially derived outwash of lighter silts and sands (giving heathland) and heavy, sticky clays of the North European Plain and into Scandinavia and the British Isles. The forest cover of oak, lime, and beech was even denser than on the loess to the south.

Existing settlements on the loess continued much as before, and with the development of the light scratch-plow farming expanded rapidly in areas of lighter, sandy soils, like central Jutland. But these light soils could not withstand prolonged cultivation, even with the application of manure; and the existence of Bronze Age tumuli under forests in many parts of the Continent show that once exhausted, the fields were abandoned forever. Elsewhere, dispersal into the higher forested interfluvial slopes and interiors signalled an expansion of stock rearing, especially sheep and, more important, a big increase in pigs, whose omnivorous foraging and rooting habits had an adverse effect on forest regeneration. There was even the occasional clearing in order to gain more land for cultivation during a period of what seems to have been substantial population increase.[31]

Plowing was advantageous because it increased fertility by aiding soil aeration and allowing the incorporation of new organic elements into the tilth (especially when stock were kept on the land), leading to greater intensification of production. On the other hand, repeated plowing and cross-plowing with the scratch ard pulverized the soil and repressed the regeneration of the natural vegetation. In time the deterioration of the lighter soils and the population expansion forced the new wave of settlers to attack the fertile but more labor-intensive heavy, sticky clays, alluviums, and loams of the Northern Plains, almost always covered with dense forest. To cope with such soils a heavier form of ard capable of turning the sod came into use. Animals now figured even more largely in the economy, not only for the production of meat, milk, and wool, but also for traction (mostly oxen but some evidence of horses) to pull ards and carts, and help in forest clearing.[32] Human labor was now augmented by a factor of up to four or five by animal power, and tasks previously too arduous to be undertaken by humans could be contemplated. Prime timbers could be selected and dragged or "skidded" out of the forest. Animal power and animal manure aided productivity on good land and made economical the preparation of marginal land from which only a poor yield might have been expected. Consequently, the dependence on floodplain habitats diminished. Plowing may also have assisted in the establishment of tree crops.[33] Accompanying these changes came the planting of winter-grown cereals and new crops such as rye, and the development of field systems.[34]

The "package" of innovations that came from the east into forested Europe was interactive and had many feedback loops. Although other areas of the world had animals integrated into their economy, it was temperate Europe that had the plow, with its implied logic of extending the area under cultivation, even at the expense of lower yields, and the sustaining of a large pastoral sector on the fallow. "It was this linkage," maintains Sherratt, "that built in a cumulative advantage to forest clearance, and made possible the expansion of livestock rearing and the integration of new practices."[35] It was no accident that horses and wool sheep spread across Europe in the wake of the plow, which again accelerated the rate of forest clearance. But the most significant development of the plow was that it enabled settlers to tackle the heavier, forested soils.

The use of the plow put a premium on large areas of cleared land and therefore trees had to be felled. From about 4000 BC onward, the simple, wedgelike, stone "shoe-last adzes" of the primary Neolithic were being replaced by a true ax technology in flint and polished stone. The mining of ax flints became common across northern, forested Europe, the output of mines being estimated as over 400,000 ax heads annually. The flint of Grand Pressigny, France, is found throughout the previously wooded areas of that country. The mines at Krzemionki, the largest of the Polish mining centers, are even more instructive (fig. 3.6). Finds for the period between 4000 and 3400 BC spread over 100 km; those between 3400 and 2800 BC spread over 800 km. This expansion is a measure of the value and utility of the high-quality flints, and gives evidence of the new scale of the attack on the forests from the mid-fourth millennium onward.[36]

Put together, then, the evidence of Neolithic occupation over the space of some 2,500 years is of a more stable, sedentary society of "considerable stability and continuity,"[37] and a more diversified economy than that thought up to now, that must have made intensive use of the dominant deciduous forest cover and its many resources. Some measure of that forest use and destruction can be gleaned from the simulation of the nutritional requirements, risks, and optimal farming strategies of a typical 6-household, 30-person settlement (fig. 3.7). Such a settlement would have needed to plant 13.2 ha of wheat and run a 40-head herd of cattle with 40 sheep/goats. Assuming a 30-year life for each of the 6 houses, the need to reconstruct one house every five years, and a 60-year forest regeneration cycle, about 4.5 ha of woodland would be reserved for houses, outbuildings, and garden plots.[38] Enormous quantities of fuelwood would have been needed: about 20 cords (a cord is a cubic measure of $4 \times 4 \times 8$ ft or 128 ft^3) to heat the house during winter, and a further 2 cords for cooking throughout the year. On the assumption that a well-managed woodlot of good burning timber could provide 2.5 cords/ha/yr, then each house would require a 8.8-ha woodlot, and the typical modal settlement of 6 families a total of 52.8 ha. Oak and beech burn well with little smoke, an advantage in

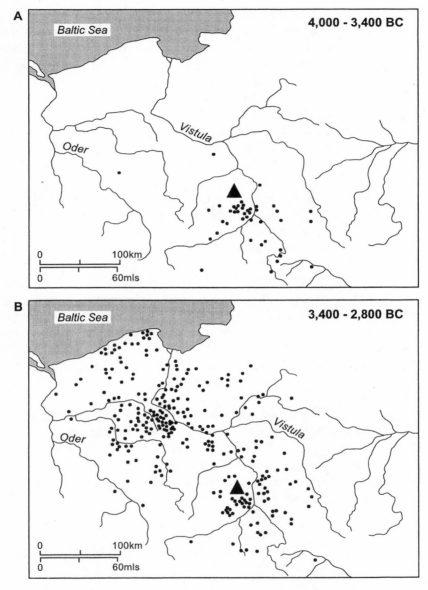

Figure 3.6 Distribution of axes of banded flint in Poland, around the mining center of Krzemionki Opatowskie: *A,* in the TRB period (4000–3400 BC); and *B,* in the Globular Amphora period (3400–2800 BC). *Source:* after Lech and Leligdowicz, 1980, and modified by Sherratt, 1986: 9.

the chimney-less longhouses; but if only wood of poor burning quality were available, then the woodlot would have been proportionately greater.[39] In addition, the livestock would require 18.18 ha of pastureland (cleared forest?), 19.66 ha of natural meadows, and 2.56 km² for forest browse, which could reasonably be doubled in size to guard against overgrazing the forest resource in a locationally fixed settlement. It is possible that

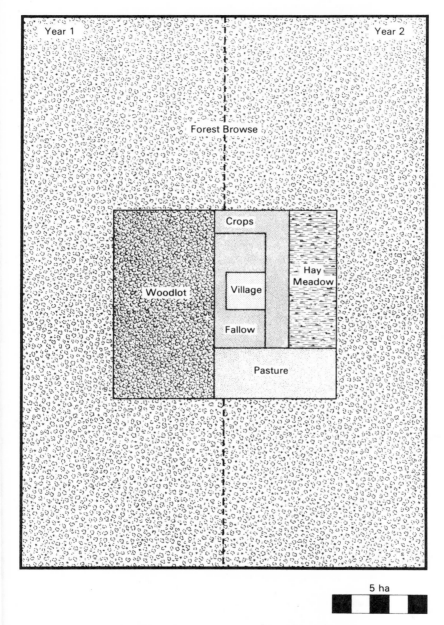

Figure 3.7 A hypothetical Neolithic village settlement in the forest and its timber needs. *Source:* based on Gregg, 1988: 165.

a cultivation cycle of one year occurred. Thus, each group of 30 persons needed a minimum of just over 6 km² of woodland to survive, a staggering 20 ha per person.[40] Even if this calculation is even only half correct, the impact on the early European forest must have been enormous.

The *Landnam* Conundrum, 2500–2200 BC

All the above evidence on Neolithic stability and continuity runs counter to Iversen's influential idea of the *landnam,* or "land-taking," phase, which typically was slash-and-burn, shifting agriculture in a roughly 50-year cycle.[41] *Landnam* had three stages (fig. 3.8). Stage 1 was marked by initial clearance, a decrease of the pollen of the high-canopy forest trees, and a brief appearance of herbaceous plants. Stage 2 was marked by a decline of lime *(Tilia)* and ash *(Franxinus excelsior)* and a low maxima for willow *(Salix)* and poplar *(Populus),* accompanied by a short burst of birch *(Betula),* which Iversen took to indicate clearing by fire rather than by ax. There was an increase in grasses and of anthropogenic indicators such as Ribwort plantain *(Plantago lanceolata).* Stage 3 was marked by a hazel *(Corylus)* maxima and the regeneration of the mixed oak forest, and as this gathered pace the cultural indicators disappear as the forest "healed." In all three stages small-scale arable cultivation and grazing is evident. The presence of *landnam* in Scandinavia was seen as evidence of its survival on the fringe of the European core, where it had been eliminated with time, and further ethno-historical documentation and pollen analysis seemed to substantiate it.[42]

But there are many unanswered questions in the *landnam* hypothesis. Foremost, its supposed widespread use in the loess and clays of the Northern Plain during the period of intensive cultivation, from the fifth- to early third-millennium-BC in Neolithic Europe has never been demonstrated as having been already in place, although Torsten Madsen claims evidence of its existence from circa 3500–2900 BC.[43] For most others the only evidence comes later, roughly 2500–2200 BC. Simply, says Andrew Sherratt, "the archaeological evidence . . . does not support such a scheme" of early shifting cultivation, and H. N. Jarman concludes that it cannot be "the dominant explanatory hypothesis" or "stage" in such a sophisticated agricultural development.[44] It is far more likely that slash-and-burn agriculture began to appear only when settlement moved into the poorer soils of the deciduous/coniferous transition on the margins of northern Europe and in upland areas such as the Carpathians during the third millennium.

In fact, *landnam* may *not have existed at all,* and if it did it might have been something other than it seemed.[45] Radiocarbon dating suggests that the typical clearing sequence stretched over at least 300 years and not 50, and that *landnam* might be an amalgam of many clearing phases. But if that were so, one would not expect the pollen curves to show such a clear regeneration sequence. Many of the original pollen diagrams were constructed on a percentage basis, but if the data are plotted on an absolute basis the picture alters completely, to such an extent that the regeneration phenomenon is illusory. In addition, the differential dispersal and filtration of pollen at lake shore sites, where most Danish *landnam* settlement sites were located, would have most likely eliminated the characteristic *landnam* frequencies.

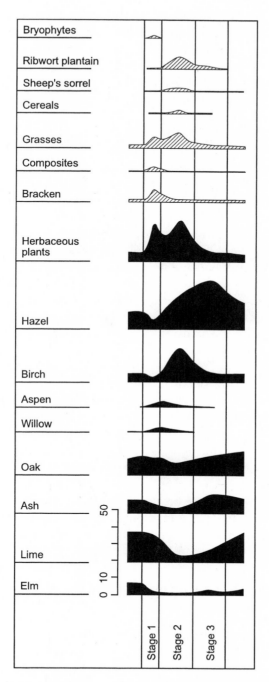

Figure 3.8 The classic *landnam* sequence. *Source:* after Iversen, 1956, modified by Bell and Walker, 1992: 165.

Also, all analogous Scandinavian historical slash-and-burn examples were on out-fields, and permanently cultivated infields always existed in conjunction with them. In the limited area of good soils in Scandinavia, continuous cereal growing was not possible without manure, but good land could not be forfeited for fodder crops for stock, which therefore had to graze on periodically fire-cleared outfields (from which an occasional crop was also taken). Recent slash-and-burn, therefore, suggests Peter Rowley-Conwy, was "one of a series of tactical solutions to a particular problem—not . . . a remnant of some once-universal stage of agriculture."

Finally, the cultivators did not have to move on because of declining yields. Cereals can be grown indefinitely on the same ground without major decline, provided the weeds are suppressed. The presence of simple scratch ards in Europe from an early date, and the presence of domesticated animals suggest that weed control by plowing and allowing stock to forage over the stubble was not impossible.

What, then, is *landnam*? Is it merely a statistical and filtration quirk of pollen? What-ever the answer, applying controlled fire in the forest to provide occasional grazing for domesticated stock or to encourage the browsing of wild ungulates, is a very likely prac-tice of the later Neolithics. Woodland management by coppicing is another possible ex-planation. Yet, while being skeptical about the supposed "stages," one must not dismiss the whole idea of weeds as anthropogenic indicators. They tell us a lot about how and when the forest was altered or cleared; they are like human footprints in the soil.[46] Burn-ing and tree felling by girdling occurred from time to time, but whether it was a part of long-term change in cultural patterns or a complex cycle within the existing farming is uncertain.

Up until the late 1970s, the dominance of the *landnam* theory colored most interpre-tations of the Neolithic encounter with the forest. Few people were as perceptive as the French historian Albert Grenier, who early on in the piece said that the great achieve-ments of the Neolithic age were "the domestication of animals, the invention of agricul-ture, and the conquest of land under forest." The concept of what Jarman has called "pre-historic man as *Homo ignoramus* has . . . been gradually eroded"; others would go so far as to say that the first farmers in Europe were "one of the most striking archaeological manifestations of later prehistory" because of the richness of their ceramic decoration, their technical achievements in building longhouses, and their introduction of a new, mixed farming economy based on introduced plants and animals in a hitherto forested environment, which they altered radically.[47]

"FROM PREDATION TO PRODUCTION": MESOAMERICA AND SOUTH AMERICA

De Candolle's suggestion that agriculture began independently in "inter-tropical Amer-ica" is supported by the impressive array of over 100 indigenous plants, including maize, potatoes, manioc/cassava, a variety of beans, squash/pumpkins, chili peppers, vanilla, sunflower, sweet potato, avocado, coca, pineapple, tomato, cacao, tobacco, and cotton. These plants and the technology used to cultivate them owed nothing to the Old World.[48]

In contrast with this wealth of edible plants, there were very few domesticated animals; only dogs (for food), muscovy duck, the turkey, some guinea pigs, and, in the central high

Andes, the camelids—the llama, the alpaca, and their wild relatives the guanaco and vicuna. Thus, the complex interaction between livestock and crops in some form of mixed farming so common in the Old World, and the developments associated with the "Secondary Products Revolution," had no counterpart here, with the exception, perhaps, of the herding of llama and alpaca in the high Andes, and the dependence on their dung for fertilizing potato patches. Everywhere the ubiquitous starchy maize was the main food, and dietary balance was achieved by the widespread consumption of high-protein beans.

Plant domestication and agriculture in the Americas had several other distinct qualities. There were multiple Centers of domestication, development was slow and evolutionary, and there was no unilinear trajectory of development. Areas were isolated from one another by mountain ranges, deserts, and broad tropical lowlands; consequently, there was great biological and cultural diversity.

There were two major independent Centers of plant domestication in the Western Hemisphere: the Andes and the cluster of subcenters in the arid and semiarid intermontane valleys of central Mexico. These have recently been joined by a new candidate—the eastern woodlands of North America.

The role of the first farmers in deforestation is difficult to piece together, and much must be inferred from the evidence of crop domestication and soil erosion. During the Preformative or Preclassic era from the sixth millennium BC onwards, and well into the Classic proper (usually defined as AD 300–900), there was a gradual move away from foraging and an increasing dependence on agriculture. It was, says Warwick Bray, an evolution "from predation to production," the ready store of wild edible plants being a major factor in this shift. The transition to a "full" agricultural society was not uniform, the arbitrary figure of a 50-percent contribution by farming to the total diet not coming until after 1000 BC in Tehuacan, about AD 1 in the drier region of southwestern Tamaulipas, and not at all in pre-Columbian times in southeastern Tamaulipas. Some form of sedentary village life seems to predate the onset of the half-and-half economy by at least 500 years, which is not inconsistent with MacNeish's Trilinear Model of development.[49]

The foraging economy had no particular effect on the vegetation. It was adapted to the flux of the seasons, and people did not stay long enough in any one place to plan a strategy of vegetation firing for thinning. In the wet season they congregated in large camps and collected cactus fruits and wild cereals, but broke up into smaller groups during the period of scarcity in the dry season, when anything that could be eaten was eaten, from mice and lizards, to snakes and grasshoppers.[50]

In time a number of significant interrelated developments appeared. It seems that humans had began to favor and select larger and more productive cultigens, including chili, manioc and beans, and particularly maize. It now "became increasingly worthwhile to clear away the wild vegetation in order to plant crops" and intensify farming with irrigation, draining, and terracing. In 3800 BC, cultivated maize produced no more calories than wild mesquite, but by 2000 BC a critical threshold was reached whereby yields in excess of 200 kilograms per hectare were achieved, an event which coincided with the appearance of the first villages and pottery makers.[51] As plants made a greater contribution to food supply, so greater population densities could be supported and remain in one place longer than before, with each change ratcheting up the change in the other to higher levels, affecting land cover as a consequence.

In the Oaxaca Valley, Anne Kirkby projected present population and agriculture back into the past.[52] Initially (circa 3000 BC) the yield of maize was no more than 90 kg–120 kg/ha, which was not sufficient for a commitment to full-time farming: the collection of wild mesquite pods would have given a superior nutritional yield. But when the critical threshold of 200 kg/ha was crossed somewhere between 2000 and 1500 BC, maize was of better value than wild foods. It was now worthwhile to clear the mesquite on the prime soils of the valley floor and replace it with maize fields, and settled agriculture became reasonable. As the cobs became larger with evolutionary selection, second-quality land could be incorporated into the agricultural system (often irrigated by elaborate water distribution schemes). By about 1000 BC, lower slopes covered by montane forest of oak and pine were being cleared, particularly for chili, avocado, and runner beans, allowing an increase in the "notional" number of people that could be supported. The territorial progression is shown in figure 3.9. In time other plants (e.g., squash) from highland Mexico,

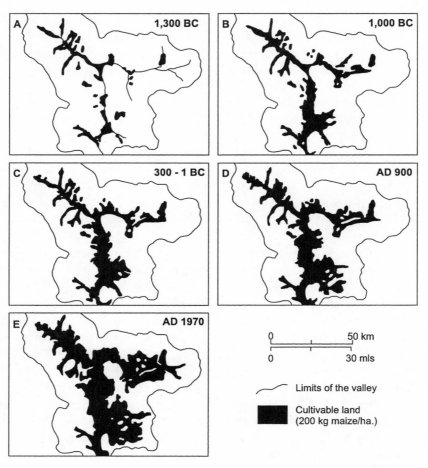

Figure 3.9 Cultivation of maize in the valley of Oaxaca, Mexico: *A,* 1300 BC; *B,* 1000 BC; *C,* 300–1 BC; *D,* AD 900; and *E,* AD 1970. *Source:* after Kirkby, 1973: 123–46.

but from outside the area, were introduced to add greater variety; and then later still, plants originating from lowland South America, such as manioc and sieva beans, appear in the system.

Highland Mexico

The gradual shift from foraging to food production was characterized by the development of villages and sedentary settlement. But the development of intensive agriculture during the late Formative or Preclassic era (circa 1000 BC–AD 300), through the Classic (AD 300–900) florescence of Aztec and related empires to the collapse of society with the Columbian encounter (circa 1520), was characterized by more dramatic cultural manifestations. The transition was now from villages to urban empires that were among the world's high civilizations, typified by the development of hieroglyphic writing, calendars, monumental architecture, complex irrigation and draining systems, ceremonial and religious centers, and the ascendancy of priestly elites sustained by oppressive political structures that wrung the most out of the land.[53] The greater variety of plants reduced risks and added greater nutritional variety to the diet; they also allowed more and more people to exist. On the eve of the Spanish Conquest, central Mexico had possibly 17 million people or more. There was a multiplicity of cultivated landscapes, and agricultural practices ranged from swidden to multicropped, hydraulically transformed wetlands.[54]

But it was the increasing tendency to intensively cultivate crops on high-rainfall steep forested slopes, with resultant degradation, that gives us some of the clearest indications of the onset of deforestation, which is almost complete in the central valley of Mexico today. Agricultural deforestation was exacerbated by the prolific use of wood in everyday life. One example comes from the Postclassical Tarascan or Purépecha culture, which had settled the basin of Lake Pátzcuaro, some 200 mi west of Mexico City, for about 3000 years. By the time of the Conquest the population had reached between 60,000 and 105,000, and there was severe overuse of the land and erosion.

The sixteenth-century chronicle *Relación de Michoacán* reveals that the Purépecha around the lake collected and milled timber for beams and boards for their temples and other buildings, gathered fuelwood for smelting metals and domestic hearths "until their backs were rubbed sore," and kept alight "huge bonfires" in the houses of priests and in temples during major religious festivals in order "to satiate with wood all the existing gods." Wood was so valuable and fire so interwoven into their culture and religion that their best timber sources were guarded, and the wood supplies of villages they planned to attack were carefully appraised beforehand. Moreover, leaders were appointed in each village whose prime duty it was to oversee the collection of wood; those who "four times had failed to bring wood for the fires when Cazonci [their ruler] had issued a general order throughout the province to gather wood" were put to death.[55]

Like the Purépecha, the inhabitants of Tenochtitlan were among those who kept ceremonial fires burning. Parts of the city were assigned to provide up to 50 youths, who, among other duties, were to serve the god Huitzilopochtli by "keeping the everlasting fire of the temple burning; bringing the wood which was to be burned." The timber depletion was such that by late Aztec times Montezuma II, the last Aztec monarch, prohibited woodcutting in a large area near San Bartolomé Coatepec.[56]

It is clear that wood cutting, selling, and working were recognized occupations in everyday pre-Hispanic life. Some hint of the complexity of wood use comes from the mid-sixteenth-century *Florentine Codex* of Fray Bernardino de Sahagún, which is the earliest and most extensive basic document that exists of pre-Hispanic life. A compendium of the life of the original Nahuatl-speaking groups of the valley of Mexico, which included the Aztec, the *Codex* reports that the wood seller was both timber procurer and timber pre-parer. He was variously

> a woodsman, a forester, a forest owner; and axe owner, a feller of trees, a wood-cutter, a user of the axe. He cuts with an axe; he fells trees—cuts them, tops them, strips them, splits them, stacks them.

A distinction was made between carpenters and woodcutters, the former selling dressed timber, the latter raw timber. Thus, the carpenter sold

> cedar, fir, pine, cypress. He sells large beams, small beams, wooden pillars, roofing, lintels, wooden columns, boards, planks, thin strips for hoops, thick boards.

The woodcutter, on the other hand, concentrated on

> oak, pine, alder, madroña; wood which produces colored flames—good burning wood; logs, toppings, kindling wood; bark—green or dry.[57]

Unfortunately, unlike many of the other occupations listed in the *Codex,* there are no il-lustrations of those based on wood.

Wood was clearly an essential commodity and entered into every aspect of Mesoamer-ican native life, in both symbolic and practical everyday ways. The peculiar tyranny of human sacrifice in their religious practices placed obligations for compulsory offerings to the gods so that documents pertaining to the age are replete with references to fire, smoke, and the labor of gathering wood.

The environmental outcome of timber stripping and collecting and the almost obses-sional scavenging for wood are revealed dramatically by radiocarbon dating for sedi-ments from the mountain-girdled Lake Pátzcuaro basin, which lies about 2,036 m above sea level. The 124-km² lake experienced three phases of massive sedimentation, which rise well above the norm of about 3,700 t–4,400 t/yr. The first phase, lasting from 3640 to 2890 BP, resulted in a rate of 5,100 t/yr and was probably associated with the intro-duction of maize cultivation. The second phase lasted from 2530 to 1190 BP and resulted in a deposit of 10,300 t/yr. The final phase, from circa 900–850 BP, shortly after the ar-rival of the Puréecha people, was marked by a massive annual sedimentation rate of 29,000 t/yr; the deposits show pine charcoal, and there is also maize *(Zea mays)* in the pollen record. What exactly triggered later phases is not known.[58]

In sum, the evidence of the effects of the first farmers on the forested landscapes of Mesoamerica, sparse as it is, is impressive. Lake Pátzcuaro was not an isolated example; timber gathering and stripping were extensive, and soil erosion was widespread in other lake basins of the central Mexican plateau. Sherburne Cook and Woodrow Borah sug-gest that the lake-basin-focused Aztec empire was on the verge of collapse from declining agriculture before European intervention, because of intense population pressure and de-forestation culminating in land degradation. Certainly, during the twentieth century the landscape of central Mexico presented a "ravaged and desolate" aspect:

Range upon range of hills appear as bare bedrock or as miniature badlands dissected by hundreds of gullies and barrancas. Forests have been cut away to give room to corn fields and great valleys lie covered with thick layers of sand and silt.

"In a general way," said Cook, "the land is in the poorest condition in those areas which formerly supported large populations." Conversely, where the destruction was worst the densest population existed.[59]

Some confirmation of this lies in the extensive distribution of *tepetate,* an indurate, substrate, caliche-like formation exposed by sheet wash, the result of intensive cultivation, overuse, and excessive erosion under population pressure in marginal land. In the Teotlalpan, north of the valley of Mexico, *tepetate* was first exposed during periods of intensive hill slope cultivation between 800 and 200 BC, reaching a peak during the fifteenth and sixteenth centuries as population densities increased. Of course, the introduction of livestock later during Hispanic times accelerated erosion and *tepetate* formation as sheep, goats, and cattle overgrazed the land; but in some parts of the plateau the Spaniards found the land so depleted that grazing was the only form of land use possible. The implication is that the worst devastation had occurred before the arrival of the Europeans and grazing was a consequence rather than a cause of land denudation. The cause went back over two millennia to the clearings of the first farmers. Contrary evidence that the major sheet erosion came *after* the Conquest with depopulation and the introduction of pastoralism has more recently been advanced.[60]

Whatever the true sequence of events, *La leyenda negra*—the Black Legend of the Spanish Conquest—is too readily evoked to explain environmental degradation in the continent, and is often juxtaposed against what may be called *La leyende verde*—the green legend—which mythologizes the environmental harmony of Amerindian cultures with their environment. But this blinkered view, say Thomas Whitmore and Billie Turner, belittles the "nature and scale of agricultural production in pre-conquest Mesoamerica and, hence the scale and magnitude of its associated environmental damage,"[61] much of which was the result of deforestation.

Lowland South American Forests

When discussing the impact of the first farmers in the European forests, we talked of "the tyranny of the ethnographic present." Contemporary, traditional, simple (often foraging) systems have been regarded as representative of the farming practices of the fourth-millennia Neolithic farmers, whereas we are becoming increasingly aware that Neolithic practices were far more sophisticated than was once thought. But it is possible that in lowland South America, specifically Amazonia, the ethnographic present has worked its tyranny in a reverse manner. The "resource modes" of the present-day Indians are shown to be elaborate, and there has been a tendency to regard them as "representative of prehistoric ones," which in reality were much less sophisticated.[62] Current food-producing practices and strategies, perhaps recorded only during the twentieth century, are probably not of great antiquity and have been changed radically in the recent past. For example, many groups in lowland Amazonia are not remnants of pre-agricultural societies but probably refugee agriculturalists who have fled from European incursions or more powerful tribes.[63] The simple and overriding fact is that few peoples anywhere in the world have been insulated from the direct or indirect impacts of the wider global economy.

Present-day traditional farming systems of shifting agriculture that seem so ideally adapted to the environment with their minimal clearing of small plots, short cropping periods, long fallows, and intricate shade arrangements, together with low population densities and small temporary settlements, may well be no more than modern, post-Conquest innovations that reflect what Alfred Métraux called perceptively "the revolution of the ax." When did the metal ax, that most basic and important of forest clearing tools, penetrate the Amazonian lowlands, and what effect did it have? "Traditional" systems probably occurred with the shift from forest clearing with stone axes to a much more efficient iron and steel ax after the Conquest which would have increased clearing efficiency by a factor of at least 10:1 or more. "In aboriginal times," says William Denevan, "forest clearing was too labor intensive to be a common or frequent agricultural strategy," especially when one considers the absence of good stone for axes.[64] Therefore, any groups living in the forest in precontact times were more likely to have been foragers than farmers, and indeed the prehistoric Indians were located predominantly in the resource-rich floodplains and adjacent uplands. Present-day Indians, in contrast, are located mainly in the *terre firme* high forests of the interfluves, where resources of soils, game, and fish are relatively poor.

If that is so, then once more we encounter the problem of overlapping ages and phases in our exploration of global deforestation. Cultural/economic change is not in synchrony with chronological change. The metal ax in the tropics came after the Conquest. But once iron was known in the lowland forests of Latin America, and its efficiency for clearing appreciated, "a return to the Stone Age was impossible."[65]

The Gulf Lowlands

In the tropical forested environment of the warm, well-watered Gulf lowlands and riverine swamps of Yucatan and adjacent areas in Guatemala and Belize, complex, full-blown agricultural societies were nurtured that lasted for nearly 2,000 years. The Olmec culture grew from about 1200 to 600 BC, only to be abandoned for unknown reasons in about 900 BC. But it was the emergence of Classic Maya civilization from about 600 BC around centers such as Tikal, Bonampak, and Altar de Sacrificios, spreading over nearly 75,000 km², that dwarfed the better-known upland cultures in the basin of Mexico which were about only one-tenth its size. The Maya population rose steadily from approximately 161,000 in 1000 BC to 242,000 in 300 BC, then to just over 1 million in AD 300 to reach a peak of between 2.6 million and 3.4 million (density 117–151 persons/km²) by 800, which is comparable to those of prehistoric Old World tropical societies—though some would double or even triple that figure.[66] Suddenly, in the early ninth century the population collapsed abruptly, dropping from its zenith in AD 825 to 536,000 in AD 1000, and from then on it kept on falling to be a mere 6,800 by 1900. The whole civilization was in disarray.

The striking image of the tops of the abandoned ceremonial buildings towering above the carpet of lush green tropical forest has tended to obscure the fact that at one time the

Plate 3.1 The ability of the forest to regenerate when human interference ceases is awesome. Here the tropical forest has completely recolonized the fields, streets, and squares around the Mayan temples at Tikal, abandoned sometime during the ninth century AD. (Tony Morrison, South American Pictures.)

forest had been removed and fields created to support this urban civilization (plate 3.1). Stone was available for axes, hence the impact of farming on the forest was enormous. Intensive research on what lies beneath the present forest canopy reveals a complex "farmscape" with thousands of settlements ranging from small courtyard "farms," to grouped farms in hamlets, to large ceremonial sites like Tikal, with over 85 courtyards, ball-playing courts, and hundreds of other buildings; and a variety of cultivation forms and sophisticated agro-engineering works.[67]

From about 1000 to 300 BC the Maya practiced swidden agriculture in the forest, chopping down trees with stone axes or burning dead, girdled trees; setting fire to the refuse and rotating the cultivation of maize; and propagating a large number of fruits, perhaps as a part of an agro-forestry system. Patches or "gardens" of unusual concentrations of "useful" tree species have survived in the middle of the present forest, often protected by low, dry stone walls. But because swiddening can rarely support more than 20 persons/km^2, gradually, and certainly after AD 300, the swidden rotation was augmented by the large-scale intensification of more "difficult" lands. These consisted of well-drained limestone slopes with shallow soils, easily eroded once exposed by clearing to the torrential rains of the wet season; and lowland wooded *bajos* (low areas) and small savannas, both of which had subsurface clays and therefore were badly drained. Accordingly, the successful extension and intensification of cultivation required either terraces on the slopes to prevent erosion, or drainage in the lowlands to be rid of surplus water. Consequently,

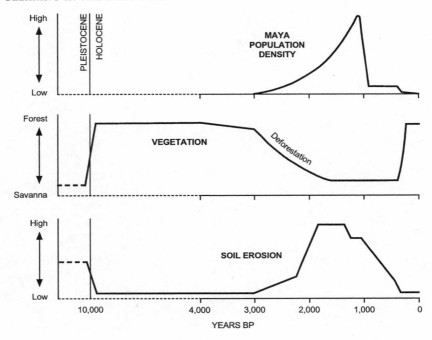

Figure 3.10 Population density, deforestation, and soil erosion associated with long-term Maya settlement on the terrestrial environment of the Peten lowlands, circa 10,000–0 BP. *Source:* after Deevy et al., 1979.

"tens of thousands" of elaborately constructed relic terraces covering over 10,000 km² have been discovered under the forest around the southeastern periphery of the lowlands. Also under forest on the eastern and northeastern periphery are over 120 km² of lattice-like patterns of ditches surrounding raised dirt platforms on which intensive cultivation and even double cropping could have been practiced, these "raised fields" being similar to the more famous *chinampa* of the Basin of Mexico. Radar imagery has detected further swathes of ditch patterns, particularly around Tikal, which amount to many more thousands of square kilometers. Both terraces and ditches were extremely labor intensive to make and to maintain, but without them it is highly doubtful if the population densities and complexities of trade and taxes in Classic Maya culture could have been maintained.[68]

The evidence of abundant agro-engineering works, the settlement remains, and lake sediments and pollen layers suggest that as population increased from circa 1000 BC onwards, deforestation gathered pace and soil erosion accelerated to reach a peak in about AD 800. In addition, in the outwardly exuberant, but potentially fragile environment of the rain forest, essential nutrients such as phosphorous were rapidly leached out of the soils; productivity must have declined dramatically[69] (fig. 3.10). In neighboring Honduras, the collapse of the Copán Mayan state between AD 850 and 1250 is attributed unequivocally to growing population, agricultural intensification, fuelwood demands, deforestation, soil erosion, and lowering agricultural productivity.[70] But was complete environmental instability triggered by soil degradation and nutrient depletion alone enough to explain the dramatic population collapse elsewhere? Other hypotheses have been put forward to explain the collapse, from "big-bang" disasters like warfare, disease, earthquakes, and drought, to more long-term reasons such as revolt and breakdown of the social system, or an interactive combination of all these. Michael Binford has suggested almost the complete opposite: that the abandonment of the very labor-intensive agriculture was a consequence of a prior population decline, or possibly, disruptive sociopolitical forces led to the collapse of the infrastructure, leading to agricultural decay.

But Billie Turner, who has authoritatively reviewed the nutritional and environmental evidence, adds a note of caution, and concludes that any linking of "Maya-induced environmental degradation to the collapse and depopulation" is too tenuous: the synchrony is there, but not the causal linkage.[71] Anyhow, even if the overuse of the environment did lead to population decline it does not explain why the decline continued in a downward spiral for the next thousand years: environments (and Neolithic societies) have far more resilience than that and would have bounded back to some sort of equilibrium long before, as perhaps the present rain forest demonstrates. Either way, however, humans did alter the forests, but in the case of the Maya, for some unknown reason it was not as permanent as it has been elsewhere in the world.

THE INDIANS AND THE NORTH AMERICAN FOREST

There are many similarities between the vast forests of eastern North America and Europe in terms of their climatic regimes and changes, physiographic zones, and vegetative changes, but perhaps one of the greatest commonalities has been the tendency to underestimate—even to deny—the human impact of the past, which has been a longer and more complex process than previously thought. Since the late 1980s the conventional wisdom about the origin and nature of agriculture in the eastern woodlands has undergone a complete revolution. Formerly, eastern North America was perceived as being "a marginal, passive, and recipient far northern fringe" under the influence of the "nuclear centers" of Meso- and even South America, which were not able to supply the trilogy of basic domestic crops of maize, beans, and squash until circa AD 900, and then by some unknown diffusion process. Once embraced, North American societies were transformed from foragers to farmers and the forests were adversely affected. But a different scenario has emerged with the advent of new techniques of analysis for archeology and paleoethnobotany. The forests of eastern North America may have sustained an independent process of plant domestication, and developed food economies for a long period of time. In fact, they may well have been the locale of an additional fourth independent Center to add to Harlan's existing three of the Near East, North China, and Mesoamerica.[72]

Three broad settlement episodes can be identified.[73] From at least 5000 BC, if not much earlier, inhabitants of the numerous river bottomlands of the watercourses that traverse the woodland (e.g., the central Mississippi, lower Illinois, Ohio, lower Missouri, Tennessee, and Kentucky and their tributaries) domesticated a series of species including sumpweed or marshelder (Iva annua), sunflower (Helianthus annus), ragweed (Ambrosia spp.), and chenopod (Chenopodium berlandieri), and may even have independently developed a species of squash (Cucurbita pepo). There is little doubt that the river-bottom environments favored a coevolutionary process between humans and plants. The violent spring floods, constant channel changes, and annual soil enrichment and disturbance created varied and changing habitats that "encouraged colonizing plants to develop attributes which preadapted them for manipulation, selection and domestication." For example, in the Little Tennessee River valley, continuous Indian population is documented for at least 10,000 years, and the amount of disturbance on the surrounding terraces grew with the growth of population. There is evidence of abundant pollens of domesticated crops and "progressive clearing and cultivation" through the middle and late Holocene, together with lithic remains.

With clearing and cultivation the dominant structure of forest communities was changed, species were extended or truncated, old fields provided open areas for native ruderals to invade, and the amount of nonforest land increased, "creating a culturally maintained landscape mosaic" in which "the natural landscape was being transformed on a new scale . . . as a result of increasing clearance of canopy level trees."[74] The fields provided a dependable, managed, and storable supply of food for the late winter and early spring, a buffer against food shortages when fishing, fowling, hunting, and foraging were impossible. Away from the rivers the use of fire to facilitate hunting and promote the growth of desirable wild plants and herbage was widespread. It was, said Joseph Caldwell, a system of "primary forest efficiency," a broad-spectrum agriculturalist-cum-forager economy making the most of the marked seasonal abundance of plant and animal resources of the forest, often moving residence with the seasonal shift in resources.[75]

Then, between circa 250 BC and AD 200, Hopewellian farming societies emerged as fully fledged food production economies, with recognizable village-type settlements. These societies possibly added erect knotweed *(Polygonum erectum)*, maygrass *(Phalaris caroliniana)*, and little barley *(Hordeum pusillum)* to the four existing domesticated crops.

Finally, between circa AD 800 and 1000, *Zea mays* was imported from the tropical areas. Initially it was a minor crop in a well-established food regime, but suddenly it took off in a "rapid and widespread" explosion across the woodland from northern Florida to Ontario, playing a central role in the evolution of complex food-producing societies across the middle latitudes, usually on easily worked terrace soils. The late adoption of maize, and the six-century lag between introduction in AD 200 and the post–AD 800 "takeoff" is a mystery. Contrary to common perceptions it is doubtful if even the settlements of the spectacular Hopewellian burial-mound cultures of the Middle Woodland times (0–AD 900) practiced agriculture. It may initially have been a controlled ceremonial crop, but it is far more likely that the massive amount of forest clearing needed to grow it, and the maintenance of those clearings, stifled adoption until demographic pressures made the labor-cost-to-food-yield ratio more attractive. Then the forest suffered.[76]

By the time Europeans landed in about 1600, then, fully fledged agriculture had only dominated as a way of life for perhaps 500 years or less on the eastern seaboard, and possibly a little longer further inland. But the imprint of agriculture and settled life was unmistakable and locally quite intensive. It was observed and recorded with some accuracy by the Europeans. Although enormous areas of "natural" forest remained, the land cover was not the vast, silent, unbroken, impenetrable tangle of vegetation inhabited by "untutored savages" so beloved by many writers in their romantic accounts of the forest wilderness. Rather, it was a mosaic of fire-altered and humanly selected species in different stages of succession, and of clearings and cultivated fields around villages and houses, to say nothing of the innumerable earthworks, ditches, and routeways, inhabited by "a people living in a society of appreciated values."[77]

Clearing Methods

Clearing was difficult and hard work. Patches were hacked out of the forest and maintained by fire. Small bushes were uprooted and burned, and the bark of larger trees was either bruised or peeled away with stone axes or burned off so that they withered and could eventually be burned. "They bruise the bark of the trees near the roote," wrote John Smith of Virginia in 1612, "then do they scorch the roots with fire that they grow no more." Occasionally, trees of up to 24 in (61 cm) in diameter were felled with stone axes, but usually the big trees (and certainly the larger stumps) were left in the cultivated area, as their removal was not worth the energy expended, whereas smaller stumps were prized out with large crooked poles. As the clearing was enlarged the women broke the soil with digging sticks or light hoes, and a mixture of crops was planted, which always included maize. The plots varied in size from a few square yards to 200 yd², and the crops were grown in mounds or sometimes in rows.[78]

Typical villages contained between 50 and 1,500 persons living in loose agglomerations of sturdy, defensible, weatherproof wooden houses, sometimes located roughly along a street, sometimes very scattered, the whole covering between 150 and 600 acres and usually surrounded by a palisade. The Huron and Iroquois, in particular, built complex longhouses and palisades that needed vast supplies of conveniently sized timber. For example, a typical Huron village of about 1,000 people needed six acres of land for its 36 longhouses. The longhouses required 16,000 poles of 4 in–5 in in diameter and 10 ft–30 ft long, 250 interior posts of 10 in in diameter and 10 ft–30 ft long, and 162,000 yd² of American elm or eastern red cedar bark for covering. The palisade needed 3,600 stakes that were 5 in in diameter and 15 ft–30 ft long. The total area of clearing would be up to 600 acres, and usually surrounded by a palisade.[79] If the density of settlement was great enough, then clearings merged into one another to make large open areas, but this was unusual unless along a riverfront.

But some settlements were much larger. Cahokia, in the Mississippi bottomland near present-day St. Louis, was not unique in size among later Mississippian settlements. It covered 1,680 acres, is estimated to have held a minimum of 10,000 people, and might have been as large as 25,000. Moreover, it was the largest settlement in the United States until it was surpassed by Philadelphia in AD 1800. Approximately 800,000 wall posts would have been needed for Cahokia's house walls, to say nothing of roofing beams and other constructional timber. In addition, the 3-km palisade would have required at least 15,000 logs the size of telegraph poles, and it was rebuilt several times. The land was cultivated up to a radius of 10 km–15 km from the center, and fuel needs would have been enormous. It is thought that overexploitation of the timber resources of areas surrounding Cahokia led to its gradual collapse between AD 1050 and 1150.[80]

The availability of fresh water and friable, fertile soil (well-drained sandy loams were favored in over two-thirds of the 137 Huron village sites) were major factors in the location of the typical Indian settlement. These preferences were well attested to by the European colonists, who said that the Indians in Virginia "fix upon the richest ground to build their houses. . . . Wherever we met with an old Indian field, or place where they have lived, we are sure of the best ground."[81]

But as indicated before, the impact of the Indians on the forest went beyond the zone of cultivation; they rarely forewent their foraging activities and continued to draw upon the forest for a great variety of products other than food crops planted in cleared land (see fig. 2.4). There were commodities such as fibers, trees, foods, medicines, and, above all, there was firewood. Beyond the fields and in the forest, fallen or dead wood was collected for fuel, mainly by the women, so that it was generally known as "squaw wood." In some groups fuel gathering was of such significance that it was an integral part of ritual activities, such as puberty rites. The quantity of wood consumed in the villages was enormous, and in time the search for wood covered an ever-increasing radius—even up to 3 mi—so that it become reasonable to fell trees in close proximity to the village rather than walk a long distance to collect such a bulky item. The older the settlement, the more likely it was that the forest was increasingly encroached on until its edge receded from the village.[82]

The zone of fuel collection was also the area for foraging for a great variety of other products such as wild fruits (persimmon, wild plums, papaws), berries, leaves, roots, and nuts—particularly acorns, which were consumed in vast quantities, along with chestnuts, pecans, hickory nuts—maple syrup, and medicinal berries like juniper and choke berry. So important and crucial to dietary needs were these products that it is thought that the unusually high proportion of nut and fruit trees in some localities at present may denote the purposeful promotion of favored species in the past. Also, the natural propagation on nutrient-deficient soil of sun-loving, aggressive colonizing trees like sumac and sassafras, commonly called "old-field trees," is a good indicator of past disturbance in the forest. Beyond the collecting zone and well away from the village lay the area for fire hunting.

The Contemporary Record

The eastern woodlands were not a homogeneous zone. The soils of the deep, fertile river bottoms differed markedly in quality from those of the interfluves and uplands. In addition, temperatures varied latitudinally, so that whereas one crop could barely be raised in the north of the region, two could be taken in the South. Thus, the form of agriculture varied too, and it is difficult to generalize.

There are dozens of contemporary descriptions of Indian villages and clearings from every state in the eastern half of the continent, but only a few can be mentioned.[83] In Virginia, John Smith described the village of the Pawhatan:

> Their houses are in the midst of their fields or gardens, which are small plots of ground. Some 20 acres, some 40 acres, some 100, some 200, some more, some less. In some places from 20 to 50 of those houses together or but little separated by groves of trees. Near their

habitations is little small wood or old trees on the ground by reason of them burning of them by fire.

This description was accompanied by a sketch (plate 3.2) that, although perhaps somewhat diagrammatic in composition, depicts clearly the arrangements in the forest which other accounts substantiate.[84] In 1620 William Strachey described the land around the present site of Hampton, Virginia, as

> ample and faire countrie indeed, an admirable pocion of land, comparatively high, wholesome, and fruietfull; the seat sometyme of a thowsand Indians and three hundred houses, as may well appeare better husbands [farmers] than in any part ells that we have observed which is the reason that so much ground is there cliered and opened, enough already prepared to receive corne and make viniards of two or three towsand acres.[85]

These examples refer only to the Tidewater area of Virginia during the early decades of the seventeenth century, but even in the back country in later years—in the Roanoke Valley and even further inland—the land was described as "by the industry of these Indians . . . very open and clear of woods." In early New England similar accounts exist. The Narragansett had cleared land for 8 to 10 mi from the coast, and the only wood found by the settlers was in the fire-protected low and damp ground. Edward Winslow and Stephen Hopkins, who rode along the banks of the Taunton River in 1621, commented on the towns and fields deserted because of disease, which had decimated the Indians. The land "was very good on both sides, it being for the most part cleared. . . . As we passed we observed that there were few places by the river but has been inhabited; by reason whereof much ground was clear, some of the weeds which grew higher than our heads." And so it went on: in the Alleghenies, the valleys of Tennessee and Kentucky, the Ohio River valley—even as far west as the Maumee River from Fort Wayne to Lake Erie in Indiana, the evidence is abundant. Some fields were mounded, while others had ridge and furrow.[86]

Two regions were particularly noteworthy: the Iroquois country in upstate New York, and the Creek country of Alabama. In New York the village of Genessee near present-day Rochester consisted of 128 houses and was said in 1779 to be "almost encircled with a cleared flat which extended for a number of miles covered by the most extensive fields of corn and every kind of vegetable that can be conceived," and there were other towns in the vicinity with fields of over 200 acres. In Georgia the descriptions contained in William Bartram's journal of 1791 and Benjamin Hawkins's *Sketch of the Creek Country* of 1798 are particularly vivid. Hawkins describes in detail the cultivation of 50 towns along the Coosa, Tallapoosa, and Chattahoochee rivers. One had fields extending "one mile and half," another "four miles down the river, from one hundred to two hundred yards wide," another "three thousand acres . . . and one third in cultivation," and so on.[87] It is probably a reasonably accurate analogue of earlier conditions, particularly the descriptions of cultivation and clearing reported by the De Soto expedition 250 years earlier which passed through fields of maize, beans, and squash often in "great fields . . . spread out as far as the eye could see across two leagues of the plain."[88] These scenes represented the culmination of a millennia of clearing.

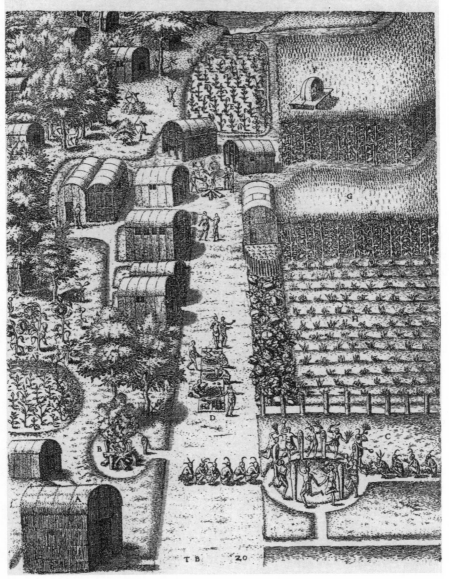

XX.

The Tovvne of Secota.

Plate 3.2 The town of Secota, Virginia. The sketch depicts various aspects of life in an actual Indian village. *H* (far right center) denotes corn in various stages of cultivation and maturity; *I* (next to the corn) depicts pumpkins, and in the top left-hand corner there is a hunting scene in the forest. John Smith, *Narrative of the First Plantation in Virginia* (1620); reproduced in Thomas Hariot, *Narrative of the First Plantation in Virginia* (1893). (State Historical Society of Wisconsin.)

Moving Fields and Settlements

Throughout North America there is evidence that cultivation and settlement was accompanied by some mobility. Even the most sedentary tribes were not stable and continued to rely on foraging for a significant part of their diet. It is thought that in some instances the surrounding forest resources became overused or worked out, while in cultivated areas yields declined; and the sheer accumulation of refuse and filth, as well as infestation by weeds and vermin, also made a move desirable, if not imperative. Such abandonment and moving meant that a significant portion of the forest was altered and therefore in different stages of regrowth and succession.

While there is evidence of the abandonment of exhausted fields to weeds for varying periods, sometimes the whole settlement was uprooted. One authentic record of such a move is that of Onondaga, the capital of the Iroquois League, which was found in nine different locations between 1610 and 1780, or an average life span of close to 20 years at each site. Father Jean de Lamberville wrote in 1682 that the then-recent move had been made by the Iroquois "in order to have nearer to them the convenience of firewood and fields more fertile than those which they abandoned." Again, in the Creek country, Hawkins described Tookabatchee on the Tallapoosa River as a town "on the decline. . . . The land is much exhausted with continued culture, and the wood for fuel is at a great and inconvenient distance, unless boats and land carriages were in use."[89] The overexploitation of wood and the need to move on to new areas was probably more common than the single well-documented example of Cahokia alone.[90]

Recently, William Doolittle has suggested that this mobility has been interpreted as a kind of shifting cultivation with a long fallow and slash-and-burn techniques. However, as he points out, the absence of any mention of field rotation and fallows in contemporary observations puts shifting cultivation in doubt, while the equally repeated references to complete clearing, long periods of cultivation, and large fields all point to an annual cultivation regime. But the suggestion has never been that all native forest cultivation was of a shifting variety, merely that *some* settlements became unwieldy and unhealthy and had to move, and that *some* fields were not in the most satisfactory location in relation to fuel supplies and continued fertility, as in the example of the Huron.[91] In any case, twenty-year shifts do not constitute shifting cultivation in the normal accepted meaning of the phrase.

Of perhaps more significance is the suggestion that with the introduction and widespread diffusion of the metal ax by the end of the eighteenth century, clearing became easier, and therefore it became more feasible for the Indians to move more frequently into unused and possibly less fertile areas of the forest. Certainly the steel ax speeded up the clearing process by a factor of possibly as much as 4.4:1 in light woodland, and many times that in dense woodland of large trees. As possible evidence of this, in the excavations along the Little Tennessee River there is an increase in pollens of upland ruderals like plantain and goosegrass, together with great sedimentation from erosion that accompanied the extensive cutting of timber for the construction of nearby Fort Loudon in 1756. As all this is in addition to the pollen of bottomland plants, it suggests that the inhabitants were clearing not only bottomland forests but large portions of upland areas as well.[92]

A Changed and Changing Forest Landscape

Whether permanent cultivation, shifting cultivation, or in some cases a technique halfway between the two, the fact remains that agriculture in eastern North America was widespread and intensive and, coupled with the foraging, firing, and hunting outlined in chapter 2, had a considerable impact on the forest. The aggregate extent of the accumulated modifications and deforestation is difficult to determine accurately, as the patches of clearing and burning were widely scattered and in various stages of regrowth. Also, there is no comprehensive record of the destruction of any considerable part of the pre-European forest to enable a calculation to be made, although the number of reports by explorers and colonists and the possibility that they saw only a small portion of Indian activity suggest that the total area involved might well be greater than the individual reports describe. In addition, there is much corroborative archeological and physical evidence in, for example, the extensive ridge and furrowed fields of Wisconsin.[93]

On the basis of population numbers and field sizes in selected examples, Alfred Kroeber suggested that one acre of cleared land on fertile soil, with mixed planting and a long growing season, might sustain one person per annum. More recently, Conrad Heidenreich has calculated that the Huron in Ontario needed 6,500 acres of cropland to support 21,000 people, about one-third of an acre per person—but that when an extended fallowing cycle is taken into account, the amount of land needed might reach 2.3 acres per person. Thus, if William Denevan's conservative estimate of a pre-Conquest population of 3.8 million for North America is accepted, then about 8.7 million acres of forest would have been affected (and that would not have included abandoned clearings), which is about 3.2 percent of the total of 278.6 million acres of cropland in the easternmost states today. Some people, like Henry Dobyns, put the population figure much higher, at double or even triple that of Denevan, and if correct, then the impact on the forest would increase proportionately. In his study of Virginia, Hu Maxwell calculated that if all the clearings that were cultivated and abandoned and all other burned areas were aggregated, a "conservative" estimate of treeless land would be between 30 and 40 acres per person, which compare with about 41 acres for Neolithics in forested Europe. Maxwell's speculation that another 500 years of Indian settlement would have reduced the eastern forests to negligible proportions is provocative, though probably exaggerated.[94] Unless population densities had grown to be so great that any mobility in agriculture had to be abandoned, with the consequence that some sort of permanent cultivation and settlement occurred everywhere, then the prodigious power of the forest to regrow would have kept a large part of the country covered in trees. The greatest modification would have occurred, as all botanical evidence suggests, in the area of the most frequent burning in the prairie ecotone, so that the grasslands together with the changed composition of the forests may have been the greatest and most enduring ecological, and even cultural, contribution of the Indians to the continent as a whole.[95]

But speculation aside, the first farmers in North America were a potent, if not crucial, ecological factor in the distribution and composition of this major forest area; and by 1600 the eastern woodlands were a changed and changing forest landscape. The Indians' farming and associated foraging activities through the millennia make the concept of "natural vegetation" a difficult one to uphold.[96] This does not mean that there was no untouched forest, or even fluctuations of climate; but the idea of the forest as being in some pristine state of equilibrium with nature, awaiting the arrival of the transforming hand of the European settler, has been all too readily accepted as a comforting generalization and as a benchmark against which to measure all subsequent change. When the Europeans came to North America, the forest had already been changed radically. Their coming did not alter the processes at work; it was merely their superior numbers and advanced technology that accomplished that. Paradoxically, their arrival may have been instrumental in causing the forests to grow more rapidly and extensively than before. The waves of disease that accompanied and then preceded the Europeans wiped out the Indians, and subsequent fire control and suppression would have limited damage. The forest of 1750 was probably thicker and more extensive than the forest had been at any time for the previous thousand years.

THE REST OF THE WORLD

Space does not permit a detailed account of the impact of the first farmers in other parts of the world, and indeed, our understanding and knowledge of other regions is less well developed. For example, in the forested Center of the Far East the sequence of development leading to rice cultivation is not clear. Domestication and agriculture seemed to have begun in China in the loessic highlands in the big bend of the Yellow River. There the remains of domesticated pigs and dogs and wild plants have been found that range from 6000 to 4000 BC. By 3000 BC slash-and-burn agriculture was present in central China, but the sequence whereby villages emerged and the way in which vegetation was affected is far from clear. The best evidence in the region comes from the peripheral area of Japan, where, like Europe and eastern North America, collecting and harvesting bands followed MacNeish's Tertiary route, making great use of the extensive resources of the lush coastal lowlands that provided food in all seasons, the process being supplemented by the repeated introduction of cultivars and domesticates from China. Again, until the research is done in detail one can only suppose that the forest vegetation was affected first by fire, foraging, and slash-and-burn impacts until horticultural villages were established. That did not occur until well into the Yoyoi period from about 1000 BC onwards, when the cultivation of dry and then wet rice introduced a permanent transformation of the land and its vegetation cover.

In all the tropical Non-Centers, such as India and Southeast Asia, the New World Tropics, and Africa (except for the Nile valley), the transformation is even less clear, if for no other reason than that in the tropics the preservation of plant remains is extremely unlikely. The forested lowlands of Southeast Asia, once thought of as one of the Centers, if not *the* hearth, of all agriculture, seem less and less likely to be so, and their development may not be all that different from other regions. What one can say is that by 2000 BC at least, if not earlier in some cases, all three regions were showing evidence of plant domestication and were following Routes 4, 5, and 12 to become Horticultural Villages with occasional cultivation.[97]

The story can be taken a little further. By the middle of the last millennia BC, southern and eastern Asia in particular displayed a flowering of civilizations in temperate and tropical forested areas. They defy easy summary, but mention must be made of, for example, the growth of the Han Empire in China (which spread into Korea and Japan), and later empires in Cambodia (Angkor Wat), Thailand, Burma (Pagan), and Java. China flourished from about 600 BC into one of the most complex, innovative, and technologically proficient societies of the time; and although we know very little about its impact on the forest, it must have been great, if only through the demands for fuel for smelting and warmth, timber use in house construction, and agricultural clearing. It is a story yet to be told by others more skilled and able in its sources than the present author.

In contrast, the full flowering of civilization in the forested lands of Southeast Asia was "neither early nor rapid."[98] The region was well populated by 1000 BC, and possessed advanced bronze and iron metalworking skills and developed agricultural systems. But its most spectacular achievements were in city building and monumental architecture, which in size and number equaled the splendors of Egypt and even Rome. These urban centers did not emerge until much later, after AD 500, and must have been based on efficient and intensive food production for surpluses (abundant suitable soils and water for rice) in nearby locations. But no record has been revealed yet that allows us to even begin to unravel the impact of these civilizations on the forest. One thing we know is that in Angkor Wat, just as in Yucatan, once the maintenance of clearing for cultivation was abandoned, the forest reasserted itself and recolonized the urban areas, which were rediscovered only during the mid-nineteenth century.

In conclusion, then, two points can be made. First, for at least the last 4000 years, and much longer in the Centers and adjacent areas, the forests of the world have been cleared, thinned, or altered by humans in their search for food, shelter, and warmth. Second, while the fact that the first farmers transformed the forest is incontrovertible, it is certainly almost totally unrecorded in detail, so the extent of clearing can only be guessed at. But without a doubt it was immense. It was the first great human change of the face of the earth.

Chapter 4

The Classical World

Clever beyond all dreams . . .
—SOPHOCLES, *Antigone*

It is for the sake of their timber that Nature has created . . . the trees.
—PLINY, *Natural History*

IN MANY WAYS it is misleading to make a division between the prehistoric world of the first farmers in Europe and the conventionally labeled "classical" world of Greece and Rome, as at an early point they were one and the same thing—the late Neolithic or Early Bronze Age, in cultural terms. In the Mediterranean coastlands, particularly around the Aegean Sea, small-scale horticultural communities had become established from early Neolithic times (e.g., 6000 BC). Cereals and pulses were grown, crops were rotated, land was manured, and stock, including sheep, cattle, and pigs, were integrated into the economy. Settlement occurred in the open woodlands along stream courses, and in the case of Greece, the thicker oak woodlands of the plains; the lower slopes were not penetrated even by Roman times. Nut and fruit trees were selected and favored, especially the fig and olive, and later the vine. In the plains of Apulia in southern Italy hundreds of complex agricultural villages flourished before and at the same time as the "farmers of the forest" were colonizing central and northern Europe.[1]

Despite the contemporaneous nature of the colonizing, cultivation, and clearing of the Mediterranean periphery with other parts of Europe, scholarship has canonized the era and area as "classical," and that holds a special place in Western culture which is difficult to ignore. But it is more than a case of historical labels alone: the changes around the Mediterranean rim were extensive and distinctive enough to warrant separate consideration.

"THEN AND NOW"

The classical and Hellenistic-Roman periods from about 1100 BC to the onset of the Byzantine age, circa AD 565—the Minoan, Mycenaean, and Helladic millennia are excluded—brought about enormous changes in thought and action, which influenced attitudes toward the resources and nature in the region. The reverberations of a growing population, rapid urbanization, extensive mineral extraction, the development of complex patterns of trade, and, above all, a vibrant intellectual life by different cultures and civilizations throughout the Mediterranean basin, but particularly on its northern rim, were enormous. Some of these changes and characteristics have a distinctly modern ring to them. From the point of view of deforestation we see for the first time how building, heating, cooking, shipbuilding, metal smelting, and brick making make enormous demands on timber resources. Perhaps one can agree with Fairfield Osborn that the history of Greece and Rome "assumes the character of a prologue to modern times. Assuredly there is an affinity between *then* and *now*." [2]

But this was not an undifferentiated 1,500 years. Fritz Heichelheim saw it as having five distinctive subphases, each with special characteristics that moved society from a state of subsistence to one of exchange/consumption, and brought a higher standard of technical civilization to all classes. [3] They throw light on our understanding of the human impact on the environment in general and on the forests in particular.

In the first subphase, from 1100 to 560 BC, iron tools (particularly the iron plow-share) infiltrated agriculture, displacing copper and bronze implements and enabling the fertile, heavy, and often more-timbered soils to be cultivated, usually for grain. For the first time population increase took place outside the "hydraulic" societies of Egypt and Mesopotamia. The Greek polis, a new type of urban unit, emerged, and by the eighth century BC Greek and Phoenician inventions in shipbuilding intensified commerce and trade around the basin, the expansion of fleets being one of the first major drains on the forests. Whereas in 1000 BC most of the Mediterranean was "effectively prehistoric," by 500 BC "it formed a series of well differentiated zones [of production and trade] within a world-system." [4]

The second subphase, from circa 560 to 333 BC, was a time of "classical refinement in all spheres of human life." [5] Attributes of mind, such as reason, logic, and analysis of cause and effect, accompanied attributes of existence, such as capital accumulation and investment, to alter life and livelihood in town and country. Workshops, the division of labor, the development of silver as a medium of exchange, and giro transfers in bookkeeping enabled and generated the burgeoning manufacturing and trade. Agricultural colonization prospered with extended knowledge of manuring, special seeds, and animal husbandry. Irrigation in Egypt and draining in southern Italy expanded the ecumene. Slavery, long a part of Greek society, was expanded to provide much of the labor for the new scale of agriculture, manufacturing, and trade.

All these trends intensified during the third subphase, from 333 to 31 BC. It coincided with the territorial expansion of Greece throughout the eastern Mediterranean and Asia Minor, as far away as the Ganges and the coast of East Africa, and the even greater expansion of Rome westward into Spain (after 209 BC), North Africa (after 146 BC), the central and northern Balkan peninsula (from 229 BC), and Gaul (from 125 BC). Everywhere, capital investment in agriculture and manufacturing reached new heights. The detail of scrub clearing, irrigating, tree planting, and cultivation at a large estate in Philadelphia, near present-day Fayum in Ptolemaic Egypt, during the third century BC, and the self-assurance, order, and conscious control displayed in the extensive Roman land subdivision, or centuriation, leave one in no doubt as to the scale and complexity of change. [6]

Trade was facilitated by a new type of money, the "bill of exchange." Roads, docks, harbors, markets, aqueducts, and splendid private dwellings, as well as houses for the less well-off in concrete and brick, accompanied town development everywhere. In the countryside, improved water mills facilitated irrigation, and wine and olive-oil presses and other agricultural tools had implications for agricultural production. New plants and animals were introduced into the Mediterranean basin from Asia.[7]

In the Roman world, land was the main source of wealth and the mainspring of political power. Agriculture and pastoral expansion depended on slavery, which became more exploitative and less humane. Agriculture became organized into bigger slave-operated units, and the small-scale, self-sufficient "Italian" peasant estates of earlier centuries were in retreat. "Many of the 'conquerors of the world,' as the Roman often called themselves, were ejected from their farms and displaced by peoples whom they had vanquished and enslaved," and the displaced peasants supplied the people for the massive Roman colonizations in the frontier provinces.[8] Everywhere, the emphasis on land and agricultural expansion put pressure on the forests. To safeguard this valuable and strategic resource, the state assumed ownership of them.

The penultimate subphase, from 31 BC to AD 284, was, as Heichelheim says, "Janus-faced" in its contrasting themes of expansion and innovation, and contraction and decline. It was the era of the pomp of imperial Rome and of a greater emphasis on urban dwelling—often at the neglect of agriculture, the livelihood of more than 90 percent of the people. But not for long: urban living declined, and imperial resources waned as the supply of coinage could not keep pace with the expansion of new territories that had blossomed as agricultural lands and become almost self-sufficient economic units. The diffusion and application of Roman technical agricultural knowledge along with new crops and livestock produced a marked human imprint on previously unsettled or only lightly settled landscapes. Largely forested lands had to be deforested in order to be cultivated. By the end of the period the large market-oriented, slave-operated estates were in decline with the gradual disintegration of slavery, and they tended to be replaced by smaller, self-sufficient holdings, best described as peasant operated. But these were not the holdings of primitive subsistence farmers; the new operators had absorbed and adopted the "semi-scientific, technical know-how, village craftsmanship, and use of a wide variety of agricultural tools, plants, and domesticated animals" that produced "a revolution in village life and village production," thereby laying the agricultural foundations for the energetic medieval civilizations that were to come later in the Western, Russian, and Islamic worlds.[9] The final subphase, from AD 284 to 565, is concerned with the decline and fall of the classical world. These brief sketches do scant justice to the complexity of the evidence of the classical period, so admirably set out in the immense and penetrating accounts of Michael Rostovtzeff's works *The Roman Empire* and *The Hellenistic World,* and Fritz Heichelheim's *Ancient Economic History.*[10]

Besides its sheer modernity, the later classical world had a number of distinctive qualities that distinguished it from anything that had gone before. Foremost, in the realm of deforestation there is the nature of evidence. It was an intensely literate world in which, for the first time, people recorded what they saw and what they did, and linked that to a conscious, known past. Perhaps even more important, they recorded what they thought and conjectured about those scenes and actions. We do not have to rely on archeology or

the inferences drawn from pollen diagrams, useful as these often are, in order to understand what was happening, but can turn to the works of, for example, Homer, Strabo,
Theophrastus, Cicero, Varro, Columella, Pliny, and others, which are replete with information about the forests, their habitats, and their utilization. Yet, although the evidence
is abundant, we can also agree with Russell Meiggs that it is "widely dispersed and much
of it very frustrating" and "opaque." Consequently, there is much conjecture.[11] Of course,
it is true that in chapter 3 we drew on the literary accounts of the human effects on the
North American forest. But these are not the contemporary accounts of the perpetrators
of change but of observers, translators, and transcribers, mostly after the event, and almost always from a different culture, with all that that meant in terms of interpretation
and meaning.

A second distinctive feature of the classical world was the people's consciousness
of their power to control and even create nature. On the one hand there was a strong belief that humans were a part of some larger, divine plan or purpose, but on the other there
was a consciousness of the power of human action, leading to order and control. It became clear that metallurgy, mining, building, trade, and, above all, agriculture and the
domestication of animals, changed the world. These changes were not an application of
any theoretical science or profound wisdom, but were the simple evidence of how the occupations, crafts, and skills of everyday life made changes possible, and also produced a
more orderly accessibility to the things humans needed. Clarence Glacken, in his masterly
survey of nature and culture, argues that early classical writing suggests that the Greeks
were not only conscious of their power over their environment but that even their mythology reinforced the idea of man as "the orderer of nature" and even "the finisher of the
creation."[12] Above all, it was the busyness and incessant restlessness of practical people
like the artisan, the farmer, and the trader that created order and stability through the
dominance of the environment, and changed nature. Through their inventiveness and energy humans had become, as Sophocles said, "clever beyond all dreams," although it
could drive them "one time or another to well or ill."[13] The evidence of that clever-
ness and its consequences were perhaps displayed nowhere more so than in the intensely
humanized and distinctive landscape of the Mediterranean basin. It was already an old
and altered landscape by the time the Greeks were writing about what they saw.

THE MEDITERRANEAN ENVIRONMENT

The Mediterranean is not only a uniting sea; it has a distinctive climate of marked wet
winters and little rain during the summer months, leading sometimes to prolonged
drought. This regime has not changed much except, perhaps, for a relatively moist period
after the Ice Age which lasted until the second millennia BC, allowing the extension of
evergreen sclerophyllous and pine forests, even into North Africa.[14] As a result of this
rainfall seasonality, the forest grows in an open formation, and once cleared it shows less
regenerative powers than do the forests to the north. However, in more well-favored,
western-facing locations, forests were, and are, dense.

For a temperate environment the Mediterranean forest is extremely varied, with over
40 major tree species and at least 50 subvarieties, whereas there are 12 and 20, respec-

tively, in denser central and northern European forests. The variety might originate from the fact that the basin was one of the Ice Age refugia, but undoubtedly the broken topography of peninsula, island, lowland, and intervening upland must have also added much local variation. Despite this variety, however, the lowland forests are composed largely of evergreen pines and oaks. Northward the forest has more deciduous oaks and some beech, elm, and chestnut as these grade into the dense deciduous forests of central and western Europe. Southward they grade into crooked, hard, thorny, and spiny shrubs of steppe and desert. Everywhere altitude has a marked influence on forest composition, which then resembles that to the north. In the Pyrenees, Apennines, and Balkan and Turkish mountains, trees range from evergreen, oak, beech, elm, and chestnut on the lower slopes up to about 2,000 ft, to deciduous oak and sweet chestnut on the intermediate slopes, to fir and black pine on the upper slopes over about 4,000 ft, and finally to prized timber like cedar on the crests of mountains in Cyprus, Lebanon, Syria, and North Africa.[15] During the marked dry season fire has always been a major danger and modifier of the drier forests. Whether the characteristic *maquis* (*macchia* in Italian) that fringes the Mediterranean—a mixture of nondeciduous bushes, shrubs, and dwarf trees that attain a height of 15 ft–20 ft—is a natural ecosystem or a result of fire coupled with prolonged human overuse and misuse, is a matter of debate,[16] as is the lower, more degraded garrigue or matorral of herbs and shrubs.

Frequent violent and cataclysmic storms accelerate processes of soil erosion; exposed soils are leached and rapidly accompanied by gullying. Consequently, the heavy valley alluvium of the Younger Fill used for cultivation now was not available until recently, and the lighter soils elsewhere must have once been considerably better structured and more fertile in the past.

The distribution and character of the forest of the past is difficult to reconstruct with certainty, though efforts have been made to do it (see fig. 4.1). The works of classical authors have been combed for references as to the presence or otherwise of forested areas; and Ellen Semple, H. Clifford Darby, Jack Thirgood, John Perlin, and Donald Hughes have copious descriptions of the ancient forested lands drawn from contemporary sources.[17] Suffice it to say that by the time of Homer in the 8th century BC, the impression is that woodland was still abundant. Certainly palynological research confirms that the country was fairly well wooded at the start of the Neolithic.[18] But woodland was not so widespread that particularly dense or extensive stands did not warrant special mention. Thus, Homer commented on "wooded Samothrace," "wooded Zacynthos," the "tall pines and oaks" of Sicily, and other "wooded country." Aristophanes wrote of "the peaks of lofty mountains crowned with trees."[19]

But these references were part of literary creations and may be purely figurative. It was not until the work of Theophrastus (370–250 BC), a pupil of Plato's and then Aristotle's, that any systematic attempt was made to classify both wild and cultivated trees, their habitats and characteristics. His *De Historia Plantarum,* or *The Enquiry into Plants* (313 BC) was based on personal observation and possibly those of his pupils.[20]

Theophrastus was struck by the importance of habitat on the type and quality of trees; "some belong more to the mountains, some to the plains. And on the mountains themselves, in proportion to the height some grow fairer and more vigorous in the lower

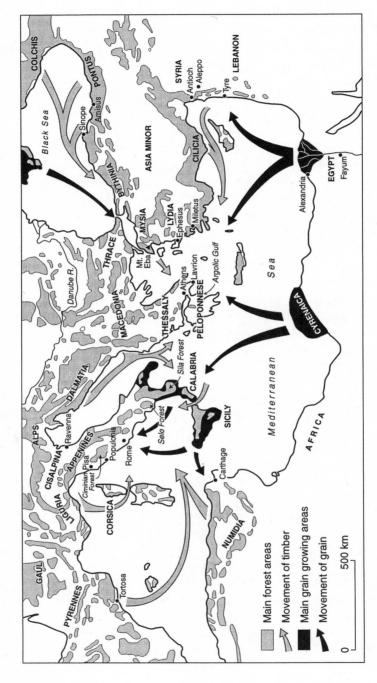

Figure 4.1 Major timber- and grain-growing areas and trade routes in the Mediterranean basin, fourth–first century BC. *Source:* after Lombard, 1959, and Sherratt and Sherratt, 1993.

regions, some about the peaks." However, wherever they grew, provided they were on a northerly aspect, their wood was "closer, more compact, and better generally." Thus it seemed clear to him that "each tree seeks an appropriate position and climate," as particular districts "bear some trees but not others." In general "locality" was "more important than cultivation and care." For this consistent questioning of the relationship between plant species and the total environment in which it flourished, he used the word *oikeios,* the root of our modern word *ecology.* Armed with this generalization he then described the forests of the mountains of Lebanon and Taurus, the ranges of Asia Minor, the Macedonian highlands, many parts of Greece, western Crete, southern Italy, and finally of Corsica, which surpassed them all in terms of quality, as well as being "thickly wooded" and "one wild forest." This work, suggests Heinrich Rubner, was possibly the beginning of forest science, and even, suggests Donald Hughes, of ecology.[21]

While Theophrastus attempted to understand the general—almost theoretical—nature of the distribution of trees, the detail comes only when the stands are discussed with reference to human use, which made the trees and their timber interesting. This anthropomorphic view complemented the belief that humans could change and thereby control nature; use and control went hand in hand. Thus, the focus on the mountain areas is explicable because they produced the most "serviceable timber"; the trees on the level parts of the mountains being "specially fair and vigorous," only to be rivaled by those growing "on the lower parts and in the hollows." During the ensuing centuries further descriptions of the Mediterranean forests, as in Starbo's second-century *Geography,* fill in the detail of the picture that Theophrastus sketched out; but similarly Strabo was incapable of description unless it was accompanied by economic value.[22]

The Hellenistic period was an active one, not only in terms of a broadening confidence in the "unlimited capabilities of man and his reason" to cope with life and the environment, but also in practical terms. Scores of expanding city-states endeavored to be self-sufficient, and stay solvent and powerful by gaining control over surrounding resources, expanding agriculture, and engaging in sea trade, which inevitably meant building ships. In this mood of "buoyant optimism" the forests were a prime resource that was going to be one of the first to suffer from human exploitation.[23] In time, Rome and its centralizing tendencies as capital of perhaps the greatest and most powerful empire seen up to that time was doing on a grand scale what the small city-states had done centuries before. Given the central importance of trees in early human existence for warmth, shelter, construction, and agricultural land, it should be no surprise that each activity was a step on the road to forest clearing, and in unison led to deforestation.

THE CAUSES OF DEFORESTATION
Cultivation and Grazing
The Mediterranean Basin

Clearing land to grow food was the primary cause of change in the forests. But, as ever, the clearing part of the agricultural operation was subsidiary to other activities. Contemporary commentators made observations on manuring, crop introductions, crop rotations, yields, and tree growing and grafting, but rarely on getting rid of the trees. Forest clearing was a negative, destructive process that was subsumed in the large practice of agriculture. Consequently we know little about it, to such an extent that one might think that it was the more extraneous, exotic activities like shipbuilding, fuel gathering, house construction, or even forest fires that were the main cause of forest denudation, not the simple, obvious, everyday, essential process of getting food. Palynological evidence helps little, as the most arid areas record little remnants of crops.

And yet, clearing for cultivation must have been happening everywhere as hoes and later iron-tipped plows tore up the plains and lower slopes of the uplands of peninsular Greece. When the chorus in Sophocles' *Antigone* wanted to exalt the power of Man they praised his success on the seas through navigation, and on land through hunting, plant and animal domestication, and home building. But above all it was his success in conquering and transforming the earth by agriculture that was most striking:

> Oh, Earth is patient, and Earth is old,
> And a mother of Gods, but he breaketh her,
> To-ing, froing, with the plough-teams going,
> Tearing the soil of her, year by year.

Only death (average life expectancy was not much beyond thirty years) and man's own nature defied his powers of mastery.[24]

Certainly, clearing was common enough for Homer to find a ready comparison between the noise of battle and "a crashing sound where woodmen fell the trees" in "mountain dells," though whether this was cutting for agriculture alone is doubtful. And in later centuries the image of the industrious plowman, who "subdues his woodland with flames and plough" and who "carted off the timber he has felled," was common enough. But on the large estates clearing was done by slaves; the heroic nature of the task of the individual proprietor was replaced by the routine tasks of servile, forced labor.[25]

Much more explicit was the comment of the Roman writer Lucretius during the early part of the first century BC:

> day by day they [agriculturalists] would constrain the woods more and more to reside up the mountains, and to give up the land beneath to tilth, that on hills and plains they might have meadows, pools, streams, crops, and glad vineyards, and the grey belt of olives might run between with its clear line, spreading over hillocks and hollows and plains: even as now you see all the land clear marked by diverse beauties.

Later, Strabo commented on the clearing of the forests of Avernian in Campania that had been "brought by the toil of man into cultivation, though in former times they were thickly covered with a wild and untrodden forest of large trees"; and the vast Ciminian forest of southern Tuscany, which Livy described during the fourth century BC as "more impassable and appalling" than the forests of Germany, had all but disappeared two centuries later. It also seems likely that the forests of the Po plain were felled systematically during the second and first centuries BC as part of the "Romanization" of the Celtic Cisalpina, and the creation of large estates within a framework of extensive centuriation.[26]

But these references are few. It seems likely that in time agricultural felling produced a gradation of clearing: extensive stripping except for woodlots on the plains, a patchwork of "fields" in the forests on the slopes, and only the most inaccessible mountain areas remaining totally wooded. The clearing of large areas of the lowlands and lower slopes was compensated for to some degree by the planting of large areas of tree crops, such as olive and later citrus—so much so that by the first century BC Varro was prompted to ask, "is not Italy so covered with trees that the whole land seems to be an orchard?"[27]

The numerous agricultural treatises of the age stress that most felling was done by axes, saws, and wedges; although it is ironic, but indicative, that in recent authoritative works on Roman farming and farm equipment, neither clearing nor any of these essential tools are mentioned. Clearing the vegetation was simply not regarded as a part of agriculture.[28] Nonetheless, single- and double-headed bronze axes appeared from Minoan times onward, and were superseded by single-headed axes, which were later cast in iron, a metal both harder and more effective. Saws up to 5.6 in. long, constructed of bronze sheets hammered into shape and cut regularly with pyramidal teeth, have been found in abundance from a similar early period, and Theophrastus (circa 300 BC) appreciated that setting saw teeth "in alternate ways, to get rid of the sawdust," aided cutting. Whether the saw was used only for crosscutting trunks and sawing planks and boards in saw pits, or also for felling trees is not known. In addition, the technique of notching a tree in order to ensure the direction of its fall might not have been understood, for guiding ropes were attached; Ovid writes of "the tree which, loosened at last by the countless blows of the axe, and drawn down by ropes, crashes to the ground."[29] Felling was timed for autumn, when the growth was over, although this was sometimes complicated by the superstition that timber would rot if cutting coincided with the end of lunar phases. The largest trees were not cut but girdled and left to die over a number of years, and the smallest trees were grubbed out. The best and largest timbers were taken out of the forest for constructional use, either dragged out by human power, mules, or oxen; hoisted up on two wheels, if the timbers were large; or floated out on accessible rivers. But much timber must have been burned on the spot and the ashes plowed into the soil in order to fertilize it. To this end, Columella (circa 116–127 BC) advised that there were two methods for "reducing a wooded area to an arable state": "either by tearing out the trees by the roots and removing them or, if they are few, by simply cutting them down, burning them, ploughing them under."[30]

Soil fertility was a prime concern to writers of the classical world, and it was to be debated as vigorously then as in later ages. The maintenance of fertility was perceived to be intimately connected with initial vegetation cover, and therefore, as such, demands some consideration, if only because different types of trees were used as indicator species. Generally, the perception was then, even as now, that the best soil was to be found "in land newly plowed where an old forest has been felled." But Pliny, who made that observation, also noted that it did not follow that the most fertile soils were those sustaining the larger, lusher trees:

> A soil in which lofty trees do brilliantly is not invariably favorable except for those trees; for what grows higher than the silver fir? Yet what other tree could have lived in the same place?[31]

But the debate went deeper than that. Whereas Lucretius had believed in the senescence of the earth—that it was a mortal body and therefore would decline in fertility and ultimately die—Columella writing at the end of the first century AD contended that soil fertility was not related to the age of the earth but to agricultural practice. He cites Tremelius, an older writer on the topic, who said, "Virginal and wooded areas, when they are first cultivated, yield abundantly, but soon thereafter are not so responsive to the toil of those who work them." Columella thought the observation correct but the interpretation wrong. The land was not fertile because it had lain idle for so long and was "younger," but because of the accumulated debris of leaves and roots that built up the humus layer in the soil. When clearing takes place and the ground is broken up by the plow, the roots that nourish the soil are severed and the soil grows infertile. Thus human action is the culprit, not senescence. It is because of "our own lack of energy that our cultivated lands yield us a less generous return. For we may reap greater harvests if the earth is quickened again by frequent, timely, and moderate manuring." Human care and activity in selecting green and animal manures were crucial to the maintenance of fertility.[32]

The debate on fertilizing shows two things. First, whatever the interpretation of the cause of fertility loss, the common, almost folk wisdom was that newly cleared ground yielded the best crops, which put a premium on forest clearing. Second, Columella's arguments showed a growing appreciation of the power of humans to alter the earth. In light of that, it seems inconceivable that the paucity of direct references to agricultural clearing is a true reflection of what was happening. A hint of the state of affairs (which may exemplify what was happening elsewhere) is given by Strabo, who quotes the description of Eratosthenes (275–195 BC) of the plains of Cyprus which were once "covered with forests, which prevented cultivation." But in time various activities altered that:

> The mines were of some service towards clearing the surface, for the trees were cut down to smelt copper and silver. Besides this timber was required for the construction of fleets, as the sea was now navigated with security and by a large naval force.

But these nonagricultural inroads made little impression on the forests, until landless peasants were given permission to occupy the land and clear it of the remaining timber, which once done could be held "as their own property, free from all payments." Such ownership by clearing in order to increase the wealth of the polis must have been common elsewhere in the forests around the Mediterranean, and indeed, by a comprehensive Roman law passed in 111 BC, anyone who occupied public land of up to thirty *jugera* (approximately 20 acres) in order to bring it into cultivation was granted ownership. It was a kind of claim staking for freehold.[33]

In emphasizing cultivation it must not be forgotten that domesticated stock were also kept and allowed to interrun with crops. Cows, pigs, goats, and horses had been kept in Crete and mainland Greece from at least the seventh millennium BC, with pigs outnumbering cattle and the proportion of sheep and goats (caprovines) ever increasing, with sheep being the predominant beast.[34] The implications for vegetation destruction were great. Land was cleared for growing pasture and fodder crops, trees were needed for green fodder, and everywhere stock stopped the regeneration of young shoots and seedlings.

To what extent stock were integrated into the total farming regime, as in the forests of northern and western Europe, is uncertain. The traditional view is that the extended dry summer period limited the quantity and quality of pasture in the lowland areas, and that only the swampy coastal lands and deltaic flats, such as those of the Po, Adige, Arno, and Guadalquiver, could support pastures. In the uplands, especially on the wetter, west-ern-facing slopes, and under the canopy of the deciduous forests, the growth of herbage was longer, and above the tree line there were the alpine pastures. Thus, the tendency was for milk cattle, horses, and working oxen to be kept on the best lowland pastures. Sheep and goats, on the other hand, entered into a seminomadic summer shift to the higher pas-tures, with the effect of depriving the cultivated lowlands of animal manure. Transhu-mance on a grand scale was particularly marked between the Apennines and their sur-rounding lowlands, with the broad *calles* or drove ways funnelling the stock from upland to lowland. But sometimes even the alpine and upland pastures were still not enough to totally sustain the animals during the summer months, and then stock would be fed on supplementary fodder of young shoots and twigs from the lower branches of the decidu-ous trees, with a devastating effect on the forests everywhere.[35]

An alternative view is that the predominance of the sheep in the stock inventory could not be primarily for their meat—swine being far more efficient converters of plant mat-ter into protein—nor for the wool, as fine wools did not appear until much later. How-ever, sheep are a "relatively good converter of plant matter into dung," producing up to ten times their own weight per annum. Without the dung, agriculture, "even on the richer soils, would not have been possible."[36] Seen in this light, flocks were essential for agri-cultural survival and transhumance was merely "a tactical adaptation" during critical pe-riods when the cereal infield was growing crops or the more rotational outfield was in al-ternative uses. In any case, upland pastures could not sustain prolonged use. Elevation reduces the growing season by about one week per 100 m; thus at 1,000 m the growing season is only 170 days, at 2000 m only 95, and the pasture yield decreases by half be-tween the lowlands and 1,200 m and 80 percent at 2,000 m.[37] Sheep, therefore, must have been integrated into the agricultural economy as fertilizing agents, and the lowland forests must have suffered accordingly.

Whatever the role of stock on cultivation, all had an effect on the forest, and the dif-ferences in browsing habits affected the type of foliage destruction. Because of their stat-ure cattle trim off the lower green fodder of the trees as well as graze the herbaceous growth on the forest floor. Varro (116–27 BC) complained that grazing cattle "do not produce what grows on the land, but tear it off with their teeth." The "raiding" goats grazed anywhere, and were blamed, perhaps erroneously, by many contemporary (and also present-day) writers as the major, if not the sole, destroyers of the forests—particu-larly because of their liking for woody vegetation and their agility even to climb trees for forage.[38] Sheep graze close to the ground and tend to favor open or disturbed patches in woodland with plenty of herbage, the growth of which would sometimes be encouraged by setting fire to the undergrowth. Pigs are essentially forest animals, and Sandor Bökönyi sees a relationship between their increase in Greece and the onset of greater wetness and coolness, leading to forest growth at the end of the Bronze Age. They are omnivorous, and excellent foragers and converters of plant matter to protein, thriving in the uncleared forest on the abundance of acorns, mast, and young shoots. Strabo reported that they roamed in vast numbers on the southern slopes of the Pyrenees, which were "well-wooded with trees of every kind and with evergreens" and produced excellent hams that "rivalled those of the famed forests of Cantabria." Meanwhile, the uncleared forests that encircled the Po lowlands produced acorns in such quantities that "Rome is fed mainly on the herds of swine that come from there." [39]

Irrespective of the grazing propensities of different stock, a vicious circle could set in whereby more clearing for whatever purpose disturbed the vegetation and promoted more low-level browse, thus encouraging more stock; and unless the stock were put out on fallowed or abandoned fields they would inhibit regeneration by eating seedlings, roots, and shoots, as well as trampling the ground and compacting the soil. Such animal impacts could be either sudden in the wake of agricultural clearing, or gradual and long term if they accompanied the gradual thinning of the forest by fuelwood gathering.

The Other Classical World

While the label "classical" straddled a vast range of time, it also straddled a vast range of space. Although the classical world is inextricably associated with Greece and Rome, as these expanded other classical worlds developed outside the immediate vicinity of the Mediterranean basin. Of these the temperate forested lands, conquered by Rome in western and south-central parts of Europe from the Danube to the Rhine and Scotland, are the most important. The northern Balkan peninsula was overcome and conquered from 229 BC onward, Spain after 209 BC, Gaul from 125 BC onward, and the occupation of the British Isles lasted from 44 BC to at least AD 400.

In the British Isles, northern France, and Germany, the usual view is that the Romans found a forest-covered landscape largely devoid of people; Britain was, according to Strabo, mostly "overgrown with forests," and "the vast expanse" of the Hercynian oak forest stood as a motif for all Germany—"untouched by the ages and coeval with the world," surpassing all wonders in its "almost immortal destiny." [40] The German forest was wilderness, the place of strange beings and wild beasts, and the abode of hostile Germanic tribal groups who were a match for the legions. Fed on the descriptions of Tacitus, the Romans regarded the German forest with a mixture of "awesome admiration as well as repugnance"—admiration at its sylvan purity, which accorded with their own founding myths, but repugnance at its uncivilized "otherness" or "outsided-ness"—in other words, for being alien and "non-Rome." [41]

But modern archeological work is challenging that view of a unbroken forest in northern Europe, just as it has challenged interpretations of Neolithic forest use, and for the same reason. Romano-British and Romano-Gallic clearing in Britain and parts of France was more widespread than thought, although Germanic lands still exhibited large tracts of untouched forest. The true ecological relationships of this age have not yet been investigated satisfactorily, but all the evidence suggests that there was less forest and far more cultivation and grazing than once thought. It was a landscape already in the process of considerable transformation at the time of the Roman occupation.

Yet we know little about rural life in these territories except for what archeology tells us, as what scraps of literary evidence exist are almost totally skewed toward urban life. Even then the preeminence of Rome and its absolute independence to govern its territories, unfettered by election or control, means that the literary evidence "bears almost wholly on the city of Rome and on the activity of the central government." Other cities barely exist in the written record and the countryside (other than Italy) even less so because the life of the ancient world is more or less identical with the life of the ancient cities. "The cities have told us their story, the country always remained silent and reserved," said Rostovtzeff.[42]

Yet one cannot read Rostovtzeff's and Heichelheim's accounts of the empire without feeling that the silence of the record masks a busy and active rural life. The accounts of the large slave-operated and tenanted estates in Italy; the affluent capitalist estates of Spain and particularly of Gaul; the rich farms of northern Gaul and on the left bank of the Rhine, particularly around Treves; and the active colonization of Roman emigrant colonists and veterans in Africa and on the Rhine and the Danube, together with the splendid cities supported in many of these fertile and highly productive agricultural regions, all add up to a picture of enormous rural activity and prosperity, and inevitably clearing.

In northern Gaul, Germany, and Britain, conquest brought peace and hence greater cultivation, and assured that markets emerged to supply the army. For example, Albert Rivet has calculated that over 106,000 acres would have been required to supply wheat to the army of occupation in Britain alone, and that the British Isles even exported wheat to Rome. On the whole it was a land "of farms and agricultural estates, . . . of villas and squires," rather than cities with surrounding peasants and small proprietors. The middle Danube region was the same. Many areas must have been like Gaul, where "enormous holes" were made in the forest as "new villas and sanctuaries were built on the fringes of the woods or even . . . in a clearing inside . . . [which was] a cause of ruin to the forest round it."[43] The remains of the large and even luxurious villas are a testimony to the scale and complexity of this new capitalistic rural life, in which cultivation and stock rearing went hand in hand.

Shipbuilding

The building of ships, and to a lesser extent, urbanization and the smelting of metals, loom large as destroyers of the forest in contemporary accounts, as in, for example, Eratosthenes' description of the denudation of Cyprus; but it is doubtful that the impact came anywhere near that of agriculture or domestic fuelwood use. Shipbuilding and smelting were extraneous, exotic activities that appeared as alien and dramatic intrusions into the rhythms of everyday life compared to the ceaseless and timeless qualities of agriculture and pastoralism, or even the now-commonplace activity of building towns. Therefore, they attracted much attention, and in this respect they were analogous to iron furnaces in seventeenth-century England or railways and iron smelting in nineteenth-century North America which were blamed erroneously for the destruction of the forest, though in reality they accounted for only a small percentage of the forest felled. Nevertheless, the importance attached to the supply of timber for building ships cannot be denied, as ship construction had become crucial to the burgeoning economic life of the Mediterranean; sea power was vital in the exercise of political control.[44]

Trade had grown rapidly during the second half of the first millennium to bring the good things of life to a large section of the population. "Command of the seas," said one anonymous writer in the late fourth century BC,

> has enabled the Athenian to . . . discover refinements of luxury. . . . Every delicacy of Sicily, Italy, Cyprus, Egypt, Lydia, the Black Sea, the Peloponnese or any other country has been accumulated in a single spot . . . [and they are in] a position to accumulate wealth.[45]

There was, suggest Andrew and Susan Sherratt, "a primary zone of capital- and labour-intensive manufacturing from the Levant to the Southern Aegean," surrounded by a zone of higher-value agricultural products (wine, oil), and beyond that a grain-growing belt in Cyrenaica, Sicily/southern Italy, and the Black Sea, with many separate centers of manufacturing and supply beyond that, particularly in the Carthaginian and Phoenician western half of the basin. In addition, timber was extracted from the forests that existed everywhere around the basin, especially the northern shores (fig. 4.1).[46] None of these regions of production could have existed without the use of silver as medium of exchange, slavery for labor, and above all, the ability to move bulky and precious goods among island, promontory, and coast in the relatively safe waters of the *Mare Internum.*

The small and largely self-sufficient poleis or city-states attempted to gain influence and power through amalgamation and control of neighboring settlements and their productive hinterlands, or even by founding new settlements. Indeed, the latter half of the second millennium BC presents a bewildering kaleidoscope of alliances and leagues as the Hellenistic kings maneuvered for power, and Rome subsequently rose as a force in the western Mediterranean. It is true that much of this colonization was land conquest—the Persian and Roman Empires being prime examples—but around the Mediterranean the influence of sea power "was rarely dormant and sometimes decisive." Thucydides' account of the prolonged and bitter wars between Athens and the Peloponnesian League was basically an account of the growth of their navies, and the search for men and the commanding of timber supplies; the same could be said for the early wars of Rome against the Carthaginians, and other confrontations. The possession of ships, for whatever purposes, was so important that Roman emperors offered privileges and tax incentives for their construction, and many a colonial enterprise was aimed at securing timber supplies.[47]

Each conflict reinforced the need for ships, and the outcome of colonization was always an increase in trade, which in turn called for more merchant ships and warships to protect them. Some idea of the size of navies is gleaned from the fact that Athenian fleets may have reached 200–300 triremes during the Persian War of 480 BC. Moreover, Rome lost 700 quinqueremes during the twenty-four years of the First Punic War; and in response, crash programs of building were undertaken, as when Rome built 120 ships in 60 days during the first war against Carthage, and a year later 220 ships in 45 days. And timber was available for their construction. The conventional trireme, in addition to the timber for the hull, needed 200 oars (170 for the three banks of rowers and 30 spares), two large steering oars, and a mast and yardarm. It might have been between 115 and 120 ft long.

Not only did the ships get more numerous, but they also got larger. By the beginning of the fourth century BC *pentereis* appeared, which one might expect to have 5 banks of oars; but this was technically impossible, especially as mysterious "fifteens" and "sixteens" appeared later. In this case the numbers probably referred not to the banks of oars, but to the number of oarsmen needed to pull each oar. Thus, a "fifteen" might have 7 persons to one oar and 8 to another, the two oars one above the other. Size became even more important when boats began to carry catapults for sinking their enemy, foregoing the previous strategy of ramming. Ptolemy IV (r. 221–203 BC) built a brobdingnagian "forty," which may have been a catamaran that needed 4,000 oarsmen, and carried 400 other crew and 2,850 marines. Later merchant ships even had a gymnasium, reading rooms, and baths on board. These were extravagant exceptions "intended for display not action." At approximately 130 tons, the norm was much smaller, making the ships more maneuverable for negotiating the multitude of small harbors and jetties that had been constructed around the Mediterranean coast.[48]

One could go on, but the important point is that the strategic demand for special types of timber was very real; a lively trade for it sprang up in peacetime, and competition was intensified during wartime. The situation was more critical in the eastern Mediterranean because of the meager and irregular distribution of trees in the Levantine, Egyptian, and Aegean regions, whereas the abundant supplies and variety of species in the west meant that competition and conflict, while not absent, were not so intense.

It is difficult to be exact about the distribution of timber resources, but Maurice Lombard's reconstruction of the early medieval forests reproduced in figure 4.1 gives us some broad appreciation of where the major forests were, and the likely routes of trade.[49] The fullest contemporary statement on strategic resources comes from Theophrastus:

> silver-fir, fir and Syrian cedar are, generally speaking, useful for ship-building; for triremes and long ships are made of silver-fir, because of its lightness, and merchant ships of fir, because it does not decay; while some make triremes of it also because they are ill-provided with silver-fir. The people of Syria and Phoenicia use Syrian cedar, since they cannot obtain much fir either; while the people of Cyprus use Aleppo pine, since their island provides this and it seems to be superior to their fir. Most parts are made of these woods.

He then continues to detail the preferred woods for keels and other parts of ships of different types and sizes.[50]

Fir *(alies alba)* was lighter than pine and grew best at or near the upper limit of tree growth on the highest mountains, over 3,000 m. Mountain pine (*Pinus nigra* in Greece and *Pinus laricio* in Italy), in contrast with the more common coastal pine, was stronger than fir and was found in more-varied locations on the intermediate mountain slopes. The parts of Mediterranean Europe that could supply these superior timbers were limited and included "the Macedonian region and certain parts of Thrace and Italy; in Asia Cilicia, Sinope, and Amisus, and also the Mysian Olympus, and Mount Ida; but in these parts it is not abundant." Syria, on the other hand, used its cedar for ships. The conflicts that arose from combatants jockeying to secure essential supplies confirm that these were indeed the prime timber areas—Sicily, the Sila forest of southern Italy, Macedonia, and Mount Ida and the Taurus Mountains of Cilicia in northwestern Asia Minor are mentioned again and again, and remained prime producing regions well into the nineteenth century. There are some hints of the conservation of strategic supplies, such as in Cyprus, where Theophrastus said, "the kings used not to cut the trees . . . because they took great care of them and managed them," adding that later rulers of the island benefited in their shipbuilding from their predecessors' foresight.[51]

Large timbers were floated down rivers to specialized ports developed at their mouths, such as Colchis on the eastern Black Sea and Ravenna and Luna on the Adriatic. Sometimes rafts were constructed and even floated across narrow seas, as in 400 BC, when Dionysus of Syracuse brought timber for shipbuilding from the Sila forest in southern

Italy and towed it across the Straits of Messina by oar-powered boats to Syracuse. By about the second century BC, specially constructed ships for carrying long timbers were developed.[52]

Strabo's descriptions of the timber sources echo and augment those of Theophrastus, but as he was writing during the period of the ascendancy of Rome, his comments pertained far more to the western half of the Mediterranean rather than the eastern half. Southeastern Spain was covered with "dense forests of tall trees" which supplied ships' timbers. The inhabitants of Marseilles were famous for their skill in shipbuilding, while the Ligurian mountains in the rich hinterland of Genoa furnished "very great quantities of timber that is suitable for ship building," with trees of up to 8 ft in diameter, as well as abundant pitch, essential for caulking ships' timbers as well as wine casks. Pliny similarly enumerated the lumber resources of the basin; his knowledge was wider, however, so he included the timber of the Alps, Jura, and Vosges on the one hand, and the Atlas Mountains on the other, in addition to the more well-known eastern ranges.[53]

The strategic use of and need for timber in times of war and peace were first adumbrated in the classical world. They were going to be elaborated even more clearly by other maritime nations in the centuries to come—regionally, with the Muslims in the seventh to eleventh centuries and the Venetian Republic in the fifteenth and sixteenth centuries, and then globally, with the great sea powers of Spain, France, Holland, and England in the sixteenth to early nineteenth centuries. Naval demands on the forest were a major reason for concern about the abundance or dearth of trees.

Urbanization

Alongside trade and commerce, urbanization was the other major, distinguishing mark of classical life. It was the age of the city which allowed a sizable proportion of the population to indulge in the higher and finer side of life, and cultivate the mind. Civilization (from *civis*, Latin for "citizen" or "city dweller") is, etymologically speaking, "citification." The concentration of such a large number of people in one spot meant a great consumption of wood for construction and fuel. Whereas country dwellers could either forage for or produce these materials as a by-product of agricultural operations with no visible short-term effect on the countryside, city dwellers could not. They were dependent on the development of a complex set of trading relationships to sustain city life, from carpenters, builders, and wood haulers, to charcoal burners and domestic wood carriers, some of whom might also have been farmers. In addition to ordinary domestic construction, the major classical cities were also the sites of large ceremonial public buildings, such as temples, circuses, theaters, palaces, baths, and assembly rooms, structures of immense size in which vast timber spans were required in order to straddle the open public spaces beneath. These needs made city requirements for carefully selected, large, straight timbers as demanding as those for shipbuilding.

The size of cities is uncertain, but it is thought that Alexandria had reached at least 300,000 by the first century BC, and that if slaves were included it might have even been double that. Below it was "a handful of cities whose total populations might have approached a quarter of a million, Pergamon, Miletus, Syrian Antioch and Athens among them and perhaps thirty or forty cities between thirty and one hundred thousand inhabitants."[54] Similar hierarchies of city size were evident in the Roman world.

Of all the classical cities, Athens and Rome provide the greatest detail about the use of timber, not only because of their size but also because of their sociopolitical importance. By the fifth century BC Plato complained that the demand for timber had denuded the hills and plains surrounding Athens and caused massive soil erosion. Most commentators are inclined to discount this as exaggerated, a combination of myth and reality, as Plato builds up a picture of a past Athens when everything was much better—a Golden Age no less. After carefully assessing the evidence, Russell Meiggs suggests that timber supply was not a critical issue at this time and that "Athenian farmers were not so senseless as to cut down all their trees." Timber on the farm was always useful for building, making tools, and supplying the "wide demand" for fuelwood and charcoal for cooking and heating.[55]

Whatever the truth of that, conditions did change later. The demands of shipbuilding; the growth of grandiose public buildings, such as the Parthenon, the Propylaea, and the Odeum; the development of pitched, gabled roofs in place of flat ones; more elaborate furnishing for houses, such as doors, lintels, windows, frames, and shutters; and the undoubted physical growth of Athens and its port, Pireaus, might have increased timber consumption "fourfold." In addition, the need for domestic fuel, that almost invisible but essential commodity for cooking and warmth, would have grown in direct proportion to the growth of population. When the industrial demands for timber for smelting silver and iron and for fusing copper and tin to make bronze are considered, then fuelwood consumption might have exceeded all other uses. Because small wood could be used for fuelwood and for making charcoal, there was a tendency to minimize transportation and scour the immediate countryside for supplies. In time the radius of gathering must have increased, and from fragmentary evidence Meiggs concludes that farmers within 20 km of Athens would have found it profitable to cut and sell wood to the city.[56] Such a conclusion accords well with the experience of urban demands for fuel in the less-developed world today.

Finer timbers for window and door furniture in the houses of the more affluent, and timber for general carpentry, were imported (see fig. 4.1). Theophrastus confirmed this when reporting the origins of the best of the timber:

> Macedonia, for it is smooth and of straight grain and it contains resin; second best is that from Pontus [northeast Turkey facing the Black Sea], third from the Rhyndakos [Bithynia].[57]

During the second century BC, Athens and the Hellenistic kingdoms were eclipsed by the growth of Rome after its victory over Carthage in the Second Punic War. Population actually declined, and for a short while Attica may have even approached self-sufficiency in wood. Rome, on the other hand, grew magnificently to become the largest city in the world (until London reached a similar size in 1801). Its population was about 463,000 in 86 BC, 1 million by 5 BC, and possibly between 1.2 million and 1.6 million by the fourth century AD, with decreases from frequent epidemics being compensated for by massive rural in-migration. Building and rebuilding (owing to destruction by floods and frequent fires, as well as pure speculative construction and stylistic whim) went on "unceasingly" and the city became filled with "many beautiful structures." The infusion of wealth and Hellenistic culture encouraged higher standards of living, and according to Strabo, people were "devising palaces of Persian magnificence."[58] Thus, like Athens before it, both private and public buildings in Rome became larger and more grandiose, requiring larger and better-quality timbers. Details of the spectacular spans needed in major buildings are abundant, but as ever, it was the unrecorded requirements of the mass of housing that led to the greatest consumption of timber and drain on the forests.

Roofing timbers, floor joists, door and window furniture, staircases, balconies, and shingles were direct users. However, the growing manufacture of tiles and bricks, which replaced shingles and mud walls in order to limit fire hazards and provide structural stability for multistoried apartment blocks, were also great consumers of wood. They had to be baked in furnaces, as indeed did the great variety of clay and ceramic tiles used for floors and mosaics. It is calculated that every cubic meter (1.0 m^3) of burnt brick required nearly 150 m^3 of wood to make. Bricks also had to be fixed to one another, and intense heat was required ($900°C–1100°C$, depending on the type of stone used) to calcinate or reduce calcium carbonate (limestone or chalk) to lime, the basis of cement, plaster, and ultimately concrete. Each ton of lime required between 5 and 10 tonnes of wood to produce, depending on the quality of the wood. By the fourth century AD, 3,000 wagonloads of lime were required in Rome annually, half for aqueduct maintenance and the other half for the repair and general construction of buildings.[59] When the development of glass manufacturing (and glassblowing) from the first century AD onward is added to that of bricks and tiles, then the energy requirement in building alone must have consumed a vast amount of wood. Even when concrete became more common—particularly for vaulting, which substituted for large beams—the demand for timber barely lessened because of its use in shuttering and scaffolding, though in such cases it could be reused a number of times and end up usefully as fuelwood.

The smaller constructional pieces were of oak, elm, and ash, as well as myrtle and beech, and came from the immediate vicinity of Rome, particularly the Alban Hills. Larger timbers for beams and bridges, however, were transported from the fir forests high in the Apennines. Strabo spoke of the "concourse of blessings" that allowed the ever-growing city to feed itself, and find building stone and timber. Foremost was the network of rivers, whereby the transportation of these materials could be focused on the city.

> First, the Anio, which flows from Alba, the Latin city next to the Marsi, through the plain that is below Alba to its confluence with the Tiber; and then the Nar and the Teneas, the rivers that run through Ombrica down to the same river, the Tiber: and also the Clanis, which, however, runs down thither through Tyrrhenia and the territory of Clusiam.

The Tyrrhenian or Etrurian timber was, he said, "very straight and very long," and that too came downriver along the west coast and up the Tiber to Rome. The competition for timber for the city was such that lumbering for shipbuilding in the hinterland of Pisa had given way to the lumbering for building construction in Rome. But where transportation was difficult there was little exploitation, which explains the survival of quite dense forests throughout the Mediterranean until the nineteenth century.[60]

The construction of buildings was not the only user of wood. Heat was needed for cooking and for house warming in the bitterly cold winter months from late November to mid-April. More affluent households had charcoal braziers that produced a steady heat, warmer and less smoky than that of open fires. But poorer households must have emulated Virgil, who in his *Ecologues* derived satisfaction and comfort from the latter:

> Here's hearth and pitch-pine billet, here's a roaring fire
> Ever alight, and door posts black with ingrained soot.

North of the Alps there is evidence that some larger houses were centrally heated, either by single pipes led around the walls and even the ceilings, or by hypocaust (literally, "fire beneath"), that is to say, the floor of the rooms being supported by short pillars and the space created filled with hot air from a furnace. Perhaps as much as 2 cords (approximately 7.2 m³) or more were used daily to maintain an adequate heat, though in Britain there is evidence of the use of coal.[61]

Two other peculiarly Roman customs or institutions consumed untold quantities of wood: cremation and hot baths. Cremation progressively supplanted burial in the later centuries BC, only to be reversed with the advent of Christianity. Its use of timber can only be surmised. However, we can be surer of the public baths and steam rooms, which held a high place in the culture of the city as social, medicinal, and hygiene centers, and which ranged from the luxurious to the mean. As the city grew in affluence and size, so the baths grew more numerous and larger. We do not know how numerous they were until much later on, in the fourth century AD, when there were said to be eleven sets of large imperial baths and 856 smaller establishments in Rome. In time public baths became common in towns throughout the empire, and private baths were attached to individual villas. The work of Fritz Kretzschmer and Anthony Rook allows one to make some reasonable calculations about the *order of magnitude* of fuel needed to warm a bath. Making a number of assumptions, the Welwyn baths in England brought to a constant requisite temperature of 70°C for the *Calarium* (hot bath) and 55°C for the *Tepidarium* (tepid bath) might have used 114 tons of wood a year, the equivalent of perhaps an acre of reasonably mature hardwood forest, or 23 acres of coppiced woodland.[62] We cannot be more precise than that.

So how much timber might an average Roman town dweller have consumed? The answer, as always, will depend on an array of variables, such as status, affluence, and local climate. But if the consumption per capita of timber for fuel for heating and cooking alone in the less developed world today is on average 0.45 m³, and can rise to as much as 0.8 m³ in rural Africa where other energy sources are absent, then consumption in the more profligate Roman world, with its many more industrial uses for wood, must have been at least double that, to be between 1.0 and 1.5 m³. The likelihood is, however, that given the central position of wood in the life and livelihood of the late classical world, we are seriously underestimating the level of consumption. The only other reasonably reliable figure from a virile, inventive wood-based economy comes for North America in the late eighteenth century, for which an annual per-capita consumption of 4.5 cords (576 ft³), or 17.3 m³, is suggested—a quantity 11.5 times greater than our calculation for Rome.[63]

But we are guessing and simply do not know; yet if the conservative estimate of consumption of Rome at the peak of its population is taken as 1.5 m³ × 1.5 million people, then 2.25 million m³ would have been consumed. If 300 m³ per acre is taken as an average density for hardwoods, then about 7,500 acres, or 11.7 mi² (30.34 km²), of woodland would have been destroyed per annum. If the consumption was greater, then the forest destruction would have been correspondingly larger. Overall it seems likely that fuelwood for all purposes may have constituted about 90 percent of all timber used in the Roman Empire.

Of course, the woodland may not have been cleared entirely. Some of the fuel could have come from coppicing, for which there is some evidence; from periodic thinning of agricultural woodlands; as the by-product of purposeful clearing for agriculture; and even from pruning, as so often happened. Cato (234–149 BC) recommended that all vine and tree cuttings be sold profitably as firewood or faggots, or, alternatively, be put to good use for the home fire and furnace. Whatever the source, however, cutting and collecting must have spread further and further afield as Rome grew and its urban influence penetrated into the surrounding countryside, aided by an ever-growing network of roads. Also broadening the scope of wood gathering was the rise of the *lignari*, possibly traders concentrating on the production and transportation of *lignum*, or fuelwood, although they may well have been involved in other wood hauling. Transportation costs and scarcity contributed to a rise in the price of wood. The Romans, said Strabo, had by valor and toil "made the country their own property"; clearing, particularly for fuel, must have been a significant part of that toil.[64]

As the centuries progressed there are indications that the very largest timbers were becoming more difficult to find, and that the demand for fuel rose as smelting and brick and lime making increased. The big beams were now coming from the Black Sea coast and the Raetian Alps. The peculiar position of the baths in Roman society adds a few final clues. Sometime before AD 235, when the emperor Alexander Severus died, he had set aside local woodlands for stoking the Roman baths, but within a hundred years, logs were being shipped by salt contractors from points along the Italian coast and up the Tiber, and even from North Africa.[65] Despite this importation, however, it is difficult to believe that all the timber in the vicinity of Rome had disappeared; it is more likely that only the readily harvested supply from unclaimed forest stands in the immediate vicinity of the city had diminished as cultivation and pastoralism domesticated, divided, and apportioned the landscape.

The urban demands for construction, fuel, heating, and all other purposes have been considered in some detail to show that even at this early date they were very great. They serve as a measure and reminder of the constant drain on the forest in all societies, and with a only few exceptions urban uses will not be dealt with in detail again.

Metal Smelting

With urbanization it is difficult to make a clear distinction between the domestic and commercial consumption of wood. Heating, cooking, and cremation were clearly domestic activities, as could be building, though the likelihood was that building was more of a commercial operation with specialized contractors. Heating water and rooms for baths was a bit of both. When it comes to the supply of constructional timber, the distinction is even less clear. Although specialized timber procurers abounded for the supply of the long, straight timbers for ships and public buildings, if classical rural society was anything like the rural societies of later times, then subsistence farmers were also part-time lumbermen. During the agricultural off-season, as Cato more than hinted, useful additions to household income could be made by cutting and carting choppings from the farm as fuel to the growing towns, or even rough timbers for construction. Some farmers may even have hired themselves out to commercial timber and fuelwood suppliers as part-time woodcutters. Either way the distinction between domestic and commercial production and consumption and agricultural and commercial cutting gets more blurred.

Mining and metal smelting, on the other hand, were definitely commercial pursuits. They were distributed widely throughout the Greek and Roman worlds, and by the latter centuries of the first millennium BC refining had become a sophisticated manufacturing process. Bronze—a fusion of tin and copper—was commonplace from archaic times in Greece, and iron was becoming more so with every century. In addition, silver was the common medium of exchange throughout the Mediterranean. Metal-smelting, together with the manufacture of glass, cement, bricks, ceramics, and concrete, was a manifestation of what Theodore Wertime has called pyrotechnology, and which required untold amounts of charcoal.[66]

Calculations have been made of the impact on the forests of smelting at notable classical mining sites,[67] but because of the many variables and uncertainties involved one cannot be too dogmatic about the amount of woodland cleared. Especially noteworthy are the factors used in the statistical transformations, such as yield of timber per tree and the density of trees per unit area, all of which have to be average estimates; the number of years over which the exploitation occurred; the regrowth regime of forests; the differing yields of metals for the same amounts of charcoal expended; and even the mixtures of other metals in ores, such as lead with silver. Some of the calculations are displayed in table 4.1, and they refer to silver smelting at Rio Tinto, in southwest Spain; iron smelting at Populonia, on the Italian mainland opposite the Isle of Elba where the ore was extracted but could no longer be smelted due to the exhaustion of fuel; copper smelting in Cyprus; and silver smelting at Laurion (Lavrion) in southern Greece. They must be treated with caution, and are only as good as the assumptions built into them.

On face value, the figures are large, but not, perhaps, as startling as they appear at first glance, especially when one realizes that they are totals that stretch over centuries. Certainly there has been a tendency toward exaggeration in some of the estimates. For example, Wertime's "20–30 million acres of cut trees" as the total deforestation caused by the metallurgical industries of Egypto-Greco-Roman civilization inexplicably became "50–70 million acres of trees" in the next year; and Constantinou's calculation that 150,000 km² of forest was needed to serve the copper mines of Cyprus—which is 16 times the size of the island—is based on a misapprehension of the process of clearing over time and the possibility of forest regeneration.[68] Even in table 4.1 the 19,195 km² of

Table 4.1 Production and estimated area of timber used in four mining locations (Rio Tinto, Populonia, Cyprus, and Lavrion) in the classical world

	Rio Tinto (Spain): Silver and Copper	Populonia (Italy): Iron and Some Bronze	Cyprus: Copper	Lavrion (Greece): Lead and Some Silver
Slag residues (tons)	30 million [1, 4]	?	4 million [3]	2.7 million [7]
Calculated metal production (tons)	?	500,000 [1]	200,000 [3]	1.4 million [7]
Charcoal needed per ton metal produced (kg)	450	4,520 [5]	300,000 [3]	450 [2]
Total charcoal (tons)	13.5 million	2.2 million	60 million	631,350 [3]
Wood needed to produce 1 ton charcoal (tons)	16 [3, 5]	16 [3, 5]	16 [3, 5]	16 [5]
Total wood needed (tons)	216 million	36.1 million	960 million	10.1 million
Yield of trees (kg)	Oak = 375	Pine = 800 [1]	Pine = 800 [1]	Pine = 800 [1]
Trees needed	575.8 million	45.2 million	1,200 million	12.6 million
Density of trees/ha	300	240	240	240
ha of trees	1.9 million	187,500	6 million	63,135
km² of forest	19.195	1,875	60,000	631
Years of operation	2,000+	500?	3,000?	2,300?

Sources: (1) Wertime and Wertime, 1979: 135; (2) Salkield 1982: 137–47; (3) Constantinou 1982: 22; (4) Salkield 1970: 94; (5) Forbes 1964, 9: 6; (6) Patterson 1972: 231–33; (7) Wertime, 1982: 356.
Note: ? denotes information that is not available.

forest cleared for Rio Tinto has to be averaged over at least 2,000 years or, if the Classical impact is isolated from the total, only half the slags over 600 years;[69] the 1,875 km² of Populonia over about 500 years; the 60,000 km² of Cyprus over 3,000 years; and the 631.5 km² in Lavrion over 550 years. If that is done, and some sort of rotational cutting is postulated, then annual totals drop dramatically, as suggested by table 12.4 on the effect of different densities of trees and rotational practices. They could be as little as 10 km²–15 km², or half that if a rotational cutting or coppicing was used. Locally it would have been devastating, but not the agent of massive change that is suggested; there were still ample reserves of timber on the mountains of Cyprus in the late Roman Empire. Perhaps Eratosthenes got it just about right in the third century BC, when he said that in ancient times the copper and silver mines "were of some service" (another translation says "helped a little")—as did shipbuilding—in the deforestation of the once wooded plains; but agricultural clearing had more effect on the forests, and even that had to be encouraged by offering free possession to anyone who cleared the land and brought it into cultivation.[70]

There is one other minutely calculated example of the demands of smelting on the forests from the "other" classical world, that of the Weald of southeast England, where the Roman military mined and smelted iron. There were perhaps 34 iron-producing sites in all, of which 6 of the largest were investigated by Henry Cleere, who also experimented with reconstructing and operating a Roman bloomery furnace in order to achieve authentic data. From slag remains and a number of statistical transformations he calculated that between AD 120 and 240 the six largest furnaces produced a total of 89,500 tonnes, or 550 tonnes annually. That resulted in the harvesting and clearing of nearly 2 km² of dense, mixed deciduous woodland, mainly oak, per annum, or about 220 km^2 over the period, which if smaller satellite furnaces were included could have been nearer 3.5 km^2/yr, or a total of 420 km^2 over 120 years, but much less if rotational felling or coppicing were resorted to.[71]

But for all these calculations it is strange that if there was so much forest devastation there is no more positive evidence. Perhaps we can agree with Meiggs, who thought that there was possibly more danger of "exaggerating rather than underestimating" the contribution of metallurgy to deforestation.[72] It was to be a common tendency everywhere through all time. Very few people would have disagreed with Pliny's observation that "it is for the sake of their timber that Nature has created . . . the trees."[73]

DEFORESTATION AND SOIL DEGRADATION

The fluctuating fortunes of great powers have fascinated observers in all ages, and Edward Gibbon's *History of the Decline and Fall of the Roman Empire* and Edgar Allan Poe's beautiful lines on "the glory that was Greece / and the grandeur that was Rome" are two works that are embedded in the Western consciousness and conscience.[74] For Donald Hughes and Jack Thirgood the connection was clear: the close link "between ruined cities and ruined land" was "inescapable," and more recently David Attenborough has seen deforestation as "the crucial blow" to settlement on the eastern and southern shores of the Mediterranean. Like Henry David Thoreau, George Perkins Marsh, Paul Sears, Walter Lowdermilk, and Fairfield Osborn before them, they are convinced that deforestation and subsequent soil degradation were major contributors to the weakening of the economic and social systems of the classical world.[75] While all note other, often unspecified, causes for decline, the one contributory cause—deforestation—slowly becomes the main cause. Repeated enough it assumes the character of truth. Arcadia becomes anarchy, ecological profligacy leads to ruin—a moral lesson that many in this environmentally conscious age would like to draw.

But it is far more complicated than that. While soil erosion most certainly occurred, and devastatingly so in places, it is more likely that constant war, ravaging epidemics, rebellion, invasion from outside, a declining population, and an excessive degree of urbanization, separately or in combination, operated in the complexity of an empire that had extended beyond its means.[76] In particular, the slender margin of surplus agricultural production needed to sustain city life could have been a crucial factor, given that over ten people were required to support one city dweller, even in a prosperous region These pressures exposed the internal fragility, instability, and weakness of the sociopolitical system, all exacerbated by compulsory work stints, overtaxation, lack of capital to invest in and improve farming, a crumbling system of slavery, and intense class divisions, many of which were created by urbanization, which engendered a privileged bourgeoisie.[77]

Over and above all this, the very existence of widespread *agricultural* decline, land abandonment, and extension of large estate farms, or *latifundia,* at the expense of the impoverishment of the free peasantry has been brought into question by Tamara Lewit after an extensive survey of over 200 villas and their economy throughout Roman Europe.

She found that there was actually a prolonged "boom period" in land occupation and farming, especially in south Gaul, southern Spain, Sicily, Pannonia, and the eastern empire during the third and fourth centuries AD, which turns the conventional interpretations on their head.[78]

What is the evidence of the deforestation/erosion argument? The starting point is the fifth-century comment of Plato in the *Critias* that in the distant past, the soil of Attica was deep and the mountains "heavily afforested." But its trees had disappeared, some to provide rafters for Athenian buildings, and the mountains could now "keep nothing but bees." As he wrote, Attica was a naked upland: "What remains of her substance is like the skeleton of a body emaciated by disease. . . . All the rich, soft soil has moulted away, leaving a country of skin and bones. . . . The annual supply of rainfall was not lost, as it is at present, through being allowed to flow over the denuded surface into the sea." The imagery is striking and has been quoted approvingly and frequently by geographers, conservationists, ecologists, and others concerned with environmental stability. But, as noted before, most commentators on the classical age are inclined to discount it as exaggerated, as Plato builds up a picture of a past Athens when everything was much better—an early example of nostalgia at work to evoke a Golden Age, which is such a perennial theme in the Western imagination. As J. Neumann suggests, it is hard to decide whether "what he writes is history, or mythology, or poetry," and for Heichelheim it is "no more reliable than his famous Atlantis myth." The naturally dry and sparsely timbered plain of Attica was certainly cultivated intensively for grain and planted with olive trees, and therefore cleared; and while there was undoubtedly overcutting in the mountains nearest to Athens, there is little evidence of the same in more distant mountains, which were still heavily forested during the nineteenth century.[79]

For Rostovtzeff the idea that soil exhaustion was a cause for a general decay of the Roman world was "unconvincing" even if there were localized pockets of degradation around Rome and Athens, as seems likely. To extend the argument to all Italy was "a generalization that cannot be accepted." In the provinces large new territories were permanently taken into cultivation throughout the second and third centuries AD. Portions of the fertile fenland of Britain were drained, as were parts of Holland. North African olive and grain cultivation expanded brilliantly, and in Egypt flood control measures and irrigation made more productive portions of land that had been previously abandoned. The story was the same throughout the Levant and Mesopotamia, and the experience seems to run counter to the general degradation thesis. Heichelheim would go so far as to say that the fertility potential of the soil was "rarely endangered" in classical antiquity, if only because the plows and other agricultural tools of the period were not "strong enough" to cause degradation; that was caused by overgrazing by large-scale cattle ranching during the Middle Ages. However, on the steep, deforested, terraced hillsides of Greece and other regions where slave raiding caused depopulation, it is likely that agricultural maintenance suffered, and the thin overlying mantle of soil was washed away.[80]

That natural processes were accelerated with tree cutting and cultivation is obvious, but all in all, it is strange that in such a literate and observant world no evidence has arisen of "consciences disturbed by the excessive exploitation of the forests," no general alarm about depletion, no treatise on forest management, nor examples of efforts to plant trees other than olive trees.[81] The numerous agricultural treatises of the age do not mention soil erosion, even as a minor problem. Equally, the maintenance of soil fertility is not explored as much as one might expect, other than by Columella, and there is no examination of soil structure. Of course, it is possible that the natural process was so slow and imperceptible that it was not noticed; natural processes are largely invisible because they are natural. But there are some hints. For example, Pliny was aware of the increased incidence of flash floods with clearing so that "devastating torrents unite when from hills has been cut away the wood that used to hold the rains and absorb them." Pausanias (circa 174 AD) compared the deposits from two river basins on the Greek Anatolian coast: the Achelous, from which the inhabitants had been driven out by the Romans, and which presumably remained largely forested or with abandoned cultivated lands; and the Maeander, "which is ploughed up each year." The former did not "bring down as much mud on the Echinades [offshore islands] as it otherwise would do," but the latter "had turned to mainland in a short time the sea that once was between Priene and Miletus." Similarly, Ephesus became landlocked with deposits from the Cyster by the third century BC, and other examples of delta formation and the herculean labors needed to dredge clogged harbors like Paestum and Ostia can be found around the eastern Mediterranean, as at the head of the Thermaic Gulf in western Macedonia (fig. 4.2). But alluviation may have happened despite deforestation, and in any case, as Meiggs points out, "[d]estruction by flood became a well-worn topos in Greek and Latin literature."[82]

In reviewing the paleo-botanical, climatic, and archeological evidence of Greece, John Bintliff argues that given its harsh natural environment, one cannot expect "vast woods of lofty trees, nor well-developed soils." In Crete, for example, steep limestone uplands cannot support woodland, but upland terraces and depressions can. Similarly, lowland soils can support forest in favorable places only. Thus, around the Minoan palace at Mallia are dense arable fields that have been cultivated for "almost uninterrupted millennia" and fine woodland in the surrounding hills. Pollen analysis in the Drama Plain, together with the corroborative evidence of travelers in the region during the last five hundred years, suggests that the forests could, and did, regenerate successfully; and that it was the massive clearances of the last couple of centuries with greater accessibility by road and rail that have created the present bare landscape, not the activities of the classical past.[83] If anything, the Roman and later medieval phase was a moist one in which woodland growth would have been encouraged. It is only during the last few centuries that there has been a return to a more "Mediterranean" climate, with natural forest recession in marginal locations.

The difficulty of disentangling the relationships among past climatic change, vegetational change, human settlement, and erosion and sedimentation phases has occupied many a learned page without definitive resolution.[84] Claudio Vita-Finzi's original hypothesis of an Older (late glacial) and Younger (essentially medieval) Fill, both caused by natural fluctuations of climate and not human action, has gone through many revisions.[85] Early work suggested that a considerable amount of the deposition was not classical or preclassical in origin but post-Roman, with C_{14} dating extending from AD 1150 to 1750,

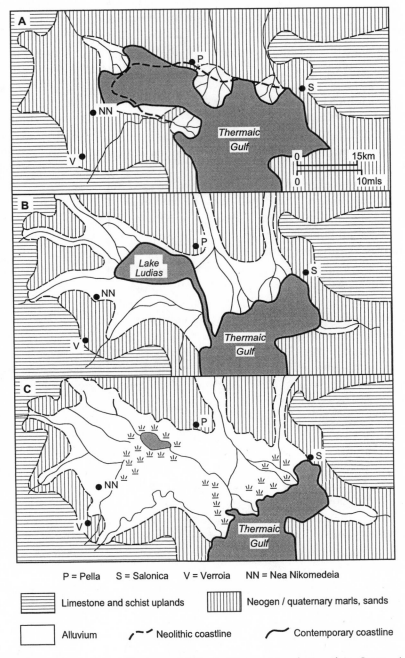

Figure 4.2 Landscape change due to siltation and fill in the Western Macedonian plain, Greece: *A*, Greco-Roman; *B* , = Late Roman; and *C*, AD 1900. *Source*: after Bintliff, 1977b: fig. 9A–D.

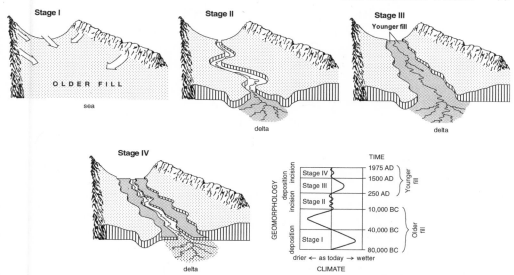

Figure 4.3 Late Quaternary development of Mediterranean river valleys, with climatic fluctuations and geomorphological phases, 80,000 BC to present. *Source:* based on Vita-Finzi, 1969, with additions by Bintliff, 1977b: fig. 8.

and that comparable deposition is not taking place today (fig. 4.3). Subsequently, Bintliff suggested that the evidence of deltaic sediments represents an earlier phase of deposition and is not connected with the Younger Fill, and that the confusion is due to a misunderstanding of the cycle of erosion and deposition in the Vita-Finzi model. Another conclusion is that the wetter the climate, the greater the erosion and hence deposition, and that the period of maximum known deforestation during the last few centuries has been marked by minimum stream aggradation and incision into previously steeply graded sediments.[86] Consequently, it is possible that the markedly wetter climate from AD 1000–1750 had caused the historical alluviation, and that classical deforestation is not the culprit. The evidence of an increase in erosion rates in river basins around Rome from 2 cm–3 cm/1000 yrs in the second century BC to 20 cm–40 cm/1000 yrs at present supports either early Roman clearing or the climatic change hypothesis.[87]

On the other hand, more recent pedological work, coupled with intensive archeological fieldwork, in the Argolid region in the Peloponnese of southeastern Greece shows that the region has been subjected to "long periods of tranquillity irregularly broken by brief events of slope destabilization and valley alluviation" that run counter to the sequence and timing of the Vita-Finzi model, but fit its idea of a "punctuated equilibrium." Clearing of oak and hornbeam forests and subsequent degradation seem to have happened around 2500 BC, between 350 and 50 BC, and between AD 950 and 1450, followed by periods of land abandonment during which soil stability and soil accumulation occurred. In particular, the "wholesale abandonment of fields in the Hellenistic and Early Roman periods is reflected in a major increase of *maquis* pollen in the sediments of the coastal lagoons." The questions are: were these changes a result of natural or human causes, and was this just a local phenomenon, or was it more widespread? We simply do not know, but we can be assured of more debate.[88]

In the classic case of the now abandoned lands of North Africa, Brent Shaw thinks it likely that Roman settlement took place under climatic conditions that were "more like those of the present than those of medieval times," which were demonstrably more humid. Many Roman wells and cisterns are still in use and any abandonment was due to neglect. Once the historical myths and proxy data are discarded the question could reasonably be put: did large-scale land use around the Mediterranean serve, "on the whole, to impede massive erosion rather than to encourage it?"[89] It is the very opposite of the received wisdom and suggests that deforestation was probably less severe than has been thought.

Nonetheless, everywhere the woodland was being thinned and removed as the population increased, cultivation was extended, and everyday life became more sophisticated. Locally, the effect was most marked in zones of intense utilization, as in the Apennines and around large cities or areas of mineral extraction, and elsewhere where strategic shipbuilding supplies were cut out. Soil erosion must have accelerated in places. The conclusion of Clifford Darby nearly fifty years ago, that

> the Mediterranean lands were then more densely wooded than they are today but that already there had been considerable clearing and that the extensive forests which remained were for the most part in the mountainous areas

might seem bland and unsatisfactory to our more quantitative frame of mind in the present day, but it is essentially correct, and is about as far as one can go in generalizing about the degree of change.[90]

CREATING A SECOND NATURE

Perhaps as important as the amount of deforestation is our knowledge about the process and differing attitudes toward it. As in every age there is conflicting evidence. The Greeks, it is suggested, "generally tended to fear and revere wild nature more, while the Romans found the landscape both friendlier and more easily subjected to various human uses." The Greeks certainly found meaning in the forest, and thought of it as the original home of humankind where humans sprang from oaks. But this ended with forest clearing, the fallen trees being likened to warriors slain in battle. Because of this we can better understand the reverence for sacred groves as the abode of the gods and tree spirits, or dryads, and as a form of temple and hence holy sanctuary. Severe penalties for desecrating a grove acted as a deterrent to clearing and a motive for the preservation of portions of the original forest, though not always adhered to. But attitudes were ambivalent; cutting trees may have been the desecration of paradise, but it could also be the dawn of civilization.[91]

Things were to change in time. Undoubtedly the classical age (particularly the Roman age) was the beginning of the modern world, but whether it was the beginning of a rational capitalism—as suggested by Max Weber—or merely a sort of protocapitalism, is argued fiercely.[92] There is evidence that nature was not being revered but being commodified, traded, and sold; and that its possession was seen as a means to wealth and capital accumulation, as witnessed in the discussion by Varro, Columella, and others on the profitability of farming. The development of private property (particularly by the latifundists); the dealing in land; the exploitation of slaves; the making of profits from trade, industry, and war; financial speculation; and the investment of surplus were all other examples of a new attitude. Avarice and an active willingness to exploit the material world and other humans for profit became common. Thus, "all the things in this world which men employ have been created and provided for the sake of men," said Cicero, and the forests were only as good as they were useful.[93]

Paralleling this view of nature was one that we have mentioned already, that of control and mastery, so that people no longer felt that they were of nature but above it. The very nature of nature was being changed by human ingenuity and industry. In his remarkably perceptive essay of 43 BC, *De Natura Deorum,* Cicero extolled the endowments of humans who had minds to invent, senses to perceive, and hands to execute, and were consequently able to achieve "the entire command of the commodities produced on land." He continued:

> We enjoy the fruits of the plains and of the mountains, the rivers and the lakes are ours, we sow corn, we plant trees, we fertilize the soil by irrigation, we confine rivers and straighten or divert their courses. In fine, by means of our hands we essay to create as it were a second world within the world of nature.[94]

Like all these other activities of humankind, the cutting of trees (and he instances that in some detail) had *become* second nature, but it had also helped to *create* a second nature in place of *first* nature. The result could be read in the land that was being changed, especially with the ever-growing population. In almost Turnerian frontier language Tertullian, a priest from the Roman province of Africa, observed at the end of the second century AD that

> [a]ll places are now accessible, all are well known, all open to commerce; most pleasant farms have obliterated all traces of what was once dreary and dangerous wastes; cultivated fields have subdued forests; flocks and herds have expelled wild beasts; sandy deserts are sown; rocks are planted; marshes are drained; and where once was hardly solitary cottages, there are now large cities.[95]

Everywhere was becoming more cultivated, more fully peopled, and more orderly, and seemed to be progressing toward some ultimate stage; indeed, everywhere in the empire seemed to becoming like the vicinity of Rome.

Chapter 5

The Medieval World

That is what it was, a chain from theology to manuring.
—CLARENCE GLACKEN, *Traces on the Rhodian Shore* (1967)

On the land . . . the economic achievement of the labouring man served to promote his social advancement . . . this appears as perhaps the most important phenomenon connected with medieval settlement and colonization.
—RICHARD KOEBNER, "The Settlement and Colonization of Europe" (1941)

IN THE ANNALS of deforestation the experience of medieval Europe must be accorded a prominent place both in terms of its extent and impact on the forests of the Continent, and in its ultimate importance in the global story. But the great clearing did not affect all Europe. If classical clearing was essentially the story of the Mediterranean lands, medieval clearing was overwhelmingly the story of temperate western and central Europe. Whereas perhaps four-fifths of the land surface of that part of the Continent had been covered with forests and swamps in about AD 500, possibly only half, or less, of that amount remained 800 years later.

Charles Higounet attempted to reconstruct the location of the major areas of "forest" on the eve of "les grands défrichements" of the eleventh to thirteenth centuries, and it is useful as a basis or starting point in discussing the great medieval onslaught.[1] The map (fig. 5.1) is useful for another reason. It reminds us that in medieval and later Europe, *forest* was a technical term. In English and German (though not in French and Italian) its meaning is not necessarily "woodland," but rather "land reserved for the use of the king, above all for his hunting." Thus, the shaded areas may not be trees because, as Christopher Wickham reminds us, "there were plenty of trees outside the forest as there were clearings inside it," and it is most likely that they represent areas of proprietorial, political, and juridical power held by royalty and the nobility, and related to hunting.[2] We also know that some of the "forest" areas are exaggerated, as in the British Isles; and that might be true for other parts of Europe, though probably to a lesser degree, as they had a denser natural tree cover. But when all was said and done, there was a lot of forest and some of it was very extensive and dense.

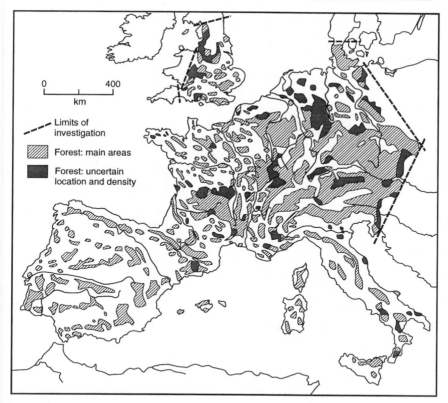

Figure 5.1 A reconstruction of the major forest areas of Europe on the eve of *les grands défrichements* of the eleventh to thirteenth centuries AD. *Source:* based on Higounet, 1966.

The evidence of the change in land cover is varied. Early documentary sources are few and are often indirect and incidental to other matters, such as rental returns, common rights, and lawsuits. But by the twelfth and thirteenth centuries, when purposeful colonization and clearing were being undertaken, the story is unmistakable, and documents "swarm" with allusions to clearing, although one must constantly bear in mind that clearing took away something visual from the landscape and therefore often went unrecorded, to be subsumed under other activities.[3] In addition to the documentary evidence there is, for the first time, the evidence of place-names and field names, and the peculiarities of forest law and usage. Most important is the tangible evidence of the fields and settlements that were created, and that have survived in the landscape or are recorded on the map.[4] Taken together, it is a formidable body of evidence on every aspect of forest use and change.

Consequently, we are confronted with both conjecture and a great amount of detailed evidence that defies easy division and easy generalization. Therefore, first, some overriding significant themes are identified and examined briefly before dealing in turn with the causes, extent and pace, and complexity of clearing.

AN ACTIVE AND ENERGETIC WORLD

The Middle Ages encapsulated an active and energetic world, which burst open after about 1100. "It was," said Kenneth Clark, "like a Russian spring. In every branch of life—action, philosophy, organization, technology—there was an extraordinary out-pouring of energy and intensification of existence."[5] To take but one example, the hundreds of magnificent cathedrals and abbeys, to say nothing of the tens of thousands of parish churches, were monuments to the new self-confidence and wealth. In France alone, several million tons of stone were quarried, Amiens cathedral was large enough to accommodate the whole town of over 10,000 people, and the top of the spire of Strasbourg cathedral was 142 m, the equivalent of a forty-floor skyscraper—and none of these examples were that unusual. On the land, humans began to make conscious and purposeful decisions about its use and about population densities. Unlike the Roman occupation, where territorial control and status seemed to be the primary aims, medieval societies wanted a fuller, more intensive use of the land in order to increase yields and promote closer settlement. Everywhere land was made more productive. Greater wealth was generated, and ultimately greater power.[6]

Of course, the same things could be said of eastern Asia at this time, where vibrant and industrious civilizations also laid to waste vast swathes of forest. But with the exception of the iron and steel industry during the Northern Sung (AD 910–1126) only a fraction of what happened in China and Japan is known to Western scholarship. Clearing remains opaque. These are truly "dark ages and dark areas."[7]

A distinctive feature of the European story that has few counterparts in any other age was the way in which the modification of the environment was linked with "ideas, ideals, and practical needs." A belief in helping to create a divine, designed earth, in which nature was likened to a book revealing the magnificence of God, was shared with a need to understand and use nature for practical ends which encompassed, for example, clearing, draining, domesticating, and fertilizing. The spread of Christianity and the cultivation of the land went hand in hand; it was, said Clarence Glacken, "a chain from theology to manuring."[8]

For Lynn White, the historian of medieval technology, understanding the Middle Ages was more complicated. It was not a matter of simply "one billiard ball striking another, of 'causes' in the narrow sense." It was more often "a process of gradual illumination of the fact to be explained by gathering around it other facts that, like lamps, seem to throw light on it."[9]

The outcome of this process was the creation of a "cultural climate" that favored and encouraged change. It consisted of an intangible melange of belief, sentiment, superstition, motivation, symbolism, and even fashion, as well as empirical experiment and technological innovation. In practical terms, a novel system of agriculture was developed in Europe during the eighth and ninth centuries that suited its ecological and physical environment. The "agricultural revolution of the Middle Ages" that was put in place shifted the focus of Europe from the south to the north, from the classical world of the Mediterranean to the great forested plains drained by the Loire, Seine, Rhine, Elbe, Danube, and

Thames.[10] It was on those plains that the distinctive features of the medieval world, and perhaps even of the modern world, developed.

In that "revolution" humans shifted from being a part of nature to being her exploiter. Nothing epitomized it more clearly than Charlemagne's renaming of months in terms of human activities—June was to be "Ploughing Month," July "Haying Month," August "Harvest Month," and so on. The change was also reflected in illustrated Carolingian calendars shortly before 830. The new calendars were very different from Byzantine and old Roman ones, and showed a "coercive attitude" toward natural resources:

> They are definitely northern in origin; for the olive, which loomed so large in the Roman cycles has disappeared. The pictures change to scenes of ploughing, harvesting, wood-chopping, people knocking-down acorns for the pigs, pig-slaughtering. Man and nature are now two things, and man is master.[11]

Whatever the truth about motives and attitudes, the upshot was that vast areas of the Continent were settled for the first time; settlement in existing areas was intensified; and the visual landscape was changed as trees were replaced by grass, crops, and farms. In fact, the clearing of the forest by individuals and great domains, both lay and ecclesiastical, and the cultivation of the ill-drained and forested land—technically the "waste"—over much of western and central Europe was one of the most dramatic changes made to human landscapes anywhere up to that time, and has been acclaimed as "one of the greatest creative achievements of medieval man."[12]

The closeness of the forest to the everyday life of ordinary people, especially the landless peasant, meant that it was not only a source of heat, materials, and arboreal by-products like honey, wax, fowl, small animals, and grazing, but also a source of land, and hence food. Historical analogies are dangerous, but in these characteristics at least, the medieval frontier of the tenth to twelfth centuries was similar to the neo-European frontier of the seventeenth to nineteenth centuries, and bears no small resemblance to the frontier facing the landless peasant in the tropical rain-forest today. The forest was then, as it is now, in the words of a Scandinavian proverb, "the mantle of the poor," and in its exploitation and probable destruction lay the means for survival, and even social and economic advancement.

In all the ferment of activity, forest clearing was the central theme around which all other modifications to the landscape revolved, because the forest occupied such a central position in medieval life as a source for light, heat, adventitious food, and construction materials. However, its destruction also meant more cultivated land, and the tremendous burst of food production, with only occasional food shortages during the High Middle Ages, seemed proof of that. Anything that altered the basic forest resource was bound to make an impression on both material, everyday life, and even on the cultural fabric of society. Consequently, as clearing progressed, conflicts arose between rights of usage—often between the poor and the rich—and rights of delimitation—often amongst the nobility and royalty—who wanted to keep the land for hunting and game. In time, other conflicts arose over the modification and preservation of the resource. These complex goals played out like antiphonal themes against the backdrop of the forest and were a marked feature of the age.[13]

Finally, in emphasizing the abundance and ubiquity of wood in medieval Europe, one should not overlook the fact that the Continent was also extraordinarily well endowed with other natural resources, most especially constantly flowing streams and diverse and abundant minerals. In various ways wood, water, and minerals become crucial to the exercise of power over the physical world, which translated into greater productivity, greater well-being, and more energy for productive purposes. It was also symptomatic of the "cultural climate" of imaginative and exploratory attitudes toward the forces of nature.

Wood was essential for smelting metals, particularly iron, which became the universal metal of the age. The medieval peasant used unprecedented amounts of iron, and "the smithy became integral to every village." Thus iron axes, plows, and implements go a long way to explain the massive extension of cultivated land from the tenth century onward.[14] The harnessing of water power in mills had long been known, and by the tenth century the combination of the Continent's many streams, together with the availability of wood and iron for construction, culminated in the erection of mills in nearly every rural settlement. First water power was applied to grinding grain; 5,624 mills in some 3,000 communities are enumerated in the Domesday Book of 1086 for England alone. But soon mills appeared throughout Europe for the mechanical fulling of cloth, the treating of hemp, and for tanning, laundering, sawing, crushing, grinding, sieving, turning, polishing, and stamping almost anything. Perhaps most significantly, from the early eleventh century onward, mechanical power was applied to operate the bellows of blast furnaces and to puddle and beat iron in blooms with trip hammers, to draw wire and to cut metal. Cranks, flywheels, pendulums, and cams were all manifestations of medieval inventiveness. The inanimate energy of water mills marked the beginning of the breakdown of the traditional world in which humans had to depend on the power of animals and on vegetable sources of energy.[15] Windmills were another manifestation of this use of inanimate nature, and it is interesting to note that the wood needed for their erection, and particularly for their vanes, was said to be one of the chief reasons for deforestation in Northamptonshire in England in 1322.[16]

All this can be seen in a wider context. In Lewis Mumford's trilogy of eras of technology—the eotechnic, the paleotechnic, and the neotechnic—the medieval was the manifestation par excellence of the eotechnic. It was the age of water, wind, wood, and stone, with some metal parts. The scale of operations was small, tools were crude and hand forged, production was restricted, and the market local.[17] But in this nexus, the forest and its products of agricultural land, timber, and fuel were the most important. As these were used, so the forest was either diminished or more valued, or both.

CAUSES OF CLEARING

The medieval age covered a vast period of time, so that the process of deforestation was, said Koebner, "an affair of centuries." Three principal periods of clearing can be identified, each with its own pulsations and shifts that were important locally, some of which were occasioned by the kaleidoscopic shifts of the great *Völkerwanderung*.[18]

The first period, from the end of the Roman Empire, circa AD 500 to circa AD 750 (the Merovingian), saw little impact on the forested landscape. The Germanic barbarian invaders, such as the Huns, Goths, Visigoths, and Vandals, had little effect. They were fairly quickly absorbed into society after the first rampage of plunder and destruction—for which they were infamous—was over. Their numbers were small, the Visigoths and Vandals probably not exceeding 80,000 in total, and most being barely one-fifth of that, although the Franks, Alemanni, and Anglo-Saxons must have been more numerous. However, they did arrive at a time when population might have already declined by up to 40 percent from a high figure of over 26 million in the fourth century due to widespread epidemics. Therefore, it is unlikely that the injection of these barbaric peoples raised the population totals very much, or that they were forced to engage in the backbreaking clearing of forested land, except here and there on a small scale. There was plenty of already cleared land for them to take over, and when they became sedentary cultivators they filled out the area worked by the former inhabitants, eventually sharing cultivation with the remnant, subject "Roman" natives. In all, the invaders were merely 2 to 5 percent of the population, and therefore the level of Roman civilization and agriculture may been have "been lowered and degraded; [but] it was not destroyed."[19] The continuity was greater than the popular image portrays.

The absence of clearing was certainly not due to technical incompetence; lack of necessity was compounded by a lack of conviction. For many Germanic tribes the primeval forest was of religious significance, and held in awe as the abode of the gods. While this did not necessarily forbid clearing, it was a hindrance. The forest was impassable and untouchable, and therefore protected "as an unchangeable thing."[20]

The second, or Carolingian, phase, from circa 700–950, was a period of economic expansion and population growth, compounded by the movement of the Scandinavian tribes into the British Isles and western Europe and the Magyars in central Europe. Population growth was probably responsible for some food shortages in the highly developed parts of western Europe.[21] Land and agricultural practices responded and began to change, in contrast with the continuity of the immediate post-Roman era. Now the forest was attacked with increasing vigor, especially during the third phase of the energetic and ebullient High Middle Ages, after 1000 to circa 1300. This was a period of purposeful change, the heroic age *des grands défrichements,* which lasted until the end of the thirteenth century, when activity began to wane and ended abruptly with the Black Death of circa 1350.

Within the general cultural climate the changes in land and society during these latter two active phases can best be divided conveniently, if not quite accurately, into three broad sorts: demographic, technological, and ideological. In many ways they are inseparable, and put together they formed a conjunction of circumstances that were uniquely favorable to the growth and expansion of settlement in the forests.

Population and Land Use

Undoubtedly the driving force or engine of change that generated such spectacular activity was the growth of population. It doubled from 18.0 million in circa AD 600 to 38.5 million in circa AD 1000 and then would double again to attain a high point of 75.5 million in the early thirteenth century, a level not equalled for another two hundred years.[22] The increase in the food supply, the improvement of diet, the reduction of famine, and therefore better health and lower mortality all contributed to this surge. Also important was the relative absence of major outbreaks of disease, coupled with a warmer and more stable climate before 1250, when temperatures rose by between 0.5 and 1°C and rainfall decreased by approximately 10 percent.[23]

In the complex interplay between land and labor, relationships were often reciprocal. Put simply, were the technological diffusions a response to population growth or its cause? It seems likely that the presence of an expanding supply of land that required only clearing must have been spur to earlier marriages for the peasantry, an increase in the birthrate, and hence larger families, and indeed, there is some evidence of that.[24] In whichever direction the relationship worked, however, the need to increase food production confronted the medieval farmer. He had two options: one was to "make" new land, the other was to shorten the fallow period.

In the making of new land the impacts on the forest were broadly twofold, and roughly sequential. First, during the early centuries (but not exclusively) there was the colonization of what Archibald Lewis has called the "Internal Frontier" of the long-occupied European heartland of northern Italy, France, western Germany, the Low Countries, and southeast England. Neglected or abandoned land was occupied first, and then more deliberate reclamation of fringing borderlands ensued. Second and latterly, the outward expansion of the "External Frontier" occurred, so that great stretches of primeval forest were cleared and incorporated into the European heartland. Sometimes the two Frontiers were coincident and coterminous, such as in the massive Germanic colonization of central and eastern Europe from the tenth to twelfth centuries.[25] By the High Middle Ages reclamation and colonization appear to have gained a momentum of their own. Multiple and positive feedback effects operated so that virtually all the wilderness zones of central and western Europe, while not necessarily cleared, were certainly incorporated into the realm of human affairs.

Everywhere on Europe's Internal Frontier the large communal fields were expanded at the expense of the lightly used "waste" of ill-drained and forested land that lay either surrounding the settlements or in the "no-man's land" between them. The "waste" was misnamed; it was a valuable resource, sometimes cultivated on an infield/outfield system, usually grazed, and always the source of fuel, wild produce, pannage, game, and fowl. Much of its use was defined by custom, and usage rights came under communal control. Consequently, as reclamation proceeded boundaries were demarcated and the communal use of resources established.

Bit by bit the existing fields were extended into the surrounding woods by making clearings (plate 5.1), or assarts (from the French *essarter,* "to grub up" or "to clear"), references to which are abundant in manorial documents from the sixth century onward.[26] Also, the periodic burning (a sort of bush fallowing) and heavier grazing in the surrounding woods intensified, which caused the degeneration of the woodlands. Eventually, the degraded forest might be cleared of its stumps and new settlements created.

Beyond the village territory on the External Frontier lay the true wilderness of unbroken forest *(silva)* which could eventually be colonized, reclaimed, and integrated into

Plate 5.1 "Cutting wood." The manuscript comes from the eleventh century AD. (By permission of the British Library, Ms. Tiberius, B.V. pt. 1, fol. 6.)

the existing community territory. Completely new settlements were created in clearings in the wilderness, often by the ecclesiastical houses, which sought solitude, and by secular lords, who wanted to expand their rent rolls. Whereas in the sixth century it is calculated that fields accounted for less than 5 percent of land use, by the later Middle Ages the figure was nearer 30 to 40 percent.[27] By implication, woodland must have diminished by a roughly equal amount.

The second option open to the medieval farmers was to shorten the fallow period, either during cropping or in grazing rotations. According to Ester Boserup, this strategy would be likely to occur when population densities reached about 30/km², which had occurred in a few localities by the seventh century. Eventually a point would be reached when a higher percentage of land was cropped for arable than not, and production would shift from pastoral to arable. The disadvantage of this shift was that the labor investment (the only spare technology available) increased substantially to compensate for the loss of fertility caused by shorter fallowing. According to William TeBrake, the fact that fallow shortening appears to have been undertaken suggests that the increase in population was a more compelling reason for the changes than technology, but this does preclude positive feedback effects of new crops and improved rotations.[28]

It is all too easy to forget that these relationships represent the lives and aspirations of real people, not some abstract, impersonal group. We have no record, as in later centuries, of what "making" the land really meant in everyday terms. But we can be assured that making a clearing in the forest was slow and arduous, the product of "a daily blinding sweat, blood at times, a backbreaking toil with axe and spade and saw."[29] It was a major part of medieval life.

Plows, Horsepower, and Fields

Somewhere between AD 650 and AD 800 three broadly "technological" developments appear that were of profound significance in allowing the European peasant to adapt to his physical ecology. These developments may partially account for the "bursting vitality" of deforestation throughout the Carolingian realm. They were the wheeled plow, the harnessing of animal power, and the three-field rotation system, which was, said Charles Parain, "the greatest agricultural novelty" of the age.[30]

The continual expansion of colonists into forestland took them out of the areas of light, well-drained sandy, chalky, and loessic soils that could be scratched open with the lightweight *ard,* to the stiff, heavier, damp (and usually heavily wooded) soils that were potentially more productive but more difficult to cultivate.[31] The solution lay in the adoption of the wheeled heavy plow that appeared in parts of Germany, the Low Countries, and northern France in the country between the Loire and the Rhine sometime during the seventh century. Because the scratch plow left a wedge of undisturbed earth between each groove, fields had to be cross-plowed, which doubled the labor and resulted in squarish fields.

The wheels of the heavy plow, on the other hand, controlled its height above the ground. Its coulter (or knife) cut the soil vertically, a plowshare sliced it horizontally, and an angled mouldboard turned it over. In one stroke, the heavy soils were conquered—weeds were buried, accumulated nutrients turned up, and labor saved. Because the plow was unwieldy and difficult to turn at the end of the furrow, land was plowed in long, narrow strips, or furlongs (furrow long), grouped in large, unfenced, "open" fields. These strips were normally plowed clockwise, with the sod being turned over and inward to the right, creating long, low ridges with an intervening depression—hence the typical "ridge and furrow" landscape of much of cultivated lowland Europe. Thus, even in the wettest years the heavy clay soils had a rudimentary artificial surface drainage system, and some crops grew successfully on dry land.

The action of the new plow in slicing and turning the sod generated increased friction, but its effectiveness was increased by the use of horses rather than oxen. The invention a little after the beginning of the ninth century of a harness with a rigid collar which rested on the shoulders and not the neck (which virtually strangled them) transformed the pulling power of horses four- or fivefold, and nailed horseshoes preserved their hooves in wet soils. As horses move faster than oxen and do about twice as much work in a day, the saving in human labor by substituting the horse for the ox was great. Moreover, the swiftness of the horse made it particularly versatile in harrowing to cover seed, break clods, and smooth fields, an advantage in the uncertain western European weather. A new form of horse-drawn spiked harrow was invented and appeared in southern Germany sometime after 1050.

The disadvantage of the new plow was that more beasts were needed to pull it—up to eight oxen or four horses, which was beyond the means of most peasants. Beasts of a settlement were consequently pooled, which reduced individualism but encouraged co-operation and a strong system of self-government.

More efficient plowing contributed to the shift from the traditional two- to the new three-field crop rotation systems, there being a close correlation between triennial rotation and the use of the horse for agriculture. This new system appeared in the ecclesiastical lands of northeast France during the ninth century and spread steadily throughout most of Europe. In place of each field sown alternately with grain in the autumn with the other left fallow, now one field was planted in autumn with winter wheat, barley, or rye; the second field was planted in spring with new crops like oats, chickpeas, peas, lentils, or broad beans; and the third field was left fallow. At a stroke, fallow was shortened from 50 to 33 percent of the total period, labor requirements were more evenly spread over the year, and oats were converted into horsepower. Leguminous crops like peas and beans fixed nitrogen in the soil and maintained its fertility, allowing larger numbers of livestock to be kept, thus reducing the chances of famine as well as providing more manure. In turn, the raised protein intake improved human nutrition and health, contributing to the explosion of population.[32]

These innovations resulted in more land being brought into cultivation. Triennial cropping could not take place unless two "old" fields could be reorganized, which was rare. It was far more likely that a third field was carved out of the standing forest and land broken up for cultivation.[33] Everywhere, improved horsepower eased and speeded up the task, and there is also some evidence of the development of an improved felling ax.[34] The growing population and farming innovations converged, enabling Europe to enter into its era of spectacular expansion into the untouched hardwood forest on its External Frontier.

Power and Piety

Population growth and farming innovation were the engines of change, but they were not the complete explanation to the great deforestation. Other factors, broadly ideological, but more accurately sociocultural and religious, also played an important part. The extension of secular power and the cult of piety gave underlying motivation to many actions and decisions: practical reality was combined with mystic idealism to produce spectacular change.

The extension of territorial organization occurred as local lay and ecclesiastical rulers connived to consolidate political control for reasons of defense and personal gain. Gradually they assumed the right to dispose of wasteland like any monarch. They allotted the wilderness under their control to groups of colonists who agreed to clear, farm, and "bring it into the realm of human affairs."[35]

But the significance of this trend was greater than territorial aggrandizement alone. The interests of these rulers were quite the opposite of those of the old manorial system who wished to keep peasants confined to traditional areas of settlement in order to control them and garner greater rents. Now, people and their labor were regarded as a source of wealth for their lords; colonizers were released from feudal constraints and offered generous terms, which included ownership and disposal of land, personal freedom, and often no restrictive requirement to clear-cut and grub out the stumps, which enabled girdling, burning, and rapid occupation to take place. Money services gradually replaced labor services and payments in kind. Thus, land reclamation contributed in a general way to a new society of free and equal agriculturalists that had more in common with many of the new urban communities than with the old rural ones. Koebner's assertion that forest clearing meant greater opportunity for advancement and freedom and was an important step in "the emancipation of the common man" seems borne out by events. In addition, with the fairly widespread adoption of primogeniture as the dominant form of inheritance, outlets had to be found for younger sons, and in this way "clearing represented for the peasants what the Crusades and wars of conquest were for the nobles." [36]

The link between Western Christian piety and land reclamation was a leitmotif running through the clearing of the medieval forest. From classical times onward the ability of humans to alter and control the environment had been prevalent; the early Christian fathers, such as Tertullian, Philo, St. Jerome, and St. Augustine, had linked it with Christianity. Like Cicero, they believed that the mind and hands of humans gave them a capacity to create their own environment through inventiveness and necessity. Consequently, they attempted to make Christianity more acceptable and less "other-worldly" by emphasizing the message of Genesis—that God had given man dominion over nature. The reconciliation of the two points of view came with the notion that man was in partnership with God, and acted as God's helper or steward on earth in finalizing creation, so that a "bridge was built from theology to farming, grazing and the forest," and a divine purpose was seen in human works. Just after AD 1000, Christian iconography showed God as a master mason measuring out the universe with T-square and compass, thereby drawing a clear parallel between the work of God and that of humans. Early Christian apologists had thus raised and exalted humans to a supreme position, so that what humans did had divine sanction; and humans, in turn, in the execution of their many accomplishments, skills, and talents, came nearer to God. This approach was a way of defending the new faith and expressing unity with humans on earth. Lynn White goes further by suggesting that Western Christianity had an even wider significance—it gave rise to the unparalleled technological creativity of medieval Europe. [37]

Onto that basis of approval of man's works was grafted the recognition of, and respect for, the concept of the dignity of labor, which was an essential and integral part of the technological change. From Carolingian times onward the monks of western Europe were less classical and bookish than their southern and eastern brethren and apologists. Physical labor was not despised and left to slaves. The Benedictines, in particular, proclaimed that "idleness is the enemy of the soul. The brethren, therefore, must be occupied in stated hours of manual labour, and again at other hours in sacred reading." [38] Work had justification in theology, even in such unsophisticated texts as Paul's exhortation to the Thessalonians (3:10): "If anyone will not work, let him not eat." Work was its own spiritual reward and especially, so it seemed, if performed away from the world and sin. St. Bernard likened the monastery to a paradise or a Jerusalem in the making:

> The cloister is a "true paradise," and the surrounding countryside shares in its dignity. Nature "in the raw," unembellished by the works of art, inspires the learned man with a sort of horror. . . . A wild spot, not hallowed by prayer and asceticism and which is not the scene of any spiritual life is, as it were, in a state of original sin. But once it has become fertile and purposeful, it takes on the utmost significance. [39]

Thus, the prayer book and the ax were the way to expiate "original sin" in man and in nature, and a way to demythologize the dark wilderness. Aided and abetted by pious monarchs who made generous grants, the early religious orders sought isolated spots in which to create a "true paradise" and glorify God. [40] If these clearings were in previously pagan areas on the margins of Christendom, as in Slavic eastern Europe, then all the better. Clearings became hearths of conversion and spiritual perfection where technical skills in agriculture combined with spiritual care, and they also helped extend secular control.

Initially the clearing work of the Benedictines on the Internal Frontier during the seventh and eighth centuries was influential, dispelling the religious awe that the Germans had to overcome before attacking the deep forest, and encouraging secular munificence. The story of Sturmi, an English missionary and student of St. Boniface's who was the systematic organizer of Christianity in Germany, exemplifies the process of selecting a monastic site in the mid-eighth century. Sturmi wished to be a hermit and examined many sites for the establishment of a cell in the forest. Because of the pagan Saxons he was urged by Boniface to go "deeper into the woods, where you can serve God." After traveling through a "frightful wilderness, seeing nothing but wild beasts, . . . birds flying, enormous trees and the rough thickets of the forests," he found "the blessed spot ordained by God." He returned to St. Boniface, who persuaded Carloman, king of the Franks, that the foundation of a monastery on the largely unsettled, pagan eastern borders of the kingdom was a desirable move; and on 12 January 744, the use of the site at Fulda in the northern Odenwald was granted, together with approximately 16 square miles of land. Two months later St. Boniface visited it with Sturmi and his followers.

> [The bishop then] ordered all the men who had accompanied him to the spot to cut down the woods and clear the undergrowth, whilst he himself climbed the brow of the hill . . . and spent his time praying to God and meditating on Sacred Scripture. . . . After a week of felling trees and clearing away the brushwood the turf was piled up ready to make lime: then the bishop gave the brethren his blessing, commended the place to God and returned home with the workmen he had brought with him.[41]

It is likely that the unimaginable remoteness of Fulda was a pious topos in order to exaggerate the spirituality and achievements of the actors. But having said that, many places were "blanks" on the map, and although the detail would vary from place to place, and from time to time, it was repeated in broad outline in St. Gallen, Lorsch, Hersfeld, and Werden-on-Ruhr and subsequently elsewhere hundreds, if not thousands, of times across the breadth of Europe. Religious houses were granted lands by the monarch; subsequently each monastery systematically allotted forestland to colonists to clear and cultivate, so that in time the countryside was transformed from forested wilderness to farmland landscape.[42]

Thus the Benedictines, and then later the Carthusians, Premonstratensians, and particularly the Cistercians, were the shock troops of clearing. Between 1098 and 1675 the Cistercians founded 742 centers of which over 95 percent were in existence by 1351, and these constituted about half of all religious houses (fig. 5.2). Each was a nucleus of clearing and farming. Daughter settlements diffused from the five founding houses, or "families," of Cîteaux, Pontigny, La Ferté, Clairviaux, and Morimond in an ever-spreading radius. Those of Cîteaux were mainly in France and south-central England, those of Pontigny and La Ferté were scattered and had no particular territory, but those of Clairvaux dominated the rest of England, eastern France, Portugal, and Italy. The most discrete territory was that of Morimond, dominating the German-speaking lands and

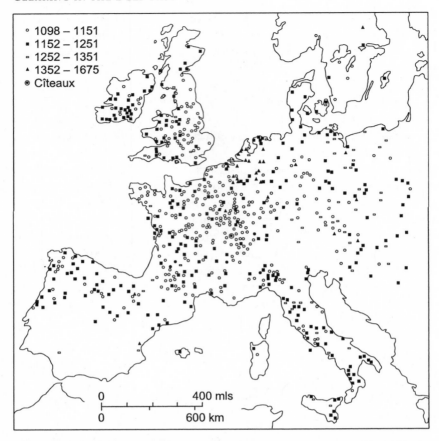

Figure 5.2 Expansion of the Cistercian order in Europe, AD 1098–1675. *Source:* Donkin, 1978.

Poland. Each house was a center of intensive forest clearing and land improvement. "Give these monks a naked moor or a wild wood;" wrote Gerald of Barri, "then let a few years pass away and you will find not only beautiful churches, but dwellings of men built around them." Piety was an accompaniment of improving zeal, and the creation of new landscapes fit for Christian settlement gave a just reward for that piety.[43]

The magnitude and fervor of the effort of the ecclesiastical houses was "far removed from the modest efforts of the laity," although they were so influential that "all the elite of society placed itself at the head of the movement." The expansion of clearing provided the rents and tithe so that the needs of the church for income harmonized admirably with "the craving of the freemen and peasants for fresh property." With time the Cistercians passed cultivation to lay brothers *(conversi)* and hired workers, often in separate out-settlements of assembled, consolidated properties or granges.[44]

The whole colonization movement, however, contained paradoxes. First, while medieval theologians stressed partnership and stewardship with nature, the destruction of the forest and the extension of cultivation was evidence of "an ethic of appropriation" and a "social commitment to the primacy of human habitation over competing interests." Second, while it cannot be denied that colonization was an act of piety, it inevitably increased the influence and fortune of the monasteries, which became politically, economically, and socially important. As they grew in size, wealth, and prestige they too became large landowners. The sacred mission gave way to the secular, solitude gave way to civilization, and toward the end of the great age of clearing in the eleventh century, monastic houses found themselves with large rent rolls. They came into conflict with neighboring lay and ecclesiastical estates, and even with the peasants, who murmured that the changes to the forest had been so drastic and clearing had gone so far as to deprive them of their valued common resource. This, together with the fact that the monasteries became more worldly—even corrupt—meant that they lost the respect they once had.[45] But for all that, nothing could take away their immense contribution to the clearing of the European landscape over three centuries. An equally spectacular story could be told of the ecclesiastical role in the draining of marshlands and reclamation of heathlands to become productive land, though neither were anywhere as extensive as forest clearing.[46]

EXTENT AND PACE OF CLEARING

Any idea of the extent and pace of clearing can fall back on what we have already called the "formidable body of evidence on every aspect of forest use and change," including documents that " swarm" with allusions to clearing,[47] place-names and field names that reveal new settlements, and details of forest law and usage. In measuring the extent, a rough but useful distinction can be made between clearing in the core of Europe—the British Isles, France, Germany, and eastern Europe—and the periphery—Russia and the Mediterranean lands.

The Core

Early Centuries

During the barbarian invasions the pace and extent of clearing is difficult to discern. There is some evidence of reversion and considerable evidence of the reoccupation of the abandoned land by the newcomers; but undoubtedly, as Clifford Darby observed, "behind the clash of warfare and the noise of political affairs, the work of clearing went on in relative silence."[48] A single settler or a group of peasants would nibble away at the edges of the woodlands around the village and then at the vast unbroken woodlands that separated one settlement from another. Then the assart, or new clearing, would be added to the existing field system. It was a process that must have been repeated thousands, possibly millions, of times across the Continent.

We get some hint of what was happening in France in the sixth and seventh centuries, when deserted properties were being resettled and new land created in the waste zones between settlements. "Brabant" was the original name for these intermediate zones, and the once wooded Belgian province of that name acquired hundreds of settlers as the great *Silva Carbonnaria,* or Charcoal-Burners' Forest, was cleared. In the time of Charlemagne the ambitions of the emperor, secular lords, and church to extend their holdings coalesced with the needs of the peasants and small holders everywhere. One of Charlemagne's decrees directed his agents as follows: "whenever there are men competent for the task, let them be given forest to cut down in order to improve our possessions."[49]

In the south, expansion of settlement moved into the forests of the alpine foreland in Bavaria and along the Danube, where a beginning was made around the new strategic settlements of Passua and Salzberg. Elsewhere, in the east, there was scattered, sporadic clearing, but nothing to compare to the lands along the middle and lower Rhine in the center of the empire, where there are indications that the forests were in rapid retreat. The Ardennes were losing their primeval character, as was much of the hill country around the upper Rhine, while further east the valleys of the great forest of the Odenwald between the Neckar and the Main, and which had been little cultivated before 800, now had many assarts, or *Bifänge*, in them. These lands also displayed the first manifestations on the Continent of the typical forest row village, or *Waldhufendorf*, with its characteristic "hufen," or long, narrow fields that were cut back into the forest behind each new holding. The *Waldhufendorf* became a sure diagnostic indication of planned clearing.[50]

The widespread and comprehensive colonization of these western forests at such an early date has usually been overlooked, as attention has tended to focus on the massive colonization east of the Elbe during the thirteenth century, but in its way it was no less spectacular. For example, the Odenwald colonization probably began in 764 with the founding of the imperial Benedictine monastery of Losch, 30 km south of Fulda. Charlemagne subdivided the royal forest among the Abbeys of Lorsch and Amorsbach, the Bishop of Worms, and half a dozen nobles in return for a variety of secular services including annual gifts, contributions to the royal budget, and most important, large numbers of mounted troops for defense. Lorsch set about methodically settling and clearing the forest with the establishment of *Waldhufendorf*. There seem to have been three sizes, which corresponded to their date of foundation and degree of independence (fig. 5.3). The earliest (ninth century) and smallest in the west were for dependent peasants who rendered services; much larger and later ones in the south and center were for independent peasants who rendered only fixed amounts of stock and harvest; and the very largest in the east and founded in the eleventh century were for the entirely free, who probably engaged in a regulated slash-and-burn tillage within the mass of smaller agricultural settlements. A systematic network of central places or *Villicatio* centers and castle settlements with manorial courts and markets were established. Thus the forested landscape was successfully transformed into a planned "cultural landscape," its many farms supplying agricultural and forest products to the densely settled lands of the Rhine to the west.

The significance of this controlled experiment of largely uniformly sized and regularly laid out settlements in the Rhineland was far reaching; it may have been the "hearth" area of experimentation and the model for the colonization of the rest of the central European forest. The *Waldhufendorf* settlement probably originated in the upper Rhine and reached its first formal perfection in Odenwald before spreading to neighboring Spessart in the east, the Black Forest, and the Augsburg plains to the south. Eventually, with variations, it was adopted even further afield in the massive forests of the Frankenwald,

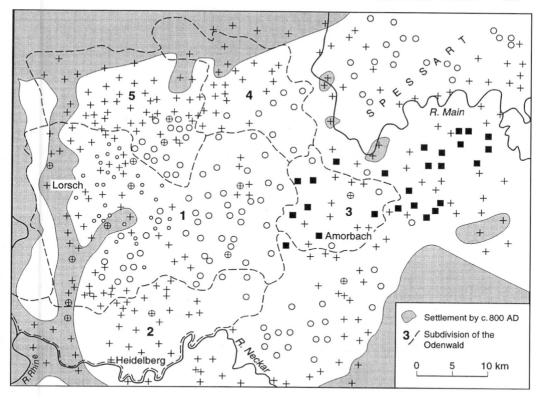

Figure 5.3 Forest clearing and village foundation in the Odenwald, eighth–eleventh centuries AD. The subdivisions of the royal forest of Odenwald as follows: 1. Abbey of Lorsch, 2. Bishop of Worms, 3. Abbey of Amorbach, 4. Abbey of Fulda, and 5. Nobility. *Source:* after Nitz, 1983a: 105–23.

Settlement by circa 800: Subdivisions of the Odenwald Settlement types

+ Irregular (Mainly early)
∘ Waldhufen—short, small "hufen" (eighth–ninth centuries)
O Waldhufen—long, large "hufen" (tenth century)
■ Waldhufen—large, disconnected "hufen" (eleventh century)
⊕ Administrative centers

Thuringia, and Lower Saxony before becoming such a distinctive feature of the trans-Elbian colonization and forest clearing.[51]

Similar, but far less systematic and extensive colonization and inroads are hinted at in fifth- to ninth-century England, where the Anglo-Saxon poet described the plowman as the "grey foe of the wood."[52] Here place-names are especially useful, as they can be divided into a relative chronology indicative of early and late stages of settlement. Names belonging to the first phase of settlement that do not indicate woodland (e.g., those ending in *-ing, -ington, -tun, -cote, -ham*) tend to occur on more easily worked light gravel and loamy soils. Names belonging to the later phase of settlement that do indicate woodland (e.g, *-leah, -feld, -wood, -holt -hurst, -weald*) occur on the deeper clays that must have been wooded and hence cleared in order to be settled. Other names indicate types of woodland, and yet others still the act of clearing such as "sarts" from "assarts," "intak" or "intake," "stubbing" or "Brentwood" for "burnt wood," and so forth.[53]

The result of this colonization on the landscape was summed up in that unique record of the medieval world, the Domesday Book of 1086. Among the many questions asked by the Commissioners was, How much woodland? The answer came in various forms— acres, overall linear dimensions by leagues, the amount of woodland available for swine, or a render or payment (expressed in actual number of swine) in return for the right of pannage. Some herds and renders numbered over 2,000. Clearly there was still a great deal of woodland left, and one estimate puts the amount at 15 percent of the country.[54] Yet, the book provides virtually no evidence of clearing, but it does show that where there was civil unrest, as when William the Conqueror subdued the last remnants of resistance in the northern and Welsh borderlands and caused much destruction, the woodland returned 20 years later to dominate over the devastated plowlands.[55]

The various strands of evidence come together nicely in Warwickshire (fig. 5.4), although other counties show the same pattern. The county was bisected from southwest to northeast by the River Avon, which divides the heavier clay from the lighter soils. To the north lay the famed Forest of Arden, to the south the open country known as the Felden. Arden shows considerable woodland in 1086, as measured by its length and breadth in leagues; a concentration of place-names such as -ley, which is indicative of clearing; and also a concentration of defensive moated farmsteads, a distinctive feature of settlement in once-forested areas, here as well as in Essex and Norfolk.[56] But the south is a complete contrast in all respects.

L'Âge des Grands Défrichements

Although there is some evidence during these early phases of clearing of the emergence of conflicts of interest between peasants who wanted land for cultivation and lords who wanted forest for hunting, these tensions seemed to melt as the eleventh century progressed and the two centuries of the great clearing began. The pace and extent of change accelerated as religious houses and lay lords actively encouraged clearing, both around villages and in the larger waste. "For historians of all countries," wrote George Duby, "but especially for Frenchmen and Germans, the age of medieval prosperity is the age of land reclamation."[57] While one must be aware of the "heroic rhetoric" in the accounts of the grand défrichements which have been accentuated in order to heighten the contrast between the natural and the newly humanized landscape, the broad outlines and many of the details have been covered accurately by a succession of writers: Aubin, Bechmann, Bloch, Darby, Devèze, Duby, Flach, Glacken, Koebner, Maury, Schlüter, Thompson, and others.[58] Many local studies fill in the picture here and there, such as Sclafert in France, and Dyer, Hart, Hatcher, and Witney in England, to mention only a few, and the same is true for Germany.[59] The local detail can be mind-numbing in its amount and complexity. But despite the detail, the exact measurement of the total clearing that changed the face of the medieval world is barely possible: it is best to look at some regional examples.

In France the early example set by the Benedictine monasteries in the Paris basin was expanded after 1125 with the massive efforts of the Cistercian order, which had a con-

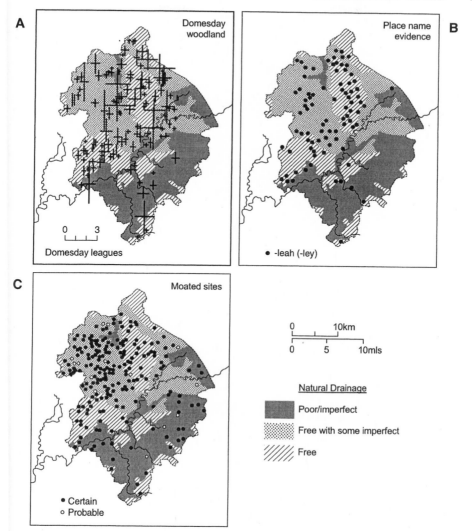

Figure 5.4 Landscapes of woodland clearing in Warwickshire, England: *A,* extent of Domesday woodland; *B,* place indicative of clearing; and *C,* moated sites. *Sources:* based on Darby and Terrett, 1971: 296; Glover and Mawer, 1936; Roberts, 1961: 41; and Whitfield, 1986.

centration of motherhouses in Burgundy in the east and north of the country from which numerous daughter settlements were founded. Often the monasteries acquired and developed land neglected by lay lords who gave it to them as an act of piety. In the Paris basin patches created by "aggressive" clearing in the forests surrounding the villages were either added to the existing fields or combined to create new ones. Documents "swarm," says George Duby, with references to clearings, or assarts; to pioneer settlements, or *hôtes;* to their crop-sharing arrangements, or *champarts;* to their tasks, or *tâches,* which were payments due from recently reclaimed land; and to *novales,* or tithes, levied on

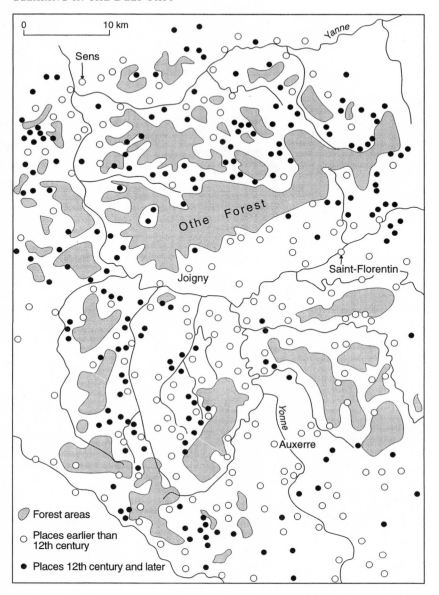

Figure 5.5 Forest clearing and settlement foundation, middle Yonne valley, France, eleventh century AD.
Source: Duby, 1974: 204.

newly broken-up areas.[60] The expansion of settlement during the twelfth century in the Middle Yonne valley, southeast of Paris, is indicative of what was happening (fig. 5.5).

Frequently, completely new settlements were created. These were the *ville-neuves* of the north, the *bourgs* of the west, and the *bastides* of the south, all basically village colonies that housed the *hopites* in groups of 30 to 80 persons. In order to encourage settlement and clearing, lords gave franchises, or freedoms of self-government, reduced dues, and abolished customary taxes, such as *chevage* (a yearly head tax), *formariage* (the prohibition of exogamy), *taille seigneuriale* (tallage), and the *corvée* (payments in labor). A kind of "megalomaniac intoxication" gripped some proprietors, wrote Marc Bloch, in their vision of the landscapes to be created out of the forest. More modestly, Abbot Suger of St. Denis boasted that he had added 20 *livres* annually to the income of a nearby manor by settling 80 new *hôtes* "on the new land next door to it." Eventually, reclamation produced a rise of property values; the obituary of 1243 of Albericus Cornu, who had been a canon at Notre-Dame de Paris, noted how in his lifetime he had founded new settlements in the forests and improved the abbey estates, which had "for long been so useless that they were a burden rather than a source of income."[61]

Sometimes the new villages, like those in Normandy, partook of the morphological characteristics of the *Waldhufendorf*, but it is the place-name elements that are so indicative of origin. For example, there are those with *rue* in their name, it meaning originally a breach in the forest *(rupta)*, hence La Rue Doré (Val-d'Oise) or Rupt-sur-Saône (Haute-Saône). Far more common are *Villeneuve, Neuville, Neufbourg, La Villeneuve, Neuvy, Neuilly,* and so forth, as part of the name, followed by the name of the founder— king, bishop, duke, or count—the saint of the founding abbey church (e.g., Neuilly-Saint-Pierre), or a neighboring town. And there are those with exotic names taken from the Crusades, such as Jerusalem, Nazareth, or Jericho, or with *assart* in the name (e.g., Essarts-le-Roi), or with the founder's own name (e.g., Beaumarchais), and there are many others.[62] Similar place-name evidence exists in other areas of western Europe. The *"-sarts"* ("assarts") in Flanders and the *"-rodes"* ("to grub up") in Brabant and Hainault were instituted by French and Flemish colonists, respectively.

Further east, in the lands between the Rhine and the Elbe, colonization was promoted vigorously by ecclesiastical and lay lords, and where it was not encouraged, or where the proprietors resisted, the peasants either encroached on the forest or took it by force. "Every motive," said Koebner, ". . . was operating in this great colonising process" of the Great Reclamation, or *Urbarmachung.* The map is peppered with ecclesiastical place-names and diagnostic place-name suffixes such as those in the land between the Weser and the Harz Mountains that end in *-hagan,* which indicate settlement by Flemish colonizers; or elsewhere, names like *-wald* ("wood") and *-holz* ("grove"), which are indicative of prior vegetation conditions; or those like *-rode* ("grubbed up"), *-swend* ("burned"), and *-ho* (cut down), which tell of the process of clearing.[63] Across the lowlands and the Alpine forelands the economy was changed and the appearance of the land transformed as fields and farms replaced forests. "Upland massifs such as the Harz, the Eifel, the Westerwald, the Thuringian Forest, and the Black Forest "were coming to look like great wooded islands in a sea of cultivation," wrote Darby. But the change did not cease; writing in 1222 of the previous century, Ceasarius of Prüm, the great monastery in the forested depths of the Eifel, recounted that "[d]uring this long space of time many forests were felled, villages founded, mills erected, taxes ordained, vines planted, and an infinite amount of land reduced to agriculture." Elsewhere in the upland forest, charcoal burners gradually chipped away and thinned the stands for their daily consumption of wood for smelting the abundant silver/lead and iron ores, particularly in the Harz Mountains.[64]

Impressive as this great colonization was, it did not equal the great movement east that occurred during the next hundred years which changed the map of the heart of central Europe, culturally and physically. Although separated by over 500 years, this migration has been compared in its extent and impact with the advance of American settlers from the eastern seaboard from first settlement to about 1810. The earlier thrust toward the southeast across the Alps, the Sudeten Mountains, and the slopes of the Erzgebirge, and down the Danube, which created Austria and culminated in many isolated pockets of German agricultural and mining settlements in Slav or Magyar territory in present-day Bohemia, Hungary, and Transylvania, was virtually over by 1150, when the other great movement from the middle and lower Elbe began to gain momentum. The advance was across the varied and poorly drained outwash sands, gravels, and clays of the northern German plain into what are now Mecklenburg, Pomerania, and Brandenberg and Silesia.[65]

The motives here were a mixture of all that we have seen before, but were also broadly economic and missionary. Old lands in Schleswig abandoned by previous Saxon settlers were occupied again, and by beating back the Slav inhabitants in adjacent areas, new lands were created out of unoccupied forest and swamp. In addition, Slavonic lords wanted to emulate German methods of cultivation and organization with the heavy plow in order to prosper. Much of the movement was the uncoordinated migration of small groups of peasants who eagerly sought land of their own and possibly greater personal liberty, although not all were landless or inexperienced farmers. Some migrants, however, were the result of deliberate colonization policies by German lay and ecclesiastical lords to populate their newfound territories with peasants and townsmen from the west. People came from all classes and from everywhere in "old" Germany; Flemings and Hollanders were especially sought out for the settlement of the swampy areas, though not exclusively so, as their reputation as pioneer colonizers made them desirable anywhere. Something of the flavor of these recruiting drives comes in a document of 1108, an appeal to "westerners" to colonize the lands east of present-day Berlin:

> These pagans are the worst of men but their land is the best, with meat, honey and flour. If it is cultivated the produce of the land will be such that none other can compare with it. That is what they say who know about it. So, O Saxons, Franconians, Lotharingians and Flemings, here you will be able to save your souls and, if you will, to acquire very good land to settle.[66]

It was like the booster literature that was used to lure settlers to the cutover lands of the Great Lakes states of the United States 700 years later.

Few of the new overlords had links with the west, and in any case, to get the best settlers and to plan the best type of settlement required an organization beyond their means. Therefore they employed "locators," middlemen whose job it was to find and negotiate with the migrants, and arrange transportation, land allotment, and settlement layout. Their reputation for organization must have been a big factor in the readiness and confidence with which so many western peasants were prepared to travel hundreds of miles into the unknown of the east. Towns were established as nodes of communication and trade, and about 1,200 villages were created in Silesia alone, though some of these must have been additions grafted onto existing settlements.[67]

Towards the end of the thirteenth century the movement had more or less played itself out. But there was one more episode of German forest colonization yet to be enacted. In the early thirteenth century the military order of the Brethren of the Sword had established an isolated outpost of fortified towns around Riga on the Baltic coast, but the penetration into the surrounding areas was not deep. Then, with the return of the Teutonic

Knights from the Crusades, the systematic colonization began of the intervening lands, by all the means already perfected on the "old frontier," so that by 1346 all the territory fringing the Baltic—through Prussia West and East, Courland, Livonia, and Estonia, almost to the Gulf of Finland—was under their control (see fig. 7.6 for these locations). With Bible and sword the land that they called *das Grosse Wildnis* was transformed into what Arnold of Lubeck, a contemporary chronicler, described as one of "fertile fields, of abundant pasture, well watered by rivers full of fish, and well covered with trees." [68] By the end of the fifteenth century some 93 cities had been established, as well as 1,400 villages, many of which can be easily traced because they are *waldhufen* or street villages in the former forest, or *marschufen* in the former marsh.

Hermann Aubin suggests that perhaps as many 150,000 settlers moved east of the Elbe-Salle line in the twelfth century, and a more recent study suggests a figure more like 200,000. Whatever the true number, the extension of the cultivated area into the forests was remarkable and very nearly reached its greatest extent ever, so that "little more land was won for agriculture" until modern times. [69]

The clearing of the forest in central and eastern Europe was not solely a function of German settlement, though these pioneers were the main spearheads of change. Slavonic lords and peasants, sometimes under coercion but often through emulation, sometimes under Slavonic law but more usually under German law, cleared forests and founded new villages, some of which were the distinctive *waldhufen* type. In the interior basin of Bohemia are over 300 villages called *Lhota,* which means approximately "freedom" or "freeing"—a reference to exemption from rents and taxes for a number of years in return for establishing a new settlement and clearing. A little further west in Slovakia the word appears about forty times as *lêhota,* and northward in eastern Poland some thirty times as *Logota,* which merge into over 1,500 places named *Wola* (again meaning "freedom") east of a line from Cracow to Kalisch. These examples could be multiplied endlessly, and added to with specifically Slavonic "clearing" names such as *kopanice, lazy,* and *paseky.* Although this clearing was more usually later and more limited in extent than the German colonization, it meant essentially the same thing: the diminution of the forest cover. [70]

How much was cleared? is a question that springs to mind but for which there will never be a definitive answer because of the long time span and the absence of unequivocal evidence. But despite the technicalities of what *forest* meant, we can be sure that there was a lot of woodland in Europe and much of it very dense. Michel Devèze estimated that from the evidence of polyptiques, 2 ha per capita of land was needed to support the population in the Middle Ages; possibly using that ratio, Roland Bechmann suggests that the forests of France were reduced from 30 million to 13 million ha between circa 800 and 1300, and still a quarter of the country remained covered. [71] In Germany and central Europe, Otto Schlüter's exhaustive and detailed enquiry into nearly 7,000 German and non-German place-names, tempered and checked against the evidence of historical documents, soils, archeology, vegetation history, and the actual sites themselves, has allowed him to produce tentative maps of the forest for over 1 million km² in central Europe in circa 900, and again a thousand years later. Perhaps 70 percent of the land was forest covered initially and about 25 percent remained by 1900 (figs. 5.6A and 5.6B). Devèze suggests that more than half the forest had been cut down between 1100 and 1350, and although some of the decrease must have happened after the Middle Ages, all the

Figure 5.6A Forest cover in central Europe, circa AD 900. *Sources:* Darby, 1956: 202, 203, after Schlüter, 1952.

evidence is that the bulk had occurred by 1500.[72] We may vary these estimates here and there, but they are certainly within the correct level of magnitude. By any calculation, the medieval European experience must rank as one of the great deforestation episodes in the world.

Britain participated in much of the experience of the continental core, but as is so often the case, it stood slightly aside and was a faint echo of the bigger story. The rapidly growing population put pressure on woodland on the edges of cultivation everywhere, yet the piecemeal clearing of previous centuries had left a patchy cover that was already exploited. For example, the Weald, one of the largest forested areas remaining, was crisscrossed by tracks from Roman times onward, large areas of its woodlands were managed through coppicing for the iron smelting industry, and most of it was systematically exploited for pannage and perhaps timber from the eighth century at the latest.[73]

There are a few references to large clearings such as the 1,000 acres in the Bishop of Winchester's manor at Witney, Oxfordshire, in the early thirteenth century, followed by a further 660 acres and 680 acres in 1256 and 1306, respectively, or the lands of Battle Abbey which grew to 1,400 acres in the fifty years after its foundation, to which was added a further 6 mi^2 of assarts out of woodland in Rotherfield manor sometime between

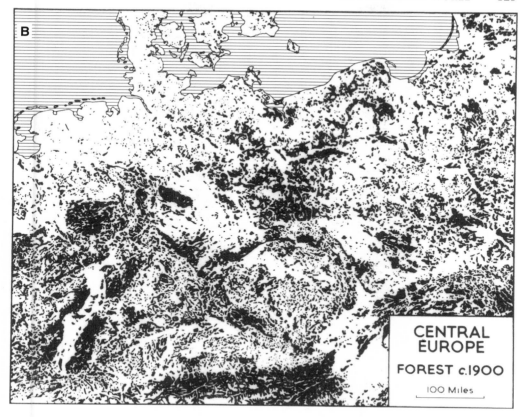

Figure 5.6B Forest cover in central Europe, circa AD 1900. *Sources:* Darby, 1956: 202, 203, after Schlüter, 1952.

1086 and 1346. But there was no concerted plan comparable to mainland Europe. Clearing was piecemeal by free peasants and tenants, some acting with a license from their lord to go ahead and open up the land, but most acting illegally.[74] References are scattered and difficult to trace, even in large woodland areas; but just occasionally the story of individual effort can be reconstructed, as in the parish of Hanbury, in northeast Worcestershire, deep in the Forest of Feckenham.[75] Figure 5.7 shows the incidence of assarts and the areas in which most clearance occurred in Hanbury, where the population rose from 266 to 725 by 1299. Small as the parish is, Hanbury must stand as a representative example of what must have happened hundreds, if not thousands, of times across Britain, and indeed the whole continent, during the great age of clearing. The detail might have varied from place to place, but the experience of clearing a small patch of woodland, breaking up the soil, and getting in and harvesting the first crop was one that millions of people shared from Land's End to the Urals.

The Periphery

Around the European core of innovation and transformation lay the peripheries: Russia to the east and northeast and the Mediterranean to the south. Clearing occurred for all

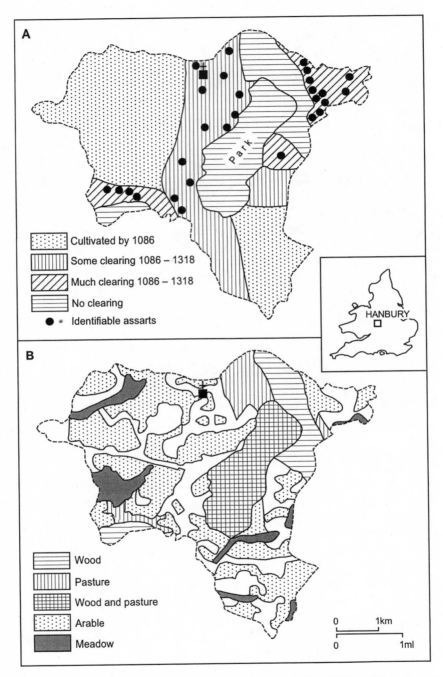

Figure 5.7 Hanbury, West Midlands, England: *A*, settlement zones, AD 400–1318; and *B*, land use circa AD 1300. *Source:* after Dyer, 1991.

the reasons explored already, but never with the same single-mindedness of purpose or overall impact.

Russia: "The Icon and the Axe"

Russia exhibited many of the characteristics of the core, but the experience was subtly different. The early history of forest clearing is murky and confused.[76] We know that the Slavs moved westward into mainland Europe from their homeland somewhere between the Carpathians and the Upper Dnieper, but they also moved eastward into the mixed-oak forest zone that lay in a great triangle pointing eastward toward Asia—its apex located on the Oka-Volga confluence (near present-day Moscow), one side bounded by a line to the Gulf of Finland, and the other side by a line to Kiev. The triangle was wedged between the almost unbroken wall of the coniferous forests to the north, and the forest/steppe zone to the south which was similar to the prairie/woodland ecotone in the United States. It is a fretted and irregular transition zone about 200 mi deep, with tongues of woodland penetrating south along river courses, projections of steppe extending north, and "islands" of woodland on the steppes. Kiev was founded in the ninth century and traditionally lay "amongst forests" but is now surrounded by open steppe, which suggests extensive clearing and the northward movement of the forest boundary.[77]

The processes whereby the settlement and clearing occurred is uncertain, but it is known that the Kievan Rus on the southern edge of the forest zone was a frontier society. It was constantly battered by invasions of barbarian nomads, particularly the Mongol invasions of 1237–40, when cultivated land was devastated and the population slaughtered "with a thoroughness the world would not see again until the twentieth century." The Slavic Orthodox Christian refugees sought the security of the forests and moved northward into the principalities, such as Moscow (founded circa 1147), which had been established in the country between the Oka and Volga during the twelfth century.[78] In the process the original Finno-Ugarian population of shifting cultivators and foragers was subdued or assimilated, or they retreated to the coniferous forest edge. They were replaced by slash-and-burn cultivators and sedentary, intensive cultivators employing 2- and 3-field crop rotation systems.

Probably nothing better illustrates the combination of material struggle and spiritual exultation that accompanied these movements into the forest than the icon and the axe—two objects that had enduring meaning to Russians and were traditionally hung together in a place of honor on the wall of every peasant hut. "The axe," said James Billington,

> was the basic implement of Great Russia: the indispensable means of subordinating the forest to the purposes of man. The icon . . . was the omnipresent reminder of the religious faith that gave the beleaguered frontiersman a sense of ultimate security and higher purpose. If the axe was used with delicacy to plane and smooth the wooden surface on which the holy pictures were painted, the icon, in turn was borne militantly before the peasantry whenever they ventured forth into the forests with axes for the more harsh business of felling trees or warding off assailants.[79]

The progress of forest clearing and settlement was slow and the extent limited and intermittent compared with the vigor and thoroughness of the trans-Elbean Germans at this time. There were reasons, of course. Civil disorder and raids by the Mongols and others had their effect; the dominance of slash-and-burn cultivation did not lead to permanent clearing; and the fact that the principalities and monasteries were intensely feudal and autocratic meant that it was not "a new frontier, but a world of clearly defined and institutionalized private property." [80] Here, there was no feeling of the freedom and emancipation that had fired the energy and ambition of the western European forest settler. The abundant religious fervor came without a concept of personal redemption, and was no substitute for material betterment. The migrant peasant had little choice but to accept dependence on his new lord and offer his labor in kind. Thus, clearing was slow and limited, other than in the immediate environs of Moscow; but even there the area of cultivation remained small by the end of the sixteenth century. And even as late as the eighteenth century Moscovy would have "struck a Western European traveller journeying from Smolensk to Moscow as one huge forest, and the towns and villages in it as mere clearings." [81] It is possible that more clearing went on with the encouragement of many religious houses in the comparative safety of the trans-Volgan lands.

In the coniferous forests further north, furs, pitch, pine, tar, and wax were funnelled through the merchant system of Novgorod, which moved increasingly into the orbit of the Hanseatic League, and from there out to the markets of the core of maritime western Europe. Small settlements developed into prosperous towns between Moscow and the White Sea, but as Darby warns, one must "not endow this northern settlement with an intensity it did not possess," for it had more in common with the slash-and-burn cropping with rye, flax, oats, and hemp of the boreal fringe lands.[82]

The Muslim Mediterranean

Once the upheaval of the barbarian invasions subsided, people on the southern Mediterranean periphery of Europe went about life as of old: settling, clearing, and cutting. The demands of an imperial Rome had no longer to be met; fleets and grandiose buildings were a thing of the past until the Muslim invasion.

Initially the Muslim conquest of the Mediterranean lands was a land-based affair, with expansion moving through Egypt and North Africa between AD 700 and 750. Generally sea power was disdained, but repeated forays and victories by Christian fleets from Byzantium against Muslim conquests in North Africa altered that, and soon the Muslims were engaged in shipbuilding. The forests of the Atlas were a particularly favored source of timber, and Tunis and Cairo became major shipbuilding centers. Soon their navies were large enough to engage not only in defense but offense. Raids from Tunis for wood occurred in Sicily, Sardinia, Corsica, and southern Italy, and from Cairo into Cyprus and Crete and the coastal areas of the Byzantine Empire during the eighth and ninth centuries. These assaults culminated in outright conquest: Spain fell in the early eighth century, then Cyprus, although the conquest of Sicily was a long, drawn-out affair between AD 800 and 902.

The new conquered territories of Sicily, the Maghreb, and Spain provided abundant sources of timber, but Syria, Mesopotamia, and Egypt had almost none. Consequently a complex network of long-distance trade for the supply of timber emerged during the seventh to eleventh centuries, complemented by trading from the Anatolian and Dalmatian coasts and even as far away as the Malabar coast, where teak for shipbuilding was obtained (fig. 5.8). Idrisi, the Arab geographer, commented on the mountains in northeast

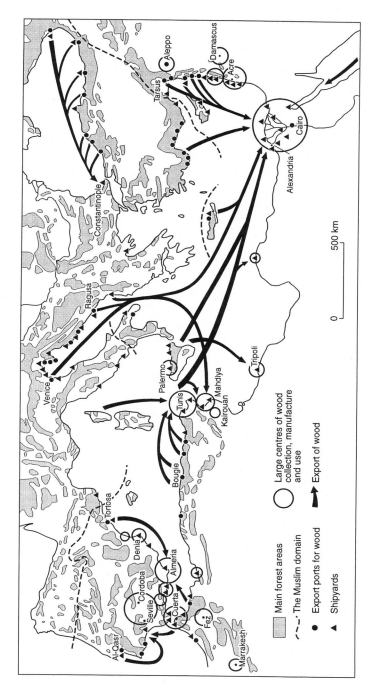

Figure 5.8 Wood and timber in the medieval Muslim Mediterranean world. *Source*: after Lombard, 1959.

Spain which "produce pine whose wood equals in beauty, thickness and length the best in the world. With wood they build great vessels."[83] The timber was floated down the River Ebro to shipbuilding yards at Tortosa, something that could not be done anywhere else in the Mediterranean, except for a few locations in southern Italy. Elsewhere, overland pack animals were used over rough terrain.

Demands for timber for construction, fuel, and artisans' workshops in Middle Eastern and North African cities such as Cairo, Baghdad, Tunis, and Acre; the Spanish cities of Seville, Cordoba, and Almeria; and new towns like Kairouan in Tunisia put a severe strain on the meager supplies. Metal smelting, sugar refining, and ceramic manufacture all placed additional enormous demands on the scarce timber resources. The silver mines of Rio Tinto, near Seville, were fed by wood from the Balearics.[84]

But Muslim domination of the Mediterranean did not last. By the thirteenth century Byzantium had reconquered Crete, Cyprus, and much of Syria, and then Sicily fell, and Spain was to follow, and their timber supplies dried up. By the thirteenth century Arabs tried to organize supplies from the rich Venetian hinterland in Dalmatia and the Alps, but they either had to pay exorbitant prices that they could ill afford (and which benefited Venice enormously), or were denied access to supplies, as the strategic nature of timber was appreciated, especially at a time when the Crusades to reoccupy the Holy Land were getting under way. By the end of the fourteenth century the Muslim world was in comparative disarray in the Mediterranean, and Venice was in the ascendancy. A new chapter in forest use in this part of the world was opening up.

COMPLEXITY AND CONFLICT IN THE FOREST

The forest was deeply embedded in the fabric of medieval life. Its size, its multiple uses, and yet its continuing diminution meant that it was involved both in the "need for change and the need for stability" which these centuries posed.[85] Thus, a complexity of uses, an ambivalence of motives, and an inevitable conflict of aims were hallmarks of the age.

These issues arose because few rural communities or towns owned the freehold of the forest: that was the prerogative of royalty, and later the nobility. Monarchs and aristocrats had reserved forest areas (whether densely treed or not) in which they had ancient and inviolable rights for their own use, particularly for game and hunting. Yet the forest was also close to the everyday life of ordinary people because of the multiplicity of its products and uses. It was not an abstract concept: it was bound up with the necessity of eating and keeping warm, of fencing land and pasturage (plate 5.2). It was a valued resource without which people could not exist. Consequently, from about the eighth and ninth centuries a vast body of rights, usages, and customary law had grown up pertaining to forest use that were gradually codified and regulated, and by the twelfth and thirteenth centuries were given precise definitions and delimitations. Nearly everyone had some rights in the forest, be it grazing for cattle or pannage for swine, the right to take firewood, or the right to take constructional timber, known collectively as "estovers."[86] Almost any medieval charter, cartulary, or rental agreement abounds with details of these customs and traditional usages.

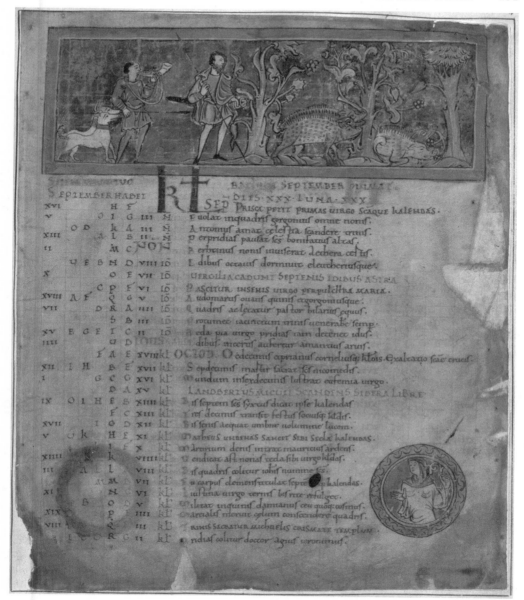

Plate 5.2 "Swine feeding in the forest." The manuscript comes from the eleventh century AD. (By permission of the British Library, Ms. Tiberius, B.V. fol. 7.)

In France, over 350 places surrounding or within the huge Forest of Orléans had codified and defined usage rights of some sort. These were usually free, or, if emanating from a religious house, granted in return for the saying of masses for the lord. There was *faucillage* or *herbage,* the right to cut grass and take it away; *champiage,* the right to graze animals on common pastures; *ramage,* the right to take branches and boughs for fences; *affouage,* the right take firewood; *maronage,* the right to cut timber for necessary repairs to buildings; and *ramas,* the right to collect litter for cattle, to name but a few. The Law of Beaumont (1182) granted free use of woodlands to over 500 mainly new towns created throughout the country, and the Law of Lorris (1108–37) did the same for over new 300 towns created in the east and south of the Parisian basin.[87]

In Britain, the forest was less extensive and all pervasive in rural society than it was in France, but even so the Domesday Book refers occasionally to forest rights.[88] Charters and assize proceedings in later centuries show that forest use was extensive, valued, and intricately controlled. Many peasants had the right to collect constructional timber *(housebote),* wood for fencing *(hayebote),* and wood for fuel *(firebote),* which was often deadwood that could be got "by hook or by crook"—that is to say, such timber as could be knocked off or pulled down from standing trees, a concession paralleling the French right of *mort-bois* or *morbois.*[89]

But hunting was a preserve of royalty and the nobility, who had a "widespread and irresistible infatuation" with it that went way beyond the attaining of meat (plate 5.3). "The symbolism of hunting," commented Christopher Wickham, "ever more clearly came to match that of royal charisma," and more broadly its history "closely mirrors that of political power and socio-political change" among the elites.[90] At one level it was a ritual display of "manners" and power because it was "encrusted with courtly ceremony that served to demonstrate the genteel manners (or exposed the pretensions) of the participants of the chase."[91] At another level it was a ritualist reenactment of the historical conquest of wilderness (literally, "the place of wild beasts"). Thus the king or lord embodied and represented in his person "the civilizing force of history," but he also harbored a savage nature that ensured the protection of the territory. In this way, concludes Robert Harrison, did the king's "sovereign nature belong to nature," and thus he would "return every so often to the sanctuaries to ritualize the law of its overcoming."[92]

These examples of forest control and use could be multiplied endlessly at different times and different places, and we have not even touched the abundant evidence of these practices for Germany and central Europe. So intricate was this body of custom and traditional rights in most rural societies that they were like strands that enmeshed individuals and institutions, and constituted, suggests Glacken, "the medieval counterpart of the modern concept of culture" that bespoke of an organized society, and which spanned the continent.[93]

Anything that lessened these rights and customs was bound to cause concern. The continued population increase during the thirteenth century, the demands of trade and towns, and the clearing and conversion of forest to farmland produced an acute pressure on the resource. In addition, seigniorial pressure on the peasantry in order to maintain income led to the demarcation and regulation, or even prohibition, of certain forest rights. Thus, a tension arose between royalty and lords, who wanted to preserve the forests for hunting and for territorial control, and between both of these and the peasants, who valued the products and privileges of forested land.[94] It was a sort of conflict of interest between preservation and modification, though at times it is difficult to know who was preserver and who was modifier—king, lord, or peasant—though we can be certain that hunting was crucial in forest conservation.

Plate 5.3 The Hunt in the Forest by Paolo Uccello, circa 1470. This unique painting depicts wealthy patricians indulging in the ritual of their favorite sport on a moonlit night. (Ashmolean Museum, Oxford.)

As early as Carolingian times in the early ninth century, royalty attempted to regulate forest use by forbidding lords to make new *forestae,* the legal term for a hunting ground, and, more commonly, lords limited peasant rights. As an example of the latter, when the count of Vendôme found unauthorized clearings in his woods he had the houses destroyed and the crops mowed off. "That was fair," said the monk who recounted the story. Such a comment was noteworthy, as the church usually showed far more appreciation of the peasant point of view than did the nobility, and often suffered too from noble imperiousness. But usually "fairness" did not seem to be a quality of the new forest laws. In England, William set up a severe forest regime with harsh penalties for poaching and assarting. Whole counties were scheduled as "forest" (fig. 5.1) and hundreds of families evicted. In time, peasants and nobles alike chaffed under the harsh restrictions, and in 1217 the nobles wrung concessions out of Henry III with the Forest Charter, which safeguarded the rights of their tenants and themselves. The charter was far reaching in its implications and "took its place," said Doris Stenton, "alongside the Great Charter [Magna Carta] as part of the foundations on which the English social scene was laid."[95] Simply, once more, the forest played a role in the development of human affairs. Not only did clearing it promote the social advancement of the common man, but the establishment of forest rights was a precursor of human rights.

The great age of clearing saw a shift in attitude as both lords and peasants alike joined in a great effort of cooperative change in the forest. For many peasants the lure of freehold overrode the privilege of usufruct. But as the colonization process waned at the end of the thirteenth century, many felt that clearing had gone far enough, if not too far. "Reclamation had come close to the reasonable limit," noted Bloch. If it continued, where would the animals graze and where would the fuel come from, especially as the development of the chimney and hearths in individual rooms in houses increased the demand for fuelwood? Now the medieval frontier had closed, and what Lewis called the "unearned increment of land" could no longer enrich monastic proprietor, seigniorial landlord, or peasant cultivator as it had in the past.[96] Forest protection began to be asserted as a desirable aim.

It is difficult to generalize about attitudes during these centuries, but there are many indicators. In France, an ever-increasing proliferation and complexity of edicts throughout the thirteenth century defined usage rights more closely, set up a special judiciary concerning forests, and culminated in 1291 in an ordinance defining the role of the new officials, the masters of *Eaux et Forêts,* that was repeated and strengthened by measures in 1317, 1319, 1346, 1355, and 1357. The agents were charged with visiting all forest areas, investigating complaints and breaches of use, and having the forests exploited with the purpose that they "may remain perpetually in a good condition." In Germany, similar, though less comprehensive measures are evident. In 1309 either side of the Pegnitz River, near Nurenberg, which was formerly forested and converted to agriculture, was ordered to be returned to forest by royal edict, and clearings in Hagenauer forest phased out. In 1331 King Ludwig of Bavaria promulgated more regulations that further restricted forest use, especially the sale of wood that might be "harmful to the city" and its industries.[97]

The significance of these glimmerings of awareness for the story of global deforestation is that the forest was becoming valued progressively, both economically and culturally. Additionally, there was an awareness that the forest environment was being changed radically (plate 5.4), and that not all change constituted "progress" or was necessarily

Plate 5.4 Mining used up vast amounts of wood for shoring up the workings and, of course, for smelting.
From G. Agricola, *De Re Metallica*, 1557.

desirable, an observation that has continued from those times to the present. Finally, there was a consciousness of the need to achieve a balance among the different and competing uses of the forest—agriculture, industry, and forestry. Timber was the indispensable raw material of metal smelting, glass-making, furniture making, cooperage, house building, and a dozen other manufacturing and fabricating processes. By about 1400 iron production alone throughout Europe was between 25,000 and 30,000 tons.[98] The ore deposits and the towns and their industries could not be moved when the supplies of wood ran out, but the supplies could be protected and growth encouraged. Simply, the forest was the lifeblood of the brisk and vigorous medieval economy, so an accommodation between various uses had to be found.

EUROPEAN EPILOGUE: PLAGUE AND REFORESTATION

The crisis in the forest never came; the exuberance of the medieval spring turned to the melancholy of dark winter. The spread of bubonic plague west and north across Europe from Constantinople between 1347 and 1353 wiped out at least one-third of the population in most of the West, and in places the proportion may have risen to one half. The death toll may have been over 20 million, and the total population fell from 73.5 million in 1340 to about 50 million in 1450. In some areas the effect was compounded by deteriorating climate and unsettled weather, first evident during the late thirteenth century, which became more obvious in time and led to crop failure, disease in stock, and settlement retreat from marginal areas. The population surplus, which had caused an "agrarian crisis" in farming, overcrowding of good lands, pressure on the forests, and conflicts over usage rights, was reduced at a stroke.[99] Across the continent, between one-fifth and one-fourth of all settlements were abandoned, the "deserted villages" of England and France being matched by the *Wüstungen* of Germany, in both the "old" south and west as well as the "new" eastern trans-Elbean settlement. The abandonment of once-cultivated land has been put as high as 25 percent, although some of the contraction may have been only temporary as part of a regrouping of settlements.[100] But in many places the forests re-advanced on the fields (figure 5.9 shows the changes in the areas around Hofgeismar in the upper Weser Basin); and many present forests in Germany came into being only after the Middle Ages.[101]

Conditions became no better in the succeeding century. War and pillage ravaged the countryside; the Hussite Wars (1419–36) devastated Bohemia economically and demographically, and similarly in the west, France suffered grievously during the Hundred Years War (1337–1453), which reduced the population by one half to one third in places. That once prosperous country was, said Petrarch in 1360, "a heap of ruins"; and about 80 years later Bishop Thomas Basin of Lisieux described the vast extent of uncultivated fields between the Loire and the Somme as being "overgrown with brambles and bushes." In the southwest, in Saintogne, between the Charente and the Dordogne, for a long time people said that "the forests came back to France with the English."[102] For a while, the forest had been reprieved.

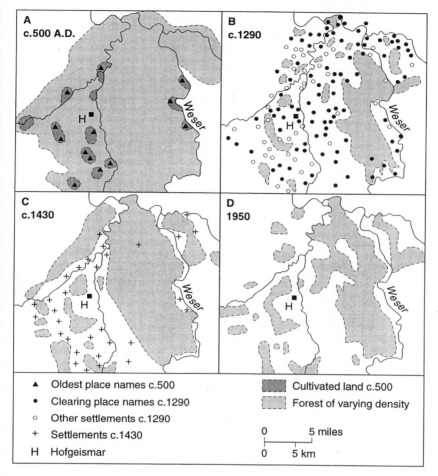

Figure 5.9 Woodland and settlement change around Hofgeismar in the upper Weser basin: *A*, circa AD 500, to *D*, AD 1950. *Source:* Jäger, 1951. Note the post-fifteenth-century settlements not shown in fig. 5.9C.

CHINA: A LAND OF "PONDEROUS UNKNOWNS"

The comparison between Europe and the even more densely populated and intensely humanized lands of China, where deforestation was going on during the equivalent of the oriental Neolithic, classical, and medieval times, could not be more stark. Whereas events and evidence in Europe are reasonably clear, the story in China before the beginning of the Ming dynasty in 1368 is truly "dark." Our knowledge of deforestation is almost wholly confined to the musings of the third-century BC philosopher Mencius on the destructive nature of grazing and tree lopping for fuel that left "bald" mountains,[103] the seventh-to tenth-century poems of the *Shih Ching,* and the workings of the iron industry. The sparsity of information prompted a leading scholar on deforestation to conclude that the information gap was "of a different order from that for other areas," making China a land of "ponderous unknowns."[104] There is a paucity of information on status, property rights, individual wealth, forest protection, and duties of individuals and even of classes, but an abundance on the working of bureaucratic government, taxation, government agricultural policies, fiscal reforms, and development plans. Thus, material for a "bottom-up" approach is missing, and it is unlikely that sinologists "will ever be able to produce regional studies or monographs of a depth or quality to match those written on Europe."[105] Historical interpretations of early Chinese rural society rarely carry the conviction of their counterparts in Europe. Nonetheless, what evidence there is hints at massive change.

The Clearing Process

The Chinese forest has a greater geographical variation than does that of Europe. It stretches from the Arctic tundra and steppes of Siberia to the tropical rain forests of Southeast Asia. The core of agricultural development was centered in the Yellow River (Huang-Ho) basin in the broad-leafed deciduous forests of the north, which merged into the loess plateau, and the grassland steppe beyond. Possible climatic change and millennia of agriculture had transformed these lands into a mosaic of different vegetation types. Thus the "original," historical landscape, says Nicholas Menzies, had

> fairly thick forest around rivers and other permanent sources of water. The plains were probably covered with rather sparse deciduous woodland, opening out into savannah grasslands with scattered trees or brush in the northwest in what is now Shensi province, and most of the Ordos plateau of Inner Mongolia. Denser deciduous woodland was found on the foothills of the mountains. . . . Coniferous forest dominated the higher elevations above about 1,500 metres with larch and spruce forming the highest forests.

The heavily forested northeast and tropical southern forests were peripheral to this core.[106]

How these lands were occupied and improved predominantly by the Han is largely unknown. Nonetheless, the seventh- to tenth-century BC poems in the *Book of Odes (Shih Ching)* give us some idea of the labors and livelihood of ordinary people as they broke in new land:

> They clear away the grass, the trees;
> Their ploughs open up the ground.
> In a thousand pairs they tug at weeds and roots,
> Along the low ground, along the ridges
> There is the master and his eldest son,
> There is the headman and overseer.
> They mark out, they plough.
>
> Truly those southern hills—
> It was Yü who fashioned them;
> Those level spaces, upland and lowland—
> The descendant tills them.
> We draw boundaries, we divide the plots,
> On southern slopes and eastern we set our acres.[107]

The extent of clearing depended on the intensity of cultivation and population density. Thus, shifting cultivation, short fallows, and permanent cultivation bore some relationship to these factors. The one unambiguous description of land clearing occurs in the *Chhi Min Yao Shu* composed by Chia Ssu-Hsien circa AD 535, and it refers to the reclamation of woodland and scrub that had grown up after decades of devastating warfare in North China in the post-Han period (after AD 220) which were to be cleared for civil and military colonies:

> When clearing land (Khai huang) in mountains or marshes for new fields, always cut down the weeds in the seventh month; the weeds should be set on fire once they have dried out. Cultivation should begin only in the spring. Larger trees and shrubs should be killed by ring-barking. Once the leaves are dead and no longer cast any shade ploughing and sowing may begin, and after three years the roots will have withered and the trunks decayed enough to be burned out.
>
> Once the ploughing of the waste is completed, draw an iron-toothed harrow across it twice. Broadcast millet and then run the bush-harrow over the field twice. By the next year it will be fit for grain land.

Roots and stumps were grubbed out with mattock and hoe. Clearing was certainly worth the effort, and it was a common saying that "even setting up in trade is not as profitable as clearing new land."[108]

In the forested hill slopes of the less densely populated tropical forests south of the Yangtze, a shifting cultivation system seems to have been practiced, in which the inhabitants were "ploughing with fire," and using axes and spades. This was satisfactory as long as the patch cleared was small and the rotation short; but problems arose after the third century AD, when the Han migrants with their clear-cutting techniques moved into the forested hill country from the overcrowded north. Overcultivation caused massive soil degradation, and siltation in the Yangtze by the thirteenth century.[109]

By the end of the innovative T'ang dynasty (circa AD 923/36) the transformation of large parts of northern China was evident. Buddhism and Confucianism had not stopped the ascendancy of culture over nature; indeed, that "most civilized of all arts"—calligraphy—had led to a demand for pine soot for making the ink for the vast Chinese bureaucracy, causing massive inroads into the pine forests of the T'ai-hang mountains between Shansi and Hopei. Paradoxically, says Yi-Fu Tuan, it was the advantages of comfort and safety of the human-made world that "translated into a greater awareness of the beauty and fragility of nature." Increasingly the government sought to protect forests against needless agricultural burning and excessive cutting in watersheds, and reinforced respect for the surroundings of temples and tombs, though often in vain. As in Europe, some forests were reserved by the nobility for hunting.[110]

In the north the strategic value of intact forest was appreciated as a barrier to the marauding hordes of horsemen from the steppes of Central Asia who plagued these agricultural societies. The Great Wall begun in 300 BC completed what the forests could not accomplish, but strategic barriers of trees on the Wu-t'ai mountains in northern Shan-shi were still in place in the sixteenth century. In the southern mountainous region the vast mixed deciduous and evergreen broad-leafed forests were barely touched, and wild elephants and the rhinoceros roamed the malaria jungles of the province of Kuang-tung in the ninth century; but that was to change with migration from the north which reached a new momentum after the tenth century.[111]

Urbanization and Industry

While clearing for agriculture was the key element in the deforestation of the countryside, the detail, as ever, is murky. In contrast the demands of urbanization and industry have some firmness, and they were immense.

In particular, an iron and steel industry flourished in the Shantung region in northeast China during the ebullient and innovative Northern Sung, between AD 910 and 1126 (fig. 5.10). In what can only be called an industrial revolution, iron production reached 125,000 to 150,000 tons by the end of the Sung (AD 1078), which compares favorably with the total western and Russian European output of 145,000 to 180,000 tons at the beginning of the eighteenth century, and was a figure only just surpassed in England and Wales in 1796. The bulk of iron went into producing farm implements and armaments, and surprisingly, into shipbuilding. The Shantung peninsula, formerly described by the Japanese monk Ennin in 845 as so "densely wooded" that the widely spaced towns "were like single mounds in the wilderness," was severely denuded a few hundred years later.[112] What woodland remained was coppiced and pollarded in order to ensure supplies. Firewood and charcoal were transported from as far afield as Schezwan, Hunan, and Fukien in a wide arc to the south, together with food from the newly colonized irrigated rice fields of the great deltas. The Grand Canal constructed between 1266–89 was the culmination of many efforts to improve waterways and so secure these southern supplies of fuel and food. In addition, the early substitution of coal for charcoal suggests not only precocious technological development but widespread forest devastation and shortages of fuel, which the manufacturing of salt, alum, bricks, porcelain, tiles, and liquor all exacerbated.[113]

Compared with the more bureaucratic past, the vibrant economy produced new, flexible social and economic structures. Local self-sufficiency turned into regional specialization and exchange. Coins and paper money entered circulation by the eleventh century; indeed, if charcoal only had been used, then a forest of 22,000 medium-sized trees would have been needed to mint the iron and copper cash needed in 1086 alone.[114] But by 1300, the Northern Sung iron production had declined by one half—whether through exhaustion of fuel, the Mongol invasions, or some other factor, is not known. Whatever the reason, the florescence of the Sung dynasty was over, and with it the glimmer of light that illuminated the deep past of the Chinese forests was extinguished.

The remarkable economic expansion of China during the Northern Sung had generated massive urbanization, which, like the iron industry, had no counterpart in the European world at this time. By 1100 at least five cities had populations exceeding one million, including K'ai-feng and Hang-Chaou, the capitals of the Northern and Southern dynasties, respectively, with a number of other trading and administrative centers on the southeast coast almost as large.[115] The demand for building materials and wood for keeping warm and for cooking was immense. Cities counted fuelwood resources as one of their major essential "imports" together with food and water, and there is some evidence that carefully managed plantations for supplies were located on the edges of some cities. Nonetheless, the accumulated evidence of this and succeeding periods points to a severe energy crisis in China from 1400 until at least the mid-nineteenth century, and that scavenging for combustible matter from stunted shrubs, grass, and leaves was a major preoccupation of the Chinese peasant until recent times.[116]

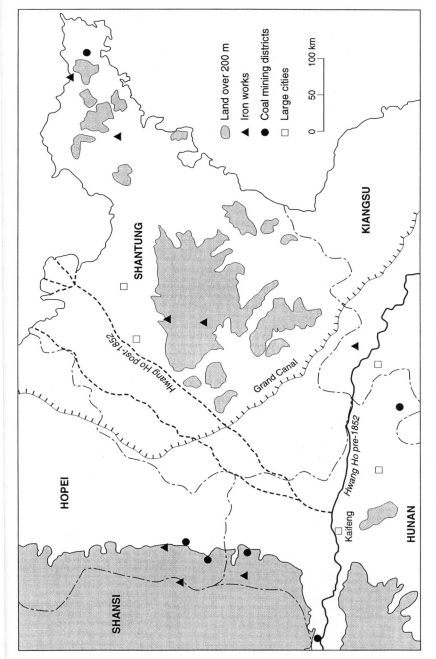

Figure 5.10 The iron industry of Sung China, circa AD 1100. *Source:* Hartwell, 1967.

When the subsequent histories of deforestation in Europe and China are compared, it is clear that the sheer press of population in China and the constant emphasis on agriculture for subsistence was to the detriment of extensive land uses, whether grazing or forests. The overwhelming peasant population had little choice but to "alter and manipulate nature for their own survival" and over the centuries changed and destroyed their environment "on a greater scale than any other part of the world" if only because there were "so many more of them at it for so much longer." [117] Europe, on the other hand, broke out of its vicious circle of subsistence when it was able to reach out and garner the resources of the wider world.

PART II

REACHING OUT: EUROPE AND THE WIDER WORLD

Chapter 6

Driving Forces and Cultural Climates, 1500–1750

Two things belong to this age [the sixteenth century] more than to all its predecessors: the discovery of the world and the discovery of man.
—JULES MICHELET, *Histoire de France* (1855)

The end . . . is the knowledge of Causes and secret motions of things, and the enlarging of the bounds of the Human Empire, to the effecting of all things possible.
—FRANCIS BACON, *The New Atlantis* (1627)

Everywhere money was on the march.
—HERMAN VAN DER WEE, "Monetary, Credit and Banking Systems" (1970)

MEDIEVAL EUROPEANS may have behaved toward their forests in an "eminently parasitic and extremely wasteful way," but they had used them to provide an expanded agriculture, an abundant source of energy, considerable construction and development of dwellings in the country and in towns, and a vibrant metallurgical industry. Land and its biological resources were the basis for the creation of an innovative, decentralized, energetic, yet comparatively stable society that enjoyed a rise in the general standard of living in which "all income levels, profits, wages, and rents, grew in real terms."[1] Indeed, before the end of the fifteenth century Europe had climbed out of the abyss of plague and depression, pulled itself together, and was preparing for the long-term economic and cumulative development that Douglass North and Robert Thomas have termed "the rise of the Western world," or, as Eric Jones has aptly labelled it, "The European Miracle."[2] Perhaps it was even the beginning of what we call today globalization.

Therefore, although the Middle Ages signaled the end of the "deep past" of deforestation in a chronological sense, in a thematic sense they were merely a prelude to an even bigger episode that was yet to come, when Europe began "reaching out" across the wider world. This was the "age of discovery" par excellence, but it was also an age of intellectual ferment that encapsulated the Renaissance and the Reformation. Michelet put it nicely when he said that two things belonged to the sixteenth century "more than to all its predecessors: the discovery of the world and the discovery of man."[3] But there was a third characteristic to this period that went hand in hand with global and personal discovery, and that was commercial expansion and enterprise, which flowered during the 250 years separating 1500 and 1750 and bridged the gap between feudal agricultural Europe and industrial Europe.[4] Now the countries of the western rim of the Continent broke out of their geographical bounds and initiated a new phase of change, far different in kind and greater in extent than anything known before. This phase was the start of what were probably the biggest transformations in natural vegetation of the world since the Ice Age. Of all the major types of land cover affected, perhaps the forest was altered most.

Two major theaters of action comprised that alteration of the forest. First, a core of intensive (usually urban-oriented) land use emerged, particularly in the sea-oriented, capitalist economies of western Europe. In the sixteenth century there were Spain and Portugal, then in the next century Britain and the Low Countries, and to a lesser extent France. Only later did the other countries of the European continent come into the picture.[5] An increasing scarcity of wood, sometimes real but sometimes imaginary, led to the search and utilization of forest resources on the European margins, and then ultimately overseas.

Second, in time, the countries of the core expanded their influence outside the confines of the continent and exploited the global periphery. Successive waves or frontiers of settlement, together with the growing of new crops by new methods, extracted the wealth and stored energy of the peripheral environment for the benefit of the core. In that expansion events were put into motion that had far-reaching consequences on the distribution of the world's peoples, plants, animals, and even diseases—but particularly on plants, because forest clearing occurred in places where it had never happened before—all of which had direct effects on soils, hydrology, and other biogeographical phenomena.

There is considerable justification for regarding these two locales of forest clearing and exploitation in Europe and its overseas territories as related themes: indeed, they are often inseparable. For example, ships were built of timber and were the means of exploration and overseas expansion, and the lack of ships' timber precipitated sea-faring nations' search for new supplies. Again, the forces that led to the European resurgence after the fifteenth century were also the forces that propelled them overseas in the sixteenth; the attitudes toward the forest that drove the desire to clear in Europe also drove clearing in the new settlements, especially in North America; and there are many more connections. Nonetheless, if only because of order and clarity, the two theaters of forest exploitation are best separated and dealt with in individual chapters, although their complementarity must be recognized. In reality, of course, Europe and the territories it affected were not the whole world; there was a third major theater of deforestation in the older civilizations of, for example, China and Japan, which were also making massive inroads into their forests.

DRIVING FORCES AND CULTURAL CLIMATES

Our knowledge about changes in the extent and composition of the forests during the 250 years between roughly 1500 and 1750 is, with few exceptions, surprisingly and tantalizingly slight. In some parts of Europe probably less is known about clearing then than during the Middle Ages, if only because two forms of evidence that were so useful—place-names and settlement morphology—are no longer diagnostic of either the time or the conditions of first settlement. In the wider world, pioneer societies and initial settlers were not great record keepers; they had more pressing tasks of simple survival to keep them occupied.

The story, however, is not only one of what happened, of the facts of where and when and the obvious relations between them, but one of why it happened. Such explanations are often obscure, because they usually lie buried deep in the past and are often difficult to link in any causal connection. But difficult or not, such explanations must be confronted because any land transformation must be placed in its particular social, economic, and intellectual context. As has been said repeatedly, deforestation is not solely a matter of hectares cleared; it is a humanly activated and humanly induced process of environmental change, and is a part of the society that does it.

It is important to sort out which of the many developments in society and economy contributed to the accelerated changes in the forests of Europe and the rest of the world. They are multilayered as well as interacting. They are also of long standing, frequently very ordinary, and part of basic survival, and have been present in most societies from time immemorial, constituting what Fernand Braudel calls "the structures of everyday life."[6] The need for wood for fuel to keep warm, to smelt metals, and to cook; the demand for wood for construction, utensils, tools, and ships; and the use of forests for "making" new land to grow food have not changed much since humans have been on earth, except inasmuch as the number of people utilizing them has grown inexorably. These processes might well be termed the sources, "driving forces," or causes of change in the forest environment.

But such an explanation of change as being an outcome of "driving forces," which in contemporary deforestation studies are isolated in order to explain, forecast, and prescribe action, is seldom that simple. Change is likely to mirror not one basic force, but many, which interact in clusters. Moreover, nonmaterial forces like motivation, sentiment, and symbolism (especially strong in forest environments)[7] are largely ignored because they cannot be quantified or factored into explanations easily, especially if some sort of modeling is envisaged. Rather, Lynn White's concept of complex "cultural climates," which favor and encourage change, is probably more realistic.[8] In the accounts of the classical and medieval worlds it is just possible to include these deeply buried streams of folk consciousness, belief, and memory into the narrative. But from the sixteenth century onward, the complexity and interaction of events, and the sheer magnitude of change, are such that separate chapters (as in this one and chapter 9) are needed in order to provide the bases of understanding and knowledge for what then ensues.

The need, then, is to concentrate on those forces that most clearly linked land and its vegetation with economic growth and social change in European society during these centuries. Some, like population numbers, are tangible and calculable, but others, like human goals and attitudes, are more difficult to grasp.[9] For the sake of brevity only four are selected here, as they seem to have either generated or facilitated significant changes, and affected underlying structures. These forces can be called conveniently, if not quite accurately, Discovery, Technology, Modernity, and Ascendancy, which go a long way to explain the cultural climate of the sixteenth to early eighteenth centuries; a quartet of themes obviously already appreciated by the opening of the seventeenth century (plate 6.1). They are not separate, independent topics with clear boundaries. For example, a great deal of interplay exists among territorial expansion and control, technology, the organization and conditions of material life, and attitudes of superiority over nature. In

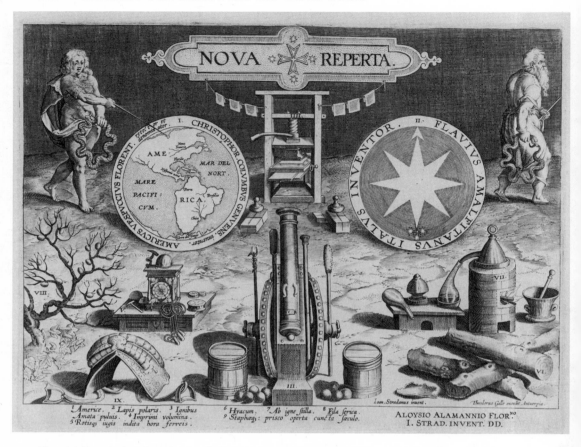

Plate 6.1 Frontispiece from Jan van de Straet's *Nova Reperta* (New discoveries). Antwerp, 1600. (By permission of the Folger Shakespeare Library, Washington, D.C.) This etching is replete with the imagery of Discovery, Technology, Modernity, and Ascendancy. The unadorned young woman on the upper left could well represent Modernity, while the bearded old man who is about to leave the stage might represent the Old order. Modernity points to a map of the newly discovered Americas encircled by the inscription "I. Christophor Columus Genuens. Inventor. Americus Vespuccius Florent. Retector et denominator." The corresponding circle to the right represents a compass and is encircled by the inscription "II. Flavius Amalfitanus Italus Inventor." Between and beneath these are an array of symbolic technical inventions or discoveries: the printing press, for dissemination of information, and the cannon, for military power, stand central. On the left the saddle with stirrups again represents military power, and the clock speaks of mechanical ingenuity and the triumph of science in ordering time and space. The apparatus of alchemy and smelting as symbol of the conquest of the material world are on the right. The logs are labeled *Hyacum* or guaiacum, a tree from the New World commonly thought to be an antidote to the one unwelcome import from the New World—syphilis.

the great ferment of activity of the age, each intertwined and reinforced the other. Together they produced a cultural climate characterized by an ever-upwardly ascending spiral of increased production and consumption, economic change, and biome modification, leading to the intensification and permanent transformation of the land cover and land use of most parts of the globe. As never before, humans could now intervene and alter nature on an unprecedented scale, increase the production of all commodities to unparalleled levels, and move commodities in unheard-of quantities, all to cater for accelerating human needs.

DISCOVERY

The encounter with the Americas in 1492 is often chosen as a convenient date for dividing the Middle Ages from the early modern era, which began with the "Great Age of Discovery," the Renaissance, and the Reformation. But like all dates it is fairly arbitrary, and the history of expansion, ideas, and science show that there was no abrupt change; "[t]he world of Ptolemy did not suddenly became the world of Mercator." Even Columbus's remarkable discovery had its roots deep in the Middle Ages.[10]

Europeans had been on the move for a long time; portents of what was to come were already in place in the fourteenth century. The *Reconquista* of the Iberian peninsula, begun in AD 800 and largely over by 1300, was dramatic evidence of land expansion. The Norse explorations to Iceland (circa AD 900?) and Greenland (AD 982) and almost certainly Newfoundland (AD 1000), while abortive in terms of permanent settlement, were spectacular evidence of what might be achieved through long-distance sea voyages. The exploits of the vigorous and aggressive politico-commercial networks of Genoa and Venice, which reached at least a thousand miles across the Aegean to outposts in the Levant and the Black Sea, where they "connected with all the great trade routes of western Asia," showed what trade could do.[11] The Crusades were also a pointer to European mobility. Most significant of all, however, were the voyages of the ambitious Portuguese prince, Henry the Navigator (1394–1460), who wanted to penetrate beyond the Muslim world of North Africa to the fabled sources of gold in Africa; capture the spice trade from the Venetians; and search for new potential allies in the "perennial Christian struggle with Islam," which the fall of Constantinople in 1453 and the engulfing of the Balkans and blocking of trade routes to the east more than emphasized.[12] By the end of the century the Portuguese had made landings all down the west coast of Africa, and were trading ivory, pepper, and gold from Guinea and the Cameroons. By 1488 Bartholomew Dias had rounded the Cape of Good Hope, and ten years later Vasco da Gama had reached Calicut, a major spice port on the Malabar coast of India, by way of the east coast of Africa. Despite opposition from established Arab traders, cinnamon was soon coming to Europe from Ceylon (Sri Lanka), cloves from the Moluccas, nutmeg and mace from the Banda Islands, and later, porcelain and brocades from China. The Western preoccupation with the Orient had begun and was to open the first global epoch in human history.[13]

None of these voyages would have been possible without the assimilation of Chinese knowledge of cartography and astronomy, and the use of the astrolabe and the compass, including the gyroscopic compass (all via the medium of the Arab world). These had greater utility in the wide oceans of the Atlantic (especially in establishing latitude) than in the narrow seas of the Mediterranean. Additionally, the improvement in shipbuilding and sailing technology during the twelfth century helped. Hinged stern rudders, and the lateen sail that allowed ships to sail much closer to the wind, were combined in the easily handled Portuguese caravel, which outperformed the contemporary square-rigged northern European cogs. Then within twenty years, during the middle of the fifteenth century, the best of both kinds of rigging were combined in the carracks, which were versatile, oceangoing ships with square sails, lateens, and jibs.[14] By 1500 good portolan maps of sailing directions aided navigation. With the development of ship-mounted guns and lightweight field artillery, Europe achieved absolute and relative superiority even where its numbers were small,[15] and it was now well placed to dominate the global seas and their coasts.

The significance of these voyages of exploration was manyfold. First, before the fifteenth century Europe was a peripheral appendage—a mere "peninsula of peninsulas"—of the civilized world, which consisted of the land-based empires of Ming China, Ottoman Middle East and North Africa, Safavid Persia, and Mughal northern India, in which contacts by sea were relatively unimportant (fig. 6.1).[16] The continents were isolated one from another, except for a few overland trading routes that linked Europe with India and Africa for the movement of high-cost goods, such as tea, porcelain, indigo, spices, and pearls. But it was Europe that leaped ahead, breaking out of its land-based territory and turning

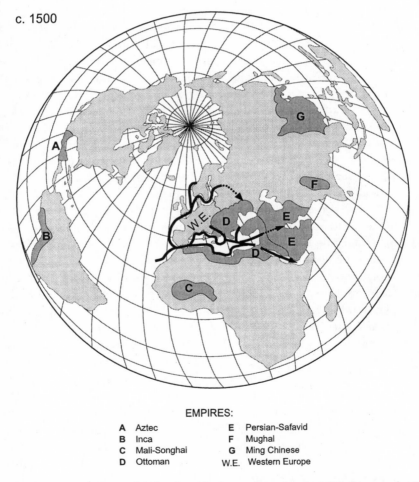

c. 1500

EMPIRES:

A	Aztec	E	Persian-Safavid
B	Inca	F	Mughal
C	Mali-Songhai	G	Ming Chinese
D	Ottoman	W.E.	Western Europe

Figure 6.1 European economy on a global scale, and other empires, circa AD 1500. *Sources:* after Braudel, 1981: 26, and Barraclough, 1978: 154–55.

c. 1775

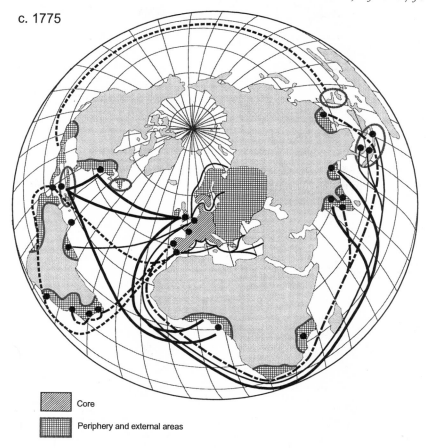

Core

Periphery and external areas

Figure 6.2 European economy on a global scale, and the emergence of a core and periphery, circa AD 1775. *Sources:* after Braudel, 1981: 27, and Barraclough, 1978: 198–99.

the continents inside out by, in effect, reorienting them to face the sea.[17] The exploits of the Portuguese established sea contacts between continents, and started a process of cultural and economic expansion and domination by Europe over much of the globe. From being on the periphery Europe now moved to be at the center, or core, of innovation, trade, and change, to become the most powerful region of the world (fig. 6.2).

Naval supremacy and trade had a powerful internal effect on the nations engaged in it, creating, suggests Peter Padfield, a more open and more entrepreneurial government and society in which merchant values, open consultative government, and greater tolerance prevailed.[18] That archetypal discoverer, entrepreneur, colonizer and adventurer, Sir Walter Ralegh, was convinced of the preeminence of those "ascendant at sea" when he coined the dictum "Hee that commaunds the sea, commaunds the trade, and hee that is Lord of the Trade is Lord of the wealth of the worlde."[19] "Lord of the wealth of the world": an awesome prediction of what was going to happen. The relative peace and harmonious relationship between the inhabitants and their environment in the peripheral parts of the world was shattered as Europe extracted the unused and stored-up potential of land and its vegetation for its own use.

But a word of caution is needed at this point. In emphasizing the undoubted success of European traders on the global seas, it should not be overlooked that when they entered the Asian realm, in particular, they found extensive and well-organized regional trading systems that were handling basic commodities as well as luxuries. How large that trade was we do not know, but the work of Janet Abu-Lughod, Kirti Chaudhuri, and others suggests that it was not inconsiderable. However, despite the recognition of the existence of this trade and the plea "to raise one's eye from the European scene," the fact remains that the global *mass movement* of bulky commodities and raw materials came only with European expansion. There was an increasing separation of areas of production from areas of consumption, and the bulk of the trade ended up in Europe.[20]

TECHNOLOGY

The technological creativity of high medieval Europe is "one of the resonant facts of history," and much of it had been born directly in the forests; the heavy plow, the new field systems, and the horse had led to forest clearing. It marked, suggests White, "the moment of crisis in the history of mankind's relationship to the natural environment: it produced the 'invention of invention' of which the practical effects were soon felt."[21] The new technology of the early modern period (the Renaissance) built on that foundation and was the beginning of a cultural climate of ever-accelerating enquiry, change, and innovation with a renewed interest in experimentation, verification, and accuracy, which led to a pervasive and thorough-going transformation of all nature. Technology was more a facilitator of change than a driving force: without technology change was less effective, and it did create a certain momentum of its own.

It has been said that Europe showed not so much an inventive ingenuity as "a remarkable capacity for assimilation," borrowing ideas and technologies and bringing them to a high pitch of perfection and practical use.[22] In 1620, Francis Bacon observed that the three greatest inventions "which had changed the appearance of the whole world" up to Stuart times—printing, gunpowder, and the compass—had all originated in China; they had been received by Islam from China and then brought to Europe from the Levant during the Crusades.[23] He might have added the astrolabe, chain mail, the crossbow, methods of rigging, papermaking, and possibly clocks (to say nothing of mathematics and trigonometry). Much play is made of this assimilation in order, perhaps to belittle the European achievement, but that is irrelevant; Europe borrowed, used, and conquered, and in the final analysis that was what mattered. Moreover, the prior existence of inventions provided many externalities and advantages, and Europe was no technical laggard, constantly improving, refining, and innovating on what it had assimilated.

Those inventions/discoveries that aided navigation, as well as gunpowder and mills, have been mentioned already, but printing and clocks have not, and they need fuller explanation.

Just as the full-rigged ship opened up the geographical world to Europe, so the printing press and cheap paper opened up the world of knowledge to the European mind. Gutenberg's invention of movable type, first used in his Bible of circa 1468, revolutionized learning and the dissemination of information. It took time to diffuse against the op-position of copyists, but by 1500 it had reached every country except Russia. Widespread and increasing literacy, the prior invention of spectacles (AD 1280), and an openness in societies that contained a large secular section and on the whole did not impose censor-ship led to the growth of printing. By 1600 about 2,000 titles were printed annually; by 1815 it was 20,000. Febvre calculates that 20 million books had been printed *before 1500* alone, an impressive number for a population that was somewhere in the region of 70 million. The retrieval and dissemination of knowledge, precision, continuity of thought, and the revision of ideas through argument were now commonplace through the agency of the written word. The result was incalculable in the story of Western intellectual and technological progress, and indeed in Western domination.[24] To imagine a world with-out books is to imagine a world without ideas; the book was a potent "force for change" that altered society, its outlook, and its technology.[25] Ultimately, of course, after the mid-nineteenth century, paper would be made from wood fiber and not rags, with devastat-ing effects on the world's forests—but that is looking too far ahead.

The scientific and intellectual ferment of the age in Europe is neatly summarized in the number of new books, the number of universities as centers of learning and innovation, and the growth of population (fig. 6.3). These developments intersected at around 1650, when there existed approximately 100 universities, 1 million books, and 100 million

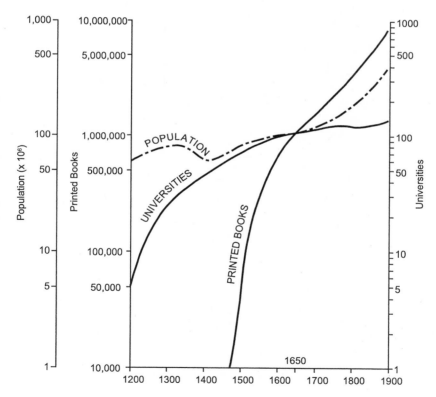

Figure 6.3 The cumulative total of population, universities, and printed books in Europe, AD 1200–1900. *Source:* after Warntz, 1989: 170.

persons. Of course, the triple intersection is contrived because of the arbitrary scaling of the graphs; but "since the three vertical scales all *are* logarithmic, growth rates (or rather rates of change) all *are* comparable." Perhaps 1650 marks the end of one epoch (the Renaissance) and the beginning of another (the modern), when the Aristotelian Scholastic-Cartesian debate peaked and the Newtonian-Cartesian controversy was "in the offing."[26] We will have reason elsewhere to note 1650 as a key marker date in the transition of cultural climates.

One other invention needs special mention. Mechanical clocks appeared in northern Italy by the middle of the fourteenth century and spread widely after that. Clocks radically affected mental and social attitudes. Their manufacture created a corps of skilled craftsmen, their existence aided the synchronization of production and processes in manufacturing generally, and they were a manifestation of "an irrepressible taste for mechanical achievements" that was a hallmark of modern European society.[27] When the spring was invented toward the beginning of the fifteenth century, the miniaturization of domestic clocks and watches was possible. Instead of nature being the clock with dusk and dawn, the day could be divided finely, especially with the development of the minute hand. A new awareness of time arose; the clock was "the prod and key to personal achievement and productivity," and the novel concept of "time thrift" was practiced. People now had

> time at home or on their own person and could order their life and work in a manner once reserved for regulated communities. In this way privatization (personalization) of time was a major stimulus to the individualism that was an ever more salient aspect of Western civilization.[28]

But clocks had a significance beyond the keeping of time, important as that was. The division of time was inseparable from the division of space on the globe, and was also the basic explanation of the solar system. To understand the latter accurately was to eventually undermine the medieval religious cosmological view of the world. Keeping time became an invaluable, if not indispensable, tool of astronomical observation, and with modification the clock became the maritime clinometer, crucial for the calculation of longitude at sea. Delays at sea were shortened, landfalls found, cargoes saved, and the loss of crews through thirst and disease eliminated. More accurate maps could be made. The story of the persistent experimentation between 1714 and 1773 by the lone, mechanical genius, Thomas Harrison, to create frictionless, carefully balanced timepieces that had no pendulum, needed no cleaning, and were not subject to temperature differences or the movement of the sea (they were made of wood) is one of the great stories of patient invention that revolutionized life. It proved beyond doubt that then, as now in the age of satellite "fixes," it is time which determines where you are.[29]

But other than the developments that aided navigation, what has all this to do with the forests and their destruction? In answer one could say, "a lot"; the end result was the development of the physical and mental equipment of the dynamic early modern capitalist world. The ever-accelerating quest for power over nature, the development of labor-saving mechanisms, the creation of new productive skills, and the evidence of dynamism and innovation, which started in about 1000, has continued ever since. By about 1450 European intellectuals regarded technological progress not as "a project" but as "an historic and happy fact." In its gadgetry as well as in its mentality, the later Middle Ages had provided the basis for the subsequent technological structure of the early modern age, which was the harbinger of the "violent changes that came about with the Industrial Revolution." [30] Lynn White has put the significance of these years more succinctly, if bluntly, by saying that the buildup of technological competence, self-confidence, and accelerated change during the Middle Ages enabled Europe after 1500 "to invade the rest of the world, conquering, looting, trading and colonizing." [31] In that process the forest was affected severely.

MODERNITY

Modernity describes those sweeping changes that began in Europe in the sixteenth century and then spread throughout the rest of the world, transcending geographical boundaries and binding disparate peoples, nations, and societies in a "paradoxical unity of disunity" under a global market. [32] Ever since the breakdown of feudalism in the late fourteenth century, Europe had been moving toward a more entrepreneurial, commercial, mercantile, profit-oriented market system—capitalism no less. [33] The economic system and means of production were interacting with each other in an upwardly ascending spiral of consumption and production.

The transition to modernity was not clear-cut. Dates as wide apart as 1510, 1600, 1650, and 1750 have been suggested, as if one could ever pick a specific year. What we are sure of is that compared to anything which had existed in medieval times, a qualitatively different social system, together with systems of production and distribution, had emerged during the late sixteenth century, and was fully in place by 1650. Also, a new sociopolitical system emerged as state structures strengthened, especially in the ability to wage large-scale war. "The organizational tasks attending the wars . . . were so vast by the late seventeenth century that even kings were obliged to attend to them, becoming in the process more like heads of corporations rather than surrogate gods." Indeed, a large part of the dynamic of the state system was "the arms race." [34] It may well be that Europe's polycentric, competitive state system was the key ingredient in the rise of the merchant empires. [35]

Thus, we see the emergence of truly capitalist states involved in a new sort of international exchange economy, first, possibly, in northern Italy during the late sixteenth century, but most certainly in the Low Countries and then Britain during the mid-seventeenth century, and the concomitant rise of Amsterdam and London as international trading, financial, and information-exchanging centers. These regions were highly urbanized, dependent to an unprecedented extent on imported food and raw materials, socially varied but predominantly middle class, and enjoying an unusually high standard of living. [36]

The vigor of the late medieval economy and the rise of urbanism meant that a monetary economy had become pervasive in Europe and was dominant by the late sixteenth century. "Everywhere," said the Dutch historian Herman Van der Wee, "money was on the march." [37] The old economic relationships that were embedded in the connection between environment and society (as in peasant economies) were dissolved as the link between where one lived and what one consumed was broken. Money brought anonymity to the process of economic exchange and allowed profit to be extended through social interactions. Thus, barter as a means of exchange gave way to a monetary economy, initially based on metallic money boosted by the huge shipments of gold and silver bullion from Latin America after 1550. While enormous effort went into establishing, stabilizing, and regularizing metallic money, it in no way hampered the development of credit, which was central to the new market economies and their dependence on both local and long-distance trade. Credit required a financial infrastructure: fairs, bills of exchange, commerce manuals, the check, marine insurance, new methods of accounting—even, possibly, double-entry bookkeeping. All of these were present from the fourteenth century, if not earlier; however, they became increasingly sophisticated and flourished as never before. Anti-usury laws, which particularly affected Catholic southern Europe, were also broken down.[38]

The need to ease the circulation of money and expand consumer credit was crucial to the new level of economic activity. This was especially so in overseas trade, where cargoes took months, if not years, to collect, dispatch, and sell.[39] Usually no actual, physical money changed hands, so trust and honesty were essential in this new system of global interchange. Credit was conducted through the development of bills of exchange, bills obligatory, notes of credit, and a host of other promissory instruments, often at the main international fairs, such as those at Lyons, Frankfurt, or Antwerp. The mobility of money was constantly being improved, both from place to place and temporally into the future.

Developing a legal and institutional framework in which transactions could function was also an important requirement for the successful working of the global interchange system. The refinement of banking, clearing, settlement days, and the fixing of exchange rates were crucial in making credit free and mobile. Institutional landmarks in the organization of money and credit were, for example, the bourses established in Antwerp (1531), London (1571), Seville (1583), and Amsterdam (1611). Epitomizing the new-style public banks were the Banco della Piazza Rialto (1587) and even more successful Banco del Giro (1619) of Venice which were the models for exchange banks elsewhere, such as the Wisselbank, Amsterdam (1609), and banks in Hamburg (1619) Rotterdam (1635), and Stockholm (1656). By 1697 there were 25 major banks in existence, of which the Wisselbank of Amsterdam was preeminent until overtaken by London in the early eighteenth century. The foundation of the Bank of England (1694) was another landmark, as it functioned as a central bank, transferring funds, discounting bills of exchange, issuing "promises to pay on demand," or bank notes, and consolidating the national debt, which all made a tangible contribution to the financing of commercial, industrial, and colonial infrastructure. At the same time, merchant law evolved to protect traders and entrepreneurs from unreasonable claims and nonpayments.

Symptomatic of the new organization needed was the rise of the trading, or joint stock, company, in which people ventured capital in hazardous overseas enterprises in return for monopolies guaranteed by royal charter. Such were the English Muscovy Company (founded in 1555 and incorporated in 1630), the East India Company (1600), the Dutch East India Company (1602), the Dutch West India Company (1621), and later the Hudson Bay Company (1670) and the Royal Africa Company (1672), as well as many minor ones. The companies were the powerful and well-organized spearheads of long-distance trade, and the precursors of colonial land empires. They were capital intensive, spread the risks and concentrated settlement, and combined the various tasks of conquest, settlement, investment, and defense all in one. In the tropical world they imported labor in the form of slaves or indentured laborers. To a greater or lesser degree they were like the Dutch Indian Company, which one observer during the next century described as

> absolute, and invested with a kind of sovereignty and dominion . . . [it] makes peace and war at pleasure, and by its own authority; administers justice to all; . . . settles colonies, builds fortifications, levies troops, maintains numerous armies and garrisons, fits out fleets and coins money." [40]

They were the transnational companies of the age.

In sum, the sixteenth century saw the adoption of efficient and flexible institutions and procedures that constantly lowered the cost of transacting, producing, and transporting goods, and thus produced a continuous growth of productivity. Capital became more mobile, uncertainty was transformed into an actuarial, ascertainable risk, information improved, and traders received better protection. Enterprise and its perpetrators, the entrepreneurs who made the decisions and took the risks, flourished in direct measure as they gained greater and more certain control of their environment, both socioeconomic and physical.[41] Each development encouraged and eased another into being, and modernity was born.

The great companies and lesser traders could only function with ships—and many of them. It is estimated that in 1600 there were between 600,000 and 700,000 tons of merchant shipping, quadrupling to 3.37 million tons by 1786, which translates into nearly as many tons of ship timber. How this tonnage was distributed between countries we do not know for certain, but of the 20,000-odd ships in 1650, three-quarters were said to be owned by the Dutch. As late as 1728 Defoe thought the Dutch were still "the Carryers of the World, the middle Persons in Trade, the Factors and Brokers of Europe," although that was an exaggeration, as Britain had usurped Dutch hegemony by the mid-eighteenth century. Perhaps two-thirds of the Dutch fleet were *fluyts,* or flyboats—light, fast, maneuverable and unarmed cargo ships of about 200 tons that were cheap to build and maximized cargo-carrying capacity. They were constantly being modified in order to increase their speed and crew-to-tonnage ratio, which made them very profitable.[42]

The expansion and improvement of the financial infrastructure and of shipping allowed the free and easy movement of goods in quantity, and facilitated the ascending spiral of consumption and production. For example, the number of European ships outward bound for Asian ports stayed stable at between 50 and 90 per decade until 1590, then rose spectacularly to over 250 per decade by 1620, stabilized, and then rose again dramatically to about 450 per decade after 1660 until the end of the century.[43]

But questions remain: what caused the increased consumption, what goods were moved, and what was the effect on global forests? Undoubtedly the increase in Europe's population from about 82 million in 1500 to about 105 million in 1600 and 140 million in 1750 was a driving force that must have stimulated consumption.[44] But rising numbers were of less significance than the increasing purchasing power of segments of the expanding and sophisticated European population, a power aided by the influx of gold and silver bullion from the New World. After an exhaustive survey of the evidence of this period, Walter Michinton concludes that for the rich of western Europe all aspects of life improved considerably, as indeed they did for the expanding urban commercial and professional classes. The intermediate group of skilled artisans and small farmers was also marginally better off, and the "fairly ordinary man as a consumer was beginning to emerge as a person of importance in the demand picture."[45] The gulf between rich and poor may have widened, but life for the bulk of the population was more stable, safer, and more law-abiding, though in eastern and southern Europe it may not necessarily have been more comfortable.

Whatever the final verdict, the fact remains that during the late sixteenth century and early seventeenth century demand for all goods rose, putting increased pressures on land resources. In particular there was a shift from the medieval preoccupation with a land-based trade in small quantities of high-value luxury goods, such as spices (though pepper was a semi-necessity and associated with the vast increase in meat eating in Europe, particularly England), perfumes, porcelain, dyestuffs, and silk clothes and rugs from Asia and Africa, to a sea-borne mass trade of far bulkier commodities or staples from Asia, the Caribbean, and the Americas. Some came in such bulk that their very names passed into everyday usage: "muslin" for high–quality, lightweight fabric from Mosul; "calico" for thicker cotton fabric from Calicut; and "china" for tableware. These were destined for an increasingly widening segment of affluent people who consumed a disproportionate amount of resources. Immanuel Wallerstein typifies this shift as a move from "preciosities" from the largely unaffected "external area" of contact in Africa and most of Asia, in contrast with the trade in lower-ranking goods from the "periphery" of the Americas and the East Indies, a trade that had led to social change, division of labor, *and* change in land use in those areas.[46]

Many of these "lower-ranking" goods were tropical products, the growing of which led directly to tropical forest clearing. Some, such as tea, coffee, chocolate, and sugar, were not essential, but they certainly varied diet; some, like silks and tobacco, were more purely optional. Later, potatoes and cotton were of more fundamental significance in that they related to basic needs for an easily cultivated, high-yielding food crop and for cheap and hygienic over- and underclothing. These tropical staples could now be added to the traditional trade staples of wheat, wood, wine, and dyes. Fernand Braudel attempted to trace the origin and diffusion of these and other commodities in everyday material life. For example, the stimulants and tonics of tea, coffee, and chocolate were introduced into Britain during the 1650s and the Low Countries a few decades earlier. What is clear is that initially, these goods were regarded in Europe as expensive, exotic products or luxuries (even as aphrodisiacs) that only the wealthy could afford. But from the mid-seventeenth century onward, rising affluence for many, better global transportation, and the consequent cheapening of commodities meant that their consumption filtered down through society, and they became the staples or commonplace necessities of the masses.[47]

The significance of these tropical products went beyond mere titillation of the palate, as they created a legacy of what Marshall Sahlins has called the West's "soft drug" culture. The impact of tea on British life was overwhelming; its acquisition was the basis of many imperialist adventures around the Pacific, and its psychological values and desirability functioned to deliver a "docile and effective working class into the maws of developing capitalism."[48] Sugar was probably even more significant. Geographically its cultivation was "a means of both financing colonial endeavours as well as a motive for the occupation of yet more territory"; socially it fostered habits of consumption, changed dietary habits, and was a source of wealth and power; economically its production on the plantation system altered the distribution of populations globally through slavery and emigration.[49] Said one eighteenth century observer:

> Whether coffee and sugar are really necessary to the happiness of Europe, is more than I can say, but I can affirm—that these two vegetables have brought wretchedness and misery upon America and Africa. The former has been depopulated, that Europeans may have land to plant them in; and the latter is stripped of its inhabitants, for hands to cultivate them.[50]

The link between production and consumption was, of course, foreign trade, which, in a favorite metaphor of the time, was "the great wheel setting the machinery of society in motion." Trade was a true driving force, and the ship was its symbol. It is impossible and probably unnecessary to look at trade in detail. Kristof Glamann has done that in terms of areas and trade flows for the period, particularly the trade of the Baltic, the Mediterranean, and the wider world, and the trade in basic commodities such as grain, cattle, copper, and textiles. It is easy to become ensnared in the tangled thickets of trade flows and tonnages around the world, but suffice it to say that these commodities domi-nated European trading patterns during these years. But there was a shift to the wider world, and import statistics give us a clue to what was happening.[51] By the early seven-teenth century, 20 and 24 percent of all imports into the Netherlands and England, re-spectively, were tropical goods. In England by the middle of the next century the pro-portion had doubled. The total imports revealed in the customs registers of 1752–54 (the only source for which reasonably complete records are available) show that 46 percent and about 17 percent of English and Dutch imports, respectively, were from tropical areas (table 6.1).[52] The table confirms the overall ascendancy of England in the colonial trade by the eighteenth century, especially in the Americas. But who would have thought that so much tea, coffee, sugar, and silk could have been consumed?

Table 6.1 Value of colonial commodities (×1,000 pesos) as percentage of total colonial imports, England and the Netherlands, 1752–54

	England		Netherlands		Total	
	Value	%	Value	%	Value	%
Asia						
Silk and calico	4,853	20.9	1,893	21.4	6,746	21.0
Pepper	404	1.7	677	7.6	1,081	3.4
Tea	1,627	7.0	1,176	13.3	2,803	8.6
Coffee	344	1.5	615	6.9	959	3.0
Other spices	156	0.7	2,116	23.8	2,272	7.1
Miscellaneous	1,475	6.3	965	10.9	2,440	7.6
Total Asia	8,743	37.7	7,442	83.9	16,301	50.7
America						
Sugar	7,135	30.7	920	10.4	8,055	25.1
Tobacco	3,689	15.9	0	0	3,689	11.5
Coffee	?	?	499	5.3	499	1.5
Miscellaneous	3,608	15.6	?	?	3,608	11.2
Total America	14,432	62.3	1,419	16.0	15,851	49.5
Total colonial	23,175		8,861		32,152	0

Source: based on Steensgaard, 1990: 148–50.
Note: ? denotes information that is not available.

When that transition in consumption got under way, the impact on the biomes of the world really began, as sugarcane, tea bushes, coffee trees, and numerous other crops replaced wild tropical vegetation. Peasant proprietors almost imperceptibly shifted from predominantly subsistence agriculture to an agriculture with a considerable cash-crop element in it; and the recent invention of the plantation (first fully developed by the British in the colonization of Ireland), with its subjugated and/or imported servile labor of slaves, "left an indelible mark on huge expanses of the world." In a word, the "look" of the tropical world changed forever:

> The wilderness was won over and converted to the fruitful and profitable production of crops, many of them not even indigenous to the region. From Java to Jamaica, Virginia to Assam, from Fiji to Malaya, Brazil to Congo, tropical regions were utterly transformed by the drive towards managed tropical agriculture.[53]

When the purposeful movement of "settler societies" to the temperate lands of North America, Argentina, and southern Brazil got under way in later years, the impact on the global forests was devastating.

ASCENDANCY

It would be surprising if the age of discovery, which opened up the map of the world, and the Renaissance and Reformation, which opened up the human mind to new concepts, questions, and relationships, did not coalesce to bring about changed ideas of the habitable world and the human ascendancy over nature. Everywhere there was a broadening and deepening of intellectual life, in which printing played no small part. In time, science and technology created a great repository of knowledge of the physical world and the means for making it useful for humans.

A major factor in this new awareness was the European encounter with the Americas, which led to an "intellectual confrontation" with the geography, natural history, and ethnography of a "new" world. Karl Butzer instances the early, but curiously overlooked, contributions of the Spanish—for example, the observational skills of Columbus, the landscape taxonomy of his son, Fernando, the biotic taxonomy of Oviedo, the cultural recording of Sahagún in the *Florentine Codex*, the scientific framework of analysis employed by Acosta—among others, which added up to "a wealth of original and empirical observation and analysis of new environments and unfamiliar peoples, all within a span of three generations."[54] It was not only a bigger world than the medieval mind had encompassed, but a more varied and complex world.

Nature

The Middle Ages had been a period of extensive environmental change, with clearing, draining, and domestication, and later hints of concern about overuse, especially of the forests. But the dominant idea, if any existed (and one must be careful of generalizing about such a varied period), was, in Clarence Glacken's words, that man, "blessed with the faculty of work, assisted God and himself in the improvement of an earthly home"—even if, in the Christian view of things, the earth was merely "a sojourners' way station."[55]

The most compelling reason for studying nature was that it led to a greater understanding of God, and together with the new discoveries, was proof of His existence, of a varied, full, and designed world, and of the truth of Christianity and final causes.

Implicit in this teleology was the physio-theological idea of The Great Chain of Being, whereby humans were seen as a part of a pyramidal hierarchy with God at the apex, followed in descending order by the angels, humans, animals, plants, metals, minerals, and the ground itself. On the face of it this was an essentially holistic, organic, and harmonious arrangement in which man was placed on earth as God's steward to tend and complete the creation, as interpreted by John Ray in his *Wisdom of God Manifest in the Works of Creation* of 1691.[56] Looked at another way, however, the Chain of Being could be interpreted as the reverse of humility to nature and an appreciation of its links, and rather as a recipe for its domination. Increasingly, humans were seen as superior or ascendant to the other elements of creation, which gave them the right to exploit it.[57]

The assumption that the earth had been created for the sake of humans appears to have grown stronger during this era, and it was rarely questioned or reflected upon. There were good precedents: classical writing from Aristotle to Cicero (now revived with the Renaissance) had urged man to use the earth because it existed in order to serve human interests of pleasure and profit, and Christianity reinforced these ideas. The narrative of Genesis (1:28) explained that the earth was a paradise prepared by God for man in which he had dominion over all living things. Admittedly, the Fall had caused God to make life more difficult with odious insects, troublesome weeds, sterile soil, wild animals, and the need for human toil, but even so, superiority over all other works of creation was assured in the divine plan. From about 1500, and well into the eighteenth century, theological writing in England (and it must have been true elsewhere in western Europe) provided a substantial moral underpinning for the ascendancy of humans over all other elements in the natural world.[58]

Nonetheless, no age is uniform in its thought, and the growth of natural science had a curious twofold, even contradictory, effect on these ideas. On the one hand it underpinned religious thought; on the other hand it strengthened and gave new justification to human domination. By the sixteenth century cracks were appearing in the unity of medieval theology. The Ptolemaic/medieval cosmological view of a geocentric universe centered on a stationary, motionless earth around which rotated the sun, planets, and stars, was shattered in 1543 by Copernicus with his simple suggestion that the position of sun and earth should be reversed, and that the earth revolved in its own orbit. In what seems in retrospect to be a dizzying spiral of inquiry, reasoning, and explanation came the work and overlapping careers of Galileo Galilei (1564–1642), Johannes Kepler (1571–1630), and René Descartes (1596–1650). From now on, nature was more likely to be written in the language of mathematics than words, matter was separated from mind, and rationality extolled over religion. Descartes was particularly influential; all nature, except the human mind, was a machine without feeling and therefore could be manipulated without scruple, and all received wisdom should be doubted systematically, as expressed succinctly in his dictum in his *Discourse on Method* (1637), "I think, therefore I am."[59] In place of the medieval unity of the trilogy of God, humans, and nature, Cartesian dualism now separated the mind from tangible, objective earthly matter; and science as a way of thinking grew in importance.[60] Suffice it to say that as the centuries unfolded, the idea grew that nature was of less relevance than before as a teacher and that "technical problems could be solved by patient, systematic experimentation," accompanied by a growing faith in quantitative progress and what John Nef has called "the multiplication of output."[61]

That the accumulation of knowledge, the waning of the human-nature unity, and the replacement of that unity by separation would increase the control of humans over nature seemed self-evident and, indeed, as we have seen, was fully underpinned by theology. But it was Francis Bacon (1561–1626) who, perhaps, first drew out the full implications. For him the most lofty and noble use of the new knowledge was not only to restore to man the dominion over creation that he had partly lost with the Fall, but also to relieve the lot of humankind: "the empire of man over things is founded on the arts and sciences alone, for nature is only to be commanded by obeying her." Like Descartes' belief in technology, Bacon's belief in science was as a means of controlling nature and changing the environment. It was an altruistic enterprise in which the "power and empire of mankind in general over the universe" was enlarged: it was a departure from the stultification of the past of Aristotle and the Scriptures, and brought order out of chaos.[62] Although Bacon was not the only one who expressed the view that the earth was made for humans, he put it particularly well:

> For the whole world works together in the service of man; and there is nothing from which he does not derive use and fruit . . . insomuch that all things seem to be going about man's business and not their own.[63]

From now on, humans viewed their role less as John Ray saw it—as God's humble stewards on earth—and more as Sir Matthew Hale perceived it, as "the Vice-Roy of the great God . . . in this inferior World . . . and reserve to himself the supreme Dominion, and the Tribute of Fidelity, Obedience, and Gratitude, as the greatest recognition or Rent for the same."[64] Instead of nature being the tyrant that subdued humans, humans were fast becoming the tyrant that subdued nature. The transformation of the cultural climate was complete.

Purposive control meant that the world was to be used and its products could be exploited, sold, and traded—in a word, commodified—particularly the tropical world, which was perceived as being a place of such "exuberance" and plenty that Europeans need no longer face scarcities.[65] The rational pursuit of profit, which was the logical end of capitalist enterprise, took Europeans a long way along the road to global domination. Perhaps, ultimately, this shift in attitude toward nature and their penchant to rationalize encounters with new lands and "to develop the resources they brought within their reach" was more important to their success than the technology, the environmental advantages, and the voyages themselves.[66] When that encounter got under way, the world and its forests were changed.

The Trees and the Forest

Of all the forms of plant life that were altered in this new, conscious domination of nature, trees and their assemblage in forests seemed to engender the most emotional comment and action. They were both detested and loved. Keith Thomas, in his brilliant survey of the human relationship to the natural world in England, makes the novel and perspicacious observation that the progression of attitudes toward trees has paralleled that towards animals, which

> had been divided into the wild, to be tamed or eliminated, the domestic, to be exploited for useful purposes, and the pet, to be cherished for emotional satisfaction. The early modern period has duly seen the elimination of many wild animals, the increased exploitation of domestic ones, and a rise in interest in the third category, the pet, maintained for non-utilitarian reasons.[67]

It is possible that the development of these attitudes was more pronounced in the lives of the well-to-do of seventeenth- to nineteenth-century England than in other countries of the European continent; that is yet to be tested. But there is evidence that in time these attitudes permeated through the population at large, and that they were most certainly transported with that population wherever it migrated, especially in the vast forests of North America.

From the time of the first farmers, almost anywhere in the world, forests had been seen as wild and hostile, and human progress had seemed to be viewed in some proportion to the amount of woodland cleared, or at least used. The Middle Ages in Europe had seen one of the greatest onslaughts on the forest ever witnessed, and although there was a hiatus in clearing during the *Wüstungen,* the attack was taken up with renewed vigor during the sixteenth century. By then religion and aesthetics found forests not only forbidding but repugnant and repulsive, and a mythology or set of cultural mores had developed in which the acts of felling, firing, grazing, and cultivating turned them into civilized abodes. Forests were dark and horrible places where there were very real dangers from wild animals, particularly bears and wolves, and, in North America, snakes and ticks. The word *wilderness* etymologically was the "place of wild beasts," and it was almost synonymous with *forest.* In addition, the forests were places of terrifying eeriness, awe, and horror, where the imagination played tricks and the limbs of trees looked like the limbs of people, especially if animated by the wind. In that chaos, the hapless peasant was first *be-wildered* and eventually succumbed to license and sin.

The accumulation of folklore and tradition attests to these deeply held feelings. For the Greeks there were the genial dryads, but there were also the malevolent satyrs and centaurs; Pan was the Lord of the Woods, and his approach produced *panic* in unwary travelers. In northern and central Europe popular folk culture abounded with trolls, sprites, dwarfs, ogres, witches, werewolves, child-eating monsters, and forest demons of all descriptions. The fears embodied in these creatures have been handed down to us in the terrifying "fairy tales" of, for example, Hansel and Gretel, Red Riding Hood, Sleeping Beauty, Tom Thumb, The Three Pigs, and even Snow White, all set in the somber, dark environment of the forest. Early Christianity, as we have seen, extolled the virtue of clearing the forest on two counts: the forest was associated with pagan gods and also equated with the devil, and was therefore the abode of natural sin. But there were contradictions. Wild country was also a place to draw nearer to God, and it became a sanctuary against evil. Many a medieval monk had been motivated to make a clearing in the wicked waste as a means of purifying his faith.[68] Yet if the forest was to be feared, its products were to be valued; piety and economic progress went hand in hand with the creation of "new" land that was akin to Paradise, an Eden, or, in North America, a New Canaan or New Jerusalem.[69]

In addition to being places of original evil and wild animals, forests were also the abode of savagery and dangerous outlaws. *Wood* may have a common root with *wild* and the word *savage* is derived from *sylva*—"a wood." The forest was dark, melancholy, and uninhabited, fit only for beasts, and therefore by implication those who lived in the forests were uncouth and barbarous. The Irish, said one Elizabethan, remained "wood-born savages, dunghill gnats," while John Locke averred that experience showed that inhabitants of cities were "civil and rational," while those from "woods and forests" were "irrational, untaught."[70] In Europe, the forests were regarded, with some justification, as the abode of outlaws, brigands, highwaymen, smugglers, poachers, and the more benign, but no less feared, blackened charcoal burners and squatters. All this is to say nothing of wolves. Because of the many postmedieval disputes over rights of forest use, the forests were also areas of resentment, social conflict, and violence. Selwood Forest in England was felled largely to eliminate a refuge for criminals, and in France many a forest, "hitherto a den of robbers," was felled alongside major highways in order to give a safe passage to travelers. In the twelfth century the Capetians had established twelve *villeneuve* and set up citadels in three established settlements along the road from Paris to Orléans— "the axis of their monarchy"—that ran through the vast Forest of Orléans, and there are many other examples.[71]

Nowhere was the notion of the relationship between forests and savagery more fully developed than in the forest settlements of seventeenth-century North America. The Plymouth colony was founded, said Governor Winthrop, in a "hideous & desolate wilderness," "where are nothing but wild beasts and beastlike men." Terror of the forest was reinforced by the way nature seemed to contrive to help the Indians in their attacks on the colonists, so that, said Increase Mather, "our Men when in that hideous place, if they did but see a Bush stir would fire presently, whereby 'tis verily feared that they sometimes unhappily shoot *English Men* instead of *Indians*." The forest was a dark and sinister symbol of man's evil where the Indians "were transformed into beasts,"[72] and where even a civilized man could revert to savagery because he was beyond the reach of redemption. The fact that the Indian inhabited the forest and did not appear to clear it (which was not true) was proof of that. His "vegetative nature," said Arnold Guyot, kept him at the "lowest grade on the scale of civilization."[73]

Thus, social order and the Christian concept of morality seemed to stop on the edge of the cleared land; and in new territories at least, without the ameliorating regulations of organized communities, social cohesion, and the ties of positive Christianity, frontier man could become less civilized and degenerate into license and even savagery. J. Hector St. John de Crèvecoeur in his celebrated essay "What is an American?" was quite explicit. In the "great woods, near the last inhabited districts" inland, dwelt the "off-casts" of society, where men "appear to be no better than carnivorous animals of a superior rank. . . . There remote from the power of example, and check of shame, many families exhibit the most hideous parts of our society." In time that "hitherto barbarous country" would be "purged" by the next wave of decent settlers and changed into a "fine, fertile, and well regulated district."[74]

It is evident in this amalgam of belief, superstition, and prejudice that the virtues of development, progress, and individual freedom were never far beneath the surface, as they were the logical outcome of the fight for survival. More and more the tamed landscape became the ideal. In England this view went so far that "moralists who condemned enclosures made an exception for taking in and grubbing up trees," and even objected to trees in hedgerows, as they might hinder the ripening of crops. Tree clearing became something of a crusade: in 1683 John Houghton advocated the destruction of all forests within 12 mi of a navigable river or the coast in order that the land could be converted to more productive uses, and in 1629 one person living near Durham, said to have "brought to the grounde . . . above 30,000 oakes in his life tyme," was still going strong, and the same was happening here and there all over Europe.[75]

In North America the experience came about a century later, but with much more intensity. The difficulties of the forested wilderness reinforced the Puritan New Englanders' belief that they were the Chosen of God and that the New Jerusalem would lie in America. Consequently, "subduing the wilderness quickly became an exalted calling" that tested and strengthened their faith. Increasingly, to fell the forest was almost to enter the kingdom of heaven on earth, as the making of new land seemed to demonstrate the direct causal relationship between it and righteous Puritan faith, and more broadly, moral effort, sobriety, frugality, industry, and material reward. Early American nature seemed full of implications for ethical and material betterment. By the early eighteenth century Benjamin Franklin identified the frontier of cultivation with opportunity and tended, said Charles Sandford, "to measure moral and spiritual progress by progress in converting the wilderness into a paradise of material plenty."[76] Half playfully, Franklin even attributed a cosmic influence to the clearing of the forest: "by *clearing America* of Woods" Americans were "*Scouring* our Planet . . . and so making this Side of our Globe reflect a brighter Light to the Eyes of the Inhabitants of *Mars or Venus*." But on the more mundane and day-to-day level the "great primary aim" of most pioneer farmers was, said William Cooper, "to cause the wilderness to bloom and fructify" so that the landscape would be converted from forest to

> fair cities, substantial villages, extensive fields, an immense country filled with decent houses, good roads, orchards, meadows, and bridges, where a hundred years ago all was wild, woody and uncultivated![77]

Thus, it is no surprise that when nearly every religious, aesthetic, practical, and even moral circumstance conspired toward the taming or elimination of the forest, great changes occurred in its composition and extent. Clearing was both a sacred and a secular process, a combination of motives that was particularly apparent in medieval Europe and early colonial North America.

The historian of medieval society and technology, Lynn White, has condemned Western Christianity as being the "most anthropocentric religion that the world has seen," and the font of the attitudes that have led to the environmental degradation of the present day. But it would be absurd to infer from all that has been said about forest clearing that western Europeans were uniquely inclined to transform, manipulate, and so abuse the environment. Certainly they were no laggards, but the history of deforestation and subsequent soil erosion by, for example, the Greeks and Romans (chapter 4), native Indian societies in Central and North America (chapter 3), and Chinese society, despite all its avowed working *with* nature (chapters 5 and 8), all without the assistance of Christianity, should effectively dispose of that notion.[78] The ambivalent messages of Christianity, with its antithetical emphases on stewardship and domination, are also ignored in that argument. The important point is that at the start of our period, exploitation, not stewardship, was the dominant theme, though in time a more reserved attitude toward the modification of nature by humans emerged as Europeans and their overseas offspring moved into the second and third stages of their relationship with trees, and began to preserve the useful and cherish the beautiful.

In summary, the Europe of the mid-eighteenth century and its place in, and impact on, the world was very different from the Europe of 1500. The little civilization of land-based states had spread across the world and was going to eventually dominate it. European rule was established in North America, Latin America, the Indian mainland, and portions of Southeast Asia and Africa; and the population of European communities overseas, particularly North America, now reached several million. Europe's ships traversed every ocean and entered every harbor, and its control over world trade was disproportionately great.

Hegemony is a word that is much in vogue to describe the dominance of Europe in world affairs and trade, and it is usually thought of as unpleasant, undesirable, and reprehensible. Much writing by "world systems" economic historians has focused on the malfunctions and inequalities of that past world, so much so that it has become conventional wisdom.[79] But two points need to be made.

First, it is too easy to overemphasize the idea of the core sucking the lifeblood out of the periphery. Europe's trade, even as late as 1800, may only have been 4 percent overseas, although it was greater for Britain and Holland; and for Britain, the preeminent maritime power, profits from commerce from the periphery probably financed less than 15 percent of gross investment made between 1750 and 1850. Undoubtedly Europe gained from the profits made abroad and found markets for its goods and manufactures, and its major sea-port cities flourished on the trade. But the periphery does not explain the dynamic economic growth of the core which must be attributed to other internal causes.[80] The periphery remained peripheral, although its forest and vegetation generally were altered radically.

Second, as Eric Jones argues cogently, those writers who project their distaste of the world of today on the world of the past miss the point that enormous progress had been made in the Continent since the Middle Ages—often, to be sure, at a great cost and misery, and often falling short of the ideal, "[b]ut the pot was half-full as well as half-empty and there were stars to be seen as well as mud." [81] There may have been setbacks, but there were rebirths, leading to, as Bacon said, "the effecting of all things possible." The improvement in agricultural, and to a lesser extent in industrial, productivity was impressive; fundamental services and security were vastly improved; and there was a general belief that order was better than chaos, prosperity was better than poverty, knowledge was better than ignorance, and creation better than destruction, all of which are pretty enviable in any place, at any time. Whatever our judgement, the history of the world during the last five centuries has of necessity been a history in very large measure of the things that Europeans (and North Americans) did to themselves and to others, and how non-Europeans reacted to them and were frequently adversely affected. That, after all, is what the rest of the world thinks is wrong and criticizes.

To a certain extent, such evaluations are beyond this enquiry into global deforestation in the past and present, except to reinforce the idea yet again that any form of land transformation must be placed in its precise social, economic, and intellectual context. Deforestation is not solely a matter of hectares cleared; it cannot be divorced from the society that begets it.

Chapter 7

Clearing in Europe, 1500–1750

No wood, no kingdome.
—Arthur Standish, *The Commons Complaint* (1611)

Trees had ceased to be a symbol of barbarism or a mere economic commodity. They had become an indispensable part of the scenery of upper-class life.
—Keith Thomas, *Man and the Natural World* (1983)

The outreach of Europe across the globe after 1500 and its eventual impact on the forests of the world did not mean that the forests of the Continent remained untouched. Everywhere people were chopping, lopping, burning, and otherwise altering the composition and extent of the forest, as well as establishing and codifying rights pertaining to its use.[1] But it is difficult to generalize about these alterations if only because the forest varied with the physical and climatic gradation of the Continent from west to east and from north to south, as well as with the human variability of economic development from the core in the northwest to the more peripheral areas elsewhere.

Before the sixteenth century, much of Europe had been covered with broad-leaved deciduous forest as far east as the plains of Germany and Poland. Beech and oak predominated, chestnut and elm were common, and ash, willow, and alder covered low and damp ground. Coniferous trees were largely confined to Alpine and other upland areas, Scandinavia, and the Baltic fringes of the northern European plain, as in Prussia and Pomerania. But the climate was changing, and the forest changed too. After the increased storminess and rain of the late Middle Ages that resulted in crop failures and famines, and even the abandonment of settlement in Greenland in 1410,[2] Europe entered its "Little Ice Age." The ice pack, glaciers, and snow spread more widely and lasted longer, and rivers froze more frequently and for longer periods, with a consequent decrease in flow and lowering of groundwater. The growing season diminished, causing a general retreat from upland areas as far apart as Norway, Scotland, and the Alps.[3] Even southern France was affected: the olives and vines of Provence suffered extensive ruination, and Languedoc's position as a grain exporting region was seriously compromised. Famine and vagrancy ensued.[4] Insolation decreased by possibly as much as one-tenth, and the deciduous trees could not cope with the colder, drier conditions and lowered water table. Their place was taken by conifers, which had spread into upland Germany and the Rhine plains by the early sixteenth century.

How much forest remained depended on where one was. Its abundance varied with the physical factors of climate and topography, and the intensity of economic activity and agriculture. It seems likely that about 7.7 percent, or perhaps a little more, of England and Wales was forest covered at the end of the seventeenth century, Scotland even less, while Ireland was still 12 percent covered in 1600.[5] Across the Channel, the Netherlands had next to none and 31 departments in northern France might have been 16.3-percent covered (Sebastian Vauban thought a typical square league in France was 18.06 percent forest covered in about 1700), with the proportion increasing the further east one went until it was over 40 percent in Prussia even in the late eighteenth century.[6] One cannot be more precise than that. Nonetheless, these estimates are important, as it seems that once the proportion of forest falls below about one-fifth of the land in any country, alarm, both real and perceived, seems to set in that clearing has gone too far. It happened in Europe in various places between the sixteenth and eighteenth centuries, and in North America in the later nineteenth century.[7]

A TIMBER CRISIS?

After the *Wüstungen* (village desertion) and retreat of cultivation during the late fourteenth and early fifteenth centuries, the attack on the European forests was renewed with vigor, largely as a response to the expanding population—from approximately 82 million in 1500 to 105 million in 1600, and then to 115 million a hundred years later.[8] The demand for land for cultivation, and wood and wood-derived products in every branch of industry, transportation, and day-to-day life, was immense. The idea of a "timber scarcity" gained ground throughout the seventeenth and early eighteenth centuries, though in many ways the scarcity was more apparent than real. More and more of the forest was being claimed and reserved for hunting and game by seigniorial lords, royalty, and the nobility, thus reducing the amount available for general use, particularly in the more feudal societies of Germany and France. There was also much exaggeration and alarm at the extent and perceived immediacy of timber shortages put out by special-interest groups.

Generally speaking, shortages appeared in the economic core, first in England and the Netherlands during the later 1500s, but the scarcity was probably more local and limited than widespread. It was certainly intense around centers of industry and large urban areas which were growing as a result of trade and commerce, such as London, Paris, Barcelona, Amsterdam, Antwerp, Milan, Venice, Naples, and Messina. By and large, there was no crisis in central and eastern Europe, where the forest was still abundant. Local demands were not as intense as in western Europe, except, perhaps, alongside the watercourses leading to the Baltic, where felling for ships' timbers, potash, and pitch served the burgeoning economy of the core.[9] Mediterranean Europe had always had less timber, and severe inroads had been made during the fifteenth and sixteenth centuries by the Venetian and Spanish shipbuilders. The forests of the Apennines, Calabria, Sicily, Monte Gargano, southern Spain, and the Dalmatian coast of the Adriatic were depleted of large timber, and only the highest and most inaccessible mountainous areas had substantial resources left.[10]

Table 7.1 Index of general prices, firewood prices, and the population of London, 1451–1702

Date	General Prices	Firewood Prices	Population London
1451–1500	100	100	40,000–50,000
1531–40	105	94	60,000 (1534)
1551–60	132	163	
1583–92	198	277	
1603–12	251	366	224,275 (1605)
1613–22	257	457	
1623–32	282	677	
1633–42	291	780	339,824 (1634)
1643–52	331	490	
1653–62	308	662	460,000 (1661)
1663–72	324	577	
1673–82	348	679	
1683–92	319	683	
1693–1702	339	683	530,000 (1698)

Source: Wiebe, 1895: 375.

Much of the evidence of an impending timber crisis and its solutions comes from the British Isles, one of the least wooded parts of Europe and the scene of some of the earliest depredations due to industrialization and urbanization. Rome at its peak never came anywhere near the timber crisis of England in the later sixteenth century, though northern China during the twelfth century was a serious contestant. For the near-hundred years of the reigns of Elizabeth I and James I (1558–1649), dozens of government commissions investigated the purported devastation of the woodlands, resulting in many legislative acts prohibiting or restricting cutting. Even in remote and reasonably well-wooded Pembrokeshire in southwest Wales, a local topographer wrote in 1603 that "this Countrie groneth with the generalle complainte of other countries of the decreasinge of wood." [11] The comment in 1600 that the national forests had been "reduced to such a sicknesse and wasting consumption, as all the physick in England cannot cure," [12] described a common perception of the situation. Two other pieces of evidence have been cited to establish the shortage: the rising importation of timber from Norway and the Baltic for general construction and even for pit props in the mines, and the rise in the price of firewood in London. [13] From a base level of 100 in 1451–1500, the price index for firewood climbed roughly in line with the general index for all goods until the decade 1583–92, when it diverged markedly to ultimately reach 780 in 1633–42, more than double the general trend of the rise in prices of all goods (table 7.1). During this time the population of London grew from between 40,000–50,000 to about 340,000. John Nef saw 1588–1649 as a period of "acute shortage . . . which . . . may be described as a national crisis," a point of view also subscribed to by Archibald and Nan Clow. [14]

However, more recent, detailed work by Michael Flinn and George Hammersley suggests that while the crisis may have been acute locally, it was not national in extent. [15] The propaganda about scarcity put out by special-interest groups was misleading and exaggerated, and the sweeping exemptions that vitiated the provisions of the many acts made them "hollow" legislation. Second, the rise of the price in wood in London, even if correct, was subject to the distinctive demands around a uniquely growing and industrializing city, and did not necessarily reflect the conditions in rural areas. In addition, as this was a period of general inflation, the fuelwood inflation cannot be isolated from the general upward drift in prices and may even have been an element in those rising prices, at least until the end of the seventeenth century.[16]

Similar revisionist arguments have been put forward about the perceived shortages in France and Germany. In France the forests had undoubtedly diminished. At the end of the seventeenth century William Brown, an Edinburgh colliery merchant traveling in search of markets for Scottish coal, reported that Flanders, Brabant, and Artois—the agricultural north of France—was "destitute of wood," and by 1701 it was said that all riverside forests in the lower Loire valley that could easily be transported had been removed. The causes of decrease were manifold and clear. An underpaid bureaucracy of foresters accepted bribes to cut and sell wood illegally; Louis XV wanted quick revenues and alienated 800,000 acres of royal forests; a growing population needed more grain and therefore cleared agricultural land; the peasants claimed their rights to use the forest to a degree greater than good silviculture could withstand; and mining and industry stripped some areas. For example, there were complaints about "déboisement" around Nevers that led to the demolition of all forges within 4–5 mi of that town.

Nonetheless, it seems that the forests provided sufficient wood for the majority of local needs well into the eighteenth century. The price of firewood in urban areas was either about the same or less than inflation, so that the spectacular climb that occurred in England after about 1600 never happened in France[17] (fig. 7.1). David Young contends that of the four major groups of users, the royal government via the navy suffered the greatest deficiency, and the peasantry experienced some hardship but only locally as in, say, Brittany, but the urban dwellers and industrialists were barely affected at all. Marcel Rouff's enquiry in 1701 into the use of coal as a substitute fuel, and general treatises on the state of the forests like those of the Contrôleur Général des Finances in 1701 and comte de Buffon in 1739 suggest concern, but a general shortage was a long way off. The minute use of the abundant supplies of coal in the country compared with Britain— 450,000 tons in 1789 compared with 15.2 million tons in the United Kingdom in 1800— is a clear indicator of this.[18]

Similarly, Joachim Radkau rejects Werner Sombart's thesis of a major timber scarcity (Holznot) in German lands. Certainly there was a scarcity of charcoal and pit props at copper and silver mines in Bavaria in 1463 and Bohemia in 1550, and the number of furnaces in the Siegerland had to be halved between 1563 and 1616 due to high wood prices;[19] but the timber debate had more to do with protecting state-controlled resources (and the jobs of foresters) than with protecting the forests per se. The shift from timber to coal did not come until the middle of nineteenth century, and then it was a response to a need for a more efficient fuel for steam engines, not a lack of fuelwood.[20] Nonetheless, there was a growing awareness that supplies were getting scarcer and prices rising, indicated by enquiries such as that of Philip Bünting in 1693.[21]

But having cast doubt on the generality of a crisis, shortages were becoming real enough in specific places and for specific sorts of wood. The evidence of that scarcity revolves around four activities that destroyed the forest: clearing for agriculture and for fuelwood supplies, which were local and domestic; shipbuilding, which was basically foreign and strategic; and charcoal supplies for iron making and industry in general, which

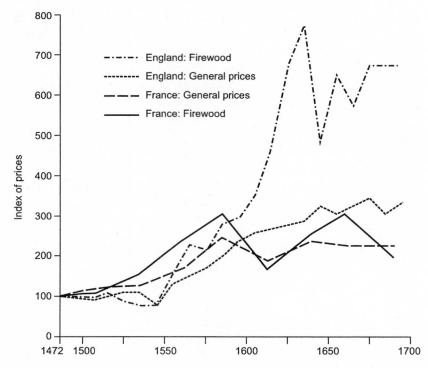

Figure 7.1 Indices of firewood and general price rises in England and France, 1451–1702. *Source:* based on Wiebe, 1895: 375, 378.

were a bit of both. But the perception of, and emphasis on, each of these activities varied, largely because of the nature of the particular evidence.

Agricultural clearing elicited little comment and even less record. It was a part of the day-to-day task of making and maintaining a farm (and getting fuel), which was scheduled for the slacker parts of the agricultural calendar, usually winter. Clearing had become a part of the natural agricultural round of preparing, plowing, sowing, and harvesting and was now depicted as one of the typical monthly tasks in Books of Hours. It did not warrant special record unless it caused an infringement of someone else's property or rights, in which case it was challenged and brought before some form of arbitration or court. Agricultural clearing was individual, piecemeal, and, above all, approved of. It was imbued with virtue as the correct and time-honored thing to do in order to either perfect God's creation or contribute to the domination of nature. Hence it was "natural."

On the other hand, clearing to make industrial charcoal and build ships was viewed differently. First, these activities represented outside interests that paid little regard to local rights and arrangements, and therefore were often resented and opposed. Second, they were regarded as new, alien, "unnatural" intrusions into the forests. Charcoal burners, who formed a new set of forest dwellers, were particularly feared because of their peripatetic habits, blackened faces, and the general air of lawlessness that seemed attached to them.[22] In sum, the popular perception was that the presence of woodland was far more agreeable than that of industry: industry used the woodland and led to its decline; therefore, industry must have destroyed the woodland.[23] Despite these sentiments and misgivings, however, these activities had to be tolerated or endured because the state dictated that they were of national and strategic importance. Without ships and armaments a country was in an inferior position in the new competitive arena that was emerging in the Europe of territorially aggressive, mercantilist nation-states, which jockeyed with one another for local, and, increasingly, global supremacy. Arthur Standish put it very pithily in 1611 when he said; "No wood, no Kingdome." [24]

Consequently, agricultural clearing and wood gathering for domestic fuel were ignored in the historical record, while iron furnaces and ships loom disproportionately large as destroyers of the forest. Glass, brick, and saltmaking and other industries were also criticized, though to a lesser extent. Unlike agricultural clearing, the record was official and published, and therefore accessible and prominent. But it seems likely that charcoal making and shipbuilding were not major elements of the bigger picture.

AGRICULTURAL CLEARING

The addition of about 60 million people between the *Wüstungen* and the end of the devastating religious wars of the seventeenth century (circa 1500–1750) undoubtedly made agricultural expansion the single greatest factor in the decrease of woodland and forest.[25] The lands of the *Wüstungen* were reoccupied, and meadows and vineyards were replaced by cropland. Everywhere, cultivation nibbled away at the edge of the forests, which in western Europe at least were now reduced to relatively isolated patches that could be attacked from all sides. Rising grain prices reflected the competition for land, which was augmented by an overall increase in the number of horses and stock and their need for fodder. The pressure did not relax until the latter half of the seventeenth century, when prices fell, some cropland passed out of cultivation, and much land moved into grass as pastoralism and animal husbandry expanded.[26]

The historical record is remarkably silent about these events, but the unique chronicle of the Zimmer family of Swabia during the early sixteenth century provides a vivid insight into what was happening, and must stand as an example of a wider experience. After commenting on the rapidly growing population in the district, the writer continued:

> [S]o they started to plough the fields and stock the meadows once more, and the place where a village had stood before began to look like a village again.

Even inferior land was being cultivated:

> Never in the memory of man has the land been so much opened up. No corner, even in the densest forests or highest hills, but is ploughed and inhabited.[27]

The patient, backbreaking drudgery of clearing a few more acres every year was still an important element in widening the margin of subsistence, creating greater income, and conferring independence on millions of small-scale farmers and their families. It represented the application of a tried-and-true method and technology, although there was very little mention of it as a deforestation activity compared with shipbuilding and iron making.

One of the clearest statements about the impact of agriculture on the forests came somewhat surprisingly from England, which is usually associated more with iron making and shipbuilding during this period. Its population had almost doubled between 1550 and 1700 to reach an overall density of about 7 persons per acre, exceeded perhaps only by Holland and China at this time. Its people were still predominantly engaged in agriculture and dependent on homegrown grain. In 1662 in *Sylva,* his celebrated enquiry into the shortage of timber and the extent of forest of England, John Evelyn was convinced that industry was of less importance in the demise of woodland than agriculture:

> [I]t has not been the late increase of shipping alone, the multiplication of glass-works, iron-furnaces, and the like from whence this impolitic diminution of our timber had proceeded; but from the disproportionate spreading of tillage, caused through that prodigious havoc made by such, as lately professing themselves against root and branch . . . were tempted not only to fell and cut down, but utterly to extirpate, demolish and raze, as it were, all those goodly woods and forests, which our more prudent ancestors left standing for the ornament and service of their country.

To correct this devastation by letting nature take its course "would cost (besides the enclosure) some entire ages repose of the plough."[28]

Probably few of Evelyn's contemporaries agreed with him, but he was only echoing the assessments of other writers and travelers such as Harrison, Norden, Camden, and Cholmeley, who were either ignored or conveniently forgotten. For example, in 1553 William Cholmeley described how "the unsatiable desyre of pasture for sheep and cattel" had resulted in the clearing of untold woodlands during the preceding thirty years.[29] With a few exceptions, as in the detailed study of Irish woodlands by Eileen McCracken, the same amnesia about agricultural clearing applies even now.[30]

Elsewhere in Europe, evidence of agricultural clearing is patchy. France had a considerable amount of forest left, firmly held by the unbreakable triad of crown, nobility, and church. Michel Devèze's reconstruction of the forests in the northern part of the country during the reign of François I at the beginning of the sixteenth century shows just how extensive they still were, accounting for nearly one-third of the land (fig. 7.2). The royal forests dominated everywhere, the nobility had extensive holdings in the western Loire valley and between the Upper Loire and Yonne, and the ecclesiastical estates were almost absent in the west but numerous in the land between the Seine and Yonne.[31]

Irrespective of ownership, it is clear that the forests were under pressure from the burgeoning peasant population, which was either denied access or allowed to use (but not clear) one-third of their total extent (the *tièrcement*). As in Germany, abandoned lands were recolonized during the fifteenth and sixteenth centuries—"we have ploughed up land that has lain waste as long as any man can remember," wrote a proprietor in the parish of d'Auzon (Yonne)[32]—but there were limits. The forest edicts issued by François I (1516, 1518, 1519) and the measures taken by the regional parliaments of Paris and Rouen to stop peasant incursions from extending beyond their current rights in the forests testify to that. Consequently, complaints of timber shortages were sporadic but frequent; for example, alarms were raised in the Franche-Comté region as early as 1588 and 1606 about the dearth of domestic supplies; wine merchants in Bordeaux complained that they did not have enough wood to make casks; and peasants blamed forges and foundries for the lack of fuelwood for baking their bread—a single forge using, it was claimed, as much wood as the whole town of Chalon-sur-Marne. The eastern borders of France were little better; the devastation and turmoil of the Thirty Years' War and the Frondist revolts of 1648–53 had left their mark. The Frondist agitation was initially

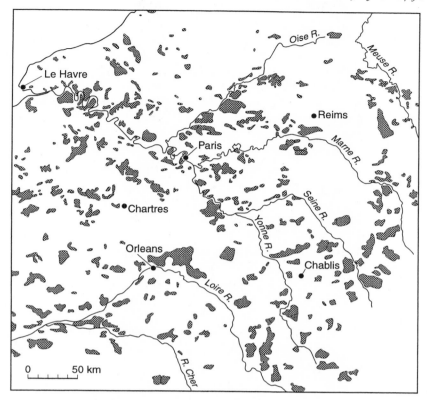

Figure 7.2 The distribution of forest estates in northern France, circa 1540. *Source:* Devèze, 1960.

a protest against excessive taxation but then became a power struggle between the nobility and the king. This led to much forest destruction, as peasants went on the rampage and took the wood they wanted, deforesting many hundreds of thousands of hectares. By the time of Cassini's reasonably accurate maps of the mid-eighteenth century, many of the forests depicted in figure 7.2 had been significantly reduced in size.[33]

Like France, the expanding peasantry of Germany chafed under the feudal oppression of the nobles and formed protest movements (especially in the Alpine district) over their loss of hunting, grazing, and fuel rights, and the inroads made into the forest by industrial uses. These grievances contributed to, and culminated in, the Peasants Revolt of 1524–26, usually thought of as purely a sociopolitical movement. Because forests were so much a part of the peasants' everyday life, their list of demands—The Twelve Articles—called for the restitution of grazing and hunting rights, condemned the emparkment of forests by the nobles, demanded that all forest not bought fairly by territorial nobles revert to the community, and evoked the common man's "divine right" to the products of the forest, among other stipulations.[34] Emboldened by the fervor of Lutheranism, the protest erupted into revolt. It was eventually suppressed, and even more forest was confiscated and removed from common use. More serious for forest use was the intense religious turmoil of the Thirty Years' War (1618–48), fought mainly in Germany and spilling over into adjacent countries, which caused widespread domestic and civil havoc, and a veritable holocaust of the population. This had two quite contrary results. Where population was decreased (by one half in places), forests reestablished themselves over much marginal and abandoned land. In other areas, however, both the act of warfare and the ensuing lawlessness resulted in much deforestation. For example, the Swedes, who needed ready money to continue fighting, cut down large areas of forest on the light soils of Pomerania which degenerated into sand dunes.[35] But generally, it is thought that the forests expanded, and although the population downswing was rather like the *Wüstungen,* it was not so severe.

All in all, the forests were more extensive and the destructive exploitation had been less than in the more-maritime west. By the middle of the seventeenth century, metallurgical and industrial uses of wood were rising again, although shortages did not appear. Some attempts were made to replace logged-over forests with quick-growing conifers around Nuremburg, and experiments were carried out around Memmingen to determine better felling methods. But the impression is that wood was abundant: large exports of hardwood timber still went to England and Holland during the eighteenth century.[36]

Rapid economic growth in the core of western Europe had a remarkable effect on the forests and grain lands of other parts of the Continent. Like the Mediterranean lands of Sicily, Andalusia, and Languedoc, the southern shores of the Baltic were what Fernand Braudel called Europe's "internal Americas,"[37] which awaited economic colonization and integration into the buoyant economy of the core. Rising demand for new grain supplies pushed up prices, so that in Poland and adjacent areas the landowning nobility responded to the opportunity for profits by subjugating the peasants to a revived manorial agricultural system of large-scale cultivation during the summer, and then mobilizing them to cut and haul timber during the winter. Between 1497 and 1660 over 200,000 ships entered and exited the Baltic Sound, and besides the timber and naval stores, the cereals carried from the Baltic averaged 60,000 tonnes/yr, with 60 percent going to the Low Countries, and later, much going to England. Between 1661 and 1787 some 560,000 ships entered and exited the Sound, and an average of 95,296 tonnes of cereals were moved per annum, with a marked falloff occurring only after the mid-eighteenth century.[38] Grain exports of this magnitude translate into between 500,000 to 700,000 ha of grain lands extra to local needs. Thus, the forests alongside the river frontages and in the hinterlands of the Oder, Vistula, and Nieman rivers and their tributaries were cleared for grain growing and acted as a giant food reserve for western Europe. In Prussia, on the edge of the new area of exploitation, clearing was confined solely to the river edges, and inland forests remained largely untouched until the late eighteenth century.[39]

In Russia the forest was even closer to peasant life than in France or Germany because it was more extensive and yielded copious supplies of deadwood for fuel, as well as furs, fish, small game, wax, honey, and quite overwhelming yields of mushrooms and berries, all of which sustained life in a harsh environment. But this "deep and multifarious generosity of the forest" was ill repaid, as peasants steadily cleared the mixed hardwood forests during the sixteenth and seventeenth centuries in much the same way as the hardwoods from the Loire to the Elbe had been cleared during the medieval period. Traditional slash-and-burn and long-fallow agriculture gave way to more sophisticated common two- and three-field systems. In Lithuania, the Forest Decree of 1557 set aside wide swathes of Crown forestland in which new settlements could be established, and peasants were given a 10-year exemption from taxes. Then the clearing of *pochinki*, or outlying fields, was undertaken, sometimes doubling the area of land cleared.[40]

Some of the most spectacular changes in forest extent occurred on the frontier south and southeast of the Muscovy heartland after the defeat of the Kazan Tartars in 1552. A large influx of Russian settlers occupied the forests in the rolling hills and plains between the Dneiper and the Volga, while Ukrainian cossacks moved east, bringing with them teams of oxen and heavy iron plows for cutting the matted sod. Forestland was parceled out to individuals, and ecclesiastical houses and clearing proceeded energetically.[41] By the mid-seventeenth century the pioneer frontier had reached the Grey Forest Earths, Black Earths, and the richer chernozum soils of the southern mixed forest and forest steppe, eventually transforming them into cultivated land. With the buildup of Tsarist military forces, especially after the campaign of Peter the Great against the Kazan Tartars in the lower Don valley in 1696, the scene was set for a massive expansion of Russian peasant agriculturalists into these areas.[42] A successive series of defensive lines (the Zaseki, Belgorod, Izyum, and Simbrisk) were established, running roughly west–east across the new territory, and the forest was cleared along them to provide barriers of fallen trees and timber for forts and stockades (as well as open and easily defensible ground in front). Next the forests behind the fortifications were cleared ruthlessly (fig. 7.3).

Gradually, the density of population and percentage of land under cultivation increased in the provinces straddling the deciduous forest, forest/steppe (parkland), and steppe zones. In table 7.2 these six provinces—Tula, Ryazan, Orel, Tambov, Kursk, and Vorenezh—are arranged in a north–south order, and are depicted in figure 7.3 against the distribution of the "natural" vegetation. Whereas in 1719 about one-third of the land was in cultivation and population densities were about 10–15/km², the comparable figures had risen to nearer one half and 20–30/km² by 1811; clearing and settlement went hand in hand.

Further north, in the coniferous forests of Russia, Finland, and Sweden, poor glacial, ill-drained soils, together with a limited growing season, restricted the urge for clearing, except in small patches of favorable soils north of Moscow. But other than that the northern lands were almost totally covered with coniferous forests, which, before the development of the pulp industry, had little commercial value compared with hardwoods. It was only after the opening of the White Sea route to the west by English Elizabethan merchants in 1533 that the forest became a source of strategic goods, such as masts, naval stores like pitch and tar, and furs. Yet here and there peasant settlers were felling and burning these northern forest margins. The system was primitive but effective—roughly four cycles of burning occurred in each century, so that in a hundred years the burned-over land would experience 20 years under grain (usually rye), perhaps 12 under rough grazing, and 68 under woodland grazing. In the long run, this practice of "burn-beating" destroyed the forest structure, and because it continued well into the twentieth century it has left permanent marks on the northern forests.[43]

In southern Europe, the decline in forest after the Middle Ages was due less to the expansion of cultivation than to extensive migratory livestock grazing. In central Spain, the powerful organization of the Meseta, promoted by the unrestricted autocracy of the

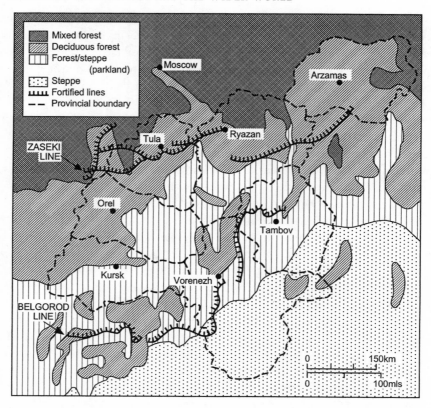

Figure 7.3 Provinces, main vegetation zones, and fortified lines, south-central Russia (note: the tsarist "governments" would have had slightly different boundaries to the postrevolutionary provinces shown here). *Sources:* natural vegetation zones based on Central Department of Geodosy and Cartography, Council of Ministers, USSR (Moscow, 1975), 1:5,000,000; political administrative map based on Central Department of Geodosy and Cartography, Ministry of Geology (Moscow: 1966), 1:5,000,000; and lines after Shaw, 1983: 123, 128.

Castilian monarchs, pastured vast flocks of sheep that ran into the millions. The hills of Castile were stripped bare of young trees for fodder; and annual burning to promote grass growth, and close grazing of the sheep, stifled tree regrowth. The annual havoc left the denuded landscape that so impressed the Venetian ambassadors and other observant travelers in the middle decades of the sixteenth century.[44] The same processes, though not so single-minded or severe, were at work in Languedoc, Provence, the Apennines, Calabria, and parts of the Balkans. Where subsequent erosion did not strip the soil, the forest vegetation was in the first stages of its degradation to the typical Mediterranean "garigue" or "maquis" scrub. In a small area of some 1,500 km² in the Pays de Sault in the foothills of the Pyrenees of southwest France, Christian Fruhauf has attempted to reconstruct the reduction of forest caused by both peasant and large-scale proprietors between 1670 and 1740.[45]

In sum, all the indications are that the agricultural landscape of Europe had undergone another period of intensive change by 1750, and that it was very different from that

Table 7.2 Population density (persons/km²) and land in cultivation (%), 1719–1912; and forest cover (%), 1696–1725, 1796, and 1914 in six provinces in south-central Russia

Province	1719	1762	1811	1861	1881	1912
Kursk						
pop. den.	15.6	18.0	29.3	36.9	51.0	70.1
% cult.	36	38	51	67	74	72
% forest	16		12			6
Orel						
pop. den.	15.1	16.0	24.9	30.2	43.5	59.1
% cult.	38	40	51	55	62	56
% forest	31		29			17
Ryazan						
pop. den.	12.0	16.6	24.8	32.5	43.0	66.1
% cult.	30	37	47	56	56	52
% forest	48		33			19
Tambov						
pop. den.	7.0	10.1	19.2	26.7	40.3	53.0
% cult.	18	25	38	60	63	62
% forest	41		28			16
Tula						
pop. den.	15.6	22.1	32.5	36.3	45.8	60.9
% cult.	39	55	69	71	73	66
% forest	24		16			8
Vorenezh						
pop. den.	4.0	8.0	17.6	27.5	38.4	55.1
% cult.	11	25	40	60	69	63
% forest	13		9			7
Region						
pop. den.	10.5	14.0	23.5	30.8	43.0	59.7
% cult.	26	34	47	61	66	63
% forest	17		13			7

Source: land and population after Stebelsky, 1983: 52 and 54; forest cover after French, 1983: 40.
Note: the % forest cover is allotted to the population density and % cultivation column closest, chronologically speaking.

of the beginning of the sixteenth century. The change during those two hundred years cannot be quantified with any certainty, but it must have been immense. But we know that by about 1700, there were about 100 million ha of cropland, one-third of that in Russia.[46] Most of it had been created out of the forestland of the western, central, and northern portions of the continent.

FUELWOOD

Wood was the indispensable raw material of everyday life, and as necessary as food in a preindustrial society. The forests provided the major raw material for buildings, mills, looms, furniture, spinning wheels, plows, carts, and wheels; wood was even used in the gear wheels of clocks and watches. All tools and machines were of wood, except for the actual cutting or striking edge, which was of iron.[47] Moreover it was calculated that a Russian farmhouse and yard took the timber of about 1.36 ha of forest to construct, and there were untold millions of farmhouses in Russia that had an average life of only 15 years.[48]

Plate 7.1 Winter Landscape by Lucas I. van Valckenborch, 1586. Collecting and carting wood was a typical occupation during the winter months, when demand was highest and agricultural tasks at a minimum. (Kunsthistorisches Museum, Vienna.)

Table 7.3 Towns in Europe of more than 40,000 inhabitants,
circa 1500–1700

Thousands	Early 16th Century	End of 16th–Early 17th Century	End of 17th Century
+400	0	0	3
200–399	0	3	1
150–199	3	3	1
100–149	2	6	7
60–99	5	10	14
40–59	16	20	22
Total	26	42	48

Source: Mols, 1977: 42–43.

It was a "wooden" age, so we have to take the ubiquitous and universal use of wood for buildings, fencing, tools, and implements as given, and concentrate rather on the use of wood for fuel.

Wood fuel was vital during the intense winters of northern, central, and eastern Europe, which had become significantly colder with the onset of the Little Ice Age; in addition, most food was unpalatable without the application of heat. Existence simply would have been impossible without wood to burn. The comfortably well-off peasant farmer in seventeenth-century southern Germany could reckon on using 50 m³ (13.8 cords) per annum, though most rural dwellers had to be content with about half that amount.[49] Cutting, gathering, and hauling wood were common wintertime activities that typified the busy countryside scenes of the late sixteenth-century Netherlandish painters Pieter Bruegel and Lucas van Valckenborch (plate 7.1).[50] But the days were gone when the mass of the population lived in villages and small towns, and fuel could be gathered freely from surrounding woodlands without payment. From the early sixteenth century onward, more and more people were living in larger and larger towns and cities. If 40,000 is taken as a reasonable measure of an urban area large enough to make significant demands on its hinterland, then there were 26 such towns at the beginning of the sixteenth century, 42 at the end, and 48 at the close of the seventeenth century, of which Amsterdam, Naples, Constantinople, Paris, and London numbered over 150,000 (table 7.3 and fig. 7.4).[51] Each urban conglomeration formed a node of collection, haulage, and consumption. The average person needed to spend about one-tenth of his annual income to get enough wood to "keep a fire burning for himself and his family for part of the day in one room during the coldest weather," and that was probably only enough to keep them alive, not comfortable. This income proportion is broadly supported by the more precise calculations of Ernest Phelps Brown and Sheila Hopkins, who suggest that about 7.5 percent of an ordinary budget was spent on lighting and heating during the sixteenth to late eighteenth centuries.[52]

Clearly, the amount of wood consumed depended not only on the climate and weather, but also on the availability of fuel and the income of the purchaser, as there was always wood to be had for a price. But the price was usually excessively high, as middlemen intervened at every stage between suppliers and dealers. Like fuel dealers anywhere and at

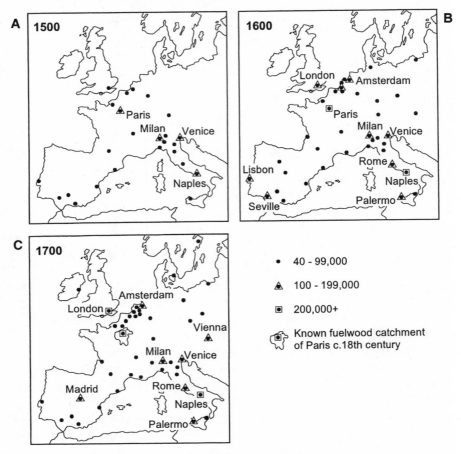

Figure 7.4 European towns whose populations exceeded 40,000, *A,* circa 1500; *B,* circa 1600; and *C,* circa 1700. *Source:* after Mols, 1977: 40–44.

any time, through "greyde, appetite, and covetousness," as one mid-sixteenth-century London Assize (court clerk) put it, they hoarded stocks, delayed deliveries, created artificial shortages, especially in times of severe cold, pushed up prices, and still sold substantial quantities to rich and poor alike. Wood shortages were manufactured in an unscrupulous fashion.[53] For the poor there was no alternative, and when one realizes that the extreme cold also brought the additional disadvantages of frozen rivers, a dearth of food supplies, and a multiplicity of epidemics, then it is not surprising that William Harrison could say at the end of the sixteenth century that the poor "often perish for cold," while in Paris at the end of the severe winter of 1709 "people died like flies."[54] Death from exposure to cold as well as famine were still realities in early eighteenth-century Europe.

General shortages of fuelwood seem first to have appeared in London, one of Europe's largest cities, as early as 1300. At that time it drew supplies of faggots (bundled small wood) from an extensive zone that reached up the Thames as far west as the wooded

Chiltern district and also encompassed the heavily wooded parts of the Weald south of the Thames, as well as parts of Essex and Hertfordshire to the north. The Black Death temporarily lessened the pressure and caused the supply zone to contract; but shortages began to appear again in the late fifteenth century, and a general air of concern about diminishing supplies arose by the 1500s.[55] The once flourishing medieval export trade of fuelwood from Essex, Kent, and Sussex across the Channel to the woodless Low Countries and agricultural northern France was long over, and Harrison's *Description of England* of 1587 referred repeatedly to timber "want" and forest "decay." He also commented that one could ride "ten or twenty miles" in many counties and find "very little [wood] or rather none at all."[56] In France and Italy, local shortages appeared around larger towns such as Montpelier, Lyons, Paris, and Naples by the later seventeenth century. Thomas Platter, a Swiss student in Montpelier, noted the absence of forests around the town as early as 1595:

> The nearest is at the Saint-Paul glass works, a good three miles in the direction of Celleneuve. The firewood is brought from there in the winter and sold by weight. One wonders where they would get it if the winter lasted a long time because they consume an enormous quantity of it in their fireplaces, while shivering beside them. Stoves are unknown in this region; unlike at home, the shortage of wood is so great that bakers fill their ovens with rosemary, kermes-oak and other bushes.

The shortage increased the further south one traveled: in Medina del Campo in Spain, fuel was more expensive than the food that it cooked in the pot.[57] Generally, the opposite was true in central and eastern Europe, where the forest was extensive enough to withstand domestic and the typically lesser industrial demands for fuel, though local shortages existed around metallurgical centers in Germany and Bohemia.

How much fuelwood was consumed is not known; no one collected statistics about an everyday necessity that literally "went without saying." In any case, much of it was the by-product of agricultural clearing and was never enumerated. But an immense amount was needed. Per capita consumption in preindustrial northern Europe was about 1.6 to 2.3 tons of dry wood, say, 2 tons. Assuming a production of about 20 to 25 tons of underwood per square kilometer of intensively managed woodland, then a town of approximately 40,000 people needed the annual yield of between 3,200 and 4,000 km² (1,235 mi²–1544 mi²) of managed woodland.[58] In France, Vauban calculated in about 1700 that 700 arpents (roughly 425 ha) of 20-year-old forest could keep about 110 households supplied with heating, cooking, and construction materials for a year, and as there were about 3.2 million households, up to 123,636 km² of woodland would be required—probably a greater area of forest than existed.[59] These figures cannot be regarded as definitive, only indicative.

Examples of the fuelwood demand in individual European towns and cities can be enumerated endlessly. St. Petersburg in the eighteenth century consumed "thousands of rafts of timber and thousands of cart loads of firewood every year. Even the boats bringing the wood were usually broken up and sold for their timbers." In Paris, wood for both construction and heating was transported down the Seine and its many tributaries from as far away as Morvan along the Cure and Yonne after the mid-1500s. But unlike London there was no subsequent access to mineral fuel, and twelve years later the radius of collection had widened from 60 km to 200 km, with supplies coming down the Marne and its tributaries. This situation brought domestic fuelwood gathering into direct conflict with the local iron industry in Lorraine, Haute-Marne, Haute-Sâone, and the edges of the Vosges forest (see fig. 10.2 below), and even possibly contributed to difficulties of food supply for the city. In the sixteenth century charcoal reached Paris by way of Sens from the forest of Othe, but two hundred years later it was coming from all over France, sometimes in carts or on pack animals, but usually by river, the boats "piled high, with hurdles along the sides of the boat to keep the charcoal in." [60] In sum, fuel supply to Paris was very different from the situation in London, so it was truly "a tale of two cities."

There were two ways around the fuelwood shortage: either improve the method of heating or find a substitute fuel. The traditional large, open hearth was used primarily for cooking, for it was a poor source of heat, irrespective of how much wood was piled upon it. Braudel notes that the two huge blazing fires in the admittedly vast Hall of Mirrors in the Palace of Versailles did not succeed in heating the room. It was advisable to wear furs for dining, and in February 1695 it was observed that "at the King's table the wine and water froze in the glasses." It was not an uncommon experience. Gradually, during the later seventeenth century, chimneys were made narrower and deeper, with the shaft curved to prevent smoke from coming back into the room; the mantle was lowered; the hearth's dual purpose of cooking and heating was restricted to one function or the other; and the fire was raised off the brick base and placed on an iron grate to enable a strong updraft through the embers. Hearths were now more heat efficient and consequently spread widely. Stoves of brick or stone—sometimes covered with ceramic tiles—that were more fuel efficient, free of fumes, and able to maintain a comfortable and even temperature, were not unknown in England or France, but they never caught on in the rest of Europe as they did in Germany and central, northern, and eastern Europe. One can begin to see the truth of the comment that by the early eighteenth century, "it was better to pass the winter in Cologne or Warsaw than Milan or Toulouse." [61] Cast-iron stoves did not appear until the end of the eighteenth century.

Coal—or sea coal, as it was more often called, to distinguish it from charcoal—had been brought by coasters from Newcastle to London and English east-coast towns since medieval times. Ease of sea and river transportation, favorable conditions of landownership, and the undoubted demand created by timber shortages gave the coal-mining industry an initial advantage and much encouragement. By the end of the seventeenth century, many coalfields had been opened, and only the most inaccessible parts of the four countries of the United Kingdom were solely dependent on wood (fig. 7.5). In round figures, coal production increased from about 210,000 tons in 1551–60 to 2.9 million tons in 1681–90, and then to 10.3 million tons in 1781–90. Elsewhere at this time, only Belgium had a colliery district of any importance, but even so it is doubtful whether by the end of the seventeenth century "the entire annual production of the Continent amounted to more than a sixth of the annual production of Great Britain." [62]

Despite its noxious smokiness, coal seems to have been well accepted for heating and cooking in the domestic households of all classes in Britain by the early seventeenth cen-

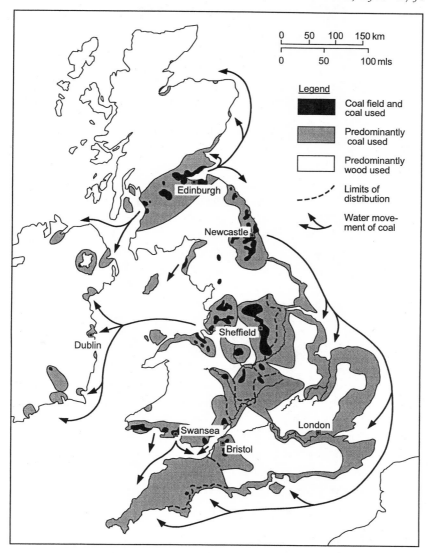

Figure 7.5 Coalfields and type of fuel used in the United Kingdom, circa 1680. *Source:* based on Nef, 1932, vol. 1, facing p.19.

tury, much to the astonishment of Continental travellers. But it was not used for domestic purposes alone: soon it was being substituted for wood in industrial processes where technical obstacles could be overcome, with the notable exception of ferrous ore smelting. As a result, other than the remarkable example of eleventh-century northern China, Britain led the world in the conversion from vegetable to mineral energy sources, the process being well under way before 1600. Industrial consumption reached about 1 million tons before the end of the century, or about one-third of total output.

The shrill cries of a timber shortage, so common in the early decades of the century, die away from about 1670 onward. Fuelwood prices stabilize, and in the name of economic efficiency, people like John Houghton in 1683 could advocate the complete stripping of forests so that land could be put to more productive use for growing food; timber could be imported, and coal used for fuel. Coal had penetrated nearly everywhere and in abundance; in 1724 Daniel Defoe commented on its widespread use in London taverns, and added, "T'is not immaterial to observe what an Alteration it makes in the Value of those Woods in *Kent,* and how many more of them, than usual are yearly grubbed up, and the Land made fit for the Plough." [63]

For the moment, at least, the pressure was off the British forests, as coal was plentiful and cheaper to produce than charcoal. In Nef's view, the transition from wood to coal as the source of heat was the mainspring of Britain's leadership in the future "Industrial Revolution." [64] He may well have a point. Eric Jones makes the provocative suggestion that analogous to the idea of the "ghost acreage" that Europe obtained with its extension into overseas territories, it also obtained a "coal acreage" when it extended its resource frontier vertically by mining coal, thereby giving its economy a massive boost. It should be possible to calculate the "additional acreage that would have been needed, with given techniques, to produce the charcoal and firewood energy and organic chemicals for which coal provided a substitute." [65] The calculation has never been done and there are many variables to consider, but if we took the simple rule of thumb that the heat generated by a ton of coal was the equivalent of the burning of 2 tons of dry wood, which might be the underwood output of an acre of well-managed woodland, then the 2.98 million tons of coal consumed as energy in Britain in 1681–90 was the equivalent of about 3 million more acres of forest than the country felled. By 1781–90 its "ghost coal acreage" would have risen in proportion to the 10.3 million tons of coal mined, or approximately 10 million acres, which was much vaster than all available woodland. This goes a long way in explaining why Britain was able to industrialize so early despite a shortage of wood.

CHARCOAL AND IRON MAKING

The collection of fuelwood was undoubtedly a drain on the forests, but many contemporary observers thought that the real culprit was not domestic fuel consumption but industrial expansion. Brick, glass, and iron making, salt evaporation, lime burning, sugar refining, soap boiling, brewing, and the charcoal (plate 7.2), brimstone, and saltpeter needed in the making of gunpowder, for example, were taking prodigious amounts of timber, and their demands were year-round and growing. A single glazier in London during the early seventeenth century burned 2,000 wagonloads of wood annually, while the average intake for a glass furnace was 60–70 cords a month. Brewers in London may have consumed as much as 20,000 wagonloads of wood a year in 1578. [66] Wood use for salt making was prodigal: one of many salt furnaces in Nantwich in Lancashire consumed 6,000 cartloads of wood a year, collected from a 75-mi radius as far south as Worcester; and the great mines of Hall in the Tyrol might have used 1 million m³ during the late fifteenth to early sixteenth centuries. Similar examples can be cited for Russia. [67]

Plate 7.2 Preparing and making charcoal. Woodcutters brought the wood to the kiln area, where the charcoal producers stacked it methodically in cone or beehive form and then covered all with a coating of clay or earth (*I*, this page). This kept the inner temperature at a minimum, so that the wood smoldered and was eventually converted to charcoal and not ash. After the cone was lit (*II*, p. 188, right foreground), the pile was progressively reduced in size until pure charcoal remained. (From D. Diderot, *Encyclopedie . . . Recueil de planches sur le sciences, les artes liberaux, et les arts méchaniques,* vol. 1 [Paris, 1763].)

When multiplied across the Continent by thousands of large towns and manufacturing units, for hundreds of years, the result is incalculable, and the drain on the forests must have been immense.

But it was metallurgy in general, and iron making in particular, that engaged the most attention as the destroyer of forests and the creator of a timber famine, largely because, unlike other forms of manufacturing, it was not easy to satisfactorily substitute coal for charcoal in the smelting process. As the universal metal of the age, iron meant tools, implements, and even machinery. Above all it was crucial for armaments, and therefore had a strategic importance out of all proportion to its domestic importance.

Plate 7.2 (continued)

Iron making was scattered across the breadth of Europe (fig. 7.6), wherever ores out-cropped on valley sides or were easily stripped, and its location barely changed significantly until the late eighteenth century. Essential to the process were running water to move a wheel for the bellows and hammers, and abundant supplies of wood. Most of the production was a low-quality, soft iron, but a few places, such as northern Spain, the Dauphiné and Franche-Comté, Liege, Lorraine, the Rhineland, central Sweden, and later the Weald and Sheffield, established a reputation for finer metals that lifted them above other regions, and that also implied a degree of specialization. The technology of production was simple. Smelting was carried out on a hearth with a bellows, and alternate heating and beating removed the impurities in the metal and made it stronger and harder. The stone-built blast furnace, first invented in the later Middle Ages, greatly increased the volume, quality, and speed of production.[68]

How much wood fuel the furnaces used, and therefore how much forest was cut down, is difficult to calculate. It depended on so many variables, such as the amount of wood

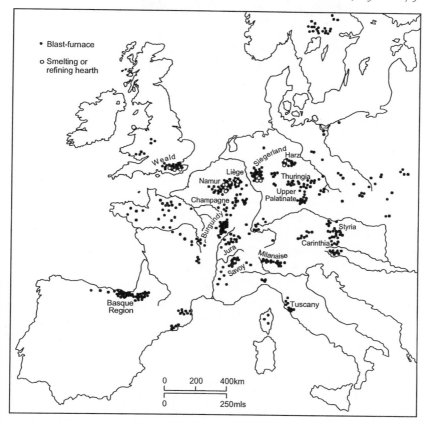

Figure 7.6 Iron making in Europe in the sixteenth century. *Source: after Pounds, 1979: 50–53.*

needed to make a load of charcoal; the quantity of charcoal used to smelt the ore and then to refine the pig iron; the amount of pig iron consumed to make a ton of bar iron; and the heat value of the wood, which could vary enormously. Another problem is to disentangle the "exaggerated, misleading, and incorrect" information put out by those with vested interests, such as shipbuilders and local inhabitants, in order to safeguard their supplies." [69] The example of Britain's iron industry is instructive. Although starting late in comparison with Germany and France, it rose spectacularly in the later sixteenth century under government encouragement for reasons of national safety and self-sufficiency, and was soon being blamed as the main destroyer of the forests. Local petitions against furnaces, and complaints at the scarcity and rising prices of domestic fuelwood in southeast England in districts near the Wealden iron industry and elsewhere, were numerous. An added complication was that the navy saw the iron industry as its main competitor for the not very extensive areas of prime oak timber in the Weald and other royal forests, so it sought to limit felling and discredit the ironmasters. Details of these accusations of wanton destruction and impending scarcity are listed in John Perlin's *A Forest Journey,* but while there was a nub of truth in them, many were alarmist, referred only to local conditions, and did not apply to the national scene.[70]

George Hammersley suggests that in Britain during the 1620s, the process of producing 1 ton of bar iron from the ore took 59.4 m³ of wood, and that by the last decades of the century fuelwood requirements were down to 50.9 m³ or less, so that during the highest output of 27,000 tons of charcoal bar iron in the mid-eighteenth century, the industry would have consumed 1,603,800 m³ of wood. The yield of the forest was variable, but early seventeenth-century Crown Surveyors-General such as Norden, Treswell, and Thorpe consistently rated coppices as yielding 30 cords/acre, which at Hammersley's own calculation that a Wealden cord equals 2.464 m³ means that each acre of coppice yielded 73.92 m³, or the equivalent of 182.85 m³/ha. We are now able to bring the two calculations together. Even at the peak annual iron ore producing period, fuelwood consumption was somewhere between 1,603,800 m³ and 1,374,300 m³, so only 8,771 to 7,516 ha of woodland would have been affected each year. Such a total is hardly enough to cause the crisis that was so often said to be imminent, especially as the wooded area at this time must have been well over 1.5 million ha, and also keeping in mind that coppiced trees are not clear felled but regrow at rates approaching 3 m³/yr.[71]

In continental Europe, greater forest cover and declining pressure from competing uses led to less comment on forest decline. Hermann Kellenbenz suggests only 4 m³ of wood was needed to produce 1 ton of pig iron and a further 9 m³ for 1 ton of wrought iron—in total, a surprising one-fourth *less* than the amount produced by Hammersley's calculations above. Nevertheless, the closure of furnaces and foundries could still occur through thoughtless cutting, and presumably a lack of coppicing. The Slovakian ironworks of Stare Hory and Harmanec were forced to shut down in 1560, and the timber shortfall was only made up with "outside" supplies floated down the River Gran to collecting points near Neusohl. The rising consumption of timber there, and in the Siegerland in the Ruhr area, caused a rise in the price of wood, and forestry corporations were formed to cultivate trees for coppicing in order to ensure a constant supply of fuel and obviate the expensive transportation of charcoal, which could amount to 70 percent of the production cost of 1 ton of wrought iron. A more extreme solution by many territorial rulers was to limit the number of foundries and forges in order to prevent forest destruction.[72]

All in all, then, the picture of the impact of metalworking on the forests is somewhat confused. Yet, the general conclusion must be that while each ironworking location (fig. 7.6) was a focus for local destruction that was often real and severe, particularly in the more treeless western and southern parts of the Continent, the overall impact was exaggerated and must have been much less than the inroads of agriculture and domestic fuel getting, which are often ignored. It is estimated that the total European production of iron (type unspecified) was 40,000 tons in 1500 and possibly 145,000 tons or a little more in 1700.[73] If Hammersley's most favorable calculations for the British iron industry are applied to these production figures, then approximately 11,135 ha of woodland would have been affected in 1500 and 40,364 ha in 1700; the effect could be dramatically less if Kellenbenz's figures are applied.

While iron and other metal smelters undoubtedly caused local destruction, closure—which was said to be another manifestation of the timber crisis—was far more likely to result from sustained production at one site rather than a national shortage of timber. The cost of carting charcoal and its friability in transit over rough tracks limited the distance it could be transported, and a 5- to 8-km radius was considered acceptable in England as in much of Europe.[74] An 8-km radius encloses approximately 20,000 ha, and a big furnace could exist on about a quarter of that if rotational coppicing was employed. Therefore, output everywhere had to adjust to the rate of regrowth in the economically accessible area of forest, and if production exceeded that, then one either waited for timber regrowth or imported roundwood for fuel at great cost.

Whichever calculation we take, the forestland affected would most likely have been cut over or coppiced, and almost certainly not totally destroyed. To have done so would have been foolish; it would have upset production stability, raised transportation costs, jeopardized the investment in the plant, and undermined profits, especially in Britain, where there was intense competition from Swedish charcoal imports. It is often forgotten that while Evelyn deplored the "prodigious waste which these voracious iron and glass works have formerly made," he asserted elsewhere that his father's forge and mills "were a means of maintaining and improving his woods, I suppose by increasing the industry of planting." This was not an isolated example; in 1667, Andrew Yarranton commented on iron making in the Forest of Dean, Gloucestershire:

> [I]f the Iron-works were not in being, these Coppices would have been stocked [pulled] up and turned into Pasture and Tillage, as is now daily done in Sussex and Surrey where the Iron-works, or most of them, are laid down . . . and so there would be neither Woods nor Timber in these places.[75]

Paradoxical as it may seem, these and many other examples point to the conclusion that while being among the first to exploit the woodland commercially, the ironmasters were also amongst the first to consider some form of forest management in the form of systematic cultivation and coppicing of hundreds of thousands of acres (plate 7.3). These practices cheapened the cost of fuel, protected the ironmasters' investment, and maintained profits. They were merely following an age-long practice since medieval times and before, when many forest areas had been managed to produce fuelwood, a frequently overlooked practice in the heroic story of cultivation, which is all too often seen as what Christopher Wickham has called the "great mythic symbol of medieval agrarian *croissance*." Unlike the agriculturalists, the ironmasters "did not plough up woodlands or uproot them, neither did they nibble the young shoots," thereby averting the fairly irrevocable clearing of the land.[76]

Finally, these figures for the amount of forest affected by iron making can be compared with those for complete clearing, primarily for agriculture. From 1650 to 1749 between 18.4 million and 24.6 million ha of forest disappeared in Europe.[77] At the greatest level of production, the area affected by iron making was only a mere 12 to 16 percent of the amount cleared annually during roughly the same period. If most iron-making impacts came through coppicing rather than the complete stripping that was done for agriculture, then iron making was a very minor element in the total picture of deforestation, accounting for a few percent, at most, of the annual wastage. Clearly much more work

Plate 7.3 Fuelwood cutters at work in a coppice. From John Perlin, *A Forest Journey: The Role of Wood in the Development of Civilization* (Cambridge, Mass.: Harvard University Press, 1991).

needs to be done to verify this, but it seems more than likely that iron was not the devourer of the woods it was made out to be.

THE DEMANDS OF THE SEA
Homegrown Timber

Shipbuilding (plate 7.4) has always exerted a powerful influence on the perception and use of the forests because of its strategic and commercial significance in the life of nations that were born through overseas expansion. In addition, the requirement for special types of timbers—those resistant to rot, naturally curved in some fashion for the construction of hulls, or supple yet strong enough for masts—meant that different timbers were sought widely. During the early Renaissance period Venice, Genoa, and Catalonia launched great fleets at the expense of the Mediterranean forest. The Venetian Republic may have held "the gorgeous east in fee," but part of the price of that domination was the stripping of the forests from the mountains around the rim of the Adriatic. By the fourteenth century, timber cutters were scouring the upper reaches of the Adige, Cadore, and Piare in the Dolomitic Alps, and Trevisana and Friuli in Istria for oak, and the timber was floated downstream on sizable rafts.[78] Oak, in particular, was quickly depleted, as its growing area was also good agricultural land. While Venice had just about enough timber from its reserved forests, the private shipbuilders did not. By the end of the sixteenth century they began to buy from Venice's emerging rival on the Adriatic, Ragussa, which had plentiful supplies of oak for the time being, and from the Dutch, who were virtually mass-producing ships from Baltic timber. A new chapter was opening in European maritime activity as trade shifted from the Mediterranean to the Atlantic, and the source of naval supplies shifted permanently to the Baltic. It was the same everywhere in the Mediterranean area; even Spain in the days of the Armada was sending North American silver to the Baltic to buy suitable timber, masts, and naval stores.[79]

Obviously, the successful expansion of the merchant and fighting fleets of the northwestern European nations depended on an adequate supply of suitable timber (plate 7.5). Estimates vary, but a large warship of about 1,000 tons required between 1,400 and 2,000 oak trees, each at least 100 years old, which could not have grown on less than 16–20 ha of woodland;[80] three masts of up to 130 feet; and numerous spars. Oaks were at a premium because of their resistance to fungal rot, and because of the way in which they grew naturally to form the variously curved timbers for the hull: the "futtocks," "knees," "crutches," "catheads," and "ribs."[81] Oak is indigenous to all the countries of western and central Europe from Spain to Poland, but firs are not; and from the thirteenth century at least, firs together with such "naval stores" as pitch and tar for waterproofing hulls and decking, turpentine for preserving rigging, hemp for making ropes, and flax for making sails, had been imported from the Baltic lands.

In Holland the supply of oak was never adequate for the vast shipbuilding program undertaken, and from a very early date the country imported timber for both hulls and masts from the south Baltic lands. In Britain supplies of oak seem to have been adequate, but concern about reserves was expressed after about the early seventeenth century. The oak came mainly from the royal forests; the three main ones on which the navy depended

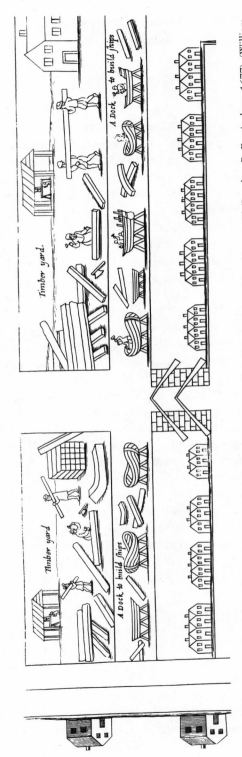

Plate 7.4 An eighteenth-century shipyard. From Andrew Yarranton, *England's Improvement by Sea and Land . . .*, p. 19 (London: R. Everingham, 1677). (William Adams Clark Memorial Library, UCLA.)

Plate 7.5 Timber being felled by ax and measured by dividiers (probably for shipbuilding) while the owner and his agent discuss the price with the timber merchant. Frontispiece to Moses Cook, *The Manner of Raising, Ordering and Improving Forest Trees*, 1717 ed. (William Andrews Clark Memorial Library, UCLA.)

were the Forest of Dean, the New Forest, and the Alice Holt forest in northwest Hampshire. But all the southeast counties were important suppliers of wood as well. Moreover, though unreliable, private parks and estates could make up deficiencies from time to time. The Dutch wars of the seventeenth century and the maritime wars of the eighteenth put a heavy and continuous strain on oak supplies. Samuel Pepys, secretary to the admiralty, could only write, "God knows where materials can be had." [82] In France the situation was better, delaying the supply crisis, but the shipyards were using up as much as 28,000 to 56,000 m³ of oak per annum. Philosopher-geographer-silviculturalist Buffon predicted in 1739, "we are threatened with absolute want of it in time to come." [83]

In both Britain and France these statements have been taken as proof of widespread scarcity, but it is probably best to regard them as "only as warnings, albeit prophetic warnings, based on awareness of local scarcity." The continuing reduction of forest led many local observers to exaggerate the extent and immediacy of deforestation, egged on by vested interests, though the steady and long-term depletion of resources cannot be denied. The admiralty's request for advice from the Royal Society, which led in 1664 to John Evelyn's *Sylva: Or, a Discourse of Forest Trees,* and the almost contemporaneous enquiry by Colbert in France, which culminated in his "Ordonnance des eaux et forêts" of 1669, were evidence of official concern. But despite the alarm and propaganda, the navies of both countries relied almost entirely on native timbers for more than another 100 years.[84] For example, 90 percent of the 66,330 m³ of timber used annually between 1760 and 1788 in English dockyards was still homegrown, and French dockyards did not import large quantities of foreign timbers until after 1783, and then only as required. The family business of Pierre Babaud de la Chaussade was able to transport millions of cubic feet of timber from the Alsace region to Holland via the Rhine, Saar, and Moselle on rafts during the short space of 10 years between 1728 and 1738, which suggests that there was abundant timber around.

All this supports Michael Flinn's view that "so far from there being a timber famine, it is abundantly clear that the supply of both timber and cordwood during the two centuries after 1550 was enormously increased" and, one might add, with surprisingly little rise in prices. Perhaps the real basis for anxiety was that the forests were not being replanted; the British experience was a dismal story of "culpable neglect" and inadequate planning on the part of successive governments that never thought beyond their term of office.[85]

The Baltic Timber Trade

Masts and naval stores were another matter. Masts demanded length, cylindrical straightness, strength, durability, and yet a certain elasticity—a combination of qualities that could only be obtained from the conifers of the Baltic forests, which set the standard of quality. But supply from the Baltic was always precarious. Each western consuming maritime nation wanted to deny supplies to its rival; each Baltic supplying nation was at pains not to alienate influential customers and lose essential revenue. Baltic timber was, said Robert Albion, "a matter for diplomats as well as traders." Moreover, the closure of the

Baltic was a constant threat; it had happened during the First Dutch War in 1652. Exacerbating matters, Prussia, Sweden, Denmark, and Russia had occasionally levied additional customs duties on masts and naval stores. Naval powers like Britain and France did not want to be dependent on foreign powers for indispensable shipping supplies, and in time looked elsewhere. France experimented with domestic sources from Auvergne, Alsace, Dauphiné, and the Pyrenees, and even trees from Quebec, although they were often of inferior quality. Britain tried its North American colonies with more success, but at the expense of raising the ire of its American colonists, with ultimately far-reaching political consequences.[86]

Masts were only a relatively small part of the development of Europe's "internal America" of the Baltic, which was also the source for other everyday bulk commodities, such as timber, potash, grain, fish, furs, flax, and iron.[87] Of these, timber was most important and needs closer examination, as the Baltic timber trade was probably the first manifestation in the world of *lumber* (i.e., crude, undressed trunks) and mass-production techniques that were to be copied later in the forests of North America and elsewhere.

The Baltic timber trade was of long standing. From the Middle Ages the Hanse had overseen a thriving trade in wood, pitch, and tar between the settlements along the river edges and the towns established by the Teutonic knights. The wave of colonization in Poland and Lithuania in the fifteenth and sixteenth centuries stimulated clearing for more extensive agricultural and urban needs, as well as for exports. Danzig, with its many water-driven sawmills, emerged as a major shipbuilding center and the hub of the export trade, which it soon dominated, dictating standards to Konigsberg, Riga, and other exporting towns in the "East Country." It was a complex story of shifting zones of exploitation, depending very much on rapidly changing political swings and alliances (see fig. 7.6). By the seventeenth century, a reasonably well-defined system for mass production appeared. A contract would be drawn up in, say, Deptford, Amsterdam, or La Rochelle, and credit advanced to a Baltic merchant house, which would engage middlemen to negotiate with forest owners to produce the required amount of timber and sometimes to transport the trunks to port, paying so much per tree. The growth of the grain trade under the Polish nobility was crucial to the new lumbering system, for armies of peasants worked in the fields during the summer and the forests during the winter. Thus, lumbering became a convenient adjunct to the feudal system, and the "lopsided development of agriculture and forestry under the massive pressure of western demand" took place in Poland and adjacent territories at the expense of local crafts and industries.[88]

Unlike the exploitation of the remaining patches of dense forest in the high, inaccessible mountainous areas of the Mediterranean basin, the exploitation of the extensive forests of the Baltic region was aided by local topographical and climatic conditions. Gradients were gentle, felling could be done in the winter months, when the sap was low, and the huge spars and trunks then hauled out of the forest easily on horse- and ox-drawn sleds on the snow cover to the edge of the many substantial rivers that flowed across the northern European plain (fig. 7.7). With the spring thaw, individual logs were thrown into the smaller streams, to be collected at some strategic point for assembly into great rafts of over a thousand logs that could be navigated downstream. These rafts were piled

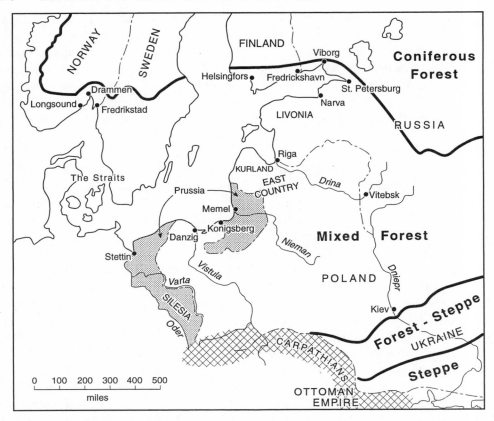

Figure 7.7 The Baltic and Scandinavian timber trade in the seventeenth and eighteenth centuries. It is impossible to show political boundaries with any certainty over this long period because of the frequent and substantial changes of states. For example, Sweden extended around the eastern Baltic and included Livonia until 1658; the two parts of Prussia were joined after 1720; and Poland did not exist as a separate state entity but was variously partitioned between neighboring states until 1810.

high with smaller sawn lumber, fuelwood, grain, and also potash, the production of which, according to the customs registers at Wloclawek, consumed over 6 million m³ of timber per annum.[89]

At the Baltic ports, the rafts were floated into mast ponds and broken up. The choicest "sticks" were reserved for masts, and the rest sawn into whatever lengths and widths the market demanded: balks, planks, deals, battens. Lumber was originally sawn laboriously by hand, but productivity was stepped up manyfold when Dutch and German wind- and water-driven multiframe mills were established, each with up to 10 multiple blades per frame. As these had already diffused further east into the Finnish/Russian towns such as Narva, Nyen, and Viborg by 1700 and Fredikshamn and Helsingfors by 1710, they must have been adopted in the main south Baltic milling centers before that date. The timber was loaded into comparatively small ships of 250 to 400 tons that drew shallow drafts and were preferred because of the many offshore spits and bars in the shallow and sandy Baltic ports.[90] The whole system was a precursor of the timber transportation that evolved in North America during the eighteenth century.

Each river had a major transshipment port at its estuary, and each tapped specific supplies in its hinterland. The Stettin trade along the Oder and Warta was almost exclusively oak from central Germany and even Silesia, but fragmented political control upstream hindered development, and it was both easier and less costly for Prussia to transport lumber from Mazovia and Lithuania. The Danzig trade along the Vistula reached into Galicia and even the Carpathian edge, from where both oak and fir were obtained. Riga on the Drina specialized in masts from Livonia and later from as far east as Vitebsk, and with connecting canals it could draw on the fir and oak from as far south as Volhynia and the Ukraine on the Dnieper beyond Kiev, from where the famous "Riga wainscot" came. Memel on the Neimen was developed in the eighteenth century to exploit the areas of oak and fir not reached from either the Vistula or Drina. St. Petersburg traded almost exclusively in fir; what little oak existed was used by the Russian navy.[91]

For over three hundred years these forests had been repeatedly cut over and culled for large mast timbers, so that by the sixteenth and seventeenth centuries, when the huge demands of the Dutch, English, and French navies came into being, the wave of exploitation was forced eastward into the less disturbed forests of the Russian borderland, and especially Finland. This shift is borne out by table 7.4, which for the sake of completeness is taken beyond our period of concern to 1785. Up until 1760 the Baltic stays dominant in

Table 7.4 Imports of masts into Britain for selected periods, 1706–1785

Period	Source	Diameter			Source As % of Total for Period
		Great (18″+)	Middling (12″–18″)	Small (8″–12″)	
1706–7	B	1,168	1,606	579	98.6
	A	48	–	–	1.4
1718–27	B	6,028	8,879	20,056	84.3
	A	2,615	1,148	2,748	15.7
1744–45	B	1,595	999	1,128	89.9
	A	419	–	–	10.1
1759–60	B	1,309	1,876	2,648	88.0
	A	603	127	58	12.0
1766–70	B	5,814	1,813	4,245	27.0
	A	3,910	2,206	2,520	20.0
	N	166	8,687	13,781	53.0
1771–75	B	8,644	3,161	3,125	25.7
	A	3,833	2,131	1,508	13.0
	N	205	10,494	17,470	61.3
1776–80	B	17,371	1,722	3,433	39.3
	A	289	596	397	2.2
	N	584	134,474	19,553	58.5
1781–85	B	5,369	3,928	3,329	23.6
	A	4,188	1,206	6,274	21.8
	N	444	12,262	16,515	54.6

Sources: Malone, 1964: 399; Lord, 1989: app. B; Albion, 1926: 283.
Note: B = Baltic; A = America; N = Norway.

the mast trade, supplying over 84 percent of all sizes of masts in every year; but it is noticeable that a substantial number of the "great sticks" of over 18 inches in diameter were coming from North America. After 1760 two things happen: total imports increase manyfold, with the bulk of the smaller spares coming from Norway, which could not be blockaded, and only the irreplaceable "greats" coming from the Baltic, which by this time meant almost exclusively Russia and its territories, and shipped mainly out of Riga. North America also supplied many "great sticks," but the War of Independence during the 1770s caused a dent in whatever trade there was. We do not know the situation for the Dutch and French mast imports, but presumably they must have followed a similar pattern.[92]

Paralleling the mast trade was the trade in the vital and strategic naval stores of pitch and tar, which came primarily from the Finnish forests and the pine forests of South Carolina. The geography of their production and trade is complex; what we do know is that in northern Europe, the prime area of extraction was in "Old Finland," deep in the hinterland of Viborg; but when Finland lost that territory to Russia in 1720 the Russians ceased producing tar in favor of timber. Then the focus of production shifted to the Bothnian coast, and as supplies of suitable trees diminished, production shifted further and further inland and up the river valleys.[93]

The efforts to procure masts and naval stores, and find substitutes for these in North America, has always tended to overshadow the very substantial imports into northwest Europe from both the southern Baltic lands and Scandinavia of timbers other than those vital to naval strategy. General sawn timber imports were not a new phenomenon of the eighteenth century; during the great boom in domestic building in England in the sixteenth century, Baltic oak paneling, or "wainscot" (which referred to the way oak logs were shipped from Danzig and Riga with two sides hewn flat to save space in the hold), estriches (East Reichs), and spruce (from "sprusia," an Old English corruption of Prussia) were common, and deals, the 12-inch planking so common in English houses built before 1880, are mentioned frequently. The need to rebuild more than half of London after the Great Fire of 1666 resulted in massive felling in Norway, so much so that it was said that the Norwegian merchants "warmed themselves well at the fire."[94]

But substantial amounts of constructional timber continued to come from Norway after 1666 via Drammen, Longsound, and Fredrikstad, where rivers reached the sea. In addition, contrary to all that was known before, exports of sawn timber came from the northern Bothnian-facing provinces of Sweden, with most of the overseas trade being funnelled through Stockholm and Kalmar. Between 1685 and 1760 it increased over sixfold and Sweden rapidly replaced the southern Baltic ports as a source of supply for western Europe.[95] It was one of the ironies of the age that because of the shortage of large timber for house construction, brick and plaster were used instead. Yet it probably took more wood to bake the bricks and burn the lime than was needed to erect a timber house. It was only with the substitution of coal for wood fuel that the drain on the forests was halted.[96]

The full flowering of the Baltic timber trade in the eighteenth century is considered later, but the important point here is that lumber was so indispensable a commodity that it was worth moving a great distance. The idea that a mast felled in the central Russian forest might be shipped to a naval yard in the Caribbean in order to refit a vessel at a distant station seems exotic, but because of its strategic and unique value we have become accustomed to it. But the idea that crude, unsawn lumber ("fir timber") might make al-most as great a journey is rarely appreciated. It was not as if lumber were a high-value product; perhaps the nearest comparable commodity moved in bulk was wheat, and that was anything between 4 and 6 times more valuable than sawn lumber and 10 to 12 times more valuable than logs per unit weight—and even wheat was said not to be worth mov-ing if the price was low. That lumber continued to be moved around the world irrespec-tive of its bulkiness and low per-unit value was a measure of its essential nature. It is salu-tary to think that prosaic English drawing rooms constructed in the late sixteenth century were paneled with oak that came from Silesia and Galicia, and occasionally with "Riga wainscot," oak that came from Kazan on the Russian forest-steppe edge. Timber had turned the bulk trade of the world upside down.

PLUNDER, PRESERVATION, AND PLANTING

Generally, the human modifications of the earth that took place during the seventeenth and early eighteenth centuries seemed to be a fulfilment and vindication of Francis Bacon's prophesy that "all things seem to be going about man's business and not their own." Hu-man actions seemed beneficent, and optimism prevailed. But the forests appeared to be an exception; the plundering of their timber threatened their very existence (plate 7.6A–D). And yet, how to stop that destruction defied solution, as the economic necessity for tim-ber and fuel overrode concern. Advances in knowledge and crop-cultivation methods were discussed, disseminated, and acted upon, but the idea that the same principles might be applied to trees—that trees were a crop—was a much rarer notion. "Wood," said George Louis-Leclerc, comte de Buffon, "appears to be a present from nature," and most people thought that they had to do "no more . . . but to receive it, just as it comes out of her hand."[97] The simplest methods of preserving forests and increasing their produce were still largely unknown, and he spoke with some knowledge as the Keeper of the Jardin de Roi in Paris.

Generally speaking, Buffon was correct in his observation, though there were notable exceptions. For example, measures had been taken in places to ensure supplies of partic-ular types of wood for shipbuilding, and also for fuel for local metal-smelting needs. In addition, a completely new element entered into the forest picture during the course of the seventeenth century, arising from a desire on the part of the English aristocracy to plant trees for a "complex mixture of social assertiveness, aesthetic sense, patriotism, and long-term profit."[98] In time, this new, multistranded motivation was to have a far-reaching influence on attitudes toward the forest in many parts of the world.

Preservation

During the fifteenth and sixteenth centuries, Venice had to confront the problem of di-minishing timber supplies for shipbuilding, leading to some of the first known measures to preserve the forest. In 1470 it reserved oak forests in Friuli and Istria, and fir trees in the upper Adige and Cadore; but inevitably, so it seemed, this policy led to dispute, eva-sion, and resentment from villagers, who long had rights in the forests, and private ship-

Plate 7.6 The consequences of deforestation, 1601. In this uniquely early set of sketches of a hypothetical mountain, Giuseppe Paulini, a forestland owner at Belluno in the mountains northwest of Venice, graphically portrayed the sequence and consequence of deforestation, especially as it affected the siltation of the Venetian lagoon. *A*, the tree-covered mountain in its pre-exploitation state. The runoff was slight and controlled. *B*, logging and fuel gathering denude the lower slopes. *C*, shepherds and agriculturalists fire the remaining forest to enrich the herbage and the soil. *D*, the hill is denuded of trees. At this point, the lack of vegetation and humus causes a rapid runoff and snowmelt. The water sweeps away the topsoil, damages the pastures, and carries huge deposits to Venice which silt up the lagoon. G. Paulini, *Un Codice Veneziano dell 1600 per le Acque e le Foreste.* (Originals in Venice State Archives.)

builders, who had previously profited from felling. The policy failed to replenish the timber supply and, in fact, may even have hastened timber destruction by the peasants who thought the possession of oak trees would become a burden due to the obligation placed on them to move timber at the arsenal's command. A complete survey and mapping of oak forests was completed in 1568, and from then until 1660 the policy was more rigidly enforced in what were, in effect, state forests. The stock of oaks grew, especially in the Val di Livenza in the foothills north and west of Istria, and in the Alpine foothills in the Val di Montona, and Montello of Treviso. But this "enlightened conception of forests management," in which the trees were regarded as a crop to be cultivated under a definite

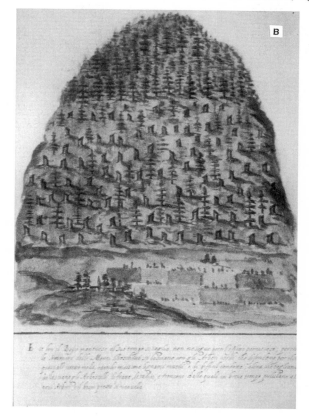

plan, rather than a mine to be exploited, was never pushed to its conclusion. It needed more policing than the state was willing to sanction, and in any case the decline of Venice as a maritime power and the availability of Baltic supplies effectively took all the resolve out of it.[99]

One moderately successful manipulation of the forest on a sustained, long-term basis came with the iron industry in Britain. The ironmasters had learned the hard way that indiscriminate cutting was a waste of their investment in furnaces and foundries, which had to close if fuelwood supplies ran out. Coppicing and crop rotation were extensive to maintain a constant supply of fuel. It was claimed in one petition that 200,000 acres in the Weald alone was so managed, and it must have been more widespread than that.[100]

Signs of purposeful, corrective action to counteract the unplanned and unsought consequences of environmental modification did not come about until the publication of Evelyn's *Sylva: Or, A Discourse of Forest Trees* (1664) and the French Forest Ordinance of 1669, associated with Colbert.[101] Both were prompted by the perceived dearth of naval timber. For Clarence Glacken, these two works represent a "divide" that separated centuries of abuse from a recognition of the need for forest conservation; they were also

"harbingers of more complex and more widely distributed conflicts." [102] Evelyn's *Sylva* was an appeal for a scientific approach to forest conservation and for a proper understanding of the competing demands of industry, agriculture, and forests. It abounds with technical details on planting, grafting, and other arboricultural advice, and was a plea to the nobility to plant oaks. But in a broader sense it was less a forest manual and more an appeal for the rational use of all land, forest or not. Portions of the royal forests were reserved and some planting went on, but the government lacked all *esprit de suite* and the program of planting lapsed by the end of the century.

The Ordinance of 1669 was different in purpose and design to *Sylva*. It sought to rationalize and codify the mass of ancient French forest law, which had become confused and unworkable, and to make forestry an autonomous branch of the state economy while ensuring the supply of timber for the navy. It was designed for the royal forests but was soon being applied to all forestland—ecclesiastical, community, and private. The details of this long document are less important than its general purpose and the fact that it was widely copied throughout continental Europe. It stipulated that kilns, furnaces, and charcoal making were to be restricted in forests, and a range of other woodworking

occupations—such as coopers, tanners, woodworkers—had to be located at least 1.5 mi (2.4 km) away from the forest edge. Cattle, sheep, and goat grazing was absolutely prohibited in forests, pannage was regulated annually by common agreement, and large trees and seed-bearing trees (the "stallions," or *balliveaux*) were marked and reserved.[103] Not unnaturally the restrictions and severe penalties imposed for infringement of the ordinance did not commend it to the mass of people, who lost privileges and individual freedoms, but the forests did prosper, or certainly got no worse.

Over most of politically fragmented Germany, forestry was still largely subordinate to hunting, but where mining was important, forest planning became a necessity by the eighteenth century. In 1713, Hans von Carlowitz, the chief mining official in Saxony, published his *Silvicultura Oeconimica* and recommended the planting of fast-growing conifers in order to replenish stocks, a policy that eventually spread through Silesia and Moravia. In the more western political units of Hesse-Darmstadt, Kassel, and Mainz, deciduous trees were favored, and many other experiments were conducted elsewhere. W. Gottfried von Moser's *Grundsätze der Forstökonomie* (Principles of forest economy) of 1757 was a landmark publication in forest science, and by the latter half of the eighteenth century a spate of forest manuals appeared. Forestry was consequently taught to cameral officials (princely advisers) as part of their science and administrative coursework in half a dozen universities.[104] These were the foundations of the reputation that Germany soon acquired throughout the world for the rational and scientific study of trees, and the development of a sustained yield from even-aged woodlands.[105]

Planting

In the preface to the 1679 edition of *Sylva,* Evelyn boasts that several million trees had been planted as a result of his book; but while its publication certainly raised awareness of the desirability of tree planting, there is reason to believe that the trend had begun earlier.[106] The reasons for planting (plate 7.7) were primarily economic. It paid well to grow large trees, if one could wait the fifty or more years it took for them to mature. Trees were a bankable asset that could be realized in times of emergency to pay unforeseen debts, as, for example, had the prodigal earl of Northumberland in 1536 who had run up a debt of £17,000, so "the axe was put to the tree" on his estates near Petworth.[107] Elsewhere, tree planting was an economic necessity for the continuance of industry. But along with these practical arguments for planting and preserving the woodland went other, less utilitarian considerations. Ever since medieval times the forests had been the hunting grounds of royalty, and large areas of the country were preserved for the recreational use of the few. Hunting, and the possession of the ground in which it could be undertaken, became an important symbol of social rank, and large landowners emulated the privileges of royalty by creating their own private deer parks, so that by the time Saxton had drawn his maps of Elizabethan England there were over 800 of them. During the period of rising prices during the sixteenth and seventeenth centuries, many of the deer reserves or parks were converted to grazing ground for cattle and sheep, but those that remained became more ornamental and nonutilitarian as the owners displayed their wealth and power by re-fashioning the landscape, mainly through planting trees. In this way the deer parks and the royal forests engendered a more "enduring reason for tree conservation, namely the belief that wood added beauty and dignity to the scene."[108] This belief was the genesis of the famed English landscaped park or garden.

To look favorably on trees as an element of landscape was a crucial point somewhere between the second and the third phases of the transition of attitudes toward trees depicted by Keith Thomas—between that of exploitation and fond appreciation. It was not that the first phase of taming and eliminating trees was over, or that the exploitation of useful trees was not still taking place; it was merely that these actions were now paralleled by a different set of values and aspirations that were to grow stronger as time progressed.

It is possible to see two strands in this development of a love of trees—or silvaphilia, if one may call it that—one rural, mentioned already in relation to the beautifying of deer parks, the other urban. In the urban sphere the cult of walking and promenading as a social exercise gathered momentum after the Restoration of Charles II in 1660, and where better to do it than along formally laid out tree-lined walks and avenues modeled on Continental examples? Fairly rapidly, the London parks and the gardens of Oxford and Cambridge colleges were transformed, and in due course

Plate 7.7 Reforestation. From G. Agricola, *A Philosophical Treatise on Husbandry*, 1721. On the left, tree stumps are being grubbed out; in the foreground, portions of roots and saplings are being prepared for replanting in pits that are protected by shields, seen on the hills in the background and to the left. (William Adams Clark Memorial Library, UCLA.)

virtually every town of any social pretension became prepared to vote money for a walk or avenue where local beaux and belles might stroll up and down under the trees to display their best clothes and exchange gossip, as a sort of outdoor assembly room.[109]

Whereas the Romans had taken off their clothes and used great quantities of wood at the baths in order to meet socially, the English donned their best clothes and planted a great number of trees to do the same.

In the country, trees were planted in hedgerows and thousands of acres of orchards established, but above all it was the scale of planting on the country estates that was so extraordinary (plate 7.8). Landowners vied with each other in the complexity and extent of their plantings of ornamental clumps and radiating avenues of trees, and in so doing

Plate 7.8 The cult of trees: "wood added beauty and dignity to the scene." Blenheim Palace, near Oxford, England, and its park, looking northwest. Built during the early eighteenth century, Blenheim was larger than most country houses. It was a gift from a grateful nation to John Churchill, first duke of Marlborough, for his decisive military victories over the French between 1704 and 1709. (Simmons Aerofilms Limited.)

subjected the surrounding countryside to the impress of the authority of the landowner himself. Trees became the way to conceal, extend, ameliorate, enhance, or otherwise manipulate the view from the great country house, and in that process to "appropriate" the view, and ultimately, one must add, the people.[110] Trees even had a symbolic, patriotic quality in that after the depredations caused by felling during the republican era of the Commonwealth, to plant trees was to express publicly and visually the planter's loyalty to the restored monarchy.[111]

From now on, trees could not be regarded simply as evidence of barbarism and a cause of savagery, nor purely as useful objects in nature. Through a complex mixture of social assertiveness, aesthetic sense, patriotism, and long-term profit, they had become, as Thomas says, "an indispensable part of the scenery of upper-class life." The important point is that here was one of the first manifestations of the value shift from extirpation, through utilitarianism, to aesthetic appreciation and a love of trees, so that ultimately trees achieved "an almost pet-like status." [112] In future years, more and more people across a broader social spectrum of the population would find pleasure in and revere trees, so that they would not only plant new ones but preserve the old—thereby starting a revolution in how the forest was viewed and used.

Chapter 8

The Wider World, 1500–1750

Hee that commaunds the sea, commaunds the trade, and hee that is Lord of the Trade of the world is lord of the wealth of the worlde.
—SIR WALTER RALEGH (ca. 1603)

The internal Americas were not enough.
—IMMANUEL WALLERSTEIN, *The Modern World System I* (1974)

Such are the means by which North-America, which one hundred years ago was nothing but a vast forest, is peopled with three million inhabitants. Four years ago, one might have travelled ten miles in the woods I traversed, without seeing a single habitation.
—MARQUIS DE CHASTELLUX, *Travels in North America* (1789)

BY THE OPENING of the sixteenth century, Europe was not the world, but it was certainly the most dynamic and potentially powerful part of it. With bursting social energy and surging economies a few countries broke out of their national confines and began to utilize the resources of the wider world. The processes of conquest, colonization, and terrestrial and cultural transformation that had created the European landscape and society during the latter Middle Ages were now applied abroad. The European Christians who sailed to the coasts of the Americas, Asia, and Africa already understood the problems of and the solutions to the settlement of new lands, learned through long apprenticeship in places like Iberia, eastern Europe, and Ireland. In addition to knowledge and techniques went an ability, suggests Robert Bartlett, to maintain cultural identity "through legal forms and nurtured attitudes, the institutions and outlook required to confront the strange or abhorrent, to repress it and live with it, the law and religion, as well as the guns and the ships."[1] The expansion was all part of what Walter Prescott Webb called the "Great Frontier" of European outward expansion, particularly in the New World, which gave it unprecedented windfalls of land, minerals, timber, and crops, as well as fish and furs. As this unmatched flow of abundant and cheap resources gathered momentum "the expansive process of land transformation in the modern world began," of which deforestation was a major part.[2]

But there were some places that the Europeans did not affect at this time. In the Asian realm of the Old World—China, Japan, and to a much lesser extent India—they remained "outsiders," and different forces were at work in these regions. In China the Treaty Ports had little effect on life inland and existed, in Richard Tawney's words, as "a fringe stitched along the hem of an ancient garment"; Japan was barely penetrated until 1865. Even the bulk of India, which was to become the model of successful western expansion in Asia, remained untouched beyond the hinterlands of Bombay, Madras, and Calcutta.[3] While external influence was restricted to the few trading points along the coasts, indigenous, internally generated change was enormous. The populations of these countries were growing rapidly, so more land was needed for food production. Large-scale forest clearance and lowland reclamation were undertaken in nearby territories as new land was "made" to accommodate the growing population and increasing urban complexity of life, and trees were cut for fuel and timber. The forest experience of China during the sixteenth and seventeenth centuries was probably more akin to Europe during the Middle Ages than to anywhere else. That of Japan, however, was unique in every way.

Although the penetration of the wider world began about 1500, it took about another 150 years for the Europeans to grasp the real novelty of the "New World."[4] The first colonists were obsessed with precious metals, the creation of landed estates, the right to collect revenues, and the sharing out of spoils—the *ecomienda*—as well as the conversion of the natives to Christianity. On the whole these activities did not greatly affect the forest. But when later colonists grasped the significance of the productive capabilities of the land they had occupied and the possibilities of trade, the impact became much greater. Perhaps the proverb of the Dutch colonial latecomers when they compared themselves to their Spanish predecessors summed it up well: "Jesus Christ is good, but trade is better." Step by step the Europeans advanced westward via the Atlantic islands, Brazil, the Caribbean, and the mainland of the Americas. Technical superiority and cultural assurance were critical in this expansion, but so too was disease, the harbinger of the new "ecological imperialism."

"ECOLOGICAL IMPERIALISM"
Disease

Before the late sixteenth century, sea contact around the globe was not very important, and the continents were relatively isolated one from another; it was a world of separate peoples. It is true that long-distance oceanic voyages were being undertaken by mercantile-maritime communities; the exploits of Cheng Ho to India and East Africa, and generally within the south China seas were an example of this.[5] But in the larger intercontinental picture the significant developments were the forays of Breton fishermen to the Grand Banks off Newfoundland for their harvest of cod, and the exploration by Spanish and Portuguese sailors down the coast of Africa and out to the Atlantic islands of the Canaries, Azores, and Madeira. They found, and got to know, the currents and winds of these regions, which, compared with those elsewhere in the world, were remarkably constant and reliable. The Northeast Trade Winds *did* carry them from Europe and down

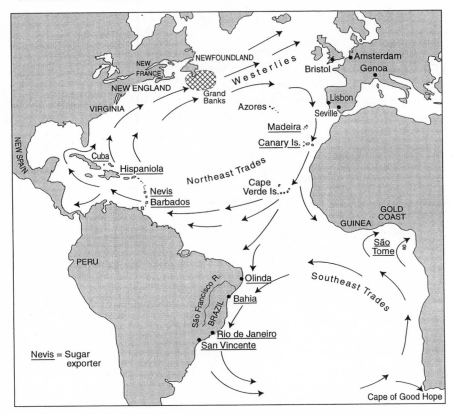

Figure 8.1 Circuits and stepping-stones across the Atlantic. *Source:* after Galloway, 1989: 49.

the coast of Africa to the Canaries and thence on to the Caribbean, and the return voyage *could* be made northward via the Westerlies and the strong sea currents, provided they first sailed northwestward in order to pick up the wind. Simply, environmental conditions aided long sea voyages from Europe to the Americas and back again, or hindered them elsewhere (fig. 8.1).[6]

Because of the assured accessibility and contact that the winds and currents gave, fresh infusions of people and supplies from the Old World were reasonably reliable, enhancing the success of the settlement process. But by the same token too, there was an equally unfailing, constant, and unrelenting infusion of biological forces, such as plants, animals, and above all diseases, which gave an overwhelming advantage to the invaders. It was, says Alfred Crosby, an "ecological imperialism" far more effective and far more terrible than an imperialism of arms.[7]

Europeans carried with them many pathogens to which the native population had no immunity. This had been evident earlier in the small island communities, like the Canaries, but it was also true of the continental Americas. For all their vastness the Americas were no more than "an enormous island" compared with the Old World, as their long isolation had excluded exposure to a whole range of Old World epidemic diseases (many of which had evolved with domesticated animals) and to which Europeans were all but immune. With these Old World pathogens the native populations met their "most hideous enemy."[8] Each new European contact brought a new wave of diseases: first influenza, smallpox, measles, which were particularly virulent and deadly, and then mumps and pneumonic plague, followed later by diphtheria, trachoma, whooping cough, chicken pox, malaria, typhoid fever, cholera, yellow fever, and scarlet fever.

The evidence is fragmentary but abundant, and it parallels the well-documented experience of the susceptibility of isolated peoples in more recent times. The first manifestation of the debilitating effect of disease occurred in the Canaries, where resistance by the native Guanches to Spanish conquest suddenly buckled during the 1480s and was overcome by 1495.[9] Then it reached its apogee in the Americas, where each new pandemic not only displaced or eliminated hundreds of cultural groups, but led to the cumulative effect of a total demographic collapse. Needless to say, all resistance to conquest was undermined. William Denevan estimates conservatively that the population for the hemisphere was 53.9 million in 1492, but only 5.6 million in 1650, a 89-percent drop; and that in North America it fell from 3.8 million in 1492 to approximately 1 million in 1800, a 74-percent drop.[10] Others would put the original population total for the hemisphere much higher at between 100 and 113 million, which would merely make the decline even more dramatic.[11] Whatever the exact numbers the fact remains that depopulation did happen on a catastrophic level. Metal weapons—to say nothing of gunpowder and horses (the Amerinds had none of these), though decisive in campaigns, were nothing compared to the biological advantages possessed by Columbus and those who followed him. "It was their germs, not the imperialists themselves, for all their brutality and callousness, that were chiefly responsible for sweeping aside the indigenes and opening the Neo-Europes to demographic takeover."[12] One could say, fancifully, that they triumphed through breath alone.

Plants and Animals

Over 50 million people cannot exist without altering their surroundings, often markedly. Aboriginal numbers in the forests of the Americas were such that densities were causing major faunal changes in certain places. Quite contrary to the denial of contemporary environmentalists, romantics, Native Americans, and marxists, the New World was not a pristine wilderness.[13] By the same token, however, the loss of up to 90 percent of the population also led to massive changes. Like depopulations everywhere, the widespread abandonment of agricultural land led to an increase in forest extent and density, so that by 1750 America was probably more forested than it had been in 1492.

In the short term, however, the upshot was that as the population was eliminated already cleared fields—and even at times, growing crops of nutritious plants such as squash, tomatoes, potatoes, and maize—were available to the newcomers. Both were a major factor in the colonists' ability to gain a successful toehold on the continent. In fact, they thought this bounty was part of a divine punishment on heathens and a God-given reward for their endeavors: said Governor John Winthrop of Massachussetts, "For the natives they are all neere dead of small Poxe, so as the Lord hathe cleared our title to what we possess." Little wonder a settler in tidewater Virginia could say, not altogether disingenuously, many years later:

> The objection that the country is overgrown by woods, and consequently not in many years to be penetrable for the plow, carried a great feebleness with it for there is an immense quantity of Indian fields cleared ready to hand by the natives, which, till we are grown overpopulous, may be every way abundantly sufficient.[14]

While nutritious food crops were readily used, other flora and fauna disappeared and were replaced by opportunistic and aggressive Old World varieties. From the St. Lawrence to the Rio de la Plate, ferns, thistles, nettles, artichokes, and plantain (weeds we would call them), as well as the more common grasses and clovers such as bluegrass and white clover, found eco-niches on the bared and eroded ground of abandoned Amerind fields or new European clearings. Plants moved with feral stock in advance of people. In more tropical locations, as in the Caribbean, soils were changed as the humus layer was leached or destroyed, with detrimental long-term effects.[15]

The ecological advantage of the Europeans over the indigenes, however, was not so much a matter of crop plants as of domesticated animals. Their multiplication was prolific, as they ran wild in a world without natural predators and competitors. In particular, pigs flourished in forested environments; they are omnivorous, and healthy sows can have litters of 10 or more piglets. The 8 pigs brought by Columbus to Hispaniola in 1492 multiplied prodigiously in the wild, spreading to mainland Mexico during the late 1490s and soon said by the Spanish to be "infinitos." Cattle were said to multiply tenfold in 3 or 4 years. Horses adapted more slowly, as did sheep. Slower they may have been, but the rate of increase was unimpeded. These feral goats, sheep, horses, pigs, mules, and cattle were the forerunners and forebears of the millions that were to populate the land from the prairies in the north to the pampas in the south. Felix Azara, an unusually keen observer of natural phenomena, calculated that the numbers of cattle in the pampas had reached 48 million in 1700—perhaps an exaggeration, but even if he got it only half, or even quarter, right, it was still a staggering number.[16]

All stock had a devastating effect on the land because of the need to create pastures and hence partially or permanently clear land, a process that had not been a part of the native economy. Stock also prevented tree regrowth by nibbling young shoots, trampling and overgrazing land, causing erosion, and, incidentally, in so doing, aiding the spread of Old World crops and weeds. Old World stock seemed to do well, if not better, in their New World situations than in their homeland, and the Europeans benefited with better nutrition.

The breaking down of the biological isolation of the continents that had existed for millennia, and the replacement of one vegetation cover by another, was the supreme example of what Columbus's voyages really meant. Although the immigrant settlers had no understanding of epidemiology, processes were set in motion and soon augmented by many purposeful changes as large areas of the earth's surface were cleared of their vegetation and either cultivated or grazed more intensively. Within 250 years, virtually all land uses, land covers, and biota in the Atlantic islands and the Americas had, or were in the process of, being changed dramatically, particularly the most prized land cover of all, the forests.[17]

STEPPING-STONES AND CIRCUITS TO THE NEW WORLD
The Atlantic Islands

Tropical islands had long held a peculiar fascination for the European mind as a part of the myth of tropical exuberance. Not only were they sources of exotic products, but they were also perceived as island Edens. The Portuguese voyages of the fifteenth century stimulated the perpetual fascination over the location of the biblical Garden of Eden, which "was removed from a distant past to a distant present, from something remote in time to something far away, but still conceivably discoverable." A literary tradition that stretched from Shakespeare's *The Tempest* and the poetry of Andrew Marvell, and subsequently to the novels of Daniel Defoe and Jean-Jacques Rousseau, bestowed tropical islands with a symbolic significance.[18] They became paradisal utopias, idealized as places of plenty, and microcosms of a seemingly simplified and less sophisticated society. Paradoxically, they were also an allegory of the whole world. If Paradise could not be attained in a tropical island, then it was recreated and encapsulated in the botanical garden, an encyclopedia of common and exotic plants displayed in the open or under glass for all to see. Such gardens began to appear throughout Europe from the sixteenth century onward.[19]

Although not truly tropical, for the European expansionists the three archipelagos of the Azores, Madeira, and Canaries in the eastern Atlantic were some or all of these things, but more importantly and practically, they were stepping-stones on the way to the New World. By 1420 the occupation of Madeira was complete; by 1429 the Azores was occupied; and by 1492 resistance in the heavily populated Canaries was all but over. The Cape Verde Islands, São Tomé, and the islands of the Caribbean were added in time (see fig. 8.1). The first three were like "pilot programs" of colonization and acted as precedents for the new settlement and plantation colonies that were to come; the lessons learned were to last for centuries.[20] Although not extensive, these pinpricks in the ocean had a significance out of all proportion to the size. They experienced intense change in a remarkably short period of time, and were microcosms of how the new, alien, commercial objectives of the Europeans, serving a worldwide market, unleashed a whole host of ecological and biogeographical changes, and of how places were changed through clearing, stocking, planting, and generally rationalizing the landscape for production.

The insatiable demand for sugar in Europe was the key to the settlers' success by providing a source of export income. The significance of sugar was far reaching; geographically it became an instrument of expansion and "a means of both financing colonial endeavours as well as a motive for the occupation of yet more territory." Its cultivation also led to extensive forest clearing, for growing both the crop and the food for the workers that tended it, as well for the fuel needed to refine it.[21] One by one the Atlantic islands embraced the new crop, and their economies flourished wonderfully.

In Madeira the settlers found a lush vegetation: "there was not a foot of ground that was not entirely covered with great trees," hence the name given to it, *madeira,* meaning "wood." Despairing of their ability to clear enough land in time to get in food crops and sugar, they set fire to the forest, and so great was the conflagration that they had to take refuge in the sea, where they stayed for two days and two nights up to their necks until the blaze burned itself out. In subsequent years, lumbering for the highly prized furniture timbers went hand in hand with sugar cultivation.[22] But sugarcane raising is arduous, and in 1540 slaves were introduced (probably Guanches from the Canaries) to clear and cultivate the land and to construct and tend the irrigation system. Besides forest destruction for clearing plots, prodigious amounts of wood were used to boil and refine the cane. On the basis that each ton of sugar required about 100 m^3 of fuelwood, then some 1,500,000 m^3 of wood was being used per annum, which, depending on the density of the trees and their timber yield, translates into between approximately 2,500 to 4,000 ha of forest cut out per annum.[23]

In contrast, the Azores were too cool for sugar and some of the islands in the Canaries too dry, but not the upland slopes and northern sides of Tenerife and Grand Canaria. Although the evidence is hazy, it seems that a flourishing plantation sugar economy existed in these islands, peaking between 1520 and 1550. Far to the south, tropical São Tomé had more in common with the Caribbean islands. There was no indigenous population, Europeans were not encouraged to emigrate and work in such a hot, enervating climate, and there was an obvious shortage of labor. In what was to be a harbinger of a social system/mode of production that was to dominate the Americas in years to come, African slaves were imported in large numbers to service the plantations.[24]

In time all the Atlantic sugar islands succumbed to the lower-cost producers in the Americas. In addition, the scarcity and expense of fuel; the progressive deforestation of the islands that led to clearing on the high, steep mountain slopes away from the mills; and the almost inevitable accompanying soil exhaustion and erosion on steep slopes and reduction of runoff, particularly in Madeira and the Canaries—to say nothing of slave revolts in São Tomé—all undermined production. The space to engage in rotational fallows was not available, nor the space for extensive stock raising to produce animal manure for fertilizer. The islands were simply too small and their resources too limited for such a burgeoning and scourging agriculture. By 1550 Madeira abandoned the sugar crop and turned to viticulture to produce the sweet dessert wine for which it has become famous, and in the Canaries the industry dwindled to be replaced by banana growing. São Tomé lingered on, but painfully. The colonies on the Atlantic stepping-stones declined in the face of the massive production coming from Brazil, where land, fuel, and slaves were plentiful.

Brazil and the Caribbean

As the consumption of sugar diffused both down the social scale and outward spatially throughout Europe, all the new production from Brazil and the Caribbean was readily absorbed.[25] Compared with the relatively small area of forests on the Atlantic and Caribbean islands, those of Brazil were among the most extensive in the world. A vast subtropical rain forest of 780,000 km^2 stretched along the Atlantic coast from Recife (Pernambuco) in the north to Rio de Janeiro and St. Vincent in the south.[26]

The pre-Columbian Tupi-Guarani Amerind population of the forest practiced a shifting, slash-and-burn, swidden cultivation, and grew crops of manioc, maize, squash, beans, peppers, and peanuts. But by 1500 the Tupi were stricken by Western diseases and slave-raiding and were gradually replaced by a mestizo population. The concomitant introduction of iron axes and machetes and the herding of pigs and cattle intensified the pre-existing shifting regime. Whereas the Tupi swiddening might have cut and burned about 1 ha per family per annum, leaving the large trees untouched, the Europeanized mestizo was capable of cultivating 3 ha, or more if the soil was fertile, with his more efficient tools, and he cleared more thoroughly. The forest did not regenerate easily under such a regime, and the open ground left as a result of periodic shifting was colonized by exotic grasses, ferns, and weeds. In addition, selective logging for the brazilwood *(Caesalpinia echinata)*, a source of dye, caused widespread destruction along riverbanks and the coast.[27] In some places this logging was the first step in the establishment of export-oriented plantation sugar.

Sugar was introduced from Madeira in about 1560, and cultivation was concentrated in a narrow coastal strip in the northeast that focused on Pernambuco, Sergipe, and Bahia, with a minor concentration around Espirito Santo and Rio de Janeiro in the south. Considering sugar "ruled" Brazil and provided the context for so many aspects of life for well over a hundred years, it is surprising that so little information survives about its extent and methods of cultivation. As in all cases where industry impinges on the forest, there are far more detailed descriptions of the process of refining, rolling, and boiling at the mill or *engenho* (and of the social life of the *senhor de engenho*) than of the more familiar and mundane agricultural tasks. Despite the many paintings and etchings of mills, especially during the Dutch period of occupation around Olinda in the northeast from 1630–54, there is only one crude drawing of an *engenho* in which the cane fields are also represented, though with over a dozen of the imposing residences, with their outhouses, mills, and unloading bays. Nevertheless, it is clear that primary forest was always favored for planting, the clearing done by ax, hoe, mattocks, and fire by slaves who were expected to clear 6.6 m² a day. Local practices for stump removal tended to affect this norm; grubbing out was common in Bahia and slowed the rate of clearing. Plows were rarely used to open up the soil, but gangs of hoe-wielding slaves worked in rows, falling back together and repeating the process through all the daylight hours until the field was turned up. Then the cane was planted in trenches, and after three or more periodic weedings the crop would mature and smother weeds by shading them out, and after about 18 months would be ready for cutting and harvesting. At every stage it was backbreaking, arduous, repetitive work that was accompanied by force and brutality, and mortality among the slaves was high.[28]

Because no thought was given to replenishing soil, fertility yields declined, but since cane is a fast-growing grass, it could be left in the ground for multiple cuttings and burned periodically in order to boost the yield. In time, however, the yield fell so low that the field was abandoned to pasture, a cycle that took between 12 and 15 years. New areas were cleared and cultivation moved on, destroying more forest.[29] Erosion on steeper slopes was also a major problem and contributed to declining yield. Sugar growing was a system of profligate use based on abundant resources of land and labor.

Demands on the forest were not confined to clearing the land for cultivation alone, as extreme heat was required for boiling the cane syrup in order to crystallize it. The supply of firewood was a central concern and expense, amounting to about 20 percent of operating costs, and only occasionally exceeded by the cost of slaves. There are various measures of the amount of wood used, with between fifteen and twenty tarefas of wood to produce ten tarefas of sugar the approximate output of 1 to 2 mills—another rule of thumb being that crystalizing 1 metric ton of cane required at least 100 m^3 of wood, and some would put it as much as 4 times higher. If anything, cutting for the mills caused more destruction than cutting to clear ground. Certainly clearing did not contribute to fuelwood, as the normal practice was to make planks for sugar crates out of the larger trees; "otherwise," said an eighteenth century observer, José da Silva Lisboa, "all is reduced to ash. . . . The smaller, remaining firewood is piled into mounds called *coviras* and fire is set to them until all the wood is consumed."[30]

By the first decade of the seventeenth century, there were over 140 *engenhos* in the northeast, and readily available fuel supplies were becoming a problem that got progressively worse as the number rose to 180 by 1758. Measures of this deteriorating situation were the illegal cutting on neighbors' property, the relocation of plantations to be nearer forested areas, the cessation of sugar refining for weeks on end, the relocation of *engenhos* to river sites in order to increase the range of wood collection, and the late seventeenth-century decree that mills were not to be built within half a league (3.3 km) of each other, which was rarely observed. The appetite for fuel at the mills was voracious, and the use of bagasse (cane stalks left after pressing) for this purpose, common in the Caribbean, did not become widespread in Brazil until the next century. In the meantime, the forests were under pressure, though the crisis was more one of accessibility than availability.[31]

The sugar industry was responsible for other clearing, as the need for oxen for carting, as well as for providing tallow for candles and meat for employees, encouraged wide-ranging cattle ranching in land in the serato, especially along the São Francisco River. Ranches were often large, exceeding 100,000 acres (approximately 41,500 ha), or 20,000 head of cattle, though usually smaller; and total numbers of cattle reached over 1.3 million by 1600. Most of the time the cattle ranged freely through the forest, altering its composition by nibbling and trampling. But around the ranch headquarters the forest was fired indiscriminately to improve feed and cleared to provide pastures and arable land.[32]

The Brazilian sugar industry was inefficient, and it wilted under the rising cost of slaves (plate 8.1) and competition from the Caribbean as the English, Dutch, and French founded their own sugar colonies in order to secure supplies of what had become both a lucrative and almost strategic crop. Locally, the discovery of gold in Minas Gerais caused a great out-migration of white and black residents alike, although the distinctive slave-sugar society on the coast lingered on into the nineteenth century. The center of gravity had now moved to the Caribbean islands, mainly in the English colonies of the little islands of Barbados and St. Nevis, where trading companies sponsored settlers on the land in order to grow sugar and stimulate trade.[33]

Although the vegetation of the individual Caribbean islands varied in detail, most had a fairly dense cover of subtropical species, with a dense, many-layered canopy of trees and lianas, which became denser in the higher center of the small islands. They were, said Andrew White, "growne over wth trees and undershrubs without any passage, except where the planters have cleared." Jamaica was larger and more lushly tropical; it also had extensive savannas "which . . . were sometimes fields of Indian Maize or Wheat, which when the Spaniards became Masters of the Isle, they converted to pasture for the feeding of their Cattel,"[34] which certainly referred to depopulation and abandonment due to disease.

Plate 8.1 A water-powered *engenho* (sugar mill) with slaves at work, Olinda, Brazil, by Frans Post, mid-seventeenth century. From Joaquim de Sousa-Leão, *Frans Post, 1612–1680* (Amsterdam: A. L. van Gendt, 1973), 150. (University of Wisconsin.)

The growing of tobacco, cotton, and sugar crops for trade, and of food crops for survival, were the aims of the new settlements, and the first season was a scramble to find food. From Barbados, the message went back to England to send able-bodied axmen with "working tools, to cut down the woods, and clear the ground." When they came, patches of forest were selected and tall trees removed either by clear-cutting or ringbarking, followed by the burning of the dried-out debris and trees toward the end of the dry season. It was essential that "every hand employ'd therein must be furnished with an Axe, a Saw, and other Instruments for felling Timber, and grubbing up it Roots." Soon, more systematic clearing got under way and vast swathes were cleared in the dense coastal semitropical forests, but as Richard Ligon, an early settler commented,

> the woods were so thick, and most of the trees so large and massie [massive], as they were not to be falne with so few hands; and when they were lay'd along, the branches were so thick and boysterous, as required more help, and those strong and active men, to lop and remove them off the ground.

Clearing proved so difficult that Indian methods of cultivation were adopted, and crops were planted "between the boughs, the trees lying along the ground; so far short was the ground then of being clear'd."[35]

By 1647, about one-fifth of the rain forest and the secondary scrub along the coasts had been cleared, and fields for vegetables and many sugar plantations had been established (fig. 8.2). Clearing opened up the view, so that "as the woods are cut down, the landscape will appear at farther distances." The selective cutting of better-timber trees for constructing pig sties, sugar mills, houses, and furniture and for export added to the toll. In time the infusion of capital and importation of African slaves ensured the rapid expansion and profitability of the plantations, and the systematic replacement of the remainder of the forest by cane fields. Slaves now took over from the white settlers, and were made

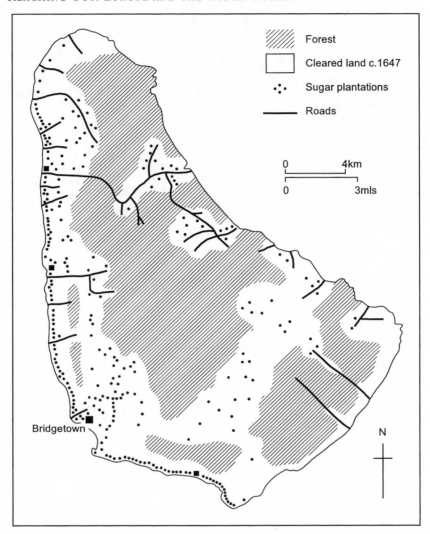

Figure 8.2 Forests and plantations in Barbados, 1647. *Source:* after Watts, 1987: 185.

to clear about 3 acres of ground a year. The method of clearing did not change—partial clearing, burning, an adventitious subsistence crop or two—leading eventually to a sugar plantation in about 7 years. By 1665 the once forest-covered landscape of Barbados was dominated by large sugar estates and almost totally open except for forest on the highest peaks. "There is not a foot of land in Barbados that is not employed even to the very sea-side," said Governor Atkins in his report to London in 1676. The extent and speed of the alteration of the land cover of the island after 1627 must have been, suggests David Watts, "without parallel in an agricultural area." Though small in area, it was a measure and portent of things to come elsewhere in the wider world when commercial plantation agriculture really got under way.[36]

Indeed, in every island colony the 15 years before 1665 had been called "The Great Clearing," and by 1672 the same devastation and transformation had happened in the neighboring islands of St. Kitts, Nevis, and Montserrat. In St. Christopher thick woods could be seen only on the mountaintops by 1672, in Nevis the ground was cleared "almost to the top of the Hill" by 1707, and Governor Staple wrote home that, "most of the Islands are destitute of timber, Antigua only excepted." By 1690 the same was true of Martinique, Guadeloupe, and Montserrat, and Jamaica was becoming that way along its coasts. Throughout the Caribbean the severity of clearing was highlighted by soil erosion, and by the scarcity and high price of timber for construction and fuelwood, particularly for refining the sugar. By the 1660s timber shortages were appearing, and by 1671 it was reported from Barbados that "all the trees are destroyed so that wanting wood to boyle their sugar, they are forc'd to send for coales from England." But that was not a satisfactory solution and soon timber was flowing from North America.[37]

In an age when raw, unaltered forested landscapes were regarded with loathing and even fear, the new man-made landscape of clearing attracted favorable comment. As Richard Ligon sailed around the shore of Barbados in 1647 he said that "the Plantations appear'd to us one above another: like several stories of stately buildings, which afforded us a large proportion of delight." Some travelers were reminded, fancifully, of England, in that it looked like a planted green garden, or "one great Citty adorned with gardens"; "Itt is," said Governor James Kendall in 1690, "the beautyfulls't spott of ground I ever saw." In St. Christopher, the neatly planted rows of bright green tobacco, pale yellow sugarcane, and dark green ginger, along with bordering groves of fruit trees, the whole dotted with the bright red roofs of the plantations, "make so delightful a Landskip," wrote Janet Schaw, "as must cause an extraordinary recreation to the unwearied eye." And yet, the vigor of nature to reclaim what had been won from it by clearing was not far away; Sir Hans Sloane stumbled on an abandoned Spanish settlement and cacao grove on the north shore of Jamaica where the cocoa trees were now 70 ft high and the town site studded with mature trees. "'Tis a very strange thing," he remarked, "to see how short a time a Plantation formerly clear'd of Trees and Shrubs, will grow foul."[38] But that was a rare sight; far more forest was being felled during these centuries than ever reverted to its natural state. The great clearing of the eighteenth century was about to begin.

The Emerging Atlantic Timber Trade

The spectacular success of the English settlements in the Caribbean initially overshadowed the ultimately larger and more significant settlements in North America. Even by 1642 the 80,000 Caribbean Englishmen outnumbered the 49,000 American Englishmen by nearly 2 to 1, a ratio that did not change much: the flow of migration to New England dried up after 1640, when conditions improved in England after the Long Parliament. Lack of constant contact and a dearth of finished goods to New England caused a local crisis, the solution to which was to export the undoubted surplus of timber that it possessed for the essential manufactured goods it lacked.[39]

The first overseas export ventures were with Spain, Portugal, Madeira, the Canaries, and the Azores, where supplies of ships' timbers and timber for wine casks were diminishing rapidly, especially the timbers that enhanced the flavor of wine. Consequently, white-oak pipe staves for wet casks were shipped east in the tens of thousands, together with some general timber cargoes, fish, and provisions. Then New Englanders turned their attention to timber-starved Barbados, exporting timber in exchange for cotton. With growing contacts many of the poorer independent and tenanted Barbadian farmers migrated from the overcrowded island to New England, especially after the introduction of slaves in the middle of the 1650s completely transformed the economy and society of the island and turned it into "one large sugar factory."[40] These changes invigorated and balanced the economy of New England because an immense market for its timber was created in the Caribbean for construction, and for refining and transporting sugar. General lumber, white oak-staves for rum casks, and red-oak pipe staves for sugar and molasses casks flowed from north to south. Although places like Jamaica had abundant timber, it was said that they could not compete, and that even finished casks could be made in Boston and sold in Barbados more cheaply than locally assembled ones.

Trade patterns strengthened and flourished throughout the seventeenth century, with less going to the "Wine Islands" over time and more to the Caribbean, together with a lively trade to Newfoundland, where over 20,000 fishermen exploiting the Grand Banks fisheries required wood supplies. Beyond lay the European market, but timber could not stand the costs of transportation across the Atlantic when compared with the cheapness of supplies from the Baltic, except for specialized woods like mahogany, brazilwood, and dyewoods, and masts, which had strategic value.

The commodities that linked the three continents in an emerging pattern of trade were basically sugar and timber, which stimulated development in all parts of the circuit. There are many examples, but one must suffice. Although it was easy for New England vessels to go out filled to capacity with timber, it was difficult for them to return fully loaded. Therefore, in order to pick up bulky cargoes they called into places like Tortunga to pick up salt or the Gulf of Campeche for logwood (mahogany), which was then re-exported from Boston. In time slaves entered into the pattern. The forests around the western Atlantic were slowly becoming enmeshed in new circuits of trade that were going to grow enormously in future years, but which, even at this early date, were contributing to their exploitation and destruction.

THE ENCOUNTER WITH THE AMERICAN FOREST

Since the early seventeenth century, political and religious refugees had sought their freedom in the land around Boston, while even earlier adventurers like Ralegh had experimented with settlement in Virginia. After some initial adjustment, the Plymouth Colony had quickly adapted to the forest environment, and once the bonus of abandoned Indian fields was exhausted, it started to clear in order to make land for farming. From these "hearths" and many others along the eastern seaboard, European settlers edged forward for the next two centuries into the vast forests that covered the interior of North America from Florida in the south to Maine and Quebec in the north. Figure 8.3 shows the spread of settlement by 1700, 1760, 1790, and 1810, when the total population reached about 0.25, 1.6, 3.9, and 7 million respectively, and the spread can be taken as a measure of the human impact on the forest at these different times. Settlers were not occupying a totally un-humanized landscape, it is true, but the prior advance of disease had ensured

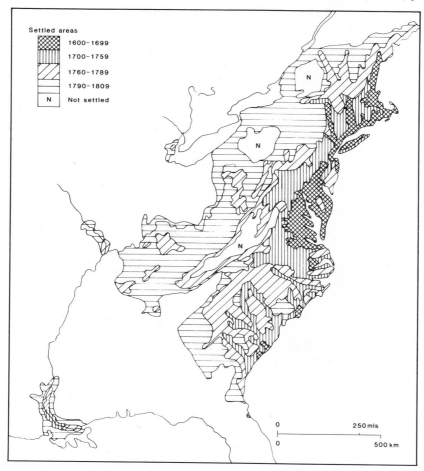

Figure 8.3 Spread of settlement, North America, 1700, 1760, 1790, and 1810. *Source: after Williams, 1989: 54.*

that it was a depopulated one, which during the seventeenth century was probably in the process of reverting to a denser forest than existed previously.

Backwoods Life

Compared to all that had gone before in the saga of European penetration overseas, the settlement of North America displayed many new characteristics that were to have a profound impact on the forests. The ideals of agricultural living, freehold tenure, dispersed settlement, "improvement," and personal and political freedom were extolled, and were novel and potent driving forces in the cultural climate of the new settler empire. The pioneer's self-sufficiency, thrift, independence, and resourcefulness were virtues that were lauded, although for them the reality, as they cleared the land, was more likely to have been isolation, drudgery, unremitting toil, and worry. A distinctive American "backwoods" culture evolved in the forests (plate 8.2), producing the largest transformation of forest landscapes seen in the world since the high Middle Ages. Also, it was probably the best documented account of forest clearance and occupation encountered until then, or even after.[41]

By the middle of the eighteenth century America was still, as Thomas Pownall put it, "as yet a new World to the Land-workers of Europe." But soon the forest experience of the "land-workers" was to become the basic element in the geography and history of the continent. The marquis de Chastellux, who travelled extensively in America, said that the sight of "the work of a single man who in the space of a single year" had cut down several acres of woodland and built himself a house in the clearing was something he had

Plate 8.2 "Backwoods Life in New England," 1770. From the anonymous work *One Hundred Years of Progress in the United States* (Hartford, Conn.: L. G. Stebbins, n.d.), 21. (University of Wisconsin.)

observed "a hundred times. . . . I have never travelled three miles without meeting a new settlement either beginning to take form or already in cultivation." The combined tasks of clearing, building a house and fences, and even of making a road to his clearing could take a settler's lifetime, during which "he was less a farmer and more a builder."[42]

Before a pioneer could clear land he had to acquire it. In the early tightly knit village communities of New England that was a carefully controlled communal affair, but with the removal of the Indian harassment after about 1760 and the relaxation of religious oversight, regular surveys were made in townships away from the villages, and settlement and clearing spread rapidly. In contrast, in the later frontier areas of New York, Pennsylvania, Tennessee, Kentucky, and Virginia, it was a relatively simple matter for an enterprising man to move into the forest beyond his neighbor in true backwoods fashion and squat without legal title, sometimes blazing a tree and establishing his claim by "tomahawk right." A cabin and a clearing of a few acres were sufficient to establish title for the land. After 1790, regular surveys by government and individuals in Ohio and western New York resulted in more orderly westward expansion, which was fortunate, as the new forest dweller was unlikely to be from the neighborhood but came from many hundreds of miles away, often from New England. He got his information about land sales from newspapers and broadsides; he even went to have preliminary look at the land he wanted, possibly buying it, going home, and returning the next winter with ax, gun, blanket, provisions, and ammunition. He would then start to clear it in preparation for his family, who might follow one or even two years later.[43] Such dissemination of information and personal mobility were without precedent, and were a foretaste of the dynamic forces being unleashed on the world's forests.

Although individuals in many parts of the South pioneered in the traditional manner, the rise of the plantation system gradually forced all other considerations into the background. The system that had developed progressively on the island stepping-stones across the Atlantic now took hold on the American mainland. Large blocks of land of 500 to 1,000 acres and more were needed for cotton and tobacco growing, and slaves replaced European pioneer farmers.

Clearing

Everywhere, old Indian fields initially reduced the amount of clearing necessary and heightened the chances of survival. Low, badly drained ground was avoided because of the prevalence of malaria. But soil quality was usually judged on tree size and, perceptively, on the prevalence of particular species. For example, pitch and other pines meant dry, sandy soils; oak, chestnut, walnut, and hickory meant good arable soils. Every region, it seemed, had its plant indicators.[44]

In the northern and middle colonies, clearing was accomplished by either clear-cutting or ringbarking, both followed by burning; the former procedure was common enough in New England and New York to be known as the "Yankee" method. There was little to recommend one method over the other, for girdling merely deferred the expenses of time and labor for some future period, though it at least allowed the pioneer to get on with cropping. Stumps were a problem with both methods, and most were left in the ground to rot, with cultivation carried on around them. Grass, potatoes, tobacco, flax, and maize were no problem, as they could be planted "indian style" on mounds between the "recently decapitated stumps of trees," and then either harvested by hand or grazed by stock. Stump clearing only became necessary once wheat or rye were sown and had to be harvested.[45]

The individual experience of clearing is difficult to capture, but the simple yet powerful poem of a Pennsylvania farmer as he clear-cut his farm in 1692 comes very near it:

> When we began to clear the Land
>   For room to sow our Seed,
> And that our Corn might grow and stand,
>   For Food in time of Need,
>
> Then with the Ax, with Might and Strength
>   The Trees so thick and strong,
> Yet on each side, such strokes at length
>   We laid them all along.
>
> So when the Trees, that grew so high
>   Were fallen to the ground
> Which we with Fire, most furiously
>   to Ashes did Confound.[46]

Pioneers rarely cleared more than 10 acres during the first year; it would have simply been too arduous, and there was so much else to do. Few cleared more than 30 acres if a comfortable subsistence was their aim; anything more than that betokened a thriving, entrepreneurial farmer with an outside market, and that achievement, said Henry Beaufoy, was "an affair of years." Either way, however, clearing was a combination of "sweat, skill and strength," and the pioneer farmer was seen as the heroic subduer of a sullen and unyielding wilderness that needed to be tamed.[47]

In the Southern colonies girdling was the most common clearing method; as William Byrd said in 1623, "the English have up to now with little difference imitated the Indians in this." But in any case, stump grubbing was rarely worthwhile because of the need for constant crop rotation. Tobacco exhausted the soil and led to soil toxicity, and cotton was only a little less demanding. Manuring was rarely resorted to: "we can buy an acre of new land cheaper than we can manure an old one," said Thomas Jefferson; and dunging was "regarded as more irksome than cutting down trees," according to Johann Schoepf. Planters calculated on getting three or four tobacco crops before turning the clearing over to a few crops of wheat or maize and then abandoning it to the forest. "After twenty or thirty years," commented one observer, "the same land would be cleared and put under a similar scourging tillage."[48]

To accommodate these constant shifts, estates had to be large and widely spaced, and the impression they created was of islands of cultivation in a sea of forests. Thomas Anburey, who traveled through the South in 1789, said the following:

> The house we reside in is situated upon an eminence commanding a prospect of nearly thirty miles around it, and the face of the country appears an immense forest, interspersed with various plantations, four or five miles distant from each other: on these there is a dwelling house in the centre with kitchen, smoke house, and out-houses and from various buildings each plantation has the appearance of a small village.[49]

The plantations had their own seasonal labor rhythm. It was a common slave task to clear 3 acres during the fall, split the timber for huts and rails, and then prepare the ground for planting in March. While the cutting of trees on 1 acre was considered "a day's task of eight slaves," lopping and burning during the evening was an extra. The cost of clearing had to take into account the cost of buying, housing, and feeding slaves, which was not inconsiderable; consequently, clearing in the South was far more commercially oriented and influenced than the essentially subsistence process in the North. What the northern farmer paid for with hard labor the southern planter paid for with hard cash.[50]

Whichever part of North America one was in, however, the process of land clearing and farm developing was widespread, universal, and an integral part of rural life, continuing well into the latter years of the nineteenth century. "Such are the means," marveled the marquis de Chastellux in 1789,

> by which North-America, which one hundred years ago was nothing but a vast forest, is peopled with three million of inhabitants. . . . Four years ago, one might have travelled ten miles in the woods I traversed, without seeing a single habitation.

The clearing in the forest on the frontier with its log cabin was the ultimate American symbol, the place where the pioneer created the world anew as if in some latter-day Genesis (plate 8.3). Perhaps Benjamin Latrobe's seemingly extravagant comment, that "the

Plate 8.3 "The Beginning." From the anonymous work *One Hundred Years of Progress in the United States* (Hartford, Conn.: L. G. Stebbins, n.d.), 19. (University of Wisconsin.)

American axe may well rank with maize and steam as one of the three things which have conquered the western world," may have more of a ring of truth in it than might first seem apparent.[51]

Other Backwoods Forest Uses

The contribution of the forest to the backwoods pioneering economy did not end with the clearing and creation of land for crops. Beyond the clearing lay the unfenced, unclaimed range of the forest that provided free feed for stock and the raw material for many of the essentials of everyday life, including houses, fences, fuel, and the generation of cash.

Overwhelmingly stock meant swine, and the wild razorback hog dominated the woodland grazing regime; cattle only challenged swine during the later nineteenth century. Consequently, pork was the most widely consumed meat, either as fresh meat or salted down and packed in barrels. The full pork barrel was a symbol of plenty, and when its bottom could be seen it was a symbol of starvation—one was literally "scraping the bottom of the barrel."[52]

Large feral cattle herds dominated the forests of the South, particularly the Carolinas. The forest and any clearings in it were fired continuously in order to maintain the growth of young grass. Cow pens were constructed in strategic places so that the wild herds would return at night to suckle their calves. With the establishment of more permanent dwellings, along with branding, rustling, and roundups (often with black "cowboys"), we can perceive the prototype for the western range, except that closed forest replaced the open grassland.[53]

The presumption was that fences were essential only if the aim was to keep the stock out of fields, not in them; therefore, the onus of responsibility lay with the cultivator, not the forest stock owner. Given the number of other tasks the pioneer farmer had to do, fencing was not too high on his list of priorities, and hence many makeshift fences of piled-up stumps or brushwood served until straight-grained logs could be split, postholes dug, and posts notched and holed for cross rails. A common and favorite pioneer expedient was the Virginia, worm, or zigzag fence, which was constructed by laying horizontally 6 to 10 slender, 12-ft poles or rails in such a way as to interlock with one another at right angles. It was expensive in its use of land and wood (for example, a square field of 160 acres required about 15,000 rails) but not in time to construct, and therefore was adopted widely in forested environments. By as late as 1850, worm fences still accounted for 79 percent of the 3.4 million mi of fencing in the United States, and post-and-rail and plank fences another 14 percent, mainly in the prairies, where timber was expensive. Wood was the overwhelming fencing material well into the nineteenth century and was not replaced by barbed wire until after the 1860s.[54]

As in fencing, the dominant building material was wood. The archetypal domestic structure was the log cabin, both an emblem of frontier life in the forest and a metaphor for pioneer hardship, hope, and virtue. So simple was this dwelling that little can be said of it, except that its origins have been traced to northwestern Europe, and that after its introduction into the Delaware area by the Swedes it diffused widely and mutated vigorously throughout the length and breadth of the country.[55] All that was needed to build a cabin were 80 or so logs between 20 and 30 ft long for the walls, split planks for the floor, and grass, straw, and mud for filling the gaps between the logs. Depending on the help received from neighbors, the whole structure could be raised in between 1 and 3 days. Not until the Indian threat diminished and sawn timber from mills became readily available did clapboard frame houses appear, generally after the mid-eighteenth century. But the log cabin took a long time to disappear; there were still over 33,000 in New York in 1855, and they housed over one-fifth of all farm families. But whatever the construction or appearance of houses, four-fifths of Americans lived in timber houses of one sort or another at the turn of the nineteenth century.[56]

The forest yielded two other "domestic" products that are difficult to calculate accurately but were of immense value: potash and fuel. Potash produced an alkali solution used for many industrial purposes, including soap and glass-making, tanning, bleaching, calico printing, medicines, and gunpowder. It sold readily, and provided a steady cash income for farmers. According to one commentator, "one-half or two-thirds of the expense of clearing land in New York is repaid from burning the wood"; the cash earned in this manner helped buy land, hire labor to clear it, and purchase the necessities that could not be produced on the farm. Potash was in great demand in Europe, and by the late eighteenth century it ranked sixth in value among American exports.[57]

Books could (and have been) written about the importance of fuel to everyday life in America. In the north of the country, fuel was basic and indispensable for the very preservation of life for 7 or 8 months, and it was scarcely less crucial during the southern winter, so that slaves never dared return from the fields "without bringing a load of firewood on their shoulders." "So much of the comfort and convenience of life," said Benjamin Franklin, "depends on the article of *fire*." The answer, said one settler, was "not to spare the wood of which there is enough," and great blazing fires halfway up the chimney were a common sight in the homes of colonial America.[58]

Fuelwood was usually measured in cords, a cubic measure of 4 by 4 by 8 ft, or a total of 128 ft^3 (3.625 m^3). Consumption varied according to the combustible quality of the wood (hardwoods usually burning warmest), the size of the house, and the habits of a family, but each year a typical rural household might well have consumed between 20 and 30 cords, which is between 72 and 109 m^3, some of which might well have been sold to urban centers for cash.[59] Undoubtedly, fuelwood demand rose markedly with the growth of cities on the eastern seaboard; by 1750 there were 435 sizable urban centers on the coast, and the populations of Boston, Philadelphia, New York, and Baltimore were all over 50,000. There are plenty of examples of measures of scarcity (and hence destruction), particularly during the punishing winter months: the emergence of fuel dealers, price increases and seasonal "gouging," municipal regulation, and wood charities for the urban poor, along with the increasing use of iron or tin-plated draught stoves, or "Franklins," as they were known after their inventor.[60] Whereas wood had once been "at every man's door," it now had to be trundled overland from pioneering districts well over a hundred miles distant, while along the coast sloops brought supplies down from Maine and New Hampshire to Boston, up from New Jersey to Philadelphia, and down the Hudson to New York. So bad was the situation that by the winter of 1775, fuelwood was said to be just as dear as it was in timber-starved England![61]

How much wood was cut for fuel will never be known precisely because of the variability of, among other things, the yield of forests, the amount of regrowth and recutting (it might be cropped 4 or 5 times in a century), and the human population, and the fact that fuelwood was a cheap and plentiful by-product of agricultural clearing. But it is possible that by the end of the eighteenth century, a total of some 812 million cords had been consumed. At a yield of 100 cords per acre (a high figure), this equals 8.12 million acres, which is more than the amount of land cleared for agriculture at the time, so there must have been a great deal of repeated tree "cropping."[62] Regrettably, we will never know the amount of land cleared purely for fuel; the wood used for fuel was as plentiful as air— and who wrote about that or collected statistics about it?

Commercial Uses of the Forest

To make a distinction between the impact of agricultural clearing in the forest and the impact of commercial cutting and exploitation is difficult, as the two overlapped in so many ways. On the one hand, the infant settlements needed to clear land in order to grow food to live; on the other they needed to export surplus products to exchange for essential manufactured goods not available in the new locations. Either way, it was no exaggeration when people talked of the riches of the forest as being "fundamental to the developing economy," that the forest was "the mainstay of the agricultural and commercial economy," that life was dominated by "The Forest and the Sea," or that the economy of the seventeenth- and eighteenth-century settler empire was "a timber economy."[63] Thus we know that potash and fuelwood, while incidental products of clearing, were crucial to the profitability of farm making, and that similarly, agriculturalists supplied much of the wood that went into the general domestic lumber business and even the export trade, and there are many more examples. The point is that at some indeterminate point the pioneer agricultural settler arranged his life and activities in such a way that he purposely supplied the outside, even distant market, rather than his own and local needs. At that point the pioneer economy shifted away from self-sufficiency, and the exploitation of the forest began to have a distinctly commercial orientation.

It is impossible to summarize the detail of the commercial use of the forest, such as naval stores, masts, shipbuilding, timber production, and charcoal making, but suffice it to say that while these products and processes were important locally, and prominent enough to be commented upon extensively, they were a mere pinpricks in the destruction of the forest compared with farm making and domestic fuel consumption. If collectively they amounted to as much as 10 percent of the drain on the forest resource by the mid-eighteenth century, it would be surprising; the percentage was probably much less.

Naval stores and masts had a strategic significance for England because of the precarious nature of supplies from the Baltic which endangered the country's burgeoning navy and growing global outreach. The gathering and manufacture of pitch, tar, turpentine, and resin for waterproofing hulls and decks and preserving rigging were fairly unsystematic, scattered, and tied in with southern plantation agriculture, and far more expensive than their Baltic counterparts. But under the stimulus of subsidies, production in the Carolinas reached over 82,000 barrels in 1718, accounting for nearly 90 percent of Britain's total imports of these commodities.[64]

While Britain's policy under the Navigation and Trade Acts of utilizing its colonies as a source for raw materials and a market for its manufactured goods worked reasonably well in the South, it went wildly astray in the North. Increasingly the Yankees were building boats and transporting timber and other products for trade (particularly to the "Wine Islands" and the West Indies), and in the process achieving some sort of economic independence. From about 1660 onward, true conflict arose over mother-country and colonial demands for shipbuilding timber and over the claim by Britain under the White Pine Act of 1722 to reserve and exploit exclusively the choicest timber for masts, the so-called Broad Arrow Policy. While the number of masts exported was very few—rarely more than 15 percent of total Royal Navy needs—most of their diameters were over 20 in, and many over 27 in, sizes that the depleted German and Russian forests could no longer supply. But to get these the British placed a blanket ban on felling all white pines growing outside the townships, irrespective of domestic and overseas trading needs. Resentment ran high at these unworkable restrictions—at the high prices the contractors received and the low prices the local woodsmen got; at the speculation in land prices that the higher value of the pines helped to promote; and at the many "paper townships" in Maine that were created by speculators in order to get the pines.

The years between 1722 and 1776 are muddled with illegal cutting on the part of the woodsmen, duplicity on the part of the Crown agents, and conniving on the part of the contractors. New England merchants carried on a thriving trade in masts and timber with Spain and Portugal even though these countries were officially at war with Britain, because better prices were to be had from those countries. What John Evelyn called the "touchy humour" of those Yankee colonies culminated in the "woodland rebellion" against the timber restrictions that had all the ingredients of the conflict of 50 years later which brought about American independence. Timber and forests were too important an ingredient in the life and livelihood of colonial North America to be dealt with lightly.[65]

From the very beginning, shipbuilding was an integral and fundamental part of the whole timber and trade economy of New England, and in scattered ports as far south as Georgia. We will never know exactly how many ships were built, but all the evidence is that it ran into many scores per annum, and that most were of small capacity (approximately 100 tons) to suit the coastal trade and the seasonal nature of the West Indies trade. Because of timber shortages at home, British merchants began to place orders in American yards for larger transatlantic vessels, and so successful were the Americans with this production that by the eve of the Revolutionary War a startling 40 percent of all British tonnage was being built on the eastern seaboard.[66]

The "woodlands revolt" highlighted the fact that indigenous American commercial timber production was well developed by the eighteenth century. Every settlement, almost without exception, had its small water-powered sawmill that was considered an indispensable adjunct to pioneering life, and it would be true to say that nearly every farmer was a part-time lumberman. Logging did not usually extend for more than 5 or 6 mi from the mill; logs were snaked out of the forest and then carted to the settlements.

The insatiable market for timber in the growing urban centers on the eastern seaboard meant that a more regular long-distance method of transportation had to be devised, and sometime during the early 1700s cooperative rafting became popular. Although rafts had been used on European rivers for centuries, it was the immense rafts on the American ones that foreign travelers and native Americans alike never ceased to comment upon. During the 1750s Anne McVickar Grant witnessed some "very amusing scenes" on the banks of the Hudson where the new settlers had cut planks and logs and brought them down to the river edge:

> [A]nd when the season arrived that swelled the stream to its greatest height, a whole neigh-bourhood assembled, and made their joint stock into a large raft, which was floated down river. . . . There is something serenely majestic in the easy progress of these large bodies on the full stream of the copious river. Some times one can see a whole family transported on this simple conveyance; the mother calmly spinning, the children sporting about her, and the father fishing at one end and watching its safety at the same time. These rafts are taken down to Albany, and put on board vessels there for conveyance to New York.

Soon raft building spread to all the east-flowing rivers and the tributaries of the St. Law-rence. "The finest timber for ship builders and architects" was conveyed downstream to the markets, as this was the "cheapest way possible to covert it into money" for pur-chasing the essential items needed in the pioneer land-clearing settlements inland.[67]

Timber production was widespread and regarded as a necessary part of everyday liv-ing that required no comment; only where timber entered into overseas trade is there a record of cutting. Every port from Falmouth in Maine to Sunbury in Georgia was ex-porting sawn lumber, staves, and shingles, mainly to the Caribbean at this time. The New England ports tended to dominate the sawn lumber trade, the southern ports the stave trade. Only the Piscataqua inlet with its felling and shipbuilding and the Albany-Glen Falls region on the Hudson with its many mills seemed to be emerging as distinctive tim-ber production centers.[68]

Like timber production, charcoal production for iron smelting was early, widespread, and commonplace in colonial America because of the huge need for equipment and tools in this energetic, pioneering economy. It is possible that pig-iron production reached 30,000 tons on the eve of the Revolution, of which 3,000 to 5,000 tons was being ex-ported to Britain. Wood fuel was rarely a locational factor in production, as it was so abundant and ubiquitous, but iron ore deposits and moving water to drive trip-hammers and bellows was locationally significant. Furnaces dotted all the Atlantic states, with ma-jor concentrations in the oak forests of northern New Jersey and adjacent southern New York, western Connecticut and Massachusetts, most of Pennsylvania, and the pine bar-rens of New Jersey.[69]

From permutations involving cords per acre, bushels per cord, and charcoal per bushel, it can be calculated that efficient high yielding–low consumption furnaces needed about 150 acres of woodland to produce 1,000 tons of pig iron, and if inefficient low yielding–high consumption furnaces were in operation, the amount of forest affected could multiply tenfold. In reality an intermediate figure of 500 acres per 1,000 tons seems more likely, and is substantiated by contemporary accounts of the size of forest reserves needed for a 20-year rotation of cutting. These estimates have to placed against the comments of Johann Schoepf, who traveled through Pennsylvania in 1783 and noted the lack of timber supplies in the country around the Schuylkill, where the forests were "everywhere thin," because the ironworks "could not but ravage the woods to their own hurt"; and there were plenty of examples of furnaces in northern New Jersey and the Housatonic valley in Connecticut said to have been abandoned because of timber depletion.[70]

The impression is that, like seventeenth-century England, local depredations could be severe but their overall impact greatly exaggerated. The alien, disruptive intrusion of industry into the quiet and traditional regimes of the forest and agricultural life was still a literary topos. At its least, charcoal making before the Revolution was destroying a mere 4,500 acres per annum and at its greatest, 45,000; the actual figure was most likely about 15,000 acres, a mere drop in the ocean of forests that clothed the eastern United States. Unlike England, the lack of interest in substitute fuels for nearly another hundred years suggests no shortages. The retention of the old fuel technology was both a reflection of the superabundance of wood and a widespread preference for the type of versatile iron that charcoal made.

CHINA: "A DARK AREA IN SPACE"

To shift attention from the tiny islands of the Atlantic and the territorially restricted toeholds of early European settlement in Brazil, Virginia, and New England, all with modest populations measured in tens of thousands, to the vast, semicontinental extent of China, with a population measured in tens, if not hundreds, of millions, requires a great effort of the imagination. Yet the Chinese realm is one of the longest settled and most intensely humanized landscapes, and as such must have been a major part of the "wider world" of deforestation. But it was slow to change and difficult to generalize about; it is "a dark area in space" in that wider story, with a "history imperfectly kept."[71]

In all the uncertainty, one basic fact stands out for consideration, and that is population figures, although the detail is being revised constantly. The population at the beginning of the Ming dynasty in circa 1400 was between 65 and 80 million, and the area cultivated about 24.7 million ha. By 1770 there were 270 million people and 63.3 million ha of cultivated land, and by 1893 385 million people and 82.7 million ha of land in cultivation—a fourfold increase from 1400 to 1770, and a five- to sixfold increase to the end of the nineteenth century.[72] The population was never well fed, but it survived disasters and multiplied, being one of the most rapidly growing of any in the early modern world, averaging 0.4–0.5 percent per annum. Given our knowledge of comparable societies at comparable times, it seems inconceivable that this huge increment of over 300 million people and 58 million ha of "new" agricultural land did not have a dramatic effect on the natural vegetation, and the reduction of the forested area must have been one of the major consequences. Of course, not all of this vast increment of people was absorbed in forested areas. It is possible that farmers were able to raise their grain output by raising the yields per hectare as well as by expanding cultivation acreage. Submarginal land on forested slopes in southern and central China, dry land on the northern fringes and Inner Mongolia, and wetland in the river bottoms and deltas were attacked first, mainly between about 1600 and 1850. The raising of yields through the selection of better seeds, double-cropping, and better water control and fertilizing tended to follow later, but the transition was never that clear-cut.[73]

On top of the vast numbers, huge spaces, and long time spans is the sparsity of information about the forest. If Rhoads Murphey could say that the extent of China's forest cover and its depletion during the nineteenth century "is not known, or discoverable by any means," then how much more so can that be said for earlier centuries? As already noted in chapter 5, the information gap is awesome, and China is a land of "ponderous unknowns," a sort of "black hole" in the story of global deforestation that is difficult to delineate.[74] One can scour works on agricultural and rural life in China and not find one reference to forests, woodland, timber, or fuelwood, yet these were absolutely essential for the very existence of the inhabitants up until recent times, and are by no means irrelevant today. Yet they have not emerged as topics to be considered in their own right except in a few works.[75]

The paucity of information on everyday rural life precludes any work comparable to that in Europe in the *Annales* tradition.[76] For most of the Ming and Qing dynasties (1368–1912), if not before, the story of deforestation can almost only be told through the medium of traditional first millennium BC poetry and the observations of foreign scientists and travelers of the late nineteenth and early twentieth centuries. It is as if one is combining Homer with the technical reports of field officers of the U.S. Department of Agriculture or some similar organization.

Mandarins and Peasants

In addition to the great number of people, the one thing about the Chinese past of which we can be reasonably sure is the form of governance, though what to call it—Oriental Despotism, Bureaucratic Feudalism, Imperial Bureaucracy, or the Asian Mode of Production—is an open question.[77] The label is of less importance than the characteristics, which had their effects on the clearing process. An all-powerful mandarin bureaucracy dominated a multitude of autonomous village communities. While the state did not attempt to interfere in the daily affairs of the villagers, it ensured its dominance over society through the management of public works, and took an active role in migration, land clearance, and reclamation, sometimes through enforcing corvée labor.[78] Despotic rule did not seem to hinder agrarian economic growth, but commercial development seemed not to occur, and the country remained obstinately feudal. The peasantry labored hard but were lightly taxed and relatively unfettered, and did much as they liked; the state directed major developments of irrigation, drainage, and clearing as part of a dynastic concern for the welfare of its subjects and the feeding of an expanding population.

The example of the 210,000 km² of Hunan Province in south-central China during the Ming dynasty (1386–1644) and the early part of the Qing (1644–1911), as it changed from an underpopulated periphery to part of the densely settled core of the country through state-encouraged immigration, helps us to focus on processes and trends in deforestation in a significantly large part of the country.[79]

At the outset of the Ming (1386), the population was between 1.87 and 2.08 million, spread over some 695,000 ha of agricultural lowlands around Donting Lake on the central Yangtze, where the Yuan, Xiang, Li, and Zi rivers meet. The lowlands comprise about 15 percent of the land surface of the province, with the remainder consisting of steeply sloping land on the interfluvial ridges and ranges that separate the main rivers and their tributaries, and the high mountains (over 1,500 m) in the fringing southern, eastern, and western edges of the province.

During the Ming period, officials encouraged in-migration from more populated areas in the lower Yangtze by giving exemptions on loans for tools, seeds, and animals as incentives to clear the land or drain it. This practice stemmed not only from a concern for the welfare of people, but also from a desire to raise the tax base of the province. The evidence is uncertain at times, but all the indications are that the population had increased to between 5.1 million–5.6 million by 1582 and cultivated land to 1,885,200 ha, but there was still room for further expansion.

The impressive progress of settlement was completely disrupted by widespread internal conflict and destruction during the transition from the Ming to Qing dynasties (circa 1640–70). There was great loss of life and total depopulation in some areas, with many fleeing to the hills; and only 27 percent of the land registered in 1581 was still being cultivated in 1679. With the restoration of peace, a standardized program of land settlement through immigration was renewed to restore the population to its pre-Qing level, again with loans for implements, seeds, and animals, and tax exemptions. Cultivation revived quickly, even bypassing previous totals. Population rose to 14.9 million by 1776, and registered cultivated land to 2.6 million ha; consequently, Hunan "filled up," with the population reaching 20 million by 1842. Land around Donting Lake was reclaimed and there was a shift in the lowlands to intensification, particularly double-cropping. Immigrants were now forced into the steeper, forested, surrounding slopes of Hunan and started extensive clearing, an experience repeated throughout the mountainous areas of southern China.[80]

While clearing for agriculture was undoubtedly the key element in the deforestation of the Chinese countryside, there can be no doubt that the demands for fuelwood were also immense, especially in the colder northern half of the country. Major cities counted fuelwood resources as one of their major essential "imports," together with food and water, and there is some evidence that carefully managed plantations for supplies were located on the edges of some urban areas. Nonetheless, everything points to the conclusion that there was a severe energy crisis in China from 1400 until at least the mid-nineteenth century, and that the collection of grass, leaves, and any other combustible matter was a major preoccupation of the Chinese peasant until recent times.[81]

The Landscape of Clearing

The term *land clearing* is used widely in both traditional and modern literature and seems to include all forms of land improvement: for example, land drainage and/or irrigation, as well as forest clearing.[82] The type of "land clearing" brought about depended on the topography. In the varied lowland/upland topography of the southern hills, lowland farmers relied on paddy rice and therefore must have built dykes and ditches to ensure an abundant water supply. On the steep mountainsides, however, farmers engaged in forest removal, periodically clearing small patches by ax and fire, and then moving on every 3 or 4 years when fertility ran out or the land was eroded beyond repair. Crops depended on rainfall, which could be either torrential or minimal, and the yield was always poor and frequently failed. The early (mid-sixteenth century) introduction of New World crops like peanuts, corn, and sweet potatoes and their widespread acceptance by the early eighteenth century further enabled the colonization of those upland areas. However, they considerably worsened erosion and lowland siltation, especially maize and potatoes, which were invariably sown in straight furrows up and down the slope.[83]

Up to a point, fertilizer provided a solution to low yields, and in the lowlands its steady supply easily maintained by the waste from hogs and humans. But in the hills the replenishment of nutrients was almost impossible, so that in those areas where lumber could not be easily shipped out as timber, lumbermen burned entire hillsides and collected the ashes to sell further downslope, with devastating effects on soil stability.

Late eighteenth-century descriptions of Hunan make it quite clear that the deforestation had been dramatic, and had upset the precarious ecological balance. Hillsides were "stripped of trees," and there was a scarcity of firewood:

> When there are too many people there is not enough land to contain them, there is not enough grain to feed them, and there are not enough wealthy people to take care of them. . . . Water rushes down violently from the mountains and the mountains became bare; earth is dug out . . . and the rocks are split; there is not an inch of cultivable land left.

With forest cover gone, the "earth was loose; when the big rains came, water rushed down from the highlands and mud and silt spread out below. Fertile areas near the mountains were ruined as they were repeatedly covered with sand and abandoned."[84]

It was little different in the north of the country. The well-wooded mountains and foothills of Shen-hsi and Shan-hsi Provinces had experienced some clearing during the economically energetic Sung dynasty (960–1127) but not enough to make a vast difference to the forest cover. In any case, officials sought to protect the forests as a barrier to the penetration of the nomadic invading horsemen from the Mongolian steppes; the Wu-t'ai mountains in northern Shan-hsi were still a wilderness in the early sixteenth century.[85] But within a few decades a Ming scholar reported:

> At the beginning of the reign of Chia-ching [1522–66] people vied with each other to build houses, and wood from the southern mountains was cut without a year's rest. The natives took advantage of the barren mountain surface and converted it into farms. . . . If heaven sends down a torrent, there is nothing to obstruct the flow of water. In the morning it falls on the southern mountains; in the evening, when it reaches the plains, its angry waves swell in volume and break embankments causing frequent changes in the course of the river. . . . Hence, Ch'i district was deprived of seven-tenths of its wealth.[86]

A gazetteer of 1596 reported the following:

> When the timber by the streams was gone the wood cutters went into the midst of the valleys in crowds of a thousand or a hundred, covering the mountains and wilderness; axes fell like rain and shouts shook the mountain. . . . [Eventually] the beautiful scenery of Ch'ing-liang became almost like a cow or horse pasture.[87]

With the erosion of land and even territorial security at risk, an imperial edict was passed in 1580, prohibiting further timber felling, and aiding in some forest regrowth.

But when imperial control waned again in the later nineteenth century, farmers and graziers moved in and stripped the timber. When in 1697 Father Gerbillon visited Ning-hsia Fu, near the point where the Great Wall crossed the western arm of the Huang Ho, he described it as a densely populated city where

> building timber . . . is very cheap, because they get it in that chain of mountains which is to the northwest [Hsi shan or Alashan Mountains] . . . where it is so abundant that from the neighbouring localities, more than 400 or 500 lys away, they come to buy it at Ning-hia.

But when the explorer Woodville Rockhill passed the same spot in 1892, it was completely deforested. He reported that "not one forest tree is to be seen, only a few poplars recently planted along the irrigation ditches." [88]

The overwhelming impression is that there was "a linear process of environmental degradation" throughout much of China. Yet while that was true overall, one must recognize the periods of respite, and examples of conscious forest protection. There were over one hundred hunting reserves, the largest of which was the great imperial hunting enclosure of the Mulan Weichang, which covered over 10,400 km² in northern China. There were also temple and monastic forests, community forests, and trees grown as a part of agro-forestry systems, particularly for silk production. [89] But these exceptions, while interesting, do not amount to much; and one must conclude that throughout the seventeenth and eighteenth centuries the Chinese moved inexorably toward the almost total deforestation of their portion of the earth—leaving forests, said Norman Shaw, only in the remote "wildly mountainous parts, which are little suited for agriculture." [90]

JAPAN: "THE FOUNDATIONS OF THE HEARTH"

The "ponderous unknowns" of forest clearance and usage in China are not repeated in Japan. That is not to say that everything was recorded and can be easily comprehended, but the picture of change in this remarkable society is much clearer, and the eventual outcome is markedly different. In stark contrast with China, Japan is one of the most densely forested countries in the world today, and the seeds of that plenitude were sown during the sixteenth century.

The impacts on the forest accelerated in pace and expanded in area as the population of the archipelago approached 12 million by 1600 and doubled to 26 million by 1720, while the amount of cultivated land rose from 1.49 to 2.94 million ha during the same period. [91] By the end of the sixteenth century an industrious society of subsistence cultivators had already occupied most of the highly restricted area of the alluvial lowlands (approximately 20 percent of all land) that were sandwiched between the high, steep mountains and the sea, and were busy clearing the forests of the lower valley sides and headwaters to make cultivation terraces. Above, the forests of the higher upland slopes were exploited widely for green fodder for stock and fertilizer for the intensively cultivated fields. For any given area of rice, between 5 and 10 times as much mountain land was needed to supply the grass, scrub brush, leaf fall, and small branches that were either trampled into the flooded paddies or fed to stock. [92] In addition, demand for forest resources was increasing in line with a growing economy and a rising level of affluence as families were consciously limited. Iron smelting, salt making, ceramic production, and building all expanded, and the demand for both domestic and industrial fuelwood grew.

Considering the importance and ubiquity of these activities to everyday life and existence it is surprising that there is comparatively little evidence of these uses, although, as we have come to expect, it is just this ubiquity and the taken-for-granted nature of agriculture and peasant subsistence that *are* the very reasons for the silence. Few records exist of fuel, fodder, and fertilizer use by the peasants, and land cover conversion is equally unrecorded, even though conflicts over essential common woodland resources were one of the most frequent causes of intervillage disputes. But a few hints about forest use can be gleaned. The unique diary of the Ishikawa family in Mushai Province for 1728 suggests that 45 person-days were spent gathering fuel on the mountainsides, but by 1804 the figure had dropped to 8 days, presumably because the family now bought most of its fuel. A similar shift in labor expenditure is seen as commercial fertilizers of dried fish, oil cakes, and night soil replaced the green fodder, and the time saved in fodder and fuel collection went into silk manufacture and more intensive arable cultivation.[93]

We are on much surer ground, however, when considering the forest used to satisfy the egos and ambitions of the ruling elites. They indulged in an almost peculiarly Japanese passion for grandiose and monumental building projects that consumed vast quantities of prime timber, and that had few counterparts other than in, perhaps, Imperial Rome, although the latter built predominantly in stone and brick.[94]

During the fifteenth and sixteenth centuries, the 250-odd major regional military and feudal lords—the *daimyō*—were constantly feuding with each other. Indeed, the early name for Japan—Sengoku—meant simply "the country at war."[95] In this ceaseless struggle for supremacy, the *daimyō* built a multitude of defensive regional fortresses with barracks, watchtowers, gates, and residences primarily of wood that often became the nuclei of urban settlements. Between 1467 and 1571 over 111 were constructed, and during the next 8 years another 90. In addition, because of the usefulness of timber and its essential military nature, many *daimyō* strengthened their control over woodland and appointed officials to ensure that timber and bamboo groves (the latter valuable as an obstacle against cavalry) were properly maintained, even to the extent of forbidding peasants to fell trees and engage in slash-and-burn agriculture. In this way military and defensive needs ensured that large areas of forest were protected, just as hunting ensured the protection of forests in medieval and later Europe. Additionally, forests were simply a ready source of wealth.

The chaos and lawlessness of the constantly feuding *daimyō* and their *samurai* warriors were replaced during the late sixteenth century by the hegemonic rule of the new shogunate, or *bakufu*. First, and outstanding, was Hideyoshi (r. 1582–98), followed by Tokugawa Ieyusa (r. 1598–1616), who established the Tokugawa or Edo period in Japanese history, which lasted from 1603 to 1868. Both rulers imposed a tight control over many of the *daimyō*, who became vassals, and by a complex system of alliances with others extended their power throughout most of the islands and demanded massive contributions of timber.

Many *daimyō* and their domains *(han)* paid a timber tribute to the shogun. Outstanding was Hideyoshi's levy for his monumental castle at Osaka and numerous grandiose temples and shrines, as well as for the building and equipping of two armadas of troop

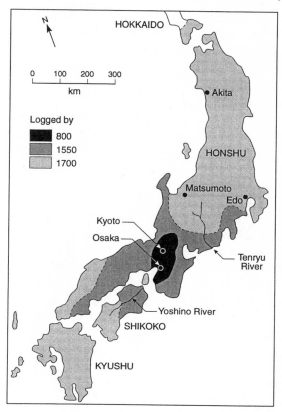

Figure 8.4 Forest exploitation in Japan. *Source:* based on Totman, 1989: fig. 2.

carriers for the conquest of Korea and China. These buildings required large, high-quality timbers that could be found only in the untouched forests. Thus, he established direct control and organized the systematic exploitation of stands on the Yoshino and Kiso river valleys in Shikuko and the east-central Honshu Islands, respectively, and placed pliant overlords to control other timber resources in the Tenryū valley and further north around Akita (fig. 8.4).

The exploits of Ieyusa were probably more spectacular than those of Hideyoshi. His monumental castles at Edo, Sunpu, and Nagyoa used wood lavishly, and Conrad Totman calculates that these three structures alone must have consumed over 2,750 ha of prime woodland, or many times that if obtained from areas of natural woodland. As supplies became more distant and more difficult to obtain, Ieyusa was forced to improve the means of long-distance timber transportation. Small timber came on horseback as usual, but larger pieces were moved along improved rivers in rafts and collected at booms, in a manner reminiscent of late eighteenth-century American logging practices.

In order to ensure *daimyō* compliance, the new *bakufu* required each warlord to keep his wife and main heir in a residence adjacent to the shogunate castle in Edo; consequently, each of the *daimyō* built ostentatious mansions (often several of them) for their families in the capital. In the country they vied with one another and with the shogunate in constructing elaborate castles, shrines, and many towns, cutting wide swathes through the mountain forests. Fairly accurate records of this destruction exist for a number of places, including Matsumoto in west-central Honshu and Tosa on eastern Shikoku.

After about 1660 a class of entrepreneurial commercial loggers emerged to supply the timber for a increasingly sophisticated urban market. Most seemed to rise from fairly humble rural beginnings and a few became spectacularly wealthy merchants, buying up stumpage and anticipating demand, especially after the devastating fires that periodically wiped out individual structures and whole cities and created a ceaseless cycle of repair and replacement.[96] The best documented of these fires are in Edo, which grew to about half a million people by 1660. There were 93 major fires between 1601 and 1866, and so frequent and spectacular were they that they earned the name "the flowers of Edo." The conflagrations of 1657 and 1772 were particularly devastating: over 100,000 people were killed in the holocaust of 1657, and because the city was rebuilt immediately, it required, by the most conservative calculation, the timber from many hundreds of thousands of hectares of forests from throughout Japan. Kyoto and Osaka were barely smaller, and sections frequently went up in flames, as did those of many a smaller town.[97]

The forests of Japan were in precipitous decline by the end of the seventeenth century. The imposition of peace among the feuding *daimiyō* had, paradoxically, allowed a long century of unbridled and profligate timber use in the construction of extravagant ecclesiastical and other monumental buildings; burgeoning urban development; a surge of population that demanded food, fuel, fertilizer, and shelter, and ever-intensified methods of tillage; and an expansion of industry. Regional examples of the deteriorating situation abound. In Matsumoto in central Honshu, agricultural products, silver, and coins were substituted for the original timber levies by the local *daimyō*; city loggers pulled out of local operations that were no longer profitable; and the *daimyō* began to reserve large individual trees, while the *han* established forest reserves that were patrolled in order to restrict access. In the Tenryū valley in eastern Honshu—which had been major source of big timbers for Ieyasu—inferior species (e.g., pine and chestnut instead of cypress, oak, and cedar) and smaller standard sizes were increasingly being accepted by lords by mid-century; tax levies in timber were written off or replaced by rice or money levies; and entry into certain forests was restricted. On the river, the number of logs sent downstream declined radically by the turn of the century (table 8.1); and the wasteful "free float" of individual logs downstream that caused great losses of timber was replaced by mass floats that were carefully supervised, and eventually even these were replaced by rafts. In Tosa on the island of Shikoku, the previous stripping at Hideyoshi's command had been so great that the local *daimyō*, Yamanouchi, answering a request to furnish timber for the rebuilding of Edo after the great fire of 1657, had the following to say:

> The mountains of our domain are exhausted; we have neither *sugi* [cryptomeria] nor *hinoki* [Japanese cypress]. We are unable to provide good lumber as requested by the shogun.

Elsewhere, as in Akita in the northwest, fuelwood was scarce, as were large constructional timbers.[98]

The last of the large, old-growth timber accessible to streams, coast, and roads had been cut out everywhere. Loggers were having to move into the interior high forests in search of exploitable timber, and employing new transportation methods in order to "log

Table 8.1 Timber shipped down the Tenryū River, Japan, 1671–1782

Period	Pieces (Ann. Average)	Raft Loads (Ann. Average)	Pieces per Raft
1671–1687	165,572	4,653	35.6
1688–1715	334,640	2,823	118.5
1716–1735	231,989	1,305	117.8
1736–1763	42,061	426	98.7
1768–1782	8,954	128	69.9

Source: Totman, 1989: 72.

the unloggable." Scarcity and price rises were common after the 1660s, which led to the substitution of inferior pieces and the use of alternative materials, a move which continued throughout the next century. These examples could be multiplied endlessly, but they all add up to an incontrovertible story of overexploitation and timber paucity.[99] As Kumazawa Banzan, a Confucian scholar and severe critic of ecclesiastical extravagance lamented, "Eight out of ten mountains in this nation are deforested." [100]

It was fortuitous for Japan that, unlike China, the pressure of population and the consequent colonization, clearing, and cultivation of the upper mountain slopes did not occur before consciousness of the need for conservation became widespread. What followed during the eighteenth century was an era of purposeful regulation, silviculture, and planting, unprecedented in Asia and, indeed, perhaps anywhere in the world.

The increasing concern about the mountain forests is captured in the remarks of Nobumasa, the fourth *daimyō* of Tsugaru *han* who wrote during the 1660s about the essential nature of forests to everyday life. They encapsulate the ethos of care and sensitivity about the forests that began to pervaded Japanese society:

> One must take care for the family line and one's heir. One's third consideration is the mountains. To elaborate, man is sustained by the five elements [wood, fire, water, earth, and metal]. In our world today neither high nor low can survive if any one of the five is missing. Among the five, water and fire [heat] are most important. Of the two fire is more crucial. However, fire cannot sustain itself; it requires wood. Hence wood is central to a person's hearth and home. And wood comes from the mountains. Wood is fundamental to the hearth; the hearth is central to the person. Whether one be high or low, when one lacks wood one lacks fire and cannot exist. One must take care that wood be abundant. To assure that wood not become scarce, one cherishes the mountains. And thus, because they are the foundations of the hearth, which nurtures the lives of all people, the mountains are to be treasured.[101]

By about the middle of the eighteenth century, the lineaments of nineteenth- and early twentieth-century global deforestation were becoming discernible. China, and to a much lesser extent southern and western Europe, were nearly bankrupt of stock; Japan was embarking on an exciting experiment in preservation; and northern Europe was still acting as a great reservoir of supplies. America was beginning the great clearing that would transform the continent and act as the model for European colonists everywhere. In the tropical areas the pinpricks of European influence were soon to grow—with less obvious impact than in their temperate settler empires, it is true, but ultimately with about just as much effect. The forest biomes of the world were changing irrevocably.

Chapter 9

Driving Forces and Cultural Climates, 1750–1900

Consumption is the sole end and purpose of all production.
—ADAM SMITH, *The Wealth of Nations* (1776)

Americans are insensible to the wonders of inanimate nature, and they may be said not to perceive the mighty forests that surround them till they fall beneath their hatchet. Their eyes are fixed upon another sight . . . peopling solitudes and subduing nature.
—ALEXIS DE TOCQUEVILLE, *Democracy in America* (1838)

For nature then to me was all in all.
—WILLIAM WORDSWORTH, *Tintern Abbey* (1793)

THE FORCES unleashed during the period of discovery, commercialism, and territorial and intellectual exploration from the early sixteenth to mid-eighteenth centuries were suddenly put into high gear after about 1750 and accelerated with the onset of the Industrial Revolution. *Revolution* is a term used liberally by historians to describe major shifts in national or world affairs, but the concept of the Industrial Revolution is perhaps a wholly justified term. Within the span of scarcely three generations from 1750 to 1830, the face of the globe changed, and the relatively simple world of plants and animals, and of water and wind power, that had existed before now became the world of machines, of inventions, of inanimate energy use, of rapid communication, and of the movement of goods in bulk as humans gained control of the world and its resources.[1] Needless to say, concomitant with these changes went intellectual ones, along with ideas and attitudes towards nature, and the forest changed in parallel with the material changes of life.

Of course, none of these changes happened overnight. Just as the previous age of commercialism had its antecedents in the medieval period, so the Industrial Revolution had its roots in the age of commercialism and early capitalism, and there was a direct line of progression between the two. Technology, in its broadest sense, had long existed in order to achieve greater human control over nature by increasing production, by extracting wealth from the earth, by going faster or lighting the darkness. That was all part of the "conquest of the material world." Technology also had another dimension: it allowed one group to gain a greater control over other groups by defeating enemies, outwitting

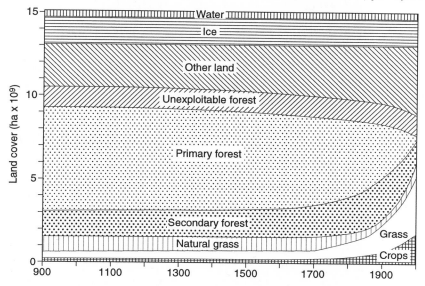

Figure 9.1 The transformation of major global land covers, AD900–2000. *Source:* after Buringh and Dudal, 1987: 15.

competitors, and controlling the vanquished.[2] By 1500, the foundation had been set for global trade and political domination by Europe, an inquisitive attitude toward all knowledge, an arrogant appropriation of the natural world, and the spread of Western peoples and their civilization over the "thinly or weakly peopled parts of the earth." [3]

The power and progress of industrial technology radically altered the pace and nature of the life and livelihood of a large number of people, and the character of their society.[4] Europe and its appendages overseas—North America, Australia, New Zealand, and select parts of Latin America—rapidly followed suit. In Asia, Africa, and the bulk of Latin America, aspects of the same technology, coupled with exploitation and domination by Europeans, had equally dramatic and ultimately devastating effects, overturning ancient ways of life, opening the way for a new global economy, and unbalancing world relations. Everywhere, land cover and land use experienced a dramatic transformation, of which, perhaps, the forest was affected most of all, followed in time by changes in grasslands (fig. 9.1). It was, as we have said before, the biggest change to the vegetation of the world since the Ice Age.

With the passing of the eighteenth century, one epoch in Western civilization's relationship with the natural world ends and another of a different order begins. It was based on machinery and energy use and informed by specialized knowledge; it resulted in the acceleration of the transformation of the natural world. So far and so fast did changes happen that by the early twentieth century there was a sense that things had gotten out of control: that technology was becoming the master of people, and that nature was being changed irrevocably. The succession of interrelated changes was, as David Landes has aptly called it, an "unbound Prometheus," whose suppressed energy and inventiveness burst upon the world.[5]

Needless to say, the significance and effect of the changes *on the forests* between 1750 and 1900 varied both in place and time. To that end the precise division between a European core and "the wider world" no longer suffice as an organizing structure, if only because parts of the periphery, such as North America, Australasia, and eventually Russia and Japan, come increasingly to be a part of the core. It is now more accurate to distinguish a temperate and a tropical world, each with their own deforestation story. There are two separate but intimately intertwined spheres of activity in which disparities became intensified, so that the core became broadly synonymous with temperate and the periphery broadly synonymous with tropical. Later the distinction gets new names: on the one hand, Developed, and on the other, Less Developed, Developing, or Third World.

As before, it is useful to sort out the new forms of environmental change from the old, but in so doing we must look only at those driving forces that can be perceived to have a direct bearing on the pace and extent of deforestation, and that created the cultural climate conducive to change. The old forms still existed, but new ones and new outcomes were in the making: "The shepherd and the goatherd are still in Cyprus, the charcoal burner is in the Ardennes, the tree girdler in New England," wrote Clarence Glacken about the end of the eighteenth century, though adding, "it will not be long before men will look on the vistas of the new Lièges, the Manchesters, and the Dusseldorfs."[6] Of the many driving forces that were formative in these new vistas, five are selected—industrialization, population and migration, colonization, transportation and communication, and domination, preservation, and regulation—each operating and being manifest on various scales, ranging from the local to the global. On the face of it, they may seem disparate, but they all add up to global domination and the transformation of the earth's forest cover.[7] Increasingly, measures of change can be displayed statistically in long time series, which in some tables in this chapter are continued up to the near-present for the sake of completeness.

INDUSTRIALIZATION

Whereas for the Middle Ages it is possible to select individual technological changes that affected forest clearing in Europe, such as plows, horses, harnesses, and field systems, it becomes less easy to do that for the middle of the eighteenth century onward, when there were more complex congeries of interrelated changes—some technological but others financial and attitudinal—that had effects on the forest. The Industrial Revolution is probably one of the most written-about topics of all time; there is a library of works about it.[8] Crucial questions are, How and why did it happen? What was the sequence of causal links that might explain why the revolution began at all, and why it began specifically in Britain?[9] The central role of the agricultural "revolution" in the century after 1750, with its fundamental changes in productivity and husbandry, is acknowledged, but many questions lie beyond that: Did the Industrial Revolution make demographic growth and capital formation possible (did it even occur?)?[10] Did rising demand for all goods make mechanization profitable, did capital enable mechanization, did demographic growth make proletarianization possible, or was it something to do with attitudes of mind and societal structure? What was the role of capital and credit, those "almost indispensable bridge[s] between demand and supply" without which industry could not grow and overseas expansion could not occur?[11] Immanuel Wallerstein finds most explanations unconvincing, but quotes approvingly the simple and straightforward contemporary statement of Natalis Briavonne as to what was going on in 1839:

> The sphere of labor grew larger; the means of production were in the process of being multiplied and simplified each day a bit more. Population grew consequently through the diminution of the mortality rate. The treasures found in the earth were exploited better and more abundantly: man produced and consumed more; he became more rich. All these changes constitute the industrial revolution.[12]

Perhaps Briavonne's summary is sufficient for our purposes, and we must be content with the idea that the revolution was basically a process of "industrialization," to which must be added massive urbanization. But how, specifically, did it affect the forests of the world?

Pace and Location

A preliminary answer to the some of the questions comes from asking where and when industrialization occurred, because its location and movement are important in the story of global deforestation. Needless to say, its progress was uneven. Table 9.1, which enumerates total industrial potential from 1750 to 1980, helps in pinpointing some of the main sequences of timing and diffusion.[13] Industrialization began in England, especially Lancashire and the Midlands, between 1750 and 1830 with one indigenous product, iron, and one exotic product, cotton. At its peak in 1880 the United Kingdom had increased manufacturing output by 36 times over 1750, and accounted for 22.9 percent of the global manufacturing total. Then, with the application of steam to stationary engines and after 1830 to locomotion, industrialization diffused into other parts of western Europe. Not until the later nineteenth century did it spread to Germany and the United

Table 9.1 Total industrial potential, 1750–1980 (index: UK = 100 in 1900)

	1750	1800	1830	1860	1880	1900	1913	1938	1953	1963	1973	1980
Developed	34	47	73	143	253	481	863	1,562	2,870	4,694	8,452	9,718
UK	2	6	18	45	73	100	127	181	258	330	462	441
Germany	4	5	7	11	27	71	138	214	180	330	550	590
France	5	6	10	18	25	37	57	74	98	194	328	362
Italy	3	4	4	6	8	14	23	46	71	150	258	319
Russia/ USSR	–	1	5	16	47	128	298	528	1,378	1,804	3,089	3,475
Japan	5	5	5	6	8	13	25	88	88	264	819	1,001
Less Developed	93	99	112	83	67	60	70	122	200	439	927	1,323
China	42	49	55	44	40	34	33	52	71	178	364	553
India	31	29	33	19	9	9	13	40	52	91	194	254
Total World Industrial Potential	127	147	184	226	320	541	933	1,684	3,074	5,138	9,359	11,041

Source: Bairoch, 1982: 292, 299.

States (13.2 and 23.6 percent, respectively, by 1900), and then later to Russia and Japan. This sequence was accompanied by a less familiar one: an absolute decline in manufacturing in the less developed world which fell from 73.0 percent of the global share in 1750 to 6.5 percent in 1953. The implications for deforestation are clear: Western imports replaced local manufactures and were paid for by exports of primary raw materials, of which timber and the plantation crops that replaced the forest were major items.

Income and Consumption

At one level it would be true to say that nearly all the inventions and changes encapsulated in industrialization had an effect, directly or indirectly, on the vegetation of the world, but from this great array we must select only those aspects of the general process that had a direct bearing on the forests. Foremost was the increased consumption that accompanied the increased wealth, itself the result of economic growth, and timber and timber products were no exception. Real incomes per head accelerated, often in fits and starts but always ascending upward, exceeding 1 percent per annum in many European countries.[14] For example, they averaged 1.25 percent in the United Kingdom after 1780; probably the same amount for France; 0.8 to 1.6 percent for Germany from the 1850s to 1880s; and 2.5 percent for a brief period in Russia from 1860 to 1914. In the United States and "Europe's overseas descendants," growth was more consistent, with the U.S. achieving a steady 1.55 to 1.76 percent increase between 1839 and 1959 on an already high base level to become "unquestionably the richest country in the world" by the 1890s, and Canada and Australia were not far behind.[15]

Increasingly affluent populations in the economic "core" consumed a rising amount of timber products for housing and construction (and, in some countries, for fuel), as well as the food and fiber products that came from the erstwhile tropical and subtropical forested environments. The one well-attested example of timber consumption was the United States, where per capita use of lumber (saw timber) rose from approximately 220 bf (0.51 m^3) in 1850 to 510 bf (1.2 m^3) in 1910. Per capita consumption for *all* timber products, which included fuelwood, was 157 ft^3 (4.445 m^3) in 1910.[16] Although this level of consumption was higher than in any other country, the general upward trend was common everywhere in the industrializing world. Britain, for example, did not build in wood or use much wood fuel after the conversion to coal in the eighteenth century, but consumption was still 40–50 percent that of the United States.[17]

Mechanization and Motive Power

The harvesting and manufacture of lumber was the perfect example of what the Industrial Revolution really meant. The scale of operations, the interrelated inventions, and business and labor organization were geared to mass consumption. Increased consumption in urban and industrial markets meant greater logging activity in the forests and the development of improved methods for handling and moving the bulky raw material. In the mills, timber needed to be processed more quickly and at a greater capacity in order to feed the demand. Consequently, a concatenation of inventions and improvements to existing machinery came into being to boost production.

Table 9.2 Increasing productivity of saws, seventeenth to nineteenth centuries

	Sawmill Output per Day (bf)
Hand-powered pit saw	100–200
Water-powered single blade (1621)	500–3,000
Water-powered single sash (1621)	2,000–3,000
Water-powered muley saw (circa 1780)	5,000–8,000
Water-powered circular saw (1844)	500–1,200
Steam-powered gang saw (circa 1850)	40,000+
Steam-powered circular saw (1863)	40,000+
Steam-powered band saw (1876)	20,000+

Sources: Van Tassel and Bluestone, 1940: 8; Bryant, 1923: 3; Defebaugh, 1906–7: 2:8, 58; Latham, 1957: 209–18.

Log handling and sawmill technology had not changed much since the Middle Ages. It is true that a marginal improvement in productivity occurred during the early seventeenth century, when the old water-powered, single-bladed, up-and-down saws that cut 500–3,000 bf a day had been replaced by finer, multibladed gang saws, and later by light, fast-moving muley saws that doubled production (table 9.2). These had been invented in Holland and/or Germany and introduced into the Baltic lumber industry in the later seventeenth century, from where they diffused widely thereafter.[18]

But the big changes came in the early nineteenth century with improved saws and steam power. Circular saws, invented and used in English shipbuilding yards as early as 1777, penetrated the lumber manufacturing industry slowly at first because they were made of thick plate iron, overheated and wobbled at high speed, had easily breakable teeth, and wasted an enormous amount of wood in the "kerf" or "bite." For example, a saw "bite" of five-sixteenths of an inch could turn 312 bf (8.83 m³) into dust for every 1,000 bf (28.3 m³) of boards sawed. If the bite could be reduced to only one-twelfth of an inch, then the waste was only 83 bf (2.39 m³). Some improvement came in 1846, when Spaulding of Sacramento, California, invented a curved ratchet that held hard-tempered replacement teeth, with the result that the saw could be easily repaired by the insertion of a new tooth. But the need for a thinner, heat-resistant steel and better welding procedures remained, and restricted the widespread adoption of the circular saw until the 1870s. When the new heat-resistant steel blades incorporating these improvements were introduced, production increased enormously. A similar story of invention and subsequent modification before widespread acceptance occurred with the band saw, which had been invented in France in the early nineteenth century, and which eventually pushed up productivity even further.[19]

Water was the main motive power, and subject to all the vagaries of climate and associated river flow, which included drought but more commonly freezing, as most major timber-producing areas were in high-latitude coniferous softwood forests. But it was the application of steam to cutting that eventually shifted productivity to a new high level, although its penetration into lumber-producing areas was perhaps later than might be expected. Of the 1,616 steam engines reported operating in the United States in 1838, only 202, or a mere eighth, were applied to woodworking of any kind, and even as late as 1870 there were still 16,562 water wheels in lumber mills generating 327,000 hp compared with 11,204 steam engines generating 314,000 hp. Even at this late stage, steam power had still not begun to dominate; it was not until the last decades of the century that its adoption became almost universal.[20]

Evidence of the adoption of steam in the timber-producing regions of northern Europe is sketchy. What is known, however, is that as production for export declined on the south side of the Baltic and shifted firmly into Scandinavia proper, the multitude of water-power sites, where the rivers tumbled off the Scandinavian Shield and Norwegian mountains, were systematically utilized to produce hydroelectricity. Consequently, steam made relatively little headway in this region, but electricity achieved the same acceleration of the manufacturing process and fed the rising demand—but later.

Saws and steam were only part of the picture of industrialized logging; there were a host of other inventions as well. Until now logs were handled manually, but the United States led the way with inventions to speed the preparation and finishing of the timber. In the mill, friction feeds, wire feeds, and direct steam-powered carriages increased the speed at which the logs were transported past the saws. New labor-saving devices included the accurate setting of head and side blocks, and a "steam-nigger"[!] for turning the logs for the saw. Now the men hardly touched the logs. In 1863 a Wisconsin lumberman patented the endless-chain method of moving logs from the sorting ponds and into the mills, and few years later the automatic carrying of the sawdust to fuel the boilers of the steam engines was perfected. Double edgers and gang (multiple) edgers expedited the finishing of the wood, and shingle-, stave-, and slab-making machines made it possible to utilize awkwardly shaped material and reduce waste.[21]

In an ever-expanding and ever-more-discriminating consuming market, the rapid and standardized finishing of timber began to assume as much importance as the quantity of raw timber produced. Edgers for squaring boards had been invented in 1825. In 1828, William Wordsworth of Poughkeepsie, New York, invented and patented a planing machine that had an impact on the lumber industry second only to that of the saw. By 1850 it had evolved into numerous specialized forms adapted to all sorts of finishing purposes and final products. Inventions and modifications to lumbering and woodworking machinery flowed through the United States. Patent Office in ever-increasing numbers, and leadership in lumber manufacturing lay unequivocally in the United States.[22] In 1854 a visiting British Parliamentary Committee of Inquiry viewed the developments and was astonished at "the wonderful energy that characterizes the wood manufacture." The extensive specialization of machinery was particularly impressive.

> Many works in various towns are occupied exclusively making doors, window frames, or staircases by means of self-acting machinery, such as planing, tenoning, mortising, and jointing machines. They are able to supply builders at a cheaper rate than they can produce them in their own workshops without the aid of machinery. In one of these manufactories twenty men were making panelling doors at the rate of 100 per day.[23]

The full potential of these inventions would not have been possible without the steam engine to provide the motive power; steam was literally the engine that drove the change. Steam also had the added tendency to centralize operations into increasingly larger mills with increasingly more workers. Mills with an average production ranging from 1.5 to

5.0 million bf/yr were the norm in the mid-1850s in Michigan, but 30 years later, 10 million bf was common, with some mills even achieving outputs of between 50 million and 60 million bf (i.e., 118,000 m³), making them among the biggest businesses of the day.[24] Generally mills were smaller in northern Europe, but almost without exception the adoption of steam led to an increase in size.

The inventions and increasing size of plant boosted production by speeding up the flow of wood through the mills to produce a better, more standardized product, at no greater cost than before; in fact, they often achieved a cheapening of the product. These developments both fed and fueled greater consumption in more-affluent and consumer-oriented populations. Change begot change in a cumulative and self-sustaining advance in technology and output. Gains in productivity in one field exerted pressures on related industrial operations. Not only was more produced faster, but products were manufactured that could not have been produced by the craft industries of the past, which were now waning.[25]

Material changes promoted nonmaterial changes as the factory system dominated lumber production. In the past, mills had usually been one-man or single-family affairs, but as the size of plant increased with the concentration of power sources and machinery, the gap between owner and worker widened, and jobs became more specialized as labor became divided. In the forest individual and neighborhood logging ventures gave way to lumber camps, which were formed to concentrate the productive labor of the male workforce. Whole lumber towns—special settlements devoted entirely to the manufacture of lumber—appeared and then disappeared as the lumber was cut out.

On the business front, there was a rapid evolution of corporations, and the establishment of monopolies and trade associations. Most significant was the vigorous pursuit of vertical and horizontal integration by acquiring large tracts of timberland, or stumpage. This ensured adequate supplies of raw material, and a continuous, uninterrupted, and profitable flow of produce from forest to retail outlet as the new mass-production methods came on stream. It also helped to eliminate rivals, as increasing size, takeovers, and amalgamations were part of the monopolizing concentration process. All this was accomplished by a relentless quest for greater efficiency, greater competition, tight contractual agreements based on the time element, and the mass production of a standardized manufactured end product.[26]

Coal became the prime source of industrial energy, and it was the direct substitute for wood as a fuel; "No nation ever began to look for fuel under ground till their woods were gone," said the bishop of Landaff in 1816, and he was about right.[27] In that year 17.6 million tons were mined in Britain, the most treeless country in Europe, compared with only 942,000 metric tons in fairly well-forested France. Generally, where wood was abundant, the urge to mine was not present. But we have to admit that the role of wood in the energy economies of most countries in the past—or for that matter, even today—is not known. One of the most thorough and up-to-date surveys of "primary" energy production during the last two centuries includes coal, brown coal, natural gas, crude oil, electricity, geothermal and nuclear electricity, and peat, but not wood, "due to insufficient statistics"; and the authors point out that even in up-to-date international publications wood is not included.[28]

Yet in some countries wood was crucial to the industrialization process. In the United States, for example, fuelwood dominated energy production in domestic hearths, charcoal furnaces, and mechanical and locomotive engines as late as the closing years of the nineteenth century, and it only became less significant when alternative sources such as coal, oil, and natural gas came onto the scene. Fuelwood still accounted for four-fifths of all energy use as late as 1867, and not until the mid-1880s did coal overtake it as the principal source. By 1900 fuelwood was probably contributing only 21 percent of the nation's energy needs, and by 1920 a mere 7.5 percent, by which time coal had passed its peak and oil and natural gas were making their impact felt. But even if the relative contribution of wood to energy needs was diminishing, it was still large in absolute terms; and even a share of 5.4 percent in 1940 was probably the equivalent of nearly 4 billion ft^3 (113.2 million m^3) of timber—still more than in any year in the nineteenth century, with the exception of 1899 (fig. 9.2).[29]

Simply , the emphasis on coal in the industrialization process must not obscure the fact that abundant wood was, and still is, a major contributory factor in the drive to industrialization. It still plays a significant role in the process in late twentieth-century Brazil, India, and China.

POPULATION AND MIGRATION

Since 1700 the population of the world has shown a nearly unbroken upward trend, and the increase in numbers has had a severe impact on the world's forests. The global total was 769 million in 1750, and within a hundred years it had nearly doubled to 1,260 million, to double again to reach 2,515 million by 1950 (table 9.3).[30] The relationship between the total number of people in a given territory and deforestation in the developmental phase has been shown time and again to be a very positive one; it is perhaps the one driving force that we can be absolutely sure about.[31] The increment of 1.7 billion

Table 9.3 World population by major regions (millions), 1700–1985 and projection to 2020

	1700	1750	1800	1850	1900	1950	1985	2020
Africa	107	106	107	111	133	224	587	1,441
Asia (total)	435	498	630	801	925	1,375	2,834	4,680
China	–	200	323	430	436	555	1,060	1,460
Japan	–	30	30	31	44	84	121	130
Rest of Asia	–	268	277	340	445	736	1,653	3,090
Europe (1)	92	109	145	208	294	393	492	514
USSR	30	35	49	79	127	180	277	343
N. America (2)	2	3	5	25	90	166	265	327
Latin America (3)	10	15	19	34	75	165	404	719
Oceania	3	3	2	2	6	13	25	37
World total	679	769	957	1,260	1,650	2,515	4,853	8,061

Source: after Demeny, 1990: 42.
(1) Less USSR.
(2) USA and Canada.
(3) South and Central America, Mexico, and the Caribbean.

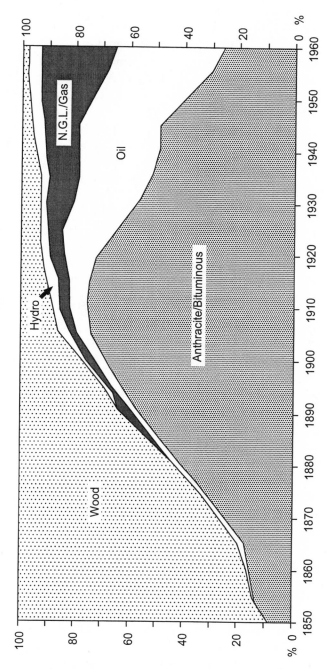

Figure 9.2 Energy sources in the United States as a percentage of total consumption by 10-year periods, 1850–1960. *Source:* based on Schurr and Netschert, 1960: 36–37.

people in 150 years and their inevitable spread meant a need for more land to grow food, more timber to provide shelter, and more fuelwood to cook food and to keep warm. Where rotational bush fallow systems were practiced, they had to be shortened and intensified, leading to greater woodland destruction, and in many places the forest was felled to make way for intensive plantation or commercial peasant cultivation. The weight of population numbers did, and still does, hang heavily on the forest.

The increase in population was first noticeable in the industrialized and urbanized countries of the world, where political stability, and improved nutritional status, was aided by more productive agriculture, an increase in imported foodstuffs and plants, and improved animal husbandry. Better sanitation, hygiene, clothing, and housing, plus better transportation and storage of foods to combat times of dearth, all added up to a major change in mortality. The old demographic regime in which high fertility and high mortality were in rough accord, leading to little increase in population, was increasingly replaced by one of lower mortality, leading to an increase in total population. As industrialization and its benefits progressed and spread during the nineteenth century, so the demographic character of populations changed. Fertility was controlled and highly responsive to changing economic conditions, but it was still high enough to cause a rapid increase in the overall population.[32] In 1750 the population of Europe and Russia was 144 million, and at each successive 50 years between then and 1900 it rose to 194, 287, and 421 million, representing 18.8, 20.3, 22.8, and 28.5 percent, respectively, of the world population. After the beginning of the twentieth century, the proportion fell off.

The increment of over 200 million people in Europe, many of whom were becoming increasingly affluent, not only put pressure on the forests of that continent but also on those overseas. Between the late 1840s and early 1930s, at least 52 million migrants left Europe and Russia. The majority went to the United States, which grew from 3 million in 1750 to 90 million in 1900, but many also went to Latin America (15 to 75 million) and Oceania (3 to 6 million) during the same span of years. There were other significant European settlements in southern and northern Africa, and eastward from European to Asiatic Russia.[33] Altogether, the area of European settlement in Europe proper and in the formerly thinly populated "neo-Europes," which comprised barely 20 percent of the world's population in 1700, rose to 36 percent of the world total by 1900.

Generally, by 1900, the shift in demographic behavior had not yet reached the rest of the world; the population of Africa barely moved, but because Asia already had a high base population, 427 million were added by 1900. Most remarkable was the spectacular expansion in China between 1750 and 1800, when its annual rate of population growth averaged 1 percent, nearly double that of Europe.[34] The expansion continued until about 1850, after which it came to a near halt. China's share of the world total had risen from 26 percent in 1750 to 34.1 percent in 1850, only to fall to 27 percent by 1900.

The population changes occurring after 1900 are left for consideration for later chapters, where they are more relevant, but the point can be made here that sometime after 1900 most of the areas suitable for human settlement under the then existing state of technology had become inhabited. Towns, of course, were going to grow or be established all over the globe,[35] but the outer edges of the great grasslands had more or less been defined, and irrigation in the semiarid areas was amenable to some, but not much, extension. The only great reserve of "unused" land capable of growing more food lay in the forests, which had the added advantage of providing a bonus of raw material and fuel. Consequently, it was the global biome of the forest that was to feel the full weight of human numbers during the twentieth century.

COLONIZATION

The nineteenth century witnessed an unprecedented escalation of change in the world's vegetation as European industrial technology interacted with European imperial territorial ambitions to colonize large areas of the world. In Europe, sharpening political rivalries, "land hunger," and the pursuit of spheres of influence led to rapid overseas expansion, either by formal annexation and colonization or by forming or imposing informal commercial ties over weaker peoples. In this competitive process for territory and global influence Britain became supreme. With the signing of the Treaty of Paris in 1763 at the end of the Seven Years' War, Britain effectively ousted France from the Western Hemisphere, and Spain and Portugal were unable to reassert their old dominance.[36] The story of that expansion is too well known to require detailed review here. Suffice it to say that at the opening of the period, Europe occupied or controlled approximately 35 percent of the world's land surface; by 1878 that proportion had risen to 67 percent; and on the eve of World War I it was 84 percent—more than four-fifths of the globe. Between 1800 and 1878 the average rate of imperial expansion was 216,000 mi^2 a year. Nowhere was too small, too remote, or too barren not to be incorporated in the new nationalistic empires. According to Landes, "This was the high-water mark of the expansion of Europe that began in the eleventh century on the Elbean plains, the plateau of Castile, and the waters of the Mediterranean."[37]

Concomitant with global territorial control went the vigorous, expansive spread of European industrial technology, with its "omnivorous demands for materials, its need for expanding markets and its development of even more efficient tools for overcoming distance and conquering peoples."[38] A dazzling array of interacting inventions and discoveries made contact with the "old" territories in the Americas and Australia easier and quicker, and the conquest of the "new" territories cheaper in cost, cheaper in lives, and more effective than ever before. These "tools of empire," as Daniel Headrick calls them aptly, were of various kinds; some used natural resources, some integrated economic systems, and some allowed a greater manipulation and control of lands.[39]

The new global territorial control was broadly of two kinds. First there was the continued settlement and exploitation of the neo-European temperate lands of the United States, Canada, southern Africa, Brazil, Argentina, and now Australia and New Zealand. For all intents and purposes these were "plantations" in the older sense, simplified social and political offshoots and replicas of the European mother countries; or, to look at this matter in another way, as A. S. Youngson suggested, "the territory utilized overseas by people of European origin in 1800, which was already more extensive than the whole of western Europe, was multiplied in area approximately eight- or nine-fold between 1800 and 1900."[40] Where the settlers were unable or unwilling to do the work themselves, as in the Caribbean, Brazil, or the U.S. South, they had imported slaves. Generally these settler empires were not places to be exploited haphazardly but places that conquest had converted into "an enduring source of wealth."[41] In rapid succession they were firmly incorporated into the periphery, and then, in time, some became an integral part of the core. Some, like the United States, freed themselves of their colonial ties, and were politically independent by the end of the eighteenth century. Brazil and the rest of Latin America were not far behind. But independent or not, they resembled one another in that they were vigorous neo-European "settler empires" that took on a life of their own. They experimented with, and exploited, their resources just as vigorously as had their ancestors back home, particularly the soil of the land and its vegetation. The United States had already shown that its lands were destined to become regions of massive deforestation.

But the significant difference of the nineteenth century compared to previous ones was the concentration of European attention on the tropical world, particularly Africa and Asia. These were the "external areas" of intermittent contact into which forays had been made in the past to create coastal way stations and trading points. These previous contacts had been shallow in depth, temporary in duration, and rarely the basis of settlement and control. They contrasted with the older "periphery" of the Americas and Caribbean, which had been an active theater of colonization and settlement, as well as exploitation. Now Europe attempted to create colonies and "nationalistic" empires in Asia and Africa that were politically submissive and economically profitable to them in crops, minerals, and other raw materials.[42]

Two overriding problems in these new tropical territories made political control and colonization difficult. In Africa disease, which up till now had so favored Europe in its expansion in the New World and Antipodes, was a major obstacle to penetration, though less so in Asia, where the major impediments were the sheer number of people and a pre-existing, organized political state system that was resistant to change. Some technological "tools" were especially significant in overcoming these problems and in creating the "new" imperialism in these tropical areas.[43] In Africa, dysentery, yellow fever, typhoid fever, and, above all, malaria caused enormous mortality among European settlers, missionaries, and traders, and death rates were in the order of 250–750/1,000. But solutions were at hand. The discovery in 1830 of the prophylactic use of quinine, extracted from cinchona bark, counteracted malaria, and between 1820 and 1840 European mortality dropped dramatically to 50–100/1,000. There were still many years to go before 1897, when the *Anopheles* mosquito would be identified as the vector of these diseases, although European mortality rates in Africa were still 10 times higher than for similar groups in Europe—but Africa was no longer "the white man's grave."[44]

Now that a territory's interior could be penetrated, its political control was facilitated by arms. In succeeding decades steamboats (often gunboats) were introduced on the navigable rivers and sheltered coastal waters of Africa and Southeast Asia, China, the Persian Gulf, and India. These were often transported in pieces to these locations (and even overland to avoid rapids, as in the case of the Nile and the Congo) and then reassembled in situ. Gunboats came into their own with devastating effect in China during the First and Second Opium Wars of the middle decades of the century, where they demonstrated their effectiveness as a "political persuader."[45] Another key tool in establishing early superiority was the development of the breech-loading gun during the 1860s, followed in time by the machine gun. The "arms gap" between colonizer and colonized was awesome. As a young subaltern, Winston Churchill witnessed the confrontation between the British under Kitchener and about 40,000 Dervishes at Omdurman, Sudan, in 1898 in one of the last great colonial wars of the century:

> [The infantry] fired steadily and stolidly, without hurry or excitement, for the enemy were far away and the officers careful. Besides, the soldiers were interested in the work and took great pains. But presently the mere physical act became tedious. . . .
> . . . on the other side bullets were shearing through flesh, smashing and splintering bone; blood spouted from terrible wounds; valiant men were struggling on through a hell of whistling metal, exploding shells, and spurting dust—suffering, despairing, dying.

At the end of that day, 20 Britons and 20 of their Egyptian allies were dead, but so too were 11,000 Dervishes.[46] Political domination had replaced political "persuasion," and the control of the Sudan was absolute.

TRANSPORTATION AND COMMUNICATION

Perhaps more than any other single factor in the Industrial Revolution the improvement in transportation and communication, both nationally and globally, was the key to its success. Space and time were compressed by steam locomotives, steamships, and eventually the electronic technology of submarine cables, to allow an integrated global exchange of people, goods, and knowledge. The vast resources of timber, grain, meat, and other products of the neo-Europes were developed and drawn into the world economy, and the previously backward, isolated subsistence economies in the tropics became primary producing areas for the consuming core. Everywhere, the network of communications meant that goods could be transported more cheaply, and electronic information flows meant instant price fluctuation, adjustment, and fine-tuning. All required financial infrastructures, banking, credit, and a reliable monetary system, which developed as fast as did production.[47]

In the tropical world, transportation facilitated political control, which usually resulted in land survey and subdivision, and the imposition of a taxation system. Taxes could only be paid by selling crops for cash (which usually meant expanding cultivation and cutting down trees) and, in time, the importation of Western expertise and technology in order to increase production and lower costs. One incidental but momentous effect of these developments in tropical territories was that greater security, more assured food supplies, and a growing demand for labor stimulated population growth, which was to have dramatic effects on the transformation of the land cover.

Transportation improvement had two broad impacts on the forest. First, it tied the new producing territories in the periphery (either wood-producing or wood-destroying) to the consumer core areas, and, second, it boosted the movement of timber out of the forest. The distinction between these two types of movement is a fine one, and there was much overlap at times; but broadly speaking, the first was global in extent, was often imposed as a part of some imperial strategy, and affected all primary commodities, from cotton to coffee, wheat to wool, and tea to timber, while the second was national in extent, was entered into voluntarily, and specifically affected the movement of lumber.

Across the World

Despite the undoubted power of gunboats and machine guns as "political persuaders" in the new colonies, ultimately they counted for nothing if the conquered territory was not connected effectively to the metropole. And global transportation was what distinguished the "new imperialism" of the later eighteenth and nineteenth centuries, whether in the settler or the nationalistic empires, from the "old imperialism" of the fifteenth to mid-eighteenth centuries. Economic networks were established and new techniques developed in order to exploit these territories. Goods, information, and reports were the lifeblood of the new global thrust, and European countries acquired the means, notes Headrick, "to communicate almost instantly with their remotest colonies, and to engage in an extensive trade in bulky goods that would never have borne the freight costs in any previous empire."[48]

On both land and sea, steam—the most characteristic and pervasive invention of the Industrial Revolution—lowered costs and made it more worthwhile to transport low-value goods over greater distances than before, often helping to decrease the price, which in turn increased consumption and encouraged greater specialization in those places of primary production that had natural advantages. Transportation became quicker, safer, more reliable, better handled, and more punctual, reducing insurance and inventory costs for goods, and ensuring greater comfort and safety for people.[49]

On land, the railway era really got under way after Stephenson's locomotive successfully operated the Stockton-to-Darlington line in 1825, and it lasted for over a hundred years. Railways were not cheap to build, but the expenditure was justified by the improvements they brought: compared with human portage and animal haulage they cheapened costs by anything from 30 to 10 times less; they sped up delivery by between 10 and 30 times; and it was variously calculated that a fairly small train did the work of between 13 and 20,000 human porters. Railways were dependable and, unlike canals and rudimentary roads, were not affected by the weather. Moreover, with their movement of goods and people their economic and social effects rippled through society, making them a spearhead for change and modernization.[50]

Table 9.4 shows the development of permanent track by continent and major country from 1840 to 1960. Railways started in northwestern Europe, diffused throughout the rest of the Continent by 1840, and made massive strides in eastern North America. Both these regions were covered by a dense web of main and feeder lines, so much so that by 1900 nearly 78 percent of the world's track was in these two continents. Elsewhere, in less industrialized and less populated territories, railways either connected main towns or, as in the case of colonial territories in Africa and parts of Asia and Latin America, simply linked coastal ports with continental interiors to create worldwide trading systems. Among these countries India was a special case, with a fairly dense network linking major centers by 1900. The transcontinental lines completed in the United States after 1869, Canada after 1885, and Russia after 1903 had a political as well as an economic significance.[51]

The same revolutionary changes occurred in the world of shipping. The opening of the Suez Canal in 1869 (itself the first major manifestation of the application of steam to

Table 9.4 Length of railway line open (in thousands of km) by continent and major country, 1840–1960

	1840	1860	1880	1900	1920	1940	1960
Europe	4.0	49.8	156.8	262.8	336.2	413.4	421.7
U.K.	2.4	14.6	25.0	30.1	32.7	32.1	29.5
Germany	0.5	11.1	33.8	51.7	57.5	62.0	52.2
France	0.4	9.2	23.1	38.1	38.2	40.6	39.0
Italy	0.2	2.4	9.2	16.4	20.4	22.6	21.3
Russia/USSR	–	1.6	22.8	53.2	71.6	106.1	125.8
Rest of Europe	0.5	10.9	42.9	73.3	115.8	150.0	153.9
North America	7.0	52.5	161.1	339.7	469.4	444.2	421.0
USA	4.5	49.2	150.1	311.2	406.9	376.1	350.1
Canada	2.5	3.3	11.0	28.5	62.5	68.5	70.9
Australia & New Zealand	–	–	7.7	25.0	46.6	50.5	47.7
Latin & Central America	–	1.4	11.1	77.5	111.5	132.9	139.6
Argentina	–	–	2.3	16.8	35.3	41.2	43.9
Rest of region	–	1.4	8.8	60.7	76.2	91.7	95.7
Asia	–	1.3	15.3	55.8	103.6	117.0	156.5
Japan	–	–	0.2	6.3	13.6	25.1	27.9
India	–	1.3	14.5	39.8	59.6	66.0	57.0
Rest of Asia	–	–	0.6	9.7	30.4	25.9	71.6
Africa	–	–	4.6	14.9	47.6	70.9	71.6
South Africa	–	–	1.6	7.0	16.3	21.4	20.5
Rest of Africa	–	–	3.0	7.9	31.3	49.5	51.1
World total	11.0	105.0	356.6	775.7	1,114.9	1,228.9	1,264.4

Sources: Mitchell, 1982: 496–508; Mitchell, 1983: 666–67; Mitchell, 1992: 655–64; Mitchell, 1993: 528–39.

earthmoving) marks a convenient watershed in the development of steam shipping. Before that steam was regarded as a fast and punctual but expensive alternative to sail.[52] But progressive improvements in multiple-cylindered engines that used less coal; the substitution of iron and then steel for wood for stronger, more durable, and more commodious hulls; and the demonstrated efficiency of the propeller over the paddle, all combined to increase speed and carrying capacity while lowering costs.[53] After 1870 and for the next forty years, world steam tonnage increased from 2.7 million to 26.2 million tons, and freight costs were halved during the same period.[54]

The days of moving only "preciosities" were well and truly over, as was the movement of only high-value products such as coffee, tea, silks, and tobacco. Now vast quantities of bulky, low-value goods such as ores, coal, wool, wheat, raw textile materials, and timber, as well as perishable commodities like fruit and meat, were worth shipping to and from distant places. For example, in 1860 alone Britain imported about 1.7 billion bf (4 million m³) of squared and sawn timber, a little under one-third of that from the Baltic and the rest from Canada, and amounts increased substantially afterward.[55] After 1880 refrigeration made it worthwhile to ship meat and butter from Australia and New Zealand, with devastating effects on their forests. All the while, consumers benefited: they paid less, consumed more, and enjoyed rising standards of living.

Together, railways and steamships increased cargo loads and reliability, made human

Table 9.5 Crossties used and estimated ha of forest cleared, world, 1840–1960

	Km of Track (thousands)	Annual Track Increment (thousands)	Ties Used in New Track (millions)[1]	Ties Renewed Annually (millions)[2]	Total Ties Used Annually (millions)[3]	Ha of Forest Cleared (thousands)[3]
1840	11	11	18	2	20	41
1860	105	94	154	23	177	358
1880	357	252	413	78	491	992
1900	776	419	688	169	857	3,414
1920	1,115	339	556	242	798	1,617
1940	1,229	114	187	267	454	1,122
1960	1,264	35	58	275	333	674

Source: based on table 9.4. Conversion factors used as in table 10.9.
(1) 1,640 ties/km of new track.
(2) 217 ties/km of track renewed.
(3) 494 ties/ha of forest.

travel comfortable, and above all reduced time and hence costs. For example, before 1830 a letter and its reply sent between London and Calcutta could have taken up to 2 years by the time the monsoons had been taken into account. With the opening of the Suez Canal, the same process took about 30 days. With the advent of the telegraph and telegram a few years later, a message and its reply would take 1 day. By 1924 the submarine cable network allowed a message to circle the globe in 80 seconds.[56] Each successive invention and development in transportation and communications facilitated or deepened contacts between parts of the globe through a constant flow of goods, people, and ideas, and buyers were put in direct contact with sellers. Isolated subsistence societies with limited trade relationships imperceptibly became part of a single world market in basic commodities that drew on natural resources, such as topsoil, timber, water, minerals, and wild game. Globalization was truly under way. Industrialization, population growth, territorial acquisition, and mechanical energy (particularly steam), together with medicine and agricultural modification of land, shattered traditional relationships and laid the foundations for a worldwide transformation of the land cover.

Railways not only speeded the flow of people, goods, and ideas, but also created a new and enormous demand for timber. Putting aside any demands for construction, rolling stock, and fuel, the railways needed crossties, and many of them. It was calculated that every new kilometer of track required 1,640 ties, which needed to be renewed approximately every 7 years or so; and that because of the special requirements for selecting ties, no more than about 494 were gathered from every hectare of forest (table 9.5). From 1865 onward there was never a year in which at least 500,000 ha of forest were not destroyed for ties; between 1881 and 1945 it never fell below 1 million; and between 1888 and 1915 it never fell below 2 million ha/yr, with the peak of 3.4 million ha coming in 1900. These are clearly average figures and could vary enormously, but even if they are only half right the effect on the world forests would have been staggering. The contemporary American view that the railroad was "the insatiable juggernaut of the vegetable world," though a little exaggerated, was essentially correct.[57]

In the Forest

Wood is a heavy and bulky commodity of intrinsically low value. It is usually found in inaccessible, uninhabited places and has to be transported many hundreds, if not thousands, of miles to its market. From the mid-eighteenth century onward, transportation costs in the large-scale lumbering areas accounted for between one-half and three-quarters of production costs, the remainder being made up of milling, sawing, and stumpage, so that the actual trees were a very small proportion of the total. Transportation controlled or influenced most other factors of production such as capital investment, forest land purchase (stumpage), and the availability of markets, finance, and labor.[58] A cheap system of transportation was therefore essential to feed the growing appetite for timber, and it also had to be flexible enough to accommodate changing sources as supplies were cut out.

Transportation was the major pivot around which revolved the entire process of converting the standing trees to lumber; and like the developments in milling and finishing machinery, the majority of modern innovations originated in the United States, which became the biggest producer and consumer of lumber in the nineteenth century—a position it has never lost—as well as the leader in the "industrialization" of the forest. Of the many new methods of getting the logs out of the forest, three deserve special mention: the log drive, the integration of the continent's rivers, and the application of steam.

The Log Drive

Rivers had always been the obvious choice for the movement of bulky timber from classical times onward. But the new mass-production methods that were emerging during the early nineteenth century demanded a more comprehensive mode of exploitation, and that was the log drive, whereby the whole river catchment and its watercourses were regarded as the venue for extraction (plate 9.1). Said to have originated in 1813 on the Schroon River, a tributary on the headwaters of the Hudson, the log drive started as a means of allowing the new high-production mills and saws to be fed adequately via a mass of individual, part-time farmer-loggers by extending the area of raw material supplies. Each logger cut during the winter and hauled and stacked his logs near the water's edge to await the spring flood. With the spring thaw the logs were thrown into the swollen rivers and carried downstream to the mill. The log drive soon became a complex and, by necessity, highly organized aspect of the lumber industry. The whole operation was analogous to cattle rearing over commons or unfenced plains. Each logger used an elaborate identifying log mark (over 20,000 were registered in Minnesota alone) for his yield, which was "driven" downstream to the millponds, where it was sorted out in enormous pens or "booms" (plate 9.2) near a mill, in order to ensure a ready supply of lumber to feed the new high-production methods (see fig. 9.3).[59]

The system required a great deal of cooperation and/or regulation. Driving, river improvement, and boomage charges were levied at the rate of so many cents per thousand board feet (hereafter mbf) delivered to the mill, and strict laws enforced the start date of the log drive, the methods of sorting, the disposal of "strays," and penalties for "log

Plate 9.1 Industrial logging: the log drive. A logjam in a river in Minnesota, the result of the unregulated felling activities of innumerable individuals and companies. (Forest History Society, Durham, N.C.)

Plate 9.2 Sometimes the products of the individual log drives could be collected within a towable boom. In this view the boom is being towed by steam tug across Rainy Lake, Ontario, to the mill of the Minnesota and Ontario Paper Company at Fort Frances. (Forest History Society, Durham, N.C.)

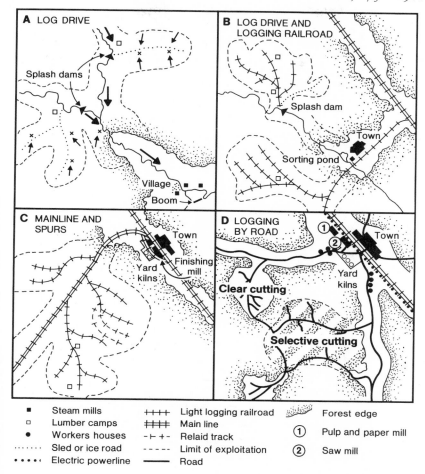

Figure 9.3 Four stages of lumber production: *A*, log drive; *B*, log drive and logging railroad; *C*, main line and spurs of the logging railroad; and *D*, logging by road. *Source:* Williams, 1988.

lifting." There were also charges for building splash dams, which stored water to be released at critical times to increase the volume of the spring flood.[60]

The first well-documented boom was built on the Androscoggin in Maine in 1789, and soon they spread to all the rivers of New England, New York, and Pennsylvania. Maine's Penobscot boom of 1825 was renowned for its size, as was Pennsylvania's Williamsport boom on the Susquehanna constructed in 1846. By 1860 booms existed on all the major rivers in the new lumber-producing areas of the Great Lakes states of Michigan, Wisconsin, and Minnesota, and later spread to rivers in Florida and Alabama that flowed into the Gulf of Mexico, when lumbering got under way in that region.[61]

Without the spatial system of the log drive as part of the new lumber production pipeline, the new high-output, steam-driven mills could not have functioned efficiently and met demand. Even if there were boomage and driving charges, and some logs were lost or damaged, the disadvantages were more than offset by the increased quantity of lumber processed.

The Continental System

While the log drive operated locally, a new river transportation system evolved at the continental level. Using major rivers to link areas of lumber surplus and lumber deficiency had been a common practice in watercourses as far apart as the Tiber, Rhine, Vistula, Seine, Adige, Pontus, and Delaware. Large individual spars, or groups, of logs were lashed together into rafts (and often piled high with smaller timber, fuel, or potash), which were floated down to the mill, market, or shipyard (plate 9.3). The continental system became best developed in the United States. By the late 1830s the industrialized and urbanized eastern seaboard states were experiencing timber deficiencies and consequently bringing in timber via the coast from Maine, then from Ottawa, Canada, then by raft and steamer from the Great Lakes states, to be off-loaded at Buffalo and Tonawanda on Lake Erie. From there it was sent by the Erie Canal to Albany, which grew to be the largest wholesale lumber center at the time, and then down the Hudson to New York.[62] To the west, Chicago after about 1845 came to be the gateway through which the lumber of eastern Wisconsin and western Michigan went into the largely treeless prairie states of the Midwest that were being settled at this time. A subsidiary arm of this western transportation system that emerged during the 1860s and 1870s was the shipment of

Plate 9.3 Industrial logging: rafting yellow poplar logs on the Big Sandy River, Ohio, circa 1920s. This was a small operation in a minor timber-producing area, but it illustrates the principle of fixing logs together, which on the larger rivers of the continent produced rafts of up to 5 acres in size, pushed and nudged along their journey by steam-powered riverboats. (Forest History Society, Durham, N.C.)

lumber from Minnesota and western Wisconsin down the Mississippi in enormous 5-acre rafts, to be broken up at west-bank ports for milling. The end product was then distributed over the plains to the emerging settlements in Kansas, Iowa, and Nebraska, and even as far west as Colorado.[63]

Steam in the Forest

In the vast forests of the cold northern continents, the log drive had disadvantages. It depended on an early freeze, heavy snow for skidding out the logs, and then the spring thaw for moving the logs down to the mills, all of which became more difficult as logging moved further away from the rivers, and certainly when it moved into warmer regions. Therefore, in time, new transportation methods were introduced into the forest in order to speed up and even out lumber production throughout the year, and thereby reduce costs.

A solution for nonsnow months was to replace the "snaking out" of individual logs by bullocks with the "go devil," a rough sled that lifted the front end of a log to stop it from digging into the ground. This was soon replaced by the "bummer cart," a self-loading skidder in which a carriage with huge wheels was linked to a long tongue that acted as a lever, so that with forward movement one end of the log was hitched up under the wheels. More applicable to the northern coniferous forests was the simple and effective solution of ice roads. Developed after 1872, these graded, permanent ways were sprinkled with water over which sleighs could be pulled with a minimum of friction by horses with spike shoes. Four horses could move 30,000 bf of timber, or 120 tons, with little effort. The power of the sleighs was improved by developing steam traction engines, with caterpillarlike treads to cope with the ice. Early experiments in Michigan in 1888 were not wholly successful, but by 1901 A. O. Lombard of Maine had managed to adapt the conventional steam locomotive to ice, and it was capable of moving loads of 120,000 bf, or about 500 tons, on linked sleds.[64]

The independence of logging from snow and ice and an even more certain and controllable means of timber supply could only come with the adaptation of the railway to the operation. If the main-line or common carriers, as they were known, had lines passing near the forests or mills, then all was well; but more often than not that was not the case, as the forests were remote from the main urban and industrial areas. Thus the construction of logging railroads as feeders to the common carriers took off in the Great Lakes states after about 1875. These logging "roads" were lightweight, small-gauge lines that could be laid quickly to exploit the forest resource thoroughly, and then pulled up and relaid in another locality when the trees were cut out. When exploitation moved into the forests of the nonfreezing South and West of the United States as well as tropical areas elsewhere in the world, the logging railroad reigned almost supreme in the industrial exploitation of the forest (fig. 9.3B).

In every way, the railroads and their versatile feeders revolutionized forest exploitation (plate 9.4). At the local level, exploitation penetrated the uttermost extreme of forest stands, evidenced by river booms becoming empty throughout the late 1880s and 1890s as more and more timber was delivered directly to the mills.[65] At the continental level, movement of timber by the river system was replaced by the main-line carriers,

Plate 9.4 The Lackawanna Valley, by George Innes, 1855. Speaking of this painting later, Innes said, "I love it more and think it more worthy of reproduction than that which is savage and untamed. It is more significant. Every act of man . . . marks itself wherever it has been." The cleared fields, the stumps, and the railroad that transported logs and hastened change are testimony to that. (Board of Trustees, National Gallery of Art, Washington.)

which linked all areas and came to dominate lumber distribution (plate 9.5). Chicago, the biggest lumber market in the United States, must stand as an example of these changes; in 1882 the railway contributed a mere 13 percent of the intake of 1.9 billion bf (4.5 million m³) to the city. As the decade progressed, however, the proportion of lumber arriving by railway increased steadily, whereas that arriving by lake and river declined, so that by 1900 more lumber was received by rail than by lake. By 1907 the railroad was supreme, responsible for 82 percent of the total of 2.4 billion bf (5.66 million m³) delivered to Chicago.[66]

There was one more stage in the transportation revolution in the forest (fig. 9.3C). In time, spur rail lines were constructed from the main lines without any break of gauge, thereby quickening and maximizing forest exploitation. Mill owners found it profitable to install drying kilns to assist in seasoning the wood, and planing mills to finish off products that could then be transported directly to the customer. They even began to produce ready-to-assemble houses, churches, stores, barns, and other buildings in a multiplicity of styles that could be ordered from a mail-order catalogue such as that produced by Sears, Roebuck and Co. Timber—and in abundance—was now one of the necessities of life, and the industrialization of the forest was complete.

Plate 9.5 The railroad provided mass movement, versatility, and speed to the industrial logging process, and was particularly important in the largely riverless areas of the South, as depicted in this photograph taken in Arkansas circa 1904. (Forest History Society, Durham, N.C.)

FOREST DOMINATION, PRESERVATION, AND REGULATION

The revolutionary economic, technological, demographic, and territorial changes of the latter half of the eighteenth and the early part of the nineteenth centuries had their intellectual and attitudinal counterparts, often labeled the Enlightenment. The age was rich in ideas and debates about a wide range of issues, such as national character, human history, culture, and environmental influences, and downplayed religious ideas, the individual, and humans in the abstract. The discovery of the wider world of natural history and ethnography by Linnaeus, Banks, Cook, and later von Humbolt and others, and the widespread dissemination of its details and peculiarities through publication, prompted endless questions about primitive peoples, the influence of the environment, and the stages of civilization. It was not that the debate about a divinely designed world was dead; physico-theologians still found evidence of God's divine plan in the creation, but they simply were unable to withstand the broadside of new ideas expressed by people like Hume, Goethe, and Kant, who questioned teleology in nature, nature's immutable laws, and the relationship of humans to it.

There were two main thrusts to this new questioning: by the middle of the eighteenth century, Montesquieu in particular (but there were others of the Physiocratic school) wondered about the influence of climate on the course and character of civilization. He suggested that the environment determined these and many other human endeavors, for nature was superior to all mortal works. The other branch of enquiry emanated from people like Condorcet and Godwin, who were enthusiastic over the political triumphs of the French Revolution, and convinced of the progress and the perfectibility of humankind in a limitless earth. But Malthus, in his first *Essay on Population* (1798), dissented from this view. The earth set limits, and checks to growth were the natural order as the weight of humankind pushed against the limits of subsistence. The ideas of Malthus are too well known to need rehearsing, but whatever one thinks about their moral and practical implications, he was the first to bring together the two facts of population numbers and resources. In his mind the former would outstrip the latter, causing human progress to be uneven and uncertain. This Malthusian "equation" is still a powerful concept with much life in it today.[67] One consequence of its initial presentation was that almost every country in Europe began to engage in inventories of natural resources, and empirical studies of forests.

This is a mere hint of the richness and volume of literature generated during these and succeeding years about human relationships and attitudes toward nature. The writings accelerated and increased throughout the nineteenth century, especially after Darwin questioned the whole edifice of Western ideas about the origins of humankind.

But there was also another dimension to the Enlightenment. Knowledge and speculation about the character and human alteration of the New World offered opportunities for comparison, of which the most striking was that between long-settled Europe and yet-to-be-settled America. In particular, the spectacular expanse of forest in the United States, and its equally spectacular clearing, gave rise to an increasingly technical literature about forests and their relationship with soils, disease, erosion, and climate. The physical environment of the New World, according to Glacken, assumed the character of a "great outdoor laboratory for scientific study."[68] It also was the place where some of the early concerns about preservation began.

Domination: "The Epoch of Man"

In the Mind

The speculations of Montesquieu, Godwin, and Condorcet (and Malthus, perhaps, a little less) could be said to have taken place in the mind, while on the ground in Europe, North America, and elsewhere in the world, the forest was still being cleared at a ferocious rate for its timber, fuel, and land. None of these writers were concerned with changes brought about by humans, nor were they specifically concerned with the forests. They recognized that humans were agents of change but gave it little further thought.

The one major exception was George-Louis Leclerc, comte de Buffon, whom we have met before in relation to the culture of trees. Buffon was a great synthesizer of the new knowledge of the natural and physical world that was unfolding during his lifetime. Between 1749 and 1804 he wrote the massive 44-volume *Histoire Naturelle Générale et Particulière,* an account of changes to the environment made by humans as a result of the growth and migration of population, the expansion of cultivation, and the domestication of plants and animals. Buffon had no romantic illusions about nature, nor for that matter about primitive societies; and while he thought nature a part of a divine creation, he also believed its power to be immense, living, inexhaustible, and even hostile. Humans brought order to nature by controlling it—by draining, clearing, diking, domesticating, and otherwise altering it. "Wild nature is hideous and dying; it is I, I alone who can make it agreeable and living," he wrote. Man was "king on earth" and master of nature, and by his activities brought order out of chaos and "improved" nature by turning forests, thickets, and swamps into meadows and arable fields. In this way the processes of nature were improved, so that it was brought to its current state of magnificence.[69]

In volume 5 of *Histoire Naturelle,* entitled "Des époques de la nature," Buffon examines what he calls the epochs of creation and change. The seventh and final epoch was "The Epoch of Man", beginning with early humans assuming control of their environment through the use of fire and clearing, thereby making lasting and widespread changes to the forest and the world. Unwittingly, with "The Epoch of Man" Buffon had written the epitaph of the coming age.[70] On the face of it the early writing of Buffon, the concerned forest cultivator, conservationist, and botanical expert, and the later writing of Buffon, the forest destroyer and extirpator, seem inconsistent. But the apparent contradiction can be explained when one realizes the degree to which his theory of the formation of the earth was influenced by the debate about the relationship of forests to other natural phenomena then going on in the New World.

Ever since Christopher Columbus had said that he knew "from experience" that the clearing of the forest cover of the Madeira, Canary, and Azores islands had reduced their rain and mist, the relationship between forests and climate had run *sotto voce* through debates about clearing, nowhere more so than in those regarding the vast forest domain of America.[71] Hugh Williamson suggested in 1770 that forest clearing had made the winters less harsh and the summers cooler during the preceding forty years. Noah Webster (of dictionary fame) in 1799 found no evidence of long-term change in climate, but conceded that clearing could make significant changes by exaggerating extremes.[72] For Buffon, the key was heat, for it was essential to life on earth, and anything that increased it was good. Forests harbored and safeguarded moisture (and possibly also harbored disease) at the expense of heat, which was necessary for the multiplication of life, so forests were inimical to nature and civilization.[73] Therefore, in the New World, large areas of forest had to be cleared to make the earth habitable, but in Europe too much had gone on already. In either case, in a "modern" country the forest had to be tended with care and foresight, and restored. Buffon's commitment to forest restoration was not in doubt, and in addition to his forest culture tracts, he was also involved in campaigns to increase the use of coal for smelting in order to lessen the demands on woodland.[74] The philosophical foundations had been set for seeing human agency as formative in the fashioning of the natural world.

On the Ground

It is doubtful if any of the immigrant or native-born pioneer settlers in North America, or, for that matter, those anywhere else in the world, whose actions on the ground were causing this debate, had heard of Buffon let alone read him; but intuitively they had come to very similar conclusions for somewhat different reasons. On a physical level the forest was an immense, hostile, and uncomfortable environment that was a threat to survival; on a symbolic level, as we have seen before, it was repugnant, being dark, sinister, devoid of order, and the abode of wild beasts and wild men. The settler had little time or value for the beauty and novelty of the untouched forest, which was worth contemplating only when it lay felled by the ax. His was a strictly utilitarian view, so the forest was good only inasmuch as it became either improved land or lumber, or the site of settlements—and quickly at that. The forest stood in the way of progress.[75]

Alexis de Tocqueville caught this mood brilliantly when he described frontier life in Michigan in 1831:

> [T]he pioneer, living in the wilds . . . only prizes the works of man. He will gladly send you off to see a road, a bridge, or a fine village, but that one should appreciate great trees and the beauties of solitude, that possibility completely passes him by.

Generally, Americans, like pioneers everywhere, were

> insensible to the wonders of inanimate nature and they may be said not to perceive the mighty forests that surround them till they fall beneath their hatchet. Their eyes are fixed upon another sight . . . peopling solitudes and subduing nature.[76]

Just like their Puritan forbears, the Promised Land or Paradise was within their grasp, provided the obstacle of trees was first cleared by backbreaking work and toil.

But even to these hard-bitten pioneers the act of clearing was not without its subconscious imagery and symbolism. Clearing was an act of redemption, and the destruction of the forest was uppermost in their minds in the making of their new, common wealth. In the clearings God could look down benevolently on their efforts to reestablish the order and morality that had gone out of their life on their departure from their native land, and to counteract the evil that always threatened on the forest edge.[77] In emphasizing the hardships and temptation of the forest environment, the pioneers fulfilled two aims: first, the struggle with the forests tempered the spiritual quality of those who faced it, and they were better, humbler beings for the trial of clearing; second, it was a reminder to later generations of the magnitude of the accomplishment and the character of those who achieved it.

Above all it was the sheer size of the forest that astonished and frustrated the New World pioneers. The forest was impersonal and lonely in its endlessness; consequently, clearing was likened to a struggle or battle between the individual and the immense obstacle that had to be overcome in order to create a new life and new society. If the immigrant Anglo-Saxon farmer in England, the ancestor of so many Americans, could be described in the chronicles of about AD 800 as "the grey foe of the wood," then within another 800 years it was the American pioneer who was reenacting the role. The image of the heroic struggle to subdue the sullen and unyielding forest by hand, and to make it something better than it was, was a legacy of feeling, thought, and imagery that was handed down over the centuries. For Francis Parkman in 1885, the forest was "an enemy to be overcome by any means, fair or foul," and Frederick Jackson Turner, the inheritor and brilliantly successful interpreter of these deeply held images, echoed these ideas and attitudes in his account of early pioneer life. The forest frontier, and subsequently the wider frontier, was the ultimate American symbol and the place where the pioneer cre-ated the world anew.[78]

Thus, although the motive for clearing the forest was virtually sacred, increasingly it came to have take on secular overtones as well. The concepts of progress, development, and ultimately of civilization itself had never been far beneath the surface even from the beginning of settlement, because they were the logical outcomes of the fight for survival. However, from the eighteenth century onward the concept of *controlling* nature and making it more *useful* gained strength. The ideal was the rural, domesticated, agrarian landscape that Crèvecouer had extolled, and the making of it was replete with ethical bet-terment, as Benjamin Franklin had suggested. The link with virtue was pointed out ex-plicitly in President Andrew Jackson's second annual address, in which he asked, not for a moment doubting the answer,

> What good man would prefer a country covered with forests, and ranged by a few thou-sand savages to our extensive Republic, studded with cities, towns, and prosperous farms, embellished with all improvements which art can devise or industry execute, occupied by more than 12,000,000 happy people, and filled with all the blessings of liberty, civilization and religion?[79]

If the forest and the Indian were swept aside in the process, then so be it. Not only was progress good; it was inevitable.

The detail of motivation and action can be varied here and there; it was writ large in North America, but for the most part it was the same whether in Europe itself, or in Aus-tralia, Canada, Siberia, in fact in all the neo-Europes and territories that were colonized. But it was not a specifically "European" phenomenon; we merely know more about it than clearing, say, in China, or elsewhere. Wherever humans needed land to grow food or timber to cook, keep warm, or to construct a shelter, the forest was in retreat.

Preservation

Destruction of the forest reached new levels of intensity and extent during this era, but there were some countervailing tendencies that would lead in time to its preservation in parts of the world. Concern about the forest focused on two broad issues: did clearing af-fect the "harmonies of nature"—in other words, did it have an environmental effect; and was the presence of forests a "tonic" for the new industrialized and urbanized popula-tion—in other words, did it have an ethical effect?

The Harmonies of Nature

The wider issues of the consequences of felling the forest did not end with the musings of Buffon. Nothing like the American environment had been experienced before, and the possible alteration of its soils and climate through agricultural clearing came under in-creasing scrutiny. Perhaps too much could be cleared with unforeseen and deleterious consequences? In 1804, Count Volney mounted a sustained inquiry into these matters. He was convinced that the alteration of the climate was "an incontestable fact" and had occurred "in proportion as the land has been cleared." Moreover, if stream flow was di-rectly related to the amount of forest cover and hence humus accumulation, then clearing, could not but reduce stream flow and bring about eventual aridity. Humans, therefore, were the agents of change who upset the harmonies of nature.[80]

More thoughtful still was John Lorain's *Nature and Reason Harmonized in the Practice of Husbandry,* published posthumously in 1825. Lorain saw nature as having a system or cycle of decomposition, growth, and change that returned humus to the soil, but continual plowing and cropping were the "hand of folly" that destroyed that cycle. Moreover, by destroying the protective vegetative cover, humans interfered in the process of runoff from the uplands and hence deposition in the lowlands. In one blow, two fundamental processes in nature were affected. To illustrate his point Lorain contrasted in some detail the clearing practices of the New England and Pennsylvania farmers. Both were destroyers of the forest, the New Englander slightly less so because he tried to increase livestock and hence grass cover and manure. However, his destructive use of burning ultimately matched the Pennsylvanian's continual cropping and lack of manuring. Lorain concluded:

> Perhaps a better method could be devised for clearing the woods, or a more profitable first course of crops be introduced, if it were not that by far the greater part of the animal and vegetable matter which nature had been accumulating for a great length of time, is destroyed in a day or two, by the destructive and truly savage practice of burning.[81]

He had come to what was really a momentous and far-reaching conclusion: whereas nature had long time processes, humans had short ones. Rather than merely conquering and controlling nature, humans were destroying it at a rate that was more rapid than their ability to adjust their activities, leading to permanent damage to the environment. Buffon's "Epoch of Man" was truly upon the world.

It was on such building blocks as these—along with the writing of Jean Baptiste Boussingault and Antoine Becquerel during the 1830s and 1850s on forests and climate, and some remarks by Alexander von Humboldt[82]—that George Perkins Marsh built his magnificent edifice published in 1864, *Man and Nature: Or, Physical Geography As Modified by Human Action.* Marsh was a sheep farmer and mill owner from Woodstock, Vermont, but he was also an extremely observant and learned man. In 1845, when was asked to address the farmers of Rutland at their annual fair, he moved beyond economic concerns about the shortage and price of fuelwood to talk of other things. Everywhere in the state, he said, "the signs of artificial improvement are mingled with the tokens of improvident waste." Denuded hilltops and slopes, dry streambeds and ravines furrowed out by torrents, had all followed agricultural clearing. If a middle-aged farmer returned to his birthplace, Marsh continued, he would look upon "another landscape than that which formed the theatre of his youthful toils and pleasures."[83] In short, the visual world had changed markedly through human action.

In 1861 Marsh was appointed U.S. ambassador to the new kingdom of Italy, and it was there that he wrote *Man and Nature.* Drawing on his early Vermont experience, stimulated by the examples of the devastated landscapes of Mediterranean Europe, and drawing on a vast historical, philosophical, and scientific literature now available to him, he compiled a highly readable account of the human impact on the environment through time. The theme of the injury to earth by humans dominates the work. More than one-third of the book deals with forests, taking the form of a painstaking review of the literature on forest influences on temperature, precipitation, soil formation, fauna and flora, and human health and disease, and the role of forests in maintaining the flow of springs and retarding erosion and flooding. Marsh's conception of the forests went far beyond their value for timber production, and he adumbrated a concern for the total forest ecosystem.

Marsh's changing the emphasis of the deforestation argument from purely economic to environmental concerns was a tremendous intellectual leap. Although humans had always intervened in nature, that intervention had always been considered "improving" the land and beneficial to it—rarely, if ever, a detrimental act. Marsh was certain that nature was in a state of equilibrium except for the disturbances made by humans, though just as humans could disturb, they could mend. He ended his book by asking "whether man is of nature or above her?"—a question that was crucial to the forest then as it is in a global sense now. Marsh's challenging query was a new facet in the relationship of humans to not only the forests, but the whole of nature. In a sense, *Man and Nature* was a philosophical treatise documented with technical details. The findings of emerging science and technology were converging with the seventeenth-century conception of nature as divinely designed harmony.[84]

Here, then, were some of the first stirrings of environmental awareness and the conservation movement, as it became known in the Western world. It started in the forest, and as we shall see in chapter 11, it drew on various experiences from around the world, including India—but it certainly came to its fullest fruition in America.

Tonics for Civilization

Trees, provided they were not in endless, gloomy forests, had always held a fascination for some people. Sacred groves, druidical temples, and individual trees associated with particular historical events and heroes had been venerated and protected for millennia. But as we have already seen, midst the general furor of destruction that characterized the age, the latter part of the seventeenth century saw the emergence of a more generally sympathetic attitude toward trees, both individually and en masse; trees were assuming an emotional importance.

The new sensibility had a number of sources. In England, the idea of tree planting as opposed to tree cutting was gaining ground. It is said to have begun with John Evelyn's *Sylva* of 1664, but for all its literary success and publicity, many landowners had already found pleasure in planting trees.[85] Moving beyond utility and the needs of the navy, construction, and fuel, important as these were, the activity was becoming an integral part of the landscape cult as well as the public display by a landowning class of its power and wealth. That power was compounded by a sense of immortality, as trees were an enduring monument of the continuity of the families that planted them, and thus provided a "visible symbol of human society." Avenues and particularly clumps of trees adorned the private parks, and new exotic species such as poplar, plane tree, cedar of Lebanon, sequoia, spruce, fir, and larch, and a variety of shrubs such as rhododendron, acacia, buddleia, and hydrangea, to mention only a few, became part of the new landscape furniture of ornament, amenity, and display. Without trees nature could not be "chastened or polished."[86]

But the significance of trees went even further than domestication, as they "gradually achieved an almost pet-like status." The gathering momentum of the Romantic movement saw grandeur, even sublimity, in trees; "The love of woods," said Joseph Addison in 1713, "seems to be a passion implanted in our natures," and William Gilpin, the arch exponent of the picturesque, thought trees "the grandest and most beautiful of all the productions of the earth." Besides their intrinsic beauty, trees—particularly oaks—symbolized continuity, strength, and even patriotism (they were the raw material of the navy, the source of British power), and these positive associations meant that they were cherished and worshipped as sources of pleasure and inspiration. In time they even assumed a religious tinge as the analogy between groves and religious architecture became firmly etched in peoples' minds.[87]

In contrast, hostility and repugnance toward the forest remained the dominant feeling in America, as the bulk of the population was still confronting it and clearing it. But in time, as in England, the forest began to find new champions among those who found aesthetic values in it and even associated its primitive, primordial condition with the works of God. The advances of eighteenth-century science had produced a new wonder and awe of nature and a feeling that God showed His power and excellence in such untouched environments. Moreover, as the proponents of the picturesque were at pains to point out, nature's "roughness" had a certain pleasing quality about it.[88]

Others went further: wild nature was sublime, and disordered, chaotic scenes could please and exalt just as easily as the comfortable, well-ordered landscapes of cleared and made land. If God and His beauty could be found in the forest, then would not humans be more perfect if they were in touch with that environment? From Daniel Defoe's *Robinson Crusoe* (1719) to Jean-Jacques Rousseau's *Emile* (1762), there had been a suggestion that the primitive life, despite its disadvantages, produced a happiness and wholesomeness that was not found in man-made agricultural landscapes, let alone cities.[89] Innocence was contrasted with sin and guile; the natural nobility of the person brought up in "nature" with the product of the new urbanized society.

Deism, sublimity, the picturesque, and the primitive fused in the multistranded Romantic movement, which also emphasized the strange, the solitary, and the melancholy. Consequently, Byron's "There is a pleasure in the pathless woods" and Wordsworth's "One impulse from a vernal wood will tell you more of man" were more than mere lines of pretty nature poetry; they were a revolution in thinking about the natural world and a substitute for moral philosophy. An early expression of romanticism in America was in the writing of the vicomte de Chateaubriand, who said that he was seized with "a sort of delirium" when he found so little evidence of civilization in his travels in 1791 and 1792. In contrast with the situation in "man-made" Europe, his imagination "could roam . . . in this deserted region, the soul delights to busy and lose itself amidst the boundless forests . . . to mix and confound . . . with the wild sublimities of Nature." And Philip Freneau was not speaking for himself alone when he said that he found "something in the woods and solitudes congenial to my nature."[90]

While the romantic gave the forests a new meaning for some people, admiration for what had once been rejected was bolstered by yet another change of attitude that can best be called the "patriotic." The quest for something distinctively and uniquely American compared to the antiquities of the Old World was fulfilled by nature and its seemingly pristine wilderness of forests, plains, and mountains. Chateaubriand touched upon this feeling when he said, "there is nothing old in America excepting the woods. . . . they are certainly the equivalent for monuments and ancestors." Diarists and naturalists, as well as fiction writers and artists, drew on this vein of feeling to contribute to "a proper feeling of nationality." [91]

By the mid-nineteenth century the significance of the uniquely American character of the continent's scenery took another twist with the writings of Ralph Waldo Emerson and particularly of Henry David Thoreau. Both expounded the transcendentalist philosophy that the experience of nature in general, and forests in particular, produced a higher awareness and sense of reality than did one's physical surroundings, particularly cities that were dominated by exploitation and expansion. Forests, on the other hand, were "God's first temples." Unlike their Puritan forebears, who thought that morality stopped on the edge of the clearing, the transcendentalists thought that it began there. The argument went further. If the forests and other wilderness areas were uniquely American, and if God's purpose was made more manifest in such places, then the very spirit of America and its creativity came from the forests, from whence came, said Thoreau, "the tonics and barks which brace mankind." "In the woods," echoed Emerson, "we return to reason and faith." In a sense this argument reflected a resuscitation of physio-theology in a new guise, and the return of teleology to the environmental agenda. [92]

Regulation

Somewhere between the domination of the forest through extirpation for agriculture and indiscriminate logging and its preservation through planting and for aesthetic enjoyment lay its regulation for the maximum production of wood. These categories correspond almost perfectly to Keith Thomas's trilogy of human approaches to the natural world: the elimination of the wild, the worship of the beautiful, and the domestication of the useful. [93] Of course, to a certain extent the forest in the older, settled parts of the world had been "domesticated" for centuries as a source of wood, wild browse, and game. An elaborate codification of uses and rights had grown up over thousands of years, but the purposeful alteration of the forest composition for maximum yield had never been attempted. However, the Enlightenment approach of quantification and rationality that flowered in Europe from the mid-eighteenth century onward was to change all that. What Henry Lowood has aptly called the "calculating forester" attempted to maximize the output of wood, an attitude and approach that was ultimately to have a global influence in later centuries. [94]

Forest regulation was very specially the product of the many princedoms of eighteenth-century Germany. Almost without exception they sought to make amends for the widespread devastation and neglect that was the outcome of the Seven Years' War (1756–63).

The specter of wood shortages, particularly fuelwood, seemed very real and caught the attention of a group of enlightened bureaucrats and conscientious foresters. A new science arose, known as the cameral sciences, a term derived from the *kammer* (chamber) in which the princes' advisors traditionally debated issues of economy, forests, finances, administration, and policing as well as manufacturing, agriculture, and trade. All these activities seemed amenable to a "rational economic regulation," and because the forests were such a significant element of the wealth of the princedoms, they were especially singled out for this treatment. Forests could be "managed" quantitatively and rationally, but that required training. Specialist schools and university courses were set up to teach "forest science" and "forest economy," thus establishing Germany's reputation for originating these approaches. The publication of Wilhelm Gottfried von Moser's *Principles of Forest-Economy* in 1757 was especially significant, and it became the bible of the new cadre of "patriotic" foresters replacing the old *jäger,* or honorary forest officials, who tended to preserve the forest primarily for hunting, with timber production a very low priority.

With the declared aim of treating the forests as a cash crop, the calculation of the mass or volume of their yield replaced the old area-based systems of measurement as the basis of quantitative forest management. The awkward shape of the tree trunk led to its being regarded as a cone, a concept that was endlessly refined statistically to become an almost abstract representation of the *Normalbaum,* or "normal tree," which was the basis of inventory, growth, and yield. From this calculation of woody fibrous mass it was a short step to regarding the standing forest as capital and its yield as interest; and one could complete the chain of conversions from wood, to units of measure, to units of currency, and then estimate the worth of a forest and predict its tax yields and future income.

The notion of a regulated forest filled with "standard" trees was soon translated into management practices that reconstructed the forest to grow only "standard" trees. This required a minimum diversity of species to simplify the calculation of the forest "balance sheet" that was in equilibrium with the state's yield projections for that forest and hence harmonized with the state financial balance sheet. Completing the trilogy of quantitative principles was the idea of sustained yield, the cutting of sufficient trees to meet the state balance sheet—a concept that became one of the cornerstones of forest management then and in the future.[95] Sustained yield also brought the element of time into forest science, so that the foresters' role moved from that of measurer to that of curator of the stock. The domestication of the trees and regulation of the forest was complete.

The monocultural, even-aged forests of Germany and many other parts of the world are the outcome of the cameral tradition. Order was imposed on disorderly nature, geometric perfection replaced the ragged edges of natural growth, and sustained yield became the forester's guiding principle. Wherever the aim was to "manage" the forests for timber production, these principles dominated, and denoted a well-managed forest. When the Americans, the French, the Australians, the British in India, and even Forestry Commission members in Britain wanted a more professional, scientific forest corps and a better conservation and management of the forest in order to stave off any impending timber "famine," they imported German ideas, and the German foresters who had the reputation for knowing what to do. In the United States it was Carl Schurz, Bernhard

Fernow, and even Gifford Pinchot, who was trained in the German school; in British India it was Dietrich Brandis, Berthold von Ribbentrop, and Robert Troup; in Britain it was William Schlicht; and in Australia it was Berthold von Ribbentrop and Frederick Mueller.

Of course, other national experiences have been subtly different from those of the United States, Britain, and Germany, and much has yet to be written about the cultural significance of the forest and trees for different peoples. But the themes that run through the British, American, and German stories, ranging from repugnance and destruction to love and protection, from the practically environmental and excessively regulatory to the irrationally aesthetic, and from the moral to the patriotic, all have their counterparts in other countries to some degree. And because of the global and intellectual dominance of these countries during the last two hundred years, their attitudes and experience have spread far and wide. Of one thing we can be certain: these conflicting attitudes and aims of preservation, domestication, and regulation will always encompass the economic, the environmental, and the ethical requirements of the society affirming them. They are always in a state of tension, and which goal dominates greatly depends on the degree to which the forest is essential to survival for a large part of the population. That is the dilemma that we must attempt to unravel in succeeding chapters.

Chapter 10

Clearing in the Temperate World, 1750–1920

The vast extension of railroads, of manufactures, and the mechanical arts, of military armaments, and especially of the commercial fleets and navies of Christendom within the present century, has greatly augmented the demand for wood.
—GEORGE PERKINS MARSH, *Man and Nature* (1864)

America is glutted with its vegetable wealth, unworked, solitary.
—ARNOLD GUYOT, *The Earth and Man* (1849)

If mere cultivation be not beauty, it is closely allied to it. . . . Every acre, reclaimed from the wilderness, is a conquest of "civilized man over uncivilized nature."
—ADAM HODGSON, *Letters from North America* (1823)

THE LATE eighteenth and the bulk of the nineteenth centuries were a period of maximum deforestation in the temperate lands of the world. All the trends and forces noted in chapter 9 were in operation, and they all worked with ever-accelerating speed, intensity, and effect as populations grew, affluence increased, and steam power and other industrial methods were applied to timber extraction, transportation, and processing. It was during these centuries that the new "settler empires" of North America, Australia, and New Zealand really came into their own, and vast areas of forest were felled and put under cultivation. Even older settled areas in Europe, particularly Russia, saw millions of hectares of forest disappear before the plow. In China, the huge expansion of the peasant population gobbled up the remaining vestiges of extensive forest. Everywhere, agriculture expanded at the expense of the forest, and industrial logging aided the process.

Some idea of the magnitude of agricultural expansion is given in table 10.1, which shows land use in the temperate areas of the world for 1700, 1850, and 1920, as far as can be reconstructed. The amount of cropland increased by 238 million ha between 1700 and 1850 and a further 243 million ha during the next 70 years to 1920; and the forest decreased by 180 million and 135 million ha, respectively, during the same periods, for a total decline of 315 million ha. The figures for forest conversion in North America are conservative, as more detailed work shows that the amount of "improved land" (plate 10.1)—in other words, cleared land in forests, which was always more than

Table 10.1 Cropland and land cover change (in millions of ha), temperate world, 1700, 1850, and 1920

	Cropland			Cropland Change		Forest Change		Grassland Change	
	1700	1850	1920	1700–1850	1850–1920	1700–1850	1850–1920	1700–1850	1850–1920
Europe	67	132	147	65	15	−25	−5	−40	11
Russia	33	94	178	61	84	−71	−80	10	−4
N. America	3	50	179	47	129	−45	−27	−1	−103
Pac. developed	5	6	19	1	13	0	−6	−1	−8
Subtotal	108	282	523	174	241	−141	−118	−32	−104
China	29	75	95	46	20	−39	−17	−7	−3
Total	137	375	618	238	243	−180	−135	−39	−107
Temperate total, 1700–1920				481		−315		−146	

Source: after Richards, 1990: 164.

Note: The estimates for 1700 were drawn from Richard A. Houghton et al., "Changes in the Carbon Content of Terrestrial Biota and Soils between 1860 and 1980: A Net Release of CO_2 to the Atmosphere," 235–62 and table 1 (p. 237). The remaining values were taken from *World Resources Review 1987*, table 18.3 "Land Use, 1850–1980" (p. 272), based upon additional modeled information supplied by Richard A. Houghton and David Skole. Besides the addition of the 1700 data, Richards's 1990 table differs from the *World Resources Review* table in three main respects: different values for grassland and pastures in North America and China, and for forest and woodland in Europe.

Plate 10.1 "Land Improvement." From George H. Andrews, *Modern Husbandry: A Practical and Scientific Treatise on Agriculture*, 1853.

cropland alone—rose by 92.2 million ha after 1850, not the mere 27 million ha listed in the table above. Before 1850 three-quarters of the cropland came out of forest and woodland areas, but after 1850 the proportion dropped to a little over one half. Increasingly greater amounts of cropland were created in the open grasslands of the prairies that were many times easier to prepare for cultivation.[1]

In all countries, shipbuilding; the refining and conversion of materials as varied as clay, lime, and metals (particularly iron); and the manufacture of beer, sugar, and bread all formed nodes of intensive wood use, drawing in their supplies from a wide radius. Of course, the discovery and increasing use of coal meant that wood was not the only fuel used, but coal substitution really affected only Britain, parts of western Europe, and the eastern seaboard of the United States. Wood still accounted for the bulk of energy needs in most parts of the world well into the twentieth century.

As the demand for constructional and general timber rose, so timber deficits occurred in western Europe and even on the eastern seaboard of the United States. They were alleviated only by the importation of timber in unprecedented quantities from the northern coniferous forest belts of Scandinavia, Russia, Canada, and the United States, meshing these countries together into a new Atlantic and Baltic system of production and consumption. In these northern forests industrial logging expanded and stands were destroyed or thinned. To a much lesser extent, the selection of mast timber and the making of potash and tar also affected the integrity and extent of the forest. In 1864 George Perkins Marsh summed up what he thought was happening:

> The vast extension of railroads, of manufactures, and the mechanical arts, of military armaments, and especially of the commercial fleets and navies of Christendom within the present century, has greatly augmented the demand for wood.[2]

Everywhere in the temperate world the toll on the forests was relentless and far reaching, and land cover and land use was transformed dramatically.

EUROPE: THREE STORIES OF CLEARING

During the late 1860s the amount of land covered by forest in European countries showed a wide variation (table 10.2). Other than the largely agriculturally untouched coniferous wildernesses of the Scandinavian countries and Russia, centuries of clearing had reduced the area of land covered by forests to less than 30 percent. Germany was just over one-quarter forest covered; France, Switzerland, and Sardinia, a little more than 12 percent; and the rest of Europe had very little woodland. Nonetheless, given the long centuries of exploitation, the surprising thing was that so much remained.[3]

The forces and cultural climates that drove and guided these biotic transformations in the temperate world varied enormously among individual countries. There was no common deforestation experience but rather a multiplicity of them, not all of which can be explored here, though some will be singled out because of the way they contribute to the wider story. In Europe, France had been long aware of the value of forests but was experiencing mounting tension about their destruction; and Russia, practiced unrestrained clearing. Moreover, Britain had little forest left, but its industrialization gener-

Table 10.2 Proportion of forest cover and acres
of forest per person, Europe, circa 1868

Country	Percent	Acres/pop.
Norway	66.0	24.61
Sweden	60.0	8.55
Russia	30.9	4.28
Germany	26.58	0.6638
Belgium	18.52	0.186
France	16.79	0.3766
Switzerland	15.00	0.396
Sardinia	12.29	0.223
Naples	9.43	0.138
Holland	7.10	0.12
Spain	5.52	0.291
Denmark	5.5	0.22
Great Britain	5.0	0.10
Portugal	4.40	0.182

Source: after USDA, *Annual Report*, 1872: 45A.

ated deficits, substitution, and trade, inextricably linking it to Scandinavia and the Baltic, where industrial logging provided copious exports. Other experiences that will not be examined are, notably, Germany, which seemed to achieve a desirable balance between forests and other land uses through "scientific" forestry methods and the creation of even-aged stands; and parts of Mediterranean Europe, Turkey, and northern Africa (particularly Tunisia, Algeria, and Morocco), where deforestation brought impoverishment and hardship.[4]

France

Agricultural Clearing

With its 8.8 million ha of forest, France was one of the best endowed countries of western Europe, although its woodland was unevenly distributed, with marked concentrations in the eastern and northern parts of the country (fig. 10.1A). Henry Colman, writing about his travels there in 1848, was "constantly impressed with the immense tracts of land which are in forest."[5] Yet large as they were, they had undoubtedly once been much more extensive: in 1750 Jean Baptiste Mirabeau had estimated their extent at a generous 17 million ha, although they must have been reduced subsequently by the edict of 1766, which exempted from taxation for 15 years any land cleared to boost food production. Whatever their true extent, however, the peasants in their excesses after the French Revolution wrought a terrible revenge on the nobility, aristocracy, and church by appropriating forests for pasturage and cultivation, or ravaging them as they had the *châteaux,* to express their fury at the old order and the symbols of authority. In the chaos that followed after 1789, even the restraints that existed over their own extensive communal forests were similarly ignored, with particularly disastrous results in the uplands. The reforms of 1791 decriminalized the usurpation of privately owned woodlands, and *défrichement* for agriculture was common, especially on lower hill slopes and in the

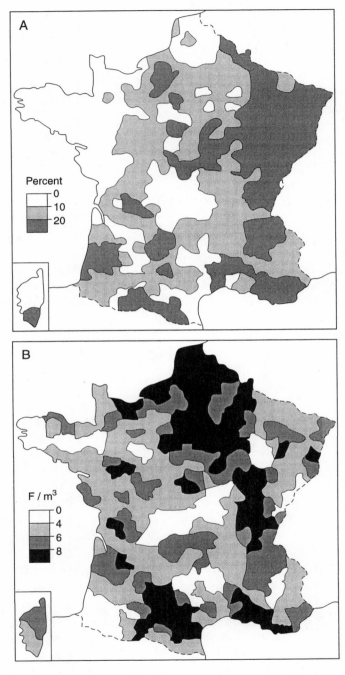

Figure 10.1A, woodland in France, 1831 (*Source:* after Clout, 1980: 73); and *B,* average price of fuelwood (F/m³), France, 1831 (*Source:* after Clout, 1980: 163).

Midi.[6] The demand for land was there: the population had increased from approximately 19 million in the early eighteenth century to 26.3 million in 1790, and 35.8 million in 1851. That increment of nearly 17 million people was not absorbed into industry, as France remained predominantly rural in livelihood throughout most of the nineteenth century, and needed to grow its own food, especially cereals. Widespread food riots and speculative prices throughout most of the later years of the ancien régime were evidence that the country was on the brink of national agricultural disaster.

The destruction of woodland was in evidence everywhere. For example, in addition to tapping the traditional sources of timber in the Vosges for shipbuilding, forests in the Upper Saône valley lowlands were stripped to supply yards in Toulon and the Mediterranean ports, while forests in Charante, and some even as far east as Burgundy, supplied yards on the Loire. Paris grew phenomenally from 524,000 in 1789 to 713,000 in 1821, and sucked in supplies of constructional timber and domestic and industrial fuel from a wide radius. Colman saw "immense arks of charcoal and wood" floating down the Seine, while there were "piles of wood in the city covering acres of ground and on a level with the highest houses." Woodlands were thinned and even eliminated around large towns like Lyon and Saint-Etienne in the south, the emerging industrial centers in the northern and cooler areas of Flanders, Picardy, Upper Normandy, and the Ardennes, and even around smaller centers of manufacture, like the glass and mulberry silk industries in small towns in Languedoc. Agricultural expansion, spurred on by a constant demand and high cereal prices, especially during the 1820s, imperceptibly nibbled away at forest edges everywhere, while some spectacular transformations occurred, as when the whole of the Bellecombe forest in Haute-Loire was felled. Woodland was even cleared to create rough pasture in Limousin, which was a poor exchange and an improvident waste of resources.[7]

How much was cleared is difficult to ascertain, as figures are contradictory and overlapping, but it could not have been more than 500,000 ha between 1800 and 1860.[8] This amount was not great by world standards, but it was important in the total land-use budget of a country with limited supplies, and signified the destruction of many of the remaining remnants of the once-great hardwood forests. As ever, the details of agricultural and pastoral expansion are ignored unless they were accompanied by other noteworthy phenomena, such as catastrophic floods, which then triggered political action. In contrast, the details of fuelwood consumption and the impacts of furnaces and forges were publicized, and loomed far larger in the record.

Iron Smelting and Fuelwood

France, which long had a thriving iron industry, produced between 78,000 and 186,000 tons in 1819, somewhat less than the United Kingdom for that year. By midcentury, production had risen to between 442,000 and 522,000 tons.[9] However, perhaps more significant than the overall output was the widespread distribution of small-scale units of production using the equally scattered woodland (fig. 10.2). There were major concentrations in Ariege in the Pyrenees, Limousin-Perigod, the Upper Loire valley (Nivernais), the heads of the Rivers Marne and Seine, Lorraine, and the Ardennes and Vosges mountains. To what extent fuel supply was critical is a matter of debate. Some argue that because of the wanton depletion of the forests during the ancien régime, the iron industry

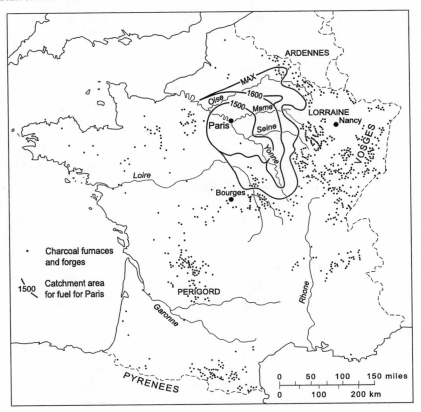

Figure 10.2 The location of furnaces and forges in early nineteenth-century France and competition for fuel-wood supplies in the Paris basin, 1500, 1600, and at its maximum in circa 1800. *Sources:* after Gille, 1947, and Boissière, 1990: 212.

was plagued by a widespread and long-lived crisis that eventually retarded the economic development of the country.[10] Others have taken the opposite view: that because of the abundance of fuelwood there was no need to mine and burn coal.[11] The answer, of course, was neither dearth nor abundance; it was not a national crisis so much as a regional one, and French ironmasters were never faced with "the choice between innovation or extinction." Admittedly, there were serious fuelwood shortfalls in places like Languedoc, Nord, and Franche-Comté, but they were of such little significance in the Ardennes, Lorraine, and the headwaters of the Marne and Seine as to be largely ignored. Initially, because of poor transportation links, coal only penetrated into nearby iron-producing districts, and costs of movement were low. But later, rapid economic expansion raised demand and prices, and coal made greater headway as a fuel, probably equalling the contribution of charcoal by the late 1820s and possibly fueling 70 percent of total iron production by 1848.[12]

Against this background, therefore, it was not surprising that the price for fuelwood formed part of a special enquiry in the French national statistical report of 1831. Price reflected factors of forest growth and yield, which varied enormously with the age and

Table 10.3 Population, fuelwood used, and per capita fuel consumption, Paris, 1815–1900

Year	Population	Fuelwood Used (m³)	Per Capita (m³)
1815	c. 670,000	1,200,000	1.80
1865	1,668,000	756,000	0.45
1900	2,661,000	552,000	0.20

Source: Clout, 1983: 132.

type of trees, and local environmental conditions as much as with the degree of prudent management and/or devastation that had occurred in the past. Royal and state forests were better managed and cutting restrictions more strictly enforced than communal forests, and consequently yields were higher. Some well-managed areas produced 13 to 16 m³/ha, others, either near large towns or in the overgrazed upland communes, a mere 1.0 to 1.5 m³/ha. The total yield cannot be computed from the figures, but we know that all departments produced more than was consumed, with the exception of four with modest deficits and Seine (Paris) with an annual deficit of 1.2 million m³. Figure 10.1B shows the price variations across the country in 1831, with the highest prices in the areas of greatest demand around Paris (16F/m³); a variety of places in the cooler, industrial north; the Lyonnais and Rhône valley and delta; and in the sparsely wooded Mediterranean peripheral around Marseilles and from Narbonne to Mountauban.[13]

The lines of waterways and rivers also stand out as areas of high fuelwood prices, not only because of the cities and industries located along their courses, but also because the canals led supplies toward them from further afield. Later, canals and then railways made the distribution easier and rectified deficits; and by the 1860s coal was being substituted for wood in the north and in Paris, as indicated by table 10.3.

However, for all that, France's energy crisis rumbled on in more remote areas throughout the nineteenth century, and many rural areas still relied on fuelwood and charcoal well into the twentieth century.

The Déboisement *of the Uplands*

Although some localities in the agricultural lowlands suffered overclearing, deforestation was much more severe in the extensive communal lands in the mountains of the Pyrenees, Alps, Causse, and even further north in the Jura and Vosges. Particularly badly affected were the provinces of Dauphine and Provence in the departments of Var, Basse-Alpes, Hautes-Alpes, Vaucluse, and Drôme in the extreme southeast of the country. Population numbers had been rising steadily since the late Middle Ages and reached a crisis point in the early eighteenth century; and that "pressure of immediate want" was not helped by the "passion for clearing" during the revolution.[14] In places, clearing was total: woodcutters took any wood fiber available, and what lopping and fire did not accomplish, goats and sheep finished off. With vegetation cover and even the roots gone, runoff accelerated; the soil moved; the steep, fragile slopes became denuded; and the once-fertile valleys became covered with coarse deposits and boulders. Heavy and sudden downpours of rain turned the once-placid streams into raging torrents. Devastation was severe far downstream as sediment clogged the lower reaches of rivers, navigation was impeded, and malaria throve around sluggish watercourses.

Owing to the endemic paucity of fuelwood, peasants trudged up to 5 hours daily to collect whatever they could, or they scraped leaves off the ground and uprooted heather to augment meager supplies. As far apart as the Haute-Alps, Provence, and Puy-de-Dôme, peasants kept warm and baked their bread with "sun-dried cow dung," and during the winter moved in with the cattle to keep warm. Descriptions of the uplands of the Jura, Pyrenees, and Alps abound with phrases and words like "landscapes of desolation," "blasted," "terrible aspect," and "terrible nudity . . . of bare and sterile rocks," and the memoirs of Henri Baudillart in 1831, Adolphe Blanqui in 1846, and many others were sprinkled with descriptions of "déboisement," "défrichement," "disaster," and "devastation." [15]

Everywhere yields and flocks decreased and the local economy went into decline. "The country," wrote André Surell, "is being depopulated day by day. . . . There may be seen on all hands cabins deserted or in ruins, and already in some localities there are more fields than labourers." The "physical deterioration" in the French, Italian, and Swiss Alps was evident to the acute observer. Whereas in 1789 Arthur Young had commented favorably on the cover of "good grass that feeds a million of emigrating sheep" and vast herds of cattle on the hills near Barcellonette, by 1843 Blanqui was lamenting their utter devastation:

> Whoever has visited the valley of Barcellonette, those of Embrun, and of Verdun, and that Arabia Petraea of the department of the Upper Alps, called Dévoluy, knows that there is no time to lose, that in fifty years from this date France will be separated from Savoy, as Egypt from Syria, by a desert.

Analogies with Algeria and Syria (then very much in the French mind because of colonial expansion), the encroaching desert, and the specter of the decline and fall of Rome permeated the imagination and the rhetoric. But bad as conditions were, it is likely that there was much overstatement in the descriptions. More often than not the situation was more a case of slow degradation (déboisement) than outright clearing (défrichement) and consequently only needed less intense use to regenerate. However, the words tended to be used interchangeably and the severity of the situation exaggerated. But no one doubted the rapidity of change. Marsh, who was not prone to exaggeration, soberly announced that "a single generation has witnessed the beginning and the end of the melancholy revolution." [16]

One of the earliest known efforts at reforestation anywhere occurred in these uplands. It was not a "protogreen" movement but a struggle between the state and the peasant, between technocracy and tradition, between private and communal property, and it was a manifestation of opposing cultural constructions of the nature of alpine France. The realities of the peasant agro-pastoral economy were not understood—and even deliberately misunderstood—by a bureaucracy of foresters and engineers who had been trained in the semimilitary atmosphere of the new École des Eaux-et-Forêts, founded in Nancy in 1822. All public forests passed under their control, and in 1827 a more efficient code of management came into force which, among other things, delimited forests more clearly, excluded destructive uses, and levied stringent fines for misdemeanors. In the atmosphere of national revival that pervaded the Second Empire (1852–70), along with the atmosphere of concern over the torrents, agricultural production, and wood supplies for construction and firewood, reforestation became almost a "moral awakening." The mountains, like the peasants, appeared disorderly and anarchic, and had to be tamed and controlled. Indeed, thinking went so far as to imply that the peasantry should be ejected, transformed, or otherwise altered so that the mountains would return to an idealized greenery.[17]

The afforestation cause was fiercely resisted by the pastoralists because they thought it would alter their way of life and reduce their livelihood even further; already, during preceding centuries, capitalist landowners had expropriated large portions of their communal lands. Open rebellion in the Guerre des Demoiselles in Ariége in the Pyrenees in 1829, when the rioters disguised themselves as women, and outbreaks of similar hostility elsewhere in the Jura, Pyrenees, and Alps, seemed a confirmation of peasant anarchy. The cause of reforestation was put back severely, and it was only at the very end of the century that significant progress was made to reforest these upland regions.[18]

Patriotic fervor for afforestation had two broad outcomes. It was greatest in the wastes of the lowland agricultural districts of Champagne in the departments of Marne and Aube in the Vosges, and particularly in the departments of Landes and Gironde, where the forest area nearly doubled from 127,000 ha in 1821 to 225,000 in the late 1830s to become the basis of what is still claimed to be the biggest human-made forest in the world.[19] Overall, France came out of its intensive and often fraught forest experiences with more forest than it had started with, and between the time of the *ancien cadastre* (variable, but mainly midcentury) to 1907 the forest area had risen from 7.6 million to 9.2 million ha. It was an impressive record for a country in timber-starved western Europe.[20]

The *déboisement* of the French uplands and the cause and possible amelioration of the torrents had a broader, more global, significance than the local area alone. Humans appeared to be at the center of a complex relationship between uplands and lowlands. Simply put, the torrents showed that social conditions, and even ancient customs, could be directly related to physical processes; humanly induced change had led to the permanent loss of soils and the irreversible change in river courses.[21] It is little wonder that the "Torrents of the Var" was the penultimate topic in Clarence Glacken's magisterial work on nature and culture in Western thought, because it signaled a new appreciation of what humans could do to the environment and contained a "far more pessimistic idea than the simple warning about damage to a single holder or a commune."[22] Knowledge about the interconnectedness of things was growing.

Russia

The richly textured detail about the French forest does not exist for the continental extent of the Russian forest. What happened where and when is largely unknown, and local motivation and causes are obscure. Nevertheless, the overall picture of destruction is reasonably clear, even if the estimates of the amount of clearing vary. A huge cropland expansion of at least 145 million ha occurred between 1700 and 1920, all of which came out of former forestlands. In a more detailed study of each province between 1696 and 1914, Tsvetkov put the figure for clearing lower at about 67.1 million ha, or 28 percent of all forests. The difference between the two estimates might be explained partly by the fact that the first refers to the whole Russian state, while Tsvetkov's concerns European Russia only. Thus about half of the difference of 78 million ha can be accounted for, but we simply cannot be more dogmatic than that.[23]

What we do know, however, is that by either measure the amount of clearing was immense, though Tsvetkov's maps pose as many questions as answers (fig. 10.3A–D). In the six sample central provinces of Tula, Ryazan, Orel, Tambov, Kursk, and Vorenezh looked at already in table 7.2 and figure 7.3, the ever-increasing density of population and percentage of land under cultivation as the forest was cleared, first evident during the eighteenth century, did not abate in the nineteenth. From roughly one-half of the land in cultivation and a population density of between 20 and 30/km^2 in 1811, two-thirds of the land was in fields and population densities had risen to 27/km^2–36/km^2 by the mid-nineteenth century. From now on, the process of clearing was little more than "a mopping-up operation." In 1847 the novelist Ivan Turgenev commented in "A Sportsman's Sketches" that in his native Orel Gubernia, "the last of the woods and copses will have disappeared five years hence"; sometime later a landowner, Golenishchev-Kutuzov, told a congress of forest owners that "the Tartar invasion did not inflict greater evil on us than we ourselves have done, robbing our descendants by the cutting and devastation of forests.[24]

The woods and copses never disappeared entirely, but toward the end of the century anything between two-thirds and three-quarters of the land was cultivated, and rural densities reached between 40 and 50/km^2. Deforestation was nearing its limits. But nothing tells the story more clearly than the pattern of changing land cover in the Arzamas region on the Volga right bank, east and slightly south of Moscow and situated almost wholly in the deciduous forest belt of oak, beech, and hornbeam. The maps (fig. 10.4A–C), which are based on the general survey of large estates of 1696 and subsequent cadastres, show the dramatic decline of forest between the mid-sixteenth and late eighteenth centuries, and again by 1947.

Some independent confirmation of this deforestation came later in 1894, when surveys to determine the role of forests in regulating water supply were carried out by the Forestry Department on the headwaters of some of the country's rivers. In the upper Oka watershed the forest cover had diminished from 15.8 to 3.6 percent during the previous 200 years, and in the Don watershed from 9.2 to 1.8 percent.[25] In contrast, the vast forests of Siberia in Asiatic Russia were an untouched "new world" that, as one writer put it, had "to be overcome" by a methodical plan of forest colonization and "by the conquests of culture and civilization" before it would be of any value.[26]

Agriculture and pastoralism were not the only causes of the forestland destruction. Fuelwood must have been cut in prodigious and almost incalculable amounts during the long, severe Russian winter. If the citizens of Paris—in the warm western periphery of Europe, where the mean January temperature did not go below freezing—needed an average of 1.80 m^3 per capita to keep life and limb together in 1815, then the citizens of Moscow—in the heart of continental Europe, where the mean January temperature was −10 to −20°C—must have needed many times that amount. By 1890 the population of

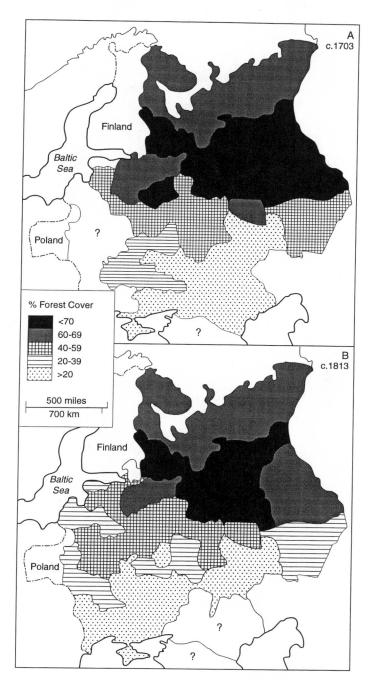

Figure 10.3A–B A, percentage of surface of European Russia covered by forest, 1696–1710 (midpoint, circa 1703); and B, percentage of surface of European Russia covered by forest at the time of the General Survey, 1782–1845 (midpoint, circa 1813). *Sources:* French, 1963: figs. 2A and B, based on calculations by Tsvetkov, 1957.

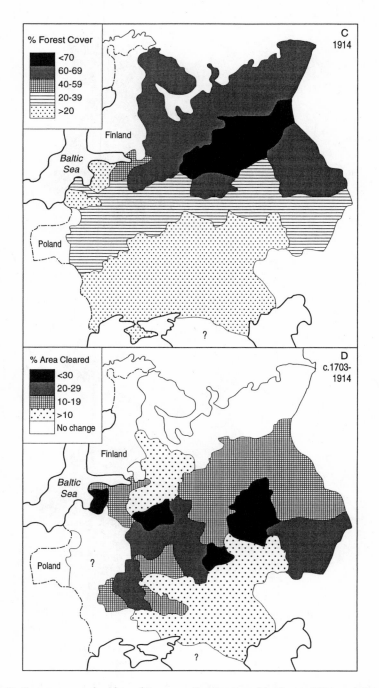

Figure 10.3C–D C, percentage of surface of European Russia covered by forest, 1914; and *D,* change in forest cover of European Russia, and percent of area cleared, circa 1703–1914. *Sources:* French, 1963: figs. 2C and D, based on calculations by Tsvetkov, 1957.

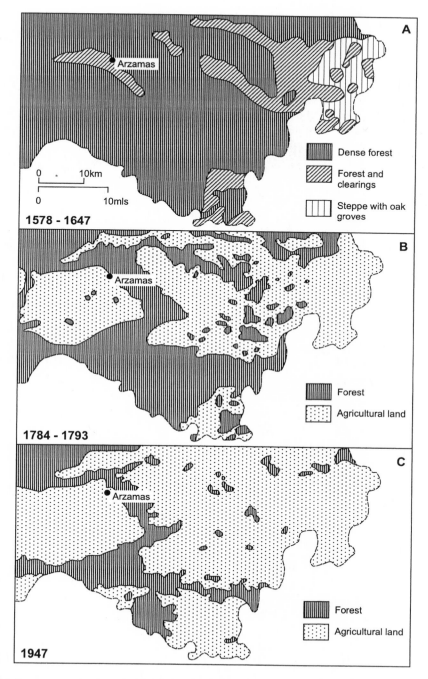

Figure 10.4 Forest cover, Arzamas region, Russia, from sources covering the period *A*, 1578–1647; *B*, 1784–93; and *C*, 1947. *Source:* after French, 1963: 47–48.

Russia was about 110 million, with all which that number implied for fuelwood consumption. In addition, nearly every building in the rural areas was made of wood and lasted not much more than 15 years. For example, in the mid-nineteenth century it was calculated that over 600,000 trees—the equivalent of the timber from 11,000 ha of dense forest—were needed per annum to build 8,080 new houses to replenish and augment the stock of 121,213 old ones in the province of Minsk alone, and there were over 50 provinces in European Russia alone. River barges, of which there were over 5,000, consumed about 500 trees each. Moreover, the Russian navy was growing in an attempt to dominate the Baltic, and iron making (using 17.5 million m^3–20.4 million m^3 of timber per annum by 1880), potash making, and salt making all took their toll on the forests.

The export of timber for ready cash increased markedly during the eighteenth century, with British merchants being in the forefront of exploitation in an effort to supply their home market. One such company, Gom, operated in the White Sea area around Archangel during most of the eighteenth century, and by 1830 was said to have caused so much destruction that the forest "wounds" would "not quickly heal." Another company, Pitt and Forster, working in the Belorussian forest along the Pripyat' from the late eighteenth century onward, stripped and exported all the merchantable timber and sold the land as cleared estates. But its speculative operations were so rapacious that local landowners protested, the tsar intervened, and the company was forced to stop operations.[27]

With the construction of railways to the Baltic and Black Sea ports, improved accessibility to western markets securely locked Russian supplies into the global timber trade. Russian timber landowners indulged in an orgy of destruction on their estates, and "strove," commented Tsvetkov, "in every way possible, as it were to overtake each other in wiping out their forests as fast as possible." The emancipation of the serfs in 1861 had undermined the economic viability of estates, and landowners also wanted to raise capital to invest in industry, railways, and the newly opened Donbas coalfields. Contractors were given the right to cut without limitation or amount over a specified period, so that most of them tried to scalp the land, a process that was usually followed by stock grazing over the cutover area, thereby stopping any regrowth: "Entire forest *dachi* [unit of forest exploitation] of hundreds of thousands of *desyatiny* [2.7 ha] have been ruthlessly cut and, if not converted into arable, it becomes for the most part waste land." By 1897 over 1.6 million tons of logs and an almost equal number of tons of sawnwood were exported annually, mainly to Britain, Germany, and Holland, a total that had risen to 2.9 million tons by 1908.[28]

One could go on recounting endlessly statistics of consumption in this and that industry, here and there, from time to time. The best summary view is that given by A. F. Rondski and N. I. Shafranov in their exhaustive enquiry into the Russian wood- and timber-using industries of 1890.[29] With a mixture of complex calculations interspersed with inspired guesses, they arrived at a total consumption of 543.9 million m^3 destroyed annually by that year, an amount that rose to 869.2 million m^3 if the higher estimate for export figures is accepted (table 10.4). Whatever the exact figures, the point was that the forest was under a widespread and sustained attack from agriculture and industry, from which it was not to recover for many decades, if at all. The maps of diminishing tree cover told it all; the late seventeenth to early twentieth centuries in Russia had witnessed one of

Table 10.4 Consumption of wood and timber products (in millions of m³), Russia, 1890–91

Use	Million m³	Total
Industrial		
Woodstuffs in chemical and mechanical operations, including shipbuilding	19.4	
Mining (salt, iron, metals)	24.2	
Railways (fuel, sleepers, and construction)	7.8	
Steamboats	2.9	
Manufactures and works	18.5	72.8
Domestic		
Domestic fuelwood @ 3.23 m³/capita	359.3	359.3
Exports		
Low estimate	436.0	
High estimate	543.7	
Total consumption (low est.)		795.3
Total consumption (high est.)		903.0

Source: Rondski and Shafranov, 1893: 334–40.
Note: original figures are in the traditional measure of sagenes³, which have been converted to m³ and rounded up to the nearest million.

the great episodes in global deforestation. Forestland in the central provinces became "a mere dwindling reminiscence of the past, and preserved as a luxury."[30]

Britain

Britain did not figure prominently in the story of European deforestation in the same way as did France or Russia; it had hardly any forest left to chop down, although here and there, as at Hainault Forest in about 1851, remnants of woodland were cleared and heavy clay lands tile-drained as part of enclosure and agricultural improvement.[31] (See plate 10.1.) But that very lack of wood supplies was vitally important in stimulating interest in inventions, substitutes, and trade as ways of making up deficiencies. Putting aside the early example of Sung China, the move to substitute fossil fuel for vegetable fuel occurred first in the British Isles, both in the domestic and industrial spheres; and Britain (and to a lesser extent, Holland) was the focus, organizer, and carrier of the world timber trade, which was a precursor of present patterns of global exploitation.

Coke for Charcoal

Contrary to popular opinion, the use of coke to smelt iron ore by Abraham Darby of Coalbrookdale in Shropshire in 1709 was neither the first attempt to smelt with it, nor did it herald the revolution in iron production that is sometimes suggested. At least twenty attempts had been made to substitute peat or coal for wood in iron making during the preceding 150 years. Coal was already being used successfully for smelting copper and making glass and bricks, so the idea of resource substitution was not revolutionary. Darby's achievement was to make three great technical discoveries: that coal could be freed from sulphur and other impurities by coking; that coke made good iron castings; and that although coke made poor pig iron, the first step had been taken toward the production of commercial pig iron.[32] George Hammersley has argued that the lack of headway made by these experiments suggests that coal and coke were no less cheaper than charcoal, and that the shortage of timber was overstated. Coke pig did not become consistently cheaper than charcoal pig until after 1770, nor coke bar cheaper than charcoal bar until about 1800. Charcoal iron persisted throughout the eighteenth and nineteenth centuries, even against cheaper Swedish imports; and as the manufacturers did not ask for "bounties on the planting of coppice, for rights of pre-emption on woodlands or even for some public encouragement for the planting and care of woods," it would seem that the supplies of timber were there to support it. By the middle of the seventeenth century, coppicing had become "almost universal in Britain" and was producing wood containing a higher calorific value than much of the small wood previously used for producing charcoal. Therefore, as already concluded in chapter 7, the ironworks were not the devourer of the woods that they were made out to be.[33]

Therefore, the proposition that scarcity was the spur to inventiveness and resource substitution clearly did not occur except on a local scale. But we are probably safe in saying that when overall demand for iron reached new heights during the industrial upheaval of the late eighteenth century, the concentrated, large, and accessible supplies of coal came into their own, and were able to compete successfully and economically with charcoal. Additionally, while charcoal iron technology did not improve, coke iron technology did—for example, readily adopting the steam engine after 1775 for blasting and forging. It was lack of organization and inertia in a new dynamic age that left the charcoal iron industry behind, so that, concluded Hammersley, it "rather fell than was pushed." The great shift occurred after 1780, when for the first time the number of coke furnaces exceeded charcoal-fueled ones, although the shift in the balance of production had occurred about 20 years earlier (table 10.5). By 1800 "charcoal . . . had been almost entirely superseded by coke."[34]

Table 10.5 Charcoal and coke furnaces and estimated total output (in thousands of tons), United Kingdom, 1750–91

	Charcoal Furnaces			Coke Furnaces				
	Number	Average Output	Total Output	Number	Average Output	Total Output	Total Industry	% Charcoal Pig Iron
circa 1750	71	375	26.6	3	500	1.5	28.1	95
circa 1760	64	400	25.6	14	700	9.8	35.4	72
circa 1775	44	450	19.8	30	800	24.0	43.8	45
circa 1780	34	500	17.0	43	850	36.6	53.6	32
circa 1785	28	500	14.0	53	900	47.7	61.7	23
1788	26	558	14.5	60	925	55.5	66.0	21
1790	25	500	12.5	81	925	74.9	87.4	14
1791	22	432	9.5	85	950	80.7	90.2	10

Source: Hyde, 1977: 67.

Note: average output is in absolute tons and is calculated by total output divided by the number of furnaces.

The "fall" occurred much earlier in Britain than elsewhere in Europe, where the problem of charcoal supplies was less acute because more wood and less industry were the norm, and it was not until after 1850 that smelting with coke became common in France and Germany. In Germany as late as 1848, in the wooded district between the Ruhr and the Sieg, coppice rotations were cut every 16 years, providing bark for tanners and charcoal for smelters, with the whole augmented by occasional crops of rye, which were sown on the newly coppiced land. Yet the evidence is that while such forest-field rotations were fairly common and widespread in the German iron-producing districts, the price of charcoal was rising rapidly and many furnace owners were turning to coke.[35]

The Hub of the World

But interesting and important as was the substitution of coke for charcoal, it was the role of Britain as a great consumer of timber to feed its metropolitan, industrial, and naval power that must command our attention. As the economic and social upheaval of the Industrial Revolution got under way it drew in vast quantities of timber and created patterns of global exploitation, permanently altering the forests of the world. In time, trade also affected the economies of the timber-growing countries, in many cases aiding development and promoting protoindustrialization.

Change did not happen overnight. The eighteenth century had been a period of steady expansion that the loss of the American Colonies, though humiliating, had not really altered economically. The importation of resources, and their subsequent re-exportation as manufactured goods, ensured growth on the edge of Europe; and all the institutions and structures of trade and commerce expanded. Almost any statistical measure one might like to take (e.g., population, income, navy tonnage, imports, exports) showed a steady expansion, which brought an extension of global influence and power, and ultimately conflict with Continental powers, particularly France. The Napoleonic Wars were a trying time, but after Waterloo in 1815 a new century of prosperity opened up: population increased from approximately 15 million in 1801 to 29 million in 1861; enhanced conditions of material life meant improved shelter, better food, and more fuel; and increased affluence turned luxuries into necessities, of which abundant timber was one. Between 1811 and 1831 alone, when it was said that half the expense of building a house was in the cost of the timber, over 750,000 new houses were built, and between 1831 and 1851 the railway extended from a few hundred miles to over 6,000.[36] Britain was becoming the driving force and hub of the world.

With the fuel problem more or less solved, the national forests had to provide sufficient timber for the two other great demands of a premier world power and industrializing society: shipbuilding and general constructional needs. There was an enormous shortfall of supplies, especially of general constructional timber, and the deficiency was made up by trade. Although it is convenient to look at shipbuilding and general construction separately, in reality they were not discrete but highly interrelated, as the source, organization, and trade of both types of timber were often identical. The major difference was that ships' timbers and masts were of strategic importance, valuable, and moved in relatively small quantities, whereas general constructional timbers were commonplace, of low cost and high bulk, and moved in vast quantities. Both were moved over great distances.

Ships and Masts

The political precariousness of the traditional Baltic countries as a source of materials for sustaining British sea power had long been appreciated, but the situation reached a new level of uncertainty and danger during the conflict and long blockade of the Revolutionary and Napoleonic Wars from 1793 to 1815. Every port in Europe was closed to British shipping, and the price of timber rose: for example, Memel fir leapt 300 percent between 1806 and 1808. Britain might just have survived on its own reserves of oak, but at roughly 50 acres (20.23 ha) of mature oak per 74-gunner, and considering the number of ships launched annually, one can understand why John Marshall said, "we are ready to tremble for the consequences." [37] More critically, it lacked the masts and naval stores that were essential to its very survival.

Of all the British possessions, Canada seemed the most promising source of supply, in particular New Brunswick, and Nova Scotia and the Maritimes generally.[38] In all these provinces the discredited Broad Arrow Policy of 1729 still applied, but it was modified so that only stands of the best pine were reserved for the Royal Navy, and the area set aside could be no more than 600 acres for every township of 6 mi^2. Inevitably, the conflict between private property and imperial strategy erupted as of old, though with nowhere near the same degree of resentment and fury as in the United States 80 years before. The landowners simply took what they needed and were fined accordingly. After the wars the Broad Arrow Policy was relaxed and provisions for the navy incorporated into the general Canadian Crown Land laws.

The forests of Nova Scotia had been culled for masts since 1721, so there were few left, and attention turned to New Brunswick and then Ontario. With the imposition of the Baltic blockade, the annual shipment of 3 or 4 mast cargoes from North America increased dramatically between 1804 and 1812. But when the blockade was lifted, the mast trade swung back to the Baltic and more or less remained there (table 10.6).

Nonetheless, during these difficult years Britain scoured the world for alternative naval supplies. Companies traded with the states of the U.S. South, where live oak and pitch pine were "discovered," but trade proved increasingly difficult owing to Jefferson's Non-Intercourse Laws. Forays were made to exploit stinkwood and yellowwood from

Table 10.6 British imports of masts and timber from the Baltic and North America for specified periods, 1799–1815

	Masts		% NA	Oak and Pine	% NA	Fir and Pine	% NA
1799–1803	B	58,192		46,757		974,323	
	NA	9,221	15.8	4,963	10.6	19,582	2.0
1804–7	B	59,363		52,691		880,470	
	NA	10,953	18.5	15,260	30.0	64,523	7.3
1808–12	B	98,786		82,887		897,518	
	NA	68,018	68.9	74,869	90.3	506,015	56.0
1812–15	B	11,827		30,521		501,306	
	NA	4,129	35.2	8,395	27.5	278,829	55.0

Source: Albion, 1926: 420–22.
Note: B = Baltic, NA = North America. Masts are by number, though a few imports from Norway and Sweden are by load, which is calculated to be approximately equivalent to a mast. Total numbers are therefore approximate. Figures for timber represent loads.

the Cape, teak from Sierra Leone and India, kauri from New Zealand, jarrah from Australia, mahogany from Honduras and Madagascar, and Demerara in British Guiana. But nearly all foundered due to imperfections in the timber, unfavorable transportation rates, or local difficulties in extraction, such as tropical disease and labor supply. It was still easier and more satisfactory to raid enemy cargoes in foreign ports like Genoa, Copenhagen, and Flushing for supplies.

Only one viable alternative existed, and that was teak from the Malabar coast of southwest India. This wood soon got a reputation for being the finest ships' timber available on account of its durability. Also, because it did not corrode iron as did oak, it allowed shipbuilding to be simplified via the use of spikes instead of wooden nails. The prize was worth war: Portuguese and Dutch interests in Malabar were eliminated; the local ruler, Tippoo Sahib, who favored the French, was deposed; and by the beginning of the century the supply of teak was strictly to the British—yet one more forest entered into world trade and was exploited. While little teak was actually moved to British yards because of protectionism at home and high transportation costs, many ships were built in Calcutta and particularly in Bombay by the expert Pharsee shipbuilder, Jamsedjee Jeejeebhoy, ensuring British supremacy in the South Seas and Southeast Asia.[39]

The timber problem remained acute for all European navies, but changes were at hand. Iron gradually began to enter more and more into ship construction, its advantages of lesser weight and greater strength, and hence bigger payloads, becoming apparent, especially since steam began to be used for propulsion after 1830. Initially, wooden frames were clad in iron for protection in warfare, or iron frames were sheathed in wood, as with the fast-sailing clippers built during the 1850s and 1860s. In both cases teak came into its own because of its noncorrosive qualities. But by 1840 wood had practically been superseded by iron except in the United States and Canada, where supplies were still abundant. One of the great icons of nineteenth-century British art, J. M. W. Turner's painting *The Fighting Temeraire* of 1838 (plate 10.2) depicts the battered, de-masted hulk of the massive wooden fighting ship being dragged up the Thames at sunset to the breaker's yard by two nondescript steam-powered iron paddle tugs. It sums up dramatically the passing of the age of wood at sea. It is doubtful that Turner ever saw the scene, but that he could imagine it and transform the dull prose of the event into the transcendent poetry of this masterpiece suggests that the end of wood and the ascendancy of steam power at sea were common knowledge. Perhaps the decisive event in the death of the wooden ship occurred on 9 March 1862. On that day the Battle of Hampton Roads in the American Civil War demonstrated the superiority of the iron-clad fighting ship. From that moment the drain on the world's forests that had gone on for thousands of years stopped suddenly and dramatically.[40]

General Constructional Timber

While strategic considerations dominated thinking about overseas sources of supply, it was inevitable that much was learned about the rest of the forests of the world by people who were exploring, expanding, and experimenting everywhere. The apparatus of exploitation set up to garner naval stores from the forests was in place to exploit them for wider commercial purposes, which now began to dominate. The great demand was for constructional timber, or lumber.[41] It was imported as large, crudely squared-off logs

Plate 10.2 The Fighting Temeraire *Tugged to Her Last Berth to Be Broken Up, 1838,* by J. M. W. Turner. (National Gallery, London.)

known as "fir timber" if from the Baltic or "ton timber" if from Canada, or as smaller planks, deals, and battens, in abundant amounts, and as cheaply as possible. A secondary, minor demand was for selected quality timbers such as mahogany, brazilwood, and rosewood for ornamentation, furniture, and interior finishing, but these came from the tropical world, and constituted barely 3 percent of imports. The general-purpose timber came initially and overwhelmingly from the Baltic, which became so enmeshed in the British trade that it became, suggests Arthur Lower, "a semi-colony" of Britain, just as Canada was to become "Great Britain's woodyard" in later years.[42]

But to get an overview of the flows and amounts is difficult. First, the prosaic planks and blocks of timber did not have the glamour and contingent interest of political events that accompanied masts and naval supplies. Therefore they have been neglected in terms of record. Second, because of the large numbers of different measures used, the discontinuity of records—whether they relate to ships cleared at the exporting port or the importing port or, in the case of the Baltic trade, through the Baltic Sound—to say nothing of the normal annual fluctuations of trade and commerce, the topic has lain unresearched for a long time. There is enough material to give a tantalizing glimpse of the patterns and flows, but not quite enough for a definitive account.[43] Of the many possible geographies of trade, only one—the export and import of deals of various sizes for 1784—is shown in figure 10.5, and it must stand as an example of the complexity of production and consumption of timber around the world.

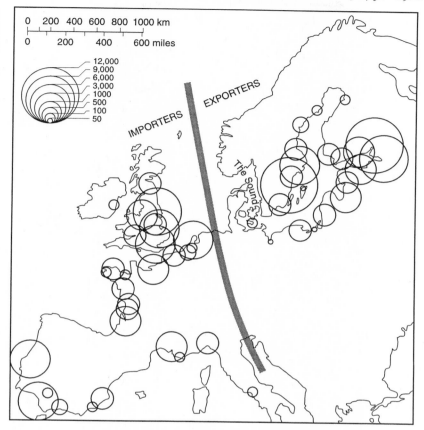

Figure 10.5 The geography of the European trade in Baltic "deals" (planks) for the year 1784. *Source:* based on Ånström, 1970: 31–32. The map shows shipments originating in the Baltic and customs-cleared through the Baltic Sound. The unit of measure is the long hundred, or 120 pieces, up to 20 ft long.

Despite the manifold and ever-changing nature of the trade, however, some trends show through. Britain was the main consumer and destination of flows, and imports of major types of wood are known for the period 1697 to 1808, although their value, which allows for comparison between different types of wood, is available only after 1720. The picture is one of gradually rising consumption of all types of wood but particularly of general-purpose fir timber after about 1750, from approximately 42,476 m³ to 223,704 m³, the total amount being initially equal to, and then surpassing by some four-fold, the imports to the Netherlands, where demand stayed relatively stable. This sharp increase was stimulated by the population increase, industrialization, and urbanization of Britain, and per-capita consumption rose steadily to 190 bf (0.45 m³) by the end of the century, although it was still only about one-half to two-fifths that of the United States. The domestic cut supplied barely a tenth or twelfth of the demand, which was made up for by imports. And yet, in the total picture of *all imports* timber did not loom large; it never exceeded 1 percent before 1820, and masts are put into perspective when one realizes how relatively unimportant they were even in that timber component. By 1871 imports had risen to 5.9 million m³ and then climbed steadily to 13.4 million m³ by 1901,

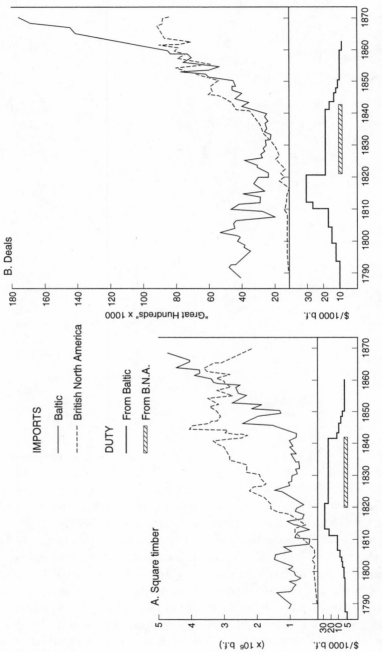

Figure 10.6 Canadian and "foreign" *A*, squared timber (in millions of bf); and *B*, deals (in thousands of "great hundreds," or long hundreds; i.e., 120 pieces) imported into Britain, and the differential tariff (in $ per 1,000 bf), circa 1785–1875. *Source*: based on Lower, 1973: 259, 260.

but despite the rising volume timber still rarely exceeded 5 percent of U.K. imports and most commonly hovered around 3–4 percent.[44]

Before 1760 all imports came primarily from Norway, that part of Scandinavia nearest to Britain and not hampered by the political vagaries of the Sound. But centuries of exploitation for the British market had taken out the big timber, and increasingly the forest could supply only smaller masts, along with deals and battens. Therefore, after 1760 fir timber and spruce deals (spruce meaning Prussia, and not necessarily *Picea abies*) came increasingly from the "East Country," which meant the rivers converging on Memel and Riga, and the hinterlands of St. Petersburg, Viborg, and Narva.[45] Like the east-flowing rivers of the United States, huge rafts with houses on them brought timber downstream. Robert Johnston saw them on the Neimen River in 1815: "They also bring along with them carts, horses, poultry, etc. When the cargo of wood is disposed of, they return, by land with the horses."[46] With low freight rates, cheap labor, and the adoption of the fine-bladed "Dutch" saw, which produced a high volume of finished timber, these forestlands leapt into prominence. Sweden did not figure much in this trade, as its mercantilist policy discouraged the export of wood products, which were kept for charcoal to produce iron, its main export. At the receiving end, London dominated the timber trade, accounting for between 40 and 60 percent of the total imports; but an increasing share was being taken by the provincial ports of Hull, Liverpool, and Newcastle, entry points adjacent to the newly emerging industrial areas of Yorkshire, Lancashire, and Durham in the North of England.

It was remarkable that despite the Napoleonic Wars and all the fiscal and political obstacles to trade in Britain, the bulk of imported timber (roughly three quarters) still found its way through the Sound. Whatever category of timber one looks at—deals under 20 ft, deals over 20 ft, fir timber, or masts—ever-increasing proportions of ever-increasing amounts from the Baltic wound up in England and Scotland. From about one-third of the total in 1780 they rose to nearly a half in 1790 and then rarely fell below two thirds or four fifths from then on. As before, the smaller deals came predominantly from Norway (57 percent), followed by Russia (19.9 percent), and those proportions were reversed for fir timber. Corresponding imports of all kinds to Amsterdam, Britain's main rival, plummeted, as affluence turned to relative decay.[47]

The other main supplier was, of course, Canada, where the British government had encouraged the investment of private capital in order to promote exploitation of strategic supplies. In Ontario in particular, private firms developed facilities and sawmills for the supply of oak timbers and masts, which rivaled those of Riga and Danzig. It was inevitable that in order to make the most of their investments they moved into the general timber trade, and soon hundreds of ships were sailing eastward with cargoes of crudely squared pine trunks, deals, and planks, and also much timber that came down the St. Lawrence from Vermont. Mindful that after the war trade might swing back to the nearer, cheaper (and generally better-quality) wood of the Baltic, as it had with masts, the Canadian firms pressured the government to impose stiff duties on Baltic timber imports (fig. 10.6) so that they were several times the cost of the wood at the port (the ratio was 5:1), and these punitive restrictions were not removed until 1857.[48] Canada concentrated on "ton" timber and deals, and dominated while the differential tariff operated between 1820 and 1846. But when the tariff was lifted, the flow of cheaper and generally better-quality Baltic supplies resumed eventually to surpass Canadian imports. Britain absorbed them all in ever-increasing quantities, especially when the railways started up with their vast demand for sleepers. Despite its prominence, Canada was "only an episode" in the history of the bulk lumber trade—a large one, to be sure, but an episode all the same.[49]

Despite the complexities and variations of what may be justly called the many different lumber trades, a number of generalizations can be made. First, timber ranked with grain, tea, sugar, cotton, and wool as a major commodity in world trade, all the more remarkable because of great bulk and low value, which attests to its indispensability. Second, in some countries, as in the Baltic lands, timber extraction did act as a general stimulus to the economy. Third, the general timber trade was very much the product of individual entrepreneurs and rarely of governments. In 1800 London had 75 timber merchants whose yards lined the Thames between Greenwich and Southwark, and later the Surrey docks. Liverpool had a score, and the same was true of all the major importing ports. Many of the firms had local agents, skilled in foreign languages and local politics, whose sole job it was to scout out supplies, arrange deals with local cutters to ship the lumber, and generally to send back intelligence of future supplies from these far-away forests.[50] The merchants were key players in the operation and dominance of the consuming market of the metropolitan core. Rarely did they engage directly in the cutting (though some founded mills at Gothenburg), only in the movement of the timber. They were the facilitators, not the producers, but they were a crucial link in the exploitation of the world's forests.

Finally, to translate the quantities of timber moved internationally into area of forest cut or thinned is almost impossible, but the outcome was most certainly depleted forests that could not supply the big timber, whether they were in Scandinavia or the Maritimes. In New Brunswick, for example,

> [l]umberers had thinned the cover and reduced the proportions of mature pine and spruce over large areas. By mid century, most of the tall pines within three miles of those streams large enough to float timber down in the spring had been felled.[51]

The destruction seemed worse in the newly settled countries, where a pioneer mentality of "cut out and get out" existed, whereas in the old, settled countries forest exploitation tended to be integrated more fully into other ways of life, and may even have proved an economic boon and an aid to protoindustrialization, as perhaps happened in Finland, southern Sweden, and parts of the south Baltic coast, in the wake of the passing of the lumber frontier.[52] But in the New World the forest was both enemy and wealth, and it was plundered. Writing about New Brunswick in 1825, one observer, Peter Fisher, speculated that a reasonable person would have expected all this trade to "produce great riches to the country; and that great and rapid improvements would be made." But instead of towns, farms, elegant houses, extensive stores, and mercantile conveniences the, "capital of the country had been wasted" and the wealth had gone elsewhere. The shippers and merchants were strangers who have taken no interest in the welfare of the country; but have merely occupied a spot in order to make what they could in the shortest time possible . . . the forests are stripped and nothing left in prospect, but the gloomy apprehension when the timber is gone, of sinking into insignificance and poverty.[53]

This picture was somewhat overdrawn: by 1850 approximately 640,000 acres had been cleared and 193,000 people lived and farmed where once forest had dominated. But although "in some areas well-cultivated fields stretched away from fertile intervales," from most other vantage points "almost unbroken forest ran back to the horizon."[54] New Brunswick was a microcosm of clearing in the temperate New World. The fact remained that lumbering meant the destruction or degradation of the forest resource, and even if a territory was lucky enough to retain some of that plundered wealth in the form of farms and settlements, it meant that the forest had gone. It was a paradox: at best, new land could only be created at the expense of the old forest; at worst, old forest was destroyed and left a wasteland.

CLEARING A CONTINENT: THE UNITED STATES

By the latter part of the eighteenth century, all the ingredients were in place in the United States for one of the greatest episodes of global deforestation ever to be enacted. Millions of immigrants swarmed into a continent so wooded that Arnold Guyot described it as "glutted with . . . vegetable wealth."[55] The population reached 23.2 million by 1850 and 74.8 million by 1899. By 1848 thirteen new states had been created in the trans-Appalachian West, and Texas was annexed. The bustling, expansive, industrial nation of the end of the nineteenth century was a very different country from the tiny agricultural one that had hugged the plains and hills of the eastern seaboard for so many generations before.

The Process and Extent of Clearing

Farm making remained in the forest and the processes stayed basically the same as in earlier centuries; it was still hard, backbreaking work that used old and well-tried methods and technology, principally the ax. The dominant agent was still the pioneer farmer, who usually went west ahead of his family to establish a clearing, and even to erect a cabin before they followed him.[56] But not all pioneer farmers stayed permanently on their cleared land; Timothy Dwight noted a class of backwoodsman who merely "prepared the way for those who came after them," and there were plenty of pioneer farmers ready to take them up. "It is considered here a small affair for a man to sell, take his family and some provisions and go into the woods upon a new farm, erect a house, and begin anew," said the Reverend John Taylor of early nineteenth-century New York.[57] Perhaps for the first time ever in the world, clearing was not a purely subsistence activity but was becoming a commercial, even speculative, proposition, characterized by high mobility and impermanence.

Obviously some farmers had capital, and the prospect of either acquiring a partially cleared farm or of hiring a labor gang to chop down the trees and prepare the land for a crop, even to build a temporary shelter and some fences, was attractive and far more common than is supposed. The "setup" men were often itinerant laborers, wandering from place to place over great distances, armed only with their axes and grubbing hoes, and usually asking about 50 cents a day, the prevailing wage in the early nineteenth century for unskilled labor. It was arduous work; some skilled axmen claimed that they could clear an acre in from 3 to 7 days, but that was the work of a professional, and a strong one at that, and the rapidity of clearing also depended on the density and size of the trees. Sometimes the "setup" men were farmers who had bought a farm but could not clear enough land in time to get in a crop and thus needed the cash to pay for food and other essentials for the family. The permutations of who was clearing for whom were endless.

The problem of "how to subdue the land," as Jeremy Belknap put it, remained, and methods of clearing did not change—it was either clear-cutting or girdling, with both involving burning. Girdling cost about 8 dollars an acre (approximately $20/ha) and took 13.5 man-days, whereas clear-cutting cost between 10 and 12 dollars an acre (approximately $25–$30/ha) but took between 16.5 and 20 man-days. Because tasks like collecting fallen timber were deferred in girdling, the conclusion is that the costs in terms of labor and cash were about the same. Both methods left stumps which were either left to rot or had to be grubbed out with axes, levers, spades, chains, and oxen, all of which took about as long as the initial tree-clearing effort. But by the end of the nineteenth century, stump removal had probably dropped to between 4 and 6 man-days as improved stump removers, primitive gasoline flamethrowers, and above all, dynamite, were brought into play. The season when clearing was done affected its cost. A summer chopping was marginally quicker and cheaper because the wood was drier and took less effort to burn. A winter chopping was cheaper still, because the sap had subsided in the trunk, and the felled logs could be slid out of the forest in the snow; it also had the advantage that it could be done during the off-peak period of farmwork. But whenever and however done, the hacking, grubbing, and burning went on until the farmer had as much land as he could handle. It was not a job of a few years, but of at least a generation.[58]

It is difficult to calculate the total amount of forest cleared. No tally was kept because, among other things, clearing was regarded as the first step in the "natural" process of land "improvement," which was so obvious and commonplace as to be barely worth comment or record. Nevertheless, in the counties of the densely forested eastern half of the country, the amount of "improved land" returned in the federal censuses after 1850 is a good indicator of the amount of land cleared (table 10.7). Before 1850 it is probable that over 113.7 million acres (46 million ha) had been cleared, the overwhelming bulk of which was carved out of the forests of the eastern half of the country, with only a very small amount coming from either natural or Indian clearings (fig. 10.7A). At the very least about 100 million acres (40.5 million ha) represents the culmination of two centuries of pioneering endeavor in the forests.

In the 20 years between 1850 and 1869 a big upswing in clearing occurred when a remarkable 59.2 million acres (24 million ha) were affected, equivalent to roughly one-half

Table 10.7 Amount of land cleared and man-years expended in forested and nonforested areas, United States, circa 1650–1909

Date	Forested		Nonforested	
	Acres (in millions)	Man-Years (in thousands)	Acres (in millions)	Man-Years (in thousands)
Before 1850	113.7	12,633	0.5	2
1850–59	39.7	4,268	9.1	48
1860–69	19.5	1,973	19.4	68
1870–79	49.3	4,243	48.7	122
1880–89	28.6	2,471	57.7	139
1890–99	31.0	2,486	41.1	68
1900–1909	22.4	1,705	51.6	86
Total	304.2	29,779	228.1	531

Source: Primack, 1963, tables 3, 4, 7, 8.

of all the clearing that had gone on before; and it was concentrated in the northeastern and northern Midwest states of New York, Ohio, Indiana, Illinois, and Wisconsin (fig. 10.7B), where "every field was won by axe and fire." [59] During the turbulent decade of the Civil War the amount of forest cleared and settled dropped to 19.5 million acres (7.9 million ha). But in the 20 years from 1870 to 1889 it rose again to its highest amount, when a colossal 77.9 million acres (31.5 million ha) were affected (fig. 10.7C).

After the 1880s got under way, more acres of open prairie land were settled than forested land. The invention of the improved steel-tipped plow by John Deere in 1837 reduced the time taken to prepare prairie ground for cultivation. A mere 1.5 man-days of labor were now needed to break and plow an acre of prairie, compared with a total of about 32 man-days to completely clear an acre of forest. Henceforth, forest clearing as an element in the formation of the landscape diminished in importance in comparison with other processes, both actually and in popular impression, as the glamour of the open range, cowboys, in fact everything that made up the amorphous concept of "the West," overshadowed the often harsh, grinding labor of forest pioneering. But what one Ohio pioneer called "the war on the woods" was by no means over: from 1880 onward, clearing continued, mainly in the southern states (nearly 29 million acres, or 11.7 million ha), with a little in the Pacific Northwest; and the old areas still contributed a significant amount to decadal totals, which still hovered between 22 million and 31 million acres (8.9 million to 12.5 million ha) (fig. 10.7D). In all, some 300 million acres (121.4 million ha) of forest were eliminated by the turn of century, after which time forest reversion became a more dominant process than forest removal.

This necessarily generalized view of clearing based on the crude statistics of counties and states gives a good overall picture of the pace and extent of the process, but it leaves little impression of the realities of everyday life for the forest pioneer, which are difficult to pinpoint and understand. Perhaps the essence of the experience is conveyed best in a series of four sketches made to illustrate Orsamus Turner's *History of the Holland Purchase of Western New York* and based on the sequence of events he had actually experienced

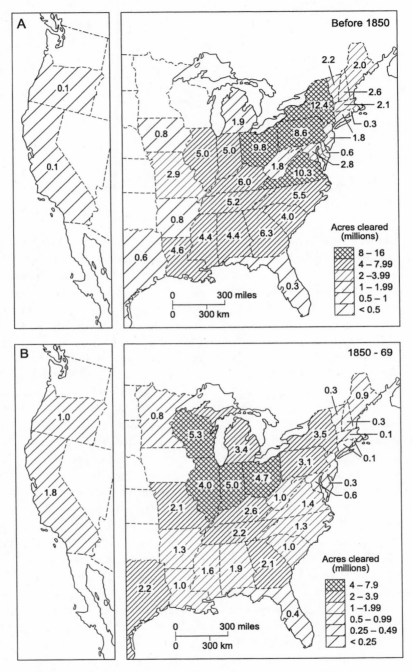

Figure 10.7A–B Millions of acres cleared in the United States, by state, *A*, before 1850; and *B*, 1850–69.
Sources: based on Primack, 1963, and U.S. Bureau of the Census for appropriate years.

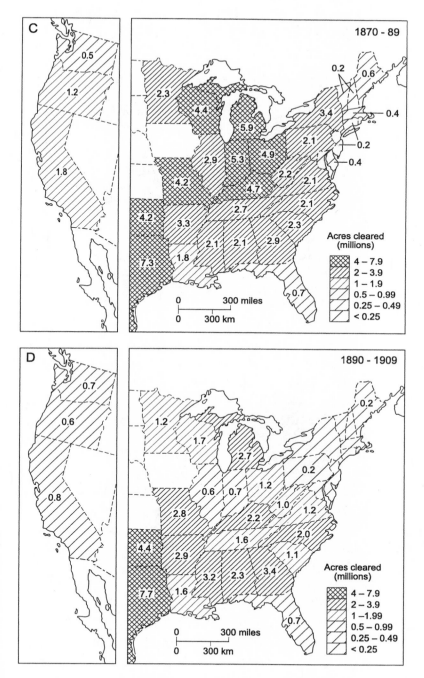

Figure 10.7C–D Millions of acres cleared in the United States, by state, *C*, 1870–89; and *D*, 1890–1909.
Sources: based on Primack, 1963, and U.S. Bureau of the Census for appropriate years.

Plate 10.3A "The First Six Months." From Orsamus Turner, *A Pioneer History of the Holland Purchase of Western New York*, 1849. (University of Wisconsin.)

Plate 10.3B "The Second Year." From Orsamus Turner, *A Pioneer History of the Holland Purchase of Western New York*, 1849. (University of Wisconsin.)

Plate 10.3C "Ten Years Later." From Orsamus Turner, *A Pioneer History of the Holland Purchase of Western New York,* 1849. (University of Wisconsin.)

and seen (plates 10.3A–D).[60] In plate 10.3A, the pioneer and his wife have been on the block for six months. He has cleared a patch to "open out" the forest and get logs for his cabin. The cows and sheep browse on whatever vegetation they can find. His nearest neighbor is miles away. After two years (plate 10.3B) the pioneer has cleared a few more acres and enclosed them with rail and brush fences. Corn, potatoes, and beans have been planted among the stumps, and in the background his scattered and distant neighbors have formed a "logging bee" to help him clear his land. In the foreground, his wife holds their first child. Ten years on (plate 10.3C), 40 acres have been cleared, and stumps in the background indicate that more clearing is under way; the fields contain crops of corn and grass. The log cabin still stands but has been expanded and improved with a new clapboard barn. In the upper left we can discern a church and schoolhouse in the nearby growing village. In the final scene—"The Work of a Lifetime" (plate 10.3D)—the surrounding forest has been cleared by the farmer and his neighbors, so that only the ridge tops remain as woodlots. The house has been extended and "beautified," and a railway passes near the village.

The detail of these four sketches, which are like "stills" clipped out of the continually moving picture of forest settlement, may be varied here and there, but the scenes portray the essential truth of an experience that was repeated many millions of times in the eastern portions of the United States until the opening years of the twentieth century. Indeed, these scenes, first recorded in the annals of deforestation, can stand as a microcosm of forest life almost anywhere in the temperate world, at almost any time during the last 300 years.

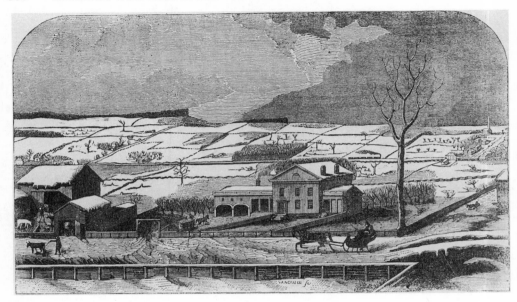

Plate 10.3D "The Work of a Lifetime." From Orsamus Turner, *A Pioneer History of the Holland Purchase of Western New York,* 1849. (University of Wisconsin.)

Rapidity of change was the overriding characteristic of American clearing, which seemed so speeded up as to achieve an almost dreamlike quality. The sudden creation of towns and farms "in the centre of the forests," said Adam Hodgson, "in whose solitudes, within a very few years, the Indian pursued his game, appears rather like an enchantment than the slow result of those progressive efforts, with which, in the old world, savage nature has been subdued." The edges of time and space were blurred, so that what was "stage" and what was "place" were difficult to disentangle. "In successive intervals of *space,*" Hodgson noted,

> I have traced society through those various stages which in most countries are exhibited only in successive periods of *time.* I have seen the roving hunter acquiring the habits of the herdsman; the pastoral state merging into agriculture; and the agricultural in the manufacturing and commercial.[61]

The sensation was overwhelming that time was being telescoped as the process of runaway clearing rapidly reduced distance and space; and rather than taking decades, new landscapes and geographies seemed to emerge overnight. If forest clearing could be described as "perhaps the greatest single factor in the evolution of the European landscape" during historical times, the same could be said without qualification for the North American landscape.[62]

The Landscape of Clearing

It was the rawness of the newly made scene and the wanton destruction of nature and prodigal waste of wood that especially struck the travelers from Europe. Of the many de-

Plate 10.4 "Newly Cleared Land in America." The scene is Oak Orchard Creek, 40 miles west of Rochester, New York. From Basil Hall, *Forty Etchings from Sketches Made with the Camera Lucida in North America in 1827 and 1828*, 1829, plate 9. (University of Wisconsin.)

scriptions perhaps that of Basil Hall, a British artist and writer, is the most revealing. The girdled forest was grotesque:

> Some of the fields were sown with wheat above which could be seen numerous ugly stumps of old trees; others allowed to lie in the grass guarded, as it were, by a set of gigantic black monsters, the girdled, scorched and withered remains of the ancient woods. Many farms are still covered with an extricable and confused mass of prostrate trunks, branches and trees, piles of split logs, and squared timbers, planks, shingles, great stacks of fuel, and often in the midst of all this could be detected a half smothered log hut, without windows or furniture, but well stocked with people. At other places we came upon ploughs, always drawn by oxen making their sturdy way amongst the stumps like a ship navigating through coral reefs, a difficult and tiresome operation.

In addition to this splendid description of cleared land, Hall later sketched the new cutover areas (plate 10.4) and appended the following caption to his etching, which taken together are a vignette of newly cleared land anywhere, at any time:

> The trees are cut over at the height of three or four feet from the ground and the stumps are left for many years till the roots rot;—the edge of the forest, opened for the first time to the light of the sun looks cold and raw;—the ground rugged and ill-dressed . . . as if nothing could ever be made to spring from it. The houses which are made from logs, lie scattered about at long intervals;—while snake fences constructed from split trees, placed in a zig-zag form, disfigure the landscape.

The scene, said Hall, had invariably a "bleak, hopeless" aspect, which had "no parallel in old countries."[63]

Yet to the American pioneer the beauty of the forest and its destruction was of little consequence. The aesthetics of the scene were subordinate to practical problems of clearing—simply, trees and stumps meant toil; cleared land meant production, food, and neighbors; and work now meant the sacrifice of current well-being for a more glorious future. "The sight of wheat field or a cabbage garden," said Isaac Weld,

> would convey pleasure far greater than the most romantic woodland views. They [American pioneers] have an unconquerable aversion to trees; and whenever a settlement is made they cut away all before them without mercy; not one is spared; all share the same fate and are involved in the same havoc. . . . The man that can cut down the largest number, and have fields about his house most clear of them, is looked upon as the most industrious citizen, and the one that is making the greatest improvements in the country.

Ever perceptive, Adam Hodgson thought that clearing was an essential step in the development of the Americans' moral imagination:

> [I]f mere cultivation be not beauty, it is closely allied to it . . . and from its intimate connection with utility, which enters into his idea of beauty, it awakens many kindred associations.
> Every acre, reclaimed from the wilderness, is a conquest of 'civilized man over uncivilized nature'; an addition to resources, which are to enable his country to stretch her moral empire to her geographical limits, and to diffuse over a vast continent the physical enjoyments, the social advantages, the political privileges, and religious institutions, the extension of which is identified with all his visions of her future greatness.[64]

But the clearing was not quite as indiscriminate as the travelers would have one believe. Remnants of forest were left on the steeper slopes, poorer ground, and the extremities of the farms. Even as late as 1900, up to half or more of the farmland in the South and the northern Great Lakes states was still in woodland, as was 10 to 20 percent in the Middle West and Middle Atlantic states. To clear more would have been ecologically impossible given the regrowth rate, and economically unsound given the value of wood to the farmer. The woodlot—depending on its size—was a valuable source of rough grazing and browsing for stock (especially in the South), shelter from cold winds and heat, construction timber, and above all, fuel. The woodlot was, and has remained, a prominent feature of the landscape.[65]

It was not until the settlers entered the Midwest, where the forest ended and the prairie began, that the value of trees was truly appreciated as a source for fuel, construction, and fencing. Initially, half a mile was said to be too much to haul timber for those settlers who had been used to trees growing at their door; but in time, 3 to 6 mi seemed reasonable. Lumber eventually came from further afield, with huge quantities being floated down the Allegheny, Ohio, and Mississippi from as far away as Upper New York State or, after 1834, coming from the newly exploited forests of southern Michigan and Wisconsin via Chicago, all at vast cost. The linking of the Illinois River with the Chicago River by the Illinois-Michigan Canal in 1847 halved prices almost overnight, and lumber now flowed easily into the largely woodless prairie lands. Yet whatever the cost of imported timber, it was more than compensated for by the absence of tree felling and by the speed and ease of breaking up the sod once the steel-tipped plow came into operation after 1837. Compared with "making" a farm in the forest, "making" one in the prairie took less than a twentieth of the time and effort, thereby signaling a massive shift in human endeavor and resources, and a partial reprieve for the forest.

Domestic Fuel

The transformation of nearly 300 million acres of forest into improved land after 1750, and the scores of millions of acres cleared as a result of industrial logging from the second half of the nineteenth century onward, provided an enormous amount of wood for energy. Admittedly, a great deal of the wood was burned on the spot; a little was used for fences, houses, and the like; and some went into the manufacture of pearl ash and potash, but most of what remained from clearing must have been burned for heating the home.[66]

Considering the magnitude of this commodity and its importance in the economy and life of the nation, it is surprising how little we know about its production, consumption, and distribution.[67] Fuelwood dominated as an energy source, domestically and industrially, until well after 1885 (see fig. 9.2 and pp. 249–50), and constituted the greatest drain on the forest until overtaken by the general timber production in about 1860 (fig. 10.8). With such a large and constant demand for fuelwood, even in the South, woodcutting was a profitable sideline for the pioneer farmer and an indispensable aid to the making of a farm. The profits were said to provide enough cash for the purchase of provisions and stock, and sometimes even the hire of "setup" men. The forest, then, was both task and

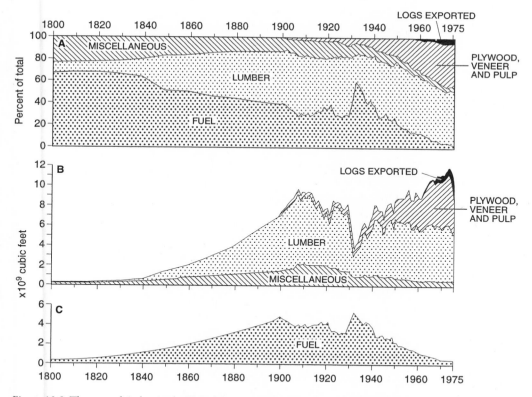

Figure 10.8 The uses of timber in the United States, 1800–1975. *A*, timber in different uses as percentage of total; *B*, all timber used, other than fuel; and *C*, timber used for fuel. Note: 1000 ft³ = 28.317 m³. *Sources:* based on Clawson, 1979: 1168–74, and Clawson, personal communication.

capital. Rural diaries suggest that anything between one-eighth and one-fourth of a farmer's time was spent in chopping, splitting, hauling, and stacking firewood. An annual consumption of 20 to 30 cords (72.5–109 m³) was common for a rural household, and larger farms used twice that amount.[68]

Fuelwood demand was everywhere—in every home, rural industry, and town. There was also an intense demand alongside the main river courses, particularly the Ohio, lower Missouri, and the Mississippi down to New Orleans, to feed the hundreds of steamboats that plied the rivers after 1820. The boats consumed about 500 tons on a 20-day, 3,000-mi voyage from New Orleans to Louisville and took on fuel twice daily, so that "wooding" stations lined the rivers, and the forests were cleared for many miles inland. Coal was not a serious substitute for wood because of its uneven distribution across the continent.[69]

But the greatest demand was undoubtedly in the urban centers on the eastern seaboard. For example, New York, which had a population of 79,000 in 1800, grew to 696,000 in 1850 and 2.5 million in 1890. Admittedly, as it was the port of entry for most immigrants, New York's growth was exceptional; but Boston, Philadelphia, and a host of other cities also showed massive growth. Thus it became profitable to haul supplies from farther and farther afield. Fuelwood came by boat along the Atlantic coast from Maine and New Jersey, down the Hudson, and increasingly along the Erie Canal, which had opened in 1825 and penetrated the forests in the Genesee country in upstate New York, the region Basil Hall had seen being cleared. By 1845 New York was said to be consuming over 4 million cords (14.5 million m³) per annum, and despite the rise in the price of fuelwood and some penetration of coal and anthracite into the domestic market, especially in Philadelphia after 1820, wood still accounted for over three-quarters of the energy used, and was still the cheapest fuel by some 12 to 25 percent.

The only other possible solution to the dearth of fuel was more efficient heating. Wide, open, roaring hearth fires lost nine-tenths of their heat up the chimney, so their replacement by more efficient enclosed stoves was advocated for heating homes. But the early stoves (known as Franklins after their inventor, Benjamin Franklin) were smoky, inefficient, and inelegant, and as long as wood was reasonably plentiful and/or cheap they made little headway. Moreover, to cut wood small enough to fit into the stove required extra effort, and time was the one commodity the pioneer did not have as he started to make a farm. Prizes and awards for improved designs proliferated in agricultural and scientific societies, and over 800 patents for stoves were taken out between 1790 and 1840, most no more than stylistic tinkerings of previous designs, although some minor improvements in efficiency were made. With the advent of better iron-casting techniques after 1820, stoves moved into mass production to become so common that they were generally accepted in urban America by 1840, and no longer a topic of comment after 1850. By 1860 nearly half a million were being manufactured annually.[70]

Anthracite was the main competitor of wood as an energy source in urban areas and came into its own after 1850, when boilers for central heating were installed in the cellars of multistoried urban buildings. Compared with anthracite, wood was bulky and heavy (by a factor of 4 to 5 times) and difficult to store in urban cellars. In time, anthracite also spread west into the less well-treed plains (fig. 10.9). However, despite the diffusion of

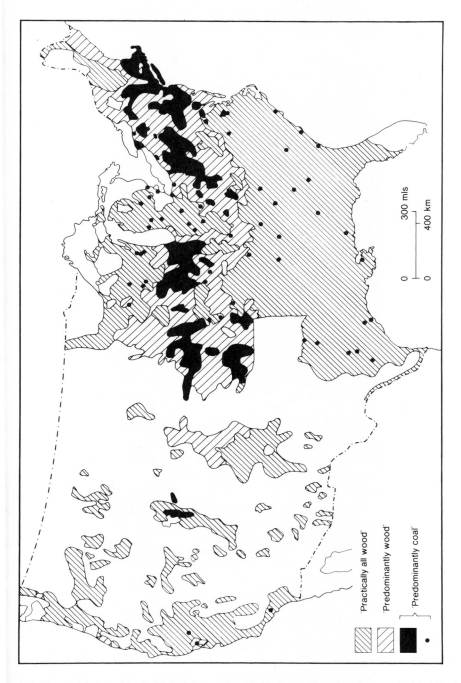

'Practically all wood'

'Predominantly wood'

'Predominantly coal'

300 mls

400 km

0

0

Figure 10.9 Types of fuel used in the United States, circa 1880. *Source:* based on Sargent, 1884: 488–89.

coal burning across the continent, wood fuel consumption continued to grow. Coal may have constituted about 60 percent of all fuel used in 1900 (fig. 9.2), but wood still comprised the bulk of the rest of the expanding energy needs. The drain on the forests continued: rural families still sat in front of their great, blazing open hearths, and with a burgeoning economy and concomitant energy needs, more wood was cut in almost every year than every year before until the late 1930s.

Railroads: "The . . . Juggernaut of the Vegetable World"

Fuelwood consumption was greatly boosted by the growth of the railroads and factories (table 10.8). The railroad in particular, that actual and symbolic agent of change and modernization, was a voracious devourer of forests. In 1866 Andrew Fuller had noted that

> even where railroads have penetrated regions abundantly supplied, we soon find all along its track timber becomes scarce. For every railroad in the country requires a continued forest from one end to the other of its line to supply it with ties, fuel, and lumber for building cars.[71]

The fuel element of the railroad's appetite for timber diminished rapidly throughout the 1870s and 1880s with the availability of coal, which was less bulky to store on the train, with about 1 ton of coal replacing 4 tons of wood. But it was gradually realized that the amount of timber needed for general railway purposes, such as buildings, stations, telegraph poles, fencing, and especially ties, would reach astronomical proportions if the length of track constructed continued to expand at the rate it had in the past. Track length tripled from 32,600 mi in 1860 to 100,000 mi in 1880, and it was set to double during the next decade and again during the next.[72] Each mile of track needed between 2,200 and 3,500 prime heart-of-oak ties, but most commonly 2,640, which had to be replaced every 6 to 7 years because of decay.

How much wood the railroads actually consumed was one of the great debates in the realms of forestry and the timber trade during the middle and latter half of the nineteenth century. Like charcoal furnaces, the railroad was singled out as a major factor in woodland destruction because it was an alien intrusion into the idyll of American rural life: it was the harbinger of rapid change and truly "the machine in the garden."[73] Others could not laud it enough; it was the spearhead of civilization in the wilderness and the uniter of the continent. In 1876, Daniel Millikin, who had lately witnessed the massive forest destruction caused by the many railroads built across his native Ohio, thought it difficult "to conceive of the demands which this new invention will make upon the woods," and five years later John Klippart thought that "this denuding process" was leading to more forest destruction in Ohio than had agriculture. The advent of the transcontinental lines that thrust across the treeless plains at a rate of up to 8 mi per day raised timber-depletion consciousness. Nathaniel Egleston, director of the fledgling Forestry Division, hazarded a guess that 3 million acres (1.2 million ha) had been destroyed for existing track and 472,400 acres (191,173 ha) were needed annually just to keep up maintenance, which estimate he raised to 567,714 acres (229,746 ha) a few years later. A more exact and sober investigation by M. G. Kern, an agent for the division, suggested that existing track had consumed 3.1 billion ft^3 (87,782.7 m^3) of timber, and that maintenance and

Table 10.8 Fuelwood consumption, United States, 1879

	Cords (in thousands)		Percentage
Domestic Use		140,537	95.5
Industrial Use			
Railways	1,972		1.3
Steamboats	788		0.5
Mineral operations	625		0.4
Manufacturing	1,856	5,241	1.3	3.5
Subtotal		145,778	99.0
Charcoal for smelting		1,459	1.0
Total		147,236	100.0

Source: Sargent, 1884, 9:489.

Table 10.9 Crossties used and acres of forest cleared, United States, 1870–1910

	Miles of Track	Ties Renewed Annually (in millions)	Ties Used on New Construction (in millions)	Total Ties Annually (in millions)	Acres of Forest Cleared (in thousands)
1870	60,000	21	18	39	195
1880	107,000	37	21	58	290
1890	200,000	70	19	89	445
1900	259,000	91		91	455
1910	357,000	124		124	620

Sources: S. Olson, 1971: 12; and U.S. Bureau of Census, 1977, vol. 2, table 392.

extension needed another 0.5 billion ft^3 (14,158 m^3), the equivalent of 300,000 acres (121,406 ha) of forest per annum.[74]

Whatever the precise figures, the preference for the heart of white and chestnut oaks—and to a lesser extent, black locust, which had the requisite qualities of strength, elasticity, and resistance to rot—meant selective but highly destructive felling throughout the hardwood forests of the Appalachians. A mere 6-ft railroad tie required a minimum of 75 ft of good timber; it was "a reckless system of forest clearing," said Kern, that was halted only when the creosoting of ties under high pressure became accepted in the later 1890s, and ultimately when railroad expansion stopped.[75] Kern's calculations were substantially upheld by the more finely worked-out estimates of the Forest Service in 1911, to which must be added the timber used in the construction and replacement of buildings, rolling stock, bridges, and so on.

If the calculations in table 10.9 are correct (and there is every indication that they are), then the railroads were using at least one-fourth to one-fifth of the annual U.S. timber production during the latter part of the century, so the contemporary view that the railroad was "the insatiable juggernaut of the vegetable world," though exaggerated, was essentially correct. Multiplied on a world scale, the effect on the forests was staggering (see table 9.5).[76]

Charcoal-Made Iron

Although the last charcoal-fueled iron furnace ceased operation in Britain in 1810, as all were being fired by coke or coal, not one coke furnace had been built in the United States, where the charcoal iron industry died a very slow death. Not until 1835 were the first experiments made with coke, and not until 1945 was the last charcoal furnace shut down. The sheer abundance of wood was an obvious factor in the survival of this traditional technology, but charcoal-made iron also had positive qualities. It was heat resistant, tough, and retained a good cutting edge, yet it was also malleable, making it a versatile all-purpose iron for use on the frontier in making boilers, tools, and implements.[77]

In 1865 there were 560 iron furnaces, of which 439, or 78 percent, were still fueled by charcoal. These were concentrated in the Hanging Rock district of southern Ohio, the Allegheny valley northeast of Pittsburgh, the Juniata valley in south-central Pennsylvania, and the Berkshires on the New York-Massachusetts-Connecticut borders. The remainder of the furnaces burned anthracite and were concentrated in eastern Pennsylvania.[78] In time, most of these charcoal furnaces were either abandoned or converted to coal of some sort, but iron making by means of charcoal did not die out entirely. It continued to flourish in the South, and particularly in northern Michigan and Wisconsin until as late as the mid-1940s, in conjunction with the mining of high-grade ores of the Lake Superior ranges.

Large supplies of wood were needed to fuel these furnaces, and iron "plantations" or estates of between 30,000 and 100,000 acres of woodland around or near the furnaces were common. These would be cut in rotational fashion, with overcutting leading to the exhaustion of supplies and the abandonment of the furnaces, as in Scioto, Jackson, and Vinton counties in southern Ohio or the Ramapos Mountains of New York and New Jersey.[79]

As ever, the amount of forest cleared for smelting iron depended on the density of the trees and the efficiency of the furnaces. But if the modest estimate already made of 150 acres for every 1,000 tons of pig iron produced is accepted, then the acres affected could have been as low as 25,000 in 1862 and as high as 94,000 in 1890, although many "iron forests" were cut over at 25- to 30-year intervals, or sometimes less. For example, a detailed survey of 837 mi^2 of Vinton and Jackson counties in the Hanging Rock district of Ohio shows that 60 percent of the forest was clear-cut down to 4-in-diameter trees between 1850 and 1860, and that trees had regenerated sufficiently for recutting to be carried out at the beginning of the twentieth century, in effect a crude form of coppicing.[80] Either way, taking the larger or the smaller estimate, the amount cut had relatively little impact on the forest as a whole. Even if we total *all* the known charcoal iron production between 1855 and 1910 (20.4 million tons), it would have consumed only 4,800 mi^2 (12,432 km^2) of woodland, or 3,000 mi^2 (7,770 km^2) if a 25-year rotation had been employed. This has to be compared with the amount of land cleared for agriculture during the same period. It is a mere 1.3 percent of that, or 0.8 percent if regrowth is considered. Having said that, however, charcoal iron production was concentrated, so the effects on the immediately surrounding forest were noticeable. Locally, the furnace and the thinned and cut forest were visually prominent, so that charcoal iron, rather like fuel for loco-motives, could be pointed to as a great destroyer of the forest. But nationally it was a mere pin-prick, as it was upon forests throughout the world.

Lumber Production

By the early decades of the nineteenth century the intertwining of lumbering activity and agricultural clearing began to unravel, and the pioneer farmer–cum–part-time lumber-man gave way to large-scale, specialized, commercial logging. New England and New York began to assume the same relationship as raw material suppliers to the urbanizing, industrializing eastern seaboard as the Baltic did to northwest Europe. But there were significant differences. Whereas the Baltic still relied on peasant cutting and protoindus-trial production methods, U.S. exploitation was the epitome of industrial capitalism in the forest. Second, U.S. sources of supply were internal and could be linked by river, lake, and canal, and eventually by rail; and while distances were often at least as great as the 1,200 mi from the Baltic to Britain, they were not separated by sea or other countries. Third, U.S. forests were supplying not only a rapidly growing and urbanizing popula-tion in the same territory, but one that after about 1840 was expanding and colonizing the vast treeless plains of the West. The population leaped from 7.2 million in 1810 to 31.5 million in 1860, and then more than doubled to 74.8 million by 1899.

Wood and wood products permeated American life so thoroughly that in 1836 James Hall could say truthfully, "Well may ours be called a *Wooden country;* not merely from the extent of the forests but because in common use wood has been substituted for a num-ber of most necessary articles, such as stone, iron, and even leather."[81] Also, from all that has been said before, its roles as a producer of energy and creator of agricultural land were paramount.

From a mere 0.5 billion bf (1.2 million m^3) cut in 1801, the amount of lumber cut rose and accelerated with each successive decade to a form a new, upwardly sloping curve that reached 20 billion bf (47.2 million m^3) in 1880 and peaked at nearly 46 billion bf (108.5 million m^3) in 1906, an amount never reached since (fig. 10.10).[82] The ability to supply these enormous quantities of lumber rested on a host of new inventions, methods of transportation, and forms of business organization, all at a new, larger scale of opera-tion. The lumber and forest products industry, like industry everywhere in the United States, was entering a new phase of vigorous expansion in an era of industrial capitalism.

Many of the technological developments affecting mechanization, transportation, and business organization have been outlined already in chapter 9, but suffice it to say that steam power meant the concentration of industrial activity, high and continuous out-put, and the beginnings of corporations and monopolies; steel meant better and more efficient tools and machinery; the railroad meant reliable, fast, and more flexible trans-portation; and all these meant increasing specialization of activity, concern for efficiency, cutthroat competition, and the mass production of a standardized manufactured end prod-uct of known quality. The factory had moved into the forest, where the systematic cut-ting of large areas replaced the cutting of individual trees, and the large-scale ownership

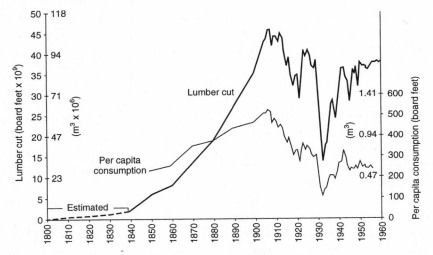

Figure 10.10 Lumber cut and per capita consumption, 1800–1960. *Source:* U.S. Bureau of the Census, 1977, tables L.87–97 and L.113–21.

of standing timber allowed monopolistic exploitation to take place.[83] The old scale and style of cutting was swept away; the only significant borrowing of a past technology was the use of river transportation, now boosted by the development of the log drive, and tugboat rafting on the continental rivers.

The vast sweep, complexity, and rapid changes of the American lumber story are difficult to encapsulate in words, but a few points can be made. Lumber was so essential to life in the United States during the nineteenth century that nothing was allowed to stand in the way of its acquisition. If stands ran out in one place, or were better and cheaper to acquire, transport, and market in another, the timber industry moved on. The continental shifts in this regard were enormous. By 1860 the supremacy of lumber production had passed from New York and New England to the Great Lakes states. Although New York, Pennsylvania, and New England were still important producers, Michigan, Wisconsin, and Minnesota now cut greater volumes and values of timber. Lumbering in the South began to achieve prominence by 1890, and carried on well into the twentieth century. And the Pacific Northwest was beginning to rank high in national production by 1900, when the Great Lakes states were in decline (fig. 10.11 A–D).

Second, each locality/phase of lumber production (they were almost one and the same thing) had its own distinctive characteristics (see fig. 9.3)—never exclusively so, to be sure, as there was much overlap, but nevertheless distinctive because of factors of terrain, climate, and technology. Each diagram in figure 9.3 is a composite picture drawn from many accounts of the salient features of each phase. The first (fig. 9.3A) was characteristic of New England, New York, and the early Great Lakes states and was common during the first half of the nineteenth century. Although the log drive dominated, it was later augmented by transport over ice roads. The second (fig. 9.3B) was common in the later Great Lakes states forest exploitation from about 1850 to 1880 and the early years

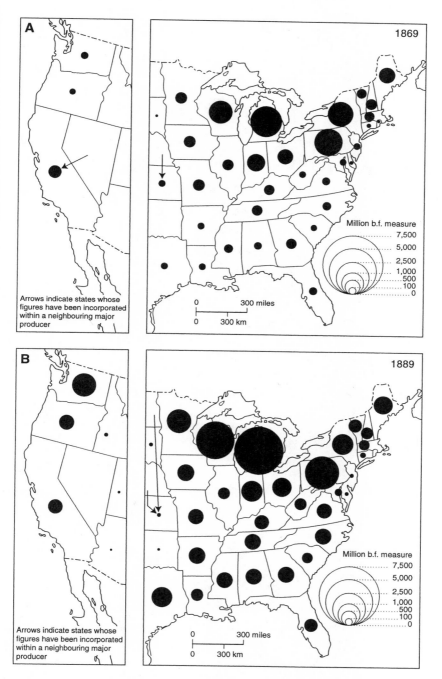

Within the maps:

A 1869

B 1889

Arrows indicate states whose figures have been incorporated within a neighbouring major producer

Million b.f. measure
7,500
5,000
2,500
1,000
500
100
0

0   300 miles
0   300 km

Figure 10.11A–B Lumber production in the United States, *A*, 1869; and *B*, 1889. *Source:* U.S. Bureau of the Census and Steer, 1948. Production is in million board feet (mbf), which equals 2,360 m³. Arrows indicate states whose figures have been incorporated within a neighbouring major producer.

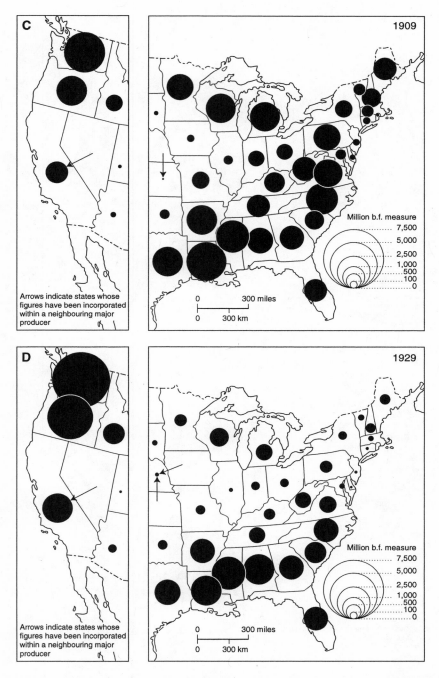

Figure 10.11C–D Lumber production in the United States, C, 1909; and D, 1929. *Source:* U.S. Bureau of the Census and Steer, 1948. Production is in million board feet (mbf), which equals 2,360 m³. Arrows indicate states whose figures have been incorporated within a neighboring major producer.

of the southern logging industry. The advent of the railroad during the 1860s caused a shift in sawmill sites to the intersections of mainline track and major river. Specialized lumber camps and lumber towns emerged to house the workers and their families. The third phase (fig. 9.3C) straddled the years 1880 to 1920 and was especially characteristic of the South. The light logging railroads were laid and relaid to ensure maximum exploitation of the stand, and in time spur lines were constructed from the main lines to overcome the break of gauge and integrate mills in order to speed up and maximize production. The fourth stage (fig 9.3D), which occurred after 1920, is dealt with later. It was characteristic of the Pacific Northwest and subsequently has become the norm everywhere.[84]

During the final decades of the century the lumber industry was exploitative in the very worst sense of the word, and the Great Lakes states, and later the South, where industrial methods of logging and transportation saw their first and fullest flowering, were the epitome of that plundering. It was the first time that the world had seen the deleterious environmental effects produced when steam, steel, and business enterprise combined with capital, rising affluence, and increased demand. It was an experience that, regretfully, was going to be repeated in one form or another in many other forests of the world in the future.

The heady boom of cutting the huge stands of the much-prized white pine in the Great Lakes states doubled lumber production from about 4 billion bf (9.4 million m³) annually in 1870 to over 9 billion bf (21.3 million m³) in 1890, only to fall from then on to a mere 1 billion bf (2.4 million m³) by 1920. The cutting left behind a landscape of depletion and devastation. Although many sawmills turned to other types of wood, especially hemlock and hardwoods, dozens of once-flourishing settlements went into decline and even disappeared. Some of the more enterprising, like Eau Claire, Oshkosh, and La Crosse in Wisconsin or Grand Rapids in Michigan, managed to diversify into manufacturing, and a whole array of wood-using industries such as door, blind, sash, and furniture making sprung up using the new industrial woodworking machinery.[85] But many more were like Cheboygan and Alpena in Michigan, which became ghosts of their former selves. During the heyday of the cutting boom in 1886, Cheboygan had been a bustling town of over 6,000 inhabitants, 16 mills, and numerous woodworking industries, but by 1916 there were only two mills left and the number of employees in the industry had fallen to barely 1,000. Alpena suffered similarly. Whereas the town had seemed once to be "made of saw dust," now it scratched for a living:

> Mills which formerly selected only the stoutest pine trunk now welcome the slender log, the crooked log, the rotten log, and the sunken log fished up from the river bottom. In place of beams for the western railway bridge or huge rafters for the Gothic church, Alpena busily turns out planks, shingles, spools, pail handles, veneering, and the wooden peg for furniture. It also makes manila paper out of hemlock pulp. It brings hemlock bark to its tannery. It combs its brains for inventions to utilize by-products, as does the Chicago pork-packer.[86]

In addition to the decline and even disappearance of the settlements, there were two other consequences of excessive logging. First, the thick carpet of combustible slash waste remained on the forest floor after the cut-out-and-get-out exploitation made the forest highly susceptible to fire. The great Peshtigo fire of 1871 in northeast Wisconsin devastated over 50 mi² and killed at least 1,500 people, and the Michigan fire of the same year consumed over 4,000 mi² of prime pine timber. In 1894 the great Hinkeley fire in Minnesota claimed 418 lives, and so it went on almost annually, and with increasing frequency.[87]

Second, there were the wastes of the aptly named cutover areas, stretching for over 600 mi across the middle and northern parts of the three Great Lakes states, from the Red River in Minnesota in the west to Lake Huron in the east, and probably totaling over 50 million acres (20.2 million ha) by the end of the century. Unlike the hardwood forests of the South, much of which had been taken up for agriculture once cleared, these lands were cut primarily for the timber and were marginal, in all senses of the word, to farming. Cutting had been careless; the ground was strewn with debris and massive stumps remained, often cut many feet above the ground. The soil was mainly poor glacial outwash sands and gravels, and the climate averaged only 100 to 130 frost-free days, a period much too short for growing corn but just sufficient for grass and hay. Most of the cutover area was simply too far north for successful agriculture.[88]

But the timber companies wanted to wring the last penny out of the land, and, moreover, wanted to get rid of it because it was liable to state taxes. It could be abandoned, of course, but that threw an intolerable burden on surrounding taxpaying areas. The railway companies wanted settlement because new farms would increase revenues, and state governments, imbued with concepts of progress and improvement, were not prepared to allow the northern portions of their states to "revert to wilderness with the passing of the lumber industry." Consequently, all three advertised the virtues of the cutover areas widely in America and Europe, particularly in Scandinavia. The literature was boosterish; it sidestepped the difficulties of the once-forested environment and promoted an image of a productive rural paradise. Thousands of unsuspecting immigrants came and struggled to make a living. There was a high rate of failure, and the survivors hung on to lead a wretched life, trying to eke out an existence.[89] The cutover areas were (and still are in places) dotted with derelict fences and sagging, unpainted farmhouses, some mere tarpaper shacks. In the deserted fields occasionally one still sees a lilac tree or heaped of stones where a chimney once stood, both markers of an abandoned homestead, the whole scene a mute and melancholy testimony to abandoned hopes in the former forested lands. The really hard sell occurred just before World War I, and it was only after the mid-1930s that efforts were made to return the land to the crop it grew best—trees.

When the output of the Great Lakes states began to decline after 1880, the wave of forest exploitation moved south to the extensive evergreen longleaf, slash, and loblolly pine forests of Georgia, Alabama, Mississippi, Louisiana, and eastern Texas. Here exploitation was possibly even more ruthless and thorough, and it was almost entirely railroad focused. Main-line railroads stretched across the continental United States from southern ports to northern markets, with many spur lines of 40 or 50 mi in length splaying into the surrounding pine forests. Mill sites would be preselected at 3- to 5-mi intervals along the spur lines, the sawmills sometimes being built ahead of the railways (the equipment trundled in by mule) so that a stock of lumber was immediately ready for market once the connection was made. The mills themselves were generally larger than they had been in the Great Lakes states and exclusively steam powered. Timber haulage was mechanized, usually by massive steam-operated skidders that ran on railway tracks. These had long grappling arms and derricks from which steel cables were run out into the surrounding forest and attached to logs, which were then dragged to the track side and hoisted onto the trucks.[90] As the skidders pulled in the logs in a circle around them, so they ripped out all the young growth that might have allowed the forest to regenerate, and scraped the thin soil bare. In one parish in Louisiana the cutover areas

> stretched wearily away from the rusting rails of the mainline track. Those nearest the mill, which had been cut last or had been gone over a second time during the recent era of high prices, were desolate indeed. No living pine tree remained on acre after acre. The extraordinary demand for every stick of timber . . . the pitiless system of taxing annually every board foot in standing trees, and the sweep of slash fires had done their work.

This description, said Reginald Forbes, was not "sensational" but "commonplace." Indeed, for some of those foresters and lumbermen who fought in the trenches in the Somme during World War I, the desolation of the shell-shattered and denuded landscape of Flanders had a familiar look—it reminded them of the cutover areas back home in the South.[91]

Just as the big lumber monopolies owned the land and the trees—in fact whole counties—so they owned the towns, and their inhabitants too. There were hundreds of little company towns featuring rows of identical houses or shacks with a central commissary, the sole, company-operated store, where the employees bought their food and goods at inflated prices, by coupons paid in lieu of wages. Most laborers were either ex-slaves or poor whites coming off low-income farms. No all-male lumberjack camps with the aura of rugged and heroic individualism existed in the South. Lumber settlements were populated instead by a docile labor force of family men in small houses and small towns who could not protest about their isolation and exploitation.[92] George Creel's description of them as a new form of "feudal" town was apt; they were mere cogs in the new machinery of industrial lumbering. With important social differences—and usually without the river—the characteristic landscape of lumber exploitation in the South conformed to the generalized pattern depicted in figure 9.3C.

When the forest was stripped bare, the lumber companies moved their mills and a few of their key workers and let the town die. The mills, once the "pulsing hearts" of the settlements, sagged at their foundations while the railroads rusted from disuse. In the towns, grass began "to grow from the middle of every street and broken window lights bespoke deserted homes." The mill had "sawed out."[93] What the skidders had not ripped out, wildfires in the slash debris finished off. How much land was left as a cutover area is difficult to calculate. In 1907 it was said to be an astounding 79 million acres (32 million ha), of which a mere one fifth was in the process of being restocked with trees. In 1920 the figure was revised downward to 55.4 million acres (29.5 million ha), of which just over one half was restocked.[94] Whatever the truth, however, one thing is certain: as in the Great Lakes states forests, logging had left a vast area of derelict land through the forests of the South. Much of the cutover areas were going to be invaded naturally by scrub oak of little commercial value; rapacious logging had led to a permanent pauperization of the forest.

The abundant detail of the North American deforestation is without parallel. At the most conservative estimate, over 350 million acres (142 million ha) of forest were cleared for agriculture and another 20 million acres (approximately 8 million ha) for industry, communications, mining, and urban sprawl. The effects of lumbering were immense. In all, by 1900 the destruction must have eliminated one-half of the original forest cover of the country, which should give us pause when we condemn the present deforestation of the tropical world. Yet, while much was lost, much was gained. Some of the first stirrings of the conservation movement as we know it in the Western world today began in the U.S. forests just prior to and just after the Civil War.[95] And there is no doubt that the widespread availability and abundance of wood and land were the mainsprings of the country's agricultural supremacy, industrial might, and high standard of living that first became evident during the second half of the nineteenth century. Simply, without its wood, the United States would not be the country it is today.

THE PACIFIC RIM: COMPLEXITY AND CONTRAST

The deforestation experience of the temperate lands around the Atlantic was very similar to each other, and even culturally and economically linked. Both North America and Europe had growing, wealthy, industrialized, urban populations that created enormous demands on their forests, and both had large areas of pioneer land settlement that led to forest destruction. In both continents, concern about woodland devastation mounted as the century neared its end, though with a few notable regional exceptions, both still had ample supplies of timber overall. In contrast, the experience of the temperate lands of the Pacific was different and disparate. Australia and New Zealand were soon to be in the throes of pioneering agricultural settlement in the forest, not dissimilar in kind to that in North America, but vastly different in scale. Japan had entered an era of purposeful regulation, silviculture, and reforestation that was unprecedented in Asia or, for that matter, anywhere in the world. China was more or less written off as a hopeless case of extreme deforestation for which there seemed neither remedy nor promise. The northwest Pacific coast of North America was gearing up to be one of the great global exporters of timber, supplementing the resource deficiencies of territories elsewhere around the Pacific. It was a complex story.

Japan

In Japan the excesses of town and monument building, illegal cutting, and cultivation on steep slopes were evident before the end of the seventeenth century. The great stands of virgin timber had gone, disputes over forest use were common, flooding and sedimentation of the cultivable lowlands were causing alarm, the quality of timber had deteriorated, and scarcity had become widespread. It was remarkable that these multiple problems were recognized so early by the shogunate and the vassal military lords, or *daimyō*, and that both took positive measures to control and alter forest use. It is difficult to generalize about the remedial measures—the Tokagawa shogunate, or *bakufu*, lasted for over 250 years and there were 250-odd *daimyō*—but in general one can say that the administration devised what Conrad Totman has called a "negative regimen."[96] Administrative rules were evolved for both the protection of the forests and the safeguarding of products. Because the concept of land "ownership" did not exist, the emphasis was on "rights," and those of the villagers and lords, and the forest domains in which exploitation could take place, were carefully delineated and codified. For example, regulations were devised to control the areas open to harvest, the number of days and number of workers who had access to the area, the size and type of tools to be used, the number of loads that could be produced, the inspection of the transportation of timber goods, and building size and timber to be used. Sumptuary regulations prohibited the use of certain prized woods such as *sugi (Cryptomeria japonica)*, *hinoki (Chamaecyparis obtusa)*, or Japanese cypress, except for specific items. It was a comprehensive, if uncoordinated, body of regulations that in toto constituted "a vast and moderately effective system of rationing." Protection was extended to lowland basins, and an Office of Erosion Control was even created to supervise excessive cutting in the Kinai basin. In many ways the "negative regimen" solved nothing during an era of growing population, but it was an essential prelude to raising awareness and knowledge. Moreover, it "bought time" for the introduction of more effective policies of silviculture and the purposeful planting of trees to produce the "green archipelago" that Japan is today, rather than the ruined land that it might have been.[97]

In an attempt to understand this remarkable precocity in forest matters, Totman dismisses explanations such as a national "love of nature" or Buddhist, Confucian, or Shinto sentiment for natural objects as facile; the Japanese sensibility toward nature was always refined and delicate, but recreational and urban in orientation, and trees were considered crude and rural. And in any case, these religious values had not saved the forests of the pre-Edo era. Rather, the concerns of the restorers were intensely practical: forests helped supply raw materials, fuel, and fertilizer, concerns that were alleviated by the natural succession of deciduous trees, which replaced coniferous trees. Also, the connection between forest cover, run-off, and erosion and the stability of the lowland paddy rice seemed to be appreciated. In all, a form of conservation ethic resulted. Additionally, for some unknown reason wheeled vehicles and crosscut saws were rarely permitted in forested areas; this constraining of technology probably helped preservation, as did the absence of sheep and goats. Finally, Totman suggests that the overriding concerns of the Tokugawa administration to preserve peace and avoid foreign contacts focused attention on the resources on hand and prevented the introduction of alien, destabilizing technology. Therefore, it was a unique social and environmental situation in which a disciplined and literate society sorted out its priorities: "The people of Tokugawa Japan, high and low alike, had to make do with what they had and what they could acquire peacefully, *and they knew it.*"[98] The fact that population increase stabilized after 1750 certainly took pressure off the forests, and the search for protein and resources shifted from the land to the ocean. As a result, the total demand for woodland actually decreased.

China

The contrast of Japan's deforestation experience with that of neighboring China could not have been starker. Everything we know about that vast country (and it is precious little for this period) suggests the existence of an impoverished peasant society, subsisting in a deforested, denuded, and eroded lunar landscape. Even during the early years of this century, China was being held up as an example of what excessive deforestation could do. "It can be concluded," wrote Walter Lowdermilk in his evocatively entitled article, "Forestry in Denuded China," "that forests formerly covered wide areas now bare or covered with grass." Substantial timber reserves remained only in the coniferous forests of Manchuria and northwest Mongolia, and the evergreen broad-leaved forests of parts of the subtropical and tropical south. These were the areas that were either remotest from the populous parts of the country or mountainous and little suited to agriculture.[99]

The primary cause of the denudation was, of course, agricultural clearing to feed a population that grew from about 300 million in the early eighteenth century to reach 430 million by 1850 and 500 million by 1900. In the northern and central lowlands rice cultivation leveled the land; in the more mountainous south the forested uplands were colonized by renewed bursts of migration during the eighteenth century. Migrants came from the overcrowded lowlands of Hunan and Szechwan into the Han uplands, and from the southern coastal mountain areas of Guangdong and Fujian into the Lower Yangzi highlands on the borders of Anhui and Zhejiang Provinces. As in the case of the Hunan colonization, the New World crops of maize and sweet and Irish potatoes were suited to and productive in these marginal highland environments where the previous crop mix was not. It was now an old story: slash-and-burn cultivation stripped the hillsides. The sequence was outlined graphically during the early nineteenth century by a local official:

> The mountain people fell trees and cultivate in the shade of the dead trees. The fertility of the soil will double the grain for one or two years. After the fourth of fifth year, the soil is already gouged and slack, the mountain is steep and the fierce water of the sudden rains in summer and autumn leave only stone "bones" everywhere. They must again seek land to cultivate. The original land, left vacant, gradually grows grasses, shrubs rot and become mud, or are felled and burned to ash; only then can it be tilled again. One cannot rely on the old forests for a steady living but must move on to seek one's livelihood; thus the mountain people cannot but wander.

These mobile "shed" or "shack" people, as they were quite accurately known, disrupted the stability of the land as surely as they disrupted the stability of existing society.[100]

The severity of deforestation was manifest in two other ways, which added greatly to the hardship of peasant life. First, soil erosion and swollen, silt-laden rivers plagued lowland agricultural productivity; and second, the scarcity of fuel was a constant worry, particularly in the cold north of the country. These problems caused a vicious downward spiral in which the grubbing-up of every piece of combustible material removed the last remnants of vegetation that held the soil together and/or helped to manure it. China's fuelwood crisis had lasted since at least 1400, and nineteenth-century observers confirmed its persistence. "Fire-wood is so scarce in the country," said Robert Fortune in 1847, "that a great portion of the straw, cotton stalks, and grass, which would go to manure the fields, are used for firing." Arthur Smith, who erroneously interpreted Chinese conditions as a quaint, rural "sense of economy" rather than the dire want and poverty that they were, noted in 1894 that wood was almost nonexistent, so that fuel "consists generally of nothing but leaves, stalks, and roots of crops, making a rapid blaze that quickly disappears." The whole village was organized to strip the land of what combustible matter was available:

> Every smallest child, who can do nothing else, can at least gather fuel. The vast army of fuel-gatherers, which in autumn or winter overspread the land, leave not a weed behind the hungry teeth of the bamboo rakes. Boys are sent into trees to beat off with clubs the autumnal leaves, as if they are chestnuts.

The alternative was to economize on domestic heating and go without hot meals, as many did, with grim consequences for health and longevity.[101]

It is clear that the overwhelmingly Confucian ethos had not stemmed deforestation in China any more than it had in pre-Edo Japan, except for the vicinity of a few temples and sacred sites. Obvious explanations for the devastation are a long history of agricultural transformation along with unremitting population growth and the consequent pressure on available land leading to an intense struggle for existence, and little substitution of wood or its importation from the wider world. But the root of the cause was more than numbers alone; Egbert Walker thought that weak government control was the culprit. The elite of the Ming and Ching dynasties were drawn "largely from the 'literati' or scholars of the country" who, though they may have found aesthetic pleasure in the temples and manicured gardens that they were fortunate enough to experience, left the mundane problems of agriculture, trees, and productivity to officials from the "lower classes, who had little or no vision beyond their narrow fields nor the means to carry out what little they did have." Whatever the reason, China's deforestation experience was the very antithesis of neighboring Japan's. The outcome by the beginning of the twentieth century was a "scarcity of timber" that was "acutely felt throughout the length and breadth of the land," and few would have disagreed with that assessment.[102]

Australia and New Zealand

In the first chapter of *Man and Nature,* George Perkins Marsh suggested optimistically that the recently settled continent of Australia would provide "the fullest elucidation of [the] difficult and disputable problems" that lead to "physical decay on new countries." However, Australia's recent settlement, bureaucratic efficiency, and seeming

Plate 10.5 A selector's homestead cleared out of the dense eucalypt forests of Victoria. From *The Illustrated Handbook of Victoria, Australia Prepared for the Colonial and Indian Exhibition, London,* 1886.

simplicity were not enough to give the unequivocal record of deforestation that he hoped was possible. Australia was no different than other new countries, where "the pioneers, whether settlers or timber-getters, cut down indiscriminately, giving no thought to anything but their immediate requirements" (plates 10.5, 10.6). According to R. Kaleski, the "war of destruction" had reduced the forests of New South Wales alone from an original 10.1 million ha to 4.5 million ha by 1900.[103]

Australia's dense eucalypt forests are located in the humid areas in the extreme southern and eastern portions of the continent. As rainfall decreases inland large trees give way to open savanna forest, which in turn merge into scrubby trees, often the distinctive mallee vegetation—multiple-stemmed, drought-resistant eucalypts with massive lignotuber roots. Beyond that again lay mulga scrub and grassland, and finally stony and sandy deserts. In round figures, between 238 and 244 million ha, or a quarter of the continent, was tree covered, of which only about 30 million ha (3–4 percent) could be considered forest in the commonly accepted sense of the word, and therefore suitable for timber exploitation. The rest was scrubby low forest and woodland. That these forested areas were also the areas suitable for agricultural settlement meant widespread destruction.[104]

Considering how basic agricultural clearing was to initial settlement, information about it is tantalizingly slight—just as in other areas of the world. There is no easy way to get an overall view of clearing, as no comprehensive statistical series exists. The one attempt has been a study of land-cover modification. Starting with a generalized map of nat-

Plate 10.6 These once mighty forests of the Gippsland region in Victoria were reduced to dairy cow pastures. From *The Illustrated Handbook of Victoria, Australia Prepared for the Colonial and Indian Exhibition, London, 1886.*

ural vegetation and land cover, changes between the two were calculated for nearly 900 statistical areas using LANDSAT (land surveillance satellite) images (fig. 10.12). Although the picture confirms in a general way what we know intuitively, the data and method have limitations, particularly the interpretation of this early satellite imagery and the generalized nature of the evidence. For example, the mallee scrub woodlands of Western Australia,

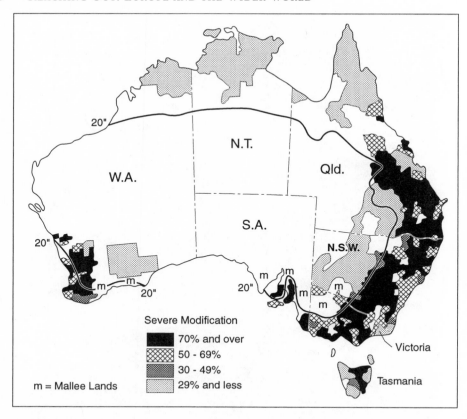

Figure 10.12 Australia: percentage of vegetation severely modified since 1780, by rural local government area. *Source:* Wells, Wood, and Laut, 1984: fold-out map and table.

South Australia, northwest Victoria, and western New South Wales are excluded because of their sparse, intermittent, and generally low level of forest, but we know that vast areas of these woodlands were cleared for wheat growing. This is acknowledged, and it is thought that South and Western Australia are greatly underrepresented. Nonetheless, the overall conclusion is that 87.6 million ha were cleared or "modified" (table 10.10), with the greatest changes occurring in the tall and medium-height forest (46–58 percent affected), and less drastic changes occurring in the woodlands and tall scrubland (29–31 percent).[105] One cannot be more precise than that.

Inevitably, the biographies of individual forests give a more detailed clue as to what was going on. Generally, clearing in Australia was an especially physically demanding task because of the dominance of hardwoods, the constant regeneration of suckers, and the ability of eucalypts to regenerate after even severe fire. Consequently, ringbarking followed by the firing of the deadened trees was the most common method of clearing, and stumps were left in the ground, either to rot or to be grubbed out when time was available. In the more open savanna forests, ringbarking was resorted to exclusively, with the gaunt skeletons being left because cultivation or pastures could be developed around them.[106]

Table 10.10 Australia: minimum area of vegetation severely modified since 1780, by State/Territory (in millions of ha)

State/Territory	Modified	Orig. wooded	% Modified
New South Wales	30.7	61.5	50
Victoria	11.3	16.3	69
Queensland	29.6	83.8	35
South Australia	2.3	5.6	41
Western Australia	11.7	36.7	32
Tasmania	2.0	5.3	37
Northern Territory	0.01	34.4	–
Australian Capital Territory	0.1	0.2	60
Total	87.6	243.9	36

Source: Wells, Wood and Laut, 1984: foldout map and table.

Clearing was brutal and complete in the high-rainfall areas containing rain forest and wet sclerophyll forest along the coasts of Queensland, New South Wales, Victoria, and Western Australia, and in the dry sclerophyll of the Western District of Victoria, the southeast of South Australia, and much of Western Australia south of Perth. The "Big Scrub" astride the New South Wales–Queensland border was a semitropical rain forest of well over 4 million ha, which was described when first encountered as "all but impenetrable jungle, a lush profusion of vegetable growth." But between 1880 and 1910, over 2.8 million ha of forest had been cleared for dairying, sugarcane growing, and lumber. At about the same time, an equally large area in the Strzelecki and Otway ranges in Victoria was also cleared for dairying. According to the authors of a state government report in 1905, "The destruction of timber is enormous." Everything was burned on the spot and nothing disposed of profitably, as transportation links to markets had not been developed. The equivalent of the American woodlot was never seen. "Here the axe is set to every tree, and often not a shrub is left for shelter or cover."[107]

The expansion of dairying and the destruction of the forest in both Victoria and New South Wales–Queensland had much to do with butter making, which flourished after the perfection of the refrigerator (1880), the cream separator (1883), and the Babcock milk-testing machine (1892), together with the railways that eventually opened up these regions. Increasingly, the technological advances in one sphere of activity had repercussions in others, so that, for example, a direct connection existed between the butter that British families spread on their toast for breakfast and the destruction of the great trees of the forests of the Otway and Strzelecki ranges, via the refrigerated holds of the fast steamships that brought the previously perishable goods from one part of the Empire to another.[108]

One might have thought that the massive eucalypt trees in the pastoral savanna lands would have been spared for shade and even fodder during times of drought, and that even the popular folk idea that trees encouraged rainfall would have favored their retention. But it was not to be, because the opposite idea gained ground: that tree destruction was the best and cheapest way of promoting good grass growth. A Mr. Abbott of the Hunter Valley in New South Wales was a spirited advocate of ringbarking, the spread of which, "in spite of the opposition of all the lovers of fine scenery and many scientific men . . .

proves that there must be a clear gain to the graziers in getting rid of the timber,"—and up to three-fourths of the purchased land in the Hunter Valley had been ringbarked. While it is true that trees competed successfully with grass during times of moisture stress, the enthusiasm of the advocates of the "murderous practice of ringbarking" went so far as to suggest that the destruction of the forests improved the flow of streams.[109] It was for actions like this that Australians came to have the unenviable reputation of being mindless tree hackers.

The radically different character of the mallee scrubland throughout much of South Australia, northwest Victoria, southwest Western Australia, southwestern New South Wales, and inland areas of Western Australia demanded a different method of clearing. Even if the many stems were axed down, the massive lignotuber root just below the surface remained fully alive and ready to sprout a thicket of saplings the next spring. Technological innovations were developed in South Australia which facilitated the clearing and cultivation of these "despised scrubs." In 1866 Joseph Mullens, a settler on the plains north of Adelaide, devised, first, a heavy horse-drawn rake-cum-harrow, then later a primitive roller, to knock down the slender scrub stems prior to burning and sowing in the ashes. Then in 1875 J. B. Smith, a settler from Yorke Peninsula, invented the stump-jump plow, whose hinged and weighted shares kicked up harmlessly over the rocks and mallee roots of the newly cleared land. These two folk inventions were the key to the opening up of the lightly wooded areas of the continent, from the mallee lands of the south to the similar brigalow scrubs of southern Queensland. Between 1870 and 1880, over 810,000 ha on Yorke Peninsula alone were cleared and cultivated, and the total in the southeast states must have reached many millions of hectares. Horse-drawn rollers could clear up to 16 ha a day, which by the next century could be achieved every hour when a heavy chain linked between two crawler tractors was dragged across the ground, knocking down all before it.[110]

The linkage between technology, food supply, global markets, and forest clearing already noted in the clearing of the Otways and Strezlecki ranges of Victoria was even more evident with the development of dairying and pastoralism in remote New Zealand, probably the furthest corner of the habitable globe from Europe. Between 1840 and 1900 the remaining forest cover of that country was reduced from just under a half to about 25 percent, most of that occurring during the last decade of the century, when 36,000 km², or approximately 14 percent of the entire country, was cleared in order to establish a pastoral economy of pioneer family farms.[111] The products of these New Zealand pastures were mutton, butter, and cheese, which became a byword of quality in England. The world was shrinking as surely as were its forests.

Agricultural and pastoral clearing were not the only inroads into the forest; it would be possible to instance the details of how fencing, railways, mining, smelting, and fuel-wood gathering in these fledgling pioneer societies of a few million—which took over continents and lands greater in size than the United States—consumed vast amounts of the best timber. But the upshot was that by the end of the century there was not enough left for housing and general construction, especially after the excesses that followed the Victoria Gold Rush of 1850. In later years the cheap and abundant timber of North America increasingly filled the shortfall of the countries around the Pacific basin. With the stimulus of railroad construction, the demand for Californian termite-resistant red-wood for ties complemented the demand for Oregon pine for general construction. In addition to Australia, China, Hawaii, and even Peru and Ecuador proved to be lucrative markets for the enterprising Pacific Coast lumber entrepreneurs. Perhaps only New Zealand was an exception with its own flourishing timber industry. Now, the Pacific basin, like the Atlantic basin, was fully enmeshed in the global timber trade.[112]

Chapter 11

Clearing in the Tropical World, 1750–1920

There is something in a tropical forest akin to the ocean in its effect on the mind. Man feels completely his insignificance there, and the vastness of nature.
—HENRY W. BATES, *The Naturalist on the River Amazon* (1863)

Nothing was heard but groaning, cracking, crunching, and splintering . . . it appeared as though the whole of the forest-world about me was tumbling to pieces.
—JOHN CAPPER, *Old Ceylon* (1878)

The lovely sloping forests are going, the forests through which elephants have trampled for we do not know how many more than 2,000 years; and the very regular but ugly coffee plantations are taking their place.
—ANTHONY TROLLOPE

BY ABOUT 1700, the temperate and tropical worlds were roughly evenly matched in terms of population totals and hectares of land in cultivation. As far as can be ascertained, the temperate world (including Japan and China) contained 324 million people and had 137 million ha in cultivation; the tropical world, 355 million people and 128 million ha in cultivation.[1] But the massive changes in Europe during the previous century, together with the vast extension its holdings overseas, dramatically changed that rough parity. By 1850 the population of the temperate world was about half as much again as that of the tropical world (775 million compared with 485 million) and the area of cultivated land was almost exactly double—357 million ha compared with 180 million ha (compare tables 10.1 and 11.1). By the closing years of the century, the population gap narrowed slightly (from 1,191 million to 1,125 million) as European and Chinese birthrates stabilized or fell, while greater survival rates in the tropical world led to an increase in population; but the difference in the area of cultivation shifted even more decisively in favor of the temperate world: 618 million compared with 295 million ha.

Most of the expansion of population and cultivation was largely at the expense of the original biomes. Between 1700 and 1920 a global total of 537 million ha of forest disappeared under cropland—315 million ha in temperate areas and 222 million ha in the tropical areas, a ratio of about 1.5 to 1 (this difference is greater if the evidence of the "land improved" in forested counties in the United States is taken into account). Of the

Table 11.1 Cropland and land-cover change (in millions of ha), tropical world, 1700, 1850, and 1920

	Cropland			Cropland Change		Forest Change		Grassland Change	
	1700	1850	1920	1700–1850	1850–1920	1700–1850	1850–1920	1700–1850	1850–1920
Tropical Africa	44	57	88	13	31	−22	−61	9	30
North Africa and Middle East	20	27	43	7	16	−4	−7	−4	−7
South Asia	53	71	98	18	27	−18	−28	0	1
Southeast Asia	4	7	21	3	14	−1	−5	−2	−9
Latin America	7	18	45	11	27	−25	−51	13	25
Tropical Total	128	180	295	52	115	−70	−152	16	40

Source: after Richards, 1990: 164.
Note: South Asia = Afghanistan, Bangladesh, Bhutan, Myanmar, India, Nepal, Pakistan, and Sri Lanka; Southeast Asia = Brunei, Cambodia, East Timor, Indonesia, Laos, Malaysia, Philippines, Thailand, and Vietnam. The data are derived from *World Resources Review, 1987.*

grasslands, 146 million ha were changed into cropland in the temperate world, whereas in the tropical world a staggering 56-million-ha net of forest was so permanently damaged by burning, grazing, and shifting cultivation that it *was transformed into grassland,* so adding to the net area of this biome in the tropics. The temperate deforestation was examined in chapter 10, but the tropical deforestation, while less, was still immense at 222 million ha, and is the focus of this chapter.

Tropical forest destruction stemmed from two broadly different sets of driving forces and processes of change: first, the expansion of indigenous agriculture, which needed to support the addition of 770 million people during this century and a half; and second, the impact of European colonialism and capitalist commercialization. Inevitably this division is blurred at the edges, as when indigenous overlords extracted tribute from the peasants; subsistence agriculture merged into the occasional cash crop when encouraged by colonial overlords; or, more commonly, when colonial "modernization" seemed to unleash a fury of peasant entrepreneurial activity. Our knowledge of these changes is sketchy at times, but is aided by the legacy of efficient colonial administrative bureaucracies and the observations of interested travelers and scientists. Thus, developments in India and to a lesser extent Southeast Asia were exceptionally well documented at an early stage, and consequently figure largely in this account. Events in Latin America occurred a bit later and were less well documented, with the exception of Brazil; like India, it looms large in this chapter. Africa was least known and latest of all to develop; its interpretation is really much more of a twentieth-century story, and consequently is best left until chapter 12.

INDIGENOUS USE OF THE FOREST

Nearly all the world's tropical forests were inhabited from earliest times. Not surprisingly, the descendants of the first dwellers wrought major changes in their surroundings, especially after the introduction of steel axes (see chapters 3 and 7). And yet the idea has grown, especially in recent decades, that the tropical forests were barely touched in extent and composition before the coming of the Europeans because the native peoples were "ecologically noble savages" who lived in perfect harmony and balance with their surroundings. Precontact America, in particular, has been perceived as "a place as close to an ecological paradise as humans are likely to come."[2] But the certainty of this early paradise on earth evaporates when confronted with the social complexity, antiquity, and obvious manipulation of the environment in the Old World, especially Asia. Here any picture of an ecological, precolonial, precapitalist golden age of common property rights, sustainable resource use, and a happy, even "merrie" peasantry are overdrawn, hopelessly romantic, and barely plausible. If a sustainable society existed, then it was dependent on a very low population density, abundance of land, and little or no involvement in a market economy, local or regional, all of which were rare. Nor does such a view of an ecological paradise credit the capability and aspirations of the indigenous inhabitants to change their environment and so better themselves.[3] Consequently, long before the supposed Eden was spoiled by the grasping, exploitative European invaders, shifting cultivators and peasant agriculturalists were chopping, cropping, burning, and grazing their forests, changing them to cropland and grassland.

Shifting Agriculture

The indigenous impacts on the tropics came mainly through the widespread use of burning to clear land for agriculture, improved grazing for domestic stock or to attract game, and driving away predatory animals and pests. But clearing in tropical environments caused problems. Leaching, iron pan formation, erosion, and weed infestation all took their toll on soil fertility; therefore, cultivators typically shifted from place to place, utilizing a method of crop raising in temporary clearings. With only minor variations this system existed throughout the tropical world. In Malaysia and Indonesia it was called *ladang;* in central America, *milpa;* in parts of Africa, *chitemene;* in India, *kumri;* and in Sri Lanka, *chena.* Only the largest trees were spared; the rest were felled or deadened, with the debris burned during the dry season and the land cultivated for one, two, or maybe four years at most before being abandoned.[4]

Only the crops were different in different parts of the world. In central and northern Latin America maize and beans were common; in Brazil, manioc; in the Southeast Asian realm the principal crop was upland rice; in Africa it was small grains usually called "millet" or sorghum—but even these differences were being obliterated by the eighteenth century with the worldwide occurrence of crop exchanges. For example, maize, manioc, sweet potatoes, pineapples, and tobacco came from the Americas to Africa and Asia, and conversely sugarcane and rice quickly established themselves in the Americas. If burning was too frequent and the "forest fallow" reduced, especially where the forest was on some marginal climatic zone and in an unstable equilibrium, then the land quickly became overgrown with tough perennial grass that inhibited further cultivation.

There are many excellent accounts of this agricultural method. In 1784, William Marsden, who was resident at Fort Marlborough, a British establishment on the western coast of south Sumatra at what is now Bengkulu, produced one of the first and best descriptions of clearing which was echoed by John Crawfurd for Java in 1820 and Peter Begbie for Malaysia in 1834.[5] The *ladang* or upland paddies were, he said, sown . . . in high grounds, and almost universally on the site of old woods, on account of the superior richness of the soil: the continual fall and rotting of leaves, forming there a bed of vegetable mould, which the open plains cannot afford, being exhausted by the powerful action of the sun's rays and the constant production of rank grass, called *lallang*.

The large trees were felled from a platform erected about 10 to 12 ft high, where the girth of the tree was smaller. When the trees were sufficiently weakened they were pulled over by rattans or creepers. Then the branches were lopped off, and with the onset of the dry weather

they are set fire to, and the country is, for the space of a month, in a general blaze, till the whole is consumed. The expiring wood, beneficent to its ungrateful destroyer, fertilizes for his use, by it's ashes and their salts, the earth from which it sprung, and which it so long adorned.

With the onset of the rainy season the ground was prodded open with a sharp stick, and a few seeds of rice dropped in each hole. Plows were rarely used, and then only in the open plains and where the original forest was comparatively scarce, as in most cases, "the stumps of the trees would entirely preclude the possibility of working them." An observant traveler could usually detect traces of this culture on the forested hillsides near the mountain villages by the presence of light green patches, which marked the abandonment and regrowth of young forest.

Unlike Asia, there appears to be no clear recognition or description of the shifting, or *milpa*, system in Central and South America until the writing of Orator Fuller Cook in the early part of the twentieth century. He was in no doubt as to what was happening. Cutting, burning, and subsequent regrowth were in evidence on every hand. "To invoke other than human agencies to account for the present lack of forests," he commented, "is superfluous, for the destructive influences of the Indians are everywhere in evidence." The great problem was that burning was not limited to areas ready for planting, but usually allowed to spread indiscriminately. "At night in the farm clearing season," he wrote, "the burning mountain slopes gleam with lines of light like the streets of distant cities. By day the sky is darkened and the air is heavy with smoke." *Milpa* agriculture had "long been at work" in destroying the forest, so that like tropical forests everywhere, those of Central and Latin America were "far from [being in] a virgin state," and bore the marks of a long history of clearing in its "many stages of reforestation." He was convinced that over-burning was the cause of the Maya decline.[6]

Other than Ivor Wilk's account of the clearing of forest (in contrast to the savanna edge) in Ashanti, evidence for Africa is sparse. However, Livingstone's records of his travels along the Upper Zambesi to the western shores of Lake Nyasa yield many examples: lighter patches in the distant forest that could only be the regrowth of clearings; forest fires and evidence of burning grasslands; and extensive tree chopping for charcoal making for the once-flourishing iron industry of the region. But, if anything, there seems to be more evidence of forest advance than forest retreat because many areas of formerly thriving agriculture had been abandoned as a result of the depopulation following slave raids by rival tribes and Arab raiders.[7]

Almost without exception, the European sensibility toward nature revolted at the unequal exchange of magnificent trees for a small plot of ground soon to be abandoned.

Shifting agriculture seemed to be not only primitive, backward, inefficient, and unproductive, but also wasteful and destructive to the point of irrationality. Thus, although Marsden was stuck by the immediate replacement within a single month of paddy by vegetation sufficient to "afford full shelter for a tiger," he fully realized the difference between that weedy growth and the magnificent ancient primary forest, the destruction of which he lamented:

> I could never behold this devastation without a strong sentiment of regret. Perhaps the prejudices of a classical education taught me to respect those aged trees, as the habitation or material frame of an order of sylvan deities, who were now deprived of existence, by the sacrilegious hand of a rude, undistinguished savage. But without having recourse to superstition, it is not difficult to account for such feelings, on the sight of a venerable wood, old as the soil it stood on, and beautiful beyond what pencil can describe, for the temporary use of the space it occupied. It appears a violation of nature in the exercise of too arbitrary right. . . . Trees whose amazing bulk, height, and straightness would excite the admiration of a traveller, compared to which the masts of men of war are diminutive, fall in the general ruin.[8]

The destruction of the forest "giants" was only mitigated for some people, like Hugh Low in Sarawak in 1848, by the spectacle of the burn, which at a distance was "awfully beautiful," even "sublime." The dark, heavy cloud of smoke that hung over the country could easily being mistaken for a thundercloud until a gust of wind "carried the flames high above the jungle, and displayed to the spectator a scene of most majestic beauty, which certainly equals, and probably surpasses, the burning of the grass of the plains of North America."[9]

The feeling that Europeans could make better use of the land was not just a matter of different cultural perceptions; it could have serious, practical ramifications. The "impossible gulf" between savagery and civilization was a potent rationale for justifying timber exploitation, and the consequent dispossession of the indigenes from their native lands, particularly in the Americas and Africa. However, the gulf was not as great in Asia, where a complex, structured society and economy already existed and there were few European settlers. Nonetheless, even here two themes dominated overlordship and affected land cover. European rule and organization were perceived to be beneficial, as they brought tranquillity, stability, and prosperity—which was frequently true—and therefore agricultural expansion was encouraged. India was the supreme example of this.[10] Second— and perhaps colored by the European experience of timber shortages—trees were thought to be more valuable than anything other than the most intensive cultivation. In India, this meant excluding the traditional users from the forests.

Permanent Agriculture

Despite difficulties of erosion, declining fertility, and iron pan formation, a considerable area of clearing existed for permanent agriculture which was largely of two kinds: the cultivation of irrigated land, and the cultivation of groves and gardens for vegetables and spices, much of which entered into world trade.

Although we do not know even vaguely the date of the origin of either of these agricultural forms, nor their exact extent or impact on the forest, all the indications are that they are of great antiquity, and that they were more extensive than thought previously.

Table 11.2 Estimate of forest felling for pepper growing, Sumatra, seventeenth through nineteenth centuries

	17th Century	18th Century	19th Century
Production (tons/annum)	5,000	7,000	20,000
Area Required (ha)	14,000	20,000	57,000
Forest Felled (ha)	120,000	165,000	475,000

Source: Reid, 1995: 101.

For example, Sumatra (Aceh Province in particular) and western Java had been supplying the Chinese, Indian, and Muslim worlds with cinnamon, mace, cloves, nutmeg, and particularly pepper for literally thousands of years, and it was only after about 1600 that the trade with Europe grew to such a great volume. Anthony Reid calculates that because of the agronomically exhausting nature of pepper growing, regular and widespread rotations had to be resorted to (see table 11.2), with the cleared land rarely reverting to forest but usually becoming grassland. If "new" forestland was not available, then the nutrient level in existing fields was kept high with animal and human excreta, vegetable "waste" from the village, and especially with green leaves from the forest. Elsewhere in Java, the forest had been so reduced by the seventeenth century that it was no longer able to sustain elephants.[11]

Irrigated rice land depended on an elaborate system of water impoundment in either valley flats or terraced hill slopes. By the early eighteenth century it was certainly well developed in the lands of South and Southeast Asia, which abounded with dense populations in favored floodplains, or where level land was limited, in spectacular rice terraces, as in Java, Sumatra, parts of south China, and the Bontoc in Luzon, which were miracles of peasant engineering. These permanent irrigated rice fields, or *sawah*, contrasted with the dry-land rice fields, or *ladang*, of the shifting agriculturists.

Often the two forms of cultivation were combined, producing mature and picturesque tropical landscapes. Ancient village centers displayed intensive horticulture, gardening, and groves

> perhaps separated by a bamboo hedge from surrounding lands in permanent *sawah* cultivation, around which the forest retains its proper place, regulating stream-flow, preventing excessive erosion, yielding forest products, and affording sanctuary to the wild animals and plants.[12]

But to achieve that landscape the devastation had to be significant. Looking from the summit of the Dempo volcano in the Pelambang region of south Sumatra in 1885, Henry Forbes was amazed at the vast extent of treeless land. The forest of Sumatra, as in Java, was "rapidly disappearing," as each year saw "immense tracts felled for rice fields" and gardens wantonly consumed by "wilful fires." Trees of the rarest and finest timber were hewn, half burned, and then left to rot, only to be replaced by worthless secondary forest and grasses. He lamented that "our children's children will search in vain in their travels for the old forest trees of which they have read in the books of their grandfathers."[13]

Contrary to accepted views, similar "busy" landscapes of cultivation were seen in West Africa. In 1839 the Reverend Dr. Savage saw rice cultivation along the rivers and near the coast in southern Liberia, "expanding far beyond [the river landing], into fields of many acres; [elsewhere] . . . the 'bush' being cleared away to the very verge of the river, unfolds to the eye an immense expanse, waving in all the luxuriance of nature"; and further east in Côte d'Ivoire, Ghana, and Togo are numerous nineteenth-century descriptions of villages and farms surrounded by fields and palm forests, both in the humid forest zone and in the savannas to the north.[14]

Although the subsistence and the commercial economies relied on the liberal use of the forest resource, the ownership and use of that common resource was vastly more complex than is commonly supposed. A few examples must suffice. Uttra Kannada was one of the successor states to Mughal rule on the southwest coast of India, and is now part of Karnatak State. It stretched about 200 mi across the forested and cultivated coastal plain, and up onto the heavily forested western Ghats to Shimoga. For most of the eighteenth century it was under the autocratic rule of Hyder Ali and then his son Tippoo Sultan before finally succumbing to British rule in 1799. During precolonial times the Muslim rulers imposed an autocratic state control on the forests to raise revenue, a control incorporating elements of military power and caste. There was a complex hierarchy of rights and access similar to that of late medieval Europe in which usage was not necessarily accompanied by legal ownership, but which, in time, implied de facto ownership, leading to greater commercialization of the resource. The sultans established their rights of timber procurement for teak (its strategic, naval value being understood and well developed in the shipbuilding yards along the coast), blackwood, sandalwood, and ebony; established teak plantations; and engaged in trading in wild and cultivated peppers and cinnamon. How representative Uttra Kannada was of the rest of India is difficult to say, but all the indications are that the forests of Travancore, Cochin, and the Maratha states bore many resemblances in their complexity of use.[15]

Across the plain, largely Hindu village chiefs and headmen *(patel)* controlled the local agriculturalist proprietors and their tenants through taxation and land allocation, and they also controlled access to the forest. The agriculturalists basically had free use of the forest for collecting firewood; cutting constructional wood for road building, housing, implements, and fencing; and grazing stock. They also chopped green fodder for cattle and for fertilizing the coastal rain-fed paddy rice fields and the irrigated, terraced paddies on the slopes. Tracts around the villages were freely burned and cleared in order to provide grazing for cattle and to create a buffer zone of safety from wild animals and fires in the forest. In some localities forest use was controlled by village councils, which limited removals; however, peasant farmers compensated for the restrictions by overexploiting forests in neighboring locations.

The rights of the agriculturalists and their tenants to small wood and green manure did not extend to the non-Hindu tribal shifting cultivators in the upland forested areas, who moved from site to site as and when fertility declined. This shifting cultivation, known locally as *kumri,* was not illegal or improper, but the "tribals" had no rights and their uncontrolled fires were always feared. Sometimes the tribals became day laborers for the permanent Hindu peasant farmers *(rhyots),* and occasionally tribal herdsmen were allowed to pasture in the woodlands of the "agriculturalists." Some tribals (Vaddars, Siddis, and others) were tree cutters and wood carriers as well as shifting cultivators.

In the vast riverine plains of the north, two contrasting examples of exploitation existed. On the lower Indus plain of northwestern India (Pakistan today), forest regulation was intense. Throughout the eighteenth and early nineteenth centuries the Muslim Amirs of Sind planted and reserved extensive forests in order to generate timber supplies, fuel, and revenue, as well as serve as game reserves *(shikargahs)*. There were probably about 87 *shikargahs* covering over 1 million acres (approximately 404,680 ha). So methodically and profitably were these administered that after the annexation of the Punjab by the British in 1847 they provided a ready-made laboratory in which to experiment with forms of colonial forest administration that became a model for the rest of India.[16] However, further east in the lands fringing the Gangetic plain, the complete opposite was happening. The forest was being pushed back on all fronts (fig. 11.1); strips and corridors of

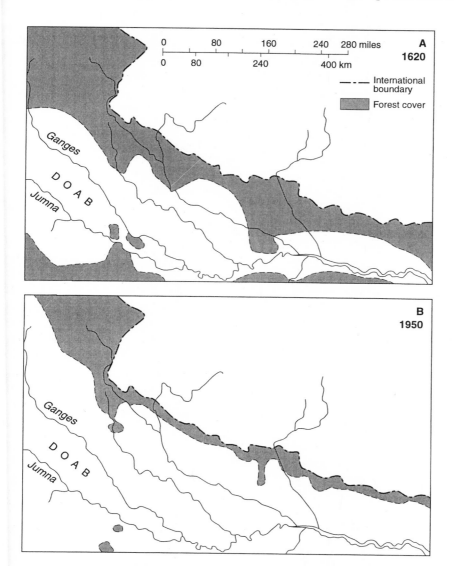

Figure 11.1 Forests of northern India, *A, 1620;* and *B, 1950. Source:* after Habib, 1982: 5. Figure 11.1 is probably based on Habib, *An Atlas of Mughal India: Political and Economic Maps with Detailed Notes, Bibliography and Index,* maps 8B (Uttar Pradesh), 10B (Bihar), and 11.B (Bengal). The presence of forest is based on the idea (p. xi) that "where there were wild elephants there must have been forest."

woodland connected with the Himalayan foothills were disappearing under a fierce agricultural onslaught of permanently cultivated cropland. Tigers had disappeared, and "similarly, elephants could only have roamed about the Rajpipla forests of Gujarat in the seventeenth century if there was an unbroken belt of forests extending to Malwa." But some time before 1760, the intervening ground had been cleared, barring the westward movement of elephants from central India.[17]

In places, clearing went too far and degradation ensued, with once-cultivated land being abandoned or subject to uncontrolled fires. For example, the country between Cuddapah and Hyderabad was littered with the ruins of villages and remnants of field divisions; in the view of naturalist Benjamin Heyne, it would "in a short time be a dessert [sic], in which no human being will be found except some straggling lombardies with their herds." He put the degradation down to the autocratic behavior of the Muslim overlords toward the vegetation: "destruction is the delight of the pious Mussleman—he is the destroying angel." The signs of ecological deterioration were to be seen on every hand.[18]

There were other examples of the precolonial hierarchical exploitation of the forest outside southern Asia, of which Madagascar was one. The "free" use of the forest resources on the eastern coastal plains and ranges was usurped by the late eighteenth- and nineteenth-century monarchies. The king allowed slaves and ex-slaves to pasture the huge royal herds in the forest and its margins, and encouraged *tavy*—the local name for slash-and-burn clearing—for small rotational plots of rice, corn, and cassava.[19]

The precolonial forest, then, was not an untouched, pristine Eden nor a community resource shared equitably by all; nor was it used by everyone in the same way. Society was stratified; those in power tried to control or own land and especially forest resources for economic and prestige purposes: lessees, servants, laborers, or slaves were allowed occasionally to use the forest but had only a tenuous grip on it. Everywhere the forest was under intense pressure, and equilibrium did not exist. As one Indian scholar has put it recently, "[a]rable expansion, elite hunting and land colonization existed long before the Company Raj and the making of the British Empire." The imposition of colonial rule and the implementation of imperial programs of timber production, as, for example, in India, while vast in their scope, were not the radical break seen by some, but rather displayed "broad continuities in the policies adopted by Indian rulers and their British successors."[20]

Grazing and Burning

Our knowledge of the impact of the First Farmers (chapter 3) should leave one in no doubt about the ability of humans to convert forests to grassland. Nonetheless, the transformation of 56 million ha of forest to grassland in the tropical world between 1750 and 1900 is one of the striking features of global land-cover change. Of that total area of grassland about 54 percent was in Africa, 45 percent in Latin America, and a mere fraction in Southeast Asia.

Many writers and observers affirmed confidently that the transformation was caused by deleterious native agricultural practices. Harley Bartlett, who reviewed a vast literature, was convinced that in normally forested tropical locations the extent of grassland was almost always to be taken as "a measure of the cumulative effect of human occupa-

tion," although the semi-arid edge of the forest presented many problems of interpretation and causation.[21] It is, of course, easy to overemphasize the process of degradation,
and many did. For them the savanna and grassland were an anthropogenic formation as
centuries of short fallows, fire, and overgrazing reduced the forest to a sea of grass or even
desert studded with remnant islands of fire-resistant trees, with changes being accelerated
by periods of climatic deterioration and stress along with edaphic factors.[22] A leading advocate of this hypothesis was André Aubréville, as evidenced by his many publications on
forest retreat in francophone West Africa. However, although he realized that the hypothesis of native degradation could not be proved historically, he could not see how else
the degraded forests had come about. Many others argued along the same lines.[23]

But the processes were far more complex than that. Many assumptions were built into
this conventional wisdom that, among other things, some "baseline" vegetation exists
against which modern change can be measured; that there was little change before circa
1900; that the climate has been deteriorating progressively; and that forest clearance has
been partly responsible for that. But much of the evidence is flawed. The processes have
not been all one way, and "what appeared to be the most undisturbed vegetation forms
turn out to be the most disturbed." Much new forest has been created, and forest composition is the result of active management of particular trees. In addition, there must
have been much regeneration of old fields *back to forest* after the depopulation consequent on the slave trade over centuries.[24]

A similar story of exaggeration and preconceived assumption leading to a dominant
discourse is true of Madagascar. The island is held up as an example of rampant deforestation and ecological mayhem through erosion. The views stem from the work of two
French botanists, Henri Perrier de la Bâthie and Henri Humbert, who, drawing on remnants of pollens and fossils (particularly of pygmy hippopotamuses and *Aepyornis,* a
large, moalike flightless bird), concluded that the whole island had once been forested but
had been denuded during the 1,500 years of human occupation by the Malagasy immigrants. But they exaggerated many aspects of the ecology: that the original forest extent
was 90 percent of the island, rather than approximately 30 percent; that the grassland
was a result of repeated burning of forestland for cattle grazing, rather than the natural
phenomenon that it is; and that the spectacular gully erosion was an outcome of misuse,
rather than the natural feature that it is. This is not to deny that deforestation occurred,
especially after colonization in 1893 let loose a spate of logging. Of the 58 million ha of
the island, by 1920 about 20 percent was said to remain in primary forest. By 1949 it
was 8.6 percent; 10.3 percent was in *savoka,* second-growth bracken fern with bamboos;
and the rest was in grass and savanna. Consequently, the Malagasy were not the ecological vandals as commonly portrayed but quite careful land managers who treasured the
forest, which they traditionally referred to as "the robe of the ancestors" because of its
multiple and essential uses. It was not the hopelessly tattered garment that it was popularly described as being, though there were some big holes and tears in it.[25]

In contrast with Africa, the ample rainfall of the tropical countries of Southeast Asia
ensured that grassland created as a consequence of deforestation did not degenerate into
semidesert, but was often utilized productively, as reflected in the small amount of land
converted to grassland in table 11.1. In fact, overall, grassland declined at the expense of
cropland. For example, in Sumatra most areas of *lalang* (*Imperata* and associates) became

productive rubber and tobacco plantations. In the Philippines grassland *(cogonales)* produced as a result of shifting agriculture *(kaigin)* was more questionable; some provided poor grazing, some was reforested, but much remained as unusable coarse grassland.[26]

But South and Southeast Asia were a mere pinprick in the process of forest conversion to grassland and savanna compared with the other major tropical region of Latin America. The *campo cerrado* (literally, "closed field") or simply *cerrado* covers an enormous area of interior Brazil and the drier northeast coast—from near the mouth of the Amazon as far west as the Tocatins River, with large fingers extending westward along the Tapajoz and other rivers. Everywhere it impinges on the Atlantic coast and Amazonian forests, and the implication is that large parts of its margins were once forest. But how much is man-made or natural, both perhaps aided by climatic changes, is not entirely clear from phytogeographic and floristic studies. While the antiquity of human occupation is only a tenth that of Africa or a quarter that of Asia, it is still sufficiently long enough to suggest the likelihood of major anthropogenic modification.[27]

The longevity of active European involvement in this region complicates the analysis of human impact. Unlike Asia and Africa, from about 1500 Brazil was a theater of active Portuguese colonization for growing sugarcane along the coast, and also for cattle ranching inland. Uniquely too, the Portuguese rapidly intermarried with the native Indian population, thereby often altering traditional Indian ways, yet frequently adopting them as well, which blurs our distinction between indigenous agricultural impacts on the forests and the impacts of colonialism and capitalism.

The Tupi-Guarani agricultural clearing and the ceaseless warfare between tribes created intense local pressure on the forest, reducing it to secondary growth and even grassland. The gradual replacement of the Indian population by a mixed mestizo population after disease and slave raiding had taken their initial toll, and the introduction of iron axes and machetes, meant that traditional swidden cultivation was intensified. Whereas the Tupi might have cut and burned about 1 ha per family per annum, leaving the large trees untouched, the Europeanized mestizo was capable of cultivating 3 ha or more, and he cleared more thoroughly. The truth of Alfred Métraux's remark—that once iron was introduced into the lowlands of Latin America, "a return to the Stone Age was impossible"—was pertinent at all times. Moreover, the beginning of the herding of pigs and cattle added a dimension to forest destruction that had been absent before. The forest did not regenerate easily, and any open ground was colonized by exotic grasses, ferns, and weeds.[28]

CAPITALIST PENETRATION:
THE PASSAGE TO INDIA, 1750–1850

The European capitalist exploitation and/or colonial expansion of the forests of the tropical world after 1750 had many motives and antecedents. One of the most important was the extension of agriculture to feed the European taste for exotic tropical products, such as cotton, tea, sugar, coffee, chocolate, and pepper, which were no longer luxuries but necessities. This trade had propelled Europeans overseas to establish plantations and trading stations on a multitude of small islands in the Caribbean and elsewhere, and to establish foothold settlements on the coasts of the tropical land masses (plates 11.1 and 11.2).

Plate 11.1 "Clearing Mahogany down the Rapids in Cuba." From Chaloner and Fleming, *The Mahogany Tree . . .* , 1851. (University of Wisconsin.)

Plate 11.2 "Cutting and Trucking Mahogany in Honduras." From Chaloner and Fleming, *The Mahogany Tree . . .* , 1851. (University of Wisconsin.)

In that burgeoning global trade, the islands, though mere pinpoints in the ocean, served many important functions. They were strategic stepping-stones; they provided fresh water and provisions for the ships of the major trading companies; they acted as experimental precedents for a wider and more penetrating settlement of the mainland masses; and by no means least, they conjured up an engaging image as Edens or paradisal utopias, places of plenty and safety, that seduced the Western mind.[29]

Ascension, St. Helena, and Mauritius—together with the Cape of Good Hope, an enclave in a vast continent and an "island" in all but name—were the crucial stepping-stones on the passage to India before the Suez Canal was excavated in 1869. What happened on them loomed large in the minds of those predisposed to think about the relationships among climate, vegetation, and the human use of the land. Because of their small size and confined area, the consequences of environmental deterioration were spotted early, and sometimes even acted upon. In St. Helena, for example, deforestation, soil erosion, and stream-flow variation were all noted, and government officials tried to protect the remaining forest and corral destructive grazing animals, but with little ultimate effect; the "paradise" which Sir Joseph Banks had known had "become a desert" by 1771. Similar problems plagued the Dutch and then the French in Mauritius, and the island's diminishing role as a supplier of ship timber added another layer of concern. The innovative and widely traveled Pierre Poivre, who was appointed Commissaire-Intendant of Mauritius in 1766, was convinced that deforestation caused a decline in rainfall and affected the incidence and spread of disease. He tried to establish reserves in order to protect plants and animals, and also created the island's celebrated botanical garden. The extinction of the dodo, while noted at the time, did not achieve notoriety as a symbol of human extirpation of species that it did in later years.

Consequently, developments on these tiny islands (to say nothing of the concern for environmental degradation in the sugar growing islands of the Caribbean) had at least three practical outcomes that were transported to the Continental colonial empires, particularly India. First, Poivre had made many observations and drawn inferences about the role of tropical forests in influencing rainfall and runoff that came to have a widespread currency, principally that their removal led to desiccation and "deserts." Second, the regulations for forest management and reservation devised for Mauritius were later applied to St. Helena, and eventually were regarded as a model throughout the tropical world, especially India. Third, the famed botanical garden (the captured Eden in miniature) of Mauritius was emulated in St. Helena, and then Calcutta in 1788, and many other tropical locations in later years. Not only were rare species brought together but there was also an increased awareness of tree growth and management, and the value or otherwise of exotic species for food and manufacturing. In short, the course of empire and the management of the Asian tropical forests owed much to the experience gained in these minuscule islands.[30]

But these islands were as nothing compared to the prize to be won in India, which must rank high as the best documented and most outstanding example of all tropical colonizations and deforestation episodes.[31] By 1805 the hegemony of the great imperial trading organization, the East India Company (EIC), was an established fact over much of the peninsula, where the population stood at about 197 million in 1800 and rose to 245 million by 1860. The EIC remained in control until the administration of the country was taken over by the British government in 1857. Increasingly, India's administration, survey and land revenue system, trade, transportation, and communications were fashioned and focused by its colonial overlords. The four presidencies based in Calcutta, Bengal, Bombay, and Madras and their surrounding territories were miniempires in themselves. (For their extent see fig. 11.5 below.) Thus it was the largest, most populous (285 million people by 1901), most diverse colonial territory the world had ever seen.[32]

Britain undoubtedly gained much economically from the control of this vast empire. It certainly engaged in the exercise of imperial power on a hitherto unparalleled scale, and Indian production contributed to the British balance of payments; some would say that it was an organized system of deliberate "resource extraction," or even one geared to getting a "free or highly subsidized supply of biomass."[33] But British imperialism was far more than narrow materialist gain, as asserted by Ramachandra Guha, or even of a cruder sentiment expressed by Edward Said, wistfully hankering after the "Oriental," a totalizing discourse which has distorted serious historical analysis of events and interactions in the "East."[34] There was another side to the coin. Vast sums of capital *were* invested in Indian infrastructure, especially railways, communications, irrigation, and public health works; and the exercise of imperial power, while authoritarian and frequently repressive, was tempered by a concern for stability, prosperity, adequate food supplies, public health, *and* an intellectual curiosity at the cultures encountered. In place of political turmoil, predatory raiding, banditry, and endemic warfare there was relative tranquility, political unity, and the stability of a reasonably predictable administration bound "by its own laws and published regulations bearing the force of law." Energies, then, were diverted to more peaceful purposes, allowing the already complex, entrepreneurial native society to respond dynamically to the imposed political framework and stability of "government encouraged incentives for enhanced economic productivity," especially within agriculture, from which many benefited.[35]

The creation of a market for land and a vast land revenue system to support the public works and the British *raj* subtly penetrated all levels of economic activity and social intercourse. A new elite was created of professionals and employees of the colonial administrators, and the rural propertied classes probably benefited at the expense of the mass of producers. It is a matter of some debate as to what extent the peasants were caught up in a vicious circle of increased revenue demands, deeper debt, greater taxation, and therefore the need to clear more land in order to raise cash crops and increase productivity. The balance of the evidence is that the forest *did* come under pressure and was reduced in size; "it was," said Bertold Ribbentrop, "the watchword of the time to bring everywhere more extensive forest areas under cultivation," and what remained was reserved for timber production.[36] One thing is certain: the reliance of both the sedentary and the traditional shifting agricultural economies on the "free" bounty and safety valve of the forest in times of stress or need was diminished.

While British political and commercial hegemony over the Indian Subcontinent was becoming an established fact and affected land cover, another, more subtle intellectual authority was emerging in the form of a certain crude environmental awareness. The "island experience," and the rise of "professional science," personified by explorer-botanists like Sir Joseph Banks and Alexander von Humboldt, together with the circumnavigational expeditions of Cook, Flinders, Bougainville, and others, were just some of the many strands in the colonial intellectual penetration of the tropical world. Additionally—and especially important in India—was the activity, writing, and "networking" of some of the 800-odd influential and botanically well-versed surgeons of the EIC (some became superintendents of botanical gardens) who were in the second rank of science. Of particular significance in the story of Indian deforestation were Edward Balfour, Hugh Cleghorn, Alexander Gibson, John McClelland, William Roxburgh, and John Stocks, the intellectual offspring of the Scottish scientific, medical, and philosophical "enlightenment" and more often than not men of a radical social and political persuasion. They had respectability and permanence in the structure of the EIC and exercised enormous local influence; ultimately, their ideas were to have international significance. They knew about St. Helena and Mauritius as well as the works of Humboldt, Boussingault, Count Volney, and early American writers on the relationship between forests and climate. Increasingly these surgeons became commentators on environmental and ecological matters in the subcontinent, and they kept up a relentless campaign to intervene and halt forest destruction, not only because it led to timber shortages but because they thought that it affected climate, health, and food supply. So concerned and confident did they become of the correctness of their cause that on several occasions they were prepared to bypass the channels of authority within the EIC—which was not only conservative but said to be "ponderous, lethargic, and determined to avoid the nineteenth century"—by either appealing directly to its directors or to scientific forum in Britain.[37]

In 1851 Hugh Cleghorn did just that, and independently reported to the British Association meeting in Ipswich about "the probable effects in an economical and physical point of view of the destruction of tropical forests." Despite the popular image of India as having "interminable jungles," much, said Cleghorn, had been cleared. His report, a catalogue of acts of "indiscriminate havoc," shortage, and impending "deficiency" and "timber famine," became the basis for most subsequent colonial responses to problems of environmental degradation in India.[38] In order to understand how this startlingly contemporary concern came about more than a hundred years before its modern counterparts, we need to look in turn at the twin questions of teak supplies and the relationship between deforestation and climate, food supply, and health.

The Teak Forests

Since at least the ninth century, Arab traders had prized the teak *(Tectona grandis)* timber of the Malabar coast for shipbuilding and general construction, and had carried planks and beams back to the Red Sea and the Gulfs of Persia and Kutch (chapter 5). In later centuries many Parsi west coast shipbuilders and traders also recognized its value, which inevitably brought them into competition and conflict with the EIC, which attempted to monopolize supplies. Between 1760 and the end of the century, the perceived shortage of teak and other timber was a major factor in the company's expansion northward to the

Nepalese border and eastward into the Maratha states. With the mounting reputation of teak for durability at sea, and the blockade of the Baltic from 1805 to 1822, the teak of the Malabar coast and later of Bengal and Burma seemed crucial for British shipbuilding. Little teak was actually shipped to Britain because of the protectionism at home and high transportation costs, but vast amounts were used in the Parsis' shipyards of Bombay, which built ships for the British, and also in Calcutta.[39]

Clearly, continued cutting of teak by local entrepreneurs and indigenous rulers deprived the EIC of valuable revenues and strategic materials. In 1805 it reserved the teak forests for its own use and appointed the first "Conservator of Forests," legitimizing the takeover by citing the previous princely control as a precedent and justification. The resultant monopoly more or less "practically annihilated . . . all private rights . . . by assuming their non-existence," and caused much resentment among local traders and shipbuilders as well as among permanent and shifting agriculturalists—a recurrent theme in the Indian forests in later years. By 1822, Sir Thomas Munro, governor of Madras, criticized the EIC severely for restricting "sensible" local trading and cutting with regulations that he thought "worthy only of the times of the Norman Forest Laws." He recommended the lifting of the conservation restrictions; if the navy needed timber for a couple of ships annually, then it could simply be purchased in the market "without any restrictive system."[40]

Munro's free-trading convictions and somewhat romanticized views of the ecologically sound nature of native agriculture overshadowed any awareness of the true extent of the cutting that had already been undertaken by the local timber merchants, shipbuilders, and traders, or of the pressures that were building up in this economically energetic part of India. With the relaxation of restrictions, the rate of deforestation accelerated. Throughout the coastal forests, exploitation was said to be "reckless"; large areas of first-class teak (and other woods) were lost, "never to be recovered," and prices rose sharply. The use of elephants—the most versatile logging machine ever devised—was a major factor in the effective removal of large trees.[41]

By the time Hugh Cleghorn reported on the destruction of Indian forests 29 years later, exports of teak were hovering between 11,000 and 18,000 tons per annum; the forests of Malabar had "fallen to a deplorable state"; the tribal *kumri* shifting agriculturalists had cleared the forests of Canara "to a most destructive extent"; and the teak of Mysore had "well nigh disappeared" as forest rentiers let out tracts for cutting to the highest bidder, and thousands of "floats" went downstream every year. Already by midcentury, the west coast forests as far east as the Ghats were said to be largely cut out of big trees, and the focus of cutting had shifted to the "glory of the Tenasserim forests" in Burma, annexed in 1826. But even there, "wanton destruction . . . by fire" and the chopping up of large timbers for ease of transport depreciated the value of the original trees to one-tenth of the amount they would have realized whole as ships' timbers. Undoubtedly this account was exaggerated in order to make a particular case for action, but there was a large measure of truth in it. Everywhere, there were endless examples of cutting, often out of necessity, but also through indiscriminate and profligate felling, and consequently the teak forests were a diminishing asset.[42]

Clearing, Rainfall, Famine, and Health

Concern about deforestation shifted from one of basic timber depletion to a more complex and sophisticated consideration of the relationship between forests and rainfall, food supply, and health. India had a large and ever-growing population, and "as in other long and early civilized countries," said Cleghorn, "the parts best adapted for agriculture have long been cleared of jungle" and "stript of their timber." The process was accelerating because food production (and the extraction of the maximum possible land revenue from the peasant) became a major concern of the EIC, despite the fact that this was in direct conflict with its timber reservation policy on the coast. But revenue expansion was tempered by a concern that deforestation might lead to serious stream flow and rainfall changes that might in turn worsen the agricultural situation; widespread famines during the late 1830s and subsequent civil unrest gave this concern a political and practical urgency. The truth of Cleghorn's aphorism that "climate concerns the whole community" was beginning to be apparent.[43]

EIC interest in these environmental relationships was stimulated by the early work of one of its surgeons, William Roxburgh, who collected meteorological data relating to the 1780 and 1789–93 famines in the Circars of the Madras Presidency (i.e., the coastal zone between Madras and Calcutta, either side of the Godavari delta). He came to the conclusion that local climatic variation (drought) seemed less significant for famine than the widespread clearing, of which there was abundant evidence, and the government policy of renting out lands, which engendered tenurial uncertainty.[44]

Those who traveled around the country seemed able to verify the thinning and deforestation, and its probable effect on rainfall. Bishop Reginald Heber commented in 1824 on the "great devastation" in the Kemaoon [Kumaon] and Siwalik hills in Uttar Pradesh, caused

> partly by the increase of population, building and agriculture, partly by the wasteful habits of travellers, who cut down multitudes of young trees to make temporary huts, and for fuel, while the cattle and goats which browse on the mountains prevent a great part of the seedlings from rising.

Unless some precautions were undertaken, he believed, "the uninhabited parts of Kemaoon will soon be wretchedly bare of wood and the country, already too arid, will not only lose its beauty, but its small space of fertility."[45] William Henry Sleeman, better known as the successful suppressor of the notorious thuggee gangs, left descriptions of deforestation during the 1820s in the foothills of the Himalayas, present-day Uttar Pradesh and Himachal Pradesh, and the Doab, the strip of land about 80–120 km wide by 500 km that lies between the Ganges and Jummna, from the Himalayas southeast to the confluence of the two rivers at Allahabad.[46]

Changes in forest cover were becoming evident in the 25,000 km² of the southeastern half of the Doab below Delhi. By 1800 thick Dhak *(Butea frondosa)* forests were said to cover over half the land surface, particularly on the low interfluvial ridges, and in wide continuous belts. Even in the agricultural areas, up to one-fifth of the land cover was still forest. With direct colonial rule after annexation in 1805, high revenue assessments were imposed and the expansion of more internationally valuable cash crops, such as cotton,

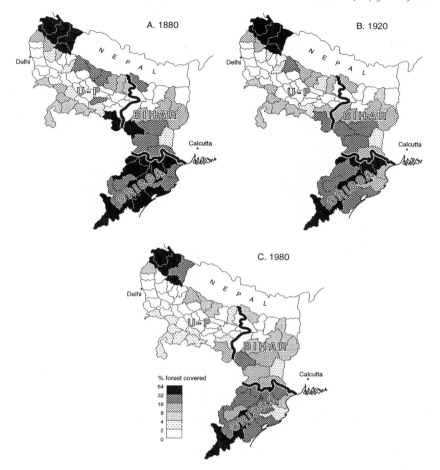

Figure 11.2 Percentage of land in forest in Uttar Pradesh, Bihar, and Orissa, *A*, 1880; *B*, 1920; and *C*, 1980. *Source:* Richards, 1984.

sugarcane, and indigo, were encouraged, often at the expense of subsistence food crops. A vicious circle arose of raised taxation, deepening debt, and expanding agriculture accompanied by forest destruction and deteriorating ecological conditions, all exacerbated by demographic pressures and increased economic activity with brick-making and general construction.

The upshot was the almost complete annihilation of the forest in about 25 years— the forest of the Alighara district in the middle third of the Doab, which was said to be 30 km wide and 200 km long in 1805, being greatly reduced by 1850, and "by the end of the 19th century, apart from a few small patches . . . every tree had been destroyed" (see figs. 11.2 A–C and 11.3A–B). With the progressive destruction of the forest, salinization became common, water tables dropped, many wells were abandoned, drainage channels dried out or were silted by moving soil, and malaria spread. The drought of 1837–38 was the final blow to the area.[47] Deforestation and colonization seemed to go hand in hand.

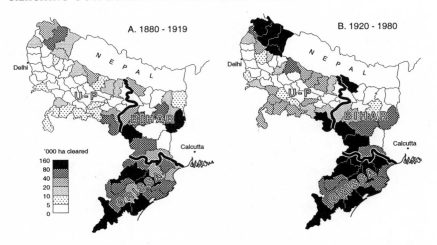

Figure 11.3 Forest decrease in Uttar Pradesh, Bihar, and Orissa, *A*, 1880–1919; and *B*, 1920–80 (in thousands of ha). *Source:* Richards, 1984.

Once more, concern swung back to the forest destruction occurring in the Madras and Bombay Presidencies. Alexander Gibson, another of the EIC's surgeons who became director of the Bombay botanical gardens, waged an energetic campaign throughout the 1840s to draw attention to the extent and effects of deforestation, and the need to establish an independent forestry department. He was particularly concerned about the forests of the Ghats, which he thought encouraged rainfall:

> the Deccan is more bare than Guzerat and the clefts of the Ghat mountains are the only situation where the trees are to be found in any quantity and even they are disappearing fast under the increased demand for land for spade husbandry . . . they are too steep for the plough. It is a matter of regret for the naturalist, perhaps also for the economist, that the woods are in such a rapid progress of destruction.[48]

Because of his status in both the EIC and scientific circles, Gibson was able to go over the heads of the Bombay and Indian governments directly to the directors of the EIC in London, and his advice was heeded. In 1847 the Bombay Presidency decided to form a Forestry Department, with Gibson as its conservator; in 1855 the Madras Presidency followed suit, appointing Hugh Cleghorn, the arch political activist in the cause of forest preservation, as its conservator.[49]

As part of his campaign, Gibson, together with Blane, collector of taxes in Canara, submitted a report on the state of the forests in that part of India. It was a powerful statement about forest destruction and deteriorating climate, calculated to cause alarm and prompt action. In Canara it was said that "within thirty or forty years the forests had receded from the coast to within a few miles of the Ghats," and large areas of country that were known to have been once forested now hardly "carried a stick large enough for firewood." In the neighborhood of Mangalore on the coast, the destruction was so great that firewood, "formerly so abundant, is now one of the chief items of expense to the poorer classes of society." The scarcity was a result of the improvidence with which the wood was treated, every tree and bush being felled at first, and the shoots and saplings which would have grown up and supplied their places being cut down every year until the roots die off, leaving nothing but the bare laterite hills which will remain for ever afterwards utterly sterile and useless.[50]

As for the "wasteful and improvident" *kumri* agriculture, Gibson and Blane recommended that the forests be protected from its ravishes by being alienated and put into reserves. The EIC obliged, established a Department of Forestry, and once more legitimized its action by arguing that it was only doing what the precolonial Indian rulers had done. The immemorial rights of the *kumri* shifting cultivators were extinguished; the ad hoc clearing of the permanent agriculturalist peasants, or *rhyots*, was banned; and private capital interests, both Indian and European, were excluded from timber felling in the valuable teak forests.[51] Clashes between the EIC and the indigenous cultivators and logging interests were to be common in later years, one of the earliest and best-documented struggles being in the Thana District of Bombay.[52]

The Gibson-Blane report disturbed the Madras government, which feared that famine would follow the deforestation so clearly evident within its confines. Like Bombay, it was anxious to establish a Forestry Department, but was thwarted in its desire by a lukewarm response from the Indian government. Consequently, it could be said to have sided with the surgeon-environmentalists by sponsoring the publication in 1849 of a report by another of their number, Edward Balfour, entitled "Notes on the Influence Exercised by Trees in Inducing Rain and Preserving Moisture," which had appeared earlier in the *Madras Journal of Literature and Science.* Balfour's report drew heavily on the work of Jean Baptiste Boussingault, Alexander von Humboldt, and his own experience in Mauritius. He explicitly affirmed that deforestation caused a cycle of drought, famine, and death, though he also developed a sustained critique of colonial revenue-raising policies as a contributing factor. He also introduced a definite public health element into the deforestation debate by asserting that deforestation increased the incidence of disease, a concern he developed later during the 1870s, when he was surgeon-general of India.

Lord Dalhousie, the new, technocratic, "modernizing" governor-general of India, was sympathetic to these arguments, and his enthusiasm found an outlet after 1849 with the annexation of the Punjab and the acquisition of the *shikargahs,* or forest and game reserves, of Sind, ready-made units in which to set up an embryonic forest administration devised by John Stocks, another surgeon-botanist. A further survey of the forests of Burma in the late 1840s by the surgeon John McClelland, and the appearance of Hugh Cleghorn's report in 1851, pushed everything into high gear.[53] India was fast on the road to becoming the first major country of the world, outside the nascent German state, to boast an efficient and widespread forest administration.

It would be possible to document in detail the deforestation and the gradual establishment of government control over the forests for other areas of the Indian Subcontinent—such as Tenasserim, the Northwest Provinces, Oudh, Punjab, Bengal, and Assam—from the copious accounts of Edward Stebbing, one-time administrator of the forests, but it would be repetitious. The important point was that forest destruction was rapid and widespread, and the establishment of government control reflected this. Undoubtedly the government was spurred on by the specter of famine and the outbreak of disease. The famines of 1837–39 in the Doab and Bengal and the start of the Irish famine of 1846 cannot but have had an effect on thinking. Additionally, the surgeon-environmentalists expressed concern at the outbreak of serious epidemics in the rapidly expanding urban centers, particularly Calcutta, and the possible connections between vegetation, runoff, and water supply. Thus, the moral duties of public health and adequate food supplies loomed large in the deforestation debate.

But there were far-reaching contradictions in what happened. While the surgeon-environmentalists and their scientific allies showed precocious and spectacular intellectual curiosity, engaged in much astute political maneuvering, and expressed admirable moral concern about the welfare of those over whom they had assumed control, with few exceptions they were blind to the long-term environmental effects of the interventionist policies they were advocating. The condemnation of *kumri*, the "settling" of people, the reservation of forest tracts, and the raising of taxes to pay for public works probably contributed in no small way to local hardship and widespread deforestation in the teak, sal, and other commercially valuable forests of the continent. The Forest Conservation Department founded in 1857, of which the Bombay, Madras, and Sind conservancies were experimental forerunners, was a remarkable achievement, but it was also going to be a source of future trouble.

COLONIAL CONSOLIDATION: INDIA, 1850–1920

The maneuvers of the surgeon-environmentalists and the setting up of the presidency forestry departments were important preludes to raising consciousness about deforestation and to more comprehensive conservation policies, but they could barely keep pace with the changes occurring in Indian life during the latter half of the century and before 1920, when the colonial enterprise reached its peak. The subcontinent occupied a pivotal position in the British imperial system, and the aim was to consolidate imperial rule. The need was to bring order, stability, and efficiency into the sprawling physical, economic, and social diversity of the subcontinent. Railway development, financed largely by British capital (and the opening of the Suez Canal in 1869), welded India together more effectively and enmeshed it in the trade of the wider world. Survey, well under way by the midcentury, created knowledge and control over the land and was the basis of the cadastre and the taxation system.[54] The halting—even reluctant—administrative developments of the EIC were now replaced by the purposeful creation of a modern judiciary and civil service composed of British officials inspired by Benthamite ideals, who intervened directly and vigorously in such matters as tenurial systems and property rights; the initiation of irrigation projects, road building, and a comprehensive forestry policy; and the prohibition of customs they considered inhumane.

There can be little doubt that the extension and intensification of the "modernization" project had a profound effect on the land cover. Better communications, more commercialized farming, and greater land control, together with an increasing population, all seemed to interact with one another to unleash "a fierce onslaught," leading to the "serious" depletion of the forest, the major natural resource and habitat left.[55] As each decade passed, rural inhabitants were pushed to extract more products out of the forest; yet the firewood, forage, green fertilizer, thatching grass, building material, honey, game, and medicinal cures, and the use of the forest for gathering, hunting, and grazing, all became less accessible and abundant. Increasingly, peasants lost access to emergency fodder and fuel supplies, and more and more found themselves "forced into the market to purchase products that they had formerly procured by their own labor at minimal cost."[56]

The Amount and Locale of Clearing

If the destruction of the forest seemed bad before 1850, it was nothing compared with what followed. The comments of Sainthill Eardley-Wilmott, who entered the Indian Forest Service in 1873 and became inspector-general in 1908, summed it all up in his memoirs:

> Nature's forces cannot be expected to contend against the cattle that destroy the seedlings, against fires that kill saplings, and against the axe that removes the seed-bearers. Persistent attacks by these enemies, ever increasing in strength with the increase in population must result in the deterioration and ultimate disappearance of the forest, and these are just those forces which have been active ever since the time when men were few and forests overwhelming. And now . . . the position is reversed, and forests are restricted while men are all-powerful.[57]

But how much forest disappeared is difficult to assess. The detail of land use found in the district and provincial gazetteers and taxation surveys begun in 1869 gives a sense of accuracy, but also some conflicting results. Table 11.1 gives a broad view of the major land-use change in the regions of the tropical world, and it shows that in South and Southeast Asia during nearly seventy-five years between 1850 and 1920, crops increased from 78 million to 119 million ha (net change of 41 million ha), forests and woodland declined by 33 million ha, and grasslands declined by a net 8 million ha.

In a later, more richly detailed study of the South and Southeast Asia region (table 11.3), John Richards and Elizabeth Flint suggest that the decline of woodland for the Indian Subcontinent alone at 7.4 million ha was not as great as that for mainland Southeast Asia (8.9 million ha) or for insular Southeast Asia (10.3 million ha).[58] But any attempt to compare table 11.1 with table 11.3 is fraught with difficulties: the latter represents a shorter period of 40 years between 1880 and 1920, different regional groups of countries, and different land-use categories. Suffice it to say that in this later calculation, all cropland rose by 24.6 million ha (compared with 41 million ha in table 11.1) and forest declined by 25.5 million ha, which, when combined with a decline of 6.8 and 4.3 million ha of interrupted woodland and wetland forest respectively, makes for the destruction of a total of 36.6 million ha of woodland of all types. Whichever figure we accept for forest destruction—33 million or 36.6 million ha—it is a vast amount of forest to disappear, but large as it is, it is probably more important to understand what forces were at work to cause this terrestrial transformation, and what it did to the landscape.

In mainland India it was the increase in the area of cultivation by some 6.7 million ha which more than anything else caused the destruction of the forests. This increase is usually attributed to three main causes, although there is lively debate about the exact and relative impact of these. They were the extension of railways; the pressure of increased

Table 11.3 Estimated total area in major land-use categories and change (in millions of ha) and population and livestock totals (millions) for three major regions of South and Southeast Asia, 1880 and 1920

	Southeast Asia Subcontinent			Mainland Southeast Asia			Insular Southeast Asia			Total Change
	1880	1920	Change	1880	1920	Change	1880	1920	Change	
Total Cultivated	110.7	117.4	6.7	8.0	16.5	8.5	8.1	17.5	9.4	24.6
Forest/ Woodland	68.5	61.1	−7.4	94.3	85.4	−8.9	160.9	150.6	−10.3	−25.5
Interupted Woodland	36.7	34.8	−1.9	49.2	45.0	−4.2	21.7	20.8	−0.9	−6.8
Forested Wetlands	3.4	3.0	−0.4	6.8	4.3	−2.5	32.8	31.4	−1.4	−4.3
Subtotal All Forest	108.6	98.9	−9.7	150.3	134.7	−15.6	215.4	202.8	−12.6	−36.6
All Other Land Use	121.8	124.8	3.0	35.6	42.7	7.1	32.9	36.1	3.2	13.3
Total	341.1	341.1		193.9	193.9		256.4	256.4		
Population	253.1	291.4	38.3	23.8	41.6	17.8	33.6	64.3	30.70	86.8
Livestock	199.7	235.3	35.6	10.3	19.0	8.7	11.2	16.8	5.60	49.90

Source: based on Richards and Flint, 1994: 20, 34, 36, tables 2, 3 and 4.

population, which rose by 236 million between 1850 and 1920; and the commercialization of agriculture (exacerbated by increased taxation). They all fed off one another in a way impossible to quantify, but all undoubtedly had an immense impact locally, if not nationally. Forest policy was not a *cause* of deforestation, but it was a response to perceived shortages and an important element in the shortfall of forest products for the Indian farmers.

The Railways and Their Impact

The construction of railways was an integral part of British colonial military and commercial policy.[59] They strengthened the control of British rule by facilitating the speedy movement of troops and armaments—a point emphasized by the Mutiny of 1857—and second, they augmented British wealth by facilitating the import of British manufactured goods and the export of Indian raw materials, which had implications for land use. The Lancashire and Glasgow cotton manufacturers were a powerful lobby group for railways, especially after the "cotton famine" of 1846, which underlined their precarious dependence on American supplies. With startling clarity and self-assurance they saw that a railway from Bombay inland was simply "nothing more than an extension of their own line from Manchester to Liverpool."[60] It would be far speedier and efficient than bullock wagons, which took months to trundle down from the Deccan, with the cotton bales often being ruined by dust and rain.

The manufacturers had a strong ally in the reformist first governor-general, Lord Dalhousie, who replaced the lethargic and ponderous administration of the EIC. He thought that the railway, together with the telegraph and uniform postage, would be one of "three great engines of social improvement"; an aid in the development of the "great tracts" of land, which he perceived were "teeming with produce which they cannot dispose of"; and the promoter of other areas, which were "scantily bearing what they would carry in abundance. If only it could be conveyed whether it is needed."[61] The internal development of the country was not an aim per se, but many railway promoters were conscious of the multiple "modernizing" effects that railways brought, which could not but be beneficial. Certainly, Indian society and economy were transformed radically as its millions took amazingly readily to the railways. Social and cultural barriers were broken down, local markets were ruptured, self-sufficiency was upset, and local handicraft industries went into decline.[62] Construction of lines began in 1852 from Bombay inland to the foot of the Ghats, and from Calcutta to the Raniganj coalfields 195 km away. The utility of these early lines was clearly evident; construction burgeoned, and by 1867 nineteen of India's 20 largest cities were linked. India's network increased rapidly, so that by 1900 its 40,396 mi were surpassed only by those of the United States, Russia, and Germany, and by 1920 its 61,957 mi were exceeded only by the United States, Russia, and Canada.[63]

It is generally thought that the new rail network allowed transportation costs to be halved and access to global markets to be guaranteed, causing shifts in cropping patterns in the interior, where profits could now be realized. Certainly land use and productivity changed, as detailed studies of northern India, from the Sind in the west across the Indo-Gangetic plain to Bengal in the east, testify.[64] However, opinion is divided as to whether the changes were beneficial and provided rising incomes, or deleterious and encouraged the cultivation of nonfood crops such as cotton and the export of crops such as wheat, thus reducing the supply of domestic food. It seems, however, that the railways did not have such a catastrophic effect on food supply as is commonly supposed; there was neither a marked rise in incomes nor a radical shift in cropping patterns. New tax regimes may have produced a far more radical change.[65] Evidence from five large sample areas scattered across the subcontinent suggests that cotton showed a slight upward trend from 6.4 to 9 percent of cultivated land, and that food grains showed no major drop by the end of the century (they increased in many cases). It is even difficult to prove that per capita food grain production fell below consumption levels, except in the more extreme famine years.[66] But undoubtedly the high price for cotton that continued after the American Civil War continued to feed into the rural system, gave slightly higher crop prices, and did encourage higher consumption and food production. The peasants did not *become* commercialized; many were *already* commercialized in the precolonial market economies of the Hindu and Muslim regimes. Thus by the time the railway came, millions of peasant proprietors were not the "passive pawns of market forces," as they are sometimes portrayed, but canny opportunists who saw the chances for profits that the new agriculture provided, and consequently were drawn into the global commercial market.[67]

One example of change was the vast upland plateau of the Deccan and Karnatak, east of Bombay, where the amount of cultivated land rose from 6.3 million to 8.3 million ha (15.5 to 20.5 million acres) between 1856/60 and 1871–75, and within that total the acreage of cotton increased from 322,125 to 614,708 ha (796,000 to 1,519 000 acres). Undoubtedly, the existing peasant entrepreneurial expertise was stimulated by the extension of the Bombay railway to Nagpur during the early 1860s, which cut costs and transportation times to the coast, the latter from 3 months to 3 days. An additional factor in other places was the revision of taxation rates to a lower level than formerly, which stimulated agricultural clearing. Some areas changed faster than others; in the 26,000-km² Khandesh subdistrict in the northern Deccan abutting the Satapura Hills, cultivation doubled, from 687,956 to 1,456,848 ha (1.7 million to 3.6 million acres) between 1856/60 and 1916/20, and cotton production rose threefold, from 11.9 to 36.9 percent of the total land cultivated. Almost imperceptibly the cover of dry deciduous *Babhul* forest *(Acacia arabica)* dwindled as the trees fell before the ax, and remnants remained only on the hill ridges, so that by 1878 it could be said that "no tracts of good land lie waste." By the latter decades of the nineteenth century, fuel, pasture, and fodder supplies were in short supply everywhere, and because of the removal of the tree cover, flooding, silting, and erosion were becoming common.[68]

In contrast with this almost imperceptible land use change, the impact on the forest and the scrub jungles and their wildlife in the immediate vicinity of the railroads was usually stark and severe. This was especially true of the early lines, which were designed to link large cities that then consumed whatever supplies of fuelwood were available, so that "the scrub jungles within the neighbourhood would soon be cut out and disappear." Ribbentrop was in no doubt about the relationship: "Railways spread and forest growth disappeared with incredible rapidity within reach of the lines," partly due to the direct demands for construction and for fuel, which were carried out in a "reckless and wasteful manner," and partly on account of the "increased impetus" given to cultivation. The railways, said Robert Wallace in 1887, had caused large areas to be "shamefully and wastefully denuded."[69] Typical was the line from Madras to the southwest coast which passed through the

> wooded country occupying the notch [The Palghat Gap in the Ghats, in reality about 20 mi wide] between the Koondah and Anaimalai ranges [which] was famous for wild elephants, but the extended cultivation along the line, and the increasing demand for wood, have jointly contributed to clear the primeval forests, and there is now only a thin scattered jungle.[70]

In the timber-scarce Punjab the situation was worsened by the competition for fuel by the riverboats on the Indus and its tributaries.[71]

As was the case everywhere in the world, the railways received far more attention as the direct destroyer of the forest than did the diffuse and difficult question of their effect on cultivation, which must have been much greater. But how much forest fell directly to the railways? Ties are probably the easiest to calculate, but even here there is much conflicting evidence. Every mile of railroad required between 1,760 and 2,000 ties, each of at least 3.5 ft³ or more, depending on whether it was narrow- or broad-gauge line.[72] But as ties rotted in the ballast or were eaten by termites, they had to be replaced regularly. The life of the ties depended on the timber used. Teak was said to last for 14 years, sal and deodar 13 years, but other timbers rotted in 6 years. The wide variation of official reports suggests that 10 years was a reasonable (if somewhat optimistic) average life,[73] and therefore one-tenth of the track had to be replaced every year (table 11.4).

Table 11.4 Estimate of sleepers (crossties) used and acres of forest cleared, India, 1850–1940

	Miles of Track	10-year Increment	Ties in New Construction (in millions)	Ties Renewed Annually (in millions)	Total Ties (in millions)	Acres of Forest Cleared (in thousands)
1850	0					
1860	1,542	1,542	2.8	0.3	3.1	15.5
1870	8,637	7,095	12.8	1.3	14.1	70.5
1880	15,764	7,127	12.8	1.3	14.1	70.5
1890	27,227	11,463	20.6	2.1	22.7	113.5
1900	40,396	13,169	23.7	2.4	26.1	130.5
1910	52,767	12,371	22.3	2.3	24.6	123.0
1920	61,957	9,190	16.5	1.7	18.2	91.0
1930	70,565	8,608	15.5	1.6	17.1	85.5
1940	72,144	1,579	2.8	0.3	3.1	15.6
Total						715.6

Source: track-miles from Morris and Dudley, 1975: 193–96.

The type of timber used for ties varied with what was available; it was a complicated geography of supply across the subcontinent. Deodar *(Cedrus deodara)* predominated in the hill forests of the northwest provinces and the Punjab, while teak predominated in Burma and to a lesser extent in south-central India, but it was expensive because of competition for other uses. Sal *(Shorea robusta)* grew on the hill slopes of the Himalayas and was floated down the many tributaries of the Jumna and Ganges to the rest of northern India. There were also extensive areas of sal on the Chota Nagpur plateau of Bihar, and most of Orissa and eastern Madhya Pradesh, which supplied Bengal and northeast India. Because sal was resistant to termites and rot it had been subjected to long-term exploitation for construction long before the railways came. As early as 1868 Edward Davidson said that the supply forests had been "so carelessly treated and so wastefully denuded" that shortages would occur inevitably. By the end of the 1870s, when the railway system was approaching 8,600 mi—a mere one-eighth of its final length—shortfalls were evident. In 1878, Dietrich Brandis, the inspector-general of forests, thought that the supply of suitable timber was "not sufficient at present to meet the requirements of construction and renewals," nor would it be so until the forests under his control had many decades to recover from past excesses.[74] The shortage was so acute that substitutes were used; Baltic pine impregnated with creosote and other chemicals (chloride of zinc, sulphate of copper) was cheap and easy to import, and indeed might have accounted for up to 25 percent of the requirements in the admittedly timber-deficient area of the Central Railway System of Rajputana, Sind, and Neemuch. But the dependence on overseas supplies seemed precarious and to undermine the purpose of the Forest Department. Iron ties were discussed by railway and forestry officials but not seriously, so that the less valuable but abundant conifers of the Himalayas such as Himalayan spruce *(Abies Smithiana)* and silver fir *(Abies Webbiana), Pinus longifolia* and *Pinus excelsia,* seemed a reasonable solution. How they were to be treated, and with what, was debated at length. The cost of importing creosote was "prohibitory," so local solutions had to be found and adapted to local timbers. An experimental treatment works at Delhi was suggested, but nothing seems to have been done until 1924, when a plant for creosoting 400,000 ties annually from less useful woods was set up in "the North West" with another smaller plant in Assam.[75]

While the debate on crosstie substitution and preservation ranged back and forth, the forest was being destroyed steadily to accommodate the necessary onward march of the railroad at a rate of some 70,000 acres (28,611 ha) per annum during the 1860s and 1870s; the deforestation rate nearly doubled to between 122,000 and 130,000 acres per annum during the 1890s and 1900s, the peak of railroad construction activity. Many variables might enter these computations to alter them one way or another, but whatever way they are looked at, the impact was nothing compared with the difficult-to-define but relentless clearing by peasant proprietors and commercial farmers. In all, about 700,000 acres (286,118 ha) of forest must have been destroyed to supply the ties, a sizable amount in one way, but a mere pinprick (about 4.5 percent) of the total destruction of 6 million ha by agriculture over the same period.

Railway fuel is even more difficult to calculate. During the late 1860s over 80 percent of engines were using firewood, and the proportion did not diminish markedly over the next few decades. Calculations of what this meant in terms of timber supply were legion, but one reasonable estimate was that with a 17-year cutting rotation, plantations devoted solely to railway fuel would be required near lines at the rate of 20 acres per mile of line.[76] At that rate about 544,000 acres (approximately 220,000 ha) were needed in 1890 and 1,056,000 acres (approximately 427,000 ha) in 1910, though coal was probably making inroads by this time. Certainly Stebbing's many accounts of efforts to secure railway fuel supplies are peppered with plans and legislative acts for setting aside 3,000- to 8,000-acre forest tracts for plantations near railway lines. Wherever there were lines, fuelwood supply was a topic of constant concern. Another consideration was that the railways came into competition not only with domestic firewood users but also with charcoal iron producers, which were said to be using up forests at the rate of 50 mi^2 (approximately 13,000 ha) per annum for every 4,380 tons produced (12 tons per day). But we do not know the total national production of iron at this time, though all the indications are that India's typically soft, poor-quality iron was all but eliminated by imports of superior British product after about 1870.[77]

Peasant Cultivation

The felled forests; the new railway earthworks, bridges, and tunnels; and the hordes of itinerant workers who provided the hard manual labor had a dramatic impact on the lands and livelihoods through which they slowly passed like some crashing, noisy juggernaut, crushing all that got in its path. But away from the lines, peasant farmers were largely untouched by it. Life went on in its inexorable and timeless way: the seasons of planting and harvesting, the cycles of birth and death, and the constant battle to provide enough food for a slowly increasing population occupied the minds and muscles of these village dwellers.

Table 11.5 Changing land cover (in millions of ha) and population (in millions) in Uttar Pradesh, Bihar, and Orissa States, North India, 1880, 1920, and 1980

	1880				1920				1980			
	U.P.	Bi.	Or.	Total	U.P.	Bi.	Or.	Total	U.P.	Bi.	Or.	Total
Cultivated	14.8	9.2	3.5	27.5	15.9	10.2	4.7	30.8	19.2	10.0	6.8	36.0
Forest	4.2	2.4	5.9	12.5	4.0	1.8	5.0	10.8	2.3	1.3	3.5	7.1
Interrupted Woodland	2.2	2.4	2.8	7.4	2.1	2.4	2.6	7.1	2.1	2.4	2.1	6.6
Grassland	3.9	1.6	2.0	7.5	3.6	1.3	2.0	6.9	1.9	1.5	1.9	5.3
Other	4.3	1.8	1.4	7.5	3.8	1.7	1.3	6.8	3.9	2.2	1.3	7.4
Total	29.4	17.4	15.6	62.4	29.4	17.4	15.6	62.4	29.4	17.4	25.6	62.4
Population	44.8	27.0	8.0	79.8	46.7	28.1	11.3	86.1	108.8	72.4	26.3	207.1

Source: J. Richards et al., 1988: 585–714, 753–82.

In the vast plain of the Ganges and its tributaries that stretched from beyond Delhi in the west to nearly Calcutta in the east—in the States of Uttar Pradesh, Bihar, and Orissa—little land was left unused by the closing decades of the nineteenth century (table 11.5).[78] The production of food reigned supreme, and by 1880 half the land was in cultivation. Uttar Pradesh was the most cultivated, with just over half the land in crops and only 14.2 percent in forest, with an additional 7.4 percent in interrupted woodland in which foraging could be carried out and firewood gathered. Bihar was about the same, but Orissa was much more forested. In the three states together, some 44 percent of the land was in cultivation, 20 percent in forest, and 12.1 percent in interrupted woodlands. There were "large tracts where trees, much less forests, are almost unknown," said Augustus Voelcker in 1893.[79] Only on the upland margins did the proportions change significantly, with forest accounting for a quarter to a third of the land, and even up to nearly all land in the Himalayan provinces of northern Uttar Pradesh, although it too was being cleared. Down the coast, through Orissa and toward Madras, forest was generally much more widespread and accounted for half or more of the land, but agricultural expansion and the cutting of the sal for the expanding railway system caused massive destruction.

During the next 40 years the population of this vast area of nearly 65,000 km² increased from 79.8 million to 86.1 million, and arable land from 27.8 million to 30.8 million ha. The bulk of this newly cultivated land was taken out of the extensive forests of Bihar and Orissa and the margins of Uttar Pradesh, which decreased from 12.5 million to 10.8 million ha. Another 0.3 million ha came out of interrupted woodland, 0.6 million out of grasslands, and another 0.7 million out of other land uses. Little expansion occurred on the plain, as there was no more forest to fell. The changes are shown in figure 11.2A–C, which shows the extent of forest in 1880, 1920, and 1980. The annual rate of clearing from 1880 to 1920 was 42,500 ha, most of this coming out of eastern Bihar and Orissa generally, where individual provinces showed declines of well over 50,000 ha (fig. 11.2A). It was a complex picture of transformation and change that hints at, but hides, many local stories of the relationship of the peasant proprietors with the forests.

Global Crops: Plantations and Commercial Farming

In contrast with the incremental and largely undetected expansion of agriculture by the millions of peasant farmers, there were a few areas where commercial plantation cropping for a global market reached spectacular proportions. These areas *did* owe their existence to rapid accessibility and cheap and efficient transportation links with the wider world, and to that extent they can be said to have been created by the railways (and steamships). In addition, they also had either settler capital or official sponsorship and encouragement. Four of these areas will be looked at in more detail. Three were on the periphery of the Indian Subcontinent—Assam for tea, the Nilgri Hills and Wynaard Plateau of Kerala for coffee and subsequently for tea, and Sri Lanka (Ceylon) for coffee and tea, the stimulants that were exported to satisfy Europe's continually expanding "soft drug" culture. Somewhat different, and in the heart of India, was the Ganges-Brahmaputra delta or Sunderbans, where rice production for domestic consumption was promoted. All were in areas that had had a dense forest cover and had previously been largely unsettled; all entailed massive forest destruction; and all (with the exception of the Sunderbans) functioned with imported indentured labor.

In favorable spots throughout the 130,000 km² of the foothills of the eastern Himalayas, from Darjeerling east to Lakhimpur, tea cultivation competed with the forest. After 1833, legislation allowed foreigners to buy land in India, and by the end of the century British speculators had amassed over 253,000 ha in about 764 large estates, of which about one third was cultivated at any one time. Tea was a lucrative crop: during the early 1850s it yielded, on average, about Rs. 445 per ha, compared with 30 for rice, 52 for cotton, and 90 for opium. Only sugarcane, at Rs. 475, exceeded it.[80] Such high profits encouraged exploitation in difficult terrain, and bridges and roads were built to aid exploitation.[81]

In Kerala the semi-independent, indigenous princes and landed elite encouraged British administrators and planters to colonize uncultivated tribal hill forests in order to increase their revenues. The Wynaard Plateau, and later the Nilgiri Hills, were favored locations for Europeans on account of their cooler climate and lush forest vegetation; said one explorer of the Wynaard forests in 1830, they are "strong, wild and beautiful" and "we discovered trees of such enormous height and magnitude, that I am fearful of mentioning my ideas of their measurement." But they were not to remain untouched. Clements Markham, who knew the area well, observed in 1865 that "within the last 20 years a great change has come over the forest-clad mountain districts, in the establishment of many English planters. . . . In all a total area of 180,000 acres of forest has been cleared for coffee, tea and chinchona plantations." Blight in coffee in 1868 caused a major shift to, and expansion of, tea cultivation. Markham had no doubt about the gains and losses of the clearing: the planters had "brought great material blessings to the natives, but in the extensive clearings of trees which they have necessarily made, [they] have brought about a deterioration of the climate," and he proceeded to resuscitate all the arguments and observations about lessening rainfall in the western Ghats region.[82] Similar arguments were presented for the Coorg in the center of the western Ghats.[83]

Plate 11.3 "The New Clearing." Plate 4 of Verken M. Hamilton and Stewart M. Fasson, *Scenes in Ceylon,* 1881. (Bodleian Library, Oxford.) This sketch had an accompanying verse:

> The ruthless flames have cleared his lands;
> No trace remains of green
> When lost in thought our Planter stands
> And views a sterile scene.
>
> In dreams he sees his Coffee spring,
> Fed by the welcome rain
> And berries many a dollar bring
> To take him home again.

Even in more distant Ceylon (Sri Lanka), the same processes were at work with ruthless efficiency (plate 11.3), and by the end of the 1880s, nearly 600,000 acres (243,000 ha) were felled for tea plantations, which had replaced those for coffee (fig. 11.4). On one of his many global journeys, novelist Anthony Trollope bemoaned the passing of the forests:

> The lovely sloping forests are going, the forests through which elephants have trampled for we do not know how many more than 2,000 years; and the very regular but ugly coffee plantations are taking their place.[84]

How those plantations were created some decades before is recounted vividly by John Capper in a splendid, if lengthy, account of clearing that must stand as an example of the "industrial" clearing of the tropical forest:

> Before us were . . . fifty acres of felled jungle in wildest disorder; just as the monsters of the forest had fallen so they lay, heap on heap, crunched, splintered into ten thousand frag-

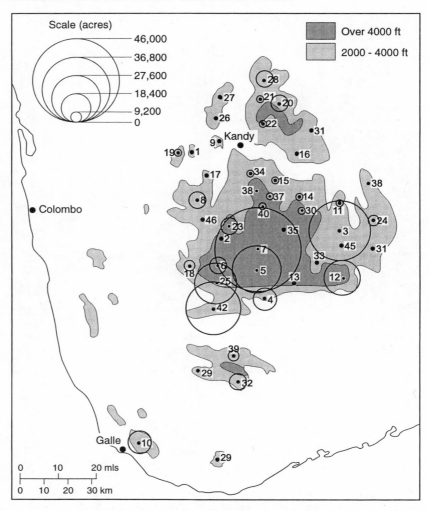

Figure 11.4 Extent of tea plantations, Sri Lanka, circa 1955. *Source:* Forrest, 1967.

ments. . . . The "fall" had taken place a good week before, and the trees would be left in this state until the end of October by which time they would be sufficiently dry for a good "burn."

He and his companions clambered through the "fall" to the steeper forested slopes, "where the heavy click of many axes told us there was a working party busily employed." In front of him were some forty Sinhalese laborers "plying their small axes with a rapidity and precision that was truly marvellous," but leaving enough of the stem uncut to keep the tree just standing upright. A few hours later, Capper climbed to the top of the slope and looked down on the vast area of almost cut-through trees that were ready to knock down one another like a series of upturned dominoes:

> [T]he manager sounded the conch sharply . . . forty bright axes gleamed high in the air, then sank deeply into as many trees, which . . . groaned heavily, waved their huge branches

to and fro, like drowning giants, then toppled over and fell with a stunning crash upon the trees below them. Nothing was heard but the groaning, cracking, crunching, and splintering . . . it appeared as though the whole of the forest-world about me was tumbling to pieces.

When he recovered from the overwhelming experience, Capper commented wryly that the small axes may have "rang out a merry chime—merrily to the planter's ear—but the death-knell of many fine old forest trees."[85]

Completely different was the colonization, reclamation, and settlement of the 18,000–20,000 km² of sparsely inhabited but potentially "cultivable wastes" of the Sunderbans of the Ganges-Brahmaputra delta (and similar but small deltas on the Mahanadi, Godavari, Krishna, and Penner rivers).[86] The seaward side of the delta was covered with the largest area of mangroves in the world, while on the inland side, and away from the river channels, were dense stands of *kanazo (Heritiera fomes)* forests, with trees up to 45 m high. It was the natural habitat of the Bengal tiger, the crocodile, and a rich assemblage of monkeys and snakes, a "sort of drowned land, covered with jungle, smitten by malaria and infested with wild beasts," said William Hunter in his report for the District Gazetteer.

As early as 1793 the land was declared "state" owned, and from 1816 onward a commissioner of the Sunderbans was appointed to oversee the extraction of fuelwood for the growing urban area of Calcutta and its jute mills. Moreover, the commissioner was to encourage private owners to settle and drain the land by embanking, clearing the forest, and growing rice in order to build up export and emergency famine stocks. Taxation and tenure were manipulated to encourage settlement; large areas were made available free of charge on long-term leases that were inheritable and transferable, provided 25 percent of the land was under cultivation within 5 years. After 20 years, 75 percent of the land was liable to normal taxation. These regulations, together with formal land survey after 1830, guaranteed private property rights and unleashed a rush of peasant entrepreneurial energy. By 1870, 2,790 km² had already been cleared and embanked, and by 1920 about another 5,000 km². The Bengal tiger was becoming as rare a beast as its watery forest habitat.

Shortages and Forest Policy

By the early 1860s, everything was moving inexorably toward a state of alarm about the reduction in the area and quality of the forest, and the pressure on its many "free" products. An extra 38.3 million people between 1880 and 1920, an almost equal addition of cows, and all-too-frequent famines showed that the quest for more land could never be relaxed. In the absence of intensification of agriculture, expansion into the forest was the only possibility, and was a deliberate part of British land policy, especially as it helped to maximize revenue. Augustus Voelcker, who had been asked to report on the state of Indian agriculture, was pessimistic: the forests, he said, were "fast disappearing before the spread of cultivation, and by the reckless destruction caused by the people."[87]

Rural life was affected in other ways. The widespread dependency on livestock in Indian society was not possible unless forested forage lands were available. But common rights to browse diminished as the area of the forest was reduced and greater restrictions were placed on its use by the colonial authorities. Fuelwood supplies were similarly affected. The spread of the railways, and their insatiable demand for timber of all kinds, caused "havoc" in the forests alongside the lines and reduced local supplies. The radius of fuelwood procurement was widened so that the demand was "so steadily on the increase that in a few years supplies will have to be drawn from remote districts as yet have hardly heard the axe." [88] This was already happening in the villages of the intensive agricultural districts.

The alternative to wood fuel was to burn cow dung, with disastrous effects on yields in existing cultivated lands; it was a vicious circle of degradation. For example, the following was reported to be the case at Ahmedabad

> firewood is scarce; it costs R.1 for four maunds of 40 lbs each, and the testimony of the cultivators is, that they gather all the stalks, etc, off their fields and would not burn any dung if they could help it. Poona is another place where firewood is expensive. It has to be carted between 30 and 40 miles, and then costs R.5 a cartload, whereas a cartload of cow-dung cakes costs R.3, and a cartload of loose cow-dung, R.1 only. It is not to be wondered at, then, that the cakes are burnt as fuel instead of wood. [89]

In highlighting the general timber shortage, and the role of the railways after 1860 as the primary cause of a nationwide forest policy, it is easy to ignore other complex official concerns and opinions. First, there was the search for teak and other useful timbers within the broader strategic view of empire which led to the reservation of particular stands of trees. Second, there was an animosity toward uncultivated land, which was regarded as "waste." Moreover, forests were perceived as the abode of the unruly and disorderly, from the murderous thuggees down to run-of-the-mill thieves, so that the elimination of the forests would mean an end to lawlessness, as well as unproductive land and population. Finally, from at least the late 1840s the surgeon-environmentalists saw the "vagabond habits" of the itinerant *kumri* cultivators in the hills and their torching of the forest as *the* prime cause of forest destruction, decreasing rainfall and increasing desiccation, famine, and declining health—not realizing that the regeneration of the timbers they prized so much was dependent on periodic burning. The suppression of *kumri* seemed essential for environmental health, and reflected the wider concern about revenue and labor supply because uncontrolled patterns of settlement and production betokened a lack of colonial control. Both actually and metaphorically, the shifting cultivators needed to be kept in their place. [90] It was a circular, self-reinforcing, and self-justifying argument that the stewardship of the forests and the control of the hill people were essential for the survival and welfare of the mass of Indians and their forests.

Therefore, in response to these pressures the British authorities began one of their great "modernizing" projects: to set aside forest reserves for preservation and management by professional foresters. The appropriate expertise was found in the German-trained Dietrich Brandis, who was appointed as the first inspector-general of Indian forests in 1864. Since 1856 Brandis had been superintendent of forests in Pegu and later in Tenasserim and Martaban, where he initiated forestry policies described as the outcome of "a master-hand and mind." An outstanding administrator, he slowly built up a massive administrative and management structure based on scientific management and sustained-yield principles. By the end of the century the Forest Department had within its remit slightly over one-fifth of the total land of the subcontinent (fig. 11.5). [91]

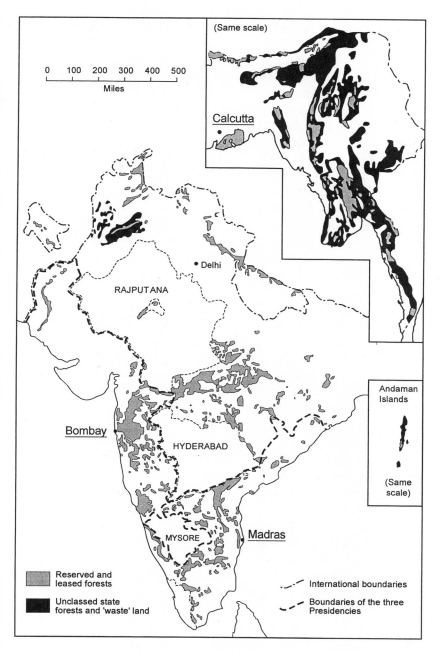

Figure 11.5 The extent of reserved and leased forests, and unclassed state forests and wasteland under British control in the three presidencies of Madras, Bombay, and Bengal (Calcutta), India, 1899. *Source:* Ribbentrop, 1900.

The Forest Act of 1865 was, said Mahesh Rangarajan, the "first step towards a rule of property for the forests of British India,"[92] but its provisions were soon a matter of fierce debate among British officials. Some leaders, like those in the Madras Presidency, took an enlightened view and resisted it vehemently until 1882, contending that it was a usurpation of native rights and a prescription for further shortages, rural hardship, and even social instability and crime. They were not alone; commentators in Britain condemned the "excessive zeal" of the Indian government which had "put on the screw in . . . limited areas," and observed that "[i]t would take a forest officer years of hard study to be even partially qualified to judge of the injury done to an agricultural population by the shutting up for forestry purposes of the land on which the cattle graze."[93] Others, like the autocratic and influential B. Henry Baden-Powell, would not countenance the idea of customary rights, and wanted the removal of all ambiguity about the "absolute propriety right of the state." Customary rights would be allowed only if "proof" were available in writing, something that even European peasants could rarely do. Like suttee or smallpox, the indiscriminate cutting of trees was "an evil that must be suppressed."[94] Brandis attempted to steer a middle course between these extremes, favoring selective annexation of areas vital for commercial or climatic purposes, but leaving village rights, in particular, untouched. But in the end Baden-Powell's views prevailed.

As far as the Forest Department was concerned, the 1865 act allowed only a tenuous control over the continent's forests. There was a need for new, stricter, and more comprehensive legislation. Brandis, with the help of his forest officers and aided by Baden-Powell's formidable knowledge of Indian land rights, drafted the New Indian Forests Act, which became law in 1878. In reality the impact of the 1878 legislation was not as devastating as feared, if only because its effect was not uniform—the government by no means annexed all uncultivated lands. In any case, the impact depended on three other widely varying conditions: the type of forest, the applicability of the legislation, and local tenure.[95] In the legislation a distinction was made between forested lands that were either reserved or protected: in the former, no rights could be acquired unless explicitly ceded by a provincial government; in the latter, rights were recorded and permitted, but land was not settled. It is true that tribal forests were still potential arable land, as in upland country of Chota Nagpur in Bihar State, southeast of Calcutta, where with the coming of the railway "vast stretches of jungle . . . disappeared, swept clean off the surface of the land, or represented only by a puny growth of saplings that will take a century to rival the magnificent trees that were there before them."[96] But forests were also protected to secure timber; it was now possible to exclude rural land users and promote the growth of commercially valuable species. And, because of the often quite severe precolonial regulation and use of the forest, the regulations were not the crucial turning point or ecological catastrophe that some would maintain.[97]

But in the end, one is left with a terrible paradox. An admirable and massive administrative edifice had been constructed for the rational use of the timber resource, which had no parallel in the world at this time or for decades to come.[98] It was one of the administrative jewels in the Imperial Crown, a model for the rest of the world, and a highly efficient and profitable enterprise.[99] But it was also going to prove to be one of the festering sores in the body of the Indian Subcontinent that has still not been healed.[100] The foresters and their regulations became the face of alien power, which pervaded Indian rural life just as surely as any military, judiciary, or political administrative framework. The process of colonization was far more complex than political domination alone. Its cultural, social, economic, and even psychological ramifications cut deeply into the fabric of traditional life—in this case the forest—carrying with them rapid and sometimes deleterious change.

MAINLAND AND INSULAR SOUTHEAST ASIA

With very few exceptions, the overwhelming wealth of detail that accompanied forest destruction and policy in India is not paralleled throughout the rest of Asia. Most of the lands did not fall under the bureaucratic, efficient, and precise administration of British officials, who bequeathed such an archive of information elsewhere, but the forces of change were different too. In 1880 in mainland Asia (Burma, Thailand, Cambodia, Laos, and Vietnam), population densities were a mere one-sixth of India's (0.12 compared with 0.73 person/ha). Production went well beyond subsistence needs, and the primary impetus for clearing lay in external rather than internal demand. Pioneer peasant farmers attacked the lowland and delta forests aggressively to grow rice and feed the greater world beyond, encouraged by an extended period of favorable terms of trade and rising land and commodity prices.[101]

Some clearance episodes are known, for example the purposeful and rapid changes that occurred in Lower Burma (significantly a British possession).[102] Initially, interest had revolved around the extraction and conservation of teak and ironwood for ship construction, first in coastal Arakan and Tenassarim and later along the Sittang and Salween rivers. Then Lower Burma was annexed in 1852 including the 35,000–40,000 km^2 of *kanazo* forests of the Irrawaddy delta. At midcentury no more than 3,200 km^2 were in cultivation, but undoubtedly with the experience of the Sunderbans in mind, officials regarded the region as ideal for growing paddy rice that would produce revenue and surpluses. When Burma became a part of the empire in 1886, a deliberate policy was undertaken to encourage pioneering peasant migrant cultivators to clear the *kanazo* and mangrove for rice growing, especially with the recurrent famine crises of Bengal in mind. In a phrase reminiscent of de Tocqueville's description of pioneering in North America over 100 years before, James Grant said, "the pioneer's axe is heard daily as the forests are cleared and prepared for the rice crop." [103] Canals, embankments, roads, railways, and mills were built, and steamship routes established. Peasant migrants flocked in, and the population of the delta area rose from 1.5 million in 1852 to over 4 million in the early 1900s, and with over 12,000 km^2 of wet rice it became one of the main rice-exporting regions of the world. So swift and complete was the deforestation that by the early 1920s "scarce a tree was to be seen" in the delta, which had once been dense jungle.

Similar stories of reclamation and deforestation of coastal deltas can be told for the 12,700 km^2 of the Chao Phraya in Thailand, the Mekong in Cambodia, and other, smaller deltas, but details are sketchy. In Thailand in particular, royal patronage and state aid, under the stimulus of British imperial hegemony, were directed toward encouraging energetic peasant rice cultivators. It was the Irrawaddy story all over again: canals were dug to facilitate communications, Dutch hydraulic expertise was brought in to plan the draining, Bangkok grew as the major rice processing and refining center, and the wetland forests disappeared.[104]

Clearing before 1920 was equally prolific in insular Southeast Asia, the third of the regions. Cultivated crops increased by a phenomenal 9.4 million ha and over 10.3 million ha of forest was cleared, the largest amount in any of the three Asian regions. But the detail of how that happened is virtually unknown. In Indonesia, for example, copious records exist of the changes in the policies and conservation measures of the Vereenigde Oostindische Campagnie (United [Dutch] East India Company [VOC]) in precolonial Java—up to 175,000 teak logs were being cut annually by the mid-1860s—but this gives only a limited view of the forest changes. We are told by Peter Boomgaard that new cash crops of coffee, indigo, tobacco, and sugar destined for the European market meant "large-scale land clearing," that "clearing for subsistence was still considerable," and that the years between 1826 and 1865 were "the age of destruction"; but the multitude of individual and incremental clearings by peasant proprietors eludes summary analysis. In addition, the 6,400 mi (9,300 km) of railway constructed between 1873 and 1920 demanded clearing for track rights-of-way, and timber for sleepers.[105]

Knowledge of clearing in the Philippines is slightly better, especially around the core of early settlement in the plains of central Luzon.[106] Here the legacy of over 300 years of Spanish settlement had created a domesticated landscape of large estates and smaller farms, which were gradually encroaching on the upland margins of the forest, the habitat of the slash-and-burn cultivators. The forest cover declined from about 90 percent of the island in 1521 to about 70 percent by 1900, and most of that in central Luzon. A rising population and the spread of commercial crops such as tobacco, abaca (manila hemp, used for ships' rigging), and sugarcane integrated the local economy into the world system. A microcosm of the process is provided by the example of the province of Nueva Ecija, just north of Manila, between 1800 and 1920, "the great era" of forest clearance. Sugar was grown on large feudal-like estates owned by elite Filipinos and Chinese mestizos, and abaca on smaller peasant farms. Sugar estates were clear-cut, and were voracious consumers of fuel for refining the sugar; abaca had no manufacturing process, and because trees were left in fields to shade plants, it had less impact on the landscape. Wherever these two plantation crops were not grown, rice and ranching took over the land.

But away from the Luzon plain, the rest of the Philippines was still almost untouched, other than by shifting cultivation. In a report of 1917 it was said that there were

> vast stretches of unmapped and sparsely inhabited forests. . . . No effort has been made to make any use of these forests. Communities living in sight of virgin forests imported timber from abroad. Near such forests were people living in houses of thatch and bamboo. The main reason for this non-development was the great lack of transportation. Far from making any commercial use of the forests of these regions the principal industry of the inhabitants seemed to be forest destruction by a system of shifting agriculture.[107]

Once more, Western perceptions were at variance with local adaptations, and the elimination of shifting agriculture and the promotion of "development" were seen as the keys to unlocking the forests. When the crucial transportation links came after 1920, the Philippine forest began its long and rapid descent to near oblivion.[108]

BRAZIL AND THE "LONG JOURNEY TO EXTINCTION"
The Continental Picture

With the notable exception of Brazil, the forests of Latin America were barely touched before 1900 and only marginally so by 1920, other than by shifting cultivation.[109] Of the 51 million ha cleared from 1850 to 1920, approximately half disappeared before 1900 and half in the following 20 years, the bulk of it in Brazil (see table 11.1). But clearing in this continent was by no means a prelude to agricultural expansion. Of the 27 million ha of cropland created by 1920, about two-thirds of it was in the temperate grasslands of Argentina, Uruguay, and Chile. Mexico and Brazil accounted for about another 12 percent each, and the rest was scattered in small amounts in all other countries.[110] Therefore, with permanent cropland constituting only a little more than one-half of the forest cleared, the bulk of clearing must have been either for grazing or an outcome of destructive exploitation by careless and/or rapacious cultivators.

To emphasize the overwhelming dominance of Brazil in this story is not to deny that clearing took place elsewhere. In every country a few tracts of 100,000 ha or more disappeared as large estate *(latifundia)* owners, and some individual pioneer settlers, lumberers, and fuel procurers, set about their work. But clearing was marginal in the development of these territories. In the Pacific-facing countries of Chile, Peru, Ecuador, and Colombia, remoteness and high transportation costs militated against lumbering and commercial cropping for overseas markets. What agriculture there was existed mainly in either the treeless Sierra upland or the irrigated coastal plains. Bolivia and Paraguay were landlocked.

The Atlantic-facing countries of Uruguay and Argentina concentrated on utilizing their extensive grasslands for cattle raising and then wheat cultivation, both for the European market. In Venezuela and Atlantic-facing Colombia, coffee and cacao cultivation had made limited inroads into the tropical forests of the plains and foothills, but it was not extensive. Of far greater impact was the plantation economy of Cuba, which became the sugar colony par excellence by the mid-nineteenth century. Sugar dominated the social and physical landscape, creating a slave society in its demand for labor, along with a deforested landscape (over 500,000 ha in sugar) because of its demand for land and fuelwood for refining. The larger area of Mexico is more of an enigma. Although an intensely peasant and agricultural society, little evidence suggests that inroads were made into the southern tropical forests before the very end of the nineteenth century. The estimated precontact population of 25 million had dropped to 3.8 million in 1650 and existing clearings had reverted to forest, thereby increasing its size. The next three centuries were a long and slow process of recovery from that demographic disaster, and the population did not regain its precontact level until roughly 1950. The only evidence of impacts on the forest was lumbering for mahogany in coastal Yucatan,[111] and the extension of railways, which climbed steadily from 1,080 km in 1880 to 20,447 km in 1912, needed sleepers, and opened up remoter forested areas to settlement—but again, not until after the turn of the century.

Brazil: Elites and Exploitation

But Brazil was utterly different. The devastation of the great Atlantic coastal forest was early, extensive, and severe, and had much to do with the peculiar social system that developed with initial colonization.[112] During the seventeenth century the racial and social makeup of the colony began to take shape, and it became stratified into a caste system. The more obviously white population sought and received royal (Portuguese) patronage over land and forest rights, and progressively they occupied land illegally (squatted). Also, if they had enough money and/or influence, they had their occupation legitimized by receiving *sesmarias,* royal land grants 1 square league (4,356 ha) in size. Ownership of land was a form of privilege confirmed through royal connivance; it had almost no monetary value and was rarely sold, which meant that little care was taken of it, but it was the basis of social position.

Those natives who survived disease and were captured, and the vastly expanded mestizo population, were segregated into *adelias* (government-sponsored villages often under the administration of missionary Jesuits and Franciscans). This captive underclass of the *adelias* formed a pool of ready labor for the large estates, supplemented after 1550 by African slaves. Consequently, the forest frontier was rarely one based on small pioneer settlers but instead was founded on *latifundia,* slave labor and coercion. The boundaries and locations of the *sesmarias* were often unknown, which led to unbridled lawlessness, fraud, and violence; and because no one could be trusted, the estates were maintained very largely by endogamy. It was recipe for future social disaster and ecological mayhem.

The enormous size of the *sesmarias* allowed for an extravagant use of the forest in a modified form of slash-and-burn agriculture. The obvious fertility of newly cleared and burned land meant that fallow could be dispensed with and plows ignored. When the soil became "tired," the next piece of forest, and even the next *sesmaria,* was occupied. This agricultural method meant a saving in labor, but in the meantime the use of the once-and-for-all fertility of the soil maintained the population at a subsistence level. Imported pigs, sheep, chicken, goats, and above all cattle ran wild and multiplied wonderfully in the absence of natural predators. They soon filled the available grasslands and invaded the forests of the *serato* (internal backwoods). It is possible that the cycle of cultivation was well under 30 years, and that the forest had little chance to grow back except as very degraded secondary woodland, or *capoeira,* especially now that animals grazed it. The usual outcome was that the woodland ended up as grassland.

By about 1700 the population in the Portuguese-controlled section of the forest probably numbered about 300,000, of which only a third were Portuguese. They occupied an astounding 65,000 km² of the forest at very low population densities (2–5/km²), all in various states and degrees of clearing. Sugar cultivation had led to the clearing of about 1,000 km² in pockets along the coast near Recife, Salvador, Espirito Santo, and Rio de Janeiro, and at least another 1,200 km² had been cleared or degraded to supply fuel for the refineries. The massive influx of people into the interior with the discovery of gold and diamonds in Minas Gerais during the early eighteenth century had far-reaching effects on the vegetation. Around the site of the mines the forest was stripped and the land scarred and eroded. "As far as the eye can see," said one contemporary observer, "the earth is turned over by human hands,"[113] and perhaps 4,000 km² ended up looking like a lunar landscape.

Over 100,000 miners moved into the area; they ate prodigious amounts of beef, which meant an expansion of herds on the natural pastures and degraded subsistence plots. Incapable of being grazed so intensively, the pastures were quickly replaced by less palatable species and less nutritious introduced African grasses. In order to encourage new succulent growth, fire was applied indiscriminately, but with devastating effects where it reached the forest edges. The cattle bred freely on the unfenced range, creating *minas de ganado*—"mines of livestock." But the cattle were prone to vampire bats and gadflies, so in order to avoid these debilitating pests they invaded the forest margins, trampling saplings and spreading grass seeds. Everything seemed to transpire to shift the cattle from grassland to forest edge, especially where forest had previously been farmed, opened up, and then abandoned on the *sesmarias*. The result, said Warren Dean, was that

> cattle raising, permanently extensive and expansive, everywhere prevented the reversion of abandoned farms to forest. Furthermore, the continual and aggressive use of fire presented a constant danger to forest margins, and in the dry season or during droughts it imperiled the forests themselves. Very likely they were a greater hazard than fires set by the hunter-gathers or by swidden farmers, because they were more frequent and on a much grander scale.

Cattle raising created a permanent change to the human landscape and its vegetation. So broad, complete, and irreversible was the removal of forest that when Karl Friedrich Martius, the renowned botanist, visited the gold and diamond region southwest of Minas Gerais and the region northwest of São Paulo in 1840, he supposed that they were natural grassland and had never been forested. Just as the sugar planters were nibbling away at the eastern edge of the great Atlantic forest, so were the graziers on its western edge. In all, mining, farming, and cattle grazing in the southeastern sector of the forest in a 300 to 400 km arc inland from Rio and Santos may have eliminated another 30,000 km² of forest. The Zona da Mata, or Forest Zone, of Minas Gerais was disappearing, and the Atlantic forest was at the beginning of its "long journey to extinction."[114]

Brazil: "Green Gold"

The late eighteenth/early nineteenth-century phenomenon of scientific curiosity about the natural world barely touched colonial Brazil because of royal suppression of any enquiring mind, which was equated with subversive political and social concepts. The prohibition of printing presses and public libraries was indicative of the insecurity and paranoia of the ruling elite. Nevertheless, some trees, plants, and forest products were identified and their commercial properties recognized—for example, brazilwood, cochineal, indigo, and rubber. Generally, however, the sentiment was that the Brazilian forest was of little value, although Brazilian plants like cashews, papaya, passion fruit, and pineapples were quickly adopted when introduced to the cuisine of Goa and India generally, and from there spread to the wider world. Greater emphasis was placed on importing, and subsequently attempting to grow and then export, exotic Eastern crops like cinnamon, hemp, and chinchona, but with little success.

Some local shipbuilding took place along the coasts, but timber suitable for ocean-going vessels was first sent to Lisbon and later commandeered for Portuguese vessels built at Bahia. In an act reminiscent of the British in North America, the Portuguese authorities tried to reserve for their own use all hardwoods suitable for shipbuilding that grew between the coast and the inland escarpment, although centuries of cutting in the forests meant that there were few hardwoods left. Faced with shortages, they also quickly learned some of the lessons of the subtropical Atlantic forest: unlike the temperate forests, trees did not grow back from stumps; they rarely grew at all unless in a forest; and their growth was so slow that generations would be born and die before the trees could be harvested again. This suggested that the replanting of hardwoods in homogeneous stands was not feasible, and that an adequate supply could come only through carefully selective logging and conservation. But such biological niceties were of little concern to the loggers who forged ahead into the forest wherever possible, and soon came into conflict with the colonial landholding elite. Exacerbating matters, because of the royal reservation policy, the landholders could no longer legally fell timber on their own land without consent, and indignant at their loss of freedom, they simply cut down as much woodland as possible to get around the restriction. The forest was always the loser.

In the end it was easier and cheaper to import wood for shipbuilding and construction from the United States, just as later, jarrah railroad ties came from Australia. There were shortages everywhere, even on the forest frontier, where it might least be expected. Here the backwoods farmer (caboclos) set fire to the woods for a few seasons of manioc raising and never considered replanting. One naturalist, the Mineiro José Vieira Couto, vividly and memorably depicted the caboclos as devastating vast areas as he held a "broadax in one hand and a firebrand in the other":

> [He] gazes upon one or two leagues of forest as though they were nought, and hardly has he reduced them to ashes but he extends his view still further to carry destruction to other parts; he harbors neither affection nor love for the land he cultivates, knowing full well that it will probably not last for his children.[115]

The rapid advance into new forest and the incessant burning left behind a "hollow" frontier, studded with stunted and pauperized woodland, sparsely settled and almost invariably changing to grassland and cattle grazing.

In 1815 Brazil became a separate kingdom from the main House in Portugal, and by 1821 an independent country; but the great political upheavals of these years did not signal a change of attitude toward the forest. If anything, the destruction became worse as the elite did everything to maintain its privileged position. Slavery was not abolished until 1888, by which time another 1.25 million African slaves had been transported, enough to service the plantation system until the end of the century; any restriction on gaining free land (which still had no monetary value) was resisted; the removal, enslavement, or servitude of indigenous peoples continued; and any restrictions on the use of the forest and its trees was opposed. The elite wanted the right to convert this vast stockpile of wood into cash as quickly as possible. Everywhere, profligacy, exploitation, shortages, and violence continued unabated.

In their search for a more enduring prosperity, the colonial aristocracy cast about for a staple crop to export to the consuming nations of the Northern Hemisphere. Experiments with tea were a failure, and the demand for rubber was not yet on the horizon.[116] Sugarcane cultivation was revived and spread south into the coastal plains around Santos, Rio, Campos, and Vitoria. It unleashed a new onslaught on the forest and may have consumed up to 7,500 km² of forest by the mid-nineteenth century, along with another 900 km² for the fuel to refine it.[117]

Because of cheaper competitors, the colonial elite's hoped-for prosperity from sugarcane never materialized. But salvation came in the form of an entirely new crop—coffee—which proved to be their "green gold." Although coffee had been introduced from East Africa in 1727, its value was not recognized until later. By the end of the eighteenth century, coffee *fazendas* covered the hills around Rio, later spreading over the Serro da Mar and into the Paraibo Sul Valley and the surrounding São Paulo highlands. By the 1840s the extensive forests of Minas Gerais and adjacent portions of Espirito Santo were succumbing to the crop.[118] Coffee became Brazil's main income source and remained the principal export commodity until 1964, reaching its apogee in 1925, when it accounted for three-quarters of the country's export earnings.

Occasionally coffee was planted on ground already thinned for either fuel gathering or sugar cultivation. More generally, however, it was planted on heavily forested ridges, as it was commonly thought that it would not yield unless grown on land originally covered by "virgin" forest. As the plant was particularly sensitive to frost damage, the bushes were planted in rows up and down the steep hills in order to facilitate the drainage of cold air. The result was devastating erosion, which hastened crop abandonment and migration to new tree-covered areas. Although the bushes could yield for many decades if tended carefully, they were usually neglected, as in the time-honored Brazilian tradition, it was easier to claim that the land was (as they put it) "tired," apply for a new *sesmaria,* and shift on to the next piece of forestland, clear it, fire it, and plant it again. The land resembled "some modern battlefield, blackened, smouldering and desolate," for the forest was felled in a restless cycle as the coffee frontier moved continuously inland.[119]

The construction of the Santos–São Paulo railway over the obstacle of the Serro do Mar in 1867 allowed a new wave of exploitation to be unleashed in the interior uplands (figs. 11.6A and 11.6B), and during the next two decades railroads fanned out in all directions from Campinas to southern Minas Gerais and the "Paulista West." The realization of the inherent fertility of the decomposed basaltic-derived red soils, or *terra roxa,* encouraged the massive expansion of the *fazenda* frontier toward Ribeirô Prêto between 1885 and 1900; but depletion of even these soils meant yet further migration west onto the interfluves of the many rivers flowing toward to Paraná River.[120]

The creation and extension of the coffee *fazenda* was founded originally on slave labor, and indeed, the newfound wealth provided by coffee was the excuse for its retention and extension. But with the construction of the railroad in 1867, major social and

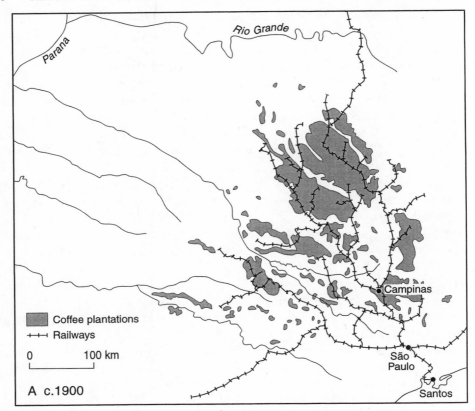

Figure 11.6A Extent of coffee plantations, Brazil, end of nineteenth century. *Source:* Monbeig, 1952.

economic changes were unleashed that led to the slow crumbling of the old regime. When the slaves were finally emancipated in 1888, their place in the labor force was taken by an influx of over half a million Italian, Spanish, and Portuguese migrants—their movement greatly facilitated by the railway. In every way the railroads led to further cycles of forest destruction. There was over 6,000 km of line by 1900 and approximately 12,000 by 1929. The migrants came in and the coffee beans went out through the new port of Santos, while the railroads gobbled up timber for rights-of-way, fuel, and ties, and the movement of fuelwood to the growing cities was facilitated. Coffee cultivation was dynamic, mobile, and wasteful. If the land in coffee is used as a surrogate measure for the area of forest destroyed, then at least 4,000 km² could have been cleared by 1900, 7,980 km² by 1920, and 140,000 km² by 1931.[121]

Throughout the southeast region the rural and urban population climbed steadily with the coffee boom, from about 1 million in 1808 to 6.4 million in 1890; Rio alone became a bustling metropolis of 500,000. The appetite for wood was immense. More land had to be cleared for food crops. Domestic fuel consumption was at least half a ton per capita per annum, or more, and with over 40,000 dwellings in Rio in 1890, about 400,000 tons

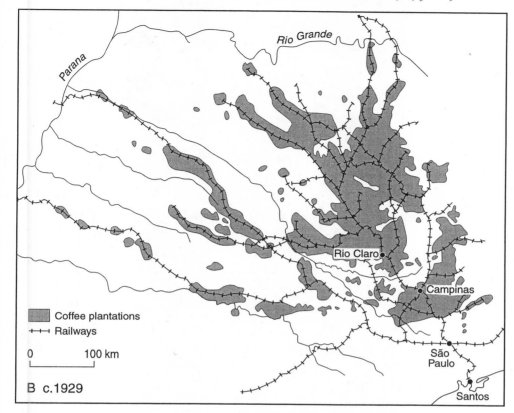

Figure 11.6B Extent of coffee plantations, Brazil, 1929. *Source:* Monbeig, 1952.

of fuel would have been needed, the equivalent of 200 km² of secondary forest, to which must be added the demands of the bakeries, forges, and numerous factories. In addition, the construction of each dwelling would have needed about 100 tons of fuel for the firing of bricks and the burning of lime for plaster. Further, the iron forges of Minas Gerais would have consumed 40 km² a year.

While the spread of the coffee plantations and the growth of cities were the "new instruments of devastation" in the elimination of the virgin forest, by no means did they entirely supplant the traditional forms of forest exploitation—rather, they accelerated them. In the vicinity of the older settlements, firewood, crops, and meat still came out of the *capoeira,* or secondary forest, causing it to become more biologically degraded or disappear entirely. The *caboclos* in the *capoeira* and the true forest remained persistently itinerant. They had no security of tenure, tenancy being discouraged by the plantation elite because it might endanger the slave society; but by being itinerant they also avoided arbitrary impressment into the military, which was employed as a means of suppressing opposition. Thus, the displaced *caboclos* moved on to the forests of the drier western frontier—cutting, burning, planting an occasional crop, and running a few stock.

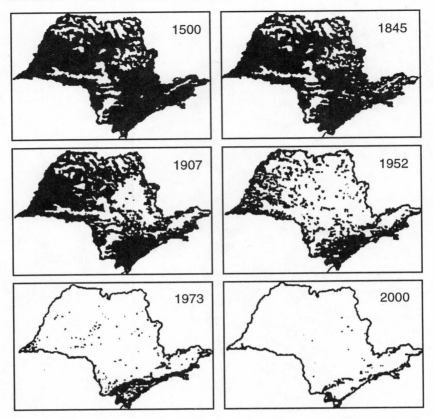

Figure 11.7 Forest clearing in São Paulo State, Brazil, 1500, 1845, 1907, 1952, 1973, and 2000. *Source:* Oedekoven, 1980: 185.

Further inland the big cattle ranchers, their trade boosted by the coffee boom, continued to transform the grassland-forest border by repeated, large-scale, and indiscriminate burning to repress woody growth, ultimately reducing the productive capacity of the grasslands as well as eliminating the western forest margin and the gallery forests that extended along the rivers.[122]

All these forces were reducing the forest, particularly in São Paulo, to a mere shadow of what it had once been (fig. 11.7).[123] The virtual elimination of the Atlantic coastal forest must rank as one of the most rapacious, complete, thorough, and ultimately perhaps needless and senseless episodes in the annals of the deforestation of the earth.

In 1776, Adam Smith said that "the discovery of America, and that of a passage to the East Indies by the Cape of Good Hope, are the two greatest and most important events recorded in the history of mankind."[124] Whether or not that was true, the two geographical events certainly meant radical changes to the societies and economies of the tropical areas of the world, and ultimately their vegetation cover. The forests of southern and southeastern Asia, and particularly those of Brazil, while still extensive, underwent massive transformations as their people and produce were drawn into the global economy. Over 222 million ha disappeared by the beginning of this century, and crops and grasslands took their place. In John Capper's memorable words, "the whole of the forest-world . . . was tumbling to pieces." It was to be nothing, however, compared to what was to follow in the second half of the twentieth century, which was the era of true tropical deforestation.

PART III

THE GLOBAL FOREST

Chapter 12

Scares and Solutions, 1900–1944

Reduction in the area under forest will undoubtedly continue in the future as it has in the past, as increasing population requires more land for agriculture, and as the forests in many regions continue to be destroyed by fires and cutting without provision for their renewal.

—RAPHAEL ZON AND WILLIAM N. SPARHAWK, *Forest Resources of the World* (1923)

If the present rate of forest destruction is allowed to continue, with nothing to offset it, a timber famine in the future is inevitable.

—THEODORE ROOSEVELT, "The Forest in the Life of the Nation" (1905)

PROBABLY ALL centuries end on a pessimistic note as people reassess the past and look toward the next century with a mixture of trepidation and hope. But compared with the hubris of the nineteenth century, the 1890s was a period of particular introspection. For Europe the space for colonization had all but gone, and the glitter and brilliance of "la belle epoch" seemed too brittle to last. For the United States a similar sense of limited space accompanied Frederick Jackson Turner's announcement that the frontier had "closed," and the Gilded Age was over. The phrase *fin de siècle* was coined; more than a reference to the last decade, it resonated: *decade, decayed, decadence*. To some it implied even worse things: in his novel, *The Picture of Dorian Gray*, Oscar Wilde wrote of "fin du globe," the end of the world as then known.[1]

Yet the signs of "progress" seemed to confute the pessimism and feelings of decline and decay. The development of railways, steamships, industry, and world trade had led to a booming world economy, with western Europe and the eastern United States as its twin cores, and imperialism and "white" expansion were at their peak.[2] The world had been neatly parceled out among the "Great Powers"; Africa had been partitioned and China seemed to be going the same way. Of course, the great discontinuity was not the end of the century but the outbreak of World War I in 1914. It produced the chasm and yet bridged the gap between the age of European predominance and a new era of global affairs and politics. When the cataclysmic events of World War II a mere 21 years later are added, then the whole era from 1914 to 1945 became a new "Thirty Years' War" that tossed the assured world of the nineteenth century upside down. It was, said Carl Sauer, "the end of what we have been pleased to call modern history [1492 to 1918], the expansion of western peoples and civilization over the thinly or weakly peopled spaces of the earth." [3]

During these years of reflection and adjustment from about 1900 to the early 1950s, there was much concern about the limits, availability, and ownership of some of the earth's key resources, particularly land, timber, soil, and water. This led to the quest for "conservation" while in addition a concern for ecology emerged in the discourse. Ecological thinking provided a coherence and focus for fusing concerns about resources and their scarcity by formulating a contextual and holistic biology that would heal the land and society's relations with it. Both of these concerns were characterized by a shift from local and regional thinking to a more global view, and earlier assumptions about the propriety and justice of the imperial role were questioned.

DESTRUCTIVE EXPLOITATION OF GLOBAL RESOURCES

The very progress that ensured the prosperity, territorial control, power, and influence of the developed Western world had also increased resource competition and exploitation. Timber and land were the greatest concerns. For all the steam, steel, and speed of the era, it was still a "wooden age" for many industrialized countries. Even up to 1950, assured supplies of timber for construction and fuel were a high priority in the political and economic planning of some countries, with timber's strategic position being akin to that of petroleum later on. It was widely believed that a predicted "timber famine" would become so severe as to undermine civilization.

Concern about natural resources in general was not new, but what distinguished the turn-of-the-century views from earlier observations was that exploitation was seen increasingly as being worldwide and deleterious. Earlier, in his seminal *Man and Nature* of 1864, George Perkins Marsh had outlined the character and extent of changes produced by humans. But for all his admonitory warnings about the imprudent use of the earth, he was optimistic that damaged areas could be rectified by "restoration," for example by reforestation. Others took an even more upbeat view. For example, the French geographer and radical socialist, Élisée Reclus, thought that the destruction caused by human action could always be turned to improvement, so his *La terre* extolled humanity's inventive power and skill and was, said Russell Whitaker, an unrealistic "eulogy to the creative power of man." Herbert Spencer thought the upward march of civilization inevitable, until the entire global population reached a state of equilibrium and all the land of the world was cultivated like a garden. [4]

But notes of disquiet could be heard. In 1901 the Russian physical geographer, Alexander Woeikof, was concerned about the emergence of a "world civilization" in the previous century which had led to "the growing disassociation of man and the earth." Humans had became more urbanized and industrialized, and consequently had lost contact with their surroundings, which were then altered unthinkingly and irrevocably. Humans exploited and transformed the earth's vegetation most of all, which in turn affected hydrology, erosion, and climate, and could well lead, he thought, to the ultimate destruction of civilization. Three years later, the German geographer, Ernst Friedrich, went further and suggested that European global expansion and resource gathering was based on an exploitative and destructive economy—or *Raubwirtschaft*—that had already destroyed the flora, fauna, and soils over vast areas. In a series of papers, Nathaniel S. Shaler speculated about the exhaustion of soils, power, and metals, and thought it inevitable that even "with the utmost economy, it requires about an acre of woodland to meet the demands of each civilized person in high latitudes [and] as much is required for food." Consequently, the complete deforestation of the globe would occur by the twenty-third century.[5]

And there the matter lay until 1938, when unexpectedly Carl Sauer produced two sustained, biting critiques of the destructive social and environmental impact resulting from Europe's predatory outreach. Marsh provided Sauer with a description and analysis of the role of humans as destructive agents "who set nature to discords," and Friedrich provided the conceptual schema of destructive exploitation, the skimming of the accrued fertility of new lands, that came with initial expansion. Sauer's experience of Latin America and knowledge of its history suggested a devastating and permanent impoverishment of land, *and* of culture and society. The Spanish Conquest had led to the ravishing of New World societies, which were devastated by disease, warfare, and enslavement, and the total disruption of their traditional value systems. Thus, humans and their culture could be abused by thoughtless exploitation at the hands of new and technologically superior societies, just as much as physical resources could be.[6]

These points were elaborated in Sauer's second essay, which considered plant-animal-soil destruction throughout human history, and concluded that any equilibrium achieved in the "older" world was only at the expense of the "younger" world. Somehow, humans had to rise above this mindless, short-term exploitative mode and acquire what Sauer later called "an ethic and aesthetic under which man, practising the qualities of prudence and moderation, may indeed pass on to posterity a good Earth".[7]

The complex idea of ecology ran *sotto voce* throughout many of the narratives. The word itself was coined in 1866 by Ernst Haeckel, a German biologist, to describe the web of linked organisms and their surrounding environment. But it is an enigmatic concept that changes as other ideas and experiences change, and it soon became loaded with multiple meanings, such as "economy," the avoidance of waste and disorder, and the efficient use of "energy." Its most obvious manifestation was in the Clementsian ecological climax–equilibrium concept within biology, which implied a steady state, stability, interacting community, and no change, which appealed because it mirrored earlier and older states of society that were supposedly more stable and happier. Aldo Leopold's "Land Ethic" added yet another dimension to this ecological mystique. The destruction of the Great Plains during the dust bowl era and the crash of Wall Street all seemed to point to the same thing—a need to sustain the community and its environment in stable equilibrium.[8]

Ecology was the one conceptual contribution of the age to resource use and environmental management. Certainly toward the end of this period, ecology and scientific conservation became a proof of right thinking, and came to represent a moral yardstick that emphasized desirable qualities such as "balance, integrity, order, harmony, stasis, diversity—all that was benign, caring, respectful, holistic," compared to the greed and grasping materialism of the production-oriented, industrialized world of the early twentieth century.

But if nature "was most fruitful where it was altered least," difficulties were going to arise with forests, which had always engendered deeply held feelings. Depending on one's point of view, the alternatives were stark—either use them and clear them or leave them alone. But experience had shown that there was a third way and that some forests, at least, had a long history of conscious, manipulative conservation management along ecological lines, and were thus capable of yielding a harvest of timber while staying intact enough to grow another day.[9] The experience of the global forests during the first half of the century revealed these contrasting philosophies in all their complexity, with the debate driven by the specter of a predicted "timber famine." From this debate eventually arose some of the first glimmerings of global awareness of forest resources.

THE COMING TIMBER FAMINE

Many countries in Europe had long since faced up to the fact that they did not possess enough timber for their needs, and had overcome their deficiencies by securing colonial supplies and/or establishing an elaborate system of reforestation. But when the specter of a timber famine hit the United States, by any measure the biggest producer and user of timber in the world, scarcity assumed both urgency and importance. Timber became the key resource issue, and it was replete with all sorts of environmental implications.

"The Day Is Coming": The United States

As early as 1865, Frederick Starr had issued a dire warning that the United States was like some giantess that

> had slept because the gnawing of want had not wakened her. She had plenty and to spare, but within thirty years she will be conscious that not only individual want is present, but that it comes to each from permanent national *famine* of wood.[10]

The next year Andrew Fuller added to the alarm: "every civilized nation," he averred, felt the need for an abundant supply of forest trees, and happily America had felt little of this. "But the day is coming," he warned, "if not already here, when her people will look to the time when forests were wantonly destroyed."[11]

By the late 1870s or early 1880s, the day seemed to have come. Whereas supplies of lumber and land had always seemed obtainable by the opening up of a new region, the public domain was closing. Admittedly, settlement was moving into the forested areas of the Rocky Mountains and Pacific Coast, which contained about one-third of the known forest stand, but this was the "last timber frontier"; there was no more after that. Increasingly, the words *extinction, timber famine,* and *timber starvation* were bandied about to describe the perceived impending crisis, and because the American economy and way of life were so dependent on wood, many were prepared to believe it. Charles Sargent's great survey of American forests of 1884 had stoked the fires of concern. It was a catalogue of destruction: maps of the nation's forests, which once extended "from the Atlantic sea-board in a nearly unbroken sheet," showed large gaps as a result of the "great and increasing drains made upon them." [12]

By the turn of the century the United States needed every bit of wood it could get. In 1906 lumber production reached 46 billion bf (108.5 million m³), nearly two-thirds of the world's output and an amount never equaled since. Per capita consumption was 525 bf (1.24 m³), which was not even remotely equaled anywhere else in the world then or since. The total U.S. consumption of *all* wood products reached its highest point of 13.38 billion ft³ (31.6 million m³) in 1907; 1906 had been the third highest and 1910 the second highest totals. Of this total consumption, over one third was fuelwood (5 billion ft³, or 11 million m³), which still accounted for about 21 percent of energy needs in 1900, and a million tons of pig iron were still being made from charcoal. At the same time as these industrial demands were being made, agricultural clearing had reduced the forests by a further 108.9 million acres (44.1 million ha) between 1869 and 1899. [13] It could not go on like this for much longer.

Although American forest policy germinated in the rich humus of experience and practice of German forestry, via the British imperial Forest Service in India, the particular response in the United States was unique. As early as 1877, Carl Schurz promoted the idea of the preservation and conservation of the forests, and with the efforts of pressure groups and forestry professionals the goal eventually came to fruition with the creation of the Division of Forestry under, successively, Frederick Hough, Nathaniel Egleston, and Bernhard Fernow. [14] Then, by a series of bizarre events (and even some illegalities) in Congress, the Forest Reserve Act was passed in 1891, conferring on the president the power to reserve land from the public domain. This legislation was followed by the Forest Management Act of 1897, which provided for forest administration. About 47 million acres (19 million ha) were reserved almost immediately (fig. 12.1), and the 1897 act allowed further reserves to be created "to improve and protect the forests" or to assist "water flow," and to provide "a continuous supply of timber." [15] Nonetheless, the country remained concerned about the rapacious laissez-faire economy and the destructive exploitation of the "cut-out-and-get-out" lumbermen. In addition, the western states were becoming anxious to preserve forested watersheds in order to promote the integrated harnessing of water for irrigation, domestic use, and hydroelectric power. The forests became an emotive issue for everyone—the tree lover, the rainmaker on the plains, the sportsman, the wilderness preservationist, the aesthete, and the western developer—while the man in the street was concerned about timber scarcity and high prices.

It was against this background of early legislation, preservation, and accelerating demand that Gifford Pinchot was appointed head of the Division of Forestry in 1898 in succession to Fernow. Pinchot was a remarkable person; he was rich, young, energetic, intensely ambitious, and displayed a great insight into issues as well as an adroitness in manipulating public and congressional opinion. The epitome of the technical "expert," Pinchot sensed brilliantly the uneasy mood of the public, and also that of the loggers themselves, who were frightened by the dwindling supply of timber, the frenetic shifts of price, output, and location, and their inability to manage the forests for a more sustained yield.

Pinchot concentrated on the forests of the western public lands in order to establish his management program of "wise use," a basically Utilitarian philosophy of resource

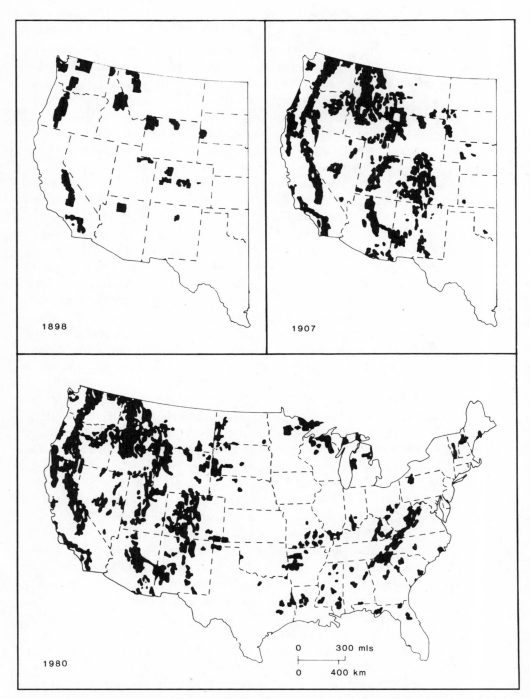

Figure 12.1 The national forests of the United States, 1898, 1907, and 1980. *Sources:* Williams, 1989: 408, based on National Archives GRG 95, container 108 and official maps.

extraction that embodied concepts of "the most productive use for the permanent good of the whole people," and of "the greatest good for the greatest number for the longest time." Conservation was simply "good business," he said; every other consideration was secondary to economics.[16] In addition he had three other aims—(1) transfer the forest reserves from the Land Office to his Division of Forestry (renamed the Forestry Bureau in 1901), (2) raise the status of the Forestry Division in the federal hierarchy, and (3) add even more forests to the reserves. Pinchot's campaign coincided with the presidency of Theodore Roosevelt, whose interests in the out-of-doors and flamboyant personality complemented those of Pinchot perfectly. They understood each other intuitively, and both were imbued with the same crusading zeal to change the current way of looking at land and its resources at the turn of the century. Roosevelt embraced the "timber-famine" thesis and used the phrase many times in his speeches—probably because Pinchot ghost-wrote them. In 1905 the president said, "If the present rate of forest destruction is allowed to continue, with nothing to offset it, a timber famine in the future is inevitable."[17] It was claimed that Roosevelt consulted Pinchot more than any other person in Washington, so Pinchot was able to behave like a benevolent autocrat, confident that he had presidential approval and a large measure of public opinion behind him.[18] The practical upshot was that Pinchot achieved all his aims, created a powerful federal agency in the Forest Bureau, and almost doubled the number of reserved forests, increasing their area to a massive 150 million acres (60.7 million ha) by 1906.[19] (See fig 12.1.)

Using his influence and his own money, he bankrolled a lavish Governors' Conference in Washington in 1907, a spectacular and unprecedented gathering of politicians, experts, and big business at which his philosophy of conservation would be proclaimed before the people, bypassing an unwilling and increasingly hostile Congress. Although stage-managed down to the last detail, Pinchot found it difficult to get recommendations out of the conference, and as a compromise steered it toward the idea of a National Resources Inventory, to be compiled by a National Resources Commission with himself as chairman. The resultant report, a massive three-volume affair divided into Water, Forests, and Land and Minerals, was perhaps the first national stocktaking of a country's resources ever attempted, and was in a format repeated in environmental literature ever since.[20]

In later years Pinchot continued to create a climate of anxiety about supplies. His assistant, Royal Kellogg, told the National Resources Commission in 1909 that the forest contained about 2,500 billion bf, that the trees were being cut "three times as fast as they were growing," and that, although the country might never reach "absolute timber exhaustion," serious disruption of life would ensue unless the federal government, the states, and individual owners cooperated in some way. Several times Pinchot himself predicted that the supply would end in 30 to 35 years' time. His most eloquent statement was in his little, but influential book of 1910, *The Fight for Conservation,* in which he brought the timber issue down to the individual home by saying that the country had "already crossed the verge of a timber famine so severe that its blighting effects will be felt in every household in the land" through scarcity and rising prices. The forests had begun to fail as "a direct result of the suicidal policy of forest destruction which the people of the United States have allowed themselves to pursue." That such dire warnings came from the chief forester, confidant of the president, a prominent public figure in the heart of government, meant that they were treated seriously.[21]

With his alarmism and actions, both autocratic and arbitrary, Pinchot made many enemies. Congress resented his overly intimate association with the president, rival federal departments were jealous of Forestry's spectacular success, and the public at large tired of his moral crusade and began to distrust his alliance with big business.[22] When Roosevelt's second term ended and Taft was elected, Pinchot lost his independence and much influence. In 1910 he was dismissed on a relatively insignificant charge of insubordination over the Alaska coal holdings case, the so-called Ballinger-Pinchot affair.[23]

Although out of federal office, never to return, Pinchot continued to act as goad, spur, and agitator for another 35 years as leading spokesman for the Progressive Party from 1910 to 1917, and as governor of Pennsylvania from 1923 to 1927 and 1931 to 1935. But he was walking an intellectual tightrope: conservation could not be both a moral crusade against materialism *and* a wise-use policy that smacked of rank materialism. Pinchot's doctrine was, as Samuel Hays has aptly called it, a philosophy of conservation coupled with "a gospel of efficiency," inevitably bringing him into conflict with aesthetics like John Muir, who drew upon the romanticism of transcendentalism and the "wilderness" experience.[24] In time, considerations of aesthetics and beauty would loom as large, if not larger, than those of utility when it came to judging the "conservation" of trees.[25]

In the immediate post–World War I period, Pinchot became increasingly authoritarian. In order to whip up support for his apocalyptic vision of shortages, he cast his successors in the Forest Service—Henry Graves and William Greeley—together with the Society of American Foresters and the lumbermen in the role of the enemies within, who were creating the "blighting famine." "Forest devastation . . . threatens our national safety and undermines our industrial welfare," thundered Pinchot, so that "without the products of the forest, civilization as we know it would stop."[26] His call for the nationalization of the forests stirred up enough support in Congress for the Senate to institute an enquiry, *Timber Depletion, Lumber Prices, Lumber Exports and Concentration of Timber Ownership,* commonly known as the Capper Report.[27] This slim report was accurate in its information, measured in its conclusions, and crucial in the subsequent formulation of positive policies to manage and protect the forests, particularly fire control (the cooperative Clark-McNary Bill of 1924 put this into place). Although its thinking and phraseology were permeated with the "five Ds"—devastation, depletion, deterioration, decay, and disappearance—it did not advocate a national takeover of the forests and the lumber industry. Knowing it had had a narrow escape, the lumber industry concluded that the report was "fair."[28]

Although attributed to Chief Forester William Greeley, the Capper Report was largely written by Earle Clapp and Raphael Zon of the newly created Research Section of the Forest Service. It was more sophisticated than previous reports in that it emphasized the dynamics of *growth* of the forest and not simply the *area.* It calculated that growth was 6 billion ft^3 but that the drain on resources was 26 billion ft^3, which meant that mature, high-volume original stands were being plundered at 4.3 times the rate of growth, and inferior timber used for fuel and smaller products was being depleted at 3.5 times the

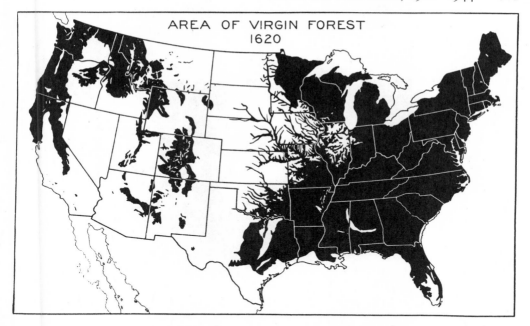

Figure 12.2 "Area of virgin forest," United States, 1620. *Source:* Greeley, 1925: 4, 5. See also Williams, 1989: 436–37.

rate of growth. It was, said Greeley, "A steady wiping out of the original forest resources of the country. Three-fifths of primeval forest are gone." In addition, about 81 million acres (32.8 million ha) of the cutover trees—an area greater than the combined forested areas of France, Germany, Belgium, Holland, Denmark, Switzerland, Spain, and Portugal—were periodically swept with fire and were contributing nothing to the growth budget; and of the 5.5 million acres (2.2 million ha) of merchantable timber being cut annually, well over half did not restock and were being added to the cutover trees. And yet, for all the emphasis on the productive dynamics of the forest, there was still an obsessive concern—particularly by Greeley—on the area of mature or virgin forest, as he called it repeatedly. For him virgin trees represented the major, perhaps the only true, resource remaining in the forest. Though it is true that virgin trees are the source of large merchantable timbers, they do not represent a source of growth; they are, as E. A. Zeigler said, "non-producing capital." But Greeley did not seem to recognize the distinction, and he stoked the fires of concern by later compiling three maps of the declining area of virgin forest, 1620, 1850 and 1920, which were alarming in their stark and seemingly simple message of denudation (figs. 12.2, 12.3, and 12.4). The mathematical precision and detail of the dots reinforced the certainty of his enterprise, and the country had to replenish "the storehouse of splendid virgin timber whose end is in sight." It looked as though the predictions of the doomsday men from Frederick Starr to Charles Sargent, from Theodore Roosevelt to Gifford Pinchot, were correct: the day was coming when the country would experience a timber famine.[29]

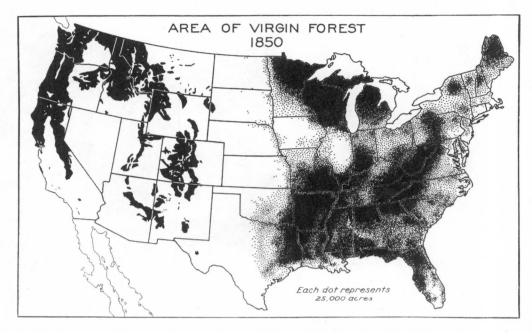

Figure 12.3 "Area of virgin forest," United States, 1850. *Source:* Greeley, 1925: 4, 5. See also Williams, 1989: 436–37.

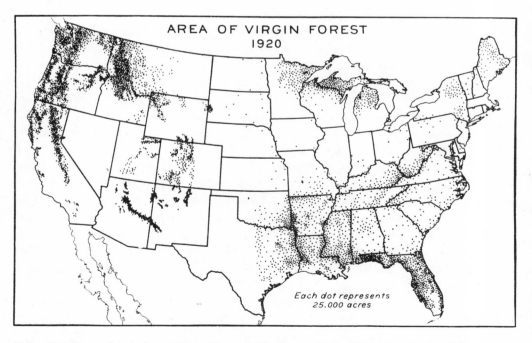

Figure 12.4 "Area of virgin forest," United States, 1920. *Source:* Greeley, 1925: 4, 5. See also Williams, 1989: 436–37.

"Segments of a Greater Whole": World Supplies

If U.S. timber needs could not be satisfied by the nation's own forests, where could the supply come from? The question had already been asked by the Research Branch of the Forest Service. By 1910, Zon had already completed a preliminary assessment of global timber resources followed by a detailed study of those of Latin America.[30] This was then followed up by *The Forest Resources of the World*, a landmark publication of 997 pages which for the first time attempted to survey the forests globally and comprehensively—a difficult task, considering the almost total absence of statistics on area, growth, consumption, and production for the bulk of the world. For the first time, maps were produced of four different types of forest (coniferous, temperate hardwood, mixed hardwood and coniferous, and tropical hardwood); calculations were made of the area, productivity in terms of growth, production (saw timber and firewood), and drain and depletion of remaining resources; and ownership, consumption, and trade were also discussed. It was not going to be replaced as a sourcebook for decades, until the publication of *A World Geography of Forest Resources* in 1956 and the *Weltforstatlas* in 1971.[31]

The provenance of Zon and Sparhawk's work was clear from the foreword by Gifford Pinchot, now governor of Pennsylvania: it was vintage stuff with its doom-laden aphorisms and slogans. The wood problem was "a world problem"; "the need for wood is increasing, the forests are decreasing"; even the "last great bodies of soft woods—those of the Pacific Coast—will soon be gone"; the deficits of America and many countries in western Europe could only be met from the "great, but little-known forests of Asiatic Russia" and the "vast, undeveloped tropical forests." Furthermore, World War I and U-boat sea warfare had shown conclusively how global conflict severely affected the movement of goods, so that the establishment of peace and the lowering or abolition of trade barriers were indispensable to the stemming of America's timber shortage. Pinchot, always with an eye to the "big show," called for an international conference to prepare an inventory of *all* global resources, with himself, no doubt, as a prime player.[32] It was his first, and last, gambol into global forests.

Zon owed much to Pinchot, who was his patron, but he did not adopt the same strident, alarmist tone, and his work was sober and methodical. He was not one for the limelight; perhaps he had had more than enough after being arrested for political activity as a student in Kazan University in tsarist Russia. Sentenced to imprisonment, he escaped, and finally made his way to the United States. He entered the Forest Service and by 1914 was appointed Head of the Office of Forest Investigations.[33]

Zon set out the interrelated economic, social, and environmental benefits of forests, which he considered seriously impaired once the area of forest fell below the magical figure of 30 percent for any territory or state. He calculated that the global area of forests was 30.3 million km², or 22 percent, of the extrapolar regions—a figure, it turned out, that was an underestimation. He was aware that the area of world forests had been drastically reduced over the ages, and that the process was continuing. The greatest decline had possibly been in China, but no one knew for sure. Next came Europe, where most of the original land area of 10.1 million km² had been forested, but now only 3.1 million km²,

Table 12.1 World forest area (in millions of ha), production (in millions of m³), and deficits (in millions of m³) by major world regions, circa 1923

	Area (in millions of ha)	Production (in millions of m³)	Avg. Annual Cut (million m³)			Excess of Growth over Consumption
			Saw Timber	Fuelwood	Total	
Developed						
North America	502.7	120.8	421.0	338.5	759.5	−638.7
Europe	132.7	272.6	142.6	133.6	276.2	−3.6
USSR	640.2	367.0	116.8	88.5	205.3	+161.7
Other	80.5	85.0	13.5	57.9	71.4	+13.6
Total Developed	1,356.0	845.4	693.9	618.5	1,312.4	−467.0
Less Developed						
Asia	346.4	95.2	25.2	79.7	104.9	−9.7
China	76.9	55.8	8.1	47.8	55.9	−0.1
Central and Latin America	524.1	15.5	7.8	53.8	61.6	−46.1
Brazil	404.7	36.8	2.8	34.0	36.8	0.0
Africa	322.1	28.0	1.8	18.5	20.5	+7.5
Other	–	0.3	0.0	0.2	0.2	0.0
Total Less Developed	1,674.2	231.6	45.7	234.0	279.7	−48.1
World	3,030.2	1,007.0	739.6	852.5	1,592.1	−515.1

Source: based on Zon and Sparhawk, 1923: 4–12, 37–43.

or about one third, remained, most of that in Scandinavia and Russia. In the United States the original forest had "shrunk more than 40 per cent in the course of three centuries."

Zon's country-by-country calculations are regrouped in table 12.1 into the two major categories of Developed and Less Developed, which correspond largely to the temperate and tropical world. The figures are undoubtedly flawed in detail, as he had little hard fact to draw on; but whatever their imperfections in absolute terms, they did pinpoint for the first time the relative magnitude of forest area, use, and destruction, and the contemporary perception of the potential of the global forests. Slightly less than half (44.75 percent) of the forest was in the Developed World, but because these forests were so well managed they were able to contribute over three-quarters of the growth. However, the drain of cutting for sawed timber and firewood was so great that the balance sheet of growth versus consumption showed a massive deficit. The annual drain was in the order of 56 billion ft³ (1592.1 million m³), of which 46.4 percent was sawed timber, and the remaining 53.6 percent was firewood. In aggregate the world cut of sawed timber exceeded growth by one half, and of that deficit the United States accounted for nine tenths. The country was clearly heading for a timber famine.

Zon was aware that the growth figures were "guesstimates," but the one statistic about which he was certain was that of the timber trade. The six western European countries of the United Kingdom, Germany, France, Netherlands, Italy, and Belgium (in order of magnitude) took nearly half of the world's imports, and the United States another 15 percent.[34] The imports were supplied largely from the coniferous forests of Russia, Canada, the three Scandinavian countries of Norway, Sweden, and Finland, *and* the United States, which, paradoxically, exported as well as imported timber. This pattern of consumption and supply was not going to vary markedly over the next half century, other than the addition of Japan, and with only minor variations will probably continue well into the twenty-first century.

Taking "a look into the future," Zon thought that the reduction in forest area would "undoubtedly continue" as world population increased (particularly in the tropics) and required more land for agriculture. Reforestation in Europe and reversion of abandoned farmland to forest in the United States did not seem that it would be great enough to compensate for clearing in these continents. On the plus side were the vast untouched reserves of timber growing in Siberia and the tropical world, enough to supply the needs of America and the rest of the world for many decades to come. But Zon was uneasy: the tropical forest areas lacked communications, and their biological diversity made extraction uneconomical and difficult—"on a single acre it is hardly possible to find two or three trees of the same kind." These factors, together with the costs of transporting weighty timbers long distances, made marketing problematic in the consuming countries. Also, the wood was so hard that softwood sawmill machinery could only achieve about one-third of the output when applied to South American timbers. In any case, as the tropical areas developed economically, as they surely would, their forests would be "exploited just as wastefully as have forests in all other regions under similar circumstances," and so bring about a reduction in their area and available quality. On top of that was evidence that the consumption of wood rose in line with a rise in standards of living. As fast as the consumption of fuelwood decreased in favor of substitute energy sources, so new uses arose, such as paper, packaging, railroad ties, and telegraph and telephone poles. The world timber famine, therefore, could be averted only by boosting the production and management of the coniferous forests, which unlike the temperate deciduous and tropical forests grew on poor and inaccessible land unlikely to be converted to agricultural land in the future.[35]

Whatever the future held, one thing was becoming abundantly clear—after 1920, forests everywhere in the world were coming under scrutiny and being assessed. What happened in one part of the world had repercussions in another part. Of course, that had always been true, but now it was clearly recognized that individual forests were "only segments of a great whole." The "forest" was now being looked at as not only a global resource but an object of knowledge, a large-scale conceptual entity that could be visualized, managed, made productive, and "economized."

CLEARING IN THE LESS-DEVELOPED WORLD

While Zon's speculations about the future of the world's forests were not all that accurate or startling, they were essentially correct and discerning. Particularly astute was his recognition that population growth in the tropical world was on a new, upward trajectory and, combined with slowly but steadily growing economies, would be likely to cause massive deforestation in the future—indeed, between 1900 and 1920 another 40 million ha was cleared. In contrast, he underestimated the extent of abandonment of farmland in

Table 12.2 Net forest change (in millions of ha) and annual rate of change
(in millions of ha), tropical and temperate worlds, 1700–1995

Date	Tropical	Temperate	Total	Rate/yr
1700–1849	109	180	−289	1.94
1850–1919	70	135	−205	2.97
1920–49	235	99	−334	11.52
1950–79	318	18	−336	11.57
1980–95	220	6	−226	15.10

Sources: Richards, 1990: 164; and amendments by Williams, 1997.

the marginal areas of the developed world and its reversion to forest, so that the 40 million to 44 million ha cleared there between 1900 and 1920 was matched almost exactly by the same amount of forestland gained, especially in Europe. Even in the eastern United States the pioneering urge had waned and forest reversion was well under way.[36] But, knowledgeable and perceptive as he was, Zon could not have foreseen the magnitude and extent of clearing during the next 30 years, when the secular trend of expansion of cultivation at the expense of all types of natural vegetation was relentless (table 12.2). In the tropical world an additional 235 million ha were cleared between 1920 and 1950, almost half as much again as the 179 million ha of the long two centuries before. Even in the temperate, developed world a net 99 million ha disappeared, most of that destruction caused by timber extraction, though the total might be offset somewhat by further land abandonment and forest reversion. In other words, the 50 years between 1900 and 1950 saw a complete reversal of the eighteenth- and nineteenth-century pattern, where the temperate world had surpassed the tropical in terms of deforestation.[37] The other startling fact was that the rate of clearing had risen from nearly 3 million ha/yr between 1850 and 1919 to a staggering 11.5 million ha/yr between 1920 and 1949, an amount only fractionally less than during the opening three decades of the highly publicized "great onslaught" after World War II.

The regional detail of clearing between 1900 and 1950 is tantalizingly difficult to come by. With few exceptions the sources seem either to be absent or fugitive and fragmentary—a classic example of what has been referred to before as a "dark age" and a "dark space" in the history and geography of deforestation, but this time the opacity is much more recent. Also, in some cases, particularly Africa, it seems that wholly wrong interpretations were being placed on the trend in forest area. In general, though, what happened seems to be more a continuation of past events and a perpetuation of the localities of deforestation evident during the later nineteenth century rather than anything startlingly new. Continuing expansion of peasant agriculture caught up increasingly in the world economy, together with plantations and commercial farming for cash, intensified and expanded. The millions of individual, incremental actions by peasant farmers to clear a few square meters of forest here and there and to include it in the cultivated habitus meant widespread destruction. The whole was driven by a massive population increase of over half a billion between 1900 and 1950, on a base of about 1.1 billion (see table 9.3). Indeed, the average annual rates of population increase were greater than any seen in the world to that time, for example, 1.6 percent in Latin Amer-

Table 12.3 Cropland and land-cover change (in millions of ha), tropical (developing) world, 1920, 1950, and 1980

	Cropland			Cropland Change		Forest Change		Grassland Change	
	1920	1950	1980	1920–50	1950–80	1920–50	1950–80	1920–50	1950–80
Tropical Africa	88	136	222	48	86	−87	−114	+39	+28
N. Africa and Middle East	43	66	107	23	41	−9	−4	−15	−37
South Asia	98	136	210	38	74	−38	−71	0	−3
Southeast Asia	21	35	55	14	20	−5	−7	−9	−13
Latin America	45	87	142	42	55	−96	−122	+54	+67
Total	295	460	735	165	276	−235	−318	+69	+42

Source: after Richards, 1990: 164.

ica, 1.3 percent in Japan, and 1 percent in Africa and India, compared with Europe's declining 0.7 percent.[38]

In summary, over 70 percent of the 235 million ha taken from the tropical forests between 1920 and 1950 went to make new cropland, with the remainder reverting to grassland (table 12.3). Cutting for firewood was rising in line with population increase, though all the past evidence from Brazil and India suggests that Zon's 234 million m³ for fuelwood cut in the less-developed world was probably an underestimate (table 12.1). In addition, lumbering could now be added to the impacts on these forests, although compared with temperate lumbering it was still a mere one-fifteenth of the volume (approximately 3.1 million m³), barely increasing until the massive export trade developed after 1950. It is true that Britain in particular, and Europe in general, had always cut special tropical timbers for special purposes, such as mahogany, rosewood, and brazilwood for furniture, and teak for ships and jetties, but now the tropical forest was beginning to be regarded simply as a source for wood regardless of type. For example, the British Forestry Commission, created in 1918 after World War I to plant and grow a strategic stock of trees on marginal uplands, was worried about the "systematic depletion" of American softwood supplies and the uncertainty of European continental supplies. It eyed the tropical forests of the Empire which were "awaiting development" and would have to be tapped in the future in order to make up the anticipated shortfall.[39] As far as the forest was concerned, it was one world.

Central and South America

In the Western Hemisphere the United States, whose economic progress and expansion was said to be "largely dependent upon an abundant wood supply," regarded the "untouched storehouse" of the "vast underdeveloped tropical forests" of its southerly tropical neighbors in Latin America and the Caribbean with more than "a mere academic and scientific interest in what these forests . . . hold, what they are good for, and how easily they can be exploited."[40] Already in 1915 Zon had made a preliminary assessment of the

Plate 12.1 A coffee plantation in Brazil. From *Emigrazione Agricola al Brasile. Relazonne della Commissione Italiana,* 1912. (University of Wisconsin.)

potential of these forests and the practical difficulties of exploiting them. Now in their global survey, Zon and Sparhawk updated these country-by-country assessments, and attempted to calculate how long supplies would last in the face of vigorous domestic agricultural clearing, something they did not do for any other part of the world. Destruction was most severe in Central America and Brazil. For example, in Costa Rica there was "much clearing"; in Guatemala clearing was "steadily though slowly going on"; in Honduras "much land has been cleared . . . and is still going on"; in Nicaragua clearing was "steadily, although not rapidly, going forward"; in El Salvador a "great deal of the original forest . . . has been swept away"; in Dominica deforestation had consumed more than half the forests; Ecuador had lost "large tracts" to plantation crops, as had the coastal areas and river valleys of Venezuela; and finally, with classic understatement, they said that in Brazil the forest was "much reduced"[41] (plates 12.1 and 12.2). There was very little hard fact about the extent of forest change, though there was a suspicion of great activity.

As part of the campaign to secure U.S. supplies, Tom Gill toured the Caribbean for three seasons to assess the forest prospects for the Charles Lathrop Pack Forestry Trust, an organization devoted to advancing public awareness of forests as economic resources.[42] Gill's book—part travelogue, part sermon on the need for conservation, and

Plate 12.2 Deforestation for a coffee plantation in São Paulo State, Brazil, with a *fazenda* plantation in the background. From *Le Brésil: Ses Richesse Naturalles ses Industries,* vol. 2, 1910. (University of Wisconsin.)

part primer for a lumber industry interested in exploiting the stands—is full of qualitative information about the forests, but again contains little quantitative data, except what he borrowed from Zon and Sparhawk's great work. However, it is significant that Gill, like many before him, did not find untouched, pristine "unbroken leagues of thick luxuriant forest," but rather a forest that was well used and severely degraded in places. Despite his trumpeting of the timber resources available for American loggers, Gill was both amazed and depressed by the devastation wrought already by indigenous and colonial agriculture. Fire and *conuco,* or shifting agriculture, had made massive inroads into the forest, always with the same result:

> [T]he land has been cleared and is now abandoned. Trees have been cut and destroyed. Usually worthless jungle takes its place; a thick growth of brush springs up that will probably prevent forestation by valuable species for many years to come. Worse still, coarse, rapidly growing grasses may capture the field and prevent any form of forest cover reestablishing itself.

The "waste" of good trees and the permanent degradation of the forest were deplored; it was an argument reminiscent of *kumri* in India, and for all the same reasons. If the native people were removed, then the forest might "slowly, but surely, regain the ground that it had lost through long centuries." However, it was far more likely that the population would multiply and "drive back the forest to the very Atlantic."

The shifting agriculturalists were not the only ones to blame. Around the cities, forests had been "cut away for miles." Along the coasts and inland along accessible rivers, American and European loggers had "laid waste" to great areas of forest:

> In Cuba only scattered remnants remain of the original forest growth. The woodlands of Puerto Rico are only a memory. The forests of Haiti, Panama and Trinidad have suffered heavily. The immediately accessible portions of southern Mexico have long been culled of many valuable species.

Only British Guiana, parts of Venezuela, Colombia, and southern Mexico possessed a "wealth of useful products" and were a source of wood for the future; the rest had gone.[43]

The great Amazonian forest was not going to be touched significantly until after 1950, but its eastern extension, the Atlantic coastal forest, was fast becoming "little more than a memory" as coffee, cotton, cattle, colonists, *caboclos,* and industrial and domestic fuel users ensured its rapid reduction during the early years of the century.[44] Its destruction must have constituted a considerable part of the 96 million ha of the Latin American forest that disappeared between 1920 and 1950 (table 12.3). The growth of population in southeast Brazil was phenomenal; between 1900 and 1950 it rose from approximately 7 million to 22 million, generating "boom" conditions. Even during the 1930s depression, when the flow of overseas migrants dried up, hordes of internal migrants from the drought-prone and impoverished northeast and others from the overcrowded southeast flocked into the cities and the countryside; everywhere people pressed heavily on the forest. The pioneer "front" disappeared before the onslaught, and all that was left were patches of the original forest, a few of which became reserves. The remnants of the native population were rounded up into reserves or eliminated, and all land was "owned" either legally or by force. There was no public forest left.

Scarcely anyone objected to the diminution of the forest, as everyone's prosperity and comfort were bound up with its exploitation, and acquiescence with irregularities accompanied the transformation. There were some slight flurries of concern that deforestation might cause a reduction of rainfall and thus affect crop productivity, but it was short-lived. Surveys in São Paulo State showed that forest decreased relentlessly, from about 34 percent of land use in 1905 to a mere 15 percent by 1950. Overall it was disappearing at rate of 3,000 km²/yr, so that in the four southeasternmost states of São Paulo, Paraná, Santa Catarina, and Rio Grande do Sul, only 158,000 km² of forest remained in 1947, a probable loss of 150 percent since 1910.

As long as it was believed that coffee growing was most productive in "virgin" forest, then the frontier of deforestation was going to advance inexorably to the south and west to the extreme limits of the forest stand. Cotton, sugar, and cattle pastures likewise made local inroads. So valuable did untouched forest become that land values were reversed; uncleared land began to command a premium in contrast with cleared land. But increasingly it was domestic and industrial fuel needs that put most pressure on the remnants of the forest. It is difficult to summarize neatly and concisely the many inroads that fuel procurement made; Warren Dean produced elaborate and reasonable statistical transformations based on the surrogate statistics of pig-iron production and other uses. For example, it took 4.5 m³ to produce a ton of pig iron, and 4.2 million tons were produced by 1950. At a reasonable growth of 200 m³ for secondary *(copoiera)* forest, that would equal 2650 km² of woodland cleared in that year alone. Similarly, if railroads used 12.5 million m³ in 1950, then that was the equivalent of 620 km² of forest. Domestic and small industrial establishments, metal works, and other uses may have amounted to at least 1,000 km², and between 7.5 and 10 percent of the population was engaged in fuelwood gathering and charcoal making. A total, then, of something approaching 4,000 km²/yr (less, if some form of rotation was in play) was a formidable drain on the forest that it simply could not sustain, especially when one realizes that even as late as 1979, 79 percent of Brazil's energy needs were still supplied by wood. Some attempt was made to reforest in order to create fuelwood supplies, especially with fast-growing Australian *Eucalypts,* and although millions were planted between 1911 and 1953, it is doubtful if even "3 hectares had been planted for every 10,000 that had been cleared."[45]

On its southernmost extremities in the states of Paraná, Santa Catarina, Rio Grande do Sul, and adjacent parts of Paraguay, the semitropical forest merged into the temperate stands of the easily worked softwood, *Araucaria augustiflora* or Paraná pine. Of the total land area of 58 million ha in these three states, about 44 percent (25.3 million ha) consisted of forests of these widely spaced (approximately 25–65 trees/ha—but at least uncomplicated by other species), tall, thick conifers. By 1980 it was estimated that this once extensive forest had been reduced to a mere 445,000 ha, mainly by immigrant European and Japanese farmers, who after 1920 or thereabouts had established small, independent, intensive, and highly mechanized holdings growing temperate crops for export. Also, the fire farming for temporary clearing and pasture improvement by the many itinerant *caboclos* frequently got out of hand, so that uncontrolled and devastating fires finished off what was not cut purposefully.[46] In addition to pioneer clearing, U.S. lumbermen had developed a thriving trade in this straight-grained and easily worked pine. The growth of local towns and more distant markets in the southern, treeless pampas, such as Montevideo and particularly Buenos Aires (up from 750,000 in 1893 to 4 million by 1940), led to the massive culling of these trees. Over 17.7 million tons of logs were exported, and probably double that amount illegally, but it was only a fraction of the potential 1.5 billion m³ that the forest could have yielded. It was a typical Brazilian story of "stupendous" waste. Similarly, to the east, in the northern Argentine provinces of Chaco, Formosa, Tucuman, Santigo del Estero, and Sante Fe, and adjacent parts of the vast Chaco Boreal of Paraguay, the easily worked hardwood, *quebracho,* was being cleared at the alarming rate of over 200,000 ha/yr.[47]

Not until the attack on the Amazonian rain forest occurred in earnest after 1950 did South America prove to be the "great storehouse" for world needs that many had hoped for. But in the meantime it provided useful supplies for the locally burgeoning economies, and as a consequence was diminished.

Africa

Although it is probable that 87 million ha of forest were cleared for agriculture in tropical Africa between 1920 and 1950 (table 12.3), little is known about it, and some of what is known might well be erroneous. With the exception of the extremes of the continent in French North Africa and British South Africa, the colonizing powers had hardly got a sufficient grip on their new territories between "the scramble" of the 1880s and the beginning of the twentieth century to know what was in the forests in terms of their character, extent, and exploitation, let alone to recognize and explain deforestation or the lack of it. Africa was a "dark continent" in more ways than one. Even as late as 1945 the second edition of Lord Hailey's influential and authoritative *An African Survey* still devoted less than *one* of its 1,800-odd pages to African forests. Forests were thought to have the primary functions of conserving water and ameliorating climatic conditions, "which is often of greater importance than that which they exercise as sources of the supply of timber." Yet there was some awareness that "progressive deforestation caused by human action" had occurred, which pointed to the need to conserve supplies, particularly firewood, the universal and only energy source, and combat erosion. By the third edition of the *Survey* in 1957, the forest occupied 23 pages; but deforestation, other than as a vague background fact, was still neither analyzed nor commented on.[48]

What early twentieth-century explanations of forest change existed revolved around pejorative views of African farming practices, which dominated debates during the colonial and immediate postcolonial periods. The conventional wisdom was that, as ever, the "greatest enemy of the forest" was the native farmer,

> who clears virgin forest to plant his crops, uses the area a few years, then passes on to the new one. Fires following at frequent intervals destroy the second growth, and gradually convert forest land into park-like savanna.

Consequently, every year "thousands of square miles of forest are ruthlessly cut down for a few years' crops."[49] Homer Shantz and Curtis Marbut guessed wildly that 1 billion ha of forest been lost already and converted to grassland by farming misuse, and that another 500 million ha would go the same way in the future.

Shifting cultivation or bush fallow was the only possibility for "races backward by modern standards," said Graham Jacks and Robert Whyte in their influential book *The Rape of the Earth*. According to climax theory, they pointed out, this practice led inevitably to the creation of grasslands in addition to causing soil erosion and exhaustion, and initiating desertification. More extreme was their view that all indigenous cultivators were environmental destroyers—"in the scientific sense, parasites, all of them." The only way to stop the "destruction" of shifting agriculture was to declare forest reserves and exclude the local population, though where they would go was never discussed.[50] For the hard-liners, the natives were likened to willful and destructive children who did not know the value of their possessions:

> A child is not allowed to play with fire, although it may very much like to see the flames; in the same way . . . [the local administration] . . . cannot allow the inhabitants . . . to play fast and loose with their priceless treasures, the African forests, well knowing that the country will be permanently injured thereby.[51]

It was the Indian story all over again but with a vengeance, always working to the detriment of the shifting agriculturalist and indigenous farming practice, and denying the peoples' livelihood and history.

Nowhere was this ignorance more pronounced than in the tropical forests and forest savannas of West Africa. The antiquity of West African culture coupled with early European contact and its consequent "modernizing" influences meant that much early writing on the forest focused on this part of the continent. The forest here was/is in three broad zones, their distribution largely conditioned by decreasing precipitation and greater rainfall variability as one moves north toward the Sahara. The dense high tropical and mangrove forests occupy a belt along the coast, varying between 200 mi wide to nothing at the Dahomey Gap, and they are bounded on the north by a forest-savanna mixture in which the forest element generally diminishes with northerly latitude. Beyond that again is a wide (250 mi) belt, which eventually grades into the almost total grasslands of the Sudan zone, where there is only occasional forest along river courses. Beyond that is the Sahel.[52]

Because of the presence of quite large "islands" of dense, lush, semideciduous forest in the forest-savanna belt, successive French botanists, such as Auguste Chevalier (1911), André Aubréville (1938, 1949), and later Jacques-George Adam (1948) and Raymond Schnell (1948), designated it a natural *forest* formation that had become degraded through constant cultivation and fire. It became, therefore, a "derived" savanna. With less trees, rainfall and air humidity were reduced, which allowed the desiccating harmattan winds to penetrate further south, creating conditions under which the forest could not reestablish itself.[53]

Such explanations of human degradation were not confined to francophone Africa. The experience of the dust bowl in the United States during the 1930s was taken up enthusiastically by British foresters, who thought that the deserts were "on the march" in northern Nigeria.[54] Edward Stebbing, former director of the Indian Forest Service, toured the West African forests during the late 1930s and was convinced that the ecological equilibrium was being upset by human overuse, and that the Sahara was encroaching southward into the grasslands.[55] By the mid-1950s Harrison Church highlighted the "desperate" problem of the loss of woodland to grassland by bush firing and grazing, which then put pressure on farmers to move into the rain forest.[56] As the forest diminished and the grasslands increased stock numbers rose and tsetse fly infestation spread; it was said that the spread of the disease was almost a surrogate measure for deforestation.[57]

All contemporary observers were convinced that little of the West African coastal forest was untouched by humans. Deforestation had been "going on for centuries" but had reached "alarming proportions" only after 1900 as shifting cultivation or bush fallowing, with its periodic cutting and burning, had reduced "almost all forest" to a "secondary" status. The pauperization was clearly evident because it took at least 75 to 100 years to reestablish a reasonably mature forest, and over 250, if ever, to get back to primary forest. For example, in Sierra Leone, Harold Unwin thought that "scarcely 1 per cent of this forest remains," and in neighboring Liberia—"the forest country *par excellence*"— the "inroads of man" had reduced the coastal equatorial forests to a "dense scrub of palm, wild coffee and low scrubby trees" by 1908, whereas inland in West Africa, the rain forests of the Fouta Djallon uplands had been "eliminated in the last century and a half, since the immigration of the Fulani."[58] The contrast between the obvious modification of the coastal zone forest and the primordial nature of inland and inaccessible areas was stark. The Gola forest, straddling the Sierra Leone–Liberian border between the Morro and Mano rivers, was still only penetrable via paths made by elephants, which roamed the area freely. In the Belgian Congo (Zaire, which later became Democratic Republic of the Congo) over seven-eighths of the country was still covered with "an almost illimitable amount of unused sylvan wealth," though near the mouth and banks of the Congo River the vegetation had been reduced to "almost savannah forest."[59]

It is evident that ever since the end of the nineteenth century, the idea of forest degradation had been reproduced and elaborated through each generation of the scientific, forestry, and eventually the administrative communities. Alarm at deforestation generally preceded any analysis of it. In a way, it was a variation of the "timber famine" thesis. The vague, age-old idea of a link among climate, soils, vegetation, and "desertification" (though the word was not coined at the time) was elaborated in more scientific terms by soil scientists and ecologists, who evoked the notion of a climatic climax—an ultimate stage of succession that represented the "natural" vegetation against which the degree of current degradation could be measured. In time it became the dominant discourse and hegemonic explanation of forest destruction in the continent. But recent work by James Fairhead and Melissa Leach has shown that in the forest-savanna mosaic, far from the forest "islands" being relics of a once greater forest that disappeared under human pressure, are the effects of intensive cultivation, settlement, and fertilization, so that fallow areas became progressively more woody. Population growth has implied more forest, not less; it is a landscape "half-filled and filling with forest, not half-emptied and emptying of it" (fig. 12.5). History has been read backwards and conventional explanations of deforestation, in this part of the world, at least, turned upside down.[60]

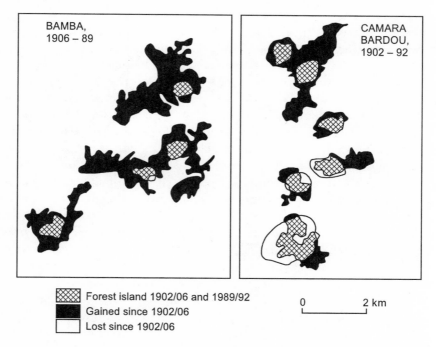

Figure 12.5 Growth of forest "islands" at Bamba (1906–89) and Camara Bardou (1902–92), Kissidougou area of Guinea. *Source:* Fairhead and Leach, 1996: 71.

Extending their critical analysis to the bulk of the West African forest belt in Sierra Leone, Liberia, Côte d'Ivoire, Ghana, Benin, and Togo, Fairhead and Leach have come to the startling conclusion that views on deforestation have been unilineal and have obscured more complex histories. The extent of the forest in the past has been grossly exaggerated, thus making any diminution appear greater. Depopulation and population shifts that have ensured forest reversal and regrowth have been ignored, recent historical climatic change favorable to tree growth has been discounted, and it is not appreciated that many forests in the open savanna are human creations based on intensive cultivation and settlement and are not relics of a forest long since gone through misuse and desiccation.[61] This is not to deny that there has been quite extensive deforestation, but it is not as great as is currently supposed. The West African story is a cautionary tale that needs to be remembered when grappling with the contemporary rhetoric about deforestation.

Just as the discourse on forest loss on the northern fringes of the West African forest belt created a predetermined mind-set for the interpretation of events, so has metal smelting. Again it has wider relevance. Time and again, whether in seventeenth- and eighteenth-century Europe or nineteenth-century United States, we have noted that the impact of metallurgy on the forests, while locally dramatic and visually spectacular, is nowhere as devastating or widespread as agricultural expansion and intensive cultivation.

The indigenous iron industry in West Africa (and tin and copper production elsewhere) had long both fascinated and perplexed observers in its antiquity, extent, technical complexity, and trade, if only because it confounded pejorative perceptions about the "level" of civilization.[62] In the Bassar region of middle Togo, for example, on the border between the equatorial forest and the savanna, there were still about 500 furnaces operating by the end of the nineteenth century, and iron goods were sent for hundreds of kilometers in all directions. Similar extensive metallurgical industry existed in the Asante region of neighboring Ghana and the plateau of Fouta Djallon, all with associated forest destruction.[63]

The demise of the once widespread iron industry has been explained as a direct result of European technological competition and the importation of cheaper and purer iron. However, imported European iron was neither cheap nor pure compared with the charcoal-derived native product, which was of high quality, easily worked, and multipurpose. The provision of that quality, it is argued by Janice Goucher, depended upon the use of dense, slow-burning hardwood trees that were suitable for charcoal making, such as *Burkea africana* (*Acacia* sp.), *Prosopis africana,* and *Zyzyphus mucronata*. Because these trees are slow-growing the suggestion is that the iron industry collapsed through lack of easily accessible fuel as trees were cut out and ecological conditions deteriorated generally.

The 26 slag heaps covering about a hectare around one furnace in Dapaa in northern Ghana would, it is claimed, have required a "staggering" minimum of 300,000 trees.[64] On the face of it, that does seem an immense amount of trees, yet if only some trees were preferred for smelting, deforestation would not have occurred—only the depletion of specific species. Even assuming all savanna trees were suitable they would not all have been felled simultaneously, so that the time scale of felling would have to be considered

Table 12.4 Area needed to produce 300,000 trees in savanna woodland under different assumptions of densities and regrowth cycles

Period of Felling (yrs.)	Tree-Growth Periods (30-Year Regrowth)				
	30	60	90	120	300
Regrowth Cycles	1	2	3	4	10
Original Density and Avg. Spacing					
2500/ha (2m × 2m)	120 ha	60 ha	40 ha	30 ha	12 ha
625/ha (4m × 4m)	480 ha	240 ha	160 ha	120 ha	48 ha
277/ha (6m × 6m)	1083 ha	541 ha	361 ha	270 ha	108 ha
156/ha (8m × 8m)	1923 ha	961 ha	641 ha	480 ha	192 ha
100/ha (10m × 10m)	3000 ha	1500 ha	1000 ha	750 ha	300 ha

Source: based on Fairhead and Leach, 1998: 130.

as well as the density of trees. Thus, at a density of 625 trees per ha or a spacing equivalent of 4 m × 4 m and a time scale of, say, 30 years—which is a reasonable interval for savanna trees to grow—then only 480 ha would have been needed, which is not large compared with the area felled annually by any village settlement (table 12.4). If some sort of woodland management through a coppicelike rotation of felling were adopted, then over a 60-year period and two cycles of growth a mere 240 ha would be required, and so it gets less with longer rotations. Even if the trees were very widely spaced, the area affected is nowhere near enough to produce deforestation, only local thinning and stripping.[65] The iron-smelting industry of the Bassar region of central Togo has been in existence for over 1,000 years, producing mainly hoe blades. Annual production has varied from as little as 7 tonnes per annum prior to the fourteenth century to possibly as much as 135 tonnes in the nineteenth century. Using a rule of thumb that each tonne of iron requires the charcoal produced from about 8 ha of land, then the amount of land cleared annually could be as little as 56 ha or as great as 1,080 ha; and if a 30-year regeneration cycle is assumed, then the total area of forest needed could be between 1,814 and 32,400 ha. So once again, fuel demand for iron is rarely a cause of deforestation.[66]

Far more destructive was land clearance for commercial crops, which replaced subsistence plots. Large-scale plantations often failed from a lack of knowledge about suitable soils, hydrographic regimes, and indigenous expertise. But where peasant proprietors experimented with commercial cropping of cotton, coffee, cocoa, palm oil, and rubber in familiar localities, production seemed to flourish. In the rain forest of Asante (Ashanti) around Kumase in Ghana, the local council became alarmed at the destruction, bemoaning in 1938 that "almost all the forests . . . have been converted to cocoa farms and that all attention has been diverted from the cultivation of foodstuffs." [67] It was the same around Ibadan and other large settlements: within two generations western Nigeria and the Benin borderlands had changed from unappropriated forestland, roamed by elephants, lions, and monkeys, "in which tribal wars were fought and hunters wandered over large tracts, to settled and cultivated land over which families and individuals claimed more or less exclusive rights." The whole process of conversion was going to accelerate rapidly after 1945.[68]

Table 12.5 Estimated total area in major land-use categories and change (in millions of ha) and population and livestock totals (in millions) for three major regions of South and Southeast Asia, 1920 and 1950

	Southeast Asia Subcontinent			Mainland Southeast Asia			Insular Southeast Asia			Total Change
	1920	1950	Change	1920	1950	Change	1920	1950	Change	
Total Cultivated	117.4	135.6	18.2	16.5	21.0	4.5	17.5	24.7	7.2	+29.9
Forest/ Woodland	61.1	53.9	−7.2	85.4	76.0	−9.4	150.6	134.1	−16.5	−33.1
Interrupted Woods	34.8	30.3	−4.5	45.0	44.1	−0.9	20.8	27.5	+6.7	+2.2
Forested Wetlands	3.0	2.2	−0.8	4.3	3.2	−1.1	31.4	28.4	−3.0	−4.9
Subtotal All Forest	98.9	86.4	−12.5	134.7	123.3	−11.4	202.8	190.0	−12.8	35.8
All Other Land Use	124.8	119.1	−5.7	42.7	49.6	6.9	36.1	41.7	5.5	6.7
Total	341.1	341.1		193.9	193.9		256.4	256.4		
Population	291.4	412.2	120.8	41.6	72.0	30.4	64.3	105.1	40.8	192
Livestock	235.3	303.9	68.6	19.0	28.9	9.9	16.8	27.7	10.9	89.4

Source: based on Richards and Flint, 1994: 20, 34, and 36, tables 2, 3, and 4.

South and Southeast Asia

Despite our emphasis here on Central and South America and Africa, which enter the picture for the first time, forest destruction was not standing still in South and Southeast Asia, and a mosaic of different patterns and motivations emerges. Between 1920 and 1950 the population of the region rose by 192 million and livestock numbers by 89.4 million. While some land began to be cropped twice, the easiest solution was to convert forestland to arable, so that 35.8 million ha of forest of all types was affected (table 12.5). In British India it was official policy to sacrifice forest for crops, even in hilly and mountainous districts, as on the Himalayan slopes and in Orissa Hills (see fig. 11.2 B), but railways and fuelwood demands continued to take an enormous toll.

In mainland Asia, pioneering peasant farmers cleared land for cultivation of wet paddies, especially in Thailand's Chao Phraya delta region and surrounding country, and because population densities were low, the resulting surplus of rice became the basis of a thriving export industry. In insular Southeast Asia, Indonesia and Malaysia expanded cultivation but also plantation crops, especially rubber, and with Borneo indulged in quite rapacious logging of timber for the export market.[69] It was a prelude to the great logging exploitation for global markets that was to come later.

CLEARING IN THE DEVELOPED WORLD

During the first half of the twentieth century, the great bulk of the world's timber came from the softwood coniferous forests that stretched across the northern parts of the Eurasian and American landmasses, encompassing Scandinavia and the USSR/Mongolia, and Alaska/Canada/northern United States, with important offshoots of other softwood production in the Pacific coast and the South of the United States. Although a little less than half (44.75 percent) of all the forests of the world, they contributed to a staggering three-quarters of all production. The experience of exploitation in three of the core countries of production, the United States, the USSR and Sweden, was very different. In the United States laissez-faire capitalism ran riot until tempered by regulation and self-interest; in the USSR a nominally planned economy resting on Marxist-Leninist ideology plundered the forests in the name of production; while in Sweden the semiregulatory, cooperative approach of a liberal socialist administration produced a forest about as regulated, artificial, and productive as any in the world. Together these three countries form a wide spectrum of experiences and approaches regarding the perception of the coming timber crisis, the attempt to sustain production, and the problem of deforestation.

The United States: Laissez-Faire Capitalism and Self-Interest

Even as Pinchot and his clique were proclaiming the coming timber famine, the forest was making its comeback in the eastern half of the country as farmland was abandoned. In addition, programs of fire suppression and afforestation and changing patterns of consumption augmented stands. Most important, investigators and commentators seriously underestimated the regenerative power of the forest and did not detect or perceive the trend toward regrowth.

The Forest Balance Sheet

In 1905 James Defebaugh had pointed out that in the past the country had been "drawing on the surplus," but now it was starting "to draw down on the capital funds."[70] His analogy of a financial statement or balance sheet in describing the forest resource was a good one because politicians, professional foresters, and the public alike wanted to be able to see the debits and credits. The debits or drains were reasonably well known; the credits or growth were a mystery. In order to produce a forest balance sheet, two major investigations had to be carried out that had a significance far beyond the United States alone. First, the location and extent of the forest had to be determined in order to calculate the stock, and second—and dependent on the first—the volume of timber and its rate of growth or depletion also had to be calculated, problems which Zon had grappled with, but not solved, in his world survey.

By the beginning of the century the mapping of the forest was almost complete and its size could be calculated with some reasonable accuracy. (table 12.6). The original forest was estimated to be between 950 million and 1,000 million acres (384 million and 405 million ha), of which 850 million acres (344 million ha) was commercial forest and 100–150 million acres (40.5 million to 60.7 million ha) noncommercial forest. By 1907 William Greeley estimated that only 515 million and 65 million acres (208 million and 26 million ha), respectively, remained, and although later estimates varied considerably, there was little doubt that the forest had diminished by between 300 million and 350 million acres (121 million to 142 million ha) by the beginning of the century. The future looked just as bleak: projections of past trends carried forward by Greeley to the year

Table 12.6 Estimated area of commercial and noncommercial
U.S. forest and standing saw-timber volume

Date	Commercial Forest (in millions of ha)	Non-Commercial Forest (in millions of ha)	Standing Saw-Timber Volume (in billions of ft³)
1630	344	40	635
"Original"	344	61	433
1895	227	–	192
1902	200	–	167
1907	208	26	–
1908	223	–	208
1920	188	61	185
1930	200	49	139
1944	187	66	133
1952	200	100	201
1962	206	101	203
1970	202	103	202
1977	197	102	214

Source: Clawson, 1979.

1950 suggested that another 100 million acres (40.5 million ha) would disappear in new farms, and that lumbering would create an unproductive cutover area of 182 million acres (74 million ha), leaving something like a mere 230 million acres (93 million ha) in forest.[71] It was an alarming prospect that struck at the very heart of America's self-image as the storehouse of boundless resources; the nation might be reduced to the state of some impoverished and denuded Mediterranean country. The message of dearth was underlined by the publication of Greeley's misleading maps depicting the diminishing acreage of "virgin" forests between 1620 and 1920. The fact that second- and third-growth forests more than compensated for the decrease in "first"-growth forest was ignored.[72]

But the area of a forest really tells one little about its productive capacity, its stock of timber, and its rate of growth. Such calculations were (and are) fraught with difficulties. Subjective assessments, differing measures, deliberate underestimates by large companies to avoid taxation or competition, and the changing value of different timbers all led to pessimistic interpretations and underestimates of the forest resources. The best estimates showed a volume of 635 billion ft³ (17.96 billion m³) of standing timber in the original forest, which was reduced to between 167 and 208 billion ft³ (4.73 billion and 5.89 billion m³) by the end of the nineteenth century (table 12.6). In these varied estimates, the work of E. A. Zeigler was important because he pointed out something that was known intuitively but rarely appreciated:[73] that timber harvest could not exceed net timber growth indefinitely, neither could net growth exceed harvest for very long because the standing timber accumulated to a level where no further net growth occurred unless young growth was stimulated after storm damage, fire, or decaying trees. Not only did Zeigler dismiss Greeley's fixation with "virgin" timber as unrealistic in terms of growth, but he went so far as to suggest that if all mature timber were removed and replaced by second growth, then yields would be raised by between 30 and 100 ft³/acre/annum, depending on the species and location.[74] In other words, careful production management

Table 12.7 Estimated forest volume and annual growth and drain, United States, 1909–77 (in billions of ft³)

	1909 Zeigler	1920 Greeley	1933 Copeland	1950 Forecast (I)	1950 Forecast (II)	1952 F.S.	1962 F.S.	1970 F.S.	1977 F.S.
Stock of All Standing Timber	545	746	486	634	634	603	648	680	711
Growth per Annum									
a) Actual	6.75	6.0	8.9	–	–	13.9	16.7	19.8	21.7
b) Potential									
Cutovers Restocked	–	19.5							
Virgin Timber Cut	–	8.2		10.6	21.4	27.5	–	–	≈36.0
All Forest Well Stocked and Managed	–	27.7							
Drain									
Firewood and Lumber	23.0	24.3	14.5	15.3	15.3	11.8	12.0	14.0	14.2
Fire and Insects	≈2.0	1.7	1.8	1.2	1.2	3.9	4.3	4.0	3.9
Total	25.0	26.0	16.3	16.5	16.5	15.7	16.3	18.0	18.1
Ratio									
Growth to Drain	1:3.5	1:4.3	1:1.8	1:1.5	1:0.77	1:1.13	1:0.97	1:0.90	1:0.83

Note: F.S.= U.S. Forest Service.

could increase yields and be the answer to the impending famine. This, of course, was not a revolutionary suggestion, having had its origins in the German tradition of total forest management; but the significance for the United States was that the "bounty" of a supposedly pristine nature could no longer be relied upon; humans would have to intervene and alter "the wilderness."

All this debate on area, stock, and growth fed into the calculation of the overall balance sheet of growth and drain. Although Zeigler had estimated that annual growth was 6.75 billion ft³—which was barely more than one-fourth of the estimated annual drain— it remained for Greeley in 1920 to refine the ideas and calculations further (table 12.7). The result was more alarming than the estimates of the number of acres being cleared. Growth was down to 6 billion ft³ and the drain was up to 26 billion ft³, or 4.3 times the rate of the growth. It was, said Greeley, "the steady wiping out of the original forests of the country," and grist for the alarmist mill of Pinchot and his associates.[75]

Greeley's gloomy scenario never eventuated, however, and the balance between growth and drain shifted by the time of the Copeland enquiry of 1933 into the nation's forests when the ratio between them was down to 1:1.8. Copeland's projections to 1950, based on various mixes of extensive and intensive management strategies, suggested that growth could exceed drain and redress the ratio to parity or even below. By 1950 the lower of the two estimates of twenty years before had been surpassed. In 1952 the actual annual growth was 13.9 billion ft³, and it rose steadily to 22.5 billion ft³ in 1986 (fig. 12.6). Pinchot's prediction of nil stock by 1940 proved wrong; the forest famine and the specter of forest death were over, and the rebirth of the forest had begun. Its potential growth is currently thought to be 36 billion ft³.[76]

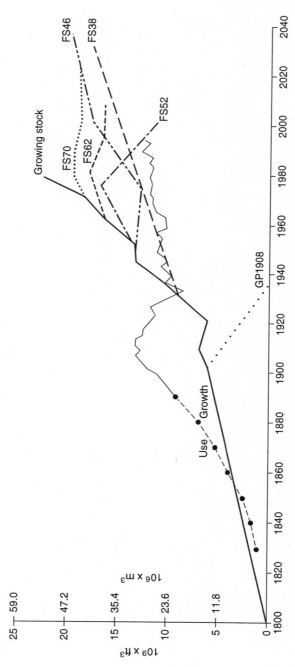

Figure 12.6 Annual net growth and use of timber in the United States, 1800–2040. *FS* denotes Forest Service; *GP*, Gifford Pinchot, followed by date of projection. *Sources*: Clawson, 1979, with additional information from USDA, Forest Service, 1982, 1990.

From Death to Rebirth

The remarkable turnaround of the forest from death to rebirth after the 1930s was a combination of many changes and trends that are representative of the changing status of forests in the developed world. First, the enormous growth of trees was possible only because the old forest had been removed and allowed to recolonize the cutover area with second growth. Second, a vigorous program of fire control was initiated under the Clark-McNary Act of 1924, which provided funds for federal and state schemes of cooperation. From a staggering annual burn of 53 million acres (21.4 million ha) in 1931 alone, the number of acres affected annually dropped steadily to less than one-tenth of that amount by the 1960s.[77] Third, reforestation was encouraged under a number of federal-state cooperative initiatives, which were also extended to private landowners under soil conservation programs. Most significant of all, the lumber companies realized that it was no longer feasible to abandon old plant and move on to new stands (even if there were any) as they had done throughout the nineteenth century; it was cheaper to maintain the expensive capital equipment and its economic and social infrastructure, and replant the surrounding forests. How much forest was replanted is hard to say, but it must have been at least 1 million acres (approximately 405,000 ha) per annum.[78] Fourth, per capita consumption of lumber has dropped phenomenally, from a peak of 82 ft³ in 1906 to a little less then one-third of that amount, with the increasing use of substitute materials such as aluminium, steel, and (later) plastics, despite a doubling of the population. Fuelwood consumption fell even more dramatically with conversions to natural gas and electricity, although plywood and pulp consumption have both risen.[79]

Most important, throughout the eastern half of the country farmland was being abandoned and reverting to forest. From as early as 1840, farmers were leaving land that was difficult to farm and either moved to better farmland further west or migrated to the urban industrial centers. The process began in the Middle Atlantic states of New York, Pennsylvania, and New Jersey after 1880 and affected the east-central states of Ohio, Indiana, and West Virginia after 1920. Later still, the same happened in the South as old cotton and tobacco fields reverted to pine forest. Knowledge about abandonment is remarkably sparse. In a society imbued with the frontier ideals of development, progress, and the virtues of forest clearance, abandonment was retrogressive, difficult to comprehend, and even sinful to contemplate, and therefore ignored tactfully.

Although there were hints in the Copeland Report of what was happening, the implications for forest growth were never spelled out. However, an analysis of census data in the 31 easternmost states shows that the net loss of cleared land between 1910 and 1959 was 17.7 million ha (43.8 million acres; see table 12.8), with 26.5 million ha (65.5 million acres) having been abandoned mainly in eastern Ohio, western Pennsylvania, New York, New England, and the whole southern Piedmont, but 8.8 million ha (21.7 million acres) gained, largely out of the forest, mainly in Florida, Minnesota, Iowa, Arkansas, and Louisiana. In other words, 362,000 ha (894,000 acres) have been lost to agriculture and added to the forest in every year between 1910 and 1959. During the next 20 years the trend has continued with another 9.55 million ha (23.6 million acres), giving a significantly higher rate of 477,500 ha (1,180,000 acres) lost to agriculture and added to the forest every year.[80]

Table 12.8 Cleared farmland, United States, 1910–79 (in millions of ha)

	Conterminous U.S.	Thirty-one Eastern States		
	Total Farmland	Total Farmland	Farm Woodland	Cleared Farmland
1910	356.7	198.4	58.4	140.0
1920	388.0	193.4	52.8	140.7
1925	374.0	180.4	44.0	136.4
1930	400.7	179.4	44.6	134.9
1935	426.7	192.0	53.5	138.5
1940	431.0	186.1	42.9	143.2
1945	462.0	189.2	48.0	141.3
1950	470.0	190.4	55.0	135.4
1954	468.7	184.1	54.0	130.1
1959	453.3	168.1	45.8	122.3
1965	447.9	160.3	38.7	121.6
1969	428.8	149.5	31.6	117.8
1975	410.2	139.0	31.4	107.5
1979	–	142.1	29.3	112.7

Sources: Hart, 1968; and U.S. Department of Agriculture, *Agricultural Census, USA,* 1910–79.

The trend still continues. These figures are mind-boggling in their millions and hundreds of thousands, and are therefore difficult to comprehend, a problem compounded by the fact that the pattern of regrowth is just as individual, piecemeal, and difficult to detect as was initial clearing in the forest during the last three centuries. A map of a single county tells the story better than any words can (fig. 12.7). Carroll County is about 30 miles southwest of Atlanta, Georgia, and between 1937 and 1974 8,496 acres of forest succumbed to agriculture and a further 515 to urban expansion; but 90,807 acres of once-agricultural land reverted to forest and a further 6,171 acres to urban uses.[81] It is a story that has been repeated thousands of times in the eastern states; after 1974 even more land has been abandoned, so that the forest is coming back.

The Soviet Union: The State Supreme

The forces of change that were unleashed in Russia during the mid-nineteenth century as landowners attempted to recoup their losses after the 1861 emancipation of the serfs (see p. 290 in chapter 10) were augmented as the country entered upon a new and unprecedented era of capitalist industrial expansion at the turn of the century. A royal edict of 1888 to conserve the forests was ignored, and at least another 3 million ha were destroyed during the next two decades as over 2 million peasant loggers and countless forced laborers (to say nothing of tens of millions rural households) hacked away at the country's wealth: "anarchy prevailed: the exchequer, the aristocracy, mining enterprises, military authorities and private landowners treated the forests with impunity and with a total disregard for conservation and replacement."[82] Undoubtedly, the sheer size and ubiquity of the country's forest, which comprises one-fifth of the world total, nearly a quarter of its growing stock, and just over half the volume of all coniferous forests, engendered a sense of their endless bounty, which encouraged profligacy and waste.

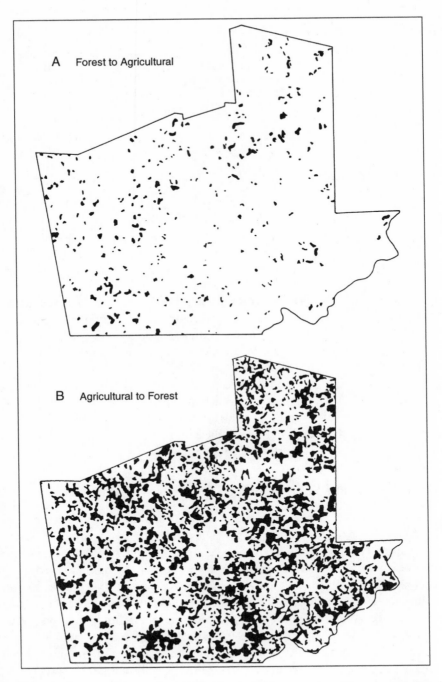

Figure 12.7 Abandonment of *B,* agricultural land to forest; and *A,* conversion of forest to agricultural land, Carroll County, Georgia, 1937–74. *Source:* Hart, 1980, 514–16.

And it got no better in revolutionary times.[83] Conflict caused destruction. The depredations of World War I and the ensuing civil war were hastily and recklessly amended by even more rapacious cutting. During World War II the wholesale logging and transport of lumber from Russia to Germany and the scorched-earth policies and general destruction, much of which occurred in the forests surrounding the Pripyat marshes and north to Leningrad, may well have led to the destruction of another 20 million ha of forest in Nazi-held territories, from the Baltic through Byelorussia to the northern Ukraine. Savage Japanese exploitative logging in Sakhalin Island (as well as in Manchuria and Inner Mongolia) must be added to this toll.[84]

But even if one puts to one side these catastrophic and unusual events, all the evidence available supports Boris Kamarov's devastating judgment that it was the Soviet system of centralized planning, introduced in 1928, that initiated a new era of state plundering that led to the widespread "destruction of nature," whether flora, fauna, or landscape.[85] With centralized planning, tsarist indifference was replaced by cynical Communist mismanagement. Doctrinaire Marxist-Leninist ideology sanctioned human interference with nature as laudable and correct, so that environmental outcomes were considered minor and temporary aberrations that were inevitable but irrelevant in the goal of a creating a superior economic and social system. In addition, the system of financial rewards and production bonuses to state managers and producers was such that there was simply no incentive to behave in the long-term interest of the resource, the state, or society at large, *or* of the ultimate efficiency of the production unit. A multiplicity of state organizations and departments (about 34), along with over 10,000 logging units, worked either in ignorance of or deliberately against each other in order to reach production targets. Targets went up with each Five-Year Plan and production rose to meet them (table 12.9), irrespective of the ability of the forest to sustain such cutting. Areas of supply (Siberia) got

Table 12.9 Industrial and domestic timber removals (in millions of m³), U.S.S.R., 1913–83

	Industrial Removals			Domestic Removals			
	Roundwood	Fuelwood	Total	Roundwood	Fuelwood	Total	All Removals
1913	27.2	33.4	60.6	28.0	204.0	232.0	292.6
1928	36.0	25.7	61.7	27.0	215.0	242.0	303.7
1930	96.7	50.5	147.2	n/a	n/a	n/a	–
1935	117.0	93.1	210.1	22.0(a)	201.0(a)	223.0(a)	433.1
1940	117.9	128.2	246.1	6.0	130.0	136.0	382.1
1945	61.6	106.8	168.4	10.0	130.0	140.0	308.4
1950	161.0	105.0	266.0	8.0	92.0	100.0	366.0
1955	212.1	122.0	334.1	7.0	63.0	70.0	404.1
1960	261.5	108.0	369.5	10.0	30.0	40.0	409.5
1965	273.6	104.5	378.1	6.0	32.0	38.0	416.5
1970	298.5	86.5	385.0	7.0	30.0	37.0	422.0
1975	312.9	82.1	395.0	6.0	29.0	35.0	425.0
1980	277.7	78.9	356.3	n/a	n/a	n/a	n/a
1983 (est.)	274.0	83.0	357.0	n/a	n/a	n/a	n/a

Source: Barr, 1988: 242.
Note: (a) Record for domestic removals is for 1932.

effectively more distant from areas of consumption (Europe); and on a more local scale, the reckless cutting of forests around new giant, expensive wood chemistry plants at Zima, Birusa, Yurty, Tulun, and Chunsky in Irkutsk Province led to reverse journeys of supplies from Europe to Siberia. Deforestation was not acknowledged, nor was it problematized, and even as late as the 1950s it appears that there was even ignorance of basic sustained-yield management. Thus, defective and divided administration, poor managerial practices, and ignorance, together with the erratic events from 1900 to 1945, with problems of war and survival interspersed with social upheaval, led to a progressive deterioration of the quality of the growing stock. As a consequence, throughout the European Soviet Union there were "extensive areas of relatively unproductive and uneconomical forest land primarily comprising poor-quality deciduous species and mixed age stands of conifers." [86]

The comparison with the United States from the 1920s to 1940s could not have been more stark. Considerations of efficient management, which had become such a constraint on capitalist entrepreneurs that sheer self-interest, guided by enlightened federal intervention, eventually promoted better forest management and conservation measures, never emerged in the USSR. Despite the superior size of the Russian forest, it was producing only a fraction of the wood of the United States. Despite comprehensive planning and legislation, and even the apparent increase in the area of forest (e.g., 738 million ha in 1961 to 792 million ha in 1978) as more distant areas were drawn into national inventories, supplies actually diminished. Even putting aside disastrous fires, about 40 percent of the annual harvest of approximately 400 million m³ was lost in various stages of production, a little less than 10 percent was used as scrap fuel, and only half reached the customer. Consequently, by 1950 the Soviet Union was suffering from a unique form of deforestation that was set to get much worse in the subsequent decades. It was not brought on by the pressure of peasants seeking land, the influx of unemployed urban dwellers into forested areas, or plantation agriculture, but by the unwieldy centralized planning apparatus, where the size and multiplicity of forest cutters caused destruction over vast areas while paralyzing production that never satisfied needs.

Little has improved in the post-Soviet era. The legacy of overuse and unsustainable exploitation, together with the collapse of the previous network of command and transaction, shortage of capital, decaying plant, and political chaos, has contributed to a plummeting output. At present the Russian forest is an underused and wasting asset. [87]

Sweden: "Negotiated Order"

At some intermediate point between the laissez-faire capitalism of the United States and the doctrinaire communism of the Soviet Union, lay the forest experience of Sweden—a mixture of state intervention and private cooperation—which produced what Per Stjernquist has called aptly "a negotiated order" of exploitation. [88]

By the end of the eighteenth century the oak, hazel, and beech forests of southern and southeastern Sweden were severely affected by the inroads of peasant agriculture and iron smelting. [89] The practice of burn-baiting to improve fertility on poor soils in order to get an occasional crop of rye and hay had reduced much of the deciduous forest to heather, which was then colonized by birch and alder. Elsewhere, fuelwood procurement and cattle grazing in commonly held forests had thinned and altered the forest.

With a rapidly expanding population after 1820, forest use grew so great that it was no longer self-replenishing as it had once been, especially as the industry augmented the inroads of agriculture. By the early nineteenth century Sweden's output of 50,000 tons of bar iron required about 1 million m³ of wood in the mines, and 3 million m³ for charcoal for smelting. Glass, lime, and tar works all added to the drain on the forest.

The lowering of the British import tariff on Swedish timber in 1840 caused a boom in the coniferous forests of Norrland as both national and particularly foreign companies indulged in a free-for-all, cut-out-and-get-out exploitation of the old-growth stands. The frontier of exploitation pushed north between 1840 and 1875; sawmills were set up on every convenient break of slope on the eastward-flowing rivers which funneled the timber to the Gulf of Bothnia.[90] So extensive and indiscriminate was the cutting in Norrland that supplies dwindled, and the lumber companies began to buy up farms and the forest common. This was particularly worrisome because it meant the gradual elimination of forest grazing, which had made farming in these northern marginal areas just about possible. The precarious nature of farming was an emotive issue striking at the very heart of the concept of being Swedish, especially from the 1880s onward, when migration of landless rural workers to North America was reaching massive proportions. The demographic vitality, skills, and talents of the nation seemed to be hemorrhaging.

Bit by bit the state intervened to counteract these trends, and by 1903 had set up regional forestry boards composed of rural landowners and staffed by trained foresters. Their job was to promote the multiple use of the forest, and stop or regulate purchases of rural land by lumber companies so that the traditional farming practices of forest grazing could be stabilized. To this end, forest ownership was "frozen" in proportions that are still in force today—namely, approximately 25 percent each to companies and to the state, and the remaining half to private owners. Gradually, the agrarian aims changed, and it was realized that the land grew trees best. Private farm owners were cajoled and persuaded to abandon forest farming and accept the forest as the single-purpose producer of wood, particularly in the south, where the time required for tree regeneration is approximately 75 years, half of what it is in Norrland. Further acts followed in 1918, 1923, and 1948, consolidating state regulation with the avowed aim of a gradual but firm "public direction of private forestry."[91] In the process, productivity has increased as deciduous woods have been replaced by coniferous forests (down from 40 percent of southern forests in 1920 to 14 percent in 1977), spruce has replaced pine *(Pinus sylvestris),* and more recently the high-yielding American Lodgepole pine *(Pinus contorta)* is replacing all other trees. The forest is no longer a wilderness of old-growth mature timber but an almost totally managed human artifact of even-aged, even-spaced exotic trees. It is manipulated by thinning and fertilizing, disease and fire control. The progressive diminishing of the number of dead trees, or "snags," as most trees that grow are productive, healthy trees, is a good summary measure of the human manipulation of the forest (fig. 12.8).[92]

Rather like the United States, with its fears of shortages and timber famine, Swedish conservation measures have been driven by anticipated dearth supported, it must be admitted, by local and regional shortages. But when reliable records became available

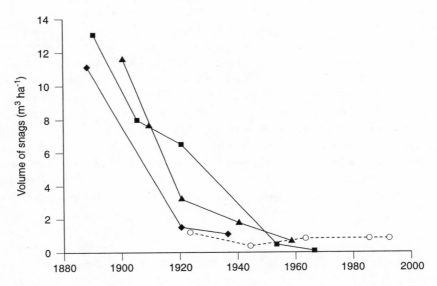

Figure 12.8 Decline in number of dead standing trees (snags) in four forests in central Sweden, 1885–1998. *Source:* Linder and Östlund, 1998: 15.

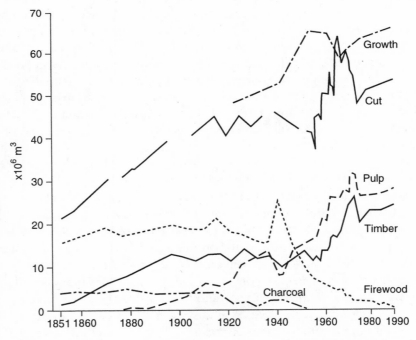

Figure 12.9 Swedish forest budget: Annual growth and cut, and wood use, 1861–1990. *Source:* Hägerstrand and Lohm, 1990: 614.

during the 1920s, it was found that the volume of wood extracted was less than the volume added by growth, something which lasted until the mid-1950s, when the regrowth of previously cut forest began to be apparent (fig. 12.9). Current growth may also be due to a higher density of introduced spruce, but others suggest controversially that the increased flow of nitrogen through atmospheric pollution may probably act as a fertilizer. Some trees may even "be forced to grow to death because other necessary nutrients are no longer able to match the intake of nitrogen," and even the acidification of the soils may be leading to the leaching out of deleterious nutrients in the bedrock, enhancing the relatively poor soil.[93]

* * *

WHEN THE midpoint of the century was reached, the world forests were broadly divided into two kinds. There were those that were managed carefully for production and/or environmental protection and leisure, though often unwittingly at great sacrifice to their ultimate diversity and ecological viability,[94] and there were those that were hacked and felled either to create land to grow food or provide a source of ready cash. There was nothing very new in this division; in some form or another it had already been in existence for several hundreds of years. What was new was the broad and fairly consistent relationship of surplus with temperate forests, and dearth with tropical forests. What the temperate world lacked it bought with its superior wealth from the tropical, often, as in the case of Japan and several European countries, in an effort to conserve national timber supplies and forests while depleting those of the exporting countries. Of all the countries of the developed world, only the United States had timber in such abundance that it was both importer and exporter at one and the same time. Global solutions had been found for the scares of a timber famine that had characterized the opening years of the century, but they were not going to suffice in the closing half of the century, when considerations other than the simple supply of timber, such as global warming and biodiversity, began to alter the whole discourse on deforestation.

Chapter 13

The Great Onslaught, 1945–95: Dimensions of Change

The destruction in modern times of a forest that is millions of years old is a major event in the world's history. It is larger in scale than the clearing of the forests in temperate Eurasia and America, and it will be accomplished in a much shorter time.
—PAUL W. RICHARDS, "The Tropical Rain Forest" (1973)

Tropical forests are among the world's least well known environments yet they are central to an understanding of fundamental problems of evolution and ecology.
—DUNCAN POORE, "The Values of Tropical Moist Forest Ecosystems" (1976)

The one process now going on that will take millions of years to correct is the loss of genetic and species diversity by the destruction of natural habitats. This is the folly our descendents are least likely to forgive us.
—EDWARD O. WILSON, *Biophilia* (1984)

THE CATACLYSMIC events of World War II altered the world's forests more surely than any "end of the century" of about 50 years before could have ever brought about. But it was not the five years of conflict, devastating as they were, that caused deforestation; rather, it was the aftermath of political, economic, technological, and demographic changes that they unleashed during subsequent decades. These changes were rapid and far-reaching, causing massive disruption to global patterns everywhere, and bringing with them a new concern about the nature and intensity of change itself. Change and the concern it provokes is not new,[1] but after 1945 it seemed to reach especially worrisome levels of pace, magnitude, and environmental significance compared to anything that had gone before.

It is commonly supposed that the biggest changes that humans have made to the earth relate to nineteenth-century industrialization and the flow of materials and energy through the chain of extraction, production, consumption, and disposal. But the human onslaught on the world's biomes has probably been equally revolutionary in its impact. Its signs were already present during the hitherto ignored 1920s and 1930s, when global clearing was just above 11 million ha, at least 70 percent of that occurring in the tropical forests.

But after 1950 the rate went up slightly and was *wholly* in the tropical forest. Paul Richards got it just about right when he said in 1973 that tropical deforestation was "a major event in the world's history" that was "larger in scale than the clearing of the forests in temperate Eurasia and America, and it will be accomplished in a much shorter time."[2] Calculations of how much forest has been lost vary enormously and are hotly debated, but it is probably safe to say that between 1950 and 1980 a total of 318 million ha[2] disappeared in the tropical world (table 12.2), and a further 11 million were cleared in China. In contrast, the forests of the developed countries of the temperate world declined by a mere net 7 million ha, those of the USSR. and the developed Pacific countries falling by 11 million and 12 million ha, respectively, but those of the United States and Europe rising by 3 million and 13 million ha so that the amount of land in forests has remained essentially the same. Thus, a global total of 336 million ha net had disappeared, almost all the clearing being accounted for by the expansion of cropland, with some conversion to pastures. Since 1980 deforestation has accelerated, so that perhaps another 220 million ha have been wiped away, at a rate of over 15 million ha (150,000 k[2]) a year. In a little under half a century, approximately 555 million ha have gone, and there is no end in sight. In the whole history of deforestation there has been nothing comparable to this rate.

The massive change to the world's forests has generated a vast amount of new information on deforestation. Whereas we struggled to find this information for past eras, the last 50 years has produced an overwhelming surfeit of data that is difficult to digest, and is being added to daily as books, articles, and satellite data, all the products of concerned and well-funded academic, environmental, and governmental enterprises, flow into the libraries and Websites of the world. Yet, as before, there is much uncertainty about where, when, how, and why deforestation is happening. These basic questions are approached in the next two chapters in much the same way as in previous parts of this book. This chapter basically addresses the driving forces and cultural climates that inform the issue of the current attack on the forests and the reactions to it, while chapter 14 explores the regional locations and incidences of that change.

The forces that drive current change in the forests and the climate of opinion that accompanies them have three major dimensions that can be summarized as cause, concern, and calibration. First, why has "The Great Onslaught" happened? Answers to that vexed question lie in the political, economic, technical, and demographic changes that have occurred since 1945, all within the context of a global system of trade, commerce, and power. Increasingly, national explanations are inadequate and the global view is the only way to understand events. Second, how and why did deforestation move from being, at best, a national concern to become a global environmental crisis? How did traditional concerns of diminishing timber supply, lack of self-sufficiency, and land destabilization that were almost wholly confined to the developed world, become augmented and even replaced by new concerns of wider significance, such as deleterious climatic change, rising sea levels, and the loss of biodiversity, which affected the developing world in particular? Finally, how is change measured, and how accurate is it? Deforestation is a seemingly simple issue, but in reality it is one fraught with difficulties. It is this intertwining of the causes, concerns, and calibrations of forest destruction that forms an essential background to the story of contemporary tropical deforestation.

THE CAUSES OF CHANGE: "A WORLD LOSING SHAPE"

The immense complexity of World War II sent out political, economic, technological, and demographic ripples that reached every part of the globe, whether it was involved in actual conflict or not. In that portion of the world ecosystem dominated by tropical rain forests, change could mean only one thing—the alteration and destruction of the dominant land cover.

Political and Economic

One of the most obvious changes after 1945 was the end of empire as the European powers retreated from their overseas possessions, which were predominantly in the tropical world. Some disengagement had already happened before World War II, but war weariness, postwar economic weakness, rising local nationalism, and a general sentiment against the colonial system turned halting moves into a general and rapid retreat after 1945.[3] Between 1947 and 1948 Britain quit its Indian empire, which became India, Pakistan, and Burma, and the Dutch quit Indonesia. The bulk of Africa and the small Caribbean and Pacific island territories shifted to self-rule between 1954 and 1965, many in the short space of the four years between 1958 and 1962. The Portuguese empire in Africa (Angola and Mozambique), the oldest of them all, was the last to collapse, in 1975.

Political independence did not necessarily bring economic independence. The power of Europe in global political and economic affairs, while still significant, was now augmented and even overshadowed by that of the United States. Additionally, the postwar rivalry between the "the West" and the Eastern bloc led to the notion of a "third world," nominally independent but courted and cajoled by both camps. With very few exceptions, third world states were African or South and Southeast Asian, excolonial, underdeveloped, and tropical. It was these newly emerging countries, with all their special problems, that saw the greatest impacts on their forests. As population soared whatever economic gains had been made since independence were reduced or swallowed up. Consequently, strains on the forest increased as it became one of the last sources of new land for the extension of cultivation and pasture, and for fuelwood for heating, cooking, and even industry. Moreover, spontaneous migration—and planned settlement schemes, as in Brazil, Indonesia, and Malaysia—ate into the forest. Latin and Central America were a little different. Although ostensibly independent, most of these countries were deeply in the thrall of the United States, but most displayed at least some of the third world characteristics of poverty and underdevelopment, all tinged with a special Latin American character of deeply polarized social classes. Added to all this, the economies of the West, which recovered after about 1960, had a voracious demand for timber and other resources for reconstruction and expansion, as did a few selected countries in the developing world (such as Japan), where rising affluence boosted consumption.

Generally, third world governments were prepared to meet the "Western" demand for timber by mining their forest stock mercilessly in the form of whole logs, sawn timber, and wood chips, in order to gain sorely needed hard currency to aid development. Trees were cash and their replacement by tropical plantation crops was perceived also as cash, but with a more frequent turnover than trees. Even if governments did not acquiesce in mining and stripping the forests, powerful minority elites, sometimes in collusion with government—and even government itself—plundered them for their own gain. Thus, deprivation, stark economic necessity and inequality, and the perceived remedies for these, were all forces that "drove" deforestation.

Technological and Demographic

The unprecedented strain on the world's forest resources was exacerbated by a few simple but significant technological changes. The development of gasoline-powered motors and their widespread use after 1945 in trucks, tractors, and chain saws introduced mobility and versatility, thereby altering the scale of production. From now on exploitation did not have to be carried out by big business and heavy capital investment, though they often were. Now the individual settler/logger with a bit of cash or credit to purchase a saw and truck could wreak high-tech havoc (plate 13.1). Consequently, almost nowhere in the world was too remote to be exploited, and because of the perfection of techniques to reconstitute vegetable fiber into boards and packaging paper/cardboard, no wood was too inferior to be harvested and used.

Far less obvious, but of far greater importance than the technological changes in forest exploitation—or, for that matter, the political and economic changes—was the wholesale implementation of improved Western medical technology in the developing world to eliminate diseases and epidemics, and alleviate obvious misery, suffering, and mortality. There was some evidence of improvements taking effect even during the pre–World War II decades. But after 1950, better medicine, improved sanitation, and pest control led to better general public health, causing a demographic explosion that was to be a major driving force underlying all change.

Although these demographic changes were gathering momentum during the 1950s and early 1960s, they were largely ignored, or if recognized, they were not viewed with much concern. By and large, population numbers were not high on international agendas, as there was a widespread faith that the science and technology which had created the increase would also cushion it. There were a few exceptions, such as Fairfield Osborn's *Our Crowded Planet* of 1962, which predicted the "wild proliferation of men" and called the "pace of reproduction . . . cancer-like, and a "threat to man's well-being"; but Fairfield Osborn, William Vogt, and like people were dismissed as "lugubrious wailing . . . Neo-Malthusian Jeremiahs" by boosters such as Earle Parker Hanson, and that was a common reaction.[4] Generally demographers seemed more preoccupied with the phenomenon of the miraculous but short-lived Western "baby-boom," which was to last for only about a decade before reproduction subsided to mere replacement level, or even below. The radical acceleration of growth, the precipitous decline of deaths, and the phenomenal rise of numbers even in the poorest countries of the developing third world were grossly underestimated and largely passed them by.

Not until the publication of the *Population Bomb* by Paul and Anne Ehrlich in 1968 was the full extent of population growth realized, and even then it was discounted by

Plate 13.1 One person with a chain saw can create high-tech havoc in a forest. Parabara, Guyana. (Jevan Berrange, South American Pictures.)

some as alarmist. The reality was that between 1950 and 1985 the world population nearly doubled, from 2,515 million to 4,853 million (see table 9.3), and the developing World's proportion of that total rose from two thirds to three quarters (67%–76%).[5] Still, the scale of change was ignored: projections of future growth were based on the assumption that the developing world would go through the same demographic transition (delayed and protracted, to be sure) as had the Western world as affluence increased and births fell. The expectation was for a relatively modest growth of population of between 1 and 1.5 percent per annum, rather than the 2–3 percent that was soon to rage across Africa, Latin America, and Southeast Asia.[6] In 1949 Fairfield Osborn had thought that the total world population might reach 3.6 billion by the end of the century, when the "limits of the earth" would be clearly visible. But even in his pessimism he was far too optimistic; it passed 6 billion in 1999, and quite credible projections to 2020 suggest that about 80 percent of the world's population of 8 billion will be in tropical countries (see table 9.3). It is commonly conceded that the increasing numbers in those countries will put further pressures on their forests.[7]

The "Multilayered Cake" of Causes

The main causes of contemporary deforestation seem simple enough and easily isolated. From time immemorial it has been expanding population numbers and increased technological abilities to promote change that has placed people in competition with all other life forms for the remaining niches of the world. More land goes into cultivation, shifting agriculture is extended, fallows are shortened, and more livestock are grazed more intensively. Timber extraction and fuelwood gathering are promoted, as are technological innovations. It is a simple land use problem and is particularly evident wherever there is a significant subsistence element in the economy.[8] And this basic demand has not changed much in recent decades, except that marginally greater affluence and the improved technology of farming, clearing, and felling has accelerated change, which leads to a greater consumption of wood products for construction, warmth, and energy.[9]

But more recently the simple central facts of numbers, affluence, and technology have been augmented by other leading or underlying causes.[10] For some it is not population numbers per se that are the cause, but the emphasis that one places on the numbers and their complex interplay with other socioeconomic factors. The debate is driven by much emotional heat along with political and intellectual agendas. Broadly speaking, neo-Malthusians see global population increase as leading to environmental degradation,[11] while cornucopians think that population growth stimulates technological and social change, and even enhances the environment.[12] Neoclassical political economists think that costs are not allocated correctly, so that effects and solutions are distorted,[13] while neo-Marxists and like-thinking political economists, in addition to totally rejecting neo-Malthusian arguments as ideologically self-serving, think that the capitalist quest for profits and accumulated capital requires unsustainable exploitation, socioeconomic difference, and the creation of inequality and poverty. Underdevelopment, then, is not merely a result of deforestation but a cause of it.[14] The differences in these positions reflect less the conflicting evidence than the conflicting interpretations of the same evidence because all approaches are ideological and underpinned by a definite set of assumptions.

But beyond population numbers, which other causes are dominant and what emphasis should be placed on them are questions that are vigorously debated. Thus, for some the blame for deforestation falls on such additional factors as the lack of employment opportunities, inequality of distribution of assets (particularly land), exploitative private enterprise and weak government control, misdirected past policies of aid agencies, national indebtedness, poverty, and corruption as the elite groups having economic and political control in society accumulate profits through the extension of commercial logging. All these factors seem well validated in many cases. "Usually," concludes Erik Eckholm, "uncontrolled deforestation is a symptom of society's inability to get a grip on other fundamental development problems." [15]

There is no doubt, also, that national and international policies toward forest use are often ill devised and imprudent, and have "failed" through undervaluing the environmental functions of the forest resource. Inadvertently—or even intentionally—they aggravate losses by encouraging inefficient forest industries, and therefore promote undue exploitation. [16]

In contrast with these largely theoretical statements, over a dozen empirical, econometric analyses support some of the relationships, particularly that of deforestation with population density. In two studies Matti Palo looked at a vast array of variables in 76 countries, as did Julia Allen and Douglas Barnes in 19 countries, and they found a positive relationship between increasing population growth and density and deforestation, and a weak relationship between agricultural expansion and deforestation. Allen and Barnes also found a positive relationship between wood use and logging and deforestation. [17] Doris Capistrano has emphasized the impact that agricultural export prices—and to a lesser extent domestic fiscal policies, such as the devaluation of exchange rates or the rising burden of repaying debts—have in inducing agricultural expansion, and James Kahn and Judith McDonald have pointed the finger at international debt. In yet another study Alan Grainger found a positive relationship not only between population density and deforestation but also with gross national product, because it leads to greater demand for food, while the Allen-Barnes and Palo studies did not. On a different tack Dal Didia found "a strong negative correlation between the rate of tropical deforestation and the level of democracy" as measured by various indices indicative of democratic institutions. [18]

Somewhere between the two extremes of the "hard" numerical data of these quantitative analyses and the "softer" social values of the qualitative explanations is the judgment of three major international organizations, the World Resources Institute, the World Bank, and the United Nations Development Programme, which cite the expansion of agriculture as the biggest cause of deforestation, exacerbated by socioeconomic inequality and unequal land distribution and pressure on land. In recent years the WRI seems to have deemphasized the sociopolitical arguments and stressed more the environmental. Degradation of land and forest stands from intensified land use on poor tropical soils and from logging are seen as the leading causes of deforestation. More recently still, it has come down on the side of population growth, buffered or increased by "government policies, the legal system, access to capital and technology, the efficiency of industrial production, inequality in the distribution of land and resources, poverty in the South and conspicuous consumption in the North," all compounding "the environmental impact of human activity." [19]

The realization that deforestation is a complex and multifaceted process operating at various scales, in various places, and with a multiplicity of variables augmenting and sometimes even canceling its impact, has induced other researchers to attempt a more holistic and global explanation rather than reliance on one, or a few, testable variables alone. One such attempt to model the process is illustrated in figure 13.1. Alan Grainger sees deforestation as an interrelated system of negative and positive feedback loops in

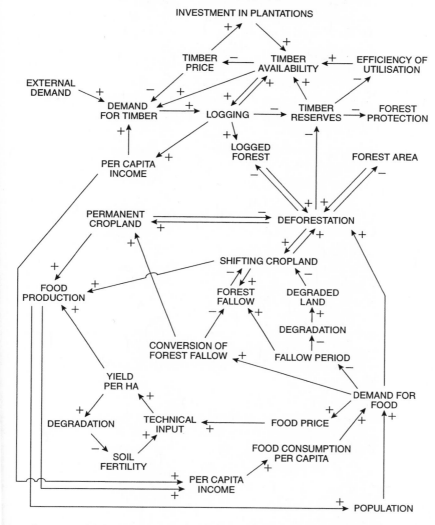

Figure 13.1 The causes of deforestation: A causal loop diagram of a systems model of national land use.
Source: Grainger, 1990: 55.

which an important two-fold distinction can made in causation: "types of forest exploita-tion" and "mechanisms of deforestation."[20] Forest exploitation consists of any form of land use that modifies or replaces forest cover, either temporarily or permanently. It could include shifting cultivation of varying fallow lengths, and even pastoralism. Permanent agriculture (cropping or ranching) and the creation of settlements are other modifiers, with the third leg of the exploitation trilogy being logging. However, all these are essen-tially a reflection of the entire socioeconomic framework that constitutes the second por-tion of the causation, the "mechanisms of deforestation." These include population in-crease, rising per capita incomes, accessibility, and environmental considerations. In Grainger's analysis it is these latter "mechanisms" that control the "types" of exploitation and hence the rate of deforestation. Thus, for example, rising per-capita consumption of food could lead to a positive response in the expansion of the cultivated area at the expense of the forest, but ultimately to a negative feedback as soil degradation culminates in cropland abandonment and reforestation.

Out of the bewildering complexity of the debate as to which human causes drive land-cover change, particularly deforestation, a number of things seem clear. First, whatever driving force is in play can either augment or lessen a deforestation change. For example, rising interest rates or an increase in agricultural prices will increase deforestation because they provide an incentive for further clearing. At the same time, however, they decrease soil erosion on cultivated land, as it pays to conserve the soil. Second, there is no global, let alone regional, uniformity of deforestation; different causes can have the same effect. For example, deforestation in Borneo and parts of the Philippines stems from logging for export; in peninsular Malaysia it is due to agricultural clearing. Third, even if the underlying causes are agreed upon, no one is prepared to agree on what constitutes a sufficient explanation for why this is so.[21]

Perhaps the last word on the complexity of the many causes and dominant cultural climates impelling deforestation can be found in the perceptive and biting critique of Nicholas Guppy during the early 1980s. He likened the attempt to explain the sudden acceleration of deforestation to "slicing into a multilayered cake." On the surface are the obvious factors—population growth, increased need of land for agriculture, stock raising and settlement, the wish to raise capital for development, and a rapidly growing demand for forest products. Yet these are not necessarily decisive or even important causes, because

> underneath are other layers—of social mores, of political expedients, of national and global economics, and of ideological conflict . . . [so that] . . . almost everywhere destroying rainforest is a means of *avoiding* tackling real problems by pursuing chimeras: a "license to print money" which yields quick cash at the cost of ultimate catastrophe.

He thought that these underlying layers included cropping of unsuitable soils, ignorance of the environmental benefits of forests, inequitable landownership, the political entrenchment and aggrandizement of local elites, and the lending policies of Western governments and financial agencies (such as the World Bank) that allowed such elites to remain in power and even to get more affluent and autocratic. In addition, the cult of giantism in development, dependency on foreign finance and expertise, the inevitable debt and then even greater plundering of the forest resource at the expense of the population at large, all generate unrest and repressive government, and inevitably environmental degradation. In short, Guppy's analysis of causes stresses the international nature of processes, and it is an indictment of the global capitalist system's quest for profits. When "the deepest layer of the cake" is reached, then "what Oscar Wilde would have called Cynicism—knowing the price of everything and the value of nothing" was encountered, as prices and values were not identical. In this way "the world loses shape," and the tropical forests dwindle.[22]

Indeed, the "multilayered cake" of deforestation is made up of a complicated mix of ingredients; it has layers of different thicknesses and different flavors, some of which peter out here and there, all of which are assessed according to the consumer's ideological

taste buds. The development of efficient policy instruments for the management and reduction of deforestation tend to fix on one or, at best, a couple of causes, but on the
whole if they have had any effect it is merely to slow down the rate of increase rather than
to stop clearing altogether. In the meantime important issues are avoided, deforestation
surges ahead, and concern about the process deepens.

CONCERN ABOUT CHANGE

In the past there was no reason for people to lament the passing of the tropical forests
unless their aesthetic senses were offended by the felling of the noble "giants" or their
economic interests were threatened by a lack of valuable timbers. To be sure, a few travelers, commentators, and foresters had expressed some concern. For example, in 1888
Henry Forbes had wondered what future generations would know of Java's once great
forests, and during the 1920s Thomas Gill had lamented "the passing of the Great
Mother Forest" of the Amazon.[23] But these were mere islands of concern within a sea of
apathy and ignorance.

   In the immediate aftermath of the destruction and devastation of World War II, utilitarian and commodity considerations dominated concern about the forest. The new Food
and Agriculture Organization, established by the United Nations, began annual inventories of resources. In 1948 it calculated that there were 3,978 million ha of forest worldwide, of which a mere two-thirds was classed as "productive." Significantly, of those
"productive" 2,612 million ha only 36 percent were softwood conifers in the temperate
regions, while the remaining 64 percent were broad-leaved forests, dominantly in the
tropical regions. But wherever located, this acreage was "in reality one forest," a unitary,
interdependent resource, something that the title of FAO's new journal—*Unasylva*—
symbolized. "Throughout history," wrote the first director, Sir John Boyd-Orr, in a foreword to the opening issue, "man has always looked to the forest for many of his necessities and comforts" of wood, fuel, paper, and other products. He barely addressed the
idea that the forests were environments, habitats, biological and aesthetic resources, or
integral parts of bigger geo-bio-chemical systems and cycles, although he did add that
forests were "now universally recognized as guardians of soil and water" and could ex-
ert "tremendous influence for good or evil" over agriculture and hence food production
in all parts of the world.[24] But it was still going to take some decades for forests to be
viewed as environments, and as aesthetic resources that "provided amenities and enhanced daily life."[25]

   The obvious economic benefits that came from felling the forest had long been appreciated. Its bounty of timber, land, trade, warmth, energy, and even (indirectly) metals
had come to be regarded as necessities of life, second only to food itself. As a consequence, the forest suffered. But with the exception of a few rumblings of concern, rarely
were any negative or malign consequences of clearing mentioned, only the progressive,
utilitarian, and benign ones. The whole history of deforestation was largely one of contributing to "improvement," "civilization," and "progress," and even, subconsciously, of
aiding in the perfection of what seemed like the imperfect wilderness in God's creation of
a designed earth.

In general, the social and environmental benefits of leaving forests untouched and unchanged were rarely appreciated, and they came late. It was not until the early 1980s that deforestation became a "problem" that moved from a fairly restricted debate in scientific and conservation journals to coverage in the large-circulation media; consequently, after 1987 the concern became general.[26]

These positive benefits of leaving the forests untouched were fivefold and emerged in a roughly chronological order. They revolved around issues of social benefits, rainfall, ecological stability, climate change, and biodiversity, the last being so crucial that it deserves special attention.

Social Benefits

The social benefits of intact forest commons, and the game, fodder, fuel, forage, and small timber they provided, had been important in the Western countries until at least the end of the eighteenth century, and much later in the rest of the world. Forests cushioned the marginality of subsistence life and augmented income by offering greater diversification and an opportunity to counter seasonal shifts in the economy and employment. But as the forest and its products were expropriated, divided, and felled, and substitutes found for some of the products, the social benefits counted for less. When Europe came to dominate the world during the nineteenth century it tended to subordinate the social benefits of "the commons" to what seemed like the more obvious economic benefits of individual ownership and the production of timber for the global market. In the Indian forests, for example, foraging by tribal groups and fringing peasant settlements was forcibly restricted by the British reserving forests for timber production. The social benefits of trees as cultural symbols and sources of aesthetic improvement and enjoyment made only marginal inroads into consciousness by the nineteenth century, although their function as a recreational milieu was to become very important after about 1875.

Rainfall and Trees

Whereas the perception of the socioeconomic benefits of forests diminished as the nineteenth century progressed, the perception of their ecological/environmental benefits grew stronger. Initially these revolved around the effect of forests in promoting rainfall, and consequently protecting the earth from excessive runoff and erosion. The trees, in other words, "kept the land together." These links had long been suspected, though never proven conclusively; but the belief in a connection was a remarkably persistent theme in the history of the attempt to comprehend the effect of humans on earth. So ancient was it that it became entrenched in folk belief, and got incorporated into conventional wisdom as the cause of the decline and fall of Rome and a contributory factor in the dimming of the "glory that was Greece." Deforestation and consequent aridity was one of the great "lessons of history" that every literate person knew about.

The idea gained new currency with the settlement of the great outdoor laboratory for scientific study of the vast forests of North America. During the late eighteenth century commentators speculated on the changes and extremes in seasonal humidity and temperature, which clearing apparently brought about. A long line of writers, from Count Volney in 1804, John Lorian in 1825, George Perkins Marsh in 1864, to Increase Lapham in 1867, equated changed runoff regimes with changed rainfall as a result of clearing.[27] The message of the relationship was not confined to North America, for it had a fairly worldwide currency. For example, the surgeon-environmentalists of early nineteenth century India and the intelligentsia in the Russian forest-steppe zone, like Dr. Astrov in Chekov's *Uncle Vanya,* knew that

> [e]very year thousands, millions of trees are cut down. . . . Our climate is being tampered with in a way we don't understand at all. Our magnificent landscape is mutilated forever. Our rivers grow shallower and will ultimately dry up. And the natural habitat of animals and birds is so disturbed that they may never be reinstated.[28]

But if the clearing of the forest caused a decrease in rainfall and a drying-out of the land, then would not the planting of trees increase rainfall? The audacious assertion of Buffon, that

> a single forest . . . in the midst of . . . parched deserts would be sufficient to render them the more temperate, and attract the waters from the atmosphere, to restore all the principles of fertility to the earth

so that the farmers would "enjoy the sweets of a temperate climate," was a message that the boosters and settlers of the North American western frontier wanted to hear. Obviously, the plains only needed trees to convert them into the "middle landscape" of well-tended land with the correct proportion of arable, pasture, and forest. Thus tree planting flourished as a means of turning the "Great American Desert" into the "Garden of the World." It culminated in the Timber Culture Act of 1873, whereby settlers were granted 160 acres free of cost provided they planted trees, and it remained in operation for 18 years. But prolonged drought in the plains during the early 1890s showed that the clumps of trees had had no effect on rainfall, and the experiment of tree planting to promote rainfall was pronounced a failure. "It was a beautiful dream," wrote Benjamin Hibbard in his classic study of public land policies, "but the substance of the dream was for the most part as unreal as such visions usually are."[29]

By the end of the century the argument that forests influenced climate was almost dead, and its scientific basis was questioned increasingly. But the forestry profession could not let it go and flirted with this will-o'-the-wisp; if only it could be proved, what a boost to forestry it would be! Raphael Zon, chief of the Research Service branch of the U.S. Forest Service, had investigated the effects of forests on flood control and found it difficult to entirely disavow the belief in the forest-rainfall relationship. In his lengthy report of 1912—"Forests and Water in the Light of Scientific Investigation"—he concluded that although forests did not prevent floods, they could ameliorate their destructiveness; and then, in an almost throwaway remark, went on to say:

> Forests increase both the abundance and frequency of local precipitation over the areas they occupy as compared with that over adjoining unforested areas, amounting in some cases to more than 25 per cent.[30]

The rainfall connection was repeated halfheartedly in an address to the Society of American Foresters on the relationship between the forests on the Atlantic plain and the humidity of the interior, and it was not amended in a 1927 reprint of the "Forests and Water" paper. Even as late as 1945 Zon was not prepared to declare the relationship dead—only "moot."[31] But that was the end of it for a while; the idea became so discredited that Zon pursued it no further.

Nonetheless, the notion will not lie down. By 1984, the prospect of widespread regional deforestation in the Amazon basin prompted scientists to predict an alteration in the regional equilibrium. Anne Henderson-Sellers and Victor Gornitz suggested a *decrease* in Amazon rainfall of up to 200 mm per annum: Eneas Salati and Peter Vose put the figure higher, at 600 mm. Any certainty over deforestation effects on rainfall still eludes the global scientific community.[32] Similar uncertainty characterizes the work of hydrologists, who are not sure if deforestation is accelerating or decreasing runoff and consequently aggravating flooding in the Amazon River, though there is much less doubt concerning the possible link between deforestation and higher sediment loads arising from soil erosion.[33]

But there is one effect that forests have on the environment about which there is little doubt, and that is shelter—protecting houses and crops from the force of the wind, stopping snowdrifts on highways and railroads, and providing shade for houses and stock during the summer. Drought in the United States during 1910–11 brought about a greater appreciation of the value of trees as windbreaks, which culminated in the Shelter Belt project of the 1930s across the Great Plains.

Ecology and Order

The forest-rainfall connection was overtaken during the 1930s by the bigger and more tangible experience of the dust bowl, one of the defining moments in American and global environmental history and thinking. Whereas the forest-rainfall connection had been a remarkably persistent but difficult to prove hypothesis of human effects, the dust bowl was the human hand on nature writ large and clear: simply, within a few decades the plains had been reduced to dust by excessive plowing, though there are divergent explanations as to the exact causes.[34]

The equilibrium model of ecology with its concept of succession-to-climax, developed by Frederic Clements and others during the 1920s, helped explain the dust bowl and other environmental disasters. Contrary to all previous research, the lesson was now found to be that technology was not necessarily benign and passive. Moreover, technology did not necessarily improve or perfect some unfinished nature, but more than likely debased and destroyed it. Interference with nature became suspect: its conservation and preservation became idealized. Thus, "nature was most fruitful where it was altered least," notes David Lowenthal, and flora and fauna consequently would reach maximum diversity and stability.[35] It was the change in primary land cover as a prelude to monoculture and destructive, exploitative clearing that threatened this beneficial climax. The records of ancient history did not need plundering for corroboration; abundant contemporary "Lessons from the Old World to the Americas," lessons of "wasteful exploitation and reckless use" that interrupted "orderly solutions to land-use problems," told the story of the link between deforestation and land degradation all too well.[36] Contemporary clearing in the tropical moist forest told a similar story: the natural rate of soil erosion could increase by anything between 7 and 50 times depending on whether the disturbance was through shifting cultivation or clear-cutting followed by cultivation with crawler tractors.[37]

The ecological climax-equilibrium suggested a steady state, stability, balance, harmony, an interacting community, and no change to the environment, and the concept appealed because it mirrored earlier states of society that were supposedly more stable and happier. Although most ecologists have abandoned these ideas as scientifically untenable, they are still embedded in ecological texts and certainly appear in much contemporary environmental rhetoric. Thus, by the end of World War II, ecology and scientific conservation became a proof of right-thinking,[38] and within that paradigm forest clearing was the quintessential environmental change having the multiple ramifications of land-cover change, agricultural practice, soil stability, climatic change, biological diversity, and landscape alteration. One ignored the rules of ecology at one's peril because "nature always had the last word," a dictum which may have been "physically painful" at times, said John S. Collis, but at least was "metaphysically inspiring," as it answered Marsh's ultimate question: "whether man is of nature or above her."[39] Put simply, the forest was perceived as most fruitful when it was altered least, but that was not possible in the world of expanding numbers and needs that ensued during the second half of the twentieth century.

Climate Change and Trace Gases

The ability of humans to alter local climate by clearing forests had long been suggested but difficult to prove. The most common effect of deforestation had always been assumed to be decreased rainfall. But more recently the idea has grown that global temperatures may be increased by the changed albedo.[40] Whereas the urban climatic effects are well substantiated, those of albedo are still being debated; at most the increase may only be a fraction of 1 percent, and even then changes in hydrology may be more important than changes in albedo.[41] In contrast, the ability of humans to affect atmospheric quality by the emission of fossil fuels has been easier to substantiate. The formation of local smog caused by petrochemical exhaust was established during the 1950s, and two decades later the long-range transport of emissions to produce acid rain seemed incontrovertible. Whereas these effects were local, or at most continental or regional, the idea of any global effect seemed unlikely, if not impossible. The conventional wisdom was voiced by one researcher: "How can little creatures like us compete with those titanic forces that drive the winds of the atmosphere and the ocean currents?"[42]

However, during the mid-1960s a sneaking suspicion arose within the scientific community that the "little creatures" en masse were in fact altering the global climate. It was established that emissions from fossil fuels *and* from land-cover change, of which deforestation was the most important component, could absorb the infrared radiation emitted by the earth's surface and by trace gases like methane (CH_4) and nitrous oxide (N_2O), both of which interact radiatively in the atmosphere. This could trigger alterations in the heat balance of the earth, and hence temperatures, atmospheric moisture amounts, and even sea levels. Predictions were made that global temperatures could rise by between 0.8 and 4.1°C (the rise being greater at the poles than at the equator), although because of the time lag they might not be evident until the end of the twenty-first century (fig. 13.2). This conjectured temperature rise is put into perspective when one realizes that the Ice Age was triggered by an approximate decrease of 4°C from the average.[43]

There was also the possibility that climatic change could have disastrous effects on biodiversity, the other new major cause for concern about forest loss, by causing the extinction of peripheral populations, geographically localized and impoverished species, poor dispersers, and some animals and communities in arctic, montane, and alpine locations. In addition, rising sea levels would engulf coastal species. That these events, in turn, could trigger humanly relevant "knock-on" effects, such as crop failure, crop shift, water shortages, and economic refugees, gave the deforestation debate a new dimension, and widened it from science alone to include decision makers considering climate change when shaping public policy.[44]

The steps whereby this suspicion grew about the power of cumulative human action have been chronicled by a number of writers.[45] Of note was the suggestion as early as 1895 by the Swedish glaciologist Svante Arrhenius that anthropogenic sources of CO_2 might lead to global warming in the future, and the prediction by Charles Van Hise in 1910 that coal burning might affect atmospheric temperatures. Crucial, however, were the annual readings of atmospheric CO_2 begun in 1956 at the Mauna Loa observatory in Hawaii, which showed that the concentration of 275 ppm–280 ppm that had prevailed since the end of the Ice Age until about 1770 had risen to 350 ppm by 1990, an increase of 25 percent, and that it is still rising at 1.5 ppm annually.[46] During the 1970s, evidence accumulated that surface temperatures in the Northern Hemisphere were rising, and an international report—*The Study of Man's Impact on Climate* of 1971—was an early and authoritative assessment of human impacts. By the mid-1980s, the so-called greenhouse effect and associated climatic change were firmly established as worldwide concerns after two major international scientific gatherings.[47] By 1990 the Intergovernmental Panel on Climate Change was set up to coordinate research and results, and after a run of the driest summers ever in the early 1990s, it declared unequivocally in 1996 that humans had altered the atmosphere to bring about the biggest changes in the global climate since the Ice Age.

The contribution of the forests to the damaging emissions and trace gases is rarely acknowledged but probably quite large. About 50 percent of all terrestrial carbon is stored in the vegetation and soils of the world's forests, with the remainder being in woodlands, grasslands, tundra, wetlands, and agricultural lands. There is, of course, an uncalculated amount of this element in the world's oceans and the atmosphere. With forest clearing, the carbon is released through decay and particularly burning, and it could constitute anything between 10 and 50 percent of the total amount sent into the atmosphere, the precise figure being much debated. Certainly land-cover change has dominated the release of

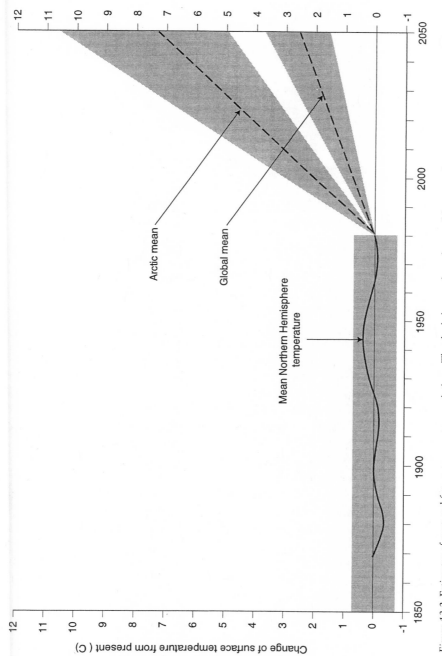

Figure 13.2 Estimates of past and future temperature variations. The shaded areas show the possible range of temperatures in the future. The shaded area at the bottom of the diagram shows the range of earth temperatures during the past 1,000 years. *Source:* Kellogg, 1987: 124.

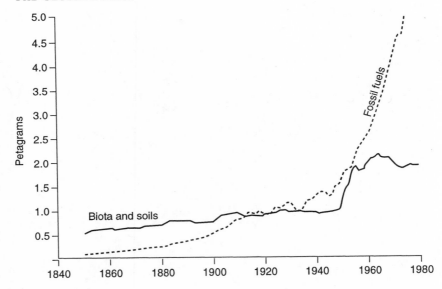

Figure 13.3 Annual releases of carbon from changes in land use and emissions from fossil fuel combustion, 1850–1980. One petagram = 1 × 10^{15} g (1 million billion grammes) = 1 billion metric tons. *Source:* Houghton and Skole, 1990: 398.

carbon throughout the bulk of human history, being surpassed only by fossil fuel emissions after about 1910 (fig. 13.3).

Of the carbon released in the past, most came from the regions that experienced massive clearing in the eighteenth and nineteenth centuries—North America, Russia, and Europe—while current carbon releases caused by land-cover change come from areas of major deforestation in South and Southeast Asia, the Russian Federation, Africa, and Latin America, regions where they still surpass fossil-fuel carbon releases.[48] Likewise, land-cover and land-use changes account for between 25 and 80 percent of all methane (CH_4) released, which has doubled since 1800, and 70 percent of nitrous oxide (N_2O) released.[49]

Given the magnitude of these emissions, the need to incorporate human land-cover change into global circulation models (GCMs) and even policy predictions was clear, and provided the rationale and resources during the past 15 years for understanding deforestation and its effects on climate.[50] The urge to calibrate change has led to an unprecedented assessment of the processes, amounts, and rates of deforestation and fuelwood use in major world regions, and the explosion of literature has been staggering.[51] Deforestation has moved from being the preserve of a few academic geographers and historians interested in the evolution and formation of landscapes and societies in the past to a matter of global scientific and governmental environmental concern.

But a note of caution is needed here. Some commentators have questioned the validity of the basic premise. First, they believe the assumptions that are built into the climate-change models are flawed and that the changes are well within the realm of natural perturbations. Their point is gaining ground. Second, they point out that the problem is socially constructed, whereas the research is politically motivated and financially driven.[52] Third, the amount of deforestation is inflated. A penetrating study of West African deforestation by James Fairhead and Melissa Leach has suggested that for complex reasons, deforestation has been exaggerated to become a new orthodoxy. Old colonial predictions of native profligacy and forest loss have become so accepted that "the tendency is for programmes to be constructed (and their funding justified) against a backdrop of decline." Consequently, deforestation may provide no more than "a cultural script for action" or a simplified narrative that facilitates action on the research-policy interface.[53] If that regional example is translated to the wider global arena, then the implications are enormous; deforestation is certainly happening, but it may not be as great as is commonly supposed, a suspicion that the following discussion on biodiversity tends to bolster.

THE RISE OF BIODIVERSITY

The destruction of the world's botanical abundance and diversity—the bulk of which probably lies in the tropical moist forests—has been the most important factor in the rising awareness and concern about deforestation. Within about 10 years, between 1986 and 1996, biodiversity moved from being an unknown term to becoming a global byword and the subject of an international convention signed by over 150 nations. Indeed, it is almost synonymous with deforestation. But unlike climatic change, the story of how and why biodiversity became an issue of global concern is untold because it has not had the full power of a vast international research machine to chart its progress.

The neat, encapsulating, "glitzy" buzzword—*biodiversity*—is, in reality, a complex concept of multiple meanings. It is the place where species, habitat, and ecosystem-based concerns meet, and where biological, economic, and socially and ethically driven motivations merge. Biodiversity is, says David Takacs,

> a tool for a zealous defence of a particular social construction of nature that recognizes, analyzes, and rues this furious destruction of life on Earth . . . [which aims] . . . to change science, conservation, cultural habits, human values, our ideas about nature, and, ultimately nature itself.[54]

In order to understand how this particular social construction has evolved, we need to appreciate how its diverse aspects have become woven together, and how they relate to forest destruction. To do that, at least three questions need answering:

1. What are the reasons for the belief that biodiversity is an important feature of nature?
2. How and why was the concept conceived? and finally,
3. How did it become linked indissolubly with the loss or retention of forests?[55]

It is suggested that the answers to these questions lie in the "archeology" of the word-concept, which reveals that new discussions, or "discourses" in a Foucaldian sense, arose during the 1940s to 1980s. Parallel, adjacent, and seemingly different but closely related events, facts, and ideas were defined, redefined, and transformed to combine and give new meaning and significance to the word.[56] In short, the knowledge of biodiversity has been socially "produced."

The origin of the concept of "biodiversity" probably lay in evolutionary biology, ecology, and conservation, and meant a scale-dependent mixture of heterogeneities essential for the functional integrity, adaptiveness, and even stability of biological systems. The germ of the idea had been about for a long time. Charles Darwin was convinced of the necessity of variability for natural selection; by 1953 Aldo Leopold felt that "keeping every cog and wheel" in nature was the "first precaution of intelligent tinkering"; by 1958 Charles Elton was advocating conservation measures based on the diversity/stability hypothesis; and by 1960 Rachel Carson was deploring the destruction via pesticides of nature's intricate processes.[57] But biodiversity was an *imprecise*, "umbrella" or pseudocognate concept with multiple meanings that created confusion because many users, then as now, "assume that everyone shares the same intuitive definition."[58]

For example, it can include the number of species, the variety of habitat, genetic variation, or the general heterogeneity of nature. It is both a *descriptive* term that explains a structurally visible and measurable variability, and an *abstract* term that describes a concept of great complexity. In its second, more abstract, meaning are at least two key ideas:

1. Variability and heterogeneity are a necessary condition for the existence of human life.
2. The significance of diversity can be reduced to two general metaphorical arguments: first, it provides buffers or *functional resilience* against unexpected shocks and perturbations; and, second, it provides the raw material for adaptive change and evolution—in other words, the *selection function*.

The arguments for these claims are many, diverse, and involved, and the answers lie deep within biological research.

But during the last 40 years the focus of the discourse has shifted from a scientific to a human concern that "truncates" the idea of "the range of biologically essential heterogeneity that is important in the conservation discourse." Simply, human disquiet over biodiversity stems from a concern to maintain a habitable earth, and to preserve its beauty and variability; it amounts, no less, to the "irreducible complexity of the totality of life." Thus, several new and interdependent discourses have arisen, of which the conservation discourse is only one and is paralleled by an

> "economic discourse" on the economic value of biodiversity, [a] "management discourse" on the methods and means of maintaining biodiversity in human-modified environments, . . . [and an] "ethical discourse" on the relevance of biodiversity to the human relationship to nature.[59]

The evolution of these discourses from the 1940s to the present has come from different sources of concern that have a roughly sequential development and over time become increasingly overlapping and interdigitating. They are the recognition of the abundance and diversity of the environment during the 1950s; an understanding of speciation and genetic diversity during the 1960s; and a recognition of the pace and irreversibility of change during the 1970s. Between 1979 and 1981, these concerns were publicized and popularized, and from the mid-1980s onward biodiversity arrived as a part of the international lexicon and environmental agenda. In the process, concepts have become polarized, so that, broadly speaking, some ideas are "good" (e.g., biodiversity) and some ideas are "bad" (e.g., deforestation).

1950s: Abundance and Diversity

The "jungle" had always been popularly described as "rich," "fertile," "prolific," "lush," "luxuriant," "complex," "teeming with life," and quick to revert if cleared, even "indestructible"; but its true species abundance, diversity, and resilience were only guessed at. One of the first people to confront these issues was Eldred J. H. Corner, a mycologist in the Singapore Botanical Gardens, who commented in 1946 on botanists' ignorance of the true variety of tropical forest. He marveled at the "hundreds of thousands" of unknown and unrecorded plants in the Malay Peninsula, and suggested that "botanical progress" might be achieved with a more thorough inventory. But time was not on one's side; during the last two or three decades,

> more primeval forest must have been destroyed *botanically*—cut over, extracted, alienated, improved, converted, to use departmental terms—than in any other generation. . . . I fear lest all the virgin lowland forest of the tropics may be destroyed before botany awakes; even our children may never see the objects of our delight which we have not cared for in their vanishing.

Much of the destruction was "wanton through careless or corrupt control, without provision for the future." In the forest the thud of the ax and the crash of the trees as they hit the ground, followed by the "silencing of birds and monkeys, and the crackle of the flames," was enough to tell one that "Artemis has fled where Plutus starts to reign." [60]

The theme of thoughtless biological loss was taken up by Paul Richards in 1952 in his classic text, *The Tropical Rain Forest*. He was, perhaps, the first person to juxtapose the idea of millions of years of stability and genetic evolution producing diversity with the short, rapid period of destruction. He observed that a 2-ha plot in the Malay Peninsula contained more than 200 tree species, compared with 10 in an equivalent area of New England and 25 in the exceptionally species-rich "cove" forests of Tennessee and South Carolina. In addition there were smaller trees, vines, orchids, herbaceous plants, ferns, epiphytes, to say nothing of uncounted mosses, liverworts, algae, fungi, and lichens. He blamed Western imperialism and the spread of plantation monoculture for forest change and destruction. Also, the growing native population under settled government gave rise to "even more widespread clearing of the forest in the interests of subsistence agriculture." With rare insight he likened the destruction of tropical forest to

> the clearing of the European forest by agricultural people beginning in the Neolithic period, except that the one process has been accomplished in a few decades, while the other lasted for thousands of years. [61]

Richards's comments went largely unheeded by those who said they were concerned with the environment. John Curtis, a respected and influential botanist, found the "running-down" of the rain-forest ecosystems by humans acceptable because "the improbability of the climax biotic community was too great to be sustained." In the 1950s it seemed as though worries about tropical rain-forest destruction were for scientific ignoramuses and crackpots only, and it is difficult to find specific elements of concern in early "environmental" texts such as those by Fairfield Osborn and William Vogt, except perhaps for the comment by Osborn about "the present terrific attack upon the natural life-giving elements of the earth."[62]

1960s: Speciation and Genetic Diversity

If the tropical rain forest had such an abundance and variety of species, then why and how had that come about? A new slant on this question came in 1964 from the Russian scientist, A. Fedorov, who suggested that species variation and the evolution of new species was not connected with habitat or site differentiation, which created variation through natural selection, but by "random genetic drift"—a completely new ecological concept. Two basic characteristics of rain-forest structure seemed to support this hypothesis: the widespread occurrence of groups of closely related species, and the observation that the most abundant species are found in relatively low densities, with individuals of any given population separated spatially. In addition, the lack of seasonality in the tropics led to irregular flowering between these sparse populations, making self-fertilization important, and the complex fauna-flora dispersal synergies were also probably significant.[63]

The response to Fedorov's hypothesis was understandably varied. Paul Richards clung to natural selection in niche or site, Thomas Ashton believed that complexity resulted from the great age of the forests in areas of climatic and geological stability which led to selection for mutual avoidance, with the increasing specialization creating increasingly narrow ecological amplitudes. J. L. Stennis suggested that the bare soil of the rain forest was a free-for-all environment for seeds that offered a moist macrobiotope in which every plant had a chance. Later, Daniel Janzen thought that the great number and mobility of herbivores affected species variation. Tim Whitmore thought speciation a combination of some or all of the above. The tropical rain forest, commented Philip Stott wryly in an extensive review, was becoming "nearly as rich in theories concerning speciation . . . as they are in species!"[64] But the variety and validity of the theories were of less importance than the fact that they had been advanced. Each opened up new hypotheses about the undoubted genetic abundance and variety which increasingly became listed and categorized, thereby stimulating research into how tropical breeding systems worked.

While this was going on, an unrelated but parallel debate arose about the need to conserve genetic resources. This was a classic case of adjacency of an independent issue with a strong "family resemblance," which ultimately crossed over, melded, and transformed the nature of concern about the tropical rain forest.[65]

By the early 1960s the rapid increase in the world's population became a matter of concern because of its implications for food supply. In 1964 an International Biological Programme (IBP) was set up to explore ways of collecting and maintaining plants and germplasm that could aid further development of plant breeding, and the propagation of higher-yielding and/or disease-resistant varieties. Otto Frankel, a leading plant scientist in the endeavor, noted that before the mid-nineteenth century, when purposeful individual plant selection was carried out, any variation had occurred in areas that were relatively stable and with a large natural variability—in fact, those very areas that 40 years before had been designated centers of agricultural domestication by Nicolai Vavilov (see chapter 3). These gene centers were mainly in low latitudes where "more than half of mankind lives under conditions of serious under-nutrition," and which, although not mentioned at the time, were in the tropical forested regions, with the exception of the Middle East. The possibility of recombining old plant varieties with new to increase productivity had been proven with improved strains of wheat from Mexico and rice from the Philippines which were to engender the "Green Revolution," but their very success highlighted the possibility of the threat that "the treasuries of variation in the centres of genetic diversity will disappear without a trace." The participation of latter-day scientists in these early explorations of the historically minded plant geneticists, notably Jack Harlan and Daniel Zohary, linked and widened the concern for diversity with that of domestication, social anthropology, and the very beginnings of agricultural endeavor on earth. At the instigation of the International Council of the Union of Scientists in 1972, the aims of the IBP had become incorporated in a *Declaration on the Human Environment* that came out of its Stockholm conference of that year, and the conservation of genetic resources was now an internationally recognized concern.[66] With the collaboration of FAO a system of germplasm banks was created, of which there are now about 40 around the world, as part of the International Board of Plant Genetic Resources. Though not germane to this argument, it is interesting to note that the current debate about genetically modified foods is a direct outcome of these concerns.

The idea that genetic diversity was connected with the very evolution of human life and likely to be of practical value gave the concept a new dimension that "truncated" the purely biological. At the simplest, utilitarian level, which could be easily grasped by the average layperson, the tropical forests were "a source-book of potential foods, drinks, medicines, contraceptives, abortifacients, gums, resins, scents, colorants, specific pesticides, and so on, of which we have scarcely turned the pages." In subsequent years the pages were being turned rapidly and detailed inventories were compiled of tropical genetic resources. Also the first tentative steps were taken in the scientific community to emphasize the desirability of in-situ conservation by indigenous peoples rather than ex-situ conservation via gene banks, however desirable the latter may have been.[67]

1970s: Pace and Irreversibility

The immediate postwar apathy about the felling of the tropical rain forests gave way to a new level of concern during the later 1960s as it became increasingly evident that "bulldozers and power saws were replacing axes and machetes" and causing massive change. Drawing on a lifetime experience of the forest, Paul Richards revoiced his concerns of nearly 15 years earlier in a popularly written school text; the forest's "wonderfully varied life" was worth saving not only for economic reasons, but for "compelling scientific reasons" because if it were destroyed before it could be studied, "whole chapters of biology may never be written."[68]

This plea was reiterated three years later in his article in *The Scientific American* targeted specifically at the scientific and thinking lay public. It was, perhaps, the first piece written in the recognizably modern idiom of "genetic diversity" and "species richness." Richards introduced an ethical/uniqueness argument and emphasized the idea that all living creatures were "a source of wonder, enjoyment and instruction to man" and should be preserved before they disappeared. He compared ancient forests to ancient buildings, which it were becoming increasingly valued by the public as structures worthy of preservation because they were a source of national pride:

> Although the cost of preservation is sometimes high, it is considered to be justified by the insight such monuments give into the life and thought of past civilizations. The tropical rain forest is also a monument, far older than the human species.[69]

It was an argument that echoed Chateaubriand's assertion in 1828 that the forests of America were "certainly the equivalent for monuments and ancestors."[70]

And there the issue might have lain had it not been for the emergence and interposition of another parallel concept that became linked to the idea of abundance and its increasingly rapid loss: the idea of nonrenewability and the long-term survival of the tropical forest, which might well be the precursor of another key concept of the era—sustainability. Most people thought that the forest was exuberant, resilient, and indestructible, but by 1972 Arturo Gómez-Pompa and his Mexican colleagues had become convinced that it was not. They admitted that they did not have all the scientific evidence to prove their case, but they were sure that if one waited for further research, "there probably will not be rain forests left to prove it." Mechanical and chemical intensification of tropical agriculture and its extension to keep up with population growth had disrupted and eliminated natural processes that favored primary species. Only favored secondary species that were preadapted to disturbance flourished, eventually leading to what Gerardo Budowski had predicted in 1958 to be the "savannaization" and "desertization" of erstwhile forests. Comparisons with sustained, long-term land-use practices in the temperate world were not tenable. All the evidence supported the idea that with the new and widespread intensive use of tropical land, "ecosystems are in danger of mass extinction." Not only did Gómez-Pompa emphasize nonrenewability, he also stressed the delicate adaptation of traditional shifting agriculture to the complex and intricate species regeneration systems that had evolved over millennia. Given these botanical conditions, shifting agriculture seemed the natural way to use the regenerative properties of the rain forest "for human benefit" because it retained "the genetic pool of primary trees" that were the main raw material of the successional process.[71] This was a revolutionary viewpoint, and it reversed the centuries-old conventional wisdom of the Western discourse on the destructive effect of "native" agricultural systems on the tropical forest. For example, as late as 1945 André Aubréville had said that shifting agriculture was "the curse that has been plaguing Africa," and unless controlled would "doom" the continent "to become unproductive grassland or even a desert."[72]

Gómez-Pompa's prediction of obliteration seemed well on the way to reality a few months later, when the geographer William Denevan forecast the seemingly outrageous idea of the "imminent demise" of the Amazon rain forest, which "within one hundred years . . . will have ceased to exist," as development projects and subsidized agricultural settlement caused the "most intensive destruction of extensive forest in the history of the world."[73] A few years later the publication of the survey of the world's tropical moist forests by Adrian Sommer seemed to provide the objective proof of these speculative assertions.[74] Sommer's assessment used FAO material and land-use and vegetation maps; and from a detailed study of 13 countries representing some 163 million ha, or 18 percent of the world's tropical forests, he calculated that 2.16 million ha were being lost annually, a figure which if extrapolated to the rest of the global rain forest would be "at least 11 million ha per annum," or 20.9 ha per minute. At this rate, the tropical forest would be irreparably damaged and would largely disappear.

1979–81: Publicization, Popularization, and Cultural Survival

Sommer's figures provided the link that united the three themes of deforestation, species loss, and nonrenewability. More and even higher estimates of forest destruction during the closing years of the 1970s (see fig. 13.4 below), together with a high-profile conference on tropical deforestation in Washington, D.C., in 1978, fueled the debate in which, by now, the various strands of concern for the environment fused and linked with climatic change to create "an extremely serious problem."[75] Tropical deforestation had now become identified and "problematized," and the "problem" was appropriated by the international research machine, which now moved into high gear.

The *publicization* and official adoption of the "problem" as part of the international research agenda was paralleled and driven by its *popularization* through emphasizing the economic and ecological value of biological diversity. The words *deforestation* and *diversity* achieved an almost sloganlike, charismatic status among an increasingly environmentally aware population, which accepted uncritically the simple and easy-to-understand associations that one was a "bad thing" and the other a "good thing." "Save the rain forest" became a rallying cry for conservationists, and in time would be taken up by "politicians, pundits and rock stars."[76] Advocacy scientists capitalized on the public's worries about uncertainty and irreversible loss. Thus, between 1978 and 1981 the debate moved from being an almost private one carried out in the journals of different disciplines and learned bodies to being a public one on the popular bookshelves. Norman Myers's *The Sinking Ark: A New Look at the Problem of Disappearing Species* (1979), and Paul and Anne Ehrlich's *Extinction: The Causes and Consequences of the Disappearance of Species* (1981), for example, explicitly made a causal link between the increase of population and the systematic modification and elimination of habitats on which species depended, thereby leading to species loss. Much of this reasoning was based on the prediction derived from island biogeography that the number of species inhabiting any environmental type (e.g., the tropical rain forest) would decline in proportion to the decrease in area, in an assumed approximately linear proportion, leading to mechanistic and alarmist predictions on extinctions, although without natural history details.[77] The rate of species loss was modestly estimated at about 3 per day, but was later raised to 11–16 per diem. In time the "numbers became tokens of faith" in one's belief, and riveted the attention of the concerned.[78]

These publications achieved wide circulation and some notoriety, especially when their neo-Malthusian message of ever-depressing impoverishment and genetic decline was linked and likened to Nuclear Winter, a much discussed idea at the height of the cold war years. Now the idea of diversity loss intersected with that of national security. Barring an actual nuclear conflict, predicted Paul Ehrlich, civilization itself would disappear before the end of the twenty-first century, "not with a bang but a whimper," in T. S. Eliot's words.[79] One way or another, mass extinction seemed around the corner. Out of this general concern conservation biology was formalized as a separate academic subdiscipline.

At about this time a previous parallel concern became prominent again. Gómez-Pompa's assertion that the native dwellers of the rain forests had a better appreciation of the variety and potential of biological diversity than did the farming immigrants, and that they indulged in more ecologically friendly and sustainable practices, blossomed with greater awareness of cultural variety. The newly dubbed *ecosystem people* had learned to live more sustainably within their natural ecosystem habitat than had the *biosphere people,* who drew on the resources of the global economy or entire biosphere. Undoubtedly a part of the belief lay in a residue from Western Romantic literature that had idealized some "primitive" societies and created the concept of the "noble savage." But during the 1970s and 1980s social anthropologists, ethnobotanists, and even plant geneticists began to argue that not only did instinctive ecological harmony make the savage noble, but that local in-situ knowledge was indispensable to plant genetic evolution. After all, coevolution had created plant variety and maintained it through conservation in the first place, and had even encouraged mutation.[80]

Studies purported to show that the greatest concentration of biological utility and diversity lay in those habitats with the greatest concentration of indigenous cultural diversity. In Latin America, for example, this "strong positive correlation" is most evident in the "base ecoregion" of the Tropical Moist Forest (table 13.1) and is also strong in Tropical Dry Broad-Leafed and Tropical and Subtropical Forests, but generally weakens as one moves to more temperate climes.[81]

Gradually, the idea grew (and with some justification) that not only were the species in danger of mass extinction from deforestation, but so were those in most contact with them—the rain forest dwellers. Thus both cultural diversity and biological diversity are endangered; the mass extinction of species was paralleled by, and connected to, the mass annihilation of cultures and languages.[82]

Up to that point the discourse on biodiversity had been fairly low key and diffuse, but now the idea became firmly established that extinction of the tropical rain forest was a major step on the road to ecological and environmental deterioration, and even ethnic elimination. The forest may have covered only 7 percent of the earth's surface, but it probably contained about half of the 1.4 million known living species (although there is much uncertainty as to numbers), and the key to further plant evolution.[83] Edward O. Wilson was convinced that the loss of diversity through the destruction of natural habitats would "take millions of years to correct" and was "the folly our descendents are least likely to forgive us." [84] Similarly the forest might only have contained a fraction of 1 percent of the world's population, but it may have contained some 30 to 40 percent of all known languages. Biological and cultural diversity now went hand in hand.

Mid-1980s: Biodiversity Arrives

This new concern about change in the forest rose rapidly during the middle and closing years of the 1980s and was increasingly described as a loss of "biodiversity" (often rendered initially as BioDiversity), a neologism, which Edward O. Wilson claims was coined by Walter G. Rosen in 1986 and incorporated in the title of the National Forum on BioDiversity sponsored by the Smithsonian Institution and the National Academy of Sciences in Washington in September of that year. Certainly before 1986 "species variety,"

Table 13.1 Cultural diversity and biodiversity, Latin America

Habitat Type	Cultural Diversity	Biodiversity Measures				
	Indigenous Populations	Base Ecoregions	Forest Tree Genetic Resources	Centers of Plant Diversity	Origin of Important Crop Species	Domesticated Animal Origins
Tropical Moist Forests	334	54	95	40	18	14
Tropical Dry Broad-Leafed Forests	89	32	70	12	12	11
Tropical and Subtropical Forests	56	15	48	9	1	0
Temperate Forests	2	4	1	2	0	1
Grassland/Savanna/ Shrubland	48	16	17	3	4	5
Flooded Grassland/ Savanna and Wetlands	21	13	5	0	2	3
Montane Grassland	13	13	7	9	1	6
Medit'n Chaparral	2	2	3	0	0	0
Deserts and Xeric Shrubland	31	27	39	9	9	7
Dunes	0	3	1	0	0	0
Mangroves	10	39	2	2	0	2

Source: Wilcox and Duin, 1995: 51.

"variety of life," "genetic diversity," and increasingly "biological diversity" (all meaning slightly different things, depending on the context in which they were used), could describe the concept. Now they were being rapidly replaced by the single word—*biodiversity*. *Biodiversity* was subsequently used throughout Edward Wilson's edited volume of the proceedings of the National Forum. The Office of Technology Assessment report of 1987, *Techniques to Maintain Biological Diversity,* prompted the Library of Congress in September 1987 to enter "Biological diversity" in its cataloguing with a cross-reference to "Biodiversity." [85] This late start in recognizing the concept is borne out by the fact that the words *biological diversity* and *biodiversity* (and then almost exclusively the former) barely figured in titles and abstracts of papers before 1984, then occurred in around 50 during the next few years, reaching about 75 (1989), then 110 (1990), then 160 (1991), and over 250 (1992), as increasingly biodiversity became less of an abstract concept and more a phenomenon of difference that could be measured.[86]

Thus, although biodiversity is an amorphous, even abstract, idea, and certainly one that has many meanings, within a few years after its circa-1986 invention it became a concept that was so firmly established in scientific and popular literature that it achieved buzzword status. Biologists are still attempting to count, measure, differentiate, and manage biodiversity,[87] while on the more human side the original utilitarian, practical concerns about the loss of "wonder drugs" have been supplemented by a new discourse in which deforestation and irreversible habitat and species loss have became defined and redefined, understood, accepted unquestionably, given an ethical dimension, and condemned. Biodiversity loss has become socially constructed and "problematized," and it has become almost synonymous with deforestation.[88] Moreover, the concept has other resonances that have led to its widespread acceptance as inherently "good." In the social sciences diversity and heterogeneity were being promoted as desirable political and social ideals for Western societies that are becoming more ethnically, culturally, and sexually pluralistic and diverse. Biologically, the rise of the idea of a global "heritage" of genes and species that demanded preservation just as surely as did the Pyramids or the Taj Mahal meant that biodiversity was an idea whose time had come.

If ecology was the token of all right-thinking people during and after World War II, then the desirability of biodiversity is the token of all right-thinking people in 1990s. It has become one of the most prominent and popularly understood environmental issues among the half a dozen or so major ones that have dominated the environmental debates during the last 20 years. Biodiversity has become officially mythologized and adopted as the charismatic cry of the environmental activist. Its acceptance has been little short of amazing; in 1992 it was the basis of the Rio International Convention designed to stem diversity loss which was signed by 158 countries.[89] With tropical deforestation as the universal metaphor for environmental and habitat change, the process of tree removal could never be the same again.

CALIBRATING CHANGE

When I started this book in Los Angeles in 1994, there was a large electronic billboard above the Hard Rock Cafe at the Beverly Center, just off Beverly Boulevard. It flashed its message day and night. Its row of figures represented the area of the global tropical rain forest in the hundreds of millions of ha. The last digit kept on flicking over and decreasing; it was counting backwards, signaling the minute-by-minute destruction of the forest. It fell at about 20 ha (approximately 50 acres) per minute, at which rate there would be no rain forest left by the end of the twenty-first century. The flashing, ever-diminishing total was an arresting and disturbing reminder of what was happening. But it induced a strange mixture of reactions—indignation, concern, but more often a shrug of the shoulders as one realized the difficulty of "doing anything" about it. Then you dived into the mall to do your shopping and get on with your own life.

Whatever one's reactions to the display, at least three questions about it need answering: was the total amount of rain forest shown correct; what exactly is "deforestation"; and is the rate of destruction true? Despite the undoubted importance and magnitude of deforestation as a key process in the transformation of the earth, our knowledge of these three elements is marked by an astonishing uncertainty and debate. Definitions are disputed; basic data are either uncertain or found wanting; and the calibration of change is contested.

Extent and Area of World Forests

Before change in the forest can be measured, its extent and area must be known; and even more basically, before either can be delineated a "forest" must be defined, something that has not been attempted until recent years. Intuitive experience suggests that a broad distinction can be made between closed and open forest, and in practice most writers make such a distinction. FAO defines *closed forest* as "land where trees cover a high proportion of the ground and where grass does not form a continuous layer on the floor," and *open forest* (sometimes called woodland) as "mixed forest/grasslands with at least 10 percent tree cover and a continuous grass layer." Alternatively, from time to time, various percentages of crown cover have been suggested as diagnostic of forest. For example, UNECE/FAO (United Nations Economic Commission for Europe) defines a forest as closed when "tree crowns cover more than 20 per cent of the area and when the area is used primarily for forestry." But more recently FAO says a *forest* is an ecological system with a minimum crown coverage of the land surface of 10 percent, and *wooded land* is a part of *nonforested* land. Neither definition is the same as a legal definition, such as where an area is proclaimed to be forest under a national forest act or ordinance.[90]

Despite conflicting definitions, attempts have been made to map the *distribution* of the world's forests and woodlands. For example, the huge *Weltforstatlas* from 1951 onward shows the distribution of forest cover and production by country and continent, as well as the breakdown of the forest into separate botanical species. Detailed as it is, however, it does not serve well the purpose of getting an accurate measure of either the extent or rate of change. Like most maps of global vegetation it is formed by aggregating small-scale map data, and incorporates implicitly all their inherent problems of diverse aims, subjective classifications, and boundary delimitation.[91]

The quest to overcome the problems inherent in qualitative maps and to get a *statistical* measure of the *area* and of *change* in the global forests has been pioneered by climatic modelers, who want objective measures to incorporate in Global Circulation Models (GCMs) and other calculations. Data sources have been analyzed digitally, with at least four attempts at statistical measure having been made during the 1980s. CLIMAP (Climate: Long-Range Investigation, Mapping, and Prediction), and John Hummel and Ruth Reck concentrated on maps to assist in surface albedo studies. These were general descriptions of land cover (e.g., tropical woodland/grassland, deciduous forest, arable land, etc.) and did not conform to generally accepted classifications of vegetation, but were files based on 2° latitude × 2° longitude cells. Subsequently, the utility of these maps was extended so as to help in the elucidation of other global issues such as carbon density or biomass for climatic modeling studies. Jerry Olson, J. A. Watts, and L. J. Allison modified the Hummel and Reck map, organizing data in a 0.5° latitude × 0.5° longitude grid, with 12 general vegetation types being designated; these were annotated further by climatic (e.g., tropical, subtropical, boreal) and elevational (e.g., lowland, montane) characteristics, resulting in 43 vegetation types. Finally, Elaine Matthews widened the utility of vegetation mapping further by making it applicable to a variety of climatically related research, such as primary productivity, surface roughness, and ground hydrology, in addition to albedo and biomass. Two separate databases were constructed, one of "natural" vegetation, the other of current land use. In the vegetation base an attempt was made to reconstruct the preagricultural vegetation, and the land-use data base was used to calculate the amount of vegetation remaining. Both databases were constructed on 1° latitude × 1° longitude cells so that they could be quantified. The vegetation classification used was the UNESCO hierarchical system based first on life form, and then subdivided into density, seasonality (evergreen or deciduous), altitude, climate, and vegetation structure, and

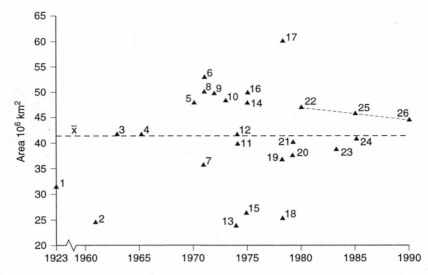

Figure 13.4 Estimates of world forest extent, 1923–90. *Sources:* The figures on the diagram refer to the following authors listed in the bibliography: (1) Zon and Sparhawk, 1923; (2) Weck and Wiebecke, 1961; (3) FAO, 1963; (4) FAO, *For. Prods. YB,* 1966; (5) Olson, 1970; (6) Bazilevich, Rodin, and Rozov, 1971; (7) Brüning, 1971; (8) Whittaker and Woodwell, 1971; (9) Lieth, 1972; (10) Whittaker and Likens, 1973; (11) Perrson, 1974; (12) Brüning, 1975; (13) Windhorst, 1974; (14) Olson, 1975; (15) Eckholm, 1975; (16) Lieth, 1975; (17) Eyre, 1978: (18) Ross-Sheriff, 1980; (19) Openshaw, 1978; (20) Steele, 1979; (21) FAO, *For. Prods. YB,* 1980; (22) WRI, 1987; (23) Matthews, 1983; (24) FAO, *For. Prods. YB,* 1985; (25) WRI, 1987; and (26) WRI, 1988–89. The three totals for 1980, 1985, and 1990 are joined by a dashed line and suggest a steady decline.

it was compiled from over 40 atlases, with all the problems inherent in that. Of the potential 225 vegetation types, 178 were used, together with 119 land-use types.[92]

As the *extent* of the forest is largely the outcome of the accurate delineation of its *distribution,* there has been little agreement about the amount of the "contemporary" forest.[93] Between 1923 and 1985 there have been at least 26 calculations of closed-forest land, and these are arranged chronologically in figure 13.4. Ranging from 60.5 million to 23.9 million km², they are randomly distributed around a mean of 41.27 million km², and show no discernible trend over time. They are estimates compiled from different sources, utilizing different definitions, and cannot, therefore, be used as an indicator of current deforestation rates. However, there is a general firming-up of the estimates during the 1980s as being between about 47 million and 37 million km², still a wide variation.[94]

The only long time-series data for forest area come from the FAO returns of land cover (not land use) for the 35 years between 1950 and 1985. However, the FAO figures from the Third and erstwhile Second Worlds must be used with caution. First, *forest* and *woodland* in the *Yearbooks* is defined as "land under natural or planted stands of trees, whether productive or not, and includes land from which forests have been cleared but will be reforested in the foreseeable future." But when is the "foreseeable future," will there be replanting, and what about regrowth? Second, it has been shown conclusively that the *Yearbooks* of 1976, 1981, and 1986 contain retrospective 10-year estimates that give different totals to each other and do not tally with the totals for *individual* years before 1975 (fig. 13.5). Until the aggregates are analyzed for each country or group of countries, then

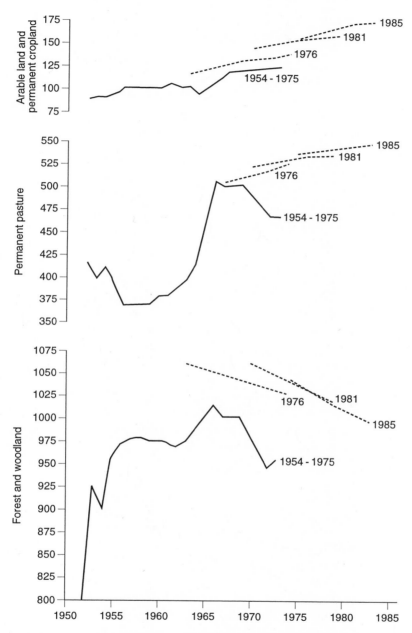

Figure 13.5 Area (in millions of ha) of three major categories of land use reported by the *Forest Products Yearbooks* of FAO (1949–87). The curves 1954–1975 are annual estimates from successive yearbooks. The curves for 1976, 1981, and 1985 are retrospective estimates from single yearbooks. They do not coincide because they are based on different terminology or methodology. *Source:* based on Houghton, Lefkowitz, and Skole, 1991: 157.

Table 13.2 Estimates of closed forest and open woodland (in millions of ha) in three continents, 1980–88

	1980	1984	1987	1988
North America				
Closed	470	470	419	459
Open	176	176	215	275
Total	646	646	670	734
Africa				
Closed	190	217	218	221
Open	570	486	500	499
Total	760	703	718	720
Latin America				
Closed	530	679	692	693
Open	150	217	250	240
Total	680	836	942	· 933

Sources: Barney, 1980: 118; Postel, 1984: 75; World Resources Institute, 1987: 59; and Postel and Heise, 1988: 8.

the FAO data must be regarded as another set of imperfect estimates.[95] On face value the data suggest that temperate forests (North America, Europe, Mainland China, USSR, and Oceania) are in a steady state with slight increase, and tropical forests are declining slightly. However, the aggregate total masks many regional fluctuations.

The problems of definition that bedeviled global estimates, particularly the distinction between closed and open forest, becomes more critical as the scale of analysis shrinks. For example, table 13.2 shows four calculations ranging between 1980 and 1987 by Gerald Barney, Sandra Postel, the *World Resources Report, 1987,* and Sandra Postel and Lori Heise, for the three major continental areas: North America, Africa, and Latin America. There is little agreement except in a most general way. Similarly, estimates of a subset of the above—tropical moist forests—range from 935 million ha by Adrian Sommer in 1976, to 1756 million ha by FAO in 1990, with a sprinkling of other estimates in between.[96]

Perhaps the most consistent view of forest extent at the present time is that of the World Resources Institute which is based on a number of recent sources from FAO and UN Economic Commission for Europe (table 13.3). The table shows that closed forests occupy 2,948 million ha (29.4 million km²) and occupy about 21 percent of the earth's surface. The other woodlands of 1,779 million ha (17.7 million km²) include open forest and forest left "fallow" after shifting cultivation, and they constitute another 13 percent of the earth's surface. The report strikes a note of caution about the latter as "estimates of open woodland are highly uncertain and the actual density of trees in such areas is often very low."[97] The extent of closed forest is greater in the temperate areas of the world than in the tropical.

Any attempt to compare this calculation with two other previous calculations of the institute for 1980 and 1985 is difficult. First, earlier calculations divided the data into Developed and Developing rather than Temperate and Tropical, as at present.[98] However, in table 13.3 China and South Africa have been moved from Developing to Temperate.

Table 13.3 Distribution of world's forest and woodlands (in millions of ha), circa 1990 and 1985 (parentheses)

Region	Land Area	Closed Forest	Other Woodland			Total Forest and Woodland	Shrubland
			Total	Open	Forest Fallow		
Temperate							
North America	1,835	459 (469)	275 (215)	x (215)	n/a	734 (684)	n/a
Europe	472	145 (153)	35 (21)	x (21)	n/a	181 (174)	n/a
USSR	2,227	792 (792)	138 (128)	x (128)	n/a	930 (920)	n/a
Other Countries	1,883	194 (194)	115 (85)	x (85)	n/a	309 (279)	(30)
Total Temperate	6,417	1,590 (1608)	563 (449)	x (449)	n/a	2,153 (2,057)	(30)
Tropical							
Africa	2,190	217 (218)	652 (660)	486 (500)	166 (160)	869 (878)	(450)
Asia & Pacific	945	306 (347)	104 (159)	31 (83)	73 (76)	410 (506)	(45)
Latin America	1,680	679 (692)	388 (420)	217 (250)	170 (170)	1,067 (1,112)	(150)
Total Tropical	4,815	1,202 (1,257)	1,144 (1,239)	734 (833)	410 (406)	2,346 (2,469)	(645)
Total World, ca. 1990	13,077	2,792	1,707	734	410	4,499	
Total World, ca. 1985	13,077	(2,865)	(1,688)	(1,282)	(406)	(4,553)	(675)
Total World, ca. 1980	13,077	2,948	1,779	1,372	407	4,727	624

Second, previous calculations included between 620 million (1980) and 675 million (1985) ha of natural "shrubland and degraded forests" that have been excluded from the recent calculation, presumably because of difficulties of interpretation. Bearing these changes in mind, the 1985 data are reassigned to the new categories and they are shown in parentheses because of their questionable nature. The world total of closed and open forests as now defined has apparently fallen from 4,727 million ha (47.27 million km) in 1980, to 4,553 million ha (45.55 million km^2) in 1985, to 4,499 million ha (44.99 million km^2) in 1990. These three totals are joined by a dashed line in figure 13.4 and suggest steady decline. But that trend must be treated with caution, as global totals of forest area cannot be used to estimate deforestation rates during the last few decades.

Definitions and Pathways of Deforestation

In the quest to understand the deforestation process, disagreement about what is "forest," and uncertainty about its global extent and area, are compounded by similar problems of definition about what constitutes "deforestation," how it happens, and how much is occurring. It is not a simple set of binary opposites of "trees" or "no trees," but everything in between. Often deforestation is qualified with words like *clearance, conversion, modification,* and *disturbance.* For example, in the FAO/UNEP (United Nations Environmental Program) report, *deforestation* refers to the "complete clearing of tree formations" either into a shifting cultivation cycle or into permanently cleared land. Curiously, it did not include logging, all the more strange as one of the primary concerns of FAO is stocks of timber. Somewhat different was the definition in the report by Norman Myers for the National Academy of Science in 1980, in which *conversion* included any modification of the forest from "marginal modification to fundamental transformation." This could be caused by a spectrum of changes ranging from permanent clearing, to logging, to selective harvesting, because the concern was about the damage to the totality of the environmental benefits performed by the forest ecosystem, from gene pools to wildlife and biomass stocks, and their effect on climate.[99] More inclusive was Myers's 1988 definition, where *deforestation* refers

> generally to the complete destruction of forest cover through clearing for agriculture . . . [so] . . . that not a tree remains, and the land is given over to non-forest purposes . . . [and where] very heavy and unduly negligent logging . . . [results in a] . . . decline of biomass and depletion of ecosystem services . . . so severe that the residual forest can no longer qualify as forest in any practical sense of the word.[100]

Equally as contentious as definitions, and indeed, part of the reason for the confusion, is the role of logging. Alan Grainger asserts that selective logging does not "lead to forest clearance and so does not constitute deforestation," whereas Norman Myers thinks that logging is crucial because, although it may only affect a small proportion of trees per hectare, it damages wide areas and is the precursor of penetration by the forest farmers:

> Along the timber tracks come subsistence peasants, able to penetrate deep into forest zones that have hitherto been closed to them. Clearing away more trees in order to plant their crops, they soon cause far more damage if not destruction than the lumberman ever did.[101]

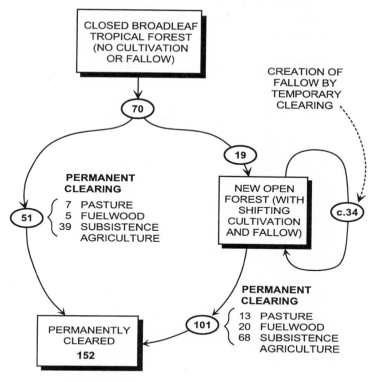

Figure 13.6 Tropical forest: annual pathways of conversion ($\times$ thousands of km^2). *Source:* based on Houghton et al., 1986: 617.

Thus, the "commercial logging/follow-on cultivator" combination is the "primary" cause of tropical forest conversion.

Perhaps an even bigger problem lies in the role of rotational, shifting agriculture in causing either permanent forest change or merely disturbance, although ultimately both lead to ecosystem change and degradation (i.e., some form of deforestation). Possibly only between 60 and 70 percent of land cleared for agriculture remains permanently without trees, with the rest becoming fallow and returning to some form of forest. When one realizes that the number of shifting and "shifted" (displaced) agriculturalists might be 250–300 million and that they may be affecting as much as 190 million ha, then their total impact on the forests is not negligible.[102] An illustration of the problem of disentangling their role is given in figure 13.6, which is based on an interpretation of pathways of change implicit in Myers's 1980 National Academy of Science report, *Conversion of Tropical Moist Forests*, with later amendments.[103] From a stock of untouched closed broadleaf forest, an annual amount of 70,000 km^2 is "deforested" annually, of which 51,000 km^2 is cleared totally and passes into the land-use category of permanently cleared, while the remaining 19,000 km^2 goes into the category of fallow (shifting) closed forest. At the same time there is some 34,000 km^2 of forest that is left fallow and open as a result of the annual cycle of shifting. But as population increases, cropland is overtaxed and fallows are shortened, so that 101,000 km^2 of that open forest is converted annually to permanently cleared land. In fact the net reduction of the fallow forest category is only 82,000 km^2 because of the annual addition of 19,000 km^2 of newly disturbed nonfallow forest. If this pathway is correct, then a total of 152,000 km^2 is being cleared annually in the tropics, with 51,000 km^2 coming from the nonfallow forests and 101,000 km^2 coming from the fallow forests that were once a part of the shifting cultivation cycle. Similar calculations of pathways can be hypothesized for the FAO/UNEP data,[104] but the information in Myers's Friends of the Earth report does not allow such interpretations.

On a larger scale analysis it seems clear that the area of forest lost does not automatically go into increased agricultural land. From raw FAO data it seems that in tropical Latin America at least one third goes into "other" categories, and in Africa only 10 percent appears in the increased agricultural area.[105] Clearly then, much forest must either become totally degraded or, more likely, become some form of open woodland or grassland. The internal dynamics of the pathways of change are critical to calculating rates of deforestation, but are imperfectly understood.

Rates of Change

When Adrian Sommer produced his inventory of tropical moist forests in 1976 along with an estimate of the rate of deforestation, it was to counter what he called the almost universal "euphoric belief" of the unlimited extent and growth of those forests. But he also fired the first shot in what was to become a vast international endeavor to turn firsthand impression and experiences of devastation into hard statistical data. But as figure 13.7 shows, a quarter of a century later on we are probably no nearer to knowing the rough—let alone the exact—rate of tropical deforestation over the globe. It is still a largely unresolved and contentious question.

Sommer had no illusions about the accuracy of his survey; it was based on "a mass of incomplete data and a number of assumptions," he said, and would ultimately yield only "rather rough results," He arrived at a figure of "approximately 11 million hectares" based on the average percentage deforestation rate for just 13 countries (Bangladesh, Colombia, Costa Rica, Ghana, Ivory Coast, Laos, Madagascar, Malaysia, Papua New Guinea, the Philippines, Thailand, Venezuela, and North Vietnam) for which *unattributed estimates* of deforestation rates were available, and then extrapolated those to all tropical moist forests.[106]

By the time of the Eighth World Forestry Congress in Jakarta in October 1978, Edouard Saouma was suggesting a rate of 12 million ha. In the same year Gerald Barney in the *Global 2000* report thought it was about 6.4 million ha, and then in a later volume of the *Report* inexplicably chose to use the high figure of 18–20 million ha, and proceeded to treat that figure as if it were totally reliable.[107] Two years later, Myers produced his report to the U.S. National Academy of Sciences, and it rapidly became a definitive study in deforestation. On the basis of unspecified estimates for 13 countries (Brazil, Burma, Colombia, Indonesia, Laos, Liberia, Madagascar, Nicaragua, Papua New Guinea, Peru, the Philippines, Thailand, and Zaire), he calculated that the rate of deforestation

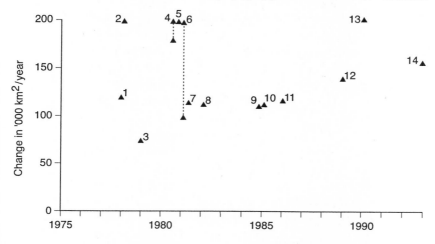

Figure 13.7 Estimates of annual rate of deforestation, 1978–93. *Sources:* The figures on the diagram refer to the following authors listed in the bibliography: (1) Sauoma, 1980; (2) Barney, 1978; (3) Lanly and Clement, 1979; (4) Robinson and Barney, 1980; (5) Myers, 1980, 1984; (6) U.S. Interagency Task Force on Tropical Forests, 1980; (7) FAO, *For. Prods. YB,* average 1968–78; (8) Lanly, 1981a, 1981b, 1981c; (9) *Tropical Forests : A Call for Action,* 1985; (10) FAO, *For. Prods. YB,* 1985; (11) FAO, *For. Prods. YB,* average 1974–84; (12) Myers, 1989; (13) WRI, 1990–91; and (14) Singh, 1993.

for them was 7.8 million ha, which he extrapolated to 11 million ha for the world, which was the same figure as Sommer's. But on the penultimate page of that report Myers opined that if forest farmers and their undoubted increase in numbers were included, then the figure might rise to over 21 million ha, which a few years later was revised to give an annual loss of 7.5 million ha of closed forest and 14.5 million ha of forest fallow.[108] The contrary assessments continued with the publication of the massive, fifteen-hundred-page FAO/UNEP report of 1981 based on deforestation rates for 76 countries, of which 13 had supplementary satellite data. This put a figure of 7.3 million ha for the clearance of closed forests between 1976 and 1980 and a forecast of 7.5 million ha for 1981–85. During the next 15 years assessments continued to fluctuate widely.[109] Suffice it to say the rough parameters of magnitude (7.5–approximately 20 million ha/yr) have been set. The lower figure is generally acknowledged to represent the complete removal of trees, with the upper figure depending upon a wider definition of deforestation, which could include modification to some degree. Thus, an area equal or even nearly double that destroyed could be severely disturbed or degraded.

Finally, the latest and most authoritative assessment is that by FAO for 1990. It is far more elaborate than anything done before, and is based on a continuous monitoring record, using a combination of ground-level and remote-sensing data and Geographical Information Systems (GIS) mapping for 90 countries. The assessment aims to draw conclusions on not only the location, amount, and shift in forest cover but also the causes and impact of deforestation. The interim data are displayed in table 13.4. This shows that between 1981 and 1990 the annual rate of deforestation (i.e., a change of land use with the depletion of the tree crown cover to less than 10 percent) has been

Table 13.4 Estimate of forest area and deforestation, tropical areas, 1980 and 1990

Continent & Subregion	No. of Countries	Total Land Area (in millions of ha)	Forest Area (in millions of ha)		Annual Deforestation (in millions of ha)	Rate of Change (%/yr.)
			1980	1990		
Africa						
West Sahelian Africa	9	528.0	43.7	40.8	0.3	−0.7
East Sahelian Africa	6	489.7	71.4	65.3	0.6	−0.8
West Africa	8	203.8	61.5	55.6	0.6	−0.8
Central Africa	6	398.3	215.5	204.1	1.1	−0.5
Tropical Southern Africa	10	558.1	159.3	145.9	1.3	−0.8
Insular Africa	1	58.2	17.1	15.8	0.1	−0.8
Total Africa	40	2,236.1	568.1	527.6	4.1	−0.7
Asia						
South Asia	6	412.2	69.4	63.0	0.6	−0.8
Continental Southeast Asia	5	190.2	88.4	75.2	1.3	−1.5
Insular Southeast Asia	5	244.4	154.7	135.4	1.9	−1.2
Pacific Islands	1	45.3	37.1	36.0	0.1	−0.3
Total Asia	17	1,650.1	349.6	310.6	3.9	−1.1
Latin America						
Central America and Mexico	7	239.6	79.2	68.1	1.1	−1.4
Caribbean	19	69.0	48.3	47.1	0.1	−0.3
Tropical S. America	7	1,341.6	864.6	802.9	6.2	−0.7
Total Latin America	33	1,650.1	992.2	918.1	7.4	−0.7
Total Tropical World	90	4,778.3	1,910.4	1,756.3	15.4	−0.8

Source: Singh, 1993: 15.

15.4 million ha (compare with the rate of 15.1 million ha in table 12.2 arrived by different calculations).[110]

By 1985, international agencies had responded to the worldwide concern about these figures of forest loss by compiling a large-scale plan setting out possible courses of action for lessening the rate of deforestation. This was followed two years later by a policy document entitled *The Tropical Forestry Action Plan*. But the main thrust was aimed at regulating forestry, so it said little about the destruction caused by subsistence agriculture.[111]

Roger Sedjo and Marion Clawson were highly critical of the assertions about the rate of deforestation and the programs that ensued, and while not denying that "local effects of rapid deforestation may be severe," resulting in the clearing of about 7 million ha per annum, they did not think that the evidence supported the view "that either the world or the tropics are experiencing rapid aggregate deforestation." Maybe it is higher than they suggest, but they are not the only commentators who are skeptical about the extreme claims.[112]

In all this debate, it is salutary to realize that between 1976 and 1998, only two primary sources of data have been produced—those made by FAO/UNEP and those made by Myers, one incorporating some objective satellite-measured data, the other relying on the expert assessment of an individual. All other estimates, including those made to date by the World Resources Institute, have been derived from these estimates, and their secondary nature makes them less reliable. Their variability depends on definitions of what is deforestation and what is conversion, the role of logging and shifting agriculture, the types of forest considered (closed or open), and whether they are specific measurements by remote sensing or subjective judgements, or a combination of both. Some are extrapolations from sample areas, some are averages, some are actual, and some potential.[113] In addition, it does not take too much imagination to realize that there may be good reasons to either exaggerate or play down the rate of deforestation for national political or economic ends, and even for personal professional reasons in the race for funding and status.

Thus, we are left with the knowledge that the exact magnitude, pace, and nature of one of the most important processes in the changing environment of large portions of the earth is largely unknown. In all this uncertainty we can be sure that the debate on the rate of deforestation is not over. As for the electronic sign over the Hard Rock Cafe, it is no more. The management dismantled it a few years ago—it had lost its appeal and impact, and someone had told them that the whole thing was suspect anyhow. Both of those are true, but we do know that if it were still functioning, even if it had been calibrated incorrectly, nothing was going to stop it counting down.

Chapter 14

The Great Onslaught, 1945–95: Patterns of Change

Peasants felling trees in a rain forest cut poignant figures in the late twentieth century. Aspiring yeoman farmers, they struggle to better themselves by destroying an ecological treasure.

—THOMAS K. RUDEL, *Tropical Deforestation: Small Farmers and Land Clearing in the Ecuadorian Amazon* (1993)

The pace of change in Amazonia has to be seen to be appreciated: 6 years at the frontier can transform an area as much as many decades or even centuries in other parts of the world.

—PHILIP M. FEARNSIDE, *Global Environmental Change* (1997)

JUST AS THE factors that drive people to cut down trees are clouded by uncertainty, the same is true about where they do it. In that respect most contemporary tropical deforestation is no different from deforestation anywhere else, at any other time. It is diffuse and difficult to detect; it is made up of the uncoordinated and unrecorded individual actions of tens of millions of small-scale decision makers and land managers. A good example of the difficulties of detection comes from a large area of roughly 45,000 km² in eastern Thailand (fig. 14.1). Between 1973 and 1976 sedentary cultivators had nibbled away at the edges of the forest in order to create more land to grow food, while in the forest itself expanding numbers of shifting cultivators had shortened crop rotations, leading to permanent clearing. While the edge of the forest succumbed first in a piecemeal fashion, the thinning from the interior of the forest was almost impossible to detect, a problem that holds true for other parts of the world.[1]

Amid all the unknowns, however, some parts of the earth do show clear and incontestable signs of massive clearing that are amply documented and in which definite forces for change appear to operate strongly—or at least have been better documented than elsewhere. Here, the rationale of the principal actors, their attitudes, prejudices, and economic strategies, are known, and this information lends understanding to the current

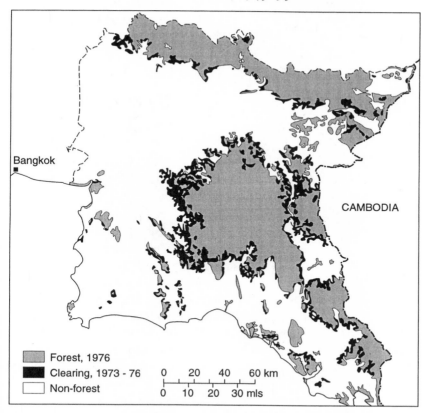

Figure 14.1 Deforestation in eastern Thailand, 1973–76. *Source:* Grainger, 1984, after Morain and Klankamsorn, 1978.

massive onslaught upon the tropical forest.[2] These examples, therefore, give the pattern of deforestation not only a reality but also a superficial regional emphasis.

Broadly speaking, deforestation is associated with four kinds of motives or forces, though in reality the forces of change are more varied and less clear-cut than this, and they tend to operate in varying combinations to produce clearing:

1. Agricultural expansion, associated with population increase/resettlement resulting in either planned or spontaneous colonization schemes, is universal, but is particularly important in Amazonia, Indonesia, and Malaysia.
2. Ranching and pasture development are significant in Central and Latin America.
3. Fuelwood gathering is most important in Africa and to a lesser extent in India.
4. Logging is noteworthy in South and Southeast Asia, and of declining importance in West Africa.

Some of these regional manifestations of predominant/proximate reasons for change will be examined in more detail below.

AGRICULTURAL DEVELOPMENT
Amazonia: "The Great Mother Forest"

Among the papers of Thomas Gill, traveler, conservationist, and American commercial timber scout, is a manuscript of an unpublished short story or popularly written article about the Amazonian forest (the genre is difficult to determine, as so much of Gill's handwriting is illegible). Written sometime in the early 1930s, it is entitled "The Passing of the Great Mother Forest." Its opening is disturbing and prophetic:

> The perfect forest, men called it, but the Amazon Indian knew it as the Great Mother. Certainly it is the richest, the most complex expression of all life, unique and certainly old. Yet in all likelihood it will become little more than a memory before the century ends. And when it is gone we will never know again the same luxuriant out flowing of life.[3]

About 25 years later not much had changed in Amazonia; this little bit of the "aggressive immensity" of 5.4 million km² of forested lowland that Bill Denevan saw in the early 1980s, extending "unbroken for hours beneath the plane" as he flew across its southwest corner from Porto Velho to La Paz in Bolivia, was still largely intact. But as he was well aware, its "demise" was only "a matter of time given present pressures."[4]

Of course, the forest was not entirely unbroken, untouched, and uninhabited. It contained about 150,000 to 200,000 Amazonian Indians, a mere remnant of the original 2–6 million that had been wiped out through disease, enslavement, and deliberate extermination from the beginning of the sixteenth century onward. Not only had the population fallen to a remnant of about 1 million in 1900, but it fell again to a mere 200,000–300,000 by 1957. More than a third of the 220 tribes had passed away during the same period, and by the late 1950s it was predicted that the native Amazonians were destined to vanish.[5] Also populating the forest were untold thousands of rubber tappers, some independent migratory workers, and some overlords with vast estates or territories of millions of hectares with thousands of Indian workers and tappers—slaves in all but name.[6] But none of these inhabitants had had any discernible *permanent* effect on the forest: their impact was small scale and intermittent, and they all worked within the natural decay and regeneration rhythms and cycles of the forest trees.[7]

But changes were already well under way around the edges of the Amazon River basin. By the mid-1960s about 4 out of every 10 ha cut in the tropics of the world was cut in this region, so its clearing burst upon Western consciousness to provide a dramatic focus of concern about deforestation. From the west and the north in the overpopulated highlands stretching from Peru to Venezuela, peasants who scratched a bare living from the thin soils began "overflowing from the Andes down to the Amazon plains . . . like a slow burning fire, concentrating along a narrow margin between the land they . . . [were] . . . destroying and . . . about to leave behind, and the forests lying ahead of them." From the south and the east, Brazilian peasants from the heavily populated coastal lands, and the drought- and poverty-stricken Northeast, were looking inward at their bigger territory. "The historical reluctance to settle the more humid life zones of the Americas is at an end," said Joseph Tosi and Robert Voertman in 1964[8] From all sides, so it seemed, everything was conspiring to attack, maim, and reduce the "Great Mother Forest."

East of the Andes

Brazil and the Amazon forest seem synonymous, but it is not commonly recognized that almost exactly one-third of the 5.4 million km² of the basin lies in the national territories of the Andean countries, which stretch from Bolivia in the south to Venezuela in the north (table 14.1). In contrast with the largely uninhabited forested lowlands, between 34 and 79 percent of the population of Peru, Bolivia, and Ecuador is located above 2,500 m (8,200 ft) in the *tierra fría,* or cold country, while the proportion in Venezuela and Colombia, though less, is still significant.

The economic, political, and social marginality of this Andean peasantry has been of long standing. Repression, violence, and poverty, either controlled or exacerbated by entrenched elites, endemic fatalism, and the fact that Spanish is still a foreign tongue to the majority, have created a critical socioeconomic situation. "The circle of life and hope has been so small and so tight," said Raymond Crist and Charles Nissly in 1973, "that it has been impossible for the individual to escape from the immemorial way of life, or even think of wanting to escape"—that is, until new roads enabled migration to the urban centers or down to the unsettled forested lands of the east.[9]

Travel eastward across one of the largest mountain chains in the world had always been difficult. Precipitous terrain, deep ravines, and raging torrents meant that it was far more difficult to go overland from, say, Lima to Pucallpa in the humid lowlands 542 km to the east, than to take a ship via the Panama Canal to Belém, transfer to river steamer, and travel over 2,600 km up the Amazon and its tributary the Ucayli, via Iquitos. Nonetheless, by the 1940s a few roads had been constructed across the high Andes to the *tierra templada,* or temperate lands, lying between about 3,000 and 6,000 ft. Fewer still had penetrated the *tierra caliente,* or hot lowlands, of the tropical rain forest to reach the eastern national boundaries in the Amazon basin proper.[10]

The eastward drive stemmed from a number of factors. Undoubtedly the urge to consolidate all territory within the national confines loomed large, especially after the bitter conflicts among Peru, Ecuador, Colombia, and Brazil over their eastern boundaries during

Table 14.1 Extent of Amazonian tropical lowland and extent of land over 2,500 m, and % of population living over 2,500 m, by country

	Amazonian Lowlands			Andean Uplands (land over 2,500 m)		
	Amazon Area (in thousands of km²)	% of Total Area	% of National Territory	% of National Territory	Population (in millions)	% of National Population
Brazil	3,560	65.9	54	–	–	–
Peru	785	14.5	61	5.6	13.6	43
Bolivia	510	9.4	47	3.7	4.7	79
Colombia	309	5.7	27	5.7	22.2	26
Ecuador	139	2.6	48	2.0	6.0	33
Venezuela	100	1.9	9	0.1	10.8	1
Total	5,403	100.0				

Source: after Moran, 1983: 5, and Little, 1981: 149.

the early 1940s. This strategic military involvement was made all the more important by valuable oil and gas discoveries in all eastern provinces during the early 1960s. Additionally, the rapidly expanding population of the high Andes (over 3 percent per annum, i.e., doubling in 21 years) after the mid-1940s, as a result of stable birthrates and tumbling death rates, strained available agricultural resources to the point of environmental deterioration, so migration and colonization seemed a reasonable solution. By 1963, President Balaúde Terry of Peru took the lead in proposing a 3,500-km highway that would link all the two dozen or so eastern trans-Andean highways from Caracas in Venezuela to Santa Cruz in Bolivia. As its name implies, the Carretera Marginal de la Selva skirted the "high jungle," or *selva*, in order to open up the *tierra templada* and act as a springboard for future colonization of the lowland humid tropical forest (fig. 14.2). Financed liberally by international backers who saw it as an imaginative developmental project to even out population pressures, the highway was constructed piecemeal over the ensuing decades.[11]

The copious commentary on the settlement and colonization that preceded and followed the Carretera from the late 1950s to the mid-1970s was couched very much in optimistic, heroic, and boosterish terms, much like Isaiah Bowman's prewar study *The Pioneer Fringe*, although Bowman had not considered (in fact, had made no mention of) the lowland tropics as a potential pioneer zone.[12] Raymond Crist and Charles Nissly's 1973 overview of migration and settlement, *East of the Andes*, implicitly adopted the same view. The rain forest was no longer "the enemy, but rather the haven for those with the will to work." They knew, as did some other writers, that farming in the tropics presented problems, and that "tens of thousands of acres of forest land are being cleared annually for cropland and pasture land." But they were not prepared to be seen to be "passing judgements" on the wisdom and efficiency of the pioneering deforestation process. Rather, they thought the damage overstated, and quoted approvingly René Dubois's article "How Man Helps Nature."[13]

In time the boosterism gave way to caution and even pessimism as the evidence steadily accumulated that many of the new settlements came at high social and ecological costs. They were "haphazard" and "ill-suited" because of lack of funds; poor social infrastructure; lack of planning, markets, and technical knowledge; and an overly bureaucratic administration, all compounded by the social upheaval and destabilization caused by the oil discoveries.[14] Moreover, directing or encouraging the spontaneous movement of ignorant peasants from the Andes to the rain forest made them no less ignorant, and they remained trapped in a peasant economy. For some commentators the fact that the peasants had come from the "treeless landscapes of the Costa or Sierra" made matters worse; it meant that when they moved into the Oriente, "their desire to create open country knows few limits," and they indulged in an orgy of clearing (plate 14.1). Further, it began to be realized that the native Amerind lowland people were "bound to suffer" in any contact, via disease, altered values, and labor coercion.

However, colonization was uncontroversial in spite of its problems, as it was a substitute for more-radical and much-needed land reform that was politically difficult to enact because of entrenched interests. But it fell far short of even its own goals; rather than creating small farms, colonization created "large, unproductive, essentially speculative"

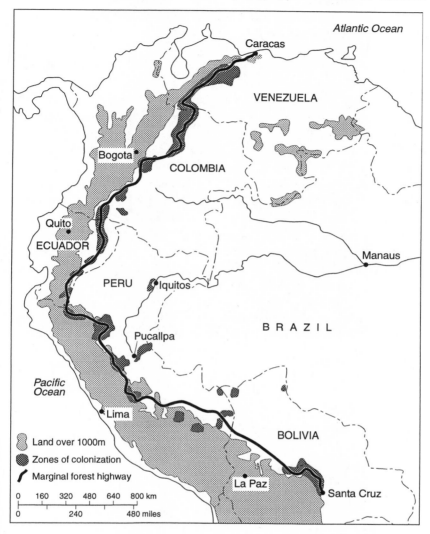

Figure 14.2 The Carretera Marginal de la Selva and areas of active colonization, east of the Andes, 1950–70.
Source: based on Crist and Nissly, 1973.

ones characterized by "semi-feudal labour relations." Moreover, as in the Brazilian Amazon, Andean Amazonian colonization was dominated by cattle raising. Ranching required little labor, did not need complex transportation infrastructure, paid well, and conferred social status. According to a perceptive observer in the mid-1960s, it was a trend that could only cause "massive deforestation and negative long-term environmental consequences."[15] Indeed, migration had already had a marked effect: between 1972 and 1987 the lowland population of the Peruvian forest had risen from 1.3 million to 2.2 million, and more than 6 million ha of forest had been cleared in addition to the 1.2 million lost prior to 1972. In the Colombian Amazon 2 million ha had been cleared (7 percent of the

Plate 14.1 East of the Andes, Bolivian Lowlands. A migrant peasant family clearing their patch of forest and erecting a crude dwelling. (Tony Morrison, South American Pictures.)

total forest), while the "humid tropical forest at the foot of the Andes had been almost completely cut down and transformed into pasture for cattle-grazing."[16]

Brazil: "Growth without Development"

Unlike their eastern neighbors, the Brazilians had always regarded the humid, moist forests of the continent as a grim fact of existence, which like an "interminable green monster. . . [shut] out the sun of heaven." From the beginning of settlement in the mid-sixteenth century, the Atlantic coastal forest had been an all-pervasive reality. Settlement had always meant the conquest of the coastal forests; the growing of sugar, cotton, cocoa, and coffee and the raising of cattle had only been possible by felling and burning the trees. The people of Brazil, thought Roy Nash in 1926, "always have considered the forests as a communal possession which they felt free to hack, burn and abandon at will," so that even then he thought that at least 30 percent of the precontact forest had disappeared:

> [I]f one could hover over Brazil in a balloon and get a bird's-eye view of forest after forest as each comes to the end of its dry season, he would see myriad smokes curl heaven-ward year after year, and century after century. Farming by fire—shifting agriculture—is as much the mode of life of the nomads of the Brazilian forests as of the Fangs of the Congo.[17]

But Brazil, in addition to its uniquely vast forest resource, was also probably in a class of its own in other ways. Settlement and territorial expansion had long been accompanied by a history of exploitative behavior and violence that had few counterparts in the world. Wide social differentiation, undemocratic politics, illegal squatting, the segregation—and even elimination—of native populations, and vast grants of land, all shot through with a staggering lawlessness, corruption, and contravention of the rule of law, were the hallmarks of Brazilian society, and did not change markedly in the later twentieth century. The forest peasantry, or *caboclos,* had always devastated large areas with "broadax in one hand and a firebrand in the other," but now the shifting backwoodsmen were aided, encouraged, and even replaced by much bigger players. The army, government agencies, transnational companies, even the state were the new *caboclos.*[18] Deforestation in the Brazilian Amazon after 1960 becomes a story of superlatives: of vast areas and long distances, of swirling population shifts by the millions, massive deforestation, breathtaking change, contradictory claims, and international reaction and condemnation.

The Generals' Plan

The impetus for Brazil's post–World War II acceleration of deforestation was its emerging obsession with economic development. The aim was to stimulate capital accumulation and industrialization through aggressive central planning in order to achieve a high rate of economic growth that would give country world-class status while promoting the positive virtues of independence, self-realization, and the banishment of backwardness and poverty. Postwar exuberance worldwide had led to the notion that the global "periphery" could compete successfully with the "core" of the industrialized world; "hot-" and "cold-" war policies from 1940 onward aided this notion and led to the propping up of the Latin American economies. "Economic development was more than a government policy," said Warren Dean; "it amounted to a social program of vast scope, energy and originality." The subsequent "high-powered public relations campaign" penetrated the consciousness of every citizen, and was made to justify everything that was done to society, nature, and the forest.[19]

But development was a chimera; the strategy did not achieve its aims. Wealth was redistributed not to the poor, but to the rich; the crucial issue of agrarian reform for the small landholder was avoided by diverting attention to the colonization of the Atlantic and Amazon forests, which tended to favor the large landholders. Brazil's unparalleled forests were squandered in an exploitative binge that undervalued the rich resource, which was bartered cheaply for "development." As far as the Amazon was concerned, it was "growth without development."[20]

Initially the transformation took place in the Atlantic coastal forest, and from about 1950 to 1970 investment and development were concentrated in and around the "industrial triangle" of São Paulo, Belo Horizonte, and Rio de Janiero, where the return on investment was high. The remnants of the Atlantic forest were further reduced. All this was achieved, however, amid much political instability and volatility, with marked swings to the Left and to the Right. In the poisoned atmosphere of the cold war years and with the specter of a Communist ascendancy raised by the Cuban Revolution of 1959, such instability could not be tolerated, and military intervention followed in 1964 with the overthrow of the government of President Goulart. For the next 24 years "the Generals" ruled supreme, obsessed with the development imperative, dreaming of national destiny, suspicious of populism or any collective action—whether by peasant farmers, environmental activists, or banks—paranoiac about foreign designs on the Amazon, and wary of overseas criticism of the loss of cultural and biological diversity.[21]

The grand strategy envisaged for the colonization of the Amazon was a combination of military-strategic and geopolitical aims designed to secure national boundaries, promote economic development, and exploit unused resources. Central to the geopolitical was the development of roads to link "vast hinterlands waiting and hoping to be moved to life and to fulfil their historic destiny" from the central or "manoeuvring platform" of the developed south. The roads would also aid in the "total war" that the Generals foresaw would have to be waged against internal and even external—particularly neighboring—subversion, which certainly had attracted U.S. aid in the Alliance for Progress program. The threat of the "internationalisation" of the Amazon voiced either in the insensitive overseas comments about relieving global population pressures and resettling tens of millions in the basin, or in lamentations over environmental degradation, also figured in their calculations.[22]

Between 1964 and 1967 the new government committed itself to developing the whole subcontinental region and integrating it into the rest of Brazil with a series of acts and decrees, known collectively as Operation Amazonia. Central to this policy was the acquisition of state land by the federal government for a road-building program, which had three aims:

1. integrating the poverty-stricken and isolated Northeast around Recife into the rest of Brazil and syphoning off the excess of the 30 million inhabitants (a severe drought in 1970 merely laid bare an agony of poverty long evident);
2. promoting colonization in the northwest in the states of Rondônia and Acre in order to counteract active colonization by Peru and Venezuela in these vast, but thinly populated upriver forested areas of the Amazon; and
3. creating a major east–west road, running roughly parallel to the River Amazon in order to protect the frontier, "inundate the Amazon forest with civilization," and link the newfound mineral resources (e.g., iron ore) with the coast.[23]

In 1960, the Amazon region had only 6,000 km of roads; two major cities, Belém and Manaus; and a scatter of small towns and villages along the major lines of communication, which consisted of the Amazon and its hundreds of tributaries. That isolation ended with the building the 1,900-km road from Belém, south along the Tocantins valley. It ran through a mixed-vegetation area of savanna, scrub, and tropical deciduous forests to the new capital, Brasília, which had been officially opened in 1960, itself a part of the overall strategy to shift the focus of the country from the overcrowded coasts to the interior (fig. 14.3). Construction of the Belém–Brasília road had actually begun in 1958 under the previous civil administration, which had also created SPVEA (Superintendency for the Economic Valorization of the Amazon), the first of the many acronymic bodies set up to develop the Amazon. SPVEA had already defined the "Legal Amazon" as an area for operations (see fig. 14.6) and set up a development bank, but it was perceived (correctly) by the Generals as corrupt and inefficient. Consequently it was replaced by SUDAM, Superintendência de Desenvolvimento da Amazônia.[24]

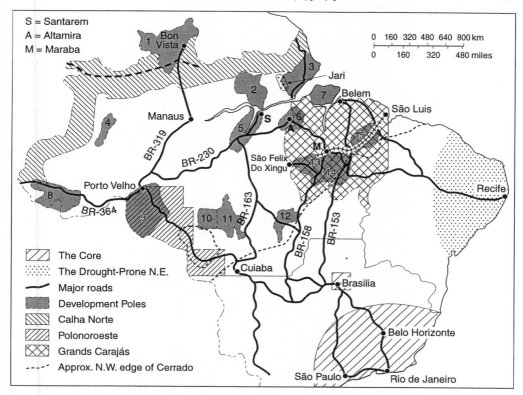

Figure 14.3 The Generals' Plan: slicing up the Amazon basin. *Source:* Hecht and Cockburn, 1989: 127–28; various. The growth poles in the Polo Amazônia and their rationale are as follows.

1. Roraima: livestock and some mining in a frontier zone.
2. Trombetas: bauxite deposits.
3. Amapa: agriculture and livestock in a frontier zone.
4. Juruá: logging and later, oil.
5. Tapajós: agriculture and livestock, later gold mining.
6. Altamira: agricultural and livestock farming on Trans-Amazonian Highway.
7. Marajó: livestock, timber, and oil.
8. Acre: agriculture and livestock in frontier area.
9. Rondônia: agriculture and livestock in frontier area.
10. Aripuná: forest research and logging.
11. Juruena: livestock and agriculture; later, gold mining.
12. Xingu-Araguaia: livestock and meat.
13. The Carajás: iron and gold mining, and center for later Projeto Grande Carajás.
14. Araguaia-Tocantins: livestock, logging, gold mining, and general commerce.
15. Livestock, but later focused on railway line, Sao Luis to Carajás iron mine.

The Belém–Brasília road and its feeders were successful in opening up the forest and linking distant parts of the country. As was to be proved again and again, the provision of paved roads unleashed the spontaneous and uncontrollable spread of settlement. Small peasant holdings, but particularly cattle ranches, sprang up everywhere on the low-quality pastures created on cheaply deforested land, bolstered by the generous tax and credit incentives offered by the government to attract private enterprise. The population increased from about 100,000 in 1960 to 2 million ten years later, and more significantly the cattle population rose from nil to over 5 million in the same period. The adjacent country was serviced by the feeder roads, and it was occupied quickly. For example, on either side of the parallel road PA-150 in southeast Pará, a stretch of 4.7 million ha (about the size of Switzerland) had 30,000 ha cleared in 1972, 170,000 ha in 1977, and 820,000 in 1985 (fig. 14.4), and must serve as an example of what some commentators later called "explosive deforestation."[25]

The array of financial incentives for settlement and clearing was astounding. For example, up to 50 percent of corporate tax liability for 12 years (later extended to 17 years) could be invested in already existing Amazonian projects, thus allowing taxes to become, in effect, venture capital. Up to 75 percent of capital costs would be supplied by the government through its special credit bank, BASA; and credit was available for the purchase of land with no repayment for between 4 to 8 years at interest rates of about 10–12 percent. Without these tax incentives the cattle ranches would not have been profitable. But with them—and given the fact that inflation was running at well over 100 percent a year—it was a license to chop down trees and print money.[26]

In addition to the incentives to invest, the costs of production were low because little labor was needed, and in any case, workers could easily be hired from the hordes of refugees from the drought-stricken Northeast. The final product—meat—could be walked to market and was always readily salable whatever its quality: as Warren Dean commented, "Brazilians were culturally addicted to beef eating." In what was to become indicative of future developments, cattle reigned supreme: of about 950 projects approved by SUDAM, 631 were in the livestock sector, mainly in South Pará and northern Mato Grosso, with at least 60 percent of the investment coming from large industrial and agro-industrial enterprises in the São Paulo region, which saw cattle raising as a tax-efficient investment. In the 8.4 million ha of SUDAM-approved cattle ranches, the average size was about 24,000 ha, and one (the Suia-Missu in northern Mato Grosso) was 560,000 ha. On every count the little farmer was being squeezed out. Without the government subsidies, deforestation rates would have been far lower.[27]

Encouraged by the success of the Belém–Brasília road, the military government moved quickly to create the Program for National Integration (PIN) with the aim of building the 1,800-km north–south Cuiabá–Santarém road (B-163). More important was the symbolically significant east–west Transamazonia highway, BR-230. Its 5,400 km (about 3,300 km in Amazonia) was to link Recife with the interior and direct the movement of the poverty-stricken Northeasterners toward the Amazon and away from the center-south around São Paulo (see fig. 14.3). Like the U.S. Homestead Act of a century before, the settlement project distributed free land with the aim of creating a class of prosperous, independent small farmers. The settlement along these new roads was planned in contrast with the spontaneous settlement along the Belém–Brasília highway, which the Generals branded as "disorderly." The aims were ambitious: a hierarchical set of planned and serviced cities *(ruropolis)* for about 1,000 families; towns *(agropolis)* for about 300 families; and agro-villages *(agrovila)* for 48–60 families were envisaged at varying distances along and around the main highways.[28] The goal was the "gradual occupying of the empty spaces" by moving 100,000 families in the first 5 years, though that would have hardly made a dent in the demographic problems of the Northeast. More strategic than these two roads was the construction of a parallel Northern Perimeter Road to stop any chance of incursion into Brazilian territory by Venezuela and Colombia, and to act as a

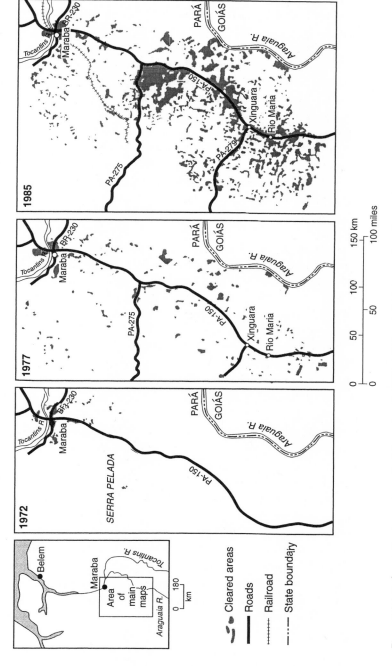

Figure 14.4 Deforestation in southeast Pará State, Brazil, 1972, 1977, and 1985. *Source:* based on Mahar, 1989: 14.

counterbalance to the developmental Marginal Forest Highway (Carretera Marginal de la Selva) built by the Andean countries.[29]

But because of the 1973 oil crisis, which severely affected Brazil, many of these plans were shelved. The Perimeter Road was never built and was replaced by the more limited and overtly strategic Calle Norte. Along the Transamazon Highway the policy of encouraging small farmers was abandoned in 1974 in favor of large-scale entrepreneurs. Of the 100,000 families that PIN had hoped to settle, perhaps only 8,000 relocated, and very few of the planned settlements eventuated. In addition, because the cost of cutting the subsidiary feeder roads was about three times greater than envisaged, thousands of kilometers were never built, which relegated the would-be settler to isolation and poverty, as the forest plots could yield no produce. In any case the initial enthusiasm about the fertility of most of the Amazonian soils was soon destroyed when their true lateritic nature was revealed after clearing. The declared aim of PIN to provide "a land without men for men without land" was all but over. All it had done was to unleash a fury of speculative clearing in the forest; it had created a land without trees but full of cattle.[30]

Rondônia

One of the most remote and inaccessible areas of the Amazon—indeed of the world—before 1970 was the border country with Bolivia and Peru, in the states of Acre, Rondônia, and northern Mato Grosso. Here were some 85 million ha of land, most of which was covered with tropical moist forest inhabited by about only 70,000 rubber tappers and an unknown number of Indian tribespeople. From the southern, populated part of the country, around Rio or São Paulo, it took about 6 weeks to reach by oceangoing ship up the Amazon to Manaus, and then by steamer 1,100 km down the Madeira River to disembark at Porto Velho. In 1968 the geography of the region was revolutionized: Highway BR-364 was constructed to link the 1,500 km between Cuiabá and Porto Velho, and the wild, remote, forested frontier could now be reached by 3 to 4 days' hard, but not unreasonable, coach journey.

As with the Belém–Brasília highway, the completion of BR-364 was followed by a wave of spontaneous migration, which rose from a few thousand per annum during the early 1970s, when the road was first opened, to a yearly average of 160,000 between 1984 and 1988. The rush into Rondônia stemmed from "pull" and "push" factors. First BR-364 traversed some areas of good soils (approximately 10 percent of the area, compared with an average of 3 percent over all Amazonia), a feature that was publicized and exaggerated. In addition, 100-ha plots with roads and services could be purchased cheaply via several colonization companies established by INCRA (National Institute for Colonization and Agrarian Reform). But as the decade progressed, migrants came not from Brazil's perennial problem area of the Northeast as had been expected, but from the rich agricultural areas of the state of Paraná, 1,300 km to the south of Cuiabá at the far southern end of the highway. These settlers had a dramatic effect on Rondônia's forests.

Paraná had been a thriving agricultural area in the immediate postwar period with a reasonably healthy mix of tree and field crops—primarily coffee and maize, rice, and beans—and by Brazilian standards, it was a prosperous and egalitarian rural society. But disease, soil erosion, and overproduction had caused severe problems in the rural areas, and the government's solution was to reduce the number of coffee trees, exacerbating the rural problems. The generous provision of compensation to the former coffee growers meant that more coffee trees were uprooted than had been anticipated: about 400 million were eliminated between 1961 and 1969, and what remained were devastated by a killing frost in 1975. As a result, the economy never recovered fully. Labor was shed as former coffee growing areas were converted to mechanized soya bean crops, for which there was a ready international market as livestock feed. Small farms (less than 50 ha) fell by 109,000 units between 1970 and 1980, with a loss of 890,000 ha of land, whereas during the same period large farms (over 1,000 ha) increased by 450 units, with a gain of more than 1,000,000 ha. As coffee acreage halved and then halved again, land in soya beans rose from a mere 172,000 ha to over 2.3 million ha.

The loss of employment was catastrophic: over 2.5 million small farmers and laborers migrating out, with at least a third going to Rondônia.[31] The establishment of a regular coach connection between Paraná and Rondônia completed the process of change. All that was needed was a ticket to ride the bus, and three or four days later the aspiring migrants arrived in the promised land, initiating one of the most rapid and extensive deforestation episodes of modern times.

The agricultural workers were given temporary accommodations and inoculated against malaria and gastrointestinal diseases and worms, which were rife.[32] Those who had money attempted to buy land. The rest waited up to 2 years to be allotted a plot, by which time they had drifted into the squatter settlements on the edge of the burgeoning towns, become sharecroppers to established landholders, or illegally staked out claims in the forest edge and hoped for an eventual title to their land. The flow of migrants was so great that INCRA soon recognized illegal settler claims, but it was overwhelmed by the demand. In an attempt to control and cope with the flood of people, a new scheme— POLONORESTE (The Northwest Brazil Integrated Development Program)—was set up in 1981 with World Bank backing to benefit an additional 20,000 families expected to come to the region, in addition to the 15,000 awaiting land. The program emphasized the planned provision of services and a sustainable system of farming consisting of protective tree crops like coffee, cacao, and rubber, along with a reduction of pasture development. But after 1984 it too was overwhelmed by migrants when BR-364 was made into an all-weather road. The flow of newcomers rose to a yearly average of 160,000, fanning out along the branch roads, chopping, burning, and planting, hoping for a brighter future (plate 14.2, fig. 14.5).[33]

The sheer press of people made the government's task unequal to the resources available, but just as important was the fact that many of the banks and SUDAM favored pasture development over small landholdings. This meant that by 1985 over a quarter of all the "improved" land was in pasture, a figure that has probably tripled since then. In fact, more land was cleared for speculative purposes than for producing food. Any land cleared of its trees was regarded as "improved" and the "improvement" could be sold, so that with the rapid rise of land prices a "frenzy of deforestation and real estate speculation" ensued. Consequently, it was possible to garner a net US$9,000 for clearing 14 ha of forest, plant some pasture, and get a few crops for a couple of years, and then sell to a new settler, a process enhanced by the fact that the 25-percent capital gains tax was rarely collected. The implication of this level of profit for small landholders, let alone those with

Plate 14.2 An aspiring migrant family in the promised land of Rondônia State, Brazil. (Tony Morrison, South American Pictures.)

tens of thousands of hectares was clear, and rising land prices were the engine that drove deforestation.[34]

As was the case almost everywhere in Brazil, everything ultimately favored the clearing of the forest for pasture, and probably as much as 85 percent of all land cleared in Rondônia is occupied by livestock (plate 14.3). The positive benefits of cattle raising, such as high social status, low labor costs, and relatively good returns, are clear, as are the credit and tax incentives. Again, with a rate of inflation that has varied between 20 and 200 percent per annum, land has served as a hedge against the faltering value of the Brazilian currency. These advantages far outweigh the abysmally low productivity of pastures, which rarely exceed one beast per 2.4 ha. But in a country of—to put it mildly— uncertain land titles, which "rest on shameless fraud" and violence, a plot cleared of its vegetation is evidence of "effective use" (which has some legal standing), and substantiates and denotes ownership. At the very least it has readily recognizable boundaries that might dissuade the gunmen of the big landowners from trying to take it over.[35] Thus cattle substitute for other traditional ways of making money—through speculation and fraud. Once government subsidies are stopped, livestock raising is abandoned, as has happened with many of the SUDAM projects.[36]

Other Schemes

Agriculture and ranching are not the only ways in which the forest is being destroyed. A naive faith in "giantism" has penetrated into other Brazilian schemes with devastating effect. The Fordlandia rubber plantation along the Tapajós River, just south of Santarém, was begun in 1927 only to be abandoned in 1945 after poor local planning, unsuitable soils, plant diseases, labor problems, and local corruption made it impossible to carry on. In an eerie replay of that experience, Daniel Ludwig, an American shipping billionaire, launched the rashly ambitious Jari scheme in 1967 with Japanese financial backing (fig. 14.3). About 2.5 million ha of forest were cleared and planted with the fast-growing *Gmelina arborea* trees from eastern India in order to supply an anticipated shortage of wood fiber. But again, poor planning, unsuitable soils, diseases to trees, labor problems, and an inability to get clear title to the land from the state government meant that the project failed, closing down in 1982.[37] Everywhere, scores of plans and schemes for dams to generate hydroelectric power have inundated many thousands of square kilometers of forest because the generally flat terrain does not provide ideal locations for effective dam building.

Finally, the massive Grande Carajás Project (see fig. 14.3), a major regional plan for some 825,000 km² south of the Transamazon Highway and east of the Xingu River, involves the development of mining, forestry, agriculture, hydroelectricity, and transportation. Mining is concentrated on the exploitation of the vast deposits of copper,

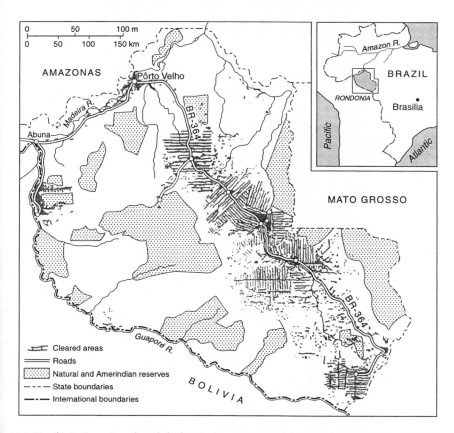

Figure 14.5 Rondônia State, Brazil, and the herringbone pattern of clearing. *Source:* Mahar, 1989: 32; see also Fearnside, 1986: 74–81.

Plate 14.3 Rondônia State, Brazil. Banana plants replace the cleared tropical forest (remnants of which are in the background) while the ubiquitous white Brahmin/Zebu cattle roam over improvised pastures and degraded scrubland. (Tony Morrison, South American Pictures.)

nickel, manganese, bauxite, and particularly iron ore. Although the mining per se has little impact on the forest (except to create some of the largest holes ever made in the ground), the 25 or so industrial furnaces use local charcoal. Plans to plant eucalypts have foundered because of their ecological unsustainability in the lowland rain forest, and fuelwood supplies are being garnered from an ever-increasing circle, consuming many hundreds of square kilometers of forest a year.[38]

Life on the Forest Frontier

Almost everywhere in the world the colonization of the forest has been the means of social advancement and improvement for the landless peasant—the "little" man and his family. It was true, for example, on the frontiers of Rome during the first centuries BC and AD, of medieval Europe, eighteenth- and nineteenth-century America, nineteenth-century New Zealand and Australia, large parts of colonial India and Burma, and even, from what little we know, of Ming China, especially in the southern part of the country. Even in Brazil, small- and medium-sized holdings were created successfully during the late nineteenth and early twentieth centuries out of the forested lands of the eastern parts of Rio Grande do Sul, west Santa Catarina, west and north Paraná, south Mato Grosso, areas of central-west São Paulo, the Doce valley in Minas Gerais, and a large part of Espírito Santo. But with very few exceptions the same has not been true of the colonization of the great Amazonian forest after about 1960. Despite the rhetoric "to give people with no land a land with no people," the reality has fallen far short of the ideal. Migrants have been lucky if they have farmed the land "for two or three years—if at all," according to Joe Foweraker in his aptly entitled 1981 study *The Struggle for Land,* which focused on south Pará, western Paraná and south Mato Grosso. "Land on the frontier is taken over by large holdings and large enterprises dedicated more often than not to cattle raising . . . the cattle grow fat . . . while the people go hungry," he says. Thus, the colonization of the forest did not result in social betterment but social impoverishment, and the situation has fared no better in the subsequent 20 years.[39]

Many of the reasons for this paradox have been mentioned already. After the early 1970s there was a unique convergence of national and international economic and political factors that distorted the aims of natives and newcomers alike. Prolonged military government and strategic aims, a drive to industrialize, insensitive and corrupt bureaucracy, conflicting policies, a collapse of sponsored colonization schemes, increasing fiscal and credit incentives to international and national enterprises—all led to the penetration by monopoly capital not people. As always it was the poor, the potential beneficiaries of the mantle of the forest, who suffered most. Colonization was beyond even the reach of those with some resources to invest. They found it impossible to secure a clear title to the land they claimed or to establish the minimum conditions for long-term investment of time and labor. Even if they did, they faced a hostile physical environment of deteriorating soils and yields, and an even more hostile social environment of violence, intimidation, takeover, and murder as cattle ranchers and land grabbers (aided and abetted by corrupt local police and administrators) made their life one of fairly unrelieved toil, poverty, and injustice. If resistance became too great the military was called in to quell "a national security problem," of which the "Araguaia War" was a notorious example. In all, many thousands were killed.[40] Thus, while the big sweep of the story of Amazonian deforestation is reasonably clear, the voices of the little people—"the men with the machetes" who "are ahead of the road builders trying, in the honest tradition of the pioneer, to carve a home from the forest"—are often difficult to hear in the din and turmoil of this new forest frontier. In fact, they have often been muted or extinguished.[41]

Books have been written attempting to explain the paradoxical nature of Brazilian agricultural development, and it would be superfluous to reiterate in detail what they have to say. One example must suffice. For 15 years Marianne Schmink and Charles Wood followed the lives and fortunes of migrants in the frontier settlement around São Felix do Xingu, a small frontier town on the Xingu River in South Pará State at the end of B-279, about 300 km west of the junction at Xinguara on the B-150 (see fig. 14.3).[42] By the middle of the 1970s most of the small farmers had been driven off the land they had cleared.

> The dispossessed faced a difficult and uncertain future. Many moved on down the road. Others ventured back into the bush, only to fall victim again to expropriation. Thousands of families drifted from one work site to another, temporarily employed by labor recruiters . . . who had been contracted by ranchers to clear land for pasture during the dry season.

If they had enough money, some went back to their home states, but many more lost their land and were too poor to return, so they sought refuge in the new shanty towns that sprang up on the outskirts of cities like Marabá, Xinguara, or Redenção. "In as little as two or three years places that held only a handful of people suddenly exploded into make-shift towns of fifteen to twenty thousand." Marabá grew at a staggering rate of 21 per-cent per annum between 1960 and 1980, and was well over 100,000 by the mid-1980s. Not surprisingly, these "boom" towns lacked sanitation, medical and educational serv-ices, regular employment, or any means of support for the uprooted.

The people of São Felix do Xingu experienced a measurable deterioration in their liv-ing standards between 1978 and 1984. Food consumption had decreased, the choice of foods had narrowed, and infant and child mortality had risen. To make matters worse, "Sao Felix was the third or fourth place where they had tried unsuccessfully to find a piece of land to support themselves." Some got employment during the dry season in the small sawmills that sprang up everywhere, but these were temporary, makeshift affairs. Once the mahogany was logged (which represented a minuscule part of the total tim-ber available), the rest of the forest was cleared, burned, and converted to grazing land. The vision of the better life that the cleared forest offered was a chimera, and the hapless settlers were now literally and metaphorically at the "end of the road."

Opposition and resistance, exemplified by the protests and subsequent murder of rub-ber tapper Chico Mendes, sparked national and international condemnation, and the presence and savvy of the Kayapó Indians on their vast reserve west of the region might impede the exploitation of people and vegetation, but Schmink and Wood have no wish "to wax romantic about grassroots movements . . . which remain small and perched at the edge of power." Nor do they have any reason to believe that "deforestation will abate, at least not as long as the incentives for it remain"—a dismal conclusion to reach, but un-doubtedly realistic.[43]

How Much Deforestation?

Given the speed and extent of clearing in the Amazon region and the evidence of large, powerful, and long-lasting forest fires, it would not be surprising if the questions "how much?" and "how fast?" were asked. Like everything else about the Amazon, the an-swers seem to come in emotive superlatives as the "dialectics of destruction" tumble out; the forest is in a state of "systematic demolition" or "imminent demise." The immigrants are "torching" the forest and creating "a burning season" (plate 14.4) while the large landholders indulge in murder and violence in order to dominate the frontier. A report by the São Paulo–based Institute for Space Research, analyzing air photography images drawn from an 80-day period during 1987, "conservatively estimated" that over 200,000 km^2 of the forest, or 4 percent of the Amazon region, were burning between July and Oc-tober. "The skies over western Brazil," reported *Time* magazine in 1989, "will soon be dark both day and night. Dark from the smoke of thousands of fires as farmers and cat-tle ranchers engage in the seasonal rite of destruction." The destruction of the Amazon rain forest was one of the "great tragedies of all history," and the country had acquired a reputation, "especially among the young" said *The Economist,* "as the world's envi-ronmental thug."[44]

The Amazon, of course, is not just an example or a microcosm of the bigger picture of tropical deforestation; it is a very sizable chunk of it, so that the pace and extent of clearing not only reflects but affects the global trend. All the problems of calibration and

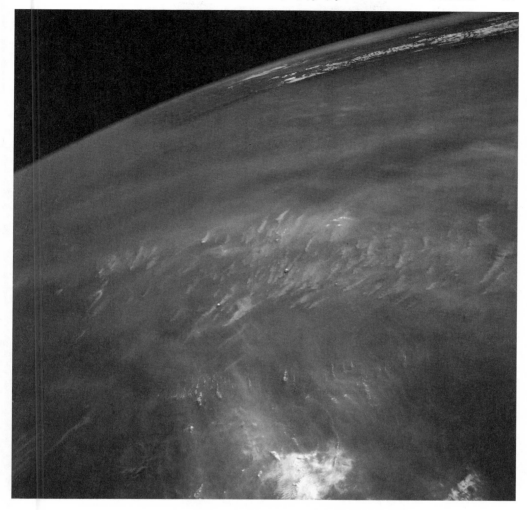

Plate 14.4 Rondônia and Mato Grosso States, Brazil, during the burning season, August 1984. The thermal plumes of smoke from clearing activity reach up above the smoke haze toward the Space Shuttle camera. On the horizon are the snow-covered peaks of the Bolivian/Peruvian Andes, which stand above the smoke pall, and Lake Titicaca beyond. (NASA STS41D-40-0022.)

accuracy noted earlier are present. Official data are incomplete and often out of date, and estimates "vary sharply" while data from different forms of satellite surveillance (e.g., LANDSAT, AVHRR [Advanced Very High Resolution Radiometer] satellite sensors) are open to different interpretation—in particular, the clearing of forest, or *cerrado,* and its regrowth are difficult to detect.[45] During the early 1980s it looked as though the rate of clearing was such that if continued it would explode exponentially. In that case, all states of the Amazon would have been completely stripped clear of trees by now, except Roraima (cleared by 2002) and Amazonas (cleared by 2003) (table 14.2; for locations see fig. 14.6). This obviously has not happened, and as the end of the century has come and gone the forest is still far from becoming what Tom Gill had predicted as "little more than

Table 14.2 Clearing (by km² and % affected) in the Legal Amazon, 1975, 1978, 1980, and 1988, and estimate of year of complete clearing

State or Territory	Area (in thousands of km²)	Area Altered (in km²) To 1975	To 1978	To 1980	To 1988	% of Area Altered To 1975	To 1978	To 1980	To 1988	Year Completely Cleared
Acre	152.6	1,166	2,465	4,627	19,500	0.8	1.6	3.0	12.8	1995
Amàpá	140.3	153	172	–	572	0.1	0.1	–	0.4	2159
Amazonas	1,587.1	784	1,791	–	105,790	0.1	0.1	–	6.8	2003
Maranhão	257.5	2,941	7,334	10,671	50,670	1.1	2.8	4.1	19.7	1990
Mato Grosso	881.0	9,871	30,309	52,786	208,000	1.1	3.4	6.0	23.6	1989
Pará	1,248.6	9,948	24,950	33,914	120,000	0.8	2.0	2.7	9.6	1991
Rondônia	243.0	1,216	4,185	7,579	58,000	0.5	1.7	3.1	23.7	1988
Roraima	230.1	55	144	1,170	3,270	0.0	0.1	0.5	1.4	2002
Tocantins	285.8	3,299	7,209	9,121	33,120	1.2	2.5	3.2	11.6	1988
Total	5,005.4	29,342	78,617	119,868	598,922	0.6	1.6	2.4	12.0	1991

Source: based on Salati et al., 1990: 486; and Fearnside, 1982: 85.

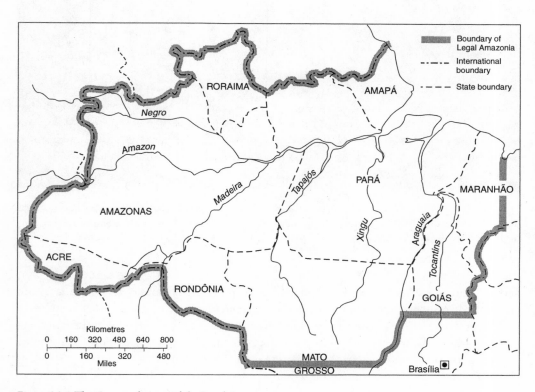

Figure 14.6 The rivers and states of the Legal Amazon.

a memory."[46] By 1985 Philip Fearnside had abandoned the exponential argument and the prediction that the forest would disappear by a particular year, saying instead that deforestation was "explosive," especially in Rondônia, where the mass migration of smaller settlers, especially after the paving of highway BR-364, made it a "laboratory for studying deforestation." Rondônia became one of the most photographed and remote-sensed patches on the earth's surface as paper after paper analyzed changes and made familiar the images of the progressively thickening herringbone pattern of clearing along main and subsidiary side roads (plates 14.5A, 14.5B), so that it became a popular and

Plate 14.5A The distinctive "herringbone" pattern of clearing in Rondônia State, Brazil, as settlers fell the forest to create pastures and agricultural plots either side of the lateral roads, has made it one of the most photographed pieces of the earth's surface from space. Here the main road, Highway B-364, snakes diagonally across the picture, and roads branch out every 2–3 mi (4–5 km) into the tropical rain forest, shown as solid dark color. June 1985. (NASA STS51G-34-0060.)

Plate 14.5B An adjacent area 7 years later. The amount of clear-cut now exceeds the remaining rain forest stands. August 1992. (NASA STS046-078-026.)

universal symbol of forest destruction.[47] Starting from virtually no land cleared in 1970 within its 230,104 km², the area of forest destruction climbed steadily to 13,995 km² in 1983, and to nearly 58,000 km² in 1988.[48]

Over the whole of the Legal Amazon (5 million km²) the picture looked only fractionally better. Despite inconsistencies, problems, and the controversy of interpreting data, "best estimates" suggested that 345,000 km² had been deforested between 1970 and 1988 (including old clearings), or 8.2 percent of the forested four-fifths of the Legal Amazon, a total which might be raised by another 115,000 km², or 9.6 percent, if the area originally under forest and in *cerrado* was included. The rate of new clearing was staggering—20,000 km²/yr or 39,000 km² if the *cerrado* was included.[49] With new data

Eneas Salati suggested that the total was even greater: up to 1988 over 598,921 km², or 12 percent, had been cleared (table 14.2).[50]

And there the matter of Amazonian deforestation lay, shrouded in uncertainty and speculation, until David Skole and Compton J. Tucker produced the most detailed and most widespread analysis ever attempted. Using photographic images from LANDSAT Thematic Mapping Data and a GIS computer program, Skole and Tucker mapped changes between 1978 and 1988 at a spatial resolution of 16 × 16 km², small enough to allow the identification of individual plots of forest, regrowth, crops, and pasture. Not only could the area of deforestation in the closed-canopy forest over the total Brazilian Amazon be identified, but also the degree to which the forest had become fragmented and degraded, that is to say, the amount of forest that became isolated and the length of forest edge that was exposed through deforestation.[51] By 1978 some 78,000 km² had been cleared, which had risen to 230,000 km² by 1988 (table 14.3), giving an average annual rate of clearing of 15,200 km² over the intervening 10 years. The amount of forest degraded or fragmented rose from 208,000 km² to 588,000 km² in 1988.

Skole and Tucker's new total of 230,000 km² by 1988 is considerably less than the 345,000 km² calculated by Fearnside, and markedly less than the 598,921 km² suggested by Salati/Mahar or, indeed, amounts put forward in a host of other more recent studies. Similarly, the rate of clearing at 15,200 km²/yr is considerably less than the 21,000 to 80,000 km²/yr suggested elsewhere, all of which has implications for the global total.[52] Wherever the truth lies about the amount and rate of deforestation, it is evident that as in the tropical world at large uncertainty reigns, and that there is much hype about it. That is not to say that the amount or rate is insignificant, but that it is not as great as was commonly thought. At a constant rate of clearing of 15,200 km²/yr, it will take about 276 years for the 4.1 million or 4.2 million km² of the "Great Mother Forest" to disappear, even assuming that abandonment and regrowth will not reclaim a considerable portion of the old forestland, as all experience shows it will. What the Skole and Tucker study does supremely well is to locate change geographically for the whole Legal Amazon in a way that has only been hinted at before, or known only for small sections of spectacular change such as Rondônia and the Belém-Brasília highway (fig. 14.7).

Beyond Amazonia there is hardly any part of the Latin American continent where there is not some evidence of clearing, both planned and spontaneous, though much of it is only know about vaguely. In the Zona Central of Paraguay, for example, it is claimed that the 40,000 km² of tropical rain forest that existed in 1945 has been reduced to about 13,000 km² today, while the borderlands with Brazil have also been cleared for agriculture and pastureland.[53] But the total continental picture remains blurred.

South and Southeast Asia

Planned and deliberate governmental schemes to promote agricultural development and resettlement for the alleviation of population pressures are not confined to the Amazon basin; they also have been prominent in South and Southeast Asia, primarily in Indonesia and Malaysia. But in neither of these countries are the agricultural development programs

Table 14.3 Predeforestation area of forest, *cerrado*, and water, and deforested and isolated and edge forest (in km²), Brazilian Amazon, 1978 and 1988

	Predeforestation				1978				1988		1988
	Forest	Cerrado	Water	Total Area	Deforested	Isolated and Edge	Total Disturbed	Deforested	Isolated and Edge	Total Disturbed	As % Total Area
Acre	152.4	0	0.4	152.8	2.6	4.5	7.1	6.4	24.1	30.5	20.0
Amàpá	137.4	1.0	1.1	139.5	0.2	0.4	0.6	0.2	0.7	0.9	0.6
Amazonas	1,531.1	14.4	29.8	1,575.3	2.3	6.5	8.8	11.8	36.9	48.7	3.1
Maranhão	145.8	114.7	1.3	261.8	9.4	13.8	23.2	32.0	30.3	62.3	23.8
Mato Grosso	527.6	368.7	4.2	900.5	21.1	26.2	47.3	47.6	73.7	121.3	13.4
Pará	1,183.6	28.6	49.5	1,261.7	30.5	52.0	82.5	95.1	123.5	218.6	17.3
Rondônia	212.2	24.6	1.5	238.3	6.2	18.7	24.9	24.0	54.8	78.8	33.0
Roraima	172.4	51.5	1.8	225.7	0.2	0.8	1.0	1.9	5.2	7.1	3.1
Tocantins	30.3	244.0	2.9	277.2	5.7	6.9	12.6	11.4	8.2	19.6	7.1
Total	4,092.8	847.5	92.5	5,032.8	78.2	129.8	208	230.4	357.8	587.8	11.7

Source: Skole and Tucker, 1993: 1906.

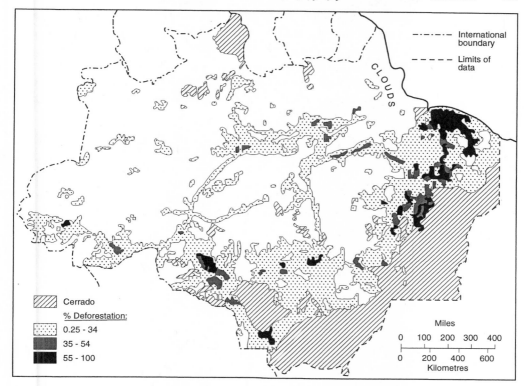

Figure 14.7 Deforestation in the Brazilian Amazon, 1988. *Source:* generalized from Skole and Tucker, 1993: 1907.

as large or subject to such grandiose plans, nor have they received the same publicity or research investigation. In any case they have been directed far more at peasant agricultural clearing.

In Indonesia the government initiated a Transmigration Project, which has attempted to shift over 2 million peasant farmers from overcrowded Java (where population densities reach as much as 3,000/km^2) to "empty" forested lands in Sumatra, Irian Jaya, and Kalimantan, although the schemes themselves have also proved to be the catalyst for larger, spontaneous migrations.[54] But the true magnitude of the schemes and the clearing is lost in the fragmented locations of change in scores of islands, the spontaneous movements within a population of over 200 million people, and the cloak of secrecy with which the government has covered its activities. An added complication in knowing what is happening is that much of the movement is not to forests, but to undrained or partially drained tidal wetlands, so we have no clear idea of the area of forest involved.[55] Nonetheless, estimates suggest that perhaps as much as 6,000 km^2 have been cleared by planned or spontaneous movement, less than a quarter of that of the Amazon deforestation.

Attracting much less attention, but equally as devastating, are the activities of the Federal Land Development Agency (FELDA) and associated government agencies in peninsular Malaysia, which have embarked on a deliberate policy of expanding primary production of food and cash crops—particularly oil palm—in order to increase national wealth and create a prosperous rural middle class. In the process some 250,000 people have been resettled.[56] The progress of deforestation in this country has been well documented. About 73 percent of the land surface of the peninsula was forested in the early 1950s; a considerable amount had already been cleared during the early years of the century for rubber plantations and small peasant farms. During the early 1960s the annual rate cleared was about 80 km²/yr, which rapidly rose to over 350 km² during the late 1970s. By 1966 the forest has been reduced to 64 percent of the peninsula (84,832 km²) and by 1982 it was 51 percent (67,351 km²) (fig. 14.8). At least another 10 percent will be cleared before government aims are fulfilled in the mid-1990s. But the ability of the government of Malaysia, or anywhere, to put a brake on associated spontaneous clearing is doubtful, and the evidence is that it has already overshot its target considerably. Already the forest, which once stretched in an almost continuous mantle over the peninsula,

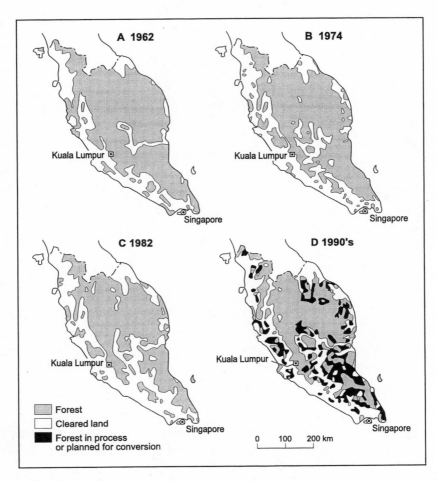

Figure 14.8 Forest clearing in peninsular Malaysia, *A*, 1962; *B*, 1974; *C*, 1982; and *D*, 1990s. *Source:* Brookfield, 1990.

Table 14.4 Estimated total area in major land-use categories and change (in millions of ha) and population and livestock totals (in millions) for three major regions of South and Southeast Asia, 1950 and 1980

	Southeast Asia Subcontinent			Mainland Southeast Asia			Insular Southeast Asia			Total Change
	1950	1980	Change	1950	1980	Change	1950	1980	Change	
Total Cultivated	135.6	155.1	19.5	21.0	36.0	15.0	24.7	42.0	17.3	51.8
Forest/ Woodland Interrupted	53.9	41.2	−12.7	76.0	61.3	−14.7	134.1	110.6	−23.5	−50.9
Woodland Forested	30.3	25.6	−4.7	44.1	44.8	−0.7	27.5	32.5	−5.0	−10.4
Wetlands	2.2	1.6	−0.6	3.2	1.7	−1.5	28.4	23.3	−5.1	−7.2
Subtotal All Forest	86.5	68.4	−18.0	123.3	107.8	−16.9	190.0	166.4	−33.6	−68.5
All Other Land Use	119.1	117.9	−1.2	49.6	50.1	−0.5	41.7	48.0	−6.3	−8.0
Total	341.1	341.1		193.9	193.9		256.4	256.4		
Population	412.2	784.8	372.6	72.0	145.2	73.2	105.1	210.4	105.3	551.1
Livestock	303.9	199.7	112.3	28.9	48.5	19.6	27.7	43.4	15.6	147.5

Source: based on Richards and Flint, 1994: 20, 34, and 36, tables 2, 3, and 4.

is fragmented into a southern remnant and two large northern blocks, and in many places the dominant landscape is no longer one of forest but of cultivation.

In all this discussion of the grand plans in Brazil, Indonesia, and Malaysia, the forest has been seen as wealth to be garnered for the advantage of the state, and its clearing is often a surrogate measure for other, more pressing, but much more difficult social reforms, as Nicholas Guppy forecast nearly 20 years ago. But in many parts of the world the peasants have taken the initiative themselves and have gone ahead and cleared the land in the time-honored fashion, bit by bit, year by year, making enough new ground to establish themselves and feed a family. In toto this massive, undocumented movement is thought to be one of the greatest impacts on the forests of the tropical world (see fig. 13.6). It is their activities that go a long way to explain the decline of forested lands by some 50.9 million ha, over half of which is in mainland and subcontinental Southeast Asia (table 14.4).

"HOOFPRINTS ON THE FOREST": RANCHING AND PASTURE DEVELOPMENT

In Central America, pasture development is probably the major cause of forest loss, and may well be the primary cause of deforestation everywhere in Latin America. Pasture establishment is a relatively new phenomenon because the lack of livestock in pre-Columbian times gave no incentive for the American Indians to establish pastures, and any clearings quickly reverted to some sort of forest. But that situation has changed, and at no time more rapidly than after 1945, with the advent of bulldozers for road making.

Even though the stated aim of many of the development and clearing projects has been the resettlement of peasant proprietors on small plots of land, a whole amalgam of economic, social, and fiscal reasons work toward the new clearings eventually being converted to pasture. By the mid-1980s, the experience of Douglas Shane, as he hiked through the Ecuadorian tropical forest for hours on end and accidentally stumbled on "a distinct line of a path" which he followed for another hour, was to become common.

> Suddenly a wall of vegetation sprung up before me. I assumed I had come to a river, for only where the forest ends at such a feature does one usually find such thick growth. I approached the green wall and pushing through the curtain of vines, branches and weeds, to my astonishment I entered into a clearing of several hectares. Directly across the clearing, over the charred stumps and logs . . . [was] . . . the shack of the colonist whose ax had felled the forest. And to my left, plodding about among the debris were a dozen cattle.

It was, as he said colorfully, the impress of these "Hoofprints on the Forest" that was so radically transforming and destroying the tropical forests in Latin America.[57]

Small farmers, as well as large, succumb to the lure of cattle. Pasture is the easiest means of keeping the land from reverting to secondary forest, cleared land has a speculative value far in excess of crop production in high-inflation economies, pastures are encouraged by tax laws, and cleared land is the surest title to ownership amid chaotic land title registration and not a little corruption.[58] Moreover, to be a cattle raiser is congenial to the Latin value system: "*Ganadero,* like *cabaltero,* is a term of respect," noted Jim Parsons. "It carries prestige, and it implies an attractive way of life that is easily entered."[59]

Practicalities support social mores: cattle provide versatility and additional income in the form of milk and calves, they even out risk, and they require much less labor inputs than rice or maize. They can be walked to market, where they are not subject to gluts in the same manner as are crops. What is more, in a way cattle raising conforms to the realities of the environment because (as even Rondônia showed) newly cleared and planted fields of crops go out of production in about 3 years, at which time they are turned over to grass because cattle provide a marginal return, which however little is crucial to the struggling small landholder. In time the declining fertility and weed invasion of his plot are compensated for by clearing a new area or letting part of a holding go to bush, then cutting and burning it to give a flush of nutrients.[60] Whatever is done, however, the result is the same: more of the forest is felled, and secondary regrowth takes over in abandoned plots or is fired constantly.

Cattle are excellent converters of cellulose to protein, and do so relatively cheaply. In Central America their number has risen phenomenally from a few thousand to millions, and much of the final product—beef—finds a ready export market, mainly in the United States for pet and fast foods. This link between deforestation and consumer lifestyles and consumption a continent away has been dubbed the "Hamburger Connection" by Norman Myers, though its magnitude may not be as great as is thought.[61]

As early as 1972 Jim Parsons warned about what was happening: "The once limitless forests of humid tropical America are rapidly being converted to grasslands," he wrote, and "it must now be considered an important question whether . . . [the forest] . . . will long endure." Wherever roads penetrated, agriculture followed, but it was only a temporary stage in the process by which the forest was converted to *potreros*. After a few years of cropping and declining soil fertility, aggressively colonizing African grasses formed "artificial" pastures. The small landholder was forced to sell out to the next wave of settlers or speculators who followed, who consolidated the small holdings into larger ones in order to raise beef cattle; or he became a laborer for the hacienda owners, who owned disproportionately large areas of land and wanted to clear and acquire even more. The change in the landscape was striking: Parsons had done fieldwork in many parts of Latin America over decades and could now barely recognize places:

> Where once stood great tracts of lowland forest—along the Pan American Highway in Mexico and Central America, the northern coast of Colombia, on the Andean spurs of eastern Venezuela, in the Interior of Brazil, on the islands of the Greater Antilles—today one sees pasture lands stretching to the horizon, interrupted only by scattered palms, remnant woodlots or rows of trees planted as live fences.[62]

The evidence of air photography and remote sensing more than supports this observation (fig. 14.9), with the situation in Costa Rica having been particularly well monitored over the decades.

Even by the mid-1970s Parsons thought that "more than enough of the forest resource has been cleared already. . . . It is time now to pause in this mad assault on nature, time to think more in terms of saving what is left. We are rapidly running out of both time and

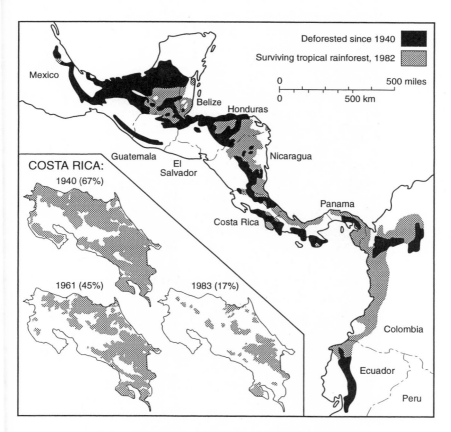

Figure 14.9 Forest clearing in Central America, 1940–82, and the detail of Costa Rica, 1940, 1961, and 1983. *Sources:* Williams, 1990: 192, after Nations and Komer, 1982.

forest." [63] But the "mad assault" never stopped, and perhaps as much as 25,000 km² have been cleared annually for cattle ranching. The transformation of the Central and South American forests continues unabated and much of the original forest cover has gone.

FUELWOOD AND CHARCOAL

Throughout the history of the human use of the forest, four broad applications of this resource have dominated: to create land for growing food, to supply timber for constructing dwellings and for building ships for the strategic and economic power they brought, and to provide fuel for warmth. In the latter half of the twentieth century the demand for land for food has risen with devastating effect. The demand for timber for construction is unabated and significant, but in the temperate world, at least, it is often replenished by reforestation. The other two uses of timber, shipbuilding and fuel, seem to have been relegated; neither wooden ships nor indeed, any ships, hold the key to world supremacy in trade and influence anymore, and in many countries coal and petroleum seem to have eliminated the need for wood burning for warmth and energy.

But the perception that fossil fuels have supplanted wood is erroneous: in the developing world, wood and charcoal for personal warmth, for the preparation of food, and even for industrial energy is of long standing and still looms large. In 1798, Mungo Park described the capital of Kaarta (present-day Mali) as being "situated in the middle of an open plain, the country of two miles round being cleared of wood by the great consumption of that article for building and fuel," [64] and the situation has not changed during the next 200 years.

It took the 1973 hike in oil prices by OPEC and the near panic in the developed world about the basis of its mobility, industry, and heating to remind people of what Erik Eckholm called in 1975 "the other energy crisis." [65] Approximately 2.5 billion to 3 billion people (40 to 50 percent of the world's population) rely on wood, not only for warmth but for the daily preparation of the very food that they eat. In fact, wood comprises more than 70 percent of the national energy consumption in more than 40 countries. Deficiencies in this resource are particularly acute in Andean Latin America, the Caribbean Islands, most of the Indian Subcontinent, and particularly Nepal (fig. 14.10), but the shortfall appears to be most marked in Africa, which depends on wood for up to 58 percent of *all* energy requirements, and where in many savanna areas depletion far exceeds the rate of growth. [66]

In these and adjacent parts of the developing world, fuel is scarcer and more expensive than food, and occasionally consumes one-fifth to one-half of the monetary budget of urban households, and up to four-fifths of the annual working year for scouring the countryside for the last remnant of woody fiber to burn. [67] This is particularly true around urban and industrial areas. For example, the closed forest cover within a 100-km radius of 30 major Indian cities was reduced from 96,625 to 72,278 km² between 1972 and 1982, although about 8,000 km² of the loss probably ended up as second-growth degraded open forest.

The collection and distribution of fuelwood and charcoal is one of the most important facets of the infrastructure of any large third-world city. Hyderabad, for example,

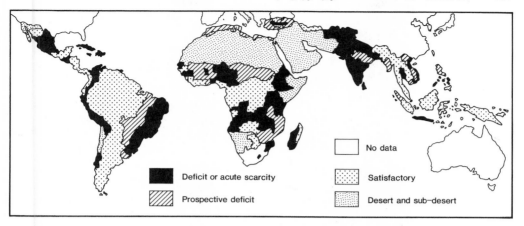

Figure 14.10 Global fuelwood deficits. *Source:* FAO, *Forest Products Yearbook, 1983.*

has 3.5 million inhabitants, and just over 100,000 tons of wood were "imported" into the urban area annually, coming from distances of up to 154 km away. Once in the city the wood was handled by 6 major wholesalers and a diverse assemblage of 472 firewood retailers, who then auctioned it out to households.[68] Rural dwellers, on the other hand, rarely cause the same sort of absolute deforestation; rather, they collect deadwood or cause a "thinning" of the forest, though in the extreme that too can become complete deforestation, especially in the drier, more open forests.

Currently just over half (55 percent) of all wood known to be extracted from the forests of the world (1.8 billion m³) is fuelwood (fig. 14.11), and just as demand has doubled during the last 20 years, so the eminently predictable increase in world population makes it unlikely that the demand will slacken in the future. Indeed, predictions are that it will reach 2.4 billion m³ by 2010.[69] Energy is essential in a developing economy,[70] as the story of fuelwood use in the industrial and transportation growth of the United States during the eighteenth and nineteenth centuries shows clearly, and which has been repeated with variations in twentieth-century Brazil.[71] As nearly 85 percent of the demand for fuelwood is in the developing world, the sharp rise of oil prices in the 1970s caused much hardship as competition for fuelwood increased; and although oil became cheaper during the 1990s, it has now risen again, causing new concerns. A switch to alternative fuels, such as petroleum and kerosene, by the 2.5 billion to 3 billion fuelwood burners is feasible in terms of the extra amount of these fuels consumed—a mere 4 percent of the current world petroleum production—however, the income and the hard currency needed to pay for this are usually difficult to come by.[72]

Although much of the fuelwood comes from trees that have in effect been coppiced and regrow in time, much comes as a byproduct of land clearing. Nevertheless, it is thought that as much as 20,000 to 25,000 km² of woodland and forest are destroyed specifically for fuelwood gathering each year. The accuracy of this estimate is open to question, but one thing is certain: cutting for fuelwood in the forests is a problem that won't go away.

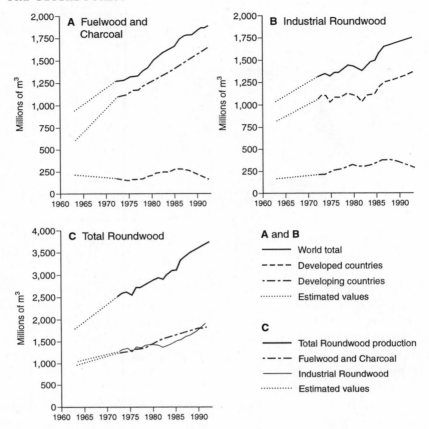

Figure 14.11 A, total roundwood production, 1963–85; *B,* fuelwood and charcoal production, 1963–85; and *C,* industrial fuelwood production, 1963–85. *Source:* FAO, *Forest Products Yearbook,* 1997.

TIMBER EXTRACTION

In the first-ever attempt to calculate the drain on global forest resources, William Sparhawk and Raphael Zon in 1923 thought that slightly less saw timber was being extracted than firewood—739.6 million m³ compared with 852.5 million m³ (see table 12.1). In the post-1945 world, the expectation was that despite an increase in world population, the rapid substitution of steel, concrete, brick, and plastic for many purposes that had previously used wood would result in a relative decline in sawnwood use compared with fuelwood use. But that has not happened; in fact the very reverse has occurred. Since 1923 sawnwood and roundwood consumption has increased 2.59 times, to 1.9 billion m³ (and that does not take into account significant new extra uses of wood for paneling and paper, amounting to 363 million m³) while fuelwood consumption has increased by only 2.18 times, to 1.8 billion m³, although it is forecast to rise rapidly again in line with world population increase. Currently about 1.8 billion m³ is cut annually, and the rate is increasing by about 25 million m³ every year. In terms of value, the world export trade in wood products was worth over $135 billion in 1997.[73] Next to petroleum and natural gas, wood is the third most valuable primary commodity in world trade.

In the developing world in particular, industrial roundwood or sawnwood is seen as the source of foreign exchange and an essential element in the quest for advancement. Regrettably, however, there are few well-managed forests and plantations, so that the extraction is at the expense of the standing stock. Also, the process is often monopolized by large companies and/or influential individuals, often in corrupt political alliances with government and the authorities. On the other hand, in the industrial economies of the developed world, extraction and regeneration are roughly in equilibrium: regrowth exceeds extraction in Canada, New Zealand, the Russian Federation, and Scandinavia, but probably only marginally so in the United States, western Europe, and Japan. But this internal conservation is often achieved at the disadvantage of producers in the tropical world who are ready to supply hardwood for hard currency, even if they do not get the full resource value of the timber.

If the major softwood exporters such as Canada, Finland, and Sweden (and the United States and Germany) are excluded, then the next largest are the hardwood tropical exporters, Indonesia, Malaysia, and Brazil. Table 14.5 gives a "still" in the ever-changing, kaleidoscopic pattern of world trade. The exporters and importers that have a *net* trade in excess of $1 billion are ranked by volume. The biggest importers are predictably the most economically advanced countries in Europe and Japan, but China (now including Hong Kong) and South Africa have entered their ranks.[74] The decline of production in Indonesia, Thailand, and the Philippines through sheer overexploitation is now being played out again in Malaysia and the Indonesian territories of Sabah and Sarawak, where the rate of extraction is roughly 2 to 4 times the natural regrowth. It is estimated that in Thailand the forest cover has fallen from 53 percent in 1961 to 25 percent or even less in 1986. In Cambodia illegal timber exports have been the means of sustaining various factions and warlords, like the infamous Khmer Rouge, while the world turns a blind eye to where the timber comes from in order to secure supplies.[75] Similarly devastating economic and political crises have torn Indonesia apart in recent years and in the resultant "resource anarchy" the "protected" forests of the bulk of lowland Indonesia are being logged mercilessly, so that it is predicted that little forest will remain in another decade.[76]

Although the valuable hardwoods account for only as little as 2 to 10 percent of any unit area of the forest, careless and indiscriminate logging destroys up to 60 percent, and the soil is compacted or eroded. For example, a study of selective logging in the Paragominas region of Pará State in Brazil found that while only 1 to 2 percent of the trees were purposefully harvested, 26 percent were killed or damaged (12 percent lost their crowns, 11 percent were uprooted by bulldozers, 3 percent suffered substantial bark scarring) and the forest canopy was reduced by almost one half. Logging roads also scar the forest and become pathways for exploitation by spontaneous migrations of slash-and-burn cultivators.[77] Further degrading the ecosystem is the threat of fire sweeping through the logged area because it "escaped" from clearings made by small landholders, logging companies were careless, or even large landholders deliberately set it, hoping to drive out small cultivators and eventually take over their land. When these occurrences coincide with drought

Table 14.5 Global export, import, and net trade of forest products,
+/− $US million, 1997 (in millions of $US)

Country	Exports	Imports	Net Trade
Net Exporters +500			
Canada	25,081	3,189	21,892
Finland	10,394	707	9,687
Sweden	10,260	1,379	8,881
Indonesia	5,093	286	4,102
Malaysia	4,025	988	3,037
Austria	4,440	2,116	2,324
Russian Federation	2,892	688	2,204
Brazil	2,874	1,294	1,580
Chile	1,431	200	1,231
New Zealand	1,376	308	1,068
Net Importers			
Mexico	440	1,463	−1,023
Germany	10,727	12,037	−1,310
Denmark	435	1,801	−1,366
Netherlands	2,759	4,725	−1,966
Spain	1,664	3,704	−2,090
Korean Republic	1,512	3,813	−2,301
France	4,049	5,257	−3,217
South Africa	1,282	5,321	−4,039
Italy	2,632	6,776	−4,144
United Kingdom	2,116	10,009	−7,893
United States	15,698	24,003	−8,305
China	3,641	12,380	−8,739
Japan	1,639	17,160	−15,521

Source: FAO, 1997.

brought on by El Niño oscillations, the result can be catastrophic. It happened in East Kalimantan in 1983, when about 3,500 km² were destroyed or heavily damaged, and again in the disastrous fires of Indonesia and Kalimantan in 1992, 1993, and especially in 1997 that put most of Southeast Asia under a pall of smoke for months on end, disrupting traffic and life, and causing a severe health hazard.[78]

Various models have been constructed to predict the worldwide consumption and extraction of wood products under a number of different assumptions or scenarios. While the results are contradictory, all predict rising demand, though some predict constant prices while others expect a doubling of price. Some models indicate that global warming will result in a more rapid tree growth in higher latitudes and hence an expansion of coniferous forests, while others predict that acid rain will cause destruction, an increase in cutting, and a short-term rise in production.[79] Generally the assumption is that in the future the world demand for timber will exceed the maximum level available from the forests on a sustainable basis.

Whatever credence one puts on these global models, more regionally specific ones seem to have greater validity. For example, Alan Grainger's TROPFORM model of trends in tropical hardwood supply, demand, trade, and natural growth over the 40-year period from 1980 to 2020 suggests that timber supplies would be more limited than assumed formerly, peaking in the first decade of this century and then falling. With a fall in supply, timber sources would shift from South and Southeast Asia as supplies are cut out and local demand rises, to untapped but expensive sources in Africa and, very significantly, Latin America. Africa's Côte d'Ivoire already is a substantial exporter.

It is possible, however, that the calculation of the scale of deforestation is based on the erroneous exaggeration of the extent of the precolonial forest, which itself was based on the conventional wisdom that the native peoples had degraded and severely reduced the forest in the past.[80] For example, the original forest cover of Côte d'Ivoire is more likely to have been approximately 7 million to 8 million ha rather than the approximately 14.5 million to 16 million ha, so that the 2.7 million ha remaining in 1990 represents a loss nearer to 130,000/yr than 330,000/yr—still great, to be sure, but nearly a third less. The same might well be true for other parts of West Africa.[81]

Whatever the exact figures in this or that country, it is thought that about 44,000 km² of the tropical forest is logged over annually and largely destroyed or degraded, in addition to the approximately 110,000 km² cleared for agriculture. Such a scale of loss will lead to a permanent diminution of the tropical forest as the "mad assault" goes on.

Backward and Forward Glances

The global problem of deforestation provokes unlikely reactions of concern these days among city dwellers, not only because of the enormity of the scale but also because in the depths of cultural memory forests remain the correlate of human transcendence. We call it the loss of nature, or the loss of wildlife habitat, or the loss of biodiversity, but underlying the ecological concern is perhaps a much deeper appreciation about the disappearance of boundaries, without which the human abode loses its grounding. . . . Without such outside domains there is no inside in which to dwell.
—ROBERT POGUE HARRISON, *Forests: The Shadow of Civilization* (1992)

TWENTY-FIVE YEARS ago, when I first visited the United States, I started to think and write about what I saw—or, perhaps more correctly, about what I could no longer see. What had happened to the forest that once covered so much of the country? How, when, and why had a people wrought such a massive change to their landscape and their environment, and with what consequences? My musings culminated in the construction of an account from many texts; *Americans and Their Forests* helped answer many of the questions I had, some satisfactorily, some less so. For the most part, I have used the same questions, methods, and inductive approaches in the present text, but this time for the whole world through all time—how satisfactorily, one can only guess.

It just so happens that I am writing these final words at the end of the year 2000. Although reason tells us that there is no significance between events and the turning points of our calendar, the round numbers of the year invite backward and forward glances. What does this account tell us about the process of deforestation? Will the next thousand years be significantly different from the last thousand years? Would an observer of even 1800 have been able to even come anywhere near visualizing the world of 2000? It is difficult enough to sum up the complexity of the past of human existence, let alone the unpredictability of its future.

Of one thing I am sure, *Deforesting the Earth: From Prehistory to Global Crisis* makes no claim to solve the profound problems of the transformation of global land cover, and can never be truly up-to-date. Books and reports on global deforestation abound and are published at a bewildering rate. A random glance at my study shelves reveals that in the first six years of the 1990s a dozen books emerged, all with arresting titles—*The End of Nature; Rainforest Politics: Ecological Destruction in South East Asia; Managing the World's Forests: Looking for Balance between Conservation and Development; Forests: Market and Intervention Failures; Who Will Save the Forests?: Knowledge, Power and Environmental Destruction; The Struggle for Land and the Fate of the Forests; Bad Harvest?: The Timber Trade and the Degradation of the World's Forests; Tropical Deforestation: A Socio-Economic Approach; The Vanishing Forest: The Human Consequences of Deforestation;* and *Logging the Globe;* and many more followed.[1] And this says nothing about, for example, the biennial *World Resources* reports of the World Resources Institute; *The State of the World's Forests,* the reports of the FAO produced roughly every five years; and the numerous articles in environmental and forestry journals. A memorable passage in the Book of Ecclesiastes more or less sums up the telling of the global deforestation story: "Of the making of books there is no end." And because there is no end to this continuous process of global transformation, many more books will be written about it in the future.

Consequently, *Deforesting the Earth: From Prehistory to Global Crisis* is just that: an account of how humans have related to their forests over at least 7 millennia. It is not a compendium of solutions for environmental degradation but an attempt to make sense of a very long, drawn-out, and momentous process of change up to the end of the twentieth century. If in the process of writing I have pointed out how various societies and cultures have managed to do something with their forests other than destroy them, then these examples will have some value in extending our knowledge about possible solutions. This book can only be an invitation for reflection, not a prescription for action. That I leave to others.

A few things about the future are reasonably certain. World population will continue to rise, and depending on a variety of assumptions will stabilize at between 9 billion and 10 billion by 2100. The bulk of those 3 billion or 4 billion extra people will be in the developing world, primarily in the tropical forest zone. It is inconceivable that they will need any less land to grow food, unless some miracle of genetic engineering of high-yielding foods comes to their (and the forest's) rescue. Simply, one of the prime driving forces of deforestation—the sheer press of people—will continue unabated, and as cultivation has always been the greatest devourer of the forests, many more millions of hectares will be destroyed. Similarly, the demand for fuelwood will remain immense for the poor of the world. Many of the additional people over the coming century will be born in urban areas or will migrate to them, but those living in or near the tropical forest will have it provide land, fuel, and shelter for as long as it lasts, and it will continue to be "the mantle of the poor." The impoverished will want to use it; others will wish to restrict its use and preserve it.

The population of the developed world will barely increase over the next century, but real incomes will do so dramatically. Steady rises of about 2 percent plus per annum are common, and during the 1990s the United States, the biggest consuming country of all, was achieving an unprecedented 4 to 5 percent. Such rates of growth cannot be sustained without even greater demands on the world's resources, of which wood and pulp are still important. More dwellings are being constructed, invariably with a large component of

Table E.1 Current and forecast global production/consumption of wood and paper products, 1996 and 2010

Products (in millions of m³)	Production/ Consumption		Total growth	
	1996	2010	1996–2010	% Increase
Wood				
Industrial roundwood	1,490	1,872	382	
Sawnwood	430	501	71	23.4
Wood-based panels	149	180	31	
Total wood products (in millions of tonnes)	2,069	2,553	484	
Pulp and paper				
Pulp	179	208	29	30.0
Paper and paperboard	284	394	110	
Total pulp and paper products	463	602	139	

Source: FAO, 1999: 50.

wood in them. Wood as a furniture and interior finishing material still has a workability and aesthetic acceptability that is unlikely to be wholly replaced by any synthetics, especially as standards of living rise. Wood-burning fires are a sign of "the good life" among many, and consumption of wood for energy is rising.

Moreover, the much-vaunted electronic age has not diminished the consumption of paper. If anything it has created new demands for the product, and a more profligate use. For example, word processors allow minute changes in texts (including this one) that would have been undreamed of even 10 years ago, when whole manuscripts would have had to have been retyped at great time and effort to accommodate even the most minor alterations. Word processing greatly facilitates text revisions, so more drafts wind up going through the desk printer. Another departure from the paperless, cyber-spaced world that had been predicted: books, newspapers, and magazines are being produced in ever-greater numbers as literacy increases. Similarly, e-commerce puts an even greater emphasis on packaging for transportation. Currently every 1,000 people in the developed world use about 160 tonnes of paper products per annum, compared with about 25 tonnes in the developing world. Just as wood has served humankind well in the past, it will continue to do so in the future.

The FAO has attempted to forecast what the demand for these wood products might be like by 2010 (table E.1). Overall global consumption of industrial roundwood, sawnwood, and panels will rise from 2,069 million to 2,553 million m³, a 23 percent increase, while pulp, paper, and cardboard will rise from 463 million to 602 million tonnes, a 30 percent increase. It is thought that the forests can meet these demands if, among other things, the older plantations of countries like Australia, Chile, New Zealand, South Africa, the United Kingdom, and the United States start to produce the saw logs needed, and all countries of the developed world recycled fibers and recovered paper in order to boost paper and pulp production.[2] The figures of this forecast are less important than the predicted magnitude of change: an increase of approximately 25 percent over a span of 15 years. Clearly, the pressure on the global forests will continue to be relentless.

In addition to more people and more products calling for wood, other threats to forests loom on the horizon and are not easy to predict or prevent. For example, acid rain pollution, caused by gaseous emissions and heavy metals, produces forest death, or *Waldsterben*. The many possible processes and biological pathways of this phenomenon are not fully understood, though many hypotheses have been developed. Nevertheless, it is incontestable that between 70,000 and 100,000 km^2 of coniferous forests in central and eastern Europe are affected, and it is highly possible that 3 times that amount are at risk—perhaps as much as one-fifth of all forests there. Climatic stress after the recent spells of exceptionally dry years and mild winters during the 1990s, accompanied by pollution from eastern Europe, has also endangered broadleaf forests throughout western Europe. Acid rain is becoming evident in Canada, as well as in the United States in the northeast, the Appalachians, and the coastal ranges of California. It has even been detected in China, Malaysia, and Brazil.[3]

The decline of the world's forest stocks has been countered, albeit slightly, by reforestation, but ascertaining the extent of this practice is difficult. Whereas deforestation is often concealed or underestimated in many countries, reforestation is publicized, exaggerated, and optimistically assessed as a positive and desirable part of public works programs. Moreover, many trees that are planted do not survive. For example, 11.7 million ha were planted in the 13 states of the American South between 1925 and 1979, but spot checks over large areas showed that anywhere between 13 and 18 percent of the replantings had failed. In addition, of the millions of hectares said to have been planted in China, it is unlikely that more than a fraction have come to maturity. Therefore, some announcements have to be treated with caution and even skepticism, so that the claim that the average annual amount of recorded reforestation during the 1980s was about 150,000 km^2, almost exactly the same as the amount of deforestation, is possibly not as comforting as it sounds. Of that total, 128,420 km^2, or 85.6 percent, were in the cool coniferous, temperate mixed, and warm temperate moist forests of the Northern Hemisphere, including China, Japan, and Korea, and the forests of South Africa, Australia, and New Zealand. In the tropical world, Brazil had an annual reforestation rate of 5,610 km^2, but the only other countries rated above 1,000 km^2 were India (1,730) and Indonesia (1,640).[4] The optimistic implication of these figures is that depletion is being matched approximately by replanting and careful forest management in the cool coniferous forests of the major exporting countries of Canada, the United States, the Russian Federation, and Scandinavia. But depletion in the tropical forests, where trees are more difficult to propagate anyhow, is not being offset by replanting.

A possible mitigating factor in the deforestation crisis is the establishment of an international tree-planting initiative to sequester carbon as an alternative or supplementation to the worldwide efforts to reduce carbon (CO_2) emissions. Although this program would not be a permanent solution, it would buy, say, five decades' worth of time while the trees grow and use up carbon, and society develops alternatives to existing fossil fuel sources. It is part of the thinking behind the United States' objections to the Kyoto Treaty negotiations that rely solely on the reduction of fossil fuel emissions. With this in mind, by early 1990 the world would have needed to plant an estimated 465 million ha of forest, an area more than 10 percent of the current global forests, to mop up its 2.9 billion tons of global emissions. Many financial, economic, and political problems are associated with this solution. For example, some reforestation sites could be found in marginal lands in the temperate areas, but anything else would be extremely expensive. There are extensive areas of degraded lands in the tropics, but who would pay for this massive outlay and maintenance, which would amount to perhaps $500 billion or more? If the current rate of reforestation is thought to be 15,000 km² (1.5 million ha) and the total area of plantations some 92 million ha, planting would have to be "at a scale that would dwarf all previous plantation efforts."[5]

So much for the future, what about the past? How does it relate to the here and now? First, the enormity of past change means that the past must be taken seriously. Too often history is dismissed as irrelevant by policymakers and publicists living in a world of the "present" as though it were stable, normal, unchanging, and unchanged. Second, this book shows that almost as much forest was cleared in the past as has been cleared in the last 50 years, so present concerns are not new. Possibly between 7.4 million and and 9.14 million km² have disappeared, perhaps up to half of that before 1950.[6] Third, the continuity of this process of terrestrial transformation does help to illuminate our understanding of what is happening.

In a reflexive way, therefore, the causes and nature of past deforestation in all its social and economic complexity and dynamism throw light on present processes, and the present situation throws light on past processes. For example, time and again we have seen that it is the underlying social, economic, and political makeup of society at any given time—its "cultural climate," no less—that causes deforestation. However, we know far less about what brings deforestation under control, except that experience suggests the need for strong government institutions to implement stated policies and resist elite groups who have traditionally pursued the exploitation of the forest. In addition, in the tropical realm (and, perhaps, post-Soviet Russia) of the modern era, such governments would also have to be responsive to popular concerns about the deleterious effects of deforestation, such as flooding, mud slides, landslides, smoke pollution, and high fuelwood prices. For a government to exhibit these qualities requires a high degree of democratic function and a certain amount of socioeconomic growth to raise standards of living. Of course, benevolent despots have existed—perhaps the Forestry Department in British colonial India was as near as one would get to that—but the likelihood is that absolute power will lead to absolute corruption, as has been true in Cambodia. What is needed are governments that are strong enough to be pluralistic, and listen to the concerns of the people.[7]

Attempts by developed countries, international agencies, and NGOs (Non-Government Organizations) to force the reforestation process are frequently viewed with suspicion by the developing countries. Criticism of deforestation seems like antidevelopment rhetoric and hypocrisy from countries that have already "made it," often on the basis of the profligate use of their forests in the past (plate E.1). Calls for conservation seem like neo-imperialism, and even debt-for-nature swaps are not immune to these negative impressions. Two items from two U.S. newspapers from March 1989, when concern about Brazilian deforestation was at its height, perhaps sum up these points of view. Regarding

Plate E.1 Deforestation is perceived differently by people and governments in developed and developing countries. (Scott Willis, Copley News Service, 1989.)

the North American historical experience, which could apply equally as well to Europe, Tom Wicker of the *New York Times* said the following:

> Now there's little left of the vast tree cover that once stretched from the Atlantic to the Mississippi and beyond.... Thus has the United States done throughout its history what a righteous world denounces Brazil for doing today: no wonder Brazilian leaders point to the United States as their role model in deforestation.

A few days earlier, another article in the *Chicago Tribune* quoted a Brazilian official:

> If the world wants oxygen, let them pay for it. We're not going to stay poor because the rest of the world wants to breathe.[8]

As revealed by the debate over deforestation rates, the whole topic of deforestation and the part it plays in the balance of forest resources is underresearched. We lack much hard data, and that which we have is open to varying forms of interpretation. But over and above all that, it is difficult to separate the rhetoric from the reality of what is happening to the global forests. This is true about *Waldsterben*, reforestation, the possible effects (let alone the reality) of climatic change, the controversy over the Kyoto Treaty, and the truth of reduced biodiversity. Moreover, in the past we have seen repeatedly how deforestation has been exaggerated in order to serve special interests and pressure groups, and the same may be true today. In the developed world the wrong culprits, such as iron making, shipbuilding, or railway enterprises, were usually the deforestation scapegoats, whereas land clearing for permanent agriculture was so normal, so essential that it was excused, overlooked, or ignored. In the developing world, the myths of wilderness and of the destructive nature of swidden agriculture by the "backward" natives have justified authoritarian conservation policies based on outdated ecological notions of climax vegetation and a mistrust of fire, which have decoupled local people from their livelihoods.

The flood of books, often by environmental advocacy groups, continues—each one with a seemingly more alarming message than the last. For example, one of the latest, arrestingly entitled *The Last Frontier Forests: Ecosystems and Economics on the Edge,* claims that only 13.5 million km² remains of the earth's 62.2 million km² of "Frontier Forest." On a casual reading it seems as though that is the only forest remaining, until one realizes that the subject is "large, ecologically intact, relatively undisturbed natural forests" harboring maximum biodiversity—a narrowly defined subset of the total remaining 33.4 million km² of all forests.[9] The other 19.9 million km² of "non-frontier forest" includes those of all of Europe, almost the whole of the United States, the southern half of Canada, most of Australia, and massive chunks of Asia, the Russian Federation, and Africa, and they are ignored. Yet, people know they see and enjoy these forests, and consequently are less impressed than perhaps they should be at the bad news. Deforestation and biodiversity loss are stories that sell, and they can leave an uneasy impression a little like Greeley's "virgin timber" maps of 1925 at the height of the "timber scare" era: amidst the concern over the environment, special interests are being served as they jockey for power, influence, and funds.

Perhaps for reasons like this, a commensurate response to many environmental statements does not seem to exist. Is the public losing interest in the issue and becoming more skeptical—or is it just accepting the inevitable? One gets the sense that with the end of the cold war and the emergence during the mid- to late 1990s of real, televisual ethnic and religious conflicts, famines, and mass global migration, a sort of "environmental crisis fatigue" has set in, so claims of disaster around the corner are being treated with some skepticism and weariness. Meanwhile, the pricing out of environmentally detrimental practices that affect peoples' comfort and mobility are meeting increasing resistance from the public. Town and rural dwellers alike are apprehensive about the new orthodoxy and discourse that tells people what to do with their lives, and smacks of a sort of "ecofascism."

Deforestation is no longer a purely economic issue, though it is supremely that, as it is also fast becoming a matter of humanitarian concerns mixed with long-term environmental ethics. Unless forests are either regarded as "sacred" in some way or another or bought and conserved, sustainability of the forest will continue to diminish. In 1923 Raphael Zon and William Sparhawk concluded their great work by saying:

> Reduction in the area under forest will undoubtedly continue in the future as it has in the past, as increasing population requires more and more land for agriculture, and as the forests in many regions so continue to be destroyed by fires and cutting, without provision for their renewal.[10]

One has to say regretfully that not much has changed. One thing the past does tell us clearly is that the process of land-cover transformation and destruction is never ending. In a decade or so, perhaps another chapter will have to be written, outlining how humans grappled with the problems of the use and abuse of their incomparable heritage, a green, global mantle of forest.

NOTES

Preface

1. Sauer correspondence, Bancroft Library Archives, University of California, Berkeley, H. Clifford Darby to P. Fejos, 19 July 1954.

2. H. Clifford Darby, "The Clearing of the Woodland in Europe," 183–216; and William G. Hoskins, *The Making of the English Landscape,* 6.

3. Richard Blome, *A Geographical Description of the Four Parts of the World,* Preface to the Reader, frontispiece.

4. The phrase is taken from E. Estyn Evans, "The Ecology of Peasant Life in Western Europe," 217, and used recently in an article I wrote, "'Dark Ages and Dark Areas': Global Deforestation in the Deep Past," 28–46.

5. Michael Williams, "Forests and Tree Cover," 97–124.

6. Charles Darwin, *The Origin of Species by Means of Natural Selection,* 166.

Chapter 1

1. For a good general overview see Neil Roberts, *The Holocene: An Environmental History,* 45–47; Martin Bell and Michael J. Walker, *Late Quaternary Environmental Change: Physical and Human Perspectives;* and Andrew S. Goudie, *Environmental Change,* 97–104, 121–31.

2. André Berger, John Imbrie, J. Hays, G. Kulka, and B. Saltzman, eds., *Milankovitch and Climate: Understanding the Response to Astronomical Forcing,* pt. 1; and John Imbrie and Katherine Imbrie, *Ice Ages: Solving the Mystery,* 113–22.

3. George H. Denton and Terance J. Hughes, eds., *The Last Great Ice Sheets,* 135–41; and William F. Ruddiman and Alexander McIntyre, "The Mode and Mechanism of the Last Deglaciation: Oceanic Evidence," 125–34.

4. For example, see the essays in A. R. Harding, ed., *Climate Change in Later Prehistory.*

5. George Perkins Marsh, *Man and Nature: Or, Physical Geography as Modified by Human Action,* 36.

6. Knut Faegri and Johannes Iversen, *Textbook of Modern Pollen Analysis;* and Peter D. Moore, J. A. Webb, and Margaret E. Collinson, *Pollen Analysis.*

7. S. T. Andersen, "The Different Productivity of Trees and Its Significance for the Interpretation of Pollen Diagrams from a Forested Region," 109–15; Paul A. Delcourt and Hazel R. Delcourt, *Long-Term Forest Dynamics of the Temperate Zone: A Case Study of the Late-Quaternary Forests of Eastern North America,* 29–61; and A. M. Solomon, "Pollen," 41–84.

8. R. Burleigh, "W. F. Libby and the Development of Radiocarbon Dating," 6–8; and Royal E. Taylor, ed., *Radiocarbon after Four Decades: An Interdisciplinary Perspective.*

9. Daniel Zohary and Maria Hopf, *Domestication of Plants in the Old World: The Origin and Spread of Cultivated Plants in West Asia, Europe and the Nile Valley,* 12–14; and G. W. Pearson, "How to Cope with Calibration," 98–103.

10. Brian J. Huntley and Hilary J. B. Birks, *An Atlas of Past and Present Pollen Maps for Europe: 0–13 000 Years Ago.*

11. Paul A. Delcourt and Hazel R. Delcourt, "Vegetation Maps for Eastern North America: 40,000 yrs BP to the Present," 123–66, and *Long-Term Forest Dynamics of the Temperate Zone,* 85–106; Patricia F. McDowell, Thompson Webb III, and Patrick J Bartlein, "Long-Term Environmental Change," 143–62; and Thompson Webb III, "Eastern North America," 85–414.

12. COHMAP Members, "Major Climatic Changes of the Last 18,000 Years: Observations and Model Simulations," 1043–52.

13. Willem van Zeist and S. Bottema, "Vegetational History of the Eastern Mediterranean and the Near East during the Last 20,000 Years," 277–321.

14. There is a good summary of these shifts of individual taxa in Delcourt and Delcourt, *Long-Term Forest Dynamics of the Temperate Zone,* 374–98.

15. Ibid., 111–291; McDowell, Webb III, and Bartlein, "Long-Term Environmental Change," 143–62; and Webb III, "Eastern North America," 385–414.

16. Andrew S. Goudie, "The Ice Age in the Tropics," 1–14.

17. Francis Aleyne Street and Alfred T. Grove, "Environmental and Climatic Implications of Late Quaternary Lake Level Fluctuations in Africa," 385–90.

18. Roberts, *The Holocene,* 86.

19. John R. Flenley, *The Equatorial Rain Forest: A Geological History,* 29–54; and Andrew S. Goudie, "The Arid Earth," 152–71.

20. John R. Flenley, "The Late Quaternary Vegetation History of the Equatorial Mountains," 488–509.

21. Huntley and Birks, *An Atlas of Past and Present Pollen,* 379.

22. Karl-Ernst Behre, "The Role of Man in European Vegetation History," 633–72; and Karl-Ernst Behre, *Anthropogenic Indications in Pollen Diagrams.*

23. For a fuller discussion see chapter 2.

24. Hazel R. Delcourt, "The Impact of Prehistoric Agriculture and Land Occupation on Natural Vegetation," 40–43. See also the discussion in chapter 3.

Chapter 2

1. E. K. Janaki Ammal, "Introduction to the Subsistence Economy of India," 327; and Carl O. Sauer, "The Agency of Man on Earth," 56.

2. Donald R. Strong Jr., Daniel Simberloff, Lawrence G. Abele, and Anne B. Thistle, eds., *Ecological Communities: Conceptual Issues and the Evidence,* esp. 3–18 and 101–12.

3. Geoffrey W. Dimbleby, "Climate, Soil and Man," 197–208.

4. Johannes Iversen, "Retrogressive Vegetational Succession in the Post-Glacial," 59–70; and Norman L. Christensen, "Fire Regimes and Ecosystem Dynamics," 233.

5. Omer C. Stewart, "Fire As the First Great Force Employed by Man," 115–33, is an early and excellent summary of fire "evidence." For the wider significance of fire in this and following paragraphs I have made use of Johann Goudsblom's thought-provoking work, "The Civilizing Process and the Domestication of Fire," and his *Fire and Civilization;* and Stephen J. Pyne, "The

Keeper of the Flame: A Survey of Anthropogenic Fire," 245–46, and his larger work, *Vestal Fire: An Environmental History, Told through Fire, of Europe, and Europe's Encounter with the World*.

6. O. Stewart, "Fire As the First Great Force," 118.

7. The literature on fire-changed and -induced vegetation is immense, but the following are a good introduction: I. F. Ahlgren and C. E. Ahlgren, "Ecological Effects of Forest Fires," 483–537; J. S. Clark and J. Robinson, "Palaeoecology of Fire," 193–94; and Theodore T. Kozlowski and C. E. Ahlgren, eds., *Fire and Ecosystems*.

8. Christensen, "Fire Regimes and Ecosystem Dynamics," 240–42.

9. Pyne, "The Keeper of the Flame," 250–51; Paul A. Mellars, "Fire Ecology, Animal Population and Man: A Study of Some Ecological Relationships in Prehistory," 18–26; Paul A. Mellars and S. C. Reinhardt, "Patterns of Mesolithic Land-Use in Southern England: A Geological Perspective," 256–59; and O. Stewart, "Fire As the First Great Force," 119.

10. Based on O. Stewart, "Fire As the First Great Force," 115–33; and Pyne, "The Keeper of the Flame," 245–66.

11. Mellars, "Fire Ecology, Animal Population, and Man," 38–39.

12. Pyne, "The Keeper of the Flame," 249–50.

13. Goudsblom, "The Civilizing Process and the Domestication of Fire," 8.

14. J. Desmond Clark and J. W. K. Harris, "Fire and Its Roles in Early Hominid Lifeways," 3–27.

15. Carl O. Sauer, "Fire and Early Man," 399–407.

16. E. V. Komarek, "Ancient Fires," 219–40, and "Lightning and Lightning Fires As Ecological Forces," 169–97.

17. For an exhaustive review see Donald K. Grayson, "Pleistocene Avifaunas and the Overkill Hypothesis," 691–92; and C. A. Reed, "Extinction of Mammalian Megafauna in the Old World Late Quaternary," 284–88.

18. Paul S. Martin and H. E. Wright Jr., eds., *Pleistocene Extinctions: The Search for a Cause*; and Paul S. Martin and Richard G. Klein, eds., *Quaternary Extinctions: A Prehistoric Revolution*.

19. For an excellent and up-to-date review of the evidence, see Anthony J. Stuart, "Mammalian Extinctions in the Late Pleistocene of Northern Eurasia and North America," esp. 456–59 and 543–52.

20. Jack Golson, "Cultural Change in Prehistoric New Zealand," 19–74.

21. For the diaspora see J. D. Jennings, ed., *The Prehistory of Polynesia*, 6–26, 323–51; and for early New Zealand see Janet M. Davidson, *The Prehistory of New Zealand*, 38–40.

22. J. R. Flenley, A. Sarah M. King, J. T. Teller, M. E. Prentice, J. Jackson, and C. Chew, "The Late Quaternary Vegetational and Climatic History of Easter Island," 112.

23. M. S. McGlone, "Polynesian Deforestation of New Zealand: A Preliminary Synthesis," 11.

24. Based on Kenneth B. Cumberland, "Moas and Men: New Zealand about A.D. 1250," 151–73, and "Climatic Change or Cultural Interference?" 88–142; and McGlone, "Polynesian Deforestation," and his authoritative summary in "The Polynesian Settlement of New Zealand in Relation to Environmental and Biotic Changes," 115–30. Other useful material is in Atholl J. Anderson, *Prodigious Birds: Moas and Moa-Hunting in Prehistoric New Zealand*, 97–109, 149–57, and 171–91, and "The Extinction of the Moa in Southern New Zealand," 728–40; and Michael M. Trotter and Beverley McCulloch, "Moas, Men and Middens," 708–27.

25. James Cook, *A Voyage Towards the South Pole and Round the World*, 2:88; and McGlone, "The Polynesian Settlement of New Zealand," 126. See also the commentary (p. 32) by Ross Cochrane on "The Impact of Man on the Natural Biota," which accompanies his four maps of change.

26. Réne Battistini and Pierre Vérin, "Man and Environment in Madagascar," 311–27.

27. R. E. Dewar, "Extinctions in Madagascar: The Loss of Subsoil Fauna," 575–87; and Battistini and Vérin, "Man and Environment," 311–37.

28. Magadalena Ralska-Jasiewiczowa and Bas Van Geel, "Early Human Disturbance of the Natural Environment Recorded in Annually Laminated Sediments in Lake Gosciaz, Central Poland," 36–37.

29. A. G. Smith, "The Influence of Mesolithic and Neolithic Man on British Vegetation: A Discussion," 81–96; and Kevin J. Edwards, "Meso-Neolithic Vegetational Impact in Scotland and Beyond: Palynological Considerations," 143–55.

30. K. D. Bennett, "A Provisional Map of Forest Types for the British Isles, 5000 Years Ago," 141–44.

31. Ian .G. Simmons, "The Earliest Cultural Landscapes of England," 113.

32. R. Jacobi, J. H. Tallis, and Paul A. Mellars, "The Southern Pennine Mesolithic and Ecological Record," 307–20; Ian G. Simmons, "Late Mesolithic Societies and the Environment of the Uplands of England and Wales," 111–29; and Ian G. Simmons, G. W. Dimbleby, and C. Grigson, "The Mesolithic," 82–124.

33. Ian G. Simmons and J. B. Innes, "Late Mesolithic Land-Use and Its Impact on the English Uplands," 7–17, and "Mid-Holocene Adaptations and Later Mesolithic Forest Disturbances in Northern England," 385–403.

34. Johannes Iversen, "The Influence of Prehistoric Man on Vegetation," 6; and J. Troels-Smith, "Ertebólletidens Fangstfolk og Bónder," 102.

35. Peter Rowley-Conwy, "Forest Grazing and Clearance in Temperate Europe with Special Reference to Denmark: An Archaeological View," 203–4.

36. T. Champion, C. Gamble, S. Shennan, and A. Whittle, eds., *Prehistoric Europe*, 109–11; and T. D. Price, "Regional Approaches to Human Adaption in the Mesolithic of the Northern European Plain," 217–34.

37. Brian J. Huntley and Hilary J. B. Birks, *An Atlas of Past and Present Pollen Maps for Europe: 0–13,000 Years Ago*, 209–11.

38. H. M. Heybroek, "Diseases and Lopping for Fodder As Possible Causes of a Prehistoric Decline in *Ulmus*," 1–11.

39. J. R. Pilcher, A. G. Smith, G. W. Pearson, and A. Crowder, "Land Clearance in the Irish Neolithic: New Evidence and Interpretation," 560–62.

40. Ralska-Jasiewiczowa and Van Geel, "Early Human Disturbance," 38; and Ralska-Jasiewiczowa, "Isopollen Maps of Poland, 0–11,000 Years B.P.," 144.

41. Peter Bogucki, *Forest Farmers and Stockherders: Early Agriculture and Its Consequences in North-Central Europe*, 33.

42. Jorgen Troels-Smith, "Ivy, Mistletoe and Elm: Climatic Indicator-Fodder Plants," 23–26; Rowley-Conwy, "Forest Grazing and Clearance in Temperate Europe," 205–6; and Oliver Rackham, *Ancient Woodland: Its History, Vegetation, and Uses in England*, 266.

43. Bogucki, *Forest Farmers and Stockherders*, 33.

44. Ibid., 34.

45. S. K. Kozlowski, *Cultural Differentiation of Europe between the 10th and 5th Millennia B.C.*, 18–19; and Boguki, *Forest Farmers and Stockherders*, 41.

46. J. Grahame D. Clark, "Starr Carr: A Case Study in Bioarchaeology," 1–42, and *Mesolithic Prelude: The Palaeolithic–Neolithic Transition in Old World Prehistory*, 42–44.

47. John M. Coles, S. V. E. Heal, and Bryony J. Orme, "The Uses of Wood in Prehistoric Britain and Ireland," 1–45. For wetland archeology in general, see Bryony Coles, "Wetlands Archaeology: A Wealth of Evidence," 145–80.

48. Of the many publications relating to the Somerset Levels Project, see in particular John M. Coles and Bryony J. Orme, "Neolithic Hurdles from Walton Heath, Somerset," 6–29. Bryony J. Coles and John M. Coles, *Sweet Track to Glastonbury,* summarizes the evidence.

49. V. Gordon Childe, *The Danube in Prehistory,* 1–16; and Graeme Barker, *Prehistoric Farming in Europe,* xiv.

50. Michael Williams, *Americans and Their Forests: A Historical Geography,* 8–17; and Martyn Bowden, "The Invention of American Tradition," 22. Since writing this and the following paragraphs, Shepard Krech's *Ecological Indian: Myth and History* has appeared, which is a penetrating study of all aspects of Indian impacts on vegetation and wildlife, and supports the thesis of major environmental manipulation.

51. For an extensive discussion and review of the "denial" syndrome, see Evan Peacock, "Historical and Applied Perspectives on Prehistoric Land Use in Eastern North America," 1–30, quotation p. 8; and Stanley Z. Guffey, "A Review and Analysis of the Effects of Pre-Columbian Man on the Eastern North American Forests," 121–23.

52. Arturo Gómez-Pompa and Andrea Kaus, "Taming the Wilderness Myth," 271–79.

53. See F. Fertig, "Child of Nature: the American Indian As Ecologist," 4–7; and J. Baird Callicott, "Traditional American Indian and Western European Attitudes towards Nature: An Overview," 293–318. Paradoxically, the same argument has been turned on its head and used as justification for gaining commercial access to protected natural resources. For a summary of the debate see Alice E. Ingerson, "Tracking and Testing the Nature-Culture Dichotomy," 43–66.

54. See Iversen, "The Influence of Prehistoric Man on Vegetation," 6; and S. Shetler, "Three Faces of Eden," 226.

55. For an extreme example of the pristine, "edenic" view, see Kirkpatrick Sale, *The Conquest of Paradise: Christopher Columbus and the Columbian Legacy.*

56. For a revaluation see William M. Denevan, "The Pristine Myth: The Landscape of the Americas in 1492," 370, et seq.; M. Williams, *Americans and Their Forests,* 32–49; and William Cronon, *Changes in the Land: Indians, Colonists, and the Ecology of New England,* 49–51.

57. Denevan, "The Pristine Myth," 370. For details of the demographic collapse see Alfred L. Crosby, *Ecological Imperialism: The Biological Expansion of Europe, 900–1900,* 195–216, and his earlier *The Columbian Exchange: Biological and Cultural Consequences of 1492,* 35–64; and George Lovell, "'Heavy Shadows and Black Night': Disease and Depopulation in Colonial Spanish America," 426–43.

58. Joan C. Taylor, "The Earliest Hunters, Gatherers and Farmers of North America," 221.

59. Denevan, "The Pristine Myth," 371; Hugh M. Raup, "Recent Changes in Climate and Vegetation in Southern New England and Adjacent New York," 79–117; and quotations from Emily W. B. Russell, "Indian-Set Fires in the Forests of the Northeastern United States," 86, and Richard T. Foreman and Emily W. B. Russell, "Evaluation of Historical Data in Ecology," 5. For rebuttals see William A. Patterson III and Kenneth E. Sassaman, "Indian Fires in the Prehistory of New England," 107–13.

60. For an exhaustive appraisal of fire in America, see Stephen J. Pyne, *Fire in America: A Cultural History of Wild Land and Rural Fire,* 74.

61. Sauer, "The Agency of Man on Earth," 54–56, and an elaboration of these themes in "Man's Dominance by Use of Fire," 1–13.

62. Particularly useful are Gordon M. Day, "The Indian As an Ecological Factor in the Northeastern Forest," 334–35; Calvin Martin, "Forest and Fire Structures in the Aboriginal Eastern Forest," 38–42; Omer C. Stewart, "Burning and Natural Vegetation in the United States," 319: and S. W. Bromley, "The Original Forest Types of Southern New England," 61–66. An up-to-date

summary of the evidence is in Guffey, "A Review and Analysis of the Effects of Pre-Columbian Man," 121–37.

63. Mark Catesby, *The Natural History of Carolina, Florida, and the Bahama Islands*, ii.

64. Thomas Morton, *The New England Canaan of Thomas Morton*, 172–73.

65. Francis H. Higginson, *New-England's Plantation: or, A Short and True Description of the Commodities and Discommodities of That Country*, 9; William Byrd, *History of the Dividing Line between Virginia and Other Tracts*, 2:15–17; Andrew White, "A Relation of the Colony of the Lord Baron of Baltimore in Maryland, near Virginia," 18; and John Smith, *Travels and Works of Captain John Smith*, 2:77–80.

66. Edward Johnson, *Johnson's Wonder-Working Providence of Sion's Saviour in New England, 1628–1681*, 5; and Adam Hodgson, *Letters from North America written during a Tour in the United States and Canada*, 1:273.

67. Hu Maxwell, "The Use and Abuse of the Forests by the Virginia Indians," 4–6; Harold J. Lutz, "The Vegetation of Heart's Content: A Virgin Forest in North Western Pennsylvania," 20; and Nathaniel S. Shaler, *Nature and Man in North America*, 186.

68. Thomas Bigelow, *Journal of a Tour to Niagra Falls in the Year 1805*, 49–51.

69. For an extensive examination of the evidence see Erhard Rostlund, "The Myth of a Natural Prairie Belt in Alabama: An Interpretation of Historical Records"; and J. Baird, *View of the Valley of the Mississippi; or, the Emigrants' and Travellers' Guide to the West*, 204.

70. Asa Gray, "Characteristics of the North American Flora," 337.

71. The "denial" syndrome has even extended to Indian hunting, but after an extensive inquiry Charles Kay comments that he could not "find any evidence that Native Americans effectively conserved ungulates," but rather hunted them. Charles E. Kay, "Aboriginal Overkill: The Role of Native Americans in Structuring Western Ecosystems," 377.

72. T. Dwight, *Travels in New-England and New-York in 1821*, 1:90; and Catesby, *The Natural History of Carolina*, xii. For many more examples of fire hunting, see Guffey, "A Review and Analysis of the Effects of Pre-Columbian Man," 125–26; and W. H. Elder, "Primeval Deer Hunting Pressures Revealed by Remains from American Indian Middens," 366–70.

73. Carl O. Sauer, "A Geographical Sketch of Early Man in America," 543–56; Pyne, *Fire in America*, 76; Douglas Branch, *The Hunting of the Buffalo*, 52–63; and F. G. Roe, *The North American Buffalo: A Critical Study of the Species in the Wild State*, 26–28, 228–82.

74. Carl O. Sauer, "Grassland Climax, Fire, and Man," 16–21, and "Man's Dominance by Use of Fire," 1–13.

75. Elizabeth Chavannes, "Written Records of Forest Succession," 76–80, for Wisconsin; and Herbert A. Gleason, "Vegetational History of the Middle West," 80–85, for Illinois. Bayard Taylor's *Colorado: A Summer Trip*, 179, has other examples.

76. Roger C. Anderson, "The Historic Role of Fire in the North American Grassland," 14.

77. K. H. Garren, "The Effects of Fire on the Vegetation of the Southeastern United States," 620–35; Elsie Quarterman and Catherine Keever, "Southern Mixed Hardwood Forest: Climax in the Southeastern Coastal Plain, USA," 168–69.

78. Arthur A. Brown and Kenneth P. Davis, *Forest Fire: Control and Use*, 31–44; and Kozlowski and Ahlgren, *Fire and Ecosystems*, 195–320.

79. Cronon, *Changes in the Land*, 51; Day, "The Indian As an Ecological Factor," 339–40.

80. Sauer, "Grassland Climax, Fire and Man," 16–21.

81. Paul Richards, *The Tropical Rain Forest: An Ecological Study*, 404; Carl O. Sauer, "Man in the Ecology of Tropical America," 106–7; and G. Budowski, "Tropical Savannas, A Sequence of Forest Felling and Repeated Burnings," 23–33.

82. Johann Georg Goldammer, *Fire in Tropical Biota: Ecosystem Processes and Global Challenges,* 4–15.

83. Robert L. Sanford, Juan Saldarriaga, Kathleen E. Clark, Christopher Uhl, and Rafael Herrera, "Amazon Rain-Forest Fires," 53–55; Horst Fölster, "Holocene Autochthonous Forest Degradation in Southeast Venezuela," 41–43; and John R. Flenley, "Palynological Evidence Relating to Disturbance and Other Ecological Phenomena of Rain Forests," 19.

84. Christopher Uhl, Daniel Nepstad, Robert Buschbacher, Kathleen Clark, Boone Kauffman, and Scott Subler, "Studies of Ecosystem Response to Natural and Anthropogenic Disturbances Provide Guidelines for Designing Sustainable Land-Use Systems in Amazonia," 30.

85. Int. al., Darrell A. Posey, "Indigenous Management of Tropical Forest Ecosystems: The Case of the Kayapó Indians of the Brazilian Amazon," 139–58; William Balée, "Indigenous Transformation of Amazonian Forests: An Example from Maranhâo, Brazil," 231–54, and "The Culture of Amazonian Forests," 1–21; A. Roosevelt, "Resource Management in Amazonia before the Conquest: Beyond Ethnographic Projection," 30–62; and Laura Rival, "The Huaorani and Their Trees: Managing and Imagining the Equadorian Rainforest," 67–78. Quotation is from Posey, p. 141. For Maya lands see Arturo Gómez-Pompa, J. S. Flores, and V. Sosa, "The 'Pet Kot': A Man-Made Tropical Forest of the Maya," 10–15.

86. Sandra Brown and Ariel Lugo, "Tropical Secondary Forests," 4.

87. Rhys Jones, "Fire-Stick Farming," 224–28, and "Hunters in the Australian Coastal Savannas," 107–46; and J. Desmond Clark, "Early Human Occupation of African Savanna Environments," 41–72.

88. Denevan, "The Pristine Myth," 372–75.

89. Fölster, "Forest Degradation in Southeast Venezuela," 25–44.

90. J. G. Myers, "Savanna and Forest Vegetation in the Interior Guiana Plateau," 162–83.

91. Geoffrey A. J. Scott, "The Role of Fire in the Creation and Maintenance of Savannas in the Montaña of Peru," 143–67, and *Grassland Development in the Gran Pajonal of Eastern Peru.*

92. Le Roy R. Gordon, *The Human Geography and Ecology of the Sinú Country of Colombia.* For other examples of fire clearings in the American tropics, see Budowski, "Tropical Savannas," 22–33, and "The Ecological Status of Fire in American Tropical Lowlands"; and Sauer, "Fire and Early Man," 399–407, and "Man's Dominance by Use of Fire," 1–13.

93. J. Grahame D. Clark, *Prehistoric Europe: The Economic Basis,* 91–92.

94. Denevan, "The Pristine Myth," 375.

Chapter 3

1. Peter Rowley-Conwy, "Sedentary Hunters: The Ertebólle Example," 111–26; Richard B. Lee and Irven DeVore, eds., *Man the Hunter;* and quotation from Robin Dennell, *European Economic Prehistory: A New Approach,* 154.

2. Based on Ivor Wilks, "Land, Labour, and the Forest Kingdom of Asante: A Model of Early Change," esp. 501–08. Also relevant is Robert L. Carneiro, "Forest Clearance among the Yanomamö: Observations and Implications," 67–73.

3. Bryony Orme, "The Advantages of Agriculture," 41–50; and Andrew G. Sherratt, "Plough and Pastoralism: Aspects of the Secondary Products Revolution," 261–306, "Wool, Wheels, and Ploughmarks: Local Developments or Outside Introductions in Northern Europe?" 1–15, and "The Secondary Exploitation of Animals in the Old World," 90–104.

4. Estyn Evans, "The Ecology of Peasant Life in Western Europe," 217.

5. Int. al., Thomas J. Meyers, "The Origins of Agriculture: An Evaluation of Three Hypothe-

ses," 101–21; Edgar Anderson, *Plants, Man and Life,* and "Man As a Maker of New Plants and New Plant Communities," 763–77; David R. Harris, "Alternative Pathways toward Agriculture," 179–237; David R. Harris and Gordon C. Hillman, eds., *Foraging and Farming: The Evolution of Plant Exploitation,* 120–31; and Charles A. Reed, ed., *Origins of Agriculture.*

6. V. Gordon Childe, *The Dawn of European Civilization,* 1–8; and Dennell, *European Economic Prehistory,* 153–55.

7. David Rindos, *The Origins of Agriculture: An Evolutionary Perspective,* 127–37.

8. Jacquetta Hawkes, "The Ecological Background of Plant Domestication," 21.

9. Edgar Anderson, *Plants, Man and Life,* 120–131 on "Rubbish Piles and the Origins of Agriculture"; and "Man As a Maker of New Plants and New Plant Communities," 763–77.

10. Hawkes, "The Ecological Background," 22.

11. Rindos, *The Origins of Agriculture,* 135–37, quotation from p. 137.

12. Ibid., 138–43.

13. Paul E. Minnis, "Paleoethnobotanical Indicators of Prehistoric Environmental Disturbance: A Case Study," 348–51.

14. Alphonse de Candolle, *Géographie botanique raisonée,* 1–50; Nikolai Vavilov, "Studies on the Origins of Cultivated Plants," 1–243; Carl O. Sauer, *Agricultural Origins and Dispersals;* Jack R. Harlan, "Agricultural Origins: Centers and Noncenters," 468–74; and Richard S. MacNeish, *The Origins of Agriculture and Settled Life.*

15. MacNeish, *The Origins of Agriculture,* 19–33.

16. There is a vast literature on agriculture and its diffusion from the "Near-East," but H. E. Wright Jr.'s "Natural Environment of Early Food Production North of Mesopotamia," 334–39, and "The Environmental Setting for Plant Domestication in the Near East," 385–89, offer succinct summaries, as does Peter I. Bogucki, "The Spread of Early Farming in Europe," esp. 242–47. For individual plants see Daniel Zohary and Maria Hopf, *Domestication of Plants in the Old World.*

17. Based on Andrew G. Sherratt, "The Beginnings of Agriculture in the Near East and Europe," 102–11, and "Early Agricultural Communities in Europe," 144–51; and Peter I. Bogucki, *Forest Farmers and Stockherders: Early Agriculture and Its Consequences in North-Central Europe,* 11–17; and Bogucki, "The Spread of Early Farming," 246–53.

18. Childe, *The Dawn of European Civilization,* 105; J. Grahame D. Clark, "Forest Clearance and Prehistoric Farming," 45–51, and quotation from his *Prehistoric Europe: The Economic Basis,* 92.

19. Johannes Iversen, "The Influence of Prehistoric Man on Vegetation," 1–23; Werner Buttler and Waldemar Haberey, *Die banderkeramische Ansiedlung bei Köln-Lindenthal;* and Ester Boserup, *The Conditions of Agricultural Growth: The Economics of Agrarian Change under Population Growth.*

20. Description based largely on James Greig, "Past and Present Lime Woods of Europe," 23–55. See also Robert Gradmann, "Das Mitteleuropäische Landschaftsbild nach seiner geschichtlichen Entwicklung," 435–47.

21. Nicholas J. Starling, "Colonization and Succession: The Earlier Neolithic of Central Europe," 41–57, which convincingly challenges the earlier work of Albert J. Ammerman and Luigi L. Carvalli-Sforza in "Measuring the Rate of Spread of Early Farming in Europe," 674–88, and "A Population Model for the Diffusion of Early Farming in Europe," 343–57. See also Bogucki, *Forest Farmers and Stockherders,* 119–20.

22. Bogucki, *Forest Farmers and Stockherders,* 59–61. The literature on Neolithic settlement and farming is vast. See in particular the syntheses by Graeme Barker, *Prehistoric Farming in Europe,* and Alisdair Whittle, *Neolithic Europe: A Survey;* and the penetrating critique of both by Andrew Sherratt, "Two New Books on Early European Agriculture," 134–37.

23. Sherratt, "Early Agricultural Communities in Europe," 144; Bogucki, *Forest Farmers and Stockherders,* 62–77.

24. Pietr J. R. Modderman, *Linearbandkeramik aus Elsloo und Stein,* and "Banderkeramiker und Wandernbauerntum," 7–9; H. N. Jarman, "Early Crop Agriculture in Europe," 116–42; and Janusz Kruk, *The Neolithic Settlement of Southern Poland,* 8.

25. Burchard Sielmann, "Die frühneolithische Besiedlung Mitteleuropas," 18; and Wolfgang Linke, *Frühestes Bauerntum und Geographische Umwelt,* 20–50.

26. Helmut Nietsch, *Wald und Seidlung im Vorgeschichtlichen Mitteleuropa,* 70.

27. Sherratt, "Plough and Pastoralism," 275–87, "The Secondary Exploitation of Animals," 94–95, and "Wool, Wheels and Ploughmarks," 5.

28. Bogucki, *Forest Farmers and Stockherders,* 85–89.

29. Susan A. Gregg, *Foragers and Farmers: Population Interaction and Agricultural Expansion in Prehistoric Europe,* 128–45.

30. Kruk, *The Neolithic Settlement of Southern Poland;* Peter Rowley-Conwy, "Slash and Burn in the Temperate European Neolithic," 85–96; and MacNeish, *The Origins of Agriculture,* 226–29.

31. Janusz Kruk sees dispersal as a shift from an intensive horticultural economy to a more extensive regime based on swidden agriculture: Janusz Kruk, *Studia Osadnicze nod Neolitem Wyzyn Lessowych,* 244–65, and *The Neolithic Settlement of Southern Poland,* 50–66. For the contrary view that is an *intensification* and not an *extensification,* see Bogucki, *Forest Farmers and Stockherders,* 168, 170–71; and H. N. Jarman, "The Lowlands," 198.

32. Sherratt, "Plough and Pastoralism," 292–93, "The Secondary Exploitation of Animals," 90–104, and "The Beginnings of Agriculture in the Near East and Europe," 102–11. The origins of the LBK culture in the steppes to the east and north of the Black Sea are marked by prominent burial mounds; in some cases the dead have been buried with carts that have solid wooden wheels.

33. Colin Clark and Margaret R.Haswell, *The Economics of Subsistence,* 55; and Daniel Zohary and Pinchas Speigel-Roy, "The Beginnings of Fruit-Growing in the Old World," 319–27.

34. Sherratt, "Early Agricultural Communities in Europe," 151; and Bogucki, *Forest Farmers and Stockherders,* 176–77.

35. Sherratt, "Wool, Wheels, and Ploughmarks," 11.

36. Andrew G. Sherratt, "Resources, Technology and Trade in Early European Metallurgy," 562–66, and "Wool, Wheels, and Ploughmarks," 8–9. Alasdair Whittle in his "Gifts from the Earth: Symbolic Dimensions of the Use and Production of Neolithic Flint and Stone Axes," argues that ax heads had a symbolic as well as practical role, encouraging participation in, commemoration of, and consciousness of nature.

37. Starling, "Colonization and Succession," 55.

38. W. Startin, "Linear Pottery Culture Houses: Reconstruction and Manpower," 158.

39. Gregg, *Foragers and Farmers,* 163–65.

40. Based on ibid., 163–67.

41. Iversen, *Landnam i Danmarks Stenalder,* 20–68, and the idea is developed in "The Influence of Prehistoric Man on Vegetation," 1–23; "Forest Clearance in the Stone Age," 36–41, and "The Development of Denmark's Nature since the Last Glacial," 1–120.

42. Boserup, *The Conditions of Agricultural Growth;* and Axel Steensberg, *Draved: An Experiment in Stone Age Agriculture. Burning, Sowing and Harvesting.* For the Finnish evidence see Irmeli Vuorela, "Palynological and Historical Evidence of Slash-and-Burn Cultivation in South Finland," 53–64; Pertti Huttunen, "Early Land Use, Especially the Slash-and-Burn Cultivation. . ."; and Karl-Ernst Behre, "The Role of Man in European Vegetation History," 633–72.

43. Torsten Madsen, "Changing Patterns of Land Use in the TRB Culture of Southern Scandinavia," 29–30.

44. Sherratt, "Plough and Pastoralism," 290; and Jarman, "The Lowlands," 134.

45. The following argument is based on Rowley-Conwy, "Slash and Burn in the Temperate European Neolithic," 85–96. See also H. Tauber, "Differential Pollen Dispersal and the Interpretation of Pollen Diagrams," 1–69.

46. Karl-Ernst Behre, "The Interpretation of Anthropogenic Indicators in Pollen Diagrams," 225–45, and "The Role of Man in European Vegetation History," 633–72.

47. Albert Grenier, "Aux origines de l'économie rurale: La conquête de sol français," 28; Jarman, "The Lowlands," 133–34; and Bogucki, *Forest Farmers and Stockherders,* 49.

48. Charles B. Heiser, "Variation in the Bottle Gourd," 121–28; and Richard S. MacNeish, "The Origin and Dispersal of New World Agriculture," 87–94.

49. Warwick Bray, "From Predation to Production: The Nature of Agricultural Evolution in Mexico and Peru," 73–96, and "From Foraging to Farming in Early Mexico," 225–47.

50. Bray, "From Foraging to Farming," 229–32, and "Early Agriculture in the Americas," 368; and Richard S. MacNeish, "Ancient Mesoamerican Civilizations," 531–37.

51. Based on Paul L. Mangelsdorf, Richard S. MacNeish, and Walton C. Galinet, "Domestication of Corn," 538–45; and and Kent V. Flannery, "The Origins of Agriculture," 271–310. Quotation is from Bray, "Early Agriculture in the Americas," 369.

52. Anne V. T. Kirkby, "The Use of Land and Water Resources in the Past and Present Valley of Oaxaca, Mexico," 123–46.

53. John E. S. Thompson, *The Rise and Fall of Maya Civilization;* and Robert E. W. Adams and T. Patrick Culbert, "The Origins of Civilization in the Maya Lowlands," 3–24.

54. Thomas M. Whitmore and Billie L. Turner II, "Landscapes of Cultivation in Mesoamerica on the Eve of the Conquest," 402–25.

55. Eugene R. Craine and Reginald C. Reindorp, eds. and trans., *The Chronicles of Michoacán,* 13, 20, 173, 130, 24–25, 11, 101. For the background to the Purépecha peoples, see Vincent H. Malmström, "Geographical Origins of the Tarascans," 31–40.

56. Fray Diego Durán, *Book of the Gods and Rites of the Ancient Calendar,* 83.

57. Fray de Bernardino Sahagún, *The Florentine Codex: General History of the Things of New Spain,* 11:80–81.

58. Sarah L. O'Hara, F. Aleyne Street-Perrott, and Timothy P. Burt, "Accelerated Soil Erosion around a Mexican Highland Lake Caused by Pre-Hispanic Agriculture," 48–51; and F. Aleyne Street-Perrott, R. A. Perrott, and D. D. Harkness, "Anthropogenic Soil Erosion around Lake Putzcuaro, Michoacan, Mexico, during the Preclassic and Late Postclassic-Hispanic Periods," 759–95.

59. For the general degradation see John H. MacAndrews, "Human Disturbance of North American Forests and Grasslands: The Fossil Pollen Record," 674–75; and Sherburne F. Cook and Woodrow Borah, *Essays in Population History: Mexico and California,* 3:129–40. Quotations are from Cook, *Soil Erosion and Population in Central Mexico,* 1, 86. For a critique of Cook's possibly erroneous interpretation of the sequences of erosion, deforestation, and pastoralism, see Elinor G. K. Melville, *A Plague of Sheep: Environmental Consequences of the Conquest of Mexico,* 56–60 n. 11.

60. Barbara J. Williams, "Tepetate in the Valley of Mexico," 618–26; and Melville, *A Plague of Sheep,* 161–66.

61. Whitmore and Turner, "Landscapes of Cultivation," 419.

62. Anna C. Roosevelt, "Resource Management in Amazonia before the Conquest: Beyond Ethnographic Projection," 31.

63. Claude Lévi-Strauss, "The Concept of Archaism in Anthropology," 95–115.

64. Alfred Métraux, "The Revolution of the Ax," 28–40; and William M. Denevan, "Stone v. Metal Axes: The Ambiguity of Shifting Cultivation in Prehistoric Amazonia," 155. For the calculation of clearing times see Robert L. Carneiro, "On the Use of the Stone Axe by the Amahuaca Indians of Eastern Peru," 107–22, and "Forest Clearance Among the Yanomamö," 69–71.

65. Métraux, "The Revolution of the Ax," 30.

66. Billie L. Turner II, "The Rise and Fall of Population and Agriculture in the Central Maya Lowlands: 300 B.C. to Present," 178–211.

67. F. M. Wiseman, "Agriculture and Vegetation Dynamics of the Maya Collapse in Central Petén, Guatemala," 63–72; and Wendy Ashmore, ed., *Lowland Maya Settlement Patterns.*

68. This account of Maya agricultural practice is based on Arturo Gómez-Pompa, José S. Flores, and Victoria Sosa, "The 'Petkot': A Man-Made Tropical Forest of the Maya," 10–15; Billie L. Turner II, "Prehistoric Intensive Agriculture in the Mayan Lowlands," 118–24; Robert E. W. Adams, W. E. Brown Jr., and T. Patrick Culbert, "Radar Mapping Archaeology and Ancient Maya Land Use," 1457–63; and Billie Lee Turner II, "Issues Related to Subsistence and Environment among the Ancient Maya," 195–209.

69. Michael W. Binford, Mark Brenner, Thomas J. Whitmore, Antonia Higuera-Grundy, E. S. Deevey, and Barbara Leyden, "Ecosystems, Palaeoecology and Human Disturbance in Subtropical and Tropical America," 115–28; Matsuo Tsukada, "The Pollen Sequence," 63–66; and Edward S. Deevey, Don S. Rice, Prudence M. Rice, H. H. Vaughan, Mark Brenner, and M. S. Flannery, "Mayan Urbanism: Impact on a Tropical Karst Environment," 298–306.

70. Elliot M. Abrams, Anncorinne Freter, David J. Rue, and John D. Wingard, "The Role of Deforestation in the Collapse of the Late Classic Copán Maya State," 55–75.

71. Robert E. W. Adams, "The Collapse of Maya Civilization: A Review of Previous Theories," 21–34; and B. Turner, "The Rise and Fall of Population," 179.

72. Based on Bruce D. Smith, *Rivers of Change: Essays on Early Agriculture in Eastern North America,* 1–16; quotation is from p. 7. For earlier interpretations see Richard I. Ford, "The Process of Plant Food Production in Prehistoric North America," 1–128; Richard A. Yarnell, "Early Plant Husbandry in Eastern North America," 265–73; and MacNeish, *The Origins of Agriculture,* 246.

73. Based on Smith, *Rivers of Change,* and particularly "Origins of Agriculture in Eastern North America," 1566–71. For greater details on individual aspects see C. Margaret Scarry, ed., *Foraging and Farming in the Eastern Woodlands,* esp. 1–90.

74. Quotations are from Hazel R. Delcourt and Paul A. Delcourt, *Quaternary Ecology: A Palaeoecological Perspective,* 87–89. See also Hazel R. Delcourt, "The Impact of Prehistoric Agriculture and Land Occupation on Natural Vegetation," 39–44; Jefferson Chapman, Paul A. Delcourt, Patricia A. Cridlebaugh, A. Shea, and Hazel R. Delcourt, "Man-Land Interaction: 10,000 Years of American Indian Impact on Native Ecosystems in the Lower Little Tennessee Valley," 115–21; and C. Wesley Cowan, "Understanding the Evolution of Plant Husbandry in Eastern North America: Lessons from Botany, Ethnography and Archaeology," 10.

75. William F. Keegan, ed., *Emergent Horticultural Economies of the Eastern Woodlands;* Bruce D. Smith, "Variations in Mississippian Settlement Patterns," 479–503; and Joseph R. Caldwell's early but penetrating analysis, "Trend and Tradition in the Prehistory of the Eastern United States," 6–14.

76. Smith, *Rivers of Change,* 291–96; quotation is from p. 292.

77. Carl O. Sauer, *Sixteenth Century North America: The Land and the People As Seen by the Europeans,* 303. Much of the following account of the Indian impact on the forest is drawn from Michael Williams, *Americans and Their Forests: A Historical Geography,* 35–43. Since writing this section, Shepard Krech's *Ecological Indian: Myth and History* has appeared, which is a pene-

trating study of all aspects of Indian impacts on vegetation and wildlife, and supports the general thesis of environmental manipulation.

78. John Smith, "Description of Virginia and Proceedings of the Colonie," in *Travels and Works of Captain John Smith,* 1:95; Gordon M. Day, "The Indian As an Ecological Factor in the Northeastern Forest," 344–46; and Bruce G. Trigger, *The Huron: Farmers of the North,* 77–78.

79. Conrad Heidenreich, *Huronia: A History and Geography of the Huron Indians, 1600– 1650,* 107–218.

80. Neal H. Lopinot and William I. Woods, "Wood Over-Exploitation and the Collapse of Cahokia," 206–31.

81. Based on Conrad Heidenreich, "The Huron," 368–88; and Hugh Jones, *The Present State of Virginia . . . ,* 55.

82. Joseph F. Lafitau, "Customs of the American Indians Compared with Those of the Customs of Primitive Times," 39; and Day, "The Indian As an Ecological Factor," 330.

83. For collected descriptions of fields see L. Ceci, "Maize Cultivation in Coastal New York: The Archaeological, Agronomical, and Documentary Evidence," 45–74; William E. Doolittle, "Agriculture in North America on the Eve of Contact: A Reassessment," 386–401; and William I. Woods, "Maize Agriculture and the Late Prehistoric; A Characterization of Settlement Location Strategies," 275–94.

84. John Smith, "Advertisements for the Inexperienced Planters of New England or Anywhere," 2:363.

85. William Strachey, *The Historie of Travelle into Virginia Britannia,* 67.

86. John Lederer, *The Discoveries of John Lederer . . . ,* 24; Winslow and Hopkins are quoted in Alexander Young, *Chronicles of the Pilgrim Fathers of the Colony of Plymouth from 1602 to 1625,* 206–7. For more details see M. Williams, *Americans and Their Forests,* 41–43.

87. Frederick Cook, ed., *Journals of the Military Expedition of General John Sullivan against the Six Nations of Indians in 1779,* 301; Benjamin Hawkins, *A Sketch of the Creek Country in the Years 1798 and 1799,* 22, 27, 33–35; and William Bartram, *The Travels of William Bartram,* 68.

88. Garcilasco de la Vega, *The Florida of the Inca: A History of Adelantado, Hernando de Soto,* 2:182.

89. John N. B. Hewitt, "The Iroquoian Cosmology," 461–62; and Hawkins, *A Sketch of the Creek Country,* 30.

90. Lopinot and Woods, "Wood Over-Exploitation and the Collapse of Cahokia," 206–31; James B. Griffin, "Timber Procurement and Village Location in the Middle Missouri Sub-Area," 177–185; and William C. MacLeod, "Fuel and Early Civilization," 344–46.

91. Doolittle, "Agriculture in North America," 392; and Trigger, *The Huron,* 27–28.

92. Ratio based on William H. Townsend, "Stone and Steel Use in a New Guinea Society," 199–205. See also Hazel Delcourt, "The Impact of Prehistoric Agriculture," 341–46.

93. See Evan Peacock, "Historical and Applied Perspectives on Prehistoric Land Use in Eastern North America," 10–11.

94. Alfred L. Kroeber, *Cultural and Natural Areas of Native North America,* 131, 166; Heidenreich, *Huronia,* 195–200; William M. Denevan, "The Pristine Myth: The Landscape of the Americas in 1492," 370–71, and *The Native Population of the Americas in 1492,* 1–7, 289–92; Henry Dobyns, "Estimating Aboriginal American Populations: An Appraisal of Techniques with a New Hemispheric Estimate," 395–449; and Hu Maxwell, "The Use and Abuse of the Forests by the Virginia Indians," 81.

95. Roger C. Anderson, "The Historic Role of Fire in the North American Grassland," 8–18; Carl O. Sauer, "Grassland Climax, Fire and Man," 16–21; and Theodore T. Kozlowski and Clifford E. Ahlgren, eds., *Fire and Ecosystems,* 179–94.

96. Omer C. Stewart, "Barriers to Understanding the Influence of the Use of Fire by Aborigines on Vegetation," 117–26.

97. Discussion on other Centers and Non-Centers based on MacNeish, *The Origins of Agriculture,* 150–70, 255–318.

98. Bennet Bronson, "South-East Asia: Civilizations of the Tropical Forests," 263.

Chapter 4

1. Based on James R. A. Greig and J. Turner, "Some Pollen Diagrams from Greece and Their Archaeological Significance," 183–86; Paul Halstead, "Counting Sheep in Neolithic and Bronze Age Greece," 307–40; Jane M. Renfrew, "Agriculture," 147–63; Andrew G. Sherratt, "The Beginnings of Agriculture in the Near East and Europe," 102–11, and "Early Agricultural Communities in Europe," 144–51; and John Bradford, "Buried Landscapes in Southern Italy," 65–72.

2. Fairfield Osborn, *The Limits of the Earth,* 17.

3. Fritz M. Heichelheim, "Effects of Classical Antiquity on the Land," 165–82. Unless otherwise acknowledged, the following paragraphs draw on Heichelheim.

4. Andrew G. Sherratt and Susan Sherratt, "The Growth of the Mediterranean Economy in the Early First Millennium BC," 374.

5. Heichelheim, "Effects of Classical Antiquity," 167.

6. Michael Rostovtzeff, *A Large Estate in Egypt in the Third Century, B.C.,* 56–92; and John Bradford, *Ancient Landscapes in Europe and Asia: Studies in Archaeology and Photography,* 145–49.

7. Heichelheim, "Effects of Classical Antiquity," 170–72.

8. For a thorough analysis of slavery and its implications on land expansion, see Keith Hopkins, *Conquerors and Slaves,* esp. 8–25, 48–63. Quotation is from p. 13.

9. Heichelheim, "Effects of Classical Antiquity," 176.

10. Michael Rostovtzeff, *The Social and Economic History of the Roman Empire,* and *The Social and Economic History of the Hellenistic World;* and Fritz M. Heichelheim, *An Ancient Economic History from the Palaeolithic Age to the Migrations of Germanic, Slavic and Arabic Nations.*

11. See Olli Makkonen, "Ancient Forestry: An Historical Study," 9–16 for the characteristics of the written record. Also see Russell Meiggs, *Trees and Timber in the Ancient Mediterranean World,* 13–14.

12. Clarence Glacken, *Traces on the Rhodian Shore: Nature and Culture in Western Thought from Ancient Times to the End of the Eighteenth Century,* 117 et seq. See also J. Donald Hughes, *Ecology in Ancient Civilizations,* 56–67, 87–98 for similar themes.

13. Glacken, *Traces,* 116–19; and Sophocles, *Antigone,* 362.

14. John L. Bintliff, *Natural Environment and Human Settlement in Prehistoric Greece,* 60–75; Pierre Quezel, "Incidences climatologique de l'utilisation des sols par l'homme dans le monde méditerranéen protohistorique," 129–33.

15. Marvin Mikesell, "The Deforestation of Mount Lebanon," 1–28; and Pierre Quezel, "Forests of the Mediterranean Basin," 9–31.

16. R. Tomaselli, "Degradation of the Mediterranean Maquis," 33–72; and Zev Naveh and Joel Dan, "The Human Degradation of Mediterranean Landscapes in Israel," 373–90.

17. Ellen Churchill Semple, *The Geography of the Mediterranean Region: Its Relation to Ancient History,* 261–97; H. Clifford Darby, "The Clearing of the Woodland in Europe," 184–86; Jack V. Thirgood, *Man and the Mediterranean Forest: A History of Resource Depletion,* 1–78; John Perlin, *A Forest Journey: The Role of Wood in the Development of Civilization,* 75–129;

and J. Donald Hughes, *Pan's Travail: Environmental Problems of the Ancient Greeks and Romans,* 73–90.

18. Bintliff, *Natural Environment and Human Settlement,* 66–83.

19. Homer, *The Iliad,* xiii, 13; xvi, 482–84; xvi, 643–46; xx, 490–92; and Aristophanes, *The Clouds,* 281–82. Renderings vary enormously with different translations.

20. Theophrastus, *Enquiry into Plants,* introduction by Sir Arthur Hort, xx–xxi.

21. Theophrastus, *Enquiry into Plants,* IV.i.4, IV.v.5, V.viii.1–2; Heinrich Rubner, "Greek Thought and Forest Science," 277–95; and J. Donald Hughes, "Theophrastus As Ecologist," 67–75.

22. Theophrastus, *Enquiry into Plants,* III.iii.2–3; and Strabo, *The Geography of Strabo.* See also Makkonen, "Ancient Forestry," 28–50 on other early ideas about the propagation, growth, and location of trees.

23. Rostovtzeff, *The Hellenistic World,* 1095.

24. Renfrew, "Agriculture," 149; Arnold J. Toynbee, ed. and trans., *Greek Historical Thought from Homer to the Age of Heraclius,* 144; Sophocles, *Antigone,* 338–41.

25. Homer, *Illiad,* XVI. 794–97; Horace, *Satires, Epistles, and Ars Poetica,* "Epistles," II.2.185–88; and Virgil, *The Geogrics,* 2:177.

26. Lucretius, *Titi Lucreti Cari de Rerum Natura Libra Sex,* 5:505; Strabo, *Geography,* 5.4.5; Livy, *History of Rome,* 9.36.1; and Claude Nicolet, "Economy and Society, 133–43 B.C.," 609, 611.

27. Marcus Terentius Varro, *De re Rustica,* 1.2.6.

28. Kenneth D. White, *Roman Farming,* and *Farm Equipment of the Roman World.*

29. Meiggs, *Trees and Timber,* 330–31, 346–47; Theophrastus, *Enquiry into Plants,* V.vi.3; and Ovid, *Metamorphoses,* 8.775.

30. Lucius Junius Moderatus Columella, *De re Rustica* (On agriculture), II.ii.8, II.ii.11–12.

31. Pliny the Elder, *Natural History,* XVII.3.39, XVII.3. 26.

32. Glacken, *Traces,* 134; Columella, *De re Rustica,* II.i.3–6.

33. Strabo, *Geography,* 14.6.5; and E. G. Hardy, *Roman Laws and Charters,* 59, clause 14.

34. Halstead, "Counting Sheep," 307–40; and Sandor Bököny, "Stockbreeding," 165–78.

35. Semple, *The Geography of the Mediterranean Region,* 298–300; and Nicolet, "Economy and Society, 133–43 B.C.," 615–16.

36. James A. R. Lewthwaite, "Plains Tails from the Hills: Transhumance in Mediterranean Archaeology," 60–61.

37. Yves Baticle, *L'elevage ovir dans les Pays Européens de la Méditerranée Occidentale.*

38. Varro, *De re Rustica,* 2, intro. 4; and John F. Kolars, "Locational Aspects of Cultural Ecology: The Case of the Goat in Non-Western Agriculture," 577–84.

39. Bökönyi, "Stockbreeding," 173; James J. Parsons, "The Acorn-Hog Economy of the Oak Woodlands of Southwestern Spain," 211–35; and Strabo, *Geography,* 3.4.11, 5.1.12.

40. Strabo, *Geography,* 4.5.2.; and Pliny, *Natural History,* XVI.ii.5.

41. Simon Schama, *Landscape and Memory,* 81–91.

42. Rostovtzeff, *The Roman Empire,* 1:138, 192.

43. Albert L. F. Rivet, *Town and Country in Roman Britain,* 197; Rostovtzeff, *The Roman Empire,* 1:229, 1:244; and Jules Toutain, *The Economic Life of the Ancient World,* 265–66.

44. Alan Chester Johnson, "Ancient Forests and Navies," 199–209.

45. Toynbee, *Greek Historical Thought,* 291–92.

46. Sherratt and Sherratt, "The Growth of the Mediterranean Economy," 375.

47. Meiggs, *Trees and Timber,* 117; Thucydides, *History of the Peloponnesian War,* e.g.,

bk. 8, yr. XIX; Johnson, "Ancient Forests and Navies," 199–209; and Rostovtzeff, *The Roman Empire,* I:223, 233, 239, 243; II:609, 672, 722.

48. Meiggs, *Trees and Timber,* 183, 121, 141; Lionel Casson, *Ships and Seamanship in the Ancient World,* 108–12.

49. Maurice Lombard, "Une carte du bois la Méditerranée musulmane (VIIe–XIe siècle)," 23–54.

50. Theophrastus, *Enquiry into Plants,* quotation from V.vii.1–3; and on sources and types of ship's timbers generally, V.viii.1–5 and V.v.5.

51. Ibid., V.viii.1.

52. Meiggs, *Trees and Timber,* 338–39; and Johnson, "Ancient Forests and Navies," 199–209.

53. Strabo, *Geography,* 3.4.2., 4.1.5., 4.6.2. Pliny is quoted in Semple, *The Geography of the Mediterranean Region,* 269.

54. Stephen Mitchell, "The Hellenistic World," 220–21, quotation is from p. 221; and Richard Duncan-Jones, *The Economy of the Roman Empire: Quantitative Studies,* 259–87.

55. For Plato's description see Toynbee, *Greek Historical Thought,* 169; and Meiggs, *Trees and Timber,* 188–91; quotation is from p. 191.

56. Meiggs, *Trees and Timber,* 193, 206.

57. Theophrastus, *Enquiry into Plants,* V.ii.1, V.vii.4–5.

58. For the size of Rome see Jerôme Carcopino, *Daily Life in Ancient Rome: The People and the City at the Height of the Empire,* 17–20; Peter Brunt, *Italian Manpower,* 376–88; J. Whitney Oates, "The Population of Rome," 101–16; and Hopkins, *Conquerors and Slaves,* 96–98. For building, see Strabo, *Geography,* 5.3.7–8, 5.2.5, 5.7.4–5; quotation is on 5.2.5.

59. Gerald Brodribb, *Roman Brick and Tile;* Eugene Ayres and Charles A. Scarlott, *Energy Sources: The Wealth of the World,* 9; and Brian Dix, "The Manufacture of Lime and Its Uses in the Western Roman Provinces," 337, 343. A simple calculation suggests that if a wagonload were 5 tons, then between 75,000 and 150,000 tonnes of wood were needed for lime alone, which translates into the timber from between approximately 660 and 1320 heavily wooded acres or 170,000 to 340,000 acres if lightly coppiced.

60. Theophrastus, *Enquiry into Plants,* V.viii.3; and Strabo, *Geography,* 5.3.7., 5.2.5., 8.8.1.

61. Virgil, *The Ecologues,* 7.49–50; and Robert J. Forbes, *Studies in Ancient Technology,* vol. 6, *Heat and Heating, Refrigeration and Light,* 6:36–67.

62. Meiggs, *Trees and Timber,* 258; Fritz Kretzschmer, "Der Betriebsversuch an einem Hypokaustum der Saalburg," 64–7, and "Hypocausten," 7–41; and Anthony Rook, "The Development and Operation of Roman Hypocausted Baths," 269–82.

63. Robert V. Reynolds and Albert H. Pierson, *Fuel Wood Used in the United States, 1630–1930,* 8–11.

64. Marcus Porcius Cato, *On Agriculture,* XXXVII.5.37–39; Meiggs, *Trees and Timber,* 423–57; and Strabo, *Geography,* 5.3.7.

65. Pliny, *Natural History,* XXXIV.96; and Meiggs, *Trees and Timber,* 253–90.

66. John F. Healy, *Mining and Metallurgy in the Greek and Roman World,* esp. 139–215; and Theodore A. Wertime, "Cypriot Metallurgy against a Backdrop of Mediterranean Pyrotechnology: Energy Reconsidered," 351 et seq. See Theophrastus, *Enquiry into Plants,* vol 1, V.ix.2–8 for a contemporary account of the value of different woods for charcoal and fuel.

67. Perlin, *A Forest Journey,* 16, 125; Wertime, "Cypriot Metallurgy," 352–55.

68. Theodore A. Wertime and Stephen F. Wertime, *The Evolution of the First Fire-Using Industries,* 135–36; and Theodore A. Wertime, "The Furnace versus the Goat: The Pyrotechnologic

Industries and Mediterranean Deforestation in Antiquity," 452. For Cyprus see Georges Constantinou, "Geological Features and Ancient Exploitation of Cupriferous Sulphide Ore Bodies in Cyprus," 22.

69. Leonard U. Salkield, "The Roman and Pre-Roman Slags of the Rio Tinto, Spain," 146, and "Ancient Slag in the South West of the Iberian Peninsula," 94.

70. Meiggs, *Trees and Timber*, 398; and Strabo, *Geography*, 14.6.5.

71. Henry Cleere, "Some Operating Parameters for Roman Ironworks," 233–47, and "Iron-making in a Roman Furnace," 203–17.

72. Meiggs, *Trees and Timber*, 380. See, for example, chap. 12 on late nineteenth-century West Africa.

73. Pliny, *Natural History*, XVI.24.62.

74. Paul Kennedy, *The Rise and Fall of Great Powers: Economic Change and Military Conflict from 1500 to 2000*; Carlo M. Cipolla, ed., *The Economic Decline of Empires*; Edward Gibbon, *The History of the Decline and Fall of the Roman Empire . . .* ; and Edgar Allan Poe, "To Helen."

75. J. Donald Hughes and Jack V. Thirgood, "Deforestation, Erosion, and Forest Management in Ancient Greece and Rome," 165; David Attenborough, *The First Eden: The Mediterranean World and Man*, 117–18; Henry David Thoreau, "Walking," 9:281; George Perkins Marsh, *Man and Nature: Or, Physical Geography As Modified by Human Action*, 9–11; Walter Clay Lowdermilk, "Lessons from the Old World to the Americas in Land Use," 413–28; Paul Sears, *Deserts on the March*, 27–30; and Osborn, *The Limits of the Earth*, 8–11. Hughes somewhat modifies his views on the importance of deforestation in his *Pan's Travail*, 181–99.

76. See Hughes, *Pan's Travail*, 186–89 for an extensive discussion on epidemics.

77. Rostovtzeff, *The Roman Empire*, 1:378–89, 480–88, 500–51; and Heichelheim, "Effects of Classical Antiquity," 177–80.

78. Tamara Lewit, *Agricultural Production in the Roman Economy, A.D. 200–400*, 85–88.

79. Toynbee, *Greek Historical Thought*, 169; Meiggs, *Trees and Timber*, 188–91; J. Neumann, "Climatic Change As a Topic in the Classical Greek and Roman Literature," 444; and Heichelheim, *An Ancient Economic History*, 2:110.

80. Rostovtzeff, *The Roman Empire*, 1:376–77, 2:134; and Heichelheim, "Effects of Classical Antiquity," 171. Aurelio Bernardi, "The Economic Problems of the Roman Empire at the Time of Its Decline," 16–83 discusses many contributory causes of decline, of which land degradation is not one.

81. Meiggs, *Trees and Timber*, 188–91, 377.

82. Pliny, *Natural History*, XXXI.30.53; Pausanias, *Description of Greece*, 8.24.11; Perlin, *A Forest Journey*, 79–80; and Meiggs, *Trees and Timber*, 376.

83. John L. Bintliff, "New Approaches to Human Geography. Prehistoric Greece: A Case Study," 75–81, quotation is from p. 75, and *Natural Environment and Human Settlement*, 73; and James R. A. Greig and J. Turner, "Some Pollen Diagrams from Greece," 177–94.

84. For a recent review of the evidence and shifts in interpretation, see John Bintliff's excellent "Erosion in the Mediterranean Lands: A Reconsideration of Patterns, Processes, and Methodology," 125–32.

85. Claudio Vita-Finzi, *The Mediterranean Valleys: Geological Changes in Historical Times*, 107–15; John L. Bintliff, "Mediterranean Alluviation: New Evidence from Archaeology," 78–84, *Natural Environment and Human Settlement*, and "New Approaches to Human Geography," 75–82; and Sheldon Judson, "Stream Changes during Historic Time in East-Central Sicily," 287–89.

86. Bintliff, "Mediterranean Alluviation," 78–84, "New Approaches to Human Geography," 77–78, and diagram on p. 76.

87. Hubert H. Lamb, "Our Changing Climate: Past and Present," 5–11; and Sheldon Judson, "Erosion Rates near Rome, Italy," 1445.

88. Tjeerd H. van Andel, Curtis N. Runnels, and Kevin O. Pope, "Five Thousand Years of Land Use and Abuse in the Southern Argolid, Greece," 103–128, quotations are from pp. 110 and 118; and Tjeerd H. van Andel and Curtis N. Runnels, *Beyond the Acropolis, A Rural Greek Past,* esp. 135–56.

89. Brent D. Shaw, "Climate, Environment and History: The Case of Roman North Africa," 379–43; quotations are from p. 395.

90. Darby, "The Clearing of the Woodland in Europe," 395. See the more recent work of Hughes, *Ecology in Ancient Civilizations,* 71, for a similar conclusion.

91. Hughes, "How the Ancients Viewed Deforestation," 437–38, quotation is from pp. 437–38, and *Pan's Travail,* 169–80. See also Henry Rushton Fairclough, *Love of Nature among Greeks and Romans.*

92. John R. Love, *Antiquity and Capitalism: Max Weber and the Sociological Foundations of Roman Civilization,* esp. 1–55, and 59–109 on "The Economic Climate of the Ancient Agricultural Estates: *Oikos* or Enterprise?"

93. Marcus Tullius Cicero, *De Natura Deorum Academica,* II.61.154.

94. Ibid., *De Natura Deorum,* II.60.151–52.

95. Tertullian, *De Anima,* vol. 3, XXX.210.

Chapter 5

1. Charles Higounet, "Les forêts de L'Europe occidentale du Vᵉ au XIᵉ siècle," 398.

2. Christopher Wickham, "European Forests in the Early Middle Ages: Landscape and Land Clearance," 485, 488. See pp. 485–90 for an exhaustive discussion on the meaning of *foresta, saltus, silva,* and other medieval terminology relating to wastes.

3. George Duby, *Rural Economy and Country Life in the Medieval West,* 68.

4. For a review of the different evidence see Richard Koebner, "The Settlement and Colonization of Europe," 6–8; and Robert Bartlett, *The Making of Europe: Conquest, Colonization, and Cultural Change, 950–1350,* 156–66. For the reconstruction of forest conditions over the center of the Continent, see Otto Schlüter, *Die Siedlungsräume Mitteleuropas in frühgeschichtlicher Zeit,* and the subsequent detailed colored map in *Atlas Ostliches Mitteleuropa,* plate 10.

5. Kenneth Clark, *Civilisation: A Personal View,* 23.

6. Jean Gimpel, *The Cathedral Builders.* See also, Francis Gies and Joseph Gies, *Cathedral, Forge, and Waterwheel: Technology and Invention in the Middle Ages,* 105–236.

7. Conrad Totman, *The Green Archipelago: Forestry in Pre-Industrial Japan,* 34–49; Yi-fu Tuan, *China,* 31–41, 78, 141–44; Vaclaf Smil, "Deforestation in China," 226–33; and Rhoads Murphey, "Deforestation in Modern China," 111–28. The quotation is from Estyn Evans, "The Ecology of Peasant Life in Western Europe," 217.

8. See Andrew M. Watson, "Towards a Denser and More Continuous Settlement: New Crops and Farming Techniques in the Early Middle Ages," 65–82; and Clarence F. Glacken, *Traces on the Rhodian Shore: Nature and Culture in Western Thought from Ancient Times to the End of the Eighteenth Century,* 288–351; quotations are from pp. 350 and 351.

9. Lynn White Jr., "Cultural Climates and Technological Advance in the Middle Ages," 171.

10. Lynn White Jr., *Medieval Technology and Social Change,* 77–78.

11. Ibid., 56–57, quotation is from p. 57; and his "Cultural Climates and Technological Advance," 199–200, in which he debates whether agricultural change and clearing is motivated by

religious attitudes or secular ones. *Man* is used and capitalized where in medieval (and later) theological contexts the word is juxtaposed as a contrast between generic humans and a divine being: God—and/or what was commonly regarded as God's work—Nature.

12. Norman J. G. Pounds, *Economic History of Medieval Europe*, 97.

13. Based on Glacken, *Traces*, 289–341.

14. John U. Nef, *The Conquest of the Material World*, 3–42; and L. White, *Medieval Technology and Social Change*, esp. 89, 41; quotation is from p. 89.

15. M. T. Hodgson, "Domesday Water Mills," 261–79; and Carlo M. Cipolla, *Before the Industrial Revolution: European Society and Economy, 1000–1700*, 161–64.

16. Lynn White, "What Accelerated Technological Progress in the Western Middle Ages?" 272–73.

17. Lewis Mumford, *Technics and Civilization*, 109–10.

18. Koebner, "The Settlement and Colonization," 3; Roger Grand and Raymond Delatouche, *L'agriculture au moyen âge de la fin de L'Empire Romain au XVIe siècle*, 237 et seq.

19. Koebner, "Settlement and Colonization," 31–33; J. C. Russell, "Late Ancient and Medieval Population," 147–48; Alfons Döpsch, *The Economic and Social Foundations of European Civilization*, 97–98; and Pounds, *Medieval Europe*, 44.

20. Koebner, "The Settlement and Colonization," 20.

21. Andi E. Verhulst, "Karolingische Agarpolitik: Das *Capitulare de villis* die Hungernöte von 792/93 und 805/06," 179–89; William H. TeBrake, *Medieval Frontier: Culture and Ecology in Rijnland*, 44–45; and Michel Rouche, "La faim à l'époque carolingienne: essaisur quelques types de rations alimentaires," 295–320.

22. J. C. Russell, "Late Ancient and Medieval Population," 147–48, and "Population in Europe, 500–1500," 34–36.

23. Duby, *Rural Economy and Country Life*, 65–67; Martin L. Parry, *Climatic Change, Agriculture and Settlement*, 65, 96–98.

24. See Eric Jones, *The European Miracle: Environments, Economies, and Geopolitics in the History of Europe and Asia*, 48–50; Pounds, *Economic History of Medieval Europe*, 130–33; and Ester Boserup, "Population and Technology in Preindustrial Europe," 692–93.

25. Archibald R. Lewis, "The Closing of the Medieval Frontier, 1250–1350," 475–83. For a wider discussion on the nature of the medieval frontier, see TeBrake, *Medieval Frontier*, 21–52; Pounds, *Economic History of Medieval Europe*, 175–83; and William S. Cooter, "Preindustrial Frontiers and Interaction Spheres: Aspects of the Human Ecology of Roman Frontier Regions in Northwest Europe." For detailed accounts of the Germanic colonization, see Koebner, "The Settlement and Colonization," 79–86; R. Kötzschke and W. Ebert, *Geschichte der Ostdeutschen Kolonisation;* James Westfall Thompson, *An Economic and Social History of the Middle Ages (300–1300)*, 517–39; and his *Feudal Germany*, 451–670.

26. Koebner, "The Settlement and Colonization," 42–43; George Duby, *The Early Growth of the European Economy: Warriors and Peasants from the Seventh to the Twelfth Century*, 72; Grand and Delatouche, *L'agriculture au moyen âge*, 237–42; and G. Des Marez, *Le problème de la colonization franque et du régime agraire en Basse Belgique*, 13–40.

27. Duby, *The Early Growth of the European Economy*, 12–13; and TeBrake, *Medieval Frontier*, 35–51.

28. Ester Boserup, *The Conditions of Agricultural Growth: The Economics of Agrarian Change under Population Growth*, 18–19; Duby, *The Early Growth of the European Economy*, 13; and TeBrake, *Medieval Frontier*, 26–34.

29. William G. Hoskins, "The English Landscape," 10.

30. L. White, *Medieval Technology and Social Change*, 54–5; and Charles Parain, "The Evolution of Agricultural Technique," 127 et seq.

31. This and the following paragraph are based on L. White, *Medieval Technology and Social Change*, 57–63, and "The Expansion of Technology, 500–1500," 149–53; Parain, "The Evolution of Agricultural Technique," 132–35; and George Duby, "Medieval Agriculture, 900–1500," 175–220.

32. William S. Cooter, "Ecological Dimensions of Medieval Agrarian Systems," 458–77; and L. White, *Medieval Technology and Social Change*, 75–76, and "The Expansion of Technology," 149.

33. T. A. M. Bishop, "Assarting and the Growth of the Open Fields," 19.

34. L. White, *Medieval Technology and Social Change*, 41; and George Duby, "La révolution agricole médiévale," 363.

35. TeBrake, *Medieval Frontier*, 49–50; Koebner, "The Settlement and Colonization," 4–6, 11; and Glacken, *Traces*, 289.

36. Glacken, *Traces*, 289, 313–14; Koebner, "The Settlement and Colonization," 4–5; and Roland Bechmann, *Trees and Man: The Forest in the Middle Ages*, 295 et seq.

37. The following paragraphs on the religious motivation draw on Glacken's brilliant analysis in *Traces*, 293–309. See also Christopher Dawson, *The Making of Europe: An Introduction to the History of European Unity*, 48–60. For "A bridge . . ." see Glacken, *Traces*, 294. L. White, "Cultural Climates and Technological Advance," 189–90, 197 also suggests that in the common imagination, God the builder was fast on his way to being God the mechanic. See Gies and Gies, *Cathedral, Forge, and Waterwheel*, 5.

38. See L. White, "Cultural Climates and Technological Advance," 191–95 for a penetrating analysis of the importance of labor in technological advance; see also Max Weber, *The Protestant Ethic and the Spirit of Capitalism*, 118–19. Quotation is from Glacken, *Traces*, 304.

39. Jean Leclercq, *The Love of Learning and the Desire for God: A Study of Monastic Culture*, 60, quoted in Glacken, *Traces*, 303.

40. Koebner, "The Settlement and Colonization," 21; and L. White, "Cultural Climates and Technological Advance," 188.

41. Charles H. Talbot, ed., *The Anglo-Saxon Missionaries in Germany . . .* , 183, 186–87, 190.

42. See Wickham, "European Forests in the Early Middle Ages," 481–84 on the founding of Fulda.

43. Robin A. Donkin, *The Cistercians: Studies in the Geography of Medieval England and Wales*, esp. 21–67. Other useful studies are F. Van der Meer, *Atlas de l'ordre Cistercien*, which has excellent illustrations and maps. Quotations are from J. W. Thompson, *An Economic and Social History of the Middle Ages*, 611.

44. Quotations are from Glacken, *Traces*, 311; Prosper Boissonnade, *Life and Work in Medieval Europe (Fifth to Fifteenth Centuries)*, 226; and Koebner, "The Settlement and Colonization," 44.

45. George Ovitt Jr., *The Restoration of Perfection: Labor and Technology in Medieval Culture*, 38–42; quotation is from p. 40. For secular growth and its problems see Glacken, *Traces*, 309, 314; and Donkin, *The Cistercians*, 37–67.

46. Int. al., Michael Williams, "Marshland and Waste," 90–108; H. Clifford Darby, *The Medieval Fenland*; and J. W. Thompson, *Feudal Germany*, 545–79.

47. George Duby, *Rural Economy and Country Life*, 68.

48. Henry Clifford Darby, "The Clearing of the Woodland in Europe," 190.

49. Koebner, "The Settlement and Colonization," 41; Des Marez, *Le problème de la colonization franque,* 35–40; Darby, "The Clearing of the Woodland in Europe," 192–93; and Glacken, *Traces,* 334.

50. Koebner, "The Settlement and Colonization," 45–46; Döpsch, *The Economic and Social Foundations of European Civilization,* 99, 106–16, 124–26, 151–52; and C. Niemeier, "Frühformen der Waldhufen," 14–27.

51. Hans-Jurgen Nitz, "The Church As Colonist: The Benedictine Abbey of Lorsch and Planned Waldhufen Colonization in the Odenwald," 105–26. For Saxony, see Nitz, "Feudal Woodland Colonization As a Strategy of the Carolingian Empire in the Conquest of Saxony—Reconstruction of the Spatial Pattern of Expansion in the Liene-Weser Region," 171–82. For its trans-Elbian manifestations see R. Bartlett, *The Making of Europe,* 139–43, 158–61.

52. Robert K. Gordon, ed., *Anglo-Saxon Poetry,* 295.

53. H. Clifford Darby, "The Clearing of the English Woodlands," 72–74, and "The Clearing of the Woodland in Europe," 191–92, using material from English Place Name Society publications. Sidney W. Wooldridge, "The Anglo-Saxon Settlement," 109–20 analyzes early, "nonwoodland" names.

54. Oliver Rackham, *Ancient Woodland: Its History, Vegetation, and Uses in England,* 111–35 and passim.

55. The classic geographical analysis is in the many regional volumes written and/or edited by H. Clifford Darby, the woodland portions of which are summarized in his *Domesday England,* 171–207. For the return of the woodlands in the north, see Reginald Lennard, "The Destruction of Woodland in the Eastern Counties under William the Conqueror," 36–43.

56. M. Williams, "Marshland and Waste," 110–11; and Frank V. Emery, "Moated Settlements in England," 378–88.

57. Duby, *Rural Economy and Country Life,* 67.

58. Wickham, "European Forests in the Early Middle Ages," 501; Hermann Aubin, "Medieval Society in Its Prime: The Lands East of the Elbe and German Colonization Eastwards," 361–97; Bechmann, *Trees and Man;* Marc Bloch, *French Rural History: An Essay on Its Basic Characteristics,* 5–20; H. Clifford Darby, "The Economic Geography of England, A.D. 1000–1250," 173–89, and "The Clearing of the Woodland in Europe," 182–216; Michel Devèze, "Forêts françaises et forêts allemandes: étude historique comparée," 347–80, 47–68; Duby, *Rural Economy and Country Life,* 65–85, 41–56, and *The Early Growth of the European Economy,* 199–210; Jacques Flach, *Les origines de l'ancienne France,* 2:139–57; Glacken, *Traces,* 288–351; Koebner, "The Settlement and Colonization," 1–88; L. F. A. Maury, *Les forêts de la France: dans l'antiqué et au moyen âge,* and *Les forêts de la Gaule et de l'ancienne France;* Otto Schlüter, *Die Siedlungsräume Mittleuropas;* and J. W. Thompson, *An Economic and Social History of the Middle Ages,* 517–39, 603–46, 756–58, *Feudal Germany,* 451–670, and "East German Colonization in the Middle Ages," 125–50.

59. For example, Thérèse Sclafert, *Le Haute-Dauphiné au moyen âge,* and *Cultures en Haute-Provence: déboisments et pâturages au moyen âge;* Christopher Dyer, *Hanbury: Settlement and Society in a Wooded Landscape;* Cyril E. Hart, *Royal Forest: A History of Dean's Woods As Producers of Timber;* John Hatcher, *Rural Economy and Society in the Duchy of Cornwall, 1300–1500,* 184–86; and K. P. Witney, "The Woodland Economy of Kent, 1066–1348," 20–39.

60. Duby, *Rural Economy and Country Life,* 68–69, and *The Early Growth of the European Economy,* 199–201.

61. For new settlements see Bechmann, *Trees and Man,* 99–105; Bloch, *French Rural History,* 5–20; Duby, *Rural Economy and Country Life,* 72–74; and Koebner, "The Settlement and Colonization," 71–72, 77. Quotations are from Bloch, p. 14, and Koebner, p. 77.

62. For these and many other examples, see Bloch, *French Rural History,* 8–11; Bechmann, *Trees and Man,* 101, 105; Darby, "The Clearing of the Woodland in Europe," 194–95; and Maury, *Les forêts de la France,* 37–45.

63. François L. Ganshof, "Medieval Society in Its Prime: France, the Low Countries and Western Germany," 279 et seq.; Koebner, "The Settlement and Colonization," 80; and Schlüter, *Die Siedlungsräume Mitteleuropas,* 23–25.

64. Darby, "The Clearing of the Woodland in Europe," 195 for both quotations. See also J. W. Thompson, *An Economic and Social History of the Middle Ages,* 758; and Nef, *Conquest of the Material World,* 435.

65. For American comparisons, see J. W. Thompson, *Feudal Germany,* 522–28. See also Pounds, *Economic History of Medieval Europe,* 176–77 et seq.

66. Aubin, "Lands East of the Elbe," 364–76; and J. W. Thompson, *Feudal Germany,* 500–12. Document quoted in R. Bartlett, *The Making of Europe,* 136–37.

67. Koebner, "The Settlement and Colonization," 83–85; and Aubin, "Lands East of the Elbe," 365–67.

68. Aubin, "Lands East of the Elbe," 371–78; Devèze, "Forêts français et forêts allemandes," 371; and J. W. Thompson, *Feudal Germany,* 526. Quotation is from Thompson, p. 526; and figures are from Aubin, 377–78. R. Bartlett, *The Making of Europe,* 134–44 is a new study of the movement, with many original documents. See also James B. Ross and Mary M. McLaughlin, *The Portable Medieval Reader,* 421–29 for translations of documents about the Knights and their exploits.

69. Otto Schlüter, "Wald, Sumpf und Seidlungsland in Altpreussen vor der Ordenszeit," 245–49. For numbers see Aubin, "Lands East of the Elbe," 396–97; and Walter Kuhn, "Die Siedlerzahlen der deutschen Ostsiedlung." See Friedrich Mager, *Der Wald in Altpreussen als Wirtschaftsraum,* 5–25 for maps of clearing.

70. Darby, "The Clearing of the Woodland in Europe," 197; Aubin, "Lands East of the Elbe," 395–96; and Pierre Deffontaines, *La vie forestière en Slovaque,* 57.

71. Devèze, "Forêts français et forêts allemandes," 369–70; and Bechmann, *Trees and Man,* 295. See also the wider study by Devèze, *Le vie de la forêt française au XVIᵉ siècle.*

72. Schlüter, *Die Siedlungsräume Mittleuropas;* Devèze, "Forêts français et forêts allemandes," 370.

73. Wickham, "European Forests in the Early Middle Ages," 502–6, 521; and Della Hooke, "Woodland Utilization in England A.D. 800–1100," 302–10, and "Pre-Conquest Woodland: Its Distribution and Usage," 113–29.

74. Williams, "Marshland and Waste," 108–9; and William G. Hoskins, *The Making of the English Landscape,* 47–48, 69–76.

75. Hart, *Royal Forest,* 39–41, 59–60; Witney, "The Woodland Economy of Kent," 35–8; and Dyer, *Hanbury,* 27–32.

76. Henryk Paszkiewicz, *The Origins of Russia,* 255–56; and Joseph L. Wieczynski, *The Russian Frontier: The Impact of Borderlands upon the Course of Early Russian History,* 10–11.

77. Vasili O. Kluchevsky, *A History of Russia,* 5:233, 241.

78. On early farming see Robert E. F. Smith, *The Origins of Farming in Russia,* 51–73; for the Mongol invasions see Wieczynski, *The Russian Frontier,* 35, on which the quotation may also be found.

79. James H. Billington, *The Icon and the Axe: An Interpretative History of Russian Culture,* 26 et seq. on the symbolism, imagery, and practical uses of the ax in Russian life.

80. R. E. F. Smith, *The Origins of Farming in Russia,* generally; and Wieczynski, *The Russian Frontier,* 40.

81. Robert E. F. Smith, *Peasant Farming in Muscovy*, 114, 117ff.; Darby, "The Clearing of the Woodland in Europe," 207; and Alexandre Eck, *Le moyen âge Russe*, 55–57, 274–77. Quotation is from Kluchevsky, *A History of Russia*, 5:244–45.

82. Darby, "The Clearing of the Woodland in Europe," 207–8.

83. For general background to the Muslim invasion of Europe, see Pounds, *Economic History of Medieval Europe*, 72–73. For the Idrisi quotation see John Perlin, *A Forest Journey: The Role of Wood in the Development of Civilization*, 137.

84. Maurice M. Lombard, "Arsenaux et bois de marine dans la Méditerranée musulmane (VIIᵉ–XIᵉ siècles)," 53–106, and "Une carte du bois la Méditerranée musulmane (VIIᵉ–XIᵉ siècle)," 234–54.

85. Glacken, *Traces*, 320, but see also the whole discussion on 320–41.

86. See Jean Birrell, "Common Rights in the Medieval Forest: Disputes and Conflicts in the Thirteenth Century," 22–49 for an extensive discussion.

87. Réne De Maulde, *Étude sur la condition forestière de L'Orléans au moyen âge et à la renaissance*, 180–210; and Bechmann, *Trees and Man*, 224–28, 275.

88. Darby, *Domesday England*, 184.

89. Doris M. Stenton, *English Society in the Early Middle Ages*, 97–119 for a thorough examination of forest rights; H. S. Bennett, *Life on the English Manor: A Study of Peasant Conditions, 1150–1400*, 57–60; and Bechmann, *Trees and Man*, 142–46.

90. Glacken, *Traces*, 346; and Wickham, "European Forests in the Early Middle Ages," 487, 488 et seq.

91. Matt Cartmill, *A View to a Death in the Morning: Hunting and Nature through History*, 61.

92. Robert Pogue Harrison, *Forests: The Shadow of Civilization*, 74–75.

93. Glacken, *Traces*, 323 et seq.

94. Koebner, "The Settlement and Colonization," 68.

95. Ibid.; Charles R. Young, *The Royal Forests of Medieval England*, esp. 60–134 for the organization of the forests; and Stenton, *English Society in the Early Middle Ages*, 106ff. on the legal implications; quotation is from p. 106.

96. Bloch, *French Rural History*, 17; Leroy Dresbeck, "Winter Climate and Society in the Northern Middle Ages: The Technological Impact," 177–200 for the development of chimneys and rooms; and Lewis, "The Closing of the Medieval Frontier," 480–81.

97. Bechmann, *Trees and Man*, 236–51, quotation is from p. 237; and Glacken, *Traces*, 330–35, 338–39, quotation is from p. 339.

98. Rolf Sprandel, "Le production du fer au moyen âge," 312–13.

99. For the various aspects of the economic downswing, see J. C. Russell, "Late Ancient and Medieval Population," 148, and "Population in Europe, 500–1500," 36; Parry, *Climatic Change, Agriculture and Settlement*, 116–23, 42–43 for Britain and Ireland, and 125–34 for Iceland and Norway; and Ian Kershaw, "The Great Famine and Agrarian Crisis in England, 1315–1322," 3–50.

100. W. Abel, "Agakonjunktur," 49–59; and Heinz Pohlendt, *Die Verbreitung der mittelalterlichen Wüstungen in Deutschland*, 1–35.

101. Helmut Jäger, *Die Entwicklung der Kulturlandschaft im Kriese Hofgeïsmar*, and "Zur Entstehung der heutigen grossen Forsten in Deutschland," 156–71.

102. Quotations are from Boissonade, *Life and Work in Medieval Europe*, 316; and Darby, "The Clearing of the Woodland in Europe," 198–99.

103. *Mencius*, 164–65.

104. Quotations are from Murphey, "Deforestation in Modern China," 111. See also Samuel A. M. Adshead, "Timber As a Factor in Chinese History: Problems, Sources, and Hypotheses," 1–6.

105. Francesca Bray, "Agriculture," 91. This conclusion is broadly supported by the most recent analysis in "Forestry" by Nicholas K. Menzies, 544–47, and certainly by his earlier *Forest and Land Management in Imperial China*.

106. Based on Menzies, "Forestry," 547–58; quotation is from p. 558.

107. *Shih Ching*, 162, 212. Yü was the legendary emperor of the Chou who presumably personally directed land clearance.

108. Quoted in Bray, "Agriculture," 96–98.

109. Ibid., 98–101; and Menzies, "Forestry," 563.

110. Edward H. Schafer, "The Conservation of Nature under the T'ang Dynasty," 299–300, and "Hunting Parks and Animal Enclosures in Ancient China," 318–43; and Tuan, *China*, 100.

111. Menzies, "Forestry," 658–59; and Tuan, *China*, 141.

112. Ennin, *Ennin's Diary: The Record of a Pilgrimage to China in Search of the Law (793–864)*, 154.

113. Robert Hartwell, "A Revolution in the Chinese Iron and Coal Industries during the Northern Sung, 960–1126 A.D.," 153–62, "Markets, Technology, and the Structure of Enterprise in the Development of the Eleventh-Century Chinese Iron Industry," 29–58, and "A Cycle of Economic Change in Imperial China: Coal and Iron in Northeast China, 750–1350," 102–59.

114. Hartwell, "A Revolution in the Chinese Iron and Coal Industries," 159.

115. Edward A. Kracke Jr., "Sung Society: Change within Tradition," esp. 480–83; and Tuan, *China*, 132–34.

116. Menzies, *Forest and Land Management*, 105–7; and Samuel A. M. Adshead, "An Energy Crisis in Early Modern China," 20–28.

117. Quotations are from Murphey, "Deforestation in Modern China," 116, 117.

Chapter 6

1. Carlo M. Cipolla, *Before the Industrial Revolution: European Society and Economy, 1000–1700*, 183–208; quotation is from p. 186. Also very useful on this period is Harry A. Miskimin, *The Economy of Later Renaissance Europe, 1460–1600*, esp. 83–122.

2. Douglass C. North and Robert P. Thomas, *The Rise of the Western World: A New Economic History*; Eric Jones, *The European Miracle: Environments, Economies, and Geopolitics in the History of Europe and Asia*; and William Woodruff, *Impact of Western Man: A Study of Europe's Role in the World Economy, 1750–1960*.

3. Jules Michelet, *Histoire de France*, 7:ii–iii.

4. Walter Minchinton, "Patterns and Structure of Demand, 1500–1750," 83.

5. Fernand Braudel, *Civilization and Capitalism, 15th–18th Century*, vol. 3, *The Perspective of the World*, 21–70.

6. Fernand Braudel, *Civilization and Capitalism, 15th–18th Century*, vol. 1, *The Structures of Everyday Life: The Limits of the Possible*.

7. Simon Schama, *Landscape and Memory*, 37–244; and Robert Pogue Harrison, *Forests: The Shadow of Civilization*.

8. Lynn White Jr., "Cultural Climates and Technological Advance in the Middle Ages," 171.

9. William B. Meyer and Billie Lee Turner II, eds., *Changes in Land Use and Land Cover: A Global Perspective*, 58–62, 261–388.

10. Quotation is from Harold Victor Livermore, "The New World: Portuguese Expansion," 420. Of the literally dozens of works on exploration, perhaps Samuel E. Morison's *European Discovery of America: The Southern Voyages, AD 1492–1616* and *The Northern Voyages, AD 500–1600* are the most authoritative and useful for the New World, together with John H. Parry, *The Age of Reconnaissance* and *The Discovery of the Sea*; Geoffrey V. Scammell, *The World Encompassed: The First Maritime Empires, c.800–1650*; and Geoffrey Barraclough, ed., *The Times Atlas of World History*.

11. Donald W. Meinig, "A Macrogeography of Western Imperialism: Some Morphologies of Moving Frontiers of Political Control," 211.

12. Colin Platt, "The Rise of Temperate Europe," 313.

13. I. A. MacGregor, "Europe and the East," 592–94.

14. J. H. Parry, *The Age of Reconnaissance*, 61–63.

15. Carlo M. Cipolla, *Guns and Sails in the Early Phase of European Expansion: 1400–1700*, 98–103; Geoffrey Parker, "Europe and the Wider World, 1500–1700: The Military Balance," 161–95; and for the wider context see William H. McNeill, *The Pursuit of Power: Technology, Armed Force, and Society since A.D. 1000*, 63–143.

16. Henry Clifford Darby, "The Face of Europe on the Eve of the Great Discoveries," 20.

17. Derwent S. Whittlesey, *The Earth and the State: A Study of Political Geography*, 59.

18. Peter Padfield, *Maritime Supremacy and the Opening of the Western Mind: Naval Campaigns that Shaped the Modern World*.

19. Sir Walter Ralegh, "Of the Art of Warre at Sea," British Museum, MSS Jones, B 60, f. 323, transcribed in Pierre Lefranc, *Sir Walter Ralegh: Érivain: L'Oeuvre et Les Idées*, app. D, p. 600.

20. For example, Janet L. Abu-Lughod, *Before European Hegemony: The World System, AD 1250–1350*, quotation is from p. 5; Kirti N. Chaudhuri, *Trade and Civilization in the Indian Ocean: An Economic History from the Rise of Islam to 1750*; Philip Curtin, *Cross-Cultural Trade in World History*; Colin G. F. Simkin, *The Traditional Trade of Asia*; Oskar H. K. Spate, *The Pacific since Magellan*, vol. 1, *The Spanish Lake*; and Michael Chisholm, "The Increasing Separation of Production and Consumption," 87.

21. L. White, "Cultural Climates and Technological Advance," 171–72.

22. Cipolla, *Before the Industrial Revolution*, quotation is from p. 160; and L. White, "Cultural Climates and Technological Advance," 172–75.

23. Francis Bacon, *Novum Organum*, bk. 1, cxxix.; and E. L. Jones, *The European Miracle*, 72–74.

24. E. L. Jones, *The European Miracle*, 60–62; and Lucien Febvre and Henri-Jean Martin, *The Coming of the Book: The Impact of Printing, 1450–1800*, esp. 176–215.

25. Febvre and Martin, *The Coming of the Book*, 262–332.

26. William Warntz, "Newton, the Newtonians, and the *Geographia Generalis Varenii*," 168.

27. Cipolla, *Before the Industrial Revolution*, 171.

28. David Landes, *Revolution in Time: Clocks and the Making of the Modern World*, 89.

29. Landes, *Revolution in Time*, 105–13, 146–57. For the incredible story of Thomas Harrison and the perfection of timepieces, see Dava Sobel, *Longitude: The True Story of a Lone Genius Who Solved the Greatest Scientific Problem of His Time*.

30. L. White, "Cultural Climates and Technological Advance," 99; and Hermann Kellenbenz, "Technology in the Age of the Scientific Revolution, 1500–1700," 264.

31. Lynn White Jr., "The Expansion of Technology, 500–1500," 143.

32. Marshall Berman, *All That Is Solid Melts into Air: The Experience of Modernity*, 15.

33. For a succinct review of the market economy, see E. L. Jones, *The European Miracle*, 85–103.

34. Charles Tilley, *Coercion, Capital, and European States, AD 990–1990,* esp. 127–91; quotations are from E. L. Jones, *The European Miracle,* 110, 119.

35. Thomas A. Brady Jr., "The Rise of Merchant Empires, 1400–1700: A European Counterpoint," 119–23; E. L. Jones, *The European Miracle,* 89–95, 104–24; and Immanuel M. Wallerstein, *The Modern World System I: Capitalist Agriculture and the Origins of the European World-Economy in the Sixteenth Century,* 15–18.

36. Immanuel M. Wallerstein, *The Modern World System II: Mercantilism and the Consolidation of the European World-Economy, 1600–1750,* 7. For the Low Countries see Jan De Vries' classic study, *The Dutch Rural Economy in the Golden Age, 1500–1700,* esp. 117ff. For an extensive and informative annotated bibliography of the rise, expansion, and workings of the "merchant empires," see James D. Tracy, ed., *The Political Economy of Merchant Empires,* 443–83.

37. Charles P. Kindleberger, *A Financial History of Western Europe,* 35–54; quotation is from Herman Van der Wee, "Monetary, Credit and Banking Systems," 290.

38. Cipolla, *Before the Industrial Revolution,* 182–87; Jacob M. Price, "Transaction Costs: A Note on Merchant Credit and the Organization of Private Trade," 276–97.

39. This and the following paragraph are based on the exhaustive and authoritative surveys of Van der Wee, "Monetary, Credit and Banking Systems," 290–393; and Geoffrey Parker, "The Emergence of Modern Finance in Europe, 1500–1730," 527–94.

40. Larry Neal, "The Dutch and English East India Companies Compared: Evidence from the Stock and Foreign Exchange Markets," 195–223 for a survey of the workings of the companies. Quotation is from p. 196.

41. Douglass C. North, "Institutions, Transaction Costs and the Rise of Merchant Empires," 20–40; and Barry Supple, "The Nature of Enterprise," 394–461.

42. Braudel, *Capitalism and Material Life, 1400–1800,* 265–66; Daniel Defoe, quoted in Charles H. Wilson, *Anglo-Dutch Commerce and Finance in the Eighteenth Century,* 4; Jonathon I. Israel, *Dutch Primacy and World Trade, 1585–1740,* 8–11, 381–82; and Jaap R. Bruijn, "Productivity, Profitability, and Costs of Private and Corporate Dutch Ship Owning in the Seventeenth and Eighteenth Centuries," 174–94.

43. Niels Steensgaard, "European Shipping to Asia, 1497–1700," 1–11.

44. John D. Durand, "Historical Estimates of World Population: An Evaluation," 253–96; Paul Demeny, "Population," 41–44; and Roger S. J. Mols, "Population in Europe, 1500–1700," 38.

45. Minchinton, "Patterns and Structure of Demand," 38–39.

46. Wallerstein, *Mercantilism and the Consolidation of the European World-Economy,* 301–2.

47. Braudel, *Capitalism and Material Life,* 124–91, 226–43; and James Walvin, *Fruits of Empire: Exotic Produce and British Taste, 1660–1800,* ix–xiii.

48. Marshall Sahlins, "Cosmologies of Capitalism: The Trans-Pacific Sector of 'The World System,'" 1–51; quotation is from p. 43. See also Agnes Repplier, *To Think of Tea!*

49. John H. Galloway, *The Sugar Cane Industry: An Historical Geography from Its Origins to 1914,* 48. See Sidney Mintz, *Sweetness and Power: The Place of Sugar in Modern History* for an excellent treatment of the importance of sugar.

50. Jean H. Bernardin de Saint-Pierre, *Voyage to Isle de France, the Isle of Bourbon, the Cape of Good Hope, etc. With Observations on Nature and Mankind by an Officer of the King,* 1:105.

51. For the wider picture see Jacob M. Price, "The Map of Commerce, 1683–1721."

52. Niels Steensgaard, "The Growth and Composition of the Long-Distance Trade of England and the Dutch Republic before 1750," 104, 147–51.

53. Walvin, *Fruits of Empire,* 132.

54. Karl W. Butzer, "From Columbus to Acosta: Science, Geography and the New World,"

543–565; quotations are from pp. 543, 558. Much of this material remained unpublished or was stifled with the onset of the orthodoxy of the Inquisition, which explains its neglect.

55. Glacken, *Traces,* 175 et seq.

56. Arthur O. Lovejoy, *The Great Chain of Being: A Study in the History of an Idea,* 67–143; and John Ray, *The Wisdom of God Manifest in the Works of Creation.*

57. Glacken, *Traces,* 482, 600; and Keith Thomas, *Man and the Natural World: A History of the Modern Sensibility,* 121–36, on hierarchies in general.

58. For an excellent account see K. Thomas, *Man and the Natural World,* 17–25.

59. René Descartes, *Discourse on Method,* discourse 4:53–54.

60. So much has been written about the history of science that it is difficult to specify a single source, but the work of A. Rupert Hall is excellent. See "Intellectual Tendencies: 2. Science," 359–86, and "Scientific Method and the Progress of Techniques," 96–154.

61. A. Rupert Hall, "Cultural, Intellectual and Social Foundations, 1600–1750," 112; and John U. Nef, "An Early Energy Crisis and Its Consequences," 140. For the links between ideas and technology see Charles Singer, E. J. Holmyard, A. Rupert Hall, and Trevor I. Williams, eds., *A History of Technology,* vol. 3, *From the Renaissance to the Industrial Revolution, c.1500–c.1750.*

62. Bacon, *Novum Organum,* bk. 1, cxxix; and Glacken, *Traces,* 478.

63. Francis Bacon, *De Sapientia Veterum,* "Prometheus," 270–71.

64. Sir Matthew Hale, *The Primitive Origination of Mankind,* 370.

65. Philip D. Curtin, "The Environment beyond Europe and the European Theory of Empire," 131, 138.

66. E. L. Jones, *The European Miracle,* 80.

67. K. Thomas, *Man and the Natural World,* 192.

68. Roderick Nash, *Wilderness and the American Mind,* 11–17; Alexander Porteous, *Forest Folklore, Mythology and Romance,* 84–148; and Glacken, *Traces,* 288–351 have excellent reviews of the symbolism and significance of medieval clearing activity. In addition to the symbolism of the forest, there is the symbolism of trees, which enters Western thought in many ways, from Christmas trees to genealogical trees. The tree symbolizes man himself: union "bears fruit"; untimely death is being "cut down in one's prime," so that death is, symbolically, an axman. The tree also figures largely in Christian thought, for God "planted a garden eastward of Eden," where he made "to grow every tree that is pleasant to the sight, and good for food; the tree of life also in the midst of the garden, and the tree of knowledge of good and evil" (Gen. 1:7–9). The Qur'an's account of the beginning of the world is very little different from that of the Bible.

69. Williams, *Americans and Their Forests,* 10; and Alan Heimert, "Puritanism, the Wilderness and the Frontier," 379–80.

70. Roderick Nash, *Wilderness and the American Mind,* 2; David B. Quinn, *The Elizabethans and the Irish,* 136; and John Locke, *Two Treatise on Government,* 201.

71. K. Thomas, *Man and the Natural World,* 194; Marc Bloch, *French Rural History: An Essay on Its Basic Characteristics,* quotation is from p. 16, and plate 2; and Bechmann, *Trees and Man: The Forest in the Middle Ages,* 264–65.

72. John Winthrop, *Winthrop's Journal: "History of New England,"* 2:83; and Increase Mather, *A Brief History of the War with the Indians in New England,* 5.

73. Roderick Nash, *Wilderness,* 28–30; Roy Harvey Pearce, *The Savages of America: A Study of the Indian and the Idea of Civilization,* 135–68; Robert F. Berkhofer Jr., *The White Man's Indian: Images of the American Indian from Columbus to the Present,* esp. 80–85, "Puritanism, the Wilderness, and Savagery as Divine Metaphors"; Charles F. Carroll, *The Timber Economy of Puritan New England,* 59–61; and Arnold Guyot, *The Earth and Man: Lectures on Comparative Physical Geography in Its Relation to the History of Mankind,* 216–18.

74. J. H. St. John de Crèvecoeur, *Letters from an American Farmer*, 55–57.

75. K. Thomas, *Man and the Natural World*, 196–97, quotation is from p. 196; John Houghton, *Husbandry and Trade Improv'd: Being a Collection of many Valuable Materials . . . ,* 1:99, 4:258–82; and *A Relation of Some Abuses which are Committed against the Commonwealth* (anonymous), 9.

76. Alan Heimert, "Puritanism, the Wilderness and the Frontier," 382; and Charles L. Sanford, *The Quest for Paradise: Europe and the American Moral Imagination,* 119.

77. Albert H. Smyth, ed., *The Writings of Benjamin Franklin,* 3:72–73; and W. Cooper, *A Guide in the Wilderness . . . ,* 6.

78. Lynn White Jr., "The Historical Roots of Our Ecologic Crisis," 1203–7; John A. Passmore, *Man's Responsibility for Nature: Ecological Problems and Western Traditions;* chap. 3, 5; Yi-fu Tuan, "Discrepancies between Environmental Attitude and Behaviour: Examples from Europe and China," 176–191. Despite the evidence, some still maintain that ecological degradation is purely a result of Western imperialism. See James Baird Callicott and Roger Ames, "Epilogue: On the Relation of Idea and Action," 279–89.

79. André Gunder Frank, *World Accumulation, 1492–1789;* Immanuel.M. Wallerstein, *The Modern World System, I: Capitalist Agriculture and the Origins of the European World-Economy in the Sixteenth Century, II: Mercantilism and the Consolidation of the European World-Economy, 1600–1750, and III: The Second Era of Great Expansion of the Capitalist World-Economy, 1730–1840s;* and Eric R. Wolf, *Europe and the People without History.*

80. Patrick O'Brien, "European Economic Development: The Contribution of the Periphery," 1–18; and Paul Bairoch, "Geographical Structure and Trade Balance of European Foreign Trade from 1800 to 1970," 557–608.

81. E. L. Jones, *The European Miracle,* 69.

Chapter 7

1. For example, Jean Birrell, "Common Rights in the Medieval Forest: Disputes and Conflicts in the Thirteenth Century," 22–49.

2. Ernst H. L. Krause, "Florenkarte von Norddeutschland für das 12. bis 15. Jahrhundert," 231–35; Johannes Hoops, *Waldbäume und Kulturpflanzen in Germanischen Altertum,* 227–53; and G. J. Marcus, "The Greenland Trade-Route," 71–80.

3. Hubert H. Lamb, "Our Changing Climate, Past and Present," 1–20; and Martin L. Parry, *Climatic Change, Agriculture, and Settlement,* 112–34.

4. Emmanuel Le Roy Ladurie, "Le climat des XIe et XVIe siècles: series comparées," 899–922, *The Peasants of Languedoc,* 135–42, and *Times of Feast, Times of Famine: A History of Climate since the Year 1000,* 50–79.

5. Gregory King, *Natural and Political Observations and Conclusions upon the State and Condition of England, 1696,* 428; and Eileen McCracken, "The Woodlands of Ireland, circa 1600," 273.

6. Michel Devèze, *La vie de la forêt Française au XVIe siècle,* 1:295; Sabastian le P. de Vauban, *Project d' une dixime royale,* 165; Friedrich Mager, *Der Wald in Altpreussen als Wirtschaftsraum,* 29 et seq.

7. These proportions are discussed at some length in U.S. Department of Agriculture, *Annual Report of the Commissioner of Agriculture,* 1872, "The Forests of the United States," 43–45; and Michael Williams, *Americans and Their Forests: A Historical Geography,* 373–75.

8. Roger S. J. Mols, "Population in Europe, 1500–1700," 38.

9. M. Marian Malowist, "L'approvisionnement des ports de la Baltique en produits forestiers pour les constructions navales aux XVe et XVIe siècles," 25–44.

10. Fredric C. Lane, *Venetian Ships and Shipbuilders of the Renaissance,* 217–33. See also Norman J. G. Pounds, *An Historical Geography of Europe, 1500–1840,* 9–11 for additional comments.

11. These commissions and acts are covered in John Nef, *The Rise of the British Coal Industry,* 1:158–61; John Perlin, *A Forest Journey: The Role of Wood in the Development of Civilization,* 168–90; and George Owen, *Description of Pembrokeshire,* 1:86.

12. Robert G. Albion, *Forests and Sea Power: The Timber Problem of the Royal Navy, 1652–1862,* 57.

13. Georg Wiebe, *Zur Geschichte der Preisrevolution des XVI und XVII Jahrhunderts,* 375–78.

14. Nef, *British Coal Industry,* 1:161; and Archibald Clow and Nan L. Clow, "The Timber Famine and the Development of Technology," 85–102.

15. Michael W. Flinn, "The Growth of the English Iron Industry, 1660–1760," 148–53; "Timber and the Advance of Technology: A Reconsideration," 109–20; and George Hammersley, "The Crown Woods and Their Exploitation in the Sixteenth and Seventeenth Centuries," 131–71; and "The Charcoal Iron Industry and Its Fuel, 1540–1750," 593–613.

16. Flinn, "Timber and the Advance of Technology," 115–16.

17. Nef, *British Coal Industry,* 1:161; and Wiebe, *Zur Geschichte der Preisrevolution,* 375–78.

18. David B. Young, "Forests, Mines, and Fuel: The Question of Wood and Coal in Eighteenth-Century France," 328–36; Marcel Rouff, *Les mines de charbon en France au XVIIIe siècle, 1742–1791.* . . For the United Kingdom tonnage see Michael W. Flinn, with David Stoker, *The History of the British Coal Industry,* 2:26.

19. Werner Sombart, *Der Moderne Kapitalismus,* 2, ii, 1145–48.

20. Int. al., J. Radkau, "Zur angeblichen Energiekrise des 18. Jahrhunderts: Revisionistische Betrachtung über de 'Holznot,'" 1–37; "Holzverknappung und Krisenbewusstsein im 18. Jahrhundert," 513–43; and W. Schenk, "Forest Development Types in Central Germany in Pre-Industrial Times: A Contribution by Historical Geography to the Solution of a Forest History Argument about the 'Wood Scarcity' in the Eighteenth Century," 201–23.

21. Nef, *British Coal Industry,* 1:162, quoting United Kingdom, Historical Manuscripts Commission, *Report on the MSS of the Earl of Mar and Kellie,* 1904: 212–13. See also Philip J. Bünting, *Sylva Subterranea* . . .

22. Pierre Goubert, *The French Peasantry in the Seventeenth Century,* 103.

23. George Hammersley, "The Charcoal Iron Industry and Its Fuel," 603; and Anne-Marie Pius, "La forêt dans l'histoire," 4–5.

24. Arthur Standish, *The Commons Complaint,* 2.

25. Mols, "Population in Europe, 1500–1700," 38–39 and table 9.4.

26. Bernard H. Slicher van Bath, *The Agrarian History of Western Europe, A.D. 500–1850,* 195–206.

27. P. Herrmann, *Zimmerische Chronik,* 209.

28. John Evelyn, *Sylva: Or, A Discourse of Forest Trees . . . ,* 1–2.

29. For Cholmeley and others see H. Clifford Darby, "The Clearing of the English Woodlands," 79.

30. Eileen McCracken, *The Irish Woods since Tudor Times: Distribution and Exploitation,* 15, 57, 95–96, 97ff. Perlin in his *A Forest Journey* would accord agriculture a minor part in woodland destruction compared with shipbuilding and charcoal manufacture.

31. Michel Devèze, "Forêts françaises et forêts allemandes: Études historique comparée," 47–

53; Arlette Brosselin, *La forêt bourguignonne: 1660–1789*, 119–24, 151–68; and Michel Devèze, "Superficie et propriété des forêts du Nord et de l'Est de la France vers la fin du règne de François 1er (1540–1547)," 485–92, and *La vie de la forêt Française au XVIe siècle*, 1:217–70. Although focusing on the medieval period, Bechmann's *Trees and Man: The Forest in the Middle Ages* has many references to this later period in France.

32. W. Abel, *Agricultural Fluctuations in Europe from the Thirteenth to the Twentieth Centuries*, 101–5.

33. Paul W. Bamford, *Forests and French Sea Power, 1660–1789*, 70; Bertrand Gille, *Les origines de la grande industrie métallurgie en France*, 67–79, esp. 69, 74. For the comparison of Devèze's and Cassini's maps, see Pounds, *Historical Geography*, 8–11.

34. Hermann Kellenbenz, *The Rise of the European Economy: An Economic History of Continental Europe from the Fifteenth to the Eighteenth Century*, 101–2.

35. Devèze, "Forêts françaises et forêts allemandes," 47–53; Fernand Braudel, *Civilization and Capitalism, 15th–18th Century*, vol. 1, *The Structures of Everyday Life*, 365.

36. Hermann Kellenbenz, *The Rise of the European Economy . . .* , 101, and "Technology in the Age of Scientific Revolution, 1500–1700," 252; and Devèze, "Forêts françaises et forêts allemandes," 55–56.

37. Fernand Braudel, *The Mediterranean and the Mediterranean World in the Age of Philip II*, 1:62.

38. Kristof Glamann, "European Trade, 1500–1700," 459–61.

39. John F. Richards, "Land Transformation," 177; and Mager, *Der Wald in Altpreussen*, particularly the comparison of the maps of the distribution of woodland.

40. R. Anthony French, "Russians and the Forest," 24–29; quotation is from p. 27.

41. R. Anthony French, "The Making of the Russian Landscape," 45–47, and "Russians and the Forest," 30.

42. Denis J. B. Shaw, "Southern Frontiers of Muscovy, 1550–1700," 117–39.

43. William R. Mead, *Farming in Finland*, 44–50; F. Skubbeltrang, "The History of the Finnish Peasant," 165–80; Arvo M. Soininen, "Burn-Beating As the Technical Basis of Colonisation in Finland during the 16th and 17th Centuries," 150–66.

44. Julius Klein, *The Meseta: A Study in Spanish Economic History: 1273–1836*, 317–21; and M. Ruiz and J. P. Ruiz, "Ecological History of Transhumance in Spain," 73–86.

45. Thérèse Sclafert, *Cultures en Haut-Provence: Déboisments et pâturages au moyen âge*, 52–56, 140–47; C. Patsch, *Historische Wanderungen im Karst und an der Adria*, 23–26; and Christian Fruhauf, *Forêt et société: de la forêt paysanne à la forêt capitaliste en pays de sault sous l' ancien régime (vers 1670–1791)*, esp. 51–60, 91–150, 205–11.

46. J. Richards, "Land Transformation," 164.

47. Braudel, *Civilization and Capitalism, 15th–18th Century*, vol. 1, *The Structures of Everyday Life: The Limits of the Possible*, 362–63.

48. French, "Russians and the Forest," 31.

49. Kellenbenz, *The Rise of the European Economy*, 99.

50. Lucas van Valkenborch, *Winter Landscape: January and February* (1586); and Pieter Bruegel, *Der Dustere Vorfrühling* (1565). Kunst Historische Museum, Vienna.

51. Mols, "Population in Europe," 40–44. Paul J. B. Bairoch and Piérre Chèvre in their *Population of European Cities, 800–1850*, uses slightly different categories, but the result is much the same. For a commentary on sizes see Clifford T. Smith, *An Historical Geography of Western Europe before 1800*, 296–340, esp. 331–33.

52. Nef, *British Coal Industry*, 2:203–4; Ernest H. Phelps Brown and Sheila V. Hopkins, "Seven Centuries of Prices and Consumables, Compared with Builders' Wage-Rates," 297.

53. Richard H. Tawney and Eileen Power, *Tudor Economic Documents . . .* , 2:239; and Nef, *British Coal Industry,* 2:101–5.

54. William Harrison, *The Description of England,* 356; and Fernand Braudel, *Capitalism and Material Life: 1400–1800,* 211. For further information of fuel supplies to Paris in the sixteenth century, see Kellenbenz, *The Rise of the European Economy,* 99.

55. James A. Galloway, Derek Keene, and Margret Murphy, "Fuelling the City: Production and Distribution of Firewood and Fuel in London's Region, 1290–1400," especially the map on p. 459. See also William H. TeBrake, "Air Pollution and Fuel Crisis in Preindustrial London, 1280–1650," 337–59.

56. Reginald A. Pelham, "Timber Exports from the Weald during the Fourteenth Century," 170–82; and W. Harrison, *The Description of England,* 275.

57. Braudel, *Civilization and Capitalism,* vol. 1, *The Structures of Everyday Life,* 366.

58. Figures from Paul Bairoch, *Cities and Economic Development from the Dawn of History to the Present,* 14. Galloway et al., "Fuelling the City," 455–56, are less conservative in their calculations for English urban areas; i.e., approximately 250 mi^2 of woodland were needed per urban square mile.

59. Vauban, *Project d' une dixime royale,* 136–39; and G. King, *Natural and Political Observations and Conclusions,* 439. The figure is arrived at by dividing 3,200,000 households by 110 = 29091 × 425 ha = 12,363,675 ha. See also Pounds, *Historical Geography,* 10, for a discussion of Vauban's calculations.

60. French, "Russians and the Forest," quotation from p. 31; Jean Bossière, "La consommation parisienne de bois et les sidèrurgies périphériques: Essai de mise en parallèle (milieu XVe–milieu XIXe siècles)," 35–37, 49; and Braudel, *Capitalism and Material Life,* 269, and *Civilization and Capitalism,* vol. 1, *The Structures of Everyday Life,* 365–66; quotation is from p. 366.

61. Braudel, *Capitalism and Material Life,* 216 et seq.; W. Harrison, *The Description of England,* 197; and Walter Minchinton, "Patterns and Structure of Demand, 1500–1750," 138.

62. Nef, *British Coal Industry,* 1:19–20; quotation is from p. 129.

63. Based on Nef, *British Coal Industry,* 1:201–3; John Houghton, *Husbandry and Trade Improv'd: Being a Collection of many Valuable Materials . . . ,* 1:99, 4:258–82; and Daniel Defoe, *A Tour thro' the Whole Island of Great Britain,* 1:129.

64. John U. Nef, "An Early Energy Crisis and Its Consequences," 140.

65. Eric Lionel Jones, *The European Miracle: Environments, Economies, and Geopolitics in the History of Europe and Asia,* 84, based on an idea in Walter Prescott Webb, *The Great Frontier,* 17, and further elaborated in George Bergstrom, *The Hungry Planet,* 70–90.

66. Nef, *British Coal Industry,* 1:192–93; and D. W. Crossley, "The Performance of the Glass Industry in Sixteenth Century England," 430–31.

67. W. Harrison, *The Description of England,* 378; Kellenbenz, *The Rise of the European Economy,* 100; and French, "Russians and the Forest," 32.

68. Based on Pounds, *Historical Geography,* 50–53.

69. Flinn, "Timber and the Advance of Technology," 110 et seq.

70. Tawney and Power, *Tudor Economic Documents,* 1:231–38; Albion, *Forests and Sea Power,* 116–18; and Perlin, *A Forest Journey,* 163–227.

71. Hammersley, "The Charcoal Iron Industry and Its Fuel," 605–8. This calculation can be compared with the only other known calculation for Europe at about this time: Kellenbenz (*The Rise of the European Economy,* 99–100) cites the example of the iron industry of Upper Palatine between 1387 and 1464 when the number of foundries grew from 77 to 200 and the annual consumption of wood from 175,000 to 400,000 m^3, which with fairly dense woodland of about 250 m^3/ha translates into between 700 and 1,600 ha of woodland consumed per annum. For further

background on the British industry see H. R. Schubert, *History of the British Iron and Steel Industry from c.450 B.C. to A.D. 1775,* 340–85.

72. Kellenbenz, "Technology in the Age of Scientific Revolution," 256–57, and *The Rise of the European Economy,* 105.

73. Rolf Sprandel, "Le production du fer au moyen âge," 311–12; and Braudel, *Capitalism and Material Life,* 283.

74. E. E. Söderlund, "The Impact of the British Industrial Revolution on the Swedish Iron Industry," 54.

75. Evelyn, *Sylva,* 209; and Andrew Yarranton, *England's Improvement by Sea and Land, to Out-do the Dutch without Fighting,* 60–61, 163. Flinn in "The Growth of the English Iron Industry," 149, has many other examples.

76. Flinn, "The Growth of the English Iron Industry," 149–51, and "Consommation du bois et développement sidérurgique en Angleterre"; G. Hammersley, "The Crown Woods and Their Exploitation," 154–59, and "The Charcoal Iron Industry and Its Fuel," 613; and Christopher Wickham, "European Forests in the Early Middle Ages: Landscape and Clearance," 537.

77. Michael Williams, "Forests," 180.

78. Mauro Agnoletti, "From the Dolomites to Venice: Rafts and River Driving along the Piare River, Italy, Thirteenth Century to Twentieth Century," 15–32.

79. Based on Lane, *Venetian Ships and Shipbuilders,* 225–50; and Albion, *Forests and Sea Power,* 183.

80. G. P. B. Naish, "Ships and Shipbuilding," 493; and *Encyclopaedia Britannica,* 1797 edition, 18:561.

81. See Albion, *Forests and Sea Power,* 8–16, for the technology and terminology of special oak pieces for naval construction.

82. Based on ibid., 183, ix, 121–38; and Darby, "The Clearing of the English Woodlands," 80.

83. Bamford, *Forests and French Sea Power,* 71; and George-Louis Leclerc, comte de Buffon, "Mémoire sur la conservation et la rétablissement des forêts," 3.

84. Bamford, *Forests and French Sea Power,* 71–72; and Albion, *Forests and Sea Power,* 96.

85. *Encyclopaedia Britannica,* 1797 edition, 18:561–62; Bamford, *Forests and French Sea Power,* 71; Paul W. Bamford, *Privilege and Profit: A Business Family in Eighteenth-Century France,* 28–60, and maps on xv and xvii; and Flinn, "Timber and the Advance of Technology," 116. For the subsequent history of neglect in England, see Albion, *Forests and Sea Power,* 95–135.

86. Albion, *Forests and Sea Power,* 140; Bamford, *Forests and French Sea Power,* 113–34; and Joseph S. Malone, *Pine Trees and Politics. The Naval Stores and Forest Policy in Colonial New England, 1691–1775,* 47–56, 82–123.

87. For the development of this trade in basic commodities see Marian M. Malowist, "The Economic and Social Development of the Baltic Countries from the Fifteenth to the Seventeenth Centuries," 177–89, and "Les produits des pays de la Baltique dans la commerce international au XVIᵉ siècle," 175–206.

88. Malowist, "Economic and Social Development of the Baltic Countries," esp. 183–89, for shipbuilding and lumber exports; and Glamann, "European Trade, 1500–1700," 459, on the Polish feudal system and for the quotation.

89. Kellenbenz, *The Rise of the European Economy,* 101. This was only a part of the potash trade; under the reign of Tsar Alexis (1629–76), Russia exported via Archangel 30,000 barrels, or 1,500 lasts, of potash—the equivalent of 800 tons, and the product of some 50,000 ha of forest.

90. Sven-Erik Åström, "Technology and Timber Exports from the Gulf of Finland, 1661–1740," 5–8; Arnold Soom, "Der Ostbaltische Holzhandel und die Holzindustrie im 17 Jahrhundert," 12–36; and Albion, *Forests and Sea Power,* 139–49.

91. Based on Malowist, "L'approvisionnement des ports de la Baltique," 25–44; and Albion, *Forests and Sea Power,* 140–42.

92. For the mast trade see Malone, *Pine Trees and Politics,* 55–56; and Eleanor Lord, *Industrial Experiments in the British Colonies of North America,* app. B, for the post-1760 data. A more extended treatment is in M. Williams, *Americans and Their Forests,* 90–92, which also covers the early pitch, tar, and turpentine manufacture and trade on 84–90.

93. Ian Layton, "The Timber and Naval Stores Supply Regions of Northern Europe during the Early Modern World-System," 269–81.

94. W. Harrison, *The Description of England,* 197; Albion, *Forests and Sea Power,* 157 et seq.; and Heinz S. K. Kent," The Anglo-Norwegian Timber Trade in the Eighteenth Century," 61–74; quotation is from p. 66.

95. Layton, "The Timber and Naval Stores Supply Regions," 281–90.

96. Nef, *British Coal Industry,* 1:201–23.

97. Buffon, "Mémoire sur la conservation," 110.

98. Keith Thomas, *Man and the Natural World: A History of Modern Sensibility,* 209ff.

99. Lane, *Venetian Ships and Shipbuilders,* 225–33; quotation is from p. 225.

100. For a definitive study on British coppicing practice, see Oliver Rackham, *Ancient Woodland: Its History, Vegetation, and Uses in England,* 137–60.

101. Evelyn is fairly readily available in many editions, but not Colbert or Moser. For the *Ordinance* see the translation in John Croumbie Brown, *French Forest Ordinance of 1669.*

102. Clarence F. Glacken, *Traces on the Rhodian Shore: Nature and Culture in Western Thought from Ancient Times to the End of the Eighteenth Century,* 484–95; quotations is from p. 495.

103. Bechmann, *Trees and Man,* 222–24, 241–58; J. Brown, *French Forest Ordinance,* 9–23; and Kellenbenz, *The Rise of the European Economy,* 223–24.

104. Kellenbenz, *The Rise of the European Economy,* 224–25; and W. Gottfried von Moser, *Grundsätze der Forstökonomie.*

105. For further elaboration see chapter 9, 273–75 of the present text.

106. Lindsay Sharp, "Timber, Science and Economic Reform in the Seventeenth Century," 51–86.

107. M. St. Clare Byrne, ed., *The Lisle Letters,* 4:57–9. "Within a few years [the woods were] . . . sold the value of £20,000 well worth £50,000, jewellers and silkmen making their nests in the branches."

108. Thomas, *Man and the Natural World,* 202 et seq.

109. This passage is from ibid., 205–6, but this whole section draws on Thomas's wider treatment of the love of trees.

110. Denis Cosgrove, *Social Formation and Symbolic Landscape,* 30–120; and Thomas, *Man and the Natural World,* 207–8.

111. Thomas, *Man and the Natural World,* 209. For more extended treatment of political symbolism of trees in this and later periods, see Stephen Daniels, "The Political Iconography of Woodland in Later Georgian England," 43–82.

112. Thomas, *Man and the Natural World,* 209, 212 et seq.; quotation is from p. 212.

Chapter 8

1. Robert Bartlett, *The Making of Europe: Conquest, Colonization, and Cultural Change;* quotation is from pp. 313–14. For a wider discussion of the achievements of material culture in

shaping Europe's sense of superiority, see Michael Adas, *Machines As the Measure of Men: Science, Technology, and Ideologies of Western Dominance.*

2. Walter Prescott Webb, *The Great Frontier;* quotation is from John F. Richards, "Land Transformation," 167. For general comments on the various "frontiers" see Eric Lionel Jones, *The European Miracle: Environments, Economies, and Geopolitics in the History of Europe and Asia,* 81–82; and for the fish "frontier" see A. R. Michell, "European Fisheries in the Early Modern Period," 134–84.

3. Rhoads Murphey, *The Outsiders: The Western Experience in India and China,* 12–35, 99–130, 221–34; and Richard H. Tawney, *Land and Labour in China,* 13.

4. John H. Elliott, *The Old World and the New, 1492–1650,* 3.

5. Pierre Chaunu, *European Expansion in the Later Middle Ages,* 51–56; for Chinese navigational exploits see Joseph Needham, "Voyages and Discovery," 487–91, 518, 524, 562–63, 567, 594–99, and map between 560 and 561.

6. John H. Parry, *The Discovery of the Sea,* 101–2. For charts of currents see Pierre and Hugette Chaunu, *Séville et l'Amérique aux XVIᵉ et XVIIᵉ siècles: Partie statistique,* vol. 7.

7. William H. McNeill, *Plagues and Peoples,* 199–216; Alfred L. Crosby, *Ecological Imperialism: The Biological Expansion of Europe, 900–1900,* 194–216; and Crosby's earlier work, *The Columbian Exchange: Biological and Cultural Consequences of 1492.*

8. Quotations are from McNeill, *Plagues and Peoples,* 199; and Crosby, *Ecological Imperialism,* 199.

9. Crosby, *Ecological Imperialism,* 79–103 for an extended treatment of the conquest of the Canaries.

10. William M Denevan, "The Pristine Myth: The Landscape of the Americas in 1492," 370–71, and *The Native Population of the Americas in 1492,* xvii–xxix.

11. Henry F. Dobyns, "Estimating Aboriginal American Populations: An Appraisal of Techniques with a New Hemispheric Estimate," 395–449, and *Their Number Became Thinned: Native American Population Dynamics in Eastern North America,* 7–32, 247–312; and W. George Lovell, "'Heavy Shadows and Black Night': Disease and Depopulation in Colonial Spanish America," 437–38.

12. Crosby, *Ecological Imperialism,* 196.

13. Denevan, "The Pristine Myth," 369–85; and Leslie E. Sponsel, "The Environmental History of Amazonia: Natural and Human Disturbances, and the Ecological Transition," 233–45. See also the discussion in chapter 2, pages 27–28 of the present text.

14. John Winthrop, *Winthrop Papers, 1631–1637,* 3:167; Virginia settler quoted in Hu Maxwell, "The Use and Abuse of the Forests by the Virginia Indians," 81.

15. Crosby, *Ecological Imperialism,* 145–70; and David Watts, *The West Indies: Patterns of Development, Culture and Environmental Change since 1492,* 222–28, 164–68, and 117–20.

16. Crosby, *Ecological Imperialism,* 173–78; and Watts, *The West Indies,* 155–56.

17. Billie Lee Turner II and Karl W. Butzer, "The Columbian Encounter and Land-Use Change," 16 and passim.

18. Richard H. Grove, *Green Imperialism: Colonial Expansion, Tropical Island Edens, and the Origins of Environmentalism, 1600–1800,* 16–72. The quotation is from John M. Prest, *The Garden of Eden: The Botanic Garden and the Re-creation of Paradise,* 30.

19. Prest, *Garden of Eden,* 38–56.

20. Crosby, *Ecological Imperialism,* 100.

21. Quotation is from John H. Galloway, *The Sugar Cane Industry: An Historical Geography from Its Origins to 1914,* 48. See also Sidney W. Mintz, *Sweetness and Power: The Place of Sugar*

in Modern History, for an excellent and readable treatment of the wider economic, social, and political significance of sugar.

22. Gerald R. Crone, ed., *The Voyages of Cadamosto and Other Documents on Western Africa in the Second Half of the Fifteenth Century,* 9; and Richard Eden, ed., *A Treatyse on the Newe India, with Other Newfounde Lands and Ilandes,* 40–41. Christopher Columbus gained early experience in Atlantic navigation by trading with Madeira, and married the daughter of a Madeira merchant.

23. Galloway, *The Sugar Cane Industry,* 50–55; Virginia Rau, "The Settlement of Madeira and the Sugar Plantations," 3–12; and Sidney M. Greenfield, "Madeira and the Beginning of New World Sugar Cane Cultivation and Plantation Slavery," 536–52. The calculation of forest cut is based on a yield of between 150 and 250 m³/acre.

24. Galloway, *The Sugar Cane Industry,* 50–51. For a discussion of the growth and significance of plantation systems and slave-owning societies, see Philip D. Curtin, "Slavery and Empire," 3–10.

25. James Walvin, *Fruits of Empire: Exotic Produce and British Taste, 1600–1800,* 117–31.

26. See Gustavo A. B. da Fonseca, "The Vanishing Brazilian Atlantic Forest," 17–21.

27. Warren Dean, "Deforestation in Southeastern Brazil," 51–56; and Raymond F. Watters, *Shifting Cultivation in Latin America,* 10–30.

28. Stuart B. Schwartz, *Sugar Plantations in the Formation of Brazilian Society: Bahia, 1550–1835,* 106–10, 139–42. Whereas *engenho* literally means "mill," it was applied to the entire production complex of cane fields, mill, and factory. For many illustrations of the *engenho* see Joaquim de Sousa-Leão, *Frans Post, 1612–1680,* esp. those on pp. 8, 22, 49, 66, 79, 80, 87, 97, 107, 150, and 151.

29. Dean, "Deforestation in Southeastern Brazil," 60.

30. See Schwartz, *Sugar Plantations,* 118–19. For calculation of wood use, see Shawn W. Miller, "Fuelwood in Colonial Brazil: The Economic and Social Consequences of Fuel Depletion for the Bahian Recôncavo, 1549–1820," 184, 186–87. A *tarefa* was an imprecise measure, variously said to be the extent of a cane field that would provide sufficient cane to feed a mill for a day; twenty paces square; or the capacity of an average oxcart: $1.7 \times 1.5 \times 0.8$ m, or 16.3 m³.

31. Schwartz, *Sugar Plantations,* 118, and "Free Labor in a Slave Economy: the Lavadores de Cana of Colonial Bahia," 170–71; and Dean, "Deforestation in Southeastern Brazil," 61.

32. James Lockhart and Stuart B. Schwartz, *Early Latin America: A History of Colonial Spanish America,* 213–14; and C. R. Boxer, *The Golden Age of Brazil, 1695–1750: Growing Pains of a Colonial Society,* 226–46.

33. See Galloway, *The Sugar Cane Industry,* 77–81; and Richard B. Sheridan, *The Development of the Plantations to 1750: A Era of West Indian Prosperity, 1750–1775,* 9–21, for the shift to the Caribbean; and Carl Bridenbaugh and Roberta Bridenbaugh, *No Peace Beyond the Line: The English in the Caribbean, 1624–1690,* 9–76, for the founding of Barbados.

34. Andrew White, "A Briefe Relation of the Voyage unto Maryland," 37.

35. Ibid.; Richard Blome, *A Description of the Island of Jamaica . . . ,* 4; Richard Ligon, *A True and Exact History of the Island of Barbadoes,* 28, 24; and Sir Dalby Thomas, *An Historical Account of the Rise and Growth of the West-India Colonies: And the Great Advantage they are to England in Respect of Trade,* 25. Quotations are from Ligon, p. 24; and Thomas, p. 35.

36. Ligon, *A True and Exact History,* 24; United Kingdom, *Calendar of State Papers, Colonial, 1675–76,* no. 973; and David Watts, *Man's Influence on the Vegetation of Barbados: 1627–1800,* 34–35, 36, 38–45.

37. Bridenbaugh and Bridenbaugh, *No Peace beyond the Line,* 268–71; Watts, *The West Indies,* 186, 142–231; Gordon Clark Merrill, *Historical Geography of St. Kitts and Nevis, The West*

Indies, 32, 37; Sir Hans Sloane, *A Voyage to the Islands of Madera, Barbadoes, Nieves, St. Christopher and Jamaica . . . ,* 1:42; Clarissa Thérèse Kimber, *Martinique Revisted: The Changing Plant Geographies of a West Indian Island,* 119–24, 128, 131–33, 182–88, 224, 228–29, 275; Blome, *A Description of the Island of Jamaica,* 3, 11, 77, 98; and Lydia M. Pulsipher, *Seventeenth Century Montserrat: An Environmental Impact Statement.* For the quote on "coales" see PRO, CO Record Group 1, vol. 21 (1667), "Memorial on the Island of Tobago," 171, quoted in Watts, *Man's Influence,* 45.

38. Ligon, *A True and Exact History,* quotation from pp. 20–21; Richard S. Dunn, *Sugar and Slaves: The Rise of the Planter Class in the English West Indies, 1624–1713,* quotation from p. 28; Evangeline W. Andrews and Charles M. Andrews, eds., *Journal of a Lady of Quality, 1774–1776,* 120–27; and Sloane, *A Voyage to the Islands of Madera, Barbadoes,* 2:294.

39. For a detailed account of early timber trade, on which this is based, see Charles F. Carroll, *The Timber Economy of Puritan New England,* esp. 75–97; and for a definitive treatment of the context and larger patterns, Donald W. Meinig, *The Shaping of America: A Geographical Perspective on 500 Years of History,* vol. 1, *Atlantic America,* 55–76, 160–72.

40. Carroll, *The Timber Economy of Puritan New England,* 87.

41. For an in-depth treatment of early clearing in North America, see Michael Williams, *Americans and Their Forests: A Historical Geography,* esp. 53–81, 111–45. Terry G. Jordan and Matti Kaups, *The American Backwoods Frontier: An Ethnic and Ecological Interpretation,* 1–18, discuss the characteristics and diffusion of backwoods culture.

42. Thomas Pownall, *A Topographical Description of the Dominions of the United States of America,* 23; François Jean, marquis de Chastellux, *Travels in North America in the Years 1780, 1781, and 1782,* 2:44; and Paul W. Gates, "Problems of Agricultural History, 1790–1840," 34.

43. For a general view of New England and New York settlement, see Charles E. Clark, *The Eastern Frontier: The Settlement of Northern New England, 1610–1763;* John R. Stilgoe, *The Common Landscape of America, 1580 to 1845,* 99–107; and Orsamus Turner, *A Pioneer History of the Holland Purchase of Western New York,* 322.

44. William Cooper, *A Guide in the Wilderness . . . ,* 22, 34–35; Stilgoe, *Common Landscape,* 143–48; and Richard G. Lillard, *The Great Forest,* 67–68.

45. Based on a variety of sources, including Jared Eliot, *Essays upon Field Husbandry in New England [1760] and Other Papers, 1748–1762,* 1; Johann D. Schoepf, *Travels in the Confederation (1783–1784),* 1:264; Timothy Dwight, *Travels in New-England and New-York in 1821,* letter 11, 2:125–26; Jeremy Belknap, *The History of New Hampshire,* 3:131–37 (p. 135 is the source of the "decapitated stumps" quotation); Carl Bridenbaugh, "Yankee Use and Abuse of the Forest in the Building of New England, 1620–1660," 3–35; and James Stuart, *Three Years in North America,* 1:260–66.

46. Richard Frame, "A Short Description of Pennsylvania by Richard Frame," 303.

47. Henry Beaufoy, *Tour through Parts of the United States and Canada by a British Subject,* 81–82, the source of the quotations; and David M. Ellis, *Landlords and Farmers in the Hudson-Mohawk Region, 1790–1850,* 73 and passim.

48. William Byrd, *Natural History of Virginia: or, The Newly Discovered Eden,* 93; Schoepf, *Travels,* 48; Edmund Ruffin, *An Essay on Calcareous Manures,* 12; and Avery O. Craven, *Soil Exhaustion As a Factor in the Agricultural History of Virginia and Maryland, 1606–1860.* Jefferson is quoted in Craven, p. 34.

49. Thomas Anburey, *Travels through the Interior Parts of America in a Series of Letters by an Officer,* 2:322.

50. For an excellent description of the slave economy see John G. W. De Brahm, "Philosophico-Historico-Hydrogeography of South Carolina, Georgia, and East Florida," 197–98. For a more

extensive discussion of forest clearing see Timothy Silver, *A New Face on the Countryside: Indians, Colonists, and Slaves in the South Atlantic Forests, 1500–1800,* 104–7.

51. Chastellux, *Travels in North America,* 1:49; and Latrobe, quoted in *The Pittsburgh Gazette,* 8 September 1838.

52. Sam Bass Hilliard, *Hogmeat and Hocake: Food Supply in the Old South, 1840–1860,* 28–56. The progenitors of the razorback swine probably escaped from the herds that accompanied the De Soto expedition of 1538.

53. Based on Samuel Wilson, "An Account of the Province of Carolina in America, together with an Abstract of the Patent," 171; Thomas Nairne, *A Letter from South Carolina: Giving an Account of the Soil, Air, Products, Trade, Government . . . of that Province,* 131; and Rupert Vance, *The Human Geography of the South: A Study in Regional Resources and Human Adequacy,* 145–60.

54. Percy W. Bidwell and John I. Falconer, *History of Agriculture in the Northern United States, 1620–1860,* 21–22; and Lewis C. Gray and Esther K. Thompson, *History of Agriculture in the Southern United States to 1860,* 145–46. For the problems and extent of fencing, see Clarence H. Danhof, "The Fencing Problem in the Eighteen-Fifties," 168–86; and Martin Primack, "Farm Formed Capital in American Agriculture, 1850–1910," 287–91. Beaufoy, *Tour,* 53–54, has an excellent description of zigzag fences. See also Jordan and Kaups, *American Backwoods Frontier,* 105–15.

55. Jordan and Kaups, *American Backwoods Frontier,* 135–211.

56. Timothy Flint, *A Condensed Geography and History of the Western States or the Mississippi Valley,* 75–76; and *New York State Census* (1855), 245–46, (1856), 271–72.

57. Thomas Cooper, *Some Information Respecting America collected by Thomas Cooper,* 119; and Tench Coxe, *A View of the United States of America . . . ,* 452–53.

58. Gray and Thompson, *Agriculture in the Southern United States,* 1:554; for the Franklin quotation see Benjamin Franklin, *An Account of the New-Invented Pennsylvania Fire-Place . . . ,* 392.

59. Robert V. Reynolds and Albert Pierson, *Fuel Wood Used in the United States, 1630–1930,* 6–11. This is at least double the amount calculated for a prosperous German peasant farmer at the same time. See chapter 7, p. 181 of the present text.

60. Carl Bridenbaugh, *Cities in the Wilderness: The First Century of Urban Life in America, 1625–1742,* 11–12, 151–52, 311–13; Pehr Kalm, *Travels into North America, Containing its Natural History and a Circumstantial Account of its Plantations and Agriculture,* 1:93–4; and Schoepf, *Travels,* 1:5, 60–61.

61. Franklin, *Account of the New-Invented Pennsylvania Fire-Place,* 392; and Charles Clark, *Eastern Frontier,* 116.

62. Reynolds and Pierson, *Fuel Wood Used,* 112–20; and Arthur H. Cole, "The Mystery of Fuel Wood Marketing in the United States," 339–59.

63. Philip L. White, *Beekmantown, New York: Forest Frontier to Farm Community,* 29; Howard S. Russell, *A Long Deep Furrow: Three Centuries of Farming in New England,* 93; Charles Clark, *Eastern Frontier,* chap 1; and Carroll, *Timber Economy.*

64. Of the many sources on naval stores manufacture and trade, the following are especially useful: Justin Williams, "England's Colonial Naval Stores Policy, 1588–1776"; Joseph J. Malone, *Pine Trees and Politics: The Naval Stores and Forest Policy in Colonial New England,* 35–38; and Eleanor L. Lord, *Industrial Experiments in the British Colonies of North America,* app. B. Also, as production was interwoven with agriculture, there are good descriptions in Gray and Thompson, *Agriculture in the Southern United States,* 159–60; and Schoepf, *Travels,* 140–43.

65. Robert G. Albion, *Forests and Sea Power: The Timber Problem of the Royal Navy,* 200–315, esp. 236–37 for mast sizes; Jay P. Kinney, *Forest Legislation in America Prior to March 4, 1789;* and Malone, *Pine Trees and Politics,* 82–143.

66. Carroll, *Timber Economy,* 69, 131–33; Bernard Bailyn and Lotte Bailyn, *Massachusetts Shipping, 1697–1714: A Statistical Study,* 42, tables 17 and 18, and pp. 102–9; and Melvin G. Herndon, "Forest Products of Colonial Georgia," 426–33.

67. Anne McVickar Grant, *Memoirs of an American Lady: With Sketches of Manners and Scenes in America, as They Existed Previous to the Revolution,* 2:258–59; and Henry Wansey, *Journal of an Excursion in the United States in the Summer of 1794,* 107–8.

68. See M. Williams, *Americans and Their Forests,* 100–4.

69. Based on, int. al., James M. Swank, *The History of the Manufacture of Iron in All Ages and Particularly in the United States from Colonial Times to 1891;* Victor S. Clark, *History of Manufactures in the United States, 1607–1914,* vol. 1, *1607–1860;* Peter Temin, *Iron and Steel in Nineteenth Century America: An Economic Inquiry,* 264–65; and Arthur C. Bining, *Pennsylvania Iron Manufacture in the Eighteenth Century,* 67–94.

70. For a full discussion of these calculations see M. Williams, *Americans and Their Forests,* 106–7 and table 4.3. For abandonment see Schoepf, *Travels,* 5:36–37; Charles S. Boyer, *Early Forges and Furnaces in New Jersey,* 48–49; and James M. Ransom, *The Vanishing Ironworks of the Ramapos: The Story of the Forges, Furnaces and Mines of the New Jersey-New York Border Area,* 102.

71. Quotations are from E. Estyn Evans, "The Ecology of Peasant Life in Western Europe," 217; and Charles Darwin, *The Origin of Species by Means of Natural Selection,* 166.

72. Dwight Perkins, *Agricultural Development in China, 1368–1968,* table 2.1, pp. 15–16, and apps. A and B, pp. 192–240. For earlier studies see Ping-ti Ho, *Studies on the Population of China, 1368–1953,* 1–97. Although Perkins's figures are different from those of Demeny, given all the uncertainties and the different marker dates, they are in the right range of magnitude.

73. Perkins, *Agricultural Development in China,* 13, 38–53; and Rhoads Murphey, "Deforestation in Modern China," n. 2.

74. Murphey, "Deforestation in Modern China," 111. See also S. A. M. Adshead, "Timber As a Factor in Chinese History: Problems, Sources, and Hypotheses," 1–6.

75. Examples of the lack of reference to forest and timber are John Lossing Buck, *Chinese Farm Economy: A Study of 2866 Farms in Seventeen Localities and Seven Provinces in China;* and Ramon H. Myers, *Agricultural Development in Hopei and Shantung, 1890–1949,* but there are many others. For those works that do deal with the forest see Norman Shaw, *Chinese Forest Trees and Timber Supply;* Peter C. Perdue, *Exhausting the Earth: State and Peasant in Hunan, 1500–1850;* and Kenneth Pomeranz, *The Making of a Hinterland: State, Society and Economy in Inland North China, 1853–1937,* 123–42.

76. Francesca Bray, "Agriculture," 91.

77. Perdue, *Exhausting the Earth,* 3–13; Karl Wittfogel, *Oriental Despotism;* Joseph Needham, "Science and Society in East and West," 190–219; and Perry Anderson, "The Asiatic Mode of Production," 462–541.

78. F. Bray, "Agriculture," 94–96.

79. The following paragraphs are based on Perdue, *Exhausting the Earth,* 41–58, 64–80, and tables 3 and 4—"Registered Population, and Land Area."

80. See Nicholas Menzies, *Forest and Land Management in Imperial China,* 19–20, and "Forestry," 543–667; and Evelyn S. Rawski, "Agricultural Development in the Han River Highlands," 63–81.

81. Menzies, *Forest and Land Management in Imperial China*, 105–7, and "Forestry", 543–667; and Adshead, "An Energy Crisis in Early Modern China," 20–28.

82. F. Bray, "Agriculture," 95–98; and Perdue, *Exhausting the Earth*, 61–62.

83. Ping-ti Ho, *Population of China*, 183–89, and "The Introduction of American Food Plants into China," 191–201; and Yi-fu Tuan, *China*, 143–44.

84. Perkins, *Agricultural Development in China*, 70–77; and Perdue, *Exhausting the Earth*, 35–36, quotations on p. 88.

85. Tuan, *China*, 141, on which this section relies.

86. Ch'ao-Ting Chi, *Key Economic Areas in Chinese History as Revealed in the Development of Public Works for Water Control*, 22.

87. Walter C. Lowdermilk and Dean R. Wickes, *History of Soil Use in the Wu T'ai Shan Area*, 4–5.

88. Jean-Baptiste Du Halde, *The General History of China*, 4:370; and W. Woodville Rockhill, "Explorations in Mongolia and Tibet," 663.

89. Menzies, *Forest and Land Management in Imperial China*, 55–87; and Edward H. Schafer, "Hunting Parks and Animal Enclosures in Ancient China," 318–43.

90. N. Shaw, *Chinese Forest Trees and Timber Supply*, 15.

91. For details of the population see Irene Taeuber, *The Population of Japan*; and for more-recent assessments of numbers, Susan B. Hanley and Kozo Yamamura, *Economic and Demographic Change in Pre-Industrial Japan, 1600–1868*, 38–68.

92. Conrad Totman, "The Forests of Tokugawa Japan: A Catastrophe That Was Avoided," 3; and Thomas C. Smith, *The Agrarian Origins of Modern Japan*, 82, 101.

93. T. C. Smith, *Agrarian Origins of Modern Japan*, 42, 82, 84–86, 101; and Conrad D. Totman, *The Green Archipelago: Forestry in Pre-Industrial Japan*, 50–51.

94. Yoshinori Yasuda, "Early Historic Forest Clearance around the Ancient Castle Site of Tagajo, Miyagi Prefecture, Japan," 42–58.

95. For a good account of Japanese life, see George Elison and L. Smith Bardwell, *Warlords, Artists and Commoners: Japan in the Sixteenth Century*, 7–23. Except where otherwise noted, this discussion on forest use is based on Totman, *The Green Archipelago*, 52–68.

96. Based on Conrad D. Totman, "Lumber Provisioning in Early Modern Japan, 1580–1850," 61–70. There was also a flourishing urban market in firewood and charcoal, serviced by small-sale entrepreneurs. See William B. Hauser, *Economic and Institutional Change in Tokugawa Japan: Osaka and the Kinai Cotton Trade*, 14, 21, 28, 38–39, 43–44, 46, 50.

97. Totman, *The Green Archipelago*, 67–68, and "Lumber Provisioning," 56, 61–70.

98. Based on Totman, *The Green Archipelago*, 68–78; quotation is from pp. 74–75.

99. Based on Totman, *The Green Archipelago*, 68–77, "The Forests of Tokugawa Japan," 6, "Logging the Unloggable: Timber Transport in Early Modern Japan," 180–91, and "From Exploitation to Plantation Forestry in Early Modern Japan," 270–72; and Masako Osako, "Forest Preservation in Tokugawa Japan," 129–36. For the story of destruction in one individual forest, see Totman's *Origins of Japan's Modern Forests: The Case of Akita*, 1–22. There is also a vast Japanese literature that is not examined here, but preeminent is Tokoro Mitsuo's monumental 858-page *Kinsei Ringyōshi no Kenkyū* (Studies in the history of early modern forestry), whose maps, tables, and diagrams alone are worth looking at.

100. James McMullen, *Idealism, Protest, and the "Tale of the Genji": The Confucianism of Kamazawa Banzan (1619–91)*, 239–45; quotation is from p. 241. It is clear that the multiple themes of Banzan's thought—intense economic conservation; fear of exhaustion of natural resources; condemnation of extravagant consumption, rationalism, environmental determinism, climatic warming, and humanitarianism; and aversion to the harsh rule of law—come together in his

extensive discussion on forestry, which would repay much deeper analysis than it is accorded here.

101. Quoted in Totman, *The Green Archipelago*, 77.

Chapter 9

1. Carlo M. Cipolla, introduction, in *The Fontana Economic History of Europe*, 7–8.

2. John U. Nef, *The Conquest of the Material World*, 3–42; and Daniel Headrick, "Technological Change," 55.

3. Carl O. Sauer, "The Prospect for Redistribution of Population," 8.

4. For a useful summary of some of these changes, see Eric E. Lampard, "The Social Impact of the Industrial Revolution," 302–24; and Nathan Rosenberg, "The Economic Consequences of Technological Change, 1830–1880," 515–31.

5. Clarence F. Glacken, *Traces on the Rhodian Shore: Nature and Culture in Western Thought from Ancient Times to the End of the Eighteenth Century*, 705; and David S. Landes, *The Unbound Prometheus: Technological Change and Industrial Development in Western Europe from 1750 to the Present*, esp. 1–40, 554–55.

6. Glacken, *Traces*, 705.

7. For an attempt to grapple with the more complex cultural forces see John W. Bennett and Kenneth A. Dahlberg, "Institutions, Social Organization, and Cultural Values," 69–86.

8. Int. al., Thomas S. Ashton, *The Industrial Revolution, 1760–1830*; Carlo M. Cipolla, ed., *The Fontana Economic History of Europe*, vol. 3, *The Industrial Revolution, 1700–1914*; Shepard B. Clough, *European Economic History: The Economic Development of Western Civilization*; Phyllis Deane, *The First Industrial Revolution*; H. John Habakkuk and Michael Postan, eds., *The Cambridge Economic History of Europe*, vol. 6, *The Industrial Revolution and After: Incomes, Population and Technological Change*; Melvin Kranzberg and Carroll W. Pursell Jr., eds., *Technology in Western Civilization*, vol. 1, *The Emergence of Modern Industrial Society—Earliest Times to 1900*; Eric L. Jones, *The European Miracle: Environments, Economies, and Geopolitics in the History of Europe and Asia*; Landes, *The Unbound Prometheus*; Lewis Mumford, *Technics and Civilization*; and Max Weber, *The Protestant Ethic and the Spirit of Capitalism*.

9. Immanuel Wallerstein, *The Modern World-System III: The Second Era of Great Expansion of the Capitalist World–Economy, 1730–1840s*, 3–33.

10. Int. al., Paul Bairoch, "Agriculture and the Industrial Revolution," 452–506; Folke Dovering, "The Transformation of European Agriculture," 604–814; Eric L. Jones, *Agriculture and Economic Growth in England, 1750–1815*; Eric Kerridge, "The Agricultural Revolution Reconsidered," 463–75; G. E. Mingay, ed., *The Agricultural Revolution: Changes in Agriculture, 1650–1880*; Patrick K. O'Brien, "Agriculture and Industrial Revolution," 166–81; Mark Overton, "Re-establishing the English Agricultural Revolution," 1–20; and Bernard H. Slicher van Bath, *The Agrarian History of Western Europe, A.D. 850–1850*, 221–309, and "Eighteenth Century Agriculture on the Continent of Europe: Evolution or Revolution?" 169–79.

11. Bertrand Gille, "Banking and Industrialization in Europe, 1730–1914," 256.

12. Natalis Briavonne, *De l'Industrie en Belgique . . .*, 185–86, quoted in I. Wallerstein, *The Modern World System III*, 15. It is interesting that Briavonne followed Francis Bacon in that he thought that the revolution had stemmed from three basic or key inventions: the printing press, the compass, and firearms.

13. Paul Bairoch, "International Industrialization Levels from 1750 to 1980," 269–333. See also William O. Henderson, *The Industrial Revolution on the Continent: Germany, France, Russia, 1800–1914*.

14. W. A. Cole and Phyllis Deane, "The Growth of National Incomes," esp. 10–17, 29–39; and Walter Minchinton, "Patterns of Demand, 1750–1914," 110–12.

15. Cole and Deane, "The Growth of National Incomes," 9–11, 17, 31–32.

16. U.S. Bureau of the Census, *Historical Statistics of the United States from Colonial Times to 1957*, tables L113–L121.

17. R. Fitzgerald and J. Grenier, *Timber: A Centenary History of the Timber Trade Federation, 1892–1992*, app. 4, p.18.

18. Sven-Erik Åström, "Technology and Timber Exports from the Gulf of Finland, 1661–1740," 6–9.

19. Sources of information about technological improvements and changes in sawmills are numerous, but the following are the most important and have been used: Joseph S. Illick, "The Story of the American Lumbering Industry," 150–98; Richard G. Wood, "A History of Lumbering in Maine, 1820–1860," 162–63; James Elliot Defebaugh, *History of the Lumber Industry in America*, 2:8, 53; Ralph Clement Bryant, *Lumber: Its Manufacture and Distribution*, 3–23; Alfred J. Van Tassel and David W. Bluestone, *Mechanization in the Lumber Industry: A Study of Technology in Relation to Resources and Employment Opportunity*, 8–11, 194; Rodney C. Loehr, "Saving the Kerf: The Introduction of the Band Saw Mill," 168–72; and Bryan Latham, *Timber: Its Development and Distribution: A Historical Survey*, 207–23.

20. U.S. Congress, Senate, *Letter from the Secretary of the Treasury Transmitting Information on Steam Engines*; U.S. Bureau of the Census, *Manufactures* (1880), "Power Used in Manufactures," 2:15.

21. Michael Williams, *Americans and Their Forests: A Historical Geography*, 202.

22. Ibid., 201–2; Nathan Rosenberg, "America's Rise to Woodworking Leadership," 48–50, and *Technology and American Economic Growth*, 26–28; and U.S. Congress, House, *Patent Office Annual Report, 1847*, 758–60.

23. "Report of the Committee on the Machinery of the United States," quoted in Nathan Rosenberg, *The American System of Manufacturing . . .* , 171, 344.

24. Robert Fries, *Empire in Pine: The Story of Lumbering in Wisconsin, 1830–1900*, 61–64; Rolland Maybee, "Michigan's White Pine Era, 1840–1900," 428; and U.S. Bureau of the Census, Fourteenth Census (1919), 10:410–40, *Manufactures: Special Reports for Selected Industries*.

25. Landes, *The Unbound Prometheus*, 3.

26. For general business organization see Mumford, *Technics and Civilization*, 109–10; Bernard A. Weisberger, *The New Industrial Society*, 12–21; U.S. Bureau of Corporations, *The Lumber Industry*, 1:pt. 1, "Standing Timber," 11–12; and David Noble, *America by Design: Science, Technology and the Rise of Corporate Capitalism*, 15–17. For forestland (stumpage) ownership see U.S. Bureau of Corporations, *The Lumber Industry*, 2: pt. 3, "Land Holdings of Timber Owners." Bryan Latham, *The Development of the American Timber Trade*, 56, 203–4 covers the growing specialization and subdivision of labor. For the growth of big firms see William G. Rector, *Log Transportation in the Lake States Lumber Industry, 1840–1918 . . .* , 22; and Defebaugh, *Lumber Industry of America*, 2:319, 407. There are many individual company histories, but the following are indicative of trends: Isaac Stephenson, *Recollections of a Long Life, 1829–1915*; Charles E. Twining, *Downriver: Orrin H. Ingram and the Empire Lumber Company*; and particularly Ralph W. Hidy, Frank E. Hill, and Alan Nevins, *Timber and Men: The Weyerhaeuser Story*, 28–206.

27. Wallerstein, *The Second Era of Great Expansion*, 27, quoting *Parliamentary History of England*, vol. 26 (1816), 545. See also Landes, *The Unbound Prometheus*, 54 for comments on different national attitudes toward coal use.

28. Bouda Etemad and Jean Luciani, *World Energy Production, 1800–1985,* xvii.

29. Sam H. Schurr and Bruce C. Netschert, *Energy in the American Economy, 1850–1975: An Economic Study of Its History and Prospects,* 35–37.

30. Paul Demeny, "Population", 42–45.

31. Julia C. Allen and Douglas F. Barnes, "The Causes of Deforestation in Developing Countries," 177–78.

32. David V. Glass and Eugene Grebenik, "World Population, 1800–1950," 70–130; and E. Anthony Wrigley and Roger S. Schofield, *The Population History of England, 1541–1871.*

33. André Armengaud, "Population in Europe, 1700–1900," 60–72.

34. Demeny, "Population," 45.

35. Sam Bass Warner, "Population Movements and Urbanization," 541–46.

36. Wallerstein, *The Second Era of Great Expansion,* 193–204.

37. David K. Fieldhouse, *Economics and Empire, 1830–1914,* 3; and Donald Meinig, "A Macrogeography of Western Imperialism: Some Morphologies of Moving Frontiers of Political Control," 233. Quotation is from from Landes, *The Unbound Prometheus,* 241.

38. Meinig, "A Macrogeography of Western Imperialism," 231.

39. Daniel Headrick, *Tools of Empire: Technology and European Imperialism in the Nineteenth Century.*

40. A. S. Youngson, "The Opening Up of New Territories," 139.

41. Landes, *The Unbound Prometheus,* 37.

42. Immanuel Wallerstein, *The Modern World System I: Capitalist Agriculture and the Origins of the European World-Economy in the Sixteenth Century,* 301–2. For an extended discussion on the nature of this later imperialism, see Fieldhouse, *Economics and Empire,* 1–88.

43. Daniel Headrick's *The Tools of Empire* and *The Tentacles of Progress: Technology Transfer in the Age of Imperialism, 1850–1940* are the classic works on this topic, and they are used in the following discussion.

44. Headrick, *The Tools of Empire,* 58–74. See also Philip D. Curtin, "'The White Man's Grave': Image and Reality, 1780–1850," 94–110.

45. For the impact of gunboats see Headrick, *The Tools of Empire,* 17–42, and for their crucial role in China, 43–54.

46. Winston Spenser Churchill, *The River War: An Historical Account of the Reconquest of the Soudan,* 2:119, 124. For the wider context of the "arms gap" see Headrick, *The Tools of Empire,* 96–126.

47. There is a vast literature on the financial implication of improved communications and transportation; for example, Gille, "Banking and Industrialization in Europe", 255–97; H. John Habakkuk, "Free Trade and Commercial Expansion, 1853–1870. II. Banking and Investment," 781–806; Herbert Fies, *Europe, The World's Banker, 1870–1914;* and Anthony J. H. Latham, *The International Economy and the Underdeveloped World, 1865–1914.* The links are made explicit in Gerald S. Graham, "Imperial Finance, Trade and Communications, 1895–1914."

48. Headrick, *The Tools of Empire,* 130. See also Michael Chisholm, "The Increasing Separation of Production and Consumption," 89–90.

49. For an overall view of transport developments see Headrick, *The Tentacles of Progress,* 18–48. For the historical background see Headrick, *The Tools of Empire,* 129–56; Eugene S. Ferguson, "Steam Transportation," 285–302; and L. Girard, "Transport," esp. 228–73.

50. Headrick, *The Tentacles of Progress,* 51–52; and Ferguson, "Steam Transportation," 296–98. On the external economies of railways, see Moses Abramovitz, "The Economic Characteristics of Railroads and the Problem of Economic Development," 169–78.

51. Based on Bruce R. Mitchell, *International Historical Statistics,* "Africa and Asia," 496–508, "The Americas and Australasia," 666–67, "Europe, 1750–1988," 655–64, and "The Americas, 1750–1988," 528–39.

52. For the revolutionary impact of the canal on distances, and the growth and improvement of shipping, see André Siegfried, *Suez and Panama,* 114–58. There is also useful material in John Marlowe, *The Making of the Suez Canal,* 235–323; and Lord Kinross, *Between Two Seas: The Creation of the Suez Canal,* 215–86.

53. There is a large literature on steamships and engines, but the main points are covered in Bernard Brodie, *Seapower in the Machine Age: Major Naval Inventions and Their Consequences on International Politics,* 149–54; Charles Ernest Fayle, *A Short History of the World's Shipping Industry,* 231–41; Ferguson, "Steam Transportation," 285–300; A. Fraser-Macdonald, *Our Ocean Railways; or, the Rise, Progress and Development of Ocean Steam Navigation,* 213–31; and Ronald Hope, *A New History of British Shipping,* 263–86.

54. Adam W. Kirkaldy, *British Shipping, Its History, Organization and Importance,* app. 17; and Leon Isserlis, "Tramp Steamer Cargoes and Freights," 122.

55. Arthur R. Lower, *Great Britain's Woodyard: British America and the Timber Trade, 1763–1867,* 257–58.

56. Quoted in Headrick, *The Tools of Empire,* 130. See also C. R. Fray, "The Movement toward Free Trade, 1820–1853," 412–13.

57. Sherry Olson, *The Depletion Myth: A History of Railway Use of Timber,* quoting Howard Miller in *The Forester* 3 (1 January 1897): 6. For greater detail of the basis for these calculations, see the discussion in chapter 10 of the present text, pp. 314–15.

58. Ralph C. Bryant, *Logging: The Principles and General Methods of Operation in the United States,* 121; and Rector, *Log Transportation,* 15–41.

59. For a colorful account of the start of the log drive, see Henry David Thoreau, *The Maine Woods,* 41–42; and John S. Springer, *Forest Life and Forest Trees* . . . For log marks see Elizabeth Bachmann, "Minnesota Log Marks," 126–37; and James E. Lundsted, "Log Marks: Forgotten Lore of the Logging Era," 44–46.

60. Wood, "A History of Lumbering in Maine, 1820–1860," 114–22; and William F. Fox, "History of the Lumber Industry of the State of New York," 23–29.

61. For booms see Franklin B. Hough, *Report upon Forestry,* 1:438–39 for New York and 465–66 for Pennsylvania; Wood, "A History of Lumbering in Maine," 188–20 for Bangor; Fries, *Empire in Pine,* 49–55 for Wisconsin; and for the great Glen Falls boom on the Hudson, see Benson Lossing, *The Hudson from the Wilderness to the Sea,* 65–66.

62. Hough, *Report upon Forestry,* 1:446–53; and Defebaugh, *Lumber Industry in America,* 2:317–18, 407, 418.

63. For exhaustive accounts see Rector, *Log Transportation,* 147–89; and Fries, *Empire in Pine,* 60–83, 141–60.

64. Bryant, *Logging,* 172–77; Illick, "The Story of the American Lumbering Industry," 24, 167–71; and Rector, *Log Transportation,* 208–14.

65. Bryant, *Logging,* 242–47; Fries, *Empire in Pine,* 64–65, 84–91; Hough, *Report upon Forestry,* 1:546–47; and Rector, *Log Transportation,* 200–22.

66. George Woodward Hotchkiss, *History of the Lumber and Forest Industry of the Northwest,* 685; and Hough, *Report upon Forestry,* 2:49.

67. Based on Glacken, *Traces,* 501–3. For greater detail on the physico-theologians see 504–50; for Montesquieu and other determinists, 552–622; and for the origins of the perfectibility, population, and environmental limits debate, 623–54.

68. Ibid., 656–7; quotation is from p. 685. See also Gilbert Chinard, "The American Philosophical Society and the Early History of Forestry in America," 452.

69. George-Louis Leclerc, comte de Buffon, *Histoire naturelle, générale et particulière,* vol. 12, "De la nature, première vue," xiii.

70. Ibid., "Des époques de la nature." For the Seventh Epoch see 5:228–37.

71. Benjamin Keen, *The Life of the Admiral Christopher Columbus by His Son Ferdinand,* 142–43. For the wider context see Kenneth Thompson, "Forests and Climate Change in America: Some Early Views," 47–64.

72. Hugh Williamson, "An Attempt to Account for the CHANGE IN CLIMATE, which has been Observed in the Middle Colonies in North America," 337–45; and Noah Webster, "Dissertation on the Supposed Change of Temperature in Modern Winters," 119–62. See also Glacken, *Traces,* 658–63, 668–69.

73. Glacken, *Traces,* 670–71. For the related issues of forest influences on soils and health, see Jared Eliot, *Essays upon Field Husbandry in New England [1760] and Other Papers, 1748–1762;* and Benjamin Rush, "An Inquiry into the Cause of the Increase of Bilious and Intermitting Fevers in Pennsilvania with Hints for Preventing Them," 206–12.

74. Glacken, *Traces,* 671.

75. Bohumil Shimek, "The Pioneer and the Forest," 97–99; and Chinard, "The American Philosophical Society," 444.

76. Alexis de Tocqueville, "A Fortnight in the Wilds," *Journey to America,* 335; and *Democracy in America,* 2:74.

77. "Wilderness evil" has been identified as a major theme in American culture by Constance M. Rourke in *The Roots of American Culture and Other Essays,* 20–21.

78. Francis Parkman, "The Forest and the Census," 836; and Frederick Jackson Turner, *The Frontier in American History,* 269–70.

79. Andrew Jackson, "Second Annual Message," in James D. Richardson, *A Compilation of the Messages and Papers of the Presidents,* 3:1084.

80. Constantinee, Count Volney, *A View of the Climate and Soil of the United States of America,* 213–16.

81. John Lorain, *Nature and Reason Harmonized in the Practice of Husbandry,* 25–27; for descriptions of clearing see 333–39; quotation is from pp. 335–36.

82. See K. Thompson, "Forests and Climate Change in America," 50–51.

83. George Perkins Marsh, *Address before the Agricultural Society of Rutland County, Sept. 30th, 1847,* 17–19. For additional details, see David Lowenthal's *George Perkins Marsh: Versatile Vermonter,* and particularly his second biography, *George Perkins Marsh: Prophet of Conservation.*

84. Clarence Glacken, "Changing Ideas of the Habitable World," 81.

85. Lindsay Sharp, "Timber, Science and Economic Reform in the Seventeenth Century," 51–54; and Keith Thomas, *Man and the Natural World: Changing Attitudes in England, 1500–1800,* 198–99.

86. K. Thomas, *Man and the Natural World,* 210–11, 219, quotation is from p. 219; and H. Clifford Darby, "The Changing English Landscape," 389.

87. K. Thomas, *Man and the Natural World,* esp. 212–13, 216, 218–19, quotation is from p. 212; Joseph Addison, *The Spectator,* 31 May 1712, p. 393; and William Gilpin, *Remarks on Forest Scenery,* 1794, 1:1.

88. Merle Curti, *The Growth of American Thought,* 150–55; and Christopher Hussey, *The Picturesque: Studies in a Point of View,* 20–37.

89. Walter J. Hipple, *The Beautiful, the Sublime, and the Picturesque in Eighteenth Century British Aesthetics;* and Marjorie Hope Nicolson, *Mountain Gloom and Mountain Glory: The Development of the Aesthetics of the Infinite.*

90. Curti, *Growth of American Thought,* 239–43; Perry Miller, *Errand into Wilderness,* 209; and Hoxie Neal Fairchild, *The Romantic Quest,* 123–40, 351–72. For the Lord Byron quotation see his *Child Harold's Pilgrimage,* canto 4, clxxvii; for Wordsworth's see William Wordsworth, *The Tables Turned;* François August René, vicomte de Chateaubriand, *Recollections of Italy, England, and America on Various Subjects,* 138–39; and Philip M. Marsh, ed., *The Prose of Philip Freneau,* esp. 196–202.

91. François August René, vicomte de Chateaubriand, *Travels in America and Italy,* quotation is from p. 98; Curti, *The Growth of American Thought,* 141–48, 238–44; Roderick Nash, *Wilderness and the American Mind,* 78–83; and Charles Leroy Sanford, "The Concept of the Sublime in the Works of Thomas Cole and William Cullen Bryant," 438–48.

92. Arthur A. Ekirch Jr., *Man and Nature in America,* 47–69; Nash, *Wilderness,* 84–95; Henry David Thoreau, "Walking," 672; and Ralph Waldo Emerson, "Nature," 1:15.

93. K. Thomas, *Man and the Natural World,* 192.

94. Henry E. Lowood, "The Calculating Forester: Quantification, Cameral Science, and the Emergence of Scientific Forestry Management in Germany," 315–42, on which this section is based; and Wilhelm Gottfried von Moser, *Grundsätze Forstöekonomie,* 1–93.

95. Harold K. Steen, *History of Sustained-Yield Forestry: A Symposium,* esp. 3–15, 170–201.

Chapter 10

1. Michael Williams, *Americans and Their Forests: A Historical Geography,* 353–61.

2. George Perkins Marsh, *Man and Nature: Or, Physical Geography As Modified by Human Action,* 251.

3. The figures from Rentzsch's *Der Wald* are quoted in U.S. Department of Agriculture, *Annual Report of the Commissioner of Agriculture,* 1872, 45. For a good review of European forest culture and preservation, see U.S. Government, *Forestry in Europe: Report from the Consuls of the United States.*

4. For an introduction to changes in German forests, see Winfried Schenk, "Fundamental Changes in the Forest Landscapes of Lower Franconia (Germany) in the 19th Century," 249–58; Ekkhard Liehl and Wolf Dieter Sick, *Der Schwarzwald: Beiträge zur Landeskunde,* 129–80; and the classic work of Franz Heske, *German Forestry.* For the Mediterranean see John R. McNeill, *The Mountains of the Mediterranean World: An Environmental History,* 286–324, 349–50.

5. H. Colman, *The Agriculture and Rural Economy of France, Belgium, Holland and Switzerland,* 23.

6. See G. Debien, *En Haut-Poitou: Défricheurs au travail, XVᵉ–XVIIIᵉ siècles;* Denis Woronoff, "La 'dévastation révolutionaire' des forêts," 44–52; and Edward A. Allen, "Deforestation and Fuel Crisis in Pre-Revolutionary Languedoc, 1720–1789," 463–68.

7. Based on Hugh D. Clout, *Agriculture in France on the Eve of the Railway Age,* 157, and *The Land of France, 1815–1914,* 124, Colman, *Agriculture and Rural Economy,* 23–24, quotations are from p. 24; Jean Bossière, "La consommation parisienne de bois et les sidèurgies périphériques: essai de mise en parallèle (milieu XVᵉ–milieu XIXᵉ siècles)," 35–37, 49; and E. Allen, "Deforestation and the Fuel Crisis," 468–71. See M. de Sainte-Colombe, "Notice sur l'instruction publique: l'agriculture et l'industrie de l'arrondissement d'Yssingeaux," 116–17, for descriptions of the destruction of Bellecombe forest and woodlands of Saint-Etienne.

8. Based on Clout, *Agriculture in France,* 159–60, and *Land of France,* 130–32.

9. Arthur Louis Dunham, *The Industrial Revolution in France, 1815–1848,* 136–37.

10. Michel Devèze, "Les forêts françaises à la veille de la Révolution de 1789," 241–72; Denis Woronoff, "La crise de la forêt française pendant la Révolution et L'Empire: L'indicateur sidérurgique," 3–17, and *L'industire sidérique en France pendant la Révolution et l'Empire;* and H. Séle, "Les forêts et la question du déboisement en Bretagne à la fin de l'ancien régime," 1–28, 360–76.

11. David B. Young, "Forests, Mines and Fuel: The Question of Wood and Coal in Eighteenth-Century France," 328–36, esp. 332; and F. Crouzet, "England and France in the Eighteenth Century: A Comparative Analysis of Two Economic Growths," 168–69.

12. Dunham, *Industrial Revolution in France,* 86–87; quotation is from p. 91.

13. Clout, *Land of France,* 132, and *Agriculture in France,* 159–65.

14. G. Marsh, *Man and Nature,* 206–7, 212, and generally 200–33; Adolphe Jérôme Blanqui, "Rapport sur la situation économique des départments de la frontière des Alpes: Isère, Hautes-Alpes, Basses-Alpes et Var," 363–64. For the continuation of these practices into more modern times, see J. Blache, "L'essartage, ancienne practique culturale dans les Alpes Dauphinoises," 553–75; and E. Liouville, "Les tailles des Ardennes," 257–67.

15. Based on G. Marsh, *Man and Nature,* 210; Clout, *Land of France* 124; Henri Joseph Baudrillart, "Mémoire sur le déboisement des montagnes," 65–78; and Blanqui, *Du déboisement des montagnes.*

16. Arthur Young, *Travels during the Years 1787, 1788, and 1789 . . . in the Kingdom of France,* 2:17; Adolphe Jérôme Blanqui, "Rapport sur la situation . . . ," 364; and G. Marsh, *Man and Nature,* 201, 210.

17. Andrée Corvol, *L'homme aux bois . . . ,* esp. 291–315; and Tamara Louise Whithed, "The Struggle for the Forests in the French Alps and Pyrenees, 1860–1940," 1–9, 84–135. For the foundation and history of the school at Nancy, see Michel Devèze, "L'Ècole Nationale des Eaux et Forêts," 237–40; and Corvol, *L'homme aux bois,* 247–48. In 2000, Whited turned her dissertation into a much fuller study entitled *Forests and Peasant Politics in Modern France.*

18. Whithed, "Struggle for the Forest," 60–74. See also Peter Sahlins, *Forest Rites: The War of the Demoiselles in Nineteenth Century France;* and John Merriman, "The Demoiselles of the Ariège, 1829–1831," 87–113. For an account of common land lost and the destruction of the pine forests, see Christian Fruhauf, *Forêt et société de la forêt paysanne à la forêt capitaliste en pays de sault sous l'ancien régime (vers 1670–1791),* 39–106; and for specific afforestation programs see Paul de Boixo, *Les forêts et le réboisement dans le Pyrénées-Orientale.*

19. Based on Clout, *Agriculture in France,* 166–67, and *Land of France,* 126–33. See also Keith Sutton, "Reclamation of Wasteland during the Eighteenth and Nineteenth Centuries," 273–85.

20. For the subsequent history of French forests, see G. Huffel, *Economie forestière;* and the highly readable account of Louis Badré, *Histoire de la forêt française,* 131–276.

21. Jean Antoine Fabre, *Essai sur la théorie des torrens et des rivières;* and Alexandre Surell, *Étude sur les torrents des Hautes-Alpes.* Extracts from these works and many other early nineteenth-century treatises on déboisement and floods are usefully extracted and translated in one of John Croumbie Brown's many compilations, *Réboisement in France: Or, Records of the Replanting of the Alps. Cevennes, and the Pyrennes with Trees, Herbage and Bush* (1880). A good case study is in C. Rabot, "Le déboisement dans la vallée d'Aspe et son influence sur le régime des cours d'eau," 207–8.

22. Clarence F. Glacken, *Traces on the Rhodian Shore: Nature and Culture in Western Thought from Ancient Times to the End of the Eighteenth Century,* 702.

23. See J. Richards, "Land Transformation," 164, and M. A. Tsvetkov, as calculated in French, "Russians and the Forest," 40.

24. Denis J. B. Shaw, "Southern Frontiers of Muscovy, 1550–1700," 119–39; I. Stebelsky, "Agriculture and Soil Erosion in the European Forest-Steppe," 46–56; and French, "Russians and the Forest," 30, for both quotations, and "The Making of the Russian Landscape," 51, for Golenishchev-Kutuzov.

25. French, "Making of the Russian Landscape," 47–48, based on the work of A. S. Fat'yanov, "Opyt analiza istorii razvitiya pochvennogo pokrova Gor'kovskoy oblsati," in *Pochvenno-geograficheskiye issledovaniya i ispol'zovamiye aerofotos'yemki v kartirovanii pochy*, 1–171 (Akadamie Nuak SSSR, 1959). For the other reconstructions see French, "Russians and the Forest," 39.

26. M. Ludwick de Tegoborski, *Commentaries on the Productive Forces of Russia*, 1:76–79; quotation is from p. 76.

27. Based on French, "Making of the Russian Landscape," 47–50, and "Russians and the Forest," 30–39, quotation on Gom is from p. 37.

28. French, "Russians and the Forest," quotation on Tsvetkov is from p. 38, and "Making of the Russian Landscape," quotation is from p. 50.

29. A. F. Rondski and N. I. Shafranov, "Forestry," 3:311–46.

30. V. O. Kluchevsky, *A History of Russia*, 5:244–45.

31. For example, G. H. Andrews, *Modern Husbandry: A Practical and Scientific Treatise on Agriculture*, 45–55.

32. Thomas Southcliffe Ashton, "The Discoveries of the Darbys of Coalbrookdale," 11–25; Michael W. Flinn, "William Wood and the Coke Smelting Process," 66–71; and John U. Nef, *The Rise of the British Coal Industry*, 1:215–23. Ashton's classic work, *Iron and Steel in the Industrial Revolution*, 1–59, although written as early as 1924, is still highly relevant. The 1968 edition has an excellent, updated bibliography.

33. George Hammersley, "The Charcoal Iron Industry and Its Fuel, 1540–1750," 611–13, quotations are from pp. 612 and 608; H. R. Schubert, *History of the British Iron and Steel Industry from c. 450 B.C. to A.D. 1775*, 218–22; C. K. Hyde, *Technological Change and the British Iron Industry, 1700–1870*, 28, 104. For an excellent study of woodland management for ironworks and the exaggeration about depletion, see J. M. Lindsay, "Charcoal Iron Smelting and Its Fuel Supply: The Example of Lorn Furnace, Argyllshire, 1753–1876," 259–82.

34. Quotations from George Hammersley, "Did It Fall or Was It Pushed? The Foleys and the End of the Charcoal Iron Industry in the Eighteenth Century," 85–86. See also Hyde, *Technological Change*, 65 et seq.; and Schubert, *History of the British Iron and Steel Industry*, 331–35.

35. T. C. Banfield, *Industry of the Rhine*, 2:65. For rising prices see 1:109–15.

36. Phyllis Deane and W. A. Cole, *British Economic Growth, 1689–1959*, 75; and Bruce R. Mitchell, *Abstract of British Historical Statistics*, 225.

37. Quoted in Noel David G. James, *A History of English Forestry*, 148. There are many additional details on forest demands and forest policy during this time on pp. 139–88.

38. The following paragraphs on naval supplies, unless otherwise stated, are based on Robert Greenhalgh Albion, *Forests and Sea Power*, 349–69.

39. A. Siddiqi, "The Business World of Jamsedjee Jeejeebhoy," 301–24.

40. J. M. W. Turner, *The Fighting Tameraire Tugged to Her Last Berth to Be Broken Up*, National Gallery, London. The painting has recently been the subject of an extensive study; see Jean Egerton, *Turner: The Fighting Temeraire*. For the Battle of Hampton Roads, see Albion, *Forests and Sea Power*, 408–9.

41. To a certain extent the words *timber* and *lumber* are interchangeable, but there were nuances of meaning: *lumber* being partly prepared timber, and *timber* being wood prepared for building, carpentry, etc. *Lumber* is favored in the United States, *timber* in Britain.

42. Arthur R. M. Lower, *Great Britain's Woodyard: British America and the Timber Trade, 1763–1867,* 18.

43. For the fraught problem of reconciling measures and standardization, the authority is J. R. McCulloch, *A Dictionary, Practical, Theoretical and Historical, of Commerce and Commercial Navigation,* which is also rich in information on harbors, trade routes, and trade treaties in the trade. A modern version is R. F. A. Mallinson and R. Grugeon, *Timber Trade Practice.* See also Sven-Erik Åström, *From Tar to Timber: Studies in Northeast European Forest Exploitation and Foreign Trade, 1660–1860,* 201–4 on "Nomenclature," and note 45 below for dimensions.

44. Based on Elizabeth Boody Schumpter, *English Overseas Trade Statistics, 1697–1808,* 52–59; and Sven-Erik Åström, "English Timber Imports from Northern Europe in the Eighteenth Century," 12–32. For nineteenth-century import figures, see R. Fitzgerald and J. Grenier, *Timber: A Centenary History of the Timber Trade Federation, 1892–1992,* app. 3 and 4, and p. 18.

45. For the Norwegian trade see Heinz S. K. Kent, *War and Trade in Northern Seas: Anglo-Scandinavian Economic Relations in the Mid-Eighteenth Century,* 39–58. So important did Memel become that it provided the standard for European prices of fir timber. Similarly, the St. Petersburg standard of 120 deals or planks of $1.5 \times 11 \times 12$ in (165 ft^3 or 4.673 m^3, or $2,750$ bf, in American terms) eclipsed the standards of Kristiana, Drammen, Gothenburg, and even Quebec, and became the international standard. Traditionally, on both sides of the Atlantic, deals were sold by the long hundred or great hundred, i.e., 120 pieces.

46. Robert Johnston, *Travels through Part of the Russian Empire and the Country of Poland along the Southern Shores of the Baltic,* 75.

47. Sven-Erik Åström, "Britain's Timber Imports from the Baltic, 1775–1830: Some New Figures and Viewpoints," 57–71. For the opposite story of the declining trade to Holland, see Jan Thomas Linblad, "Structural Change in the Dutch Trade with the Baltic in the Eighteenth Century," 193–207.

48. J. Potter, "The British Timber Duties, 1815–1860," 122–36. For good summaries of the duties and their effect on Canadian exports, see Graeme Wynne, *Timber Colony: A Historical Geography of Early Nineteenth Century New Brunswick,* 30–33; and Lower, *Great Britain's Woodyard,* 45–96.

49. Åström, "English Timber Imports," 30.

50. For example, D. R. Williams, "Merchanting in the First Half of the Nineteenth Century: The Liverpool Timber Trade," 103–21, and "Bulk Carriers and Timber Imports: The British North American Trade and the Shipping Boom of 1824–5," 373–82. Bryan Latham, *Timber: Its Development and Distribution: A Historical Survey,* has much useful information.

51. Wynne, *Timber Colony,* 152.

52. For Finland see Åström, *From Tar to Timber,* esp. 9–11, 183–87, and "British Timber Imports," 67; for Sweden see Lars Östlund, "Exploitation and Structural Changes in the North Swedish Boreal Forest," *1800–1992,* 6–22.

53. Peter Fisher, *History of New Brunswick,* 72.

54. Wynne, *Timber Colony,* 150.

55. Arnold Guyot, *The Earth and Man: Lectures on Comparative Physical Geography in Its Relation to the History of Mankind,* 208.

56. Unless otherwise acknowledged, the following pages on clearing and wood use in North America are based on M. Williams, *Americans and Their Forests.*

57. Timothy Dwight, *Travels in New-England and New-York in 1821*, letter 13, 2:321–22; John Taylor, "Journal of Rev. John Taylor, Missionary, on Tour through the Mohawk and Black River Counties, in 1802," 3:1148.

58. Jeremy Belknap, *The History of New Hampshire*, 3:95. For calculations on the time expended in clearing, see Martin I. Primack, "Land Clearing under Nineteenth Century Techniques: Some Preliminary Calculations," 485–96. For later nineteenth–century developments see Harry Thompson, *Costs and Methods of Clearing Land in Western Washington*, 13–59; and F. M. White and E. R. Jones, *Getting Rid of Stumps*, 5–31.

59. Daniel Millikin, "The Best Practical Means of Preserving and Restoring the Forests of Ohio," 319.

60. Orsamus Turner, *Pioneer History of the Holland Purchase of Western New York*, plates opposite 562, 564, 565, 566.

61. Adam Hodgson, *Letters from North America written during a Tour in the United States and Canada*, 1:339–40, 2:318–19. Not until the clearing of the Amazonian forests in the later twentieth century have similar sensations of unreality been voiced. See chapter 14 of the present text.

62. H. Clifford Darby, "The Clearing of the Woodland in Europe," 183.

63. Basil Hall, *Travels in North America in the Years 1827 and 1828*, 2:135, and *Forty Etchings from Sketches made with the Camera Lucida in North America in 1827 and 1829*.

64. Isaac Weld, *Travels through the States of North America and Provinces of Upper and Lower Canada during the Years 1795, 1796, and 1797*, 1:31–41, 231–3, quotation is from 1:232–33; and Hodgson, *Letters from North America*, 1:396–97.

65. Earl H. Frothingham, *The Status and Value of Farm Woodlots in the Eastern United States*; and John Fraser Hart, "Loss and Abandonment of Cleared Farm Land in the Eastern United States," 58:417–40.

66. Reynolds and Pierson, *Fuel Wood Used in the United States, 1630–1930*. For other calculations, see Sam H. Schurr and Bruce C. Netschert, *Energy in the American Economy, 1850–1975: An Economic History of Its Study and Prospects*, 50 n. 6.

67. Arthur H. Cole, "The Mystery of Fuel Wood Marketing in the United States," 339–40.

68. Paul W. Gates, "Problems in Agricultural History," 34–6.

69. Erik F. Haites, James Mak, and Gary M. Walton, *Western River Transportation: The Era of Early Internal Development, 1810–1860*, 144–47; and David F. Schob, "Woodhawks and Cordwood: Steamboat Fuel on the Ohio and Mississippi Rivers, 1820–1860," 124–32.

70. A. William Hoglund, "Forest Conservation and Stove Inventions, 1789–1850," 2–8.

71. Andrew Fuller, *The Forest Tree Culturist: A Treatise on the Cultivation of American Forest Trees*, 12.

72. Bruce R. Mitchell, *International Historical Statistics: The Americas, 1750–1988*, 528–39; and U.S. Bureau of the Census, *Historical Statistics of the United States from Colonial Times to 1957*, 2:372 and tables Q323, Q288.

73. Leo Marx, *The Machine in the Garden: Technology and the Pastoral Ideal in America*.

74. Millikin, "Preserving and Restoring the Forests of Ohio," 532–36; John H. Klippart, "Condition of Agriculture in Ohio in 1876," 577; Nathaniel Egleston in USDA, *Annual Report of the Commissioner of Agriculture* (1883), 445, and (1885), 185; and M. G. Kern, *The Relation of Railroads to Forest Supplies and Forestry*, 14.

75. For an authoritative discussion on the railroad tie question, see Sherry Olson, *The Depletion Myth: A History of the Railway Use of Timber*; and Kern, *Relation of Railroads to Forest Supplies*, 40.

76. Olson, *Depletion Myth*, 6, quoting H. Miller in *The Forester* 3 (1 January 1897).

77. Richard H. Schallenberg, "Evolution, Adaption, and Survival: The Very Slow Death of the American Charcoal Iron Industry," 341–59.

78. Based on J. Peter Lesley, *The Iron Manufacturer's Guide to the Furnaces, Forges, and Rolling Mills of the United States,* 30–37, 129–30, 249–50; with additional information from Ken Warren, *The American Steel Industry, 1850–1970: A Geographical Interpretation,* 20–62.

79. See Janice Carson Beatley, "The Primary Forests of Vinton and Jackson Counties, Ohio," 96–108; and James M. Ransom, *The Vanishing Ironworks of the Ramapos: The Story of the Forges, Furnace, and Mines of the New Jersey-New York Border Area.*

80. See chapter 7, p. 191 of the present text. See also Beatley, "The Primary Forests," 96–108.

81. James Hall, *Statistics of the West,* 100–101. For the importance of wood in American life see Brooke Hindle, ed., *America's Wooden Age: Aspects of Its Early Technology;* and Charles Van Ravenswaay, "America's Age of Wood," 49–66. John Perlin, *A Forest Journey: The Role of Wood in the Development of Civilization,* 324–61 has some additional details on wood use in America after the Revolutionary War.

82. Henry B. Steer, *Lumber Production in the United States, 1799–1946.* A board foot (bf) is a common measure of timber in the United States. It is 1 ft × 1 ft × 1 in, and 12 bf equals 1 ft³, or 0.02832 m³.

83. See chapter 9, pp. 259–64 of the present text. The working out of these developments on the ground are dealt with in Evelyn M. Dinsdale, "Spatial Patterns of Technological Change: The Lumber Industry of Northern New York," 258–65.

84. For a fuller explanation of these stages see Michael Williams, "The Clearing of the Forests," 156–57.

85. Robert F. Fries, *Empire in Pine: The Story of Lumbering in Wisconsin, 1830–1900,* 243–44; Barbara E. Benson, "Logs and Lumber: The Development of the Lumber Industry in Michigan's Lower Peninsula, 1837–1870"; and James B. Smith, "Lumbertowns in the Cutover: A Comparative Study of the Stage Hypothesis of Urban Growth."

86. Rollin Lynde Hartt, "Notes on a Michigan Lumber Town," 107.

87. The classic reviews are Stewart H. Holbrook, *Burning an Empire: The Story of American Forest Fires;* and Stephen J. Pyne, *Fire in America: A Cultural History of Wild Land and Rural Fire,* esp. 199–218. In his *Report on the Forests of North America (Exclusive of Mexico)* of 1880, Charles Sprague Sargent calculated (pp. 491–92) that 110.3 million acres were burned, and damage to property totaled $25.4 million in that year alone.

88. W. A. Hartman and J. D. Black, *Economic Aspects of Land Settlement in the Cut-Over Region of the Great Lakes States.*

89. Int. al., Vernon R. Carstenson, *Farms or Forests: Evolution of State Land Policy in Northern Wisconsin, 1850–1932;* James I. Clark, *Farming the Cutover: The Settlement of Northern Wisconsin;* and Lucile Kane, "Selling the Cut-Over Lands in Wisconsin," 236–47.

90. Ralph Clement Bryant, *Logging: The Principles and General Methods of Operation in the United States,* 172–80, 196–260, 343–93; and Nollie W. Hickman, *Mississippi Harvest: Lumbering in the Longleaf Pine Belt, 1840–1915,* 153–83, 212–32.

91. Reginald D. Forbes, "The Passing of the Piney Woods," 133.

92. Ruth A. Allen, *East Texas Lumber Workers: An Economic and Social Picture, 1870–1950;* and George Creel, "The Feudal Towns of Texas," 76–78.

93. Forbes, "Passing of the Piney Woods," 131–36, 185, quotation is from p. 136; and George A. Stokes, "Lumbering and Western Louisiana Landscapes," 250–66.

94. U.S. Congress, Senate, *Report of the National Conservation Commission,* 2:639; and U.S. Forest Service, *Timber Depletion, Lumber Prices, Lumber Exports, and Concentration of Timber Ownership,* 20.

95. But see the evidence of environmental concern in early nineteenth-century colonial India in chapter 11.

96. See Totman, *The Green Archipelago: Forestry in Pre-Industrial Japan,* 83–115. For developments in silviculture and plantations, see 116–48.

97. Ibid., 83–115; quotation is from p. 89.

98. Ibid., 184; italics in the original.

99. Walter Clay Lowdermilk and T. L. Li, "Forestry in Denuded China," 127; and Ernest Henry Wilson, *A Naturalist in Western China with Vasculum, Camera and Gun,* 2:15.

100. Quotation from Evelyn S. Rawski, "Agricultural Development in the Han River Highlands," 68.

101. Samuel Adrian M. Adshead, "An Energy Crisis in Early Modern China," 20–28; Robert Fortune, *Three Years' Wanderings in the Northern Provinces of China,* 312; and Arthur H. Smith, *Chinese Characteristics* 22.

102. Egbert H. Walker, "The Plants of China and Their Usefulness to Man," 351; and E. H. Wilson, *A Naturalist in Western China,* 15. For a deeper discussion on aesthetics and nature in China, see Edward H. Schafer, "The Conservation of Nature under the T'ang Dynasty," 279–308.

103. G. Marsh, *Man and Nature,* 49; T. A. Coghlan, *The Timber Resources of New South Wales,* 1; and R. Kaleski, "Our Forests in Earlier Days: Some Political History," 323–26. Unless otherwise stated, the following paragraphs on Australia are based on Michael Williams, "Clearing the Woods," 115–26.

104. For the distribution of forests and their characteristics see Geoffrey W. Leeper, ed., *The Australian Environment,* 44–67, 120–30; and D. A. N. Cromer, "Australia," 573–90. The lower figure of 238 million ha is from Leeper, *Australian Environment;* the higher of 243.88 million ha from K. F. Wells, N. H. Wood, and Peter Laut, *Loss of Forests and Woodlands in Australia: A Summary by State, Based on Rural Local Government Areas,* fold-out map.

105. Wells, Wood, and Laut, *Loss of Forests and Woodlands in Australia.*

106. R. T. Archer and P. J. Carrol, "Dairy Framing," 297–333; and Samuel M. Wadham and G. L. Wood, *Land Utilization in Australia,* 61–73, 111–12.

107. Archer and Carrol, "Dairy Farming," 303.

108. T. A. Coghlan, *Picturesque New South Wales: An Illustrated Guide for the Settler and the Tourist,* 90; and A. M. Laughton and T. S. Hall, *Handbook to Victoria,* 41, 331.

109. W. E. Abbott, "Ringbarking and Its Effects," 41; and "Forest Destruction in New South Wales," 49–54.

110. For a thorough discussion of mallee clearing, see Michael Williams, *The Making of the South Australian Landscape,* 124–77.

111. Kenneth B. Cumberland, " A Century's Change: Natural to Cultural Vegetation in New Zealand," 531. Andrew H. Clark's *Invasion of New Zealand by People, Plants and Animals* is full of details on aspects of the revolutionary changes to the landscape of these islands.

112. M. Williams, "Clearing the Woods," 122–25; Thomas R. Cox, *Mills and Markets: A History of the Pacific Coast Lumber Industry to 1900,* 81–100, 130–37; and Michael M. Roche, "The New Zealand Timber Economy, 1840–1935," 295–313.

Chapter 11

1. These and the following figures are based on John F. Richards, "Land Transformation," 164; and Paul Demeny, "Population," 42.

2. Kent H. Redford, "The Ecologically Noble Savage," 24–29; Murdo J. Macleod, "Ex-

ploitation of Natural Resources in Colonial Central America: Indian and Spanish Approaches," quotation is from p. 31.

3. Leslie E. Sponsel, "The Environmental History of Amazonia: Natural and Human Disturbances, and the Ecological Transition," 233–35. The revisionist view of a "golden age" is put forward in, for example, Ramachandra Guha and Madhav Gadgil, "State Forestry and Social Conflict in British India," 141–77; and Gadgil and Guha, *This Fissured Land: An Ecological History of India*, 113–15.

4. For a thorough discussion of regional names and variations in agricultural technique, see Harley Harris Bartlett, "Fire, Primitive Agriculture and Grazing in the Tropics," 693–94. See also his massive compilation of literary evidence in *Fire in Relation to Primitive Agriculture and Grazing in the Tropics: Annotated Bibliography*.

5. William Marsden, *The History of Sumatra, Containing an Account of the Government, Laws, Customs . . .* , 61–64. See also Peter James Begbie, *The Malayan Peninsula Embracing its History, Customs, Manners, and Customs of the Inhabitants . . .* , 439–41; and John Crawfurd, *History of the Indian Archipelago*, 1:344.

6. Orator Fuller Cook, "Vegetation Affected by Agriculture in Central America," 1–30, quotation is from p. 6, and "Milpa Agriculture, a Primitive Tropical System," quotation is from p. 307.

7. Ivor Wilks, "Land, Labour, and the Forest Kingdom of Asante: A Model of Early Change," 487–534; David and Charles Livingstone, *Narrative of an Expedition to the Zambesi and its Tributaries; and of the Discovery of Lakes Shirwa and Nyasa, 1858–64*, 112, 468–69, 572; and David Livingstone, *The Last Journals of David Livingstone in Central Africa . . .* , 30, 60, 64, 76, 82, 116.

8. Marsden, *The History of Sumatra*, 61, 62. For more contemporary views in the same vein, see John Bodley, ed., *Tribal Peoples and Development Issues: A Global Overview*, and his *Victims of Progress*, 12–21.

9. Hugh Low, *Sarawak: Its Inhabitants and Production, being Notes during a Residence in that Country with His Excellency Mr Brooke*, 225–26.

10. For America see William T. Hagan, "Justifying Dispossession of the Indian: The Land Utilization Argument," 65–80; Christopher Vecsey and Robert W. Venables, eds., *American Indian Environments: Ecological Issues in Native American History*, xix, 3–5; Robert A. F. Berkhofer Jr., *The White Man's Indian: Images of the American Indian from Columbus to the Present*, 44–49; and Roy Harvey Pearce, *Savages and Civilization: A Study of the Indian and the American Mind*, 135–68. For attitudes on "progress" in Asia see Begbie, *Malayan Peninsula*, 154–55; and J. Baird Callicott and Roger T. Ames, eds., "Epilogue: On the Relation of Idea and Action," 279–89.

11. Anthony Reid, "Humans and Forests in Pre-Colonial Southeast Asia," 93–111.

12. H. Bartlett, "Fire, Primitive Agriculture and Grazing," 696.

13. Henry O. Forbes, *A Naturalist's Wanderings in the Eastern Archipelago: A Narrative of Travel and Exploration from 1878 to 1883*, 214, 132.

14. Quoted in James Fairhead and Melissa Leach, *Reframing Deforestation: Global Analysis and Local Realities: Studies in West Africa*, 50. For other descriptions see 69–75, 112–18.

15. Mangesh Venktesh Nadkarni, Syed Ajmal Pasha, and L. S. Prabhakar, *Political Economy of Forest Use and Management*, 30–36, with additional material from Richard Tucker, "Forest Management and Imperial Politics: Thana District, Bombay, 1823–1887," 275–76; and Das Dipakranjan, *Economic History of the Deccan from the First to the Sixth Century A.D.*, 105–15. For other examples in the Maratha states, see John F. Richards and Michelle B. McAlpin, "Cotton Cultivating and Land Clearing in the Bombay Deccan and Karnatak: 1818–1920," 71–5; and H. B. Vashishta, *Land Revenue and Public Finance in Maratha Administration*, 138–46, for precolonial forest regulations and taxation.

16. Edward Backhouse Eastwick, *A Glance at Sind before Napier; or, Dry Leaves from Young Egypt,* 24. For the subsequent history and significance of the *shikargahs,* see Richard H. Grove, *Green Imperialism: Colonial Expansion, Tropical Island Edens, and the Origins of Environmentalism, 1600–1800,* 455–60.

17. Ifran Habib, "The Geographical Background," 4–6; quotation is from p. 5.

18. Benjamin Heyne, *Tracts, Historical and Statistical, on India . . . Tract XIX, Cuddapa to Hyderabad in the Year 1809,* 302. Hugh Cleghorn, who was a surgeon based at Shimoga, commented in 1848 on the wholesale destruction of forests by shifting cultivators. See also Dietrich Brandis, *Indian Forestry,* 16; and Edward Percy Stebbing, *The Forests of India,* 1:38.

19. Sherry H. Olson, "The Robe of the Ancestors: Forests in the History of Madagascar," 177–79; and Hubert Jules Deschamps, *Histoire de Madagascar,* 37–45. For fuller details, see the treatment in Stephen J. Pyne, *Vestal Fire: An Environmental History Told through Fire, of Europe and Europe's Encounter with the World,* 436–42.

20. Mahesh Rangarajan, "Production, Desiccation and Forest Management in the Central Provinces, 1850–1930," 588–89.

21. H. Bartlett, "Fire, Primitive Agriculture and Grazing," 700, 703.

22. André Aubréville, *Contribution à la paleohistoire des forêts de l'Afrique tropicale,* 37–38.

23. André Aubréville, "Dix années d'expériences sylvicoles en Côte d'Ivoire," 1–4, 289–302, and *Climats, forêts et désertification de l'Afrique tropicale,* 313–17, 323. Other works in a similar vein are James Robert Ainslie, *The Physiography of Southern Nigeria and Its Effect on the Forest Flora of the Country,* 14, 22–25, 28, 30–32; Jean-Paul Harroy, *Afrique: Terre qui meurt. La dégradation des sols africains sous l'influences de la colonisation,* 71–88, 385–415; Pierre Gourou, *Les pays tropicaux: Principes d'une géographie humaine et economique,* 29, 48; and Edward P. Stebbing, *The Encroaching Sahara: The Threat to the West African Colonies.*

24. Fairhead and Leach, *Reframing Deforestation,* 1–22, 182–97; quotation is from 21. See chapter 12 of the present text for a fuller analysis of the arguments.

25. Henri Humbert, "Principaux aspects de la végétation à Madagascar. La destruction d'une flore insulaire par le feu," 1–79; and Henri Perrier de la Bâthie, "La végétation malgache," 1–266. For the revisionist interpretation see Christian A. Kull, "Deforestation, Erosion, and Fire: Degradation Myths in the Environmental History of Madagascar," which questions the severity of the deforestation. Quotation is from S. Olson, "Robe of the Ancestors," 174.

26. H. Bartlett, "Fire, Primitive Agriculture and Grazing," 700–2.

27. Ibid., 702. See also chapters 2 and 3 of the present text, which address human changes to tropical vegetation in the Amazon region.

28. Warren Dean, *With Broadax and Firebrand: The Destruction of the Brazilian Atlantic Forest,* 39–40; and Alfred Métraux, "The Revolution of the Ax," 30. As late as 1914, Algot Lange (*The Lower Amazon,* 1:228) found some Indians of Tupi linguistic stock on the Moju River: "Until last year," he wrote, "the work of felling trees had been performed with diorite axes, shaped from the stones found in the rapids, but after the visit of the rubber workers the Indians acquired through their hunters a few good steel axes of good make, and they were quite expert in handling them"—with devastating effect on the forest.

29. For a fuller discussion on colonial trade and the role of islands see pp. 156–60 of chapter 6 and p. 215 of chapter 8.

30. For Banks's comments on St. Helena see J. C. Beaglehole, ed., *The "Endeavour" Journal of Sir Joseph Banks, 1768–1772,* 2:265–66; and for the wider context see Richard H. Grove, "Conserving Eden: The (European) East India Companies and Their Environmental Policies on St. Helena, Mauritius, and in Western India, 1660 to 1854," 327–38. For a more detailed treatment see Grove, *Green Imperialism,* 168–263, 309–79.

31. Since this chapter was written, the massive 1,036-page volume *Nature and the Orient: The Environmental History of South and Southeast Asia,* edited by Richard H. Grove, Vinita Damodoran, and Satpal Sangwan, has appeared. Despite its wide-ranging title, over four-fifths of the work is concerned with forest policy in India, and some of the chapters have been published before. I have not been inclined to change anything in my original account, but have benefited from some additional perspectives contained in the chapters by Rajan, Flint, and Rangarajan, and have added references to chapters that exemplify points already made.

32. For the general administrative spread see Barraclough, ed., *The Times Atlas of World History,* 234–35; for population calculations see Morris David Morris, "The Population of All-India, 1800–1951," 309–13.

33. Richard P. Tucker, "The Depletion of Indian Forests under British Imperialism: Plantations, Foresters, and Peasants in Assam and Kerala," 118; and A. Singh Rawat, *History of Forestry in India,* 37.

34. See Mahesh Rangarajan, "Imperial Agendas and India's Forests: The Early History of Indian Forestry, 1800–1878," 147–49; and Edward W. Said, *Orientalism.* For similar conclusions see Grove, Damodaran, and Sangwan, eds., *Nature and the Orient,* 3.

35. Quoted from Richards and McAlpin, "Cotton Cultivating and Land Clearing," 75.

36. Berthold Ribbentrop, *Forestry in British India,* 60. For details see A. Siddiqi, "Agrarian Depression in Uttar Pradesh," 175, 177, and *Agrarian Change in a Northern Indian State: Uttar Pradesh, 1819–1833,* 173; and Kirti N. Chaudhuri, "Indian International Economy in the Nineteenth Century," 41.

37. The role of the surgeon-environmentalists in India is pursued exhaustively in Grove, *Green Imperialism,* 380–473, quotation is from p. 392; and Satpal Sangwan, "From Gentlemen Amateurs to Professionals: Reassessing the Natural Science Tradition in Colonial India, 1780–1840," 210–36, for other perspectives. For Boussingault see his "Memoir concerning the Effect of which Clearing the Land has in Diminishing the Quantity of Water in the Streams of a District," 85–106; and for Volney and others in North America see chapter 9, pages 269–71 in the present text. For comments on the EIC, see Daniel R. Headrick, *The Tentacles of Progress: Technology Transfer in the Age of Imperialism, 1850–1940;* quotation is from p. 59.

38. Hugh Cleghorn, Forbes Royle, R. Baird Smith, and R. Strachey, "Report of the Committee appointed by the British Association to Consider the probable Effects in a Oeconomical and Physical Point of View of the Destruction of Tropical Forests," quotations are from pp. 80, 86, 82, and 85; and Grove, *Green Imperialism,* 453. But see the cautionary note of David Lowenthal regarding claims about the origins of conservation in India versus the United States in "Nature and Morality from George Perkins Marsh to the Millennium," 14.

39. Sir Thomas Munro, "Timber Monopoly in Malabar and Canara," 1:178–87. For the earlier shipbuilding precedents see A. Jan Qaisar, "Shipbuilding in the Mughal Empire during the Seventeenth Century," 149–70; Ruttonji Ardeshir Wadia, *The Bombay Dockyard and the Wadia Master Builders;* and A. Siddiqi, "The Business World of Jamsedjee Jeejeebhoy," 320–23.

40. Ribbentrop, *Forestry in British India,* 65–66; and Munro, "Timber Monopoly in Malabar and Canara," 1:185.

41. For the 1822 to 1850 history of the regulation and exploitation in the Madras and Bombay Presidencies, see Stebbing, *The Forests of India,* 1:71–87; quotations are from p. 71.

42. Cleghorn et al., "Report of the Committee"; quotations are from pp. 82, 83, 87, and 88–89. For additional details on the teak forests see the many reports reprinted in Stebbing, *The Forests of India,* 1:125–91, 231–64; and for a detailed case study see Ajay Skaria, "Timber Conservancy, Desiccation, and Scientific Forestry: The Dangs, 1840–1920," 591–635.

43. Cleghorn et al., "Report of the Committee," 80, 91.

44. Grove, *Green Imperialism,* 399–407.

45. Reginald Heber, *Narrative of a Journey through the Upper Provinces of India from Calcutta to Bombay, 1824–5 . . . ,* 1:406, 497.

46. William Henry Sleeman, *Rambles and Recollections of an Indian Official,* 1:73–77, 196–97, 433–52.

47. Michael Mann, "Ecological Change in North India: Deforestation and Agrarian Distress in the Ganges-Jamna Doab, 1800–1850," 201–20; quotation is from p. 211. For other examples of forest destruction in northern India at this time, see Richard P. Tucker, "The British Colonial System and the Forests of the Western Himalayas, 1815–1914," 150–56.

48. Letter, A. Gibson to J. D. Hooker, 1 March 1841, quoted in Grove, *Green Imperialism,* 343.

49. Grove, *Green Imperialism,* 431–36.

50. Stebbing, *The Forests of India,* 1:120–21. Stebbing's four volumes are a compendious collection of many of the basic documents on Indian forests.

51. Jacques Pouchepadass, "British Attitudes towards Shifting Cultivation in Colonial South India: A Case Study of South Canara District 1800–1920," 123–51.

52. R. Tucker, "Forest Management and Imperial Politics," 272–85; and Indra Munshi Saladanha, "Colonial Forest Regulations and Collective Resistance: Nineteenth-Century Thana District," 708–33.

53. Grove, *Green Imperialism,* 441–62, with additional details from Stebbing, *The Forests of India,* 1:205–325.

54. See the brilliant recent work by Martin H. Edney, *Mapping an Empire: The Geographical Construction of British India, 1765–1843.*

55. Quotation from Evelyn A. Smythies, *India's Forest Wealth,* 6. Other examples of forest destruction abound in Cleghorn, *The Forests and Gardens of South India.*

56. John F. Richards, Edward S. Haynes, and James R. Hagen, "Changes in the Land and Human Productivity in Northern India, 1870–1970," 534.

57. Sainthill Eardly-Wilmot, *Forest Life and Sport in India,* 9.

58. John F. Richards and Elizabeth P. Flint, "A Century of Land-Use Change in South and Southeast Asia," tables on 17, 20, 34, and 36. The regions used in this study are as follows: *South Asia* = Bangladesh, India, and Sri Lanka; *Mainland Southeast Asia* = Myanmar (Burma), Thailand, Cambodia, Laos, and Vietnam; *Insular Southeast Asia* = Malaysia, Brunei, Singapore, Indonesia, and the Philippines.

The regions used in the 1990 study by Richards and reproduced in table 11.1 are: *South Asia* = Afghanistan, Bangladesh, Bhutan, Myanmar, India, Nepal, Pakistan, and Sri Lanka; and *South East Asia* = Brunei, Cambodia, East Timor, Indonesia, Laos, Malaysia, Philippines, Thailand, and Vietnam. The data are derived from *World Resources Review, 1987.*

59. All aspects of the railways of India have been analyzed in great detail. The most accessible general accounts are in Vinod Dubey, "Railways," 327–47; John M. Hurd, "Railways," 737–61; and Headrick, *The Tentacles of Progress,* 49–95.

60. Quoted in Daniel Thorner, "Investment in Empire: British Railway and Steam Shipping Enterprises in India, 1825–1849," 96.

61. Quoted in Headrick, *The Tentacles of Progress,* 64; and United Kingdom, House of Commons, "Minute by the Most Noble, the Governor-General; dated 20th April, 1853: Railways in India," *Parliamentary Papers* 76 (1852–53): 595.

62. Headrick, *The Tentacles of Progress,* 59; and Dubey, "Railways," 329, 334–35.

63. Based on Hurd, "Railways," 739; and Headrick, *The Tentacles of Progress,* 55, with ad-

ditional information from Morris D. Morris and Clyde B. Dudley, "Selected Railway Statistics for the Indian Subcontinent (India, Pakistan, Bangladesh), 1853–1946/7," 193–96.

64. Richards, Haynes, and Hagen, "Changes in the Land and Human Productivity," 523–48; and Richards, Hagen, and Haynes, "Changing Land Use in Bihar, Punjab and Haryana, 1850–1970," 699–732.

65. Michelle B. McAlpin, "Railroads, Prices, and Peasant Rationality: India, 1860–1900," 662–63, 683. See also John M. Hurd, "Railways and Expansion of Markets in India," 737–61; and Mukul Mukherjee, "Railways and Their Impact on Bengal's Economy, 1879–1920," 191–210, for the ironing out of commodity price fluctuations.

66. Michelle B. McAlpin, "Railroads, Cultivation Patterns, and Foodgrain Availability: India, 1860–1900," 46–47, 52–53.

67. McAlpin, "Railroads, Prices, and Peasant Rationality," 683; and Richards and McAlpin, "Cotton Cultivating and Land Clearing," 80.

68. Richards and McAlpin, "Cotton Cultivating and Land Clearing," 82–94; quotation is from p. 89, where the authors are quoting p. 297 of the *Gazetteer of the Bombay Presidency— Khandesh.* For other examples see Richards, Hagen, and Haynes, "Changing Land Use in Bihar, Punjab and Haryana," 699–732; and Richards, Haynes, and Hagen, "Changes in the Land and Human Productivity," 523–48.

69. Stebbing, *The Forests of India,* 2:99; Ribbentrop, *Forestry in British India,* 61; and Robert Wallace, *India in 1887 as Seen by Robert Wallace,* 296.

70. Quoted in Stebbing, *The Forests of India,* 2:99.

71. Richards, Hagen, and Haynes, "Changing Land Use in Bihar, Punjab and Haryana," 720.

72. The number of sleepers per mile varies. Dietrich Brandis in his "Memorandum on the Supply of Railway Sleepers of the Himalayan Pines impregnated in India," 373, calculates 1,800 per mile; Stebbing, in *The Forests of India,* 2:175, 311, calculates between 2,000 and 2,200; and Edward Davidson, in *Railways of India: With an Account of their Rise, Progress and Construction, Written with the Aid of Records of the India Office,* says 1760.

73. G. L. Molesworth, "Durability of Indian Railway Sleepers, and the Rules for Marking Them," 97.

74. E. Davidson, *Railways of India,* 108–9; and Brandis, "Memorandum on the Supply of Railway Sleepers," 365.

75. Based on Brandis, "Memorandum on the Supply of Railway Sleepers," 365–85; and Stebbing, *The Forests of India,* 3:373–74.

76. Stebbing, *The Forests of India,* 3:51 for the Sind; see also 2:284–85.

77. "Iron-Making in India," 207; and Hitesranjan Sanyal, "The Indigenous Iron Industry of Birbhum," 101–8.

78. Figures in this section and table 11.5 are based on John Richards, Edward Haynes, James Hagen, Elizabeth Flint, Joseph Arlinghaus, Judith B. Dillon, and A. Lindsey Reber, *Changing Land Use in Pakistan, Northern India, Bangladesh, Burma, Malaysia, and Brunei, 1880–1980,* 585–714, 753–82.

79. John Augustus Voelcker, *Report on the Improvement of Indian Agriculture,* 237.

80. R. Tucker, "The Depletion of Indian Forests," 121–28, with additional information from Amalendu Guha, "Colonisation of Assam: Second Phase, 1840–1859," 289–317, and "A Big Push without a Take-Off: A Case Study of Assam, 1871–1901," 201–20.

81. J. Sykes Gamble, "The Darjeerling Forests." The fold-out map shows how the hill forest of Darjeerling was being altered.

82. R. Tucker, "The Depletion of Indian Forests," 128–40, with additional information from

James Welsh, *Military Reminiscences: Extracted from a Journal of Nearly Forty Years' Active Service in the East Indies,* 2:14–15; and Clements R. Markham, "On the Effect of the Destruction of the Forests in the Western Ghats of India on the Water Supply," 266. For a more extended discussion on the effect of clearing on rainfall, see Markham's fuller paper in *Journal of the Royal Geographical Society,* 1866. Contemporary studies of the Nilgiri Hills suggest that Markham's ideas were essentially correct. See V. M. Meher-Homji, "Repercussions of Deforestation on Precipitation in Western Karnataka, India," 385–400.

83. George Bidie in "On the Effects of Forest Destruction in Coorg," 74–83, and his extended treatment in the *Journal of the Royal Geographical Society,* 77–90.

84. Quoted in Victoria Glendinning, *Trollope,* 437.

85. John Capper, *Old Ceylon—Sketches of Ceylon in Olden Times,* 32–34.

86. Based on John F. Richards, "Agricultural Impacts in Tropical Wetlands: Rice Paddies for Mangroves in South and South East Asia," 219–24, with additional details from William Wilson Hunter, *A Statistical Account of Bengal,* 1:285–309. Quotation is from p. xiii. For fuelwood collection see 1:309–14, and for reclamation, 1:328–35. It is possible that Hunter's account was exaggerated; see Paul Greenough, "Hunter's Drowned Land: An Environmental Fantasy of the Victorian Sunderbans," 237–72.

87. Voelcker, *Indian Agriculture,* 135.

88. Bidie, "Effects of Forest Destruction," 88.

89. Voelcker, *Indian Agriculture,* 102. For other remarks on the use of dung for fuel, see 151–52.

90. For a detailed view of the "problem" of shifting cultivation, see Guha and Gadgil, "State Forestry and Social Conflict," 151–57; and a very balanced view in Rangarajan, "Imperial Agendas and India's Forests," 152–58.

91. Ribbentrop, *Forestry in British India,* 72. See also 76 et seq. for the subsequent organization of the department. Elizabeth Flint, "Deforestation and Land Use in Northern India, with a Focus on Sal *(Shorea robusta)* Forests, 1880–1980," 440–41 has a good summary of the department.

92. Rangarajan, "Imperial Agendas and India's Forests," 162.

93. Ramachandra Guha, "An Environmental Debate: The Making of the 1878 Forest Act," 65–82; quotations are from Wallace, *India in 1887,* 297, 302.

94. B. Henry Baden-Powell, "The Political Value of Forest Conservancy," 280–88; quotations are from pp. 280 and 285. Baden-Powell was the author of the massive and authoritative *Land Systems of British India,* which appeared in 1892.

95. Voelcker, *Indian Agriculture,* 140; and Ribbentrop, *Forestry in British India,* 97–105.

96. Vinita Damodaran, "Famine in a Forest Tract: Ecological Change and the Causes of the 1897 Famine in Chota Nagpur, Northern India," 132–7; quotation is from p. 133. See also the discussion on pp. 360–61 and figure 11.1 above.

97. Guha and Gadgil, "State Forestry and Social Conflict," 141–51; and Rangarajan, "Imperial Agendas and India's Forests," 147–67.

98. For greater details see chapter 9 of the present text, and also Ravi Rajan, "Imperial Environmentalism or Environmental Imperialism? European Forestry, Colonial Foresters and the Agendas of Forest Management in British India, 1800–1900," 343–72.

99. For the importance of the revenue motive see Smythies, *India's Forest Wealth,* 8–9; and Ribbentrop, *Forestry in British India,* 223–26.

100. K. Sivaramakrishnan, "Colonialism and Forestry in India: Imagining the Past in Present Politics," 3–40.

101. Paul Bairoch, *The Economic Development of the Third World since 1900,* 93–94, 121–22.

102. Michael Adas, "Colonization, Commercial Agriculture and the Destruction of the Deltaic Rainforests of British Burma in the late Nineteenth Century," 95–111; and additional material from J. F. Richards, "Agricultural Impacts in Tropical Wetlands," 304–15, 331–35.

103. James W. Grant, *The Rice Crops of Burma*, 203–4.

104. J. F. Richards, "Agricultural Impacts in Tropical Wetlands," 228–31.

105. Peter Boomgaard, "Forest Management and Exploitation in Colonial Java, 1677–1879," 11–12. See also Nancy L. Peluso, "The History of State Forest Management in Colonial Java," 65–69, and her larger work, *Rich Forests, Poor People: Resources Control and Resistance in Java*, for additional material.

106. Based on Dennis M. Roth, "Philippines Forests and Forestry: 1565–1920," 31–37; and Frederick L. Wernstedt and Joseph E. Spenser, *The Philippine Island World*, 43–47.

107. George P. Ahern, "The Lesson of Forestry in the Philippine Islands," 492.

108. David M. Kummer, *Deforestation in the Postwar Philippines*, 39–73.

109. Raymond F. Watters, *Shifting Cultivation in Latin America*, 3–49.

110. Based on table 11.1. Also useful is Richard A. Houghton, D. S. Lefkovitz, and David L. Skole, "Change in the Landscape of Latin America between 1850 and 1985. I. Progressive Loss of Forests," 143–72.

111. For an informative essay by timber merchants on getting mahogany throughout the Central American isthmus and Caribbean, see Chaloner and Fleming, *The Mahogany Tree: Its Botanical Character, Qualities and Uses . . . in the West Indies and Central America*, 19–36.

112. Except where otherwise noted or where there are specific quotations, the following paragraphs are based on Warren Dean's preliminary study of the region, "Deforestation in Southeastern Brazil," 50–67, and his posthumous masterpiece, *With Broadax and Firebrand*, esp. 70–90, 112–16, 119–20, 134–38, 144–67, 191–212. John R. McNeill's short overview, "Agriculture, Forests, and Ecological History, Brazil, 1500–1984," 122–33, is useful also.

113. Quoted in Dean, *With Broadax and Firebrand*, 97.

114. Karl Friedrich P. von Martius, *Flora Brasiliensis: Enumeratio plantarum in Brasilia hactenus detectarum . . . Argumentum fasciculorum*, LXXVI–LXXVII; and Gustavo A. B. da Fonseca, "The Vanishing Brazilian Atlantic Forest," 21–22. Quotations are from Dean, *With Broadax and Firebrand*, 114–15, 116.

115. Quoted in Dean, *With Broadax and Firebrand*, 138.

116. Warren Dean, *Brazil and the Struggle for Rubber: A Study in Environmental History*, 4–36. Rubber was not really viable until after 1940.

117. These destruction rates are from Dean, *With Broadax and Firebrand*, 176–77, and are based on (1) a production of 2.6 million tons over a period of 150 years, at 50 tons per ha = 1,000 km^2 × a 20-year cycle = 7,500 km^2; and (2) approx. 7 kg of wood fuel per kg of sugar = 18,000,000 tons @ 200 tons per ha = 900 km^2.

118. Dean, "Deforestation in Southeastern Brazil," 61–63; and Preston E. James, "The Coffee Lands of Southeastern Brazil," 225–43.

119. For details of the cycle and techniques of cultivation see Warren Dean, *Rio Claro: A Brazilian Plantation System, 1820–1920*, 24–46; and Stanley J. Stein, *Vassouras: A Brazilian Coffee County, 1850–1900*, 29–53. Quotation is from Dean, *With Broadax and Firebrand*, 185.

120. The classic account of the expanding coffee frontier is Pierre Monbeig, *Pionniers et planteurs de São Paulo*, 148–73, 191–200.

121. Dean (*With Broadax and Firebrand*, 188) calculates a similar figure of 7,200 km^2 for the earlier date of 1888, "the equivalent of 300 million tons of forest biomass gone up in smoke"; but in his "Deforestation in Southeastern Brazil," 63, he calculates that 30,000 km^2 may have been affected "over the course of the nineteenth century."

122. Dean, *With Broadax and Firebrand*, 191, 211.

123. K. Oedekoven, "The Vanishing Forest," 184–85.

124. Adam Smith, *An Inquiry into the Nature and Causes of the Wealth of Nations*, 590.

Chapter 12

1. Asa Briggs and Daniel Snowman, eds., *Fins de Siècle: How Centuries End, 1400–2000*, 157–96; E. Louis Peffer, *The Closing of the Public Domain: Disposal and Reservation Policies, 1900–1950*; and Oscar F. O. Wilde, *The Picture of Dorian Gray*, 19.

2. D. K. Fieldhouse, *Economics and Empire, 1830–1914*; David S. Landes, *The Unbound Prometheus: Technological Change and Industrial Development in Western Europe from 1750 to the Present*; and Donald W. Meinig, "A Macrogeography of Western Imperialism: Some Morphologies of Moving Frontiers of Political Control," 213–40.

3. Carl O. Sauer, "The Prospect for Redistribution of Population," 8. See also Michael Williams, "The End of Modern History?" 275–300.

4. Élisée Reclus, *La Terre*; J. R. Whitaker, "World View of Destruction and Conservation of Natural Resources," 149; and Herbert Spencer, *The Principles of Biology*, 506–7. For a review of this period, 1900–1950, see Clarence Glacken, "Changing Ideas of the Habitable World," 81–88; and M. Williams, "The End of Modern History?" 275–300.

5. Alexandre Woeikof, "De l'influence de l'homme sur la terre," 97–114, 193–215, quotation is from p. 97; Ernst Friedrich, "Wesen und Geographische Verbreitung der 'Raubwirtschaft,'" 68–72, 92–95; and Nathaniel S. Shaler, "The Economic Aspects of Soil Erosion," "Earth and Man: An Economic Forecast," and "The Exhaustion of the World's Metals." Quotation is from "The Future of Power," 31.

6. Carl O. Sauer, "Destructive Exploitation in Modern Colonial Expansion," 494–99. See also William W. Speth, "Carl Ortwin Sauer on Destructive Exploitation," 145–60.

7. Carl O. Sauer, "Theme of Plant and Animal Destruction in Economic History," 765–75 and "The Agency of Man on Earth," 68.

8. Donald Worster, *Nature's Economy: A History of Ecological Ideas*, 378; and Aldo Leopold, "The Land Ethic," 224–25. Frederic Clements was professor of biology at the University of Nebraska and, with Henry C. Cowles of the University of Chicago, dominated thinking about ecology between about 1915 and 1940. Cowles's theories of plant succession were paralleled by Clements's theories of dynamic ecological succession and the organismic character of plant formations, leading to a vaguely stable, final climax type of vegetation. For the formative ideas about ecology that came out of Nazi Germany during the 1930s, see Anna Bramwell, *Ecology in the 20th Century: A History*, 104–32.

9. David Lowenthal, "Awareness of Human Impacts: Changing Attitudes and Emphases," quotation is from p. 124. See also M. Williams, "The End of Modern History?" 293–96.

10. Frederick Starr, "American Forests: Their Destruction and Preservation," 219.

11. Andrew S. Fuller, *The Forest Tree Culturist: A Treatise on the Cultivation of American Forest Trees*, 5.

12. See Roy M. Robbins, *Our Landed Heritage: The Public Domain, 1776–1936*, 302; U.S. Department of Agriculture, *Annual Report of the Commissioner of Agriculture*, 1872, 45; 1878, 245; Michael Williams, "The Last Lumber Frontier," 224–50; and Charles S. Sargent, *Report on the Forests of North America (Exclusive of Mexico)*, 10.

13. See Michael Williams, *Americans and Their Forests: A Historical Geography*, 331–52 for industrial impacts and 357–61 for agricultural clearing. The raw consumption figures that under-

lay the diagrams in Marion Clawson, "Forests in the Long Sweep of American History," were kindly supplied to the author by Dr. Clawson.

14. M. Williams, *Americans and Their Forests*, 395–409; and Gregory A. Barton, "Empire Forestry and American Environmentalism," 187–204.

15. Robbins, *Our Landed Heritage*, 320–24 for the bills; A. D. Rodgers, *Bernhard Edward Fernow: A Story of North American Forestry*, 223–24; and *Statutes at Large*, 2:34–36. Other comments are in Peffer, *Closing of the Public Domain*, 14–17; Samuel P. Hays, *Conservation and the Gospel of Efficiency: The Progressive Conservation Movement, 1890–1920*, 36–37; and John Ise, *The United States Forest Policy*, 119–42.

16. The phrases are contained in a letter to Pinchot from the Secretary of Agriculture, James Wilson, in Hays, *Conservation and the Gospel of Efficiency*, 1–4. See also Jenks Cameron, *The Development of Governmental Forest Control in the United States*, 239–40.

17. Theodore Roosevelt, "The Forest in the Life of the Nation," 8–9.

18. William B. Greeley, *Forests and Men*, 64; Robbins, *Our Landed Heritage*, 337; and Martin N. McGeary, *Gifford Pinchot, Forester-Politician*, 54–55.

19. M. Williams, *Americans and Their Forests*, 417–21.

20. U.S. Congress, Senate, *Report of the National Conservation Commission*, esp. vol. 2; and Ise, *Forest Policy*, 153.

21. U.S. Congress, Senate, *Report of the National Conservation Commission*, 2:188–89; and Gifford Pinchot, *The Fight for Conservation*, 14–15, 74.

22. For "The moral issue," see Pinchot, *The Fight for Conservation*, 79–80; and Hays, *Conservation and the Gospel of Efficiency*, 122–27.

23. The Ballinger-Pinchot controversy, its context, and wider administrative implications must be among the most written-about episodes in American conservation history. See especially James L. Bates, "Fulfilling American Democracy: The Conservation Movement, 1907–1921"; Alpheus T. Mason, *Bureaucracy Convicts Itself: The Ballinger-Pinchot Controversy of 1910*; James L. Penick, *Progressive Politics and Conservation: The Ballinger-Pinchot Affair*; Harold T. Pinkett, *Gifford Pinchot: Public and Private Forester*; and Rose M. Stahl, *The Ballinger-Pinchot Controversy*. For Pinchot's own account see his *Breaking New Ground*, 430–33.

24. M. Williams, *Americans and Their Forests*, 423–24; and Hays, *Conservation and the Gospel of Efficiency*, 42.

25. Roderick Nash, *Wilderness and the American Mind*, 161–81.

26. Gifford Pinchot, "Forest Devastation: A National Danger and a Plan to Meet It," 925, 914, 922, 915. For the wider context of Pinchot's broadside see M. Williams, *Americans and Their Forests*, 443–44.

27. U.S. Forest Service, *Timber Depletion, Lumber Prices, Lumber Exports, and Concentration of Timber Ownership*. See Samuel Trask Dana, *Forest and Range Policy: Its Development in the United States*, 125–26.

28. M. Williams, *Americans and their Forests*, 446.

29. U.S. Forest Service, *Timber Depletion, Lumber Prices*, 70; E. A. Zeigler, "Rate of Forest Growth," 2:203–69; M. Williams, *Americans and Their Forests*, 438–40; and William B. Greeley, "The Relation of Geography to Timber Supply," caption to fig. 1, p. 3. The three maps were first produced in Greeley's article, and subsequently included in Charles Paullin, ed., *Atlas of the Historical Geography of the United States*, plates 3A–C.

30. Raphael Zon, *The Forest Resources of the World*, esp. 3–15, and "South American Forest Resources and Their Relation to the World's Timber Supply," 483–92.

31. Raphael Zon and William N. Sparhawk, *The Forest Resources of the World*; Stephen

Haden-Guest, John K. Wright, and Eileen M. Teclaff, eds., *A World Geography of Forest Resources;* and Richard Torunsky, ed., *Weltforstatlas—World Forestry Atlas—Atlas des forêts du monde—Atlas forestal del mundo.*

32. Gifford Pinchot, foreword to Zon and Sparhawk, *Forest Resources,* vii–viii.

33. Norman J. Schmaltz, "Raphael Zon: Forest Researcher," 24–39. In 1923 Zon became head of the Lake States Forest Experiment Station in St. Paul, Minnesota, where he remained for the rest of his professional life.

34. Zon and Sparhawk, *Forest Resources,* 1–44, quotation is from p. 3; and Bruno F. A. Dietrich, "European Forests and Their Utilization," 143–45.

35. Zon and Sparhawk, *Forest Resources,* 68–73, quotation is from p. 68; and Zon, "South American Forest Resources," 484–85, quotation is from p. 485.

36. The figures for the temperate world between 1900 and 1920 need to be treated with some caution, as surprisingly there is disagreement as to the exact figures for 1900, which is used as the basis of change. World Resources Institute, *World Resources* 1987:272 gives 2,208 × 10⁶ ha in 1900, falling to 2,168 × 10⁶ ha in 1920; J. F. Richards's figures ("Land Transformation," p. 164) jump between 1850 and 1920. For independent evidence of reversion in the eastern United States in the early decades of the twentieth century, see C. I. Hendrickson, "The Agricultural Land Available for Forestry," 1:151–69.

37. See chapter 11, pp. 1–3.

38. Paul Demeny, "Population," table 3.2, p. 43. These comparisons ignore North America's annual increment of population, which was 2 to 3 percent during the nineteenth century because of mass immigration.

39. Jan G. Laarman, "Export of Tropical Hardwoods in the Twentieth Century," 148–50; and United Kingdom, Forestry Commission, *Fourth Annual Report of the Forestry Commissioners,* 33–34.

40. Pinchot, in the foreword to Zon and Sparhawk, *Forest Resources,* viii; and Tom H. Gill, *Tropical Forests of the Caribbean,* 285, 10.

41. Zon, "South American Forest Resources"; and Zon and Sparhawk, *Forest Resources,* 563, 568, 573, 579, 594, 657, 769, 789, 692.

42. Charles Lathrop Pack (1857–1937) had made much money from southern pine investments, and was one of Pinchot's "old crusaders," acting as advisor to the Conference of Governors in 1908 and generally endowing and supporting forestry and conservation issues. With Tom H. Gill he coauthored *Forests and Mankind.*

43. Gill, *Tropical Forests;* quotations are from pp. 59, 60, 67, 66, and 73, respectively.

44. The following paragraphs on Brazil are based on Warren Dean, *With Broadax and Firebrand: The Destruction of the Brazilian Atlantic Forest,* 239–64, unless otherwise stated.

45. Ibid., 255.

46. D. R. Heinsdjik, O. Soares, and H. Haufe, "The Future of Brazilian Pine Forests," 1:669–73; M. S. Lowden, "Fire Crisis in Brazil," 42–44, 46; R. Maack, "Devastação das matas do Paraná," 22–32; and Hilgard O'Reilly Sternberg, "Man and Environmental Change in South America," 413–45.

47. John R. McNeill, "Deforestation in the Araucaria Zone of Southern Brazil, 1900–1983," 15–32; and Zon, "South American Forest Resources," 486.

48. Lord Hailey, *An African Survey: A Study of Problems Arising in Africa South of the Sahara,* 1652.

49. Zon and Sparhawk, *Forest Resources,* 814; and Homer L. Shantz and C. F. Marbut, *The Vegetation and Soils of Africa,* 6, 30–1.

50. Graham Vernon Jacks and Robert Orr Whyte, *The Rape of the Earth: A World Survey of Soil Erosion,* esp. 247–63; quotations are from pp. 249 and 257.

51. A. Harold Unwin, *West African Forests and Forestry,* 160; quotation is from p. 92.

52. For full descriptions of West African vegetation, see Brian Hopkins, *Forest and Savanna: An Introduction to Tropical Plant Ecology with Special Reference to West Africa,* 20–57; and R. J. Harrison Church, *West Africa: A Study of the Environment and of Man's Use of It,* 65–79.

53. A. Chevalier, "Essai d'une carte botanique forestière et pastorale de l'A. O .F."; André Aubréville, "La forêt coloniale: les forêts de l'Afrique-Occidentale française," and *Climats, forêts et désertification de l'Afrique tropicale,* 311; Jaques-George Adam, "Les reliques boisés et les essences des savanes dans la zone préforestière en Guinée française," 22–66; and Raymond Schnell, "Essai de synthèse biogéographie sur la région forestière d'Afrique occidentale," 29–35.

54. Paul Sears, *Deserts on the March.*

55. Edward P. Stebbing, "The Encroaching Sahara: The Threat to the West African Colonies," 506–24, *The Forests of West Africa and the Sahara: A Study of Modern Conditions,* 22–9, and "The Man-Made Desert of Africa: Erosion and Drought." For contrary views see L. Dudley Stamp, "The Southern Margins of the Sahara: Comments on some Recent Studies of the Question of Desiccation in West Africa," 297–300, which pointed out that although the sand did move, it was not the menacing advance from "outside" that Stebbing made out, but was caused by desiccation that took place from "within" as a result of overclearing in the areas of forested light soils.

56. Church, *West Africa,* 82.

57. Douglas C. Dorward and A. I. Payne, "Deforestation, the Decline of the Horse, and the Spread of the Tsetse Fly and Trypanosomiasis *(nagana)* in Nineteenth-Century Sierre Leone," 239–56; and C. G. Knight, "The Ecology of African Sleeping Sickness," 23–44.

58. Based on Virginia Thompson and Richard Adloff, *French West Africa,* 342; Unwin, *West African Forests,* 25; Sir Harry Johnston, *Liberia,* 2:524; Church, *West Africa,* 72; and B. Hopkins, *Forest and Savanna,* 39–42, 54–57.

59. Unwin, *West African Forests,* 66, 424.

60. James Fairhead and Melissa Leach, "Rethinking the Forest-Savanna Mosaic," 105–21, and their larger, more detailed work, *Misreading the African Landscape: Society and Ecology in a Forest-Savanna Mosaic,* esp. 1–54, 237–78.

61. James Fairhead and Melissa Leach, *Reframing Deforestation: Global Analysis and Local Realities: Studies in West Africa.*

62. For the broader picture of metallurgy see W. Cline, *Mining and Metallurgy in Negro Africa;* and Duncan E. Miller and Nikolaas J. Van de Merwe, "Early Metal Working in Sub-Saharan Africa: A Review of Recent Research," 1–36.

63. Robert Sutherland Rattray, "The Iron Workers of Akpafu," 431–35; and Ivor Wilks, "Land, Labour, and the Forest Kingdom of Asante: A Model of Early Change," 272.

64. Candice Goucher, "Iron is Iron 'til It Is Rust: Trade and Ecology in the Decline of West African Iron Smelting," 179–83, and "The Impact of German Colonial Rule on the Forests of Togo," 60.

65. The main conclusions of this critique were arrived at by the author in a draft of this chapter in 1996, but have benefited from the penetrating comments of Fairhead and Leach in their *Reframing Deforestation,* 129–33, especially the inclusion of data on the effect of timescales.

66. Based on Fairhead and Leach, *Reframing Deforestation,* 133–35.

67. For failures in Togoland see Goucher, "The Impact of German Colonial Rule." Ashanti quotation is from K. Boaten, "Commercial Agriculture in Asante," 46–47.

68. Henry Ward-Price, *Land Tenure in the Yoruba Provinces,* par. 139, 149 et seq.; and Robert Galleti, K. D. S. Baldwin, and I. O. Dina, *Nigerian Cocoa Farmers: An Economic Survey of Yoruba Cocoa Farming Families,* 19, 107.

69. For greater detail see John F. Richards and Elizabeth P. Flint, "A Century of Land-Use Change in South and Southeast Asia," 31–39; and B. Bowonder, "Deforestation in India," 223–38.

70. James Elliott Defebaugh, *History of the Lumber Industry in America,* 1:272.

71. M. Clawson, "Forests in the Long Sweep," 1168–74; and William B. Greeley, "Reduction of the Timber Supply through Abandonment or Clearing of Forest Lands," 633–44.

72. See p. 389 above.

73. Zeigler, "Rate of Forest Growth," 203–69.

74. M. Clawson, "Forests in the Long Sweep," 4; and Zeigler, "Rate of Forest Growth," 219, 222–23.

75. William B. Greeley, "Timber: Mine or Crop ?" 84–93; quotation is from p. 86.

76. USDA Forest Service, *A National Plan for American Forestry,* 1:222–25, 242; and USDA Forest Service, *An Analysis of the Timber Situation in the United States, 1952–2030,* 134 (table 6.13), 136 (table 6.14), and 137, and *An Analysis of the Timber Situation in the United States, 1989–2040,* 53 (table 43), 54 (table 45).

77. Greeley, *Forests and Men,* 15–29; and U.S. Bureau of the Census, *Historical Statistics of the United States from Colonial Times to 1957,* pt. 1: tables L48 and L49.

78. U.S. Bureau of the Census, *Historical Statistics,* tables L32–L43 and accompanying notes.

79. M. Clawson, "Forests in the Long Sweep," 5.

80. Hendrickson, "Agricultural Land Available," 1:151–69; John Fraser Hart, "Loss and Abandonment of Cleared Farm Land in the Eastern United States," 417–40 for the situation 1910 to 1959; and the author's own calculations for 1959 to 1979.

81. John Fraser Hart, "Land Use Change in a Piedmont County," 514–16.

82. V. P. Tseplyaev, *Lesnoye Khozyaystvo SSSR,* 144, quoted in Brenton Barr, "Perspectives on Deforestation in the U.S.S.R," 245.

83. Unless otherwise acknowledged, the following paragraphs are based on Barr, "Deforestation in the U.S.S.R," 230–61.

84. J. W. Miller Jr., "Forest Fighting on the Eastern Front in World War II," 186–202.

85. Boris Kamarov, *The Destruction of Nature in the Soviet Union,* 217–18.

86. For a good discussion on neglect in resource management, see Philip R. Pryde, *Conservation in the Soviet Union,* 92–100; and W. R. J. Sutton, "The Forest Resources of the U.S.S.R.: Their Exploitation and Their Potential," 110–38.

87. For contemporary trends see Charles A. Backman, *The Forest Industrial Sector of Russia: Opportunity Awaiting.*

88. Per Stjernquist, *Laws in the Forests: A Study of Public Direction of Private Forestry,* 68–113; quotation is from p. 69.

89. Unless otherwise acknowledged, the following paragraphs are based on Torsten Hägerstrand and Ulrik Lohm, "Sweden," 614–17.

90. Lars Östlund, "Exploitation and Structural Changes in the North Swedish Boreal Forest, 1800–1992," 13–23, and especially fig. 4 on p. 17.

91. For greater detail of the local arrangement, see Sven Gaunitz, "Resource Exploitation on the North Swedish Timber Frontier in the Nineteenth and the Beginning of the Twentieth Centuries," 140–44; and Stjernquist, *Laws in the Forests.*

92. See Per Linder and Lars Östlund, "Structural Changes in Three Mid-Boreal Swedish Forest Landscapes, 1885–1996," 9–19; Lars Östlund, L. Zackrisson, and A.-L. Axelsson, "The His-

tory and Transformation of Scandinavian Boreal Forest Landscape since the Nineteenth Century," 1198–1206; and Östlund, "Exploitation and Structural Changes."

93. Haägerstrand and Lohm, "Sweden," 620.

94. For an excellent case study of ecological changes through over management in the Blue Mountains, Washington, U.S.A., see Nancy Langston, *Forest Dreams, Forest Nightmares: The Paradox of Old Growth in the Inland West*, 157–24.

Chapter 13

1. Peter Munz, *Our Knowledge of the Growth of Knowledge: Popper or Wittgenstein?* 316.

2. Paul. W. Richards, "The Tropical Rain Forest," 59.

3. Which of the many causes was crucial is hotly debated. See John Darwin, *The End of the British Empire: The Historical Debate.*

4. Fairfield H. Osborn, "Over-Population and Genetic Selection," 43; André Maurois, "The Good Life," 178–79; Earle Parker Hanson, *New Worlds Emerging*, x–xi; and David Lowenthal, "Awareness of Human Impacts: Changing Attitudes and Emphases," 125–26.

5. Paul R. Ehrlich and Anne H. Ehrlich, *The Population Bomb;* and Paul Demeny, "Population," 47.

6. Warren S. Thompson, "The Spiral of Population," 985.

7. Fairfield Osborn, *The Limits of the Earth*, 153, 164; and Norman Myers, "Tropical Deforestation; Rates and Patterns," 37.

8. Ester Boserup, *The Conditions of Agricultural Growth: The Economics of Agrarian Change under Population Growth*, and *Population and Technological Change: A Study of Long Term Trends.*

9. B. Bowonder, "Deforestation in Developing Countries," 171–92; Norman Myers, *Conversion of Tropical Moist Forests,* and *Deforestation Rates in Tropical Forests and their Climatic Implications*, 13–52; and Alan Grainger, *Controlling Tropical Deforestation*, 49–68.

10. For an excellent overview see William B. Meyer and Billie L. Turner II, "Human Population Growth and Global Land-Use/Cover Change," 51–56. David M. Kummer, *Deforestation in the Postwar Philippines*, 9–37; and Thomas K. Rudel, *Tropical Deforestation: Small Farmers and Land Clearing in the Ecuadorian Amazon*, 13–41 on "A Theory of Tropical Deforestation," also have extensive analyses of causes.

11. For example, Ehrlich and Ehrlich, *The Population Bomb;* and Paul R. Ehrlich and John P. Holdren, eds., *The Cassandra Conference: Resources and the Human Predicament.*

12. For example, Roger A. Sedjo and Marion Clawson, "Global Forests," 128–67; Julian Simon, *The Ultimate Resource;* and Robert Repetto, ed., *The Global Possible: Resources, Development and the New Century.*

13. W. J. Baumol and W. E. Oates, *The Theory of Environmental Policy*, 22–56.

14. Piers M. Blaikie, *The Political Economy of Soil Erosion in Developing Countries;* Piers M. Blaikie and Harold C. Brookfield, *Land Degradation and Society*, esp. 157–85, 239–50; David Harvey, "Population, Resources and the Ideology of Science," 256–77; Peter D. Little, Michael M. Horowitz, and A. Endre Nyerges, eds., *Lands at Risk in the Third World: Local-Level Perspectives*, 5–13 and passim; Michael Redclift, *Sustainable Development: Exploring the Contradictions*, 52–78; and Paul Sweezy and Harry Magdoff, "Capitalism and the Environment," esp. 7–10 on the destructive role of capitalism.

15. Int. al., Val Plumwood and R. Routley, "World Rainforest Destruction: The Social Factors," 4–22; and Erik Eckholm, *Losing Ground: Environmental Stress and World Food Prospects,* 42. For more recent reviews see Grainger, *Controlling Tropical Deforestation*, 92–102; and

Katrina Brown and David W. Pearce, eds., *The Causes of Tropical Deforestation,* esp. 10–21. Quotation is from Erik Eckholm, *Planting for the Future: Forestry for Human Needs,* 16.

16. Robert Repetto, *Forests for the Trees?: Government Policies and the Misuse of Forest Resources;* Robert Repetto and Malcolm Gillis, eds., *Public Policies and the Misuse of Forest Resources,* esp. 1–41; and Jack Westoby, *The Purpose of Forests: Follies of Development.*

17. Julia C. Allen and Douglas F. Barnes, "The Causes of Deforestation in Developing Countries," 163–84; Matti Palo, G. Mery, and J. Salmi, "Deforestation in the Tropics: Pilot Scenarios Based on Quantitative Analyses," 1:53–106; and Matti Palo, "Population and Deforestation," 42–56. See also Brown and Pearce, *Causes of Tropical Deforestation,* 18–21, for a list of over a dozen other econometric analyses exploring relationships.

18. Ana Doris Capistrano, "Tropical Forest Depletion and the Changing Macroeconomy, 1967–85," 68–85; James Kahn and Judith McDonald, "International Debt and Deforestation," 56–67; Alan Grainger, "Modelling Deforestation in the Humid Tropics," 3:51–67; and Dal O. Didia, "Democracy, Political Instability, and Tropical Deforestation," 74.

19. World Resources Institute, *World Resources* 1986:70–75, 1988–9:71, and 1994–5:27–28, quotation is from p. 28.

20. Alan Grainger, "Modelling Deforestation in the Humid Tropics," 51–67.

21. Douglas Southgate, "The Causes of Land Degradation along 'Spontaneously' Expanding Agricultural Frontiers in the Third World," 93–101; Harold C. Brookfield, Francis J. Lian, Kwai-Sim Low, and Lesley Potter, "Borneo and the Malay Peninsula," 500, 506–7; and Kummer, *Deforestation in the Postwar Philippines,* 93–100.

22. Nicholas Guppy, "Tropical Deforestation: A Global View"; quotations are from pp. 932, 964.

23. Forest History Society, Durham, N.C., Gill MSS, box 10, 1931–36.

24. "Forest Resources of the World," 161–70; and John Boyd-Orr, "One World—One Forest," 2. Also useful for an immediate postwar view of global forests are Erich W. Zimmermann, "The Forest and Its Products," 398–420; and E. I. Kotok, "America's Role in Meeting World Timber Needs," 418–22.

25. Samuel P. Hays, *Beauty, Health and Permanence: Environmental Politics in the United States, 1955–1985,* 17.

26. Emilio F. Moran, "Deforestation and Land Use in the Brazilian Amazon," 8–11.

27. See chapter 9, pp. 269–71; Michael Williams, *Americans and Their Forests: A Historical Geography,* 370–72, 379–86; and Kenneth Thompson, "Forests and Climate Change in America: Some Early Views," 47–55.

28. See chapter 11 and Anton Chekov, *Uncle Vanya,* act 1.

29. George-Louis Leclerc, comte de Buffon, *Natural History, General and Particular: The History of Man and the Quadrupeds,* 2:341; M. Williams, *Americans and Their Forests,* 383–86; USDA Forestry Division, *Forest Influences,* 9–22, 23–186 passim, 187–91; and Benjamin Hibbard, *A History of Public Land Policies,* 411–23; quotation is from p. 421. See also Walter Kollmorgen, "The Woodsman's Assault on the Domain of the Cattleman," 221–23; William F. Raney, "The Timber Culture Acts," 209–19; and C. Barron McIntosh, "Use and Abuse of the Timber Culture Acts," 347–62.

30. Raphael Zon, "Forests and Water in the Light of Scientific Investigations," 51–55; quotation is from p. 55.

31. Raphael Zon, "The Relation of Forests in the Atlantic Plain to the Humidity of the Central States and Prairie Region," 139–53, and "Forests in Relation to Soil and Water," 399.

32. The prediction of Eneas Salati and Peter B. Vose in "Amazon Basin: A System in Equi-

librium," 129–38 was based on a mistaken interpretation of the preliminary work by Anne Henderson-Sellers and Victor Gornitz, "Possible Climatic Impacts of Land Cover Transformations, with Particular Emphasis on Tropical Deforestation," 231–57, which put the figure lower at 200 mm. For a full discussion of the debate see Anne Henderson-Sellers, "Effects of Change in Land Use on Climate in the Humid Tropics," 485.

33. Hilgard O'Reilly Sternberg, "Aggravation of Floods in the Amazon River As a Consequence of Deforestation?" 201–19. For the claim and counterclaim of flooding in the Peruvian Amazon see A. H. Gentry and J. Lopez-Parodi, "Deforestation and Increased Flooding in the Upper Amazon," 1354–56 and C. F. Nurdin and R. H. Meade, "Deforestation and Increased Flooding of the Upper Amazon," 426–47.

34. Paul B. Sears, *Deserts on the March,* and James C. Malin, "The Grassland of North America: Its Occupance and the Challenge of Continuous Reappraisals," 350–66, for traditional explanations. For different interpretations see Donald Worster, *Dustbowl: The Southern Plains in the 1930s;* and Mathew P. Bonnifield, *The Dust Bowl: Men, Dirt and Depression.* On the interpretation and narration of the evidence see William Cronon, "A Place for Stories: Nature, History, and Narrative," 1347–76.

35. Lowenthal, "Awareness of Human Impacts: Changing Attitudes and Emphases," 124. My debt to Lowenthal's perceptive work in the next few paragraphs is greater than this sole reference alone indicates. For an exhaustive examination of the Clementian paradigm, see Worster, *Nature's Economy,* 205–53.

36. Walter Clay Lowdermilk, "Lessons from the Old World to the Americas in Land Use," 413–15, 425–26; quotations are from pp. 413, 425. See also Lowdermilk and T. L. Li, "Forestry in Denuded China," 127–41, which had as its subtext a similar lesson for America of the consequences of profligate resource use.

37. M. C. Kellman, "Some Environmental Components of Shifting Cultivation in Upland Mindanao," 40–56; and R. Lal, "Deforestation of Tropical Rainforest and Hydrological Problems," 13140, "Deforestation and Soil Erosion," 299–315, and "Soil Degradation and Conversion of Tropical Rainforests," 137–54.

38. Lowenthal, "Awareness of Human Impacts," 124.

39. John S. Collis, *The Triumph of the Tree,* 246; and George Perkins Marsh, *Man and Nature: Or, Physical Geography As Modified by Human Action,* 465.

40. Carl Sagan, O. B. Toon, and J. B. Pollack, "Anthropogenic Albedo Changes and the Earth's Climate," 1365–66; Henderson-Sellers and Gornitz, "Possible Climatic Impacts of Land Cover Transformations," 231–57; Anne Henderson-Sellers and A. Wilson, "Surface Albedo Data for Climate Modeling," 1743–48; and Anne Henderson-Sellers, "A Commentary on Tropical Deforestation, Albedo and the Surface-Energy Balance," 135–38. For urban heat islands the classic study is H. E. Landsberg, *The Urban Climate.*

41. Jill Jäger and Roger G. Barry, "Climate," 345–46; and Henderson-Sellers, "Effects of Changes in Land Use on Climate," 475–87.

42. Sandra Postel, *Air Pollution, Acid Rain and the Future of Forests,* 7–22; quotation is from William W. Kellogg, "Mankind's Impact on Climate: The Evolution of Awareness," 113.

43. World Meteorological Organization, *Report of The International Assessment of the Role of Carbon Dioxide and Other Greenhouse Gases in Climatic Variation and Associated Impacts.*

44. Robert L. Peters and Joan D. S. Darling, "The Greenhouse Effect and Nature Reserves," 707–17; and Stephen H. Schneider, "The Greenhouse Effect: Science and Policy," 771–81.

45. Kellogg, "Mankind's Impact on Climate," 113–36; M. D. H. Jones and Anne Henderson-Sellers, "History of the Greenhouse Effect," 1–18; and Mark D. Handel and James S. Risbey,

"An Annotated Bibliography on the Greenhouse Effect and Climate Change," 91–255; the editorial on pp. 91–95, "Reflections of More than a Century of Climate Change Research," is particularly useful.

46. A. Neftel, E. Moor, H. Oeschger, and B. Stauffer, "Evidence from Polar Ice Cores for the Increase in Atmospheric CO_2 in the Past Two Centuries," 45–47; and C. D. Keeling et al., "Atmospheric Carbon Dioxide Variations at Mauna Loa Observatory, Hawaii," 538–51. For authoritative and accessible summaries on carbon accumulation, see Richard A. Houghton and David L. Skole, "Carbon," 400; and R. A. Houghton, "Tropical Deforestation and Atmospheric Carbon Dioxide," 99–118.

47. The Study of Man's Impact on Climate (SMIC), *Inadvertent Climate Modification,* especially 12, 18, 63, and 170–73; Kellogg, "Mankind's Impact on Climate," 126–27; and P. D. Jones, T. M. L. Wrigley, and P. B. Wright, "Global Temperature Variations between 1861 and 1984," 430–34.

48. Houghton and Skole, "Carbon," 394–95, 398–400.

49. Joyce E. Penner, "Atmospheric Chemistry and Air Quality," 175–77, 180, 183–86.

50. Anne Henderson-Sellers, Robert E. Dickinson, and M. F. Wilson, "Tropical Deforestation: Important Processes for Climate Models," 43–67.

51. For example, of which there are many: Victor Gornitz and NASA, "A Survey of Anthropogenic Vegetation Changes in West Africa during the Last Century—Climatic Implications," 285–325; R. A. Houghton, "Estimating Changes in the Carbon Content of Terrestrial Ecosystems from Historical Data," 175–93; R. A. Houghton, "Releases of Carbon to the Atmosphere from Degradation of Forests in Tropical Asia," 132–42; R. A. Houghton, D. S. Lefkowitz, and David L. Skole, "Changes in the Landscape of Latin America between 1850 and 1985: 1. Progressive Loss of Forests," 143–72; John F. Richards and Elizabeth P. Flint, "A Century of Land Use Change in South and Southeast Asia," 15–67; and Ralph M. Rotty, "Estimates of CO_2 from Wood Fuel based on Forest Harvest Data," 312–25."

52. For a flavor of this complex debate see David Demeritt, "The Construction of Global Warming and the Politics of Science," 307–37; and the response by Stephen H. Schneider, "A Constructive Deconstruction of Deconstructionists: A Response to Demeritt," 338–34.

53. James Fairhead and Melissa Leach, *Reframing Deforestation: Global Analysis and Local Realities: Studies in West Africa,* 180, 190.

54. David Takacs, *The Idea of Biodiversity: Philosophies of Paradise,* 1–2. When this section on biodiversity was written, I was unaware of Takacs's work, but I have the satisfaction of knowing that we were on the same track; consequently, I have not altered my text. What he does *not* deal with is the peculiarly important role of tropical deforestation in driving the debate; that is ignored.

55. The following discussion owes much to Yrjö Haila and Jari Kouki, "The Phenomenon of Biodiversity in Conservation Biology," 6–11.

56. Michel Foucault, *The Archaeology of Knowledge,* 136–40, 189–95. See also Paul A. Bové, "Discourse," 5–65, for the nature of "discourse"; and Joseph Rouse, "Interpretation in Natural and Human Science," 42–56, for the philosophical context.

57. Quoted in Bryan G. Norton, "On the Inherent Danger of Undervaluing Species," 113. See also Takacs, *Idea of Biodiversity,* 9–40, for a fuller development of the ideas of Darwin, Leopold, and Elton, and also of those of David Ehrenfeld.

58. Kevin J Gaston, "What Is Biodiversity?" 1.

59. P. H. Williams, Kevin J. Gaston, and C. J. Humphreys, "Do Conservationists and Molecular Scientists Value Differences between Organisms in the Same Way?" 67–78; and Haila and Kouki, "Phenomenon of Biodiversity," quotations are from pp. 9, 15.

60. Edred J. H. Corner, "Suggestions for Botanical Progress," 185–86; emphasis by Corner.

61. Paul W. Richards, *The Tropical Rain Forest: An Ecological Study,* 404, 406–7. The species contrast came from p. 60 of his article "The Tropical Rain Forest," written twenty years later.

62. John T. Curtis, "The Modification of Mid-Latitude Grasslands and Forests by Man," 734–35; Fairfield H. Osborn, *Our Plundered Planet,* 177; and William Vogt, *Road to Survival.* Vogt was the chief of the conservation section of the Pan-American Union, Washington, D.C.

63. An. A. Fedorov, "The Structure of the Tropical Rain Forest and Speciation in the Humid Tropics," 8–9. The idea that species associations were correlated with site factors dates at least to 1938, in André Aubréville's "La forêt coloniale: Les forêts de L'Afrique-Occidentale française," and was also known as the "mosaic" or "cyclical" theory of regeneration.

64. Philip A. Stott, "Tropical Rainforest in Recent Ecological Thought: The Reassessment of a Non-Renewable Resource," 84; for further summaries of the debate on speciation see Timothy C. Whitmore, *Tropical Rain Forests of the Far East,* 237–42.

65. Foucault, *Archaeology of Knowledge,* 136–40.

66. See in particular Otto H. Frankel and Erna Bennett, eds., *Genetic Resources in Plants— Their Exploration and Conservation,* 1–17, quotations from p. 9; and Otto H. Frankel and John G. Hawkes, eds., *Crop Genetic Resources for Today and Tomorrow,* 1–10. The subsequent proliferation of literature on the topic is vast, e.g., Anthony H. D. Brown, Otto H. Frankel, D. R. Marshall, and J. T. Williams, eds., *The Use of Plant Genetic Resources,* 1–48; Brian Ford-Lloyd and Michael Jackson, *Plant Genetic Resources: An Introduction to Their Conservation and Use;* and Otto H. Frankel, Anthony H. D. Brown, and Jeremy J. Burdon, eds., *The Conservation of Plant Diversity,* give a hint of the burgeoning field.

67. M. E. Duncan Poore, "The Values of Tropical Moist Forest Ecosystems," quotation is from p. 138; and Margery L. Oldfield, "Tropical Deforestation and Genetic Resources Conservation," 277–346. The practical, utilitarian uses were amplified in Norman Myers, *A Wealth of Wild Species: Storehouse for Human Welfare.*

68. Paul W. Richards, *The Life of the Jungle,* 194, 196, 199.

69. Paul W. Richards, "The Tropical Rain Forest," 67.

70. See p. 272 in chapter 9.

71. Based on Arturo Gómez-Pompa, C. Vázquaz-Yanes, and S. Guevara, "The Tropical Rainforest: A Non-Renewable Resource," 762–65, quotations are from p. 763.

72. André Aubréville, "The Disappearance of the Tropical Forests of Africa," 10–11.

73. William M. Denevan, "Development and the Imminent Demise of the Amazon Rain Forest," 130. It is clear that Denevan had been influenced by Paul Richards's warnings of 1970.

74. Adrian Sommer, "Attempt at an Assessment of the World's Tropical Forests," 5–25.

75. U.S. Interagency Task Force on Tropical Forests, *The World's Tropical Forests: A Policy Strategy and Program for the United States,* 7.

76. Eugene Linden, "Torching the Amazon: Playing with Fire," 44.

77. Norman Myers, *The Sinking Ark: A New Look at the Problem of Disappearing Species;* Paul R. Ehrlich and Anne H. Ehrlich, *Extinction: The Causes and Consequences of the Disappearance of Species;* and Haila and Kouki, "Phenomenon of Biodiversity," 9–10.

78. Myers, *Sinking Ark,* 4–5. For the higher estimate see Edward O. Wilson, "Threats to Biodiversity," 64. Quotation from Lowenthal, "Awareness of Human Impacts," 128.

79. Paul R. Ehrlich, "The Loss of Diversity: Causes and Consequences," 25. In much the same vein were Norman Myers's later publications, for example, "Questions of Mass Extinction," 2–17; and Edward C. Wolf's *On the Brink of Extinction: Conserving the Diversity of Life.*

80. The origins of this idea probably lay in Margery Oldfield's 1980 essay, "Tropical Deforestation and Genetic Resources Conversion," which has been amplified more recently in Margery Oldfield and Janis B. Alcorn, eds., *Biodiversity: Culture, Conservation and Ecodevelopment.*

81. Bruce A. Wilcox and Kristin N. Duin, "Indigenous Cultural and Biological Diversity: Overlapping Values of Latin American Ecoregions," 49–53.

82. Edward O. Wilson, foreword, to *Biodiviersity, Culture, Conservation and Ecodevelopment,* xviii. Also useful is Kent H. Redford and J. A. Mansour, *Traditional People and Biological Conservation in Large Tropical Landscapes;* Kent H. Redford and Christine Padoch, *Conservation of Neotropical Forests: Working from Traditional Resource Use;* and Leslie E. Sponsel, Thomas N. Headland, and Robert C. Bailey, eds., *Tropical Deforestation: The Human Dimension.*

83. Based on Edward O. Wilson, ed., *Biodiversity,* 3–5. Of these 1.4 million, approximately 750,000 are insects, 41,000 are vertebrates, and 250,000 are plants. Some estimates put the number of species at over 5 million, while Wolf ("On the Brink of Extinction," 8) suggests as many as 30 million.

84. Edward O. Wilson, *Biophilia,* 121.

85. The reference to Rosen is in Wilson, *Biodiversity,* xxx, and confirmed in an interview in Takacs, *Idea of Biodiversity,* 37, where Wilson says he thought originally that the word was "too glitzy" but later admitted that Rosen was "completely right." Office of Technology Assessment (OTA), *Technologies to Maintain Biodiversity.* I am indebted to Linda Atkinson, librarian, School of Geography, Oxford, for information on the Library of Congress classification.

86. For the incidence of the term see Haila and Kouki, "Phenomenon of Biodiversity," 9–10; also J. L. Harper and D. L. Hawksworth, "Biodiversity. Measurement and Estimation. Preface," 5–12. On measurement see Gaston, "What Is Biodiversity?" 1–8.

87. See Kevin J. Gaston, ed., *Biodiversity: A Biology of Numbers and Difference.*

88. Timothy C. Whitmore, *Tropical Deforestation and Species Extinction.*

89. The United Nations Conference on Environment and Development (UNCED) held in Rio de Janeiro in June 1992, discussed tropical deforestation. It produced *Global Diversity Strategy: Guidelines for Action to Save, Study, and Use Earth's Biotic Wealth Sustainably and Equitably* and concluded treaties to protect global climate, biodiversity, and Agenda 21, an action plan for sustainable development. See World Resources Institute, *World Resources* 1994–95:154–62.

90. Definitions taken from World Resources Institute, *World Resources* 1992–93:292; and Food and Agriculture Organization, *Forest Resources Assessment, 1990: Guidelines for Assessment,* 5–9. For a fuller discussion see Michael Williams, "Forests and Tree Cover," 97–102.

91. Richard Torunsky, ed., *Weltforstatlas—World Forestry Atlas—Atlas des forêts du monde—Atlas forestal del mundo;* Heinz Ellenberg and Dieter Mueller-Dombois, "Tentative Physiognomic-Ecological Classification of Plant Formations of the Earth," 37–55; Raymond F. Fosberg, "A Classification of Vegetation for General Purposes," 1–28; and UNESCO, *International Classification and Mapping of Vegetation.*

92. CLIMAP, "Seasonal Reconstructions of the Earth's Surface at the Last Glacial Maximum," 172–229; J. Hummel and R. Reck, "Global Surface Albedo Model," 239–53; Jerry Olson, J. A. Watts, and L. J. Allison, *Major World Ecosystem Complexes Ranked by Carbon in Live Vegetation;* and Elaine Matthews, "Global Vegetation and Land Use: New High-Resolution Data Bases for Climate Studies," 474–87.

93. Andrew S. Mather, "Global Trends in Forest Resources," 1–15.

94. Sedjo and Clawson, "Global Forests," 156–58.

95. Houghton, Lefkowitz, and Skole, "Changes in the Landscape of Latin America between 1850 and 1985," 156–58.

96. Bruce Ross-Sheriff, "Forest Projections," 118; Sandra Postel, "Protecting Forests," 75; Sandra Postel and Lori Heise, *Reforesting the Earth,* 8; and World Resources Institute, *World Resources* 1987:59. For estimates of tropical rain forest see Alan Grainger, "Rates of Deforestation

in the Humid Tropics: Estimates and Measurements," 37–38; and for 1993 see K. D. Singh, "The Tropical Forests Resources Assessment," 15–16.

97. World Resources Institute, *World Resources* 1988–9:70.

98. Ibid., 1987:58.

99. Jean-Paul P. Lanly, "Tropical Forest Resources," 74; and N. Myers, *Conversion of Tropical Moist Forests,* 7–8.

100. N. Myers, *Deforestation Rates in Tropical Forests,* 5.

101. Grainger, "Rates of Deforestation in the Humid Tropics," 34; and Norman Myers, "Conversion Rates in Tropical Moist Forests," 292, 296, quotation is from p. 292.

102. Sommer, "Attempt at an Assessment of the World's Tropical Forests," 20.

103. Richard A. Houghton, R. D. Boone, J. M. Melillo, C. A. Palm, George M. Woodwell, Norman Myers, Berrien Moore III, and David L. Skole, "Net Flux of Carbon Dioxide from Tropical Forests in 1980," 617–18.

104. Jerry M. Melillo, C. A. Palm, Richard A. Houghton, George M. Woodwell, and Norman Myers, "A Comparison of Recent Estimates of Disturbance in Tropical Forests," 12:38–39.

105. Houghton, Lefkowitz, and Skole, "Changes in the Landscape of Latin America," 159–65.

106. Sommer, "Attempt at an Assessment of the World's Tropical Forests," 5, 23.

107. As reported in U.S. Interagency Task Force on Tropical Forests, *The World's Tropical Forests,* 15, though Norman Myers, who attended the congress, reports that Saouma offered a figure of 40 ha per minute, or 21 million ha per annum (*Conversion of Tropical Moist Forests,* 4, 26). Barney's 1978 estimate is in Gerald O. Barney, "The Nature of the Deforestation Problem — Trends and Policy Implications," 15. His later estimates are in Jennifer Robinson and Gerald O. Barney, eds., "The Forestry Projections and the Environment," 318–19.

108. N. Myers, *Conversion of Tropical Moist Forests,* 23–50, 175; and Melillo et al., "A Comparison of Recent Estimates of Disturbance," 40.

109. Jean-Paul Lanly, ed., *Tropical Forest Resources Assessment Project (GEMS): Tropical Africa, Tropical Asia, Tropical America,* and the summary paper also by Lanly, "Tropical Forest Resources," 77–90. For an attempt to reconcile the irreconcilable in 1986, see Jane Molofsky, Charles A. S. Hall, and Norman Myers, *A Comparison of Tropical Forest Surveys.*

110. Singh, "The Tropical Forests Resources Assessment," 10–17. See also the commentary by Reidar Perrson, "Deforestation in the Tropics," 36–42.

111. *Tropical Forests: A Call for Action;* and Food and Agriculture Organization et al., *The Tropical Forestry Action Plan.*

112. Roger A. Sedjo and Marion Clawson, "How Serious Is Tropical Deforestation?" 792–94, and "Global Forests," 155–59. There are similar comments by Ariel E. Lugo and Sandra Brown, "Conversion of Tropical Moist Forests: A Critique," 89–93; and Grainger, "Rates of Deforestation in the Humid Tropics," 33–43.

113. Grainger, "Rates of Deforestation in the Humid Tropics," 38–40.

Chapter 14

1. S. A. Morain and B. Klankamsorn, "Forest Mapping and Inventory Techniques through Visual Analysis of LANDSAT Imagery: Examples from Thailand," 417–26; and Eneas Salati and Peter B. Vose, "The Depletion of Tropical Rain Forests," 67–71.

2. Robert Repetto, "Deforestation in the Tropics," 18–24; and P. Aldous, "Tropical Deforestation Not Just a Problem in Amazonia," 1390.

3. Forest History Society, Durham, N.C., Gill MSS, box 10, 1931–36.

4. William M. Denevan, foreword to *Hoofprints on the Forest: Cattle Ranching and the Destruction of Latin America's Tropical Forests,* by Douglas R. Shane, vii.

5. William M. Denevan (ed., *The Native Population of the Americas in 1492,* 205–34) conservatively estimates 6.6 million as the preconquest Indian population, but some archeologists have nearly tripled that total. See also John Hemming, *Red Gold: The Conquest of the Brazilian Indians,* particularly 3–64; Alcida R. Ramos, "Frontier Expansion and Indian Peoples in the Brazilian Amazon," 83–90; and Edwin J. Brooks, "Twilight of Brazilian Tribes," 310.

6. See Susanna Hecht and Alexander Cockburn, *The Fate of the Forest: Developers, Destroyers, and Defenders of the Amazon,* 61–62, 77–93; and Warren Dean, *Brazil and the Struggle for Rubber: A Study in Environmental History.*

7. Leslie E. Sponsel, "The Environmental History of Amazonia: Natural and Human Disturbances, and the Ecological Transition," 233–51; and Betty J. Meggers, "Aboriginal Adaptations to Amazonia," 307–27.

8. Marc J. Dourojeanni, quoted in Thomas K. Rudel, *Tropical Deforestation: Small Farmers and Land Clearing in the Ecuadorian Amazon,* 7; and Joseph A. Tosi and Robert F. Voertman, "Some Environmental Factors in the Economic Development of the Tropics," 196.

9. Raymond E. Crist and Charles M. Nissly, *East from the Andes: Pioneer Settlements in the South American Heartland,* 1–8; quotation is from p. i. For a more recent and penetrating analysis of land use, history, and social status, see David L. Clawson and Raymond E. Crist, "Evolution of Land-Use Patterns and Agricultural Systems," 265–72.

10. Crist and Nissly, *East from the Andes,* 13–14, 93.

11. David E. Snyder, "The 'Carretera Marginal de la Selva': A Geographical Review and Appraisal," 87–100; Crist and Nissly, *East from the Andes,* 113–21; and R. J. Bromley, "Agricultural Colonization in the Upper Amazon Basin: The Impact of Oil Discoveries," 278–94. For the demographic increase see Michael A. Little, "Human Populations in the Andes: The Human Science Basis for Research Planning," 160–62.

12. Among the dozens of publications on this movement, the following are significant, but there are many more: D. Brunnschweiler, *The Llanos Frontier of Colombia: Environment and Changing Land Use in Meta;* Bromley, "Agricultural Colonization in the Upper Amazon Basin," 278–94; Gilbert J. Butland, "Frontiers of Settlement in South America," 93–108; Raymond E. Crist, "Along the Llanos-Andean Border in Venezuela: Then and Now!" 187–208; Crist, "Go East, Young Man," 3–9; Raymond E. Crist and Ernesto Guhl, "Pioneer Settlement in Eastern Colombia"; Craig L. Dozier, *Land Development and Colonization in Latin America: Case Studies in Peru, Bolivia and Mexico;* Robert C. Eidt, "Pioneer Settlement in Eastern Peru," 255–78; Eidt, "Agrarian Reform and the Growth of New Rural Settlements in Venezuela," 120–32; Earl P. Hanson, "New Conquistadors in the Amazon Jungle," 1–8; E. E. Hegen, *Highways in the Upper Amazon Basin: Pioneer Lands in Southern Colombia, Ecuador and Northern Peru;* J. M. Kirby, "Colombian Land-Use Changes and the Settlement of the Oriente," 1–25; and N. R. Stewart, "Some Problems in the Development of Agricultural Colonization in the Andean Oriente," 33–38.

13. Crist and Nissly, *East from the Andes,* iv, vi, and vii, quoting René Dubois, "How Man Helps Nature," 20. These comments can be contrasted with those of William Denevan in his "Development and the Imminent Demise of the Amazon Rain Forest," which was published in the same year and much castigated at the time, for example in Janet D. Henshall and Richard P. Momsen Jr., *A Geography of Brazilian Development,* 259–63. For an update of Denevan's views in 1981 see William M. Denevan, "Swiddens and Cattle versus Forest: Development and the Imminent Demise of the Amazon Rain Forest Reexamined," 25–44.

14. Mario Hiraoka and Shozo Yamamato, "Agricultural Development in the Upper Amazon of Ecuador," 444–45; Carlos E. Aramburú, "Expansion of the Agrarian and Demographic Fron-

tier in the Peruvian Selva," 153–79; Sutti Ortiz, "Colonization of the Colombian Amazon," 204–30; J. Uquillas, "Colonization and Spontaneous Settlement in the Ecuadorian Amazon," 261–84; and Rudel, *Tropical Deforestation,* 1–42.

15. Quotations from Hiraoka and Yamamoto, "Agricultural Development in the Upper Amazon," 429, 445; Eidt, "Pioneer Settlement in Eastern Peru," 277; and R. Bromley, "Agricultural Colonization in the Upper Amazon Basin," 292.

16. Eneas Salati, Marc J. Dourojeanni, Fernando C. Novaes, Adélia Engrácia de Oliveira, Richard W. Perritt, Herbert Otto, Roger Schubart, and Julio C. Umana, "Amazonia," 487–89; quotation is from p. 489.

17. Roy Nash, *The Conquest of Brazil,* 287–288. The "nomads" were, of course, the forest peasantry, or *caboclos.* See Stephen Nugent, *Amazonian Caboclo Society: An Essay on Invisibility and Peasant Economy,* esp. 93–136.

18. Attributed to The Mineiro José Vieira Couto, a late eighteenth century author, quoted in Warren Dean, *With Broadax and Firebrand: The Destruction of the Brazilian Atlantic Forest,* 139.

19. Dean, *With Broadax and Firebrand,* 266; and Thomas E. Skidmore, *The Politics of Military Rule in Brazil, 1964–85,* 147.

20. Emilio F. Moran, "Growth without Development: Past and Present Development Efforts in Amazonia," 3–23.

21. Dean, *With Broadax and Firebrand,* 265–91, for the demise of the Atlantic coast forest; and Thomas E. Skidmore, *Politics in Brazil, 1930–1964: An Experiment in Democracy,* 205 and passim, and *The Politics of Military Rule,* 133–6, 144–50.

22. Hecht and Cockburn, *The Fate of the Forest,* 100–108; quotations are from 102, 103; and Dennis J. Mahar, *Frontier Development Policy in Brazil: A Study of Amazonia,* 1–39. For more succinct overviews see Emilio Moran, "Deforestation and Land Use in the Brazilian Amazon," 1–8, and "Deforestation in the Brazilian Amazon," 149–64.

23. Mahar, *Frontier Development Policy in Brazil,* 10–35. See also Marianne Schmink and Charles H. Wood, eds., *Contested Frontiers in Amazonia,* 58–94 (quotation is from p. 59) on "Militarizing Amazonia, 1964–1985."

24. The Legal Amazon is the administrative area defined as "The Amazon" by the Brazilian government, and is not coterminous with the Amazon River basin. It consists of the federal territories of Rondônia and Amapá, and the states of Pará, Roaraima, Maranhão (part only), Goiás (part only, and sometimes known as Tocantins), Acre, Rondônia, Mato Grosso, and Amazonas. See figure 14.6. Particularly authoritative on these developments is Dennis J. Mahar, *Government Policies and Deforestation in Brazil's Amazon Region,* 9–13.

25. Ibid., 13–14 (for details of the migration flows and types of settlements mainly in the region of Altamira, see Emilio Moran, *Developing the Amazon,* 68–96); and Philip M. Fearnside and Eneas Salati, "Explosive Deforestation in Rondônia, Brazil," 355–56.

26. Mahar, *Government Policies and Deforestation,* 13–23; and Hecht and Cockburn, *The Fate of the Forest,* 106–7.

27. Based on Dean, *With Broadax and Firebrand,* 270; Mahar, *Government Policies and Deforestation,* 15; Hecht and Cockburn, *The Fate of the Forest,* 107; and Moran, "Deforestation and Land Use," 6. For the wider issues raised by the emphasis on cattle, see Susanna B. Hecht, "Cattle Ranching in the Eastern Amazon: Environmental and Social Implications," 155–88, and "Cattle Ranching in Amazonia: Political and Ecological Considerations," 366–400.

28. Moran, "Deforestation in the Brazilian Amazon," 150; Mahar, *Government Policies and Deforestation,* 26; and Moran, *Developing the Amazon,* 14–17. For a plan of the hierarchical urban arrangement see Neil J. H. Smith, *Rainfall Corridors: The Transamazon Colonisation Scheme,* 20.

29. Moran, *Developing the Amazon,* 1–18 and passim, 75–83; Moran, "Deforestation in the Brazilian Amazon," 150–52; and Niel J. H. Smith, *Rainfall Corridors: The Transamazon Colonization Scheme,* 50–75.

30. Hecht and Cockburn, *The Fate of the Forest,* 108; Emilio F. Moran, "Colonization in the Transamazon and Rondônia," 287–92; and J. M. G. Kleinpenning, *The Integration and Colonization of the Brazilian Portion of the Amazon Basin,* 3–39.

31. Based on Mahar, *Government Policies and Deforestation,* 30–31.

32. For health problems in the newly colonized areas see Moran, *Developing the Amazon,* 183–212; and N. J. H. Smith, *Rainfall Corridors,* 93–139.

33. Dennis J. Mahar, *Brazil: Integrated Development of the Northwest Frontier,* 27–68; Mahar, *Government Policies and Deforestation,* 33–40; and C. C. Mueller, "Frontier-Based Agricultural Expansion: The Case of Rondônia," 141–53.

34. Mahar, *Government Policies and Deforestation,* 33–34.

35. For examples of the precariousness of titles and the endemic violence used by hired gunmen, see Joe Foweraker, *The Struggle for Land: A Political Economy of the Pioneer Frontier in Brazil from 1930 to the Present Day,* 13–26; and Schmink and Wood, *Contested Frontiers,* 10–20, 78–83, 172–76, 186–90, 302–6.

36. Hecht and Cockburn, *The Fate of the Forest,* 148–50; Hecht, "Cattle Ranching in the Eastern Amazon," 158–88; and Mahar, *Brazil: Integrated Development,* 118–29.

37. Hecht and Cockburn, *The Fate of the Forest,* 85, 114–15; Philip M. Fearnside, "Jari Development in the Brazilian Amazon," 145–56, and "Jari Revisited: Changes and the Outlook for Sustainability in Amazonia's Largest Silvicultural Estate," 121–29.

38. Anthony L. Hall, *Developing Amazonia: Deforestation and Social Conflict in Brazil's Carajás Programme.*

39. Foweraker, *The Struggle for Land,* 5.

40. Ibid., 65; and Schmink and Wood, *Contested Frontiers,* 4, 72–74, quotation is from p. 73.

41. Tosi and Voertman, "Some Environmental Factors," 205.

42. The following paragraphs are based on Schmink and Wood, *Contested Frontiers,* 2–4, 348, 353, 354. These extracts do scant justice to the harrowing detail of this book. See also Brian J. Godfrey, "Boom Towns of the Amazon," 103–17, which deals with the same towns.

43. Andrew Revkin, *The Burning Season: The Murder of Chico Mendes and the Fight for the Amazon Rainforest;* and Hecht and Cockburn, *The Fate of the Forest,* 192–209. Quotations are from Schmink and Wood, *Contested Frontiers,* 353, 354.

44. Denevan, "Development and the Imminent Demise of the Amazon Rain Forest," 130–35; "Threat from Amazon Burn-Off," *The* (London) *Times,* 6 September 1988; Eugene Linden, "Torching the Amazon," *Time,* 18 September 1989, 44–50, quotation is from p. 44; Revkin, *The Burning Season;* and "The Month Amazonia Burns," *The Economist,* 9 September 1989, 15.

45. Philip M. Fearnside, "Deforestation in the Brazilian Amazon: How Fast Is It Occurring?" 82–88; and "A Floresta vai Acabar?" 42–52. There are many studies on interpreting imagery. There is a good summary in Compton J. Tucker, J. R. G. Townshend, T. E. Goff, and B. N. Holben, "Continental and Global Scale Remote Sensing of Land Cover," 221–41.

46. Fearnside, "Deforestation in the Brazilian Amazon."

47. Mueller, "Frontier-Based Agricultural Expansion," 141–53; and Fearnside and Salati, "Explosive Deforestation in Rondônia, Brazil," 355–56. For the remote sensing see, for example, Compton J. Tucker, B. N. Holben, and T. E. Goff, "Intensive Forest Clearing in Rondonia, Brazil, As Detected by Satellite Remote Sensing," 255–61; George M. Woodwell, Richard A. Houghton, Thomas A. Stone, and Archibald B. Park, "Changes in the Area of Forests in Rondônia, Amazon Basin, Measured by Satellite Imagery," 242–57; Jean-Paul Malingreau and Compton J. Tucker,

"Large-Scale Deforestation in the Southeastern Amazon Basin of Brazil," 49–55; and George M. Woodwell, Richard A. Houghton, Thomas A. Stone, R. F. Nelson, and W. Kovalick, "Deforestation in the Tropics: New Measurements in the Amazon Basin Using Landsat and NOAA Advanced Very High Resolution Radiometer Imagery," 2157–63.

48. Salati et al., "Amazonia," 486.

49. Philip M. Fearnside, "The Rate and Extent of Deforestation in Brazilian Amazonia," 213–26.

50. The conflict over claims of deforestation and the "borrowing" of estimates is illustrated by the figure of 598,921 km². It appears in Salati et al., "Amazonia," 486 (1990) and is attributed to Brazil's Institute for Forestry and the National Space Research Institute; but it also appears one year earlier in Mahar, *Government Policies and Deforestation,* 6 (1989) and is attributed to Philip M. Fearnside, *Human Carrying Capacity of the Brazilian Rainforest* (1986), and "World Bank estimates."

51. David Skole and Compton J. Tucker, "Tropical Deforestation and Habitat Fragmentation in the Amazon: Satellite Data from 1978 to 1988," 1905–10.

52. For other estimates see Skole and Tucker, "Tropical Deforestation and Habitat Fragmentation," 1909–10.

53. J. M. G. Kleinpenning and E. B. Zoomers, "Environmental Degradation in Latin America: The Example of Paraguay," 242–50; and R. A. Nickson, "Brazilian Colonization of the Eastern Border Region of Paraguay," 111–31.

54. Joan M. Hardjano, "Transmigration: Looking to the Future," 28–53; Kuswata Kartawinata, S. Adisoemarto, S. Riswan, and A. D. Vayda, "The Impact of Man on a Tropical Forest of Indonesia," 115–119; M. K. Ranjitsinh, "Forest Destruction in Asia and the South Pacific," 192–201; B. M. Rich, "The World Bank's Indonesia Transmigration Project: Potential for Disaster," 2–5; and C. Secrett, "The Environmental Impact of Transmigration," 77–88.

55. Michael Williams, "Protection and Retrospection," 339–42.

56. Tunku S. Barhin and P. D. A. Perera, *FELDA. 21 Years of Land Development;* and Harold C. Brookfield et al., "Borneo and the Malay Peninsula," 506–8.

57. Shane, *Hoofprints on the Forest;* quotation is from p. xii.

58. The best overall views are in Shane, *Hoofprints on the Forest;* and Theodore E. Downing, Susanna B. Hecht, Harry A. Pearson, and Carmen Garcia-Downing, eds., *Destruction or Development: The Conversion of Tropical Forest to Pasture in Latin America.* For more localized accounts see Robert J. Buschbacher, "Tropical Deforestation and Pasture Development," 22–28; Philip M. Fearnside, "Land-Use Trends in the Brazilian Amazon Region As Factors in Accelerating Deforestation," 141–48; and Laercio L. Leite and Peter A. Furley, "Land Development in the Brazilian Amazon Region with Particular Reference to Rondônia and the Ouro Prêto Colonization Project," 119–39.

59. James J. Parsons, "Forest to Pasture: Development or Destruction?" 126.

60. Hecht, "Cattle Ranching in Amazonia," 366–400, and "Deforestation in the Amazon Basin: Magnitude, Dynamics, and Soil Resource Effects," 66–108 for soil depletion characteristics; and James J. Parsons, "Spread of African Pasture Grasses to the American Tropics," 12–17.

61. Billie R. Dewalt, "The Cattle Are Eating the Forest," 18–23; George Guess, "Pasture Expansion, Forestry and Development Contradictions: The Case of Costa Rica," 42–55; Norman Myers, "The Hamburger Connection: How Central America's Forests Become North America's Hamburgers," 3–8; Norman Myers and Richard Tucker, "Deforestation in Central America: Spanish Legacy and North American Consumers," 55–71; James D. Nations and Daniel I. Komer, "Indians, Immigrants and Beef Exports: Deforestation in Central America," 8–12; and Shane, *Hoofprints on the Forest,* 77–97.

62. Parsons, "Spread of African Pasture Grasses to the American Tropics," quotations are from p. 12, and further details in "Forest to Pasture," 121–37. For major regional accounts of pasture development and deforestation see Karen L. O'Brien, *Sacrificing the Forest: Environmental and Social Struggles in Chiapas*, 24–30, 110–32; Stanley Moreno Heckadon and Alberto McKay, eds., *Colonización y destruccion de bosques en Panamá*; and Silvia Rodriguez and Emilio Vargas, *El Recurso Forestal en Costa Rica: Politicas y Sociedad*.

63. Parsons, "Forest to Pasture," 132.

64. Mungo Park, *Mungo Park's Travels in the Interior of Africa: The First Journey*, 70.

65. Erik P. Eckholm, *The Other Energy Crisis: Firewood*.

66. Dennis Anderson and Robert Fishwick, *Fuelwood Consumption and Deforestation in African Countries*; Elizabeth Cecelski, Joy Dunkerley, and William Ramsey, *Household Energy and the Poor in the Third World*; Erik P. Eckholm, Gerald Foley, and G. Bernard, *Fuelwood: The Energy Crisis That Won't Go Away*; Barry Munslow, Yemi Katerere, Adriaan Ferf, and Philip O'Keefe, *The Fuelwood Trap: A Study of the SADCC Region*; and Food and Agriculture Organization, *The State of the World's Forests, 1995*, 24. For examples of the problems in the savanna regions, see Henri Chauvin, "When an African City Runs Out of Fuel," 11–20; and Jacqueline Ki-Zerboi, "Women and the Energy Crisis in the Sahel," 5–10.

67. J. E. M. Arnold and Jules Jogma, "Fuel and Charcoal in Developing Countries," 2–9; Food and Agriculture Organization, *Wood for Energy*; and Philip Wardle and Massimo Palmieri, "What Does Fuelwood Really Cost?"

68. B. Bowonder, S. S. R. Prasad, and N. V. M. Unni, "Deforestation around Urban Centres in India," 23–28; and Manzoor Alam, Joy Dunkerley, K. N. Gopi, William Ramsey, and Elizabeth Davis, *Fuelwood in Urban Markets: A Case Study of Hyderabad*.

69. Food and Agriculture Organization, *State of World Forests, 1995*, 26.

70. Derek E. Earl, *Forest Energy and Economic Development*.

71. Michael Williams, *Americans and Their Forests: A Historical Geography*, 78–81, 133–39, 146–59, 332–52. In the mid-1960s 40 percent of Brazil's 3 million tons of pig-iron production was still based on charcoal. See Werner Baer, *The Development of the Brazilian Steel Industry*, 85, 110–13.

72. Gerald Foley, "Wood Fuel and Conventional Fuel Demands in the Developing World," 253–58.

73. Exports are worth $135 billion; imports, $144.3 billion (Food and Agriculture Organization, *Yearbook of Forest Products, 1993–1997*).

74. François Nectoux and Yiochi Kuroda, *Timber from the South Seas: An Analysis of Japan's Tropical Environmental Impact*; and Patricia M. Marchak, *Logging the Globe*.

75. Philip Hirsch, "Deforestation and Development in Thailand," 129–38; Victor T. King, "Politik Pembangunan: The Political Economy of Rainforest Exploitation and Destruction in Sarawak, East Malaysia," 235–44; Rodolphe De Koninck, "Forest Policies in Southeast Asia: Taming Nature or Taming People?" 33–48; Frédéric Durand, *Les forêts en asie du sud-est: Recul et exploitation: Le cas de l'Indonésie*, 261–304; and Global Witness, *Corruption, War, and Forest Policy: The Unsustainable Exploitation of Cambodia's Forests*, 1–35.

76. Paul Jepson, James K. Jarvie, Kathy MacKinnon, and Kathryn A. Monk, "The End for Indonesia's Lowland Forests?" 859–61.

77. Christopher Uhl and Ima C. G. Vieira, "Ecological Impacts of Selective Logging in the Brazilian Amazon: A Case Study from the Paragominas Region of the State of Pará," 98–106.

78. Jean-Paul Malingreau, G. Stephens, and L. Fellows, "Remote Sensing and Forest Fires: Kalimantan and North Borneo in 1982–83," 314–21; T. Tomich, "Indonesia's Fires: Smoke As a Problem, Smoke As a Symptom," 8; and J. Vidal, "The Thousand Mile Shroud."

79. Dennis P. Dykstra and Markku Kallio, "Scenario Analysis," 613–72.

80. For example, Jean-Paul Lanly, "Regression de la forêt dense en Côte-d'Ivoire," 45–9.

81. James Fairhead and Melissa Leach, *Reframing Deforestation: Global Analysis and Local Realities: Studies in West Africa,* 22–41 on Côte d'Ivoire.

Epilogue

1. Bill McKibben, *The End of Nature;* Philip Hurst, *Rainforest Politics: Ecological Destruction in South East Asia;* Narenda P. Sharma, ed., *Managing the World's Forests: Looking for Balance between Conservation and Development;* Sören Wibe and Tom Jones, *Forests: Market and Intervention Failures;* Tariq Banuri and Frédérique A. Marglin, eds., *Who Will Save the Forests?: Knowledge, Power and Environmental Destruction;* Marcus Colchester and Larry Lohmann, eds., *The Struggle for Land and the Fate of the Forests;* Nigel Dudley, Jean-Paul Jeanrenaud, and Francis Sullivan, *Bad Harvest?: The Timber Trade and the Degradation of the World's Forests;* Catrinus J. Jepma, *Tropical Deforestation: A Socio-Economic Approach;* H. Beer and Z. Rizvi, *The Vanishing Forest: The Human Consequences of Deforestation;* and Marchak, *Logging the Globe.*

2. Food and Agriculture Organization, *The State of the World's Forests, 1999,* 50–57.

3. Christopher Park, *Acid Rain: Rhetoric and Reality.*

4. World Resources Institute and International Institute for Environment and Development, *World Resources, 1990–91,* 292–93; Hamlin L. Williston, *A Statistical History of Tree Planting in the South, 1925–79.*

5. Roger A. Sedjo, "Forests to Offset the Greenhouse Effect," 12–15, quotation is from p. 13; and Sandra Postel and Lori Heise, *Reforesting the Earth.*

6. For these calculations see Michael Williams, "Forests," 179–80.

7. Alan Grainger, *Controlling Tropical Deforestation.* For the example of Cambodia see Global Witness, *Corruption, War, and Forest Policy.*

8. J. P. Resor, "Debt for Nature Swaps: A Decade of Experience and New Directions for the Future," 15–22; *New York Times,* 24 March 1989, p. 21; and *Chicago Tribune,* 12 March 1989, p. 29.

9. Dirk Bryant, Daniel Nielsen, and Laura Tangley, *The Last Frontier Forests: Ecosystem and Economics on the Edge,* 5 and table on 9.

10. Raphael Zon and William Sparhawk, *Forest Resources of the World,* 68.

BIBLIOGRAPHY

Abel, W. "Agakonjuntur." In *Hand wörterbuch der Sozialwissenschaften,* edited by E. von Beck-enrath et al., 49–59. Stuttgart: G.Fischer, 1956.

———. *Agricultural Fluctuations in Europe from the Thirteenth to the Twentieth Centuries.* Translated from the German by Olive Ordish. 1966. Reprint, London: Methuen, 1980.

Abbott, W. E. "Ringbarking and Its Effects." *Journal and Proceedings of Royal Society of New South Wales* 14 (1880): 41–66.

———. "Forest Destruction in New South Wales." *Journal and Proceedings of Royal Society of New South Wales* 22 (1888): 47–54.

Abramovitz, Moses. "The Economic Characteristics of Railroads and the Problem of Economic Development." *Far Eastern Quarterly* 14 (1955): 169–78.

Abrams, Elliot M., Anncorinne Freter, David J. Rue, and John D. Wingard. "The Role of Defor-estation in the Collapse of the Late Classic Copán Maya State." In *Tropical Deforestation: The Human Dimension,* ed. Leslie E. Sponsel, Thomas N. Headland, and Robert C. Bailey, 55–75. New York: Columbia University Press, 1996.

Abu-Lughod, Janet L. *Before European Hegemony: The World System, A.D. 1250–1350.* New York: Oxford University Press, 1989.

Adam, Jacques-George. "Les reliques boisés et les essences des savanes dans la zone préforestière en Guinée française." *Bulletin de la Société Botanique Française* 98 (1948): 22–26.

Adams, Robert E. W. 1973. "The Collapse of Maya Civilization: A Review of Previous Theories." In *The Classic Maya Collapse,* edited by T. Patrick Culbert, 21–34. Albuquerque: University of New Mexico Press, 1973.

Adams, Robert E. W., W. E. Brown Jr., and T. Patrick Culbert. "Radar Mapping Archaeology and Ancient Maya Land Use." *Science* 213 (1981), 1457–63.

Adams, Robert E. W., and Thomas P. Culbert. "The Origins of Civilization in the Maya Low-lands." In *The Origins of Maya Lowland Civilization,* edited by Robert E. W. Adams, 3–34. Albuquerque: University of New Mexico Press, 1977.

Adas, Michael. "Colonization, Commercial Agriculture and the Destruction of the Deltaic Rain-forests of British Burma in the Late Nineteenth Century." In *Global Deforestation and the Nineteenth Century World Economy,* edited by Richard P. Tucker and John F. Richards, 95–110. Duke Press Policy Studies. Durham, N.C.: Duke University Press, 1983.

———. *Machines As the Measure of Men: Science, Technology, and Ideologies of Western Domi-nance.* Ithaca, N.Y.: Cornell University Press, 1989.

Addison, Joseph. *The Spectator,* 31 May 1712, 393.

Adshead, Samuel Adrian M. "An Energy Crisis in Early Modern China." *Late Imperial China* [formerly *Ching-shih wan-t'-i*] 3, no. 4 (1974): 20–28.

———. "Timber As a Factor in Chinese History: Problems, Sources, and Hypotheses." In *Proceedings of the First International Symposium on Asian Studies,* vol. 1, *China,* 1–6. Hong Kong: Hong Kong University Press, 1979.

Agnoletti, Mauro. "From the Dolomites to Venice: Rafts and River Driving along the Piare River, Italy, Thirteenth to Twentieth Century." *Journal of Society for Industrial Archaeology* 21 (1995): 15–32.

Ahern, George P. "The Lesson of Forestry in the Philippine Islands." *Proceedings of the Second American Scientific Congress.* 3 vols. Washington, D.C.: Government Printing Office, 1917.

Ahlgren, I. F., and Clifford E. Ahlgren. "Ecological Effects of Forest Fires." *Botanical Review* 26 (1960): 483–537.

Ainslie, James Robert. *The Physiography of Southern Nigeria and Its Effect on the Forest Flora of the Country.* Oxford Forestry Memoirs, no 5. Oxford: The Clarendon Press, 1926.

Alam, Manzoor, Joy Dunkerley, K. N. Gopi, William Ramsey, and Elizabeth Davis. *Fuelwood in Urban Markets: A Case Study of Hyderabad.* New Delhi: Concept Publishing Company, 1985.

Albion, Robert Greenhalgh. *Forests and Sea Power: The Timber Problem of the Royal Navy, 1652–1862.* Cambridge, Mass.: Havard University Press, 1926.

Aldous, P. "Tropical Deforestation Is Not Just a Problem in Amazonia." *Science* 259 (1993): 1390–91.

Allen, Edward A. "Deforestation and the Fuel Crisis in Pre-Revolutionary Languedoc, 1720–1789." *French Historical Studies* 13 (1984): 455–73.

Allen, Julia C., and Douglas F. Barnes. "The Causes of Deforestation in Developing Countries." *Annals, Association of American Geographers* 75 (1985): 163–84.

Allen, Ruth A. *East Texas Lumber Workers: An Economic and Social Picture, 1870–1950.* Austin: University of Texas Press, 1961.

"The Amazon." *Chicago Tribune,* 12 March 1989, sec. 1, p. 29.

Ammal, E. K. Janaki. "Introduction to the Subsistence Economy of India." In *Man's Role in Changing the Face of the Earth,* edited by William L. Thomas, 324–35. Chicago: University of Chicago Press, 1956.

Ammerman, Albert J., and Luigi L. Cavalli-Sforza. "Measuring the Rate of Spread of Early Farming in Europe." *Man,* n.s., 6 (1971): 674–88.

———. "A Population Model for the Diffusion of Early Farming in Europe." In *The Explanation of Cultural Change: Models in Prehistory,* edited by Colin Renfrew, 343–57. London: Duckworth, 1973.

Anburey, Thomas. *Travels through the Interior Parts of America in a Series of Letters by an Officer.* 2 vols. London, 1791. Reprint, Boston: Houghton Mifflin, 1923.

Andel, Tjeerd H. van, and Curtis Runnels. *Beyond the Acropolis: A Rural Greek Past.* Stanford Calif.: Stanford University Press, 1987.

Andel, Tjeerd H. van, Curtis Runnels, and Kevin O. Pope. "Five Thousand Years of Land Use and Abuse in the Southern Argolid, Greece." *Hesperia* 55 (1986): 103–28.

Andersen, S. T. "The Different Productivity of Trees and Its Significance for the Interpretation of Pollen Diagrams from a Forested Region." In *Quaternary Plant Ecology,* edited by Harry J. B. Birks and R. G.West, 109–15. Oxford: Basil Blackwell, 1973.

Anderson, Atholl J. "The Extinction of the Moa in Southern New Zealand." In *Quaternary Extinctions: A Prehistoric Revolution,* edited by Paul S. Martin and Richard G. Klein, 728–40. Tucson: University of Arizona Press, 1984.

————. *Prodigious Birds: Moas and Moa-Hunting in Prehistoric New Zealand*. Cambridge: Cambridge University Press, 1989.

Anderson, Dennis, and Robert Fishwick. *Fuelwood Consumption and Deforestation in African Countries*. World Bank Staff Working Paper no. 704. Washington, D.C.: World Bank, 1984.

Anderson, Edgar. "Man As a Maker of New Plants and Plant Communities." In *Man's Role in Changing the Face of the Earth,* ed. William L. Thomas, 763–77. Chicago: University of Chicago Press, 1956.

————. *Plants, Man and Life*. Boston: Little, Brown, 1952. Reprint, Berkeley and Los Angeles: University of California Press, 1969.

Anderson, Perry. "The Asiatic Mode of Production." In *Lineages of the Absolutist State,* note B, 462, 541. London: Verso, 1979.

Anderson, Roger C. "The Historic Role of Fire in the North American Grassland." In *Fire in North American Tallgrass Prairies,* edited by Scott L. Collins and Linda L. Wallace, 8–18. Norman: University of Oklahoma Press, 1990.

Andrews, Evangeline Walker, and Charles McLean Andrews, eds. *Journal of a Lady of Quality, 1774–1776*. New Haven, Conn.: Yale University Press, 1923.

Andrews, George Henry. *Modern Husbandry: A Practical and Scientific Treatise on Agriculture*. London: Nathaniel Cooke, 1830.

Andrews, Kenneth R. *Trade, Plunder, and Settlement: Maritime Enterprise and the Genesis of the British Empire, 1480–1630*. Cambridge: Cambridge University Press, 1994.

Aramburú, Carlos E. "Expansion of the Agrarian and Demographic Frontier in the Peruvian Selva." In *Frontier Expansion in Amazonia,* edited by Marianne Schmink and Charles H. Wood, 153–79. Gainesville: University of Florida Press, 1984.

Archer, R. T., and P. J. Carrol. "Dairy Farming." In *Victoria: The Yearbook of Agriculture for 1905,* 297–333. Melbourne: Government Printer, 1905.

Aristophanes. *The Clouds*. translated by Alan H. Sommerstein. Warminster, England: Aries and Philips, 1982.

Armengaud, André. "Population in Europe, 1700–1900." In *The Fontana Economic History of Europe,* edited by Carlo M. Cipolla, vol. 3, *The Industrial Revolution, 1700–1914,* 22–77. Brighton: Harvester Press, 1976.

Arnold, J. E. M., and Jules Jogma. "Fuel and Charcoal in Developing Countries." *Unasylva* 29 (1978): 2–9.

Ashmore, Wendy, ed. *Lowland Maya Settlement Patterns*. Albuquerque: University of New Mexico Press, 1981.

Ashton, Thomas Southcliffe. "The Discovery of the Darbys of Coalbrookdale." *Transactions of the Newcommen Society* 5 (1925): 11–25.

————. *The Industrial Revolution, 1760–1830*. London: Oxford University Press, 1948.

————. *Iron and Steel in the Industrial Revolution*. Manchester: Manchester University Press, 1924; 4th ed. with updated bibliography, 1968.

Åström, Sven-Erik. "English Timber Imports from Northern Europe in the Eighteenth Century." *Scandinavian Economic History Review* 18 (1970): 12–32.

————. "Technology and Timber Exports from the Gulf of Finland, 1661–1740." *Scandinavian Economic History Review* 23 (1975): 4–14.

————. *From Tar to Timber: Studies in Northeast European Forest Exploitation and Foreign Trade, 1660–1860*. Helsinki: Societas Scientiarum Fennica. Commentationes Humanarum Litterarum, no. 89, 1988.

————. "Britain's Timber Imports from the Baltic, 1775–1830: Some New Figures and Viewpoints." *Scandinavian Economic History Review* 37 (1989): 57–61.

Attenborough, David. *The First Eden: The Mediterranean World and Man.* Boston: Little, Brown and Co., 1987.

Aubin, Hermann. "Medieval Society in Its Prime: The Lands East of the Elbe and German Colonization Eastwards." In *The Cambridge Economic History of Europe,* vol. 1, *Agrarian Life in the Middle Ages,* edited by John H. Clapham and Eileen Power, 361–97. Cambridge: Cambridge University Press, 1941.

Aubréville, André. "Dix années d'expériences sylvicoles en Côte d'Ivoire." *Revue des Eaux et Forêts* 75, no. 4 (1937): 289–302.

———. "La forêt coloniale: les forêts de l'Afrique-Occidentale française." *Annales d'Académie des Sciences Coloniales* IX, 1–245. Paris: Société d'Editions Géographiques, Maritimes et Colonial, 1938.

———. "The Disappearance of the Tropical Forests of Africa." *Unasylva* 1 (1947): 5–11.

———. *Climats, forêts et désertification de l'Afrique tropicale.* Paris: Sociéte d'Éditions Géographiques, Maritimes et Coloniales, 1949.

———. *Contribution à la paléohistoire des forêts de l'Afrique tropicale.* Paris: Sociéte d'Éditions Géographiques, Maritimes et Coloniales, 1949.

Ayres, Eugene, and Charles A. Scarlott. *Energy Sources: The Wealth of the World.* New York: McGraw-Hill Book Comp. Inc, 1952.

Bachmann, Elizabeth. "Minnesota Log Marks." *Minnesota History* 26 (1945): 126–37.

Backman, Charles A. *The Forest Industrial Sector of Russia: Opportunity Awaiting.* New York and London. Parthenon Publishing Group, 1998.

Bacon, Francis. *De Sapientia Veterum* (Of the wisdom of the ancients) [1609]. Printed in *The Essays,* edited by John Pitcher. Harmondsworth, England: Penguin Books, 1985.

———. *Novum Organum* [1620]. Printed in *The Physical and Metaphysical Works of Lord Bacon,* ed. Joseph Devey. London: G. Bell and Sons, 1911.

———. *The New Atlantis* [1627]. Printed in *The Advancement of Learning and New Atlantis,* edited by Arthur Johnston. Oxford: Clarendon Press, 1974.

Baden-Powell, B. Henry. "The Political Value of Forest Conservancy." *Indian Forester* 2 (1876): 280–88.

———. *The Land-Systems of British India, Being a Manual of the Land-Tenures and of the Systems of Land-Revenue.* Oxford: Clarendon Press, 1892.

Badré, Louis. *Histoire de la forêt française.* Paris: Les Éditions Arthaud, 1983.

Baer, Werner. *The Development of the Brazilian Steel Industry.* Knoxville, Tenn.: Vanderbilt University Press, 1969.

Bailyn, Bernard, and Lotte Bailyn. *Massachusetts Shipping, 1697–1714: A Statistical Study.* Cambridge, Mass.: Harvard University Press, 1959.

Baird, J. *View of the Valley of the Mississippi; or, the Emigrants' and Travellers' Guide to the West.* Philadelphia: H. S.Tanner, 1832.

Bairoch, Paul. "Geographical Structure and Trade Balance of European Foreign Trade from 1800 to 1970." *Journal of European Economic History* 3 (1974): 557–608.

———. *The Economic Development of the Third World since 1900.* Translated by Cynthia Postan. London: Methuen, 1975.

———. "Agriculture and the Industrial Revolution." In *The Fontana Economic History of Europe,* edited by Carlo M. Cipolla, vol. 3, *The Industrial Revolution, 1700–1914, 452–506.* Brighton: Harvester Press, 1976.

———. "International Industrialization Levels from 1750 to 1980." *Journal of European Economic History* 11 (1982), 269–333.

Bairoch, Paul, J.B., and Jean Batou. *Cities and Economic Development from the Dawn of History to the Present.* Translated by Christopher Braider. London: Mansell Publishing, 1988. Originally published under the title *De Jéricho à Mexico: Villes et économie dans l'histoire* (Paris: Gallimard, 1985).

Bairoch, Paul, Jean Batou, and Piérre Chèvre. *The Population of European Cities, 800–1850.* Geneva: Librairée Droz, 1988.

Balée, William. "The Culture of Amazonian Forests." In *Advances in Economic Botany, vol. 7, Resource Management in Amazonia: Indigenous and Folk Strategies,* edited by Darrell A. Posey and William Balée, 1–21. New York: New York Botanical Gardens, 1987.

———. "Indigenous Transformation of Amazonian Forests: An Example from Maranhâo, Brazil." *L'Homme* 126–28, no. 33 (1993): 231–54.

Bamford, Paul Waldon. *Forests and French Sea Power, 1660–1789* [1956]. Reprint, Toronto: Toronto University Press, 1971.

———. *Privilege and Profit: A Business Family in Eighteenth-Century France.* Philadelphia: University of Pennsylvania Press, 1988.

Banfield, Thomas C. *Industry of the Rhine.* London: Charles Knight & Co., 1846–48.

Banuri, Tariq, and Frédérique A. Marglin, eds. *Who Will Save the Forests?: Knowledge, Power and Environmental Destruction.* London: Zed Books, 1993.

Barhin, Tunku S., and P. D. A. Perera. *FELDA. 21 Years of Land Development.* Kuala Lumpur: Federal Land Development Authority, 1977.

Barker, Graeme. *Prehistoric Farming in Europe.* Cambridge: Cambridge University Press, 1985.

Barney, Gerald O. "The Nature of the Deforestation Problem—Trends and Policy Implications." *Proceedings of the U.S. Strategy Conference on Tropical Deforestation,* 12–14 June, 1978, 25–34. Washington, D.C.: Department of State and U.S. Agency for International Development, 1978.

———. *Technical Report.* Vol. 2 of *Global 2000 Report to the President: Entering the Twenty-First Century,* Council of Environmental Quality and U.S. Department of State, edited by Gerald O. Barney. Washington, D.C.: GPO, 1980.

Barr, Brenton. "Perspectives on Deforestation in the U.S.S.R." In *World Deforestation in the Twentieth Century,* edited by John F. Richards and Richard P. Tucker, 230–61. Duke Press Policy Studies. Durham, N.C.: Duke University Press, 1988.

Barraclough, Geoffrey, ed. *The Times Atlas of World History.* London: The Times Publishing Company, 1978.

Bartlett, Harley Harris. "Fire, Primitive Agriculture and Grazing in the Tropics." In *Man's Role in Changing the Face of the Earth,* edited by William L. Thomas, 652–720. Chicago: University of Chicago Press, 1956.

———. *Fire in Relation to Primitive Agriculture and Grazing in the Tropics: Annotated Bibliography.* 3 vols. Ann Arbor: University of Michigan Botanical Gardens, 1955–61.

Bartlett, Robert. *The Making of Europe: Conquest, Colonization, and Cultural Change, 950–1350.* Princeton, N.J.: Princeton University Press, 1993.

Barton, Gregory A. "Empire Forestry and American Environmentalism." *Environmental History* 6 (2000): 187–204.

Bartram, William. *The Travels of William Bartram.* Edited by Mark van Doren. New York: Facsimile Library, 1940.

Bates, Henry Walter. *The Naturalist on the River Amazon.* London: John Murray, 1863.

Bates, James Leonard. "Fulfilling American Democracy: The Conservation Movement, 1907–1921." *Mississippi Valley Historical Review* 44 (1957): 29–57.

Baticle, Yves. *L'elevage ovir dans les Pays Européens de la Méditerranée Occidentale.* Publication no. 47. Dijon: Universitaires de Dijon, 1974.

Battistini, Réne, and Pierre Vérin. "Man and Environment in Madagascar: Past Problems and Problems of Today." In *Biogeography and Ecology in Madagascar,* edited by Réne Battistini and G. Richard-Vinard, 311–37. The Hague: Dr. W. Junk, 1972.

Baudrillart, Henri Joseph. "Mémoire sur le déboisement des montagnes." *Annals de l'Agriculture Français* 8 (1831): 65–78.

Baumol, William J., and Wallace E. Oates. *The Theory of Environmental Policy.* New York: Cambridge University Press, 1988.

Bazilevich, N. E., L. F. Rodin, and N. N. Roznov. "Geographical Aspects of Biological Productivity." *Soviet Geography, Review and Translation* 12 (1971): 293–317.

Beaglehole, John Cawte, ed. *The "Endeavour" Journal of Sir Joseph Banks, 1768–1772.* 2 vols. Sydney: Trustees of the Public Library of New South Wales and Angus and Robertson, 1963.

Beatley, Janice Carson. "The Primary Forests of Vinton and Jackson Counties, Ohio." Ph.D. diss., Ohio State University, 1953.

Beaufoy, Henry. *Tour through Parts of the United States and Canada by a British Subject.* London: Longman, Rees, Orme, Browne and Green, 1828.

Bechmann, Roland. *Trees and Man: The Forest in the Middle Ages* [1984]. Translated from the French by Katharyn Dunham. New York: Paragon House, 1990.

Beer, H., and Z. Rizvi. *The Vanishing Forest: The Human Consequences of Deforestation.* Report of the Independent Commission on International Human Rights. London: Zed Books, 1986.

Begbie, Peter James. *The Malayan Peninsula Embracing Its History, Customs, Manners and Customs of the Inhabitants, Politics, Natural History, etc., from the Earliest Records.* 2 vols. N.p.: Printed for the author at the Vepery Mission Press, 1835.

Behre, Karl-Ernst. "The Interpretation of Anthropogenic Indicators in Pollen Diagrams." *Pollen et Spores* 23 (1981): 225–45.

———. *Anthropogenic Indications in Pollen Diagrams.* Rotterdam: A. A.Balkema, 1986.

———. "The Role of Man in European Vegetation History." In *Vegetation History,* edited by Brian Huntely and Thomas Webb III, 633–72. Dordrecht: Kluwer Academic Publishers, 1988.

Belknap, Jeremy. *The History of New Hampshire.* 3 vols. Boston: Printed for the author, n.p., 1791–92.

Bell, Martin, and Michael J. Walker. *Late Quaternary Environmental Change: Physical and Human Perspectives.* Harlow, England: Longmans Scientific and Technical, 1992.

Bennett, H. S. *Life on the English Manor: A Study of Peasant Conditions, 1150–1400.* Cambridge: Cambridge University Press, 1937.

Bennett, John W., and Kenneth A. Dahlberg. "Institutions, Social Organization, and Cultural Values." In *The Earth As Transformed by Human Action: Global and Regional Changes in the Biosphere over the Past 300 Years,* edited by Billie Lee Turner II, William C. Clark, Robert W. Kates, John F. Richards, Jessica T. Mathews, and William B. Meyer, 69–86. New York: Cambridge University Press, 1990.

Bennett, K. D. "A Provisional Map of Forest Types for the British Isles, 5000 Years Ago." *Journal of Quaternary Science* 4 (1989): 141–44.

Benson, Barbara E. "Logs and Lumber: The Development of the Lumber Industry in Michigan's Lower Peninsula, 1837–1870." Ph.D. diss., Indiana University, 1976.

Berger, André, John Imbrie, J. Hays, G. Kulka, and B. Saltzman, eds. *Milankovitch and Climate: Understanding the Response to Astronomical Forcing.* Part I. Dordrecht: Reidel , 1979.

Bergstrom, George. *The Hungry Planet.* New York: Collier, 1972.

Berkhofer, Robert A. F. Jr. *The White Man's Indian: Images of the American Indian from Columbus to the Present*. New York: Alfred Knopf, 1978.

Berman, Marshall. *All That Is Solid Melts into Air: The Experience of Modernity*. London: Verso, 1981.

Bernardi, Aurelio. "The Economic Problems of the Roman Empire at the Time of Its Decline." In *The Economic Decline of Empires,* edited by Carlo M. Cipolla, 16–83. London: Methuen and Co., 1970.

Bidie, George. "On the Effects of Forest Destruction in Coorg." *Proceedings of the Royal Geographical Society* 13 (1869): 74–83. For an extended treatment see the *Journal of the Royal Geographical Society* 39 (1869): 77–90.

Bidwell, Percy W., and John I. Falconer. *History of Agriculture in the Northern United States, 1620–1860* [1925]. Carnegie Institute Publication no 358. Reprint, New York: P. S. Smith, 1941.

Bigelow, Thomas. *Journal of a Tour to Niagra Falls in the Year 1805*. Boston: J.Wilson, 1876.

Billington, James H. *The Icon and the Axe: An Interpretative History of Russian Culture*. London: Weidenfeld and Nicolson, 1966.

Binford, Michael W., Mark Brenner, Thomas J. Whitmore, Antonia Higuera-Gundy, E. S. Deevey, and Barbara Leyden. "Ecosystems, Paleoecology and Human Disturbance in Subtropical and Tropical America." *Quaternary Sciences Review* 6 (1987): 115–28.

Bining, Arthur C. *Pennsylvania Iron Manufacture in the Eighteenth Century*. Publication no. 4. Harrisburg: Pennsylvania Historical Commission, 1938.

Bintliff, John L. "Mediterranean Alluviation: New Evidence from Archaeology." *Proceedings of the Prehistorical Society* 41 (1975): 78–84.

———. *Natural Environment and Human Settlement in Prehistoric Greece*. 2 vols. British Archaeological Reports, suppl. ser. 28. Oxford: Tempus Reparatum, 1977.

———. "New Approaches to Human Geography. Prehistoric Greece: A Case Study." In *An Historical Geography of the Balkans,* edited by Frank W. Carter, 59–114. London: Academic Press, 1977.

———. "Erosion in the Mediterranean Lands: A Reconsideration of Patterns, Processes, and Methodology." In *Past and Present Soil Erosion: Archaeological and Geographical Perspectives,* edited by Martin Bell and John Boardman, 125–32. Oxbow Monographs 22. Oxford: Oxbow Books, 1992.

Birrell, Jean. "Common Rights in the Medieval Forest: Disputes and Conflicts in the Thirteenth Century." *Past and Present* 117 (1987): 22–49.

Bishop, T. A. M. "Assarting and the Growth of the Open Fields." *Economic History Review* 6 (1935): 19–29.

Blache, Jacques. "L'essartage, ancienne practique culturale dans les Alpes Dauphinoises." *Revue de géographie alpine* 11 (1923): 553–75.

Blaikie. Piers M. *The Political Economy of Soil Erosion in Developing Countries*. Harlow, England: Longmans Science and Technology, 1985.

Blaikie, Piers M., and Harold C. Brookfield. *Land Degradation and Society*. London: Methuen, 1987.

Blanqui, Adolphe Jérôme. *Du déboisement des montagnes*. Paris: L'Hachette, 1838.

———. "Rapport sur la situation économique des départments de la frontiére des Alpes: Isère, Hautes-Alpes, Basses-Alpes et Var." *Académie des Sciences Morales et Politiques, Sèances et Travaux* 4 (1843): 353–64.

Bloch, Marc L. B. *French Rural History: An Essay on Its Basic Characteristics* [1932]. Translated from the French by Janet Sondheimer. Berkeley and Los Angeles: University of California Press, 1970.

Blome, Richard. *A Geographical Description of the Four Parts of the World*. London: Printed by T. N. for R. Blome, 1670.

———. *A Description of the Island of Jamaica with Other Isles and Territories in America to which the English are Related . . .* London: Printed by J. B. for Dorman Newman, 1672.

Boaten, K. "Commercial Agriculture in Asante," *Ghana Geographical Association Bulletin* 15 (1973), 40–49.

Bodley, John. *Victims of Progress*. Mountain View, Mass.: Mayfield Publishing Co., 1990.

———, ed. *Tribal Peoples and Development Issues: A Global Overview*. Mountain View, Mass.: Mayfield Publishing Co., 1988.

Bogucki, Peter I. *Forest Farmers and Stockherders: Early Agriculture and Its Consequences in North-Central Europe*. Cambridge: Cambridge University Press, 1988.

———. "The Spread of Early Farming in Europe." *American Scientist* 84 (May-June 1991): 242–53.

Boissonnade, Prosper. *Life and Work in Medieval Europe (Fifth to Fifteenth Centuries)*. Translated from the French with an introduction by Eileen Power. New York: Alfred A. Knopf, 1927.

Boixo, Paul de. *Les forêts et la réboisement dans les Pyrénées-Orientales*. Paris: J. Rothschild, 1894.

Bökönyi, Sandor. "Stockbreeding." In *Neolithic Greece*, edited by Demetrios R. Theocaris, 165–78. Athens: National Bank of Greece, 1973.

Bonnifield, Mathew Paul. *The Dust Bowl: Men, Dirt and Depression*. Albuquerque: University of New Mexico Press, 1979.

Boomgaard, Peter. "Forest Management and Exploitation in Colonial Java, 1677–1879." *Forest and Conservation History* 36 (1992): 1–14.

Boserup, Ester. *The Conditions of Agricultural Growth: The Economics of Agrarian Change under Population Growth*. Chicago: Aldine Publishing Co., 1965.

———. *Population and Technological Change: A Study of Long Term Trends*. Chicago: University of Chicago Press, 1981.

———. "Population and Technology in Preindustrial Europe." *Population and Development Review* 13 (1987): 691–700.

Bossière, Jean. "La consommation parisienne de bois et les sidèrurgies périphériques: essai de mise en parallèle (milieu XVᵉ–milieu XIXᵉ siècles)." In *Forges et forêts: Recherches sur la consummation proto industrie de bois,* edited by Denis Woronoff, 29–55. Paris: L'École des Haute Études en Sciences Sociales, 1990.

Boussingault, Jean Baptiste. "Memoir Concerning the Effect of which Clearing the Land has in Diminishing the Quantity of Water in the Streams of a District." *Edinburgh New Philosophical Journal* 24 (1838): 85–106.

Bové, Paul A. "Discourse." In *Critical Terms for Literary Theory,* edited by Frank Lentricchia and Thomas McLaughlin, 50–65. Chicago: University of Chicago Press, 1990.

Bowden, Martyn J. "The Invention of American Tradition." *Journal of Historical Geography* 18 (1992), 3–26.

Bowonder, B. "Deforestation in India." *International Journal of Environmental Studies* 18 (1982): 223–38.

———. "Deforestation in Developing Countries." *Journal of Environmental Systems* 15 (1986): 171–92.

Bowonder, B., S. S. R. Prasad, and N. V. M. Unni. "Deforestation around Urban Centres in India." *Environmental Conservation* 14 (1987): 23–28.

Boxer, Charles Ralph. *The Golden Age of Brazil, 1695–1750: Growing Pains of a Colonial Society*. Berkeley and Los Angeles: University of California Press in cooperation with the Sociedade de Estudos Histórics Dom Pedro Segundo, Rio De Janeiro, 1962.

Boyd-Orr, Sir John. "One World—One Forest." *Unasylva* 1 (1947): 2–3.

Boyer, Charles Shimer. *Early Forges and Furnaces in New Jersey*. Philadelphia: University of Pennsylvania Press, 1931.

Bradford, John. "Buried Landscapes in Southern Italy." *Antiquity* 23 (1949): 65–72.

———. *Ancient Landscapes in Europe and Asia: Studies in Archaeology and Photography*. Oxford: Oxford University Press, 1965.

Brady, Thomas A. Jr. "The Rise of Merchant Empires, 1400–1700: A European Counterpoint." In *The Political Economy of Merchant Empires,* edited by James D. Tracy, 117–60. Cambridge: Cambridge University Press, 1991.

Bramwell, Anna. *Ecology in the 20th Century: A History*. New Haven, Conn.: Yale University Press, 1989.

Branch, Douglas. *The Hunting of the Buffalo*. Lincoln: University of Nebraska Press, 1962.

Brandis, Dietrich. "Memorandum on the Supply of Railway Sleepers of the Himalayan Pines impregnated in India." *Indian Forester* 4 (1879): 365–83.

———. *Indian Forestry*. Woking, England: Oriental University Institute, 1897.

Braudel, Fernand. *The Mediterranean and the Mediterranean World in the Age of Philip II*. Translated from the French by Siân Reynolds. New York: Harper Collins, 1972.

———. *Capitalism and Material Life, 1400–1800* [1967]. Translated from the French by Miriam Kochan. New York: Harper and Row, 1973.

———. *Capitalism and Material Life, 15ᵗʰ to 18ᵗʰ Century*. Vol. 1, *1400–1800* [1967]. Translated from the French by Miriam Kochan. New York: Harper and Row, 1973.

———. *Civilization and Capitalism, 15th–18th Century*. Vol. 1, *The Structures of Everyday Life: The Limits of the Possible*. Translated from the French by Siân Reynolds. New York: Harper and Row, 1981.

———. *Civilization and Capitalism, 15th–18th Century*. Vol. 3, *The Perspective of the World* [1981]. Translated from the French by Siân Reynolds. New York: Harper and Row, 1984.

Bray, Francesca. "Agriculture." In *Science and Civilization in China,* edited by Joseph Needham, vol. 6., *Biology and Biological Technology,* part 2, *Agriculture*. Cambridge: Cambridge University Press, 1984.

Bray, Warwick. "From Predation to Production: The Nature of Agricultural Evolution in Mexico and Peru." In *Problems in Economic and Social Archaeology,* edited by Gale de Giberne Sieveking, Ian H. Longworth, and K. E. Wilson, 73–96. London: Duckworth, 1976.

———. "From Foraging to Farming in Early Mexico." In *Hunters, Gatherers, and First Farmers beyond Europe,* edited by John V. S. Megaw, 225–47. Leicester: Leicester University Press, 1977.

———. "Early Agriculture in the Americas." In *The Cambridge Encyclopedia of Archaeology,* edited by Andrew Sherratt, 365–74. Cambridge: Cambridge University Press, 1980.

Briavonne, Natalis. *De l'Industrie en Belgique, causes de décadence et de prosperité, sa situation actuelle*. Vol. 1. Bruxelles: Eugene Dubois, 1839.

Bridenbaugh, Carl. *Cities in the Wilderness: The First Century of Urban Life in America, 1625–1742*. New York: Rowland Press, 1938.

———. "Yankee Use and Abuse of the Forest in the Building of New England, 1620–1660." *Proceedings of the Massachusetts Historical Society* 89 (1977): 3–35.

Bridenbaugh, Carl, and Roberta Bridenbaugh. *No Peace beyond the Line: The English in the Caribbean, 1624–1690*. New York: Oxford University Press, 1972.

Briggs, Asa, and David Snowman, eds. *Fins de Siècle: How Centuries End, 1400–2000.* New Haven, Conn.: Yale University Press, 1996.

Brodie, Bernard. *Seapower in the Machine Age: Major Naval Inventions and Their Consequences on International Politics, 1814–1940.* Princeton, N.J.: Princeton University Press, 1941.

Brodribb, Gerald. *Roman Brick and Tile.* Gloucester: Allan Sutton, 1987.

Bromley, R. J. "Agricultural Colonization in the Upper Amazon Basin: The Impact of Oil Discoveries." *Tijdschrift voor Economisch en Sociale Geografie* 63 (1972): 278–94.

Bromley, S. W. "The Original Forest Types of Southern New England." *Ecological Monographs* 5 (1955): 61–89.

Bronson, Bennet. "South-East Asia: Civilizations of the Tropical Forests." In *The Cambridge Encyclopedia of Archaeology,* edited by Andrew Sherratt, 262–66. Cambridge: Cambridge University Press, 1980.

Brookfield, Harold C., Frances Jane Lian, Kwai-Sim Low, and Lesley Potter. "Borneo and the Malay Peninsula." In *The Earth As Transformed by Human Action: Global and Regional Changes in the Biosphere over the Past 300 Years,* edited by Billie Lee Turner II, William C. Clark, Robert W. Kates, John F. Richards, Jessica T. Mathews, and William B. Meyer, 495–512. New York: Cambridge University Press, 1990.

Brooks, Edwin J. "Twilight of Brazilian Tribes." *Geographical Magazine* 45, no. 4 (1973): 304–10.

Brosselin, Arlette. *La forêt bourguignonne: 1660–1789.* Dijon: Editions Universitaires de Dijon, 1987.

Brown, Anthony H. D., Otto H. Frankel, D. R. Marshall, and J. T. Williams, eds. *The Use of Plant Genetic Resources.* Cambridge: Cambridge University Press, 1989.

Brown, Arthur A., and Kenneth P. Davis. *Forest Fire: Control and Use.* 2d ed. New York: McGraw-Hill, 1973.

Brown, John Croumbie. *Réboisement in France: Or, Records of the Replanting of the Alps, Cevennes, and the Pyrenees with Trees, Herbage and Bush.* London: Kegan Paul, 1880.

———. *French Forest Ordinance of 1669.* Translated from the French by J. C. Brown. Edinburgh: Oliver and Boyd, 1883.

Brown, Katrina, and David W. Pearce, eds. *The Causes of Tropical Deforestation.* London: University College Press, 1994.

Brown, Sandra, and Ariel Lugo. "Tropical Secondary Forests." *Journal of Tropical Ecology* 6 (1990): 1–32.

Bruijn, Jaap R. "Productivity, Profitability, and Costs of Private and Corporate Dutch Ship Owning in the Seventeenth and Eighteenth Centuries." In *The Rise of Merchant Empires: Long Distance Trade in the Early Modern World, 1350–1750,* edited by James D. Tracy, 174–94. Cambridge: Cambridge University Press, 1990.

Brüning, E. F. "Förstliche Produktionslehre." *Europäische Hochschulschriften* 25, no. 1 (1971): 1–23. Bern: Frankfurt.

———. "Ökosysteme in den Tropen." *Umschau* 47 (1975): 405–10.

Brunnschweller, D. *The Llanos Frontier of Colombia: Environment and Changing Land Use in Meta.* Latin American Studies Center Monograph no 9. East Lansing: Michigan State University, 1972.

Brunt, Peter A. *Italian Manpower, 225 BC—AD 14.* Oxford: Oxford University Press, 1971.

Bryant, Dirk, Daniel Nielsen, and Laura Tangley. *The Last Frontier Forests: Ecosystem and Economics on the Edge.* Washington, D.C.: World Resources Institute, 1997.

Bryant, Ralph Clement. *Logging: The Principles and General Methods of Operation in the United States* [1913], 2d ed. New York: John Wiley, 1923.

————. *Lumber: Its Manufacture and Distribution* [1922], 2d ed. New York: John Wiley and Sons, 1934.

Buck, John Lossing. *Chinese Farm Economy: A Study of 2866 Farms in Seventeen Localities and Seven Provinces in China.* Chicago: University of Chicago Press for the University of Nanking and the China Council of the Institute of Pacific Relations, 1930.

Budowski, Gerardo. "Tropical Savannas, a Sequence of Forest Felling and Repeated Burnings." *Turrialba* 6 (1956): 22–33.

————. "The Ecological Status of Fire in American Tropical Lowlands." *Actas 33º Congreso Internacional de Americanistas, San José, Costa Rica, 1958* 1 (1959): 264–78.

Buffon, George-Louis Leclerc, comte de. "Mémoire sur la conservation et la rétablissement des forêts." *Mémoires de l'Académie Royale des Sciences.* Paris, 1739. Translated and printed in *A Treatise on the Manner of Raising Forest Trees, etc. to which is added Two Memoirs . . . on Preserving and Repairing Forests and the Culture of Forests,* 83–105, 109–29. Edinburgh: G. Hamilton and J. Balfour, 1761.

————. *Histoire naturelle, générale et particulière.* 44 vols. Paris, 1749–1804. Another edition: W. Wood, ed., *Comte de Buffon, Natural History, General and Particular: The History of Man and the Quadrupeds.* Translated with notes and observations by William Smellie. 10 vols. London: T. Cadell and W. Davis, 1812.

Bünting, Philip Johan. *Sylva Subterranea, oder vortreffliche Nützbarkeit des unterirdischen Waldes der Stein-Kohlen.* Halle: n.p., 1693.

Buringh, P., and R. Dudal. "Agricultural Land Use in Space and Time." In *Land Transformation in Agriculture,* edited by M. Gordon Wolman and F. G. A. Fournier, 9–44. Scope Publication no. 32. Chichester: John Wiley and Sons, 1987.

Burleigh, R. "W. F. Libby and the Development of Radiocarbon Dating." *Antiquity* 55 (1981): 6–8.

Buschbacher, Robert J. "Tropical Deforestation and Pasture Development." *BioScience* 36 (1986): 22–28.

Butland, Gilbert J. "Frontiers of Settlement in South America." *Revista Geografica* 65 (1966): 93–108.

Buttler, Werner, and Waldemar Haberey. *Die Banderkeramische Ansiedlung bei Köln-Lindenthal.* Römisch-Germanische Forschungen no. 11. Berlin: Walter de Gruyter, 1936.

Butzer, Karl W. "From Columbus to Acosta: Science, Geography and the New World." *Annals, Association of American Geographers* 82 (1992): 543–65.

Byrd, William. *History of the Dividing Line between Virginia and Other Tracts: 1728–1736: From the Papers of William Byrd, Virginia, Esq.* Edited by T. H. Wynne. Richmond, Va.: n.p., 1866.

————. *William Byrd's Natural History of Virginia: or, The Newly Discovered Eden* [n.d.]. Edited and translated from a German version by Richard C. Beatty and W. J. Mulloy. Richmond, Va.: Dietz Press, 1940.

Byrne, Muriel St. Clare. *The Lisle Letters.* 6 vols. Chicago: University of Chicago Press, 1981.

Caldwell, Joseph R. "Trend and Tradition in the Prehistory of the Eastern United States." Scientific Paper no. 10. *American Anthropologist,* Memoir 88, 1958.

Callicott, James Baird. "Traditional American Indian and Western European Attitudes towards Nature: An Overview." *Environmental Ethics* 4 (1982): 293–318.

Callicott, James Baird, and Roger T. Ames, eds. *Nature in Asian Traditions of Thought: Essays in Environmental Philosophy.* New York: State University of New York Press, 1989.

Callicott, James Baird, and Roger T. Ames. "Epilogue: On the Relation of Idea and Action." In *Nature in Asian Traditions of Thought: Essays in Environmental Philosophy,* edited by James Baird Callicott and Roger T. Ames, 279–89. New York: State University of New York Press, 1989.

Cameron, Jenks. *The Development of Governmental Forest Control in the United States* [1928]. Institute for Government Research, Studies in Administration. Baltimore: Johns Hopkins University Press. Reprint, New York: De Capo Press, 1972.

Candolle, Alphonse de. *Géographie botanique raisonée*. Paris: de Candolle 1855. English translation published under the title *Origin of Cultivated Plants* (London, 1884).

Capistrano, Ana Doris. "Tropical Forest Depletion and the Changing Macro-Economy, 1967–85." In *The Causes of Tropical Deforestation,* edited by Katrina Brown and David W. Pearce, 68–85. London: University College Press, 1994.

Capper, John. *Old Ceylon—Sketches of Ceylon in Olden Times*. London: W. B. Whittingham, 1878.

Carcopino, Jerôme. *Daily Life in Ancient Rome: The People and the City at the Height of the Empire* [1940]. Translated from the French by E. O.Lorimer. New Haven: Yale University Press, 1960.

Carneiro, Robert L. "On the Use of the Stone Axe by the Amahuaca Indians of Eastern Peru." *Ethnologische Zeitschrift Zürich* 1 (1974): 107–22.

———. "Forest Clearance among the Yanomamö: Observations and Implications." *Antropológica* 52 (1979): 39–76.

Carroll, Charles F. *The Timber Economy of Puritan New England*. Providence, R.I.: Brown University Press, 1973.

Carstenson, Vernon R. *Farms or Forests: Evolution of State Land Policy in Northern Wisconsin, 1850–1932*. Madison: University of Wisconsin, College of Agriculture, 1958.

Cartmill, Matt. *A View to a Death in the Morning: Hunting and Nature through History*. Cambridge, Mass.: Harvard University Press, 1993.

Casson, Lionel. *Ships and Seamanship in the Ancient World*. Princeton, N.J.: Princeton University Press, 1971.

Catesby, Mark. *The Natural History of Carolina, Florida and the Bahama Islands*. 2 vols. London: Benjamin White, 1747.

Cato, Marcus Porcius. *On Agriculture*. Translated from the Latin by William D. Hooper; revised by Harrison B. Ash. Loeb Classical Library. Cambridge, Mass.: Harvard University Press, 1936.

Cecelski, Elizabeth, Joy Dunkerley, and William Ramsey. *Household Energy and the Poor in the Third World*. Washington, D.C.: Resources for the Future, 1979.

Ceci, L. "Maize Cultivation in Coastal New York: The Archaeological, Agronomical, and Documentary Evidence." *North American Archaeologist* 1 (1979): 45–74.

Chaloner and Fleming [No initials]. *The Mahogany Tree: Its Botanical Character, Qualities and Uses . . . in the West Indies and Central America*. Liverpool: Rockriff and Sons, 1851.

Champion, T., Clive Gamble, Stephen Shennan, and Alastair Whittle, eds. *Prehistoric Europe*. London: Academic Press, 1984.

Chapman, Jefferson, Paul A. Delcourt, Patricia A. Cridlebaugh, A. Shea, and Hazel R. Delcourt. "Man-Land Interaction: 10,000 Years of American Indian Impact on Native Ecosystems in the Lower Little Tennessee Valley." *Southeastern Archaeology* 1 (1982): 115–21.

Chastellux, François Jean, marquis de. *Travels in North America in the Years 1780, 1781, and 1782*. 2 vols. New York: White, Gallacher, and White, 1789.

Chateaubriand, François Auguste René, vicomte de. *Recollections of Italy, England, and America on Various Subjects*. Philadelphia: M. Carey, 1816.

———. *Travels in America and Italy*. 2 vols. London: H. Colburn, 1828.

Chaudhuri, Kirti N. *The English East India Company. The Study of an Early Joint-Stock Company, 1600–1640*. London: Frank Cass, 1965.

———. "Indian International Economy in the Nineteenth Century." *Modern Asian Studies.* 2 (1968): 31–50.

———. *Trade and Civilization in the Indian Ocean: An Economic History of the Rise of Islam to 1750.* Cambridge: Cambridge University Press, 1985.

Chaunu, Pierre. *European Expansion in the Later Middle Ages.* Translated from the French by Katherine Bertram. Amsterdam: N. Holland Publishing Co., 1979.

Chaunu, Pierre, and Hugette Chaunu. *Séville et l'Amérique aux XVIe et XVIIe siècles. Partie interprétive,* 4 vols., and *Partie statistique,* 7 parts in 8 vols. Paris: Flammarion, 1977.

Chauvin, Henri. "When an African City Runs Out of Fuel." *Unasylva* 33, no. 133 (1981): 11–20.

Chavannes, Elizabeth. "Written Records of Forest Succession." *Scientific American* 53 (1941): 76–80.

Chekov, Anton P. *Uncle Vanya* (1900). In *Chekov's Plays,* edited by Elisaveta Fen. Harmondsworth, England: Penguin Classics, 1954.

Chevalier, A. "Essai d'une carte botanique forestière et pastorale de l'A. O. F." *Compte Rendus de l'Académie des Sciences* 152, no. 6 (June 1911).

Chi, Ch'ao-Ting. *Key Economic Areas in Chinese History, as Revealed in the Development of Public Works for Water Control* [1936], 2d ed. London: Allen and Unwin Ltd, 1963.

Childe, V. Gordon. *The Dawn of European Civilization.* London: Kegan Paul, Trench, Trubner and Co. Ltd, 1925.

———. *The Danube in Prehistory.* London: Oxford University Press, 1929.

Chinard, Gilbert. "The American Philosophical Society and the Early History of Forestry in America." *Proceedings, American Philosophical Society* 89 (1945): 444–88.

Chisholm, Michael. "The Increasing Separation of Production and Consumption." In *The Earth As Transformed by Human Action: Global and Regional Changes in the Biosphere over the Past 300 Years,* edited by Billie Lee Turner II, William C. Clark, Robert W. Kates, John F. Richards, Jessica T. Mathews, and William B. Meyer, 87–101. New York: Cambridge University Press, 1990.

Christensen, Norman L. "Fire Regimes and Ecosystem Dynamics." In *Fire in the Environment: The Ecological, Atmospheric and Climatic Importance of Vegetation Fires,* edited by Paul J. Crutzen, and Johann Georg Goldammer, 233–44. Chichester: John Wiley, 1993.

Christian Science Monitor, 10 October 1988.

Church, R. J. Harrison. *West Africa: A Study of the Environment and of Man's Use of It* [1957], 5th ed. London: Longmans, 1966.

Churchill, Winston Spencer. *The River War: An Historical Account of the Reconquest of the Soudan.* Edited by Col. F. Rhodes. 2 vols. London: Longmans Green and Co., 1899.

Cicero, Marcus Tullius. *De Natura Deorum Academica.* Translated from the Latin by H. Rackham. Loeb Classical Library. London: William Heinemann, 1933.

Cipolla, Carlo M. *Guns and Sails in the Early Phase of European Expansion: 1400–1700.* London: Collins, 1965.

———. *Before the Industrial Revolution: European Society and Economy, 1000–1700.* 3d ed. London: Routledge, 1993.

———. Introduction in *The Fontana Economic History of Europe,* edited by Carlo Cipolla, vol. 3, *The Industrial Revolution, 1700–1914,* 8–21. Brighton: Harvester Press, 1976.

———, ed. *The Economic Decline of Empires.* London: Methuen and Co., 1970.

———. *The Fontana Economic History of Europe.* Vol. 2, *The Sixteenth and Seventeenth Centuries.* Brighton: Harvester Press, 1972.

———. *The Fontana Economic History of Europe.* Vol. 3, *The Industrial Revolution, 1700–1914.* Brighton: Harvester Press, 1976.

Clapham, John H., and Eileen Power, eds. *The Cambridge Economic History of Europe from the Decline of the Roman Empire.* Vol. 1, *The Agrarian Life of the Middle Ages.* Cambridge: Cambridge University Press, 1941; 2d rev. ed., 1966.

Clark, Andrew H. *The Invasion of New Zealand by People, Plants and Animals.* New Brunswick, N.J.: Rutgers University Press, 1944.

Clark, Charles E. *The Eastern Frontier: The Settlement of Northern New England, 1610–1763.* New York: Alfred A.Knopf, 1977.

Clark, Colin, and Margaret Haswell. *The Economics of Subsistence Agriculture,* 4th ed. London: Macmilllan, 1970.

Clark, J. Desmond. "Early Human Occupation of African Savanna Environments." In *Human Ecology in Savanna Environments,* edited by David R. Harris, 41–72. London: Academic Press, 1978.

Clark, J. Desmond, and J. W. K. Harris. "Fire and Its Roles in Early Hominid Lifeways." *African Archaeological Review* 3 (1985): 3–27.

Clark, J. Grahame D. "Forest Clearance and Prehistoric Farming." *Economic History Review* 17 (1947): 45–51.

———. *Prehistoric Europe: The Economic Basis.* London: Methuen and Co., 1952.

———. "Starr Carr: A Case Study in Bioarchaeology." *Addison-Wesley Module in Anthropology* 10 (1972): 1–42.

———. *Mesolithic Prelude: The Palaeolithic–Neolithic Transition in Old World Prehistory.* Robert Munro Foundation Lectures. Edinburgh: Edinburgh University Press, 1980.

Clark, James I. *Farming the Cutover: The Settlement of Northern Wisconsin.* Madison, Wis.: State Historical Society, 1956.

Clark, J. S., and Robinson, J. "Paleoecology of Fire." In *Fire in the Environment: The Ecological, Atmospheric and Climatic Importance of Vegetation in the Environment,.* edited by Paul J. Crutzen and Johann Georg Goldammer, 193–214. Chichester: John Wiley, 1993.

Clark, Kenneth. *Civilisation: A Personal View.* New York: Harper and Row Publishers, 1969.

Clark, Victor S. *History of Manufactures in the United States, 1607–1914* [1929]. 3 vols. Carnegie Institute Publication no. 215B. Washington, D.C.: Carnegie Institute. Reprint, New York: Arno Press, 1949.

Clawson, David L., and Raymond E. Crist. "Evolution of Land-Use Patterns and Agricultural Systems." *Mountain Research and Development* 2 (1982): 265–72.

Clawson, Marion. "Forests in the Long Sweep of American History." *Science* 204 (1979): 1168–74. Reprint, Washington, D.C.: Resources for the Future, Reprint no. 164, 1979.

Cleere, Henry. "Ironmaking in a Roman Furnace." *Britannia* 2 (1971), 203–17.

———. "Some Operating Parameters for Roman Ironworks." *London University, Bulletin of the Institute of Archaeology* 13 (1976), 233–247.

Cleghorn, Hugh. *The Forests and Gardens of South India.* London: W. H. Allen and Co., 1861.

Cleghorn, Hugh, Forbes Royle, R. Baird Smith, and R. Strachey. "Report of the Committee Appointed by the British Association to Consider the Probable Effects in a Oeconomical and Physical Point of View of the Destruction of Tropical Forests." *21st Meeting of the British Association,* Ipswich, 1851, 78–102. London: British Association, 1852.

CLIMAP Project Members. "Seasonal Reconstructions of the Earth's Surface at the Last Glacial Maximum." *GSA Maps and Charts Series, MC-36,* 179–229. Boulder, Colo.: Geological Society of America, 1981.

Cline, W. *Mining and Metallurgy in Negro Africa.* General Series in Anthropology, no. 5. Menasha, Wis.: George Banta Publishing Co., 1937.

Clough, Shepard Bancroft. *European Economic History: The Economic Development of Western Civilization.* New York: McGraw-Hill, 1959.

Clout, Hugh D. *Agriculture in France on the Eve of the Railway Age.* London: Croom Helm, 1980.

———. *The Land of France, 1815–1914.* London: George Allen and Unwin, 1983.

Clow, Archibold, and Nan L. Clow. "The Timber Famine and the Development of Technology." *Annals of Science* 12 (1956): 85–102.

Cochrane, G. Ross. "The Impact of Man on the Natural Biota." In *New Zealand in Maps,* edited by A. Grant Anderson and Don Brunch, 32–33. London: Hodder and Straughton, 1977.

Coghlan, T. A. *The Timber Resources of New South Wales.* Sydney: Government Printer, 1900.

———. *Picturesque New South Wales: An Illustrated Guide for the Settler and the Tourist.* Sydney: Government Printer, 1901.

COHMAP Members. "Major Climatic Changes of the Last 18,000 Years: Observations and Model Simulations." *Science* 241 (1988): 1043–52.

Colchester, Marcus, and Larry Lohmann, eds. *The Struggle for Land and the Fate of the Forests.* Penang, Malaysia: World Rainforest Movement, 1993.

Cole, Arthur H. "The Mystery of Fuel Wood Marketing in the United States." *Business History Review* 44 (1970): 339–59.

Cole, W. A., and Phyllis Deane. "The Growth of National Incomes." In *The Cambridge Economic History of Europe,* vol. 6, *The Industrial Revolution and After: Incomes, Population and Technological Change,* edited by H. John Habakkuk and Michael Postan, 1–59. Cambridge: Cambridge University Press, 1965.

Coles, Bryony J. "Wetlands Archaeology: A Wealth of Evidence," In *Wetlands: A Threatened Landscape,* edited by Michael Williams, 145–80. Oxford: Basil Blackwell, 1990.

Coles, Bryony J., and John M. Coles. *Sweet Track to Glastonbury.* London: Thames and Hudson, 1986.

Coles, John M., and Bryony J. Orme. "Neolithic Hurdles from Walton Heath, Somerset." *Somerset Levels Papers* 3 (1977): 6–29.

Coles, John M., S. V. E. Heal, and Bryony J. Orme. "The Uses of Wood in Prehistoric Britain and Ireland." *Proc. Prehistoric Society* 44 (1977): 1–45.

Collis, John S. *The Triumph of the Tree.* London: Jonathon Cape, 1950.

Colman, Henry. *The Agriculture and Rural Economy of France, Belgium, Holland and Switzerland.* London: Petheram, 1848.

Columella, Lucius Junius Moderatus. *De re Rustica* (On agriculture), books 1–4. Translated from the Latin by Harrison B. Ash. 3 vols. Loeb Classical Library. London: William Heinemann, 1941–55.

Constantinou, Georges. "Geological Features and Ancient Exploitation of Cupriferous Sulphide Ore Bodies in Cyprus." In *Early Metallurgy in Cyprus, 4000–500 B.C.,* edited by James D. Muhly, Robert Maddin, and Vassos Karageorghis, 13–24. Nicosia, Cyprus: Pierides Foundation in collaboration with the Department of Antiquities, Nicosia, 1982.

Cook, F., ed. *Journals of the Military Expedition of General John Sullivan against the Six Nations of Indians in 1779.* Auburn, N.Y.: Knapp, Peck and Thompson, 1887.

Cook, James. *A Voyage Towards the South Pole, and Round the World, Performed in His Majesty's Ships the RESOLUTION and ADVENTURE in the Years 1772, 1773, 1774, and 1775.* London: Printed for W. Strahan and T. Cadell in the Strand, 1777.

Cook, Orator Fuller. "Vegetation Affected by Agriculture in Central America." U.S. Department of Agriculture, Bureau of Plant Industry Bulletin no. 145. Washington, D.C.: GPO, 1909.

———. "Milpa Agriculture, a Primitive Tropical System." *Annual Report of the Smithsonian Institution for 1919,* 307–26. Washington, D.C.: GPO, 1921.

Cook, Sherburne F. *Soil Erosion and Population in Central Mexico.* Ibero-Americana, no. 34. Berkeley and Los Angeles: University of California Press, 1949.

Cook, Sherburne F., and Woodrow Borah. *Essays in Population History: Mexico and California.* Vol. 3. Berkeley and Los Angeles: University of California Press, 1979.

Cooper, Thomas. *Some Information Respecting America collected by Thomas Cooper* [Dublin: P. Wogan, 1774], 2d ed. London: J. Johnston, 1794.

Cooper, William. *A Guide in the Wilderness, or, the History of the First Settlements in the Western Counties of New York, with Useful Information for Future Settlers* [1810]. Dublin: Gilbert and Hodge. Reprint, Rochester, N.Y.: G. P. Humphrey, 1897.

Cooter, William S. "Preindustrial Frontiers and Interaction Spheres: Aspects of the Human Ecology of Roman Frontier Regions in Northwest Europe." Ph.D. diss., University of Oklahoma, 1976.

———. "Ecological Dimensions of Medieval Agrarian Systems." *Agricultural History* 52 (1978): 458–77.

Corner, Edred J. H. "Suggestions for Botanical Progress." *New Phytologist* 45 (1946): 185–92.

Corvol, Andrée. *L'homme aux bois: histoire des relations de l'homme et de la forêt, XVIIIe–XXe siècles.* Paris: Fayard, 1987.

Cosgrove, Denis. *Social Formation and Symbolic Landscape.* London: Croom Helm, 1984.

Cowan, C. Wesley. "Understanding the Evolution of Plant Husbandry in Eastern North America: Lesson from Botany, Ethnography and Archaeology." In *Prehistoric Food Production in North America,* ed. Richard Ford, 205–243. Museum of Anthropology, Anthropological Papers no. 75, 205–43. Ann Arbor: University of Michigan, 1985.

Cox, Thomas R. *Mills and Markets: A History of the Pacific Coast Lumber Industry to 1900.* Seattle: University of Seattle Press, 1974.

Coxe, Tench. *A View of the United States of America, in a Series of Papers Written at Various Times between the Years 1787 and 1794* [1794]. Philadelphia: William Hall and Wrigley and Berriman. Reprint, New York: Augustus M. Kelley, 1965.

Craine, Eugene R., and Reginald C. Reindorp, eds. and trans. *The Chronicles of Michoacán (Relaciòn de Michoacán,* 1541). Norman: University of Oklahoma Press, 1970.

Craven, Avery O. *Soil Exhaustion As a Factor in the Agricultural History of Virginia and Maryland, 1606–1860.* Urbana: University of Illinois Press, 1926.

Crawfurd, John. *History of the Indian Archipelago.* 3 vols. Edinburgh: A. Constable and Co., 1820.

Creel, George. "The Feudal Towns of Texas." *Harper's Weekly* 60 (23 July 1915): 76–78.

Crèvecoeur, J. Hector St. John de. *Letters from an American Farmer.* London: Thomas Davies, 1782.

Crist, Raymond E. "Along the Llanos-Andean Border in Venezuela: Then and Now!" *Geographical Review* 46 (1956): 187–208.

———. "Go East, Young Man." *Américas* 13, no. 6 (June 1961): 3–9.

Crist, Raymond E., and Ernesto Guhl. "Pioneer Settlement in Eastern Colombia." *Smithsonian Institution Report for 1956.* Washington, D.C.: Smithsonian Institution, 1956.

Crist, Raymond E., and Charles M. Nissly. *East from the Andes: Pioneer Settlements in the South American Heartland.* Gainesville: University of Florida Press, 1973.

Cromer, D. A. N. "Australia." In *A World Geography of Forest Resources,* edited by Stephen Haden-Guest, John K. Wright, and Eileen M. Teclaff, 573–90. American Geographical Society Special Publication, no. 33. New York: Ronald Press Company, 1956.

Crone, Gerald Roe, ed. *The Voyages of Cadamosto and Other Documents on Western Africa in the Second Half of the Fifteenth Century.* Hakluyt Society, ser. 2, vol. 80. London: The Hakluyt Society, 1937.

Cronon, William. *Changes in the Land: Indians, Colonists, and the Ecology of New England*. New York: Hill and Wang, 1983.

———. "A Place for Stories: Nature, History, and Narrative." *Journal of American History* 78, no. 4 (1992): 1347–76.

Crosby, Alfred L. *The Columbian Exchange: Biological and Cultural Consequences of 1492*. Westport, Conn.: Greenwood Press, 1976.

———. *Ecological Imperialism: The Biological Expansion of Europe, 900–1900*. Cambridge: Cambridge University Press, 1986.

Crossley, D. W. "The Performance of the Glass Industry in Sixteenth Century England." *Economic History Review* 25 (1972): 421–33.

Crouzet, François. "England and France in the Eighteenth Century: A Comparative Analysis of Two Economic Growths." In *The Causes of the Industrial Revolution in England*, edited by Roland M. Hartwell, 139–74. London: Methuen, 1967. Originally published in *Annales, Economies, Sociétés, Civilisations* 21, no. 2 (1966): 254–91.

Crystal, David. *Language Death*. Cambridge: Cambridge University Press, 2000.

Cumberland, Kenneth B. "A Century's Change: Natural to Cultural Vegetation in New Zealand." *Geographical Review* 31 (1941): 529–54.

———. "Climatic Change or Cultural Interference?" In *Land and Livelihood: Geographical Essays in Honour of George Jobberns*, edited by Murray McCaskill, 88–142. Auckland: New Zealand Geographical Society, 1962.

———. "Moas and Men: New Zealand about A.D. 1250." *Geographical Review* 52 (1962): 151–73.

Curti, Merle. *The Growth of American Thought*. New York: Harper and Row, 1943.

Curtin, Philip D. "The White Man's Grave: Image and Reality, 1780–1850." *Journal of British Studies* 1 (1961): 94–110.

———. "Slavery and Empire." In *Comparative Perspectives on Slavery in New World Plantation Societies*, edited by V. Rubin and Arthur Tudin, 292 (1977): 3–10. New York: New York Academy of Sciences, 1977.

———. *Cross-Cultural Trade in World History*. Cambridge: Cambridge University Press, 1984.

———. "The Environment beyond Europe and the European Theory of Empire." *Journal of World History* 1 (1990): 131–50.

Curtis, John T. "The Modification of Mid-Latitude Grasslands and Forests by Man." In *Man's Role in Changing the Face of the Earth*, edited by William L. Thomas, 721–36. Chicago: University of Chicago Press, 1956.

da Fonseca, Gustavo A. B. "The Vanishing Brazilian Atlantic Forest." *Biological Conservation* 34 (1985): 17–34.

Damodaran, Vinita. "Famine in a Forest Tract: Ecological Change and the Causes of the 1897 Famine in Chota Nagpur, Northern India." *Environment and History* 1 (1995): 129–58.

Dana, Samuel Trask. *Forest and Range Policy: Its Development in the United States*. American Forestry Series. New York: McGraw-Hill. Revised and enlarged by Sally K. Fairfax, 1980.

Danhof, Clarence H. "The Fencing Problem in the Eighteen-Fifties." *Agricultural History* 18 (1944): 168–86.

Daniels, Stephen. "The Political Iconography of Woodland in Later Georgian England." In *The Iconography of Landscape: Essays on the Symbolic Representation, Design and Use of Past Environments*, edited by Denis Cosgrove and Stephen Daniels, 43–82. Cambridge: Cambridge University Press, 1988.

Darby, Henry Clifford. "The Economic Geography of England, A.D. 1000–1250." In *An Histori-*

cal Geography of England before A.D. 1800, edited by H. Clifford Darby, 165–230. Cambridge: Cambridge University Press, 1936.

———. *The Medieval Fenland.* Cambridge: Cambridge University Press, 1940.

———. "The Changing English Landscape." *Geographical Journal* 117 (1951): 377–98.

———. "The Clearing of the English Woodlands." *Geography* 36 (1951): 71–83.

———. "The Clearing of the Woodland in Europe." In *Man's Role in Changing the Face of the Earth,* edited by William L. Thomas, 183–216. Chicago: University of Chicago Press, 1956.

———. "The Face of Europe on the Eve of the Great Discoveries." In *The New Cambridge Modern History,* vol. 1, *The Renaissance, 1493–1520,* edited by George Richard Potter, 20–49. Cambridge: Cambridge University Press, 1961.

———. *Domesday England.* Cambridge: Cambridge University Press, 1977.

Darby, Henry Clifford, and I. B. Terrett, eds. *The Domesday Geography of Midland England.* Cambridge: Cambridge University Press, 1971.

Darwin, Charles. *The Origin of Species by Means of Natural Selection* [1859]. Edited by William Benton. Chicago: University of Chicago Press, 1952.

Darwin, John. *The End of the British Empire: The Historical Debate.* Oxford: Basil Blackwell, 1991.

Davidson, Edward. *Railways of India: With an Account of their Rise, Progress and Construction: Written with Aid of the Records of the India Office.* London: E & F. N. Spon., 1868.

Davidson, Janet M. *The Prehistory of New Zealand.* Auckland: Longman Paul Ltd., 1984.

Dawson, Christopher. *The Making of Europe: An Introduction to the History of European Unity* [1932]. New York: Sheed and Ward, 1952.

Day, Gordon M. "The Indian As an Ecological Factor in the Northeastern Forest." *Ecology* 34 (1953): 329–46.

Dean, Warren I. *Rio Claro: A Brazilian Plantation System, 1820–1920.* Stanford, Calif.: Stanford University Press, 1976.

———. "Deforestation in Southeastern Brazil." In *Global Deforestation and the Nineteenth Century World Economy,* edited by Richard P. Tucker and John F. Richards, 50–67. Duke Press Policy Studies. Durham, N.C.: Duke University Press, 1983.

———. *Brazil and the Struggle for Rubber: A Study in Environmental History.* Cambridge: Cambridge University Press, 1987.

———. *With Broadax and Firebrand: The Destruction of the Brazilian Atlantic Forest.* Berkeley and Los Angeles: University of California Press, 1995.

Deane, Phyllis. *The First Industrial Revolution,* 2d ed. Cambridge: Cambridge University Press, 1979.

Deane, Phyllis, and William A. Cole. *British Economic Growth, 1689–1959.* Cambridge: Cambridge University Press, 1962.

Debien, G. *En Haute-Poitou: Défricheurs au travail, XVe–XVIIe siècles.* Paris: Armand Colin, 1952.

De Brahm, John Gerar William. "Philosophico-Historico-Hydrogeography of South Carolina, Georgia, and East Florida." In *Documents Connected with the History of South Carolina,* edited by P. C. J. Weston, 155–227. London: n.p., 1856.

Deevey, Edward S., Don S. Rice, Prudence M. Rice, H. H. Vaughan, Mark Brenner, and M. S. Flannery. "Mayan Urbanism: Impact on a Tropical Karst Environment." *Science* 206 (1979): 298–306.

Defebaugh, James Elliott. *History of the Lumber Industry in America.* 2 vols. Chicago: American Lumberman, 1906–7.

Deffontaines, Pierre. *La vie forestière en Slovaque.* Paris: Libraire Ancienne Honoré Champion, 1932.

Defoe, Daniel. *A Tour thro' the Whole Island of Great Britain.* 4 vols. London: J. Osborn et al., 1742.

De Koninck, Rodolphe. "Forest Policies in Southeast Asia: Taming Nature or Taming People?" In *The Challange of the Forest in Southeast Asia,* edited by Rodolphe De Koninck, Stéphane Bernard, Lyne Chabot, Christine Veilleux, Jean Michaud, and Steve Déry, 33–48. *Documents du Gérac,* 7 (1994). Quebec: University of Laval.

Delcourt, Hazel R. "The Impact of Prehistoric Agriculture and Land Occupation on Natural Vegetation." *Trends in Ecology and Evolution* 2 (1987): 39–44.

Delcourt, Hazel R., and Paul A. Delcourt. *Quaternary Ecology: A Palaeoecological Perspective.* London: Chapman Hall, 1991.

Delcourt, Paul A., and Hazel R. Delcourt. "Vegetation Maps for Eastern North America: 40,000 yrs BP to the Present." In *Geobotany II,* edited by Robert C. Romans, 123–66. New York: Plenum Press, 1981.

———. *Long-Term Forest Dynamics of the Temperate Zone: A Case Study of the Late-Quaternary Forests of Eastern North America.* Ecological Monographs no. 63. New York: Springer-Verlag, 1987.

De Maulde, Réne. *Étude sur la condition forestière de l'Orléans au moyen âge et à la renaissance.* Orléans: Herluison, 1871.

Demeny, Paul. "Population." In *The Earth As Transformed by Human Action: Global and Regional Changes in the Biosphere over the Past 300 Years,* edited by Billie Lee Turner II, William C. Clark, Robert W. Kates, John F. Richards, Jessica T. Mathews, and Wiliam B. Meyer, 41–54. New York: Cambridge University Press, 1990.

Demeritt, David. "The Construction of Global Warming and the Politics of Science." *Annals, Association of American Geographers* 91 (2001): 307–37.

Denevan, William M. "Development and the Imminent Demise of the Amazon Rain Forest." *Professional Geographer* 25 (1973): 130–35.

———. "Swiddens and Cattle Versus Forest: Development and the Imminent Demise of the Amazon Rain Forest Reexamined." In *Where Have all the Flowers Gone?: Deforestation in the Third World,* edited by Vinson H. Sutlive Jr., 25–44. Studies in Third World Societies, no. 13. Williamsburg, Va: William and Mary College Department of Anthropology, 1981.

———. "The Pristine Myth: The Landscape of the Americas in 1492." *Annals, Association of American Geographers* 82 (1992): 369–85.

———. "Stone v. Metal Axes: The Ambiguity of Shifting Cultivation in Prehistoric Amazonia." *Journal of the Steward Anthropological Society* 20 (1992): 153–65.

———, ed. *The Native Population of the Americas in 1492* [1976]. Madison: University of Wisconsin Press, 1992.

Dennell, Robin. *European Economic Prehistory: A New Approach.* London: Academic Press, 1983.

Denton, George H., and Terance J. Hughes, eds. *The Last Great Ice Sheets.* New York: John Wiley and Sons, 1981.

Des Marez, G. *Le problème de la colonization franque et du régime agraire en Basse-Belgique.* Académie Royale de Belgique, classe de lettres, mémoires, collection en quarto, 2d ser., vol. 9, fasc. 4. Brussels: Maurice Lemertin, 1926.

Descartes, René. *Discourse on Method* [1623]. Translated from the French by F. E. Sutcliffe under the title *Discourse on Method and Meditations* (Harmondsworth, England: Penguin Books, 1968).

Deschamps, Hubert Jules. *Histoire de Madagascar* [1960], 3d ed. Paris: Berger-Levrault, 1965.

Devèze, Michel. "Superficie et propriété des forêts du Nord et de l'est de la France vers la fin du règne de François 1ᵉʳ (1540–1547)." *Annales, Économies, Sociétiés, Civilisations* 15, no. 3 (May-June 1960): 485–92.

———. *La vie de la forêt Française au XVIᵉ siècle.* 2 vols. Ecole Practique des Haute Étude VIᵉ Section. Centre de Recherches Historiques. Paris: S.E.V.P.E.N., 1961.

———. "Forêts françaises et forêts allemandes: études historique comparée." *Revue Historique.* Part 1, vol. 235 (1966):347–80; Part 2, vol. 236 (1966):47–68.

———. "Les forêts françaises à la veille de la révolution de 1789." *Revue d'Histoire Moderne et Contemporaire* 8 (1966): 241–72.

———. "L'École Nationale des Eaux et Forêts (1844–1966)." In *La forêts et les communautés rurales, xviᵉ–xviiiᵉ siècles: Recueil d'articles,* edited by Michel Devèze, 237–49. Paris: Publications de la Sorbonne, 1982.

De Vries, Jan. *The Dutch Rural Economy in the Gold Age, 1500–1700.* New Haven, Conn.: Yale University Press, 1974.

Dewalt, Billie R. "The Cattle Are Eating the Forest." *Bulletin of Atomic Scientists* 39 (1983): 18–23.

Dewar, Robert E. "Extinctions in Madagascar: The Loss of Subfossil Fauna." In *Quaternary Extinctions,* edited by Paul S. Martin and Richard G. Klein, 574–93. Tucson: University of Arizona Press, 1984.

Dickinson, William R. "The Times Are Always Changing: The Holocene Saga." *Geological Society of America* 107, no. 1 (1995): 1–7.

Didia, Dal O. "Democracy, Political Instability and Tropical Deforestation." *Global Environmental Change* 7 (1997): 63–76.

Dietrich, Bruno F. A. "European Forests and Their Utilization." *Economic Geography* 4 (1928): 140–58.

Dimbleby, Geoffrey W. "Climate, Soil and Man." *Philosophical Transactions of the Royal Society, London* B275 (1976): 197–208.

Dinsdale, Evelyn M. "Spatial Patterns of Technological Change: The Lumber Industry of Northern New York." *Economic Geography* 41 (1965): 258–65.

Dipakranjan, Das. *Economic History of the Deccan from the First to the Sixth Century A.D.* Delhi: Munshiram Manoharlal, 1969.

Dix, Brian. "The Manufacture of Lime and Its Uses in the Western Roman Provinces." *Oxford Journal of Archaeology* 1 (1982): 331–45.

Dobyns, Henry F. "Estimating Aboriginal American Populations: An Appraisal of Techniques with a New Hemispheric Estimate." *Current Anthropology* 7 (1966): 395–449.

———. *Their Numbers Became Thinned: Native American Population Dynamics in Eastern North America.* Knoxville: University of Tennessee Press, 1983.

Donkin, Robin A. *The Cistercians: Studies in the Geography of Medieval England and Wales.* Toronto: Pontifical Institute of Medieval Studies, 1978.

Doolittle, William E. "Agriculture in North America on the Eve of Contact: A Reassessment." *Annals, Association of American Geographers* 82 (1992): 386–401.

Döpsch, Alfons. *The Economic and Social Foundations of European Civilization* [1923]. Translated from the German by Erna Patzelt. London: Routledge and Kegan Paul, 1937.

Dorward, D. C., and A. I. Payne. "Deforestation, the Decline of the Horse, and the Spread of the Tsetse Fly and Trypanosomiasis (*nagana*) in Nineteenth Century Sierra Leone." *Journal of African Studies* 16 (1975): 239–56.

Dovering, Folke. "The Transformation of European Agriculture." In *The Cambridge Economic History of Europe,* vol. 6, *The Industrial Revolution and After: Incomes, Population and Tech-*

nological Change, edited by H. John Habakkuk and Michael Postan, 604–72. Cambridge: Cambridge University Press, 1965.

Downing, Theodore E., Susanna B. Hecht, Harry A. Pearson, and Carmen Garcia-Downing, eds. *Destruction or Development: The Conversion of Tropical Forest to Pasture in Latin America.* Boulder, Colo.: Westview Press, 1992.

Dozier, Craig L. *Land Development and Colonization in Latin America: Case Studies in Peru, Bolivia and Mexico.* New York: Praeger, 1969.

Dresbeck, LeRoy. "Winter Climate and Society in the Northern Middle Ages: The Technological Impact." In *On Pre-Modern Technology and Science: A Volume of Studies in Honor of Lynn White Jr,* edited by Bert S. Hall and Delno C. West, 177–200. Malibu, Calif.: Udena Publications, 1976.

Du Halde, Jean-Baptiste. *The General History of China.* 4 vols. London: J. Watts, 1736.

Dubey, Vinod. "Railways." In *The Economic History of India,* edited by V. B. Singh, 327–47. New Delhi: Allied Publishers Private Limited, 1965.

Dubois, René. "How Man Helps Nature." *Smithsonian* (December 1972), 20.

Duby, George. "La révolution agricole médiévale." *Revue de geographie Lyon* 29 (1954): 361–66.

———. *Rural Economy and Country Life in the Medieval West* [1962]. Translated from the French by Cynthia Postan. London: Edward Arnold, 1968.

———. *The Early Growth of the European Economy: Warriors and Peasants from the Seventh to the Twelfth Century* [1973]. Translated from the French by H. B.Clarke. Ithaca, N.Y.: Cornell University Press, 1974.

———. "Medieval Agriculture, 900–1500," In *The Fontana Economic History of Europe,* edited by Carlo Cipolla, vol. 1, *The Middle Ages,* 175–273. Brighton: Harvester Press, 1976.

Dudley, Nigel. *The Death of Trees.* London and Sydney: Pluto Press, 1985.

Dudley, Nigel, Jean-Paul Jeanrenaud, and Francis Sullivan. *Bad Harvest?: The Timber Trade and the Degradation of the World's Forests.* London: Earthscan, 1995.

Duncan-Jones, Richard. *The Economy of the Roman Empire: Quantitative Studies.* London: Cambridge University Press, 1974.

Dunham, Arthur Louis. *The Industrial Revolution in France, 1815–1848.* New York: Exposition Press, 1955.

Dunn, Richard S. *Sugar and Slaves: The Rise of the Planter Class in the English West Indies, 1624–1713.* Chapel Hill: University of North Carolina Press for the Institute of Early American History and Culture, Williamsburg, Va., 1972.

Durán, Fray Diego. *Book of the Gods and Rites of the Ancient Calendar.* Translated and edited by Frenando Horcasitas and Doris Heyden. Norman: University of Oklahoma Press, 1971.

Durand, Frédéric. *Les forêts en asie du sud-est: Recul et exploitation: Le cas de l'Indonésie,* Paris: L'Harmattan, 1994.

Durand, John D. "Historical Estimates of World Population: An Evaluation." *Population and Development Review* 3 (1977): 253–96.

Dwight, Timothy. *Travels in New-England and New-York in 1821.* 4 vols. New Haven, Conn.: T. Dwight, 1821–22.

Dyer, Christopher. *Hanbury: Settlement and Society in a Wooded Landscape.* Dept. of Local History, Occasional Papers, 4th ser., no. 4. Leicester: Leicester University Press, 1991.

Dykstra, Dennis P., and Markku Kallio. "Scenario Analysis." In *The Global Forest Sector: An Analytical Perspective,* edited by Markku Kallio, Dennis P. Dykstra, and Clark S. Binkley, 613–72. New York: Wiley, 1987.

Eardly-Wilmot, Sainthill. *Forest Life and Sport in India.* London: Edward Arnold, 1910.

Earl, Derek E. *Forest Energy and Economic Development*. Oxford: Clarendon Press, 1975.

Eastwick, Edward Backhouse. *A Glance at Sind before Napier; or, Dry Leaves from Young Egypt* [1849]. Reprint, Karachi: Oxford University Press, 1973.

Eck, Alexandre. *Le moyen âge Russe*. Paris: Maison du Livre Etranger, 1933.

Eckholm, Erik P. *The Other Energy Crisis: Firewood*. Worldwatch Paper no. 1. Washington, D.C.: Worldwatch Institute, 1975.

———. *Losing Ground: Environmental Stress and World Food Prospects*. Worldwatch Institute with the support of United Nations Environment Program. New York: W. W. Norton and Company, 1976.

———. *Planting for the Future: Forestry for Human Needs*. Worldwatch Paper no. 26. Washington, D.C.: Worldwatch Institute, 1979.

Eckholm, Erik P., Gerald Foley, and G. Bernard. *Fuelwood: The Energy Crisis That Won't Go Away*. London: Earthscan, 1984.

Eden, Richard, ed. *A Treatyse on the Newe India, with Other Newfounde Lands and Ilandes* [1553]. In *The First Three English Books on America*, edited by E. Arber, 3–42. Edinburgh: Turnball and Spears, 1885.

Edney, Matthew H. *Mapping an Empire: The Geographical Construction of British India, 1765–1843*. Chicago: University of Chicago Press, 1998.

Edwards, Kevin J. "Meso-Neolithic Vegetational Impact in Scotland and Beyond: Palynological Considerations." In *The Mesolithic in Europe*, edited by Clive Bonsall, 143–55. Edinburgh: Donald, 1989.

Egerton, Jean. *Turner: The Fighting Temeraire*. New Haven, Conn.: Yale University Press, 1995.

Egleston, Nathaniel H. *USDA, Annual Report*. Washington, D.C.: GPO, 1883.

Ehrlich, Paul R. "The Loss of Diversity: Causes and Consequences." In *Biodiversity*, edited by Edward O. Wilson, 21–27. Washington, D.C.: National Academy Press, 1986.

Ehrlich, Paul R., and Anne H. Ehrlich. *The Population Bomb*. New York: Ballantine, 1968.

———. *Exinction: The Causes and Consequences of the Disappearance of Species*. New York: Random House, 1982.

Ehrlich, Paul R., and John P. Holdren, eds. *The Cassandra Conference: Resources and the Human Predicament*. College Station: Texas A. & M. University Press, 1985.

Eidt, Robert C., "Pioneer Settlement in Eastern Peru." *Annals, Association of American Geographers* 52 (1962): 255–78.

———. "Agrarian Reform and the Growth of New Rural Settlements in Venezuela." *Erkunde* 29 (1975): 120–32.

Ekirch, Arthur A. Jr. *Man and Nature in America*. New York: Columbia University Press, 1963.

Elder, W. H. "Primeval Deer Hunting Pressures Revealed by Remains from American Indian Middens." *Journal of Wildlife Management* 29 (1965): 366–70.

Eliot, Jared. *Essays upon Field Husbandry in New England [1760] and Other Papers, 1748–1762*. Edited by Henry J. Carver and Rexford Tugwell. New York: Columbia University Press, 1934.

Elison, George, and L. Smith Bardwell. *Warlords, Artists and Commoners: Japan in the Sixteenth Century*. Honolulu: University of Hawaii Press, 1981.

Ellenberg, Heinz, and Dieter Mueller-Dombois. "Tentative Physiognomic-Ecological Classification of Plant Formations of the Earth." *Berichte—Geobotanischen Institutes der Eidgenossischen Technischen Hochschule Stiftung Rübel* 37 (1967): 21–55.

Elliott, John H. *The Old World and the New, 1492–1650*. Cambridge: Cambridge University Press, 1970.

———. *Spain and Its World, 1500–1700: Selected Essays*. New Haven, Conn.: Yale University Press, 1989.

Ellis, David Maldwyn. *Landlords and Farmers in the Hudson-Mohawk Region, 1790–1850.* Ithaca, N.Y.: Cornell University Press, 1946.

Emerson, Ralph Waldo. "Nature." In *Nature, Addresses, and Lectures,* edited by J. E. Cabot, vol. 1. Boston: Houghton Mifflin and Co., 1876.

Emery, Frank V. "Moated Settlements in England." *Geography* 47 (1962): 378–88.

Encyclopaedia Britannica, 1797 edition. Vol. 18, s.v. "Trees."

Ennin. *Ennin's Diary: The Record of a Pilgrimage to China in Search of the Law (793–864).* Translated by Edwin O. Reischauer. New York: The Roland Press, 1955.

Etemad, Bouda, and Jean Luciani (under the direction of Paul Bairoch and Jean-Claude Toutain. *World Energy Production, 1800–1985.* Publications du centre d'histoire economique internationale de l'universite de Genève. Genève: Librairie Droz, 1991.

Evans, E. Estyn. "The Ecology of Peasant Life in Western Europe." In *Man's Role in Changing the Face of the Earth,* edited by William L. Thomas, 217–40. Chicago: University of Chicago Press, 1956.

Evelyn, John. *Sylva: Or, a Discourse of Forest Trees, and the Propogation of Timber in His Majesty's Dominion . . .* [1666]. York: A. Ward, 1786.

Eyre, Samuel R. *The Real Wealth of Nations.* New York: St Martin's Press, 1978.

Fabre, Jean Antoine. *Essai sur la théorie des torrens et des rivières.* Paris: Chez Bidault (an. 6), 1797.

Faegri, Knut, and Johannes Iversen. *Textbook of Pollen Analysis,* 2d ed. revised by K. Faegri. Copenhagen: Munksgaard, 1975.

Fairchild, Hoxie Neal. *The Romantic Quest.* New York: Columbia University Press, 1931.

Fairclough, Henry Rushton. *Love of Nature among Greeks and Romans.* London: Longmans, Green, 1930.

Fairhead, James, and Melissa Leach. *Misreading the African Landscape: Society and Ecology in a Forest-Savanna Mosaic.* Cambridge: Cambridge University Press, 1996.

———. "Rethinking the Forest-Savanna Mosiac." In *The Lie of the Land: Challenging Received Wisdom on the African Environment,* edited by Melissa Leach and Robin Mearns, 105–21. Oxford: The International African Institute in association with James Curry, Ltd., 1996.

———. *Reframing Deforestation: Global Analysis and Local Realities: Studies in West Africa.* London: Routledge, 1998.

Fayle, Charles Ernst. *A Short History of the World's Shipping Industry.* London: George Allen and Unwin Ltd., 1933.

Fearnside, Philip M. "Jari Development in the Brazilian Amazon." *Interciencia* 5 (1980): 145–56.

———. "Deforestation in the Brazilian Amazon: How Fast Is It Occurring?" *Ambio* 7 (1982): 82–88.

———. "Land-Use Trends in the Brazilian Amazon As Factors in Accelerating Deforestation." *Environmental Conservation* 10 (1983): 141–48.

———. "A Floresta vai Acabar?" *Cincia Hoje* 2 (1984): 42–52.

———. "Jari Revisted: Changes and the Outlook for Sustainability in Amazonia's Largest Silvicultural Estate." *Interciencia* 10 (1985): 121–29.

———. *Human Carrying Capacity of the Brazilian Rainforest.* New York: Columbia University Press, 1986.

———. "Spatial Concentration of Deforestation in the Brazilian Amazon." *Ambio* 15 (1986): 74–81.

———. "The Rate and Extent of Deforestation in Brazilian Amazonia." *Environmental Conservation* 17 (1990): 213–26.

Fearnside, Philip M., and Eneas Salati. "Explosive Deforestation in Rondônia, Brazil." *Environmental Conservation* 12 (1985): 355–56.

Febvre, Lucien, and Henri-Jean Martin. *The Coming of the Book: The Impact of Printing, 1450–1800* [1958]. Translated from the French by David Gerard. London: New Left Books, 1976.

Fedorov, An. A. "The Structure of the Tropical Rain Forest and Speciation in the Humid Tropics." *Journal of Ecology* 54 (1966): 1–11.

Ferguson, Eugene S. "Steam Transportation." In *Technology in Western Civilization,* edited by Melvin Kranzberg and Carroll W. Pursell Jr., vol. 1, *The Emergence of Modern Industrial Society—Earliest Times to 1900,* 285–302. New York: Oxford University Press, 1967.

Fertig, F. "Child of Nature: The American Indian As Ecologist." *Sierra Club Bulletin* 55 (1970): 4–7.

Fieldhouse, David K. *Economics and Empire, 1830–1914.* Ithaca, N.Y.: Cornell University Press, 1969.

Fies, Herbert. *Europe: The World's Banker, 1870–1914* [1930]. Published for the Council on Foreign Relations. New Haven, Conn.: Yale University Press, 1965.

Fisher, Peter. *Sketches of New Brunswick* [1825]. St. John: Chubb & Sears. Reprint, St. John, under the title *History of New Brunswick:* Government of New Brunswick and William Shives Fisher, under the auspices of New Brunswick Historical Society, 1921.

Fitzgerald, Robert, and Janet Grenier. *Timber: A Centenary History of the Timber Trade Federation, 1892–1992.* London: B. T. Batsford, 1992.

Flach, Jacques. *Les origines de l'ancienne France.* Vol. 2. Paris: Librairie du Recueil Générale de Lois et des Arrêts, 1893.

Flannery, Kent V. "The Origins of Agriculture." *Annual Review of Anthropology* 2 (1973): 271–310.

Flenley, John R. *The Equatorial Rain Forest: A Geological History.* London: Butterworth, 1979.

———. "The Late Quaternary Vegetation History of the Equatorial Mountains." *Progress in Physical Geography* 3 (1979): 488–509.

———. "Palynological Evidence Relating to Disturbance and Other Ecological Phenomena in Rain Forests." In *Tropical Forests in Transition: Ecology of Natural and Anthropogenic Disturbance Processes,* edited by Johann G. Goldammer, 17–24. Basel: Birkäuser Verlag, 1992.

Flenley, John R., A. Sarah King, J. T. Teller, M. E. Prentice, J. Jackson, and C. Chew. "The Late Quaternary Vegetational and Climatic History of Easter Island." *Journal of Quaternary Studies* 6 (1991): 85–115.

Flinn, Michael W. "The Growth of the English Iron Industry, 1660–1760." *Economic History Review* 11 (1958): 144–53.

———. "Timber and the Advance of Technology: A Reconsideration." *Annals of Science* 15 (1959): 109–20.

———. "William Wood and the Coke Smelting Process." *Transactions of the Newcommen Society* 34 (1961): 66–71.

———. "Consommation du bois et développement sidérurgique en Angleterre." *Actes du colloque sur la forêt bescançon.* Paris, 1966.

Flinn, Michael W., with David Stoker. *The History of the British Coal Industry.* Vol. 2, *1700–1830. The Industrial Revolution.* Oxford: Clarendon Press, 1984.

Flint, Elizabeth P. "Deforestation and Land Use in Northern India, with a Focus on Sal (*Shorea robusta*) Forests, 1880–1980." In *Nature and the Orient: The Environmental History of South and Southeast Asia,* edited by Richard H. Grove, Vinita Damodaran, and Satpul Sangwan,. 575–95. Delhi: Oxford University Press, 1998.

Flint, Timothy. *A Condensed Geography and History of the Western States or the Mississippi Valley.* 2 vols. Cincinnati: W. M. Farnsworth, 1828.

Foley, Gerald. "Wood Fuel and Conventional Fuel Demands in the Developing World." *Ambio* 14 (1985): 253–58.

Fölster, Horst. "Holocene Autochthonous Forest Degradation in Southeastern Venezuela." In *Tropical Forests in Transition: Ecology of Natural and Anthropogenic Processes,* edited by Johann Georg Goldammer, 25–44. Basel: Birkäuser Verlag, 1992.

Food and Agriculture Organization. *Yearbook of Forest Products.* Rome: FAO, 1949 and annually.

———. *World Forest Inventory.* Rome: FAO, 1963.

———. *Wood for Energy.* Forest Topics Report no. 1. Rome: FAO, 1975.

———. *Forest Product Prices, 1961–1980.* Rome: FAO, 1981.

———. *Forest Resources Assessment 1990: Guidelines for Assessment.* Rome: FAO, 1990.

———. *The State of the World's Forests, 1995.* Rome: FAO, 1995.

———. *State of the World's Forests, 1999.* Rome: FAO, 1999.

Food and Agriculture Organization, in cooperation with the World Resources Institute, The World Bank, and the UN Development Program. *The Tropical Forestry Action Plan.* Rome: FAO, 1987.

Forbes, Henry O. *A Naturalist's Wanderings in the Eastern Archipelago: A Narrative of Travel and Exploration from 1878 to 1883.* London: Mason, Low, Marston, Searle and Rivington, 1885.

Forbes, Reginald D. "The Passing of the Piney Woods." *American Forestry* 29 (March 1923): 131–36, 185.

Forbes, Robert J. *Studies in Ancient Technology.* Vol. 6, *Heat and Heating, Refrigeration and Light.* Leiden: E. J. Brill, 1955–64.

Ford, Richard I. 1985. "The Process of Plant Food Production in Prehistoric North America." In *Prehistoric Food Production in North America,* edited by Richard I. Ford. Anthropological Paper no. 75. Ann Arbor, Mich.: University of Michigan Museum of Anthropology, 1985.

Ford-Lloyd, Brian, and Michael Jackson. *Plant Genetic Resources: An Introduction to Their Conservation and Use.* London: Arnold, 1986.

Foreman, Richard T., and Emily W. B. Russell. "Evaluation of Historical Data in Ecology." *Bulletin of the Ecological Society of America* 64 (1983): 5–7.

"Forest Resources of the World." *Unasylva* 2 (1948): 161–70.

Forrest, Denys. *A Hundred Years of Ceylon Tea, 1867–1967.* London: Chatto & Windus, 1967.

Fortune, Robert. *Three Years' Wanderings in the Northern Provinces of China.* London: John Murray, 1847.

Fosberg, Raymond F. "A Classification of Vegetation for General Purposes." *Tropical Ecology* 2 (1961): 1–28.

Foucault, Michel. *The Archaeology of Knowledge.* Translated by Alan M. Sheridan. London: Tavistock Publications, 1972.

Foweraker, Joe. *The Struggle for Land: A Political Economy of the Pioneer Frontier in Brazil from 1930 to the Present Day.* New York: Cambridge University Press, 1981.

Fox, William F. "A History of the Lumber Industry of the State of New York." USDA Bureau of Forestry, Bulletin 34. Washington, D.C.: GPO, 1902.

Frame, Richard. "A Short Description of Pennsilvania by Richard Frame." In *Original Narratives of Early American History: Narratives of Early Pennsylvania, West New Jersey, and Delaware, 1630–1709* [1692], edited by A. C. Myers. New York: C. Scribner and Sons, 1912.

Frank, André Gunder. *World Accumulation, 1492–1789.* New York: Monthly Review Press, 1978.

Frankel, Otto H., and Erna Bennett, eds. *Genetic Resources in Plants: Their Exploration and Conservation.* IBP Handbook 11. Oxford: Blackwell Scientific Publications, 1970.

Frankel, Otto H., and John G. Hawkes, eds. *Crop Genetic Resources for Today and Tomorrow.* Cambridge: Cambridge University Press, 1975.

Frankel, Otto H., Anthony H. D. Brown, and Jeremy James Burdon, eds. *The Conservation of Plant Diversity.* Cambridge: Cambridge University Press, 1995.

Franklin, Benjamin. *An Account of the New-Invented Pennsylvania Fire-Place: Wherein Their Construction and Manner of Operation, Particularly Explained.* Philadelphia: B. Franklin, 1744.

Fraser-Macdonald, A. *Our Ocean Railways; or, the Rise, Progress and Development of Ocean Steam Navigation.* London: Chapman Hall, 1893.

Fray, C. R. "The Movement toward Free Trade, 1820–1853." In *Cambridge History of the British Empire,* edited by J. H. Rose, A. P. Newton, and E. A. Benians, vol. 2, *The Growth of the New Empire, 1783–1870,* 412–63. Cambridge: Cambridge University Press, 1940.

French, R. Anthony. "The Making of the Russian Landscape." *Advancement of Science* 20 (1963): 44–56.

———. "Russians and the Forest." In *Studies in Russian Historical Geography,* edited by James H. Bater and R. Anthony French, 1:23–44. London: Academic Press, 1983.

Friedrich, Ernst. "Wesen und Geographische Verbreitung der 'Raubwirtschaft.'" *Petermanns Meiteilungen* 50 (1904): 68–79, 92–95.

Fries, Robert F. *Empire in Pine: The Story of Lumbering in Wisconsin, 1830–1900.* Madison: State Historical Society of Wisconsin, 1951.

Frothingham, Earl H. *The State and Value of Farm Woodlots in the Eastern United States.* USDA Bulletin no. 481. Washington, D.C.: GPO, 1917.

Fruhauf, Christian. *Forêt et société: de la forêt paysanne à la forêt capitaliste en pays de sault sous l'ancien régime (vers 1670–1791).* Centre Nationale de la Recherche scientifique. Centre Régional de Publications de Tolouse, Midi-Pyrénées. Paris: Editions du C.N.R.S, 1980.

Fuller, Andrew S. *The Forest Tree Culturist: A Treatise on the Cultivation of American Forest Trees.* New York: Geo. and F. W. Woodward, 1866.

Gadgil, Madhav, and Ramachandra Guha. *This Fissured Land: An Ecological History of India.* New Delhi: Oxford University Press, 1992.

Galleti, R., K. D. S. Baldwin, and I. O. Dina. *Nigerian Cocoa Farmers: An Economic Survey of Yoruba Cocoa Farming Families.* London: Oxford University Press, 1956.

Galloway, James A., Derek Keene, and Margret Murphy. "Fuelling the City: Production and Distribution of Firewood and Fuel in London's Region, 1290–1400." *Economic History Review* 49 (1996): 447–72.

Galloway, John H. *The Sugar Cane Industry: An Historical Geography from Its Origins to 1914.* Cambridge: Cambridge University Press, 1989.

Gamble, J. Sykes. "The Darjeerling Forests." *Indian Forester* 1 (1875): 73–99.

Ganshof, François Louis. "Medieval Society in Its Prime: France, The Low Countries and Western Germany." In *The Cambridge Economic History of Europe,* vol. 1, *Agrarian Life in the Middle Ages,* edited by John H. Clapham and Eileen Power, 278–322. Cambridge: Cambridge University Press, 1941.

Garren, K. H. "The Effects of Fire on the Vegetation of the Southeastern United States." *Botanical Review* 9 (1943): 617–54.

Gaston, Kevin J. "What Is Biodiversity?" In *Biodiversity: A Biology of Numbers and Difference,* edited by Kevin J. Gaston, 1–9. Oxford: Blackwell Science, 1996.

———, ed. *Biodiversity: A Biology of Numbers and Difference.* Oxford: Blackwell Science, 1996.

Gates, Paul W. "Problems in Agricultural History, 1790–1840." *Agricultural History* 46 (1972): 33–51.

Gaunitz, Sven. "Resource Exploitation on the North Swedish Timber Frontier in the Nineteenth and the Beginning of the Twentieth Centuries." In *History of Sustain-Yield Forestry: A Sym-*

posium, edited by Harold K. Steen, 134–44. Durham, N.C.: Forest History Society/IUFRO, 1984.

Gentry, Alwyn H., and J. Lopez-Parodi. "Deforestation and Increased Flooding in the Upper Amazon." *Science* 210 (1980): 1354–56. (See also *Science* 215 (1982): 426–27.)

Gibbon, Edward. *The History of the Decline and Fall of the Roman Empire, with Notes by the Rev. H. H. Milman* [1776]. 6 vols. New York: Harper and Brothers, 1850.

Gies, Francis, and Joseph Gies. *Cathedral, Forge, and Waterwheel: Technology and Invention in the Middle Ages.* New York: Harper Collins, 1994.

Gill, Tom H. *The Tropical Forests of the Caribbean.* Tropical Plant Research Foundation: Charles Lawthrop Pack Forestry Trust. Baltimore: Read Taylor, 1931.

Gille, Bertrand. 1947. *Les origines de la grande industrie métallurgie en France.* Paris: Éditions Domat Montchrestien, 1947.

———. "Banking and Industrialization in Europe, 1730–1914." In *The Fontana Economic History of Europe,* edited by Carlo M. Cipolla, vol. 3, *The Industrial Revolution, 1700–1914,* 255–97. Brighton: Harvester Press, 1976.

Gilpin, William. *Remarks on Forest Scenery.* London: R. Blamire, 1794.

Gimpel, Jean. *The Cathedral Builders* [1961]. Translated by Teresa Waugh. New York: Grove Press, 1983.

Girard, L. "Transport." In *The Cambridge Economic History of Europe,* vol. 6, *The Industrial Revolution and After: Incomes, Population and Technological Change,* edited by H. John Habakkuk and Michael Postan, 212–73. Cambridge: Cambridge University Press, 1965.

Glacken, Clarence F. "Changing Ideas of the Habitable World." In *Man's Role in Changing the Face of the Earth,* edited by William L. Thomas, 70–92. Chicago: University of Chicago Press, 1956.

———. *Traces on the Rhodian Shore: Nature and Culture in Western Thought from Ancient Times to the End of the Eighteenth Century.* Berkeley and Los Angeles: University of California Press, 1967.

Glamann, Kristof. "The Changing Patterns of Trade." In *The Cambridge Economic History of Europe. Vol.5. The Economic Organization of Early Modern Europe,* 185–289. Cambridge: Cambridge University Press, 1970.

———. "European Trade, 1500–1700." In Cipolla, Carlo M. (ed.) *The Fontana Economic History of Europe,* vol. 2, *The Sixteenth and Seventeenth Centuries,* edited by Edwin Earnest Rich and Charles Henry Wilson, 427–526. Brighton: Harvester Press, 1977.

Glass, Daniel Victor, and Eugene Grebenik. "World Population, 1800–1950." In *The Cambridge Economic History of Europe,* vol. 6, *The Industrial Revolution and After: Incomes, Population and Technological Change,* edited by H. John Habakkuk and Michael Postan, 60–138. Cambridge: Cambridge University Press, 1965.

Gleason, Herbert A. "Vegetational History of the Middle West." *Annals, Association of American Geographers* 12 (1922), 78–85.

Glendinning, Victoria. *Trollope.* London: Hutchinson, 1992.

Glesinger, Egon. *The Coming Age of Wood.* London: Secker and Warburg, 1947.

Global Witness. *Corruption, War, and Forest Policy: The Unsustainable Exploitation of Cambodia's Forests.* London: Global Witness, Ltd. 1996.

Godfrey, Brian J. "Boom Towns of the Amazon." *Geographical Review* 80 (1990): 103–117.

Goldammer, Johann Georg. "Tropical Forests in Transition: Ecology of Natural and Anthropogenic Disturbance Processes—An Introduction." In *Tropical Forests in Transition: Ecology of Natural and Anthropogenic Processes,* edited by Johann Georg Goldammer, 1–16. Basel: Birkhäuser Verlag, 1992.

————, ed. *Fire in the Tropical Biota: Ecosystem Processes and Global Challenges.* Ecological Studies 84. Berlin: Springer-Verlag, 1990.

Golson, Jack. "Cultural Change in Prehistoric New Zealand." In *Anthropology in the South Seas,* edited by J. D. Freeman and W. R. Geddes, 29–74. New Plymouth, New Zealand: Avery, 1959.

Gómez-Pompa, Arturo, C. Vásquez-Yanes, and S. Guevara. "The Tropical Rainforest: A Non-Renewable Resource." *Science* 177 (1972): 762–65.

Gómez-Pompa, Arturo, José S. Flores, and Victoria Sosa. "The 'Pet Kot': A Man-Made Tropical Forest of the Maya." *Interciencia* 12 (1987): 10–15.

Gómez-Pompa, Arturo, and Andrea Kaus. "Taming the Wilderness Myth." *Bioscience* 42 (1992): 271–99.

Gordon, Le Roy. *The Human Geography and Ecology of the Sinú Country of Colombia.* Ibero-Americana, no. 39. Berkeley and Los Angeles: University of California Press, 1957.

Gordon, Robert K., ed. *Anglo-Saxon Poetry.* London: Dent and Sons, 1954.

Gornitz, Victor, and NASA. "A Survey of Anthropogenic Vegetation Changes in West Africa during the Last Century—Climatic Implications." *Climatic Change* 7 (1985): 285–325.

Goubert, Pierre. *The French Peasantry in the Seventeenth Century.* Translated from the French by Ian Patterson. Cambridge: Cambridge University Press, 1986.

Goucher, Candice L. "Iron Is Iron 'til It Is Rust: Trade and Ecology in the Decline of West African Iron Smelting." *Journal of African History* 22 (1981): 179–89.

————. "The Impact of German Colonial Rule on the Forests of Togo." In *World Deforestation in the Twentieth Century,* edited by John F. Richards and Richard P. Tucker, 56–69. Durham, N.C.: Duke University Policy Stduies, 1988.

Goudie, Andrew S. "The Arid Earth." In *Mega-Geomorphology,* edited by Rita Gardner and Helen Scoging, 152–71. Oxford: Clarendon Press, 1983.

————. *Environmental Change.* Oxford: Clarendon Press, Oxford. 1992.

————. "The Ice Age in the Tropics." In *Environments and Historical Change,* edited by Paul Slack, 2–32. Oxford: Oxford University Press, 1999.

Goudsblom, Johann. "The Civilizing Process and the Domestication of Fire." *World History* 3 (1992): 1–12.

————. *Fire and Civilization.* London: Penguin Books, 1992.

Gourou, Pierre. *Les pays tropicaux: Principes d'une géographie humaine et économique.* Paris: Presses Universitaires de France, 1947.

Gover, John Eric B., and Alan Mawer. *The Place-Names of Warwickshire.* Cambridge: Cambridge University Press, 1936.

Gradmann, Robert. "Das Mitteleuropäische Landschaftsbild nach seiner geschichtlichen Entwicklung." *Geographische Zeitschrift* 7 (1901): 361–77, 435–47.

Graham, Gerald S. "Imperial Finance, Trade and Communications, 1895–1914." In *The Cambridge History of the British Empire,* edited by E. A. Benians and C. E. Carrington, vol. 3, *The Empire-Commonwealth, 1870–1919,* 438–89. Cambridge: Cambridge University Press, 1959.

Grainger, Alan. *Controlling Tropical Deforestation.* London: Earthscan, 1990.

————. "Modelling Deforestation in the Humid Tropics." In *Deforestation or Development in the Third World?* edited by Matti Palo and G. Mery, vol. 3, Bulletin no. 349, 51–67. Helsinki: Finnish Forest Research Institute, 1990.

————. "Rates of Deforestation in the Humid Tropics: Estimates and Measurements." *Geographical Journal* 159 (1993): 33–44.

Grand, Roger, and Raymond Delatouche. *L'agriculture au moyen âge de la fin L'Empire Romain au XVIᵉ sièle.* Vol, 3, *L'agriculture à travers les âges.* Collection Fondée par Emile Savoy. Paris: E.De Boccard, 1950.

Grant, Anne McVickar. *Memoirs of an American Lady: With Sketches of Manners and Scenes in America, as They Existed Previous to the Revolution* [1808], 2d ed. New York: D. Appleton, 1846.

Grant, James W. *The Rice Crops of Burma*. Rangoon: Superintendent, Government Printing and Stationery, 1932.

Gray, Asa. "Characteristics of the North American Flora." *American Journal of Science*, 3d ser., 28 (1884): 323–40.

Gray, Lewis C., and Esther K. Thompson. *History of Agriculture in the Southern United States to 1860*. 2 vols. Carnegie Institute Publication no. 430. Washington, D.C.: Carnegie Institute, 1933.

Grayson, Donald K. "Pleistocene Avifaunas and the Overkill Hypothesis." *Science* 195 (1977): 691–92.

Greeley, William B. "Reduction of the Timber Supply through Abandonment or Clearing of Forest Lands." *Report of the National Conservation Commission*. 60th Cong., 2d sess., S. Doc. 676: 633–44, ser. no. 5397. Washington, D.C.: GPO, 1909.

———. "Timber: Mine or Crop?" U.S. Department of Agriculture, *Yearbook, 1922*, 83–180. Washington, D.C.: GPO, 1923.

———. "The Relation of Geography to Timber Supply." *Economic Geography* 1 (1925): 1–11.

———. *Forests and Men*. Garden City, N.Y.: Doubleday, 1951.

Greenfield, Sidney M. "Madeira and the Beginning of New World Sugar Cane Cultivation and Plantation Slavery." In *Comparative Perspectives on Slavery in New World Plantation Societies*, ed. Vera Rubin and Arthur Tuden, 536–52. Annals of New York Academy of Sciences, no. 293. New York: New York Academy of Sciences, 1977.

Greenough, Paul. "Hunter's Drowned Land: An Environmental Fantasy of the Victorian Sundererbans." In *Nature and the Orient: The Environmental History of South and Southeast Asia*, edited by Richard H. Grove, Vinita Damodaran, and Satpal Sangwan, 237–72. Delhi: Oxford University Press, 1998.

Gregg, Susan A. *Foragers and Farmers: Population Interaction and Agricultural Expansion in Prehistoric Europe*. Chicago: University of Chicago Press, 1988.

Greig, James. "Past and Present Lime Woods of Europe." In *Archaeological Aspects of Woodland Ecology*, edited by Martin Bell and Susan Limbrey, 23–55. Interl. series 146. Oxford: BAR, 1982.

Greig, James, and J. Turner. "Some Pollen Diagrams from Greece and Their Archaeological Significance." *Journal of Archaeological Science* 1 (1974): 177–94.

Grenier, Albert. "Aux origines de l'économie rurale: La conquête de sol français." *Annales d'histoire économique et sociale* 2 (1930): 26–47.

Griffin, James B. "Timber Procurement and Village Location in the Middle Missouri Sub-Area." *Plains Anthropological Memoir* 13 (1977): 177–85.

Grove, Richard H. "Conserving Eden: The (European) East India Companies and Their Environmental Policies on St. Helena, Mauritius, and in Western India, 1660 to 1854." *Comparative Studies in Society and History* 35 (1993): 318–51.

———. *Green Imperialism: Colonial Expansion, Tropical Island Edens, and the Origins of Environmentalism, 1600–1800*. Cambridge: Cambridge University Press, 1995.

Grove, Richard H., Vinita Damodaran, and Satpal Sangwan, eds. *Nature and the Orient: The Environmental History of South and Southeast Asia*. Delhi: Oxford University Press, 1998.

Guess, George. "Pasture Expansion, Forestry and Development Contradictions: The Case of Costa Rica." *Studies in Comparative International Development* 14 (1979): 42–55.

Guffey, Stanley Z. "A Review and Analysis of the Effects of Pre-Columbian Man on the Eastern North American Forests." *Tennessee Anthropologist* 2 (1977): 121–37.

Guha, Amalendu. "Colonization of Assam: Second Phase, 1840–1859." *Indian Economic and Social History Review* 4 (1967): 289–317.

———. "A Big Push without a Take-off: A Case Study of Assam, 1871–1901." *Indian Economic and Social History Review* 5 (1968): 201–21.

Guha, Ramachandra. "An Early Environmental Debate: The Making of the 1878 Forest Act." *Indian Economic and Social History Review* 27 (1990): 65–84.

Guha, Ramachandra, and Madhav Gadgil. "State Forestry and Social Conflict in British India." *Past and Present* 123 (1989): 141–77.

Guppy, Nicholas. "Tropical Deforestation: A Global View." *Foreign Affairs* 52 (1984): 928–65.

Guyot, Arnold. *The Earth and Man: Lectures on Comparative Physical Geography in Its Relation to the History of Mankind.* Translated from the French by C. Felton. Boston: Gould, Kendall, and Lincoln, 1849.

Habakkuk, H. John. "Free Trade and Commercial Expansion, 1853–1870. II. Banking and Investment." In *Cambridge History of the British Empire,* edited by J. Holland Rose, A. P. Newton, and E. A. Benians, vol. 2, *The Growth of the New Empire, 1783–1870,* 781–806. Cambridge: Cambridge University Press, 1981.

Habakkuk, H. John, and Michael Postan, eds. *The Cambridge Economic History of Europe.* Vol. 6, *The Industrial Revolution and After: Incomes, Population and Technological Change.* Cambridge: Cambridge University Press, 1965.

Habib, Ifran. *An Atlas of Mughal India. Political and Economic Maps, with Detailed Notes, Bibliography and Index.* Aligarh: Centre for Advanced Study in History, Aligarh Muslim Univesity; and Delhi: Oxford University Press, 1982.

———. "The Geographical Background." In *Cambridge Economic History of India,* edited by Tapan Raychaudhuri and Irfan Habib, vol. 1, *c. 1200–c.1750,* 4–14. Cambridge: Cambridge University Press, 1982.

Haden-Guest, Stephen, John K. Wright, and Eileen M. Teclaff, eds. *A World Geography of Forest Resources.* New York: The Roland Press Company, 1956.

Hagan, William T. "Justifying Dispossession of the Indian: The Land Utilization Argument." In *American Indian Environments: Ecological Issues in Native American History,* edited by Christopher Vecsey and Robert W. Venebles, 65–80. Syracuse, N.Y.: Syracuse University Press, 1980.

Hägerstrand, Torsten, and Ulrik Lohm. "Sweden." In *The Earth As Transformed by Human Action: Global and Regional Change in the Biosphere over the Past 300 Years,* edited by Billie Lee Turner II, William C. Clark, Robert W. Kates, John F. Richards, Jessica T. Mathews, and William B. Meyer, 605–22. New York: Cambridge University Press, 1990.

Haila, Yrjö, and Jari Kouki. "The Phenomenon of Biodiversity in Conservation Biology." *Annales Zoologici Fennici* 31 (1994): 5–18.

Hailey, William Malcolm Hailey, Baron. *An African Survey: A Study of Problems Arising in Africa South of the Sahara* [1938], rev. eds. London: Oxford University Press, 1945, 1957.

Haites, Erik F., James Mak, and Gary M. Walton. *Western River Transportation: The Era of Early Internal Development, 1810–1860.* Baltimore: Johns Hopkins University Press, 1975.

Hale, Sir Matthew. *The Primitive Origination of Mankind.* London: W. Godbid for W. Shrowsbery, 1677.

Hall, A. Rupert. "Intellectual Tendencies: 2. Science." In *The New Cambridge Modern History,* vol. 2., *The Reformation, 1520–1559,* edited by Geoffrey R. Elton, 359–86. Cambridge: Cambridge University Press, 1958.

————. "Cultural, Intellectual and Social Foundations, 1600–1750." In *Technology in Western Civilization,* edited by Melvin Kranzberg and Carroll W. Pursell Jr., vol. 1, *The Emergence of Modern Industrial Society, Earliest Times to 1900,* 107–17. New York: Oxford University Press, 1967.

————. "Scientific Method and the Progress of Techniques." In *The Cambridge Economic History of Europe,* vol. 4, *The Economy of Expanding Europe in the Sixteenth and Seventeenth Centuries,* edited by Edwin Earnest Rich and Charles Henry Wilson, 96–154. Cambridge: Cambridge University Press, 1967.

Hall, Anthony L. *Developing Amazonia: Deforestation and Social Conflict in Brazil's Carajás Programme.* Manchester: Manchester University Press, 1991.

Hall, Basil. *Forty Etchings from Sketches made with the Camera Lucida in North America in 1827 and 1829.* Edinburgh: Cadell, 1829.

————. *Travels in North America in the Years 1827 and 1828.* 3 vols. Philadelphia: Cary, Lea and Carey, 1829.

Hall, James. *Statistics of the West.* Cincinnati: J. A. James, 1836.

Halstead, Paul. "Counting Sheep in Neolithic and Bronze Age Greece." In *Patterns of the Past: Studies in Honour of David Clarke,* edited by Ian Hodder, G. Issac, and Norman Hammond, 307–39. Cambridge: Cambridge University Press, 1981.

Hammersley, George. "The Crown Woods and Their Exploitation during the Sixteenth and Seventeenth Centuries." *Bulletin of Institute of Historical Research* 30 (1957): 136–61.

————. "The Charcoal Iron Industry and Its Fuel, 1540–1750." *Economic History Review,* 2d ser., 26 (1973): 593–613.

————. "Did It Fall or Was It Pushed? The Foleys and the End of the Charcoal Iron Industry in the Eighteenth Century." In *The Search for Wealth and Stability: Essays in Economic and Social History Presented to M. W. Flinn,* edited by T. C. Smout, 67–90. London: Macmillan, 1979.

Handel, Mark D., and James S. Risbey. "An Annotated Bibliography on the Greenhouse Effect and Climate Change." *Climatic Change* 21 (1992): 97–225.

Hanley, Susan B., and Kono Yamamura. *Economic and Demographic Change in Pre-Industrial Japan, 1600–1868.* Princeton, N.J.: Princeton University Press, 1977.

Hanson, Earl Parker. *New Worlds Emerging.* London: Victor Gollancz, 1950.

————. "New Conquistadors in the Amazon Jungle." *Américas* 17, no. 9 (September 1965): 1–8.

Harding, A. F., ed. *Climate Change in Later Prehistory.* Edinburgh: Edinburgh University Press, 1982.

Hardjano, Joan M. "Transmigration: Looking to the Future." *Bulletin of Indonesian Economic Studies* 22, no. 2 (1986): 28–53.

Hardy, Ernest George. *Roman Laws and Charters.* Oxford: Clarendon Press, 1912.

Harlan, Jack R. "Agricultural Origins: Centers and Noncenters." *Science* 174 (1971): 468–74.

Harlow, Vincent Todd, ed. *Colonising Expeditions to the West Indies and Guiana, 1623–1667.* Hakluyt Society, ser. 2, vol. 56. London: The Hakluyt Society, 1925.

Harper, J. L., and Hawksworth, D. L. "Biodiversity: Measurement and Estimation. Preface." *Philosophical Transactions of the Royal Society, London,* ser. B, no. 345 (1994): 5–12.

Harris, David R. "Alternative Pathways towards Agriculture." In *The Origins of Agriculture,* edited by Charles A. Reed, 179–244. The Hague: Mouton Publishers, 1977.

Harris, David R., and Gordon C. Hillman, eds. *Foraging and Farming: The Evolution of Plant Exploitation.* London: Allen and Unwin, 1988.

Harrison, Robert Pogue. *Forests: The Shadow of Civilization.* Chicago: University of Chicago Press, 1992.

Harrison, William. *The Description of England* [1587]. Edited by G. Edelen. Ithaca, N.Y.: Cornell University Press for the Folger Shakespeare Library, 1968.

Harroy, Jean-Paul. *Afrique: Terre qui meurt: La dégradation des sols africains sous l'influence de la colonisation,* 2d ed. Brussels: Marcel Hayes, 1944.

Hart, Cyril E. *Royal Forest: A History of Dean's Woods As Producers of Timber.* Oxford: Clarendon Press, 1966.

Hart, John Fraser. "Loss and Abandonment of Cleared Farm Land in the Eastern United States." *Annals, Association of American Geographers* 58 (1968): 417–40.

———. "Land Use Change in a Piedmont County." *Annals, Association of American Geographers* 70 (1980): 492–527.

Hartman, W. A., and J. D. Black. *Economic Aspects of Land Settlement in the Cut-Over Region of the Great Lakes States.* USDA Circular no. 160. Washington, D.C.: GP0, 1931.

Hartt, Rollin Lynde. "Notes on a Michigan Lumber Town." *Atlantic Monthly* 85 (January 1900): 101–9.

Hartwell, Robert. "A Revolution in the Chinese Iron and Coal Industries during the Northern Sung, 960–1126 A.D." *Journal of Asian Studies* 21 (1961): 153–62.

———. "Markets, Technology, and the Structure of Enterprise in the Development of the Eleventh-Century Chinese Iron Industry." *Journal of Economic History* 26 (1966): 29–58.

———. "A Cycle of Economic Change in Imperial China: Coal and Iron in Northeast China, 750–1350." *Journal of Economic and Social History of the Orient* 10 (1967): 102–59.

Harvey, David. "Population, Resources and the Ideology of Science." *Economic Geography* 50 (1974): 256–77.

Hatcher, John. *Rural Economy and Society in the Duchy of Cornwall, 1300–1500.* Cambridge: Cambridge University Press, 1970.

Hauser, William B. *Economic and Institutional Change in Tokugawa, Japan: Osaka and the Kinai Cotton Trade.* Cambridge: Cambridge University Press, 1974.

Hawkes, Jacquetta G. "The Ecological Background of Plant Domestication." In *The Domestication of Plants and Animals,* edited by Peter J. Ucko and Geoffrey W. Dimbleby, 17–29. London: Duckworth, 1969.

Hawkins, Benjamin. *A Sketch of the Creek Country in the Years 1798 and 1799.* Reprint, Savannah: Collections of the Georgia Historical Society, vol. 3, pt.1, 1848.

Hays, Samuel P. *Conservation and the Gospel of Efficiency: The Progressive Conservation Movement, 1890–1920.* Harvard Historical Monographs, no. 40. Cambridge, Mass.: Harvard University Press, 1959.

———. *Beauty, Health and Permanence: Environmental Politics in the United States, 1955–1985.* New York: Cambridge University Press, 1987.

Headrick, Daniel R. *The Tools of Empire: Technology and European Imperialism in the Nineteenth Century.* New York: Oxford University Press, 1981.

———. *The Tentacles of Progress: Technology Transfer in the Age of Imperialism, 1850–1940.* Oxford: Oxford University Press, 1988.

———. "Technological Change." In *The Earth As Transformed by Human Action: Global and Regional Changes in the Biosphere over the Past 300 Years,* edited by Billie Lee Turner II, William C. Clark, Robert W. Kates, John F. Richards, Jessica T. Mathews, and William B. Meyer, 55–67. New York: Cambridge University Press, 1991.

Healy, John F. *Mining and Metallurgy in the Greek and Roman World.* London: Thames and Hudson, 1978.

Heber, Reginald. *Narrative of a Journey through the Upper Provinces from Calcutta to Bombay,*

1824–5 (With Notes upon Ceylon) and of a Journey to Madras and the Southern Provinces, 1826, with Letters Written in India. 2 vols. London: John Murray, 1828.

Hecht, Susanna B. "Deforestation in the Amazon Basin: Magnitude, Dynamics, and Soil Resource Effects." *Studies in Third World Societies* 13 (1980): 61–108.

———. "Cattle Ranching in the Eastern Amazon: Environmental and Social Implications." In *The Dilemma of Amazonian Development,* edited by Emilio F. Moran, 158–88. Boulder, Colo.: Westview Press, 1983.

———. "Cattle Ranching in Amazonia: Political and Ecological Considerations." In *Frontier Expansion in Amazonia,* edited by Marianne Schmink and Charles H. Wood, 366–400. Gainesville: University of Florida Press, 1984.

Hecht, Susanna B., and Alexander Cockburn. *The Fate of the Forest: Developers, Destroyers, and Defenders of the Amazon.* London: Verso, 1989.

Heckadon, Stanley Moreno, and Alberto McKay, eds. *Colonización y destruccion de bosques en Panamá.* Panamá: Panamá Asociación Panameña de Antropologia, 1982.

Hegen, E. E. *Highways in the Upper Amazon Basin: Pioneer Lands in Southern Colombia, Equador and Northern Peru.* Gainesville: University of Florida Press, 1966.

Heichelheim, Fritz M. "Effects of Classical Antiquity on the Land." In *Man's Role in Changing the Face of the Earth,* edited by William L. Thomas, 165–82. Chicago: University of Chicago Press, 1956.

———. *An Ancient Economic History from the Palaeolithic Age to the Migrations of Germanic, Slavic and Arabic Nations.* 3 vols. Leiden: A. W. Sijthoff, 1958.

Heidenreich, Conrad. *Huronia: A History and Geography of the Huron Indians, 1600–1650.* Ontario: McClelland and Stewart, 1971.

———. "The Huron." In *The Handbook of North American Indians,* edited by C. William Sturtevant, vol. 15, *The North East,* edited by Bruce C. Trigger, 368–88. Washington, D.C.: Smithsonian Institution, 1978.

Heimert, Alan. "Puritanism, the Wilderness and the Frontier." *New England Quarterly* 26 (1953): 361–82.

Heinsdjik, D. R., O. Soares, and H. Haufe. "The Future of the Brazilian Pine Forests." *Proceedings: Fifth World Forestry Congress, 1960* 1:669–73. Seattle: University of Washington Press, 1960.

Heiser, Charles B. "Variation in the Bottle Gourd." In *Tropical Forest Ecosystems in Africa and South America: A Comparative Review,* edited by Betty J. Meggers, Edward S. Ayensu, and W. Donald Duckworth, 121–28. Washington, D.C.: Smithsonian Institution, 1973.

Hemming, John. *Red Gold: The Conquest of the Brazilian Indians.* London: Macmillan, 1978.

Henderson, William Otto. *The Industrial Revolution on the Continent: Germany, France, Russia, 1800–1914.* London: Frank Cass and Co. Ltd., 1961.

Henderson-Sellers, Anne. "Effects of Change in Land Use on Climate in the Humid Tropics." In *The Geophysics of Amazonia,* edited by Robert E. Dickinson, 463–93. Chicester: Wiley, 1986.

———. "A Commentary on Tropical Deforestation, Albedo and the Surface-Energy Balance." *Climatic Change* 19 (1991): 135–38.

Henderson-Sellers, Anne, Robert E. Dickinson, and M. F. Wilson. "Tropical Deforestation: Important Processes for Climate Models." *Climatic Change* 13 (1988): 43–67.

Henderson-Sellers, Anne and Victor Gornitz. "Possible Climatic Impacts of Land Cover Transformations, with Particular Emphasis on Tropical Deforestation." *Climatic Change* 6 (1984): 231–57.

Henderson-Sellers, Anne, and A. Wilson. "Surface Albedo Data for Climate Modeling." *Review, Geophysics and Space Physics* 21 (1983): 1743–48.

Hendrickson, C. I. "The Agricultural Land Available for Forestry." In *A National Plan for American Forestry* [The Copeland Report]. 73d Cong., 1st sess., S. Doc. 12, 1:151–69, ser. no. 9740. Washington, D.C.: GPO, 1933.

Henshall, Janet D., and Richard P. Momsen Jr. *A Geography of Brazilian Development.* G. Bell and Sons, London, 1974.

Herndon, Melvin G. "The Forest Products of Colonial Georgia." *Georgia Historical Quarterly* 52 (1968): 426–33.

Herrmann, P., ed. *Zimmerische Chronik.* Vol. 4. Leipzig: F. Hendel, 1932.

Heske, Franz. *German Forestry.* Published by the Oberlander Trust of the Carl Schurz Foundation. New Haven, Conn.: Yale University Press, 1938.

Hewitt, John N. B. "The Iroquoian Cosmology." *43rd Annual Report of the Bureau of American Ethnology, 1925.* Part 2: 449–63. Washington, D.C.: GPO, 1926.

Heybroek, H. M. "Disease and Lopping for Fodder As Possible Causes of a Prehistoric Decline in *Ulmus.*" *Acta Botanica Neerlandica* 12 (1963): 1–11.

Heyne, Benjamin. *Tracts, Historical and Statistical, on India with Journals of Several Tours through Various Parts of the Peninsula and also an Account of Sumatra, in a Series of Letters: Tract XIX, Cuddapa to Hyderabad in the Year 1809.* London: Printed for Robert Baldwin and Black, Parry and Co., Booksellers to the East India Company, 1814.

Hibbard, Benjamin H. *A History of Public Land Policies.* New York: Macmillan, 1924. Reprinted with a foreword by Paul W. Gates, Madison: University of Wisconsin Press, 1965.

Hickman, Nollie W. *Mississippi Harvest: Lumbering in the Longleaf Pine Belt, 1840–1915.* University: University of Mississippi Press, 1962.

Hidy, Ralph W., Frank E. Hill, and Alan Nevins. *Timber and Men: The Weyerhaeuser Story.* New York: Macmillan, 1963.

Higginson, Francis H. *New-England's Plantation: or, A Short and True Description of the Commodities and Discommodities of That Country.* London: T. C. and R. C., for M. Sparke, 1830. Reprinted in *Tracts and Other Papers,* edited by Peter Force, vol. 1, no. 12. Washington, D.C.: Peter Force, 1836–41.

Higounet, Charles. "Les forêts de L'Europe occidentale du Vᵉ au XIᵉ siècle." In *Agricultura e mondo rurale in Occidente nell'alto medioevo.* Spoleto: Setimane di studio del centro italiano di studi sull'alto medioevo, 13 (1966): 343–98.

Hilliard, Sam Bass. *Hogmeat and Hocake: Food Supply in the Old South, 1840–1860.* Carbondale: Southern Illinois University Press, 1972.

Hindle, Brooke, ed. *America's Wooden Age: Aspects of Its Early Technology.* Tarrytown, N.Y.: Sleepy Hollow Restorations, 1975.

Hipple, Walter J. *The Beautiful, the Sublime, and the Picturesque in Eighteenth Century British Aesthetics.* Carbondale: Southern Illinois University Press, 1957.

Hiraoka, Mario, and Shozo Yamamoto. "Agricultural Development in the Upper Amazon of Ecuador." *Geographical Review* 52 (1982): 423–45.

Hirsch, Philip. "Deforestation and Development in Thailand." *Singapore Journal of Tropical Geography* 8 (1987): 129–38.

Ho, Ping-ti. "The Introduction of American Food Plants into China." *American Anthropologist* 57 (1955): 191–210.

———. *Studies on the Population of China, 1386–1953.* Cambridge, Mass.: Harvard University Press, 1959.

Hodgson, Adam. *Letters from North America written during a Tour in the United States and Canada.* 2 vols. New York: Samuel Whiting, 1823.

Hodgson, M. T. "Domesday Water Mills." *Antiquity* 13 (1939): 261–79.

Hoglund, A. William. "Forest Conservation and Stove Inventions, 1789–1850." *Forest History* 5 (1962): 2–8.

Holbrook, Stewart H. *Burning an Empire: The Story of American Forest Fires.* New York: Macmillan, 1943.

Homer. *The Iliad of Homer.* Translated by William Cullen Bryant. Boston: Houghton Mifflin and Company, 1895.

Hooke, Della. "Woodland Utilization in England A.D. 800–1100." In *Human Influences on Forest Ecosystems Development in Europe,* edited by Fabio Salbitano, 301–31. ESF FERN-CNR. Bologna: Piagora Editrice, 1988.

———. "Pre-Conquest Woodland: Its Distribution and Usage." *Agricultural History Review* 37 (1989): 113–29.

Hoops, Johannes. *Waldbaüme und Kulturpflanzen in Germanischen Altertum.* Strasbourg: Verlag von Karl J. Trübner, 1905.

Hope, Ronald. *A New History of British Shipping.* London: John Murray, 1990.

Hopkins, Brian. *Forest and Savanna: An Introduction to Tropical Plant Ecology with Special Reference to West Africa.* London: Heinemann, 1965.

Hopkins, Keith. *Conquerors and Slaves.* Cambridge: Cambridge University Press, 1978.

Horace. *Satires, Epistles, and Ars Poetica.* With an English translation by H. Rushton Fairclough. Loeb Classical Library. London: William Heinemann, 1926.

Hoskins, William G. *The Making of the English Landscape.* London: Hodder and Stoughton, 1951.

———. "The English Landscape." In *Medieval England,* edited by A. L. Poole, 1:1–36. Oxford: Oxford Univesity Press, 1958.

Hotchkiss, George Woodward. *History of the Lumber and Forest Industry of the Northwest.* Chicago: G. W. Hotchkiss, 1898.

Hough, Franklin B. *Report upon Forestry.* Submitted to Congress by the Commissioner of Agriculture. Vol. 1 (1878); vol. 2 (1880); and vol. 3 (1882). Vol. 4 was prepared by N. H. Egleston. Washington, D.C.: GPO, 1884.

Houghton, John. *Husbandry and Trade Improv'd: Being a Collection of many Valuable Materials . . .* 4 vols. London: Woodman and Lyon, 1681–83.

Houghton, Richard A. "Estimating Changes in the Carbon Content of Terrestrial Ecosystems from Historical Data." In *The Changing Carbon Cycle: A Global Analysis,* edited by John R. Trabalka and David E. Reichle, 175–93. New York: Springer-Verlag, 1986.

———. "Releases of Carbon to the Atmosphere from Degradation of Forests in Tropical Asia." *Canadian Journal of Forest Research* 21 (1991): 132–42.

———. "Tropical Deforestation and Atmospheric Carbon Dioxide." *Climatic Change* 19 (1991): 99–118.

Houghton, Richard A., et al. "Changes in the Carbon Content of Terrestrial Biota and Soils between 1860–1980: A Net Release of CO_2 to the Atmosphere." *Ecological Monographs* 53 (1983): 235–62.

Houghton, Richard A., R. D. Boone, J. M. Melillo, C. A. Palm, George A. Woodwell, Norman Myers, Berrien Moore III, and David L. Skole. "Net Flux of Carbon Dioxide from Tropical Forests in 1980." *Nature* 316 no. 6029 (1986): 617–20.

Houghton, Richard A., D. S. Lefkowitz, and David L. Skole. "Changes in the Landscape of Latin America between 1850 and 1985: I. Progressive Loss of Forests." *Forest Ecology and Management* 38 (1991): 143–72.

Houghton, Richard A., and David L. Skole. "Carbon." In *The Earth As Transformed by Human Action: Global and Regional Changes in the Biosphere over the Past 300 Years,* edited by

Billie Lee Turner II, William C. Clark, Robert W. Kates, John F. Richards, Jesicca T. Mathews, and William B. Meyer, 393–408. New York: Cambridge University Press, 1990.

Howard, Stephen. "The Burning Season." *The World Today* (July 1998): 172–75.

Huffel, Gustave. *Economie forestière.* 3 vols. Paris: Laveur, 1904–7.

Hughes, J. Donald. *Ecology in Ancient Civilizations.* Albuquerque: University of New Mexico Press, 1975.

———. "How the Ancients Viewed Deforestation." *Journal of Field Archaeology* 10 (1983): 437–45.

———. "Theophrastus As Ecologist." *Environmental Review* 4 (1985): 291–307. Reprinted in *Theophrastean Studies,* vol. 3, *On Natural Science, Physics, Metaphysics, Ethics, Religion, and Rhetoric,* edited by William W. Fortenbaugh and Robert W. Sharples, 67–75. Rutgers University Studies in Classical Humanities. New Brunswick, N.J. Transaction Books, 1988.

———. *Pan's Travail: Environmental Problems of the Ancient Greeks and Romans.* Baltimore: Johns Hopkins University Press, 1994.

Hughes, J. Donald, and Thirgood, Jack V. "Deforestation, Erosion, and Forest Management in Ancient Greece and Rome." *Journal of Forest History* 26 (1982): 60–75. Reprinted under the title "Deforestation in Ancient Greece and Rome: A Cause of Collapse" (*The Ecologist* 12 [1982]: 196–208).

Humbert, Henri. "Principaux aspects de la végétation à Madagascar. La destruction d'une flore insulaire par le feu." *Mémoires de L'Academie Malgache* 5 (1927): 1–79.

Hummel, John R., and Ruth Reck. "Global Surface Albedo Model." *Journal of Applied Meteorology* 18 (1979): 239–53.

Hunter, William Wilson. *A Statistical Account of Bengal.* Vol. 1, *Sunderbans.* London: Trubner, 1875–78.

Huntley, Brian J., and Hilary J. B. Birks. *An Atlas of Past and Present Pollen Maps for Europe: 0–13,000 Years Ago.* Cambridge: Cambridge University Press, 1983.

Hurd, John M. "Railways and Expansion of Markets in India." *Explorations in Economic History* 12 (1975): 263–88.

———. "Railways." In *The Cambridge Economic History of India,* edited by Dharma Kumar, vol. 2, *c.1752–c.1970,* 737–61. Cambridge: Cambridge University Press, 1983.

Hurst, Philip. *Rainforest Politics: Ecological Destruction in South East Asia.* London: Zed Books, 1990.

Hussey, Christopher. *The Pictureseque: Studies in a Point of View* [1927], 2d ed. London: Frank Cass, 1967.

Huttunen, Pertti. "Early Land Use, Especially the Slash-and-Burn Cultivation in the Commune of Lammi, Southern Finland, Interpreted Mainly Using Pollen and Charcoal Analysis." *Acta Botanica Fennica* 113 (1980): 1–45.

Hyde, C. K. *Technological Change and the British Iron Industry, 1700–1870.* Princeton, N.J.: Princeton University Press, 1977.

Illick, Joseph S. "The Story of the American Lumbering Industry." In *A Popular History of American Invention,* edited by W. Kaempffert, 2:150–98. New York: Charles Scribner and Sons, 1924.

Imbrie, John, and Katherine P. Imbrie. *Ice Ages: Solving the Mystery.* London: Macmillan, 1979.

Ingerson, Alice E. "Tracking and Testing the Nature-Culture Dichotomy." In *Historical Ecology: Cultural Knowledge and Changing Landscapes,* edited by C. L. Crumley, 43–66. Sante Fe, N.M.: School of American Research Press, 1994.

"Iron-Making in India." *Indian Forester* 6 (1881): 202–11.

Ise, John. *The United States Forest Policy.* New Haven, Conn.: Yale University Press, 1920.

Israel, Jonathan I. *Dutch Primacy and World Trade, 1585–1740.* Oxford: Clarendon Press, 1989.

Isserlis, Leon. "Tramp Steamer Cargoes and Freights." *Journal of Royal Statistical Society* 101 (1938): pt. 1, p. 122, table 8.

Iversen, Johannes. *Landnam i Danmarks Stenalder.* (Land occupation in Denmark's Stone Age). Danmarks Geologiske Undersógelse, ser. 2, vol. 3, no. 66 (1941): 1–68.

———. "The Influence of Prehistoric Man on Vegetation." Danmarks Geologiske Undersógelse, ser. 4, vol. 3, no. 6 (1949): 1–23.

———. "Forest Clearance in the Stone Age." *Scientific American* 194 (March 1956): 36–41.

———. "The Bearing of Glacial and Interglacial Epochs on the Formation and Extinction of Plant Taxa." *Uppsala Universiteit Arssk* 6 (1958): 210–15.

———. "Retrogressive Vegetational Succession in the Post-Glacial." *Journal of Ecology* 52 (1964): 59–70.

———. "The Development of Denmark's Nature since the Last Glacial." Danmarks Geologiske Undersógelse, ser. 5, no. 7-C (1973): 1–120.

Jacks, Graham Vernon, and Robert Orr Whyte. *The Rape of the Earth: A World Survey of Soil Erosion.* London: Faber and Faber, 1939.

Jacobi, R., J. H. Tallis, and Paul A. Mellars. "The Southern Pennine Mesolithic and the Ecological Record." *Journal of Archaeological Science* 3 (1979): 307–20.

Jäger, Helmut. *Die Entwicklung der Kulturlandschaft im Kriese Hofgeïsmar.* Göttinger Geographische Abhandlung no. 8. Göttingen: Department of Geography, 1951.

———. "Zur Entstehung der heutigen grossen Forsten in Deutschland." *Berichte zur Deutschen Landeskunde* 13 (1954): 156–71.

Jäger, Jill, and Roger G. Barry. "Climate." In *The Earth As Transformed by Human Action: Global and Regional Changes in the Biosphere over the Past 300 Years,* edited by Billie Lee Turner II, William C. Clark, Robert W. Kates, John F. Richards, Jessica T. Mathews, and William B. Meyer, 335–51. New York: Cambridge University Press, 1990.

James, Noel David G. *A History of English Forestry.* Oxford: Basil Blackwell, 1981.

James, Preston E. "The Coffee Lands of Southeastern Brazil." *Geographical Review* 22 (1932): 225–43.

Jarman, H. N. "Early Crop Agriculture in Europe." In *Origine de l'élevage et de la domestication,* edited by Eric Higgs, 116–42. Nice: Union International des Sciences Préhistoriques et Protohistoriques (Collogue XX, IX Congrés), 1976.

———. "The Lowlands." In *Early European Agriculture: Its Foundation and Development,* edited by M. R. Jarman, G. N. Bailey, and H. N. Jarman, 131–202. Cambridge: Cambridge University Press, 1982.

Jennings, Jesse David, ed. *The Prehistory of Polynesia.* Cambridge, Mass.: Harvard University Press, 1979.

Jepma, Catrinus J. *Tropical Deforestation: A Socio-Economic Approach.* London: Earthscan, 1995.

Jepson, Paul, James K. Jarvie, Kathy MacKinnon, and Kathryn A. Monk. "The End for Indonesia's Lowland Forests?" *Science* 292 (May 2001): 859–61.

Johnson, Alan Chester. "Ancient Forests and Navies." *Transactions and Proceedings, American Philological Society* 58 (1927): 199–209.

Johnson, Edward. *Johnson's Wonder-Working Providence of Sion's Saviour in New England, 1628–1681* [1864]. In *Original Documents of Early American History,* edited by J. F. Jameson. New York: Charles Scribner and Sons, 1910.

Johnston, Sir Harry. *Liberia.* 2 vols. London: Hutchinson and Co., 1906.

Johnston, Robert. *Travels through Part of the Russian Empire and the Country of Poland along the Southern Shores of the Baltic.* London: J. S. Stockdale, 1815.

Jones, Eric Lionel. *Agriculture and Economic Growth in England, 1750–1815.* London: Methuen, 1967.

———. *The European Miracle: Environments, Economies, and Geopolitics in the History of Europe and Asia,* 2d ed. Cambridge: Cambridge University Press, 1987.

Jones, Hugh. *The Present State of Virginia from whence is Inferred a Shorter View of Maryland and North America* [1753]. Edited by Richard L. Morton. Chapel Hill: University of North Carolina Press for the Virginia Historical Society, 1956.

Jones, M. D. H., and Anne Henderson-Sellers. "History of the Greenhouse Effect." *Progress in Physical Geography* 14 (1990): 1–18.

Jones, P. D., T. M. L. Wrigley, and P. B. Wright. "Global Temperature Variation between 1861 and 1984." *Nature* 322 (1986): 430–34.

Jones, Rhys. "Fire-Stick Farming." *Australian Natural History* 16 (1969): 224–28.

———. "Hunters in the Australian Coastal Savannas." In *Human Ecology in Savanna Environments,* edited by David R. Harris, 107–46. London: Academic Press, 1980.

Jordan, Terry G., and Matti Kaups. *The American Backwoods Frontier: An Ethnic and Ecological Interpretation.* Baltimore: Johns Hopkins University Press, 1989.

Judson, Sheldon. "Stream Changes during Historic Time in East-Central Sicily." *American Journal of Archaeology* 67 (1963): 287–89.

———. "Erosion Rates near Rome, Italy." *Science* 160 (1968): 1444–46.

Kahn, James, and Judith McDonald. "International Debt and Deforestation." In *The Causes of Tropical Deforestation,* edited by Katrina Brown and David W. Pearce, 57–67. London: University College Press, 1994.

Kaleski, R. "Our Forests in Earlier Days: Some Political History." *Australian Forestry Journal* 8 (1925): 323–26.

Kalm, Pehr. *Travels into N. America, Containing its Natural History and a Circumstantial Account of its Plantations and Agriculture.* Translated from the Finnish by John R. Forster. 3 vols. London: William Eyres, 1770–71.

Kamarov, Boris. *The Destruction of Nature in the Soviet Union.* White Plains, N.Y.: M. E. Sharpe Inc., 1981.

Kane, Lucile. "Selling the Cut-Over Lands in Wisconsin." *Business History Review* 28 (1954): 236–47.

Kartawinata, Kuswata, S. Adisoemarto, S. Riswan, and A. D. Vayda. "The Impact of Man on a Tropical Forest of Indonesia." *Ambio* 10 (1981): 115–19.

Kay, Charles E. "Aboriginal Overkill: The Role of Native Americans in Structuring Western Ecosystems." *Human Nature* 5 (1994): 359–98.

Keegan, William F., ed. *Emergent Horticultural Economies of the Eastern Woodlands.* Center for Archaeological Investigations Occasional Paper no. 7. Carbondale: Southern Illinois University, 1987.

Keeling, C. D., R. B. Bacastow, A. E. Bainbridge, C. A. Ekdahl, P. A. Guenther, L. S. Waterman, and J. F. S. Chin. "Atmospheric Carbon Dioxide Variations at Mauna Loa Observatory, Hawaii." *Tellus* 28 (1976): 538–51.

Keen, Benjamin. *The Life of the Admiral Christopher Columbus by His Son Ferdinand.* New Brunswick, N.J.: Rutgers University Press, 1959.

Kellenbenz, Hermann. *The Rise of the European Economy: An Economic History of Continental Europe from the Fifteenth to the Eighteenth Century.* London: Weidenfeld and Nicolson, 1976.

————. "Technology in the Age of Scientific Revolution, 1500–1700." In *The Fontana Economic History of Europe,* edited by Carlo M. Cipolla, vol. 2, *The Sixteenth and Seventeenth Centuries,* 171–272. Brighton: Harvester Press, 1977.

Kellman, M. C. "Some Environmental Components of Shifting Cultivation in Upland Mindanao." *Journal of Tropical Geography* 28 (1969): 40–56.

Kellogg, William W. "Mankind's Impact on Climate: The Evolution of Awareness." *Climatic Change* 10 (1987): 113–36.

Kennedy, Paul. *The Rise and Fall of Great Powers: Economic Change and Military Conflict from 1500 to 2000.* New York: Random House, 1987.

Kent, Heinz S. K. "The Anglo-Norwegian Timber Trade in the Eighteenth Century." *Economic History Review,* 2d. ser., 7 (1955): 61–74.

————. *War and Trade in Northern Seas: Anglo-Scandinavian Economic Relations in the Mid-Eighteenth Century.* Cambridge: Cambridge University Press, 1973.

Kern, M. G. *The Relation of Railroads to Forest Supplies and Forestry.* USDA, Forestry Division, Bulletin no.1. Washington, D.C.: GPO, 1887.

Kerridge, Eric. "The Agricultural Revolution Reconsidered." *Agricultural History* 43 (1969): 463–75.

Kershaw, Ian. "The Great Famine and Agrarian Crisis in England, 1315–1322." *Past and Present* 59 (1973): 3–50.

Kimber, Clarissa Thérèse. *Martinique: The Plant Geographies of a West Indian Island.* College Station: Texas A & M University Press, 1968.

Kindleberger, Charles P. *A Financial History of Western Europe.* London: George Allen and Unwin, 1984.

King, Gregory. *Natural and Political Observations and Conclusions upon the State and Condition of England, 1696.* Printed as an appendix to *An Estimate of the Comparative Strength of Great-Britain during the Present and the Four Preceding Reigns,* by G. Chalmers. London: J. Stockdale, 1804.

King, Victor T. "Politik Pembangunan: The Political Economy of Rainforest Exploitation and Development in Sarawak, East Malaysia." *Global Ecology and Biogeography Letters.* 3 (1993): 235–44.

Kinney, Jay P. *Forest Legislation in America Prior to March 4, 1789.* Cornell University Agricultural Experimental Station of New York College of Agriculture. Department of Forestry Bulletin no. 370, 359–405. Ithaca, N.Y: Cornell University, 1916.

Kinross, Lord. *Between Two Seas: The Creation of the Suez Canal.* London: John Murray, 1968.

Kirby, J. M. "Colombian Land-Use Changes and the Settlement of the Oriente." *Pacific Viewpoint* 19 (1978): 1–25.

Kirkaldy, Adam W. *British Shipping: Its History, Organization and Importance* [1914]. London: Kegan Paul, Trench and Trübner and Co. Ltd. New York: Reissued by A. M. Kelley, 1970.

Kirkby, Anne V. T. "The Use of Land and Water Resources in the Past and Present Valley of Oaxaca, Mexico." *Memoirs of the Museum of Anthropology, University of Michigan,* no. 5. Ann Arbor: University of Michigan, 1973.

Ki-Zerboi, Jacqueline. "Women and the Energy Crisis in the Sahel." *Unasylva* 33, no. 133 (1981): 5–10.

Klein, Julius. *The Mesta: A Study in Spanish Economic History, 1273–1836.* Cambridge, Mass.: Harvard University Press, 1920.

Kleinpenning, J. M. G. *The Integration and Colonization of the Brazilian Portion of the Amazon Basin.* Nijmeegse Geografische Cahiers, 4. Nijmeigen, Netherlands: Geografisch en Planologisch Institut Katholieke Universiteit Nijmeigen, 1975.

Kleinpenning, J. M. G., and E. B. Zoomers. "Environmental Degradation in Latin America: The Example of Paraguay." *Tijdschrift voor Economische en Sociale Geografie* 78 (1987): 242–50.

Klippart, John H. "Condition of Agriculture in Ohio in 1876." *Ohio Agricultural Report*, 2d ser. (1876): 549–77. Columbus, Ohio: Department of Agriculture.

Kluchevsky, Vasili Osipovich. *A History of Russia*. Translated from the Russian by C. J. Hogarth. 5 Vols. London: J. M. Dent and Sons, 1911–13.

Knight, C. G. "The Ecology of African Sleeping Sickness," *Annals, Association of American Geographers* 61 (1971): 23–44.

Koebner, Richard. "The Settlement and Colonization of Europe." In *The Cambridge Economic History of Europe*, vol. 1, *Agrarian Life in the Middle Ages*, edited by John H. Clapham and Eileen Power, 1–88. Cambridge: Cambridge University Press, 1941.

Kolars, John F. "Locational Aspects of Cultural Ecology: The Case of the Goat in Non-Western Agriculture." *Geographical Review* 56 (1966): 577–84.

Kollmorgen, Walter M. "The Woodsman's Assault on the Domain of the Cattleman." *Annals, Association of American Geographers* 59 (1969): 215–39.

Komarek, E. V. "Lightning and Lightning Fires as Ecological Forces." *Proceedings, Tall Timbers Fire Ecology Conference* 8 (1968): 169–97. Tallahassee, Fla.: Tall Timbers Research Station.

———. "Ancient Fires." *Proceedings, Tall Timbers Fire Ecology Conference* 12 (1972): 219–40. Tallahassee: Tall Timbers Research Station.

Kotok, E. I. "America's Role in Meeting World Timber Needs." *Symposium on Forestry and Public Welfare: Proceedings, American Philosophical Society* 89, no. 2 (1945): 418–22.

Kötzschke, Rudolf, and Wolfgang Ebert. *Geschichte der Ostdeutschen Kolonisation*. Leipzig: Bibliograpisches Institut, 1937.

Kozlowski, S. K. *Cultural Differentiation of Europe between the 10th and 5th Millennia B.C.* Warsaw: Warsaw University Press, 1975.

Kozlowski, Theodore T., and Clifford Elmer Ahlgren, eds. *Fire and Ecosytems*. New York, Academic Press, 1974.

Kracke, Edward A. Jr. "Sung Society: Change within Tradition." *Far Eastern Quarterly* 14 (1954): 479–88.

Kranzberg, Melvin, and Carroll W. Pursell Jr., eds. *Technology in Western Civilization*. Vol. 1, *The Emergence of Modern Industrial Society—Earliest Times to 1900*. New York: Oxford University Press, 1967.

Krause, Ernst H. L. "Florenkarte von Norddeutschland für das 12. bis 15. Jahrhundert." *Petermanns Geographische Mitteilungen* 38 (1892): 231–35.

Krech, Shepard. *The Ecological Indian: Myth and History*. New York: W. W. Norton and Company, 1999.

Kretzschmer, Fritz. "Der Betriebsversuch an einem Hypokaustum der Saalburg." *Germania* 31 (1953): 64–67.

———. "Hypocausten." *Saalburg-Jahrbuch* 12 (1953): 7–41.

Kroeber, Alfred L. *Cultural and Natural Areas of Native North America*. University of California Publications in American Archaeology and Ethnology, no. 38. Berkeley: University of California, 1939.

Kruk, Janusz. *Studia Osadnicze nad Neolitem Wyżym Lessowych* [1973]. Wroclaw: Zaklad Narodowy Imienia Ossoliskick. Translated from the Polish by M. Hejwowska and edited by John M. Howelland Nicholas J. Startling under the title *The Neolithic Settlement of Southern Poland*. British Archaeological Reports, International Series, 93. Oxford: B.A.R., 1980.

Kuhn, Walter. "Die Siedlerzahlen der deutschen Ostsiedlung." In *Stadium Sociale. Karl Valentin Müller dargebracht*, 131–54. Cologne: Springer Verlag, 1963.

Kull, Christian A. "Deforestation, Erosion and Fire: Degradation Myths in the Environmental History of Madagascar." *Environment and History* 6 (2000): 423–50.

Kummer, David M. *Deforestation in the Postwar Philippines.* University of Chicago, Department of Geography, Research Paper no. 234. Chicago: University of Chicago Press, 1992.

Laarman, Jan. "Export of Tropical Hardwoods in the Twentieth Century." In *World Deforestation in the Twentieth Century,* edited by John F. Richards and Richard P. Tucker, 147–63. Duke Press Policy Studies. Durham, N.C.: Duke University Press, 1988.

Lafitau, Joseph Françoise. *Customs of the American Indians Compared with Those of the Customs of Primitive Times.* Edited by W. N. Fenton and E. L. Moore. 2 vols. Toronto: Champlain Society, 1974. Based on *Mouers, des sauvages Ameriquains, compares aux moeurs des premier temps* (Paris, 1724).

Lal, R. "Deforestation of Tropical Rainforest and Hydrological Problems." In *Tropical Agricultural Hydrology,* edited by R. Lal and E. W. Russell, 131–40. New York: John Wiley, 1981.

———. "Deforestation and Soil Erosion." In *Land Clearing and Development in the Tropics,* edited by R. Lal, Pedro A. Sanchez, and R. W. Cummings Jr., 299–315. Rotterdam: A. A. Balkema, 1988.

———. "Soil Degradation and Conservation of Tropical Rainforests." In *Changing the Global Environment,* edited by David B. Botkin, Joan Estes, Margaret Cresswell, and Angelo A. Orio, 137–54. New York: Academic Press, 1989.

Lamb, Hubert H. "Our Changing Climate: Past and Present." In *The Changing Climate,* edited by Hubert H. Lamb, 1–20. London: Methuen and Co., 1966.

Lampard, Eric E. "The Social Impact of the Industrial Revolution." In *Technology in Western Civilization,* edited by Melvin Kranzberg and Carroll W. Pursell Jr., vol. 1, *The Emergence of Modern Industrial Society—Earliest Times to 1900,* 302–24. New York: Oxford University Press, 1967.

Landes, David S. *The Unbound Prometheus: Technological Change and Industrial Development in Western Europe from 1750 to the Present.* Cambridge: Cambridge University Press, 1969.

———. *Revolution in Time: Clocks and the Making of the Modern World.* Cambridge, Mass.: Belknap Press of Harvard University Press, 1983.

Landsberg, Helmut E. *The Urban Climate.* New York: Academic Press, 1981.

Lane, Frederic C. *Venetian Ships and Shipbuilders of the Renaissance.* Baltimore: Johns Hopkins University Press, 1934.

Lange, Algot. *The Lower Amazon.* New York: G. P. Putnam's Sons, 1914.

Langston, Nancy. *Forest Dreams, Forest Nightmares: The Paradox of Old Growth in the Inland West.* Seattle and London: University of Washington Press, 1995.

Lanly, Jean-Paul. "Regression de la forêt dese en Côte-d'Ivoire." *Bois et Forêts de Tropiques* 127 (1969): 45–49.

———. "Tropical Forest Resources." Forest Paper no. 30. Rome: FAO, 1982.

Lanly, Jean-Paul, and J. Clement. "Present and Future Natural Forest and Planatation Areas in the Tropics." *Unasylva* 31 (1979): 2–20.

Lanly, Jean-Paul, ed. *Tropical Forest Resources Assessment Project (GEMS): Tropical Africa* (1981a), *Tropical Asia* (1981b), *Tropical America* (1981c). 4 vols. Rome: FAO and UNEP, 1981.

Latham, Anthony J. H. *The International Economy and the Underdeveloped World, 1865–1914.* Totowa, N.J.: Rowan and Littlefield, 1978.

Latham, Bryan. *Timber: Its Development and Distribution: A Historical Survey.* London: G. C. Harrap, 1957.

———. *The Development of the American Timber Trade.* 1957.

Laughton, A. M. and Hall, T. S. *Handbook to Victoria*. Melbourne: Government Printer, 1914.

Layton, Ian. "The Timber and Naval Stores Supply Regions of Northern Europe during the Early Modern World-System." In *The Early Modern World-System in Geographical Perspective*, edited by Hans-Jürgen Nitz, 265–95. Stuttgart: Franz Steiner Verlag, 1993.

Le Roy Ladurie, Emmanuel. "Le climat des XIᵉ et XVIᵉ siècles: series comparées." *Annales, Économies, Sociétiés, Civilisations* 20 (1965): 899–922 and charts.

———. *The Peasants of Languedoc* [1969]. Translated from the French by John Day. Urbana: University of Illinois Press, 1974.

———. *Times of Feast, Times of Famine: A History of Climate since the Year 1000* [1967]. Translated from the French by Barbara Bray. New York: The Noonday Press, Farrar, Straus and Giroux, 1988.

Lech, J., and A. Leligdowicz. "Die Methoden der Versorgung mit Feuerstein und die lokalen Bezlehungen zwischen den Siedlungen und Bergwerken im Weichselgebiet während des 5.bis 2 Jt. v.u.z." In *Ungerschichliche Besiedlung im ihrer Beziehung zur natürlichen Umwelt*, edited by F. Schlette, 151–84. Halle: Wissenschaftliche Beeiträge der Martin-Luther Universität Halle-Wittenburg, 1980.

Leclercq, Jean. *The Love of Learning and the Desire for God: A Study of Monastic Culture* [1957]. Translated from the French by Catherine Misrahi. London: S.P.C.K., 1978.

Lederer, John. *The Discoveries of John Lederer in Three Marches from Virginia to the West of Carolina and Other Parts of the Continent, 1669 and 1670* [1672]. Collected and translated by Sir William Talbot. Reprint, Rochester, N.Y.: n.p., 1902.

Lee, James. "Migration and Expansion in Chinese History." In *Human Migration: Patterns and Policies*, edited by William H. McNeill, 20–47. Bloomington: University of Indiana Press, 1979.

Lee, Richard B., and Irven DeVore, eds. *Man the Hunter*. Chicago: Aldine, 1968.

Leeper, Geoffrey, ed. *The Australian Environment*, 4th rev. ed. Melbourne: CSIRO and Melbourne University Press, 1970.

Lefranc, Pierre. *Sir Walter Ralegh: Écrivain: l'oeuvre etles Idées*. Paris: Armand, 1980.

Leite, Laercio L., and Peter A. Furley. "Land Development in the Brazilian Amazon Region with Particular Reference to Rondônia and the Ouro Prêto Colonization Project." In *Change in the Amazon Basin: The Frontier after a Decade of Colonization*, edited by John Hemming, 119–39. Manchester: Manchester University Press, 1985.

Lennard, Reginald. "The Destruction of Woodland in the Eastern Counties under William the Conqueror." *Economic History Review* 15 (1945): 36–43.

Leopold, Aldo. "The Land Ethic." In *A Sand County Almanac, and Sketches Here and There*, 201–26. New York: Oxford University Press, 1949.

Lesley, J. Peter. *The Iron Manufacturer's Guide to the Furnaces, Forges, and Rolling Mills of the United States*. New York: J. Wiley, 1859.

Lévi-Strauss, Claude. "The Concept of Archaism in Anthropology." In *Structural Anthropology*, 97–115. New York: Anchor Books, 1963.

Lewis, Archibald R. "The Closing of the Medieval Frontier, 1250–1350." *Speculum* 33 (1958): 475–83.

Lewit, Tamara. *Agricultural Production in the Roman Economy, A.D. 200–400*. British Archaeological Reports, International Series, 568. Oxford: Tempus Repartum, 1991.

Lewthwaite, James A. R. "Plains Tails from the Hills: Transhumance in Mediterranean Archaeology." In *Economic Archaeology: Towards an Integration of Ecological and Social Approaches*, edited by Alison Sheridan and Geoffrey Bailey, 55–66. British Archaeological Reports, International Series, 96. Oxford: B.A.R., 1981.

Liehl, Ekkhard, and Wolf Dieter Sick. *Der Schwarzwalde: Beiträge zur Landskunde.* Frieburg: Veröffentlichung des Alemannischen Institut Freiburg, no. 47, 1980.

Lieth, Helmut. "Über die Primerproduktion der Pflanzendecke der Erde." *Angewandte Botantik* 46 (1972): 1–37.

———. "Primary Production of the Major Vegetation Units of the World." In *Primary Productivity of the Biosphere,* edited by Helmut Lieth and Robert H. Whittaker, 203–5. Ecological Studies no. 14. Berlin: Springer-Verlag, 1975.

Ligon, Richard. *A True and Exact History of the Island of Barbadoes* [1673]. London: Cass, 1970.

Lillard, Richard G. *The Great Forest.* New York: Alfred A. Knopf, 1948.

Linblad, Jan Thomas. "Structural Change in the Dutch Trade with the Baltic in the Eighteenth Century." *Scandinavian Economic History Review* 33 (1985): 193–207.

Linden, Eugene. "Torching the Amazon: Playing with Fire." *Time,* 18 September 1989, 44–50.

Linder, Per, and Lars Östlund. "Structural Changes in Three Mid-Boreal Swedish Forest Landscapes, 1885–1996." *Biological Conservation* 85 (1998): 9–19.

Lindsay, J. M. "Charcoal Iron Smelting and Its Fuel Supply: The Example of the Lorn Furnace, Argyllshire, 1753–1876." *Journal of Historical Geography* 1 (1975), 283–98.

Linke, Wolfgang. *Frühestes Bauerntum und Geographische Umwelt.* Bochumer Geographische Arbeiten 28. Paderborn: Schöningh, 1976.

Liouville, E. "Les tailles des Ardennes." *Revue des Eaux et Forêts* 36 (1897): 257–67.

Little, Michael A. "Human Populations in the Andes: The Human Science Basis for Research Planning." *Mountain Research and Development* 1 (1981): 14570.

Little, Peter D., Michael M. Horowitz, and A. Endre Nyerges, eds. *Lands at Risk in the Third World: Local-Level Perspectives.* Boulder, Colo.: Westview Press, 1987.

Livermore, Harold Victor. "The New World: Portuguese Expansion." In *The New Cambridge Modern History,* vol. 1, *The Renaissance, 1493–1520,* edited by George Richard Potter, 420–29. Cambridge: Cambridge University Press, 1961.

Livingstone, David. *The Last Journals of David Livingstone in Central Africa, from Eighteen Hundred and Sixty-Five to his Death: Continued by a Narrative by Horace Weller.* Chicago: Jansen McClurg and Co., 1875.

Livingstone, David, and Charles Livingstone. *Narrative of an Expedition to the Zambesi and its Tributaries; and of the Discovery of Lakes Shirwa and Nyasa, 1858–64.* New York: Harper Brothers, 1866.

Livy. *History of Rome.* Translated from the Latin by B. O. Foster. 5 vols. Loeb Classical Library. Cambridge, Mass.: Harvard University Press, 1924–29.

Locke, John. *Two Treatises on Government.* Edited by Peter Laslett. Cambridge: Cambridge University Press, 1960.

Lockhart, James, and Stuart B. Schwartz. *Early Latin America: A History of Colonial Spanish America.* Cambridge: Cambridge University Press, 1983.

Loehr, Rodney C. "Saving the Kerf. The Introduction of the Band Saw Mill." *Agricultural History* 26 (1949): 168–72.

Lombard, Maurice M. "Arsenaux et bois de marine dans la Méditerranée musulmane (VIIᵉ–XIᵉ siècles)." In *La navire et l'économie maritime du moyen-age au xviiᵉ siècle principalement en Méditerranée,* edited by Michel Mollat, 53–106. Bibliothêque Générale de L'École Practique des Hautes Études. VIᵉ Section. Paris: S.E.V.P.E.N., 1958.

———. "Une carte du bois la Méditerranée musulmane (VIIᵉ–XIᵉ siècle)." *Annales, Economies, Sociétés, Civilisations* 14 (1959): 23–54.

Lopinot, Neal H., and William I. Woods. "Wood Over-Exploitation and the Collapse of Cahokia."

In *Foraging and Farming in the Eastern Woodlands,* edited by C. Margaret Scarry, 206–31. Gainesville: University of Florida Press, 1993.

Lorain, John. *Nature and Reason Harmonized in the Practice of Husbandry.* Philadelphia: H. C. Carey and I. Lea, 1825.

Lord, Eleanor L. *Industrial Experiments in the British Colonies of North America.* Johns Hopkins University Studies in Historical and Political Science, extra vol. 17. Baltimore: Johns Hopkins Univesity Press, 1898.

Lossing, Benson J. *The Hudson from the Wilderness to the Sea.* New York: Virtue and Yorston, 1866.

Love, John R. *Antiquity and Capitalism: Max Weber and the Sociological Foundations of Roman Civilization.* London: Routledge, 1991.

Lovejoy, Arthur O. *The Great Chain of Being: A Study in the History of an Idea.* Cambridge, Mass.: Harvard University Press, 1936.

Lovell, W. George. "'Heavy Shadows and Black Night': Disease and Depopulation in Colonial Spanish America." *Annals, Association of American Geographers* 82 (1992): 426–43.

Low, Hugh. *Sarawak: Its Inhabitants and Production, being Notes during a Residence in that Country with His Excellency Mr Brooke.* London: Richard Bentley, 1846.

Lowden, M. S. "Fire Crisis in Brazil." *American Forests* 71 (1965): 42–44, 46.

Lowdermilk, Walter Clay. "Lessons from the Old World to the Americas in Land Use." *Smithsonian Institution: Annual Report,* 1943, 413–28. Washington, D.C.: GPO, 1944.

Lowdermilk, Walter Clay, and T. L. Li. "Forestry in Denuded China." *Annals of the American Academy of Political and Social Science,* no. 152, "China," edited by H. F. James, 127–41. Philadelphia: American Academy of Political and Social Science, 1930.

Lowdermilk, Walter Clay, and Dean R. Wickes. *History of Soil Use in the Wu T'ai Shan Area.* Monograph, Royal Asiatic Society, N. China Branch. London: R.A.S., 1938.

Lowenthal, David. *George Perkins Marsh: Versatile Vermonter.* New York: Columbia University Press, 1958.

———. "Awareness of Human Impacts: Changing Attitudes and Emphases." In *The Earth As Transformed by Human Action: Global and Regional Changes in the Biosphere over the Past 300 Years,* edited by Billie Lee Turner II, William C. Clark, Robert W. Kates, John F. Richards, Jessica T. Mathews, and William B. Meyer, 121–35. New York: Cambridge University Press, 1990.

———. *George Perkins Marsh: Prophet of Conservation.* Seattle: University of Washington Press, 2000.

———. "Nature and Morality from George Perkins Marsh to the Millennium." *Journal of Historical Geography* 26 (2000): 3–23.

Lower, Arthur M. *Great Britain's Woodyard: British America and the Timber Trade, 1763–1867.* Montreal: McGill-Queen's University Press, 1973.

Lowood, Henry E. "The Calculating Forester: Quantification, Cameral Science, and the Emergence of Scientific Forestry Management in Germany." In *The Quantifying Spirit in the Eighteenth Century,* edited by Tore Fränsmyr, J. H. Heilbron, and Robin C. Ryder, 315–42. Berkeley and Los Angeles: University of California Press, 1990.

Lucretius, Carus Titus. *Titi Lucreti Cari de Rerum Natura Libri Sex. Ed. with Prolegomena, Critical Apparatus, Translation and Commentary,* by Cyril Bailey. 3 vols. Oxford: Clarendon Press, 1947.

Lugo, Ariel E., and Sandra Brown. "Conversion of Tropical Moist Forests: A Critique." *Interciencia* 7, no. 2 (1982): 89–93.

Lundsted, James E. "Log Marks: Forgotten Lore of the Logging Era." *Wisconsin Magazine of History* 25 (1955): 44–46.

Lutz, Harold J. "The Vegetation of Heart's Content: A Virgin Forest in North Western Pennsylvania." *Ecology* 11 (1930): 1–29.

Maack, Reinhard. "Devastação das matas do Paraná." *Revue Conservation Nationale Economic* 13 (1953): 22–32.

MacAndrews, John H. "Human Disturbance of North American Forests and Grasslands: The Fossil Pollen Record." In *Vegetation History*, edited by Brian Huntley and Thompson Webb III, 673–98. Dordrecht: Kluwer Academic Publishers, 1988.

MacGregor, I. A. "Europe and the East." In *The New Cambridge Modern History*, vol. 2, *The Reformation, 1520–59*, edited by Geoffrey R. Elton, 591–614. Cambridge: Cambridge University Press, 1958.

MacLeod, Murdo J. "Exploitation of Natural Resources in Colonial Central America: Indian and Spanish Approaches." In *Changing Tropical Forests: Historical Perspectives on To-Day's Challenges in Central and South America*, edited by Harold K. Steen and Richard P. Tucker, 31–39. Durham, N.C.: Forest History Society, 1992.

MacLeod, William C. "Fuel and Early Civilization." *American Anthropologist* 37 (1925): 344–46.

MacNeish, Richard S. "Ancient Mesoamerica Civilizations." *Science* 143 (1964): 531–37.

———. "The Origin and Dispersal of New World Agriculture." *Antiquity* 39 (1965): 87–94.

———. *The Origins of Agriculture and Settled Life*. Norman: University of Oklahoma Press, 1992.

Madsen, Torsten. "Changing Patterns of Land Use in the TRB Culture of Southern Scandinavia." In *Die Trichterbecherkultur: Neve Forchungen und Hypothesen*, edited by Dobrochna Jankowska, 25–41. Poznan, Poland: Institut. Prahistorii Universytetu im Adam Mickiewicza, 1990.

Mager, Friedrich. *Der Wald in Altpreussen als Wirtschaftsraum*. Koln-Graz: Böhlau Verlag, 1960.

Mahar, Dennis J. *Frontier Development Policy in Brazil: A Study of Amazonia*. New York: Praeger, 1979.

———. *Brazil: Integrated Development of the Northwest Frontier*. World Bank Country Study. Washington, D.C.: World Bank, 1981.

———. *Government Policies and Deforestation in Brazil's Amazon Region*. Washington, D.C.: World Bank, 1989.

Makkonen, Olli. "Ancient Forestry: An Historical Study." *Acta Forestalia Fennica* 82 (1968): 1–84; 95 (1969): 1–46.

Malin, James C. "The Grassland of North America: Its Occupance and the Challenge of Continuous Reappraisal." In *Man's Role in Changing the Face of the Earth*, edited by William Thomas Jr., 350–66. Chicago: University of Chicago Press, 1956.

Malingreau, Jean-Paul, and Compton J. Tucker. "Large-Scale Deforestation in the Southern Amazon Basin of Brazil." *Ambio* 17 (1988): 49–55.

Malingreau, Jean-Paul, G. Stephens, and L. Fellows, "Remote Sensing and Forest Fires: Kalimantan and North Borneo in 1982–83." *Ambio* 14 (1985): 314–21.

Mallinson, R. F. A. and Roland Grugeon. *Timber Trade Practice*. London: Cleaver-Hume Press, 1965.

Malmström, Vincent H. "Geographical Origins of the Tarascans." *Geographical Review* 85 (1995): 31–40.

Malone, Joseph J. *Pine Trees and Politics: The Naval Stores and Forest Policy in Colonial New England, 1691–1775*. Seattle: University of Washington Press, 1964.

Malowist, Marian. "The Economic and Social Development of the Baltic Countries from the Fifteenth to the Seventeenth Centuries." *Economic History Review* 12 (1959): 177–89.

————. "L'approvisionnement des ports de la Baltique en produits forestiers pour les constructions navales aux XVe et XVIe-siècles." In *Le navire et l'économie maritime du nord de l'Europe du moyen-âge au xviiie siècle,* edited by M. Mollat, 25–44. Paris: S.E.V.P.E.N, 1960.

————. "Les produits des pays de la Baltique dans la commerce international au XVIe siècle." *Revue Nord* 42 (1960): 175–206.

Mangelsdorf, Paul L., Richard S. MacNeish, and Walton C. Galinet. "Domestication of Corn." *Science* 143 (1964): 538–45.

Mann, Michael. "Ecological Change in North India: Deforestation and Agrarian Distress in the Ganges—Jamna Doab, 1800–1850." *Environment and History* 1 (1995): 201–20.

Marby, Hedrun. *Tea in Ceylon: An Attempt at a Regional and Temporal Differentiation of the Tea Growing Areas in Ceylon.* Geo-Ecological Research, vol. 1. Weisbaden: Franz Steiner Verlag GMBH, 1972.

Marchak, Patricia M. *Logging the Globe.* London: McGill-Queen's University Press, 1996.

Marcus, G. J. "The Greenland Trade-Route." *Economic History Review* 7 (1954–55): 71–80.

Markham, Clements R. "On the Effect of the Destruction of the Forests in the Western Ghats of India on the Water Supply." *Proceedings of the Royal Geographical Society* 10 (1865): 266–69. For an extended treatment see the *Journal of the Royal Geographical Society* 36 (1866): 180–95.

Marlowe, John. *The Making of the Suez Canal.* London: Cresset Press, 1964.

Marsden, William. *The History of Sumatra, Containing an Account of the Government, Laws, Customs, and Manners of the Native Inhabitants, with a Description of the Natural Productions, and a Relation to the Ancient Political State of That Island.* London: Printed for the author, 1783. 3d ed., London: J. McCreery, 1811.

Marsh, George Perkins. *Address before the Agricultural Society of Rutland County, Sept. 30th, 1847.* Rutland, Vt.: Rutland Herald, 1848.

————. *Man and Nature: Or, Physical Geography As Modified by Human Action.* New York: G. Scribner's Sons, 1884. Another edition with an introduction by David Lowenthal, Cambridge, Mass.: Harvard University Press (Belknap Press), 1965.

Marsh, Philip M., ed. *The Prose of Philip Freneau.* New Brunswick, N.J.: Scarecrow Press, 1955.

Martin, Calvin. "Forest and Fire Structures in the Aboriginal Eastern Forest." *Indian Historian* 6 (1973): 23–26, 38–42, 54.

Martin, Paul S., and Richard G. Klein, eds. *Quaternary Extinctions: A Prehistoric Revolution.* Tucson: University of Arizona Press, 1984.

Martin, Paul S., and Herbert E. Wright Jr. *Pleistocene Extinctions: The Search for a Cause.* New Haven, Conn.: Yale University Press, 1967.

Martius, Karl Friedrich P. von. *Flora Brasiliensis: Enumeratio plantarum in Brasilia hactenus detectarum . . . Argumentum fasciculorum I–XL.* Leipzig: F. Fleischer, 1840–65.

Marx, Leo. *The Machine in the Garden: Technology and the Pastoral Ideal in America.* New York: Oxford University Press, 1964.

Mason, Alpheus T. *Bureaucracy Convicts Itself: The Ballinger-Pinchot Controversy of 1910.* New York: Viking Press, 1941.

Mather, Andrew S. "Global Trends in Forest Resources." *Geography* 77 (1987): 1–15.

Mather, Increase. *A Brief History of the War with the Indians in New England.* Boston: John Foster, 1676.

Matthews, Elaine. "Global Vegetation and Land Use: New High-Resolution Data Bases for Climate Studies." *Journal of Climate and Applied Meteorology* 22 (1983): 474–87.

Maurois, André. "The Good Life." In *Our Crowded Planet: Essays on the Pressures of Population*, edited by Fairfield H. Osborn, 175–79. London: Allen and Unwin, 1962.

Maury, Louis Ferdinand Alfred. *Les forêts de la France: dans l'antiqué et au moyen âge*. Mémoires présentés par divers savants a L'Académie des Inscriptions et Belles Lettres. 2d ser., vol. 4, 1860. Paris: Imprimerie Impériale, 1860.

———. *Les forêts de la Gaule et de l'ancienne France*. Paris: Ladrange, 1867.

Maxwell, Hu. "The Use and Abuse of the Forests by the Virginia Indians." *William and Mary College Quarterly* 19 (1910): 73–104.

Maybee, Rolland. "Michigan's White Pine Era, 1840–1900." *Michigan History* 34 (1959): 385–431.

McAlpin, Michelle Burge. "Railroads, Prices, and Peasant Rationality: India, 1860–1890." *Journal of Economic History* 34 (1974): 662–84.

———. "Railroads, Cultivation Patterns, and Foodgrain Availability: India, 1860–1900." *Indian Economic and Social History Review* 12 (1975): 43–60.

McCracken, Eileen. "The Woodlands of Ireland, circa 1600." *Irish Historical Studies* 11 (1959): 271–96.

———. *The Irish Woods since Tudor Times: Distribution and Exploitation*. Newton Abbot, England: David and Charles, 1971.

McCulloch, John R. *A Dictionary, Practical, Theoretical and Historical, of Commerce and Commercial Navigation*. London: Murray, 1832.

McDowell, Patricia F., Thompson Webb III, and Patrick J. Bartlein. "Long-Term Environmental Change." In *The Earth As Transformed by Human Action: Global and Regional Changes in the Biosphere over the Past 300 Years*, edited by Billie Lee Turner II, William C. Clark, Robert W. Kates, John F. Richards, Jessica T. Mathews, and William B. Meyer, 143–62. New York: Cambridge University Press, 1990.

McGeary, Martin N. *Gifford Pinchot, Forester-Politican*. Princeton, N.J.: Princeton University Press, 1960.

McGlone, M. S. "Polynesian Deforestation of New Zealand: A Preliminary Synthesis." *Archaeology in Oceania* 18 (1983): 11–25.

———. "The Polynesian Settlement of New Zealand in Relation to Environmental and Biotic Changes." In "Moas, Mammals, and Climate in the Ecological History of New Zealand," supplement to *New Zealand Journal of Ecology* 12 (1989): 115–30.

McIntosh, C. Barron. "Use and Abuse of the Timber Culture Acts." *Annals, Association of American Geographers,* 65 (1975): 347–62.

McKibben, Bill. *The End of Nature*. London: Viking Books, 1990.

McMullen, James. *Idealism, Protest and the "Tale of the Genji": The Confucianism of Kamazawa Banzan (1619–91)*. Oxford: Clarendon Press, 1999.

McNeill, John R. "Agriculture, Forests and Ecological History, Brazil, 1500–1984." *Environmental Review* 10 (1986): 122–33.

———. "Deforestation in the Araucaria Zone of Southern Brazil, 1900–1983." In *World Deforestation in the Twentieth Century*, edited by John F. Richards and Richard P. Tucker, 15–32. Duke Press Policy Studies. Durham, N.C.: Duke University Press, 1988.

———. *The Mountains of the Mediterranean World: An Environmental History*. New York: Cambridge University Press, 1992.

McNeill, William H. *Plagues and Peoples*. Garden City, N.Y.: Anchor Press, Doubleday, 1976.

———. *The Pursuit of Power: Technology, Armed Force, and Society since A.D. 1000*. Chicago: University of Chicago Press, 1982.

Mead, William Richard. *Farming in Finland*. London: Athlone Press, 1953.

Meggers, Betty J. "Aboriginal Adaptation to Amazonia." In *Key Environments: Amazonia,* edited by Ghillean T. Prance and Thomas E. Lovejoy, 307–27. Oxford: Pergamon Press, 1985.

Meher-Homji, V. M. "Repercussions of Deforestation on Precipitation in Western Karnataka, India." *Archiv. für Meteorologie Geophysik und Bioklimatologie,* ser. b, 28 (1980): 385–400.

Meiggs, Russell. *Trees and Timber in the Ancient Mediterranean World.* Oxford: The Clarendon Press, 1982.

Meinig, Donald William. "A Macrogeography of Western Imperialism: Some Morphologies of Moving Frontiers of Political Control." In *Settlement and Encounter: Geographical Essays Presented to Sir Grenfell Price,* edited by Fay G. Gale and Graham L. Lawton, 213–40. Melbourne: Oxford University Press, 1969.

———. *The Shaping of America: A Geographical Perspective on 500 Years of History.* Vol. 1, *Atlantic America, 1492–1800.* New Haven, Conn.: Yale University Press, 1986.

Melillo, Jerry M., C. A. Palm, Richard A. Houghton, George M. Woodwell, and Norman Myers. "A Comparison of Recent Estimates of Disturbance in Tropical Forests." *Environmental Conservation* 12 (1985): 37–40.

Mellars, Paul A. "Fire Ecology, Animal Population and Man: A Study of Some Ecological Relationships in Prehistory." *Proceedings of the Prehistorical Society* 42 (1976): 15–46.

Mellars, Paul A., and S. C. Reinhardt. "Patterns of Mesolithic Land-Use in Southern England: A Geological Perspective." In *The Early Postglacial Settlement of Northern Europe,* edited by Paul A. Mellars, 243–93. London: Duckworth, 1978.

Melville, Elinor G. K. *A Plague of Sheep: Environmental Consequences of the Conquest of Mexico.* Cambridge: Cambridge University Press, 1994.

Mencius. Translated from the Chinese with an introduction by D. C. Lau. Harmondsworth, England: Penguin Books, 1970.

Menzies, Nicholas K. *Forest and Land Management in Imperial China.* New York: St Martin's Press, 1994.

———. "Forestry." In *Science and Civilization in China,.* edited by Joseph Needham and Christophe Habsmere, vol. 6, *Biology and Biological Technology. Part III, Agro-Industries and Forestry,* 543–667. Cambridge: Cambridge University Press, 1996.

Merrill, Gordon Clark. *The Historical Geography of St. Kitts and Nevis, the West Indies.* Pan American Institute of Geography and History, Publication no. 232. Mexico City: Pan American Institute of Geography and History, 1958.

Merriman, John. "The Demoiselles of the Ariège, 1829–1831." In *1830 in France,* edited by John Merriman, 319–33. New York: New Viewpoints, 1975.

Métraux, Alfred. "The Revolution of the Ax." *Diogenes* 25 (1959): 28–40.

Meyer, William B., and Billie Lee Turner II. "Human Population Growth and Global Land-Use/Cover Change." *Annual Review of Ecological Systems* 23 (1992): 39–61.

———, eds. *Changes in Land Use and Land Cover: A Global Perspective.* New York: Cambridge University Press, 1994.

Meyers, Thomas J. "The Origins of Agriculture: An Evaluation of Three Hypotheses." In *Prehistoric Agriculture,* edited by Stuart Struever, 101–21 (American Museum Sourcebooks in Anthropology). Garden City, N.Y.: The Natural History Press, 1971.

Michelet, Jules. *Histoire de France: Vol. 7. Renaissance.* Paris: Chamerot, Libraire-Editor, 1855.

Michell, A. R. "European Fisheries in the Early Modern Period." In *The Cambridge Economic History of Europe,* vol. 5, *The Economic Organization of Early Modern Europe,* edited by Edwin Ernest Rich and Charles Henry Wilson, 134–84. Cambridge: Cambridge University Press, 1977.

Mikesell, Marvin W. "The Deforestation of Mount Lebanon." *Geographical Review* 59 (1969): 1–28.

Miller, Duncan E., and Nikolaas J. Van de Merwe. "Early Metal Working in Sub-Saharan Africa: A Review of Recent Research." *Journal of African History* 35 (1994): 1–36.

Miller, J. W. Jr. "Forest Fighting on the Eastern Front in World War II." *Geographical Review* 62 (1972): 186–202.

Miller, Perry. *Errand into Wilderness.* Cambridge, Mass.: Harvard University Press (Belknap Press), 1956.

Miller, Shawn W. "Fuelwood in Colonial Brazil: The Economic and Social Consequences of Fuel Depletion for the Bahian Recôncavo, 1549–1820." *Journal of Forest History* 38 (1994): 181–92.

Millikin, Daniel. "The Best Practical Means of Preserving and Restoring the Forests of Ohio." *Ohio Agricultural Report,* 2d ser. (1871): 319–33.

Minchinton, Walter. "Patterns of Demand, 1750–1914." In *The Fontana Economic History of Europe,* edited by Carlo M. Cipolla, vol. 3, *The Industrial Revolution, 1700–1914,* 77–186. Brighton: Harvester Press, 1976.

———. "Patterns and Structure of Demand, 1500–1750." In *The Fontana Economic History of Europe,* edited by Carlo M. Cipolla, vol. 2, *The Sixteenth and Seventeenth Centuries,* 83–176. Brighton: Harvester Press, 1977.

Mingay, Gordon E., ed. *The Agricultural Revolution: Changes in Agriculture, 1650–1880.* London: A. and C. Black, 1977.

Minnis, Paul E. "Paleoethnobotanical Indicators of Prehistoric Environmental Disturbance: A Case Study." In *The Nature and Status of Ethnobotany,* edited by Richard I. Ford, 347–66. Anthropological Paper no. 67. Ann Arbor: Museum of Anthropology, University of Michigan, 1978.

Mintz, Sidney W. *Sweetness and Power: The Place of Sugar in Modern History.* Harmondsworth, England: Penguin Books, 1985.

Miskimin, Harry A. *The Economy of Later Renaissance Europe, 1460–1600.* Cambridge: Cambridge University Press, 1977.

Mitchell, Bruce R. *Abstract of British Historical Statistics.* Cambridge: Cambridge University Press, 1962.

———. *International Historical Statistics.* (1) *Africa and Asia.* New York: New York University Press, 1982; (2) *The Americas and Australasia.* Detroit: Gale Research Company, 1983; (3) *Europe, 1750–1988* [1975]. New York: Stockton Press, 1992; (4) *The Americas, 1750–1988.* New York: Stockton Press, 1993.

Mitchell, Stephen. "The Hellenistic World." In *The Cambridge Encyclopedia of Archaeology,* edited by Andrew G. Sherratt, 216–21. Cambridge: Cambridge University Press, 1980.

Mitsuo, Tokoro. *Kinsei Ringyôshi no Kenkyû* (Studies in the history of early modern forestry). Tokyo: Yoshikawa Kôbunkan, 1980.

Modderman, Pietr Jan Remeer. *Linearbandkeramik aus Elsloo und Stein.* Leiden, Institute of Prehistory (Analecta Praehistorica Leidensia, vol. 3), 1970.

———. "Banderkeramiker und Wandernbauerntum." *Archölogisches Korrespondenzblatt* 1 (1971): 7–9.

Molesworth, G. L. "Durability of Indian Railway Sleepers, and the Rules for Marking Them." *Indian Forester* 6 (1881): 97–99.

Molofsky, Jane, Charles A. S. Hall, and Norman Meyers. *A Comparison of Tropical Forest Surveys.* Washington, D.C.: U.S. Department of Energy, 1986.

Mols, Roger S. J. "Population in Europe, 1500–1700." In *The Fontana Economic History of Europe,* edited by Carlo M. Cipolla, vol. 2, *The Sixteenth and Seventeenth Centuries,* 15–82. Brighton: Harvester Press, 1977.

Monbeig, Pierre. *Pionniers et planteurs de São Paulo.* Paris: Librarie Armand Colin, 1952.

"The Month Amazonia Burns." *Economist* 312, no. 7619 (9–14 September 1989): 15–16.

Moore, Peter D., J. A. Webb, and Margaret E. Collinson. *Pollen Analysis.* London: Hodder and Stoughton, 1991.

Morain, S. A., and B. Klankamsorn. "Forest Mapping and Inventory Techniques through Visual Analysis of LANDSAT Imagery: Examples from Thailand." *Proceedings, 12th Symposium on Remote Sensing of the Environment,* 417–26. Manila: Remote Sensing Society, 1978.

Moran, Emilio F. "The Adaptive System of the Amazonian Caboclo." In *Man in the Amazon,* edited by Charles Wagley, 169–89. Gainesville: University of Florida Press, 1974.

———. *Developing the Amazon.* Bloomington: Indiana University Press, 1981.

———. "Growth without Development: Past and Present Development Efforts in Amazonia." In *The Dilemma of Amazonian Development,* edited by Emilio F. Moran, 3–23. Boulder, Colo.: Westview Press, 1983.

———. "Colonization in the Transamazon and Rondônia." In *Frontier Expansion in Amazonia,* edited by Marianne Schmink and Charles H. Wood, 287–92. Gainesville: University of Florida Press, 1984.

———. "Deforestation and Land Use in the Brazilian Amazon." *Human Ecology* 21 (1993): 1–21.

———. "Deforestation in the Brazilian Amazon." In *Tropical Deforestation: The Human Dimension,* edited by Lesley Sponsel, Thomas N. Headland, and R. C. Bailey, 149–64. New York: Columbia University Press, 1996.

Morison, Samuel E. *The European Discovery of America: The Northern Voyages, AD 500–1600.* New York: Oxford University Press, 1971.

———. *The European Discovery of America: The Southern Voyages, AD 1492–1616.* New York: Oxford University Press, 1974.

Morris, Morris David. "The Population of All-India, 1800–1951." *Indian Economic and Social History Review* 9 (1974): 309–13.

Morris, Morris David, and Clyde B. Dudley. "Selected Railway Statistics for the Indian Subcontinent (India, Pakistan, Bangladesh), 1853–1946/7." *Artha Vijnana* 17 (1975): 187–298.

Morton, Thomas. *The New English Canaan of Thomas Morton* [1627]. Edited by C. Adams Jr. Publications of the Prince Society. Boston: John Wilson and Sons, 1883.

Moser, Wilhelm Gottfried von. *Grundsätze Forstökonomie* (Principles of forest economy). Frankfurt: H. L. Brönner, 1757.

Mueller, Charles C. "Frontier-Based Agricultural Expansion: The Case of Rondônia." In *Land, People and Planning in Contemporary Amazon,* edited by Françoise Barbira-Freedman, 141–53. Occasional Paper no. 3, Cambridge University Centre for Latin American Studies. Cambridge: Cambridge University Centre for Latin American Studies, 1980.

Mukherjee, Mukul. "Railways and Their Impact on Bengal's Economy, 1879–1920." *Indian Economic and Social History Review* 17 (1980): 191–210.

Mumford, Lewis. *Technics and Civilization* [1934]. New York: Harcourt Brace, 1963.

Munro, Sir Thomas. "Timber Monopoly in Malabar and Canara." In *Major-General Sir Thomas Munro Bart: A Memoir,* edited by A. J. Arbuthnot. 2 vols. 1:178–87. London: C. Kegan Paul, 1881.

Munslow, Barry, Yemi Katerere, Adriaan Ferf, and Philip O'Keefe. *The Fuelwood Trap: A Study of the SADCC Region.* London: Earthscan Publications, 1988.

Munz, Peter. *Our Knowledge of the Growth of Knowledge: Popper or Wittgenstein?* London: Routledge and Kegan Paul, 1985.

Murphey, Rhoads. *The Outsiders: The Western Experience in India and China.* Ann Arbor: University of Michigan Press, 1977.

———. "Deforestation in Modern China." In *Global Deforestation and the Nineteenth Century World Economy,* edited by Richard P. Tucker and John F. Richards, 111–28. Durham, N.C.: Duke University Press, 1983.

Myers, J. G. "Savanna and Forest Vegetation in the Interior Guiana Plateau." *Journal of Ecology* 24 (1936): 162–83.

Myers, Norman. *The Sinking Ark: A New Look at the Problem of Disappearing Species.* Oxford: Pergamon Press, 1979.

———. *Conversion of Tropical Moist Forests.* Report prepared for the National Research Council, Committee on Research Priorities on Tropical Biology. Washington, D.C.: National Academy of Sciences, 1980.

———. "The Hamburger Connection: How Central America's Forests Become North America's Hamburgers." *Ambio* 10 (1981): 3–8.

———. "Conversion Rates in Tropical Moist Forests." In *Tropical Rainforest Ecosystems: Structure and Function,* edited by Fred Golley, 289–300. Ecosystems of the World, no. 14A. Amsterdam: Elsevier Scientific Publishing Company, 1983.

———. *A Wealth of Wild Species: Storehouse for Human Welfare.* Boulder, Colo.: Westview Press, 1983.

———. *The Primary Source: Tropical Forests and Our Future.* New York: W. W. Norton and Company, 1984.

———. *Deforestation Rates in Tropical Forests and Their Climatic Implications.* London: Friends of the Earth, 1989.

———. "Questions of Mass Extinction." *Biodiversity and Conservation* 2 (1993): 2–17.

———. "Tropical Deforestation: Rates and Patterns." In *The Causes of Tropical Deforestation,* edited by Katrina Brown and David W. Pearce, 27–81. London: University College Press, 1994.

Myers, Norman, and Richard Tucker. "Deforestation in Central America: Spanish Legacy and North American Consumers." *Environmental Review* 11 (1981): 5–71.

Myers, Ramon H. *Agricultural Development in Hopei and Shantung, 1890–1949.* Cambridge, Mass.: Harvard University Press, 1970.

Nadkarni, Mangesh, Syed Ajmal Pasha, and L. S. Prabhakar. *The Political Economy of Forest Use and Management.* New Delhi: Sage Publications, 1989.

Nairne, Thomas. *A Letter from South Carolina: Giving an Account of the Soil, Air, Products, Trade, Government, Laws, Religions, People, Military Strength of that Province.* London: A.Baldwin, 1710.

Naish, G. P. B. "Ships and Shipbuilding." In *A History of Technology,* edited by Charles Joseph Singer, E. J. Holmyard, A. Rupert Hall, and Trevor I. Williams, vol 3, *From the Renaissance to the Industrial Revolution. c.1500–c.1750,* 471–500. Oxford: Clarendon Press, 1957.

Nash, Roderick. *Wilderness and the American Mind.* New Haven, Conn.: Yale University Press, 1967.

Nash, Roy. *The Conquest of Brazil.* London: Jonathon Cape, 1928.

Nations, James D., and Komer, Daniel I. "Indians, Immigrants and Beef Exports: Deforestation in Central America." *Cultural Survival Quarterly* 6 (1982): 8–12.

Naveh, Zev, and Joel Dan. "The Human Degradation of Mediterranean Landscapes in Israel." In *Mediterranean Type Ecosystems: Origin and Structure,* edited by Francesco di Castri and Harold A. Mooney, 373–90. New York: Springer Verlag, 1973.

Neal, Larry. "The Dutch and English East India Companies Compared: Evidence from the Stock and Foreign Exchange Markets." In *The Rise of Merchant Empires: Long-Distance Trade in the Early Modern World, 1350–1750,* edited by James D. Tracy, 195–223. Cambridge: Cambridge University Press, 1990.

Nectoux, François, and Yiochi Kuroda. *Timber from the South Seas: An Analysis of Japan's Tropical Environmental Impact.* Gland, Swtizerland: World Wildlife Fund International, 1989.

Needham, Joseph. "Science and Society in East and West." In *The Grand Titration: Science and Society in East and West,* 190–219. Toronto: University of Toronto Press, 1969.

———. "Voyages and Discovery." In *Science and Civilization in China,* edited by Joseph Needham, vol. 4, *Physics and Physical Chemistry, Part III, Civil Engineering and Nautics,* 486–553. Cambridge: Cambridge University Press, 1971.

Nef, John Ulrich. *The Rise of the British Coal Industry.* 2 vols. London: George Routledge and Sons, Ltd., 1932.

———. *The Conquest of the Material World.* Chicago: University of Chicago Press, 1964.

———. "An Early Energy Crisis and Its Consequences." *Scientific American* 237 (November 1977): 140–51.

Neftel, A., E. Moor, H. Oeschger, and B. Stauffer. "Evidence from Polar Ice Cores for the Increase in Atmospheric CO_2 in the Past Two Centuries." *Nature* 315 (1985): 45–47.

Neimeier, C. "Frühformen der Waldhufen." *Petermanns Geographische Mitteilungen* 93 (1949): 14–27.

Neumann, J. "Climate Change As a Topic in the Classical Greek and Roman Literature." *Climatic Change* 7 (1985): 441–54.

New York State Census, 1855, 1856.

Nickson, R. A. "Brazilian Colonization of the Eastern Border Region of Paraguay." *Journal of Latin American Studies* 13 (1981): 11–131.

Nicolet, Claude. "Economy and Society, 133–43 B.C." In *The Cambridge Ancient History,*. vol. 9, *The Last Age of the Roman Republic, 146–43 B.C.,* edited by John A. Cook, Andrew Lintott, and Elizabeth Rawson, 600–643. Cambridge: Cambridge University Press, 1994.

Nicolson, Marjorie Hope. *Mountain Gloom and Mountain Glory: The Development of the Aesthetics of the Infinite.* Ithaca, N.Y.: Cornell Univeristy Press, 1959.

Nietsch, Helmut. *Wald und Seidlung im Vorgeschichtlichen Mitteleuropa.* Leipzig, Mannus-Bucherei, 1939.

Nitz, Hans-Jurgen. "The Church As Colonist: The Benedictine Abbey of Lorsch and Planned Waldhufen Colonization in the Oldenwald." *Journal of Historical Geography* 9 (1983): 105–23.

———. "Feudal Woodland Colonization As a Strategy of the Carolingian Empire in the Conquest of Saxony—Reconstruction of the Spatial Pattern of Expansion in the Liene-Weser Region." In *Villages, Fields, and Frontiers: Studies in European Rural Settlement in the Medieval and Early Modern Period,* edited by Brian K. Roberts and Robin E. Glasscock, 171–84. British Archaeological Reports, International Series, 185. Oxford: B.A.R., 1983.

Noble, David. *America by Design: Science, Technology and the Rise of Corporate Capitalism.* New York: Oxford University Press, 1977.

North, Douglass C. "Institutions, Transaction Costs, and the Rise of Merchant Empires." In *The Political Economy of Merchant Empires,* edited by James D. Tracy, 22–40. Cambridge: Cambridge University Press, 1991.

North, Douglass C., and Robert Paul Thomas. *The Rise of the Western World: A New Economic History.* Cambridge: Cambridge University Press, 1973.

Norton, Byran G. "On the Inherent Danger of Undervaluing Species." In *The Preservation of Spe-*

cies: The Value of Biological Diversity, edited by Bryan G. Norton, 11–137. Princeton, N.J.: Princeton University Press, 1986.

Nugent, Stephen. *Amazonian Caboclo Society: An Essay on Invisibility and Peasant Economy.* Oxford: Berg, 1993.

Nurdin, C. F., and R. H. Meade. "Deforestation and Increased Flooding of the Upper Amazon." *Science* 215 (1982): 426–7.

Oates, J. Whitney. "The Population of Rome." *Classical Philology* 29 (1934): 101–16.

O'Brien, Karen L. *Sacrificing the Forest: Environmental and Social Struggles in Chiapas.* Boulder, Colo.: Westview Press, 1997.

O'Brien, Patrick K. "Agriculture and the Industrial Revolution." *Economic History Review* 30 (1977): 166–81.

———. "European Economic Development: The Contribution of the Periphery." *Economic History Review* 35 (1982): 1–18.

Oedekoven, Karl. "The Vanishing Forest." *Environmental Policy and Law* 6 (1980): 184–85.

O'Hara, Sarah L., F. Aleyne Street-Perrott, and Timothy P. Burt. "Accelerated Soil Erosion around a Mexican Highland Lake Caused by Prehispanic Agriculture." *Nature* 362 (1993): 48–51.

Oldfield, Margery L. "Tropical Deforestation and Genetic Resources Conversion." In *Blowing in the Wind: Deforestation and Long Range Implications,* edited by Vinson Sutlive, Nathan Altshuler, and Mario D. Zamora, 277–346. Studies in Third World Societies, Publication no. 14. Williamsburg, Va.: William and Mary College, 1980.

Oldfield, Margery L., and Janis B. Alcorn, eds. *Biodiversity, Culture, Conservation and Ecodevelopment.* Boulder, Colo.: Westview Press, 1991.

Olson, Jerry S. "Carbon Cycles and Temperate Woodlands." In *Ecological Studies,* edited by David E. Riechle, 226–41. London: Chapman Hall, 1970.

———. *World Ecosystems.* Seattle, Wash.: Seattle Symposium, 1975.

Olson, Jerry S., J. A. Watts, and L. J. Allsion. *Major World Ecosystem Complexes Ranked by Carbon in Live Vegetation.* NDP-017. Oak Ridge, Tenn.: Oak Ridge National Laboratory, 1985.

Olson, Sherry H. *The Depletion Myth: A History of the Railway Use of Timber.* Cambridge, Mass.: Harvard University Press, 1971.

———. "The Robe of the Ancestors: Forests in the History of Madagascar." *Journal of Forest History* 28 (1984): 174–81.

Openshaw, K. "Woodfuel—A Time for Re-assessment." *Natural Resources Forum* 3, no. 1 (1978): 35–51.

Orme, Bryony. "The Advantages of Agriculture." In *Hunters, Gatherers and First Farmers beyond Europe,* edited by John V. S. Megaw. Leicester: Leicester University Press, 1977.

Ortiz, Sutti. "Colonization of the Colombian Amazon," In *Frontier Expansion in Amazonia,* edited by Marianne Schmink and Charles H. Wood, 204–30. Gainesville: University of Florida Press, 1984.

Osako, Masako M. "Forest Preservation in Tokugawa Japan." In *Global Deforestation and the Nineteenth Century World Economy,* edited by Richard P. Tucker and John F. Richards, 129–45. Durham, N.C.: Duke University Press, 1983.

Osborn, Fairfield H. *Our Plundered Planet.* London: Faber and Faber, 1948.

———. *The Limits of Earth.* Boston: Little, Brown, and Company, 1954.

———. "Over-Population and Genetic Selection." In *Our Crowded Planet: Essays on the Pressures of Population,* edited by Fairfield H. Osborn, 43–55. London: Allen and Unwin, 1962.

Östlund, Lars. "Exploitation and Structural Changes in the North Swedish Boreal Forest, 1800–1992." *Dissertations in Forest Vegetation Ecology,* vol. 4. Umeä: Swedish University of Agricultural Sciences, 1993.

Östlund, Lars, L. Zackrisson, and A.-L. Axelsson. "The History and Transformation of Scandinavian Boreal Forest Landscape since the Nineteenth Century." *Canadian Journal of Forest Research* 27 (1997): 1198–1206.

Overton, Mark. "Re-establishing the English Agricultural Revolution." *Agricultural History Review* 44 (1996): 1–20.

Ovid. *Metamorphoses*. Translated from the Latin by Frank J. Miller. Loeb Classical Library. 2 vols. London: Heinemann, 1916.

Ovitt, George Jr. *The Restoration of Perfection: Labor and Technology in Medieval Culture*. New Brunswick, N.J.: Rutgers University Press, 1987.

Owen, George. *Description of Pembrokeshire* [1603]. Edited by Henry Owen. Cymmrodorian Record Society Series 1, pt. 2. London: Charles J. Clark, 1892, 1897.

Pack, Charles Lathrop, and Tom H. Gill. *Forests and Mankind*. New York: The MacMillan Company, 1929.

Padfield, Peter. *Maritime Supremacy and the Opening of the Western Mind: Naval Campaigns That Shaped the Modern World*. London: J. Murray, 1999.

Palo, Matti. "Population and Deforestation." In *The Causes of Tropical Deforestation,* edited by Katrina Brown and David W. Pearce, 42–56. London: University College Press, 1994.

Palo, Matti, G. Mery, and J. Salmi. "Deforestation in the Tropics: Pilot Scenarios Based on Quantitative Analyses." In *Deforestation or Development in the Third World?* edited by Matti Palo and J. Salmi, 1:53–106. Research Bulletin no. 349. Helsinki: Finnish Forest Research Institute, 1987.

Parain, Charles. "The Evolution of Agricultural Technique." In *The Cambridge Economic History of Europe,* vol. 1, *Agrarian Life in the Middle Ages,* edited by John H. Clapham and Eileen Power, 118–68. Cambridge: Cambridge University Press, 1941.

Park, Christopher. *Acid Rain: Rhetoric and Reality*. London: Routledge, 1985.

Park, Mungo. *Mungo Park's Travels in the Interior of Africa: The First Journey* [1816]. London: J. M. Dent, 1954.

Parker, Geoffrey. "The Emergence of Modern Finance in Europe, 1500–1730." In *The Fontana Economic History of Europe,* edited by Carlo M. Cipolla, vol. 2, *The Sixteenth and Seventeenth Centuries,* 527–94. Brighton: Harvester Press, 1977.

———. "Europe and the Wider World, 1500–1700: The Military Balance." In *The Political Economy of Merchant Empires,* edited by James D. Tracy, 161–95. Cambridge: Cambridge University Press, 1977.

Parkman, Francis. "The Forest and the Census." *Atlantic Monthly* 55 (1885): 835–39.

Parry, John H. *The Age of Reconnaissance*. Cleveland: World Publications Co., 1964.

———. *The Discovery of the Sea*. New York: Dial Press, 1974.

Parry, Martin L. *Climatic Change, Agriculture, and Settlement*. Folkstone: David and Charles, 1978.

Parsons, James J. "The Acorn-Hog Economy of the Oak Woodlands of Southwestern Spain." *Geographical Review* 52 (1962): 211–35.

———. "Spread of African Pasture Grasses to the American Tropics." *Journal of Range Management* 25 (1972): 12–17.

———. "Forest to Pasture: Development or Destruction?" *Revista de Biologica Tropical* 24 (suppl.1, 1976): 121–38.

Passmore, John A. *Man's Responsibility for Nature: Ecological Problems and Western Traditions*. New York: Charles Scribner's Sons, 1974.

Paszkiewicz, Henryk. *The Origins of Russia*. London: George Allen and Unwin Ltd., 1954.

Patsch, Carl. *Historische Wanderungen im Karst und an der Adria*. Vienna: Verlag des Forschungensinstitutes für Oten und Orient, 1922.

Patterson, C. "Silver Stocks and Losses in Ancient and Medieval Times." *Economic History Review* 25 (1972): 223–31.

Patterson, William A. III, and Kenneth E. Sassaman. "Indian Fires in the Prehistory of New England." In *Holocene Human Ecology in Northeastern North America*, edited by G. P. Nicholas, 107–36. New York: Plenum Press, 1988.

Paullin, Charles, ed. *Atlas of the Historical Geography of the United States*. Washington, D.C.: GPO, 1932.

Pausanias. *Description of Greece*. Translated by W. H. S. Jones. Loeb Classical Library. 5 vols. London: William Heinemann, 1935.

Peacock, Evan. "Historical and Applied Perspectives on Prehistoric Land Use in Eastern North America." *Environment and History* 4 (1998): 1–30.

Pearce, Roy Harvey. *The Savages of America. A Study of the Indian and the Idea of Civilization*. Baltimore: Johns Hopkins University Press, 1953.

———. *Savages and Civilization: A Study of the Indian and the American Mind*. Baltimore: Johns Hopkins University Press, 1965.

Pearson, G. W. "How to Cope with Calibration." *Antiquity*. 61 (1987): 98–103.

Peffer, E. Louis. *The Closing of the Public Domain: Disposal and Reservation Policies, 1900–1950*. Stanford, Calif.: Stanford University Press, 1951.

Pelham, Reginald A. "Timber Exports from the Weald during the Fourteenth Century." *Sussex Archaeological Collections* 69 (1928): 170–82.

Peluso, Nancy L. "The History of State Forest Management in Colonial Java." *Journal of Forest and Conservation History* 35 (1991): 65–75.

———. *Rich Forests, Poor People: Resources Control and Resistance in Java*. Berkeley and Los Angeles: University of California Press, 1992.

Penick, James L. *Progressive Politics and Conservation: The Ballinger-Pinchot Affair*. Chicago: University of Chicago Press, 1968.

Penner, Joyce E. "Atmospheric Chemistry and Air Quality." In *Changes in Land Use and Land Cover: A Global Perspective*, edited by William B. Meyer and Billie Lee Turner II, 175–209. Cambridge: Cambridge University Press, 1994.

Perdue, Peter C. *Exhausting the Earth: State and Peasant in Hunan, 1500–1850*. Cambridge, Mass.: Harvard University Press, 1987.

Perkins, Dwight H. *Agricultural Development in China, 1368–1968*. Chicago: Aldine Press, 1969.

Perlin, John. *A Forest Journey: The Role of Wood in the Development of Civilization*. Cambridge, Mass.: Harvard University Press, 1991.

Perrier de la Bâthie, Henri. "Au sujet des troubières de Marotampona." *Bulletin de L'Académie Malagache,* n.s., vol. 1 (1917): 137–38.

———. "La végétation malagache." *Annales du Musée Colonial de Marseille*, ser. 3, vol. 9 (1922): 1–266.

Perrson, Reidar. *World Forest Resources: Review of the World's Forest Resources in the Early 1970s*. Department of Forestry Research Note 17. Stockholm: Royal College of Forestry, 1974.

———. "Deforestation in the Tropics." *Scientific American* 264, no. 4 (1990): 36–42.

Peters, Robert L., and Joan D. S. Darling. "The Greenhouse Effect and Nature Reserves." *Bioscience* 35 (1985): 707–17.

Phelps Brown, Ernest H., and Sheila V. Hopkins. "Seven Centuries of Prices and Consumables, Compared with Builders' Wage-Rates." *Economica*, n.s., 23 (1956): 296–314.

Pilcher, J. R., A. G. Smith, G. W. Pearson, and A. Crowder. "Land Clearance in the Irish Neolithic: New Evidence and Interpretation." *Science* 172 (1971): 560–62.

Pinchot, Gifford. *The Fight for Conservation.* New York: Doubleday, Page, 1910. Reprint, Seattle: University of Washington Press, 1967.

———. "Forest Devastation: A National Danger and a Plan to Meet it." *Journal of Forestry* 17 (1919): 911–45.

———. *Breaking New Ground.* New York: Harcourt Brace, 1947.

Pinkett, Harold T. *Gifford Pinchot: Private and Public Forester.* Urbana: University of Illinois Press, 1970.

Pittsburgh Gazette. 8 September 1838, p. 3. Editorial comment.

Pius, Anne-Marie. "La forêt dans l'histoire." *Revue, Suisse d'histoire* 17 (1967): 4–12.

Platt, Colin. "The Rise of Temperate Europe." In *The Cambridge Encyclopedia of Archaeology,* edited by Andrew Sherratt, 304–13. Cambridge: Cambridge University Press, 1980.

Pliny the Elder. *Natural History.* Translated from the Latin by H. Rackham. Loeb Classical Library. 10 vols. London: William Heinemann, 1960.

Plumwood, Val, and R. Routley. "World Rainforest Destruction: The Social Factors." *The Ecologist* 12 (1982): 4–22.

Poe, Edgar Allan. "To Helen" [1831]. In *The Complete Poems and Stories of Edgar Allan Poe with Selections from His Critical Writings, with Introduction and Explanatory Notes by Arthur Hobson Quinn.* 8 vols. (New York: Alfred A. Knopf, 1946,) 1:42.

Pohlendt, Heinz. *Die Verbreitung der mittelalterlichen Wüstungen in Deutschland.* Göttinger Geographische Abhandlungen no. 3. Göttingen: Department of Geography, 1950.

Pomeranz, Kenneth. *The Making of a Hinterland: State, Society, and Economy in Inland North China, 1853–1937.* Berkeley and Los Angeles: University of California Press, 1993.

Poore, M. E. Duncan. "The Values of Tropical Moist Forest Ecosystems." *Unasylva* 28 (1976): 127–43.

Porteous, Alexander. *Forest Folklore, Mythology and Romance.* London: George Allen and Unwin, 1928.

Posey, Darrell A. "Indigenous Management of Tropical Forest Ecosystems: The Case of the Kayapó Indians of the Brazilian Amazon." *Agroforestry Systems* 3 (1985): 139–58.

Postel, Sandra. *Air Pollution, Acid Rain and the Future of Forests.* Worldwatch Paper no. 58. Washington, D.C.: Worldwatch Institute, 1984.

———. "Protecting Forests." In *The State of the World, 1984,* edited by Lester Brown, 70–83. Worldwatch Institute. New York: W. W. Norton, 1985.

Postel, Sandra, and Lori Heise. *Reforesting the Earth.* Worldwatch Paper no. 83. Washington, D.C.: Worldwatch Institute, 1988.

Potter, J. "The British Timber Duties, 1815–1860." *Economica,* n.s., 22 (1955): 122–36.

Pouchepadass, Jacques. "British Attitudes towards Shifting Cultivation in Colonial South India: A Case Study of South Canara District 1800–1920." In *Nature, Culture, Imperialism: Essays on the Environmental History of South Asia,* edited by David Arnold and Ramachandra Guha, 123–51. Delhi: Oxford University Press, 1995.

Pounds, Norman J. G. *Economic History of Medieval Europe.* London: Longmans, 1974.

———. *An Historical Geography of Europe, 1500–1840.* Cambridge: Cambridge University Press, 1979.

Pownall, Thomas. *A Topographical Description of the Dominions of the United States of America* [1783]. Edited by L. Mulkearn. Pittsburgh: Pittsburgh University Press, 1949.

Prest, John M. *The Garden of Eden: The Botanic Garden and the Re-creation of Paradise.* New Haven, Conn.: Yale University Press, 1981.

Price, Jacob M. "The Map of Commerce, 1683–1721." In *The New Cambridge Modern History*, vol. 6, *The Rise of Great Britain and Russia, 1688–1715/25*, edited by J. S. Bromley, 834–73. Cambridge: Cambridge University Press, 1970.

———. "Transaction Costs: A Note on Merchant Credit and the Organization of Private Trade." In *The Political Economy of Merchant Empires*, edited by James D. Tracy, 276–97. Cambridge: Cambridge University Press, 1991.

Price, T. D. "Regional Approaches to Human Adaption in the Mesolithic of the Northern European Plain." In *Mesolithikum in Europa*, edited by B. Gramsch, 14/15, 217–34. Potsdam: Museum für Ur-und Frühgeschichte, Veroffentlichungen, 1981.

Primack, Martin I. "Land Clearing under Nineteenth Century Techniques: Some Preliminary Calculations." *Journal of Economic History* 22 (1962): 485–96.

———. "Farm Formed Capital in American Agriculture, 1850–1910." Ph.D. diss. University of North Carolina, 1963.

Pryde, Philip R. *Conservation in the Soviet Union*. Cambridge: Cambridge University Press, 1972.

Pulsipher, Lydia M. *Seventeenth Century Monserrat: An Environmental Impact Statement*. Historical Geography Research Group Publication no. 17. London: Historical Geography Research Group, 1985.

Pyne, Stephen J. *Fire in America: A Cultural History of Wild Land and Rural Fire*. Princeton, N.J.: Princeton University Press, 1982.

———. "The Keeper of the Flame: A Survey of Anthropogenic Fire." In *Fire in the Environment: The Ecological, Atmospheric and Climatic Importance of Vegetation Fire*, edited by Paul J. Crutzen and Johannes Georg Goldammer, 245–66. Chichester: John Wiley and Sons, 1993.

———. *Vestal Fire: An Environmental History, Told through Fire, of Europe, and Europe's Encounter with the World*. Seattle: University of Washington Press, 1997.

Qaisar, A. Jan. "Shipbuilding in the Mughal Empire during the Seventeenth Century." *Indian Economic and Social History Review* 5 (1968): 149–76.

Quarterman, Elsie, and Catherine Keever. "Southern Mixed Hardwood Forest: Climax in the Southern Coastal Plain, USA." *Ecological Monographs* 32 (1962): 167–85.

Quezel, Pierre. "Incidences climatologique de l'utilisation des sols par l'homme dans le monde méditerranéen protohistorique." *Mediterranea* 2 (1964): 129–33.

———. "Forests of the Mediterranean Basin." In UNESCO, *Mediterranean Forests and Maquis: Ecology, Conservation and Management*, 9–31. MAB Technical Notes, 2. Paris: UNESCO, 1977.

Quinn, David B. *The Elizabethans and the Irish*. Ithaca, N.Y.: Cornell University Press, 1966.

Rabot, C. "Le déboisement dans la vallée d'Aspe et son influence sur le régime des cours d'eau." *La Géographie* 11 (1905): 207–8.

Rackham, Oliver. *Ancient Woodland: Its History, Vegetation, and Uses in England*. London: Edward Arnold, 1980.

———. *The Last Forest: The Story of Hatfield Forest*. J. M. Dent and Sons, 1989.

Radkau, Joachim. "Zur angeblichen Energiekrise des 18 Jahrhunderts: Revisionistische Betrachtung über de 'Holznot.'" *Vierteljahresschrift fur Sozial-und Wirtschaftsgeschichte* 73 (1981): 1–37.

———. "Holzverknappung und Krisenbewusstsein im 18 Jahrhundert." *Geschichte und Gesellschaft* 9 (1983): 513–43.

Rae, John B. "The Invention of Invention." In *Technology in Western Civilization*, edited by Melvin Kranzberg and Carroll Pursell Jr., vol. 1, *The Emergence of Modern Industrial Society—Earliest Times to 1900*, 325–35. New York: Oxford University Press, 1967.

Rajan, Ravi. "Imperial Environmentalism or Environmental Imperialism? European Forestry,

Colonial Foresters and the Agendas of Forest Management in British India, 1800–1900." In *Nature and the Orient: The Environmental History of South and Southeast Asia,* edited by Richard H. Grove, Vinita Damodaran, and Satpal Sangwan, 324–72. Delhi: Oxford University Press, 1998.

Ralegh, Sir Walter. *History of the World.* London: Stansbury for W. Burre, 1603.

Ralska-Jasiewiczowa, Magadalena. "Isopollen Maps of Poland, 0–11,000 Years B.P." *New Phytologist* 94 (1983): 133–75.

Ralska-Jasiewiczowa, Magadalena, and Bas Van Geel. "Early Human Disturbance of the Natural Environment Recorded in Annually Laminated Sediments in Lake Gosciaz, Central Poland." *Vegetation History and Archaeobotany* 1 (1992): 33–40.

Ramos, Alcida R. "Frontier Expansion and Indian Peoples in the Brazilian Amazon." In *Frontier Expansion in Amazonia,* edited by Marianne Schmink and Charles H. Wood, 83–104. Gainesville: University of Florida Press, 1984.

Raney, William F. "The Timber Culture Acts." *Mississippi Valley Historical Association Proceedings* 10 (1919–20): 219–29.

Rangarajan, Mahesh. "Imperial Agendas and India's Forests: The Early History of Indian Forestry, 1800–1878." *Indian Economic and Social History Review* 31 (1994): 147–67.

———. "Production, Dessication and Forest Management in the Central Provinces, 1850–1930." In *Nature and the Orient: The Environmental History of South and Southeast Asia,* edited by Richard H. Grove, Vinita Damodaran, and Satpal Sangwan, 575–95. Delhi: Oxford University Press, 1998.

Ranjitsinh, M. K. "Forest Destruction in Asia and the South Pacific." *Ambio* 8 (1979): 192–201.

Ransom, James Maxwell. *The Vanishing Ironworks of the Ramapos: The Story of the Forges, Furnaces and Mines of the New Jersey-New York Border Area.* New Brunswick, N.J.: Rutgers University Press, 1966.

Rattray, Robert Sutherland. "The Iron Workers of Akpafu." *Journal of Royal Anthropological Institute,* n.s. 19 (1916): 431–35.

Rau, V. "The Settlement of Madeira and the Sugar Cane Plantations." *Afdeling Agarische Geschiedenis Bijragen* 11 (1964): 3–12.

Raup, Hugh M. "Recent Changes in Climate and Vegetation in Southern New England and Adjacent New York." *Journal of the Arnold Arboretum* 18 (1937): 79–117.

Rawat, Ajay Singh. *History of Forestry in India.* New Delhi: Indus Publishing Company, 1991.

Rawksi, Evelyn S. "Agricultural Development in the Han River Highlands." *Late Imperial China* [formerly *Ching-shih wan-t'-i*] 3, no. 4 (1975): 63–81.

Ray, John. *The Wisdom of God Manifest in the Works of Creation,* 12th ed. London: John Ward and Joseph Rivington, 1691.

Reclus, Élisée. *La Terre* [1868]. English translation published under the title *A New Physical Geography,* edited by A. Keane (New York: Harper Brothers, 1874).

Rector, William G. *Log Transportation in the Lake States Lumber Industry, 1840–1918: The Movement of Logs and Its Relationship to Land Settlement, Water Way Development, Railroad Construction, Lumber Production and Prices.* American Waterways Series, no. 4. Glendale, Calif.: Arthur H. Clark, 1953.

Redclift, Michael. *Sustainable Development: Exploring the Contradictions.* London: Methuen, 1987.

Redford, Kent H. "The Ecologically Noble Savage." *Orion Nature Quarterly* 9, no. 3 (1990): 24–29.

Redford, Kent H., and J. A. Mansour. *Traditional People and Biological Conservation in Large Tropical Landscapes.* Arlington, Va.: American Verde Publications, 1996.

Redford, Kent H., and Christine Padoch. *Conservation of Neotropical Forests: Working from Traditional Resource Use.* New York: Columbia University Press, 1992.

Reed, C. A. "Extinction of Mammalian Megafauna in the Old World Late Quaternary." *Bioscience* 20 (1970): 284–88.

Reed, Charles A., ed. *Origins of Agriculture.* The Hague: Mouton Publishers, 1977.

Reid, Anthony. "Humans and Forests in Pre-Colonial Southeast Asia." *Environment and History* 1 (1995): 93–111.

A Relation of Some Abuses which are Committed Against the Common-wealth [1629]. In *Camden Miscellany* 3 (1855), edited by Frederic Madden. London: Camden Society.

Renfrew, Jane M. "Agriculture." In *Neolithic Greece,* edited by Demetrios Theocharis, 147–64. Athens: National Bank of Greece, 1973.

Repetto, Robert. *The Global Possible: Resources, Development and the New Century.* New Haven, Conn.: Yale University Press, 1985.

———. *Forest for the Trees?: Government Policies and the Misuse of Forest Resources.* Washington, D.C.: World Resources Institute, 1988.

———. "Deforestation in the Tropics." *Scientific American* 262 (April 1990): 18–24.

Repetto, Robert, and Malcolm Gillis, eds. *Public Policies and the Misuse of Forest Resources.* New York: Cambridge University Press, 1988.

Repplier, Agnes. *To Think of Tea!* Boston: Houghton Mifflin, 1932.

Resor, J. P. "Debt for Nature Swaps: A Decade of Experience and New Directions for the Future." *Unasylva* 48, no. 188 (1997): 15–22.

Revkin, Andrew. *The Burning Season: The Murder of Chico Mendes and the Fight for the Amazon Rainforest.* London: Collins, 1990.

Reynolds, Robert V., and Albert H. Pierson. *Fuel Wood Used in the United States, 1630–1930.* USDA Circular 641. Washington, D.C.: GPO, 1942.

Ribbentrop, Berthold. *Forestry in British India.* Calcutta: Office of the Superintendent of Government Printing, India, 1900.

Rich, B. M. "The World Bank's Indonesia Transmigration Project: Potential for Disaster." *Indonesia Reports* 15 (1986): 2–5.

Richards, John F. "Agricultural Impacts in Tropical Wetlands: Rice Paddies for Mangroves in South and South East Asia." In *Wetlands: A Threatened Landscape,* edited by Michael Williams, 217–33. Oxford: Basil Blackwell, 1990.

———. "Land Transformation." In *The Earth As Transformed by Human Action: Global and Regional Changes in the Biosphere over the Past 300 Years,* edited by Billie L. Turner II, William C. Clark, Robert W. Kates, John F. Richards, Jessica T. Mathews, and William B. Meyer, 163–78. New York: Cambridge University Press, 1990.

Richards, John F., and Elizabeth P. Flint. "A Century of Land-Use Change in South and Southeast Asia." In *Effects of Land-Use Change on Atmospheric CO_2 Concentrations. South and Southeast Asia As a Case Study,* edited by Virginia H. Dale, 16–66. New York: Springer-Verlag, 1994.

Richards, John F., James R. Hagen, and Edward S. Haynes. "Changing Land Use in Bihar, Punjab and Haryana, 1850–1970." *Modern Asian Studies* 19 (1985): 699–732.

Richards, John F., Edward S. Haynes, and James R. Hagen. "Changes in the Land and Human Productivity in Northern India, 1870–1970." *Agricultural History* 59 (1985): 523–48.

Richards, John F., Edward S. Haynes, James R. Hagen, Elizabeth P. Flint, Joseph Arlinghaus, Judith B. Dillon, and A. Lindsey Reber. *Changing Land Use in Pakistan, Northern India, Bangladesh, Burma, Malaysia, and Brunei, 1880–1980.* Unpublished report to Carbon Dioxide Research Division, Office of Basic Energy Sciences, U.S. Department of Energy. Washington, D.C., 1988.

Richards, John F., and Michelle B. McAlpin. "Cotton Cultivating and Land Clearing in the Bombay Deccan and Karnatak: 1818–1920." In *Global Deforestation and the Nineteenth Century World Economy,* edited by Richard P. Tucker and John F. Richards, 68–94. Duke Press Policy Studies. Durham, N.C.: Duke University Press, 1983.

Richards, Paul W. *The Tropical Rain Forest: An Ecological Study* [1952], rev. ed. Cambridge: Cambridge University Press, 1996.

———. *The Life of the Jungle.* Our Living World of Nature Series. New York: McGraw-Hill and Co., 1970.

———. "The Tropical Rain Forest." *Scientific American* 229 (December 1973): 58–67.

Richardson, James D., ed. *A Compilation of the Messages and Papers of the Presidents.* 10 vols. Washington, D.C.: Bureau of National Literature, 1897.

Rindos, David. *The Origins of Agriculture: An Evolutionary Perspective.* London: Academic Press, 1984.

Rival, Laura. "The Huaorani and Their Trees: Managing and Imagining the Ecuadorian Rainforest." In *Nature Is Culture: Indigenous Knowledge and Socio-Cultural Aspects of Trees and Forests in Non-European Cultures,* edited by Klaus Seeland, 67–78. London: Intermediate Technology Publications, Ltd., 1997.

Rivet, Albert L. F. *Town and Country in Roman Britain.* London: Hutchinson, University Library, 1958.

Robbins, Roy M. *Our Landed Heritage: The Public Domain, 1776–1936.* Princeton, N.J.: Princeton University Press, 1942.

Roberts, Bryan K. "Moated Sites." *Amateur Historian* [later *Local History*] 5 (1961–63): 34–40, 42.

Roberts, Neil. *The Holocene: An Environmental History.* Oxford: Basil Blackwell. 1989.

Robinson, Jennifer, and Gerald O. Barney, eds. "The Forestry Projections and the Environment." In *The Global 2000 Report to the President: Entering the Twenty-First Century. Part 1: Environmental Projections,* 318–27. Report prepared by the Council of Environmental Quality and the Department of State. Washington, D.C.: GPO, 1980.

Roche, Michael M. "The New Zealand Timber Economy, 1840–1935." *Journal of Historical Geography* 16 (1990): 295–313.

Rochefort, Cesar de. *The History of the Carriby-Islands, Viz. Barbados, St Christopher, St Vincent . . .* Rendered into English by John Davis. 2 vols. London: J. M. for T. Dring and J. Starkey, 1666.

Rockhill, W. Woodville. "Explorations in Mongolia and Tibet." In *Smithsonian Institution Annual Report, 1892.* Pt. 2: 659–79.

Rodgers, Andrew Dennie. *Bernhard Edward Fernow: A Story of North American Forestry.* Princeton, N.J.: Princeton University Press, 1951.

Rodriguez, Silvia, and Emilio Vargas. *El Recurso Forestal en Costa Rica: Politicas Publicas y Sociedad, 1970–1984.* Heredia, Costa Rica: Editorial de la Universidad Nacional, 1988.

Roe, Frank Gilbert. *The North American Buffalo: A Critical Study of the Species in the Wild State.* Toronto: Toronto University Press, 1951.

Rondski, A. F., and N. I. Shafranov. "Forestry." In *The Industries of Russia,* edited and translated by John Martin, vol. 3, *Agriculture and Forestry,* 311–52. Prepared for the World's Columbian Exposition at Chicago. St Petersburg: Department of Agriculture, Ministry of Crown Domains, 1893.

Rook, Anthony. "The Development and Operation of Roman Hypocausted Baths." *Journal of Archaeological Science* 5 (1978): 269–82.

Roosevelt, Anna. "Resource Management in Amazonia before the Conquest: Beyond Ethno-graphic Projection." In *Resource Management in Amazonia: Indigenes and Folk Strategies,* edited by Darrell A. Posey and William Balée, 30–62. Advances in Economic Botany 7. New York: New York Botanical Garden, 1989.

Roosevelt, Theodore. "The Forest in the Life of the Nation." *Proceedings of the American Forest Congress,* 3–12. Washington, D.C.: H. M. Suter, 1905.

Rosenberg, Nathan. "The Economic Consequences of Technological Change, 1830–1850." In *Technology in Western Civilization,* edited by Melvin Kranzberg and C. W. Pursell Jr., vol. 1, *The Emergence of Modern Industrial Society—Earliest Times to 1900,* 515–31. New York: Oxford University Press, 1967.

———. *Technology and American Economic Growth.* New York: Harper and Row, 1972.

———. "America's Rise to Woodworking Leadership." In *America's Wooden Age: Aspects of Its Early Technology,* edited by Brooke Hindle. Tarrytown, N.Y.: Sleepy Hollow Press, 1975.

———, ed. *The American System of Manufacturing: The Report of the Committee on the Ma-chinery of the United States, 1855, and the Special Report of George Walters and Joseph Went-worth, 1854.* Edinburgh: Edinburgh University Press, 1969.

Ross, James B., and Mary M. McLaughlin, eds. *The Portable Medieval Reader.* New York: The Viking Press, 1949.

Ross-Sheriff, Bruce. "Forest Projections." In *Global 2000 Report to the President: Entering the Twenty-First Century. Part 1: The Projections,* edited by Jennifer Robinson and Gerald O. Bar-ney, 117–35. Council of Environmental Quality and U.S. Department of State. Washington, D.C.: GPO, 1980.

Rostlund, Erhard. "The Myth of a Natural Prairie Belt in Alabama: An Interpretation of Histori-cal Records." *Annals, Association of American Geographers* 47 (1957): 392–411.

Rostovtzeff, Michael. *A Large Estate in Egypt in the Third Century BC: A Study in Economic His-tory.* University of Wisconsin Studies in Social Sciences and History, 6. Madison: University of Wisconsin, 1922.

———. *The Social and Economic History of the Hellenistic World.* 3 vols. Oxford: Clarendon Press, 1941.

———. *The Social and Economic History of the Roman Empire* [1924], 2d ed. 2 vols. Oxford: The Clarendon Press, 1957.

Roth, Dennis M. "Philippines Forests and Forestry, 1565–1920." In *Global Deforestation and the Nineteenth Century World Economy,* edited by Richard P. Tucker and John F. Richards, 30–49. Duke Press Policy Studies. Durham, N.C.: Duke University Press, 1983.

Rotty, Ralph M. "Estimates of CO_2 from Wood Fuel Based on Forest Harvest Data." *Climatic Change* 9 (1986): 312–26.

Rouche, Michel. "La faim à l'époque carolingienne: essai sur quelques types de rations alimen-taires." *Revue historique* 250 (1973): 295–320.

Rouff, Marcel. *Les mines de charbon en France au XVIIIᵉ siècle, 1742–1791: Étude d'histoire economique et sociale.* Paris: E. Rieder, 1922.

Rourke, Constance M. *The Roots of American Culture and Other Essays.* Edited with a preface by Van Wyck Brooks. New York: Harcourt Brace, 1942.

Rouse, Joseph. "Interpretation in Natural and Human Science." In *The Interpretative Turn: Phi-losophy, Science and Culture,* edited by David R. Hiley, James F. Bohman, and Richard Schus-terman, 42–56. Ithaca, N.Y.: Cornell University Press, 1991.

Rowley-Conwy, Peter. "Sedentary Hunters: The Ertebólle Example." In *Hunter-Gatherer Economy in Prehistory,* edited by Geoffrey Bailey, 111–26. Cambridge: Cambridge University Press, 1981.

―――. "Slash and Burn in the Temperate European Neolithic." In *Farming Practices in British Prehistory,* edited by Roger T. Mercer, 85–96. Edinburgh: Edinburgh University Press, 1981.

―――. "Forest Grazing and Clearance in Temperate Europe with Special Reference to Denmark: An Archaeological View." In *Archaeological Aspects of Woodland Ecology,* edited by Susan Limbrey and Martin Bell, 199–215. British Archaeological Reports, International Series, 146. Oxford: B.A.R., 1982.

Rubner, Heinrich. "Greek Thought and Forest Science." *Environmental Review* 9 (1985): 277–95.

Ruddiman, William F., and Alexander McIntyre. "The Mode and Mechanism of the Last Deglaciation: Oceanic Evidence." *Quaternary Research* 16 (1981): 125–34.

Rudel, Thomas K., with Bruce Horowitz. *Tropical Deforestation: Small Farmers and Land Clearing in the Ecuadorian Amazon.* New York: Columbia University Press, 1993.

Ruffin, Edmund. *An Essay on Calcareous Manures,* 2d ed. Shellbanks, Va: Farmers' Register, 1835.

Ruiz, M., and J. P. Ruiz. "Ecological History of Transhumance in Spain." *Biological Conservation* 37 (1986): 73–86.

Rush, Benjamin. "An Enquiry into the Cause of the Increase of Bilious and Intermitting Fevers in Pennsylvania with Hints for Preventing Them." *Transactions, American Philosophical Society* 2, no. 25 (1786): 206–12. Also printed in Benjamin Rush, *Medical Enquiries and Observations* 2:265–76. Philadelphia, 1799.

Russell, Emily W. B. "Indian-Set Fires in the Forests of the Northeastern United States." *Ecology* 64 (1983): 78–88.

Russell, Howard S. *A Long Deep Furrow: Three Centuries of Farming in New England.* Hanover, N.H.: University Press of New England, 1976.

Russell, J. C. "Late Ancient and Medieval Population." *Transactions of the American Philosophical Society* 48, no. 3 (1958): 131–48.

―――. "Population in Europe, 500–1500." In *The Fontana Economic History of Europe,* edited by Carlo M. Cipolla, vol. 1, *The Middle Ages,* 25–70. Brighton: Harvester Press, 1976.

Sagan, Carl, O. B. Toon, and J. B. Pollack. "Anthropological Albedo Changes and the Earth's Climate." *Science* 206 (1979): 1363–68.

Sahagún, Fray de Bernardino. *The Florentine Codex: General History of the Things of New Spain.* Translated by Charles E. Dibble and Arthur J. O. Anderson. . Vol. 10, "The People." Santa Fé: The School of American Research and the University of Utah, 1950–71; Monograph 14 of the School of American Research and the Museum of New Mexico, Santa Fé, 1961.

Sahlins, Marshall. "Cosmologies of Capitalism: The Trans-Pacific Sector of 'The World System.'" *Proceedings of the British Academy* 74 (1988): 1–51.

Sahlins, Peter. *Forest Rites: The War of the Demoiselles in Nineteenth Century France.* Cambridge, Mass.: Harvard University Press, 1994.

Said, Edward, W. *Orientalism.* London: Routledge and Kegan Paul, 1978.

Saint-Pierre, Jean H. Bernadin de. *Voyage to the Isle de France, the Isle of Bourbon, the Cape of Good Hope, etc. With Observations and Reflections on Nature and Mankind by an Officer of the King* [1773]. 2 vols. London: W. Griffin, 1775.

Sainte-Colombe, Michel de. "Notice sur l'instruction publique: l'agriculture et l'industrie de l'arrondissment d'Yssingeaux." *Annales de la Société d'Agriculture, Sciences, Arts et Commerce du Puys* 3 (1828): 80–151.

Saladanha, Indra Munshi. "Colonial Forest Regulations and Collective Resistance: Nineteenth-Century Thana District." In *Nature and the Orient: The Environmental History of South and Southeast Asia,* edited by Richard H. Grove, Vinita Damodaran, and Satpal Sangwan, 708–33. Delhi: Oxford University Press, 1998.

Salati, Eneas, Marc J. Dourojeanni, Fernando C. Novaes, Adélia E. de Oliveira, Richard W. Perritt, Herbert Otto, Roger Schubart, and Julio C. Umana. "Amazonia." In *The Earth As Transformed by Human Action: Global and Regional Changes in the Biosphere over the Past 300 Years,* edited by Billie Lee Turner II, William C. Clark, Robert W. Kates, John F. Richards, Jessica T. Mathews, and William B. Meyer, 479–93. New York: Cambridge University Press, 1990.

Salati, Eneas, and Peter B. Vose. "The Depletion of Tropical Rain Forests." *Ambio* 12 (1983): 67–71.

———. "Amazon Basin: A System in Equilibrium." *Science* 225 (1984): 129–38.

Sale, Kirkpatrick. *The Conquest of Paradise: Christopher Columbus and the Columbian Legacy.* New York: Alfred A. Knopf, 1990.

Salkield, Leonard U. "Ancient Slag in the South West of the Iberian Peninsula." *La Mineria Hispanica e Ibero-Americana* 1 (1970): 94.

———. "The Roman and Pre-Roman Slags of the Rio Tinto, Spain." In *The Evolution of the First Fire-Using Industries,* edited by Theodore A. Wertime and Steven F. Wertime, 137–47. Papers presented at a seminar on early pyrotechnology held at the Smithsonian Institution, Washington, D.C., and the National Bureau of Standards, Gaithersburg, Md., 19–20 April 1979. Washington, D.C.: Smithsonian Institution Press, microfiche, 1982.

Sanford, Charles Leroy. "The Concept of the Sublime in the Works of Thomas Cole and William Cullen Bryant." *American Literature* 28 (1957): 434–48.

———. *The Quest for Paradise: Europe and the American Moral Imagination.* Urbana: University of Illinois Press, 1961.

Sanford, Robert L., Juan Saldarriaga, Kathleen E. Clark, Christopher Uhl, and Rafael Herrera. "Amazon Rain-Forest Fires." *Science* 227 (1985): 53–55.

Sangwan, Satpal. "From Gentlemen Amateurs to Professionals: Reassessing the Natural Science Tradition in Colonial India 1780–1840." In *Nature and the Orient: The Environmental History of South and Southeast Asia,* edited by Richard H. Grove, Vinita Damodaran, and Satpal Sangwan, 210–37. Delhi: Oxford University Press, 1998.

Sanyal, Hitesranjan. "The Indigenous Iron Industry of Birbhum." *Social History Review* 5 (1968): 101–8.

Sargent, Charles Sprague. *Report on the Forests of North America (Exclusive of Mexico).* Vol. 9 of *Tenth Census of the United States* (1880). Accompanied by a *Folio Atlas of Forest Trees of North America,* 1880. Washington, D.C.: GPO, 1884.

Sauer, Carl O. "Destructive Exploitation in Modern Colonial Expansion." *Comptes Rendus du Congres International de Geographie, Amsterdam, 1938,* 2 (sec. 3c): 494–99.

———. "Theme of Plant and Animal Destruction in Economic History." *Journal of Farm Economics* 20 (1938): 765–75.

———. "The Prospect for Redistribution of Population." In *Limits of Land Settlement: A Report on Present-Day Possibilities,* edited by Isaiah Bowman, 7–24. New York: Council for Foreign Relations and the American Geographical Society, 1939.

———. "A Geographical Sketch of Early Man in America." *Geographical Review* 34 (1944): 529–73.

———. "Grassland Climax, Fire, and Man." *Journal of Range Management* 3 (1950): 16–21.

———. *Agricultural Origins and Dispersals.* New York: American Geographical Society, 1952.

———. "The Agency of Man on Earth." In *Man's Role in Changing the Face of the Earth,* edited by William L. Thomas, 49–69. Chicago: University of Chicago Press, 1956.

———. "Age and Area of American Cultivated Plants." *Actas del 33° Congreso Internacional de Americanistas, San José, Costa Rica, 1958* 1 (1959): 264–78.

———. "Fire and Early Man." *Paideuma* 7 (1961): 399–407. Reprinted in *Land and Life: A*

Selection of the Writings of Carl Ortwin Sauer, edited by John Leighly, 288–99. Berkeley and Los Angeles: University of California Press, 1963.

———. "Man in the Ecology of Tropical America." *Proceedings of the Ninth Pacific Science Congress, 1957* 20 (1958): 104–10. Reprinted in *Land and Life: A Selection of the Writings of Carl Ortwin Sauer,* edited by John Leighly, 182–94. Berkeley and Los Angeles: University of California Press, 1963.

———. *Sixteenth Century North America: The Land and the People As Seen by the Europeans.* Berkeley and Los Angeles: University of California Press, 1971.

———. "Man's Dominance by Use of Fire." *Geoscience and Man* 10 (1975): 1–13.

Sauoma, Edouard. Keynote Address to Eighth World Forestry Congress, Jakarta, 1978. Reported in U.S. Interagency Task Force on Tropical Forests, *The World's Forests: A Policy Strategy and Program for the United States* 8. Report to the President, Department of State Publication 9117. Washington, D.C.: GPO, 1980.

Scammel, Geoffrey V. *The World Encompassed: The First Maritime Empires, c. 800–1650.* Berkeley and Los Angeles: University of California Press, 1981.

Scarry, C. Margaret, ed. *Foraging and Farming in the Eastern Woodlands.* Gainesville: University of Florida Press, 1993.

Schafer, Edward H. "The Conservation of Nature under the T'ang Dynasty." *Journal of the Economic and Social History of the Orient* 5 (1962): 279–308.

———. "Hunting Parks and Animal Enclosures in Ancient China." *Journal of Economic and Social History of the Orient* 11 (1968): 318–43.

Schallenberg, Richard . "Evolution, Adaption, and Survival: The Very Slow Death of the American Charcoal Iron Industry." *Annals of Science* 32 (1975): 341–59.

Schama, Simon. *Landscape and Memory.* London: Harper Collins, 1995.

Schenk, Winfried. "Fundamental Changes in the Forest Landscapes of Lower Franconia (Germany) in the 19th Century." In *The Transformation of the European Rural Landscape: Methodological Issues and Agrarian Change, 1770–1914,* edited by Antoon Verhoere and Jelier Vervloet. Proceedings of Conference for the Study of Rural Landscapes. Brussels: NFWO: FNRS, 1992.

———. "Forest Development Types in Central Germany in Pre-Industrial Times: A Contribution by Historical Geography to the Solution of a Forest History Argument about 'Wood Scarcity' in the Eighteenth Century." In *L'uomo la foresta. Secc. XIII – XVIII,* edited by Simonetta Cavaciocchi, ser. 2: Atti della Settimane di Studi'e altri Convegni 27, 201–23. Prato, Italy: Istituto intern. di storia econom: F. Datini, 1996.

Schlüter, Otto. "Wald, Sumpf und Seidlungsland in Altpreussen vor der Ordenszeit." *Geograpischer Anzeiger* 21 (1920): 245–49.

———. *Die Seidlungsräume Mittleuropas in frühgeschichtlicher Zeit. Pt. 1. Erläuterungen zu einer Karte.* Forschungen zur Deutschen Landeskunde, 63. Hamburg: Atlantik Verlag, Amtes für Landeskunde, 1952.

———. Plate 10 in *Atlas Ostliches Mittleuropa.* Belefield: Velhagen und Klasing, 1952.

Schmaltz, Norman J. "Raphael Zon: Forest Researcher." *Journal of Forest History* 24 (1980): 24–39.

Schmink, Marianne, and Charles H. Wood, eds. *Frontier Expansion in Amazonia.* Gainesville: Florida University Press, 1984.

———. *Contested Frontiers in Amazonia.* New York: Columbia University Press, 1992.

Schneider, Stephen H. "The Greenhouse Effect: Science and Policy." *Science* 243 (1989): 771–81.

———. "A Constructive Deconstruction of Deconstructionists: A Response to Demeritt." *Annals, Association of American Geographers* 91 (2001): 338–44.

Schnell, Raymond. "Essai de synthèse biogéographie sur la région forestière d'Afrique occidentale." *Notes Africaines*, no. 52 (October 1949): 29–35.

Schob, David F. "Woodhawks and Cordwood: Steamboat Fuel on the Ohio and Mississippi Rivers, 1820–1860." *Journal of Forest History* 21 (1977): 124–32.

Schoepf, Johann David. *Travels in the Confederation (1783–1784).* Reproduced under the title *Schoepf's Travels in the Confederation, 1783–84,* translated and edited by Alfred J. Morrison (Philadelphia: W. J.Campbell, 1911).

Schubert, H. R. *History of the British Iron and Steel Industry from c. 450 B.C. to A.D. 1775.* London: Routledge and Kegan Paul, 1957.

Schulte-Bisping, Hubert, Michael Bredemeir, and Friedrich Beese. "Global Availability of Wood and Energy Supply from Fuelwood and Charcoal." *Ambio* 28 (1999): 592–94.

Schumpter, Elizabeth Boody. *English Overseas Trade Statistics, 1697–1808.* Oxford: Clarendon Press, 1960.

Schurr, Sam H., and Bruce C. Netschert. *Energy in the American Economy, 1850–1975: An Economic Study of Its History and Prospects.* Baltimore: Johns Hopkins University Press for Resources for the Future, 1960.

Schwartz, Stuart B. "Free Labor in a Slave Economy: The Lavadores de Cana of Colonial Bahia." In *Colonial Roots of Modern Brazil: Papers of the Newberry Library Conference,* edited by D. Alden, 147–97. Berkeley and Los Angeles: University of California Press, 1977.

———. *Sugar Plantations in the Formation of Brazilian Society: Bahia, 1550–1835.* Cambridge: Cambridge University Press, 1985.

Sclafert, Thérèse. *Le Haut-Dauphiné au moyen âge.* Paris: Société Anonyme de Recueil Sirey, 1926.

———. *Cultures en Haut-Provence: déboisments et pâturages au moyen âge.* Vol.4, *Les hommes et la terre.* École Pratique des Hautes Études—VIᵉ Section Centre de Recherches Historiques. Paris: S.E.V.P.E.N., 1959.

Scott, Geoffrey A. J. "The Role of Fire in the Creation and Maintenance of Savannas in the Montaña of Peru." *Journal of Biogeography* 4 (1977): 143–67.

———. *Grassland Development in the Gran Pajonal of Eastern Peru.* Hawaii Monographs in Geography, 1. Honolulu: University of Hawaii, 1979.

Sears, Paul B. *Deserts on the March.* Norman: University of Oklahoma Press, 1935.

Secrett, C. "The Environmental Impact of Transmigration." *The Ecologist* 16 (1986): 77–88.

Sedjo, Roger A. "Forests to Offset the Greenhouse Effect." *Journal of Forestry* (July 1989): 12–15.

Sedjo, Roger A., and Marion Clawson. "How Serious Is Tropical Deforestation?" *Journal of Forestry* 83 (1983): 792–94.

———. "Global Forests." In *The Resourceful Earth: A Response to Global 2000,* edited by Julian L. Simon and Herman Kahn, 128–71. Oxford: Basil Blackwell, 1984.

Séle, Henri. "Les forêts et la question du déboisement en Bretagne à la fin de l'ancien régime," *Annales de Bretagne* 26 (1924): 1–28, 355–79.

Semple, Ellen Churchill. *The Geography of the Mediterranean Region: Its Relation to Ancient History.* New York: Henry Holt and Co., 1931.

Shaler, Nathaniel S. "The Economic Aspects of Soil Erosion." *National Geographical Magazine* 79 (1896): 328–30, 79 (1896): 368–77.

———. *Nature and Man in North America.* New York: Charles Scribner and Sons, 1899.

———. "Earth and Man: An Economic Forecast." *International Quarterly* 10 (1904–5): 227–39.

———. "The Exhaustion of the World's Metals." *International Quarterly* 11 (1905): 230–47.

———. "The Future of Power." *International Quarterly* 11 (1905): 24–38.

Shane, Douglas R. *Hoofprints on the Forest: Cattle Ranching and the Destruction of Latin America's Tropical Forests*. Philadephia: Institute for the Study of Human Relations, 1986.

Shantz, Homer L., and Curtis Fletcher Marbut. *The Vegetation and Soils of Africa*. American Geographical Research Series, no. 13. New York: National Council and the American Geographical Society, 1923.

Sharma, Narenda P., ed. *Managing the World's Forests: Looking for Balance between Conservation and Development*. Dubuque, Iowa: Kendall/Hunt Publishing Co., 1992.

Sharp, Lindsay. "Timber, Science and Economic Reform in the Seventeenth Century." *Forestry* 48 (1975): 51–86.

Shaw, Brent D. "Climate, Environment and History: The Case of Roman North Africa." In *Climate and History: Studies in Past Climates and Their Impact on Man,* 379–403, edited by T. M. L. Wigley, M. J. Ingram, and G. Farmer. Cambridge: Cambridge University Press, 1981.

Shaw, Denis J. B. "Southern Frontiers of Muscovy, 1550–1700." In *Studies in Russian Historical Geography,* edited by J. H. Bater and R. A. French, 1:117–42. London: Academic Press, 1983.

Shaw, Norman. *Chinese Forest Trees and Timber Supply*. London: T. Fisher Unwin, 1914.

Sheridan, Richard B. *The Development of the Plantations to 1750: An Era of West Indian Prosperity, 1750–1775*. Kingston, Jamaica: Caribbean Universities Press, 1970.

Sherratt, Andrew G. "Resources, Technology and Trade in Early European Metallurgy." In *Problems in Economic and Social Archaeology,* edited by Gale de Giverne Sieveking, Ian H. Longworth, and K. E. Wilson, 557–82. London: Duckworth, 1976.

———. "The Beginnings of Agriculture in the Near East and Europe" and "Early Agricultural Communities in Europe." In *The Cambridge Encyclopedia of Archaeology,* edited by Andrew G. Sherratt, 102–111, 144–51. Cambridge: Cambridge University Press, 1980.

———. "Plough and Pastoralism: Aspects of the Secondary Products Revolution." In *Patterns in the Past: Studies in Honour of David Clarke,* edited by Ian Hodder, Glynn Issac, and Norman Hammond, 261–306. Cambridge: Cambridge University Press, 1981.

———. "The Secondary Exploitation of Animals in the Old World." *World Archaeology* 15 (1983): 90–104.

———. "Wool, Wheels, and Ploughmarks: Local Developments or Outside Introductions in Neolithic Europe?" *Bulletin of London Univ. Institute of Archaeology* 23 (1986): 1–15.

———. "Two New Books on Early European Agriculture." *Scottish Archaeological Review* 4 (1987): 134–37.

———. *Economy and Society in Prehistoric Europe: Changing Perspectives*. Edinburgh: Edinburgh University Press, 1997.

Sherratt, Andrew G., and Susan Sherratt. "The Growth of the Mediterranean Economy in the Early First Millennium BC." *World Archaeology* 24 (1993): 361–78.

Shetler, S. "Three Faces of Eden." In *Seeds of Change: A Quincentennial Commemoration,* edited by H. J. Viola and C. Margolis, 255–47. Washington, D.C.: Smithsonian Institution Press, 1991.

Shih Ching, The Book of Songs: The Ancient Chinese Classic of Poetry. Translated from the Chinese by Arthur Waley. New York: Grove Press, 1960.

Shimek, Bohumil. "The Pioneer and the Forest." *Proceedings, Mississippi Valley Historical Association* 3 (1971): 96–105.

Siddiqi, A. "Agrarian Depression in Uttar Pradesh." *Indian Economic and Social History Review* 6 (1969): 175–77.

———. *Agrarian Change in a Northern Indian State: Uttar Pradesh, 1819–1833*. Oxford: Oxford University Press, 1973.

———. "The Business World of Jamsedjee Jeejeebhoy." *Indian Economic and Social History Review* 19 (1982): 301–24.

Siegfreid, André. *Suez and Panama*. Translated from the French by Henry Harold and Doris Hemming. London: Jonathan Cape, 1940.

Sielmann, Burchard. "Die frühneolithische Besiedlung Mitteleuropas." In *Die Anfänge de Neolithickums vom Orient bis Nordeuropa*, edited by Herman Schwabedissen, pt. 5a, 1–65. Cologne: Böhlau Verlag, 1972.

Silver, Timothy. *A New Face on the Countryside: Indians, Colonists, and Slaves in the South Atlantic Forests, 1500–1800*. Cambridge: Cambridge University Press, 1990.

Simkin, Colin G. F. *The Traditional Trade of Asia*. Oxford: Oxford University Press, 1968.

Simmons, Ian G. "Late Mesolithic Societies and the Environment of the Uplands of England and Wales." *Bulletin of the Institute of Archaeology, University of London* 16 (1979): 11–129.

———. "The Earliest Cultural Landscapes of England." *Environmental Review* 12 (1988): 105–16. Reprinted in *Out of the Woods: Essays in Environmental History*, edited by C. Miller and H. Rothman (Pittsburgh: Pittsburgh University Press, 1997), 53–63, 324–25.)

Simmons, Ian G., Geoffrey W. Dimbleby, and C. Grigson. "The Mesolithic." In *The Environment in British Prehistory*, edited by Ian G. Simmons and M. J. Tooley, 82–124. London: Duckworth, 1981.

Simmons, Ian G., and Innes, J. B. "Later Mesolithic Land-Use and Its Impact in the English Uplands." *Biogeographical Monographs* 2 (1985): 7–17.

———. "Mid-Holocene Adaptions and Later Mesolithic Forest Disturbances in Northern England." *Journal of Archaeological Science* 14 (1987): 385–403.

Simon, Julian L. *The Ultimate Resource*. Princeton, N.J.: Princeton University Press, 1981.

Simon, Julian L., and Herman Kahn, eds. *The Resourceful Earth: A Response to Global 2000*. Oxford: Basil Blackwell, 1984.

Singer, Charles, E. J. Holmyard, A. Rupert Hall, and Trevor I. Williams, eds. *A History of Technology*. Vol. 3, *From the Renaissance to the Industrial Revolution c.1500–c.1750*. Oxford: Clarendon Press, 1957.

Singh, K. D. "The Tropical Forest Resources Assessment." *Unasylva* 44 (1993): 10–19.

Sivaramakrishnan, K. "Colonialism and Forestry in India: Imagining the Past in Present Politics." *Comparative Studies in Society and History* 37 (1995): 3–40.

Skaria, Ajay. "Timber Conservancy, Desiccation, and Scientific Forestry: The Dangs, 1840–1920." In *Nature and the Orient: The Environmental History of South and Southeast Asia*, edited by Richard H. Grove, Vinita Damodaran, and Satpal Sangwan, 591–635. Delhi: Oxford University Press, 1998.

Skidmore, Thomas E. *Politics in Brazil, 1930–1964: An Experiment in Democracy*. New York: Oxford University Press, 1967.

———. *The Politics of Military Rule in Brazil, 1964–85*. New York: Oxford University Press, 1988.

Skole, David, and Compton J. Tucker. "Tropical Deforestation and Habitat Fragmentation in the Amazon: Satellite Data from 1978 to 1988." *Science* 260 (1993): 1905–10.

Skubbeltrang, F. "The History of the Finnish Peasant." *Scandinavian Economic History Review* 12 (1964): 165–80.

Sleeman, William Henry. *Rambles and Recollections of an Indian Official*. 2 vols. London: J. Hatchard and Son, 1844.

Slicher van Bath, Bernard Hendrick. *The Agrarian History of Western Europe, A.D. 500–1850*. Translated from the Dutch by Oliver Ordish. London: Edward Arnold, 1963.

————. "Eighteenth Century Agriculture on the Continent of Europe: Evolution or Revolution?" *Agricultural History* 43 (1969): 169–79.

Sloane, Sir Hans. *A Voyage to the Islands of Madera, Barbadoes, Nieves, St. Christopher and Jamaica . . .* London: Printed for the author by B. M., circa 1707–25.

Smil, Vaclav. "Deforestation in China." *Ambio* 12 (1983): 226–33.

Smith, A. G. "The Influence of Mesolithic and Neolithic Man on British Vegetation: A Discussion." In *Studies in the Vegetational History of the British Isles: Essays in Honour of Harry Godwin,* edited by Donald Walker and R. G. West, 81–96. Cambridge: Cambridge University Press, 1970.

Smith, Adam. *An Inquiry into the Nature and Causes of the Wealth of Nations* [1776]. Edited by Edwin Cannan. New York: Random House, 1937.

Smith, Arthur H. *Chinese Characteristics.* New York: Flemming H. Revell Company, 1894.

Smith, Bruce D. "Variations in Mississippian Settlement Patterns." In *Mississippian Settlement Systems,* edited by Bruce D. Smith, 479–503. New York: Academic Press, 1978.

————. "Origins of Agriculture in Eastern North America." *Science* 246 (1989): 1566–71.

Smith, Bruce D., with contributions by C. Wesley Cowan and Michael P. Hoffman. *Rivers of Change: Essays on Early Agriculture in Eastern North America.* Washington, D.C.: Smithsonian Institution Press, 1992.

Smith, Clifford Thorpe. *An Historical Geography of Western Europe before 1800* [1967]. London: Longman, 1978.

Smith, James B. "Lumbertowns in the Cutover: A Comparative Study of the Stage Hypothesis of Urban Growth." Ph.D. diss., Univerity of Wisconsin-Madison, 1973.

Smith, John. "Advertisements for the Inexperienced Planters of New England or Anywhere." *Massachusetts Historical Society Collections,* 3d ser., 3 (1833): 1–54.

————. *Travels and Works of Captain John Smith.* Edited by Edward Arber. 2 vols. Birmingham: n.p., 1884. New edition by A. G. Bradly, Burt Franklin Research and Source Works Series, no. 130. Philadelphia: Burt Franklin Co.

Smith, Niel J. H.: *Rainfall Corridors: The Transamazon Colonization Scheme.* Berkeley and Los Angeles: University of California Press, 1982.

Smith, Robert E. F. *The Origins of Farming in Russia.* École Pratique des Hautes Études—Sorbonne. VIe Section. Paris: Mouton & Co., 1959.

————. *Peasant Farming in Muscovy.* Cambridge: Cambridge University Press, 1977.

Smith, Thomas C. *The Agrarian Origins of Modern Japan.* Stanford, Calif.: Stanford University Press, 1959.

Smyth, Albert H., ed. *The Writings of Benjamin Franklin.* 10 Vols. Collected and Edited with a Life and Introduction by M. M. Smythe. New York: Macmillan 1905–7.

Smythies, Evelyn A. *India's Forest Wealth,* 2d ed. London: Oxford University Press, 1925.

Snyder, David E. "The 'Carretera Marginal de la Selva': A Geographical Revue and Appraisal." *Revista Geografica,* no. 67 (1967): 87–100.

Sobel, Dava. *Longitude: The True Story of a Lone Genius Who Solved the Greatest Scientific Problem of His Time.* New York: Walker and Co., 1995.

Soininen, Arvo M. "Burn-Beating As the Technical Basis of Colonisation in Finland during the 16th and 17th Centuries." *Scandinavian Economic History Review* 7 (1959): 150–66.

Solomon, A. M. "Pollen." In *Aerobiology: The Ecological Systems Approach,* edited by Robert L. Edmonds, 41–84. Stroudsburg, Pa.: Dowden, Hutchinson and Ross, 1979.

Sombart, Werner. *Der Moderne Kapitalismus* [1902], 2d ed. 4 vols. Leipzig: Verlag von Duncker & Humblot, 1916–27.

Sommer, Adrian. "Attempt at an Assessment of the World's Tropical Forests." *Unasylva* 28 (1976): 5–25.

Söderlund, E. F. "The Impact of the British Industrial Revolution on the Swedish Iron Industry." In *Studies in the Industrial Revolution: Presented to T. S. Ashton,* edited by Leslie Seddon Presnell, 52–66. London: Athlone Press, 1960.

Soom, Arnold. "Der Ostbaltische Holzhandel und die Holzindustrie im 17 Jahrhundert." *Hansisch Geschichtblätter* (1961): 17–49.

Sophocles. *Antigone.* In *The Complete Greek Tragedies,* edited by David Grene and Richmond Lattimore. Vol. 2. Chicago: University of Chicago Press, 1959.

Sousa-Leão, Joaquim de. *Frans Post, 1612–1680.* Amsterdam: A. L. van Gendt, 1973.

Southgate, Douglas. "The Causes of Land Degradation along 'Spontaneously' Expanding Agricultural Frontiers in the Third World." *Land Economics* 66 (1990): 93–101.

Spate, Oskar H. K. *The Pacific since Magellan.* Vol. 1, *The Spanish Lake.* Canberra: Australian National University Press, 1979.

Spencer, Herbert. *The Principles of Biology.* 2 vols. New York: D. Appleton and Co., 1866–67.

Speth, William W. "Carl Ortwin Sauer on Destructive Exploitation." *Biological Conservation* 11 (1977): 145–60.

Sponsel, Leslie E. "The Environmental History of Amazonia: Natural and Human Disturbances, and the Ecological Transition." In *Changing Tropical Forests: Historical Perspectives on Today's Challenges in Central and South America,* edited by Harold K. Steen and Richard P. Tucker, 233–51. Durham, N.C.: Forest History Society, 1992.

Sponsel, Leslie E., Thomas N. Headland, and Robert C. Bailey, eds. *Tropical Deforestation: The Human Dimension.* New York: Columbia University Press, 1996.

Sprandel, Rolf. "Le production du fer au moyen âge." *Annales, Economiés, Sociétés, Civilisations* 24 (1969): 305–32.

Springer, John S. *Forest Life and Forest Trees: Comprising Winter Camp-Life among the Loggers and Wild-Wood Adventure, with Descriptions of Lumbering Operations on Various Rivers of Maine and New Brunswick.* New York: Harper and Brothers, 1851. Reprint, Somersworth, N.H.: New Hampshire Publishing, 1971.

Stahl, Rose M. *The Ballinger-Pinchot Controversy.* Smith College Studies in History, vol. 11, pt. 2. Northampton, Mass.: New Hampshire Publishing, 1971.

Stamp, L. Dudley. "The Southern Margins of the Sahara: Comments on some Recent Studies of the Question of Dessication in West Africa." *Geographical Review* 30 (1940), 297–300.

Standish, Arthur. *The Commons Complaint.* London: W. Stansby, 1611.

Starling, Nicholas J. "Colonization and Succession: The Earlier Neolithic of Central Europe." *Proceedings of the Prehistoric Society* 51 (1985), 41–57.

Starr, Frederick. "American Forests: Their Destruction and Preservation." USDA, *Annual Report* 1865: 210–34.

Startin, W. "Linear Pottery Culture Houses: Reconstruction and Manpower." *Proceedings of the Prehistoric Society* 44 (1978), 143–59.

Statutes at Large (United States). Washington, D.C.: GPO, 1923.

Stebbing, Edward Percy. *The Forests of India.* 4 vols. London: John Lane, The Bodley Head Ltd., 1922–26, 1962.

———. "The Encroaching Sahara: The Threat to the West African Colonies." *Geographical Journal* 85 (1935): 506–24.

———. *The Forests of West Africa and the Sahara: A Study of Modern Conditions.* London: W. and R. Chambers, 1937.

———. "The Man-Made Desert of Africa: Erosion and Drought." *Supplement of the Journal of the Royal African Society*. London and New York: Macmillan and Co., 1938.

Stebelsky, I. "Agriculture and Soil Erosion in the European Forest-Steppe." In *Studies in Russian Historical Geography*, edited by James.H. Bater and R. Anthony French, 1:45–63. London: Academic Press. 1983.

Steele, R. C. "Some Social and Economic Constraints to the Use of Forests for Energy and Organics in Great Britain." In *Biological and Sociological Basis for Rational Use of Forest Resources for Energy and Organics*, edited by Stephen G. Boyce. Proceedings of the Man and Biosphere Workshop, Michigan State University, 6–11 May 1979. Rome: FAO, 1979.

Steen, Harold H., ed. *History of Susutained–Yield Forestry: A Symposium*. Durham, N.C.: Forest History Society, 1984.

Steensberg, Axel. *Draved: An Experiment in Stone Age Agriculture. Burning, Sowing and Harvesting*. Copenhagen: National Museum of Denmark, 1979.

Steensgaard, Niels. "European Shipping to Asia, 1497–1700." *Scandinavian Economic History Review* 18 (1970): 1–11.

———. "The Growth and Composition of the Long-Distance Trade of England and the Dutch Republic before 1750." In *The Rise of Merchant Empires: Long Distance Trade in the Early Modern World, 1350–1750*, edited by James D. Tracy, 102–54. Cambridge: Cambridge University Press, 1990.

Steer, Henry B. *Lumber Production in the United States, 1799–1946*. USDA Miscellaneous Publications, no. 669. Washington, D.C.: GPO, 1948.

Stein, Stanley J. *Vassouras: A Brazilian Coffee County, 1850–1900*. Cambridge, Mass.: Harvard University Press, 1957.

Stenton, Doris M. *English Society in the Early Middle Ages*. Harmondsworth, England: Penguin Books, 1952.

Stephenson, Isaac. *Recollections of a Long Life, 1829–1915*. Chicago: Published privately, 1915.

Sternberg, Hilgard O'Reilly. "Man and Environmental Change in South America." In *Biogeography and Ecology in South America*, edited by E. J. Fittkau, J. Illies, H. Klinge, G. H. Scwabe, and H. Sioli, 413–45. The Hague: W. Junk, 1968.

———. "Aggravation of Floods in the Amazon River As a Consequence of Deforestation?" *Geografiska Annaler*, ser. a, 69 (1987): 201–19.

Stewart, N. R. "Some Problems in the Development of Agricultural Colonization in the Andean Oriente." *Professional Geographer* 20 (1968): 33–38.

Stewart, Omer C. "Burning and Natural Vegetation in the United States." *Geographical Review* 41 (1951): 317–20.

———. "Fire As the First Great Force Employed by Man." In *Man's Role in Changing the Face of the Earth*, edited by W. L. Thomas, 115–33. Chicago: University of Chicago Press, 1956.

———. "Barriers to Understanding the Influence of the Use of Fire by Aborigines on Vegetation." *Proceedings, 2nd Annual Tall Timbers Fire Ecology Conference*, 117–26. Tallahassee, Fla.: Tall Timbers Research Station, 1963.

Stilgoe, John R. *The Common Landscape of America, 1580 to 1845*. New Haven, Conn.: Yale University Press, 1982.

Stjernquist, Per. *Laws in the Forests: A Study of Public Direction of Private Forestry*. Acta Societatis Humanorum Litterarum Lundensis, no. 69. Lund: C. W. K. Gleerup, 1973.

Stokes, George A. "Lumbering and Western Lousiana Landscapes." *Annals, Association of American Geographers* 47 (1957): 250–66.

Stott, Philip A. "Tropical Rainforest in Recent Ecological Thought: The Reassessment of a Non-Renewable Resource." *Progress in Physical Geography* 2 (1979): 80–98.

Strabo. *The Geography of Strabo*. With an English translation by Horace Leonard Jones. 8 vols. Loeb Classical Library. London: William Heinemann, 1923.

Strachey, William. *The Historie of Travelle into Virginia Britannia* [1612]. Edited by Louis B. Wright and Virginia Freund. Hayluyt Society, ser. 2, vol. 103. London: The Hakluyt Society, 1953.

Street, Francis Aleyne, and Alfred T. Grove. "Environmental and Climatic Implications of the Late Quaternary Lake Level Fluctuations in Africa." *Nature* 261 (1976): 385–90.

Street-Perrott, Francis Aleyne, R. A. Perrott, and D. D. Harkness. "Anthropogenic Soil Erosion around Lake Putzcuaro, Michoacan, Mexico during the Preclassic and Postclassic-Hispanic Periods." *American Antiquity* 54 (1989): 759–65.

Strong, Doland R. Jr., Daniel Simberloff, Lawrence G. Abele, and Anne B. Thistle, eds. *Ecological Communities: Conceptual Issues and the Evidence*. Princeton, N.J.: Princeton University Press, 1984.

Stuart, Anthony J. "Mammalian Extinctions in the Late Pleistocene of Northern Eurasia and North America." *Biological Reviews* 66 (1991): 453–62.

Stuart, James. *Three Years in North America*, 2d rev. ed. 2 vols. Edinburgh: R. Cadell, 1833.

Study of Man's Impact on Climate (SMIC). *Inadvertent Climate Modification*. Cambridge, Mass.: MIT Press, 1971.

Supple, Barry. "The Nature of Enterprise." In *The Cambridge Economic History of Europe*, vol. 5, *The Economic Organization of Early Modern Europe*, edited by Edwin Earnest Rich and Charles Henry Wilson, 394–461. Cambridge: Cambridge University Press, 1970.

Surell, Alexandre C. *Étude sur les torrents des Hautes-Alpes* [1841]. Reprint, Paris: Dunod, 1870.

Sutton, Keith. "Reclamation of Wasteland during the Eighteenth and Nineteenth Centuries." In *Themes in the Historical Geography of France*, edited by Hugh D. Clout, 247–300. London: Academic Press, 1977.

Sutton, W. R. J. "The Forest Resources of the U.S.S.R.: Their Exploitation and Their Potential." *Commonwealth Forestry Review* 54 (1956): 110–38.

Swank, James M. *The History of the Manufacture of Iron in All Ages and Particularly in the United States from Colonial Times to 1891*, 2d ed. Philadelphia: American Iron and Steel Association, 1892.

Sweezy, Paul M., and Harry Magdoff. "Capitalism and the Environment." *Monthly Review* 41, no. 2 (1989): 1–10.

Taeuber, Irene. *The Population of Japan*. Princeton, N.J.: Princeton University Press, 1958.

Takacs, David. *The Idea of Biodiversity: Philosophies of Paradise*. Baltimore: Johns Hopkins University Press, 1996.

Talbot, Charles H., ed. *The Anglo-Saxon Missionaries in Germany: Being the Lives of SS. Willibrord, Boniface, Sturm, Leoba, and Lebuin, together with the Hodoeporicon of St Willibald and a Selection from the Correspondence of St Boniface*. New York: Sheed and Ward, 1954.

Tauber, Henrik. "Differential Pollen Dispersal and the Interpretation of Pollen Diagrams." *Danmarks Geologiske Undersógelse*, ser. 2, 89 (1965): 1–69.

Tawney, Richard H. *Land and Labour in China*. London: G. Allen and Unwin, Ltd., 1932.

Tawney, Richard Henry, and Eileen Power. *Tudor Economic Documents: Being Select Documents Illustrating the Economic and Social History of Tudor England*. 3 vols. London: Longmans Green and Co., 1924.

Taylor, Bayard. *Colorado: A Summer Trip*. New York: G. P. Putnam and Sons, 1867.

Taylor, Joan C. "The Earliest Hunters, Gatherers and Farmers of North America." In *Hunters, Gatherers and First Farmers beyond Europe*, edited by J. V. S. Megaw, 119–224. Leicester: Leicester University Press, 1977.

Taylor, John. "Journal of Rev. John Taylor, Missionary, on Tour through the Mohawk and Black River Counties, in 1802." In *History of the State of New York,* edited by Edmund B. O'Callaghan, 3:1107–50. Albany, N.Y.: Weed Parsons, 1854.

Taylor, Royal E., ed. *Radiocarbon after Four Decades: An Interdisciplinary Perspective.* New York: Springer Verlag, 1992.

TeBrake, William H. "Air Pollution and Fuel Crises in Preindustrial London, 1280–1650." *Technology and Culture* 16 (1975): 337–59.

———. *Medieval Frontier: Culture and Ecology in Rijnland.* College Station: Texas A. & M. Press, 1985.

Tegoborski, M. Ludwick. *Commentaries on the Productive Forces of Russia.* 2 vols. London: Longman, Brown, Green and Longman, 1855.

Temin, Peter. *Iron and Steel in Nineteenth Century America: An Economic Inquiry.* Cambridge, Mass.: MIT Press, 1964.

Tertullian. "A Treatise on the Soul" (*De Anima*). Translated by Peter Holmes. In *The Ante-Nicene Fathers: Translations of the Writings of the Fathers down to A.D. 325,* edited by Alexander Roberts and James Donaldson, vol. 3, *Latin Christianity: Its Founder, Tertullian,* 181–235. Grand Rapids, Mich.: William B. Eerdmans Publishing Company, 1908.

Theophrastus. *Enquiry into Plants.* Translated from the Greek by Sir Arthur Hort. 2 vols. Loeb Classical Library. New York: G. P. Putnam's Sons, 1916.

Thirgood, Jack V. *Man and the Mediterranean Forest: A History of Resource Depletion.* London: Academic Press, 1981.

Thomas, Sir Dalby. *An Historical Account of the Rise and Growth of the West-India Colonies: And of the Great Advantage They are to England in Respect of Trade.* London: Printed for J. Hindmarsh, 1690.

Thomas, Keith. *Man and the Natural World: Changing Attitudes in England, 1500–1800.* London: Allan Lane, 1983. Also published under the title *Man and the Natural World: A History of the Modern Sensibility* (New York: Pantheon Books, 1983).

Thompson, Harry. *Costs and Methods of Clearing Land in Western Washington.* USDA, Bureau of Plant Industry, Bulletin no. 239. Washington, D.C.: GPO, 1912.

Thompson, James Westfall. "East German Colonization in the Middle Ages." *Annual Report and Proceedings of the American Historical Association for the year 1915* (1917): 125–50.

———. *An Economic and Social History of the Middle Ages (300–1300).* New York: The Century Co., 1928.

———. *Feudal Germany.* Chicago: University of Chicago Press, 1928.

Thompson, John E. S. *The Rise and Fall of Maya Civilization,* 2d ed. Norman: University of Oklahoma Press, 1966.

Thompson, Kenneth. "Forests and Climate Change in America: Some Early Views." *Climate Change* 3 (1983): 47–64.

Thompson, Virginia, and Richard Adloff. *French West Africa.* London: George Allen and Unwin, 1958.

Thompson, Warren S. "The Spiral of Population." In *Man's Role in Changing the Face of the Earth,* edited by William L. Thomas, 970–87. Chicago: University of Chicago Press, 1956.

Thomson, J. T. "The Precolonial Woodstock in Sahelien West Africa: The Example of Central Niger (Damagaram, Damergu Aïr)." In *Global Deforestation and the Nineteenth-Century World Economy,* edited by Richard P. Tucker and John F. Richards, 167–77. Duke Press Policy Studies. Durham, N.C.: Duke University Press, 1983.

———. "Deforestation and Desertification in Twentieth-Century Arid Sahelien Africa." In *World*

Deforestation in the Twentieth Century, edited by John F. Richards and Richard P. Tucker, 70–90. Duke Press Policy Studies. Durham, N.C.: Duke University Press, 1988.

Thoreau, Henry David. "Walking." In *The Writings of Henry David Thoreau,* edited by E. Scudder, vol. 9, *Excursions,* 251–304. Boston: Houghton Mifflin and Co., 1866.

———. *The Maine Woods* [1877]. Edited by Joseph J. Moldenhauer. Princeton, N.J.: Princeton University Press, 1972.

Thorner, Daniel. *Investment in Empire: British Railway and Steam Shipping Enterprises in India, 1825–1849.* Philadelphia: University of Pennsylvania Press, 1950.

"Threat from Amazon Burn-Off." *The* (London) *Times,* 6 August 1988.

Thucydides. *The History of the Peloponnesian War.* Translated from the Greek by William Smith. London: Jones and Co., 1832.

Tilley, Charles. *Coercion, Capital and European States, AD 990–1990.* Oxford: Basil Blackwell, 1990.

Tocqueville, Alexis de. *Democracy in America,* 3d ed. Translated by H. Reeves. 4 vols. London: Saundars and Otley, 1838.

———. *Journey to America.* Comprising 14 notebooks, including "A Fortnight in the Wilds." Translated by G. Lawrence and edited by J. P. Mayer. London: Faber and Faber, 1959.

Tomaselli, R. "Degradation of the Mediterranean Maquis." In UNESCO, *Mediterranean Forests and Maquis: Ecology, Conservation and Management,* 33–72. MAB Technical Notes, 2. Paris: UNESCO, 1977.

Tomich, T. "Indonesia's Fires: Smoke As a Problem: Smoke As a Symptom." *Agroforestry Today* 10, no 1 (1998), 13–17.

Torunsky, Richard, ed. *Weltforstatlas—World Forestry Atlas—Atlas des forêts du monde—Atlas forestal del mundo.* Herausgegeben von der Bundesforschungsanstalt für Forst-und Holzwirtschaft, Reinbek bei Hamburg. 2 vols. Hamburg: Verlag Paul Parey, 1951.

Tosi, Joseph A., and Voertman, Robert F. "Some Environmental Factors in the Economic Development of the Tropics." *Economic Geography* 40 (1964): 189–205.

Totman, Conrad D. "The Forests of Tokugawa Japan: A Catastrophe That Was Avoided." *Transactions of the Asiatic Society of Japan,* 3d ser., 18 (1983): 1–15.

———. "Logging the Unloggable: Timber Transport in Early Modern Japan." *Journal of Forest History* 27 (1983): 180–91.

———. "From Exploitation to Plantation Forestry in Early Modern Japan." In *History of Sustained Forestry: A Symposium,* edited by Harold K. Steen, 270–80. Durham N.C.: Forest History Society, 1984.

———. *The Origins of Japan's Modern Forests: The Case of Akita.* Honolulu: University of Hawaii Press, 1985.

———. "Lumber Provisioning in Early Modern Japan, 1580–1850." *Journal of Forest History* 31 (1987): 56–70.

———. *The Green Archipelago: Forestry in Pre-Industrial Japan.* Berkeley and Los Angeles: University of California Press, 1989.

Toutain, Jules F. *The Economic Life of the Ancient World.* London: Kegan Paul, Trench, Trubner and Co., Ltd., 1930.

Townsend, William H. "Stone and Steel Tool Use in a New Guinea Society." *Ethnology* 8 (1969): 199–205.

Toynbee, Arnold J., ed. and trans. *Greek Historical Thought from Homer to the Age of Heraclius.* London: J. M. Dent and Sons, 1924.

Tracy, James D., ed. *The Rise of Merchant Empires: Long Distance Trade in the Early Modern World, 1350–1750.* Cambridge: Cambridge University Press, 1990.

————. *The Political Economy of Merchant Empires*. Cambridge: Cambridge University Press, 1991.

Trigger, Bruce G. *The Huron: Farmers of the North*. New York: Holt, Rinehart and Winston, 1969.

Troels-Smith, Jorgen A. "Ertebólletidens Fangstfolk og Bónder." *Fra Nationalmuseets Arbejdsmark* (1960): 95–119.

————. "Ivy, Mistletoe and Elm: Climatic Indicator-Fodder Plants." *Danmarks Geologiske Undersógelse*, ser. 4, vol. 4, no. 4 (1960): 1–32.

Tropical Forests: A Call for Action. Report of an International Task Force convened by the World Resources Institute, The World Bank, and the United Nations Development Programme. 3 vols. Washington, D.C.: World Resources Institute, 1985.

Trotter, Michael M., and Beverley McCulloch. "Moas, Men and Middens." In *Quaternary Extinctions*, edited by Paul S. Martin and Richard G. Klein, 708–27. Tucson: University of Arizona Press, 1984.

Tseplyaev, V. P. *Lesnoye Khozyaystvo SSR*. Moscow: Lesnaya Promyshlennost, 1965.

Tsukada, Matduo. "The Pollen Sequence." In *The History of Laguna de Petenxil*, edited by Ursula M. Cowgill and G. Evelyn Hutchinson. *Memoirs if the Connecticut Academy of Arts and Sciences* 17 (1966): 63–66.

Tuan, Yi-fu. *China*. London: Longman, 1966.

————. "Discrepancies between Environmental Attitude and Behaviour: Examples from China." *Canadian Geographer* 12 (1968): 176–91.

Tucker, Compton J., B. N. Holben, and T. E. Goff. "Intensive Forest Clearing in Rondonia, Brazil, As Detected by Satellite Remote Sensing." *Remote Sensing Environment* 15 (1984): 255–61.

Tucker, Compton J., J. R. G. Townsend, T. E. Goff, and B. N. Holben. "Continental and Global Scale Remote Sensing of Land Cover." In *The Changing Carbon Cycle: A Global Analysis*, edited by John R. Trabalka and Dale E. Reichle, 221–41. New York: Springer-Verlag, 1986.

Tucker, Richard P. "Forest Management and Imperial Politics: Thana District, Bombay, 1823–1887." *Indian Economic and Social History Review* 16 (1979): 273–300.

————. "The British Colonial System and the Forests of the Western Himalayas, 1815–1914." In *Global Deforestation and the Nineteenth Century World Economy*, edited by Richard P. Tucker and John F. Richards, 146–66. Duke Press Policy Studies. Durham, N.C.: Duke University Press, 1983.

————. "The Depletion of Indian Forests under British Imperialism: Planters, Foresters, and Peasants in Assam and Kerala." In *The Ends of Earth: Essays in Environmental History*, edited by Don Worster, 118–41. Cambridge: Cambridge University Press, 1988.

Turner, Billie Lee II. "Prehistoric Intensive Agriculture in the Mayan Lowlands." *Science* 185 (1974): 118–24.

————. "Issues Related to Subsistence and Environment among the Ancient Maya." In *Prehistoric Lowland Maya Environment and Subsistence Economy*, edited by Mary Pohl. Papers of the Peabody Museum, Harvard University, vol. 77. Cambridge, Mass.: Harvard University Press, 1985.

————. "The Rise and Fall of Population and Agriculture in the Central Maya Lowlands: 300 B.C. to Present." In *Hunger in History: Food Shortage, Poverty and Deprivation*, edited by Lucile F. Newman, 178–211. Oxford: Basil Blackwell, 1990.

Turner, Billie Lee II, and Karl W. Butzer. "The Columbian Encounter and Land-Use Change." *Environment* 34, no.8 (1992): 16–44.

Turner, Frederick Jackson. *The Frontier in American History*, New York: Holt, 1920.

Turner, Orsamus. *A Pioneer History of the Holland Purchase of Western New York*. Buffalo, N.Y.: Jewett Thomas, 1849.

Twining, Charles E. *Downriver: Orrin H. Ingram and the Empire Lumber Company.* Madison: State Historical Society of Wisconsin, 1975.

Ucko, Peter J., and Geoffrey W. Dimbleby, eds. *The Domestication and Exploitation of Plants and Animals.* London: G. Duckworth, 1969.

Uhl, Christopher, Daniel Nepstad, Robert Buschbacher, Kathleen Clark, Boone Kauffman, and Scott Subler. "Studies of Ecosystem Response to Natural and Anthropogenic Disturbances Provide Guidelines for Designing Sustainable Land-Use Systems in Amazonia." In *Alternatives to Deforestation: Steps toward Sustainable Use of the Amazon Rain Forest,* edited by Anthony B. Andrews, 24–42. New York: Columbia University Press, 1990.

Uhl, Christopher, and Ima C. G. Vieira. "Ecological Impacts of Selective Logging in the Brazilian Amazon: A Case Study from the Paragominas Region of the State of Pará." *Biotropica* 21 (1989): 98–106.

UNESCO. *International Classification and Mapping of Vegetation.* Paris: UNESCO, 1973.

United Kingdom. *Calendar of State Papers, Colonial, 1675–76.* London: HMSO.

———. Forestry Commission. *Fourth Annual Report of the Forestry Commissioners, 1923.* London: H.M.S.O., 1924.

———. Historical Manuscripts Commission. *Report of the MSS of the Earl of Mar and Kellie,* 212–73. London: H.M.S.O., 1904.

———. House of Commons. "Minute by the Most Noble, the Governor-General; dated 20th April, 1853: Railways in India." *Parliamentary Papers* 76 (1852–53), 593–622.

Unwin, Harold A. *West African Forests and Forestry.* London: T. Fisher Unwin, 1920.

Uquillas, J. "Colonization and Spontaneous Settlement in the Ecuadoran Amazon." In *Frontier Expansion in Amazonia,* edited by Marianne Schmink and Charles H. Wood, 261–84. Gainesville: University of Florida Press, 1984.

U.S. Bureau of the Census. *Manufactures.* "Power Used in Manufactures." Tenth Census (1880), 2:13–18.

———. *Manufactures: Special Reports for Selected Industries.* Fourteenth Census (1919), 10: 410–40.

———. *Historical Statistics of the United States from Colonial Times to 1957.* A statistical abstract supplement prepared by the Bureau of the Census with the cooperation of the Social Science Research Council. Washington, D.C.: G.P.O., 1960. Revised, updated and reprinted, 1977.

U.S. Bureau of Corporations. *The Lumber Industry.* 3 vols. Vol. 1, pt. 1, "Standing Timber" (1913); vol. 2, pt. 2, "Concentration of Timber Ownership in Important Selected Regions"; pt. 3, "Land Holdings of the Large Timber Owners" (1914); and vol. 3, pt. 4, "Conditions in Production and Wholesale Distribution Including Wholesale Prices" (1914). Washington, D.C.: GPO. Also in U.S. Congress, Senate, 61st Cong., 3d sess., S. Doc. 818, serial no. 5943. Washington, D.C.: GPO, 1910–11.

U.S. Congress. House. *Patent Office Annual Report, 1847.* 30th Cong., 1st sess., H. Doc. 54, serial no. 519. Washington, D.C.: GPO, 1848.

U.S. Congress. Office of Technology Assessment. *Technologies to Maintain Biological Diversity.* Washington, D.C.: GPO, 1987.

U.S. Congress. Senate. *Letter from the Secretary of the Treasury Transmitting Information on Steam Engines.* 25th Cong., 3d sess., S. Ex. Doc. 21, serial no. 345. Washington, D.C.: GPO, 1838.

U.S. Congress, Senate. *Report of the National Conservation Commission.* Edited by Henry Gannett. 3 vols. 60th Cong., 2d sess., S. Doc. 676, serial no. 5397–99. Washington, D.C.: GPO, 1909.

USDA Forest Service. *A National Plan for American Forestry* (The Copeland Report). 73d Cong., 1st sess., S. Doc. 12, serial nos. 9740, 9741. 2 vols. Washington, D.C.: GPO, 1933.

———. *An Analysis of the Timber Situation in the United States, 1952–2030.* Forest Resources Report no. 23. Washington, D.C.: GPO, 1982.

———. *An Analysis of the Timber Situation in the United States, 1989–2040.* A Technical document supporting the 1989 USDA Forest Service RPA Assessment. Rocky Mountain Forest and Range Experiment Station, General Technical Report RM-199. Fort Collins, Colo.: Rocky Mountain Forest and Range Experiment Station, 1990.

USDA Forestry Division. *Forest Influences.* Forestry Division Bulletin no. 7. Washington, D.C.: GPO, 1893.

U.S. Department of Agriculture. *Annual Report of the Commissioner of Agriculture, 1862–.* Washington, D.C.: GPO, 1862–.

———. *Agriultural Census, 1910–1979.* Washington, D.C.: GPO.

———. *Annual Report of the Commissioner of Agriculture, 1872–.* Washington, D.C.: GPO, 1872–.

U.S. Forest Service. *Timber Depletion, Lumber Prices, Lumber Exports and Concentration of Timber Ownership* [Capper Report]. U.S. Congress, Senate, 66th Cong., 2d sess. Report on S. Res. 11. Washington, D.C.: GPO, 1920.

U.S. Government. *Forestry in Europe: Reports from the Consuls of the United States.* Washington, D.C.: GPO, 1887.

U.S. Interagency Task Force on Tropical Forests. *The World's Tropical Forests: A Policy Strategy and Program for the United States.* Report to the president, Department of State Publication 9117. Washington, D.C.: GPO, 1980.

Van der Meer, Frederik. *Atlas de l'ordre Cistercien.* Paris: Editions Sequoia, 1965. Esp. plates 1, 2–13.

Van der Wee, Herman. "Monetary, Credit and Banking Systems." In *The Cambridge Economic History of Europe,* vol. 5, *The Economic Organization of Early Modern Europe,* edited by Edwin Earnest Rich and Charles Henry Wilson, 290–393. Cambridge: Cambridge University Press, 1970.

Van Ravenswaay, Charles. "America's Age of Wood." *Proceedings, American Antiquarian Society* 80 (1970): 49–66.

Van Tassel, Alfred J., and David W. Bluestone. *Mechanization in the Lumber Industry: A Study in Technology in Relation to Resources and Employment Opportunity.* National Research Project Report no. M-5. Philadelphia: Works Project Administration, 1940.

Vance, Rupert B. *The Human Geography of the South: A Study in Regional Resources and Human Adequacy.* Chapel Hill: University of North Carolina Press, 1932.

Varro, Marcus Terentius. *De re Rustica* (On agriculture). Translated from the Latin by William Hooper; revised by Harrison B. Ash. Loeb Classical Library. Cambridge, Mass., Harvard University Press, 1936.

Vashishta, H. B. *Land Revenue and Public Finance in Maratha Administration.* Delhi: Oriental Publishers and Distributors, 1975.

Vauban, Sebastian le Prestre de. *Project d'une dixime royale* [1705]. Translated and reprinted, London, as Anonymous under the title *An Essay for a General Tax; or a Project for a Royal Tythe:* John Matthews for Geo. Strahan, 1710.

Vavilov, Nikolai I. "Studies on the Origins of Cultivated Plants." *Bulletin of Applied Botany and Plant Breeding* 16 (1926): 1–245.

Vecsey, Christopher, and Venables, Robert W., eds. *American Indian Environments: Ecological Issues in Native American History.* Syracuse, N.Y.: Syracuse University Press, 1980.

Vega, Garcilaso de la. *The Florida of the Inca: A History of Adelantado, Hernando de Soto* [1608].

Translated and edited by John G. Varner and Jeannatta J. Varner. 2. vols. Austin: University of Texas Press, 1980.

Verhulst, Andi E. "Karolingische Agarpolitik: Das *Capitulare de villis* und die Hungernöte von 792/93 und 805/06." *Zeitschrift für Agrargeschichte und Agrarsoziologie* 13 (1965): 175–89.

Vidal, J. "The Thousand Mile Shroud." Manchester *Guardian Weekend,* 8 September 1997, Foreign News, p. 5.

Virgil. *The Georgics.* Translated by L. P. Wilkinson. Harmondsworth, England: Penguin Books, 1982.

———. *The Ecologues.* Latin text with a verse translation by Guy Lee. Harmondsworth, England: Penguin Books, 1984.

Vita-Finzi, Claudio. *The Mediterranean Valleys: Geological Changes in Historical Times.* Cambridge: Cambridge University Press, 1969.

Voelcker, John Augustus. *Report on the Improvement of Indian Agriculture.* London: Eyre and Spottiswood, 1893.

Vogt, William. *Road to Survival.* London: Victo Gollancz, 1949.

Volney, Constantine François Chasseboeuf. *A View of the Climate and Soil of the United States of America.* London: J.Johnson, 1804.

Vuorela, Irmeli. "Palynological and Historical Evidence of Slash and Burn Cultivation in South Finland." In *Anthropogenic Indicators in Pollen Diagrams,* edited by Karl-Ernst Behre, 53–64. Rotterdam: Balkema, 1986.

Wadham, Samuel M., and G. L. Wood. *Land Utilization in Australia.* Melbourne: Melbourne University Press, 1939.

Wadia, Ruttonji Ardeshir. *The Bombay Dockyard and Wadia Master Builders.* Bombay: R. A. Wadia, 1955.

Walker, Egbert H. "The Plants of China and Their Usefulness to Man." In *Smithsonian Institution Annual Report,* 1943, 325–62. Washington, D.C.: Smithsonian Institution, 1944.

Wallace, Robert. *India in 1887 as Seen by Robert Wallace.* Edinburgh: Oliver and Boyd, 1888.

Wallerstein, Immanuel M. *The Modern World System I: Capitalist Agriculture and the Origins of the European World-Economy in the Sixteenth Century.* London: Academic Press, 1974.

———. *The Modern World System II: Mercantilism and the Consolidation of the European World-Economy, 1600–1750.* New York: Academic Press, 1980.

———. *The Modern World System III: The Second Era of Great Expansion of the Capitalist World-Economy, 1730–1840s.* New York: Academic Press, 1989.

Walvin, James. *Fruits of Empire: Exotic Produce and British Taste, 1600–1800.* Basingstoke, England: MacMillan, 1997.

Wansey, Henry. *Journal of an Excursion in the United States in the Summer of 1794.* London: G. T. Wilkie, 1796.

Wardle, Philip, and Massimo Palmieri. "What Does Fuelwood Really Cost?" *Unasylva* 33, no. 131 (1981): 20–23.

Ward-Price, Henry L. *Land Tenure in the Yoruba Provinces.* London: Jarrolds, 1939.

Warner, Sam Bass. "Population Movements and Urbanization." In *Technology in Western Civilization,* edited by Melvin Kranzberg and Carroll W. Pursell Jr., vol. 1, *The Emergence of Modern Industrial Society—Earliest Times to 1900,* 532–46. New York: Oxford University Press, 1967.

Warntz, William. "Newton, the Newtonians, and the *Geographica Generalis Varenii*." *Annals, Association of American Geographers* 79 (1989): 165–91.

Warren, Kenneth. *The American Steel Industry, 1850–1970: A Geographical Interpretation.* Oxford: Oxford University Press, 1973.

Watson, Andrew M. "Towards a Denser and More Continuous Settlement: New Crops and Farming Techniques in the Early Middle Ages." In *Pathways to Medieval Peasants,* edited by James Ambrose Raftis, 65–82. Toronto: Pontifical Institute of Medieval Studies, 1981.

Watters, Raymond Frederick. *Shifting Cultivation in Latin America.* FAO Forestry Development Paper no. 17. Rome: FAO, 1971.

Watts, David. *Man's Influence on the Vegetation of Barbados: 1627–1800.* Occasional Papers in Geography, no.4. Hull, England: University of Hull Department of Geography, 1966.

———. *The West Indies: Patterns of Development, Culture, and Environmental Change since 1492.* Cambridge: Cambridge University Press, 1987.

Webb, Thompson III. "Eastern North America." In *Vegetation History,* edited by Brian Huntley and Thompson Webb IIII, 385–414. Dordrecht: Kluwer Academic Publishers, 1988.

Webb, Walter Prescott. *The Great Frontier.* Boston: Houghton Mifflin, 1952.

Weber, Max. *The Protestant Ethic and the Spirit of Capitalism.* Translated from the German by Talcott Parsons. New York: Scribners, 1952.

Webster, Noah. "Dissertation on the Supposed Change of Temperature in Modern Winters" [1799]. Printed in Webster, *A Collection of Papers on Political, Literary, and Moral Subjects,* 119–62. New York: Webster and Clark, 1843.

Weck, Johannes, and C. Wiebecke. *Weltforstwirtschaft und Deutschlands Forst—und Holzwirtschaft.* Munich: BLU Verlagsgesellschaft, 1961.

Weisberger, Bernard A. *The New Industrial Society.* New York: John Wiley, 1969.

Weld, Issac. *Travels through the States of North America and Provinces of Upper and Lower Canada during the Years 1795, 1796, and 1797,* 2d ed. 2 vols. London: John Stockdale, 1799.

Wells, K. F., N. H. Wood, and Peter Laut. *Loss of Forests and Woodlands in Australia: A Summary by State, Based on Rural Local Government Areas.* CSIRO Technical Memorandum 84/4. Canberra: CSIRO, Institute of Resources, Division of Water and Land Resources, 1984.

Welsh, James. *Military Reminiscences: Extracted from a Journal of Nearly Forty Years' Active Service in the East Indies,* 2d ed. 2 vols. London: Smith Elder and Co., 1830.

Wernstedt, Frederick L., and Joseph E. Spenser. *The Philippine Island World.* Berkeley and Los Angeles: University of California Press, 1967.

Wertime, Theodore A. "Cypriot Metallurgy against the Backdrop of Mediterranean Pyrotechnology: Energy Reconsidered." In *Early Metallurgy in Cyprus, 4000–500 B.C.,* edited by James Muhly, Robert Maddin, and Vassos Karageorghis, 351–62. Nicosià, Cyprus: Pierides Foundation in collaboration with the Department of Antiquities, Nicosia, 1982.

———. "The Furnace versus the Goat: The Pyrotechnologic Industries and Mediterranean Deforestation in Antiquity." *Journal of Field Archaeology* 10 (1983): 445–52.

Wertime, Theodore A., and Stephen F. Wertime, eds. *The Evolution of the First Fire-Using Industries,* 135–156. Papers presented at a seminar on early pyrotechnology held at the Smithsonian Institution, Washington, D.C. and the National Bureau of Standards, Gaithersburg, Md. 19–20 April 1979. Washington , D.C.: Smithsonian Institution Press Microfiche, 1982.

Westoby, Jack. *The Purpose of Forests: Follies of Development.* Oxford: Basil Blackwell, 1989.

Whitaker, J. R. "World View of Destruction and Conservation of Natural Resources." *Annals, Association of American Geographers* 30 (1940): 143–62.

White, Andrew. "A Relation of the Colony of the Lord Baron of Baltimore in Maryland, near Virginia." In *A Narrative of the Voyage to Maryland by Father Andrew White* [1644]. In *Tracts and Other Papers,* edited by P. Force, vol. 4, no. 12. Washington, D.C.: P. Force, 1836.

——. "A Briefe Relation of the Voyage unto Maryland" [1634]. In *Narratives of Early Maryland, 1633–1684,* edited by C. C. Hall, 25–46. New York: C.Scribner's Sons 1910.

White, F. M., and E. R. Jones. *Getting Rid of Stumps.* University of Wisconsin Agricultural Experimental Station Bulletin no. 295. Madison: University of Wisconsin, 1918.

White, Kenneth D. *Roman Farming.* London: Thames and Hudson, 1970.

——. *Farm Equipment of the Roman World.* Cambridge: Cambridge University Press, 1975.

White, Lynn Jr. "Technology and Invention in the Middle Ages." *Speculum* 15 (1940): 141–59.

——. *Medieval Technology and Social Change.* Oxford: Clarendon Press, 1962.

——. "What Accelerated Technological Progress in the Western Middle Ages?" In *Scientific Change: Historical Studies in the Intellectual, Social, and Technical Conditions for Scientific Discovery and Technical Invention, from Antiquity to the Present,* edited by A. C. Crombie, 272–91. London: Heinemann, 1963.

——. "The Historical Roots of Our Ecologic Crisis." *Science* 156 (1967): 1203–7.

——. "Cultural Climates and Technological Advance in the Middle Ages." *Viator: Medieval and Renaissance Studies* 2 (1971): 171–201.

——. "The Expansion of Technology, 500–1500." In *The Fontana Economic History of Europe,* edited by Carlo M. Cipolla, vol. 1, *The Middle Ages,* 143–74. Brighton: Harvester Press, 1976

White, Philip L. *Beekmantown, New York: Forest Frontier to Farm Community.* Austin: University of Texas Press, 1978.

Whitfield, William A. D. *Soil Survey of England and Wales: The Soils of Warwickshire, VI.* Soil Survey Record no. 101. Harpenden, England: Soil Survey of England and Wales.

Whithed, Tamara Louise. "The Struggle for the Forest in the French Alps and Pyrenees, 1860–1940." Ph.D. diss., University of California, Berkeley, 1994.

——. *Forests and Peasant Politics in Modern France.* New Haven, Conn.: Yale University Press, 2000.

Whitmore, Thomas M., and Billie Lee Turner II. "Landscapes of Cultivation in Mesoamerica on the Eve of the Conquest." *Annals, Association of American Geographers* 82 (1992): 402–25.

Whitmore, Timothy C. *Tropical Rain Forests of the Far East* (with a chapter on soils by C. P. Burnham). Oxford: Clarendon Press, 1984.

——. *Tropical Deforestation and Species Extinction.* IUCN Forest Conservation Programme. London: Chapman Hall, 1992.

Whittaker, Robert H., and G. E. Likens. "Primary Productivity: The Biosphere and Man." *Human Ecology* 1 (1973): 357–69.

Whittaker, Robert H., and George M. Woodwell. "Measurement of Net Primary Productivity in Forests." In *Symposium on the Productivity of Forest Ecosystems,* edited by Paul Duvigneaud, 159–75. Paris: UNESCO, 1971.

Whittle, Alasdair. *Neolithic Europe: A Survey.* Cambridge: Cambridge University Press, 1985.

——. "Gifts from the Earth: Symbolic Dimensions of the Use and Production of Neolithic Flint and Stone Axes." *Archaelogia Polona* 33 (1995): 247–59.

Whittlesey, Derwent S. *The Earth and the State: A Study of Political Geography.* New York: Holt, 1944.

Wibe, Sören, and Tom Jones. *Forests: Market and Intervention Failures.* London: Earthscan, 1992.

Wickham, Christopher. "European Forests in the Early Middle Ages: Landscape and Clearance." *L'ambiente vegetale nell'alto medioevo* 37 (1990): 479–545. Spoleto, Italy: Setimane di studio del Centro italiano di studi sull'alto medioevo.

Wiebe, Georg. *Zur Geschichte der Preisrevolution des XVI und XVII Jahrhunderts.* Leipzig: Dunder and Humblot, 1895.

Wieczynski, Joseph L. *The Russian Frontier: The Impact of Borderlands upon the Course of Early Russian History.* Charlottesville: University Press of Virginia, 1976.

Wilcox, Bruce A., and Kristin N. Duin. "Indigenous Cultural and Biological Diversity: Overlapping Values of Latin American Ecoregions." *Cultural Survival Quarterly* (winter 1995): 49–53.

Wilde, Oscar. *The Picture of Dorian Gray* [1891]. London: Peerage Books, 1991.

Wilks, Ivor. "Land, Labour and the Forest Kingdom of Asante: A Model of Early Change." In *The Evolution of Social Systems,* edited by John Friedmann and Michael J. Rowlands, 487–534. London: Duckworth, 1978.

Williams, Barbara J. "Tepetate in the Valley of Mexico." *Annals, Association of American Geographers* 62 (1972): 618–26.

Williams, D. R. "Merchanting in the First Half of the Nineteenth Century: The Liverpool Timber Trade." *Business History* 8 (1966), 103–21.

———. "Bulk Carriers and Timber Imports: The British North America Trade and the Shipping Boom of 1824–5." *Mariner's Mirror* 54 (1968): 373–82.

Williams, Justin. "England's Colonial Naval Stores Policy, 1588–1776." *University of Iowa Studies in the Social Sciences,* 10, no. 3 (1934): 32–45.

Williams, Michael. *The Making of the South Australian Landscape.* London: Academic Press, 1974.

———. "Marshland and Waste." In *The English Medieval Landscape,* edited by Leonard M. Cantor, 86–125. London: Croom Helm, 1982.

———. "Clearing the Woods." In *The Australian Experience,* edited by R. Leslie Heathcote, 115–26. Melbourne: Longmans Cheshire, 1988.

———. *Americans and Their Forests: A Historical Geography.* New York: Cambridge University Press, 1989.

———. "The Clearing of the Forests." In *The Making of the American Landscape,* edited by Michael P. Conzen, 146–68. London: Unwin Hyman, 1990.

———. "Forests." In *The Earth As Transformed by Human Action: Global and Regional Changes in the Biosphere over the Past 300 Years,* edited by Billie Lee Turner II, William C. Clark, Robert W. Kates, John F. Richards, Jessica T. Mathews, and William B. Meyer, 179–201. New York: Cambridge University Press, 1990.

——— "Protection and Retrospection." In *Wetlands: A Threatened Landscape,* edited by Michael Williams, 323–53. Oxford: Blackwell, 1990.

———. "Forests and Tree Cover." In *Changes in Land Use and Land Cover: A Global Perspective,* edited by William B. Meyer and Billie Lee Turner II, 97–124. Cambridge: Cambridge University Press, 1994.

———. "The Last Lumber Frontier." In *The Historical Geography of the Mountainous West,* edited by William Wykoff and Larry Dilsalver, 224–50. Lincoln: University of Nebraska Press, 1995.

———. "The End of Modern History?" *Geographical Review* 88 (1998): 275–300.

———. "'Dark Ages and Dark Areas': Global Deforestation in the Deep Past." *Journal of Historical Geography* 26 (2000): 28–46.

Williams, P. H., Kevin J. Gaston, and C. J. Humphreys. "Do Conservationists and Molecular Biologists Value Differences between Organisms in the Same Way?" *Biodiversity Letters* 2 (1994): 67–78.

Williamson, Hugh. "An Attempt to Account for the CHANGE IN CLIMATE, which has been Observed in the Middle Colonies in North America." *Transactions of the Amerian Philosophical Society* 1 (1789): 337–45 (2d ed., corrected).

Williston, Hamlin L. *A Statistical History of Tree Planting in the South, 1925–79.* Atlanta: USDA Forest Service, 1979.

Wilson, Charles H. *Anglo-Dutch Commerce and Finance in the Eighteenth Century.* Cambridge: Cambridge University Press, 1941.

Wilson, Edward O. *Biophilia.* Cambridge, Mass.: Harvard University Press, 1984.

———. "Threats to Biodiversity." *Scientific American* 261 (September 1989): 60, 62–66.

———. Foreword in *Biodiversity, Culture, Conservation and Ecodevelopment,* edited by Margery L. Oldfield and James B. Alcorn. Boulder, Colo.: Westview Press, 1991.

———, ed. *Biodiversity.* Washington, D.C.: National Academy Press, 1988.

Wilson, Ernest Henry. *A Naturalist in Western China with Vasculum, Camera and Gun.* 2 vols. New York: Doubleday, Page and Co., 1913.

Wilson, Samuel. "An Account of the Province of Carolina in America, together with an Abstract of the Patent" [1682]. In *Narratives of Early Carolina, 1650–1708,* edited by Alexander S. Saley, 161–76. New York: Charles Scribner's Sons, 1911.

Windhorst, H. W. "Das Ertagspotential der Wälder der Erde." *Studien zur Walkwirtschaffgeographic* (special issue of *Geographischen Zeitschrift*) 39 (1974): 40–49.

Winthrop, John. *Winthrop Papers, 1631–37.* Vol. 3 (1943). Boston: Massachusetts Historical Society, 1929–47.

———. *Winthrop's Journal: "History of New England"* [1630–49]. Edited by J. H. Hosmer. 2 vols. New York: Barnes and Noble, 1966.

Wiseman, F. M. "Agriculture and Vegetation Dynamics of the Maya Collapse in Central Petén, Guatemala." In *Prehistoric Lowland Maya Environment and Subsistence Economy,* edited by Mary Pohl, 63–72. Papers of the Peabody Museum, Harvard University, vol. 77. Cambridge, Mass.: Harvard University Press, 1985.

Witney, K. P. "The Woodland Economy of Kent, 1066–1348." *Agricultural History Review* 38 (1990): 20–39.

Wittfogel, Karl. *Oriental Despotism.* New Haven, Conn.: Yale University Press, 1953.

Woeikof, Alexandre. "De l'influence de l'homme sur la terre." *Annales de géographie* 10 (1901): 97–114, 193–215.

Wolf, Edward C. *On the Brink of Extinction: Conserving the Diversity of Life.* Worldwatch Paper no. 78. Washington, D.C.: Worldwatch Institute, 1987.

Wolf, Eric R. *Europe and the People without History.* Berkeley and Los Angeles: University of California Press, 1982.

Wood, Richard G. "A History of Lumbering in Maine, 1820–1860." University of Maine Studies in History and Government, 2d ser., 33. Orono: University of Maine Press, 1935.

Woodruff, William. *The Impact of Western Man: A Study of Europe's Role in the World Economy, 1750–1960.* New York: St. Martin's Press, 1967.

Woods, William I. "Maize Agriculture and the Late Prehistoric: A Characterization of Settlement Location Strategies." In *Emergent Horticultural Economies of the Eastern Woodlands,* edited by F. W. Keegan, 275–94. Southern Illinois University Center for Archaeological Investigations Occasional Paper no. 7. Carbondale: Southern Illinois University, 1987.

Woodwell, George M., Richard A. Houghton, Thomas A. Stone, R. F. Nelson, and W. Kovalick. "Deforestation in the Tropics: New Measurements in the Amazon Basin Using Landsat and NOAA Advanced Very High Resolution Radiometer Imagery." *Journal of Geophysical Research* 92, no. D2 (1987): 2157–63.

Woodwell, George M., Richard A. Houghton, Thomas A. Stone, and Archibald B. Park. "Changes in the Area of Forests in Rondônia, Amazon Basin, Measured by Satellite Imagery." In *The*

Changing Carbon Cycle: A Global Analysis, edited by John R. Trabalka and David E. Reichle, 242–57. New York: Springer-Verlag, 1986.

Wooldridge, Sidney W. "The Anglo-Saxon Settlement." In *An Historical Geography of England before A.D. 1800,* edited by H. Clifford Darby, 88–132. Cambridge: Cambridge University Press, 1936.

World Meteorological Organization (WMO). *Report of the International Assessment of the Role of Carbon Dioxide and Other Greenhouse Gases in Climate Variation and Associated Impacts.* WMO no. 661. WMO, Villach, Austria, 9 to 15 October 1985. Geneva: WMO, 1985.

World Resources Institute (WRI) and International Institute for Environment and Development. *World Resources: An Assessment of the Resource Base That Supports the Global Economy.* New York: Basic Books and Oxford University Press, 1986, 1987, 1988–89 1990–91, 1992–93, 1994–95, and 1998–99.

Woronoff, Denis. "La crise de la forêt française pendant la Révolution et L'Empire: L'indicateur sidérurgique." *Cahiers d'historie* 24 (1979): 3–17.

———. *L'industire sidérurgique en France pendant la Révolution et l'Empire.* Paris: École des Hautes Études en Sciences Social, Centre de Recherches Historiques, 1984.

———. "La 'dévastation révolutionnaire' des forêts." In *Révolution et espaces forestiers,* edited by Denis Woronoff, 44–52. Paris: Éditions L'Harmattan, 1988.

Worster, Donald. *Dustbowl: The Southern Plains in the 1930s.* New York: Oxford University Press, 1979.

———. *Nature's Economy: A History of Ecological Ideas.* Cambridge: Cambridge University Press, 1985.

Wright, H. E. Jr. "Natural Environment of Early Food Production North of Mesopotamia." *Science* 161 (1968): 334–39.

———. "The Environmental Setting for Plant Domestication in the Near East." *Science* 194 (1976): 385–89.

Wrigley, Edward Anthony, and Roger S. Schofield. *The Population History of England, 1541–1871.* Cambridge, Mass.: Harvard University Press, 1981.

Wynne, Graeme. *Timber Colony: A Historical Geography of Early Nineteenth Century New Brunswick.* Toronto: Toronto University Press, 1981.

Yarnell, Richard A. "Early Plant Husbandry in Eastern North America." In *Cultural Change and Continuity: Essays in Honor of James Bennett Griffin,* edited by Charles E. Cleland, 265–73. New York: Academic Press, 1976.

Yarranton, Andrew. *England's Improvement by Sea and Land, to out-do the Dutch without Fighting.* London: R. Everingham, 1677.

Yasuda, Yoshinori. "Early Historic Forest Clearance around the Ancient Castle Site of Tagajo, Miyagi Prefecture, Japan." *Asian Perspectives* 19 (1978): 42–58.

Young, Alexander. *Chronicles of the Pilgrim Fathers of the Colony of Plymouth from 1602 to 1625.* Boston: C. C. Little and J. Brown, 1841.

Young, Arthur. *Travels During the Years 1787, 1788 and 1789 . . . in the Kingdom of France.* 2 vols. Dublin: S. Powell, 1793.

Young, Charles. *The Royal Forests of Medieval England.* Philadelphia: Pennsylvania University Press, 1979.

Young, David Bruce. "Forests, Mines and Fuel: The Question of Wood and Coal in Eighteenth-Century France." *Proceedings of the Third Annual Meeting of the Western Society for French History,* Santa Barbara, Calif., 4–6 December 1975: 328–37.

Youngson, A. S. "The Opening up of New Territories." In *The Cambridge Economic History of Europe,* vol. 6, *The Industrial Revolution and After: Incomes, Population and Technological*

Change, edited by H. John Habakkuk Michael Postan, 139–221. Cambridge: Cambridge University Press, 1965.

Zeigler, E. A. "Rate of Forest Growth." In U.S.Congress, Senate, *Report of the National Conservation Commission,* 60th Cong., 2d sess., S. Doc. 676, serial no. 5398, vol. 2, 203–69. Washington, D.C.: GPO, 1909.

Zeist, Willem van, and S. Bottema. "Vegetational History of the Eastern Mediterranean and the Near East during the Last 20,000 Years." In *Palaeoclimates, Palaeoenvironments and Human Communities in the Eastern Mediterranean Region in Later Prehistory,* edited by John L. Bintliff and Willem van Zeist, 277–321. British Archaeological Reports, International Series, no. 133. Oxford: B.A.R., 1982.

Zimmermann, Erich W. "The Forest and Its Products." In *World Resources and Industries,* edited by Erich W. Zimmermann. New York: Harper and Row, 1951.

Zohary, Daniel, and Maria Hopf. *Domestication of Plants in the Old World: The Origin and Spread of Cultivated Plants in West Asia, Europe and the Nile Valley,* 2d ed. Oxford: Clarendon Press, 1993.

Zohary, Daniel, and Pinchas Spiegel-Roy. "The Beginnings of Fruit-Growing in the Old World." *Science* 187 (1975): 319–27.

Zon, Raphael. *The Forest Resources of the World.* USFS Bulletin 83. Washington, D.C.: GPO, 1910.

———. "South American Forest Resources and Their Relation to the World's Timber Supply." In *Proceedings, Second Pan-American Scientific Congress,* edited by G. L. Swiggett, vol. 3, *Conservation of Natural Resources,* 483–92. Washington D.C: GPO, 1915–16.

———. "Forests and Water in the Light of Scientific Investigations." Appendix 5, Final Report of the National Waterways Commission. U.S. Congress, Senate, 62d Cong., 2d sess., 1912, S. Doc. 469. Reprint, Washington, D.C.: U.S. Department of Agriculture Forest Service, 1927.

———. "The Relation of Forests in the Atlantic Plain to the Humidity of the Central States and Prairie Region." *Proceedings: Society of American Foresters* 8 (1913): 139–53.

———. "Forests in Relation to Soil and Water." *Symposium on Forestry and Public Welfare: Proceedings, American Philosophical Society* 89, no. 2 (1945): 399–403.

Zon, Raphael, and William N. Sparhawk. *Forest Resources of the World.* New York: McGraw-Hill Book Company, Inc., 1923.

INDEX

Note: Italicized page numbers indicate illustrations.